Bella Akhmadulina
Yehuda Amichai
Margaret Atwood
W. H. Auden
Jimmy Santiago Baca
Miriam Baruch
William Blake
Jorge Luis Borges
Anne Bradstreet
Bertolt Brecht
Grace Caroline Bridges
Elizabeth Barrett Browning
Robert Browning
Rahel Chalfi
Kelly Cherry
Gregory Corso
Léon Damas
Diana Der Hovanessian
Robert Desnos
Emily Dickinson
Rita Dove
Martín Espada
Carolyn Forché
Eleni Fourtouni
Robert Frost
Xu Gang
Nikki Giovanni
Francis E.W. Harper
Robert Hayden
Linda Hogan
Garrett Hongo
Gerard Manley Hopkins
Chenjerai Hove
Ted Hughes
Alfred Jarry
Ben Jonson
Mascha Kaleko
Anna Kamieńska
Maurice Kenny
Barbara Kingsolver
Henry Wadsworth Longfellow
Wing Tek Lum
Edna St. Vincent Millay
Czeslaw Milosz
John Milton
Les A. Murray
John Frederick Nims
Naomi Shihab Nye
Sharon Olds
Mary Oliver
Wilfred Owen
Linda Pastan
Octavio Paz
Marge Piercy
Vasko Popa
Muriel Rukeyser
Ira Sadoff
William Shakespeare
Lennart Sjögren
Cathy Song
Gary Soto
Bruce Springsteen
Sara Teasdale
Dylan Thomas
Fadwa Tuqan
Diane Wakoski
Walt Whitman
William Wordsworth
William Butler Yeats

Drama

Kōbō Abe
Tewfik al-Hakim
Christopher Durang
Dario Fo
Susan Glaspell
Václav Havel
David Ives
Betty Keller
William Shakespeare
Tennessee Williams

Discovering the Many Worlds of Literature

Discovering the Many Worlds of Literature

Literature for Composition

Stuart Hirschberg
Rutgers, The State University of New Jersey
Terry Hirschberg

New York Boston San Francisco
London Toronto Sydney Tokyo Singapore Madrid
Mexico City Munich Paris Cape Town Hong Kong Montreal

For our beloved cousin, Ruth Mirsky,
who we thank for so many years of wonderful memories.

Vice President and Editor-in-Chief: Joseph Terry
Senior Development Editor: Judith Fifer
Senior Marketing Manager: Melanie Craig
Senior Supplements Editor: Donna Campion
Production Manager: Douglas Bell
Project Coordination, Text Design, and Electronic Page Makeup: Nesbitt Graphics, Inc.
Cover Design Manager: Wendy Ann Fredericks
Cover Designer: Nancy Sacks
Cover Illustration: Mural at Queen Victoria Market, Melbourne; Photo credit: Kristi Bressert (383184) Index Stock
Manufacturing Manager: Dennis J. Para
Manufacturing Buyer: Roy L. Pickering Jr.
Printer and Binder: Quebecor World, Taunton
Cover Printer: Phoenix Color Corporation

For permission to use copyrighted material, grateful acknowledgment is made to the copyright holders on pp. 1069–1074, which are hereby made part of this copyright page.

Library of Congress Cataloging-in-Publication Data

Discovering the many worlds of literature : literature for composition/[compiled by] Stuart Hirschberg, Terry Hirschberg
p. cm.
Includes indexes.
ISBN 0-321-10212-6
1. College readers. 2. English language—Rhetoric—Problems, exercises, etc. 3. Criticism—Authorship—Problems, exercises, etc. 4. Academic writing—Problems, exercises, etc. 5. Literature—Collections. I. Hirschberg, Stuart. II. Hirschberg, Terry.

PE1417.D575 2003
808'.0427–dc21 2003051773

Please visit our website at http://www.ablongman.com

ISBN 0-321-10212-6

1 2 3 4 5 6 7 8 9 10—WCT—06 05 04 03

Brief Contents

Detailed Contents

Poems

Poems

Drama

Poems

Preface

Literature is news that stays news.

Ezra Pound, American poet and critic (1885–1972)

Discovering the Many Worlds of Literature: Literature for Composition is a global anthology of classic and contemporary works whose international and multicultural selections offer a new direction for freshman composition, introduction to literature, and contemporary world literature courses. The stories, poems, essays, and plays represent a wide variety of cultural and ethnic backgrounds. Writers, past and present, from 38 countries are represented by 158 works of fiction, nonfiction, poetry, and drama. Over forty percent of the selections are by women writers and approximately one third are by minority authors. Although classic authors are well represented, a sizeable percentage of the works were written since World War II and acquaint readers with the new directions literature has taken.

We believe that reading is one of the great pleasures that life affords—up there with eating chocolate, listening to music, and watching movies. Reading is an activity that does not require a partner or friend, electronic gear, wearing the correct clothes, having money, a particular time or season, or indeed any other precondition. We feel that the selections in *Discovering the Many Worlds of Literature* can begin a lifetime acquaintance with many authors and kinds of literature that will be a permanent source of enjoyment. Reading can be fun, as Charles Schultz illustrates in the following cartoon where Snoopy is reading a novel by Tolstoy.

Charles Schultz, PEANUTS reprinted with permission of United Features Syndicate, Inc.

We designed this text to integrate writing instruction with an emphasis on argumentation with the study of literature. We believe that in formulating and substantiating one's opinion about a literary work, we refine our skills in communicating while at the same time gain a deeper enjoyment of the profound artistry of these works. We have chosen interesting and exciting works that will produce strong responses and are genuinely capable of opening new worlds for students. The kind of reading we encourage is thorough and critical, although we recognize many readers might agree with film producer Samuel Goldwyn, who said, "I read part of it all the way through."

Organization of the Text

Chapter 1, "Reading and Writing About Literature," shows students how to approach all four genres represented in this anthology and provides guidance in writing effective argumentative essays. We discuss the processes of critical reading, note taking, journal keeping, invention strategies, arriving at a thesis, drafting and revising essays, as well as evaluating source materials and correct procedures for quoting and documenting based on the sixth edition of the MLA guidelines.

Chapter 2, "Topics for Literary Analysis," discusses important elements in the study of literature. It also introduces students (in the section "Arguing for an Interpretation of a Literary Work") to the influential Stephen Toulmin model of argumentation and shows how to use this approach to construct their own literary arguments.

The next seven thematic chapters (Chapters 3 to 9) are organized to move outward from the most personal sphere to encompass social and spiritual dimensions. Readers are encouraged to relate the selections to their personal experiences and to see commonalities between their own lives and those of others in radically different cultural circumstances. Compelling and provocative writings by authors from the Caribbean, Africa, Asia, South America, and Central America reflect the cultural and ethnic heritage of increasing numbers of student-readers.

- Chapter 3, "Family and Cultural Ties," features selections by writers who show us the common and unique elements that define family life in many countries around the world. These works also show how our identity is shaped by those attitudes, traditions, and customs that make up the ethnic and cultural heritage we often take for granted.
- Chapter 4, "Coming of Age," offers insights into the need people have in growing up to assert their own sense of individuality—often by defining themselves in opposition to the values held by their parents and society.
- Chapter 5, "Gender," presents classic and contemporary works by writers around the world that illuminate the complexities of the interactions between the sexes.
- Chapter 6, "Class, Race, and Ethnicity," takes up the crucial and often unrecognized relationships involving race, sense of identity, and class and caste conflicts through stories, essays, poems, and plays that explore positions of power and powerlessness.
- Chapter 7, "Politics and Power," reflects the ordeals faced by ordinary citizens trying to survive in repressive military and political regimes.

- Chapter 8, "Outcasts, Scapegoats, and Exiles" investigates the condition of exiles—whether refugees, immigrants, or travelers—who are caught between two cultures, at home in neither. Works in this chapter address the need of those who have left home to make sense of their lives in a new place.
- Chapter 9, "Nature and the Spirit," shows how people in many different cultures throughout the world look at themselves in relationship to the natural world, the eternal, the cosmic, and the supernatural.

The Editorial Apparatus

The editorial apparatus is designed to highlight both the themes of the selections and important elements in the study of literature. Chapter introductions discuss the theme of each chapter as it relates to the individual selections. Biographical sketches preceding each selection give background information on the writer's life and identify the cultural, historical, and personal contexts in which the selection was written.

The end-of-selection questions are of several varieties:

- "Analyzing the Text" asks students to think critically about the meaning of important aspects of the work by directing their attention to specific details, characters, events, and circumstances.
- "Understanding [the writer's] Techniques" focuses attention on significant single elements (plot, character, point of view, symbol, tone, irony) as they relate to the entire work. Important literary terms are keyed to the preceding discussion in Chapter 2, "Topics for Literary Analysis," and are included in the "Glossary of Literary Terms."
- "Arguing for an Interpretation" provides students with opportunities for writing persuasive interpretations of the works they read (based on guidelines in Chapter 1, "Reading and Writing About Literature"). These questions afford opportunities for personal and expressive writing, as well as for expository and persuasive writing, and include suggestions for library and Internet research.

Questions following each chapter, "Connections," encourage readers to consider relationships among selections within the chapter and to compare how short story writers, essayists, poets, and playwrights adapt techniques within a particular genre and treat the same theme. A filmography section at the end of each chapter is provided for instructors who wish to use films and videos related to the theme or to particular selections.

A section on "film criticism" in Appendix A enhances the usefulness of these filmographies. Overall, these assignments draw on the thematic organization of the text and ask readers to enter empathetically into viewpoints of the writer and to bring their own experiences into relationship with those of writers around the world.

We have provided two Appendixes: "Critical Approaches to Literature" and "Documenting Sources." The Appendixes go beyond the traditional elements of character, setting, point of view, conflict and plot structure, and myth and symbol, to reflect recent developments in literary theory such as "eco-criticism." These approaches should prove helpful in introducing students to the different schools of thought in literary criticism.

Instructor's Manual

The *Instructor's Manual* provides guidelines for using the text, sample syllabi, prompts for approaching all the selections, supplemental bibliographies of books and periodicals, suggested answers to questions in the text, additional writing and discussion questions, and a complete list of Web sites connected to particular authors and selections.

Additional Resources for Students and Instructors

Resources for Instructors

The Longman Electronic Testbank for Literature, by Heidi LM Jacobs. This test bank features various objective questions on major works of fiction, short fiction, poetry, and drama. A versatile and handy resource, this easy-to-use test bank can be used for all quizzing and testing needs. Available free to adopters. ISBN for Print: 0-321-14312-4 or Electronic/CD: 0-321-14314-0.

Teaching Literature On-line, Second Edition, by Daniel Kline. Concise and practical, *Teaching Literature On-line* provides instructors with strategies and advice for incorporating elements of computer technology into the literature classroom. Offering a range of information and examples, this manual provides ideas and activities for enhancing literature courses with the help of technology. Available free to adopters. ISBN 0-321-10618-0.

Video Program. For qualified adopters, an impressive selection of videotapes is available to enrich students' experience of literature. Contact your sales representative to learn how to qualify.

Resources for Students

MLA Documentation Style: A Concise Guide for Students, by Michael Greer. Replete with examples and clear explanations, this straightforward and accessible manual helps students understand and properly use the basic principles of MLA documentation. This brief guide includes a section on Frequently Asked Questions about MLA documentation style, provides all of the information students need to properly cite works and avoid plagiarism, and offers helpful guidelines on formatting papers. Available free when packaged with this text. ISBN 0-321-10337-8.

Glossary of Literary and Critical Terms, by Heidi LM Jacobs. This is a quick, reliable and portable resource for students of literature. This easy-to-use glossary includes definitions, explanations, and examples for over 100 literary and critical terms that students commonly encounter in their readings or hear in their lectures and class discussions. In addition to basic terms related to form and genre, the glossary also includes terms and explanations related to literary history, criticism, and theory. Available free when packaged with this text. ISBN 0-321-12691-2.

Literature Timeline, by Heidi LM Jacobs. This accessible and visually appealing timeline provides students with a chronological overview of major literary works; the timeline also lists major sociocultural and political events, to provide students with insight into the impact of historical events on writers and their works. Available free when packaged with this text. ISBN 0-321-14315-9.

Responding to Literature: A Writer's Journal, by Daniel Kline. This free journal provides students with their own personal space for writing. Helpful writing prompts for responding to fiction, poetry, and drama are also included. Available free when packaged with this text. ISBN 0-321-09542-1.

Evaluating a Performance, by Mike Greenwald. Perfect for the student assigned to review a local production, this supplement offers students a convenient place to record their evaluation. Useful tips and suggestions of things to consider when evaluating a production are included. Available free when packaged with this text. ISBN 0-321-09541-3.

Merriam Webster's Reader's Handbook: Your Complete Guide to Literary Terms This *Handbook* Includes nearly 2,000 entries, including Greek and Latin terminology, descriptions for every major genre, style, and era of writing, and assured authority from the combined resources of Merriam-Webster and Encyclopedia Britannica. Available at a significant discount when packaged with this text. ISBN 0-321-10541-9.

Analyzing Literature, Second Edition, by Sharon McGee. This brief supplement provides critical reading strategies, writing advice, and sample student papers to help students interpret and discuss literary works in a variety of genres. Suggestions for collaborative activities and online research on literary topics are also featured, as well as numerous exercises and writing assignments. Available free when packaged with this text. ISBN 0-321-09338-0.

Research Navigator Guide for English, by H. Eric Branscomb and Doug Gotthoffer. This guide to online research features the Longman Internet Guide and access to the Research Navigator Database. The guide gives students and instructors instant access to thousands of academic journals and periodicals any time from any computer with an Internet connection. Starting the research process has never been easier, with helpful tips on the writing process, online research, and finding and citing valid sources. Available free when packaged with this text. ISBN 0-321-20277-5.

The New American Webster Handy College Dictionary. This is a paperback reference text with more than 100,000 entries. Available free when packaged with this text. ISBN 0-451-18166-2.

Merriam-Webster Collegiate Dictionary. This hardcover comprehensive dictionary is available at a significant discount when packaged with any Longman text. ISBN 0-87779-709-9.

Penguin Discount Novel Program. In cooperation with Penguin Putnam, Inc., Longman is proud to offer a variety of Penguin paperbacks at a significant discount when packaged with any Longman title. Excellent additions to any literature course, Penguin titles give students the opportunity to explore contemporary and classical fiction and drama. The available titles include works by authors as diverse as Toni Morrison, Julia Alvarez, Mary Shelley, and Shakespeare. To review the complete list of titles available, visit the Longman-Penguin-Putnam Website: *http://www.ablongman.com/penguin.* Discounted prices of individual Penguin novels are available on the Website.

Coursecompass Generic Site. Longman English Resources for Introduction to Literature, Fiction, Creative Writing, and Drama Access Code Card, Second Edition. This course provides a number of guides that will help students analyze literature, evaluate plays, critique and write about literature and conduct research online. This course also includes a journal for writing about literature as well as a journal for creative writing. Instructors will find various additional resources, such as guides to teaching literature online and teaching multicultural literature. Available free when packaged with this text. ISBN 0-321-14311-6; Blackboard Content 0-321-14313-2.

Acknowledgments

Much appreciation goes to our editor at Longman, Joe Terry, who enthusiastically encouraged us from the onset, and to Judy Fifer, our developmental editor.

We especially want to thank Douglas Bell, production manager at Longman, for helping turn our manuscript into such a beautiful book, and our project editor, Lois Lombardo at Nesbitt Graphics, for her patience and good humor. Also, we thank Don S. Lawson for assisting with the filmography sections, Fred Courtright for obtaining the permissions, and Teresa Ward and Carol Barnette for their able assistance with the instructor's manual.

Thanks are due to the reviewers of this text, who provided helpful feedback and suggestions: Frances Secco Davidson, Mercer County Community College; Ron DiCostanzo, Long Beach City College; John C. Dobelbower, Ball State University; Thomas Dukes, University of Akron; Ralph Edsell, Southwestern College; Simone Gers, Pima Community College; Martha K. Goodman, Central Virginia Community College; Phillip Jacowitz, Embry-Riddle Aeronautical University; Rhonda Knight, Coker College; Don S. Lawson, Lander University; Philip Mayfield, Fullerton College; Eric Otto, University of Florida; Lolly Smith, Everett Community College; Will Tomory, Southwestern Michigan College; Betty Weldon, Jefferson Community College-Southwest; and Arthur Wohlgemuth, Miami Dade Community College.

Stuart Hirschberg
Terry Hirschberg

Chapter 1

Reading and Writing About Literature

Reading Essays

The literary or personal essay can serve as an ideal bridge from the world of nonfiction to the imaginary realms of fiction, poetry, and drama. Many of the same qualities we value in short stories, poems, and plays are embodied in the personal essay. As a genre, the essay was invented 400 years ago by the French writer Michel Montaigne, who called his writings *essais* (French for "attempts") because they were intended less as accounts of objective truth than as a quest to discover his own attitudes on a diverse range of subjects.

The Personal Essay

The idea that one's own life is an appropriate object of self-examination can be said to have started with *The Confessions of St. Augustine* (circa A.D. 397–401), which demonstrated a new method for exploring the mysteries of the interior life. Because writing an autobiographical essay is an interpretive act, the motives for refashioning oneself through imagination can serve many purposes.

Essays are especially interesting to read when the writer engages us in his or her own personal struggle. For example, Nawal El Saadawi, in "The Mutilated Half" (Chapter 5), offers a graphic account of the female circumcision she experienced when she was six years old. She tells how this event changed her relationship with her parents, and goes on to describe the hostility she later encountered when, as a physician in Egypt, she investigated the reasons for this practice and documented its physical and emotional effects on women.

Personal essays in which the reader can see how the acquisition of language helps create the writer's identity are particularly fascinating. For example, in the account by Amy Tan ("The Language of Discretion," Chapter 3) we can observe how English and Chinese are not simply languages that one speaks, but ways of perceiving the world that one acquires along with the language.

Autobiographical or personal essays also offer a means by which writers can define themselves as individuals, distinct from the self-images fostered by social or cultural stereotyping. Narratives by Jill Nelson ("Number One!" Chapter 3), Judith Ortiz Cofer ("The Myth of the Latin Woman," Chapter 5), Mary Crow Dog and Richard Erdoes ("Civilize Them with a Stick," Chapter 6), and James Baldwin ("Letter to My Nephew," Chapter 6) chart decisive moments when each writer came to terms with being African American, Native American, or Hispanic within a culture that marginalizes minorities. For other writers, the process of writing a personal essay can have a cathartic or therapeutic function as it does for Paul Monette in "Borrowed Time: An AIDS Memoir" (Chapter 8).

Personal essays can also serve as persuasive eyewitness accounts to historical events. For example, Luis Sepulveda's "Daisy" (Chapter 7) testifies to his imprisonment, interrogation, and torture in a Chilean prison and George Orwell denounces British imperialism from the vantage point of an officer in Burma ("Shooting an Elephant," Chapter 7).

Essays that contain detailed observations of the natural world (based on personal experience) are invaluable sources in understanding the environment and can be traced back to a tradition in American literature dating from Henry David Thoreau's *Walden* (1845). Reflections on the complex interactions of living things, the study of animal behavior, and ecological concerns inform a rich body of work represented by Ursula K. Le Guin's "A Very Warm Mountain" (Chapter 9) and Aldo Leopold's "Thinking Like a Mountain" (Chapter 9).

The 19 essayists in this book embark on voyages of self-discovery as they reflect on topics including relationships with their families and other people important in their lives, historical events, ethnic and cultural values, pressing social issues, sexual identity, and religious, spiritual and environmental themes.

Reading Critically

When you read the essays in this text, you will respond to and interact with them in ways that are unique according to your experiences. As you read, try to locate and analyze the important ideas the writer communicates and, at the same time, compare these ideas with your own values. Critical reading also involves comparing what one writer says to the observations and claims of other writers.

The process of reading literary essays differs from ordinary reading (e.g., articles in newspapers and popular magazines) in an important way. You need to read selections a second and even a third time to look beyond the immediately observable features (the topic of the essay, its length, or the author's stance) to a deeper understanding of the subordinate, but related, ideas and the underlying organization of the entire essay.

Critical reading (and writing) might be new terms and concepts for you, but they form the basis for the way in which you become a successful reader and writer. Each skill depends on the other because much of what you write in college is based on your response to what others have written. During the writing process you learn how to explore the ideas of others and to form and support your own opinions. Many of the works you read can serve as models for your own writing, but first you must be able to identify the organizational strategies the writers use to present their thoughts. When you read critically, you also develop the ability to distinguish statements that are facts (and can be verified) from those that are simply opinions.

Reading for Ideas and Organization

The process of critically reading an essay before writing about it requires you to read the selection several times to understand both the immediately observable features (such as the topic and length) and to gain a deeper understanding of the ideas as well as the overall organization. As you read, you can annotate the text and even record your observations in a reading journal. The methods you use (circling main ideas, looking up unfamiliar words, underlying key phrases) matter less than your beginning a dialogue with the author. As in a real conversation, you can pose questions, ask for clarification of a point, or start your own line of reasoning.

On the first, and in subsequent readings of the essays in this text, especially the longer ones, pay particular attention to the title, look for the introductory and concluding paragraphs (which emphasize the author's initial statement or summary of key ideas), identify headings and subheadings (and determine the relationship between these and the title), and define any unusual or foreign terms necessary to fully understand the author's concepts.

Finding a Thesis If possible, locate the author's thesis (whether stated specifically or implied) and underline it or state it in your own words. Then work your way through fairly rapidly, identifying the main ideas and the sequence in which they are presented. As you identify an important idea, ask yourself how this idea relates to the thesis statement you identified or to the idea expressed in the title. The thesis is often stated in the form of a single sentence asserting the author's response to an issue that others might respond to in different ways. For example, in "Fiesta," reprinted on pages 7–12, Octavio Paz expresses his opinion that:

> By means of the fiesta, society frees itself from the norms it has established.

The thesis or claim represents the writer's view of the subject from a certain perspective.

Transitions To better see the connections between the divisions within an essay, pay particular attention to transitional words and phrases that show relationships between ideas. These transitions may express chronological relationships ("now," "when," "before," "after") or causal relationships ("because," "therefore,") or they may signal additional information ("furthermore," "moreover") or qualifying information ("although," "however"). Also look for section summaries, where the author draws together several preceding ideas.

Evaluating Tone Tone or "voice" plays a crucial element in establishing a writer's credibility. Tone is produced by the combined effect of word choice, sentence structure, and the writer's success in adapting his or her particular "voice" to suit the subject, the audience, and the occasion. When we try to identify and analyze the tone of a work, we are seeking to hear the actual "voice" of the author, to understand how he or she intended the work to be perceived.

Humor, Irony, and Satire

Different theories have been proposed to explain what we find to be funny. One explanation put forward by Plato, Aristotle, and others is that we laugh at the misfortune of others and thereby feel superior. Another view is that we laugh at something we find incongruous. Sigmund Freud believed that we laugh to relieve nervous tension. Although it may be hard to define humor, we all seem to know when something is funny and laugh at the same things. Humor is an essential, but often underappreciated, element that enhances the reader's pleasure in many of the essays in this anthology. For example, see Fritz Peter's "Boyhood with Gurdjieff" (Chapter 3), Jill Nelson's "Number One!" (Chapter 3), and Luis Alberto Urrea's "Border Story" (Chapter 8). Laughing at oneself would seem to be a precondition for laughing at others, as does Luis Sepulveda in "Daisy" (Chapter 7). After being put into solitary confinement for pointing out to a prison guard (who had begged him to review his work) that his poems were copied verbatim from a famous Mexican poet, Sepulveda concludes:

> I swore over and over again never to become a literary critic.

Irony Irony is a a particular kind of tone encountered in many essays (as well as in short fiction, drama, and poetry). Writers use this strategy to express a discrepancy between appearance and reality. Sometimes it is difficult to tell that not everything the writer says is intended to be taken literally. Authors will occasionally say the opposite of what they mean to provoke the reader's curiosity. One clear signal that the author is being ironic is a noticeable disparity between the tone and the subject. For example, Langston Hughes (in "Salvation," Chapter 9) concludes:

> So I decided that maybe to save further trouble, I'd better lie, too, and say that Jesus had come, and get up and be saved.

The clash between the subject (a public declaration of religious fervor), and Hughes's iconoclastic comment alerts the reader that the writer is being ironic.

Satire Irony is especially important in satire, an enduring form of argument that uses parody and caricature to poke fun at a subject, idea, or person. The satirist can create a "mask" or *persona* that is very different from the author's real self to shock the audience into a new awareness about an established institution or custom. For example, in "A Modest Proposal" (1729) Jonathan Swift (Chapter 6) uses the persona of a reasonable, seemingly well-intentioned bureaucrat who proposes that Ireland solve both its economic and overpopulation problems by encouraging poor people to sell their small children as food to the wealthy:

> I have been assured by a very knowing American of my acquaintance in London, that a young healthy child well nursed is at a year old a most delicious, nourishing, and wholesome food, whether stewed, roasted, baked, or boiled, and I make no doubt that it will equally serve in a fricassee, or a ragout.

The practical, down-to-earth, and understated voice with which the narrator enumerates the financial and culinary advantages of his proposed solution is far more effective in reflecting Swift's views on the exploitation of Irish resources by English landlords, than a diatribe would have been. The discrepancy between the matter-of-fact tone and the outrageous content signals the reader as to Swift's real intention. Satirical works assail folly, greed, corruption, pride, self-righteous complacency, and private and public hypocrisy. Over the cen-

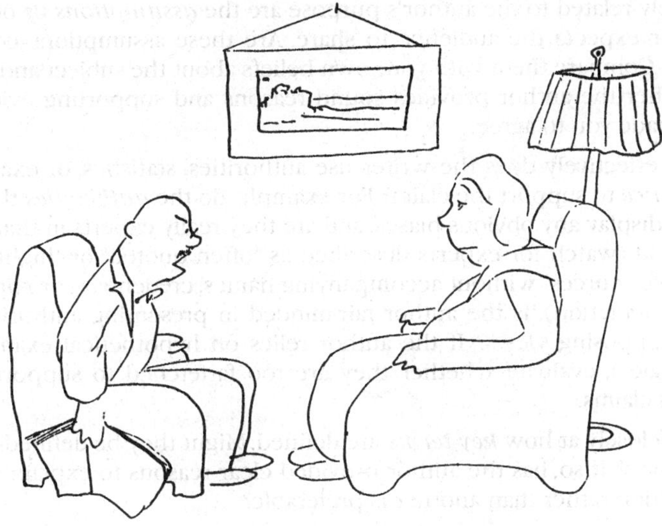

"I assume, then, that you regard yourself as omniscient.
If I am wrong, correct me!"

turies, great satirical works have included Aristophanes' *The Birds,* Voltaire's *Candide,* Swift's *Gulliver's Travels,* Mark Twain's *A Connecticut Yankee in King Arthur's Court,* and Joseph Heller's *Catch 22.*

Although we have discussed humor, irony, and satire as separate elements, they often work together, as in the cartoon by the American writer, James Thurber.

Analyzing Essays

The most effective way to think about what you read is to make notes and ask questions as you go along. Making notes as you read encourages you to think carefully about the meaning of each sentence.There are as many styles of annotating as there are readers, and you will discover your own preferred method once you have done it a few times. Some readers underline major points or statements and jot down their reactions in the margins. Others prefer to summarize each paragraph or section to help them follow the author's line of thought. Still others circle key words or phrases that help them understand the main ideas.Your notes are a conversation with the author in which you can ask questions and make observations. Be sure to mark unfamiliar words or phrases to look up later. Try to distinguish the main ideas from supporting points and examples. Use the following guidelines to evaluate whether the author makes a credible case for the conclusions reached.

Guidelines for Annotating

- When evaluating an essay, consider what the author's *purpose* is in writing it.Was it to inform, explain, solve a problem, make a recommendation, amuse, enlighten, or achieve some combination of these goals? How is the tone, or voice, the author projects related to the purpose in writing the essay?

- Closely related to the author's purpose are the *assumptions* or beliefs the writer expects the audience to share. Are these assumptions commonly held? Compare them with your own beliefs about the subject and evaluate whether the author provides sound reasons and supporting evidence to persuade you to agree.
- How effectively does the writer use authorities, statistics, or examples as *evidence* to support the claim? For example, do the *authorities* the author cites display any obvious biases, and are they really experts in that particular field (watch for experts described as "often quoted" or "highly placed reliable sources" without accompanying names, credentials, or appropriate documentation). Is the author fair-minded in presenting authorities who hold opposing views? If the author relies on hypothetical examples (or analogies), evaluate whether they are too farfetched to support the author's claims.
- Look closely at how *key terms* are defined. Might they be defined in different ways? If so, has the author provided clear reasons to explain why one definition rather than another is preferable?
- One last point—take a close look at the idea expressed in the *title* before and after you read the essay to see how it relates to the main idea.

Keeping a Reading Journal

The most effective way to keep track of your thoughts and impressions and to review what you have learned is to keep a reading journal. The comments you record in your journal may express your reflections, observations, questions, and reactions to the essays you read. You can write down questions that occur to you as you read, copy interesting or memorable phrases or sentences from the selection, give your opinion, and agree or disagree with the author's points.

Summarizing Summarizing is valuable because it requires you to pay close attention to the reading in order to distinguish the main points from the supporting details. Summarizing tests your understanding of the material by requiring you to restate concisely the author's main ideas in your own words.

> First, create a list composed of sentences that express in your own words the essential idea of each paragraph, or each group of related paragraphs. Your previous underlining of topic sentences, main ideas, and key terms (as part of the process of critical reading) will help you follow the author's line of thought. Next, whittle down this list still further by eliminating repetitive ideas. Then, formulate a thesis statement that expresses the main idea behind the article. Start your summary with this thesis statement, and combine your notes so that the summary flows together and reads easily.

Summaries should be much shorter (usually no longer than half a page) than the original text (whether the original is one page or twenty pages long) and should accurately reflect the central ideas of the article in as few words as possible. Try not to interject your own opinions or critical evaluations into the summary. Besides requiring you to read the original piece more closely, summaries are necessary first steps in developing papers that synthesize materials from different sources. The test for a good summary, of course, is whether a person reading it without having read the original article would get an accurate, balanced, and complete account of the original material.

Opening a Dialogue

The writing you do in your college courses requires you to enter a conversation with the authors whose works you read. While we don't mean conversation in a literal sense, we do ask you to open a dialogue between yourself and the text. As in a real conversation, imagine that you are free to pose questions, ask for clarification of a point, or start your own line of reasoning in response to what you have read. You can agree or disagree, defend your point of view, and even argue as long as you interact with the text. In this sense, you are the latest arrival at an ongoing conversation between the writer and all previous sources to which his or her essay is responding. You might think of it as being invited to a party where you can participate in many fascinating discussions that have started before you arrived. For example, what other observations and comments would you add to those reprinted below for Octavio Paz's essay "Fiesta."

OCTAVIO PAZ

Octavio Paz (1914–1998), born in Mexico City, was a poet, essayist, and unequalled observer of Mexican society. He served as a Mexican diplomat in France and Japan and as Ambassador to India before resigning from the diplomatic service to protest the Tlatelolco Massacre (government massacre of 300 students in Mexico City) in 1968. His many volumes of poetry include Sun Stone *(1958), a new reading of the Aztec myths;* Marcel Duchamp *(1968);* The Children of the Mire *(1974); and* The Monkey Grammarian *(1981). In 1990, Paz was awarded the Nobel Prize for Literature. As an essayist whose works have helped redefine the concept of Latin American culture, Paz wrote* The Other Mexico *(1972) and* The Labyrinth of Solitude, *translated by Lysander Kemp (1961), from which "Fiesta" is taken. In the following essay, Paz offers insight, conveyed with his typical stylistic grace and erudition, into the deep psychological needs met by fiestas in Mexican culture.*

Fiesta

The solitary Mexican loves fiestas and public gatherings. Any occasion for getting together will serve, any pretext to stop the flow of time and commemorate men and events with festivals and ceremonies. We are a ritual people, and this characteristic enriches both our imaginations and our sensibilities, which are equally sharp and alert. The art of the fiesta has been debased almost everywhere else, but not in Mexico. There are few places in the world where it is possible to take part in a spectacle like our great religious fiestas with their violent primary colors, their bizarre costumes and dances, their fireworks and ceremonies and their inexhaustible welter of surprises: the fruit, candy, toys and other objects sold on these days in the plazas and open-air markets.

analysis of factors that explain number of fiestas in Mexico and national character

Our calendar is crowded with fiestas. There are certain days when the whole country, from the most remote villages to the largest cities, prays, shouts, feasts, gets drunk and kills, in honor of the Virgin of Guadalupe or Benito Juaréz. Each year on the fifteenth of September, at eleven o'clock at night, we celebrate the fiesta of the *Grito*[1] in all the plazas of the Republic, and the excited crowds actually shout for a whole hour . . . the better, perhaps, to remain silent for the rest of the year. During the days before and after the twelfth of December,[2] time comes to a full stop, and instead of pushing us toward a deceptive tomorrow that is always beyond our reach, offers us a complete and perfect today of dancing and revelry, of communion with the most ancient and secret Mexico. Time is no longer succession, and becomes what it originally was and is: the present, in which past and future are reconciled.

fiestas are time out when people lose themselves in the moment

But the fiestas which the Church and State provide for the country as a whole are not enough. The life of every city and village is ruled by a patron saint whose blessing is celebrated with devout regularity. Neighborhoods and trades also have their annual fiestas, their ceremonies and fairs. And each one of us—atheist, Catholic, or merely indifferent—has his own saint's day, which he observes every year. It is impossible to calculate how many fiestas we have and how much time and money we spend on them. I remember asking the mayor of a village near Mitla, several years ago, "What is the income of the village government?" "About 3,000 pesos a year. We are very poor. But the Governor and the Federal Government always help us to meet our expenses." "And how are the 3,000 pesos spent?" "Mostly on fiestas, señor. We are a small village, but we have two patron saints."

towns spend more on fiestas than they can afford

This reply is not surprising. Our poverty can be measured by the frequency and luxuriousness of our holidays. Wealthy countries have very few: there is neither the time nor the desire for them, and they are not necessary. The people have other things to do, and when they amuse themselves they do so in small groups. The modern masses are agglomerations of solitary individuals. On great occasions in Paris or New York, when the populace gathers in the squares or stadiums, the absence of people, in the sense of *a* people, is remarkable: there are couples and small groups, but they never form a living community in which the individual is at once dissolved and redeemed. But how could a poor Mexican live without the two

purges pent up emotional release from depression of poverty

---

[1] Padre Hildalgo's call-to-arms against Spain, 1810.—*Tr.*
[2] Fiesta of the Virgin of Guadalupe.—*Tr.*

or three annual fiestas that make up for his poverty and misery? Fiestas are our only luxury. They replace, and are perhaps better than, the theater and vacations, Anglo-Saxon weekends and cocktail parties, the bourgeois reception, the Mediterranean café.

In all of these ceremonies—national or local, trade or family—the Mexican opens out. They all give him a chance to reveal himself and to converse with God, country, friends or relations. During these days the silent Mexican whistles, shouts, sings, shoots off fireworks, discharges his pistol into the air. He discharges his soul. And his shout, like the rockets we love so much, ascends to the heavens, explodes into green, red, blue, and white lights, and falls dizzily, to earth with a trail of golden sparks. This is the night when friends who have not exchanged more than the prescribed courtesies for months get drunk together, trade confidences, weep over the same troubles, discover that they are brothers, and sometimes, to prove it, kill each other. The night is full of songs and loud cries. The lover wakes up his sweetheart with an orchestra. There are jokes and conversations from balcony to balcony, sidewalk to sidewalk. Nobody talks quietly. Hats fly in the air. Laughter and curses ring like silver pesos. Guitars are brought out. Now and then, it is true, the happiness ends badly, in quarrels, insults, pistol shots, stabbings. But these too are part of the fiesta, for the Mexican does not seek amusement: he seeks to escape from himself, to leap over the wall of solitude that confines him during the rest of the year. All are possessed by violence and frenzy. Their souls explode like the colors and voices and emotions. Do they forget themselves and show their true faces? Nobody knows. The important thing is to go out, open a way, get drunk on noise, people, colors. Mexico is celebrating a fiesta. And this fiesta, shot through with lightning and delirium, is the brilliant reverse to our silence and apathy, our reticence and gloom.

Paz's style captures exuberance and chaotic mood of fiestas

mask of composure and propriety disgarded during fiestas

According to the interpretation of French sociologists, the fiesta is an excess, an expense. By means of this squandering the community protects itself against the envy of the gods or of men. Sacrifices and offerings placate or buy off the gods and the patron saints. Wasting money and expending energy affirms the community's wealth in both. This luxury is a proof of health, a show of abundance and power. Or a magic trap. For squandering is an effort to attract abundance by contagion. Money calls to money. When life is thrown away it increases; the orgy, which is sexual expenditure, is also a ceremony of regeneration; waste gives strength. New Year celebrations, in every culture, signify something beyond the mere observance of a date on the calendar. The day is a pause: time is stopped, is actually annihilated. The rites that celebrate its death are intended to provoke its rebirth, because they mark not only the end of an old year but also the beginning of a new. Everything attracts its opposite. The fiesta's function, then, is more utilitarian than we think: waste attracts or promotes wealth, and is an

French sociologists theorize extravagance as ritual sacrifice

conspicuous squandering of wealth precedes regeneration

investment like any other, except that the returns on it cannot be measured or counted. What is sought is potency, life, health. In this sense the fiesta, like the gift and the offering, is one of the most ancient of economic forms.

This interpretation has always seemed to me to be incomplete. The fiesta is by nature sacred, literally or figuratively, and above all it is the advent of the unusual. It is governed by its own special rules, that set it apart from other days, and it has a logic, an ethic and even an economy that are often in conflict with everyday norms. It all occurs in an enchanted world: time is transformed to a mythical past or a total present; space, the scene of the fiesta, is turned into a gaily decorated world of its own; and the persons taking part cast off all human or social rank and become, for the moment, living images. And everything takes place as if it were not so, as if it were a dream. But whatever happens, our actions have a greater lightness, a different gravity. They take on other meanings and with them we contract new obligations. We throw down our burdens of time and reason.

ritual time during fiestas differs from "normal" time

In certain fiestas the very notion of order disappears. Chaos comes back and license rules. Anything is permitted: the customary hierarchies vanish, along with all social, sex, caste, and trade distinctions. Men disguise themselves as women, gentlemen as slaves, the poor as the rich. The army, the clergy, and the law are ridiculed. Obligatory sacrilege, ritual profanation is committed. Love becomes promiscuity. Sometimes the fiesta becomes a Black Mass. Regulations, habits and customs are violated. Respectable people put away the dignified expressions and conservative clothes that isolate them, dress up in gaudy colors, hide behind a mask, and escape from themselves.

constraints in relationships between the sexes and social classes disgarded

Therefore the fiesta is not only an excess, a ritual squandering of the goods painfully accumulated during the rest of the year; it is also a revolt, a sudden immersion in the formless, in pure being. By means of the fiesta society frees itself from the norms it has established. It ridicules its gods, its principles, and its laws: it denies its own self.

The fiesta is a revolution in the most literal sense of the word. In the confusion that it generates, society is dissolved, is drowned, insofar as it is an organism ruled according to certain laws and principles. But it drowns in itself, in its own original chaos or liberty. Everything is united: good and evil, day and night, the sacred and the profane. Everything merges, loses shape and individuality and returns to the primordial mass. The fiesta is a cosmic experiment, an experiment in disorder, reuniting contradictory elements and principles in order to bring about a renascence of life. Ritual death promotes a rebirth; vomiting increases the appetite; the orgy, sterile in itself, renews the fertility of the mother or of the earth. The fiesta is a return to a remote and undifferentiated state, prenatal or presocial. It is a return that is also a beginning, in accordance with the dialectic that is inherent in social processes.

The group emerges purified and strengthened from this plunge into chaos. It has immersed itself in its own origins, in the womb from which it came. To express it in another way, the fiesta denies society as an organic system of differentiated forms and principles, but affirms it as a source of creative energy. It is a true "re-creation," the opposite of the "recreation" characterizing modern vacations, which do not entail any rites or ceremonies whatever and are as individualistic and sterile as the world that invented them.

Society communes with itself during the fiesta. Its members return to original chaos and freedom. Social structures break down and new relationships, unexpected rules, capricious hierarchies are created. In the general disorder everybody forgets himself and enters into otherwise forbidden situations and places. The bounds between audience and actors, officials and servants, are erased. Everybody takes part in the fiesta, everybody is caught up in its whirlwind. Whatever its mood, its character, its meaning, the fiesta is participation, and this trait distinguishes it from all other ceremonies and social phenomena. Lay or religious, orgy or saturnalia, the fiesta is a social act based on the full participation of all its celebrants.

barriers between social classes drop

Thanks to the fiesta the Mexican opens out, participates, communes with his fellows and with the values that give meaning to his religious or political existence. And it is significant that a country as sorrowful as ours should have so many and such joyous fiestas. Their frequency, their brilliance and excitement, the enthusiasm with which we take part, all suggest that without them we would explode. They free us, if only momentarily, from the thwarted impulses, the inflammable desires that we carry within us. But the Mexican fiesta is not merely a return to an original state of formless and normless liberty: the Mexican is not seeking to return, but to escape from himself, to exceed himself. Our fiestas are explosions. Life and death, joy and sorrow, music and mere noise are united, not to re-create or recognize themselves, but to swallow each other up. There is nothing so joyous as a Mexican fiesta, but there is also nothing so sorrowful. Fiesta night is also a night of mourning.

thesis: fiestas are a release from solitude and regenerate social, economic, and sexual aspects of life

If we hide within ourselves in our daily lives, we discharge ourselves in the whirlwind of the fiesta. It is more than an opening out: we rend ourselves open. Everything—music, love, friendship—ends in tumult and violence. The frenzy of our festivals shows the extent to which our solitude closes us off from communication with the world. We are familiar with delirium, with songs and shouts, with the monologue . . . but not with the dialogue. Our fiestas, like our confidences, our loves, our attempts to reorder our society, are violent breaks with the old or the established. Each time we try to express ourselves we have to break with ourselves. And the fiesta is only one example, perhaps the most typical, of this violent break. It is not difficult to name others, equally revealing: our games, which are always a going to extremes, often mortal; our profligate spending, the reverse of our timid investments and business enterprises; our confessions. The somber Mexican, closed up in himself, suddenly explodes, tears open his breast and reveals himself, though not without a certain complacency, and not without a

although demonstrative and seemingly open, Mexicans are reserved—fiestas are an outlet

> stopping place in the shameful or terrible mazes of his intimacy. We are not frank, but our sincerity can reach extremes that horrify a European. The explosive, dramatic, sometimes even suicidal manner in which we strip ourselves, surrender ourselves, is evidence that something inhibits and suffocates us. Something impedes us from being. And since we cannot or dare not confront our own selves, we resort to the fiesta. It fires us into the void; it is a drunken rapture that burns itself out, a pistol shot in the air, a skyrocket.

attitudes and practices opposite of Europeans

Writing About Essays

An analytical essay is one of the basic forms of writing you will most often be expected to produce in college level literature courses. In it, you build on previously developed critical thinking and reading skills in understanding a text and evaluating its effectiveness. The simplest way to do this is to find a question about any aspect of an essay you read (for example, the author's claims, use of evidence, chain of reasoning, organization or style) that you want to answer. The "Arguing for an Interpretation" assignments are designed to stimulate these kinds of questions. The question you formulate becomes the topic or subject of your paper.

The idea that expresses your opinion is called the thesis and contains a specific claim that your essay will propose and defend. For example, after reading and having annotated Octavio Paz's "Fiesta," a student wondered why fiestas were such a significant social phenomenon in Mexican culture. Based on her analysis of Paz's argument, she formulated an interpretation that could be expressed as a claim or thesis:

> **Thesis:** Fiestas in Mexican society provide a much needed "time-out" from the solitude of everyday life and from pervasive poverty.

The thesis or claim is an assertion that must be genuinely debatable; that is, there should be some alternative, or opposing opinion (such as "fiestas are a pleasant albeit meaningless pasttime").

Pre-writing Techniques

Discovering how best to approach your topic is easier if you try one or several of the pre-writing, or invention strategies (such as free-writing, the five Ws, and mapping) many writers have found helpful.

Free-writing In free-writing, you set down whatever occurs to you on the topic within a few minutes without considering spelling, punctuation, or grammar. The objective is to perceive key aspects of the issue and to discover how to focus your argument.

The Five Ws These are questions that journalists use to determine what can be known about the topic (such as fiestas in Paz's essay):

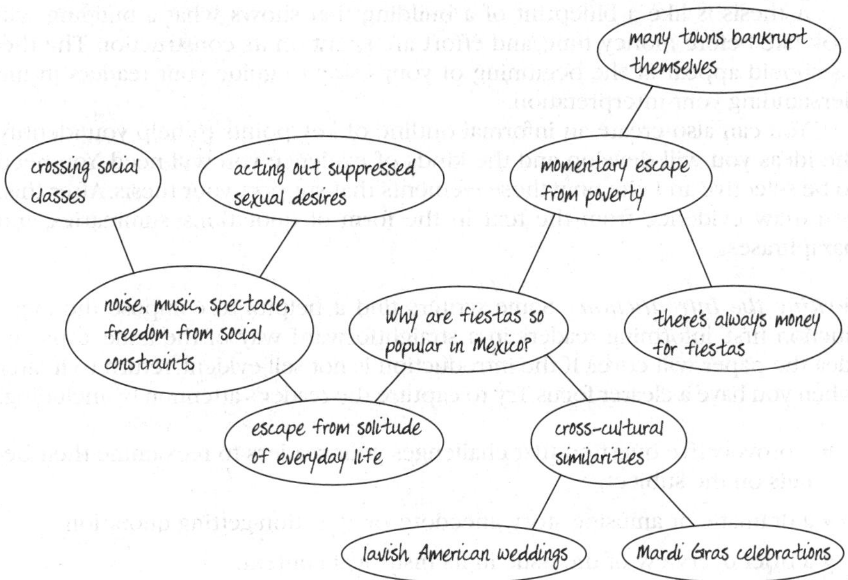

FIGURE 1 ■ An example of mapping.

- **Who** is involved in the situation? Average citizens
- **What** is at stake? Creating a lavish display
- **Where** does the action occur? Throughout Mexico
- **When** does it occur? Between September and December
- **Why** is it important? As a release from everyday life

Mapping In mapping you visually observe the relationship between important ideas. You first write down the key idea and circle it, and then jot down related ideas and draw lines between these and the key idea to create a map that shows which ideas are central and which are subordinate. Your map will show you any possible thesis and the ideas, details, and examples that can be used to support it (as in Figure 1).

Creating a Rough Draft

In a rough draft you explore ideas that draw on your annotations, reading journal, pre-writing strategies, and informal outline, if any. Write one section of the paper at a time and concentrate on the details within that section to determine if they really support your thesis. The thesis is a contract that obligates you to interpret aspects of the essay to clarify and support your opinion. The thesis can be revised later when you have a clearer focus on what you can reasonably establish. Your assertion should be stated as a single sentence. It will suggest how to organize your essay and what rhetorical strategies will prove most effective when you write your essay.

A thesis is like a blueprint of a building that shows what a building will look like before money, time, and effort are spent on its construction. The thesis should appear at the beginning of your essay to guide your readers in understanding your interpretation.

You can also create an informal outline of key points to help you identify the ideas you will develop and the kinds of evidence you will need. You need to be selective and cite only those elements that support your thesis. After this, you draw evidence from the text in the form of quotations, summaries, and paraphrases.

Writing the Introduction Some writers find it helpful to compose the introduction first, informing readers in a straightforward way of the issue, topic, or idea the paper will cover. If the introduction is not self-evident, return to it later when you have a clearer focus. Try to capture the reader's attention by including:

- a provocative question that challenges your readers to reexamine their beliefs on the subject,
- a dramatic or amusing story, anecdote, or attention-getting quotation,
- a brief overview of the issue in its historical context,
- a striking statistic,
- a brief description of both sides of a debate, or
- a description of a central person, place, or event.

Writing the Middle of the Essay Each paragraph within the body of the essay also contains a topic sentence that relates to the thesis and serves as the focus for that paragraph. Supporting material (summaries, paraphrases, or quotes) illustrates and clarifies the topic sentence. Use clear transitional sentences to draw attention to important relationships.

Writing the Conclusion The conclusion should draw together important points and relate them to the thesis. You can round off your essay by referring to points presented in the opening paragraph and by summarizing the key points made in the body of the paper.

Revising Your Essay

You will probably revise several times, and may wish to read your paper aloud to discover errors in grammar, syntax, or style. Many campuses have writing centers or tutoring services that can help you.

First examine your essay's structure. Is the introduction effective? Do the sections follow each other in a logical manner? Would the reader need more examples to clarify an idea? Do your transitions help readers to perceive relationships between different sections of your paper? Have you explained your assumptions? Have you unintentionally contradicted yourself? What new information could you add to make your argument more persuasive?

Does each paragraph have enough supporting evidence (quotations, paraphrases, examples) and is it clearly related to your thesis? You can improve your essay's grammar and style by recasting passive sentences into the active voice. To improve your style, substitute single words for roundabout phrases, such as "because" for "due to the fact that," "after" for "at the conclusion of," and "now" for "at this point in time." Consider how you might improve your choice of words, and try to avoid mixed metaphors, such as, "the hand that rocks the cradle has kicked the bucket," abstract jargon (if technical terms are necessary, define them the first time you use them), and clichés or trite phrases, such as "cool as a cucumber" or "fair and square." Lastly, rework your title to more accurately reflect your claim.

Proofreading Watch for inconsistencies in syntax, grammar, or usage. Keep a list of words you often misspell and check it as you proofread. Document the source of every quote, paraphrase, and summary (we describe the method of in-text citation and documentation in the Appendix). Check your in-text citations against the list of "Works Cited" and make sure you did not change any words or punctuation.

Revising with a Computer Revising with a computer allows you to try out different configurations by cutting and pasting sentences and paragraphs. Some computer programs also provide outline tools and spell-checkers that can help you edit your paper. Keep in mind that spell-check programs cannot sense if a word is incorrectly used if that word is spelled correctly (for example, "too" for "to" or "two," or "their" for "there"). Keep a printed version and create a backup file after each session.

Formatting

Papers are formatted in the Modern Language Association style described in the *MLA Handbook for Writers of Research Papers,* 6th ed. (New York: Modern Language Association of America, 2003) and on the MLA Web site at <http://www.mla.org>. First, document the sources in the body of the paper that you quote, paraphrase, or summarize. Then create a separate list of "Works Cited" for the end of your paper. Students in the social sciences (such as psychology and sociology) use the style manual of the American Psychological Association (APA); those in the life sciences follow the style recommended by the Council of Biology Editors (CBE).

Unless your instructor specifies otherwise, the following format is standard:

- Provide 1-inch margins on the top, bottom, and sides of each page.
- Number each page (and any running heads).
- Indent the first line of each paragraph ½ inch.
- Double space the text in standard 12-point font.
- Provide a separate list of works cited.
- Put your name, title of the essay, course, and date on the first page.

Drawing on Additional Sources for Evidence

Some papers may require additional research, using books and journals from your library, or information found on the Internet. You can search your library's online catalog with combinations of key words (for example, "fiestas" AND "Mexico") that will turn up only those sources that you will be able to use. The Library of Congress call numbers will lead you to the section of the library where other books on the subject may be found.

Bibliographies, Indexes, and Encyclopedias Bibliographies that are published annually offer useful listings of scholarly books and journal articles. They are usually kept in the reference area and also may be available online. The most comprehensive of these are *The MLA International Bibliography* and the *Readers' Guide to Periodical Literature,* especially for research in the fields of literature and the humanities. As you narrow your topic, you may need to search more specialized bibliographies and indexes (which contain alphabetical listings of subject and author entries used to locate articles and periodicals) such as the *Humanities Index* or *Humanities Abstracts.* Libraries also contain encyclopedias (available as well on CD-ROM), biographical dictionaries, and handbooks in specific subject areas.

Many libraries have extensive collections of periodicals. Although you may not be able to check these out, you can photocopy what you need from them. The *Book Review Digest,* the *Library Journal,* and *The New York Times Index* are other valuable resources. The best way to find out about a new reference tool, such as an index, is to read its preface. Reading the preface will tell you how the index is organized and what materials, subjects, and time periods it includes. When you use these reference tools, always begin with the current year and work your way backward to be sure you include the latest research.

Whatever sources you use, however, you need to think critically about them and make sure they are relevant and reliable. Skim your potential sources and ask these questions to decide if they will be useful:

- What qualifies the author as an expert on the subject?
- Is the author likely to have a particular bias?
- If your topic requires current information, is your source up to date?
- Who is the audience for the source? What level of knowledge is assumed of them?
- What kind of evidence does the author use? Is it sufficient? Is it credible?

Electronic Sources

The Internet also makes it possible to search the online catalogs of other libraries that may contain sources your library does not. You can then request your library to get these sources for you through an interlibrary loan service. The most comprehensive of these online library sources is the Library of Congress at <http://www.loc.gov/>. If you use sources from the Internet, you must be especially careful to verify their validity because anyone can create a Web page and post information on it. The information printed in articles found in scholarly journals and books has gone through a process of review by experts in the field, whereas the information posted on Web pages may need additional checking and cross-referencing to confirm these sources. Ideally, information found on the Internet should be able to be corroborated by print sources.

Directories and E-texts There are authoritative Web resources such as "The Voice of the Shuttle" at <http://vos.ucsb.edu/> that provide links to thousands of sites with useful information on every aspect of literary study. For more general searches, you can use Yahoo at <http://www.yahoo.com/>, Google at <http://www.google.com/>, or AltaVista at <http://www.altavista.com/>, and then to narrow your focus, use Infoseek at <http://www.infoseek.com/>.

E-texts are another valuable category of resources that you can access online. These are older literary texts in public domain (not covered by copyright laws) and include plays by Shakespeare and other Renaissance playwrights, editions of the Bible, and many pre-twentieth-century works of literature. These can be found at *The English Server* (Carnegie Mellon University) at <http://english-www.hss.cmu.edu/> and at *The Electronic Text Center at the University of Virginia* at <http://etext.lib.virginia.edu/>.

Locating and Evaluating Information Before you begin searching on the Internet, it is important that you focus the topic of your research as exactly as possible. Conduct your search using a sequence or string of search terms (for example, "Mexican fiestas" and "expenditures") that will narrow the list of Web pages that most closely match your request. When you find a site that you wish to quote, make a careful note of the specific address because you will need to acknowledge it both within your paper and in the List of Works Cited (for information on documenting electronic sources, see Appendix B).

Remember that a great deal of valuable information is not available on the Web because many scholarly journals have not been translated into a digital format. Web pages must be evaluated in terms of their (1) timeliness (when was the content posted?), (2) relevance (can the information be verified by other sources?), (3) authoritativeness (what are the author's credentials?), and (4) lack of bias (is the purpose to persuade you to believe or do something?). The most reliable Web pages have links that provide information about the creator or at least give the e-mail address of the creator or web master.

Sample Student Essay

Notice how each section of the following student essay, "Fiestas Are a 'Time-Out' for Mexicans" on Octavio Paz's "Fiesta" (reprinted earlier in this chapter), develops ideas that support the thesis. We have annotated it to identify key rhetorical elements and to show the connections between assertions and evidence.

Fiestas Are a "Time-Out" for Mexicans

Fiestas are enjoyed by every social class and strata in Mexican society but seem to mean the most to those who have the least. The popularity of the fiesta can be understood, says Octavio Paz in his essay "Fiesta," if we realize that the Mexicans are "a ritual people." Although they are demonstrative and exhibit an openness foreign to other nationalities, this openness is a facade, a personality Mexicans adopt in order to function in society while their true selves are normally reserved and solitary. Perhaps the true meaning of fiestas

introduction identifies the work to be discussed and presents an interpretation or claim

can be seen in their role as a much needed "time-out" from the solitude of everyday life and from pervasive poverty.

Paz says that the mask of composure and propriety in which individual Mexicans disguise themselves is discarded during the extravagance of fiestas. All inhibitions and constraints that are part of normal Mexican life are shed at the inception of a fiesta and reassumed once it is over. It is the time, says Paz, when barriers between social classes and constraints in the relationships between the sexes are ritually discarded and people can express their suppressed identities. Paz's grasp of the psychological and cultural motivations for fiestas is quite extraordinary, and his style communicates the exuberance and chaotic mood of these celebrations.

support for the thesis or claim in the form of an analysis of the psychological reasons for the popularity of fiestas

observation of how Paz's style matches the content of his essay

The French sociologists who studied fiestas believe they owe their appeal to ritual sacrifice in which squandering produces regeneration to the fullest. The conspicuous display of fertility, life, and strength achieved at the expense of energy, money, and time, is comparable to a purging that allows new strength to manifest itself--"regeneration produces strength," says Paz. Comparable celebrations in American culture might include lavish weddings that reduce couples and their families to states of indebtedness for years to present a spectacle in which everyone can enjoy luxuries that they will conceivably never afford to do again. It is for this reason that couples who elope or marry in a quiet civil ceremony are not approved of as heartily as those who incur the expenses of a lavish reception with musicians, flowers, limousines, bridal parties and endless food and liquor.

alternative explanations for the popularity of fiestas

comparison of role fiestas play with lavish American weddings to show cross-cultural similarities

During fiestas, towns whose economies border on bankruptcy think nothing of squandering all their income for an evening's celebration.

support for the thesis or claim in the form of an analysis of the paradox of expenditure to forget poverty

Clearly no culture, says Paz, would spend so much time and money on events that were not integrally vital to its psychological and cultural well-being. The fiesta is an event apart from normal economic considerations. Money is spent as though it is in ample supply, although the Mexican economy is not healthy. In fact, several towns attribute their economic misery to the fact that since they have several patron saints, they must have several fiestas each year (and spend more money than they can ever accumulate in any one year). The excess of fiestas is a means by which communities can reassure themselves that all will be well in the next year.

During fiestas individuals lose themselves in the music, spectacle, and freedom from day-to-day restrictions on behavior. In this sense, fiestas can be seen as similar to the carnival of Mardi Gras celebrations in Brazil, Trinidad, and New Orleans. A person who lives in modest circumstances may enjoy a temporary illusion of wealth and carelessness. The rules that govern ordinary life are temporarily forgotten. In this metamorphosis, the average person may externalize desires and act on them without incurring consequences that would result during non-fiesta time.

comparison of role fiestas play with other similar celebrations in other countries

conclusion sums up essay's main points, restates thesis, and emphasizes the idea in the title

Reading Fiction

Works of literature communicate intense, complex, deeply felt responses to human experiences that speak to the heart, mind, body, and imagination.

Although the range of situations that stories can offer are limitless, what makes any particular story enjoyable depends on the writer's capacity to present an interesting plot, believable characters, and convincing dialogue. The nature of the original events matters less than the writer's ability to make us feel the impact of this experience intellectually, physically, and emotionally. The writer who uses language in skillful and precise ways allows us to share the perceptions and feelings of people different from ourselves. Works of fiction not only can take us to parts of the world we never have had the opportunity to visit, but deepen our emotional capacity to understand what life is like for others in conditions very different from our own. We become more conscious of ourselves as individual human beings when our imaginations and emotions are fully involved. We value a story when through it, we touch the aspirations, motives, and feelings of other people in diverse personal and cultural situations.

Works of fiction, as distinct from biographies and historical accounts, are imaginative works that tell a story. Fiction writers use language to recreate the emotional flavor of experiences and are free to restructure their accounts in ways that will create conflict and even build suspense. They can add to or take away from the known facts, expand or compress time, invent additional imaginative details, or even invent new characters or a narrator through whose eyes the story is told. Sometimes this narrator is the thinly disguised projection of the author, and the process of telling the story provides a chance to relive and understand events whose importance may not have been appreciated when they occurred. The narrators in these works function as an alter ego and allow the writer, through this persona, to be candid while seeming to simply be an imagined character in a fictionalized work (for example, Amy Tan's "Two Kinds," Chapter 3; and F. Scott Fitzgerald's "Winter Dreams," Chapter 6).

Evolution of the Short Story

The oldest works of fiction took the form of myths and legends that described the exploits of heroes and heroines, gods and goddesses, and supernatural beings. Other ancient forms of literature were *fables* (stating explicit lessons using animal characters) and *parables* (using analogies to suggest rather than state moral points or complex philosophical concepts) of the kind related by Jesus in *The New Testament.*

The modern short story differs from earlier narrative forms in emphasizing life as most people know it. The short story originated in the 19th century as a brief fictional prose narrative that was designed to be read in a single sitting. In a short story all the literary elements of plot, character, setting, and the author's distinctive use of language work together to create a single effect. Short stories usually describe the experiences of one or two characters over the course of a series of related events.

Realistic Stories This traditional kind of story presents sharply etched pictures of characters in real settings reacting to crises with which readers can identify. The emotions, reactions, perceptions, and motivations of the characters are explored in great detail. We can see these realistic elements in short stories ranging from Kate Chopin's "Désirée's Baby" (1899) to a recent story, "This Blessed House," written 100 years later (1999) by Jhumpa Lahiri.

Modern Fiction

Modern writers offer many different kinds of representations of reality. These can take the form of fact-based accounts of everyday life, as in Bessie Head's "Looking for a Rain God" (1977), or the story may reflect everyday relationships, as in Monique Proulx's "Feint of Heart" (1995). Stories can present realistic portraits of cultural conflict of the kind seen in the works of Tayeb Salih ("A Handful of Dates," 1978) and Sembene Ousmane ("Her Three Days," 1974). We can enjoy realistic comedies of social manners in works by Kurt Vonnegut, Jr. ("Who Am I This Time?" 1961) and Alberto Moravia ("Jewellery," 1956). Some writers address themselves to momentous historical events in the 20th century as does P'an Jen-mu in her depiction of the Cultural Revolution in China ("A Pair of Socks with Love," 1985). Other writers, reacting to the prevailing conventions of realistic fiction, create stories in which reality is not presented directly but is filtered through the perceptions, associations, and emotions of the main character.

Nonrealistic Stories In these nontraditional kinds of stories, the normal chronology of events is displaced by a psychological narrative that reflects the ebb and flow of the character's feelings and associations, as does Charlotte Perkins Gilman in "The Yellow Wallpaper" (1892). Nonrealistic stories may include fantastic, bizarre, or supernatural elements as well. We can see this alternative tradition illustrated in short fiction ranging from Edgar Allen Poe's "The Masque of the Red Death" (1842) through Machado de Assis's "A Canary's Ideas" (1895) to Olaf Stapledon's "Star Maker" (1937).

Postmodernist Fiction

This text offers works drawn from many different cultural contexts reflecting diverse styles and perspectives. Fiction produced in the second half of the 20th century differs in a number of important ways from that produced before World War II. Writers in this postmodern period avoid seeing events as having only one meaning and produce works that represent reality in unique, complex, and highly individual ways. Writers in the first half of the century, such as Katherine Mansfield ("Her First Ball" 1922), Ernest Hemingway ("Hills Like White Elephants" 1927), James Joyce ("Eveline" 1914), Eudora Welty ("A Worn Path" 1941), and F. Scott Fitzgerald ("Winter Dreams" 1922) saw artistic works of fiction as self-contained worlds governed by a central theme, idea, or principle. By contrast, postmodernist writers produce works that involve the reader in the interpretation of the text.

Suspicious of claims of a set reality, postmodernist fiction offers works which suggest reality is not capable of being reduced to a single meaning. Stories can take the form of a confusing or ambiguous reality, as in Milorad Pavić's "The Wedgwood Tea Set" (1998). Or, they may appear as hallucinatory episodes, as in Inés Arredondo's "The Shunammite" (1986). In other stories, history and fantasy merge so that magical or impossible scenes occur in the middle of apparently realistic narratives, as in Robert Fox's "A Fable" (1986), and Naguib Mahfouz's "Half a Day" (1989). Other works offer oblique descriptions, ambiguously related events, gaps, and frustatingly spare dialogue that call on the reader to interpret events. We can see these features in Kazuo Ishiguro's "A Family Supper" (1982).

Although the objectives and methods of writers in the second half of the 20th century vary widely, what identifies these works as postmodernist is a shift toward the concept of identity as being continously redefined and constructed through interactions in different social and cultural contexts. Not only are postmodernist works different in kind, but they encourage the reader to participate in ways that traditional stories do not. Whereas traditional works tended to guide, manipulate, and control the reader's response, putting the audience into a passive role, postmodernist writers create open works that encourage the reader to participate in interpreting the text. For example, in "Neighbors" by Raymond Carver (1989) and in "Where Are You Going, Where Have You Been?" (1965) by Joyce Carol Oates, the authors avoid using traditional omniscient narration in favor of producing a sense of open-endedness, leaving the reader free to interpret the future lives of the characters. These works suggest that reality is not capable of being reduced to a single predetermined meaning.

Characters in postmodern fiction must be understood in terms of specific situations, through interactions that can be construed in different ways by different readers. For example, in Albert Camus's "The Guest" (1957), the protagonist's identity is constantly redefined through interactions that depend on the moment-by-moment circumstances described in the story.

Postmodernists often reject defined characters and disrupt traditional narrative points-of-view through flashbacks (by contrast, traditional authors used flashbacks to bring out a consistent psychological characterization) that emphasize how reality shifts as the observer's position changes from moment to moment. We can see this approach in Louise Erdrich's "The Red Convertible" (1984) and in Inés Arredondo's "The Shunammite" (1986).

Gender, Class, and Culture Contemporary writers have a great deal to say about the forces that shape ethnic, sexual, and racial identity in different cultural contexts. Unlike traditional works that presented social dilemmas in order to resolve them, postmodernist works underscore the difficulty of integrating competing ethnic, sexual, and racial identities within a single culture. This is especially apparent in Amy Tan's "Two Kinds" (1989) and in Jhumpa Lahiri's "This Blessed House" (1999). Other writers address themselves to how different cultures define gender roles and class relationships in terms of power and powerlessness. These issues are explored in Margaret Atwood's "Happy Endings" (1983) and in Liliana Heker's "The Stolen Party" (1985). Works by contemporary writers reflect the pluralism and diversity of 21st-century society.

Analyzing a Work of Short Fiction

When you first read a literary text, you want to become aware of how you feel about the story (or poem or play) and try to discover why you feel the way you do. What challenges you, perplexes you, confuses you, or intrigues you? Would you want to read it again? What unanswered questions does the work raise? In what important ways does your view of the world differ from that of the author, and what might explain this difference?

Two techniques are quite useful in helping you discover the important connections you will focus on in your essay: annotating and freewriting. Annotations create a dialogue between you and the writer. By asking questions and making observations about any features of the text that strike you as interesting, you can begin to develop your own assertions about some aspect of the work that would not be obvious to most casual readers. The most interesting arguments about works of literature reveal this personal interpretation and substantiate what otherwise would be simply opinion by citing details that demonstrate the existence of this hitherto unnoticed pattern of meaning.

Your analysis can focus on almost any aspect of the story—plot, characters, setting, point of view, tone, style, symbolism or theme—as long as you support your interpretation by building a case that demonstrates a pattern of relationships. The key questions to ask about each literary feature include:

1. Characters—Who is the main character and what motivates his or her actions? With which other characters do their desires bring them into conflict?
2. Setting—How does the location in which the story is set amplify or underscore its meaning?
3. Point of view (voice and tone)—Who is telling the story? How would you characterize the voice you hear—as a participant or as an observer? How

much does this person seem to know about what goes on in the mind(s) of one or more of the characters? What is their attitude toward the events they describe?

4. Language (style)—Is the style in which the story is written accessible or artificial? Does the author use words that are mostly literal or highly metaphorical? What images and metaphors accentuate the meaning of the story and add significance?
5. Plot (conflict and how it is expressed in the title)—What elements in the story are designed to enhance suspense or at least make the reader curious as to what will happen next? How is the story shaped to build up to a moment of crisis? How is this crisis related to the idea expressed in the title?
6. Symbolism—Do any objects or elements in the story stand out from their literal contexts and suggest additional dimensions of meaning (political, cultural, religious, psychological)?
7. Theme—How do the experiences undergone by the characters, and their reactions to them, illuminate the idea expressed in the title?

For example, consider the following story "Cairo Is a Small City" by Nabil Gorgy, along with the marginal notes (or student annotations) that raise questions and identify details that suggest the existence of a pattern that might be stated as a thesis.

Nabil Gorgy

Nabil Gorgy was born in Cairo in 1944 and studied civil engineering at Cairo University. After working as an engineer in New York City, he returned to Cairo, where he runs his own art gallery and writes. His interests in mysticism, Egyptology, and Sufi traditions are reflected in his novel, The Door *(1981). More recently, he has written a collection of short fiction* The Slave's Dream and Other Stories *(1991) reissued in 1998. In "Cairo Is a Small City," translated by Denys Johnson-Davies (1983), an upper-class Egyptian engineer falls victim to an age-old Bedouin tradition. Derived from the Arabic word* bedu, *the name Bedouin means "inhabitant of the desert" and refers to nomadic tribes who live in the vast expanses of the deserts of Arabia, as well as in the Sinai and in the Negev. They follow a traditional way of life, based on Islam, journeying by camel from oasis to oasis, accompanied by herds of sheep and goats, and migrate continuously in the quest to survive. The hardships of the desert have produced a people who both value hospitality and view breaches of trust as not easily forgiven.*

in what sense is Cairo "small" since actually it is quite large?

Cairo Is a Small City

On the balcony of his luxury flat Engineer Adil Salim stood watching some workmen putting up a new building across the wide street along the centre of which was a spacious garden. The building was at the foundations stage, only the concrete foundations and some of the first-floor columns having been completed. A young ironworker with long hair was engaged on bending iron rods of various dimensions. Adil noticed that the young man had carefully leant his Jawa motorcycle against a giant crane that crouched at rest awaiting its future tasks. "How the scene has changed!" Adil could still remember the picture of old-time master craftsmen, and of the workers who used to carry large bowls of mixed cement on their calloused shoulders.

The sun was about to set and the concrete columns of a number of new constructions showed up as dark frameworks against the light in this quiet district at the end of Heliopolis.

As on every day at this time there came down into the garden dividing the street a flock of sheep and goats that grazed on its grass, and behind them two bedouin women, one of whom rode a donkey, while the younger one walked beside her. As was his habit each day, Adil fixed his gaze on the woman walking in her black gown that not so much hid as emphasized the attractions of her body, her waist being tied round with a red band. It could be seen that she wore green plastic slippers on her feet. He wished that she would catch sight of him on the balcony of his luxurious flat; even if she did so, Adil was thinking, those bedouin had a special code of behaviour that differed greatly from what he was used to and rendered it difficult to make contact with them. What, then, was the reason, the motive, for wanting to think up some way of talking to her? It was thus that he was thinking, following her with his gaze as she occasionally chased after a lamb that was going to be run over by a car or a goat left far behind the flock.

the customs of the Bedouins are not those of the urbanites of Cairo

Adil, who was experienced in attracting society women, was aware of his spirit being enthralled: days would pass with him on the balcony, sunset after sunset, as he watched her without her even knowing of his existence.

Adil character-ized as confi-dent, a ladies' man, in charge of his own fate

Had it not been for that day on which he had been buying some fruit and vegetables from one of the shopkeepers on Metro Street, and had not the shopkeeper seen another bedouin woman walking behind another flock, and had he not called out to her by name, and had she not come, and had he not thrown her a huge bundle of waste from the shop, after having flirted with her and fondled her body—had it not been for that day, Adil's mind would not have given birth to the plan he was determined, whatever the cost, to put through, because of that woman who had bewitched his heart.

As every man, according to Adil's philosophy of life, had within him a devil, it was sometimes better to follow this devil in order to placate him and avoid his tyranny. Therefore Engineer Adil Salim finally decided to embark upon the terrible, the unthinkable. He remembered from his personal history during the past forty years that such a temporary alliance with this devil of his had gained him a courage that had set him apart from the rest of his colleagues, and through it he had succeeded in attaining this social position that had enabled him to become the owner of this flat whose value had reached a fig-

Adil's courage in establishing con-tact with the Bedouin girl rests on his past acts of daring

ure which he avoided mentioning even in front of his family lest they might be upset or feel envy.

Thus, from his balcony on the second floor in Tirmidhi Street, Engineer Adil Salim called out in a loud voice "Hey, girl!" as he summoned the one who was walking at the rear of the convoy. When the flock continued on its way without paying any attention, he shouted again: "Hey, girl—you who sell sheep," and before the girl moved far away he repeated the word "sheep." Adil paid no attention to the astonishment of the doorman, who had risen from the place where he had been sitting at the entrance, thinking that he was being called. In fact he quietly told him to run after the two bedouin women and to let them know that he had some bread left over which he wanted to give them for their sheep.

From the balcony Adil listened to the doorman calling to the two women in his authoritative Upper Egyptian accent, at which they came to a stop and the one who was riding the donkey looked back at him. Very quickly Adil was able to make out her face as she looked towards him, seeking to discover what the matter was. As for the young girl, she continued on behind the flock. The woman was no longer young and had a corpulent body and a commanding look which she did not seek to hide from him. Turning her donkey round, she crossed the street separating the garden from his building and waited in front of the gate for some new development. Adil collected up all the bread in the house and hurried down with it on a brass tray. Having descended to the street, he went straight up to the woman and looked at her. When she opened a saddlebag close by her leg, he emptied all the bread into it.

"Thanks," said the woman as she made off without turning towards him. He, though, raising his voice so that she would hear, called out, "And tomorrow too."

During a period that extended to a month Adil began to buy bread which he did not eat. Even on those days when he had to travel away or to spend the whole day far from the house, he would leave a large paper parcel with the doorman for him to give to the bedouin woman who rode the donkey and behind whom walked she for whom the engineer's heart craved.

Adil acts to maintain contact

Because Adil had a special sense of the expected and the probable, and after the passing of one lunar month, and in his place in front of the building, with the bread on the brass tray, there occurred that which he had been wishing would happen, for the woman riding the donkey had continued on her way and he saw the other, looking around her carefully before crossing the road, ahead of him, walking towards him. She was the most beautiful thing he had set eyes on. The speed of his pulse almost brought his heart to a stop. How was it that such beauty was to be found without it feeling embarrassed at ugliness, for after it any and every thing must needs be so described? When she was directly in front of him, and her kohl-painted eyes were scrutinizing him, he sensed a danger which he attributed to her age, which was no more than twenty. How was it that she was so tall, her waist so slim, her breasts so full, and how was it that her buttocks swayed so enticingly as she turned away and went off with the bread, having thanked him? His imagination became frozen even though she was still close to him: her pretty face with the high cheekbones, the fine nose and delicate lips, the silver, crescent-shaped earrings, and the necklace that graced her bosom? Because such beauty was "beyond the permissible," Adil went on thinking about Salma—for he had got to know her name, her mother having called her by it in order to hurry her back lest the meeting between the lovers be prolonged.

Adil disregards recurring feelings of danger that things are not as they appear

Adil no longer troubled about the whistles of the workers who had now risen floor by floor in the building opposite him, being in a state of infatuation, his heart captured by this moonlike creature. After the affair, in relation to himself, having been one of boldness, to end in seeing or greeting her, it now became a matter of necessity that she turn up before sunset at the house so that he might not be deprived of the chance of seeing her. So it was that Engineer Adil Salim fell in love with the beautiful bedouin girl Salma. And just as history is written by historians, so it was that Adil and his engineering work determined the history of this passion in the form of a building each of whose columns represented a day and each of whose floors was a month. He noted that, at the completion of twenty-eight days and exactly at full moon, Salma would come to him in place of her mother to take the bread. And so, being a structural engineer, he began to observe the moon, his yearning increasing when it was in eclipse and his spirits sparkling as its fullness drew near till, at full moon, the happiness of the lover was completed by seeing the beloved's face.

construction project represents in material form his seven-month quest of the girl

During seven months he saw her seven times, each time seeing in her the same look she had given him the first time: his heart would melt, all resolution would be squeezed out of him and that fear for which he knew no reason would be awakened. She alone was now capable of granting him his antidote. After the seventh month Salma, without any preamble, had talked to him at length, informing him that she lived with her parents around a spring at a distance of an hour's walk to the north of the airport, and that it consisted of a brackish spring alongside which was a sweet one, so that she would bathe in the first and rinse herself clean in the other, and that there were date palms around the two springs, also grass and pasturage. Her father, the owner of the springs and the land around them, had decided to invite him and so tomorrow "he'll pass by you and invite you to our place, for tomorrow we attend to the shearing of the sheep."

Adil gave the lie to what he was hearing, for it was more than any stretch of the imagination could conceive might happen.

the shearing of the sheep could be considered ironic once we know Adil's fate

The following day Adil arrived at a number of beautifully made tents where a vast area of sand was spread out below date palms that stretched to the edge of a spring. Around the spring was gathered a large herd of camels, sheep and goats that spoke of the great wealth of the father. It was difficult to believe that such a place existed so close to the city of Cairo. If Adil's astonishment was great when Salma's father passed by him driving a new Peugeot, he was yet further amazed at the beauty of the area surrounding this spring. "It's the land of the future," thought Adil to himself. If he were able to buy a few *feddans* now he'd become a millionaire in a flash, for this was the Cairo of the future. "This is the deal of a lifetime," he told himself.

the world of the Bedouins seems outside the world of Cairo

feddan = approximately one acre

Adil's desire for Salma and greed for her tribe's landholdings

On the way the father asked a lot of questions about Adil's work and where he had previously lived and about his knowledge of the desert and its people. Though Adil noticed in the father's tone something more than curiosity, he attributed this to the nature of the bedouin and their traditions.

As the car approached the tents Adil noticed that a number of men were gathered under a tent whose sides were open, and as the father and his guest got out of the car the men turned round, seated in the form of a horse-shoe. With the father sitting down and seating Engineer Adil Salim alongside him, one of the sides of the horse-shoe was completed. In front of them sat three men on whose faces could be seen the marks of time in the form of interlaced wrinkles.

The situation so held Adil's attention that he was unaware of Salma except when she passed from one tent to another in the direction he was looking and he caught sight of her gazing towards him.

what makes the story ironic and sad is that Adil truly loves Salma

The man who was sitting in a squatting position among the three others spoke. Adil heard him talking about the desert, water and sheep, about the roads that went between the oases and the *wadi,* the towns and the springs of water, about the bedouin tribes and blood ties; he heard him talking about the importance of protecting these roads and springs, and the palm trees and the dates, the goats and the milk upon which the suckling child would be fed; he also heard him talk about how small the *wadi* was in comparison to this desert that stretched out endlessly.

wadi = a streambed which fills up during the rainy season

In the same way as Adil had previously built the seven-storey building that represented the seven months, each month containing twenty-eight days, till he would see Salma's face whenever it was full moon, he likewise sensed that this was the tribunal which had been set up to make an enquiry with him into the killing of the man whom he had one day come across on the tracks between the oases of Kharga and Farshout. It had been shortly after sunset when he and a friend, having visited the iron ore mines in the oases of Kharga had, instead of taking the asphalt road to Assiout, proceeded along a rough track that took them down towards Farshout near to Kena, as his friend had to make a report about the possibility of repairing the road and of extending the railway line to the oases. Going down from

the contrast between Adil's impulsive murder and the careful consideration by the Bedouins of his crime

Adil's daring stems from his sense of having evaded punishment

the high land towards the *wadi,* the land at a distance showing up green, two armed men had appeared before them. Adil remembered how, in a spasm of fear and astonishment, of belief and disbelief, and with a speed that at the time he thought was imposed upon him, a shot had been fired as he pressed his finger on the trigger of the revolver which he was using for the first time. A man had fallen to the ground in front of him and, as happens in films, the other had fled. As for him and his friend, they had rushed off to their car in order to put an end to the memory of the incident by reaching the *wadi.* It was perhaps because Adil had once killed a man that he had found the courage to accept Salma's father's invitation.

Adil's tragic flaw of conceit

they used the girl as bait to trap Adil into coming to them

"That day," Adil heard the man address him, "with a friend in a car, you killed Mubarak bin Rabia when he went out to you, Ziyad al-Mihrab being with him."

This was the manner in which Engineer Adil Salim was executed in the desert north-west of the city of Cairo: one of the men held back his head across a marble-like piece of stone, then another man plunged the point of a tapered dagger into the spot that lies at the bottom of the neck between the two bones of the clavicle.

the paradox of the "small city" is that Adil was actually a pawn in the Bedouin's plan for revenge

Writing About Fiction

After this first reading, you may wish to free-write for a few minutes to explore the relationship between details you discovered or read the story a second time and make additional annotations that illuminate any aspect of the story in terms of the list of literary elements (described on pages 22–23). Based on the first and second readings of the story and the annotations, a student believed she had discovered an interesting pattern of details to support the following claim or thesis:

> **Thesis:** Gorgy utilizes the title, foreshadowing, and the characterization of Adil Salim to prepare the reader to accept a surprise ending.

She noted that her annotations raised some interesting points and suggested how an interpretive essay on Gorgy's story might be developed. She noted that her observations grouped themselves into different categories having to do with (1) the meaning of the title, (2) Gorgy's characterization of his protagonist, Adil Salim, and (3) the motivation of the Bedouins to capture and punish a murderer of one of their own.

These categories proved useful in helping to organize the annotations in order to write her first draft. Each of the divisions presents one phase of the argument that supports the thesis or claim stated in the introduction of the final paper (see the sample student essay, "Two Different Worlds in Nabil Gorgy's 'Cairo Is a Small City.'")

Using Paraphrases and Quotes as Evidence

The most typical and useful pattern to follow is to state the reason why you believe your interpretation is credible, and then present evidence in the form of quotes or paraphrases from the work that prove and explain your points.

Paraphrases Paraphrasing is a restatement of an author's ideas in your own words. Unlike a plot summary, which is a concise description of the characters and events in the story, paraphrases attempt to convey the complexity and flavor of the ideas in the original text. Paraphrasing is something of an art because it involves representing a passage in your own words without projecting your own spin onto the original. A paraphrase from the work serves as evidence that proves and explains your interpretation.

For example, a student paraphrased the following statement, "It was perhaps because Adil had once killed a man that he had found the courage to accept Salma's father's invitation," as evidence to explain her claim that Gorgy uses foreshadowing to signal a surprise ending:

> Adil believes he is beyond the reach of Bedouin justice and is the master of his own fate.

Quotations Quotations from the work are indispensable in proving and explaining the points you wish to make. They let your readers hear the voice of the writer at key points in your argument. Be careful not to overuse quotations as you do not want your paper to become a patchwork of stitched-together quotations. The quotes you choose should demonstrate a pattern of evidence that supports your interpretation. For example, the student's claim that Gorgy foreshadows the outcome of the story is supported by an analysis of the main character Adil's reaction to the Bedouin girl, illustrated by a short quote:

> . . . the feeling of danger did not stop there, since every time Adil saw Salma in the next seven months, that feeling of fear for which he knew no reason would be awakened.

Brief quotations (of no more than four lines) are normally run into the text and enclosed in double quotation marks. Longer quotations (more than four lines) are separated from the text, indented 1 inch from the left margin, and reproduced without quotation marks. These block quotations are normally introduced with a colon (:). Quotations must be accurate. If you need to omit part of a passage to integrate it into your text, replace the omitted segment with an ellipsis mark, or three spaced periods. Here is an example from the student's paper:

> Gorgy lets the reader know that Adil had no control over the situation when he tells us "had it not been for that day on which he had been buying fruit . . . and had not the shopkeeper seen another Bedouin woman. . . ."

Outlining Before Writing a Rough Draft

To see more clearly how the analysis and interpretation of key passages can support your claim, it is often helpful to prepare a short outline stating the points you wish to make, and identifying the specific sources within the text that will serve as evidence. Here is the outline a student prepared for her essay, "Two Different Worlds in Nabil Gorgy's 'Cairo Is a Small City'":

1. Introduction: plot summary of the story--Gorgy's use of three literary elements (title, foreshadowing, characterization) to suggest the surprise ending.
2. Section 1: the paradox implicit in the title--Cairo is "small" because Adil Salim cannot escape his fate.
3. Section 2: psychology of Adil Salim, guilty and fearful--shown in his meetings with Salma and her father.
4. Section 3: Gorgy's ironic characterization of Adil Salim--revealed as a victim who believed himself to be in control of his fate.
5. Conclusion: restating claim--supported by analysis of strategies Gorgy uses to make readers empathize with Adil, be surprised at the ending, but agree he deserves his fate.

Notice how the final paper develops the claim stated in the introduction by drawing on the annotations, the observations that refer to the literary elements, supporting paraphrases and quotations, and the outline:

"Two Different Worlds in Nabil Gorgy's 'Cairo Is a Small City'"

"Cairo Is a Small City," by Nabil Gorgy, is the tale of Adil Salim, an engineer in the booming city of Cairo. Over time, Adil falls in love with a young Bedouin woman named Salma. However, this love eventually leads to the death of Adil at the hands of a Bedouin tribe. Gorgy utilizes the title, foreshadowing, and the characterization of Adil Salim to alert the reader to the ultimate outcome of the story.

plot summary of story

claim emphasizes technical elements that alert the reader to ultimate outcome

The title of a story can alert the reader to what the story is about. "Cairo Is a Small City" is no exception. By calling Cairo a "small city," Gorgy creates a paradox that sparks the interest of the reader. At first glance, the title "Cairo Is a Small City" seems

title significant in shedding light on surprising consequences

odd, given that Cairo is quite large. However, after analyzing the story, the reader discovers Gorgy's true meaning of a "small city." When Adil is taken to the Bedouin encampment, the tribesman talks about "how small the *wadi* was in comparison to this desert that stretched out endlessly." By mentioning this detail, Gorgy suggests that although Adil thinks the modern city of Cairo is all there is (and that he is all-important) he is actually insignificant in the grand scheme of things. This insignificance is shown by the impersonal, matter of fact way that Gorgy describes Adil's execution: "one of the men held back his head across a marble-like piece of stone, then another man plunged the point of a tapered dagger into the spot that lies at the bottom of the neck between the two bones of the clavicle."

The second literary technique Gorgy uses to alert the reader to the ultimate outcome of the story is foreshadowing. Authors use foreshadowing to subliminally signal the reader about the events to follow and to accept an otherwise shocking ending. The first example of foreshadowing is the recurrent presence of a feeling of danger or fear whenever Adil comes in contact with Salma. The first time Adil came close to Salma, "he sensed a danger which he attributed to her age, which was no more than twenty." The feeling of danger did not stop there, since every time Adil saw Salma in the next seven months, "that feeling of fear for which he knew no reason would be awakened." These feelings of fear alert the reader that this story will not have a happy ending. The second example of foreshadowing that Gorgy uses was when he describes Adil's ride over to the Bedouin camp. Along the way, Salma's father interrogates Adil and, "though Adil noticed in the father's tone something more than curiosity, he attributed this to the nature of the Bedouin and their

two instances where foreshadowing suggests a crime has been committed and punishment is awaiting Adil

first example—Adil's inexplicable anxiety over seven months when seeing Salma

second example—Adil treated as a suspect being interrogated rather than prospective bridegroom

traditions." By telling the reader there was "something more than curiosity" in the father's tone, Gorgy alerts the reader that the Bedouins have ulterior motives.

Gorgy's characterization of Adil is that of someone who believes he is master of his fate but is merely a pawn

The final technique Gorgy uses to alert the reader to the outcome of the story is through the characterization of Adil. Gorgy portrays him as a victim of fate, that is, as someone with no control over the events in his life.

The effect of this depiction is to make the reader empathize with Adil. This is first evident when Gorgy describes the circumstances in which Adil hatched the plan to meet the beautiful Bedouin girl (a relationship that ultimately leads to his death). Gorgy lets the reader know that Adil had no control over the situation when he tells us "had it not been for that day on which he had been buying fruit . . . and had not the shopkeeper seen another Bedouin woman . . . and had he not called out to her by name, and had she not come. . . ."

Another way that Gorgy depicts Adil as a victim of fate is by leading the reader to conclude that the Bedouins were in control the whole time and that Adil was merely a pawn in their plan for revenge. The reader thus becomes like Adil and represses contradictory clues because he or she wants a happy ending. At the end, the reader learns that the Bedouins lured Adil to their camp in order to kill him for murdering one of their tribesmen. Throughout the story Adil believed he had a "special sense of the expected and the probable" but in reality, the Bedouins were setting him up for over seven months. The shock of the ending stems from the readers' sense of complacency in identifying with Adil. Although we may feel his fate is warranted, we come to see him as an amoral adventurer who nonetheless is truly in love. Ironically, Adil believes he is beyond the reach of Bedouin justice and the master of

conclusion restates the pattern stated in the thesis or claim and accentuates the irony of the surprise ending

his own fate, but because of Gorgy's skill in creating his title, use of foreshadowing, and his characterization of Adil, we come to see him as merely a pawn in the Bedouin's game.

Reading Poetry

Poetry differs from other genres by achieving its effects with fewer words, compressing details into carefully organized forms in which each sound, word, and image must work together to create a single intense experience. Poetry uses language in ways that communicate experience rather than simply giving information.

Differences Between Poetry and Prose

The difference between prose and poetry emerges quite clearly when you compare a stanza from Grace Caroline Bridges's poem, "Lisa's Ritual, Age 10" (Chapter 5) with the same words punctuated as a sentence in prose:

> The wall is steady while she falls away: first the hands lost arms dissolving feet gone the legs disjointed body cracking down the center like a fault she falls inside slides down like dust like kitchen dirt slips off the dustpan into noplace a place where nothing happens, nothing ever happened.

Notice how in a stanza from the poem the arrangement of the words and lines creates an entirely different relationship:

The wall is steady
while she falls   away:
first the hands   lost
arms dissolving   feet gone
the legs dis-   jointed
body cracking down
the center like a fault
she falls inside
slides down like
dust   like kitchen dirt
slips off
the dustpan into
noplace
a place where
nothing happens,
nothing ever happened.

The way the words are arranged communicates the experience of the child's detachment, alienation, and sense of shock while the same words in prose merely describe it. Each detail, coupled with the way the words are arranged on the page, stands for feelings and ideas too complex for direct statement.

Because it communicates an extraordinarily compressed moment of thought, feeling, or experience, poetry relies on figurative language, connotation, imagery, sound, and rhythm. Poetry evokes emotional associations through images whose importance is underscored by a rhythmic beat or pulse. Most people are familiar with poetry in the form of song lyrics such as Bruce Springsteen's "Streets of Philadelphia" (Chapter 8) without realizing that many of the qualities we appreciate (intricate patterns of sound and rhyme, amplified by the music in the verse, that tell a story and communicate emotion) are the same as in traditional poetry.

Patterns of sounds and images emphasize and underscore distinct thoughts and emotions, appealing simultaneously to the heart, mind, and imagination. The rhythmic beat provides the sensuous element, coupled with imagery that appeals to the senses and touches the heart. At the same time, the imagination is stimulated through the unexpected combinations and perceptions through figurative language (similes, metaphors, personification) that allow the reader to see things in new ways. Because these effects work simultaneously, the experience of reading a poem is concentrated and intense.

Kinds of Poetry

Like fiction, poems may have a narrator (called a speaker), a particular point of view, and a distinctive tone and style. Every poem is a projection of a single human voice with unifying properties that hold it together. The speaker's relationship with the events and scenes described in the poem may be of several kinds.

1. In *lyric* or *reflective poetry* we seem to overhear the thoughts of the speaker. This poetry is subjective, psychological, and personal and usually takes the form of a brief intense expression of the speaker's mood. The personality of the speaker is created through the music of the verse, its diction and imagery. For example, in Rita Dove's "The Wake" (Chapter 3), we experience directly and intimately how much the speaker misses her mother. This focus on feelings and perception from the inside is characteristic of lyric poetry. Although most lyric poems relate crises of a very personal nature, in some poems, such as "A Worker Reads History" by Bertolt Brecht (Chapter 6), the voice we hear speaks for a group rather than for an individual.

   So too, in Marge Piercy's "The Nine of Cups" (Chapter 6), the repeated incantations transcend the merely personal and bring about an identification with those who are oppressed. Whether the voice we hear represents an individual or a whole community, we get a very precise sense of the speaker's personality, mood, and reactions.

2. *Narrative poems* tend to be objective, centering around important events, and tell a story about an event that has changed the speaker's perspective or relationship with others. Narrative poems preserve a certain emotional detachment by relating events that have occurred in the past. For example, Cathy Song's poem "The Youngest Daughter" (Chapter 3) is shaped as an account of a long-brewing crisis in the life of the speaker as to whether she should continue caring for her mother or seek independence.

   Narrative poems hark back to the older forms of epics, romances, and ballads. For example, we can see features of the ballad in the repeated refrains, varied repetition, and tag-lines of Bruce Springsteen's "Streets of Philadelphia" (Chapter 8). Typically, the narrative structure of these poems enables us to understand how the events described in them have changed the lives of the characters.

3. The *descriptive* elements of poetry become dominant in poems where the speaker describes things in terms of what the eye sees such as colors, shapes, and other visual details. The intensity and depth with which the scene is described suggests that the physical sensuous elements of the environment and the faculty of seeing things as exactly as possible is a virtue in itself. In these poems, it is the speaker's response to the setting or the aspect of the speaker's sensibility that emerges through the description that is most important. In "Red Azalea on the Cliff" by Xu Gang (Chapter 4), the speaker responds with awe to the sight of a delicate red azalea surviving on a wind-whipped mountainside. The effects of descriptive poetry range from simple visual images stated directly, as in Xu Gang's poem, to the complex descriptive effects of a poem by Garrett Hongo, "Who Among You Knows the Essence of Garlic?" (Chapter 3) that depend on transposing sense impressions achieved by presenting an appeal to one sense in terms of another.

4. Whereas lyric poetry focuses on personal reflections, narrative poetry tells a story through actions and events, and descriptive poetry sees the external world in realistic terms, *dramatic poetry* includes characters in addition to the speaker, and dialogue that often takes the form of confrontations that are "staged" in ways that suggest events are happening at the moment. In these poems, we feel that we have begun to eavesdrop in the middle of a dramatic situation. For example, in Muriel Rukeyser's "Myth" (Chapter 5), we hear two voices arguing in a moment of dramatic conflict that highlight the sexist attitude of the tragic hero, Oedipus, and the sarcastic comments of the legendary Sphinx.

   Dramatic poems are constructed to lead up to a climax by building up suspense, as does Gregory Corso in "Marriage" (Chapter 5). He creates an illusion of reality that presents living figures who move, converse, and affect one another (would be in-laws, friends, and other interested spectators discussing the likelihood of the speaker getting married) and engage the reader's interest more effectively than would a narrative account of the same situation.

Although it has a public use, poetry mainly unfolds private joys, tragedies, and challenges common to all people such as the power of friendship, value of self-discovery, bondage of outworn traditions, delight in nature's beauty, devastation of war, achievement of self-respect, and despair of failed dreams. The universal elements in poetry bridge gaps in time and space and tie us together by expressing emotions shared by all people in different times, places, and cultures.

Analyzing Poetry

Learning to enjoy what poetry has to offer requires the reader to pay close attention to specific linguistic details of sound and rhythm, connotations of words, and the sensations, feelings, memories, and associations that these words evoke. After reading a poem, preferably aloud, try to determine who the speaker is. What situation does the poem describe? How might the title provide insight into the speaker's predicament? What attitude do you feel the poet projects toward the events described in the poem? Observe the language used by the speaker. What emotional state of mind is depicted? You might look for recurrent references to a particular subject and see whether these references illuminate some psychological truth. What follows is Ted Hughes's "Pike" (that a student has annotated):

a pike is a large slender voracious fresh-water fish (dictionary)

Pike

TED HUGHES

voice you hear is that of a naturalist

alludes to jungle predator the tiger

Pike, three inches long, perfect
Pike in all parts, green tigering the gold.
Killers from the egg: the malevolent aged grin.
They dance on the surface among the flies.

details emphasize malevolence as a principle in nature

the pike described scientifically-dimensions, habitat,

Or move, stunned by their own grandeur,
Over a bed of emerald, silhouette
Of submarine delicacy and horror.
A hundred feet long in their world.

In ponds, under the heat-struck lily pads—
Gloom of their stillness:
Logged on last year's black leaves, watching upwards.
Or hung in an amber cavern of weeds

the grin anthropomorphizes the pike

The jaws' hooked clamp and fangs
Not to be changed at this date;
A life subdued to its instrument;
The gills kneading quietly, and the pectorals.

the experience of keeping pike behind glass shifts the speaker's point of view

pike become predatory and cannibalistic

Three we kept behind glass,
Jungled in weed: three inches, four,
And four and a half: fed fry to them—
Suddenly there were two. Finally one

With a sag belly and the grin it was born with.
And indeed they spare nobody.
Two, six pounds each, over two feet long,
High and dry and dead in the willow-herb—

speaker finds two dead pike by lake side, one half consumed by the other

One jammed past its gills down the other's gullet:
The outside eye stared: as a vice locks—
The same iron in this eye
Though its film shrank in death.

pike symbolizes nature not subject to human values

speaker describes nighttime fishing on a pond

primitive outlasts civilized structures and religion

A pond I fished, fifty yards across,
Whose lilies and muscular tench
Had outlasted every visible stone
Of the monastery that planted them—

speaker becomes terrified and is almost paralyzed with the thought of the pike's immensity

Stilled legendary depth:
It was as deep as England. It held
Pike too immense to stir, so immense and old
That past nightfall I dared not cast

geometrical proportion three inches equals one hundred feet

But silently cast and fished
With the hair frozen on my head
For what might move, for what eye might move.
The still splashes on the dark pond,

speaker brought into their world

staccato phrasing equals primitive

Owls hushing the floating woods
Frail on my ear against the dream
Darkness beneath night's darkness had freed,
That rose slowly towards me, watching.

predator (fisherman) becomes the prey, watcher now watched

takes us from detached objective viewpoint to terrified proximity

Writing About Poetry

Often the most useful way to approach an unfamiliar poem is to read and annotate it, and then summarize the action in your own words. This summary, combined with the annotations on details of imagery and structure, provides a good basis for formulating a thesis or claim. Consider the following summary a student wrote based on her reading of "Pike":

> Initially the speaker describes the small 3-inch pike that are being kept in some sort of fish tank and watches with amazement and horror as they devour each other. Their voracious behavior is so alarming that it suggests that they are many times more menacing in their world than they appear to us. Next, the speaker describes two fairly large pike he has discovered beside a lake where one has half eaten the other. Thus far the action of the poem still takes place on land, but in the last stanzas, the speaker describes a nighttime fishing expedition on a medium sized pond that is all that remains from an ancient monastery. As he sits there in the boat at night he imagines how large and old the pike must be in this pond and begins to feel apprehensive and thinks they are watching him.

Based on her annotations and summary, the student formulated the following thesis or claim:

Thesis: Ted Hughes's "Pike" focuses on an encounter between man and animal in order to dramatize the presence of dark, irrational forces at the edge of man's awareness.

After formulating this claim, she prepared a brief outline of the points she wanted to touch on in her analysis in roughly the same order she planned to develop her argument. The details drawn from her annotations and summary are necessary to support her claim and make her analysis more than simply an expression of her opinion.

1. Starts by being quite rational and scientific about the pike--details suggest careful observation.
2. Pike symbolize malevolence as a principle in nature--3-inch pike are 400 times more menacing in their world.
3. Speaker leaves the safe civilized world and moves from land into the pike's world--the first person pronoun reveals defensive stance.
4. Pike symbolize nature not subject to human values--speaker horrified while fishing at night--one-syllable words suggest being frozen in terror.

Notice how her final paper (which we have annotated to show the relationship between her thesis and the evidence she cites) closely follows the outline of points she planned to touch on.

An Encounter with the Irrational: An Explication of Ted Hughes's "Pike"

Ted Hughes's "Pike" (1960) focuses on an encounter between man and animal in order to dramatize the presence of dark, irrational forces at the edge of man's awareness. For Hughes, the universe presents a predatory visage of irrationality and violent death for which the cannibalistic pike are an apt symbol.

overview of the poem and thesis statement

Hughes proceeds for eight stanzas to give precise naturalistic details oncerning the various pike he has observed (e.g., "The jaws' hooked clamp and fangs"). Primarily, he relies on exact numerical descriptions ("Pike, three

evidence supporting the claim in the form of line-by-line analysis showing close observation of nature

inches long") to stress that he is an accurate observer; throughout the imagery is very concrete. Hughes meticulously records the various colors ("green tigering the gold") and types of vegetation ("last year's black leaves"). His careful choice of verb forms ensures that the pike are presented in characteristic actions from birth to cannibalism:

> Three we kept behind glass,
> Jungled in weed: three inches, four,
> And four and a half: fed fry to them--
> Suddenly there were two. Finally one
>
> With a sag belly and the grin it was born
> with.
> And indeed they spare nobody.

evidence in the form of analysis of the poem's structure

With the shift to more generalized images in the final three stanzas of "Pike," this rationalistic response to natural phenomena fails. The pike transcend scientific classification and become symbolic of a malevolent universe. The narrator's view of nature as subject to human standards and circumscribed by human concepts cannot be maintained before his intuitive perception of nature as a vastly superior and essentially inscrutable force totally alien and indifferent to man. These characteristics are already apparent in the first stanza of "Pike." The rest of the poem extends these qualities in proportion to the increasing uncontrollable dimensions of the pike. Immediately at birth, the pike are "killers from the egg." These voracious predators rise to the surface of the pond in a dance of death "among the flies." The mention of flies not only extends the image of death, but also magnifies the diabolic element of their world.

analysis of how the pike becomes symbolic

analysis of the mythic dimension to support the thesis

In the second stanza, Hughes adds another disturbing, yet fascinating dimension to the myth he is creating. In the pond, the pike are four-hundred times as destructive ("A hundred feet long in their world") as their actual size ("three inches long") suggests. If a similar scale holds to the end of the poem where the pike are "too immense to stir," the corresponding power they embody would be of a satanic and overwhelming proportion.

Since man's role, for Hughes, is diminished and his efforts are futile and weak when compared with the malevolence of the universe, the speaker's "I" appears only in the eighth stanza ("A pond I fished") and plays a very limited role. To convey his sense of a hostile universe of brute power, Hughes employs stark, terse phrasing in a staccato rhythm ("perfect/Pike in all parts") reminiscent of primitive incantations. He augments this atavistic quality by using numerous one-syllable words ("For what might move, for what eye might move") and entangles the entire poem in a heavy net of assonance and consonance ("that past nightfall I dared not cast").

stylistic analysis to support the thesis

Hughes sees the mystery in the pike as revealing a dynamism of the natural world which forms a barrier against man's egocentric and rationalistic tendencies. And, although the universe revealed by Hughes is an alien and terrifying one characterized by incessant violence and sinister permanence, he calls upon the reader to face the hellish nature of existence without faltering.

conclusion summarizing the analysis and restating the thesis

Reading Drama

Drama, unlike fiction and poetry, is meant to be performed on a stage. The text of a play includes dialogue (conversation between two or more characters)—or a monologue (lines spoken by a single character to the audience)—and the playwright's stage directions.

Although the dramatist makes use of plot, characters, setting, and language, the nature of drama limits the playwright to presenting the events from an objective point of view. There are other important differences between fiction and drama as well. The dramatist must restrict the action in the play to what can be shown on the stage in two or three hours. Because plays must hold the attention of an audience, playwrights prefer obvious rather than subtle conflicts, clearly defined sequences of action, and fast-paced exposition that is not weighed down by long descriptive or narrative passages. Everything in drama has to be shown directly, concretely, through vivid images of human behavior.

Dramatic Structure

The structure of most plays begins with an *introduction* or *exposition* that introduces the characters, shows their relationship to one another, and provides background information necessary for the audience (or reader) to understand the main conflict of the play. The essence of drama is conflict. Conflict is produced when an individual pursuing an objective meets with resistance either from another person, from society, or from nature, or is opposed by an internal aspect of his or her own personality. In the most effective plays, the audience can see the central conflict through the eyes of each character in the play. As the play proceeds, complications make the problem more difficult to solve and increase suspense as to whether the *protagonist* (main character) or the opposing force (referred to as the *antagonist*) will triumph. In the climax of the play, the conflict reaches the height of emotional intensity and one side achieves a decisive advantage over the other. This is often the moment of truth when characters must confront reality and cope with the crisis that has been developing. The end of the play (or conclusion) then explores the implications of the nature of the truth that has been realized and the consequences that will flow from this.

Origins of Western Drama

Drama in ancient Greece evolved from religious rituals to honor Dionysus, the god of wine and fertility. These festivals were held every December when the planting season was over. It first involved groups of perhaps 50 men and boys who sang and danced as a chorus circling about a temporary altar erected in the center of the threshing floor. The drama took the form of singing about the adventures of Dionysus and the startling and noble events associated with him. Somewhat later, the chorus acquired a leader, probably a local priest of the Cult of Dionysus, who impersonated the god. By the fifth century B.C., these rituals became more complex, had attracted spectators, and evolved into dramatic presentations that were the central feature of the annual festivals held in Athens. These religious origins of Western drama become important when we consider that the same emotions of awe and respect are hallmarks of ancient Greek tragedy. Aristotle (384–323 B.C.), in his *Poetics,* was the first to point out tragedy's ritual functions—to purge spectators of their own emotions of pity and fear through a vicarious identification with the fate of the characters, especially the tragic hero. These tragedies were based on the legends and characters in Greek mythology with which the audience was familiar. Because the spectators already knew the outcome, the focus of the drama shifted to more profound inquiries into psychological motivation and the nature of the "tragic flaw" that led to the hero's demise.

Plays were performed in open-air amphitheaters that were built into hillsides and could hold thousands of spectators. The circular area in which the actors performed was called the orchestra. Behind it was a raised platform that functioned as a stage, and a building called a skene that was used for costume changes and storing scenery. The skene could also serve as a temple or a house as part of the play's setting. In Athens, attendance at these plays was both a religious and civic duty, and the enormous size of these theaters suggest that most of the citizens did attend. Even businesses and courts were closed, and admission was subsidized for those who could not afford to pay. Dramas were presented over a three-day competition, beginning at dawn, and each dramatist presented four plays—three tragedies and one satyr play (a short spoof or comic burlesque on a Greek myth).

By modern standards, the way the actors (who were all men) appeared on stage looked unnatural because they wore masks carved from wood or fabricated from cloth, cork, or linen with facial expressions suited to the role they were playing, including those of the female characters. Inside these masks were small megaphones that allowed the actors to project their voices to the top levels of the amphitheater, over a quarter of a mile away. They also wore high-platform, thick-soled boots and large flowing robes to amplify their appearance. The best known dramatists of this period include Aeschylus, Sophocles, and Euripides.

Conflict as a Dramatic Device

The nature of the conflict embodied in plays varies from age to age and reveals underlying social values. Greek tragedies dramatize conflicts between human beings and the gods and led to the recognition of the role fate plays in preserving an underlying order of the universe. For example, an audience watching Sophocles's play, *Oedipus, the King,* would see how the workings of destiny combine with the protagonist's flawed judgment and excessive pride (referred to as a "tragic flaw") to precipitate his downfall. The action of Greek tragedies was confined, for the most part, to one location and a time span that rarely exceeded a day.

By contrast, the action in Shakespeare's plays can span years and can encompass places at great distances from each other within the same play. The emphasis in Shakespeare's tragedies is less on the inexorable workings of fate than on the tragic weaknesses within human beings that not only destroy them but those they love. Othello's jealousy and Hamlet's excessive intellectualizing are familiar examples of Shakespeare's depiction of human beings at war with themselves. Shakespeare saw dramatic conflict as being between strengths and weaknesses within a person's character, rather than between human beings and fate or between good and evil. These plays are compelling because we experience the predicament and emotions of the protagonist and at the same time gain an objective understanding of the situation as it appears to the other characters.

The focus of theater on the French and English stage in the next two centuries emphasizes the conflict between individuals and prevailing social norms and customs. Plays by Molière (*The Misanthrope,* 1666) and Richard Brinsley Sheridan (*School for Scandal,* 1777) satirize people whose eccentricities and personality flaws make them unable to fit into established society. The characters in these works are dramatized as social beings with humorous rather than tragic flaws. The conflicts in these plays assure the audience of a happy ending in which quarreling factions are reconciled and the values of society are reaffirmed.

Modern drama began as a reaction to the stilted conventions and superficial tone of 19th-century plays. Henrik Ibsen and George Bernard Shaw created realistic plays set in recognizable everyday environments that explored conflicts in the lives of ordinary people struggling with social institutions. In *A*

Doll's House (1879), *Ghosts* (1881), and *Hedda Gabler* (1890), Ibsen portrayed women protagonists as oppressed by the male-dominated societies in which they lived. In *Arms and the Man* (1894), *Major Barbara* (1905), and *Saint Joan* (1924), Shaw explored conflicts between individuals, usually women, and legal, political, economic, and military authorities of that era. The German playwright Bertolt Brecht continued to explore the conflict between individuals and the less-than-ideal world by assailing the economic and political causes and consequences of totalitarianism, war, and poverty in such well-known works as *The Three Penny Opera* (1928), *The Caucasian Chalk Circle* (1947), and *Mother Courage and Her Children* (1940). Unlike Ibsen and Shaw, Brecht sought to make the audience aware of the representational nature of what they were watching on the stage. In 19th-century Russia, Anton Chekhov created dramas (for example, *The Cherry Orchard,* 1904) that explored the psychological conflicts people experienced as they yearned to make real their personal visions of happiness. Later, American playwrights, including Eugene O'Neill, Tennessee Williams, Lorraine Hansberry, Arthur Miller, and Edward Albee, and recently John Guare, August Wilson, David Mamet, David Henry Hwang, Christopher Durang, and Wendy Wasserstein, among others, continue to explore the conflicts between personal dreams and reality.

Watching Versus Reading Dramas

Reading a script of a play or the screenplay for a film is a very different kind of experience from seeing these works performed on the stage or screen. When watching a play or movie, you are part of an audience whose collective reactions, whether tears or laughter, enhance your experience. Reading a play engages your imagination by requiring you to visualize what characters look like, how they move or speak, what their facial expressions, intonations, and gestures are, as well as the details of the setting that are already created in a theatrical production. So, in effect, you become all the actors as well as the director, set designer, and even the playwright. But, of course, reading a play can never replace watching a live stage production or a video of a performance.

When reading a play, you rely on what is essentially a script with dialogue and some description. From this, you can try to visualize what the characters look like and sound like, how they relate to one another, and how an audience might react to them. For example, try to imagine the following scene from *Hamlet, the Prince of Denmark* (the complete text is in Chapter 9), by William Shakespeare (Act I, Scene ii, lines 176–185):

HORATIO
My lord, I came to see your father's funeral.

HAMLET
I pray thee do not mock me, fellow student.
I think it was to see my mother's wedding.

HORATIO
Indeed, my lord, it followed hard upon.

HAMLET
Thrift, thrift, Horatio! The funeral baked meats
Did coldly furnish forth the marriage tables.
Would I had met my dearest foe in Heaven
Or ever I had seen that day, Horatio!
My father!—Methinks I see my father.

HORATIO
Oh, where, my lord?

HAMLET
In my mind's eye, Horatio.

How do you stage the scene in your mind? What do Hamlet and his friend Horatio look like? What reaction passes across Horatio's face when Hamlet appears, for a moment, to suggest that he actually sees his father, the deceased king? Previously, Horatio saw what he believed to be the ghost of Hamlet's father and now must decide whether to tell Hamlet. What do you imagine their voices sound like? How are they dressed and where do you imagine the action takes place? By visualizing each aspect of the scene, you bring it to life, becoming in effect, the actors, the producer, the director, set designer, and costume designer, and even to some extent, the playwright.

The ten plays (including the sample play for analysis, *Tea Party*) presented in this book will challenge you to enter the lives of people in greatly different cultures and historical eras, set in locations as diverse as Canada, Japan, the southern United States, Italy, the Czech Republic, Egypt, and ninth-century Denmark (by way of Elizabethan England).

Analyzing Drama

As with short fiction and poetry, the first reading should focus on your personal reactions that the play elicits. Toward which character did you feel most sympathetic? What intrigued, moved, or alarmed you about his or her predicament? When did you laugh or feel sad? Were there aspects about the situation that you found confusing? At the next level of analysis, you might begin to notice how the playwright defines the characters by the way they look or are described, how they speak, and how they dress. Most importantly, pay close attention to their reactions to whatever crisis (major or minor) confronts them and to the opinions and statements of other characters. As with fiction and poetry, you should feel free to annotate the text (jotting down your reactions in the margins), wonder about the characters' motivations, background, or history, and identify elements you think might transcend their literal function in the play and be symbolic.

Because every drama is based on a conflict, the single most useful exercise in reading an unfamiliar play is to formulate a sentence for each character stating (from their perspective) what they most desire, want to achieve, or seek to accomplish.

For example, in *Tea Party,* by Betty Keller (reprinted here), each of the two characters, Alma and Hester, share a common objective—to prolong the visits of casual acquaintances such as the paperboy and meter man, to provide some respite from their loneliness. Yet, embedded in this basic dramatic situation, Keller individualizes the sisters and provides insight into their motivations and perceptions.

Once the desires, intentions, and objectives of the characters have been identified, determine whether these goals bring the characters into conflict with each other, or whether there is some external force that prevents them from achieving what they wish. The presentation of this conflict may be apparent in the first few lines of the play or gradually may become apparent as new characters enter or as new facts are discovered. For example, here is how a student annotated Keller's play *Tea Party:*

Betty Keller

Betty Keller (1930–) has served as the founder and producer of the western Canadian writers' festival and workshop program, the Festival of the Written Arts, from 1983 to 1994. Her many unusual work experiences include jobs as a farmer, an insurance adjuster, and a prison matron. She has also taught at Simon Fraser University and the University of British Columbia. Tea Party *was originally included in a collection of short plays titled* Improvisations and Creative Drama *(1974). Keller has also written biographical and historical works, including* Sea Silver *(1996) and* Bright Seas and Pioneer Spirits *(1996). The predicament confronting the characters in this play occurs more frequently than we might think. Keller's most recent work is* Pauline Johnson: First Aboriginal Voice of Canada *(1999).*

Tea Party

Characters

ALMA EVANS: Seventy-five years old, small and spare framed. Her clothing is simple but not outdated, her grey hair cut short and neat. She walks with the aid of a cane, although she would not be classed as a cripple.

HESTER EVANS: Seventy-nine years old. There is little to distinguish her physically from her sister, except perhaps a face a little more pinched and pain-worn. She sits in a wheelchair; but although her legs may be crippled, her mind certainly is not.

sisters are handicapped to elicit sympathy and explains their dependency on visits from strangers

THE BOY: In his early teens, seen only fleetingly.

SCENE. *The sitting room of the Evans sisters' home. The door to the street is on the rear wall Upstage Left,*[1] *a large window faces the street Upstage Center. On the right wall is the door to the kitchen; on the left, a door to the remainder of the house. Downstage Left is an easy chair, Upstage Right a sofa, Downstage Right a tea trolley. The room is crowded with the knickknacks gathered by its inhabitants in three-quarters of a century of living.*

the set being one room shows how confined the sisters are—the window is their only link to the outside

(*At rise, Alma is positioning Hester's wheelchair Upstage Left. Alma's cane is on Hester's lap.*)

---

[1] *Upstage Left:* Stage directions refer to the actor's vantage point. "Right" refers to the left of the audience and "Left" refers to the right of the audience. The term "Downstage" refers to the front of the stage; "Upstage" refers to the back. The terms *down* and *up* originated when stages were tilted toward the audience in order to provide a full view for all spectators. [ed.]

HESTER. That's it.

> *(Alma takes her cane from Hester. They both survey the room.)*

ALMA. I think I'll sit on the sofa . . . at the far end.

HESTER. Yes. That will be cosy. Then he can sit on this end between us.

> *(Alma sits on the Downstage Right end of the sofa. They both study the effect.)*

ALMA. But then he's too close to the door, Hester!

> *(Hester nods, absorbed in the problem.)*

ALMA *(Moving to the Upstage Left end of sofa.)* Then I'd better sit here.

HESTER. But now he's too far away from me, Alma.

> *(Alma stands; both of them study the room again.)*

ALMA. But if I push the tea trolley in front of you, he'll have to come to you, won't he?

Alma reassures Hester's insecurities

HESTER. Oh, all right, Alma. You're sure it's today?

ALMA *(Pushing the tea trolley laden with cups and napkins, etc. to Hester.)* The first Thursday of the month.

connotations of the title are of a lost upper-class childhood they wish to perpetuate

HESTER. You haven't forgotten the chocolate biscuits?[2]

ALMA. No dear, they're on the plate. I'll bring them in with the tea.

> *(Goes to window, peering up the street to the Right.)*

HESTER. And cocoa?

ALMA. I remembered.

HESTER. You didn't remember for Charlie's visit.

ALMA. Charlie drinks tea, Hester. I didn't make cocoa for him because he drinks tea.

HESTER. Oh. He didn't stay last time anyway.

argument about the name of the ship reveals sibling rivalry

ALMA. It was a busy day. . . .

HESTER. Rushing in and out like that. I was going to tell him about father and the *Bainbridge* . . . and he didn't stay.

ALMA. What about the *Bainbridge?*

HESTER. Her maiden voyage out of Liverpool . . . when father was gone three months and we thought he'd gone down with her.

ALMA. That wasn't the *Bainbridge.*

details that show sisters live in the past

HESTER. Yes, it was. It was the *Bainbridge.* I remember standing on the dock in the snow when she finally came in. That was the year I'd begun first form, and I could spell out the letters on her side.

two ships are like the two sisters—one's engine is gone and the other limps into port

ALMA. It was her sister ship, the *Heddingham.*

HESTER. The *Bainbridge.* You were too young to remember. Let's see, the year was . . .

ALMA. Mother often told the story. It was the *Heddingham* and her engine broke down off Cape Wrath beyond the Hebrides.

---

[2] *chocolate biscuits:* chocolate cookies. [ed.]

HESTER. It was 1902 and you were just four years old.

ALMA. The *Heddingham,* and she limped into port on January the fifth.

HESTER. January the fourth just after nine in the morning, and we stood in the snow and watched the *Bainbridge* nudge the pier, and I cried and the tears froze on my cheeks.

ALMA. The *Heddingham.*

> despite their petty quarrel we get the impression they really care about each other

HESTER. Alma, mother didn't cry, you know. I don't think she ever cried. My memory of names and places is sharp so that I don't confuse them as some others I could mention, but sometimes I can't remember things like how people reacted. But I remember that day. There were tears frozen on my cheeks but mother didn't cry.

> mother doesn't show emotion sisters always had to depend on each other

ALMA (*Nodding.*) She said he didn't offer a word of explanation. Just marched home beside her.

HESTER (*Smiling.*) He never did say much. . . . Is he coming yet?

ALMA. No, can't be much longer though. Almost half past four.

HESTER. Perhaps you'd better bring in the tea. Then it will seem natural.

> they pretend they always have tea but it is really staged just for the visitor

ALMA. Yes dear, I know. (*Exits out door Upstage Right.*) Everything's ready.

HESTER. What will you talk about?

ALMA (*Re-entering with the teapot.*) I thought perhaps . . . (*Carefully putting down the teapot.*) . . . perhaps brother George!

HESTER. And the torpedo? No, Alma, he's not old enough for that story!

ALMA. He's old enough to know about courage. I thought I'd show him the medal, too.

> consider telling the story of their brother's tragic war experience but feel he won't appreciate it

(***She goes to the window, peers both ways worriedly, then carries on towards the kitchen.***)

HESTER. Not yet? He's late to-night. You're sure it's today?

ALMA. He'll come. It's the first Thursday. (*Exit.*)

HESTER. You have his money?

ALMA (*Returning with the plate of biscuits.*) I've got a twenty dollar bill, Hester.

> planning every detail of the paperboy's visit so he will have to return with change

HESTER. Alma!

ALMA. Well, we haven't used that one on him. It was Dennis, the last one, who always had change. We could get two visits this way, Hester.

HESTER. Maybe Dennis warned him to carry change for a twenty.

ALMA. It seemed worth a try. (*Goes to the window again.*) Are you going to tell him about the *Heddingham?*

HESTER. The *Bainbridge.* Maybe . . . or maybe I'll tell him about the day the Great War ended. Remember, Alma, all the noise, the paper streamers . . .

> their brother George was the one who mattered the most

ALMA. And father sitting silent in his chair.

HESTER. It wasn't the same for him with George gone. Is he coming yet?

ALMA. No dear, maybe he's stopped to talk somewhere. (*Looking to the right.*) ... No ... no, there he is, on the Davis' porch now!

HESTER. I'll pour then. You get the cocoa, Alma.

ALMA (*Going out.*) It's all ready, I just have to add hot water.

HESTER. Don't forget the marshmallows!

ALMA (*Reappearing.*) Oh, Hester, what if he comes in and just sits down closest to the door? He'll never stay!

HESTER. You'll have to prod him along. For goodness sakes, Alma, get his cocoa!

(*Alma disappears.*)

HESTER. He must be nearly here. He doesn't go to the Leschynskis, and the Blackburns don't get home till after six.

ALMA (*Returning with the cocoa.*) Here we are! Just in ...

(*The Boy passes the window. There is a slapping sound as the newspaper lands on the porch.*)

(*Alma and Hester look at the door and wait, hoping to hear a knock, but they both know the truth. Finally, Alma goes to the door, opens it and looks down at the newspaper.*)

ALMA. He's gone on by.

HESTER. You must have had the day wrong.

ALMA. No, he collected at the Davis'.

HESTER (*After a long pause.*) He couldn't have forgotten us.

ALMA (*Still holding the cocoa, she turns from the door.*) He's collecting at the Kerighan's now. (*She closes the door and stands forlornly.*)

HESTER. Well, don't stand there with that cocoa! You look silly. (*Alma brings the cocoa to the tea trolley.*) Here's your tea. (*Alma takes the cup, sits on the Upstage Left of the end sofa. There is a long silence.*)

HESTER. I think I'll save that story for the meter man.

ALMA. The *Heddingham*?

HESTER. The *Bainbridge*.

ALMA (*After a pause.*) They don't read the meters for two more weeks.

SLOW BLACKOUT

when paperboy passes by without stopping Hester and Alma decide to save the stories for the meter man

sisters live only in the few moments they expect a visitor

Contextual Elements

Notice how these annotations reveal how Keller gradually discloses more and more about the sisters' predicament. After this initial reading, it is often helpful to read the play a second or even a third time using the following *contextual elements* (for a fuller discussion, see "Writing About Works in Context" in Chapter 2) as a way to discover significant patterns of meaning that can lead to the formulation of a claim or thesis:

- **Psychological Context**—what insights does the playwright offer into the needs and desires of the characters that would explain why they behave as they do? What do we know about their family backgrounds, relationships with each other, parents, siblings, friends, and acquaintances?

- **Social Context**—what does the play tell us about the society in which the characters are living? What attitudes toward them might that society have? How difficult or easy would these characters find it to live in that particular society?
- **Symbolic Context**—what features of the set, scenery, props, or other visible or audible aspects of the production have more than a literal function and serve as a sign of the drama's theme?
- **Historical and Cultural Context**—when and where was the play written, and how does this information help you understand the characters, conflicts, and events depicted in the play? What unique cultural values does the play embody that link it to its time and place of origin?

Writing About Drama

Upon a second or third reading, any or all of these four perspectives will serve a similar function as do literary elements (fully discussed in Chapter 2—plot, character, setting, point of view, tone, style, symbolism, and theme) in analyzing short fiction. These methods of inquiry can be used to generate free-writing that will help you discover your claim or thesis.

Free-writing

Free-writing is a strategy in which you generate ideas and explore them in an informal way. Take a few minutes and write, without stopping to edit or correct—simply free-associate to bring to the surface thoughts you have about the work. For example, here is a student's free-writing based on her annotations of *Tea Party:*

> Because the play is so short it doesn't allow Keller to develop characters in great depth, but their situation is communicated with great poignancy. From the stories they consider telling their "visitor"--and their elaborate plans for a tea party for a young man they barely know--we can infer that they are quite lonely. Into the bare-bones situation of the play, Keller drops a number of hints that explain the past, present, and probable future of the two sisters (an amazing feat in only three pages). Their parents were stern, self-controlled, and did not show emotion toward each other or Alma and Hester. They may have only loved their brother George who died

a hero in World War I. From this, we conclude they only have had each other to depend on since childhood and throughout their adult lives. Everything centers on their plans as to how to hold the attention of their "visitor," keep him listening, persuade him to stay and possibly even return. The fact that Keller has the paper boy not stop at their house shows his indifference, and even unkindness, and adds to the pathos of their situation. Draw attention to the last line "they don't read the meters for two more weeks" to stress the suspended "time-in-a-bottle" flavor of the sisters' lives. They only come to life when they expect a "visitor" (paper boy or meter man).

Developing a Thesis

From the annotations and free-writing, a student felt that she had discovered an intriguing angle to the play and formulated this claim:

Thesis: Without ever physically appearing on stage, the paper boy is very much a part of the play because everything that is said and done pivots around his expected arrival.

The claim is an interesting one and led to the following list of points to be developed, illustrated by specific incidents in the play that could help her support the claim. When drawing up a list to serve this function, it is important to first state your assertion and then specify the reference in the text that you will use to support your analysis.

1. The first impression of the characters and the physical environment suggests isolation and is designed to elicit sympathy.

   The first impressions of Alma and Hester are of their age, physical disabilities, and isolation in a one-room set with only a window as the link to the outside world.

2. Everything they do is for a young man they barely know to hold his attention and keep him interested in staying to visit. This makes their situation more poignant and makes the paperboy, although unseen, a major character.

   Shown by their insecurities as to which story to tell and which drink to serve, and how to seat him, so he won't be able to leave easily, and having only a 20-dollar bill so he will have to return with change, reveal a desperate need for company.

3. They have only had each other to depend on since childhood and are in desperate need for contact with other people.

   We learn that the mother didn't show emotion, and the father seemed to love only their brother George, who died as a war hero in the Great War (World War I).

4. Their relationship is based on correcting each other's memories of the past and reassuring each other about the future.

   Shown by arguments as to which ship came into port and when--the pathos of an inconsequential detail having such importance. Underscored by symbolism of two incapacitated sister ships.

5. Alma and Hester interpret the paperboy passing their house as having "forgotten" them, yet really know that he is trying to avoid them.

   Shown when the paperboy leaves the paper on the porch without stopping to collect money in person, as he did at their neighbors, and doesn't attend the "tea party." His action sums up the entire play and reinforces his importance as a major character.

Notice how the student's final paper, "The Unattended Tea Party" (which we have annotated to show the relationship between the assertions and supporting details), develops the thesis stated in the introduction by drawing on her annotations, free-writing, and the five controlling ideas stated above.

The "Unattended" Tea Party

The first impression of the characters and of their physical environment suggests that Alma, who is seventy-five (and walks with a cane), and Hester, who is seventy-nine (and is in a wheelchair), are isolated from the rest of society. They discuss elaborate plans that are designed to get their paperboy to have tea with them. Although he is a peripheral character, the paperboy can be considered the most important character in the play. Ultimately we come to see the sisters the way they must appear to him and can understand his seemingly unkind action.

introduction leading up to the thesis or claim

We first witness their desperate attempts to select the drink he might prefer (cocoa or tea), and decide which stories from their childhood might prove the most compelling (sad or heroic), where to seat him (so he will not be able to leave easily), and how to pay him (with a twenty-dollar bill) so he will have to return with change. His importance to them can be estimated from the amount of effort and thought they give to every detail of his hoped-for visit.

evidence in the form of specific incidents and actions of the sisters that support the claim

The play offers many insights that explain why the sisters are so desperate for company. Hester describes their mother as cold and indifferent ("Alma, mother didn't cry, you know. I don't think she ever cried"). Their father is described as a somewhat stoic figure ("father sitting silent in a chair") who endured the loss of their brother George who went down on a torpedoed ship in World War I.

evidence in the form of Hester and Alma's memories

We gather that they have only had each other for emotional support since childhood. Hester, the elder sister, has taken on the role of correcting Alma's mistaken memories of the distant past (circa 1902). Although their relationship consists of petty bickering, they do seem to care for one another (as Alma says, "yes dear,

analysis of the sisters' relationship and possible symbolic parallel to understand their actions

I know"). Keller may be symbolically underscoring the wounded nature of the sisters' lives by paralleling them with the incapacitated "sister ships" (the Heddingham and the Bainbridge) that they struggle to remember.

reasons why the paperboy can be considered the most important character and restatement of the claim

In the final action of the play, the paperboy passes by, throws their newspaper on the porch without stopping to collect the money they owe him (as he had done with their neighbors), and they realize that their plans for a "tea party" have failed. His action becomes the crucial one in the play that can be interpreted as indifference or even as unkindness. Yet, we are aware that the sisters are manipulative (Alma had said, "well, we haven't used that one on him") and the audience may now begin to see the sisters in the way they must appear to the paperboy.

Thus, the main conflict can be understood as the attempt by the sisters to entrap the paperboy and his choice not to stop and subject himself to another "tea party." Although we still feel sorry for the sisters, we cannot blame him for his decision. Paradoxically, the audience may now see the sisters from the point of view of this character who never actually appears on stage. After the paperboy passes by, the sisters decide they will save their stories for the meter man, a truly pathetic note implicit in Alma's statement, "they don't read the meters for two more weeks."

Chapter 2

Topics for Literary Analysis

Writing About Characterization and Setting

Characterization in Short Fiction

The study of *character* in fiction, drama, and poetry involves discovering clues and significant details that the author has provided to understand the forces shaping the characters. This term refers not only to individuals in a fictional work, but to the whole matrix of characteristics that an individual possesses. In writing about characterization we seek to discover how these character traits reveal themselves through specific consequences, and the means that writers use to create and develop these fictional characters.

An author can use direct methods of revealing character through statements made by an all-knowing or *omniscient narrator* (for more on narration, see Writing About Point of View). The author's attitude toward the character(s) may be directly expressed through comments about the character's personality or mental state, as in Bessie Head's "Looking for a Rain God":

> The men sat quiet and self-controlled; it was important for men to contain their self-control at all times but their nerve was breaking too. They knew the women were haunted by the starvation of the coming year.

More typically, authors use indirect methods to reveal character. These include descriptions of physical appearance, dress, and mannerisms, and names that have metaphorical or associative significance, as does Eudora Welty in describing the protagonist in her story "A Worn Path":

> Her name was Phoenix Jackson. She was very old and small and she walked slowly in the dark pine shadows, moving a little from side to side in her steps, with the balanced heaviness and lightness of a pendulum in a grandfather clock.

The character's relationships with other people, places, and things, as well as the character's thoughts and feelings (including those as overheard by the reader or commented on by the author) and the opinions and judgments of other characters, expressed in dialogue, also offer important indirect clues to understand the forces shaping crucial personality traits. For example, in "Reunion" John Cheever offers subtle clues about the main character's feelings toward his father:

> He was a stranger to me—my mother divorced him three years ago, and I hadn't been with him since—but as soon as I saw him I felt that he was my father, my flesh and blood, my future and my doom.

Cheever suggests, through the boy's reactions, the sense of awkwardness that surrounds their first meeting in several years and his apprehension that he may become like his father.

Characters presented through one facet are referred to as *one-dimensional,* or *stock,* or *stereotyped characters.* For example, in Louise Erdrich's "The Red Convertible," Lyman's younger sister enters the story only as a minor character who takes a picture of the brothers that will prove important in the story ("my only sister, Bonita, who is just eleven years old, came out and made us stand together for a picture"). She only speaks one word ("smile") and reenters the house ("after Bonita took the picture, she went into the house and we got into the car").

By contrast, major characters are presented less as types and more as individuals capable of complex motivations and reactions who change in response to a crisis or conflict in ways that make them seem like real people.

An essay that analyzes character in a work of fiction should first identify the individual, define that character's dominant personality traits, or unique features, discuss key incidents that reveal these traits, and describe the important changes that occur in this character between the beginning and the end of the story. By understanding the nature of the change (in terms of the character's attitude, status, or relationships), we can create a plausible interpretation of why this change takes place and what its significance might be.

The analysis should consider whether the evidence of the change is external (through action, dialogue, or behavior) and/or internal (through self-revelation). We must also consider whether the change is foreshadowed or suggested by any clues, hints, or indications at an earlier point in the story. We can also evaluate whether this change is consistent with what we already know about the character, and whether it is believable.

In organizing the essay, the introduction should define central character traits. The main section should pinpoint key incidents that reveal these character traits, and isolate those moments that clearly suggest the character has changed as a result of the events the story describes. The conclusion should elaborate on the significance of the character's change as it relates to an important idea or theme in the work.

Frequently, the title proves helpful in signaling the reason for the change in the main character and may refer to the crisis or conflict that brings about the change. For example, "The Red Convertible" focuses our attention on the important role that this automobile plays as a catalyst and symbol of the different stages in the relationship between the two brothers, Lyman and Henry.

Another approach is to ask how characters represent opposing points of view or different attitudes or values. For example, Amy Tan's "Two Kinds" explores the conflicts between different cultures and generations of Chinese mothers and daughters. The story describes how Jing Mei Woo's search for her identity brings her into conflict with her mother's desire that she become a child prodigy to fulfill the American dream. This conflict is reflected in almost every aspect of the story (including the title and the two complementary pieces of music described at the end).

In writing about character, it is important to think carefully about the often complex relationships between changes in the main character and the reasons for these changes. You can use free-writing and mapping techniques to explore the possible causes (and effects) of a character's transformation or development. The analysis can follow the chronological pattern that discusses causes and effects in the order that they occur, or can emphasize the single most significant reasons for a character's change.

The thesis of the essay should clearly signal whether the paper will emphasize the causes and/or effects of a character's transformation or development. For example, the thesis of a paper on John Cheever's story "Reunion" might be:

```
The title ("Reunion") is ironic in view of
the increasing discomfort the boy experiences
as his father attempts to befriend him.
```

The evidence for this claim would be drawn from the interpretation of specific incidents where the boy's father's rough language, disparaging comments, obvious prejudice, and drunkenness progressively alienate the boy. A counterargument might consider that the father displays these traits as he feels he is losing the chance for a relationship with his son.

Setting in Short Fiction

The time and place in which a work is set, as well as the sights, sounds, and details of the location, collectively make up the *setting*. Setting anchors the work, imbues it with a specific reality, and lends credibility to the experiences of the characters. Setting can play a role in creating a specific mood or emotional tone and can even foreshadow events. For example, Inés Arrendondo's description of the change in the weather in "The Shunammite" alerts the reader to the ominous events to follow:

> One afternoon of menacing dark clouds, when I was bringing in the clothes hanging out to dry in the courtyard, I heard Maria cry out. I stood still, listening to her cry as if it were a peal of thunder, the first of the storm to come.

Setting can symbolize the values, ideals, attitudes, and emotional states of the characters and can reveal much about the social and cultural forces that shape their lives. For example, in Kazuo Ishiguro's "A Family Supper," the ominous nature of a meal at which the main food (*fugu* fish) can prove lethal (if not prepared correctly) communicates the personal and cultural problems that could destroy the relationship between family members.

Setting can also enter the story as an active force and almost play the part of a character, as it does in "Looking for a Rain God," where the persistent drought makes a family resort to taking measures they would normally not even consider. The descriptions of the blistering heat and desiccated landscape symbolize the corrosion of the family's physical strength and moral values. The importance of setting can be appreciated when we consider that no story would remain the same if its actions and events occurred in an entirely different location.

An essay that focuses on setting (either by itself or in relationship to characterization, plot, theme, or symbolism) might analyze how a character's response to the setting reveals important things about him or her. The introduction should identify where the action takes place and offer examples that illustrate the dominant impression the author creates. Identify key phrases that evoke the look, sound, touch, and feel of the environment, and correlate these with the reactions of the characters or incidents in the plot. The main portion of the essay should discuss the methods the author uses (precise details, comparisons, allusions, or sensory images) and illuminate the role the setting plays in enabling the reader to better understand the action of the story and the emotions of the characters. The discussion might investigate whether the environment becomes an active force in the story and determines the fate of the characters.

Characterization and Setting in Poetry

In poetry, we use the word *speaker* to identify the character whose voice we hear in the poem. The speaker is not necessarily the same person as the poet. She or he may represent one facet, or *persona,* of the poet's personality or may be a wholly imaginary character.

The point of view the poet chooses to adopt colors our perception of the events in the poem. *Lyric* poems, which are intensely personal expressions of a speaker's mood, are most likely to be perceived as expressing feelings identical to the poet's. For example, the voice we hear in Robert Hayden's "Those Winter Sundays" ("Sundays too my father got up early . . .") reflects on the past in ways that seem to be indistinguishable from the poet.

The speaker in *narrative* poems (which tell a story) undergoes a transformation in ways that closely parallel what happens in fiction. For example, Cathy Song in "The Youngest Daughter" leads us through a series of events that take place between a mother and daughter and lead up to a moment of decision, much as we would expect in a short story.

In *descriptive* poems, such as "Who Among You Knows the Essence of Garlic?" by Garrett Hongo, the feelings of the speaker are revealed through images that evoke the sight, sound, touch, taste, and smell of foods unique to Hawaiian culture.

Dramatic poetry employs more characters than simply the speaker and uses dialogue to intensify conflict. We can see these dramatic elements in the anonymous 17th-century folk ballad "Edward, Edward," which builds to a shocking ending implicit in the suspenseful conversations the poem relates.

The major difference in the way characters are portrayed in fiction and in poetry is that the greater part of characterization in a poem springs from the way a character speaks (as opposed to the way he or she acts). Speakers reveal themselves—their emotions, beliefs, attitudes, values, and desires—in the process of articulating their response to a particular emotional conflict, crisis, or situation.

An essay on character in poetry should concentrate on this shift in emotional attitude (which is equivalent to the more overt changes in characters in short fiction). To appreciate this change, we must be able to identify the kind of voice we first hear—ironic, amused, incensed—and note important differences in the speaker's attitude between the beginning and the end of the poem. Often the title alludes to the reason why this change has taken place. For example, Rita Dove's "The Wake" begins with the arrival of friends and relatives whose presence makes the absence of the speaker's mother all the more painful. By the end of the poem, the speaker has retreated to her childhood room (which may also symbolize the mother's womb).

As in short fiction, the setting in poems can function literally and symbolically. For example, the actual storm howling outside in William Butler Yeats's "A Prayer for My Daughter" becomes symbolic of the turbulent civil disorder that Yeats feared would engulf Ireland.

Writing about setting in poetry entails discovering how the descriptive images help establish the situation in which the speaker finds himself or herself, and how these images set the stage for and reflect the speaker's evolution thoughout the poem. In a longer poem, you might investigate how change of setting from stanza to stanza brings out important facets of the speaker's personality. Thus, in "A Prayer for My Daughter" the threatening storm in the initial stanzas gives way to a contrasting image of a "flourishing hidden tree" that symbolizes what the speaker hopes his daughter will become.

Characterization and Setting in Drama

Characters in drama define themselves through what they say and what they do, as well as through their appearance and gestures. Unlike fiction, we must infer what characters are thinking without direct access to their minds, because we do not have a narrator who tells us what they are thinking and feeling. Playwrights reveal the personality of characters through methods of characterization adapted to the limitations of the dramatic form. We experience a drama quite differently from the way we read fiction. First of all, we watch actors play the part of the characters. We cannot request that they replay a particular scene if we lose our place. Also, dramas must compress the action into what can be shown on the stage in two or three hours. Therefore, every moment in the play must communicate something important about the person speaking and make it possible for the audience to infer why the characters act as they do. The *conflict*(s) in drama are overt, rather than subtle as they may be in fiction and poetry. The audience needs to see these conflicts enacted on the stage. For this reason, the playwright's methods of characterization must bring to light unmistakable differences between one character and another.

Every speech and action must divulge something about the characters, their backgrounds, intentions, and desires as they relate to other characters in the play. Consider what we can tell about the protagonist simply referred to as "Man" in Kōbō Abe's play *Friends* from the following speech:

> MAN (*nearly screaming*). I've had enough! I'm quite happy being alone. I'll thank you to stop your uncalled for meddling. I don't want your sympathy. I'm enjoying my life just the way it is.

These lines reveal someone in a state of near hysteria, who is defensive and somewhat incredulous that he should have to defend his right to live alone without having to share his apartment and provisions with eight strangers. The playwright's suggestion as to what tone of voice and gestures should accompany the speech provides necessary information that will enable the audience to more clearly grasp the protagonist's state of mind.

To create credibility, characters must be depicted in ways that are consistent—even if they change over the course of the play. For example, each of the characters in *Friends* is defined in terms of an easily grasped personality trait. The younger son is depicted as aggressive and intimidating; the middle daughter is flirtatious and sympathetic to the protagonist's plight; and the main character becomes increasingly frustrated and outraged because he is unable to get the police, or indeed anyone, to acknowledge his predicament.

Writing about character in drama requires you to focus on a significant figure, formulate a *thesis* or claim that expresses an opinion about an important aspect of that character's role in the play, and refer to points in the play that support your interpretation. The thesis should also refer to the central conflict in the play, either as an internal dilemma experienced by one of the characters, or as the conflict between characters, or between a character and the surrounding society or nature. A useful technique to generate relevant details for your analysis is to ask the journalist's traditional five questions:

What happened?

When did it happen?

Where did it happen?

Who was involved? and most importantly,

Why did it happen?

This technique will help you focus on essential details that will support your thesis, since the interplay of character and action is the essence of drama.

In the world of the play, props, costumes, and scenery all help to establish the prevailing values as well as the actual time and place in which the events of the play occur. The setting also plays a subliminal role in establishing what the audience perceives as being the status quo, which provides a sense of what is normal and usual. In this way, the opening scenes of a play establish a frame of reference that serves as a background against which the playwright can dramatize an emerging conflict. For example, in *Friends,* the audience watching Abe's play should be able to understand how unusual it would be for an individual to have a large apartment to oneself in an overpopulated city like Tokyo and in a society that valued conformity.

An essay in which the analysis of setting plays an important role should pay close attention to the descriptions and stage directions. How much detail do the stage directions give in describing the setting? If the stage directions are sparse, can the setting be reconstructed from the dialogue? To what extent is the setting literal and realistic or symbolic and representational? If it is symbolic, what do the objects and artifacts in the play represent? For example, in *Friends,* the cage within which the man finds himself aptly symbolizes his isolation, because no one he turns to for help, including the superintendent, police, a reporter, or even his fiancée, takes his side against the "family."

Writing About Point of View

Point of View in Short Fiction

The vantage point from which the author chooses to tell about the events that take place in a story determines its *point of view.* The point of view influences every other aspect of the story because it sets up the basic relationship between the voice we hear telling about the events and the events themselves.

It also limits what readers can and cannot know about these events. The personality of the narrator also acts as a filter through which the reader perceives the characters and events.

Although readers tend to identify the voice they hear telling of the events as that of the writer, we must remember that the narrator is simply another character who the author creates to tell the story. There are four basic vantage points from which the narrator can tell the story: omniscient, limited omniscient, first person, and objective (or dramatic). The particular point of view depends on who this narrator is, and how he or she is related to the characters and events being described.

In *omniscient narration,* the most traditional form of telling a story, the author creates an all-knowing narrator or storyteller who knows everything there is to know about every character and event in the story. The voice that we hear in omniscient narration is clearly not one of the characters, but seems to encompass and be privy to the thoughts and feelings of all the characters. The omniscient narrator is free to divulge anything that goes on in the minds of the characters, and can easily move from the consciousness of one character to another, giving the reader insight into each character's innermost thoughts and feelings. For example, in Kate Chopin's "Désirée's Baby" (Chapter 6) we move without restriction from Madame Valmondé's thoughts ("Madame Valmondé abandoned every speculation but the one that Désirée had been sent to her by a beneficient providence") through Armand's feelings ("seeing her there [he] had fallen in love with her") into Désirée's inner consciousness ("when he frowned she trembled, but loved him").

The advantage of omniscient narration is that it offers the reader a sense of knowing more than we ever could possibly know through mere observation. The disadvantage of this traditional mode of storytelling is that it tends to distance readers from the characters, and makes it impossible to share their feelings except by way of the narrator's commentary and judgments. The revolution in storytelling that took place in the early part of the 20th century in the work of writers such as James Joyce and Virginia Woolf was due to their dissatisfaction with this sense of the reader being at arm's length from the character's reactions at the instant they took place.

The mode of storytelling that succeeded omniscient narration is known as the *limited omniscient* point of view. In this form, the author employs a narrator who describes events in the third person, but limits our awareness to a single, or at most two, characters' view of events. The narrator does not reveal what is going on in the minds of all the characters, but rather focuses our attention on one character. This encourages the reader to identify with that character and experience unfolding events as they appear to that character as the story progresses. For example, in Joyce Carol Oates's "Where Are You Going, Where Have You Been?" we are privy to the thoughts of Connie ("her mother had been pretty once too, if you could believe those old snapshots in the album") and share her growing terror when Arnold Friend arrives.

The advantage of the limited omniscient point of view is that it creates an extremely strong sense of empathy and involvement. By restricting our perspective to a single character's consciousness, the story seems to be more coherent and attains a sense of unity without the distraction of shifting into the minds of other characters. For example, Kate Chopin in "The Story of an Hour" uses this third-person perspective to allow us to share the feelings, thoughts, and emotions of Mrs. Mallard, who discovers a yearning for freedom, upon learning of her husband's death, that is as surprising to her as it is to the readers ("But she saw beyond that bitter moment a long procession of years to come that would belong to her absolutely").

Like the limited omniscient vantage point, the *first-person point of view* provides a single unified view of events, but with some important differences. In the first-person point of view (grammatically signaled by the use of "I"), the author further limits what we can know by having the narrator be one of the characters (either the protagonist or a minor character) who tells the story. In stories told through the first person, we are encouraged to accept the character's view of events as he or she reports them.

At the same time, the use of a first-person narrator who is so deeply involved in the events may cause the reader to question the reliability of the narrator's perceptions. These stories restrict us to the interpretation of events, however incorrect, naive, or biased the narrator/character's assessment might be. Unlike limited omniscience, the first-person narrator remains the reader's sole source of information. For example, think how differently the events the narrator describes might look from the point of view of the miller or his wife in Jerzy Kosinski's "The Miller's Tale." Or, to cite a more whimsical example, how might the events related by the unnamed narrator/cat in Natsume Soseki's "I Am A Cat" appear to the professor who has adopted him?

The question to ask is whether the narrator/character's reports of the events and commentary on them are to be taken as trustworthy and reliable, or are they to some extent self-serving rationalizations.

The fourth, relatively rare, vantage point the author can adopt is the *objective* (or "fly on the wall") *point of view.* Much of Ernest Hemingway's fiction exemplifies this approach (see "Hills Like White Elephants," Chapter 5). We view the characters and incidents as we would in a play. Because the author shows us events without commenting on them or filtering them through the personality of a particular character, we must form our opinions based solely on what the characters do and say and how they interact with others. This point of view produces a sense of immediacy and the illusion of reality.

In writing about point of view, the first question to ask is through whose consciousness or from whose vantage point are the events of the story experienced. Determine whether the narrator is a character or participant in the story or an outside commentator. If the point of view is omniscient, does the author clearly distinguish his or her perspective from that of the characters? If the author adopts a third-person limited omniscient point of view, what do we discover about the character's thoughts and feelings? If the point of view is first person, what clues suggest that the narrator's view of things is reliable? Are there clues to the contrary? The most interesting essays on point of view investigate how the author's choice of narrator affects the reader's perception of the characters and plot. Has the writer chosen the most effective point of view for the story he or she tells? What other points of view might work as well? You might choose to rewrite one of the stories in this book as it might appear from another point of view.

Point of View in Poetry

The point of view in poetry depends on the relationship between the speaker (or the voice you hear) and the events described. As a genre, poetry seems to be more intimate and personal than short fiction. In most poems, we hear a voice that we often take to be the poet's, but as in fiction, the speaker may be an invented personality or character. In *lyric* poetry especially, the speaker represents one aspect or a *persona* of the poet who expresses a personal and intense reaction to a particular problem or situation. For example, when the speaker in Fadwa Tuqan's "I Found It" says "I found it on a radiant day/after a long drifting," we share her exaltation directly (even if we understand that the speaker may represent Tuqan's self at an earlier time in her life). Lyric poems communicate a sense of confessional intimacy, as we see in Sara Teasdale's "The Solitary," where we experience a sense of direct connection and share the speaker's thoughts at a crucial moment in her life ("My heart has grown rich with the passing of years").

In poems where the *narrative* element predominates, the emphasis is less on the speaker's feelings than on the story the poem tells. For example, in Maurice Kenny's "Sometimes . . . Injustice" the speaker tells how events outside his control have shaped his life ("The day I was born my father bought me a 22").

In *descriptive* poems the lyric or narrative elements are subordinated to panoramic or scenic images that indirectly suggest the speaker's perceptions and sensibilities. A good instance of this is Octavio Paz's "The Street," in which we enter a surrealistic landscape that becomes inseparable from the speaker's fate ("I always find myself on the same street").

Poetry written from an *objective* or a *dramatic* point of view, such as Robert Desnos's "Midway," is the furthest from the personal, subjective lyric poems. The objective impact of Desnos's poem is created through the presence of different characters and vivid contrasts, which depict a dramatic illusion of a scene that is witnessed and reported ("A woman—her hair stylish and stocking loose at the ankles—/Shows up at the corner").

Point of View in Drama

The playwright's way of telling a story differs from fiction or poetry in one important respect: we do not have a narrator who comments on events, explains the motivation of the characters, or interprets the significance of the actions the characters perform on the stage. The audience (or reader) must draw inferences based solely on what the characters do and say. When we watch a drama, we feel that we are witnessing events as they unfold and that we are listening to the conversations (dialogue) between the characters at that very moment.

The most effective dramas are those that make it possible for the audience to understand what every event or complication means from each character's point of view. These multiple perspectives are crucial if we are to appreciate how the conflict at the core of the play affects the lives of all the characters. The way the play is directed also subtly influences the way the audience sees the action on stage. Unlike films, where the point of view shifts dramatically as the camera moves from a long shot to a close up, or pans across the entire scene, dramatic works give the audience the ultimate option as to which character(s) to focus on and how to view the events happening on the stage.

The point of view through which we perceive a play also depends on whether we look through the lens of tragedy or comedy. For example, both Tennessee Williams in *The Glass Menagerie* and Christopher Durang in *For Whom the Southern Belle Tolls* offer insight into human nature in their portrayals of a southern family who represent universal character types. Williams is entirely sympathetic toward the flaws and tragic weaknesses within the Wingfield family that destroy their capacity to live in the world. Durang, by contrast, treats these same flaws from a satiric perspective by greatly exaggerating the eccentricities and personality traits that make it impossible for them to fit into modern society.

Writing About Language

Language in Short Fiction

Style embodies the author's unique vision of his or her material and is established by the writer's choice of words, or *diction*; *syntax,* or how the author arranges phrases, sentences, and paragraphs; and *figurative language,* or how he or she uses *imagery* and *metaphors.* The expressive and emotional qualities of language result from the use of figurative rather than literal images, sensitivity to the sounds of words and rhythm of phrases, and an emphasis on the *connotative* rather than the *denotative* meaning of words.

Although style encompasses a complete range of linguistic resources of diction, syntax, rhythm, and imagery, *tone* refers to the narrator's or speaker's attitude toward the characters and events depicted in the story. Whether sympathetic, indifferent, amused, disapproving, or outraged, the tone encourages the reader to feel a certain way about the work, and even a slight shift in tone may alter the reader's perception. For example, when the omniscient narrator in Monique Proulx's "Feint of Heart" says that "whether you like it or not I'm going to tell you the story of Françoise and Benoît in love: because you're a bunch of hopeless romantics," we are very well aware that the narrator is opinionated and intrusive, but probably well-meaning. Also, Proulx's unusual title uses a pun on "faint" (as in the phrase "faint-hearted") to suggest the protagonists' lack of courage in pursuing their love affair. The actual word in the title refers to a maneuver in fencing designed to distract one's opponent from the real point of attack. The relevance of this title would not have been immediately clear, but Proulx's ingenuity can be appreciated after you have read the story. It is always a good idea to take a close look at titles both before and after you read the piece.

Tone invites the reader to share the writer's response to the subject. It can be communicated directly, as it is in Proulx's story, or through imagery, or irony. For example, when the first-person narrator in Alberto Moravia's story "Jewellery" says that "later on I heard that Rinaldo had married Lucrezia; I was told that, at the church, she was more thickly covered with jewellery than a statue of the Madonna," we feel the narrator's scorn for his former friend, Rinaldo, and ironic disdain for his newly jewelry-bedecked bride.

Irony is one of the most easily recognizable expressions of tone. Irony results from a clash between appearance and reality, expectation and outcome, or when there is a discrepancy between the literal meaning of words and the intent. *Verbal irony* conveys the opposite of what is said, either through *understatement* or *overstatement* (*hyperbole*). For example, when the narrator in Margaret Atwood's "Happy Endings" opines that "John and Mary have a stimulating and challenging sex life and worthwhile friends," we know that the understated sarcasm calls into question the pompous cliché and encourages the reader to think about stereotyped plot scenarios.

Stories can also develop *situational* or *dramatic irony,* such as James Joyce does in "Eveline," where a girl who has set her heart on running away with her lover inexplicably is unable to do so at the very last moment.

One useful approach in planning an essay on language, style, and tone is first to define the characteristics of the writer's style and then to analyze the extent to which the writer's diction, syntax, rhythm, and imagery contribute to our impression of the characters and incidents. The essay can be purely informative—and acquaint the reader with unique features of the writer's style (for example, does it depend on analogies, metaphors, similes)—or persuasive, and argue as to how this style plays a role in the total effect of the story. Your essay should first identify the characteristics that distinguish a particular writer's style, and offer typical instances or illustrative examples that demonstrate your thesis.

Language in Poetry

Effective poetry has the capacity to reveal new insights into common human emotions and to open new vistas of perception in ways that are both compelling and artistically satisfying. Poems rely on the carefully selected, concentrated use of words that appeal to the senses and are capable of evoking a range of emotional associations. That is, poets rely on *connotative* rather than simply the *denotative* meaning of words. For example, the connotations of "the house blinked out" (in Jimmy Santiago Baca's poem "Spliced Wire") suggests the impression of futility and hopelessness more than would the factually correct denotative phrase "the lights in the house went out."

Another way poets use language to communicate the emotional overtones of experiences is through *imagery.* Images can be either *literal* or *figurative.* Literal images convey sensory impressions through straightforward, concrete representations through which the reader shares the sight, taste, touch, and sound described (for example, when Baca writes "but often the lights will dim weakly/in storms"). By contrast, when the poet compares a literal image to something else, the writer is using language figuratively to express an abstract idea through concrete means. If the comparison is explicit and involves the words "like" or "as," it is called a *simile.* If the comparison equates things that are essentially unlike each other but eliminates comparative words, it is called a *metaphor.* We can see both operating in Baca's poem ("my words I gave you/like soft warm toast in the early morning./I brewed your tongue to a rich dark coffee, and drank my fill"). Imagery acts as a kind of bridge to make the abstract tangible, the unfamiliar accessible, and opens the subjective realm of feeling to empathetic imagination. Imagery enables the reader to participate in the emotions of the speaker.

A single image that dominates an entire poem is called a *controlling image* as, for example, in Robert Browning's "My Last Duchess" the image of the Duchess (her portrait) frames the callous ongoing negotiation for the forthcoming marriage ("I gave commands;/Then all smiles stopped together. There she stands/As if alive").

In creating the overall effect of the poem, the sound the words create is as important as the imagery and the emotional associations these images call to mind. The stylistic analysis of sound and rhythm in poetry is known as *prosody.* Poets use patterns of sound and rhythm to create emotional involvement.

They do this in four ways: (1) by varying the pitch, tempo, and intensity of sounds; (2) by introducing patterns of repetition of consonants and vowels known respectively as *alliteration* (as in the line "I only know that *s*ummer *s*ang in me" in Edna St. Vincent Millay's poem) and *assonance* (as in the phrase "l*o*bby z*o*mbies" in Gregory Corso's poem); (3) by using *rhyme* and *meter* in various forms (such as the ballad, couplet, and sonnets, for example, by Shakespeare and Elizabeth Barrett Browning); and (4) by introducing pauses known as *caesurae* and strategically placed moments of emphasis, as Elizabeth Barrett Browning does in the lines "Smiles, tears, of all my life! — and, if God/choose. . . ."

In writing about language in poetry, try to understand why the poem affects you the way it does. Explain the feelings or ideas the poem communicates, and discuss why the poet's use of language is striking or memorable. Is the poem one you feel you will remember for a long time? Explain your reactions, quoting from the poem to support your statements. What connotations heighten the emotional impact of the poem? You might consider the connection between the subject of the poem and the imagery through which the subject is depicted. Which images are literal, and which are figurative? Does the poem contain a controlling image to which other images are subordinated? When you read the poem aloud, does it have a definite rhythm? You might wish to mark stressed syllables in each line and underline repetitive sound patterns. How do they create a sense of progression and movement and make the poem more effective?

Language in Drama

In drama, the language the audience hears as the conversation between characters is known as dramatic *dialogue*. To be effective, dialogue must give full and coherent expression to each character's thoughts and feelings, thereby delineating that particular character to the audience. Through the dialogue, the playwright presents the conflict that advances the plot. As one character converses or argues with another, the dialogue sets up a pattern of assertion and counterassertion that reveals the conflict at the heart of the play. For example, the conversations between Betty and Bill in David Ives's *Sure Thing* dramatize the difficulty Bill has in presenting himself in an acceptable manner to Betty:

BETTY.

Where was college?

BILL.

I was lying. I never really went to college. I just like to party. (*Bell.*)

Ives shrewdly demonstrates that both Betty and Bill are apprehensive about revealing aspects of themselves that might discourage the other from pursuing a relationship.

In writing an essay that analyzes the playwright's use of language, you might wish to concentrate on how the dialogue acts to define the characters, and how each character's speech is particularly suited to him or her. For example, in Susan Glaspell's *Trifles,* the language the County Attorney uses suggests that he is officious and chauvinistic ("And yet, for all their worries, what would we do without the ladies?"), character traits that place him in conflict with Mrs. Peters and Mrs. Hale. You might choose to analyze one scene in depth to show how the pattern of assertion and denial reveals the conflict between opposing motivations, views, and desires of the characters in ways that advance the plot.

You might also explore how the characters' use of certain figures of speech, metaphors, or images defines them as individuals (as when Mrs. Hale characterizes John Wright, the murder victim: "But he was a hard man, Mrs. Peters. Just to pass the time of day with him— [*shivers.*] Like a raw wind that gets to the bone").

In Glaspell's play especially, it might be instructive to compare whether the differences in social status and power between the sexes is reflected in the differences in the speech of the male and female characters. Do the women in the play avoid confrontation, phrase observations in a passive, rather than active, voice, or talk around the issues as a way of negotiating with the authoritative male characters? This connection between language and gender can become an interesting subject for analysis.

Writing About Reader Expectation

Reader Expectation in Short Fiction

Although it is something we have done most of our lives, when we look at it closely, reading is a rather mysterious activity. The individual interpretations readers bring to characters and events in the text make every story mean something slightly different to every reader. There are, however, some strategies all readers use: we instinctively draw on our own knowledge of human relationships in interpreting characters and incidents, we simultaneously draw on clues in the text to anticipate what will happen next, and we continously revise our past impressions as we encounter new information.

This process operates to some extent in nonfiction; for example, we want to know how the school authorities react to the underground newspaper in Mary Crow Dog and Richard Erdoes's account, "Civilize Them with a Stick": "We put together a newspaper which we called the *Red Panther.* In it we wrote how bad the school was . . . ." But it is really at the heart of what fiction writers do. They engage our imagination in ways that make it irresistible to speculate on what is going to happen and how the characters are going to react.

Sometimes we encounter a writer such as Guy de Maupassant who draws the reader into speculating about the meaning of the main character's perceptions, as we inevitably do in "The Necklace" ("I am vexed not to have a jewel, not one stone, nothing to adorn myself with. I shall have such a poverty-laden look. I would prefer not to go to this party"). We know that Mme. Loisel (the wife of the government clerk) feels ashamed that she cannot dress as well as the other women who will attend this party, and we can only imagine how eager she might be to borrow jewels from her wealthy friend.

We refer to this process of filling in gaps, making speculations, and drawing inferences as involving the reader's expectation. It is precisely this process of active involvement that makes reading imaginative literature such an enjoyable activity. In this way, we see that the reader plays a vital role in creating the meaning for any short story, poem, or play. Anyone who has ever returned to a favorite story, poem, or play only to discover something new in it can see how much the reader contributes to creating a meaning for any work; the text remains the same, and any new insights must be attributable to changes in the reader. Reading, thus, is a cooperative venture between the reader and the text.

Every text embodies particular ideas, experiences, and assumptions that reflect the personal attitudes of the author as well as the societal norms and literary conventions of the time and place in which the work was written. These assumptions, beliefs, and perspectives may be quite different from your own. For example, the hardships described by Mahdokht Kashkuli in "The Button" that compel a family in Iran to place one of their children in an orphanage ("This way, we'll have one less mouth to feed") would be a difficult decision for most readers to understand and accept.

In addition to differences in personal backgrounds and cultural perspectives, readers also differ in their assumptions about what function literature should serve. Some readers view fiction as an escape from reality and enjoy the twists and turns of a suspenseful plot. Other readers find fiction especially rewarding when it provides insights into human behavior.

Reader Expectation in Poetry

When it comes to poetry, some readers associate poems with what is high minded and beautiful, and believe a poem has to rhyme. Those readers might have trouble with a poem like Léon Damas's "Hiccup," whose form and content challenge conventional assumptions about poetry. However, most of us cannot resist speculating on the next disaster the speaker would be accused of by his berating mother:

> I understand that once again you missed
> your vi-o-lin lesson
> A banjo
> You said a banjo
> Is that what you said

In poetry, as well as in fiction, we project ourselves into the work by imagining what will come next, and draw from our own memories (in this case, from similar incidents from childhood) in interpreting the characters and events the poem describes.

Reader Expectation in Drama

Plays offer many opportunities for readers (or the audience) to anticipate how a character will respond to a surprising turn of events. For example, in *We Won't Pay! We Won't Pay!*, by Dario Fo, part of the humor is in his characterization of Giovanni, who at one point, believes that the juice from a jar of olives is his friend's pregnant wife's water breaking:

> LUIGI.
> You wiped up my wife's water?
>
> GÌOVANNI.
> Well, water . . . Maybe it would be more accurate to call it "juice" with an olive or two which actually you've just eaten.

By focusing on what readers would expect, the reasons why they would do so, and the specific elements within the work that provoke this involvement, we can create a particular kind of analysis called a *response statement*.

Writing a Response Statement

An essay in which you explore the personal, literary, and cultural assumptions you bring to a particular text may be written as a first-person statement, describing your interaction with the text in terms of how it made you feel, and what particular thoughts, memories, and associations it triggered. An essay of this kind goes beyond expressing why you like or dislike the work, and accounts for your reaction in terms of a close analysis of important literary elements: characterization, setting, point of view, language, tone, style, and the effective use of imagery.

The first step in writing an essay of this kind is to generate examples that might illustrate your thesis using the pre-writing techniques discussed in Chapter 1. You can adapt these to ask the questions that illuminate your understanding of the readers' expectations. For example, at what points in the work did you imagine or anticipate what would happen next? How did you make use of the information the author gave you to generate a hypothesis about what lay ahead? To what extent do your own past experiences—gender, age, race, class, and culture—differ from those of the characters in the story, poem, or play? How might your reading of the text differ from that of other readers? Has the writer explored all the possibilities raised within the work? Has she or he missed any opportunities that you as the writer would have explored? Was the narrative logic of the story (chronological, associative, surreal, and so on) sustained? For example, if ghosts can't pass through walls in the beginning of the story, has the author forgotten this by the end of the story?

Keep in mind that your thesis and the examples you generate must fit, so that if your examples contradict each other, you will have to recast your thesis to match your examples. Select only the strongest examples that actually support your thesis; the most convincing examples are likely to interest your readers and clarify the point of your essay. Strong examples are relevant, interesting, convincing, representative, accurate, and specific.

Because you are presenting an interpretation of the ways in which readers' interest would be engaged by the particular work, you should not only present your own opinion, but also provide a fair reassessment of contrary opinions. For example, after reading "Winter Dreams," your opinion may be that F. Scott Fitzgerald had not adequately prepared the reader for the shock of Dexter's crushing disillusionment on learning of Judy Jones's fate ("The dream was gone. Something had been taken from him"). But, you should make an effort to acknowledge and accommodate different viewpoints or at least empathize with those who hold the opposing viewpoint (and claim effective foreshadowing on Fitzgerald's part), and state their positions in a fair manner.

Writing About Plot, Conflict, and Structure

Plot, Conflict, and Structure in Short Fiction

The storyline, or sequence of interrelated incidents that happen to characters in fiction, is known as the *plot.* Rather than occurring randomly, these incidents are causally connected. Moreover, the particular sequence of incidents of which the story is composed is meaningful because of the changes it produces in a character's situation, self-awareness, or relationships with others. To be effective, plot must lead readers to speculate on both the causes and consequences of the character's motivations and actions. By seeing plot as a set of events capable of changing the lives of the characters caught in those events, we can better understand the intrinsic dramatic structure of most stories.

The most effective arrangement of events is the one that allows the author to generate and sustain the elements of *conflict.* In most stories, the *introduction* provides necessary background information, establishes the setting, introduces the reader to the major characters, and frames the dramatic situation in which the conflict of the story will occur. Then a *complication* instigates a clash between one character and another, or between a character and the forces of nature or society, that sets the plot in motion. The character with whom we are encouraged to identify is known as the *protagonist,* and the opposing character or force is called the *antagonist.* Succeeding complications escalate what is at stake for the protagonist by creating more obstacles for him or her to overcome in pursuing the desired goal. These obstacles may be external or based on an inner psychological conflict. An important means writers use to prepare readers for a significant future event in the story is *foreshadowing.* Foreshadowing not only heightens suspense in a story, but imbues it with a sense of artistic unity.

In the *climax* of the story, the opposing forces reach a *turning point* or *crisis,* that is, the moment of truth for the protagonist. Before this point, it is possible for events to go one way or the other, for or against the protagonist. After this crucial point, the situation can never return to what it was at the beginning of the story. Events have led to an irreversible change in a character's situation, knowledge, relationships with others, or insight into his or her motivation. The *resolution* of a story settles the crisis, and the *conclusion* then ties up loose ends or clarifies the implications of the events that have been resolved.

Looking at Luisa Valenzuela's story, "The Censors," in this way, we see that it presents a conflict, or crisis, in the life of Juan, the protagonist. Valenzuela first establishes the setting of the story in Argentina during a time of political repression, introduces the major character, Juan, and provides essential background information that allows the reader to understand how concerned Juan is over the letter he has written to his friend Mariana in Paris. The complication that sets the plot in motion occurs when Juan decides to become a government censor in hopes of retrieving this letter. Complications escalate as Juan is promoted from one department to another (because he proves so adept at discerning censorable contents in the letters of others). Finally, the moment of greatest tension occurs when he confronts his own letter and is faced with the choice of betraying his newfound vocation as censor, to which he has become zealously committed, or concealing the letter's existence. Both the resolution of the crisis and the inexorable conclusion quickly follow: "Naturally, he censored it without regret. And just as naturally, he couldn't stop them from executing him the following morning, another victim of his devotion to his work." Notice how Valenzuela focuses on a single conflict in one character's life rather than a series of dilemmas.

The *structure,* or form, of a literary work reflects the author's decision about what organization of events and scenes will best reveal the interplay between character and action. A plot develops *chronologically* if incidents unfold or are related in the order in which they occurred, as in Valenzuela's "The Censors," and in other stories such as Gloria Anzaldúa's "Cervicide." Stories that are told retrospectively, through *flashbacks,* shift the action to events that happened earlier, such as in Ernesto Cardenal's "The Swede," Panos Ioannides's "Gregory," and P'an Jen-mu's "A Pair of Socks with Love."

Another traditional variation in plot structure (which can be traced back to Homer's *The Iliad,* where he alternates between events on the Greek side and on the Trojan side) is the *oscillating* pattern. We see this in Ambrose Bierce's story "An Occurrence at Owl Creek Bridge" where he juxtaposes the scene of a hanging as it appears to an observer with the event from the perspective of the man being hanged.

Structure is less important for its own sake, but rather serves to make it easier for the reader to discern the pattern of emerging conflicts more clearly. In order to discover how all the parts of a work are mutually interrelated, identify the main *conflict,* the *protagonist* (or hero), and the *antagonist,* and which conflicts are external and which are internal and psychological. Does the work focus on a conflict between individuals (as in Ernesto Cardenal's "The Swede"), between an individual and the community (as in Gloria Anzaldúa's "Cervicide"), or on a conflict within the speaker's mind (as in Panos Ioannides's "Gregory")? What elements of foreshadowing permit the reader to foresee the eventual outcome of the action? Where does the main climax of the work occur? How is it resolved?

Plot, Conflict, and Structure in Poetry

In poetry, writing about plot, conflict, and structure involves understanding how the form of the poem sharpens the dilemma the poem explores. For example, consider how Margaret Atwood divides the action of her poem "At First I Was Given Centuries" into separate stanzas that create an arena in which the action of the poem occurs. Atwood generates suspense by revealing how the interval between the time when soldiers leave for war and the moment when the women left behind grieve for them has grown shorter and shorter. Each stanza increases the dramatic tension as the action of the poem moves into the present; thus, the form of the poem reinforces the theme and presents the conflict in easily discernible stages. Diana Der Hovanessian, W. H. Auden, Carolyn Forché, Eleni Fourtouni, Ira Sadoff, and Yehuda Amichai do this in less formal ways; however, each of these poets sets up a basic situation, and then introduces a complication that escalates to a crisis, which leads to a change, however subtle, in the speaker's situation or self-awareness. For example, the speaker in Diana Der Hovanessian's poem ("Looking at Cambodian News Photos") will never again repress her awareness of the Armenian holocaust to save herself anguish. The Jewish father and the Arab shepherd in Yehuda Amichai's poem ("An Arab Shepherd Is Searching for His Goat on Mount Zion") have permanently altered their views of one another in order to cooperate for their mutual self-interest. As you analyze a poem, try to identify how the poet uses stanzas, line lengths, and rhyme schemes to emphasize the issue the poem explores. Look for the pattern of a developing conflict that is resolved by the end of the poem.

Plot, Conflict, and Structure in Drama

As in fiction, the sequence of interrelated incidents and actions that constitute the plot in drama lead audiences through a typical progression of *exposition, complication, climax,* and *resolution.* We can discern these elements in the construction of any play, whether of one, two, three, or more acts. In addition, each scene within a play not only advances the plot but displays its own pattern of developing and resolving conflict.

For example, in Václav Havel's one-act play *Protest,* Staněk, a writer who has sold out to the government and has been rewarded with a large house and lavish lifestyle, solicits the help of his old friend Vaněk to circulate a letter of protest to free his incarcerated son-in-law. Staněk first tries to convince Vaněk by bribing him in overt and subtle ways. By contrast, Vaněk still upholds the values he and Staněk once shared, and lives in a small cottage, and is in constant trouble with the authorities. Staněk's attempts to convince Vaněk that he has an obligation to free his son-in-law are the source of much of the ironic humor in the play.

Although not divided into scenes, each separate conversation functions as a miniature play that contributes to the overall structure: that is, each interchange develops a mini-conflict with its own crisis that feeds into the larger issues in the play. The climactic moment occurs during Staněk's final long monologue, in which his blatant hypocrisy is displayed in an irrevocable manner. His guilty conscience for deserting the movement embarrasses even Vaněk (who previously disclosed that he had already written the petition Staněk needs because it was the right thing to do).

In writing about conflict and structure, your essay should clarify how each distinct part, whether act or scene, contributes to the central conflict at the core of the play. How does the playwright set the stage for the action to follow, and then initiate the conflict? What sort of conflict does the play explore? Who is the protagonist? What is his or her objective? What opposing forces—other characters, nature, society, or some aspect of the protagonist's self—create obstacles, problems, or difficulties that impede the protagonist's desire to pursue a goal? How does the dialogue in individual scenes dramatize this collision of opposing forces as well as advance the overall plot? What means does the playwright use to keep the balance between protagonist and antagonist nearly equal to produce suspense (as Havel does in waiting until the very last moment to reveal that not only had Vaněk already written the letter, but that Javurek, Staněk's son-in-law, has been released from prison)?

Most importantly, where does the climactic moment of truth and recognition occur, and in what way have events led to a change in the protagonist's situation, knowledge, or self-awareness? What consequences result from this insight?

Writing About Works in Context

Because no short story, poem, drama, or essay is written in a vacuum, another useful way of studying works of literature entails discovering the extent to which a work reflects or incorporates the historical, cultural, literary, and personal context in which it was written. Although works vary in what they require readers to know in advance, in most cases knowing more about the contexts in which the work was written will enhance a reader's pleasure and understanding.

Psychological Context

Investigating the biographical or psychological context in which the work was written assumes that the facts of an author's life are particularly relevant to a full understanding of the work. In the essays written by Paul Monette ("Borrowed Time: An AIDS Memoir") and Luis Alberto Urrea ("Border Story"), we can assume that the voices we hear are direct expressions of the authors' views. In works of fiction and poetry, the relationship between the author's life and the events depicted may be just as real, but presented more obliquely. Alice Walker's haunting tale "Flowers" may reflect the author's experiences growing up in a region of the United States where blacks had been lynched. The speaker in Czeslaw Milosz's poem, "My Faithful Mother Tongue," articulates a problem as an exile ("But without you, who am I?") that the poet most likely confronted in his own life. Similarly, we can assume that the acerbic look at Anglo culture expressed by the speaker in Wing Tek Lum's "Minority Poem" grew out of the experiences and feelings of the author ("we're just as American/as apple pie—that is, if you count/the leftover peelings"). So too, Rahel Chalfi, as an Israeli, almost certainly had experiences ("why this need for endless wariness") similar to those described in her poem "Porcupine Fish."

The presumed relevance of an author's life notwithstanding (especially if the work seems highly autobiographical), we should remember that literature doesn't simply report events, but imaginatively recreates experience.

Literary Context

You can better understand a single story, poem, or play by comparing how the same author treated similar subjects and concerns in other works. Speeches, interviews, lectures, and essays by authors often provide important insights into the contexts in which a particular literary work was created. For example, Albert Camus's classic nonfiction work *The Rebel* (1951) would provide the necessary background on the meaning of alienation that enters so significantly into his short story "The Guest" ("in this vast landscape he had loved so much, he was alone").

Placing individual works within the author's total repertoire is another way of studying works in their context. You can compare different works by the same author, or compare different stages in the composition of the same work by studying subsequent revisions or different published versions of a story, poem, or play. For example, many of Jhumpa Lahiri's stories (such as "This Blessed House") in her collection *The Interpreter of Maladies* (1999) deal with problems of adjusting to American life by immigrants from India ("'We're not Christian,' Sanjeev said. Lately he had begun noticing the need to state the obvious to Twinkle"). By studying how she develops this theme using different characters and events, we can understand how her stories dramatize this predicament from different perspectives.

Social Context

Authors often address themselves to the important political and social developments of their time. For example, Mahasweta Devi has for many years lived and worked among the tribal and outcast communities in southwest Bengal, India. Her stories reflect the information she has gleaned directly from the lives of the rural and urban underclass. We can see this is her unique style of narrative realism. Her story "Giribala" is based on observations drawn from real life situations, and accurately reflects social values in Bengal. Her work can be understood as a reaction to the appalling social attitudes that keep women from being treated as human beings in Bengali culture.

In studying the social context of the work, you might choose to analyze how the author describes or draws upon the manners, mores, customs, rituals, or codes of conduct of the particular society in which the work is set. Ask yourself what dominant social or religious values the work dramatizes, and try to determine whether the author approves or disapproves of these values according to how the characters are portrayed. For example, Kelly Cherry's poem "Alzheimer's" was written during a period (the late 1990s) when the general public became aware of the widespread impact and nature of this debilitating disease.

Historical Context

Studying the historical context within which a work is written means identifying how features of the work reveal important historical, political, economic, social, intellectual, or religious currents and problems of the time. Think how useful it would be, for example, to know the important issues in the conflict between France and Algeria that are reflected in Albert Camus's "The Guest."

So, too, in "The Wedgwood Tea Set," the Balkans (*balkan* means "forested mountain" in Turkish) to which Milorad Pavíc, who is Serbian, refers at the end of the story, have a complex and interesting history. The term refers to a mountainous peninsula in southeastern Europe that was once part of the Ottoman Empire, usually considered to include Albania, Bulgaria, Greece, Rumania, European Turkey, and the states that were formerly part of Yugoslavia. "Balkanization" has entered common usage to mean the disintegration of a geographic area into politically contentious groups. Pavíc uses the disparity in political power between Europe and the Balkans as a subject of his ingenious allegory. When you approach works to discover the historical circumstances in which they were written, you can obtain deeper insight than you otherwise might gain.

An essay that explores personal, social, or historical contexts can determine which elements in a work were preexisting, and which represent the author's original contribution. In analyzing any work, the title, names of charcters, references to places and events, or topical allusions may provide important clues to the work's original sources. Simply knowing more about the circumstances under which a work was written will add to your enjoyment and give you a broader understanding of the short story, poem, or play.

Writing About Symbolism and Myth

Symbolism in Short Fiction

Symbols in literary works refer to people, places, objects, or events that have their own meaning in the context of the work, but that also point beyond themselves to greater and more complex meanings. To determine whether any element in a literary work is symbolic, judge whether it consistently refers beyond itself to a significant idea, emotion, or quality.

Some symbols (such as a skull and crossbones; or the caduceus that serves as an emblem of the medical profession) have universally recognized meanings that derive their significance from shared historical, cultural, or religious frameworks. For example, Edgar Allan Poe, in "The Masque of the Red Death," draws on the traditional associations of the elaborate parties, or balls, the wealthy held as an escape from the bubonic plague that ravaged Europe in the Middle Ages. Other symbols do not have universally recognized significance, but develop their symbolic meanings within the context of the specific work. These are often referred to as private, authorial, or contextual symbols. For example, in Naguib Mahfouz's "Half a Day," the image of fire at the conclusion symbolizes the narrator's perception of the consuming and destructive effects of time.

How are we to know when an author intends something to serve as a symbol? Clearly, not every work of fiction uses symbols and not every character, incident, or object in a work has symbolic value. Symbols evolve within the context of the work when images of people, places, things, ideas, or events become so saturated with meaning that they begin to connect with more complex meanings beyond the confines of the story.

In order to write an essay on symbolism in a short story, you need to look for incidents, actions, objects, situations, or ideas that recur within the story in ways that suggest the author intends this feature to be taken symbolically rather than literally. For example, the impenetrable tree trunk "on which a great many devotees had previously tried their strength," in "Deliverance" by Premchand, plays an important part in the story and is referred to repeatedly.

Because the main character, an untouchable, dies in his attempt to chop it down for firewood, it comes to symbolize the intractable resistance of the caste system in India. Details that are placed in a conspicuous position, such as in the opening or closing of the story, or those that are emphasized by repetition, may come to serve as symbols. To be symbolic, the detail or feature must suggest a meaning that transcends its literal function in the story (as the tree trunk does in Premchand's tale).

To understand how an image becomes a symbol, we might examine Machado de Assis's whimsical story "A Canary's Ideas." The canary plays a central role in the story and is referred to in the title. At every stage, it serves as a foil to the narrator's quest for fame and fortune. On each occasion when the canary appears, it not only speaks, but represents a unique way of perceiving the world. By the end of the story, it has decisively changed the life of the narrator/main character Macedo, and has become a symbol encompassing a range of complex and elusive meanings.

When you interpret a symbol in a work of short fiction, it is important to discuss what it might mean without distorting the pattern in which the author has placed it. In Assis's story, you might think of canaries as decorative, mindless creatures; but be careful not to impose your own interpretation based on these associations, because the author may have symbolic associations quite different from yours. This is especially true when the symbol is personal to the author and builds its meaning over the course of the story.

Symbolism in Poetry

Poets are more likely to use symbolism because the concise nature of poetry compresses meaning into relatively few words. Ordinarily a metaphor or simile clarifies the nature of something (an emotion, or an abstract idea) by comparing it to something that is tangible and more easily understood. For example, Anna Kamieńska's poem "Funny" is developed as a series of metaphorical equivalences ("it's being held prisoner by your skin/while reaching infinity") that answer the question "what's it like to be a human/the bird asked."

By contrast, a symbol is an image that points beyond itself to an entire range of complex, not easily defined meanings, as we can see from the following famous lines from William Butler Yeats's "The Second Coming":

> And what rough beast, its hour come round at last,
> Slouches towards Bethlehem to be born?

We can certainly read this poem as an hallucinatory vision that overwhelms the speaker's consciousness. In other words, the image of the "rough beast" functions literally. But it also functions symbolically by suggesting possibilities that extend beyond the literal. Although we cannot say exactly what Yeats had in mind, the symbol suggests a range of qualities that refer to the destruction of what is normal, decent, traditional, and innocent, and the ascendancy of an inhuman bestial power that will displace Christianity. The range of meaning extends outward from the symbol and adds another dimension to the poem. Symbols serve as a shorthand to bridge the gap between the poet's vision of the world and that of the reader. As in fiction, symbols may take on unique private meanings or tap into preexisting cultural or religious meanings. For example, in Vasco Popa's "The Lost Red Boot," the title alludes to a personal symbol that evokes his great-grandmother's free-spirited nature. In "The

Windhover," Gerard Manley Hopkins uses the image of a kestrel buffeted by high winds as a symbol for self-sacrificing Christian devotion.

An essay on symbolism in poetry should carefully examine the language used by the speaker. Try to identify recurrent references that invest a person, place, or thing with a special significance. Look at the diction, sentence rhythms, and imagery. Do these repeated references cumulatively throw light on a psychological truth at the center of the poem? Is there some charged or resonant image at the heart of the poem that clarifies the particular associations the imagery of the poem expresses?

Symbolism in Drama

In drama, as with fiction and poetry, characters, objects, actions, events, or situations can function as symbols. All dramas require the playwright (and set designer) to present the audience with certain stylized representations of the world beyond the theater that the audience is asked to accept as reality. Because the playwright must communicate the meaning of the play only through what the audience can see and hear on the stage, ordinary objects are more likely to be invested with special significance.

In Shakespeare's play, *Hamlet, Prince of Denmark,* for example, what ordinarily would be a cup of wine intended to quench the thirst becomes a poisoned chalice that symbolizes treachery. So, too, a fencing match intended to be a pleasant diversion is actually a murderous design on Hamlet's life, to which he naively succumbs. Shakespeare uses these traditional props and theatrical devices to express the theme that things are not what they seem to be. Hamlet's growing disillusionment extends to his mother, his uncle, the girl he loves, her father, his friends from school, and virtually everyone else, with the exception of his friend Horatio and the traveling players. He even doubts whether the ghost he has seen is truly that of his father.

Shakespeare also uses the image of poisoning (which kills Hamlet's father and ultimately Hamlet himself) to symbolize the corrosive distrust that destroys almost all of Hamlet's relationships. The play furnishes clues that these and related details are to be taken symbolically. They accrue their meaning and gather momentum as the play develops.

An essay on symbolism in drama should determine if any characters, actions, objects, details of the setting, elements of dialogue, costumes, props, sounds, music, or lighting might serve as symbols. Do they convey generally recognized meanings or do the meanings evolve in the context of the play? To what extent does the symbolism shape the overall meaning of the play? For example, has the playwright assigned names to characters that suggest something about their nature or their roles? You are looking for any element that recurs from scene to scene that accrues an extraordinary significance as the play develops. Your essay might answer the question of how symbolism in the play directs the audience's attention to something beyond the drama that enhances the meaning and theatrical effect of the play.

Myth in Short Fiction, Poetry, and Drama

When an entire story is symbolic, it is sometimes called a myth. Whereas a symbolic story may be personal or private, a myth relates to a communal, cultural, or group experience that aims at providing explanations or interpretations of nature, the universe, and humanity. Myths satisfy a basic need to organize, explain, and humanize events or conditions that might otherwise remain mysterious. For this reason, myths are often associated with religion because they attempt to explain aspects of life that are complex and not easily understood. Myths also embody the cultural and social values of the civilizations in which they are created.

Because myths usually are symbolic and extensive, they use plot and/or character elements that recur in the imaginative works of many civilizations, across cultures, from age to age. For example, in popular culture, the well-known story of Superman can be understood as a recasting of key elements in the life of Christ. In this modern myth, Jorel (from the planet Krypton, which means "hidden" in Greek), rather than Jehovah, gives his only begotten son who travels across time and space and is raised by earthly parents, John and Martha Kent (their name means "church" in middle English). Superman's antagonist is not the fallen angel, Lucifer, but rather the archcriminal, Lex Luthor. Temptation is present not as Mary Magdalene, but rather as his coworker on *The Daily Planet,* Lois Lane, whom he resurrects. Many other elements (such as Superman's ability to see through everything except lead, which suggests the impenetrable nature of sin) enable us to understand how myths come to life in ways appropriate to particular times and cultures.

Archetypes frequently present themselves as sets of opposing values represented symbolically: if water represents creativity, rebirth, and life, then its opposite, drought and desertlike conditions, would represent sterility and death. For example, in "The Garden" Bella Akhmadulina uses oppositions between the natural world and the imagination to symbolize the difference between the literal world of prose and the figurative world of poetry.

There are several ways to analyze the literary treatment of archetypes. You might identify and examine the presence of archetypal characters. Some frequently encountered archetypes include the hero, witch, scapegoat (for example, the boy sacrificed in Achebe's story), virgin, earth mother, *femme fatale*, star-crossed lovers, saint, martyr, or tyrant.

You might also examine the literary portrayal of archetypal situations, such as an extensive journey (as in Olaf Stapledon's "Star Maker"), the rite of passage or initiation (which might be seen in Naguib Mahfouz's "Half a Day"), an animal that serves as a guide (as the canary might in Machado de Assis's "A Canary's Ideas"), or the completion of an arduous task that symbolizes death and rebirth (as in Alfred Jarry's "The Passion of Jesus Considered as an Uphill Race"). Your essay might investigate how the presence of any of these archetypal characters and situations adds an extra dimension of meaning to the work.

Arguing for an Interpretation of a Literary Work

The difficult part in an argument is not to defend one's opinion, but rather to know it.

Andre Maurois (1885–1967)
French author and critic

Writers and researchers in all academic disciplines attempt to convince others of the validity of their ideas and discoveries. Formal arguments differ from assertions based on likes and dislikes or personal opinion. Unlike questions of personal taste, arguments rest on evidence, including facts, examples, expert testimony, and logical reasoning, which can be used to prove the validity of the proposition, claim, or thesis. Effective arguments also involve persuasion. Whereas argument presents reasons and evidence to gain an audience's intellectual agreement, persuasion uses emotional appeals to connect to the needs and values of the audience.

We usually think of arguments in terms of debates over public policy or social issues such as gun control, abortion, free speech, genetic engineering, and other hot topics. Writers in the liberal arts often argue for interpretations and evaluations of works of literature (as well as music, dance, art, and film). These interpretations are designed to enhance the audience's understanding and can appear in a variety of forms as critiques, reviews, or scholarly studies.

Literary arguments about the meaning of a work of nonfiction or fiction should express a position that is genuinely debatable, is not immediately self-evident, and does not simply summarize the work. These arguments are similar to nonliterary arguments in that they consist of three main elements:

1. The claim or proposition the audience is to consider.
2. The evidence, support, or grounds the writer will have to produce to back up the claim.
3. The underlying assumption or warrant[1] that justifies how the evidence can be used to support the claim.

Your paper will present a critical evaluation or judgment, and you must express your opinion in a thesis statement. Because the goal of an interpretation is to convince your readers that it makes sense, you should cite elements from the work—by quoting from it, summarizing it, or paraphrasing it—that will allow your readers to understand your assertion as it relates to the entire work. Literary arguments can include qualifiers (such as "presumably," "in all probability," "apparently") that make the claim less sweeping and more realistic.

Ideally, your interpretation should offer an insight that would not be obvious, and identify the methods that the author uses to express this idea (in terms of characterization, setting, point of view, conflict and structure, dialogue, tone, symbolism, or any other essential literary technique). Different kinds of literary arguments seek to accomplish different kinds of objectives.

The issues about which people disagree in literary criticism can be classified according to the four basic claims arguments can make. Although we can more clearly see the distinctive issues that these claims entail by discussing them separately, literary arguments frequently rely on more than one type of claim. We will discuss each type using William Faulkner's short story "A Rose for Emily" (Chapter 9) to illustrate the different kinds of arguments that can be generated.

---

[1]One of the most innovative researchers in the field of argumentation is the British philosopher Stephen Toulmin, who identified the way in which people reason in their everyday lives. Our discussion reflects Toulmin's scheme, described in his book *The Uses of Argument* (1958).

Arguments That Define and Draw Distinctions

People can disagree about

1. The essential nature of the literary work or any elements within it,
2. What it is similar to or dissimilar to, or
3. How it should be defined.

These factual arguments (which define and draw distinctions) must identify the unique properties of the work and put forth assertions that the work and the elements within it should be characterized in a certain way. The different forms this kind of argument can take include

1. Disputes over the gaps, blanks, or inconsistencies in the work,
2. Conjectures about how an author intended a particular word or phrase to be understood,
3. Questions about the meaning and purpose of a particular image and what it might symbolize, and
4. How one might classify the work according to a particular genre.

For example, if we asked these kinds of questions about "A Rose for Emily" we might generate the following assertions:

1. "The narrator's use of figurative images that compare Miss Emily to a fallen monument, an idol in a niche, a lighthouse-keeper's face, and a strained flag, underscores how separate and aloof she was from the townspeople."
2. "Many features of the story signal that it should be seen as an example of the ghost story genre."
3. "The fact that we never really know the exact sequence of events that led to Homer Barron's death adds to the story's sense of mystery."

> To develop any of these factual claims, you would need to add several clauses beginning with the word "because" that express your reasons for holding this view and show how any of the work's literary elements, such as how the characters are developed, or their actions and what they say, or the work's overall structure, supports your interpretation or claim.

Arguments That Establish Causes and Draw Consequences

Even if critics agree about the essential nature of a work, they may still disagree about the relationship between elements within the work, or between outside influences and how they manifest themselves in the work. Claims about causation assert that two elements do not merely appear together, but, in fact, are causally connected. These arguments aim at offering plausible explanations for inner connections within the work as well as explanations for the effects produced by an external cause.

The different forms this kind of argument can take include

1. Analyses of why a character behaves as she or he does or why an event takes place,

2. Discussions about significant patterns within the text (such as repetition of words or images), and
3. The relationship between form (as in a sonnet) and content.

Statements about the theme or overall meaning of a work are often phrased as causal claims and require the writer to show how different literary techniques, such as characterization, setting, point of view, conflict and structure, dialogue, tone, symbolism, and plot structure, support the major idea or theme of the work. This kind of argument must demonstrate the means the author uses to express this theme through an analysis of these techniques.

Causal arguments can also explore the impact of external events through an analysis of the historical and cultural contexts in which the work was written and a demonstration of how they are revealed in the work. Of course, this kind of argument also takes into account debates over the influence of events in the author's life (as far as they can be known) and the way they manifest themselves in the story, poem, or play.

In the case of "A Rose for Emily," these kinds of inquiries might result in the following causal claims:

1. "It is quite likely that Emily takes up with Homer Barron, despite his being a Northerner from a lower social class, as a reaction to her father driving away suitors when she was young."
2. "Through the five-part structure of the story, Faulkner makes us wait along with the townspeople until the door to Emily's house is opened, but in the meantime, we come to understand what Miss Emily represents to them."
3. "The story reflects the post Civil War Reconstruction period in American history, and the southern reaction to northern cultural incursions."

> To develop any of these causal claims, you need to demonstrate that correlations exist between causes and effects, and to evaluate and reject competing explanations. Your causal analysis may delve into the remote, indirect, or background causes as well as the immediate or precipitating causes likely to have triggered the event you identify. Your analysis can get off track when you confuse sequence with causation. Simply because A preceded B does not mean that A caused B (this is referred to as the *posthoc fallacy*).

Arguments That Make Value Judgments

Critics who disagree about questions of value are not merely expressing personal taste, but are making a reasoned judgment based on identifiable standards. They should demonstrate that the ethical, moral, or aesthetic standard they use is an appropriate one, and they must provide convincing arguments with reasons and evidence to persuade their readers. These writers frequently use comparison and contrast as a rhetorical strategy to organize their arguments.

The forms this kind of argument can take include

1. Discussions whether the actions or views the author promotes are sound or useful,
2. Disputes whether the work is morally or ethically acceptable, and

3. Debates as to the overall aesthetic impact of the work and whether it can be considered art (as opposed to, let's say, propaganda).

Because questions of value are so subjective, writers must be sensitive to those who bring different value systems to the work and perceive and understand it in radically different ways. Value arguments are important because they challenge us to examine underlying assumptions that ordinarily remain unquestioned.

For example, if we apply ethical or moral criteria to the character's actions and the narrator's account in "A Rose for Emily," we might generate the following value claims:

1. "The way the rising generation is depicted suggests a decline in civility and literacy and a general coarsening of the manners and morals of the town."
2. "By calling the story 'A Rose for Emily,' Faulkner shows that he privately sympathizes with everything that she represents despite her bizarre behavior."
3. "By remaining by the side of her deceased lover as a nightly ritual, Emily most likely was serving penance for her crime."

> To develop a value claim, we must consider the extent to which our own values and assumptions shape our interpretation. By examining our assumptions and asking why we believe what we do, we are testing the *warrant* or generalization that links the claim and the evidence in any argument.

Writers who make value arguments may need to make underlying assumptions explicit and not take for granted that they and the audience share a common point of view. For example, in the third claim, the writer would probably need to make explicit the assumption that Miss Emily as a girl wanted to have a normal life, but was prevented from getting married and having a family by her tyrannical father. The writer might argue that above all, she was a Grierson, one who adhered to a strict social code of right and wrong and would have held herself accountable for her crime in a manner that only she would know to be a private penance. The *warrant* that the writer would make explicit is that she was not a depraved woman, but one who was frustrated and anguished. The writer could point to a pattern in Emily's earlier unwillingness to part with her dead father's body that she then reenacted with the body of Homer Barron. The relationship of claim, warrant, and evidence in a diagram might appear as shown in Figure 1.

Arguments That Propose Solutions

In addition to arguments that characterize literary works or elements within them, make value judgments about them, or establish causal connections, there are arguments that bring the literary work into the real world by exploring the social and political issues and implications the work suggests. In fact, many of the thematic chapters in this anthology are designed to sensitize readers to important social concerns having to do with gender, race, class, politics, immigration, and the environment. This kind of argument often takes the form of offering a solution to a problem inherent in the work or suggested by it. The works

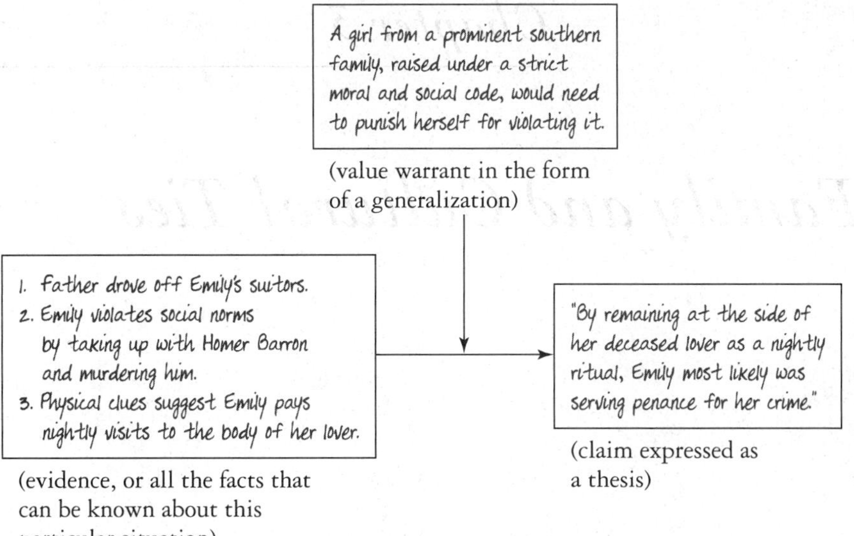

FIGURE 1 ■ Diagram of elements in a value argument.

can be seen as offering a perspective on important social or political issues, and the thesis or claim can take the form of a recommendation.

For example, in "A Rose for Emily" one might link issues in the story with social and political concerns of today as follows:

1. "If one exempts the privileged class from paying their fair share of taxes, one sets the stage for consequences no less perverse than those in Faulkner's story."
2. "Although seemingly a world away from modern times, we can ask what contemporary racial and gender stereotypes are the equivalent of Colonel Sartoris's edict that 'no Negro woman should appear on the streets without an apron.'"

> To develop either of these positions, one would have to demonstrate that harmful consequences followed from abuse of social privilege or that subtle forms of racism and sexism are as injurious as are more overt forms of discrimination.

Each of the preceding four kinds of arguments (about facts, causes, values, and policies) would be more persuasive if the writer anticipated opposing viewpoints, summarized them fairly, and pointed out their inadequacies.

Chapter 3

Family and Cultural Ties

Some people are your relatives, but others are your ancestors, and you choose the ones you want to have as ancestors. You create yourself out of those values.

Ralph Ellison

Shared practices, ceremonies, customs, beliefs, and values make up a cultural heritage that connects the present with the traditions of the past. A cultural heritage serves as a collective memory that provides a link to one's forebears. The folktales, art, music, institutions, rituals, and traditions shared by a group are a social, rather than biological, inheritance that guides people within a culture by providing common assumptions about the world that are passed on from generation to generation.

This chapter explores the extent to which our identity is shaped by all those attitudes, traditions, and customs that we often take for granted. The works of fiction and nonfiction presented here dramatize a wide range of cultural attitudes. We learn of the role traditions play in Botswana, Mexico, Japan, Lebanon, Ireland, and Zimbabwe, and, in the United States, among the Hawaiian, Chinese-American, African American, and Chippewa Indian communities.

The essays by Amy Tan ("The Language of Discretion") and Jill Nelson ("Number One!") dramatize the tension between continuing allegiance to traditional values and ambivalence toward those traditions as something antiquated to be transcended. Fritz Peters in "Boyhood with Gurdjieff" testifies to the importance of a mentor's influence on his life and the lesson he learned about compassion.

Each story in this chapter dramatizes the influence of family and the link to one's culture in a variety of situations and settings. The pressures on second-generation Chinese children to succeed are treated with candor and wit in Amy Tan's "Two Kinds." A father's boorish insensitivity undermines what was to have been a happy reunion between a son and his father in John Cheever's "Reunion." In Bessie Head's "Looking for a Rain God," a desperate family in Botswana resorts to a primitive ritual to end a seven-year drought. The events of history intrude upon a relationship between two Native American brothers in Louise Erdrich's "The Red Convertible." Inés Arredondo in "The Shunammite" dramatizes the conflict between the flesh and the spirit in a modern retelling, in Mexico, of an ancient biblical story. The mystery surrounding familial devotion is at the core of Eudora Welty's "A Worn Path." From Japan, in Kazuo Ishiguro's "A Family Supper" we observe how the cumulative effects of estrangement within a family threaten to turn tragic.

The poems in this chapter present a variety of responses toward one's cultural heritage and family. A mother's advice leads to tragic consequences and denunciation by her son in the traditional ballad "Edward, Edward." In Naomi Shihab Nye's "Where Children Live" we encounter a universal sentiment about children. The unusual accomplishment of a woman writer, Anne Bradstreet, during the Puritan era speaks to us over the centuries in "The Author to Her Book." The psychological costs of independence are confronted in "The Youngest Daughter," by the Chinese-American writer Cathy Song. The speaker in Sharon Olds's "The Planned Child," much to her surprise, feels wanted and welcomed. The speaker tries to fend off the trauma of losing his child in Ben Jonson's "On My First Son." In Robert Hayden's poem "Those Winter Sundays," the speaker regrets that he failed to appreciate his father's devotion. The Irish poet William Butler Yeats, in "A Prayer for My Daughter," expresses a hope that his newborn child will escape the bitterness and turmoil of Irish history. "The Wake," by Rita Dove, embodies the poet's heartfelt response to her mother's death. In "Who Among You Knows the Essence of Garlic?" Garrett Hongo explores the interrelationship between particular foods and one's cultural heritage. Chenjerai Hove, in "You Will Forget," sums up the consequences of losing contact with one's roots.

One of the most penetrating and original works of the Japanese theater, *Friends,* by Kōbō Abe, explores the question of whether individual freedom can coexist with family life in modern society.

Essays

FRITZ PETERS

Fritz Peters's (1916–1979) association with the philosopher and mystic George Gurdjieff began when Peters attended a school founded by Gurdjieff in Fontainebleau, France, where he spent four and a half years between 1924 and 1929. His experiences with Gurdjieff were always unpredictable and often enigmatic and rewarding. Peters wrote two books about his experiences, Boyhood with Gurdjieff *(1964) and* Gurdjieff Remembered *(1965). In the following essay, Peters reveals the highly unconventional methods Gurdjieff used to compel his protégé to develop compassion.*

Boyhood with Gurdjieff

The Saturday evening after Gurdjieff's return from America, which had been in the middle of the week, was the first general "assembly" of everyone at the Prieuré[1] in the study-house. The study-house was a separate building, originally an airplane hangar. There was a linoleum-covered raised stage at one end. Directly in front of the stage there was a small, hexagonal fountain, equipped electrically so that various coloured lights played on the water. The fountain was generally used only during the playing of music on the piano which was to the left of the stage as one faced it.

The main part of the building, from the stage to the entrance at the opposite end, was carpeted with oriental rugs of various sizes, surrounded by a small fence which made a large, rectangular open space. Cushions, covered by fur rugs, surrounded the sides of this rectangle in front of the fence, and it was here that most of the students would normally sit. Behind the fence, at a higher level, were built-up benches, also covered with Oriental rugs, for spectators. Near the entrance of the building there was a small cubicle, raised a few feet from the floor, in which Gurdjieff habitually sat, and above this there was a balcony which was rarely used and then only for "important" guests. The cross-wise beams of the ceiling had painted material nailed to them, and the material hung down in billows, creating a cloud-like effect. It was an impressive interior—with a church-like feeling about it. One had the impression that it would be improper, even when it was empty, to speak above a whisper inside the building.

On that particular Saturday evening, Gurdjieff sat in his accustomed cubicle, Miss Madison sat near him on the floor with her little black book on her lap, and most of the students sat around, inside the fence, on the fur rugs. New arrivals and "spectators" or guests were on the higher benches behind the fence. Mr. Gurdjieff announced that Miss Madison would go over all the "offences" of all the students and that proper "punishments" would be meted out to the offenders. All of the children, and perhaps I, especially, waited with bated breath as Miss Madison read from her book, which seemed to have been arranged, not alphabetically, but according to the number of offences committed. As Miss Madison had warned me, I led the list, and the recitation of my crimes and offences was a lengthy one.

Gurdjieff listened impassively, occasionally glancing at one or another of the offenders, sometimes smiling at the recital of a particular misdemeanour, and interrupting Miss Madison only to take down, personally, the actual number of individual black marks. When she had completed her reading, there was a solemn, breathless silence in the room and Gurdjieff said, with a heavy sigh, that we had all created a great burden for him. He said then that he would give out punishments according to the number of offences committed. Naturally, I was the first one to be called. He motioned to me to sit on the floor before him and then had Miss Madison re-read my offences in detail. When she had finished, he asked me if I admitted all of them. I was tempted to refute some of them, at least in part, and to argue extenuating circumstances, but the solemnity of the proceedings and the silence in the room prevented me from doing so. Every word that

[1]*Prieuré:* a priory; a large chateau in Fountainebleau, France, where G. I. Gurdjieff conducted his school.

had been uttered had dropped on the assemblage with the clarity of a bell. I did not have the courage to voice any weak defence that might have come to my mind, and I admitted that the list was accurate.

With another sigh, and shaking his head at me as if he was very much put upon, he reached into his pocket and pulled out an enormous roll of bills. Once again, he enumerated the number of my crimes, and then laboriously peeled off an equal number of notes. I do not remember exactly how much he gave me—I think it was ten francs for each offence—but when he had finished counting, he handed me a sizeable roll of francs. During this process, the entire room practically screamed with silence. There was not a murmur from anyone in the entire group, and I did not even dare to glance in Miss Madison's direction.

When my money had been handed to me, he dismissed me and called up the next offender and went through the same process. As there were a great many of us, and there was not one individual who had not done something, violated some rule during his absence, the process took a long time. When he had gone through the list, he turned to Miss Madison and handed her some small sum—perhaps ten francs, or the equivalent of one "crime" payment—for her, as he put it, "conscientious fulfilment of her obligations as director of the Prieuré."

We were all aghast; we had been taken completely by surprise, of course. But the main thing we all felt was a tremendous compassion for Miss Madison. It seemed to me a senselessly cruel, heartless act against her. I have never known Miss Madison's feelings about this performance; except for blushing furiously when I was paid, she showed no obvious reaction to anything at all, and even thanked him for the pittance he had given her.

The money that I had received amazed me. It was, literally, more money than I had ever had at one time in my life. But it also repelled me. I could not bring myself to do anything with it. It was not until a few days later, one evening when I had been summoned to bring coffee to Gurdjieff's room, that the subject came up again. I had had no private, personal contact with him—in the sense of actually talking to him, for instance—since his return. That evening—he was alone—when I had served him his coffee, he asked me how I was getting along; how I felt. I blurted out my feelings about Miss Madison and about the money that I felt unable to spend.

He laughed at me and said cheerfully that there was no reason why I should not spend the money any way I chose. It was my money, and it was a reward for my activity of the past winter. I said I could not understand why I should have been rewarded for having been dilatory about my jobs and having created only trouble.

Gurdjieff laughed again and told me that I had much to learn.

"What you not understand," he said, "is that not everyone can be troublemaker, like you. This important in life—is ingredient, like yeast for making bread. Without trouble, conflict, life become dead. People live in status-quo, live only by habit, automatically, and without conscience. You good for Miss Madison. You irritate Miss Madison all time—more than anyone else, which is why you get most reward. Without you, possibility for Miss Madison's conscience fall asleep. This money should really be reward from Miss Madison, not from me. You help keep Miss Madison alive."

I understood the actual, serious sense in which he meant what he was saying, but I said that I felt sorry for Miss Madison, that it must have been a terrible experience for her when she saw us all receiving those rewards.

He shook his head at me, still laughing. "You not see or understand important thing that happen to Miss Madison when give money. How you feel at time? You feel pity for Miss Madison, no? All other people also feel pity for Miss Madison, too."

I agreed that this was so.

"People not understand about learning," he went on. "Think necessary talk all time, that learn through mind, through words. Not so. Many things can only learn with feeling, even from sensation. But because man talk all time—use only formulatory centre—people not understand this. What you not see other night in study-house is that Miss Madison have new experience for her. Is poor woman, people not like, people think she funny—they laugh at. But other night, people not laugh. True, Miss Madison feel uncomfortable, feel embarrassed when I give money, feel shame perhaps. But when many people also feel for her sympathy, pity, compassion, even love, she understand this but not right away with mind. She feel, for first time in life, sympathy from many people. She not even know then that she feel this, but her life change; with you, I use you like example, last summer you hate Miss Madison. Now you not hate, you not think funny, you feel sorry. You even like Miss Madison. This good for her even if she not know right away—you will show; you cannot hide this from her, even if wish, cannot hide. So she now have friend, when used to be enemy. This good thing which I do for Miss Madison. I not concerned she understand this now—someday she understand and make her feel warm in heart. This unusual experience—this warm feeling—for such personality as Miss Madison who not have charm, who not friendly in self. Someday, perhaps even soon, she have good feeling because many people feel sorry, feel compassion for her. Someday she even understand what I do and even like me for this. But this kind learning take long time."

I understood him completely and was very moved by his words. But he had not finished.

"Also good thing for you in this," he said. "You young, only boy still, you not care about other people, care for self. I do this to Miss Madison and you think I do bad thing. You feel sorry, you not forget, you think I do bad thing to her. But now you understand not so. Also, good for you, because you feel about other person—you identify with Miss Madison, put self in her place, also regret what you do. Is necessary put self in place of other person if wish understand and help. This good for your conscience, this way is possibility for you learn not hate Miss Madison. All people same—stupid, blind, human. If I do bad thing, this make you learn love other people, not just self."

Analyzing the Text

1. How did Gurdjieff's allotment of rewards violate conventional expectations? What consequences did this have in changing Peters's view of Miss Madison?
2. What knowledge of human nature is implied in Gurdjieff's ability to create such an emotionally challenging event?

Understanding Peters's Techniques

1. How does Peters's description of the elaborate ritual Gurdjieff follows in doling out rewards and punishments add to the suspense of Peters's narrative?
2. How is Gurdjieff depicted in ways that emphasize why Peters was so shocked at Gurdjieff's "unfair" system of rewards?

Arguing for an Interpretation

1. Making someone feel sorry for another who is being publicly humiliated to teach a lesson in compassion is an interesting tactic, but are the benefits of this lesson offset by the harm done to Miss Madison? Keep this in mind and argue for or against Gurdjieff's actions.
2. In a short essay, discuss what Peters learns about himself from Gurdjieff's unusual actions. Few people can create conditions under which another person can learn something important about themselves. If you were to conduct such an experiment, who would be the beneficiary, what lesson would they learn, and how would the experiment work?

Jill Nelson

Jill Nelson, born in 1952, is a native New Yorker and a graduate of the City College of New York and Columbia University's School of Journalism. A journalist for fifteen years, she is a frequent contributor to Essence, U.S.A. Weekend, The Village Voice, *and* Ms. *In 1986 she went to work for* The Washington Post's *new Sunday magazine as the only black woman reporter in a bastion of elite journalism, an experience she described in* Volunteer Slavery: My Authentic Negro Experience *(1993). Her latest book is* Straight, No Chaser: How I became a Grown-Up Black Woman *(1997). In "Number One!" she reflects on the importance of her father's influence on her life.*

Number One!

That night I dream about my father, but it is really more a memory than a dream.

"Number one! Not two! Number one!" my father intones from the head of the breakfast table. The four of us sit at attention, two on each side of the ten-foot teak expanse, our brown faces rigid. At the foot, my mother looks up at my father, the expression on her face a mixture of pride, anxiety, and, could it be, boredom? I am twelve. It is 1965.

"You kids have got to be, not number two," he roars, his dark face turning darker from the effort to communicate. He holds up his index and middle fingers. "But number—" here, he pauses dramatically, a preacher going for revelation, his four children a rapt congregation, my mother a smitten church sister. "Number one!"

These last words he shouts while lowering his index finger. My father has great, big black hands, long, perfectly shaped fingers with oval nails so vast they seem landscapes all their own. The half moons leading to the cuticle take up most of the nail and seem ever encroaching, threatening to swallow up first his fingertips, then his whole hand. I always wondered if he became a dentist just to mess with people by putting those enormous fingers in their mouths, each day surprising his patients and himself by the delicacy of the work he did.

Years later my father told me that when a woman came to him with an 5
infant she asserted was his, he simply looked at the baby's hands. If they lacked the size, enormous nails, and half-moon cuticles like an ocean eroding the shore of the fingers, he dismissed them.

Early on, what I remember of my father were Sunday morning breakfasts and those hands, index finger coyly lowering, leaving the middle finger standing alone.

When he shouted "Number one!" that finger seemed to grow, thicken and harden, thrust up and at us, a phallic symbol to spur us, my sister Lynn, fifteen, brothers Stanley and Ralph, thirteen and nine, on to greatness, to number oneness. My father's rich, heavy voice rolled down the length of the table, breaking and washing over our four trembling bodies.

When I wake up I am trembling again, but it's because the air conditioner, a luxury in New York but a necessity in D.C., is set too high. I turn it down, check on Misu,[1] light a cigarette, and think about the dream.

It wasn't until my parents had separated and Sunday breakfasts were no more that I faced the fact that my father's symbol for number one was the world's sign language for "fuck you." I know my father knew this, but I still haven't figured out what he meant by it. Were we to become number one and go out and fuck the world? If we didn't, would life fuck us? Was he intentionally sending his children a mixed message? If so, what was he trying to say?

I never went to church with my family. While other black middle-class 10
families journeyed to Baptist church on Sundays, both to thank the Lord for their prosperity and donate a few dollars to the less fortunate brethren they'd left behind, we had what was reverentially known as "Sunday breakfast." That was our church.

In the dining room of the eleven-room apartment we lived in, the only black family in a building my father had threatened to file a discrimination suit to get into, my father delivered the gospel according to him. The recurring theme was the necessity that each of us be "number one," but my father preached about whatever was on his mind: current events, great black heroes, lousy black sell-outs, our responsibility as privileged children, his personal family history.

His requirements were the same as those at church: that we be on time, not fidget, hear and heed the gospel, and give generously. But Daddy's church boasted no collection plate; dropping a few nickels into a bowl would have been too easy. Instead, my father asked that we absorb his lessons and become what he wanted us to be, number one. He never told us what that meant or how to get there. It was years before I was able to forgive my father for not being more specific. It was even longer before I understood and accepted that he couldn't be.

Like most preachers, my father was stronger on imagery, oratory, and instilling fear than he was on process. I came away from fifteen years of

[1]*Misu:* Nelson's daughter.

Sunday breakfasts knowing that to be number two was not enough, and having no idea what number one was or how to become it, only that it was better.

When I was a kid, I just listened, kept a sober face, and tried to understand what was going on. Thanks to my father, my older sister Lynn and I, usually at odds, found spiritual communion. The family dishwashers, our spirits met wordlessly as my father talked. We shared each other's anguish as we watched egg yolk harden on plates, sausage fat congeal, chicken livers separate silently from gravy.

15 We all had our favorite sermons. Mine was the "Rockefeller wouldn't let his dog shit in our dining room" sermon.

"You think we're doing well?" my father would begin, looking into each of our four faces. We knew better than to venture a response. For my father, even now, conversations are lectures. Please save your applause—and questions—until the end.

"And we are," he'd answer his own query. "We live on West End Avenue, I'm a professional, your mother doesn't *have* to work, you all go to private school, we go to Martha's Vineyard in the summer. But what we have, we have because 100,000 other black people haven't made it. Have nothing! Live like dogs!"

My father has a wonderfully expressive voice. When he said dogs, you could almost hear them whimpering. In my head, I saw an uncountable mass of black faces attached to the bodies of mutts, scrambling to elevate themselves to a better life. For some reason, they were always on 125th Street, under the Apollo Theatre marquee. Years later, when I got political and decided to be the number-one black nationalist, I was thrilled by the notion that my father might have been inspired by Claude McKay's[2] poem that begins, "If we must die, let it not be like dogs."

"There is a quota system in this country for black folks, and your mother and me were allowed to make it," my father went on. It was hard to imagine anyone allowing my six-foot-three, suave, smart, take-no-shit father to do anything. Maybe his use of the word was a rhetorical device.

20 "Look around you," he continued. With the long arm that supported his heavy hand he indicated the dining room. I looked around. At the eight-foot china cabinet gleaming from the weekly oiling administered by Margie, our housekeeper, filled to bursting with my maternal grandmother's china and silver. At the lush green carpeting, the sideboard that on holidays sagged from the weight of cakes, pies, and cookies, at the paintings on the walls. We were living kind of good, I thought. That notion lasted only an instant.

My father's arm slashed left. It was as though he had stripped the room bare. I could almost hear the china crashing to the floor, all that teak splintering, silver clanging.

"Nelson Rockefeller wouldn't let his dog shit in here!" my father roared. "What we have, compared to what Rockefeller and the people who rule the world have, is nothing. Nothing! Not even good enough for his dog. You four have to remember that and do better than I have. Not just for yourselves, but for our people, black people. You have to be number one."

My father went on, but right about there was where my mind usually started drifting. I was entranced by the image of Rockefeller's dog—which

---

[2]*Claude McKay (1889–1948):* African American poet.

I imagined to be a Corgi or Afghan or Scottish Terrier—bladder and rectum full to bursting, sniffing around the green carpet of our dining room, refusing to relieve himself.

The possible reasons for this fascinated me. Didn't he like green carpets? Was he used to defecating on rare Persian rugs and our 100 percent wool carpeting wasn't good enough? Was it because we were black? But weren't dogs colorblind?

I've spent a good part of my life trying to figure out what my father 25
meant by number one. Born poor and dark in Washington, I think he was trying, in his own way, to protect us from the crushing assumptions of failure that he and his generation grew up with. I like to think he was simply saying, like the army, "Be all that you can be," but I'm still not sure. For years, I was haunted by the specter of number two gaining on me, of never having a house nice enough for Rockefeller dog shit, of my father's middle finger admonishing me. It's hard to move forward when you're looking over your shoulder.

When I was younger, I didn't ask my father what he meant. By the time I was confident enough to ask, my father had been through so many transformations—from dentist to hippie to lay guru—that he'd managed to forget, or convince himself he'd forgotten, those Sunday morning sermons. When I brought them up he'd look blank, his eyes would glaze over, and he'd say something like, "Jill, what are you talking about? With your dramatic imagination you should have been an actress."

But I'm not an actress. I'm a journalist, my father's daughter. I've spent a good portion of my life trying to be a good race woman and number one at the same time. Tomorrow, I go to work at the *Washington Post* magazine, a first. Falling asleep, I wonder if that's the same as being number one.

Analyzing the Text

1. What message did Nelson's father wish to instill during their Sunday breakfasts?
2. How has Nelson's life been influenced by her attempt to understand and act upon her father's advice?

Understanding Nelson's Techniques

1. What portrait does Nelson create of her father in terms of his strengths and weaknesses?
2. How does the setting—a Sunday family breakfast—add to the effectiveness of this piece?

Arguing for an Interpretation

1. In your view, was Nelson's father correct in his assessment of race and class relationships in the United States? Why or why not?
2. What "messages" did you receive from parents or grandparents that played a decisive role in creating your expectations about success and failure? If you did not have a Nelson's father type in your family, do you wish you had? Why or why not?

Amy Tan

Amy Tan was born in Oakland, California, in 1952. She studied linguistics and worked with disabled children. Tan's first novel,* The Joy Luck Club *(1989), was widely praised for its depiction of the relationship between Chinese mothers and their American-born daughters. Tan has also written* The Kitchen God's Wife *(1991),* The Hundred Secret Senses *(1995), and* The Bonesetter's Daughter *(2001). "The Language of Discretion" was published in 1990.

The Language of Discretion

At a recent family dinner in San Francisco, my mother whispered to me: "Sau-sau [Brother's Wife] pretends too hard to be polite! Why bother? In the end, she always takes everything."

My mother thinks like a *waixiao,* an expatriate, temporarily away from China since 1949, no longer patient with ritual courtesies. As if to prove her point, she reached across the table to offer my elderly aunt from Beijing the last scallop from the Happy Family seafood dish.

Sau-sau scowled. *"B'yao, zhen b'yao!"* (I don't want it, really I don't!) she cried, patting her plump stomach.

"Take it! Take it!" scolded my mother in Chinese.

"Full, I'm already full," Sau-sau protested weakly, eyeing the beloved 5
scallop.

"Ai!" exclaimed my mother, completely exasperated. "Nobody else wants it. If you don't take it, it will only rot!"

At this point, Sau-sau sighed, acting as if she were doing my mother a big favor by taking the wretched scrap off her hands.

My mother turned to her brother, a high-ranking communist official who was visiting her in California for the first time: "In America a Chinese person could starve to death. If you say you don't want it, they won't ask you again forever."

My uncle nodded and said he understood fully: Americans take things quickly because they have no time to be polite.

I thought about this misunderstanding again—of social contexts fail- 10
ing in translation—when a friend sent me an article from the *New York Times Magazine* (24 April 1988). The article, on changes in New York's Chinatown, made passing reference to the inherent ambivalence of the Chinese language.

Chinese people are so "discreet and modest," the article stated, there aren't even words for "yes" and "no."

That's not true, I thought, although I can see why an outsider might think that. I continued reading.

If one is Chinese, the article went on to say, "One compromises, one doesn't hazard a loss of face by an overemphatic response."

My throat seized. Why do people keep saying these things? As if we truly were those little dolls sold in Chinatown tourist shops, heads bobbing up and down in complacent agreement to anything said!

15 I worry about the effect of one-dimensional statements on the unwary and guileless. When they read about this so-called vocabulary deficit, do they also conclude that Chinese people evolved into a mild-mannered lot because the language only allowed them to hobble forth with minced words?

Something enormous is always lost in translation. Something insidious seeps into the gaps, especially when amateur linguists continue to compare, one-for-one, language differences and then put forth notions wide open to misinterpretation: that Chinese people have no direct linguistic means to make decisions, assert or deny, affirm or negate, just say no to drug dealers, or behave properly on the witness stand when told, "Please answer yes or no."

Yet one can argue, with the help of renowned linguists, that the Chinese are indeed up a creek without "yes" and "no." Take any number of variations on the old language-and-reality theory stated years ago by Edward Sapir: "Human beings . . . are very much at the mercy of the particular language which has become the medium for their society. . . . The fact of the matter is that the 'real world' is to a large extent built up on the language habits of the group."[1]

This notion was further bolstered by the famous Sapir-Whorf hypothesis, which roughly states that one's perception of the world and how one functions in it depends a great deal on the language used. As Sapir, Whorf, and new carriers of the banner would have us believe, language shapes our thinking, channels us along certain patterns embedded in words, syntactic structures, and intonation patterns. Language has become the peg and the shelf that enables us to sort out and categorize the world. In English, we see "cats" and "dogs"; what if the language had also specified *glatz,* meaning "animals that leave fur on the sofa," and *glotz,* meaning "animals that leave fur and drool on the sofa"? How would language, the enabler, have changed our perceptions with slight vocabulary variations?

And if this were the case—of language being the master of destined thought—think of the opportunities lost from failure to evolve two little words, *yes* and *no,* the simplest of opposites! Ghenghis Khan could have been sent back to Mongolia. Opium wars might have been averted. The Cultural Revolution could have been sidestepped.

20 There are still many, from serious linguists to pop psychology cultists, who view language and reality as inextricably tied, one being the consequence of the other. We have traversed the range from the Sapir-Whorf hypothesis to est[2] and neurolinguistic programming, which tell us "you are what you say."

I too have been intrigued by the theories. I can summarize, albeit badly, ages-old empirical evidence: of Eskimos and their infinite ways to say "snow," their ability to *see* the differences in snowflake configurations, thanks to the richness of their vocabulary, while non-Eskimo speakers like myself founder in "snow," "more snow," and "lots more where that came from."

---

[1]Edward Sapir, *Selected Writings,* ed. D. G. Mandelbaum (Berkeley and Los Angeles: University of California Press, 1949).

[2]est, group therapy, founded by Werner Erhard.

I too have experienced dramatic cognitive awakenings via the word. Once I added "mauve" to my vocabulary I began to see it everywhere. When I learned how to pronounce *prix fixe,* I ate French food at prices better than the easier-to-say *a la carte* choices.

But just how seriously are we supposed to take this?

Sapir said something else about language and reality. It is the part that often gets left behind in the dot-dot-dots of quotes: ". . . No two languages are ever sufficiently similar to be considered as representing the same social reality. The worlds in which different societies live are distinct worlds, not merely the same world with different labels attached."

When I first read this, I thought, Here at last is validity for the dilem- 25
mas I felt growing up in a bicultural, bilingual family! As any child of immigrant parents knows, there's a special kind of double bind attached to knowing two languages. My parents, for example, spoke to me in both Chinese and English; I spoke back to them in English.

"Amy-ah!" they'd call to me.

"What?" I'd mumble back.

"Do not question us when we call," they scolded me in Chinese. "It is not respectful."

"What do you mean?"

"Ai! Didn't we just tell you not to question?" 30

To this day, I wonder which parts of my behavior were shaped by Chinese, which by English. I am tempted to think, for example, that if I am of two minds on some matter it is due to the richness of my linguistic experiences, not to any personal tendencies toward wishy-washiness. But which mind says what?

Was it perhaps patience—developed through years of deciphering my mother's fractured English—that had me listening politely while a woman announced over the phone that I had won one of five valuable prizes? Was it respect—pounded in by the Chinese imperative to accept convoluted explanations—that had me agreeing that I might find it worth-while to drive seventy-five miles to view a time-share resort? Could I have been at a loss for words when asked, "Wouldn't you like to win a Hawaiian cruise or perhaps a fabulous Star of India designed exclusively by Carter and Van Arpels?"

And when this same woman called back a week later, this time complaining that I had missed my appointment, obviously it was my type A language that kicked into gear and interrupted her. Certainly, my blunt denial—"Frankly I'm not interested"—was as American as apple pie. And when she said, "But it's in Morgan Hill," and I shouted, "Read my lips. I don't care if it's Timbuktu," you can be sure I said it with the precise intonation expressing both cynicism and disgust.

It's dangerous business, this sorting out of language and behavior. Which one is English? Which is Chinese? The categories manifest themselves: passive and aggressive, tentative and assertive, indirect and direct. And I realize they are just variations of the same theme: that Chinese people are discreet and modest.

Reject them all! 35

If my reaction is overly strident, it is because I cannot come across as too emphatic. I grew up listening to the same lines over and over again, like so many rote expressions repeated in an English phrasebook. And I too almost came to believe them.

Yet if I consider my upbringing more carefully, I find there was nothing discreet about the Chinese language I grew up with. My parents made everything abundantly clear. Nothing wishy-washy in their demands, no compromises accepted: "Of course you will become a famous neurosurgeon," they told me. "And yes, a concert pianist on the side."

In fact, now that I remember, it seems that the more emphatic outbursts always spilled over into Chinese: "Not that way! You must wash rice so not a single grain spills out."

I do not believe that my parents—both immigrants from mainland China—are an exception to the modest-and-discreet rule. I have only to look at the number of Chinese engineering students skewing minority ratios at Berkeley, MIT, and Yale. Certainly they were not raised by passive mothers and fathers who said, "It is up to you, my daughter. Writer, welfare recipient, masseuse, or molecular engineer—you decide."

And my American mind says, See, those engineering students weren't 40
able to say no to their parents' demands. But then my Chinese mind remembers: Ah, but those parents all wanted their sons and daughters to be *pre-med.*

Having listened to both Chinese and English, I also tend to be suspicious of any comparisons between the two languages. Typically, one language—that of the person doing the comparing—is often used as the standard, the benchmark for a logical form of expression. And so the language being compared is always in danger of being judged deficient or superfluous, simplistic or unnecessarily complex, melodious or cacophonous. English speakers point out that Chinese is extremely difficult because it relies on variations in tone barely discernible to the human ear. By the same token, Chinese speakers tell me English is extremely difficult because it is inconsistent, a language of too many broken rules, of Mickey Mice and Donald Ducks.

Even more dangerous to my mind is the temptation to compare both language and behavior *in translation.* To listen to my mother speak English, one might think she has no concept of past or future tense, that she doesn't see the difference between singular and plural, that she is gender blind because she calls my husband "she." If one were not careful, one might also generalize that, based on the way my mother talks, all Chinese people take a circumlocutory route to get to the point. It is, in fact, my mother's idiosyncratic behavior to ramble a bit.

Sapir was right about differences between two languages and their realities. I can illustrate why word-for-word translation is not enough to translate meaning and intent. I once received a letter from China which I read to non-Chinese speaking friends. The letter, originally written in Chinese, had been translated by my brother-in law in Beijing. One portion described the time when my uncle at age ten discovered his widowed mother (my grandmother) had remarried—as a number three concubine, the ultimate disgrace for an honorable family. The translated version of my uncle's letter read in part:

> In 1925, I met my mother in Shanghai. When she came to me, I didn't have greeting to her as if seeing nothing. She pull me to a corner secretly and asked me why didn't have greeting to her. I couldn't control myself and cried, "Ma! Why did you leave us?

> People told me: one day you ate a beancake yourself. Your sister in-law found it and sweared at you, called your names. So . . . is it true?" She clasped my hand and answered immediately, "It's not true, don't say what like this." After this time, there was a few chance to meet her.

"What!" cried my friends. "Was eating a beancake so terrible?"

Of course not. The beancake was simply a euphemism; a ten-year-old 45
boy did not dare question his mother on something as shocking as concubinage. Eating a beancake was his equivalent for committing this selfish act, something inconsiderate of all family members, hence, my grandmother's despairing response to what seemed like a ludicrous charge of gluttony. And sure enough, she was banished from the family, and my uncle saw her only a few times before her death.

While the above may fuel people's argument that Chinese is indeed a language of extreme discretion, it does not mean that Chinese people speak in secrets and riddles. The contexts are fully understood. It is only to those on the *outside* that the language seems cryptic, the behavior inscrutable.

I am, evidently, one of the outsiders. My nephew in Shanghai, who recently started taking English lessons, has been writing me letters in English. I had told him I was a fiction writer, and so in one letter he wrote, "Congratulate to you on your writing. Perhaps one day I should like to read it." I took it in the same vein as "Perhaps one day we can get together for lunch." I sent back a cheery note. A month went by and another letter arrived from Shanghai. "Last one perhaps I hadn't writing distinctly," he said. "In the future, you'll send a copy of your works for me."

I try to explain to my English-speaking friends that Chinese language use is more *strategic* in manner, whereas English tends to be more direct; an American business executive may say, "Let's make a deal," and the Chinese manager may reply, "Is your son interested in learning about your widget business?" Each to his or her own purpose, each with his or her own linguistic path. But I hesitate to add more to the pile of generalizations, because no matter how many examples I provide and explain, I fear that it appears defensive and only reinforces the image: that Chinese people are "discreet and modest"—and it takes an American to explain what they really mean.

Why am I complaining? The description seems harmless enough (after all, the *New York Times Magazine* writer did not say "slippery and evasive"). It is precisely the bland, easy acceptability of the phrase that worries me.

I worry that the dominant society may see Chinese people from a lim- 50
ited—and limiting—perspective. I worry that seemingly benign stereotypes may be part of the reason there are few Chinese in top management positions, in mainstream political roles. I worry about the power of language: that if one says anything enough times—in *any* language—it might become true.

Could this be why Chinese friends of my parents' generation are willing to accept the generalization?

"Why are you complaining?" one of them said to me. "If people think we are modest and polite, let them think that. Wouldn't Americans be pleased to admit they are thought of as polite?"

And I do believe anyone would take the description as a compliment—at first. But after a while, it annoys, as if the only things that people heard one say were phatic remarks: "I'm so pleased to meet you. I've heard many wonderful things about you. For me? You shouldn't have!"

These remarks are not representative of new ideas, honest emotions, or considered thought. They are what is said from the polite distance of social contexts: of greetings, farewells, wedding thank-you notes, convenient excuses, and the like.

It makes me wonder though. How many anthropologists, how many 55
sociologists, how many travel journalists have documented so-called "natural interactions" in foreign lands, all observed with spiral notebook in hand? How many other cases are there of the long-lost primitive tribe, people who turned out to be sophisticated enough to put on the stone-age show that ethnologists had come to see?

And how many tourists fresh off the bus have wandered into Chinatown expecting the self-effacing shopkeeper to admit under duress that the goods are not worth the price asked? I have witnessed it.

"I don't know," the tourist said to the shopkeeper, a Cantonese woman in her fifties. "It doesn't look genuine to me. I'll give you three dollars."

"You don't like my price, go somewhere else," said the shopkeeper.

"You are not a nice person," cried the shocked tourist, "not a nice person at all!"

"Who say I have to be nice," snapped the shopkeeper. 60

"So how does one say 'yes' and 'no' in Chinese?" ask my friends a bit warily.

And here I do agree in part with the *New York Times Magazine* article. There is no one word for "yes" or "no"—but not out of necessity to be discreet. If anything, I would say the Chinese equivalent of answering "yes" or "no" is dis*crete,* that is, specific to what is asked.

Ask a Chinese person if he or she has eaten, and he or she might say *chrle* (eaten already) or perhaps *meiyou* (have not).

Ask, "So you had insurance at the time of the accident?" and the response would be *dwei* (correct) or *meiyou* (did not have).

Ask, "Have you stopped beating your wife?" and the answer refers di- 65
rectly to the proposition being asserted or denied: stopped already, still have not, never beat, have no wife.

What could be clearer?

As for those who are still wondering how to translate the language of discretion, I offer this personal example.

My aunt and uncle were about to return to Beijing after a three-month visit to the United States. On their last night I announced I wanted to take them out to dinner.

"Are you hungry?" I asked in Chinese.

"Not hungry," said my uncle promptly, the same response he once gave 70
me ten minutes before he suffered a low-blood-sugar attack.

"Not too hungry," said my aunt. "Perhaps you're hungry?"

"A little," I admitted.

"We can eat, we can eat," they both consented.

"What kind of food?" I asked.

"Oh, doesn't matter. Anything will do. Nothing fancy, just some simple 75
food is fine."

"Do you like Japanese food? We haven't had that yet," I suggested.

They looked at each other.

"We can eat it," said my uncle bravely, this survivor of the Long March.

"We have eaten it before," added my aunt. "Raw fish."

"Oh, you don't like it?" I said. "Don't be polite. We can go somewhere else."

"We are not being polite. We can eat it," my aunt insisted.

So I drove them to Japantown and we walked past several restaurants featuring colorful plastic displays of sushi.

"Not this one, not this one either," I continued to say, as if searching for a Japanese restaurant similar to the last. "Here it is," I finally said, turning into a restaurant famous for its Chinese fish dishes from Shandong.

"Oh, Chinese food!" cried my aunt, obviously relieved.

My uncle patted my arm. "You think Chinese."

"It's your last night here in America," I said. "So don't be polite. Act like an American."

And that night we ate a banquet.

Analyzing the Text

1. What conventional positive stereotype about the Chinese does Tan dispute? How did this stereotype get started?
2. How seriously does Tan take the Sapir-Whorf hypothesis? Does she believe, for example, that the lack of words for "yes" and "no" in Chinese makes Chinese people discreet and modest?

Understanding Tan's Techniques

1. Why does Tan differentiate between the terms "discreet" and "discrete"? How does she use this distinction to develop her argument?
2. Which of the examples cited by Tan—how people's interpretation of events is influenced by different cultural contexts—effectively illustrate her thesis?

Arguing for an Interpretation

1. The Sapir-Whorf hypothesis states that our perception of the world and how we function in it depends a great deal on the language we use. To what extent does Tan believe that language influences our perceptions, beliefs, and social behavior? Do you agree with her? Why or why not?
2. American-born children of immigrant parents play out the tensions of their ethnic and racial identities in terms of language. Has Tan done an adequate job in conveying this predicament?

Short Fiction

Amy Tan

Amy Tan was born in Oakland, California, in 1952 to Chinese immigrants. She received a B.A. in English and an M.A. in linguistics from San Jose State University. She has worked as a consultant to programs for disabled

children and as a freelance writer. Of her first visit to China in 1984, she says, "As soon as my feet touched China, I became Chinese."

"Two Kinds" is from Tan's first book, The Joy Luck Club *(1989), a work that explores conflicts between different cultures, and generations, of Chinese mothers and daughters in the United States. She has also written* The Kitchen God's Wife *(1991),* The Hundred Secret Senses *(1995), and* The Bonesetter's Daughter *(2001). This amusing story from the 1989 book reflects Tan's own experiences. In real life Tan's parents anticipated that she would become, as she says, "a neurosurgeon by trade and a concert pianist by hobby."*

Two Kinds

My mother believed you could be anything you wanted to be in America. You could open a restaurant. You could work for the government and get good retirement. You could buy a house with almost no money down. You could become rich. You could become instantly famous.

"Of course you can be prodigy, too," my mother told me when I was nine. "You can be best anything. What does Auntie Lindo know? Her daughter, she is only best tricky."

America was where all my mother's hopes lay. She had come here in 1949 after losing everything in China: her mother and father, her family home, her first husband, and two daughters, twin baby girls. But she never looked back with regret. There were so many ways for things to get better.

We didn't immediately pick the right kind of prodigy. At first my mother thought I could be a Chinese Shirley Temple. We'd watch Shirley's old movies on TV as though they were training films. My mother would poke my arm and say, *"Ni kan"*—You watch. And I would see Shirley tapping her feet, or singing a sailor song, or pursing her lips into a very round O while saying, "Oh my goodness."

"Ni kan," said my mother as Shirley's eyes flooded with tears. "You already know how. Don't need talent for crying!"

Soon after my mother got this idea about Shirley Temple, she took me 5
to a beauty training school in the Mission district and put me in the hands of a student who could barely hold the scissors without shaking. Instead of getting big fat curls, I emerged with an uneven mass of crinkly black fuzz. My mother dragged me off to the bathroom and tried to wet down my hair.

"You look like Negro Chinese," she lamented, as if I had done this on purpose.

The instructor of the beauty training school had to lop off these soggy clumps to make my hair even again. "Peter Pan is very popular these days," the instructor assured my mother. I now had hair the length of a boy's, with straight-across bangs that hung at a slant two inches above my eyebrows. I liked the haircut and it made me actually look forward to my future fame.

In fact, in the beginning, I was just as excited as my mother, maybe even more so. I pictured this prodigy part of me as many different images, trying each one on for size. I was a dainty ballerina girl standing by the curtains, waiting to hear the right music that would send me floating on my tiptoes. I was like the Christ child lifted out of the straw manger, crying with holy indignity. I was Cinderella stepping from her pumpkin carriage with sparkly cartoon music filling the air.

In all of my imaginings, I was filled with a sense that I would soon become *perfect.* My mother and father would adore me. I would be beyond reproach. I would never feel the need to sulk for anything.

But sometimes the prodigy in me became impatient. "If you don't 10
hurry up and get me out of here, I'm disappearing for good," it warned. "And then you'll always be nothing."

Every night after dinner, my mother and I would sit at the Formica kitchen table. She would present new tests, taking her examples from stories of amazing children she had read in *Ripley's Believe It or Not,* or *Good Housekeeping, Reader's Digest,* and a dozen other magazines she kept in a pile in our bathroom. My mother got these magazines from people whose houses she cleaned. And since she cleaned many houses each week, we had a great assortment. She would look through them all, searching for stories about remarkable children.

The first night she brought out a story about a three-year-old boy who knew the capitals of all the states and even most of the European countries. A teacher was quoted as saying the little boy could also pronounce the names of the foreign cities correctly.

"What's the capital of Finland?" my mother asked me, looking at the magazine story.

All I knew was the capital of California, because Sacramento was the name of the street we lived on in Chinatown. "Nairobi!" I guessed, saying the most foreign word I could think of. She checked to see if that was possibly one way to pronounce "Helsinki" before showing me the answer.

The tests got harder—multiplying numbers in my head, finding the 15
queen of hearts in a deck of cards, trying to stand on my head without using my hands, predicting the daily temperatures in Los Angeles, New York, and London.

One night I had to look at a page from the Bible for three minutes and then report everything I could remember. "Now Jehoshaphat had riches and honor in abundance and . . . that's all I remember, Ma," I said.

And after seeing my mother's disappointed face once again, something inside of me began to die. I hated the tests, the raised hopes and failed expectations. Before going to bed that night, I looked in the mirror above the bathroom sink and when I saw only my face staring back—and that it would always be this ordinary face—I began to cry. Such a sad, ugly girl! I made high-pitched noises like a crazed animal, trying to scratch out the face in the mirror.

And then I saw what seemed to be the prodigy side of me—because I had never seen that face before. I looked at my reflection, blinking so I could see more clearly. The girl staring back at me was angry, powerful. This girl and I were the same. I had new thoughts, willful thoughts, or rather thoughts filled with lots of won'ts. I won't let her change me, I promised myself. I won't be what I'm not.

So now on nights when my mother presented her tests, I performed listlessly, my head propped on one arm. I pretended to be bored. And I was. I got so bored I started counting the bellows of the foghorns out on the bay while my mother drilled me in other areas. The sound was comforting and reminded me of the cow jumping over the moon. And the next day, I played a game with myself, seeing if my mother would give up on me before eight bellows. After a while I usually counted only one, maybe two bellows at most. At least she was beginning to give up hope.

Two or three months had gone by without any mention of my being a 20
prodigy again. And then one day my mother was watching *The Ed Sullivan Show* on TV. The TV was old and the sound kept shorting out. Every time my mother got halfway up from the sofa to adjust the set, the sound would go back on and Ed would be talking. As soon as she sat down, Ed would go silent again. She got up, the TV broke into loud piano music. She sat down. Silence. Up and down, back and forth, quiet and loud. It was like a stiff embraceless dance between her and the TV set. Finally she stood by the set with her hand on the sound dial.

She seemed entranced by the music, a little frenzied piano piece with this mesmerizing quality, sort of quick passages and then teasing lilting ones before it returned to the quick playful parts.

"Ni kan," my mother said, calling me over with hurried hand gestures, "Look here."

I could see why my mother was fascinated by the music. It was being pounded out by a little Chinese girl, about nine years old, with a Peter Pan haircut. The girl had the sauciness of a Shirley Temple. She was proudly modest like a proper Chinese child. And she also did this fancy sweep of a curtsy, so that the fluffy skirt of her white dress cascaded slowly to the floor like the petals of a large carnation.

In spite of these warning signs, I wasn't worried. Our family had no piano and we couldn't afford to buy one, let alone reams of sheet music and piano lessons. So I could be generous in my comments when my mother bad-mouthed the little girl on TV.

"Play note right, but doesn't sound good! No singing sound," com- 25
plained my mother.

"What are you picking on her for?" I said carelessly. "She's pretty good. Maybe she's not the best, but she's trying hard." I knew almost immediately I would be sorry I said that.

"Just like you," she said. "Not the best. Because you not trying." She gave a little huff as she let go of the sound dial and sat down on the sofa.

The little Chinese girl sat down also to play an encore of "Anitra's Dance" by Grieg. I remember the song, because later on I had to learn how to play it.

Three days after watching *The Ed Sullivan Show,* my mother told me what my schedule would be for piano lessons and piano practice. She had talked to Mr. Chong, who lived on the first floor of our apartment building. Mr. Chong was a retired piano teacher and my mother had traded housecleaning services for weekly lessons and a piano for me to practice on every day, two hours a day, from four until six.

When my mother told me this, I felt as though I had been sent to hell. I 30
whined and then kicked my foot a little when I couldn't stand it anymore.

"Why don't you like me the way I am? I'm *not* a genius! I can't play the piano. And even if I could I wouldn't go on TV if you paid me a million dollars!" I cried.

My mother slapped me. "Who ask you be genius?" she shouted. "Only ask you be your best. For you sake. You think I want you be genius? Hnnh! What for! Who ask you!"

"So ungrateful," I heard her mutter in Chinese. "If she had as much talent as she has temper, she would be famous now."

Mr. Chong, whom I secretly nicknamed Old Chong, was very strange, always tapping his fingers to the silent music of an invisible orchestra. He looked ancient in my eyes. He had lost most of the hair on top of his head and he wore thick glasses and had eyes that always looked tired and sleepy. But he must have been younger than I thought, since he lived with his mother and was not yet married.

35 I met Old Lady Chong once and that was enough. She had this peculiar smell like a baby that had done something in its pants. And her fingers felt like a dead person's, like an old peach I once found in the back of the refrigerator; the skin just slid off the meat when I picked it up.

I soon found out why Old Chong had retired from teaching piano. He was deaf. "Like Beethoven!" he shouted to me. "We're both listening only in our head!" And he would start to conduct his frantic silent sonatas.

Our lessons went like this. He would open the book and point to different things, explaining their purpose: "Key! Treble! Bass! No sharps or flats! So this is C major! Listen now and play after me!"

And then he would play the C scale a few times, a simple chord, and then, as if inspired by an old, unreachable itch, he gradually added more notes and running trills and a pounding bass until the music was really something quite grand.

I would play after him, the simple scale, the simple chord, and then I just played some nonsense that sounded like a cat running up and down on top of garbage cans. Old Chong smiled and applauded and then said, "Very good! But now you must learn to keep time!"

40 So that's how I discovered that Old Chong's eyes were too slow to keep up with the wrong notes I was playing. He went through the motions in half-time. To help me keep rhythm, he stood behind me, pushing down on my right shoulder for every beat. He balanced pennies on top of my wrists so I would keep them still as I slowly played scales and arpeggios. He had me curve my hand around an apple and keep that shape when playing chords. He marched stiffly to show me how to make each finger dance up and down, staccato like an obedient little soldier.

He taught me all these things, and that was how I also learned I could be lazy and get away with mistakes, lots of mistakes. If I hit the wrong notes because I hadn't practiced enough, I never corrected myself. I just kept playing in rhythm. And Old Chong kept conducting his own private reverie.

So maybe I never really gave myself a fair chance. I did pick up the basics pretty quickly, and I might have become a good pianist at that young age. But I was so determined not to try, not to be anybody different that I learned to play only the most ear-splitting preludes, the most discordant hymns.

Over the next year, I practiced like this, dutifully in my own way. And then one day I heard my mother and her friend Lindo Jong both talking in a loud bragging tone of voice so others could hear. It was after church, and I was leaning against the brick wall wearing a dress with stiff white petticoats. Auntie Lindo's daughter, Waverly, who was about my age, was standing farther down the wall about five feet away. We had grown up together and shared all the closeness of two sisters squabbling over crayons and dolls. In other words, for the most part, we hated each other. I thought she was snotty. Waverly Jong had gained a certain amount of fame as "Chinatown's Littlest Chinese Chess Champion."

"She bring home too many trophy," lamented Auntie Lindo that Sunday. "All day she play chess. All day I have no time do nothing but dust off her winnings." She threw a scolding look at Waverly, who pretended not to see her.

"You lucky you don't have this problem," said Auntie Lindo with a sigh to my mother.

And my mother squared her shoulders and bragged: "Our problem worser than yours. If we ask Jing-Mei wash dish, she hear nothing but music. It's like you can't stop this natural talent."

And right then, I was determined to put a stop to her foolish pride.

A few weeks later, Old Chong and my mother conspired to have me play in a talent show which would be held in the church hall. By then, my parents had saved up enough to buy me a secondhand piano, a black Wurlitzer spinet with a scarred bench. It was the showpiece of our living room.

For the talent show, I was to play a piece called "Pleading Child" from Schumann's *Scenes from Childhood.* It was a simple, moody piece that sounded more difficult than it was. I was supposed to memorize the whole thing, playing the repeat parts twice to make the piece sound longer. But I dawdled over it, playing a few bars and then cheating, looking up to see what notes followed. I never really listened to what I was playing. I daydreamed about being somewhere else, about being someone else.

The part I liked to practice best was the fancy curtsy: right foot out, touch the rose on the carpet with a pointed foot, sweep to the side, left leg bends, look up and smile.

My parents invited all the couples from the Joy Luck Club to witness my debut. Auntie Lindo and Uncle Tin were there. Waverly and her two older brothers had also come. The first two rows were filled with children both younger and older than I was. The littlest ones got to go first. They recited simple nursery rhymes, squawked out tunes on miniature violins, twirled Hula Hoops, pranced in pink ballet tutus, and when they bowed or curtsied, the audience would sigh in unison, "Awww," and then clap enthusiastically.

When my turn came, I was very confident. I remember my childish excitement. It was as if I knew, without a doubt, that the prodigy side of me really did exist. I had no fear whatsoever, no nervousness. I remember thinking to myself, This is it! This is it! I looked out over the audience, at my mother's blank face, my father's yawn, Auntie Lindo's stiff-lipped smile, Waverly's sulky expression. I had on a white dress layered with sheets of lace, and a pink bow in my Peter Pan haircut. As I sat down I envisioned people jumping to their feet and Ed Sullivan rushing up to introduce me to everyone on TV.

And I started to play. It was so beautiful. I was so caught up in how lovely I looked that at first I didn't worry how I would sound. So it was a surprise to me when I hit the first wrong note and I realized something didn't sound quite right. And then I hit another and another followed that. A chill started at the top of my head and began to trickle down. Yet I couldn't stop playing, as though my hands were bewitched. I kept thinking my fingers would adjust themselves back, like a train switching to the right track. I played this strange jumble through two repeats, the sour notes staying with me all the way to the end.

When I stood up, I discovered my legs were shaking. Maybe I had just been nervous and the audience, like Old Chong, had seen me go through the right motions and had not heard anything wrong at all. I swept my right foot out, went down on my knee, looked up and smiled. The room was quiet, except for Old Chong, who was beaming and shouting, "Bravo! Bravo! Well done!" But then I saw my mother's face, her stricken face. The audience clapped weakly, and as I walked back to my chair, with my whole face quivering as I tried not to cry, I heard a little boy whisper loudly to his mother, "That was awful," and the mother whispered back, "Well, she certainly tried."

And now I realized how many people were in the audience, the whole 55
world it seemed. I was aware of eyes burning into my back. I felt the shame of my mother and father as they sat stiffly throughout the rest of the show.

We could have escaped during intermission. Pride and some strange sense of humor must have anchored my parents to their chairs. And so we watched it all: the eighteen-year-old boy with a fake mustache who did a magic show and juggled flaming hoops while riding a unicycle. The breasted girl with white makeup who sang from *Madame Butterfly* and got honorable mention. And the eleven-year-old boy who won first prize playing a tricky violin song that sounded like a busy bee.

After the show, the Hsus, the Jongs, and the St. Clairs from the Joy Luck Club came up to my mother and father.

"Lots of talented kids," Auntie Lindo said vaguely, smiling broadly.

"That was somethin' else," said my father, and I wondered if he was referring to me in a humorous way, or whether he even remembered what I had done.

Waverly looked at me and shrugged her shoulders. "You aren't a genius 60
like me," she said matter-of-factly. And if I hadn't felt so bad, I would have pulled her braids and punched her stomach.

But my mother's expression was what devastated me: a quiet, blank look that said she had lost everything. I felt the same way, and it seemed as if everybody were now coming up, like gawkers at the scene of an accident, to see what parts were actually missing. When we got on the bus to go home, my father was humming the busy-bee tune and my mother was silent. I kept thinking she wanted to wait until we got home before shouting at me. But when my father unlocked the door to our apartment, my mother walked in and then went to the back, into the bedroom. No accusations. No blame. And in a way, I felt disappointed. I had been waiting for her to start shouting, so I could shout back and cry and blame her for all my misery.

I assumed my talent-show fiasco meant I never had to play the piano again. But two days later, after school, my mother came out of the kitchen and saw me watching TV.

"Four clock," she reminded me as if it were any other day. I was stunned, as though she were asking me to go through the talent-show torture again. I wedged myself more tightly in front of the TV.

"Turn off TV," she called from the kitchen five minutes later.

I didn't budge. And then I decided. I didn't have to do what my mother 65
said anymore. I wasn't her slave. This wasn't China. I had listened to her before and look what happened. She was the stupid one.

She came out from the kitchen and stood in the arched entryway of the living room. "Four clock," she said once again, louder.

"I'm not going to play anymore," I said nonchalantly. "Why should I? I'm not a genius."

She walked over and stood in front of the TV. I saw her chest was heaving up and down in an angry way.

"No!" I said, and I now felt stronger, as if my true self had finally emerged. So this was what had been inside me all along.

"No! I won't!" I screamed. 70

She yanked me by the arm, pulled me off the floor, snapped off the TV. She was frighteningly strong, half pulling, half carrying me toward the piano as I kicked the throw rugs under my feet. She lifted me up and onto the hard bench. I was sobbing by now, looking at her bitterly. Her chest was heaving even more and her mouth was open, smiling crazily as if she were pleased I was crying.

"You want me to be someone that I'm not!" I sobbed. "I'll never be the kind of daughter you want me to be!"

"Only two kinds of daughters," she shouted in Chinese. "Those who are obedient and those who follow their own mind! Only one kind of daughter can live in this house. Obedient daughter!"

"Then I wish I wasn't your daughter. I wish you weren't my mother," I shouted. As I said these things I got scared. It felt like worms and toads and slimy things crawling out of my chest, but it also felt good, as if this awful side of me had surfaced, at last.

"Too late change this," said my mother shrilly. 75

And I could sense her anger rising to its breaking point. I wanted to see it spill over. And that's when I remembered the babies she had lost in China, the ones we never talked about. "Then I wish I'd never been born!" I shouted. "I wish I were dead! Like them."

It was as if I had said the magic words. Alakazam!—and her face went blank, her mouth closed, her arms went slack, and she backed out of the room, stunned, as if she were blowing away like a small brown leaf, thin, brittle, lifeless.

It was not the only disappointment my mother felt in me. In the years that followed, I failed her so many times, each time asserting my own will, my right to fall short of expectations. I didn't get straight As. I didn't become class president. I didn't get into Stanford. I dropped out of college.

For unlike my mother, I did not believe I could be anything I wanted to be. I could only be me.

And for all those years, we never talked about the disaster at the recital 80
or my terrible accusations afterward at the piano bench. All that remained unchecked, like a betrayal that was now unspeakable. So I never found a way to ask her why she had hoped for something so large that failure was inevitable.

And even worse, I never asked her what frightened me the most: Why had she given up hope?

For after our struggle at the piano, she never mentioned my playing again. The lessons stopped. The lid to the piano was closed, shutting out the dust, my misery, and her dreams.

So she surprised me. A few years ago, she offered to give me the piano, for my thirtieth birthday. I had not played in all those years. I saw the offer as a sign of forgiveness, a tremendous burden removed.

"Are you sure?" I asked shyly. "I mean, won't you and Dad miss it?"

"No, this your piano," she said firmly. "Always your piano. You only one can play."

"Well, I probably can't play anymore," I said. "It's been years."

"You pick up fast," said my mother, as if she knew this was certain. "You have natural talent. You could been genius if you want to."

"No I couldn't."

"You just not trying," said my mother. And she was neither angry nor sad. She said it as if to announce a fact that could never be disproved. "Take it," she said.

But I didn't at first. It was enough that she had offered it to me. And after that, every time I saw it in my parents' living room, standing in front of the bay windows, it made me feel proud, as if it were a shiny trophy I had won back.

Last week I sent a tuner over to my parents' apartment and had the piano reconditioned, for purely sentimental reasons. My mother had died a few months before and I had been getting things in order for my father, a little bit at a time. I put the jewelry in special silk pouches. The sweaters she had knitted in yellow, pink, bright orange—all the colors I hated—I put those in moth-proof boxes. I found some old Chinese silk dresses, the kind with little slits up the sides. I rubbed the old silk against my skin, then wrapped them in tissue and decided to take them home with me.

After I had the piano tuned, I opened the lid and touched the keys. It sounded even richer than I remembered. Really, it was a very good piano. Inside the bench were the same exercise notes with handwritten scales, the same secondhand music books with their covers held together with yellow tape.

I opened up the Schumann book to the dark little piece I had played at the recital. It was on the left-hand side of the page, "Pleading Child." It looked more difficult than I remembered. I played a few bars, surprised at how easily the notes came back to me.

And the first time, or so it seemed, I noticed the piece on the right-hand side. It was called "Perfectly Contented." I tried to play this one as well. It had a lighter melody but the same flowing rhythm and turned out to be quite easy. "Pleading Child" was shorter but slower; "Perfectly Contented" was longer, but faster. And after I played them both a few times, I realized they were two halves of the same song.

Analyzing the Text

1. Why is it so important to Jing-Mei's mother to have her daughter become a prodigy of some kind and how does Jing-Mei react to her mother's expectations?
2. How do we know that Jing-Mei came to understand her mother's wishes for her in a much different way than she had when she was a child?

Understanding Tan's Techniques

1. What are some of the different ways in which the idea of "two kinds" underscores the choices that faced Jing-Mei?
2. In what sense does the piano and its fate symbolize Jing-Mei's changing attitude toward her mother's aspirations?

Arguing for an Interpretation

1. Do you think Jing-Mei misunderstood what her mother expected of her? What evidence, if any, in the story might support this interpretation?
2. In what sense might this story be viewed as a parable of the immigrant experience and the kinds of pressures that faced the children of immigrants to succeed as a way of making up for their parents' sacrifices?

John Cheever

John Cheever (1912–1982) was born in Quincy, Massachusetts. His parents had planned for him to attend Harvard, but he was expelled at seventeen from the Thayer Academy for smoking, which marked the end of his formal education. Although he wrote five novels, he is best known for his deftly constructed short stories of suburban affluent America that frequently appeared in The New Yorker. *Collections of his work include* The Enormous Radio *(1953),* The House Breaker of Shady Hill *(1958),* The Brigadier and the Golf Widow *(1964), and* The Stories of John Cheever *(1978), which won a Pulitzer Prize, and from which "Reunion" is reprinted.*

Reunion

The last time I saw my father was in Grand Central Station. I was going from my grandmother's in the Adirondacks to a cottage on the Cape that my mother had rented, and I wrote my father that I would be in New York between trains for an hour and a half and asked if we could have lunch together. His secretary wrote to say that he would meet me at the information booth at noon, and at twelve o'clock sharp I saw him coming through the crowd. He was a stranger to me—my mother divorced him three years ago, and I hadn't been with him since—but as soon as I saw him I felt that he was my father, my flesh and blood, my future and my doom. I knew that when I was grown I would be something like him; I would have to plan my campaigns within his limitations. He was a big, good-looking man, and I was terribly happy to see him again. He struck me on the back and shook my hand. "Hi, Charlie," he said. "Hi, boy. I'd like to take you up to my club, but it's in the Sixties, and if you have to catch an early train I guess we'd better get something to eat around here." He put his arm around me, and I smelled my father the way my mother sniffs a rose. It was a rich compound of whiskey, aftershave lotion, shoe polish, woolens, and the rankness of a mature male. I hoped that someone would see us together. I wished that we could be photographed. I wanted some record of our having been together.

We went out of the station and up a side street to a restaurant. It was still early, and the place was empty. The bartender was quarreling with a delivery boy, and there was one very old waiter in a red coat down by the kitchen door. We sat down, and my father hailed the waiter in a loud voice. *"Kellner!"* he shouted. *"Garçon! Cameriere! You!"* His boisterousness in the empty restaurant seemed out of place. "Could we have a little service here!" he shouted. "Chop-chop." Then he clapped his hands. This caught the waiter's attention, and he shuffled over to our table.

"Were you clapping your hands at me?" he asked.

"Calm down, calm down, *sommelier,*" my father said. "If it isn't too much to ask of you—if it wouldn't be too much above and beyond the call of duty, we would like a couple of Beefeater Gibsons."

"I don't like to be clapped at," the waiter said. 5

"I should have brought my whistle," my father said. "I have a whistle that is audible only to the ears of old waiters. Now, take out your little pad and your little pencil and see if you can get this straight: two Beefeater Gibsons. Repeat after me: two Beefeater Gibsons."

"I think you'd better go somewhere else," the waiter said quietly.

"That," said my father, "is one of the most brilliant suggestions I have ever heard. Come on, Charlie, let's get the hell out of here."

I followed my father out of that restaurant into another. He was not so boisterous this time. Our drinks came, and he cross-questioned me about the baseball season. He then struck the edge of his empty glass with his knife and began shouting again. "*Garçon! Kellner! You!* Could we trouble you to bring us two more of the same."

"How old is the boy?" the waiter asked. 10

"That," my father said, "is none of your goddamned business."

"I'm sorry, sir," the waiter said, "but I won't serve the boy another drink."

"Well, I have some news for you," my father said. "I have some very interesting news for you. This doesn't happen to be the only restaurant in New York. They've opened another on the corner. Come on, Charlie."

He paid the bill, and I followed him out of that restaurant into another. Here the waiters wore pink jackets like hunting coats, and there was a lot of horse tack on the walls. We sat down, and my father began to shout again. "Master of the hounds! Tallyhoo and all that sort of thing. We'd like a little something in the way of a stirrup cup. Namely, two Bibson Geefeaters."

"Two Bibson Geefeaters?" the waiter asked, smiling. 15

"You know damned well what I want," my father said angrily. "I want two Beefeater Gibsons, and make it snappy. Things have changed in jolly old England. So my friend the duke tells me. Let's see what England can produce in the way of a cocktail."

"This isn't England," the waiter said.

"Don't argue with me," my father said. "Just do as you're told."

"I just thought you might like to know where you are," the waiter said.

"If there is one thing I cannot tolerate," my father said, "it is an impu- 20
dent domestic. Come on, Charlie."

The fourth place we went to was Italian. "*Buon giorno,*" my father said. "*Per favore, possiamo avere due cocktail americani, forti, forti. Molto gin, poco vermut.*"

"I don't understand Italian," the waiter said.

"Oh, come off it," my father said. "You understand Italian, and you know damned well you do. *Vogliamo due cocktail americani. Subito.*"

The waiter left us and spoke with the captain, who came over to our table and said, "I'm sorry, sir, but this table is reserved."

"All right," my father said. "Get us another table."

"All the tables are reserved," the captain said.

"I get it," my father said. "You don't desire our patronage. Is that it? Well, the hell with you. *Vada all' inferno.* Let's go, Charlie."

"I have to get my train," I said.

"I'm sorry, sonny," my father said. "I'm terribly sorry." He put his arm around me and pressed me against him. "I'll walk you back to the station. If there had only been time to go up to my club."

"That's all right, Daddy," I said.

"I'll get you a paper," he said. "I'll get you a paper to read on the train."

Then he went up to a newsstand and said, "Kind sir, will you be good enough to favor me with one of your goddamned, no-good, ten-cent afternoon papers?" The clerk turned away from him and stared at a magazine cover. "Is it asking too much, kind sir," my father said, "is it asking too much for you to sell me one of your disgusting specimens of yellow journalism?"

"I have to go, Daddy," I said. "It's late."

"Now, just wait a second, sonny," he said. "Just wait a second. I want to get a rise out of this chap."

"Goodbye, Daddy," I said, and I went down the stairs and got my train, and that was the last time I saw my father.

Analyzing the Text

1. What clues tell the reader how much the anticipated meeting with his father means to Charlie?
2. How would you characterize the father's attitude toward those of other nationalities and different social classes?

Understanding Cheever's Techniques

1. How does Cheever's sequencing of episodes make clear why Charlie would never wish to see his father again?
2. To what extent does the kind of language the father uses toward those he perceives as socially inferior contribute to his son's sense of alienation?

Arguing for an Interpretation

1. To what extent are Charlie's dashed expectations and decision to never see his father again the result of his thinking when he grows up he will be like him?
2. Although Cheever is best known for his deftly constructed stories of WASP (White Anglo-Saxon Protestant) suburban society, he is clearly not sympathetic to the elitist racial and social values of the father in the story. However, in a short paper, consider the opposite possibility: that the father's boorish behavior is caused by a desperate desire to impress his son and that Charlie is heartless in rejecting him?

Bessie Head

Bessie Head (1937–1986) was born in Pietermaritzburg, South Africa, the daughter of a black father and a white mother. She suffered the childhood trauma of being "re-classified"; she was taken from her mother at birth and brought up by foster parents as a Coloured. Her mother was treated as insane because of her relationship with a black man. Head was raised by her foster parents until she was thirteen, when she was placed in a mission orphanage. The emotional scars of her childhood are powerfully recorded in the widely acclaimed A Question of Power *(1973), a fictional study of madness produced by the violence of the apartheid system. After completing her education, she taught grammar school and wrote fiction for a local newspaper. In 1963, Head moved to a farm commune in Serowe, Botswana, with her son. She lived there, working as a teacher and a gardener in a local village until her death.*

Head's writing grows directly out of her experience of village life. Her first novel, When Rain Clouds Gather *(1968), presents the epic struggle of a village trying to survive a devastating drought. Her next two novels,* Maru *(1971) and* A Question of Power *(1973), depict women struggling to overcome oppression in their societies and earned her the distinction of being one of Africa's major female writers. As a chronicler of village life, Head wrote two histories,* Serowe: Village of the Rain Wind *(1981) and* A Bewitched Crossroad *(1985). "Looking for a Rain God," from* The Collector of Treasures and Other Botswana Village Tales *(1977), is based on a shocking local incident revealing how an ancient tribal ritual resurfaced after years of drought in modern-day Botswana.*

Looking for a Rain God

It is lonely at the lands where the people go to plough. These lands are vast clearings in the bush, and the wild bush is lonely too. Nearly all the lands are within walking distance from the village. In some parts of the bush where the underground water is very near the surface, people made little rest camps for themselves and dug shallow wells to quench their thirst while on their journey to their own lands. They experienced all kinds of things once they left the village. They could rest at shady watering places full of lush, tangled trees with delicate pale-gold and purple wildflowers springing up between soft green moss and the children could hunt around for wild figs and any berries that might be in season. But from 1958, a seven-year drought fell upon the land and even the watering places began to look as dismal as the dry open thorn-bush country; the leaves of the trees curled up and withered; the moss became dry and hard and, under the shade of the tangled trees, the ground turned a powdery black and white, because there was no rain. People said rather humorously that if you tried to catch the rain in a cup it would only fill a teaspoon. Toward the beginning of the seventh year of drought, the summer had become an anguish to live through. The air was so dry and moisture-free that it burned the skin. No one knew what to do to escape the heat and tragedy was in the air. At the beginning of that summer, a number of men just went out of their homes and hung themselves to death from trees. The majority of the people had lived off crops, but for two years past they had all returned from the lands with only their rolled-up skin blankets and cooking utensils. Only the charlatans, incanters, and witch doctors made a pile of money during this time because people were always turning to them in desperation for little talismans and herbs to rub on the plough for the crops to grow and the rain to fall.

The rains were late that year. They came in early November, with a promise of good rain. It wasn't the full, steady downpour of the years of good rain but thin, scanty, misty rain. It softened the earth and a rich growth of green things sprang up everywhere for the animals to eat. People were called to the center of the village to hear the proclamation of the beginning of the ploughing season; they stirred themselves and whole families began to move off to the lands to plough.

The family of the old man, Mokgobja, were among those who left early for the lands. They had a donkey cart and piled everything onto it, Mokgobja—who was over seventy years old; two girls, Neo and Boseyong; their mother Tiro and an unmarried sister, Nesta; and the father and supporter of the family, Ramadi, who drove the donkey cart. In the rush of the first hope of rain, the man, Ramadi, and the two women, cleared the land of thornbush and then hedged their vast ploughing area with this same thornbush to protect the future crop from the goats they had brought along for milk. They cleared out and deepened the old well with its pool of muddy water and still in this light, misty rain, Ramadi inspanned two oxen and turned the earth over with a hand plough.

The land was ready and ploughed, waiting for the crops. At night, the earth was alive with insects singing and rustling about in search of food. But suddenly, by mid-November, the rain flew away; the rain clouds fled away and left the sky bare. The sun danced dizzily in the skin, with a strange cruelty. Each day the land was covered in a haze of mist as the sun sucked up the last drop of moisture out of the earth. The family sat down in despair, waiting and waiting. Their hopes had run so high; the goats had started producing milk, which they had eagerly poured on their porridge; now they ate plain porridge with no milk. It was impossible to plant the corn, maize, pumpkin, and watermelon seeds in the dry earth. They sat the whole day in the shadow of the huts and even stopped thinking, for the rain had fled away. Only the children, Neo and Boseyong, were quite happy in their little-girl world. They carried on with their game of making house like their mother and chattered to each other in light, soft tones. They made children from sticks around which they tied rags, and scolded them severely in an exact imitation of their own mother. Their voices could be heard scolding the day long. "You stupid thing, when I send you to draw water, why do you spill half of it out of the bucket!" "You stupid thing! Can't you mind the porridge pot without letting the porridge burn!" And then they would beat the rag dolls on their bottoms with severe expressions.

The adults paid no attention to this; they did not even hear the funny chatter; they sat waiting for rain; their nerves were stretched to breaking-point willing the rain to fall out of the sky. Nothing was important, beyond that. All their animals had been sold during the bad years to purchase food, and of all their herd only two goats were left. It was the women of the family who finally broke down under the strain of waiting for rain. It was really the two women who caused the death of the little girls. Each night they started a weird, high-pitched wailing that began on a low, mournful note and whipped up to a frenzy. Then they would stamp their feet and shout as though they had lost their heads. The men sat quiet and self-controlled; it was important for men to maintain their self control at all times but their nerve was breaking too. They knew the women were haunted by the starvation of the coming year.

Finally, an ancient memory stirred in the old man, Mokgobja. When he was very young and the customs of the ancestors still ruled the land, he had been witness to a rain-making ceremony. And he came alive a little, struggling to recall the details which had been buried by years and years of prayer in a Christian church. As soon as the mists cleared a little, he began consulting in whispers with his youngest son, Ramadi. There was, he said, a certain rain god who accepted only the sacrifice of the bodies of children. Then the rain would fall; then the crops would grow, he said. He explained the ritual and as he talked, his memory became a conviction and he began to talk with unshakable authority. Ramadi's nerves were smashed by the nightly wailing of the women and soon the two men began whispering with the two women. The children continued their game: "You stupid thing! How could you have lost the money on the way to the shop! You must have been playing again!"

After it was all over and the bodies of the two little girls had been spread across the land, the rain did not fall. Instead, there was a deathly silence at night and the devouring heat of the sun by day. A terror, extreme and deep, overwhelmed the whole family. They packed, rolling up their skin blankets and pots, and fled back to the village.

People in the village soon noted the absence of the two little girls. They had died at the lands and were buried there, the family said. But people noted their ashen, terror-stricken faces and a murmur arose. What had killed the children, they wanted to know? And the family replied that they had just died. And people said amongst themselves that it was strange that the two deaths had occurred at the same time. And there was a feeling of great unease at the unnatural looks of the family. Soon the police came around. The family told them the same story of death and burial at the lands. They did not know what the children had died of. So the police asked to see the graves. At this, the mother of the children broke down and told everything.

Throughout that terrible summer the story of the children hung like a dark cloud of sorrow over the village, and the sorrow was not assuaged when the old man and Ramadi were sentenced to death for ritual murder. All they had on the statute books was that ritual murder was against the law and must be stamped out with the death penalty. The subtle story of strain and starvation and breakdown was inadmissible evidence at court; but all the people who lived off crops knew in their hearts that only a hair's breadth had saved them from sharing a fate similar to that of the Mokgobja family. They could have killed something to make the rain fall.

Analyzing the Text

1. In what ways does the unceasing drought reactivate beliefs that lead to the slaughter of the girls?
2. How does the story make it possible to understand the statement that other villagers "could have killed something to make the rain fall"? What does this imply about Head's attitude toward the murderers?

Understanding Head's Techniques

1. How does Head lay the psychological groundwork for what otherwise would come as a shock—the choice of two young girls as sacrificial victims? How do the girls appear to other members of the family at a time when everyone must conserve food and water?
2. Why doesn't Head wait to reveal the fact that the girls have been murdered? How does knowing this early on encourage readers to want to know how it came about?

Arguing for an Interpretation

1. How is the story constructed to make you sympathetic to the parents despite their horrendous behavior? Did it have this effect on you? Why or why not?
2. In what ways do Head's descriptions of the blistering heat and desiccated landscape serve to symbolize the destruction of the bonds between family members that allow the ritual sacrifice to occur? Does nature itself become a character in this story? Explain your answer.

Louise Erdrich

Louise Erdrich is of Chippewa Indian and German heritage. Born in 1954 in Little Falls, Minnesota, Erdrich grew up as part of the Turtle Mountain band of Chippewa in Wahpeton, North Dakota, where her grandfather was tribal chair of the reservation. While attending Dartmouth College, she received several awards for her poetry and fiction, including the American Academy of Poets Prize. After graduating, she returned to North Dakota to teach in the Poetry in the Schools Program. Her poetry has been published in Jacklight *(1984). Her first novel* Love Medicine *won the 1984 National Book Critic Circle Award for Fiction and is part of an ongoing series of novels exploring Native American life in North Dakota. Novels continuing the saga of the Chippewa clan are* Beet Queen *(1986) and* Tracks *(1988). Erdrich was married to the author Michael Dorris (1945–1997), a professor of Native American Studies at Dartmouth, with whom she collaborated on Dorris's* The Broken Cord: A Family's On-going Struggle with Fetal Alcohol Syndrome *(1989) and on a novel called* The Crown of Columbus *(1991). Her recent works include* The Antelope Wife *(1998), which received the World Fantasy Award for Best Novel,* The Last Report on the Miracles at Little No Horse *(2001), which was a finalist for the National Book Award for Fiction, and* The Master Butchers' Singing Club *(2002). Erdrich's work has been praised for the sensitivity and psychological depth of her depiction of the lives of contemporary Native Americans. "The Red Convertible," drawn from* Love Medicine, *is one of fourteen related stories in that novel.*

The Red Convertible

Lyman Lamartine

I was the first one to drive a convertible on my reservation. And of course it was red, a red Olds. I owned that car along with my brother Henry Junior. We owned it together until his boots filled with water on a windy night and he bought out my share. Now Henry owns the whole car, and his youngest brother Lyman (that's myself), Lyman walks everywhere he goes.

How did I earn enough money to buy my share in the first place? My own talent was I could always make money. I had a touch for it, unusual in a Chippewa. From the first I was different that way, and everyone recognized it. I was the only kid they let in the American Legion Hall to shine shoes, for example, and one Christmas I sold spiritual bouquets for the mission door to door. The nuns let me keep a percentage. Once I started, it seemed the more money I made the easier the money came. Everyone encouraged it. When I was fifteen I got a job washing dishes at the Joliet Café, and that was where my first big break happened.

It wasn't long before I was promoted to busing tables, and then the short-order cook quit and I was hired to take her place. No sooner than you know it I was managing the Joliet. The rest is history. I went on managing. I soon became part owner, and of course there was no stopping me then. It wasn't long before the whole thing was mine.

After I'd owned the Joliet for one year, it blew over in the worst tornado ever seen around here. The whole operation was smashed to bits. A total loss. The fryalator was up in a tree, the grill torn in half like it was paper. I was only sixteen. I had it all in my mother's name, and I lost it quick, but before I lost it I had every one of my relatives, and their relatives, to dinner, and I also bought that red Olds I mentioned, along with Henry.

The first time we saw it! I'll tell you when we first saw it. We had gotten a ride up to Winnipeg, and both of us had money. Don't ask me why, because we never mentioned a car or anything, we just had all our money. Mine was cash, a big bankroll from the Joliet's insurance. Henry had two 5 checks—a week's extra pay for being laid off, and his regular check from the Jewel Bearing Plant.

We were walking down Portage anyway, seeing the sights, when we saw it. There it was, parked, large as life. Really as *if* it was alive. I thought of the word *repose,* because the car wasn't simply stopped, parked, or whatever. That car reposed, calm and gleaming, a FOR SALE sign in its left front window. Then, before we had thought it over at all, the car belonged to us and our pockets were empty. We had just enough money for gas back home.

We went places in that car, me and Henry. We took off driving all one whole summer. We started off toward the Little Knife River and Mandaree in Fort Berthold and then we found ourselves down in Wakpala somehow, and then suddenly we were over in Montana on the Rocky Boys, and yet the summer was not even half over. Some people hang on to details when they travel, but we didn't let them bother us and just lived our everyday lives here to there.

I do remember this one place with willows. I remember I laid under those trees and it was comfortable. So comfortable. The branches bent down all around me like a tent or a stable. And quiet, it was quiet, even though there was a powwow close enough so I could see it going on. The air was not too still, not too windy either. When the dust rises up and hangs in the air around the dancers like that, I feel good. Henry was asleep with his arms thrown wide. Later on, he woke up and we started driving again. We were somewhere in Montana, or maybe on the Blood Reserve—it could have been anywhere. Anyway it was where we met the girl.

All her hair was in buns around her ears, that's the first thing I noticed about her. She was posed alongside the road with her arm out, so we stopped. That girl was short, so short her lumber shirt looked comical on her, like a nightgown. She had jeans on and fancy moccasins and she carried a little suitcase.

"Hop on in," says Henry. So she climbs in between us.

"We'll take you home," I says. "Where do you live?"

"Chicken," she says.

"Where the hell's that?" I ask her.

"Alaska."

"Okay," says Henry, and we drive.

We got up there and never wanted to leave. The sun doesn't truly set there in summer, and the night is more a soft dusk. You might doze off, sometimes, but before you know it you're up again, like an animal in nature. You never feel like you have to sleep hard or put away the world. And things would grow up there. One day just dirt or moss, the next day flowers and long grass. The girl's name was Susy. Her family really took to us. They fed us and put us up. We had our own tent to live in by their house, and the kids would be in and out of there all day and night. They couldn't get over me and Henry being brothers, we looked so different. We told them we knew we had the same mother, anyway.

One night Susy came in to visit us. We sat around in the tent talking of this thing and that. The season was changing. It was getting darker by that time, and the cold was even getting just a little mean. I told her it was time for us to go. She stood up on a chair.

"You never seen my hair," Susy said.

That was true. She was standing on a chair, but still, when she unclipped her buns the hair reached all the way to the ground. Our eyes opened. You couldn't tell how much hair she had when it was rolled up so neatly. Then my brother Henry did something funny. He went up to the chair and said, "Jump on my shoulders." So she did that, and her hair reached down past his waist, and he started twirling, this way and that, so her hair was flung out from side to side.

"I always wondered what it was like to have long pretty hair," Henry 20
says. Well we laughed. It was a funny sight, the way he did it. The next morning we got up and took leave of those people.

On to greener pastures, as they say. It was down through Spokane and across Idaho then Montana and very soon we were racing the weather right along under the Canadian border through Columbus, Des Lacs, and then we were in Bottineau County and soon home. We'd made most of the trip, that summer, without putting up the car hood at all. We got home just in time, it turned out, for the army to remember Henry had signed up to join it.

I don't wonder that the army was so glad to get my brother that they turned him into a Marine. He was built like a brick outhouse anyway. We liked to tease him that they really wanted him for his Indian nose. He had a nose big and sharp as a hatchet, like the nose on Red Tomahawk, the Indian who killed Sitting Bull, whose profile is on signs all along the North Dakota highways. Henry went off to training camp, came home once during Christmas, then the next thing you know we got an overseas letter from him. It was 1970, and he said he was stationed up in the northern hill country. Whereabouts I did not know. He wasn't such a hot letter writer, and only got off two before the enemy caught him. I could never keep it straight, which direction those good Vietnam soldiers were from.

I wrote him back several times, even though I didn't know if those letters would get through. I kept him informed all about the car. Most of the time I had it up on blocks in the yard or half taken apart, because that long trip did a hard job on it under the hood.

I always had good luck with numbers, and never worried about the draft myself. I never even had to think about what my number was. But Henry was never lucky in the same way as me. It was at least three years before Henry came home. By then I guess the whole war was solved in the government's mind, but for him it would keep on going. In those years I'd put his car into almost perfect shape. I always thought of it as his car while he was gone, even though when he left he said, "Now it's yours," and threw me his key.

"Thanks for the extra key," I'd say. "I'll put it up in your drawer just in 25
case I need it." He laughed.

When he came home, though, Henry was very different, and I'll say this: the change was no good. You could hardly expect him to change for the better, I know. But he was quiet, so quiet, and never comfortable sitting still anywhere but always up and moving around. I thought back to times we'd sat still for whole afternoons, never moving a muscle, just shifting our weight along the ground, talking to whoever sat with us, watching things. He'd always had a joke, then, too, and now you couldn't get him to laugh, or when he did it was more the sound of a man choking, a sound that stopped up the throats of other people around him. They got to leaving him alone most of the time, and I didn't blame them. It was a fact: Henry was jumpy and mean.

I'd bought a color TV set for my mom and the rest of us while Henry was away. Money still came very easy. I was sorry I'd ever bought it though, because of Henry. I was also sorry I'd bought color, because with black-and-white the pictures seem older and farther away. But what are you going to do? He sat in front of it, watching it, and that was the only time he was completely still. But it was the kind of stillness that you see in a rabbit when it freezes and before it will bolt. He was not easy. He sat in his chair gripping the armrests with all his might, as if the chair itself was moving at a high speed and if he let go at all he would rocket forward and maybe crash right through the set.

Once I was in the room watching TV with Henry and I heard his teeth click at something. I looked over, and he'd bitten through his lip. Blood was going down his chin. I tell you right then I wanted to smash that tube to pieces. I went over to it but Henry must have known what I was up to. He rushed from his chair and shoved me out of the way, against the wall. I told myself he didn't know what he was doing.

My mom came in, turned the set off real quiet, and told us she had made something for supper. So we went and sat down. There was still blood going down Henry's chin, but he didn't notice it and no one said anything, even though every time he took a bit of bread his blood fell onto it until he was eating his own blood mixed in with the food.

While Henry was not around we talked about what was going to happen to him. There were no Indian doctors on the reservation, and my mom was afraid of trusting Old Man Pillager because he courted her long ago and was jealous of her husbands. He might take revenge through her son. We were afraid that if we brought Henry to a regular hospital they would keep him.

"They don't fix them in those places," Mom said; "they just give them drugs."

"We wouldn't get him there in the first place," I agreed, "so let's just forget about it."

Then I thought about the car.

Henry had not even looked at the car since he'd gotten home, though like I said, it was in tip-top condition and ready to drive. I thought the car might bring the old Henry back somehow. So I bided my time and waited for my chance to interest him in the vehicle.

One night Henry was off somewhere. I took myself a hammer. I went out to that car and I did a number on its underside. Whacked it up. Bent the tail pipe double. Ripped the muffler loose. By the time I was done with the car it looked worse than any typical Indian car that has been driven all its life on reservation roads, which they always say are like government promises—full of holes. It just about hurt me, I'll tell you that! I threw dirt in the carburetor and I ripped all the electric tape off the seats. I made it look just as beat up as I could. Then I sat back and waited for Henry to find it.

Still, it took him over a month. That was all right, because it was just getting warm enough, not melting, but warm enough to work outside.

"Lyman," he says, walking in one day, "that red car looks like shit."

"Well it's old," I says. "You got to expect that."

"No way!" says Henry. "That car's a classic! But you went and ran the piss right out of it, Lyman, and you know it don't deserve that. I kept that car in A-one shape. You don't remember. You're too young. But when I left, that car was running like a watch. Now I don't even know if I can get it to start again, let alone get it anywhere near its old condition."

"Well you try," I said, like I was getting mad, "but I say it's a piece of 40
junk."

Then I walked out before he could realize I knew he'd strung together more than six words at once.

After that I thought he'd freeze himself to death working on that car. He was out there all day, and at night he rigged up a little lamp, ran a cord out the window, and had himself some light to see by while he worked. He was better than he had been before, but that's still not saying much. It was easier for him to do the things the rest of us did. He ate more slowly and didn't jump up and down during the meal to get this or that or look out the window. I put my hand in the back of the TV set, I admit, and fiddled around with it good, so that it was almost impossible now to get a clear picture. He didn't look at it very often anyway. He was always out with that car or going off to get parts for it. By the time it was really melting outside, he had it fixed.

I had been feeling down in the dumps about Henry around this time. We had always been together before. Henry and Lyman. But he was such a loner now that I didn't know how to take it. So I jumped at the chance one day when Henry seemed friendly. It's not that he smiled or anything. He just said, "Let's take that old shitbox for a spin." Just the way he said it made me think he could be coming around.

We went out to the car. It was spring. The sun was shining very bright. My only sister, Bonita, who was just eleven years old, came out and made us stand together for a picture. Henry leaned his elbow on the red car's windshield, and he took his other arm and put it over my shoulder, very carefully, as though it was heavy for him to lift and he didn't want to bring the weight down all at once.

"Smile," Bonita said, and he did. 45

That picture, I never look at it anymore. A few months ago, I don't know why, I got his picture out and tacked it on the wall. I felt good about Henry at the time, close to him. I felt good having his picture on the wall, until one night when I was looking at television. I was a little drunk and stoned. I looked up at the wall and Henry was staring at me. I don't know what it was, but his smile had changed, or maybe it was gone. All I know is I couldn't stay in the same room with that picture. I was shaking. I got up, closed the door, and went into the kitchen. A little later my friend Ray came over and we both went back into that room. We put the picture in a brown bag, folded the bag over and over tightly, then put it way back in a closet.

I still see that picture now, as if it tugs at me, whenever I pass that closet door. The picture is very clear in my mind. It was so sunny that day Henry had to squint against the glare. Or maybe the camera Bonita held flashed like a mirror, blinding him, before she snapped the picture. My face is right out in the sun, big and round. But he might have drawn back, because the shadows on his face are deep as holes. There are two shadows curved like little hooks around the ends of his smile, as if to frame it and try to keep it there—that one, first smile that looked like it might have hurt his face. He had his field jacket on and the worn-in clothes he'd come back in and kept wearing ever since. After Bonita took the picture, she went into the house and we got into the car. There was a full cooler in the trunk. We started off, east, toward Pembina and the Red River because Henry said he wanted to see the high water.

The trip over there was beautiful. When everything starts changing, drying up, clearing off, you feel like your whole life is starting. Henry felt it, too. The top was down and the car hummed like a top. He'd really put it back in shape, even the tape on the seats was very carefully put down and glued back in layers. It's not that he smiled again or even joked, but his face looked to me as if it was clear, more peaceful. It looked as though he wasn't thinking of anything in particular except the bare fields and windbreaks and houses we were passing.

The river was high and full of winter trash when we got there. The sun was still out, but it was colder by the river. There was still little clumps of dirty snow here and there on the banks. The water hadn't gone over the banks yet, but it would, you could tell. It was just at its limit, hard swollen glossy like an old gray scar. We made ourselves a fire, and we sat down and watched the current go. As I watched it I felt something squeezing inside me and tightening and trying to let go all at the same time. I knew I was not just feeling it myself; I knew I was feeling what Henry was going through at that moment. Except that I couldn't stand it, the closing and opening. I jumped to my feet. I took Henry by the shoulders and I started shaking him. "Wake up," I says, "wake up, wake up, wake up!" I didn't know what had come over me. I sat down beside him again.

His face was totally white and hard. Then it broke, like stones break all 50
of a sudden when water boils up inside them.

"I know it," he says. "I know it. I can't help it. It's no use."

We start talking. He said he knew what I'd done with the car. It was obvious it had been whacked out of shape and not just neglected. He said he wanted to give the car to me for good now, it was no use. He said he'd fixed it just to give it back and I should take it.

"No way," I says, "I don't want it."

"That's okay," he says, "you take it."

"I don't want it, though," I says back to him, and then to emphasize, 55
just to emphasize, you understand, I touch his shoulder. He slaps my hand off.

"Take the car," he says.

"No," I say, "make me," I say, and then he grabs my jacket and rips the arm loose. That jacket is a class act, suede with tags and zippers. I push Henry backwards, off the log. He jumps up and bowls me over. We go down in a clinch and come up swinging hard, for all we're worth, with our fists. He socks my jaw so hard I feel like it swings loose. Then I'm at his ribcage and land a good one under his chin so his head snaps back. He's dazzled. He looks at me and I look at him and then his eyes are full of tears and blood and at first I think he's crying. But no, he's laughing. "Ha! Ha!" he says. "Ha! Ha! Take good care of it."

"Okay," I says, "okay, no problem. Ha! Ha!"

I can't help it, and I start laughing, too. My face feels fat and strange, and after a while I get a beer from the cooler in the trunk, and when I hand it to Henry he takes his shirt and wipes my germs off. "Hoof-and-mouth disease," he says. For some reason this cracks me up, and so we're really laughing for a while, and then we drink all the rest of the beers one by one and throw them in the river and see how far, how fast, the current takes them before they fill up and sink.

"You want to go on back?" I ask after a while. "Maybe we could snag a 60
couple nice Kashpaw girls."

He says nothing. But I can tell his mood is turning again.

"They're all crazy, the girls up here, every damn one of them."

"You're crazy too," I say, to jolly him up. "Crazy Lamartine boys!"

He looks as though he will take this wrong at first. His face twists, then clears, and he jumps up on his feet. "That's right!" he says. "Crazier 'n hell. Crazy Indians!"

I think it's the old Henry again. He throws off his jacket and starts 65
swinging his legs out from the knees like a fancy dancer. He's down doing something between a grouse dance and a bunny hop, no kind of dance I ever saw before, but neither has anyone else on all this green growing earth. He's wild. He wants to pitch whoopee! He's up and at me and all over. All this time I'm laughing so hard, so hard my belly is getting tied up in a knot.

"Got to cool me off!" he shouts all of a sudden. Then he runs over to the river and jumps in.

There's boards and other things in the current. It's so high. No sound comes from the river after the splash he makes, so I run right over. I look around. It's getting dark. I see he's halfway across the water already, and I know he didn't swim there but the current took him. It's far. I hear his voice, though, very clearly across it.

"My boots are filling," he says.

He says this in a normal voice, like he just noticed and he doesn't know what to think of it. Then he's gone. A branch comes by. Another branch. And I go in.

By the time I get out of the river, off the snag I pulled myself onto, the 70
sun is down. I walk back to the car, turn on the high beams, and drive it up the bank. I put it in first gear and then I take my foot off the clutch. I get out, close the door, and watch it plow softly into the water. The headlights reach in as they go down, searching, still lighted after the water swirls over the back end. I wait. The wires short out. It is all finally dark. And then there is only the water, the sound of it going and running and going and running and running.

Analyzing the Text

1. How would you characterize the narrator's relationship with his brother Henry? How does it change after Henry returns from Vietnam?
2. What elements in the story help you understand how completely separate experiences of Native Americans are compared to those in mainstream society?

Understanding Erdrich's Techniques

1. What role does the red convertible play (including the phases the car goes through) in reflecting the changes in the relationship between Henry and Lyman?

2. What clues does Erdrich give the reader about how the story will end without telling us exactly what will take place? Why do you think Lyman sends the car into the water with its lights still on?

Arguing for an Interpretation

1. Why do Lyman's efforts to bring Henry back to his former self fail? How does the symbolism of the red convertible mirror what is possible and not possible in the lives of the brothers?
2. What insight does the story offer into the pressures to which Native Americans are subjected, which became more acute during the war in Vietnam?

Inés Arredondo

The Mexican writer Inés Arredondo (1928–1989) has written extensively about the north coast of the San Lorenzo River, especially in her collection of stories titled La Senal *(The Sign) (1965). As a short story writer, her work has been strongly influenced by D. H. Lawrence. Although Arredondo explores the extent to which women in Mexico become sacrificial victims in a male-dominated society, she often creates stories that bring to life archetypal female figures such as Eve, Jocasta, and Medea. In "The Shunammite," translated by Albert Manguel (1986), Arredondo recasts the biblical story in a modern context. A volume of her stories was published posthumously as* Underground River and Other Stories *(1996).*

The Shunammite

So they sought for a fair damsel throughout all the coasts of Israel, and found Abishag, a Shunammite, and brought her to the king. . . .

And the damsel was very fair, and cherished the king, and ministered to him; but the king knew her not.

—Kings I: 1, 3–4

The summer had been a fiery furnace. The last summer of my youth.

Tense, concentrated in the arrogance that precedes combustion, the city shone in a dry and dazzling light. I stood in the very midst of the light, dressed in mourning, proud, feeding the flames with my blonde hair, alone. Men's sly glances slid over my body without soiling it, and my haughty modesty forced them to barely nod at me, full of respect. I was certain of having the power to dominate passions, to purify anything in the scorching air that surrounded but did not singe me.

Nothing changed when I received the telegram; the sadness it brought me did not affect in the least my feelings towards the world. My uncle Apolonio was dying at the age of seventy-odd years and wanted to see me. I had lived as a daughter in his house for many years and I sincerely felt pain at the thought of his inevitable death. All this was perfectly normal, and not a single omen, not a single shiver made me suspect anything. Quickly I made arrangements for the journey, in the very same untouchable midst of the motionless summer.

I arrived at the village during the hour of siesta.

Walking down the empty streets with my small suitcase, I fell to daydreaming, in that dusky zone between reality and time, born of the excessive heat. I was not remembering; I was almost reliving things as they had been. "Look, Licha, the *amapas* are blooming again." The clear voice, almost childish. "I want you to get yourself a dress like that of Margarita Ibarra to wear on the sixteenth." I could hear her, feel her walking by my side, her shoulders bent a little forwards, light in spite of her plumpness, happy and old. I carried on walking in the company of my aunt Panchita, my mother's sister. "Well, my dear, if you *really* don't like Pepe . . . but he's such a *nice* boy. . . ." Yes, she had used those exact words, here, in front of Tichi Valenzuela's window, with her gay smile, innocent and impish. I walked a little further, where the paving stones seemed to fade away in the haze, and when the bells rang, heavy and real, ending the siesta and announcing the Rosary, I opened my eyes and gave the village a good, long look: it was not the same. The *amapas* had not bloomed and I was crying, in my mourning dress, at the door of my uncle's house.

The front gate was open, as always, and at the end of the courtyard rose the bougainvillea. As always: but not the same. I dried my tears, and felt that I was not arriving: I was leaving. Everything looked motionless, pinioned in my memory, and the heat and the silence seemed to wither it all. My footsteps echoed with a new sound, and Maria came out to greet me.

"Why didn't you let us know? We'd have sent . . ."

We went straight into the sick man's room. As I entered, I felt cold. Silence and gloom preceded death.

"Luisa, is that you?"

The dear voice was dying out and would soon be silent for ever.

"I'm here, uncle."

"God be praised! I won't die alone."

"Don't say that; you'll soon be much better."

He smiled sadly; he knew I was lying but he did not want to make me cry.

"Yes, my daughter. Yes. Now have a rest, make yourself at home and then come and keep me company. I'll try to sleep a little."

Shrivelled, wizened, toothless, lost in the immense bed and floating senselessly in whatever was left of his life, he was painful to be with, like something superfluous, out of place, like so many others at the point of death. Stepping out of the overheated passageway, one would take a deep breath, instinctively, hungry for light and air.

I began to nurse him and I felt happy doing it. This house was *my* house, and in the morning, while tidying up, I would sing long-forgotten songs. The peace that surrounded me came perhaps from the fact that my uncle no longer awaited death as something imminent and terrible, but instead let himself be carried by the passing days towards a more or less distant or nearby future, with the unconscious tenderness of a child. He would go over his past life with great pleasure and enjoy imagining that he was bequeathing me his images, as grandparents do with their children.

"Bring me that small chest, there, in the large wardrobe. Yes, that one. The key is underneath the mat, next to Saint Anthony. Bring the key as well."

And his sunken eyes would shine once again at the sight of all his treasures.

"Look: this necklace—I gave it to your aunt for our tenth wedding an- 20
niversary. I bought it in Mazatlan from a Polish jeweller who told me God-knows-what story about an Austrian princess, and asked an impossible price for it. I brought it back hidden in my pistol-holder and didn't sleep a wink in the stagecoach—I was so afraid someone would steal it!"

The light of dusk made the young, living stones glitter in his callused hands.

". . . this ring, so old, belonged to my mother; look carefully at the miniature in the other room and you'll see her wearing it. Cousin Begona would mutter behind her back that a sweetheart of hers . . ."

The ladies in the portraits would move their lips and speak, once again, would breathe again—all these ladies he had seen, he had touched. I would picture them in my mind and understand the meaning of these jewels.

"Have I told you about the time we travelled to Europe, in 1908, before the Revolution? You had to take a ship to Colima. . . . And in Venice your aunt Panchita fell in love with a certain pair of ear-rings. They were much too expensive, and I told her so. They are fit for a queen.' . . . Next day I bought them for her. You just can't imagine what it was like because all this took place long, long before you were born, in 1908, in Venice, when your aunt was so young, so . . ."

"Uncle, you're getting tired, you should rest." 25

"You're right, I'm tired. Leave me a while and take the small chest to your room. It's yours."

"But, uncle . . ."

"It's all yours, that's all! I trust I can give away whatever I want!"

His voice broke into a sob: the illusion was vanishing and he found himself again on the point of dying, of saying good-bye to the things he had loved. He turned to the wall and I left with the box in my hands, not knowing what to do.

On other occasions he would tell me about "the year of the famine," or 30
"the year of the yellow corn," or "the year of the plague," and very old tales of murderers and ghosts. Once he even tried to sing a *corrido*[1] from his youth, but it shattered in his jagged voice. He was leaving me his life, and he was happy. The doctor said that yes, he could see some recovery, but that we were not to raise our hopes, there was no cure, it was merely a matter of a few days more or less.

One afternoon of menacing dark clouds, when I was bringing in the clothes hanging out to dry in the courtyard, I heard Maria cry out. I stood still, listening to her cry as if it were a peal of thunder, the first of the storm to come. Then silence, and I was left alone in the courtyard, motionless. A bee buzzed by and the rain did not fall. No one knows as well as I do how awful a foreboding can be, a premonition hanging above a head turned towards the sky.

---

[1]*corrido:* Mexican folk ballad.

"Lichita, he's dying! He's gasping for air!"

"Go get the doctor. . . . No! I'll go. . . . But call Dona Clara to stay with you till I'm back."

"And the priest . . . fetch the priest."

I ran, I ran away from that unbearable moment, blunt and asphyxiat- 35
ing. I ran, hurried back, entered the house, made coffee; I greeted the relatives who began to arrive dressed in half-mourning; I ordered candles; I asked for a few holy relics; I kept on feverishly trying to fulfill my only obligation at the time, to be with my uncle. I asked the doctor: he had given him an injection, so as not to leave anything untried, but he knew it was useless. I saw the priest arrive with the Eucharist, even then I lacked the courage to enter. I knew I would regret it afterwards. *Thank God, now I won't die alone*—but I couldn't. I covered my face with my hands and prayed.

The priest came and touched my shoulder. I thought that all was over and I shivered.

"He's calling you. Come in."

I don't know how I reached the door. Night had fallen and the room, lit by a bedside lamp, seemed enormous. The furniture, larger than life, looked black, and a strange clogging atmosphere hung about the bed. Trembling, I felt I was inhaling death.

"Stand next to him," said the priest.

I obeyed, moving towards the foot of the bed, unable to look even at 40
the sheets.

"Your uncle's wish, unless you say otherwise, is to marry you *in articulo mortis,* so that you may inherit his possessions. Do you accept?"

I stifled a cry of horror. I opened my eyes wide enough to let in the whole terrible room. "Why does he want to drag me into his grave?" I felt death touching my skin.

"Luisa . . ."

It was uncle Apolonio. Now I had to look at him. He could barely mouth the words, his jaw seemed slack and he spoke moving his face like that of a ventriloquist's doll.

". . . please." 45

And he fell silent with exhaustion.

I could take no more. I left the room. That was not my uncle, it did not even look like him. Leave everything to me, yes, but not only his possessions, his stories, his life . . . I didn't want it, his life, his death. I didn't want it. When I opened my eyes I was standing again in the courtyard and the sky was still overcast. I breathed in deeply, painfully.

"Already? . ." The relatives drew near to ask, seeing me so distraught.

I shook my head. Behind me, the priest explained.

"Don Apolonio wants to marry her with his last breath, so that she 50
may inherit him."

"And you won't?" the old servant asked anxiously. "Don't be silly, you are the only one to deserve it. You were a daughter to them, and you have worked very hard looking after him. If you don't marry him, the cousins in Mexico City will leave you without a cent. Don't be silly!"

"It's a fine gesture on his part. . . ."

"And afterwards you'll be left a rich widow, as untouched as you are now." A young cousin laughed nervously.

"It's a considerable fortune, and I, as your uncle several times removed, would advise you to ..."

"If you think about it, not accepting shows a lack of both charity and humility."

"That's true, that's absolutely true."

I did not want to give an old man his last pleasure, a pleasure I should, after all, be thankful for, because my youthful body, of which I felt so proud, had not dwelt in any of the regions of death. I was overcome by nausea. That was my last clear thought that night. I woke from a kind of hypnotic slumber as they forced me to hold his hand covered in cold sweat. I felt nauseous again, but said "yes."

I remember vaguely that they hovered over me all the time, talking all at once, taking me over there, bringing me over here, making me sign, making me answer. The taste of that night—a taste that has stayed with me for the rest of my life—was that of an evil ring-around-the-rosies turning vertiginously around me, while everyone laughed and sang grotesquely

> This is the way the widow is wed,
> The widow is wed, the widow is wed

while I stood, a slave, in the middle. Something inside me hurt, and I could not lift my eyes.

When I came to my senses, all was over, and on my hand shone the braided ring which I had seen so many times on my aunt Panchita's finger: there had been no time for anything else.

The guests began to leave.

"If you need me, don't hesitate to call. In the meantime give him these drops every six hours."

"May God bless you and give you strength."

"Happy honeymoon," whispered the young cousin in my ear, with a nasty laugh.

I returned to the sickbed. "Nothing has changed, nothing has changed." My fear certainly had not changed. I convinced Maria to stay and help me look after uncle Apolonio. I only calmed down once I saw dawn was breaking. It had started to rain, but without thunder or lightning, very still.

It kept on drizzling that day and the next, and the day after. Four days of anguish. Nobody came to visit, nobody other than the doctor and the priest. On days like these no one goes out, everyone stays indoors and waits for life to start again. These are the days of the spirit, sacred days.

If at least the sick man had needed plenty of attention my hours would have seemed shorter, but there was little that could be done for him.

On the fourth night Maria went to bed in a room close by, and I stayed alone with the dying man. I was listening to the monotonous rain and praying unconsciously, half asleep and unafraid, waiting. My fingers stopped working, turning the rosary, and as I held the beads I could feel through my fingertips a peculiar warmth, a warmth both alien and intimate, the warmth we leave in things and which is returned to us transformed, a comrade, a brother foreshadowing the warmth of others, a warmth both unknown and recollected, never quite grasped and yet inhabiting the core of my bones. Softly, deliciously, my nerves relaxed, my fingers felt light, I fell asleep.

I must have slept many hours: it was dawn when I woke up. I knew because the lights had been switched off and the electric plant stops working at two in the morning. The room, barely lit by an oil lamp at the feet of the Holy Virgin on the chest of drawers, made me think of the wedding night, my wedding night. . . . It was so long ago, an empty eternity.

From the depth of the gloomy darkness don Apolonio's broken and tired breathing reached me. There he still was, not the man himself, simply the persistent and incomprehensible shred that hangs on, with no goal, with no apparent motive. Death is frightening, but life mingled with death, soaked in death, is horrible in a way that owes little to either life or death. Silence, corruption of the flesh, the stench, the monstrous transformation, the final vanishing act, all this is painful, but it reaches a climax and then gives way, dissolves into the earth, into memory, into history. But not this: this arrangement worked out between life and death—echoed in the useless exhaling and inhaling—could carry on forever. I would hear him trying to clear his anaesthetized throat and it occurred to me that air was not entering that body, or rather, that it was not a human body breathing the air: it was a machine, puffing and panting, stopping in a curious game, a game to kill time without end. That thing was no human being: it was somebody playing with huffs and snores. And the horror of it all won me over: I began to breathe to the rhythm of his panting; to inhale, stop suddenly, choke, breathe, choke again . . . unable to control myself, until I realized I had been deceived by what I thought was the sense of the game. What I really felt was the pain and shortness of breath of an animal in pain. But I kept on, on, until there was one single breathing, one single inhuman breath, one single agony. I felt calmer, terrified but calmer: I had lifted the barrier, I could let myself go and simply wait for the common end. It seemed to me that by abandoning myself, by giving myself up unconditionally, the end would happen quickly, would not be allowed to continue. It would have fulfilled its purpose and its persistent search in the world.

Not a hint of farewell, not a glimmer of pity towards me. I carried on the mortal game for a long, long while, from someplace where time had ceased to matter.

The shared breathing became less agitated, more peaceful, but also weaker. I seemed to be drifting back. I felt so tired I could barely move, exhaustion nestling in forever inside my body. I opened my eyes. Nothing had changed.

No: far away, in the shadows, is a rose. Alone, unique, alive. There it is, cut out against the darkness, clear as day, with its fleshy, luminous petals, shining. I look at it and my hand moves and I remember its touch and the simple act of putting it in a vase. I looked at it then, but I only understand it now. I stir, I blink, and the rose is still there, in full bloom, identical to itself.

I breathe freely, with my own breath. I pray, I remember, I doze off, and the untouched rose mounts guard over the dawning light and my secret. Death and hope suffer change.

And now day begins to break and in the clean sky I see that at last the days of rain are over. I stay at the window a long time, watching everything change in the sun. A strong ray enters me and the suffering seems a lie. Unjustified bliss fills my lungs and unwittingly I smile. I turn to the rose as if to an accomplice but I can't find it: the sun has withered it.

Clear days came again, and maddening heat. The people went to work, and sang, but don Apolonio would not die; in fact he seemed to get better.

I kept on looking after him, but no longer in a cheerful mood—my eyes downcast, I turned the guilt I felt into hard work. My wish, now clearly, was that it all end, that he die. The fear, the horror I felt looking at him, at his touch, his voice, were unjustified because the link between us was not real, could never be real, and yet he felt like a dead weight upon me. Through politeness and shame I wanted to get rid of it.

Yes, don Apolonio was visibly improving. Even the doctor was surprised and offered no explanation.

On the very first morning I sat him up among the pillows, I noticed that certain look in my uncle's eyes. The heat was stifling and I had to lift him all by myself. Once I had propped him up I noticed: the old man was staring as dazed at my heaving chest, his face distorted and his trembling hands unconsciously moving towards me. I drew back instinctively and turned my head away.

"Please close the blinds, it's too hot."

His almost dead body was growing warm.

"Come here, Luisa, sit by my side. Come." 80

"Yes, uncle." I sat, my knees drawn up, at the foot of the bed, without looking at him.

"Polo, you must call me Polo." His voice was again sweet and soft. "You'll have a lot to forgive me. I'm old and sick, and a man in my condition is like a child."

"Yes."

"Let's see. Try saying, 'Yes, Polo.'"

"Yes, Polo." 85

The name on my lips seemed to me an aberration, made me nauseated.

Polo got better, but became fussy and irritable. I realized he was fighting to be the man he had once been, and yet the resurrected self was not the same, but another.

"Luisa, bring me . . . Luisa, give me . . . Luisa, plump up my pillows . . . pour me some water . . . prop up my leg. . . ."

He wanted me to be there all day long, always by his side, seeing to his needs, touching him. And the fixed look and distorted face kept coming back, more and more frequently, growing over his features like a mask.

"Pick up my book. It fell underneath the bed, on this side." 90

I kneeled and stuck my head and almost half my body underneath the bed, and had to stretch my arm as far as it would go, to reach it. At first I thought it had been my own movements, or maybe the bedclothes, but once I had the book in my hand and was shuffling to get out, I froze, stunned by what I had long foreseen, even expected: the outburst, the scream, the thunder. A rage never before felt raced through me when the realization of what was happening reached my consciousness, when his shaking hand, taking advantage of my amazement, became surer and heavier, and enjoyed itself, adventuring with no restraints, feeling and exploring my thighs—a fleshless hand glued to my skin, fingering my body with delight, a dead hand searching impatiently between my legs, a bodyless hand.

I rose as quickly as I could, my face burning with shame and determination, but when I saw him I forgot myself: he had become a figure in a nightmare. Polo was laughing softly, through his toothless mouth. And then, suddenly serious, with a coolness that terrified me, he said:

"What? Aren't you my wife before God and men? Come here, I'm cold, heat my bed. But first take off your dress, you don't want to get it creased."

What followed, I know, is my story, my life, but I can barely remember it, like a disgusting dream I can't even tell whether it was long or short. Only one thought kept me sane during the early days: "This can't go on, it can't go on." I imagined that God would not allow it, would prevent it in some way or another. He, personally, God, would interfere. Death, once dreaded, seemed my only hope. Not Apolonio's—he was a demon of death—but mine, the just and necessary death for my corrupted flesh. But nothing happened. Everything stayed on, suspended in time, without future. Then, one morning, taking nothing with me, I left.

It was useless. Three days later they let me know that my husband was dying, and they called me back. I went to see the father confessor and told him my story.

"What keeps him alive is lust, the most horrible of all sins. This isn't life, Father, it's death. Let him die!"

"He would die in despair. I can't allow it."

"And I?"

"I understand, but if you don't go to him, it would be like murder. Try not to arouse him, pray to the Blessed Virgin, and keep your mind on your duties. . . ."

I went back. And lust drew him out of the grave once more. Fighting, endlessly fighting, I managed, after several years, to overcome my hatred, and finally, at the very end, I even conquered the beast: Apolonio died in peace, sweetly, his old self again.

But I was not able to go back to who I was. Now wickedness, malice, shine in the eyes of the men who look at me, and I feel I have become an occasion of sin for all, I, the vilest of harlots. Alone, a sinner, totally engulfed by the never-ending flames of this cruel summer which surrounds us all, like an army of ants.

Analyzing the Text

1. Why does Luisa agree to marry her uncle despite her initial qualms about doing so? What details suggest that Apolonio's recovery is unnatural?
2. How do Luisa's experiences change her from the person that she was at the beginning of the story? How do the changes in the rose symbolize her transformation?

Understanding Arredondo's Techniques

1. How does the quotation from the Bible about the Shunammite foreshadow Luisa's fate?
2. How do jewelry and other material treasures the uncle has acquired function as a symbol for his greed, not only for wealth, but in desiring to unnaturally extend his life?

Arguing for an Interpretation

1. In your opinion, what factors are more to blame—Uncle Apolonio's greed, Luisa's naiveté, or the parish priest's advice? Substantiate your choice with examples and quotes from the story.
2. Does framing the story with the quote from the Bible transform it from a simple bizarre and tawdry tale into a universal fable of innocence, self-betrayal, and the war between the flesh and the spirit? Explain your answer.

EUDORA WELTY

Eudora Welty (1909–2001) was born in Jackson, Mississippi, and attended the Mississippi State College for Women and the University of Wisconsin. Her first of many published volumes of short stories was A Curtain of Green *(1941), in which "A Worn Path" originally appeared. This story won an O. Henry Award for that year. "A Worn Path" blends aspects of fantasy and reality and presents an eccentric, sometimes grotesque and humorous, picture of human relationships that projects a symbolic or mythic impact. One of her most widely known works was* Delta Wedding *(1946). She was awarded the Pulitzer Prize for her short novel* The Optimist's Daughter *(1973) and received the Presidential Medal of Freedom in 1980. In 1981, she received the American Book Award for* The Collected Stories of Eudora Welty. *Her nonfiction account* One Writer's Beginning *(1984) garnered an immense audience. Welty's fame extends to the modern day. In 1990, Steve Dorner, an avid Welty fan, named a computer program after her* (Eudora, the Basis of e-mail) *after he read her 1941 story "Why I Live at the P.O."*

A Worn Path

It was December—a bright frozen day in the early morning. Far out in the country there was an old Negro woman with her head tied in a red rag, coming along a path through the pinewoods. Her name was Phoenix Jackson. She was very old and small and she walked slowly in the dark pine shadows, moving a little from side to side in her steps, with the balanced heaviness and lightness of a pendulum in a grandfather clock. She carried a thin, small cane made from an umbrella, and with this she kept tapping the frozen earth in front of her. This made a grave and persistent noise in the still air, that seemed meditative like the chirping of a solitary little bird.

She wore a dark striped dress reaching down to her shoe tops, and an equally long apron of bleached sugar sacks, with a full pocket: all neat and tidy, but every time she took a step she might have fallen over her shoelaces, which dragged from her unlaced shoes. She looked straight ahead. Her eyes were blue with age. Her skin had a pattern all its own of numberless branching wrinkles and as though a whole little tree stood in the middle of her forehead, but a golden color ran underneath, and the two knobs of her cheeks were illuminated by a yellow burning under the dark. Under the rag her hair came down on her neck in the frailest of ringlets, still black, and with an odor like copper.

Now and then there was a quivering in the thicket. Old Phoenix said, "Out of my way, all you foxes, owls, beetles, jack rabbits, coons and wild animals! . . . Keep out from under these feet, little bob-whites. . . . Keep the big wild hogs out of my path. Don't let none of those come running my direction. I got a long way." Under her small black-freckled hand her cane, limber as a buggy whip, would switch at the brush as if to rouse up any hiding things.

On she went. The woods were deep and still. The sun made the pine needles almost too bright to look at, up where the wind rocked. The cones dropped as light as feathers. Down in the hollow was the mourning dove—it was not too late for him.

The path ran up a hill. "Seem like there is chains about my feet, time I 5
get this far," she said, in the voice of argument old people keep to use with themselves. "Something always take a hold of me on this hill—pleads I should stay."

After she got to the top she turned and gave a full, severe look behind her where she had come. "Up through pines," she said at length. "Now down through oaks."

Her eyes opened their widest, and she started down gently. But before she got to the bottom of the hill a bush caught her dress.

Her fingers were busy and intent, but her skirts were full and long, so that before she could pull them free in one place they were caught in another. It was not possible to allow the dress to tear. "I in the thorny bush," she said. "Thorns, you doing your appointed work. Never want to let folks pass, no sir. Old eyes thought you was a pretty little *green* bush."

Finally, trembling all over, she stood free, and after a moment dared to stoop for her cane.

"Sun so high!" she cried, leaning back and looking, while the thick 10
tears went over her eyes. "The time getting all gone here."

At the foot of this hill was a place where a log was laid across the creek.

"Now comes the trial," said Phoenix.

Putting her right foot out, she mounted the log and shut her eyes. Lifting her skirt, leveling her cane fiercely before her, like a festival figure in some parade, she began to march across. Then she opened her eyes and she was safe on the other side.

"I wasn't as old as I thought," she said.

But she sat down to rest. She spread her skirts on the bank around her 15
and folded her hands over her knees. Up above her was a tree in a pearly cloud of mistletoe. She did not dare to close her eyes, and when a little boy brought her a plate with a slice of marble-cake on it she spoke to him. "That would be acceptable," she said. But when she went to take it there was just her own hand in the air.

So she left that tree, and had to go through a barbed-wire fence. There she had to creep and crawl, spreading her knees and stretching her fingers like a baby trying to climb the steps. But she talked loudly to herself: she could not let her dress be torn now, so late in the day, and she could not pay for having her arm or leg sawed off if she got caught fast where she was.

At last she was safe through the fence and risen up out in the clearing. Big dead trees, like black men with one arm, were standing in the purple stalks of the withered cotton field. There sat a buzzard.

"Who you watching?"

In the furrow she made her way along.

"Glad this is not the season for bulls," she said, looking sideways, "and 20
the good Lord made his snakes to curl up and sleep in the winter. A pleasure I don't see no two-headed snake coming around that tree, where it come once. It took a while to get by him, back in the summer."

She passed through the old cotton and went into a field of dead corn. It whispered and shook and was taller than her head. "Through the maze now," she said, for there was no path.

Then there was something tall, black, and skinny there, moving before her.

At first she took it for a man. It could have been a man dancing in the field. But she stood still and listened, and it did not make a sound. It was as silent as a ghost.

"Ghost," she said sharply, "who be you the ghost of? For I have heard of nary death close by."

But there was no answer—only the ragged dancing in the wind.

She shut her eyes, reached out her hand, and touched a sleeve. She found a coat and inside that an emptiness, cold as ice.

"You scarecrow," she said. Her face lighted. "I ought to be shut up for good," she said with laughter. "My senses is gone. I too old, I the oldest people I ever know. Dance, old scarecrow," she said, "while I dancing with you."

She kicked her foot over the furrow, and with mouth drawn down, shook her head once or twice in a little strutting way. Some husks blew down and whirled in steamers about her skirts.

Then she went on, parting her way from side to side with the cane, through the whispering field. At last she came to the end, to a wagon track where the silver grass blew between the red ruts. The quail were walking around like pullets, seeming all dainty and unseen.

"Walk pretty," she said. "This is the easy place. This the easy going."

She followed the track, swaying through the quiet bare fields, through the little strings of trees silver in their dead leaves, past cabins silver from weather, with the doors and windows boarded shut, all like old women under a spell sitting there. "I walking in their sleep," she said, nodding her head vigorously.

In a ravine she went where a spring was silently flowing through a hollow log. Old Phoenix bent and drank. "Sweet-gum makes the water sweet," she said, and drank more. "Nobody know who made this well, for it was here when I was born."

The track crossed a swampy part where the moss hung as white as lace from every limb. "Sleep on, alligators, and blow your bubbles." Then the track went into the road.

Deep, deep the road went down between the high green-colored banks. Overhead the live-oaks met, and it was as dark as a cave.

A black dog with a lolling tongue came up out of the weeds by the ditch. She was meditating, and not ready, and when he came at her she only hit him a little with her cane. Over she went in the ditch, like a little puff of milkweed.

Down there, her sense drifted away. A dream visited her, and she reached her hand up, but nothing reached down and gave her a pull. So she lay there and presently went to talking. "Old woman," she said to herself, "that black dog come up out of the weeds to stall you off, and now there he sitting on his fine tail smiling at you."

A white man finally came along and found her—a hunter, a young man, with his dog on a chain.

"Well, Granny!" he laughed. "What are you doing there?"

"Lying on my back like a June-bug waiting to be turned over, mister," she said, reaching up her hand.

He lifted her up, gave her a swing in the air, and set her down. 40
"Anything broken, Granny?"

"No sir, them old dead weeds is springy enough," said Phoenix, when she had got her breath. "I thank you for your trouble."

"Where do you live, Granny?" he asked, while the two dogs were growling at each other.

"Away back yonder, sir, behind the ridge. You can't even see it from here."

"On your way home?"

"No sir, I goin to town." 45

"Why, that's too far! That's as far as I walk when I come out myself, and I get something for my trouble." He patted the stuffed bag he carried, and there hung down a little closed claw. It was one of the bob-whites, with its beak hooked bitterly to show it was dead. "Now you go on home, Granny!"

"I bound to go to town, mister," said Phoenix. "The time come around."

He gave another laugh, filling the whole landscape. "I know you old colored people! Wouldn't miss going to town to see Santa Claus!"

But something held old Phoenix very still. The deep lines in her face went into a fierce and different radiation. Without warning, she had seen with her own eyes a flashing nickel fall out of the man's pocket onto the ground.

"How old are you, Granny?" he was saying. 50

"There is no telling, mister," she said, "no telling."

Then she gave a little cry and clapped her hands and said, "Git on away from here, dog! Look! Look at that dog!" She laughed as if in admiration. "He ain't scared of nobody. He a big black dog." She whispered, "Sic him!"

"Watch me get rid of that cur," said the man. "Sic him, Pete! Sic him!"

Phoenix heard the dogs fighting, and heard the man running and throwing sticks. She even heard a gunshot. But she was slowly bending forward by that time, further and further forward, the lids stretched down over her eyes, as if she were doing this in her sleep. Her chin was lowered almost to her knees. The yellow palm of her hand came out from the fold of her apron. Her fingers slid down and along the ground under the piece of money with the grace and care they would have in lifting an egg from under a setting hen. Then she slowly straightened up, she stood erect, and the nickel was in her apron pocket. A bird flew by. Her lips moved. "God watching me the whole time. I come to stealing."

The man came back, and his own dog panted about them. "Well, I 55
scared him off that time," he said, and then he laughed and lifted his gun and pointed it at Phoenix.

She stood straight and faced him.

"Doesn't the gun scare you?" he said, still pointing it.

"No, sir. I seen plenty go off closer by, in my day, and for less than what I done," she said, holding utterly still.

He smiled, and shouldered the gun. "Well, Granny," he said, "you must be a hundred years old, and scared of nothing. I'd give you a dime if I had any money with me. But you take my advice and stay home, and nothing will happen to you."

"I bound to go on my way, mister," said Phoenix. She inclined her head 60
in the red rag. Then they went in different directions, but she could hear the gun shooting again and again over the hill.

She walked on. The shadows hung from the oak trees to the road like curtains. Then she smelled wood-smoke, and smelled the river, and she saw a steeple and the cabins on their steep steps. Dozens of little black children whirled around her. There ahead was Natchez shining. Bells were ringing. She walked on.

In the paved city it was Christmas time. There were red and green electric lights strung and crisscrossed everywhere, and all turned on in the daytime. Old Phoenix would have been lost if she had not distrusted her eyesight and depended on her feet to know where to take her.

She paused quietly on the sidewalk where people were passing by. A lady came along in the crowd, carrying an armful of red-, green-, and silver-wrapped presents; she gave off perfume like the red roses in hot summer, and Phoenix stopped her.

"Please, missy, will you lace up my shoe?" She held up her foot.

"What do you want, Grandma?"

"See my shoe," said Phoenix. "Do all right for out in the country, but wouldn't look right to go in a big building."

"Stand still then, Grandma," said the lady. She put her packages down on the sidewalk beside her and laced and tied both shoes tightly.

"Can't lace 'em with a cane," said Phoenix. "Thank you, missy. I doesn't mind asking a nice lady to tie up my shoe, when I gets out on the street."

Moving slowly and from side to side, she went into the big building, and into a tower of steps, where she walked up and around and around until her feet knew to stop.

She entered a door, and there she saw nailed up on the wall the document that had been stamped with the gold seal and framed in the gold frame, which matched the dream that was hung up in her head.

"Here I be," she said. There was a fixed and ceremonial stiffness over her body.

"A charity case, I suppose," said an attendant who sat at the desk before her.

But Phoenix only looked above her head. There was sweat on her face, the wrinkles in her skin shone like a bright net.

"Speak up, Grandma," the woman said, "What's your name? We must have your history, you know. Have you been here before? What seems to be the trouble with you?"

Old Phoenix only gave a twitch to her face as if a fly were bothering her.

"Are you deaf?" cried the attendant.

But then the nurse came in.

"Oh, that's just old Aunt Phoenix," she said. "She doesn't come for herself—she has a little grandson. She makes these trips just as regular as clockwork. She lives away back off the Old Natchez Trace." She bent down. "Well, Aunt Phoenix, why don't you just take a seat? We won't keep you standing after your long trip." She pointed.

The old woman sat down, bolt upright in the chair.

"Now, how is the boy?" asked the nurse.

Old Phoenix did not speak.

"I said, how is the boy?"

But Phoenix only waited and stared straight ahead, her face very solemn and withdrawn into rigidity.

"Is his throat any better?" asked the nurse. "Aunt Phoenix, don't you hear me? Is your grandson's throat any better since the last time you came for the medicine?"

85 With her hands on her knees, the old woman waited, silent, erect, and motionless, just as if she were in armor.

"You mustn't take up our time this way, Aunt Phoenix," the nurse said. "Tell us quickly about your grandson, and get it over. He isn't dead, is he?"

At last there came a flicker and then a flame of comprehension across her face, and she spoke.

"My grandson. It was my memory had left me. There I sat and forgot why I made my long trip."

"Forgot?" the nurse frowned. "After you came so far?"

90 Then Phoenix was like an old woman begging a dignified forgiveness for waking up frightened in the night. "I never did go to school, I was too old at the Surrender," she said in a soft voice. "I'm an old woman without an education. It was my memory fail me. My little grandson, he is just the same, and I forgot it in the coming."

"Throat never heals, does it?" said the nurse, speaking in a loud, sure voice to old Phoenix. By now she had a card with something written on it, a little list. "Yes. Swallowed lye. When was it—January—two, three years ago—"

Phoenix spoke unasked now. "No missy, he not dead, he just the same. Every little while his throat begin to close up again, and he not able to swallow. He not get his breath. He not able to help himself. So the time come around, and I go on another trip for the soothing medicine."

"All right. The doctor said as long as you came to get it, you could have it," said the nurse. "But it's an obstinate case."

"My little grandson, he sit up there in the house all wrapped up, waiting by himself," Phoenix went on. "We is the only two left in the world. He suffer and it don't seem to put him back at all. He got a sweet look. He going to last. He wear a little patch quilt and peep out holding his mouth open like a little bird. I remembers so plain now. I not going to forget him again, no, the whole enduring time. I could tell him from all the others in creation."

95 "All right." The nurse was trying to hush her now. She brought her a bottle of medicine. "Charity," she said, making a check mark in a book.

Old Phoenix held the bottle close to her eyes, and then carefully put it into her pocket.

"I thank you," she said.

"It's Christmas time, Grandma," said the attendant. "Could I give you a few pennies out of my purse?"

"Five pennies is a nickel," said Phoenix stiffly.

100 "Here's a nickel," said the attendant.

Phoenix rose carefully and held out her hand. She received the nickel and then fished the other nickel out of her pocket and laid it beside the new one. She stared at her palm closely, with her head on one side.

Then she gave a tap with her cane on the floor.

"This is what come to me to do," she said, "I going to the store and buy my child a little windmill they sells, made out of paper. He going to find it hard to believe there such a thing in the world. I'll march myself back where he waiting, holding it straight up in this hand."

She lifted her free hand, gave a little nod, turned around, and walked out of the doctor's office. Then her slow step began on the stairs, going down.

Analyzing the Text

1. As we accompany Phoenix Jackson on her journey and see the way she interacts with others, what kind of an impression does she convey? How does your view of her change once you discover her motive for her solitary trek?
2. What does the nature of Phoenix's planned purchase for her grandson suggest about their relationship?

Understanding Welty's Technique

1. How does the concept of a "worn path," both literal and metaphorical, enter into the story?
2. Why do you think Welty withholds the information about Phoenix's motive until the very end?

Arguing for an Interpretation

1. How do the regional and local color aspects of the story (speech, dress, mannerisms, geography) make Welty's insights into human nature more universal? For example, what significance does the name "Phoenix" have, and why is this an apt name for Welty's main character?
2. In your opinion, is Phoenix's grandson alive or dead? Make a case for either and support your view with details from the story, such as the windmill as a symbol and how it can be interpreted.

KAZUO ISHIGURO

Kazuo Ishiguro was born in Nagasaki, Japan, in 1954 and moved to England in 1960 where he spent most of his life. As a young man, he had a variety of jobs, including being the grouse beater for the Queen Mother at Balmoral Castle in Aberdeen, Scotland. Because his parents had intended to return to Japan, they raised him as both Japanese and English, a bicultural emphasis that underlies "A Family Supper" (from Firebird 2, *1982). His novels include* A Pale View of Hills *(1982),* An Artist of the Floating World *(1986), and* The Remains of the Day *(1989), which won Britain's highest literary award, the Booker Prize, and was later made into a 1993 film starring Anthony Hopkins and Emma Thompson. His recent works include* The Unconsoled *(1995) and* When We Were Orphans *(2001).*

A Family Supper

Fugu is a fish caught off the Pacific shores of Japan. The fish has held a special significance for me ever since my mother died after eating one. The poison resides in the sex glands of the fish, inside two fragile bags. These bags must be removed with caution when preparing the fish, for any clumsiness will result in the poison leaking into the veins. Regrettably, it is not easy to tell whether or not this operation has been carried out successfully. The proof is, as it were, in the eating.

Fugu poisoning is hideously painful and almost always fatal. If the fish has been eaten during the evening, the victim is usually overtaken by pain during his sleep. He rolls about in agony for a few hours and is dead by morning. The fish became extremely popular in Japan after the war. Until stricter regulations were imposed, it was all the rage to perform the hazardous gutting operation in one's own kitchen, then to invite neighbors and friends round for the feast.

At the time of my mother's death, I was living in California. My relationship with my parents had become somewhat strained around that period and consequently I did not learn of the circumstances of her death until I returned to Tokyo two years later. Apparently, my mother had always refused to eat fugu, but on this particular occasion she had made an exception, having been invited by an old school friend whom she was anxious not to offend. It was my father who supplied me with the details as we drove from the airport to his house in the Kamakura district. When we finally arrived, it was nearing the end of a sunny autumn day.

"Did you eat on the plane?" my father asked. We were sitting on the tatami floor of his tearoom.

"They gave me a light snack."

"You must be hungry. We'll eat as soon as Kikuko arrives."

My father was a formidable-looking man with a large stony jaw and furious black eyebrows. I think now, in retrospect, that he much resembled [Chinese Communist leader] Chou En-lai, although he would not have cherished such a comparison, being particularly proud of the pure samurai blood that ran in the family. His general presence was not one that encouraged relaxed conversation; neither were things helped much by his odd way of stating each remark as if it were the concluding one. In fact, as I sat opposite him that afternoon, a boyhood memory came back to me of the time he had struck me several times around the head for "chattering like an old woman." Inevitably, our conversation since my arrival at the airport had been punctuated by long pauses.

"I'm sorry to hear about the firm," I said when neither of us had spoken for some time. He nodded gravely.

"In fact, the story didn't end there," he said. "After the firm's collapse, Watanabe killed himself. He didn't wish to live with the disgrace."

"I see."

"We were partners for seventeen years. A man of principle and honor. I respected him very much."

"Will you go into business again?" I asked.

"I am . . . in retirement. I'm too old to involve myself in new ventures now. Business these days has become so different. Dealing with foreigners.

Doing things their way. I don't understand how we've come to this. Neither did Watanabe." He sighed. "A fine man. A man of principle."

The tearoom looked out over the garden. From where I sat I could make out the ancient well that as a child I had believed to be haunted. It was just visible now through the thick foliage. The sun had sunk low and much of the garden had fallen into shadow.

"I'm glad in any case that you've decided to come back," my father said. "More than a short visit, I hope."

"I'm not sure what my plans will be."

"I, for one, am prepared to forget the past. Your mother, too, was always ready to welcome you back—upset as she was by your behavior."

"I appreciate your sympathy. As I say, I'm not sure what my plans are."

"I've come to believe now that there were no evil intentions in your mind," my father continued. "You were swayed by certain . . . influences. Like so many others."

"Perhaps we should forget it, as you suggest."

"As you will. More tea?"

Just then a girl's voice came echoing through the house.

"At last." My father rose to his feet. "Kikuko has arrived."

Despite our difference in years, my sister and I had always been close. Seeing me again seemed to make her excessively excited, and for a while she did nothing but giggle nervously. But she calmed down somewhat when my father started to question her about Osaka and her university. She answered him with short, formal replies. She in turn asked me a few questions, but she seemed inhibited by the fear that her questions might lead to awkward topics. After a while, the conversation had become even sparser than prior to Kikuko's arrival. Then my father stood up, saying: "I must attend to the supper. Please excuse me for being burdened by such matters. Kikuko will look after you."

My sister relaxed quite visibly once he had left the room. Within a few minutes, she was chatting freely about her friends in Osaka and about her classes at university. Then quite suddenly she decided we should walk in the garden and went striding out onto the veranda. We put on some straw sandals that had been left along the veranda rail and stepped out into the garden. The light in the garden had grown very dim.

"I've been dying for a smoke for the last half hour," she said, lighting a cigarette.

"Then why didn't you smoke?"

She made a furtive gesture back toward the house, then grinned mischievously.

"Oh, I see," I said.

"Guess what? I've got a boyfriend now."

"Oh, yes?"

"Except I'm wondering what to do. I haven't made up my mind yet."

"Quite understandable."

"You see, he's making plans to go to America. He wants me to go with him as soon as I finish studying."

"I see. And you want to go to America?"

"If we go, we're going to hitchhike." Kikuko waved a thumb in front of my face. "People say it's dangerous, but I've done it in Osaka and it's fine."

"I see. So what is it you're unsure about?"

We were following a narrow path that wound through the shrubs and finished by the old well. As we walked, Kikuko persisted in taking unnecessarily theatrical puffs on her cigarette.

"Well, I've got lots of friends now in Osaka. I like it there. I'm not sure I want to leave them all behind just yet. And Suichi . . . I like him, but I'm not sure I want to spend so much time with him. Do you understand?"

"Oh, perfectly."

She grinned again, then skipped on ahead of me until she had reached the well. "Do you remember," she said as I came walking up to her, "how you used to say this well was haunted?"

"Yes, I remember."

We both peered over the side.

"Mother always told me it was the old woman from the vegetable store you'd seen that night," she said. "But I never believed her and never came out here alone."

"Mother used to tell me that too. She even told me once the old woman had confessed to being the ghost. Apparently, she'd been taking a shortcut through our garden. I imagine she had some trouble clambering over these walls."

Kikuko gave a giggle. She then turned her back to the well, casting her gaze about the garden.

"Mother never really blamed you, you know," she said, in a new voice. I remained silent. "She always used to say to me how it was their fault, hers and Father's, for not bringing you up correctly. She used to tell me how much more careful they'd been with me, and that's why I was so good." She looked up and the mischievous grin had returned to her face. "Poor Mother," she said.

"Yes. Poor Mother."

"Are you going back to California?"

"I don't know. I'll have to see."

"What happened to . . . to her? To Vicki?"

"That's all finished with," I said. "There's nothing much left for me now in California."

"Do you think I ought to go there?"

"Why not? I don't know. You'll probably like it." I glanced toward the house. "Perhaps we'd better go in soon. Father might need a hand with the supper."

But my sister was once more peering down into the well. "I can't see any ghosts," she said. Her voice echoed a little.

"Is Father very upset about his firm collapsing?"

"Don't know. You never can tell with Father." Then suddenly she straightened up and turned to me. "Did he tell you about old Watanabe? What he did?"

"I heard he committed suicide."

"Well, that wasn't all. He took his whole family with him. His wife and his two little girls."

"Oh, yes?"

"Those two beautiful little girls. He turned on the gas while they were all asleep. Then he cut his stomach with a meat knife."

"Yes, Father was just telling me how Watanabe was a man of principle."

"Sick." My sister turned back to the well.

"Careful. You'll fall right in."

"I can't see any ghost," she said. "You were lying to me all that time."

"But I never said it lived down the well."

"Where is it then?"

We both looked around at the trees and shrubs. The daylight had almost gone. Eventually I pointed to a small clearing some ten yards away.

"Just there I saw it. Just there."

We stared at the spot. 70

"What did it look like?"

"I couldn't see very well. It was dark."

"But you must have seen something."

"It was an old woman. She was just standing there, watching me."

We kept staring at the spot as if mesmerized. 75

"She was wearing a white kimono," I said. "Some of her hair came undone. It was blowing around a little."

Kikuko pushed her elbow against my arm. "Oh, be quiet. You're trying to frighten me all over again." She trod on the remains of her cigarette, then for a brief moment stood regarding it with a perplexed expression. She kicked some pine needles over it, then once more displayed her grin. "Let's see if supper's ready," she said.

We found my father in the kitchen. He gave us a quick glance, then carried on with what he was doing.

"Father's become quite a chef since he's had to manage on his own," Kikuko said with a laugh.

He turned and looked at my sister coldly. "Hardly a skill I'm proud of," 80
he said. "Kikuko, come here and help."

For some moments my sister did not move. Then she stepped forward and took an apron hanging from a drawer.

"Just these vegetables need cooking now," he said to her. "The rest just needs watching." Then he looked up and regarded me strangely for some seconds. "I expect you want to look around the house," he said eventually. He put down the chopsticks he had been holding. "It's a long time since you've seen it."

As we left the kitchen I glanced toward Kikuko, but her back was turned.

"She's a good girl," my father said.

I followed my father from room to room. I had forgotten how large the 85
house was. A panel would slide open and another room would appear. But the rooms were all startlingly empty. In one of the rooms the lights did not come on, and we stared at the stark walls and tatami in the pale light that came from the windows.

"This house is too large for a man to live in alone," my father said. "I don't have much use for most of these rooms now."

But eventually my father opened the door to a room packed full of books and papers. There were flowers in vases and pictures on the walls. Then I noticed something on a low table in the corner of the room. I came nearer and saw it was a plastic model of a battleship, the kind constructed by children. It had been placed on some newspaper; scattered around it were assorted pieces of gray plastic.

My father gave a laugh. He came up to the table and picked up the model.

"Since the firm folded," he said, "I have a little more time on my hands." He laughed again, rather strangely. For a moment his face looked almost gentle. "A little more time."

"That seems odd," I said. "You were always so busy." 90

"Too busy, perhaps." He looked at me with a small smile. "Perhaps I should have been a more attentive father."

I laughed. He went on contemplating his battleship. Then he looked up. "I hadn't meant to tell you this, but perhaps it's best that I do. It's my belief that your mother's death was no accident. She had many worries. And some disappointments."

We both gazed at the plastic battleship.

"Surely," I said eventually, "my mother didn't expect me to live here forever."

"Obviously you don't see. You don't see how it is for some parents. Not only must they lose their children, they must lose them to things they don't understand." He spun the battleship in his fingers. "These little gunboats here could have been better glued, don't you think?"

"Perhaps. I think it looks fine."

"During the war I spent some time on a ship rather like this. But my ambition was always the air force. I figured it like this: If your ship was struck by the enemy, all you could do was struggle in the water hoping for a lifeline. But in an airplane—well, there was always the final weapon." He put the model back onto the table. "I don't suppose you believe in war."

"Not particularly."

He cast an eye around the room. "Supper should be ready by now," he said. "You must be hungry."

Supper was waiting in a dimly lit room next to the kitchen. The only source of light was a big lantern that hung over the table, casting the rest of the room in shadow. We bowed to each other before starting the meal.

There was little conversation. When I made some polite comment about the food, Kikuko giggled a little. Her earlier nervousness seemed to have returned to her. My father did not speak for several minutes. Finally he said:

"It must feel strange for you, being back in Japan."

"Yes, it is a little strange."

"Already, perhaps, you regret leaving America."

"A little. Not so much. I didn't leave behind much. Just some empty rooms."

"I see."

I glanced across the table. My father's face looked stony and forbidding in the half-light. We ate on in silence.

Then my eye caught something at the back of the room. At first I continued eating, then my hands became still. The others noticed and looked at me. I went on gazing into the darkness past my father's shoulder.

"Who is that? In that photograph there?"

"Which photograph?" My father turned slightly, trying to follow my gaze.

"The lowest one. The old woman in the white kimono."

My father put down his chopsticks. He looked first at the photograph, then at me.

"Your mother." His voice had become very hard. "Can't you recognize your own mother?"

"My mother. You see, it's dark. I can't see it very well."

No one spoke for a few seconds, then Kikuko rose to her feet. She took the photograph down from the wall, came back to the table, and gave it to me.

"She looks a lot older," I said.

"It was taken shortly before her death," said my father.

"It was dark. I couldn't see very well."

I looked up and noticed my father holding out a hand. I gave him the photograph. He looked at it intently, then held it toward Kikuko. Obediently, my sister rose to her feet once more and returned the picture to the wall.

There was a large pot left unopened at the center of the table. When Kikuko had seated herself again, my father reached forward and lifted the lid. A cloud of steam rose up and curled toward the lantern. He pushed the pot a little toward me.

"You must be hungry," he said. One side of his face had fallen into shadow.

"Thank you." I reached forward with my chopsticks. The steam was almost scalding. "What is it?"

"Fish."

"It smells very good."

In the soup were strips of fish that had curled almost into balls. I picked one out and brought it to my bowl.

"Help yourself. There's plenty."

"Thank you." I took a little more, then pushed the pot toward my father. I watched him take several pieces to his bowl. Then we both watched as Kikuko served herself.

My father bowed slightly. "You must be hungry," he said again. He took some fish to his mouth and started to eat. Then I, too, chose a piece and put it in my mouth. It felt soft, quite fleshy against my tongue.

The three of us ate in silence. Several minutes went by. My father lifted the lid and once more steam rose up. We all reached forward and helped ourselves.

"Here," I said to my father, "you have this last piece."

"Thank you."

When we had finished the meal, my father stretched out his arms and yawned with an air of satisfaction. "Kikuko," he said, "prepare a pot of tea, please."

My sister looked at him, then left the room without comment. My father stood up.

"Let's retire to the other room. It's rather warm in here."

I got to my feet and followed him into the tearoom. The large sliding windows had been left open, bringing in a breeze from the garden. For a while we sat in silence.

"Father," I said, finally.

"Yes?"

"Kikuko tells me Watanabe-san took his whole family with him."

My father lowered his eyes and nodded. For some moments he seemed deep in thought. "Watanabe was very devoted to his work," he said at last. "The collapse of the firm was a great blow to him. I fear it must have weakened his judgment."

"You think what he did . . . it was a mistake?"

"Why, of course. Do you see it otherwise?"

"No, no. Of course not."

"There are other things besides work," my father said.

"Yes."

We fell silent again. The sound of locusts came in from the garden. I looked out into the darkness. The well was no longer visible.

"What do you think you will do now?" my father asked. "Will you stay in Japan for a while?"

"To be honest, I hadn't thought that far ahead."

"If you wish to stay here, I mean here in this house, you would be very welcome. That is, if you don't mind living with an old man."

"Thank you. I'll have to think about it."

I gazed out once more into the darkness.

"But of course," said my father, "this house is so dreary now. You'll no doubt return to America before long."

"Perhaps. I don't know yet."

"No doubt you will."

For some time my father seemed to be studying the back of his hands. Then he looked up and sighed.

"Kikuko is due to complete her studies next spring," he said. "Perhaps she will want to come home then. She's a good girl."

"Perhaps she will."

"Things will improve then."

"Yes, I'm sure they will."

We fell silent once more, waiting for Kikuko to bring the tea.

Analyzing the Text

1. What unsolved questions in this story create suspense as to the father's true intentions when he serves his family the meal of *fugu* fish?
2. What role does the son's statement "surely my mother didn't expect me to live here forever" play in bringing to the surface the conflicts between Japanese and American assumptions?

Understanding Ishiguro's Techniques

1. How do the potentially lethal effects of the *fugu* fish serve as an apt image for the events that occur during the family supper or that are referred to in the story?
2. How do the references to murder and suicide that over hang the story complicate what otherwise would have been a pleasant homecoming?

Arguing for an Interpretation

1. Make the case that the father is so disappointed with his children that he has assembled them together to kill them (as Watanabe had done) with a dinner of *fugu* fish.
2. Argue that the father is preparing for a new life where the son will now visit him. Your paper should explore how food in the story is used to symbolize both positive and negative relationships of the family members.

Poems

ANONYMOUS

English and Scottish popular ballads (of which "Edward, Edward" is one of the most famous examples) were transmitted orally for centuries by common people. They are often tragic in tone and usually brief and anonymous. Most

were probably composed in the late Middle Ages on the border between Scotland and England. Because they were passed down through generations, many variations of words and phrases appear for the same ballad. Ballads are structured as narratives with repeated words, phrases, or lines (called a refrain) that build to a dramatic climax. The most important collection of ballads was undertaken by Bishop Thomas Percy (1729–1811) based on a manuscript he found dating from about 1650. It was published under the title Reliques of Ancient English Poetry *(1765) in which "Edward, Edward" first appeared. The story it tells is a complex family tragedy of murder and recrimination.*

Edward, Edward

I

"WHY DOES your brand[1] sae drop wi' blude,
Edward, Edward?
Why does your brand sae drop wi' blude,
And why sae sad gang[2] ye, O?"—
"O I hae kill'd my hawk sae gude,
Mither, mither;
O I hae kill'd my hawk sae gude,
And I had nae mair but he, O."

II

"Your hawk's blude was never sae red,
Edward, Edward;
Your hawk's blude was never sae red,
My dear son, I tell thee, O."—
"O I hae kill'd my red-roan steed,
Mither, mither;
O I hae kill'd my red-roan steed,
That erst was sae fair and free, O."

III

"Your steed was auld, and ye hae got mair,
Edward, Edward;
Your steed was auld, and ye hae got mair;
Some other dule ye dree,[3] O."
"Oh I hae kill'd my father dear,
Mither, mither;
O I hae kill'd my father dear,
Alas, and wae is me, O!"

---

[1]sword
[2]go
[3]grief ("dule") you suffer ("dree")

IV

"And whatten penance will ye dree for that,
Edward, Edward?
Whatten penance will ye dree for that?
My dear son, now tell me, O."—
"I'll set my feet in yonder boat,
Mither, mither;
I'll set my feet in yonder boat,
And I'll fare over the sea, O."

V

"And what will ye do wi' your tow'rs and your ha',
Edward, Edward?
And what will ye do wi' your tow'rs and your ha',
That were sae fair to see, O?"—
"I'll let them stand till they doun fa',
Mither, mither;
I'll let them stand till they doun fa',
For here never mair maun I be, O."

VI

"And what will ye leave to your bairns and your wife,
Edward, Edward?
And what will ye leave to your bairns and your wife,
When ye gang owre the sea, O?"—
"The warld's room: let them beg through life,
Mither, mither;
The warld's room: let them beg through life;
For them never mair will I see, O."

VII

"And what will ye leave to your ain mither dear,
Edward, Edward?
And what will ye leave to your ain mither dear,
My dear son, now tell me, O?"—
"The curse of hell frae me sall ye bear,
Mither, mither;
The curse of hell frae me sall ye bear:
Sic counsels ye gave to me, O!"

Analyzing the Text

1. What surprises both midway and at the end await the reader of this unusual ballad?
2. How would you characterize Edward's emotional state as it unfolds?

Understanding the Techniques

1. How do the repeated lines or refrains build suspense, provide insight into the nature of the mother–son relationship, and add to the tragic dimension of the ballad?
2. How does this ballad rapidly sketch in background information in the interest of creating a dramatic scenario?

Arguing for an Interpretation

1. In your opinion, who bears the greater responsibility, Edward or his mother? Explain your answer.
2. This is considered a classic example of the folk ballad genre (transmitted orally by uneducated people). Do you find this poem more or less satisfactory than other more polished literary efforts?

NAOMI SHIHAB NYE

Naomi Shihab Nye was born in 1952 in St. Louis, Missouri, but moved with her family to Jerusalem (which was then part of Jordan) where she attended high school. They then moved to San Antonio, Texas, where she presently lives with her husband and children. Nye's poetry celebrates the events of ordinary everyday life. Her themes and images draw upon her diverse cultural background and experiences. Collections of her poetry include Hugging the Jukebox *(1984), in which "Where Children Live" first appeared,* Words Under the Words: Selected Poems *(1995), and* Come With Me: Poems for a Journey *(2000). She is also the author of* Habibi *(1997), a novel for young adults, which is set in Jerusalem.*

Where Children Live

Homes where children live exude a pleasant rumpledness,
like a bed made by a child, or a yard littered with balloons.

To be a child again one would need to shed details
till the heart found itself dressed in the coat with a hood.
Now the heart has taken on gloves and mufflers,
the heart never goes outside to find something to "do."
And the house takes on a new face, dignified.
No lost shoes blooming under bushes.
No chipped trucks in the drive.
Grown-ups like swings, leafy plants, slow-motion back and forth.
While the yard of a child is strewn with the corpses
of bottle-rockets and whistles,
anything whizzing and spectacular, brilliantly short-lived.

Trees in children's yards speak in clearer tongues.
Ants have more hope. Squirrels dance as well as hide.
The fence has a reason to be there, so children can go in
and out.
Even when the children are at school, the yards glow
with the leftovers of their affection,
the roots of the tiniest grasses curl toward one another
like secret smiles.

Analyzing the Text

1. In what respects do "homes where children live" differ from those where they do not? Why, in the speaker's view, are "homes where children live" preferable?
2. How does the child's view of what makes a house fun to live in differ from that of adults?

Understanding Nye's Techniques

1. What images in the poem communicate the radically different perception of time and space of children from that of adults?
2. How does Nye use the concept of dressing a child up for cold weather to suggest that play for children is in and of itself a valued activity?

Arguing for an Interpretation

1. Does this poem verge on the overly sentimental in the sense of longing for an imaginary childhood? Why or why not?
2. How effectively does the poem communicate the atmosphere of congenial chaos that defines the world of children? What additional details would you add?

Anne Bradstreet

Anne Bradstreet (1612?-1672) was born in England and received a far fuller education than was usual for a young woman at that time. At the age of sixteen she married Simon Bradstreet, and in 1630 the couple sailed to America with the first group of Massachusetts Bay settlers. Both her father and her husband later became governors of the colony. Despite the heavy demands placed on her as a housewife, mother of eight, and hostess at state affairs, Bradstreet wrote poems that her brother-in-law had published in London (without her knowledge) in 1650. This volume, The Tenth Muse Lately Sprung Up in America, *presents Bradstreet as an ironic addition to the traditional nine muses of Greek mythology and was the first book of poetry published by a woman writer in colonial America. The following poem was composed in anticipation of a second edition of this volume (which appeared six years after her death).*

The Author to Her Book

Thou ill-formed offspring of my feeble brain,
Who after birth did'st by my side remain,
Till snatched from thence by friends, less wise than true,
Who thee abroad exposed to public view;
Made thee in rags, halting, to the press to trudge,
Where errors were not lessened, all may judge.
At thy return my blushing was not small,
My rambling brat[1] (in print) should mother call;
I cast thee by as one unfit for light,
Thy visage was so irksome in my sight;
Yet being mine own, at length affection would
Thy blemishes amend, if so I could:
I washed thy face, but more defects I saw,
And rubbing off a spot, still made a flaw.
I stretched thy joints to make thee even feet,[2]
Yet still thou run'st more hobbling than is meet;
In better dress to trim thee was my mind,
But nought save homespun cloth, in the house I find.
In this array, 'mongst vulgars may'st thou roam;
In critics' hands beware thou dost not come;
And take thy way where yet thou art not known.
If for thy Father asked, say thou had'st none;
And for thy Mother; she alas is poor,
Which caused her thus to send thee out of door.

Analyzing the Text

1. What is the speaker's attitude toward her "friends" who circulated her poems without her consent? How does she defend her decision to publish her book of poetry on her own?
2. How does Bradstreet forestall possible criticism by the way in which she characterizes her book of poetry?

Understanding Bradstreet's Techniques

1. How does Bradstreet develop the extended metaphor of her book as a child in order to express her feelings of pride and embarrassment?
2. What inferences can you draw about Bradstreet's everyday life from the homespun metaphors she applies to her writing?

Arguing for an Interpretation

1. To what extent does Bradstreet have to adopt a falsely humble posture in order to diffuse criticism by the community of Puritan New England who might disapprove of a wife wanting to be something more?

---

[1] *brat:* The word playfully characterizes her book/child.
[2] *feet:* Basic metrical units in a regular rhythm.

2. Since most of Bradstreet's poems were written about her everyday life with her husband and children, might she have felt embarrassed to speak about her work as the first American writer? How might conceit of that kind run counter to her deeply felt Puritan faith, which condemned egotism?

Cathy Song

Born in 1955 in Honolulu, Hawaii, of Chinese and Korean ancestry, Cathy Song was educated at Wellesley and Boston University. Her poetry is collected in Picture Bride *(1983), in which "The Youngest Daughter" first appeared. Song's work focuses on family relationships, and in this poem she explores the intricacies of a mother-daughter relationship. Her most recent collection of poetry is* School Figures *(1994).*

The Youngest Daughter

The sky has been dark
for many years.
My skin has become as damp
and pale as rice paper
and feels the way
mother's used to before the drying sun
parched it out there in the fields.

Lately, when I touch my eyelids,
my hands react as if
I had just touched something
hot enough to burn.
My skin, aspirin colored,
tingles with migraine. Mother
has been massaging the left side of my face
especially in the evenings
when the pain flares up.

This morning
her breathing was graveled,
her voice gruff with affection
when I wheeled her into the bath.
She was in a good humor,
making jokes about her great breasts,
floating in the milky water
like two walruses,
flaccid and whiskered around the nipples.
I scrubbed them with a sour taste
in my mouth, thinking:

six children and an old man
have sucked from those brown nipples.

I was almost tender
when I came to the blue bruises
that freckle her body,
places where she had been injecting insulin
for thirty years. I soaped her slowly,
she sighed deeply, her eyes closed.
It seems it has always
been like this: the two of us
in this sunless room,
the splashing of the bathwater.

In the afternoons
when she has rested,
she prepares our ritual of tea and rice,
garnished with a shred of gingered fish,
a slice of pickled turnip,
a token for my white body.
We eat in the familiar silence.
She knows I am not to be trusted,
even now planning my escape.
As I toast to her health
with the tea she has poured,
a thousand cranes curtain the window,
fly up in a sudden breeze.

Analyzing the Text

1. In what way is the poem shaped as an account of the long-brewing crisis between the speaker and her mother? Why is the title especially significant in light of the conflict described in the poem?
2. What clues does Song provide that might help explain why the daughter has submerged her own identity for so long to care for her mother?

Understanding Song's Techniques

1. What images in the poem underscore the mixture of affection and anguish that the speaker feels? What is the significance of the last image ("a thousand cranes curtain the window,/fly up in a sudden breeze")?
2. Evaluate Song's choice in relating this story from the point of view of the daughter rather than the mother or as a third-person account?

Arguing for an Interpretation

1. Based on the ending of the poem, is it clear whether or not the daughter has definitely decided to leave? Explain your answer.
2. How do the images with which the daughter describes herself, her skin, and her body communicate the distress and ambivalence she experiences? Who actually is caring for whom?

Sharon Olds

Sharon Olds was born in 1942 in San Francisco and was educated at Stanford University (B.A., 1964) and Columbia University (Ph.D., 1972). Her poetry candidly unfolds personal family life and psychological truths in ways that have made her work appeal to a wide audience. Her book The Dead and the Living *(1984) sold more than fifty thousand copies (an astonishing achievement for a poet). "The Planned Child" first appeared in* The Wellspring: Poems *(1996). Her recent works include* Blood-Tin-Straw *(1999) and* The Unswept Room *(2002), which was nominated for the National Book Award in Poetry.*

The Planned Child

I hated the fact that they had planned me, she had taken
a cardboard out of his shirt from the laundry
as if sliding the backbone up out of his body,
and made a chart of the month and put
her temperature on it, rising and falling
to know the day to make me—I would have
liked to have been conceived in heat,
in haste, by mistake, in love, in sex,
not on cardboard, the little x on the
rising line that did not fall again.

But when a friend was pouring wine
and said that I seem to have been a child who had been
  wanted,
I took the wine against my lips
as if my mouth were moving along
that valved wall in my mother's body, she was
bearing down, and then breathing from the mask, and then
bearing down, pressing me out into
the world that was not enough for her without me in it,
not the moon, the sun, Orion
cartwheeling across the dark, not
the earth, the sea—none of it
was enough, for her, without me.

Analyzing the Text

1. How does the speaker's attitude change over the course of the poem? Why does she now appreciate what she earlier had resented?

2. What kind of cosmic perception does the speaker attain, and how does this contrast with the rather mundane and tepid reality described in the first stanza?

Understanding Olds's Techniques

1. In what sense does the poem use a contrast between male imagery (in the first stanza) and female imagery (in the second stanza) to underscore the speaker's growing sense of identification with her mother?
2. How does Olds mimic the contractions of the birth process through repetition of certain words and phrases?

Arguing for an Interpretation

1. Discuss what you think causes the speaker's anger (which is so apparent in the first stanza) to dissipate in the second.
2. Why would hearing a chance remark by a friend, who commented that she seemed to be a child who was wanted, so radically change the speaker's feelings? To what extent are the sentiments about the importance of chance made in the first stanza illustrated by the circumstances under which this "conversion" takes place?

BEN JONSON

Ben Jonson (1572–1637) is without question one of the great poets of the English Renaissance. His work is noted for its wit, elegance, and clarity. He attended the Westminster School in London, where he acquired a great proficiency in classical literatures. Because he was too poor to attend either Oxford or Cambridge, he worked as a bricklayer with his stepfather and then enlisted in the army, where he fought in the war against Spain. After returning to England in 1595, he was employed as an actor and an apprentice playwright. His play Every Man in His Humor *(1598), in which Shakespeare played a role, was a popular success, and influenced English theater through the notion that each comic character is motivated by a quirk or personality trait. Among his best-known comedies are* Volpone *(1606) and* The Alchemist *(1610). Jonson's insight into the way a person's nature could be dominated by a single trait may have sprung from his own splenetic disposition. He killed an actor in a duel and barely escaped hanging by reciting a "neck verse" (a translation into English of a Latin passage) that entitled him to plead his case in a Church court; the court was suitably impressed by his classical learning and released him (after branding him on the left thumb to show he was a convicted felon). He was buried in Poets' Corner in Westminster Abbey. At the time Jonson learned of his son's death, he was staying in the country and had a vision of his young son (who was then in London) as an adult with "the mark of a bloody cross on his forehead." The next morning Jonson received news of his son's death and wrote the following poem. The lyric "On My First Son" is not only a heartfelt tribute, but reflects the high mortality rate of children in Elizabethan times because of disease and lack of sanitation and medical care.*

On My First Son

FAREWELL, THOU child of my right hand,[1] and joy;
  My sin was too much hope of thee, lov'd boy.
Seven years thou wert lent to me, and I thee pay,
  Exacted by thy fate, on the just day.[2]
O, could I lose all father,[3] now! For why
  Will man lament the state he should envy—
To have so soon scap'd world's, and flesh's rage,
  And, if no other misery, yet age?
Rest in soft peace, and, ask'd, say here doth lie
  BEN. JONSON his best piece of *poetry.*[4]
For whose sake, henceforth, all his vows be such
  As what he loves may never like too much.

Analyzing the Text

1. What features of the poem suggest that although Jonson initially attempts to write a conventional memorial, his real grief quickly overwhelms him?
2. To what extent does Jonson's use of the word "sin" ("my sin was too much hope of thee") suggest that he brings a Christian framework to try to understand the death of his son? How does this help explain his final vow?

Understanding Jonson's Techniques

1. How does Jonson's ending of the first two lines with a direct address (after a comma) suggest an overflowing emotion that he wishes to contain?
2. How does the epitaph ("here doth lie/Ben Jonson his best piece of poetry") convey Jonson's valuation both of his son and of his poetry?

Arguing for an Interpretation

1. The depth of anguish expressed in this poem for a child who has died from the plague is literally at war with the elegant grace of the poem's exterior. How does the conflict between the emotional content and form make the poem more dramatic?

---

[1]*child of my right hand:* This phrase is the literal translation of the Hebrew name Benjamin, Jonson's eldest son, who died of the plague in 1603.
[2]*just day:* Jonson's son died on his seventh birthday.
[3]*lose all father:* relinquish the connection between a father and a son so that he will not be tormented by his grief.
[4]*his best piece of poetry:* his most perfect creation.

2. To what extent does Jonson appear to believe that his son's death was a punishment for his excessive ambition and hopes for the boy?

Robert Hayden

Robert Hayden (1913–1980) was born in Detroit and educated at Wayne State University and the University of Michigan. He taught for more than twenty years at Fisk University before becoming a professor of English at the University of Michigan. He was elected to the National Academy of American Poets in 1975 and served twice as the poetry consultant to the Library of Congress, the first African American to hold the post. His volumes of poetry include A Ballad of Remembrance *(1962),* Words in Mourning Time *(1970), and* Angle of Ascent *(1975). "Those Winter Sundays" (1962) is a finely etched depiction of the speaker's change in attitude toward his father.*

Those Winter Sundays

Sundays too my father got up early
and put his clothes on in the blueblack cold,
then with cracked hands that ached
from labor in the weekday weather made
banked fires blaze. No one ever thanked him.

I'd wake and hear the cold splintering, breaking,
When the rooms were warm, he'd call,
and slowly I would rise and dress,
fearing the chronic angers of that house,

Speaking indifferently to him,
who had driven out the cold
and polished my good shoes as well.
What did I know, what did I know
of love's austere and lonely offices?

Analyzing the Text

1. How has the speaker's attitude toward his father changed from the time when he was a child?
2. What part does remorse or regret play in the way the speaker feels now?

Understanding Hayden's Techniques

1. Why is it significant that the poem begins with the phrase "Sundays too" in emphasizing the unwavering care shown by the speaker's father for his son?

2. How does Hayden use images of cold and warmth to emphasize the contrast between the physical and emotional environments the speaker experiences?

Arguing for an Interpretation

1. What insight does the phrase "the chronic angers of that house" provide in explaining the destructive cycle of unappreciated effort the poem describes?
2. Is the father a sympathetic or unsympathetic (but admirable) figure? Explain your answer.

W. B. YEATS

William Butler Yeats (1865–1939), an Irish poet and playwright, was the son of the artist John Yeats. William initially studied painting and lived in London and in Sligo, where many of his poems are set. Fascinated by Irish legend and the occult, he became a leader of the Irish Literary Renaissance. The long poems in his early book, The Wanderings of Oisin *(1889), show an intense nationalism, a feeling strengthened by his hopeless passion for the Irish patriot Maude Gonne. In 1898 he helped to found the Irish Literary Theatre and later the Abbey Theatre. As he grew older, Yeats's poetry moved from transcendentalism to a more physical realism, and polarities between the physical and the spiritual are central in poems like "Sailing to Byzantium" and the "Crazy Jane" sequence. Some of his best work came late, in* The Tower *(1928) and* Last Poems *(1940). Yeats received the Nobel Prize for literature in 1923 and is widely considered the greatest poet of the twentieth century. The extraordinary vibrancy of Yeats's poetry can be seen in "A Prayer for my Daughter" (1919).*

A Prayer for my Daughter

Once more the storm is howling, and half hid
Under this cradle-hood and coverlid
My child sleeps on. There is no obstacle
But Gregory's wood and one bare hill
Whereby the haystack- and roof-levelling wind,
Bred on the Atlantic, can be stayed;
And for an hour I have walked and prayed
Because of the great gloom that is in my mind.

I have walked and prayed for this young child an hour
And heard the sea-wind scream upon the tower,
And under the arches of the bridge, and scream

In the elms above the flooded stream;
Imagining in excited reverie
That the future years had come,
Dancing to a frenzied drum,
Out of the murderous innocence of the sea.

May she be granted beauty and yet not
Beauty to make a stranger's eye distraught,
Or hers before a looking-glass, for such,
Being made beautiful overmuch,
Consider beauty a sufficient end,
Lose natural kindness and maybe
The heart-revealing intimacy
That chooses right, and never find a friend.

Helen being chosen found life flat and dull
And later had much trouble from a fool,
While that great Queen, that rose out of the spray,
Being fatherless could have her way
Yet chose a bandy-leggèd smith for man.
It's certain that fine women eat
A crazy salad with their meat
Whereby the Horn of Plenty is undone.

In courtesy I'd have her chiefly learned;
Hearts are not had as a gift but hearts are earned
By those that are not entirely beautiful;
Yet many, that have played the fool
For beauty's very self, has charm made wise,
And many a poor man that has roved,
Loved and thought himself beloved,
From a glad kindness cannot take his eyes.

May she become a flourishing hidden tree
That all her thoughts may like the linnet be,
And have no business but dispensing round
Their magnanimities of sound,
Nor but in merriment begin a chase,
Nor but in merriment a quarrel.
O may she live like some green laurel
Rooted in one dear perpetual place.

My mind, because the minds that I have loved,
The sort of beauty that I have approved,
Prosper but little, has dried up of late,
Yet knows that to be choked with hate
May well be of all evil chances chief.
If there's no hatred in a mind
Assault and battery of the wind
Can never tear the linnet from the leaf.

An intellectual hatred is the worst,
So let her think opinions are accursed.

Have I not seen the loveliest woman born
Out of the mouth of Plenty's horn,
Because of her opinionated mind
Barter that horn and every good
By quiet natures understood
For an old bellows full of angry wind?

Considering that, all hatred driven hence,
The soul recovers radical innocence
And learns at last that it is self-delighting,
Self-appeasing, self-affrighting,
And that its own sweet will is Heaven's will;
She can, though every face should scowl
And every windy quarter howl
Or every bellows burst, be happy still.

And may her bridegroom bring her to a house
Where all's accustomed, ceremonious;
For arrogance and hatred are the wares
Peddled in the thoroughfares.
How but in custom and in ceremony
Are innocence and beauty born?
Ceremony's a name for the rich horn,
And custom for the spreading laurel tree.

Analyzing the Text

1. In what ways does Yeats create an idealized image of his daughter as an accomplished young woman who will embody the values he cherishes?
2. How do Yeats's hopes for his daughter become all the more poignant in view of the turbulent, destructive trends in the modern world that Yeats decries?

Understanding Yeats's Techniques

1. Yeats places a great deal of value on "custom" and "ceremony." What do you think he means by these terms? What trends in the modern world threaten to submerge them?
2. How does Yeats use the images of the laurel tree and the cornucopia in the last lines to symbolize the virtues he hopes his daughter will possess?

Arguing for an Interpretation

1. In what sense can this poem be considered as telling the reader more about Yeats than his daughter (since the daughter he speaks of is only an infant)?
2. As a research project, investigate Yeats's relationship with Maude Gonne and the reasons why he depicts her as "an old bellows full of angry wind" that he does not want his daughter to become. What other images in the poem support Yeats's sustained critique of a world that has become full of argument, opinion, commercialism, and controversy?

Rita Dove

Rita Dove was born in 1952, in Akron, Ohio. She went to Miami University in Ohio as a Presidential Scholar, graduated summa cum laude in English, and was awarded a Fulbright Fellowship to the University of Tübingen in Germany in 1974. She is currently professor of English at the University of Virginia. Her first collection of poems, The Yellow House on the Corner, *was published in 1980, followed by* Museum *(1983) and* Thomas and Beulah *(1986). The latter was a book of poetry about the history of blacks who migrated, as her own family did, from the South to the North, for which she was awarded the 1987 Pulitzer Prize. After Gwendolyn Brooks, Dove became only the second black poet to win the Pulitzer Prize. She is also the author of a collection of short stories,* Fifth Sunday *(1985). Her recent works include* Through the Ivory Gate *(1993),* The Darker Face of the Earth: A Verse Play in Fourteen Scenes *(1994),* Selected Poems *(1994),* Mother Love *(1995), and* On the Bus with Rosa Parks: Poems *(1999). As a poet, Dove has the unique ability to explore the lyrical possibilities of events that take place over a long period by bringing them together into a single moment. "The Wake," drawn from* Grace Notes *(1989), is a touching tribute to her mother.*

The Wake

Your absence distributed itself
like an invitation.
Friends and relatives
kept coming, trying
to fill up the house.
But the rooms still gaped—
the green hanger swang empty, and
the head of the table
demanded a plate.

When I sat down in the armchair
your warm breath fell
over my shoulder.
When I climbed to bed I walked
through your blind departure.
The others stayed downstairs,
trying to cover
the silence with weeping.

When I lay down between the sheets
I lay down in the cool waters

of my own womb
and became the child
inside, innocuous
as a button, helplessly growing.
I slept because it was the only
thing I could do. I even dreamed.
I couldn't stop myself.

Analyzing the Text

1. In what sense is the speaker's reaction to her mother's death a kind of "wake"? In what ways does the mother seem to become a presence as the poem develops?
2. How does the speaker's response to her mother's death change over the course of the three stanzas?

Understanding Dove's Techniques

1. How does the imagery of the poem present itself as a contrast between images of waking and sleeping?
2. What effect does Dove achieve through the increasing frequency with which the pronoun "I" is used?

Arguing for an Interpretation

1. What do the last lines imply about the speaker's way of coping with her mother's death? In your opinion, has she come to terms with it? Why or why not?
2. In Dove's view, does the presence of others and the formal rituals of grieving ease the pain of loss? Explain your answer.

Garrett Hongo

Garrett Hongo was born in 1951 in Volcano, Hawaii. His family moved to the San Fernando Valley in California where he and his brother were the only Japanese in the school. The family finally moved to Gardena, a Japanese-American community in south Los Angeles. He graduated from Claremont College, traveled to Japan on a Thomas J. Watson Fellowship, and returned to do graduate work at the University of Michigan. He received an M.F.A. from the University of California, Irvine, then taught at the universities of Washington and Southern California before taking a post at the University of Missouri at Columbia where he was poetry editor of the Missouri Review. *Hongo studied with poets Donald Hall and Philip Levine, among others, but was most influenced by the writing of Frank Chin, the first Asian-American playwright, and Lawson Inada, a pioneer Japanese-American poet. In 1976 Hongo founded, and until 1978 directed, a theater group in Seattle, The Asian Exclusion Act, which staged Frank Chin's* The Year of the

Dragon *and premiered Wakako Yamauchi's* And the Soul Shall Dance. *Hongo has received numerous awards, including the Hopwood Prize for Poetry, the Pushcart Prize, and the Wesleyan University Press Poetry Competition award. Hongo's poetry has been motivated by his quest for authentic roots of cultural identity in Japanese, Hawaiian, and southern Californian contexts. His collected books of poetry include* The Buddha Bandits Down Highway 99, *with Lawson Inada and Alan Lau (1978),* Yellow Light *(1982),* The River of Heaven *(1988), and* Volcano: A Memoir of Hawaii *(1995). "Who Among You Knows the Essence of Garlic" (1982) continues Hongo's exploration of ethnic roots and cultural identity through the associations evoked by specific foods.*

Who Among You Knows the Essence of Garlic?

Can your foreigner's nose smell mullets
roasting in a glaze of brown bean paste
and sprinkled with novas of sea salt?
Can you hear my grandmother
chant the mushroom's sutra?

Can you hear the papayas crying
as they bleed in porcelain plates?

I'm telling you that the bamboo
slips the long pliant shoots
of its myriad soft tongues
into your mouth that is full of oranges.

I'm saying that the silver waterfalls
of bean threads will burst in hot oil
and stain your lips like zinc.

The marbled skin of the blue mackerel
works good for men.The purple oils
from its flesh perfume the tongues of women.

If you swallow them whole, the rice cakes
soaking in a broth of coconut milk and brown sugar
will never leave the bottom of your stomach.

Flukes of giant black mushrooms
leap from their murky tubs
and strangle the toes of young carrots.

Broiling chickens ooze grease,
yellow tears of fat collect
and spatter in the smoking pot.

Soft ripe pears, blushing
on the kitchen window sill,
kneel like plump women
taking a long luxurious shampoo,
and invite you to bite their hips.

Why not grab basketfuls of steaming noodles,
lush and slick as the hair of a fine lady,
and squeeze?

The shrimps, big as Portuguese thumbs,
stew among cut guavas, red onions,
ginger root, and rosemary in lemon juice,
the palm oil bubbling to the top,
breaking through layers and layers
of shredded coconut and sliced cashews.

Who among you knows the essence
of garlic and black lotus root,
of red and green peppers sizzling
among squads of oysters in the skillet,
of crushed ginger, fresh green onions,
and pale-blue rice wine simmering
in the stomach of a big red fish?

Analyzing the Text

1. What associations are triggered in the speaker's memory when he describes the sensuous features of foods with ethnic and cultual qualities?
2. How are these qualities used to suggest a richness and diversity of which Anglo culture is unaware?

Understanding Hongo's Techniques

1. How do the complex descriptive effects of the poem depend on transposing sense impressions—that is, presenting an appeal to one sense in terms of another? What images best illustrate this?
2. How does the title of the poem and the way in which the speaker presents his unusual perceptions suggest someone who is knowledgeable about his native cuisine and wishes to make people want to know more about it?

Arguing for an Interpretation

1. How is Hongo's use of outrageous images designed to prove to the readers that they know very little about his culture?
2. Is Hongo's use of unusual foods, about which the audience might be presumed to know little, an effective tactic in making the case for his culture? Why or why not?

Chenjerai Hove

Chenjerai Hove, born in Zimbabwe in 1956, is currently a cultural journalist based in Harare, Zimbabwe, whose poetry is part of an emerging tradition in recent African poetry. He has sought to make his novels and poems a vehicle to celebrate the cultural heritage of a continent that has suffered centuries of colonial oppression. Hove differs from other African writers (most notably Ngũgĩ wa Thiong'o, the Kenyan novelist) who feel the continued use of European languages—English, French, Portuguese—perpetuates a colonial dependency. Hove chooses to use English to express an alternative vision of the African world. His novel Bones *(1988) won the Zimbabwean Publishers/Writers Literary Award. His volume of poetry,* Red Hills of Home *(1985), received special mention in the 1986 Noma Awards. Hove is also the author of* Poems Inspired by the Struggle in Zimbabwe *(1985) and a collection of essays* Palaver Finish *(2002). "You Will Forget" (1990) describes the psychological costs of losing touch with one's cultural heritage.*

You Will Forget

If you stay in comfort too long
you will not know
the weight of a water pot
on the bald head of the village woman

You will forget
the weight of three bundles of thatch grass
on the sinewy neck of the woman
whose baby cries on her back
for a blade of grass in its eyes.

Sure, if you stay in comfort too long
you will not know the pain
of child birth without a nurse in white

You will forget
the thirst, the cracked dusty lips
of the woman in the valley
on her way to the headman who isn't there

You will forget
the pouring pain of a thorn prick
with a load on the head.
If you stay in comfort too long

You will forget
the wailing in the valley
of women losing a husband in the mines

You will forget
the rough handshake of coarse palms
full of teary sorrow at the funeral.

If you stay in comfort too long
You will not hear
the shrieky voice of old warriors sing
the songs of fresh stored battlefields.

You will forget
the unfeeling bare feet
gripping the warm soil turned by the plough

You will forget
the voice of the season talking to the oxen.

Analyzing the Text

1. How does the speaker's description of the kinds of things that would be forgotten evoke the circumstances of tribal life?
2. What are the values the speaker claims are most in danger of being lost as a consequence of staying "in comfort too long"?

Understanding Hove's Techniques

1. What elements in the poem suggest that the voice we hear speaks for collective rather than simply personal values?
2. Why is the catalogue or inventory more effective than a single extended description?

Arguing for an Interpretation

1. How might Hove's poem be read as a form of social criticism? What hardships must the people in the tribe endure?
2. Could Hove's case be made about our culture? Why or why not?

Drama

Kōbō Abe

Kōbō Abe (1924–1993), the dramatist, short story writer, and novelist, was born in Tokyo but grew up in Mukden, Manchuria, then a possession of Japan. He returned to

Tokyo to prepare to become a doctor, like his father, but by 1948, when he graduated from the medical school of Tokyo University, his father had died and Abe had already decided upon a career in literature rather than medicine. He is best known for his ironic, meticulously detailed avant-garde novels that include The Woman in the Dunes *(1964),* The Face of Another *(1966),* The Ruined Map *(1969), and* The Box Man *(1974). All of these works deal with the themes of isolation and urban alienation. Much of Abe's energy has been devoted to writing for stage and screen: notably, adapting* The Woman in the Dunes *and later novels for the brilliant films directed by Teshigahara Hiroshi. In recent years, Abe founded an acting company and produced and directed a number of innovative plays including* Friends, *which was first presented in 1967 in Tokyo. This play, a tragicomedy, translated into English by Donald Keene, combines elements of the bizarre with realistic details to satirize the precarious state of the individual in contemporary Japanese society.*

Friends

Cast

MIDDLE DAUGHTER, twenty-four years old; a trim-looking, sweet girl who gives the impression of being a crystallization of good will

GRANDMOTHER, eighty years old

FATHER, a gentleman who at first glance might be taken for a clergyman; he wears a worn but quite respectable suit and carries a briefcase

MOTHER, her old-fashioned hat and glasses become her

YOUNGER SON, he once won a prize as an amateur boxer; he carries a guitar under one arm and a suitcase in the other

ELDER SON, clever, but frail-looking and rather gloomy; formerly a private detective; he carries suitcases in both hands when he enters

ELDEST DAUGHTER, thirty years old; a prospective old maid who still preserves her dreams of being raped by some man

MAN, thirty-one years old; section head in a commercial firm

YOUNGEST DAUGHTER, a little devil, though she doesn't look it

MIDDLE-AGED POLICEMAN

YOUNG POLICEMAN

BUILDING SUPERINTENDENT, a woman

FIANCÉE, she works in the same office as MAN; looks like a city girl

REPORTER, formerly on the staff of a weekly magazine

Scene One

The curtain rises to the sweetly seductive melody of "The Broken Necklace" (music by Inomata Takeshi).

Night time in the big city—
Now that the string is broken, the beads of the necklace
Scatter here and scatter there
In every direction.
Poor broken necklace, where is the breast that warmed you once?
When did you leave it, where has it gone?
Little lost beads, little lost beads.

Two large, partitionlike walls meet in a "V" at the middle of the stage. Shadows of human figures, four each from left and right, appear on the walls and, to the rhythm of the music, gradually grow larger, until in the end they seem to loom like giants over the audience.

As the music comes to an end, the owners of the shadows reveal themselves from the wings on both sides. The composition of this family of eight could hardly be more average, but one senses something peculiar about its members. They move mechanically, nobody as yet showing any expression on his face.

Middle Daughter steps forth from the group and advances to the center of the stage. The music should continue, but without words.

MIDDLE DAUGHTER (*taking up the words of the song that has been heard, her voice pleading and romantic*) But we can't just leave them to their fate. We'll gather up those poor little beads. Yes, we'll gather them up and run a new string through them. (*She turns to Grandmother.*) We can do it, Grandma, can't we?

GRANDMOTHER (*in a completely matter-of-fact tone*). Of course we can. That's our job, isn't it?

MIDDLE DAUGHTER (*turning back to audience and continuing her previous remarks*). It's wrong for there to be lost children and lonely people. It's all wrong. But you can't make a necklace without running a string through the beads. (*She turns to Father.*) We'll be the string for the necklace. Won't we, Father?

FATHER (*with a look of having heard this before*). Don't you think I know it already, that being a string is our job?

MIDDLE DAUGHTER (*singing to the music*).

Where is the breast that warmed you once?
When did you leave it, where has it gone?
Little lost beads, little lost beads.

Youngest Daughter suddenly gives a loud sneeze that stops the music.

MOTHER. My poor darling. (*To the others, reproachfully.*) If we don't settle down somewhere soon, it'll be ten o'clock before we know it.

YOUNGER SON. That's right. (*He yawns ostentatiously.*) I for one have had enough of this gabbing.

ELDER SON (*sharply*). Don't talk like a fool. It's our job, isn't it?

ELDEST DAUGHTER (*without expression*). That's right. It's our job.

The music begins again.

MIDDLE DAUGHTER (*resuming her exalted tone*). And that's why we must go on. We must search out all the lonely people and offer them our love and friendship. We are the messengers of love who can heal their loneliness. We must sniff out the faint wisps of sadness that escape like drops of starlight from the windows of the city, and go there with our gift of joy. (*She spreads her arms open as if introducing the family to the audience.*) Yes, we are the angels of broken necklaces.

Each member of the family simultaneously shines a flashlight from below on his face and smiles timidly. The contrast with the mood of what has preceded should be as strong as possible.

Blackout.

Scene Two

The partitions are drawn aside to reveal Man's room. The furniture and household accessories should all be of one color, either a reddish brown or gray.

A door leads to the kitchen at stage-right front. At stage-left rear a door leads to another room. The entrance door to the apartment is at stage-left front. Next to the door, in the hall, is a rather elaborate coat rack. (This rack will later be used as a cage; it must therefore have suitable vertical and horizontal supports.) All the furnishings, including the doors, should be simplified and abbreviated as much as possible.

Man sits at the desk. He wears a jacket and jiggles his leg as he telephones. The telephone is the only real object in the room.

MAN. Well, that's about all for now. I'll call you later on to say good night . . . What? It has yellow spots? Sounds like an alley cat, doesn't it? . . . No, I'm sorry. I assure you, I have absolute confidence in your taste . . . Oh, just a second. (*He removes the receiver from his ear and listens.*) No, it wasn't anything. I can't imagine anyone coming to see me now, at this hour of the night . . . Yes, isn't that what I've been saying all along? Next payday I'd like you to move in here for good. You should have your things packed and ready by then.

The eight members of the family approach slowly and hesitantly, walking on tiptoe.

It sounds like rain? Yes, maybe it is raining. It couldn't be foot steps—It'd take too many people for that. You know, the insurance agent in the apartment below mine is a nut for poker . . . Of course the noise has nothing to do with me.

The footsteps suddenly grow louder. Man cocks his head and listens. The family enters from stage right and crosses stage front in a single line. Younger Son, who has in the meantime passed his guitar to Elder Son, goes past the entrance to Man's apartment, then turns back; at which all the others stop in their tracks. Father and Younger Son stand on either side of the entrance. Father takes out a notebook and, after thumbing through the pages, compares what he finds with the name on the door. He nods and gives the signal to Middle Daughter, who is standing behind him. She comes forward and stands at the door, then knocks gently.

MAN. Say, it's at my door! (*He glances hurriedly at his watch.*) Must be a telegram, at this hour of the night. (*Middle Daughter knocks again and he calls to other side of the door.*) I'll be with you in a minute! (*The family is visibly relieved. He speaks into the telephone.*) I'll go out and have a look. I'll call you later. Here's a kiss. (*He makes a noise with his lips and puts down the telephone.*)

Scene Three

Grandmother, having slipped around from behind Middle Daughter, peeps through the keyhole. She sees Man coming to the door.

GRANDMOTHER. Goodness—what a handsome man!

FATHER. Shhh! (*He takes Grandmother by her sleeve and pulls her back.*)

MAN. Who is it? Who's there?

MIDDLE DAUGHTER (*in a girlish voice*). Excuse me, please. I'm sorry to bother you so late.

MAN. Who is it, please? (*He is disarmed to discover the visitor is a young woman, but is all the more suspicious.*)

MIDDLE DAUGHTER. I'm so sorry. I intended to come earlier.

Man shakes his head doubtfully, but eventually yields to curiosity and opens the door a little. Instantly Younger Son inserts his foot into the opening. Father takes the doorknob and pulls the door open. The family, moving into action, assembles before the door. Man, dumfounded, stands rooted.

MIDDLE DAUGHTER. Oh, that's a relief! You hadn't gone to bed yet, had you?

FATHER (*in the tone of an old friend*). Of course not! The young folks these days are night owls, all of them.

MOTHER (*pushing Grandmother from behind*). Shall we go inside, Grandma? The night air is bad for you.

MAN (*his voice choked*). Who are you anyway?

GRANDMOTHER (*ignoring Man and starting to go in*). Oh, dear, it's pretty bare, isn't it?

ELDEST DAUGHTER (*exhibiting strong curiosity*). What do you expect? It's a bachelor apartment, after all.

MIDDLE DAUGHTER. That's right. And that's why it's so important somebody come and help him.

MAN (*baffled*). Just a minute, please. I wonder if you haven't got the wrong party.

ELDER SON (*with a melancholy smile*). I used to work for a detective agency, you know.

MAN. But still—

YOUNGEST DAUGHTER. I'm cold.

MOTHER. Poor darling. You'll take an aspirin and get to bed early.

Mother, her arms around Youngest Daughter, propels Grandmother into the apartment. Man tries to prevent her, but Younger Son sees an opening and darts inside.

MAN. What do you mean, breaking in, without even taking off your shoes?
YOUNGER SON. Oh—sorry. (*He removes his shoes.*)

The family takes advantage of Man's distraction to surge into the apartment in one wave. Father, the last in, shuts the door behind him and turns the key. Man, in face of the concerted action of the eight of them, is powerless to resist. The members of the family scatter around the room with a kind of professional competence, neatly surrounding Man. They flash at him their usual bashful smiles. They seem to have got the better of him.

MAN. What's the big idea? It's enough to give a man the creeps.
FATHER (*unruffled*). Please, I beg you, don't get so upset.
MAN. If you've got some business with me, how about explaining exactly what it is?
FATHER. It puts us in an awkward position if you're going to turn on us that way . . . (*He looks around from one to another of the family as if enlisting their support.*)
MAN (*excitedly*). Puts you in an awkward position! You break in, without warning, on a total stranger, and you say it puts you in an awkward position! I'm the one who has something to complain about.
ELDER SON (*taps on the wall*). Pretty good! The walls have been soundproofed.
ELDEST DAUGHTER. It's freezing in here. Doesn't he have an electric heater, I wonder.
MAN (*unable to take any more*). Stop loitering around my apartment! All of you, get out of here! Now!
YOUNGER SON (*coolly*). Why, I feel as if we weren't wanted.
MAN. That's not surprising, is it? Of all the crassness!

Youngest Daughter peeps into the back room.

YOUNGEST DAUGHTER. Look, there's another room here.
GRANDMOTHER. It won't be easy dividing the space with only two rooms for nine people. (*She goes up beside Youngest Daughter and examines the other room with her.*)
MIDDLE DAUGHTER. We can't be fussy, you know. We didn't come here for our amusement.

Man stands at the door to the back room, blocking it. He is bewildered and uneasy.

MAN. Out with all of you, and right now! If you refuse to go, I'll charge you with trespassing.
YOUNGEST DAUGHTER (*with an exaggerated show of terror*). Oh, he scares me!
MOTHER (*admonishingly*). There's nothing for you to be afraid of. He's really a very nice man. There, just look at this face. He's just pretending to frighten you, that's all.
GRANDMOTHER. That's right. He's what I'd call a handsome man. If I were only ten years younger . . .
MAN. I've had all I can stand! (*He starts to lift the telephone.*)

FATHER (*quietly restraining him*). Now calm yourself. You seem to be under some terrible misapprehension. You're making such a fuss anybody might think we intended to do you some harm.

MAN. What *do* you intend, if not to harm me?

FATHER. Why should you say such a thing?

MAN. You're in a stranger's home here.

FATHER (*with an expression of dismay*). A stranger's home?

ELDER SON (*contemptuously*). A stranger's home! He certainly takes a very narrow view of things.

MAN. But, as a matter of fact, we are strangers, aren't we?

FATHER (*soothing him*). You mustn't get so worked up over each little thing. Have you never heard the saying that being brothers marks the first step on the way to being strangers? That means, if you trace strangers back far enough you'll find they were once brothers. What difference does it make if we're strangers? A little thing like that shouldn't upset you.

MOTHER. Yes, when you get to know us better you'll see we're just so relaxed and easygoing it's positively funny. (*She laughs.*)

MAN. Don't act silly. Whatever you may think, the fact is, this is my apartment.

ELDEST DAUGHTER. That's obvious, isn't it? If it weren't your apartment, you wouldn't be here.

YOUNGER SON. And, if it weren't your apartment do you suppose we'd have listened in silence all this time to your bellyaching?

MIDDLE DAUGHTER. I thought I told you to lay off him.

YOUNGER SON. I apologize. The fact is, I have a wee bit of a hangover. Damn it!

Younger Son shadowboxes briefly to cover his confusion. Middle Daughter, acting as if she has suddenly noticed it, puts out her hand to remove a bit of wool fluff from Man's jacket. Eldest Daughter tries to beat her to it. But Man shrinks back from both of them, and neither is successful. Youngest Daughter chooses this moment to disappear into the kitchen.

ELDEST DAUGHTER. I'm going to take off my coat, if you don't mind.

FATHER. Yes, we can't go on standing around this way indefinitely. Why don't we sit down and discuss things in a more relaxed mood?

They all remove their coats and hats. Younger Son also removes his jacket. Eldest Daughter's dress rather emphasizes her physique.

Man steps forward resolutely, pushes Father aside, and picks up the telephone and dials with an air of determination.

MAN. One, one, zero. (*He pauses, his finger inserted in the zero.*) Leave at once! Otherwise, I have only to release my finger and I'll be connected.

YOUNGER SON. To the police?

ELDEST DAUGHTER. Aren't you carrying things a bit too far?

FATHER (*perplexed*). It's a misunderstanding . . . a complete misunderstanding.

MAN. I have no time to bandy words with you. I'll give you until I count ten, that's all. I advise you to start getting ready. (*He starts to count slowly.*)

Younger Son stands menacingly before Man. He looks at the family to see whether they want him to go ahead.

FATHER (*sharply*). Stop! I forbid you to use violence.

MOTHER. Yes, we don't want people saying bad things about us. Stop it!

ELDER SON. How about, as a last resort, abiding by the will of the majority?

Man's attention is caught by the words "will of the majority." *He slows down the speed of his counting.*

ELDEST DAUGHTER. Even if we win a majority decision, it'd still be picking on someone weaker than us, wouldn't it?

ELDER SON. Don't be an idiot. The will of the majority means . . .

FATHER. Let's drop the whole matter. We know which side is going to win anyway. There aren't any thrills in this game.

GRANDMOTHER. Where might is master, justice is servant.

MIDDLE DAUGHTER (*somewhat uneasy*). What do you intend to do, anyway?

MAN. That's what I'd like to know. When I count one more, that'll make ten.

FATHER. It can't be helped. If you think it's absolutely necessary, do whatever you think best. It won't be very pleasant, but who knows?—it may prove more effective in bringing you to your senses than repeating the same old arguments.

MAN. Don't try to intimidate me! You're prepared, I take it? I'm really phoning the police.

FATHER. Go right ahead.

MAN (*releasing his finger from the dial emphatically*). Don't say I didn't warn you!

MOTHER (*sighs*). It's true, just as they say, a child never knows its parent's love.

MIDDLE DAUGHTER (*sighs*). This is the test run.

Scene Four

The telephone rings at the other end, then stops as the call is put through. The members of the family betray their tension in their expressions as they stand around the telephone. Younger Son puts a cigarette in his mouth. Grandmother, with an obsequious smile, tries to snatch away the cigarette, but Younger Son brusquely pushes his hand aside and lights the cigarette. Man is worked up, but he keeps himself on guard against the family.

MAN. I'm sorry to bother you, but I've been intruded on by a crazy outfit . . . No, it's not exactly a burglary . . . But there are eight of them. I've tried in every way I know to persuade them to leave, but they absolutely refuse to listen . . . No, it's not a vendetta or anything like that. They're total strangers . . . Yes, forced entry would be about right. I suppose you could call it a kind of burglary in that sense . . . That's right, eight of them . . . I? I'm all alone . . . Will you? Sorry to bother you. The place—it's a little hard to explain. Would you mind telephoning 467-0436 and asking the superintendent for directions? That's her number. My name is Homma and I'm in Apartment 12 . . . No, I don't think there's any immediate danger of violence, but there's no telling under the circumstances . . . Yes, I'd appreciate that. I'll be waiting for you . . . (*He heaves a sigh and puts down the telephone.*)

Elder Son, Younger Son, and Eldest Daughter smile to themselves, each with obvious satisfaction.

FATHER (*admonishingly*). There's nothing to smile about! I'm sure he was quite in earnest in doing what he did.

ELDER SON. But how can I help smiling? Burglary, he called it! Burglary! If a cat denounced a mouse as a burglar you couldn't keep the mouse from smiling just by telling him he shouldn't.

ELDEST DAUGHTER. I realize of course he doesn't mean any harm.

YOUNGER SON (*imitating Man's voice*). Yes, sir. There are eight of them, but I am all alone.

The members of the family start giggling again.

MAN (*challenging them*). Don't be so stubborn. You still have a few minutes left before the patrol car comes. I advise you not to waste your last chance.

Youngest Daughter sticks her head out from the kitchen. Her face is smeared around the mouth with something she has been eating. Grandmother quickly surmises what has happened.

GRANDMOTHER. Look at that! She's been nibbling something in the kitchen.

YOUNGEST DAUGHTER (*wiping her mouth and singing out*). The menu for tonight is two bottles of milk, six eggs, a loaf of bread, one bag of popcorn, one slice of mackerel, a pickle and some relish, two slices of frozen whalemeat, salad oil, and the usual spices.

YOUNGER SON. Quite a sweet tooth, hasn't he? Is there nothing in the way of liquor?

YOUNGEST DAUGHTER. Now that you mention it, there were two bottles of beer. That's all, I think.

YOUNGER SON. That's fine. I wanted a hair of the dog that bit me. (*He claps his hands in anticipation.*)

MOTHER. You can't drink it alone. We've got to save it to drink a toast to our new friendship.

ELDER SON. It's certainly not much of a menu in any case. You could find a better selection at a roadside diner.

MIDDLE DAUGHTER. Leave worrying about dinner to me. Those ingredients are more than enough for me to make quite a decent soup. (*She goes to the kitchen.*)

MAN. At last you've shown yourselves in your true colors. Out-and-out robbery is what I'd call it. The police will be here any minute. How do you plan to explain yourselves?

FATHER (*calmly*). You'll find out soon enough, when the time comes.

MAN. What will I find out?

ELDEST DAUGHTER. There's nothing for us to explain, is there? We're not doing anything we feel especially ashamed of.

MAN. Well, can you beat that? You talk as if you have the right to install yourselves in here. On what grounds can you justify—

Mother pauses in her unpacking of her suitcase.

MOTHER. But you're all alone here, aren't you?

MIDDLE DAUGHTER (*through the kitchen door*). It's terrible being alone. It's the worst thing that can happen to anybody.

ELDEST DAUGHTER. Yes, loneliness is bad for a person. In the first place, it makes you lose all resilience.

MAN. Supposing that's true, what business is it of yours?

FATHER. We're your friends. We can't abandon you, can we?

MAN. My friends?

FATHER. Of course we are. There are millions, even tens of millions of people in this city. And all of them are total strangers . . . Everywhere you look you see nothing but strangers . . . Don't you think that's frightening? There's no getting around it, we all need friends. Friends to help us, friends to encourage us.

GRANDMOTHER. In traveling, a companion; in life, sympathy. A wonderful thing, isn't it?

YOUNGER SON (*to Father*). Can't I have just one bottle of beer?

MAN (*nearly screaming*). I've had enough! I'm quite happy being alone. I'll thank you to stop your uncalled-for meddling. I don't want your sympathy. I'm enjoying my life just the way it is.

FATHER (*hesitantly*). But in general it's true, isn't it, that lunatics claim that they alone are sane?

MAN. Lunatics?

FATHER. Forgive me. I was using the word entirely by way of a simile.

MAN. As long as you're on the subject of lunatics, the description suits you all very well.

FATHER. Of course, it's difficult to define what we mean by a lunatic.

Mother sits before the mirror and begins to apply vanishing cream.

MOTHER. Nobody actually knows himself as well as he *thinks* he does.

ELDEST DAUGHTER (*suddenly clapping her hands*). That's right! I just remembered, I know a shop where they sell neckties that would look marvelous on you. I'll take you there the next time I go.

MOTHER (*reproving*). Instead of talking about such things you'd do better if you started helping in the kitchen. My stomach is beginning to tell me I need something to eat.

ELDEST DAUGHTER (*sulking*). Lend me your nail-polish remover, will you?

GRANDMOTHER. I'm in charge of dividing up the jam!

MAN. Who the hell *are* you all anyway?

YOUNGER SON (*with an air of arrogant assurance*). I'll tell you this once and for all—the most important thing for anybody to learn is how to get along with other people. A man who can get along with other people will stay out of trouble.

ELDER SON. It has been proven statistically that most criminals are antisocial.

FATHER. Be that as it may, please trust in us, and feel secure in your trust as a passenger on a great ocean liner. I'm certain that one day you'll need us and be grateful to us.

MAN. I've had all I can stand of your high-pressure salesmanship. Of all the colossal nerve!

FATHER. But we have no choice. You consider yourself to be a human being, don't you? It stands to reason, then, that it is your privilege, and also your duty, to live in a manner worthy of a human being.

Younger Son begins to strum the melody of "The Broken Necklace" on his guitar.

Middle Daughter emerges from the kitchen and begins to sing the song, still peeling a carrot. The peel hangs down to the floor in a long, unbroken coil.

MIDDLE DAUGHTER.

Night time in the big city—
Now that the string is broken, the beads of the necklace
Scatter here and scatter there
In every direction.
Poor broken necklace, where is the breast that warmed you once?

When did you leave it, where has it gone?
Little lost beads, little lost beads.

Scene Five

Two policemen are led to the door of the apartment by the Superintendent, who is a woman. The policemen have apparently been dropped some sort of hint by the Superintendent; at any rate, they seem uncommonly lax in their demeanor.

It may be that the Superintendent has been on bad terms with the Man, or that she may already have been bought over by the family; or it simply may be that she is pretending to be neutral for fear of getting involved—this is not clear.

The Superintendent points out the door of the Man's apartment and starts to make a hurried exit, but the Middle-aged Policeman, with a wry smile, plucks her back by the sleeve, his gesture suggesting a man catching a bug. The Young Policeman puts his ear to the door and listens to the sounds emanating from within, consulting his wristwatch as he does so. Then, with great deliberation, he presses the bell next to the door.

Man rushes to the door in response to the bell, all but knocking down the members of the family nearest to him (probably Grandmother and Middle Daughter), and pushes the door open. This action barely misses causing the Young Policeman to fall on his ear.

MAN (*flurried, but with great eagerness*). Oh, I'm sorry. Well, this will give you an idea of the situation. Come in, please, and have a look for yourself. The culprits are still holding out. I'm glad you got here in time. Oh, there are two of you? (*He notices Superintendent.*) It's good to have you along too, to back me up. Please step right in. Don't mind about me.

The policemen and Superintendent, at his urging, go inside. The Middle-aged Policeman, standing at center, runs his eyes professionally over the family. They betray no noticeable agitation. With absolute self-possession, they all stop whatever they were doing and return the policeman's suspicious stare with smiles and nods that all but overflow with a sincerity that could only come from the heart.

MAN (*excitedly*). They're eight of them altogether. The other one's in the kitchen.

Youngest Daughter enters from the kitchen, wiping her mouth. She obviously has been nibbling again. Grandmother gives the girl a severe look and starts to scold, but Father and Elder Son restrain her casually.

YOUNGEST DAUGHTER. Here I am.
MOTHER. Say hello to the gentlemen.
YOUNGEST DAUGHTER (*in a childish, bashful manner*). Good evening.
MIDDLE-AGED POLICEMAN (*confused*). Hmmm. Well then, what's the offense?
MAN (*failing to catch the words*). Excuse me?
YOUNG POLICEMAN. Their offense—what specific injury have you suffered?

MAN (*indignant*). I don't have to specify, do I? You've caught them red-handed in the act.

The members of the family continue to smile, quite unperturbed. Their smiles are confident and beyond all suspicion. Man, however, has become so upset by the passive attitude of the policemen that he is flustered and does not seem to have become aware of the performance the family is putting on. Middle-aged Policeman looks as if the smile tactics of the family have got the better of him. He lowers his eyes to his notebook and reads as he speaks.

MIDDLE-AGED POLICEMAN. According to the complaint, illegal entry has occurred on these premises.

MAN. That's it precisely!

MIDDLE-AGED POLICEMAN. In other words, even though you, the injured party, have plainly indicated to the parties responsible for the injury your wish that they not intrude into your apartment.

MAN. Naturally I've indicated it.

MIDDLE-AGED POLICEMAN. . . . . the offenders have brutally ignored or resisted the wishes of the injured party . . .

MAN. Ignored is a mild word for it.

MIDDLE-AGED POLICEMAN. Have you got any proof?

MAN. Proof?

YOUNG POLICEMAN. Have you any evidence of violence a doctor might be able to put in a medical certificate—broken bones or bruises?

MAN (*losing his temper*). I don't need any such evidence. All you have to do is look. They're eight against one.

MIDDLE-AGED POLICEMAN (*considers this seriously*). Eight against one and not a single bone broken? That makes it a little harder to prove violence, doesn't it?

Man does not speak and the Young Policeman lets his glance run over the smiling faces of the members of the family.

YOUNG POLICEMAN (*to Middle-aged Policeman*). The question would seem to arise, rather, why the complainant should have conceived such hostility toward these people—his motives, I mean.

MAN (*dumfounded*). Do you suspect *me?*

MIDDLE-AGED POLICEMAN. It's not that we *suspect* you. But complaints lodged over private, family matters often create a lot of trouble for us.

MAN (*in earnest*). This is preposterous. These people are complete strangers!

The members of the family, exchanging glances, smile sadly; one or two rub their chins as much as to say, "There he goes again!" and others wink at the policemen, enlisting their support. All remain silent as before.

MIDDLE-AGED POLICEMAN (*to Young Policeman*). What are we to do about this, anyway?

YOUNG POLICEMAN (*to Man*). I'd be glad to offer my services in helping to patch up the difficulties amicably.

MAN (*almost writhing with impatience*). Why can't you accept what I say? I tell you I have absolutely no connection with these people. It doesn't make sense to talk of patching up our difficulties amicably.

YOUNG POLICEMAN. That's a little hard to believe.

MIDDLE-AGED POLICEMAN. Have you any positive evidence that these people are strangers, as you claim?

MAN. Why don't you ask them?

The members of the family maintain their smiles intact. They even contrive to mingle a subtle suggestion of embarrassment in their smiles, exactly as if they were sympathizing with the policemen's predicament, or feeling embarrassment themselves over the deranged behavior of one of their own family.

MIDDLE-AGED POLICEMAN. That won't be necessary. I think I've got a pretty good idea of the essential points. It's my conclusion that there has been no injury to speak of.

MAN (*so enraged he stammers*). I'm disgusted. What more can I say to convince you? . . . And if you go on insisting that there has been no injury, even after what's happened, well, there's nothing left for me to say.

MIDDLE-AGED POLICEMAN. Excuse me for mentioning it, but you wouldn't be suffering from a persecution complex, would you?

MAN (*to Superintendent*). You can tell them, ma'am, can't you? You know I'm the one who's always paid the rent. And the name—the apartment is registered in my name, and letters are delivered regularly here to me, under my name. That's right, isn't it? This is my apartment. There's no doubt about it. I'm the only one with any rights here. That's correct, isn't it? You can surely vouch for me, can't you?

SUPERINTENDENT (*irritated*). Well, I can't say for sure.

MAN. You can't say for sure?

SUPERINTENDENT. I've always made it my practice, as long as a tenant pays the rent promptly each month, never to butt into his private life.

MAN. But at least I can ask you to vouch for the fact that I am the tenant.

SUPERINTENDENT. I'd rather not go into such things, but you know, in a place like this the person living in an apartment isn't always the same as the person who pays the rent.

MIDDLE-AGED POLICEMAN. I can imagine.

SUPERINTENDENT. Take the case of a young, unmarried woman, living alone . . .

At once Father and Younger Son react, but they restrain each other and instantly revert to the virtuous smiles they have displayed up to now. Grandmother begins to search the desk drawer.

MIDDLE-AGED POLICEMAN. Hmmm. I see.

SUPERINTENDENT. In extreme cases we may be sent money orders without even the sender's name.

MAN (*furious*). But I . . . I signed and sealed the contract, didn't I?

MIDDLE-AGED POLICEMAN. Come, now. You mustn't get so excited. Of course I understand your problem, but if there's no injury worth reporting at this stage . . .

MAN. But it's illegal entry, isn't it? It's trespassing, isn't it?

YOUNG POLICEMAN. We always ask the concerned parties in such private disputes to try to settle them among themselves. The police have their hands full as it is, what with the shortage of men.

MAN. I've told you, haven't I, these people are total strangers.

MIDDLE-AGED POLICEMAN. Well, in the event you suffer any specific injuries, please don't hesitate to get in touch with us again. (*He winks to the family, as much as to say that he has sized up the situation perfectly.*) It doesn't look as if I can write a charge—it won't make a case. I'm sorry to have bothered you all.

MOTHER (*as if the thought has suddenly struck her*). Oh, are you leaving so soon? And to think I haven't even offered you so much as a cup of tea.

MIDDLE-AGED POLICEMAN. Please don't bother.

MAN (*utterly bewildered*). But . . . just a second . . . what do you mean by . . . I've never heard of such a damned stupid . . . What am I going to . . . It's crazy. No matter how you look at it.

The Superintendent and the policemen ignore Man, who runs after them as if to implore their help. They go out very quickly and shut the door behind them. Once outside, they exchange sarcastic grimaces and exit at once.

Scene Six

Younger Son strikes a chord on his guitar, as if by way of a signal. The smiles that seemed to have been imprinted on the eight faces of the family are instantly replaced by their normal expressions.

FATHER (*consolingly*). That, my friend, is what people mean when they talk of good, common sense.

ELDER SON. Good, common sense, and at the same time, accomplished fact.

GRANDMOTHER. The proof of the pudding is in the eating.

ELDEST DAUGHTER. It seems to come as quite a shock to him. He's still standing there in a daze.

MOTHER. It'll do him good to have such an experience once.

YOUNGEST DAUGHTER. I don't understand him. Why, even a child knows how lonely it is to be without friends.

YOUNGER SON. His whole outlook's warped. He's bluffing, that's all.

MIDDLE DAUGHTER. I wish it wouldn't take him so long to understand what a miserable thing loneliness is, and how lucky he is to have us . . . (*She seems to be addressing herself to Man only. She wraps the long peel from the carrot around her neck.*)

MAN (*suddenly turning on her*). I've had all I can stand of your meddling.

FATHER (*as if reasoning with himself*). It's certainly irritating, but this is no time to lose my temper. Patient care is the only way to treat the sick.

MIDDLE DAUGHTER. Would you like a glass of water?

MAN (*unmoved*). Stop bothering me! I swear, I'll get rid of you, if it's the last thing I do. You can make up your minds to that! I tell you I won't stand being humiliated this way!

MIDDLE DAUGHTER (*unwrapping the carrot peel around her neck*). If we don't do something about it, the broken necklace will never be the same again. Isn't there anything we can do to convince him of our sincerity?

ELDEST DAUGHTER. Humpf. Such exquisite sensitivity!

MIDDLE DAUGHTER (*with an abrupt shift of mood*). Don't act so sour!

FATHER. Now, now—don't forget, anybody who creates dissension or starts a quarrel must pay a fine.

GRANDMOTHER (*still rummaging through the desk, but her tone is magnanimous*). It's a long lane that has no turning . . . There's nothing worth making a fuss over.

MIDDLE DAUGHTER (*to Youngest Daughter*). Come on, help me in the kitchen.

GRANDMOTHER (*sharply*). This time don't do any nibbling on the sly. It's disgraceful.

Youngest Daughter sticks out her tongue, then exits with Middle Daughter.

MAN (*suddenly becoming aware of Grandmother's suspicious activities*). It's all very well for you to talk, but what are you doing there, anyway?

GRANDMOTHER. I was just looking for a cigarette.

MAN. Cut it out! Stop acting like a sneak thief!

GRANDMOTHER (*with exaggerated dismay*). Oh—I'm a sneak thief, am I?

FATHER. Of course you're not a sneak thief. I ask you all to refrain from making remarks that might cast aspersions on anyone else's character.

ELDER SON. How about setting a fine of a hundred yen on any remark which is decided by majority vote to be offensive?

FATHER. An excellent suggestion. Yes, that appeals to me. There's no such thing as being too discreet when it concerns a person's character, is there?

GRANDMOTHER (*more engrossed than ever in her search for cigarettes*). Imagine calling me a sneak thief! A cigarette only turns to smoke, no matter who smokes it.

MAN. Stop rummaging that way through my desk!

Man, thinking he will stop Grandmother, steps forward automatically, only for Elder Son to stick out his foot and trip him. Man flops down magnificently.

ELDER SON. Oops—excuse me!

The family at once rushes over to Man in a body and surrounds him, lifting him to his feet, massaging his back, brushing the dust from his suit, and otherwise showering him with extreme attentions.

ELDEST DAUGHTER. Are you sure you're all right?

MOTHER. You haven't hurt yourself?

YOUNGER SON. Can you stand okay?

GRANDMOTHER. No pain anywhere?

FATHER. No broken bones?

MAN (*freeing himself*). Lay off, for God's sake!

ELDER SON (*apologetically*). I'm sorry. I was just worried you might get so carried away by your feelings you would resort to violence.

MAN. Wouldn't you describe what you did as violence?

ELDER SON. Not in the least. It was a precaution against violence.

YOUNGER SON (*cheerfully*). We won't let you get away with that! Allowing yourself to get involved in a quarrel is just the same as starting one. You'll have to pay a fine. Or would you rather make amends in kind?

ELDER SON (*dejectedly*). I don't have to tell you how hard up I am for money.

ELDEST DAUGHTER. But even if he prefers to make amends in kind, it won't be easy. How can anybody trip himself?

YOUNGER SON. Can't you think of anything better to do than butt into other people's business? Do you plan to go on removing nail polish forever? It's just a matter of time before you dissolve your finger-tips. (*To Man.*) I wonder if you'd mind tripping my brother back?

MAN (*angrily*). Don't be an idiot!

YOUNGER SON. It can't be helped, then. I'll take over as your substitute.

As soon as Younger Son finishes speaking he gets up and deftly trips Elder Son, who tumbles over with a loud groan. Younger Son at once drags Elder Son to his feet, only to trip him again, without allowing him an instant's respite. He repeats this a third time, and is about to trip him a fourth time when Man, unable to endure any more, cries out.

MAN. That's enough, for God's sake!

MOTHER (*relieved*). At last, he's forgiven you.

ELDER SON (*grimacing with pain and rubbing the small of his back*). Thanks.

YOUNGER SON. Well, what do you know? Perspiring seems to have relieved my hangover a little.

GRANDMOTHER (*suddenly*). I've found them!

(*She clutches a package of cigarettes.*)

Man takes a step in her direction only to remember immediately what happened to him the last time. He stops in his tracks. Father can't quite allow Grandmother to get away with it and takes away the cigarettes.

FATHER. That's going too far, Mother.

MAN. Sneaking around my desk like a cat. She's a regular cat burglar! (*He puts out his hand, expecting to get back his cigarettes as a matter of course.*)

FATHER (withdrawing his hand, sounding surprised). What did you just say?

Man does not speak.

GRANDMOTHER. He called me a cat burglar!

FATHER. A cat burglar!

ELDER SON (*calmly*). That calls for a fine. Number one, right?

FATHER (*his voice is strained*). I see . . . Without warning, it's come to this . . . I may seem a little too much of a stickler for the rules, but if we hope to live together amicably . . .

ELDER SON. Yes, a rule's a rule . . .

ELDEST DAUGHTER (*massaging her face*). Just a minute. There's nothing to get so upset about.

GRANDMOTHER (*getting angry*). You're always trying to be different from everyone else.

ELDEST DAUGHTER (*ignoring her*). I think cats are sweet. I adore them. They're the most aristocratic of all animals.

ELDER SON. But there's a big difference between cats and cat burglars, isn't there?

ELDEST DAUGHTER. And there's also a big difference between burglars and cat burglars.

GRANDMOTHER (*excited*). Then you say I'm a cat?

ELDEST DAUGHTER. Don't be conceited, Grandmother!

GRANDMOTHER. But that's what he said . . . He plainly called me a cat burglar.

ELDEST DAUGHTER. I'm sure he meant it as a compliment.

FATHER. Now wait, please. The meaning is quite different, depending on whether the emphasis was on burglar or on cat. In other words, did he mean a cat that resembled a burglar, or a burglar that resembled a cat?

GRANDMOTHER. I don't care what he said, I'm not a cat.

YOUNGER SON. That's so, I guess. If you were a cat, Grandma, that'd make us all half-breed cats.

FATHER. Therefore the logical meaning must be a catlike burglar.

ELDER SON. That rates a fine, doesn't it?

ELDEST DAUGHTER (*persisting*). Why should it? He didn't say she was a burglar plain and simple, but a catlike burglar.

ELDER SON. But a burglar's a burglar. The only difference is whether or not the word has an adjective before it.

GRANDMOTHER (*moaning*). I'm not a burglar!

ELDEST DAUGHTER. Do you mean to say that applying a different adjective doesn't change the meaning of a word? Well, that's the first I've ever heard of *that* argument! If a big fish and a little fish, a sunny day and a cloudy day, a decrepit old man and a snotty-faced kid, a brand-new car and an old buggy, a smiling face and a crying face all amount to the same thing, then there's no distinction either between a burglar man and a burglarized man. I've never heard such a funny story.

YOUNGER SON. It looks as if you've lost the first round, Brother. Eh?

ELDER SON. A woman's superficial cleverness, that's all it is.

ELDEST DAUGHTER (*assertively*). A cat is a superb animal.

MOTHER (indifferently). I don't like cats.

ELDEST DAUGHTER (*her tone is extremely objective*). They say that a dislike of cats is the mark of an egoist.

YOUNGEST DAUGHTER (*sticking her head in from the kitchen*). But people who don't like cats often like them.

YOUNGER SON. You don't say! That's not bad, you know.

MOTHER (*to Youngest Daughter*). Children should be seen and not heard.

YOUNGEST DAUGHTER. Hurry up and help us in the kitchen.

ELDEST DAUGHTER. I have more important things to do. We're having a serious discussion.

GRANDMOTHER. Anyway, I'm not a cat.

ELDEST DAUGHTER (*her tone becoming hysterical*). Stop it, won't you? I can't stand you speaking so sneeringly about cats.

MAN (*finally having had all he can take*). Won't you drop the whole thing, for pity's sake? I can settle this by paying a hundred yen—right? It's too ridiculous. (*He starts to look in his pockets for his wallet.*)

ELDEST DAUGHTER (*coquettishly*). Oh? But that's cheating . . . After I went to all the trouble of taking your side . . .

FATHER (*recovering himself*). That's right. You don't leave us much to say if you're going to talk in such extremes . . . We still haven't reached any conclusion, after all . . . The situation has become unexpectedly complicated.

MAN. What's so complicated? (*He continues to search his pockets.*)

FATHER. I meant merely that our opinions continue to be opposed.

ELDEST DAUGHTER. Yes. You must remember you aren't alone any more. There's someone on your side. Anyway, cats are absolutely marvelous animals.

MOTHER. But I don't like them.

GRANDMOTHER. I told you I wasn't a cat!

FATHER. There you have the problem.

MAN. What difference does it make? The long and short of it is that I have to pay a fine. Right?

FATHER. But the basic principle of communal living is respect for the opinions of each person.

MAN (*his voice dropping sarcastically*). Is that so? I'm delighted to hear it. I'll be sure to remember that. (*He is still unable to find his wallet, and begins to look rather worried. He takes his coat from its hook on the wall and starts to search the pockets.*)

FATHER (*to the others*). What do you say, all of you? Wouldn't this be a good point to try to put some order into the discussion? Now, if you'll permit me to express my opinion, the question, it seems to me, is whether the animal known as the cat—when, for example, it is compared with the dog ...

ELDEST DAUGHTER. There's no comparison!

YOUNGER SON. Still, nobody ever talks of a dog burglar.

ELDEST DAUGHTER. That's because dogs are stupid.

ELDER SON. That's a lie.

ELDEST DAUGHTER. What do you know about it?

ELDER SON. There are police dogs, but I've never heard of police cats.

ELDEST DAUGHTER. Of course not. Cats have a higher social status.

MOTHER. But, it seems to me, cats are lazy.

YOUNGER SON. Wait a second. Hard workers don't necessarily get very far.

ELDEST DAUGHTER. That's precisely it.

YOUNGER SON. But if you'll permit me to express my own preferences, I like dogs better.

ELDEST DAUGHTER. They certainly suit you. Let sleeping dogs lie. Go to the dogs. Lead a dog's life ...

YOUNGER SON. Don't be too sure of yourself with cats, you caterwauling, cat-calling, caterpillar ...

ELDEST DAUGHTER. Every dog has his day.

YOUNGEST SON. Catnip is to a cat as cash to a whore in a cathouse.

ELDEST DAUGHTER. Dog eat dog. Die like a dog. Dog in the manger.

ELDER SON. You see—friends and foes are all confused. A majority decision is the only way, Father.

MAN. I wish you'd drop the whole thing. A majority decision! (*He is still searching frantically.*)

ELDER SON. At this rate we'll never get to eat dinner.

MIDDLE DAUGHTER (*emerging from the kitchen with a frying pan in her hand*). Sorry to keep you waiting. Dinner will be ready in just a few minutes. Sis, please help me dish out the food.

MAN (*pauses in his search, with vehemence*). Dinner—of all the crazy nonsense! What crass nerve, here, in my house! Listen, I warn you, I intend to use every means at my disposal to obstruct anything you do. (*To Middle Daughter.*) Get rid of that mess. Throw it in the garbage can, now!

MIDDLE DAUGHTER (*recoiling*). But that would be a terrible waste!

FATHER. (*looks into the frying pan*). Mmm. It certainly smells good.

ELDER SON. I'm convinced that food is meant to be eaten with lots of company. Nothing is drearier than shoveling in a quick meal. I can tell you that from my own personal experience.

MAN. Unfortunately, there are some people whose temperament is such that they prefer to live alone.

ELDER SON. Well, I can see that once you've argued yourself into a point of view you'd want to stick to it.

While they are talking Middle Daughter exits.

ELDEST DAUGHTER. My sister used to take a course in cooking. (*At last she gets up and starts toward the kitchen.*)

GRANDMOTHER (*to Eldest Daughter*). I'm in charge of dividing up the jam.

ELDEST DAUGHTER. It's quite something to have been able to make a curry with the ingredients she had. (*She exits.*)

YOUNGER SON (*stifling a yawn*). I feel more like sleeping than eating now ... My hangover is beginning to take its toll.

GRANDMOTHER. I'm no good without my food. I can't get to sleep without first putting my tapeworm to bed.

MAN (*strangely self-possessed*). In that case, you should stay awake all the time. Stay awake for years, or maybe dozens of years, as long as you like. I warned you, didn't I, that I intend to do everything in my power to obstruct you? That wasn't an empty threat. I assure you I intend to carry it out. I'll make sure you don't get to eat even a slice of bread.

GRANDMOTHER. Why won't we?

ELDER SON (*with a faint smile*). He talks exactly as if he's turned into a magician or something, doesn't he?

MAN (*walking toward the kitchen*). You're going to laugh on the wrong side of your faces!

MOTHER (*to the people in the kitchen, in a casual voice*). You've put away everything harmful, haven't you?

MIDDLE DAUGHTER (*from the kitchen*). Of course we have. I've hidden everything—the tile cleanser, the rat poison, the cockroach spray. They're in a safe place.

YOUNGER SON (*in a loud voice*). It might be a good idea, while you're at it, to stow away the detergents and soap powder too.

MIDDLE DAUGHTER. Right.

Man stops in his tracks in dumb confusion at the kitchen door.

ELDER SON. You see! He intended to use one of them.

YOUNGER SON (*to Man*). You planned to use a spray to squirt foam over the dinner, didn't you?

FATHER (*a consoling expression on his face*). For good or for evil, everybody tends to think, more or less, along the same lines.

YOUNGER SON. Foam—that reminds me—beer! (*As if appealing for sympathy he looks up at ceiling.*)

While the preceding conversation has been going on, Mother has at last finished removing her makeup. She puts away her beauty aids and, rising to her feet, turns to face the others. All of a sudden she takes hold of her hair and pulls up, to reveal she is wearing a wig. She blows into the wig, fans it with her hand, and after shaking it out thoroughly, puts it back on her head.

MOTHER (*to Man, with an artificial laugh*). You don't mind, do you? You're not a stranger any more, after all. (*Abruptly changing her tone.*) By the way, what ever happened to the fine we were talking about?

FATHER (*perplexed*). We didn't seem to be able to reach any conclusion in our discussion of cats, and the person in question doesn't seem very enthusiastic about a majority decision.

MAN (*searching frantically through all his pockets, and even in the cuffs of his trousers, with an intense display of determination*). I'll pay, I tell you. You don't suppose I want to be in your debt for a mere hundred yen! I'm paying, not because I recognize I was at fault, but simply because I don't feel like arguing over anything so extremely stupid.

The attention of the entire family is at last attracted by his distraught actions, and they observe him carefully. Man suddenly stops searching, as if he found what he was looking for.

MAN. Damn it! That's funny . . .

MOTHER. Was it your wallet? Or do you carry your money loose?

MAN. I carried it in a wallet with my monthly pass ... I can't imagine ...

The glances of the others converge at the same moment in accord on Elder Son. He returns their gaze. There is a moment of silence.

ELDER SON. What's the matter with you all? Have I done something wrong?

YOUNGER SON (*crooking his index finger to suggest a robber with a gun*). Did you do it, Brother?

ELDER SON (*with feigned innocence*). What are you talking about, anyway?

FATHER (*uneasily*). It's not true, is it? I'm sure you wouldn't stoop to that sort of thing ... At a critical moment like this we must, above all, show the greatest respect for the integrity of the individual.

YOUNGER SON. But he's got a criminal record, you know.

ELDER SON. Stop it! You're ruining my reputation!

At this juncture the people in the kitchen begin to stick out their heads and observe what is going on.

YOUNGER SON. Everybody of course has committed youthful indiscretions.

ELDER SON. Haven't I told you I've completely given up all that?

MOTHER. Please. Look into Mother's eyes. Yes, look straight into my eyes.

ELDER SON. I've come back to you, haven't I? You can see that I have ... I learned, so well it hurt me, how wonderful it is when people can trust one another and what a blessing it is when people who trust one another can live together. So I came back to you, from that horrible world where every man is a stranger ... Do you think I'd betray you all? No, stop it, please ... As far as I'm concerned, the one thing that makes life worth living is being together, hand in hand.

GRANDMOTHER (*apparently unimpressed*). You aren't trying to make us cry, are you?

ELDER SON. I'm serious, I assure you.

YOUNGER SON. I'll bet if ever I tried to lie seriously I could really warm up to it.

ELDER SON (*uncertain how he should react to this comment, betraying his confusion momentarily*). I understand the situation perfectly ... And I'm glad ... I don't feel in the least offended. I'm flattered you should retain such a high opinion of my former skill.

MOTHER (*brooding*). Then, you mean ...

ELDER SON. I leave it to your imagination.

FATHER (*embarrassed*). That won't do ... You, better than anyone else, are in the position to put the matter straight. How can you speak of leaving it to our imagination? I thought we had promised not to recognize private prerogatives when it came to money.

ELDEST DAUGHTER. Yes, he himself was the first to propose that.

YOUNGER SON (*as if reading aloud*). As previously agreed, in cases where suspicions have been aroused with respect to monetary matters, no one, whosoever he may be, for whatever reason, may refuse a request for a body search.

GRANDMOTHER. Love flies out the window when poverty comes in at the door.

FATHER. I can't understand it. You have the best brains of the lot of us, there's no getting around it. And you're amenable to reason. We all depend on you. It's intolerable that we should have to treat you like a defendant in court.

ELDER SON (*laughs*). You have nothing to worry about.

FATHER (*relieved*). Then you're innocent?

MOTHER. You should have set our minds at rest sooner.

ELDER SON. I mean, I haven't done anything that warrants a physical examination.

Elder Son suddenly raises his hand and reveals that he is holding Man's wallet. The following dialogue by members of the family occurs almost simultaneously.

MOTHER. You took it, then!

ELDEST DAUGHTER. You've got to keep your eye on him every minute.

YOUNGEST DAUGHTER. Take me on as your apprentice, won't you?

YOUNGER SON. Now I know why you're never short of cigarette money.

MOTHER (*firmly*). Hand it over, here!

As Mother steps forward, Man springs to his feet with an incomprehensible cry and makes a grab for Elder Son's hand. The wallet instantly disappears.

MAN (*carried away, searching Elder Son's pockets*). What've you done with it? Give it back!

ELDER SON. Oh, you're tickling me!

(*He holds up his hands, as before a gunman, and twists himself free.*)

MOTHER (*severely*). You know the rules, don't you? I take charge of the safe.

ELDER SON (*to Man*). I surrender! If you would kindly look in the righthand pocket of your pants . . .

Man doubtfully puts his hand into his pocket and with an incredulous expression he produces the wallet.

MAN. This is it, all right.

YOUNGEST DAUGHTER (*clapping her hands*). He's a regular wizard!

MIDDLE DAUGHTER (*reproving*). You mustn't say that! You're not to admire him.

MOTHER (*to Elder Son, angrily*). Haven't you done quite enough? Surely you can't have forgotten all about your own family.

MAN (*turning wallet, upside down and shaking it*). Not a thing. There's not a penny in it . . .

(*He stands there glaring at Elder Son, grinding his teeth, for the moment unable to find even words of protest.*)

ELDER SON (*apparently enjoying it*). A pro who couldn't do that much wouldn't be worthy of the name.

MOTHER. I won't allow it—sneaking off with other people's money.

GRANDMOTHER. Like a cat burglar?

MOTHER (*to Man*). How much was in it?

MAN. How should I know?

MOTHER (*to Father*). Don't just stand there, without saying anything. Don't you think it'll set a bad example if we shut our eyes to this sort of thing?

FATHER. That's right, a very bad example . . . Still, I don't understand it . . . I thought we'd thrashed the whole thing out, only to find you're still keeping secrets from us. Why do you do it? It's not like you.

MOTHER. I beg you, don't make your mother any unhappier than she already is.

ELDER SON (*blandly*). That's what you say, Mother, but were you really so confident you could fleece this guy out of his money entirely by persuasive tactics?

MOTHER. Fleece him out of his money? I was going to take custody of it!

ELDER SON (*to Man*). Are you willing to let my mother take custody of your property?

MAN. Take custody of my property? She could ask till she was blue in the face and I'd still refuse!

FATHER. There's no getting around it. Money troubles are the worst cause of disharmony among friends.

MAN (*his anger returning*). Can it! You've got no reason to call me one of your friends . . . And as for taking custody of my property . . . I'm getting nauseous. You give me cold chills.

ELDER SON (*to the others*). Now you have a pretty good idea of the situation. You couldn't call him exceptionally cooperative. And he's just as attached to his money as the next man. He wants to have his cake and eat it. You'll find he's a hard customer to deal with. Supposing I hadn't used my special talents . . . I can't help being rather skeptical about whether that money would've ended up, as we hoped, in Mother's safe.

FATHER. That doesn't mean you have the right to grab it for yourself.

ELDEST DAUGHTER. That's right. Stealing a march on the rest of us is unfair.

MOTHER. I wonder if a person who always tries to get the lion's share for himself hasn't got something twisted inside him? It makes me unhappy.

YOUNGER SON (*whispering into his brother's ear*). I'll go to your defense, if you like, for a service charge of twenty percent.

ELDER SON. Don't underestimate me.

MIDDLE DAUGHTER (*hesitantly*). What do you intend to do about dinner?

GRANDMOTHER. I'm in charge of dividing up the jam.

MAN (*suddenly bursting into a rage*). Are you still yattering on about such things? To talk about dinner, in the midst of this crazy farce! Listen to me. I'm the original victim. Nobody else has a claim on my money, and I want it back. What possible difference does it make whether he takes sole possession of the money or two of you take it? It's illegal either way. The fact is, it's mine, and I'm the only one qualified to investigate what's happened to it. (*Suddenly he has an idea.*) That's right! The situation has assumed a completely new aspect. My friend, you've pulled a real blunder. You have enabled me to file a formal complaint. A flagrant act of pickpocketing has occurred. This time there's no doubt about it. Even the members of your family will testify. Well, are you going to give back my money? Or will I have to bother the police again?

FATHER. There's something in what he says . . . As things stand, your old tricks have boiled down to nothing more than theft, plain and simple.

MOTHER (*sighs*). You've really done a dreadful thing.

FATHER. You've ruined everything. In order to carry out our mission of spreading love for our neighbors, we ourselves must be models of neighborly love.

Middle Daughter steps forward, seemingly unable to bear what is happening.

MIDDLE DAUGHTER (*to Elder Son*). Why don't you say something? You must've had some reason, surely? Say something. Don't just grin that way.

YOUNGER SON. There are some things about which all you can do is grin. Wouldn't you agree, Brother?

MAN. It looks as if the wolves have finally shed their sheep's clothing. The salesmen for Neighborly Love, Incorporated!

ELDEST DAUGHTER (*fiercely*). I'm sick of it. After all we've gone through, I don't want the bother of moving again. (*To Elder Brother.*) I suppose you think you're the only one with the privilege of doing exactly what you please?

YOUNGEST DAUGHTER (*in a low voice*). There's a cold wind blowing outside.

GRANDMOTHER. I don't understand it. What devil got into him that he should have done such a thing?

ELDER SON (*his expression becomes severe*). Your own shortcomings don't seem to bother you.

FATHER (*soothing him*). Believe me, I understand what you've been going through . . . I understand perfectly . . . I'm sure you need more pocket money . . . You'd like to lead a more cheerful life . . . But you must recognize the eternal law that happiness which is for yourself alone is certainly not true happiness . . .

ELDER SON. I am gradually losing my amiability.

MOTHER. The brazen nerve of the thief!

ELDER SON. But, Mother, haven't I been following the ideal of neighborly love? Anything I have is yours, and anything you have is mine . . . Aren't you overdoing it a bit when you treat me like a pickpocket or a thief?

FATHER. I understand . . . I understand perfectly.

ELDEST DAUGHTER. It doesn't help much, no matter how well you understand him. We're the ones who suffer in the end.

ELDER SON. You wouldn't be jaundiced because you can't do as much yourself?

Eldest Daughter flares up; Father quiets her with a gesture.

FATHER. Depending on the end, a certain leeway is permitted in the means. But the fundamental thing, of course, is the end. Neighborly love is a splendid ideal, but if it is only an ideal, it's a little too abstract, isn't it? Why don't we think it through together? What is the common end we all share?

ELDER SON. I wonder if any of you know how many times altogether I have been insulted in the course of this argument?

FATHER. "Insulted" is an exaggeration. It distresses me to have you take it that way. My only hope was that I might rouse you somehow from your errors.

ELDER SON. Would you like to know? Don't be too surprised—fifty-three times!

YOUNGER SON. Fifty-three times? That's a little too precise!

ELDER SON. I assure you, there's been no padding. I made a careful count.

ELDEST DAUGHTER. Isn't that silly? He has nothing better to do with his time, it would seem.

ELDER SON. There! That makes fifty-four times.

MOTHER. When someone of your age tramples the peace of the family underfoot, it's not surprising that he should be insulted a hundred times, or even a thousand times.

ELDER SON. Fifty-five times.

Younger Son apparently has a glimmering of what his brother has in mind.

YOUNGER SON. Ah-hah. I'm beginning to see . . .

ELDER SON. Now it's my turn to ask you a question. What are these ends you keep talking about that seem to justify everything?

MOTHER. The family safe is one of them. (*She holds up an unusually large purse that she takes from her suitcase.*)

ELDER SON. What's this? (*He pretends to peep inside.*) Mother . . . there's quite a bulge in the pocket of that purse.

MOTHER (*surprised, looking inside the purse*). Dear me, why it's . . . (*Bewildered, she takes out a handful of bills and change.*) Oh . . . how shocking! (*She gives a forced laugh.*)

The next instant the faces of everybody present except Man change completely in expression. Now they are all smiling.

YOUNGER SON. I was completely taken in, I must say.

ELDEST DAUGHTER. You certainly more than live up to your reputation.

FATHER. I have to apologize . . .

MIDDLE DAUGHTER. Oh, I'm so glad. (*She looks around the family.*) We're all good people, aren't we?

YOUNGEST DAUGHTER. I wonder if I should start practicing too. (*She flexes her fingers.*)

MOTHER. Really, it's enough to take a person aback. He was always a mischievous child, but I never expected . . . (*She removes her glasses and starts to count the money with an air of efficiency.*)

MAN. Hey! Stop it! That's my money! You can deduct the hundred yen for the fine.

Elder Son blocks Man, who starts to make a rush for the money.

ELDER SON. You're wasting your time. I don't suppose you noted down the numbers of the bills or marked them?

At the same time Father, Younger Son, Eldest Daughter, Youngest Daughter, and even Grandmother form a kind of defensive setup around Mother. It might be effective for Youngest Daughter to brandish a cleaver.

YOUNGER SON. You see how easy it is for trouble to arise over money.

YOUNGEST DAUGHTER. A clever burglar absolutely refuses to touch anything except cash.

MAN (*to Elder Son*). Your own words prove that you yourself admit that you've picked my pocket.

ELDER SON (*playing the innocent*). I picked your pocket? (*He turns to family.*) Did I say anything like that?

MAN. You weren't the only one. The whole lot of you, without exception, all admitted it.

ELDEST DAUGHTER. I don't know anything about it!

GRANDMOTHER. Do you think any grandchild of mine would ever do such a wicked thing? I wouldn't let him, even if he tried to.

MAN. You're all in cahoots to cover up for him, aren't you? And just a minute ago you were denouncing him so!

MOTHER (*paying no attention to the arguments around her; to Man*). Tell me, how much did you have?

MAN. I have no idea.

ELDEST DAUGHTER. Pretty careless of him not to know how much he has in his own wallet.

MIDDLE DAUGHTER. A little carelessness makes a man more attractive.

ELDEST DAUGHTER (*darting a sidelong glance at her*). Doing your best to make a hit with him, aren't you?

FATHER (*looking onto Mother's hands*). Well, how much is there, anyway?

MOTHER (*complaining*). Not much, 5,600 yen. That's all.

FATHER (*frowns*). 5,600 yen . . .

ELDER SON. I suppose it's just before his payday.

MOTHER (*sarcastically*). I see. I'm sure that explanation suits your convenience.

ELDER SON. There's something disturbing about your tone.

MAN (*not missing the chance*). You see! You're admitting to one another that you swiped the money from me.

FATHER. Young man, if you're going to jump to such conclusions, you'll make it hard for all of us. People often conduct discussions on a purely hypothetical basis.

MAN. Stop quibbling!

FATHER. Well then, shall I concede a point and admit that the money was yours? But you don't even seem to know the amount of this valuable commodity. Don't you realize that the world is swarming with sinister people who have their eye on other people's wallets? The thought of it makes me shudder.

MAN. Wouldn't you yourselves qualify without any trouble for membership in that gang of sinister people?

FATHER. Don't be absurd! We've acted entirely out of good will. We felt it our duty to protect your money by taking custody of it.

MAN (*excitedly*). What right have you anyway . . . without even asking me . . .

FATHER (*emphatically*). It's a duty, a *duty.* I have no intention of insisting on any rights.

MIDDLE DAUGHTER (*heatedly*). Yes. It's true even of companies—they're all making mergers and amalgamations, aren't they? And the same thing applies to human beings too, I'm sure. Two is better than one, three is better than two. The more people put their strength together, the more . . .

GRANDMOTHER. Little drops of water, little grains of sand, make the mighty ocean . . .

MOTHER (*still looking suspiciously at Elder Son*). But there's only 5,600 yen altogether. That won't last for two days, feeding nine people.

ELDER SON (*angrily*). You talk just as if it were my fault.

MOTHER. I didn't mean it that way.

ELDER SON. After I tried to be smart, and save you some trouble . . . (*In a self-mocking tone.*) This is what they mean when they talk of a man who's fallen so low in the world his artistic accomplishments learned in happier days are his only support.

FATHER (*trying to save the situation*). What do you mean? Haven't we all been praising your skill, without uttering so much as a word of complaint?

ELDER SON (*going up to Mother*). If that's the case, I wish you'd stop giving me that look.

MOTHER (*turning aside and wiping her glasses*). It's a lot harder than you suppose, trying to make ends meet for a family of nine . . .

ELDER SON (*sits beside Mother*). I *do* understand, Ma. But I wanted you, if nobody else, to believe in me. In the course of less than ten minutes I was insulted fifty-five times . . . and that by the people I trusted most in the whole world, my own family . . . It was painful, I tell you.

MOTHER (*hesitantly*). Talking that way won't do any good . . .

ELDER SON (*ignoring her; to Man*). Payday in your company must come the day after tomorrow or the next day, doesn't it?

Man is taken by surprise. He is unable either to affirm or deny this.

ELDER SON (*standing abruptly; speaking as he goes away from Mother*). So you see, Ma, there's no need for you to worry over such a paltry sum of money, is there? If people can't live a little more expansively . . .

MOTHER (*with an expression that suggests she hasn't grasped the situation very well*). I know, but no matter how much money you have, it always seems to sprout wings and fly away. (*Suddenly noticing something*). Ohh . . . it's gone!

FATHER. What's gone?

MOTHER (*to Elder Son*). You've done it again, haven't you? (*As she stands a 100 yen coin drops from her lap.*)

Elder Son, flashing the bills ostentatiously, folds them and puts them in his pocket.

ELDER SON. Received with thanks the sum of 5,500 yen, representing fines collected from all of you for those fifty-five insults. Look, Ma, the missing hundred yen coin dropped on the floor. That's his share of the fine (*points at Man*). It's wonderful how exactly the accounts have balanced.

They all stand motionless, too dumfounded to say a word. A fairly long pause.

MOTHER (*her voice is like a moan*). Dreadful, dreadful . . .

ELDER SON (*perfectly self-possessed*). Words, like chickens, come home to roost. (*Turns back to Man*). I hope it's been a good lesson for you too. Now you know how severe the penalty is for betraying another person's trust . . . But of course, I owe this extra income all to you. It's too late today, but I'll treat you to a drink, tomorrow if you like. There's nothing to feel squeamish about. I got the money completely legally . . . You see, nobody can say a word against it . . . Yes, it really serves as an object lesson.

MAN (*suddenly shouting*). Get out of here! I'll give you the money, only get out of here, now! If it's not money you want, I'll give you anything else, only go!

YOUNGEST DAUGHTER (*playfully*). Do you really mean it?

GRANDMOTHER (*hurrying to the kitchen*). The jam is for me. You promised from the start.

MAN. Go ahead. Take anything you like. Only go.

They begin to take their pick of the things in the room excitedly. But nobody as yet does anything positive.

YOUNGER SON. He's certainly become a lot more generous, hasn't he?

ELDEST DAUGHTER. Do you mind if I look in the other room?

MAN. Go right ahead. Don't mind me. If you'd like the rats in the ceiling, you can have them too. But all this is on one condition—you leave at once. I'll give you five—no, ten minutes, that's the limit. I won't make allowances for even one minute beyond the deadline.

FATHER (*timidly*). I appreciate your kind intentions, but I wonder if two different questions aren't involved?

MAN. Two different questions?

FATHER. Your offer to turn over all your possessions to us, without holding anything back, is more than we dared hope for. That is precisely the way that true communal living is to be brought about . . . But when you tell us that in return we must leave you, aren't you guilty of something like a logical contradiction?

MIDDLE DAUGHTER. That's right. Living together is what gives meaning to the act of sharing.

YOUNGER SON. What's yours is mine, what's mine is yours.

ELDEST DAUGHTER. You smell of liquor!

YOUNGER SON. That's why I've been pleading with you to let me have a quick pick-me-up.

MAN (*turning on Father*). You can't have forgotten it was you yourself who claimed you respect the wishes of the individual.

FATHER. Of course I respect them. But you're not the only individual, are you?

MOTHER (*to nobody in particular*). If you ask me, there's nothing here anybody'd want. The place lacks the bare necessities. It's take a bit of doing even to make it habitable.

MAN. This is *my* apartment!

ELDER SON (*coldly*). This is the apartment *we've* chosen.

YOUNGER SON (*trying on Man's shoes, which have been left at the entrance*). Well, what do you know? These shoes fit me perfectly!

Man suddenly kneels on the floor. His voice, completely altered, sounds pathetic.

MAN. Please, I beg you. Please don't torture me any more . . . Of course I understand it's all a joke—it is one, isn't it—but I'm exhausted . . . I just don't feel like joking . . . Maybe something I've said has offended you, but please, I beg you, leave me here alone.

Man, continuing to kneel, bows his head, like a victim awaiting his sentence.

The members of the family, struck speechless, exchange glances. But their expressions are not merely of surprise—heartfelt sympathy and pity seem to have shaken them.

FATHER. Stand up please, young man. (*He places his hand on Man's elbow and helps him to his feet, then dusts his knees.*) It's embarrassing for us if you're going to act that way. Our only wish is to promote your happiness in whatever way we can, to serve you somehow . . . That's what first led us to come here.

ELDER SON. Or, it occurs to me, you may have subjectively interpreted our actions as being in some way opposed to your wishes—clearly, a misunderstanding . . . In other words, there may exist a difference of opinion concerning means.

MIDDLE DAUGHTER (*enthusiastically*). But hasn't it become warm in here, just because we're all together this way? It feels just like spring, even without having our soup.

ELDEST DAUGHTER. Spring? It feels more like summer. Oh, it's hot! (*She removes her jacket and exposes her bare throat and arms.*)

MAN (*weakly*). But I like being alone . . .

MIDDLE DAUGHTER. Why must you say such cruel things?

YOUNGER SON (*sounds at the end of his patience*). It can't be helped. Everybody's sick until his sickness gets better.

So saying, Younger Son begins to strum his guitar. The following dialogue is declaimed to the rhythm of the guitar.

MIDDLE DAUGHTER.

The streets are full of people,
So full of people, they're ready to burst.

YOUNGER SON.

But everywhere you go,
There're nothing but strangers.

MIDDLE DAUGHTER.

I'm still not discouraged,
I go on searching—
My friends, where are you now,
My loved ones, where are you now?

ELDER SON.

They've gone to the pinball parlor.

FATHER.

They've gone to a bar.

MOTHER.

To the beauty parlor or the department store.

GRANDMOTHER.

They're eating eels and rice.

YOUNGEST DAUGHTER.

They're riding escalators,
They're going to an amusement park.

ELDEST DAUGHTER (*meditatively; if necessary, can be sung to music*). And I have dreams. I dream of a streetcar on tracks that stretch far, far away. A streetcar packed with people goes running away over the tracks. Under the weight of all those strangers packed inside, it shoots off sparks. And in the sparks thrown off by all those innumerable strangers, I am burnt to a crisp, like a little fish forgotten in the oven.

YOUNGER SON (*in a soft voice*). Like a dried sardine, with only little bones.

MIDDLE DAUGHTER.

I'm still not discouraged,
I go on searching.
My shining sun, where have you gone?
Come back and melt away my loneliness!

FATHER (*whispering confidentially to Man*). That's why we've come all the way here. We heard your voice crying for help and we searched till we found you through the long dark tunnel they call other people. We wanted to bring you, if not the sun, at least the light from a glowing lump of coal.

MAN (*driven into a corner*). I never cried for help. I . . . It refreshes me to be alone.

ELDER SON. That's conceit! Why, in prison the thing that hits you hardest is solitary confinement. (*An expression of recollection crosses his face.*)

ELDEST DAUGHTER. I'm *completely* hopeless when I'm alone. Even when I'm left to look after the house, as soon as I'm by myself I feel as if I'll go out of my mind.

GRANDMOTHER. It's all written down in Mother Goose. Let me see, how did it go again? (*To Mother*). You remember, don't you?

MAN. I don't interfere with other people and I don't want to be interfered with myself.

Younger Son begins to play with feeling "The Broken Necklace." Middle Daughter sings to the tune. When they reach the second verse the telephone rings suddenly. For a moment they are all startled into attitudes of tableaux vivants.

ELDEST DAUGHTER. Shall I answer?

MAN (*confused*). It's all right. I'll go. (*He runs to the telephone and grabs it, but he does not lift the receiver at once.*) Will you do me a favor? At least while I'm talking on the phone, will you please keep quiet?

YOUNGER SON. At least while you're talking on the phone? Have we been making so much noise?

FATHER. Shhh. (*He puts his hand to his lips and silences Younger Son.*) Go right ahead. Don't worry about us. (*He looks to the side. At the same time the other members of the family strike poses of ostentatious indifference.*)

After another brief hesitation, Man resolutely lifts the receiver. But he is still worried about the family, and his voice is extremely tentative.

MAN. Hello, yes, it's me. (*Pause.*) No, nothing special. No, I mean it, it's nothing . . . All right, then, good night . . . The day after tomorrow? It's not necessary, I tell you. There's nothing I need your help on at this stage . . . Well, good night. You're going to bed, aren't you? No, it's not that. We can talk when I see you again tomorrow.

Suddenly Youngest Daughter emits a protracted strange noise in the process of stifling a great sneeze. Man, alarmed, covers the mouthpiece and glares at Youngest Daughter.

FATHER. Shh!

MOTHER. Do be quiet!

YOUNGER SON. Stupid, isn't she?

(*He picks up his guitar without thinking, and the guitar, bumping against something, resounds.*)

ELDER SON. You're the one that should be more careful.

YOUNGER SON. You're making more noise scolding me . . .

MAN. I beg you, stop it please!

GRANDMOTHER. I don't understand. Why do you have to act so secret? We're not hiding from the police, after all.

ELDER SON. It's from his girl.

ELDEST DAUGHTER (*reacting sharply*). His girl?

ELDER SON. I've surveyed the whole situation.

ELDEST DAUGHTER. But isn't that strange? It's a complete contradiction. After all his insisting that he prefers to be alone . . .

MAN (*desperately*). I beg you, keep quiet, please! (*Into the telephone.*) I'm terribly sorry. There was a funny noise in the kitchen . . . What? Of course I'm alone . . . A sneeze? A woman's sneeze? Don't be silly.

ELDER SON. I've never heard anything so disgraceful. Stumbling all over the place.

FATHER (*simultaneously*). Shhh!

MAN (*instantly covering the mouthpiece*). I thought I told you to please shut up.

ELDEST DAUGHTER. It may be your girlfriend, or I don't care who, but why must you keep our being here a secret? It's insulting.

MAN (*into the telephone*). Just a second, please. There's that funny noise again in the kitchen. (*He covers the mouthpiece.*) Think a minute and you'll see why. How can I possibly explain such a thing so that an outsider could understand? It's crazy . . . It'll only make things more complicated if I make a mess of explaining.

YOUNGER SON. Would you like us to explain for you?

FATHER. A good suggestion. We'll have to make it clear, sooner or later, whether we're to ask her to join us or to break with him.

ELDER SON. Making things clear is my specialty.

ELDEST DAUGHTER. It's easier for a woman to talk to another woman.

MAN (*protecting the telephone from Elder Son and Eldest Daughter, both of whom come forward at the same time*). I give up. I surrender. But won't you please let me deal with her? In return, yes, I agree to let you stay here for tonight only. That's fair enough, isn't it? You can use any and all of my apartment, as you please . . . I promise not to interfere in any way with your meals . . . All I ask is that you keep quiet while I'm making this call.

FATHER (*looking around at the others*). He hasn't made any conditions that present special difficulties, has he?

ELDER SON AND ELDEST DAUGHTER (*simultaneously moving back*). I suppose not.

MAN (*hastily returning to the telephone*). It wasn't anything. It must have been the wind . . . Hello . . . Hello . . .

(*He realizes that the other party has hung up on him and dazedly puts down the telephone.*)

ELDEST DAUGHTER. Did she hang up on you?

MIDDLE DAUGHTER. That wasn't nice of her, was it?

Man, unable to say a word, crouches beside the telephone, his head in his hands.

YOUNGEST DAUGHTER. He must really be in love with her.

MOTHER. Don't butt into grownups' affairs.

FATHER (*to Man*). You know her phone number, don't you?

ELDER SON. I know it.

FATHER. Should we call and apologize?

MAN (*moaning*). I beg you, please leave things as they are.

MIDDLE DAUGHTER. Why don't you get to bed?

MOTHER. That's right. It must be about time.

MAN. I don't want you worrying about me. You don't suppose, in the first place, I could get to sleep with all the noise going on here.

FATHER. Of course we intend to retire to the other room. Come on, everybody, get ready!

Hardly has he spoken than the members of the family throw themselves into furious activity. Elder Son and Younger Son take a hammock from their suitcase and suspend it. Mother and Youngest Daughter bring blankets in from the next room. Grandmother inflates an air pillow. Eldest Daughter and Middle Daughter swiftly remove Man's outer clothes. Then the whole family lifts Man willy-nilly onto the hammock. Man shows some resistance, but in the end proves no match for their organized activity. By the time Man sits up in the hammock the family has already withdrawn to the next room. They peep in and throw Man their radiant smiles.

FAMILY (*whispering in unison*). Good night!

Middle Daughter sticks out her hand and switches off the light in Man's room. The stage becomes dark with only a spotlight on Man. Younger Son enters on tiptoe and crosses the room on his way to the kitchen.

YOUNGER SON (in a low voice). Beer!

Slow curtain.

Scene Seven (*Intermission*)

The music of "The Broken Necklace" is played in the lobby during the intermission. Presently, the actress who has appeared as Superintendent, still dressed in the costume for the part, makes her way among the spectators, both in the lobby and in the auditorium, distributing the following leaflet.

An Appeal

Some people, it would seem, have been critical of my attitude toward the tenant in Apartment 12. Unpleasant rumors are being spread that I was bought over by the visitors or (what's worse) that I reached some sort of understanding with one or the other of the two brothers and gave him a passkey to the apartment.

I realize, having had the misfortune to lose my husband only a few years ago, there is nothing I can do about it if people, meaning to be sympathetic, say, "She must've needed money," or "She must've been lonely." But I will take an oath that I am speaking the absolute truth when I say that the first time I ever laid eyes on those people was when I saw them in Apartment 12. But in my business you get to be a pretty good judge of character, and I could see at once that there was nothing particularly suspicious about those people. The tenants in this building are all my valued guests, and the guests of my guests, you might say, are also my guests. That's why, as I'm sure you'll understand, I couldn't very well make uncalled-for remarks simply because there's been some sort of misunderstanding.

I wish also to take advantage of this occasion to confide a secret, in all candor.To the tell the truth, situations of this kind are not in the least unusual. When you're in my business you see this kind of thing happening all the time. I wonder if all the commotion hasn't simply proved the gentleman doesn't know much about people? I beg you, ladies and gentlemen, not to be deceived by any false rumors or to let your confidence be shaken in our apartment house.

THE SUPERINTENDENT

Scene Eight

The curtain rises to disclose the benches in a public park somewhere. Sounds of cars and people passing make it clear that the park is in the city. The sounds, however, are filtered and the buildings surrounding the park are concealed by trees (or something suggesting trees); the spot is somehow isolated from the outside world. The woman sitting on a bench who seems to be waiting for someone is the person with whom Man was talking on the telephone, his Fiancée. She glances at her wristwatch, then looks left and right. Her expression suggests she is immersed in thought.

Youngest Daughter enters from stage right, skipping along in a way that suggests she is kicking a stone. She strolls past Fiancée. When she reaches far stage left she gestures as if looking off to the other side of the trees. She strikes a peculiar pose and exits, still maintaining the pose.

As she leaves, Elder Son enters from stage left. Evidently Youngest Daughter's pose was a signal to him. Elder Son struts up to Fiancée.

ELDER SON (*with a slight bow of the head*). Excuse me. (*He starts to seat himself beside Fiancée, indifferent to her reactions.*)

FIANCÉE. I'm sorry, but I'm waiting for somebody.

ELDER SON. Oh, I see. (*He decides not to sit, but shows no sign of going away. He continues to stare boldly at the woman.*) I was impressed even by your picture, but you're far more charming in the flesh. Oh, you've changed the way you do your hair, haven't you? A natural effect looks better on you than fancy styling.That only goes to show how good the foundations are.

FIANCÉE. I don't think we've met . . . (*Her expression reveals mingled caution and curiosity.*)

ELDER SON. But I know all about you . . . Of course, you make such an impression that nobody who ever saw you once could forget you the second time. It's only natural, I suppose.

FIANCÉE. I wonder where I've had the pleasure . . .?

ELDER SON. Last night, in the drawer of your fiancé's desk.

FIANCÉE (*at last catching on*). Then it was you last night . . .

ELDER SON (*nods*). Yes, it was. Against my own inclinations I interrupted you in the midst of your telephone call.

FIANCÉE (*sharply*). Have you come as his stand-in?

ELDER SON. Heaven forbid! I wouldn't do such a thing even if he asked me. To tell the truth, he and I have had a slight difference of opinion concerning what happened last night.

FIANCÉE. And you've come to tell on him?

ELDER SON. How severe you are! I wonder what he could've told you about us? I gather from your tone he hasn't been too friendly. I suppose he's trying to clean up the mess left behind by shifting the blame onto us for that telephone call.

FIANCÉE. What happened anyway?

ELDER SON. How can I answer unless I know the nature of his explanation?

FIANCÉE (*finally induced to discuss the matter on his terms*). I couldn't make the least sense out of him. He was so vague that I . . .

ELDER SON (*with a suppressed laugh that does not seem malicious*). I can well imagine . . . I wonder if the problem is that he's timid, or clumsy at expressing himself, or can never get to the point, or that he's too earnest or too good-natured or too inflexible, or that he's stubborn or an introvert or self-centered . . .

FIANCÉE (*mustering her courage*). Were there also women present?

ELDER SON. Yes, four—no, five.

FIANCÉE. Five!

ELDER SON. But there were men there, too—three of us, besides him.

FIANCÉE. What were you all doing, so many of you?

ELDER SON. It's a little hard to explain.

FIANCÉE (*rather irritated*). But generally speaking, when people have gathered together for a purpose there's some sort of name for their activity. Would you describe it as a meeting, or a card game, or a drinking party? Is there anything that can't be given a name?

ELDER SON. That's the crux of the problem. (*He takes out a comb and smooths his hair.*) I'd really be most interested to hear how *he* would answer that question. (*He puts away the comb.*) But I've been making a great nuisance of myself, when you've more important things on your mind. (*He bows and starts to leave.*)

FIANCÉE (*standing before she realizes*). Wait a moment! What is it you came to tell, anyway? You and he make a good pair—one's just as vague as the other. I don't suppose you could have come for the express purpose of mystifying me.

ELDER SON (*sanctimoniously, his eyes lowered*). Of course not. But when I meet you face to face this way I suddenly lose my courage.

FIANCÉE. Go ahead. You're not bothering me.

ELDER SON (*lighting a cigarette; slowly*). To be perfectly honest, I don't really understand his feelings . . . Correct me if I'm wrong, but I gather he's engaged to you and has been planning to hold the wedding in the near future.

FIANCÉE. Yes, he only recently managed at last to rent that apartment. It's more than he could afford, but we needed it to get married.

ELDER SON. In other words, he and you are already as good as married. Right? Why, then, should he have had to keep things a secret from you, of all people, in such a furtive way? If I may cite a rather vulgar example, you often see in the advice to the lovelorn column how a man is extremely reluctant to introduce the girl he's interested in to his parents or his family . . . In such cases is it not fair to assume in general that the man's sincerity is to be doubted?

FIANCÉE. You mean you and your family are in that relationship with him?

ELDER SON. Of course, I don't know how he would answer you.

FIANCÉE (*reduced to supplication*). For heaven's sake, please tell me! Who are you all and what is your connection with him?

ELDER SON (*avoiding the issue*). Oh, yes. I've just remembered. It was something he let slip in the course of the conversation last night, but I wonder if it doesn't give us a clue to his intentions. He seems to hold extremely prejudiced views against any form of communal living, and even with respect to family life he seems to be feeling something close to dread.

FIANCÉE. I can't believe that.

ELDER SON. He went so far as to say that it actually refreshed him to be all alone in a crowd of total strangers.

FIANCÉE. But he's even made arrangements with the movers to have my furniture taken to his place at the end of the month.

ELDER SON. I'd like to believe that he got carried away by his own words. Or maybe he was just bluffing . . . After all, with such a pretty girl as you . . .

FIANCÉE. You still haven't answered my question.

ELDER SON. Oh—you mean our relationship with him? I wonder if it wouldn't be better, though, for you to get him to verify it with his own mouth. I wouldn't want my words to have the effect of implanting any preconceptions . . . It's not that I'm trying to pretend to be more of a gentleman than I am, but I just wouldn't want to make a sneak attack, or anything like that . . . I realize that it must be hard for you to understand, but basically speaking, we're closer to him than blood relations.

FIANCÉE. You must have known him a long time, then?

ELDER SON (*calmly*). We don't set too much store by the past. The same holds true of a marriage, doesn't it? The real problems are always in the future.

FIANCÉE (*again withdrawing into her shell*). Then was it something like a political meeting?

ELDER SON (*looking at his watch*). I'm sure he has no intention of trying to strengthen his position by lying to you . . . He may in fact be planning to use this opportunity to reveal to you his true feelings. Anyway, I advise you to sound him out. Maybe we'll meet again, depending on how your interview turns out.

FIANCÉE (*looking stage left*). Oh, there he is now.

ELDER SON (*showing no special embarrassment*). I hope and pray that all goes well. But I suppose I'm also half-hoping that things don't go well. In that case I'll get to see you again. (*Suddenly, as if he had remembered something urgent.*) Excuse me, but would you mind sitting there again? Just the way you were before . . . Hurry!

Fiancée overcome by his urgency, sits as requested.

ELDER SON (*with a conspiratorial smile*). That's right. Now I can see the dimples in your knees . . . Aren't they sweet? I could eat them up, those dimples.

Fiancée, flustered, brings together the hems of her coat. At the same moment Man hurriedly enters from stage left. He catches sight of Elder Son, and stops in his tracks with an expression of amazement.

Scene Nine

Fiancée, noticing Man approach, stands and turns toward him as he speaks. In other words, her actions should be simultaneous with the beginning of Man's dialogue.

MAN (*to Elder Son, sharply*). What are *you* doing here?

Elder Son turns to Man as if having become aware of his presence only then. Far from showing any embarrassment, he smiles broadly, as if greeting an old friend.

ELDER SON. Late, aren't you? This will never do!

Man looks from Fiancée to Elder Son and back, then steps forward aggressively.

MAN. What's the meaning of this, anyway?

FIANCÉE (*unable to hide her guilty conscience*). It was a complete coincidence.

ELDER SON. But as far as I'm concerned, an accidental meeting that only a marvelous necessity could have brought about.

MAN (*angrily*). I don't know what mischief you've been up to, but you're to get the hell out of here, right now.

ELDER SON (*still smiling*). Don't be uncouth. Well, I'll be saying good-by. (*He winks secretly at Fiancée.*) Go to it now, the both of you.

(*He makes a clownish gesture with his hand, then saunters off to stage left.*)

The couple stands for a time in silence, still looking off in the direction Elder Son has gone. They slowly turn and exchange glances, only to avert their eyes. Fiancée sits down on the bench, and Man then also sits. Each occupies an end of the bench.)

MAN (*gloomily*). What was he filling your ear with?

FIANCÉE (*looking at Man reproachfully*). Before we go into that, it seems to me you have a lot of explaining to do.

MAN. Explaining? There's nothing worth explaining. It's just as I told you on the phone this morning. I'm the victim. I'm sorry I worried you with that call last night. But even that was their fault, if you get right down to it.

FIANCÉE. So it would seem. It's pretty hard to keep someone from guessing, even over the phone, when you have eight people in the room with you. But tell me, why was it necessary for you to act so secretly, as if you were playing hide-and-seek with me?

MAN. I thought I'd told you. I couldn't think of any way of explaining in an intelligible manner who those people were or what they were doing.

FIANCÉE. And you're going to explain now, is that it?

MAN. Unfortunately, I still don't know what happened, even now.

FIANCÉE (*a little defiantly*). But I thought you asked me here in order to explain.

MAN (*bearing up under the confusion*). Yes, that's so . . . But my real purpose was not so much to explain as to get you to understand how difficult it is to make an explanation. Maybe I won't succeed in making you understand . . . How could you understand an outfit like that? I suppose that if it happened that I had been on the receiving end of this story, I wouldn't have been able to believe it either . . . I don't know where to start. The only way to describe what happened is to say it was plain crazy.

FIANCÉE (*losing her temper*). That certainly doesn't seem to be an explanation of anything.

MAN. But have you ever heard anything like it—a bunch of complete strangers suddenly march in on me without warning, and install themselves in my apartment, exactly as if it were their natural right?

FIANCÉE (*coldly*). It *is* a little unusual.

MAN. It certainly is. As a matter of fact, even the policemen who came after I called refused to take it seriously. (*His voice becomes more emphatic.*) But I assure you, it happened. This impossible thing has befallen me.

FIANCÉE. That man who was just here also thought it was strange. He couldn't figure out what your motive was in keeping their presence such a secret.

MAN. A secret? It's simply that I couldn't think how to explain; don't you see? So he encouraged you to act suspicious. But you're carrying your foolishness too far. Tell me, what possible advantage could there be in it for me to cover up for that bunch of parasites?

FIANCÉE. For a parasite, that man just now certainly acted like a gentleman. Unlike you, he didn't say one harsh thing. Why, he didn't even try to justify himself.

MAN. Yes, that's their technique.

FIANCÉE. I understand, by the way, that five of them are women.

MAN. Five of them? (*He bursts into derisive laughter. His voice takes on a triumphant note.*) Five women? That's a good one. Gradually I'm beginning to catch on to their tactics.

FIANCÉE. Was he lying, then?

MAN. No, it wasn't a lie. The five women include a seventy-year-old grandmother, a housewife of fifty, and a junior-high-school student.

FIANCÉE (*beginning to lose her confidence*). They certainly make an odd group of people.

MAN. No, there's nothing odd about them. Didn't he tell you? They're all one family—five children, the parents, and the grandmother, a family of eight. Five women . . . that's good. You couldn't call it a lie, and it was effective as a trick. You must've been imagining I was involved with some sort of secret society.

FIANCÉE. You were the one who first gave me that impression.

MAN (*with an expression of relief*). When you've seen what the facts really are, they don't amount to much, do they?

FIANCÉE. You can't blame me. You exaggerated so much.

MAN (*resuming his subdued tone*). It would've been easier to explain if they had actually been a secret society or a gang. But when they look so absurdly and indisputably like a family, it makes it impossible to complain to anybody.

FIANCÉE (*dubious again*). But are you sure these people have no relationship to you at all?

MAN. Absolutely none.

FIANCÉE. I can't understand it. Are you sure there wasn't some reason behind it, however slight? It's hard to imagine otherwise that they'd move in on you like that.

MAN. They say that I'm lonely and that they intend to envelop and warm me in their neighborly love.

FIANCÉE. They've ignored me completely, then?

MAN. No, I'm sure that, as long as you were willing, they'd be delighted to have you join them.

FIANCÉE (*with intensity*). This is no laughing matter.

MAN (*holding his head between his hands*). That's why I told you they were monstrous parasites.

FIANCÉE. Why don't you tell them to leave?

MAN. I have, of course.

FIANCÉE. Firmly? And clearly?

MAN. In a voice so loud it hurt my throat. (*Weakly.*) But it still didn't do any good. It made no impression on them. They have the nerve to say that occupying our apartment is not merely their privilege but their duty.

FIANCÉE (*after a pause, uncertainly*). Is that really all? Is that all there is to it?

MAN. As far as I know.

FIANCÉE. You've explained three of the five women, but what about the other two?

MAN. Stop it! If you'd only seen how I struggled with them.

FIANCÉE. It's funny . . . my engagement ring doesn't seem to fit my finger any more . . . I wonder if I should take it off.

MAN (*bewildered*). What do you mean?

FIANCÉE. I want you to be frank with me. If you've been putting on a show in order to get rid of me, you needn't go to all the trouble.

MAN. There you go again, tormenting me with your groundless accusations.

FIANCÉE. But what else can I do, as long as you're unable to take back our apartment from those people?

MAN. Insult added to injury! If I'm to be deserted even by you, I'll lose the will to fight altogether.

FIANCÉE (*suddenly sharp*). Then I can really trust what you say?

MAN. Of course! Haven't I been begging you over and over, till I'm hoarse, to do just that?

FIANCÉE. Then how would it be if I visited the apartment tomorrow with a friend?

MAN. A friend?

FIANCÉE. A man who used to be a feature writer for a weekly magazine. Exposés were always his strong suit, so I'm sure he's one person who'll be able to tell what's going on.

MAN. Are you trying to spite me?

FIANCÉE. Let the chips fall where they may. I'm only after the guilty party. If things are the way you've described them, I'm sure the family will be the ones to suffer. You understand, don't you? I desperately want to believe you.

MAN. In that case, I have no objections. There's nothing more I want than to have you believe me.

FIANCÉE. I do want to believe you.

MAN. And I want to be believed.

Suddenly Youngest Daughter pops up from behind the bench and starts tip-toeing off to stage right. Man, sensing somebody is there, turns around, and, with a shout, grabs her arm.

MAN. Wait!

YOUNGEST DAUGHTER (*letting out a scream*). Murder!

Man, surprised, releases her arm. Youngest Daughter sticks out her tongue and runs off.

FIANCÉE. Who was that?

MAN. One of the five women in the case.

The stage darkens.

Scene Ten

A strangely shaped male head emerges from the darkness. The left and right sides of the face do not seem to match, giving an impression of madness. This is the Reporter who has come at Fiancée's request. (By changing the lighting, however, it is possible to make the expression change to one of extreme gentleness.)

REPORTER (*abruptly, all but shouting*). Marvelous, isn't it? I mean it, it's really marvelous. This is what I've dreamt of for years, the model of what family life should be, solid and generous as the earth itself.

In another corner of the stage the faces of the members of the family are revealed, forming a group. They begin to sing a chorus of "The Broken Necklace" to the accompaniment of Younger Son's guitar. The chorus gives way to a solo by Middle Daughter and the stage gradually becomes lighter. Fiancée stands in another part of the stage, looking utterly baffled. Reporter goes up to Middle Daughter, applauding.

REPORTER. I'm impressed. Yes, impressed. That one word "impressed" sums up my feelings. Tell me, young lady, what is your philosophy of life? (*He takes out a notebook and holds his pencil poised.*)

MIDDLE DAUGHTER. My philosophy?

REPORTER. I mean, what you believe in . . .

MIDDLE DAUGHTER. Let me see . . . Maybe it is to forget myself.

REPORTER. Marvelous! Not to believe in your own existence is infinitely more of a strain on rationalism than believing in something that doesn't exist. (*To Fiancée.*) Thank you. Thank you for having introduced me to such wonderful people. I'm grateful to you from the bottom of my heart.

Reporter, overcome by emotion, spreads open his arms and all but embraces Fiancée. She steps back in confusion.

FIANCÉE. But it isn't as if we'd especially asked them to stay here.

REPORTER. Well, ask them now. They're not the kind of people to insist on formalities. (*To family.*) That's right, isn't it?

FATHER. Go right ahead.

FIANCÉE. But I don't think it's necessary any more.

Elder Son has been combing his hair and winking at Fiancée. Now, seeing his chance, he steps forward with a theatrical gesture.

ELDER SON. Young lady, why do you disappoint us by saying such things? Your adorable lips were never meant to pronounce such uncouth words as "necessary" or "unnecessary."

YOUNGER SON (*singing to the accompaniment of his guitar*). Chase him, chase him, but still he trots after you, that pooch is really sweet . . . (*He suddenly gets down on all fours at Fiancée's feet.*) Lady, I'm your pooch!

Fiancée is driven into a corner of the stage, but ends up by bursting into giggles.

REPORTER (*suddenly cries out*). No! This'll never do! I mustn't go on procrastinating any more. (*To Father.*) I've definitely made up my mind. I'm going to join you. I'd like you to include me in your group. Where are the headquarters? Where should I apply for membership? What are the prerequisites? The entrance fees? The conditions?

The members of the family exchange meaningful glances.

FATHER. It's hard, after having been praised so enthusiastically, to know how to answer.

REPORTER. Please believe me! I'll keep it an absolute secret.

MOTHER. A secret? We haven't any secrets, have we?

GRANDMOTHER. We're honest people, we are.

REPORTER. I don't mean to suggest I suspect you of anything. But surely your family couldn't be the only people carrying on this great movement?

FATHER. Well, of course . . . The world is not such a hopeless place.

REPORTER (*greatly in earnest*). I understand. You're saying that it's presumptuous for anyone like myself to hope to be admitted to your ranks.

ELDER SON. Somehow I think you're overestimating us a little . . .

REPORTER. Such modesty!

FATHER. What we've been doing is just plain, ordinary . . . Let's put it this way. All we're doing is what anybody with the least grain of normal human decency couldn't help but do.

MOTHER. You might say we're knitting a fabric, not out of yarn but out of people.

REPORTER. Such humility! That fabric will spread as it is knitted, from village to village, from town to town, until soon it grows into an enormous jacket covering and warming the country and the entire people. This is magnificent! Such magnificence, and such humility! I will become your disciple. Yes, I will sit at your feet. But at least you can tell me where I can find the headquarters of your knitting club.

FATHER. If you'll forgive me for saying so, you should act more spontaneously, as the voices within you command.

REPORTER. Then it's all right if I go right ahead as I please, without any license or authorization?

FATHER. Why should you hesitate? When what you want to do is right, you should throw yourself into it, with full confidence.

REPORTER. Thank you!

FATHER. As long as you perform your services with sincerity and devotion, one of these days you're sure to receive word from headquarters recognizing your work.

REPORTER. Then there is a headquarters?

ELDEST DAUGHTER. I wonder.

FATHER. I'm sure there must be one. It stands to reason . . .

ELDEST DAUGHTER. But we've never once received word from headquarters, have we?

REPORTER (*surprised*). Not even you?

FATHER. Society is demanding. But that's no reason to doubt the existence of a headquarters—it doesn't get you anywhere. If you want to believe in a headquarters, why, there's no harm in that.

REPORTER. I see . . .

ELDEST DAUGHTER. I don't mean to deny it myself. Either way, it doesn't affect my beliefs.

REPORTER. Ah? Your beliefs? (*He gets his notebook ready.*) I wonder if I might trouble you to tell me a little about them.

ELDEST DAUGHTER (*emphasizing the importance of her words*). Ask not, but give . . . That sums them up in a nutshell.

REPORTER. Ask not, but give . . . That's quite something . . . Ask not, but give . . . Isn't that splendid? How can any man be so obstinate, even after you've said *that* to him? It beats me. A feast is set before him and he refuses to eat! What a disgrace! Something must have happened to his head!

Suddenly Man, who has been lying in the hammock, sits up.

MAN. Give? Don't make me laugh! What have they ever given me? The dirty swine!

REPORTER. Who's that?

FATHER. You might call him a kind of blotting paper, I suppose.

REPORTER. Blotting paper?

ELDEST DAUGHTER (*going up to Man*). That's right. I've never seen anyone so unresponsive.

REPORTER. Repulsive, isn't he?

The stage becomes dark again, leaving light only on Man and Eldest Daughter. She produces a small bottle of whisky from the pocket of her dressing gown and takes a swig.

ELDEST DAUGHTER. Come on down, Mr. Blotting Paper.

MAN. At your service, Miss Parasite.

ELDEST DAUGHTER. Do you know why I've never married?

MAN. Today I made the most terrible blunder. I absent-mindedly sent the carpool manager some papers that were supposed to be delivered to the chief of the planning department.

ELDEST DAUGHTER. Speaking of your company, that reminds me—you took your time coming home from work today. Did you stop off somewhere?

MAN. Are you kidding? You and your family took away my pay check, envelope and all. There's no chance of my stopping off anywhere.

ELDEST DAUGHTER. Don't try to fool me. I know all about it. You stopped off to see—what was his name?—the lawyer, didn't you?

Man does not respond.

ELDEST DAUGHTER. He telephoned us immediately afterwards. And we all had a good laugh. (*She giggles.*) Why, even the lawyer . . . (*She hurriedly changes her tone.*) But you mustn't be offended. We're . . . how shall I say it . . . we're considerate. That's why, even after we had our big laugh, we decided not to tell you.

MAN. Then, there's nothing more to say, is there?

ELDEST DAUGHTER. I suppose not. Of course we should have said something, if only to induce you to reconsider your attitude, but we refrained.

MAN. You keep saying you haven't told me, but aren't you telling me now?

ELDEST DAUGHTER. I must be drunk!

MAN. You're running around like a broken-down neon sign.

ELDEST DAUGHTER. What a thing to say!

MAN. Damn him! And he calls himself a lawyer!

ELDEST DAUGHTER (*to herself*). I mustn't be over-eager.

MAN. Anyway, it isn't easy talking to you. There's no getting around it, you're one of the family.

ELDEST DAUGHTER (*in a syrupy voice*). Then, you have some feeling for me?

MAN. Heaven forbid!

ELDEST DAUGHTER. If you're still interested in that girl, I'm sorry for you, but you'd better forget her. My brother's talents as a thief aren't restricted to the contents of people's pockets.

MAN. I can't believe in anything any more.

ELDEST DAUGHTER. Doubt is the door to progress . . . Talking about doors, I can't help feeling all the time as if I'm a door that's been left permanently ajar . . . Please, come down from there. Hurry!

MAN. You know, the lawyer was in tears . . .

ELDEST DAUGHTER (*suddenly laughs*). I gather he was wearing a bandage on his head?

MAN. It's a wonder he can still stay in business!

ELDEST DAUGHTER. It's just a matter of getting used to it. Nowadays it's not all that unusual for a man to be visited by friends like us.

MAN. But the bandage clearly shows there's been violence.

ELDEST DAUGHTER. Even love has its whips, hasn't it?

MAN. The lawyer said eleven parasites had descended on him!

ELDEST DAUGHTER. He must be an even better quality of blotting paper than you.

MAN. What the devil's the matter with this hammock?

ELDEST DAUGHTER. Excuse me, but I'm taking off my clothes. I feel unbearably hot. I suppose it must be the whisky . . .

(*She is wearing under her dressing gown only net tights and a short negligee.*)

MAN. If such a thing as hot ice existed—there may be, for all I know, in fact I'm sure there is—a snowstorm in midsummer, sun stroke in midwinter . . .

ELDEST DAUGHTER. The bottle will be empty if you don't hurry.

MAN (*writhing*). That's funny. What's happened to this hammock?

ELDEST DAUGHTER (*as if she has made a surprising discovery*). Just feel me . . . I really seem to be hot and cold at the same time. I wonder why.

MAN. But what the hell's wrong with this hammock?

Scene Eleven

Lights are suddenly turned on in the room. Eldest Daughter wheels around in astonishment. Middle Daughter stands in pajamas by the wall, near the door of the adjoining room. Her hand is still on the wall switch.

ELDEST DAUGHTER (*angrily*). So you were listening!

MIDDLE DAUGHTER (*quietly and calmly*). Yes, I heard everything.

ELDEST DAUGHTER (*retrieving her gown and putting it back on*). What a way to talk? Not a scrap of respect for other people's feelings . . . I've never known anyone less lovable than you.

MIDDLE DAUGHTER. But it's something important.

ELDEST DAUGHTER. I don't care how important it is. Who ever heard of leaving the lights burning indefinitely? Why even he looks as if the light's too strong for him.

MAN (seems rather dazed). Yes, it'll soon be morning.

MIDDLE DAUGHTER (*ignoring him; to Eldest Daughter.*) Are you drunk?

ELDEST DAUGHTER (*losing her temper*). I tell you, I'm going to give you a piece of my mind if you keep tormenting me with such stupid tricks. I don't care how important you think it is, eavesdropping is still eavesdropping. You didn't listen because it was important. You listened and then you found out something that happened to be important. Why don't you at least pretend to be a little embarrassed? (*To Man, still fiddling with the hammock, unable to get out.*) I'm sorry, really I am . . .

MIDDLE DAUGHTER. Hmmm. Isn't what you really have to apologize for something quite different?

ELDEST DAUGHTER (*worsted in the argument, she adjusts the front of her gown*). I don't know what you're talking about, but there's something weird about you. (*She goes toward the door.*) Anyway, with your permission, I'd like to get a little sleep.

MIDDLE DAUGHTER (*showing her first emotional reaction*). No, you can't! Stay right where you are! You're an important witness. (*She calls through the door to the next room.*) Father, Brother . . . would you come here a minute?

ELDEST DAUGHTER (*agitated*). What are you up to, anyway?

YOUNGER SON (*calling from offstage*). Which brother do you want?

MIDDLE DAUGHTER. Both of you! Hurry! It's extremely important.

Noises from the next room—sleepy murmurs, fits of coughing, and the like—suggest people getting out of bed reluctantly.

MAN (*becoming uneasy*). Isn't there some sort of misunderstanding? Well, misunderstandings get cleared up sooner or later. There's nothing to be so excited about . . . But what the devil's happened to this hammock?

ELDEST DAUGHTER (*glaring at Middle Daughter*). After all this uproar I'm sure we'll discover that the mountain labored to bring forth a mouse. You're not going to get away with paying a hundred yen fine this time . . . I trust you've got a good stock of pin money.

MIDDLE DAUGHTER (*quietly*). It hurts me to tell you, but this is no mouse. You mean to say you haven't caught on yet?

Elder Son, Father, and Younger Son, in that order, appear from the next room. All look groggy, as if they just got out of bed. Each is muttering to himself.

YOUNGER SON. Damn it! I've got another corker of a hangover.

Eldest Daughter starts to make a sneering remark, but Middle Daughter interrupts at once.

MIDDLE DAUGHTER. He was planning an escape!

FATHER (*at once wide awake*). Escape?

They all show reactions of astonishment.

MIDDLE DAUGHTER (*slowly goes up to Man's hammock*). He was just about to try running away.

FATHER (*turning to the sons*). Running away! Things have taken a serious turn.

ELDER SON (*extremely confused*). I can see that everything has not been arranged exactly as he might have wished, but still.

MAN (*apprehensive*). That's an exaggeration. The fact is, I'm here now. Right? Run away? Fat chance I'd have, when I'm wrapped up in this crazy hammock like a tent caterpillar. (*With an unnatural, forced *laugh.*) Run away . . . why I can't even get out to take a leak. I'm suffering, I tell you!

Middle Daughter takes the cord at one end of the hammock and jerks it loose. The hammock at once opens out, and in the recoil Man drops to the floor. Man makes feeble sounds of laughter, but none of the others so much as smile.

MIDDLE DAUGHTER (*helping Man to his feet*). I'm sorry. Did you hurt yourself?

ELDEST DAUGHTER (*aggressively*). So, it was your handiwork, was it?

MIDDLE DAUGHTER. I didn't want to mention it, but you've been flirting with him for the past three days, haven't you?

ELDEST DAUGHTER. Don't say anything you'll regret! For the past three days? Go ahead, be as jealous as you like—that's your privilege—but if you get carried away to any such wild conclusions, the rest of us will be the ones to suffer.

MIDDLE DAUGHTER (*cool; to Father and the others*). I had a feeling tonight would be the crisis. So, just to be on the safe side, I tied up the hammock after he went to sleep.

ELDEST DAUGHTER. That's a lie! An out-and-out lie! Ask him to his face. He'll say which of us is telling the truth. (*To Man, seeking his assent.*) That's right, isn't it?

MAN (*hesitates before answering*). It's true she's kindly come here every evening for the last three days to keep me company, but . . .

ELDEST DAUGHTER (*unabashed*). I've no intention of hiding anything. I've been trying my best to advertise myself, hoping he'd respond to my overtures. But to hear you talk, I was inducing him to run away! That's going too far, even for a false accusation.

MIDDLE DAUGHTER (*spitefully*). It's quite possible tonight was the first time you resorted to open inducement. But how about hints?

ELDEST DAUGHTER. Mystification doesn't become you.

GRANDMOTHER (*imitating Eldest Daughter's manner of speech*). "There's nothing to be worried about. This place and time exist just for the two of us . . . If you pretend that nobody else is here, why it's just the same as if nobody were actually here. Think of the others as being insubstantial as the air . . ."

ELDEST DAUGHTER (*bursts into laughter*). How disgusting! Aren't those the usual clichés every woman uses when seducing a man? Didn't you even know that?

FATHER. What was this direct incitement she resorted to tonight?

MIDDLE DAUGHTER (*again imitating Eldest Daughter; with passion*). "You must give up all hope of getting rid of them. You'll just exhaust yourself with useless efforts. Yes, it'd be better to run away than try to chase them out. We'll run far, far away to some distant place where nobody knows us."

ELDEST DAUGHTER. That's enough!

FATHER. Mm. That was pretty direct.

YOUNGER SON. Even with my hangover I can't help being impressed.

ELDER SON. And what was his reaction to her incitement?

MIDDLE DAUGHTER (*severely*). I felt it was certainly a good thing I had tied the hammock so he couldn't get out.

ELDER SON. What a mess!

MAN (*in confused tone*). But don't you think it's unfair to base your judgments on such a one-sided . . .

FATHER (*reassuringly*). It's all right. It's all right. Please don't worry about it any more.

ELDER SON (*to Eldest Daughter*). But were you serious in trying to tempt him into such a thing?

ELDEST DAUGHTER (*sulkily*). What makes you think I was serious? Don't insult me. It doesn't take much common sense to see that there's absolutely no likelihood of his running away. This is the most disgusting thing I've ever heard of, making such a fuss, so early in the morning.

MIDDLE DAUGHTER. What makes you so sure he can't run away?

ELDEST DAUGHTER. You don't see?

MIDDLE DAUGHTER. I certainly don't.

ELDEST DAUGHTER. He's the acting department head. His fortune's assured—he's a rising star. He knows better than anyone else, I should think, how important his work is to him. He can talk all he wants about how he likes to be alone, or how he longs for freedom, but one thing he can never in the world do is to give up his job.

ELDER SON. That sounds logical, all right.

ELDEST DAUGHTER. Supposing he ran away from here without giving up his job. He'd have to find somewhere else to stay, and it'd be simple enough for us to find out where he went.

ELDER SON. Yes, that'd be no problem.

ELDEST DAUGHTER. And once we found him we surely wouldn't spare ourselves the trouble of moving in with him, would we? We'd go to help him again, as our natural duty, wouldn't we?

FATHER. Of course. We couldn't neglect our duty. That would be out of the question.

ELDEST DAUGHTER (*her self-confidence quite recovered*). And even he must be fully convinced, after living with us for almost two weeks, how strong our sense of duty is. (*To Man.*) Am I wrong?

MAN. No, I am deeply aware of it.

ELDEST DAUGHTER (*triumphantly*). Well, there you have it, ladies and gentlemen.

They all strike various attitudes which suggest they are ruminating on the above. Eldest Daughter throws Middle Daughter an unconcealed smile of derision.

FATHER. In that case, the incident is not as serious as we had imagined.

YOUNGER SON. Then, I hope you'll pardon me if I go back to bed before the rest of you. I may vomit at any minute.

MIDDLE DAUGHTER. I can't help being worried, all the same.

ELDEST DAUGHTER. The more you talk, the more shame you bring on yourself. Pretending to be an innocent little girl is all very well, but it's exhausting for the rest of us to play your game.

MIDDLE DAUGHTER. But when I heard him say, "All right, let's run away!" I was so frightened I shuddered with fear. I wonder if a man can talk in that tone of voice if he doesn't mean it.

ELDEST DAUGHTER. A mere impression, even from someone as bright as you, is not sufficient evidence.

ELDER SON. Yes, if it was nothing more than impression.

YOUNGER SON. O.K. That settles it. (*He exits, staggering, to the next room.*) It's probably my liver.

FATHER (*cautiously, observing Man*). Finally, just as a formality, I'd like to ask the subject of our discussion his opinion. Then I'll adjourn the meeting.

MAN (*gradually regaining his self-confidence*). My opinion? After all we've gone through? (*He laughs.*) That's no longer of any importance, is it? How shall I put it? To tell the truth, it's as if some devil got into me tonight . . . Or rather, as if I'd been bewitched by a goddess . . . I felt when I was talking as if I were singing the words of a song . . . (*To Eldest Daughter.*) I'm not the kind to flatter people, but I really felt as if I were swimming in a pool of whisky . . . When I proposed that we run away I wonder if I wasn't expressing, in spite of myself, the reverse of what I actually felt—my desire to hold fast to you. (*To Father.*) People sometimes say precisely the opposite of what they're thinking.

In the course of the above dialogue Grandmother, Mother, and Youngest Daughter, in that order, stick their heads in from the next room. They observe what is happening with expressions of intense curiosity.

FATHER (*reflectively*). I see . . . Well, now we seem to have heard the opinions of everyone. (*He looks from Middle Daughter to Eldest Daughter.*) How about it—will you agree to leave the final judgment to me?

ELDEST DAUGHTER (*in good spirits, now that Man has flattered her*). That's fine with me.

MIDDLE DAUGHTER. I don't suppose I have much choice.

FATHER (*abruptly gives order to Elder Son*). Prepare the cage!

They all look astonished. But Elder Son instantly moves into action. The other members of the family follow him, displaying remarkable teamwork: one arranges the coat rack in the hall, another produces a lock, another overpowers Man, still another throws a blanket over him. Finally, Man, wrapped in the blanket, is shut up inside the coat rack, which has been converted into a cage. A large lock is hung on the outside.

Man at length manages to stick his head out from inside the blanket.

MAN. What're you doing? Didn't I promise you I wouldn't run away? This is inhuman! There's no excuse for it. It's inhuman!

ELDEST DAUGHTER (*with an expression of inability to understand it herself*). Yes, really, what's happened? After he assured us so positively he had no intention of running away . . .

MAN. That's right. You tell them . . . There must be some mistake!

FATHER. The thing is, you insisted a little too emphatically that you wouldn't run away.

MAN. It's natural for a man to be emphatic when he's speaking from the heart.

FATHER. You yourself were just expressing the view that sometimes people say the opposite of what they feel.

MAN. That's a false accusation!

GRANDMOTHER. The blind man envies the one-eyed man.

FATHER. In a matter of this gravity there's no such thing as taking too many precautions.

Youngest Daughter looks into the cage as if she were watching a monkey at the zoo. Man spits at youngest daughter.

MAN. Get the hell away!

YOUNGEST DAUGHTER. Isn't he awful? Even a chimpanzee wouldn't be so rude.

MOTHER. Don't get too close to him. He's still overexcited.

MAN. Damn it! All your clever talk about neighborly love and the rest was a lot of bunk . . . Not even a slave would endure such treatment.

MIDDLE DAUGHTER (*severely*). There's been a misunderstanding. A terrible misunderstanding. You've taken everything in the wrong spirit.

MAN. Shut up! I don't even want to see your face!

FATHER. Yes, the misunderstanding was definitely on your side. And you still don't seem to understand that these measures have been taken because we earnestly desire your safety and security.

MAN. Understand! You don't suppose there's any chance I would understand that!

MIDDLE DAUGHTER. But running away means disappearing. And that's a much more frightening thing than you seem to suppose. You don't think we could expose you to such a danger, knowing how frightening it is to disappear.

ELDEST DAUGHTER (*still not satisfied*). I think you're overrating him.

ELDER SON. It seems to be our fate always to have our efforts rewarded by enmity.

MOTHER. In short, the world's fallen on evil days.

MAN (*gasping*). But if I can't go to the office, you'll be the ones to suffer. I wonder if you've thought about that.

FATHER. We don't intend to keep you in there forever. Just as soon as your frame of mind improves, of course we'll let you out.

MAN. Isn't that nice? You expect my frame of mind to improve? You amaze me. Don't you think it's a lot more likely to boomerang on you? Don't you realize I'll get to hate this place more and more?

FATHER. Please, just leave things to me. While you're meditating over your solitude in there, the pleasures of your ordinary everyday life, how you used to go to the office each morning, will come back and the happy memories will gush forth inside you like a fountain.

MOTHER. That's right. Happy memories are generally of quite ordinary things. They leave the deepest impression.

FATHER. And then your desire to escape will drop from you like the scab from a wound that has healed.

MIDDLE DAUGHTER. And your peace of mind will come back again.

FATHER. Now for the blankets.

The instant after Father speaks several blankets are draped over the cage. The stage darkens at once.

Scene Twelve

The stage blacks out completely for a moment, but almost immediately afterwards the inside of the cage is illuminated. Man sits, his knees cradled in his arms, and his face pressed against his knees.

He suddenly raises his head and looks uneasily around him. He listens attentively. Then he lies down on his side in a fetal posture. The next moment he gets on all fours like a dog. He starts to imitate a dog's howling, at which the howling of a real dog is heard from a loudspeaker. Man again lies on his side in a fetal posture.

Scene Thirteen

Now light and dark are reversed: inside the cage is dark and outside is light. It is daytime. Middle Daughter enters from the kitchen carrying a breakfast tray.

MIDDLE DAUGHTER (*standing before cage*). Are you awake? I've brought your breakfast.

MAN (*dispiritedly*). Thanks.

She puts the tray on the floor for the moment, removes the blanket covering the cage, then slips the tray into the cage from the end.

MIDDLE DAUGHTER. How do you feel?

MAN. How do you expect?

(*He stares at the food, then begins to eat little by little, but without enjoyment.*)

MIDDLE DAUGHTER. You don't seem to have much of an appetite . . . If you don't go out and get some exercise soon—

MAN. What's the weather like today?

MIDDLE DAUGHTER. It seems to be clearing gradually.

MAN. The place is strangely silent. Is nobody here?

MIDDLE DAUGHTER (*sitting down and staring at Man through the bars of the cage*). Father has gone to the miniature golf links. My older sister's at the beauty parlor and the younger one at school. The rest are out shopping, I suppose.

MAN (*entreatingly*). Couldn't you let me have a look at the newspaper, even if it's only the headlines?

MIDDLE DAUGHTER. Nothing doing. We must keep you quiet while you're convalescing.

MAN. You're certainly a hard girl to figure out. Sometimes I think you're kind, only for you to act just as much of a stickler for the rules as the others. Sometimes you seem affectionate, but then you're just as stubborn as the others.

MIDDLE DAUGHTER (*smiling*). That's because you only think about yourself.

MAN (*laughing faintly*). I know, that's what you say. But surely not even you pretend that shutting me up this way is for my own good.

MIDDLE DAUGHTER. But it's the truth.

MAN. I don't believe it.

MIDDLE DAUGHTER. It's strange, isn't it? My head is so full of you that I've never even given a thought to anything else.

MAN (*taken aback*). If that's the case, how can you fail so completely to understand my feelings? I have you and your family to thank for the opportunity to study to my heart's content the blessings of neighborly love.

MIDDLE DAUGHTER (*suddenly dejected*). I do understand. I understand much better than you suppose.

MAN. What do you understand?

MIDDLE DAUGHTER (*speaking hesitantly*). Well, for example . . .

MAN. For example?

MIDDLE DAUGHTER. The fact that your sickness has not in the least improved.

MAN (*his interest aroused*). I see . . . You may be right.

MIDDLE DAUGHTER. If I listen very carefully I can hear it, the sound of your heart flying far, far away.

MAN. Just like a bird.

MIDDLE DAUGHTER. And the commuter's train, your time card, the desk with your nameplate on it, the street corner with your company's building—they're all gradually melting away like sculpture carved of ice.

MAN. You do understand.

MIDDLE DAUGHTER (*changing her tone*). Oh, that's right. I was forgetting something important. Here. (*She takes a little packet wrapped in paper from her pocket.*) My brother asked me to give this to you.

MAN (*unwrapping the packet*). From your brother, is it? I see.

MIDDLE DAUGHTER. That's an engagement ring, isn't it?

MAN. It's a kind of metal object. It used to be an engagement ring once.

MIDDLE DAUGHTER (*staring at Man with great earnestness*). Oh, I'm so worried.

MAN. About what?

MIDDLE DAUGHTER. You seem already to have gone farther away than I had thought.

MAN (*laughing cynically*). How sentimental we've become!

MIDDLE DAUGHTER. Sentimental? That's not it at all. I meant to say you're a traitor!

MAN. A traitor!

MIDDLE DAUGHTER. How about a glass of milk?

MAN. Yes, I'd like one. The food today was a little too salty.

Middle Daughter hurries into the kitchen and returns immediately with a glass of milk. She watches affectionately as Man, with a word of thanks, drains the glass with one gulp.

MIDDLE DAUGHTER (*holding out her fist; she has something in it*). If I give you the key to this lock, will you promise not to scold me even if I tell you I love you?

(*She opens her hand. The key glitters in her palm.*)

MAN (*at a loss for words before this too-sudden realization of his wishes*). That's the easiest thing in the world. Why, if you hadn't been a member of your family, I'm sure I would have spoken first, and told you I was in love with you . . . I'm not saying this just to please you . . . I'm sure I would have.

(*He starts to shake.*)

MIDDLE DAUGHTER. Are you cold?

MAN. It must be an excess of joy. And now, for the key . . .

Man tries to take the key, but his shaking has become so violent that he cannot manage to grasp it. Suddenly Man's face is shot with fear.

MIDDLE DAUGHTER. If only you hadn't turned against us, we would have been no more than company for you . . .

Man's shaking suddenly stops. He lies motionless. Middle Daughter tenderly drapes a blanket over the cage and, kneeling beside him, quietly sobs.

MIDDLE DAUGHTER. There's no need any more to run away . . . Nobody will bother you now . . . It's quiet, isn't it? You look so well . . . Your sickness must be better.

Younger Son appears without warning from the next room.

YOUNGER SON (*putting on his shirt*). Hey, what're you bawling about?

MIDDLE DAUGHTER. Oh, were you there all the time?

YOUNGER SON (*having sized up the situation from Middle Daughter's appearance*). So, you've done it again.

MIDDLE DAUGHTER. What else could I do?

YOUNGER SON. You're hopeless . . . But there's no use crying over spilt milk . . . Well, we're going to be busy again, what with one thing and another.

MIDDLE DAUGHTER. He was such a nice man. Really sweet. And so sensitive. At the slightest touch his heart would start to pound.

YOUNGER SON (*brushing the dandruff from his head*). We borrowed in advance on his retirement pay. We've got nothing to complain about as far as our balance sheet is concerned.

MIDDLE DAUGHTER. Show a little more tact in what you say. What I lost and what you lost are not the same things.

YOUNGER SON (*looking around the room; to no one in particular*). It's funny with belongings. I don't know why it is, but every time we move we seem to have more and more of them.

MIDDLE DAUGHTER (throwing her arms around the cage and caressing it). If only you hadn't turned against us, we would have been no more than company for you.

The melody of "The Broken Necklace" begins to sound, this time in a melancholy key. The members of the family return in full strength and arrange themselves in a line. They are already dressed for travel. They all take out handkerchiefs and press them to their eyes.

FATHER. The deceased was always a good friend to us. Friend, why were you destined for such a fate? Probably you yourself do not know. Naturally, we do not know either. (*He opens the newspaper.*) Here is the newspaper you were waiting for. Please listen as I read, without the least anxiety. (*He begins to read snatches from the main news items of that day's newspaper, ranging from international events to advertisements.*) Yes, the world is a big place. A big place and a complicated one. (*To Middle Daughter.*) Come, be more cheerful. (*He lifts her to her feet.*) They're all waiting for us. (*To Man.*) Good-by.

They all wave their handkerchiefs and put them back into their pockets.

FATHER. Nobody's forgotten anything?

They begin to march off. The curtain falls slowly. Halfway off the lighting is extinguished, and all that can be recognized is the laughter of the family.

Analyzing the Text

1. What can we infer about the life of "Man" before the family enters his apartment? From the family's point of view, what justifies them in usurping his apartment, his possessions, and even his life?
2. Why is it significant that no one the protagonist turns to for help—including the superintendent, the police, the reporter, or even his fiancée—takes his side over that of the family?

Understanding Abe's Techniques

1. How does the song "The Broken Necklace" express the family's mission?
2. How are members of the family defined in terms of the roles they play in society? How does Abe use the middle daughter's sympathy for the protagonist to generate suspense about his fate?

Arguing for an Interpretation

1. What attitudes toward modern Japanese society does Abe express in this play in terms of the rights of the collective versus those of the individual?
2. In your opinion, does "Man's" reaction to the family contribute to his fate? How would you have responded if you found yourself in his predicament?

Connections

1. Compare the way shame and money operate as themes both in Fritz Peters's essay "Boyhood with Gurdjieff" and in Inés Arredondo's story "The Shunammite."
2. Compare the expectations parents and children have for each other in Jill Nelson's "Number One!," in Amy Tan's story "Two Kinds," and in John Cheever's "Reunion."
3. In what way do Amy Tan's story ("Two Kinds") and the poems by Sharon Olds ("The Planned Child) and Naomi Shihab Nye ("Where Children Live") present different perspectives on childhood?
4. Compare the theme of murder (ritual or spontaneous) in families in the stories by Bessie Head ("Looking for a Rain God") and Kazuo Ishiguro ("A Family Supper"), and in Kōbō Abe's play, *Friends*, and the poem "Edward, Edward."
5. How does the imminent war in Ireland as expressed in "A Prayer for my Daughter" and the Vietnam War dramatized in Louise Erdrich's story express the difficulties of living a normal life under these circumstances?
6. Discuss the theme of devotion in black culture as it is depicted in Eudora Welty's story ("A Worn Path") and in Robert Hayden's poem ("Those Winter Sundays").

7. Discuss the ways in which Kazuo Ishiguro's story "A Family Supper," Cathy Song's poem "The Youngest Daughter," and Amy Tan's essay "The Language of Discretion" display the conflict between traditional Asian cultures and New World values.
8. Compare how both Anne Bradstreet and Ben Jonson metaphorically link children and literary works in their poems, albeit for different reasons.
9. Compare the eulogies written by Ben Jonson for his son and Rita Dove for her mother in terms of the aspects they emphasize.
10. Discuss the theme of estrangement and delayed appreciation in Robert Hayden's poem "Those Winter Sundays" and in Amy Tan's story "Two Kinds."
11. How do both William Butler Yeats in "A Prayer for my Daughter" and Rita Dove in "The Wake" create idealized portraits?
12. How do the poems by Garrett Hongo ("Who Among You Knows the Essence of Garlic?") and Chenjerai Hove ("You Will Forget") touch on the theme of lost cultural roots?

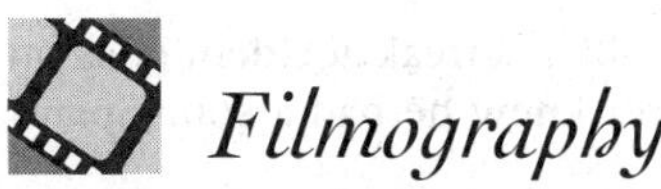

Filmography

Broken Blossoms (1919) Director: D. W. Griffith. Performers: Lillian Gish, Richard Barthelmess.
An emotionally and physically abused teenaged girl forms a bond with an elderly Chinese man in turn of the century London.

The Kid (1920) Director: Charles Chaplin. Performers: Charles Chaplin, Edna Purviance, Jackie Coogan.
A poor, unwed mother abandons her newborn son in hopes that others can give him a better life only to have the child "adopted" by Chaplin's Tramp in this film, which examines the question of what constitutes proper love and care for a child.

The 400 Blows (1959) Director: François Truffaut. Performers: Jean-Pierre Leaud, Albert Remy.
In this autobiographical film, a lonely, abused boy seeks freedom and sympathy in an indifferent world. [France]

The Godfather (1972) Director: Francis Ford Coppola. Performers: Marlon Brando, Al Pacino.
The story of an Italian crime dynasty and the complex interrelationships between family, business, and violence.

Meetings with Remarkable Men (1979) Director: Peter Brook. Performers: Dragan Maksimovic, Terence Stamp.
A film based on the memoir by George Gurdjieff about a period in his life when he searched for spiritual truth in his journeys through Asia and the Middle East.

Ordinary People (1980) Director: Robert Redford. Performers: Mary Tyler Moore, Donald Sutherland, Timothy Hutton.
This troubling, powerful story of a family's struggle to cope with a son's accidental death is based on the novel by Judith Guest.

Fanny and Alexander (1983) Director: Ingmar Bergman Performer: Pernilla Allwyn.
A year in the life of a Swedish family as seen through the eyes of two young children. [Sweden]

The Hanging Garden (1988) Director: Thom Fitzgerald. Performers: Kerry Fox, Chris Leavins.

In this magic realist film a young gay man sees two different possibilities as to what his life could be, based on an important decision he makes at a crossroads in his life. [Canada]

The Joy Luck Club (1993) Director: Wayne Wang. Performers: France Nuyen, Lisa Lu, Ming-Na.

The life histories of four Asian women and their daughters reveal universal themes; based on Amy Tan's novel.

Antonia's Line (1995) Director: Marleen Gorris. Performer: Willeke Van Ammelrooy.

Ninety-year-old Antonia begins a fifty-year-old flashback of her life as a nonconformist in a Dutch village on the day she has decided to die. [The Netherlands]

Kolya (1996) Director: Jan Sverak. Performer: Zdenek Sverak.

A womanizing cellist marries for money and finds himself left with her five-year-old son in the days just before the Velvet Revolution in 1989. [The Czech Republic]

All About My Mother (1999) Director: Pedro Almodovar. Performers: Cecelia Roth, Marisa Parades, Penelope Cruz.

A young woman who has recently lost her only child in a freak accident goes on a journey to find the boy's dying father, who never knew he had a son. [Spain]

Chapter 4

Coming of Age

The old believe everything. The middle aged suspect everything. The young know everything.

Oscar Wilde

In everyone's life there are moments of psychological insight, self-knowledge, and self-definition when you see yourself as being a certain kind of person. Sometimes these moments correspond with doing away with a false image of yourself. Sometimes it is when you see yourself, not as you would wish, but as you actually appear to others. Frequently, the experiences you have while in college are decisive in this psychological turning point, this emerging sense of your real self. It is a moment when you define yourself apart from your family and reconcile often-conflicting roles you may have been playing in trying on different identities. A sense of self develops by establishing a connection among who you are now, who you were in the past, and who you would like to be in the future. These moments of insight may be private psychological turning points or they may occur in the context of ceremonies that initiate the individual into adulthood within a community.

These crucial moments in which individuals move from childhood innocence to adult awareness often involve learning a particular society's rules governing values, knowledge, what should or should not be done under different circumstances, and expectations of how the individual should present herself or himself in a wide variety of situations. Because this chapter is rich in different perspectives, it invites you to make discoveries about turning points in your own life.

This chapter features stories that provide insight into the need people have in growing up to assert their own sense of individuality—often by defining themselves in opposition to the values held by the societies in which they live. The German writer Sabine Reichel, in her essay "Learning What Was Never Taught," tells of the difficulties she faced in finding out about the Holocaust from her teachers. An American teacher in China, Mark Salzman, relates in "Lessons" the unusual bargain he struck with the renowned martial arts master, Pan Qingfu, to exchange English lessons for instruction in the Chinese martial arts.

James Joyce captures the mood of adolescent infatuation that gives way to disillusionment in "Araby." In "Her First Ball" by Katherine Mansfield, a young girl's first dance provides a glimpse into her future, which she promptly represses. A child in Lebanon discovers the truth behind her mother's divorce in Hanan al-Shaykh's "The Persian Carpet." In Joyce Carol Oates's "Where Are You Going, Where Have You Been?" a teenager confronts the question of good versus evil when she meets a mysterious new boyfriend. In Kate Chopin's "The Story of an Hour," the protagonist experiences an entire lifetime in 60 minutes. Jerzy Kosinski describes a young boy's first experience with the consequences of jealousy and revenge in "The Miller's Tale," which is set in Poland during World War II. In "I Am A Cat," Natsume Soseki provides insight into the life of a Japanese family from a most unusual viewpoint. Last, the Sudanese writer Tayeb Salih tells a story, "A Handful of Dates," of a moment during the harvest of date palms that permanently alters the relationship between a boy and his grandfather.

Poetry is one of the most powerful ways in which people come to know themselves, externalizing thoughts, memories, and associations. The works of poetry in this chapter are intended to offer insight into the role poetry can play in developing self-awareness. In "Ethics," Linda Pastan shows how the experiences of a lifetime deepen the paradox of what was a childhood puzzle. Robert Frost in "The Road Not Taken" revisits the choices that he confronted as a young man. In "I Found It," Fadwa Tuqan, one of the Arab world's best-known poets, draws on imagery from the Sufi tradition to express her sense of self-realization. Xu Gang finds an apt image to express the idea that we must struggle to attain what is just beyond our grasp in "Red Azalea on the Cliff." An Israeli poet, Miriam Baruch, in "Sunflower," suggests that being appreciated is as important for people as the sun is for the sunflower. The great English poet William Blake, in "Ah! Sun-flower," presents a contrasting perspective by suggesting that only in eternity can we discover what we search for in life. Maurice Kenny, a Mohawk Indian, in "Sometimes . . . Injustice" depicts the quixotic circumstances that shaped his destiny. From Mexico, Octavio Paz, in "The Street," enters an eerie twilight land where pursuer and pursued are different aspects of the speaker's personality. In "Tell All the Truth but Tell It Slant," Emily Dickinson, who led a sheltered life, expresses her artistic credo that truth must be revealed in small increments so that the listener is not overwhelmed. Known for his surreal images, the French poet Robert Desnos in "Midway" opens our eyes to the bountiful impressions that await the spirit who awakes at the midpoint of life. Then, Sara Teasdale in "The Solitary" relates how she relishes her new-found independence in later life.

The plays in this chapter explore the boundary between fantasy and reality from serious and comic perspectives. Tennessee Williams, in his play *The Glass Menagerie,* evokes the appeal of a family whose life has been caught in a timeless dream of grace and gentility. Christopher Durang, in *For Whom the Southern Belle Tolls,* creates a wicked parody by inverting the themes, characters, and even the language and images of Williams's classic drama.

Essays

Sabine Reichel

Sabine Reichel was born in Hamburg, Germany, in 1946, to a German actor and a Lithuanian artist. She grew up in West Germany (now Germany) and since 1965 has had a varied career as clothing designer, free-lance journalist, contributor of film criticism, lecturer, filmmaker, and social worker active in projects caring for homeless children. She immigrated to the United States in 1976. Dissatisfied with the silence she and others of her generation encountered concerning the systematic slaughter of European Jews by Hitler and the Nazis, Reichel spent six months interviewing soldiers and teachers whose lives seemed to her to represent Germany's amnesia. The autobiographical essay that resulted was published under the title What Did You Do in the War, Daddy? *(1989). In this chapter from that book, Reichel describes the moral complacency of those of her parents' generation who refused to acknowledge the realities of the Nazi era and its lingering effects in contemporary Germany.*

Learning What Was Never Taught

I remember Herr Stock and Fräulein Lange without much affection. Partly because they weren't extraordinary people, partly because they failed their profession. They were my history teachers, ordinary civil servants, singled out to bring the tumultuous events of European history into perspective for a classroom of bored German schoolkids.

As it happened, Hitler and the Third Reich were the subjects under discussion when we were about fourteen years old, which is not to say that we discussed anything at all. I always thought that the decision to study the subject then was the result of a carefully calculated estimate by the school officials—as if German students were emotionally and intellectually ready to comprehend and digest the facts about Nazi Germany at exactly the age of 14.3. I learned much later that it had nothing to do with calculation; it was a matter of sequence. German history is taught chronologically, and Hitler was there when we were fourteen, whether we were ready or not.

Teaching this particular period was a thankless, though unavoidable, task. It was accompanied by sudden speech impediments, hoarse voices, uncontrollable coughs, and sweaty upper lips. A shift of mood would creep into the expansive lectures about kings and conquerors from the old ages, and once the Weimar Republic came to an end our teachers lost their proud diction.

We knew what it meant. We could feel the impending disaster. Only a few more pages in the history book, one last nervous swallowing, and then in a casual but controlled voice, maybe a touch too loud, Fräulein Lange would ask, "We are now getting to a dark chapter in German history. I'm sure you all know what I mean?"

We did, because each of us had already skimmed through the whole 5
book countless times in search of exotic material and, naturally, had come across the man with the mustache. We knew that she was referring to the terrible time between 1933 and 1945 when Germany fell prey to a devil in brown disguise. There were fifteen pages devoted to the Third Reich, and they were filled with incredible stories about a mass movement called National Socialism which started out splendidly and ended in a catastrophe for the whole world.

And then there was an extra chapter, about three-quarters of a page long. It was titled "The Extermination of the Jews," and I had read it in my room at home many times. I always locked the door because I didn't want anybody to know what I was reading. Six million Jews were killed in concentration camps, and as I read about Auschwitz and the gas chambers a wave of feelings—fearful fascination mingled with disgust—rushed over me. But I kept quiet. What monsters must have existed then. I was glad it had all happened in the past and that the cruel Germans were gone, because, as the book pointed out, the ones responsible were punished. I couldn't help feeling alarmed by something I couldn't put my finger on. How could so many innocent people be murdered?

There was no explanation for my unspoken questions, no answers in Fräulein Lange's helpless face. She seemed embarrassed and distraught, biting her lip and looking down at her orthopedic shoes while trying to summarize the Third Reich in fifty minutes. That worked out to one minute for every one million people killed in World War II . . . and twenty-six lines for six million Jews, printed on cheap, yellowish paper in a German history book published in 1960. An efficient timesaver, the German way.

We never read that particular chapter aloud with our teacher as we did with so many other ones. It was the untouchable subject, isolated and open to everyone's personal interpretation. There was a subtle, unspoken agreement between teacher and student not to dig into something that would cause discomfort on all sides. Besides, wanting to have known more about concentration camps as a student would have been looked upon as sick.

All things must come to an end, however, and once the Third Reich crumbled in our classroom to the sound of hastily turning pages, the suffocating silence was lifted. Everybody seemed relieved, especially Fräulein Lange, who became her jolly old self again. She had survived two world wars, she would survive a bunch of unappreciative teenagers.

In her late fifties in 1960, Fräulein Lange was a tiny, wrinkled woman 10
who matched my idea of the institutional matron right down to her baggy skirt, steel-gray bun at the nape of her neck, and seamed stockings. She also had a trying predilection for Gutenberg, the inventer of movable type, whom we got to know more intimately than Hitler. But she did her duty, more or less. German teachers had to teach history whether they liked it or not.

The teachers of my time had all been citizens of the Third Reich and therefore participants in an epoch that only a few years after its bitter collapse had to be discussed in a neutral fashion. But what could they possibly have said about this undigested, shameful subject to a partly shocked, partly bored class of adolescents? They had to preserve their authority in order to appear credible as teachers. Yet they were never put to the test. A critical imagination and unreasonable curiosity were unwelcome traits in all the classrooms of my twelve years in school. There was no danger that a precocious student would ever corner a teacher and demand more facts about the Nazis; they could walk away unscathed. We didn't ask our parents at home about the Nazis; nor did we behave differently in school.

The truth was that teachers were not allowed to indulge in private views of the Nazi past. There were nationwide guidelines for handling this topic, including one basic rule: The Third Reich and Adolf Hitler should be condemned unequivocally, without any specific criticism or praise. In reality, however, there were basically three ways to deal with the German past: (1) to go through the chapter as fast as possible, thereby avoiding any questions and answers; (2) to condemn the past passionately in order to deflate any suspicion about personal involvement; (3) to subtly legitimate the Third Reich by pointing out that it wasn't really as bad as it seemed; after all, there were the *Autobahnen.*

But no matter what the style of prevarication, the German past was always presented as an isolated, fatal accident, and so the possibility of investigating the cause of such a disaster was, of course, eliminated. Investigating crimes reinforces guilt. If something is programmatically depicted as black and bad, one doesn't look for different shades and angles. The Third Reich was out of reach for us; it couldn't be cut down to size.

I wonder now what could have been accomplished by a teacher who had taken part in the war—as a soldier, or a Nazi, or an anti-Nazi—and who talked candidly about his personal experience. But that never happened. Instead we were showered with numbers and dates. A few million dead bodies are impossible to relate to; raw numbers don't evoke emotions. Understanding is always personal. Only stories that humanized the numbers might have reached us. Had we been allowed to draw a connection between ourselves and the lives of other people, we might have been able to identify and feel compassion. But we were not aware of how blatantly insufficiently the past was handled in school because we resented the subject as much as the teacher who was somewhat entangled in it. Teenagers generally have little interest in history lessons; we learned facts and dates in order to pass a test or get a good grade and weren't convinced that comprehension of the warp and woof of historical events made any difference to the world or anybody in particular.

Another history teacher in a new school I attended in 1962 took an ac- 15
tivist approach, mixing pathos and drama into a highly entertaining theatrical performance. To introduce highlights of the Third Reich there was no finer actor than Herr Stock. His voice was angry, his brows furrowed, and his fist was raised when he talked about the Führer's ferocious reign. Some of the more outgoing male teachers might even mimic parts of a Hitler speech. Yet when it came time to discuss the war itself, everything went downhill. His hands stopped moving, his voice became reproachful—no more victories to report. His saddest expression was reserved for

the tragic end of "Germany under National Socialist dictatorship." It was time for the untouchable chapter again, the chapter that made Herr Stock nervously run his hands over his bald head, clear his throat, and mumble something about "six million Jews." It was the chapter that made him close the book with a clap, turn his back to the class, and announce with a palpable sigh of relief, "Recess."

In our next history lesson that chapter was usually forgotten, and nobody followed up with any questions. Happy to have escaped interrogation, Herr Stock turned the pages quickly, ignoring "unpleasantries" like capitulation, denazification, and the humiliating aftermath of a defeated nation. The dark clouds were gone, the past had been left behind, and he turned jocular and voluble again.

But Herr Stock wasn't really talking to us, he was rather trying to convince us of something, assuming the stance of a prosecutor. For him, the scandal wasn't the casualties of World War II, but the resulting partition of Germany and the malevolence of the Russians. Rage, anger, and disappointment over the lost war, always repressed or directed at others, could be openly displayed now, disguised as righteousness. "They" had stolen parts of Germany—no word of what we stole from other countries. The Russians were war criminals; the Germans were victims.

If I had been unexpectedly curious about Nazi Germany, I would have received little help from my history books. The conclusions to be drawn from a twelve-year catastrophe packed with enough dramatic material to fill a library were reduced to a few cryptic phrases: "The Germans showed very little insight" and "No real feelings of contrition were expressed." Teachers and history books were their own best examples of how to eviscerate the Nazi terror without ever really trying to come to terms with it.

But a new chapter, a new era, and a magic word—*Wirtschaftswunder*—soon revived our classroom and inspired another patriotic performance by Herr Stock. The undisputed star of German history education in the sixties was the remarkable reconstruction of postwar Germany. Now here was something an old schoolteacher could sink his teeth into. Gone were stutters and coughs. A nation of survivors had rolled up its sleeves, and Herr Stock had certainly been one of them. Here was a chance to rehabilitate Germany and put some gloss over its rotten core. Postwar Germany was a genuine communal construction, a well-made product, mass-manufactured by and for the tastes of the former citizens of the Reich. Every German with two functioning hands had taken part in rebuilding Germany, and history teachers all over the country waxed nostalgic about the united strength, the grim determination, and the close camaraderie that had helped build up Germany brick by brick.

We schoolchildren couldn't have cared less about these achievements. 20
We were all born under occupation; the postwar years were ours too and the memories of ruins and poverty were just as indelible—if not as traumatic—as they had been for our parents. But in his enthusiasm he overlooked the fact that his words were falling on deaf ears: we didn't like Herr Stock; nor did we trust or admire him. In all this excitement about the "economic miracle," another, even greater miracle was conveniently left unexplained. On page 219 of my history book, Germany was described as a nation living happily under National Socialism and a seemingly accepted Führer without any visible crisis of conscience. Yet only fourteen pages later the same *Volk* is depicted in the midst of an entirely different world,

miraculously denazified and retrained, its murderous past neatly tucked away behind a tattered but nevertheless impenetrable veil of forgetfulness.

How did they do it? The existing Federal Republic of Germany is only one state away from the Nazi Reich. Where did they unload the brown ballast? The role change from obedient Nazi citizen to obedient *Bundes* citizen went too smoothly from "*Sieg Heil!*" to democracy, and from marching brown uniforms to marching gray flannel suits. Where was the genuine substance which had initially constituted the basic foundation and ideology of the Third Reich? Could it still be there, hidden, repressed, put on ice?

Such questions were never asked, or encouraged. The schoolteachers that I encountered were a uniformly intimidating group of people (with one glorious exception): older men and women who demanded respect, order, and obedience. They were always curbing my curiosity with the clobbering logic of people who get paid for controlling outbursts of independent thinking. Their assessment of my character in report cards read: "She talks too much and could accomplish more if she would be more diligent."

Even though prohibited when I went to school, corporal punishment in many forms was still practiced with parental support, and my own classroom recollections are thick with thin-lipped, hawk-eyed, bespectacled men and women with mercilessly firm hands ready to take up the switch.

I always felt powerless toward teachers, and all of these emotions crystallized in 1983, when I was preparing to interview one of them. I couldn't help feeling a little triumphant. I was asking the questions now because I had discovered a slight spot on their white vests, something I couldn't see clearly when I was young and under their control. Now I had the power to make them nervous. My victory over German authority seemed complete. A schoolgirl's revenge?

But that wasn't all. I had a genuine interest in finding out how teachers in Germany feel today about their past failures. Had they found new ways to justify their damaging elisions, euphemisms, and omissions? More than any other age group, my generation was in desperate need not only of historical education but also of some form of emotional assistance from the adults who were linked to that not so distant yet unspeakable past.

In a way, I was looking for Herr Stock. But teachers as mediocre as he and Fräulein Lange had little to contribute to the kind of discussion I had in mind. I wanted the perspective of a teacher who had at least attempted to come to grips with his past. I was lucky to find one in Cäsar Hagener, a seventy-six-year-old former teacher and history professor. Hagener lives with his wife in a cozy, old-fashioned house with a garden in a suburb of Hamburg, in a quiet, safe neighborhood with lots of trees, many dachshunds, and little activity. He owns the type of one-family house, surrounded by a fence, that was commonly built in the thirties. A German house must have a fence. A house without a fence is disorderly, like a coat with a missing button.

Cäsar Hagener exuded integrity and an appealing friendliness—yet I found it impossible to forget that he had also been a teacher in the Third Reich. Hitler had envisioned a training program that would make every German youth "resilient as leather, fast as a weasel, and hard as Krupp steel." He believed that "too much education spoils the youth." (Not surprisingly, after a few years of dictatorship 30 percent of the university professors, including Jews, had left the country.)

In 1933, Cäsar Hagener was a teacher of pedagogy and history at a liberal school in Hamburg, and when he heard that Hitler was appointed Reichs Chancellor he happened to be studying *Das Kapital* together with some left-wing colleagues. "My friend said to me, 'It'll be over in no time. When you and I write a history book in twenty years, the Nazis will only be a footnote.'"

Even a skillful dictator like Hitler couldn't turn a country upside down overnight, and school life changed slowly under the Nazis. "But after 1934, the Nazis began to investigate the teachers' adaptation to the new order. Some were fired, and some were retrained in special camps. We had, of course, some 'overnight' Nazis who were strutting around in uniform, which didn't impress the students, who were quite critical. Later, in 1937, the young teachers were told to join the Nazi Party or else, so I joined the Party. Still, the first years of National Socialism were almost bearable."

However, at least once a week, teachers and students had to muster for the raising of the swastika flag and the singing of the "Horst-Wessel-Lied" or other Nazi songs. The Führer's speeches were required listening on the popular *Volksempfänger* for teachers and older students, while the nazified text in the new schoolbooks read like this: "If a mental patient costs 4 Reichsmarks a day in maintenance, a cripple 5.50, and a criminal 3.50, and about 50,000 of these people are in our institutions, how much does it cost our state at a daily rate of 4 Reichsmarks—and how many marriage loans of 1,000 Reichsmarks per couple could have been given out instead?"

The new features of Nazi education like race hygiene and heredity theory were given different degrees of importance in different schools. Hagener prepared himself: "I made sure to get a class with school beginners because children of that age weren't taught history or any of that Nazi nonsense. Besides, as a teacher, you were pretty much independent in your classroom and could make your own decision about what to say and what to skip. There were ways of getting around the obnoxious Nazi ideology."

The first public action by the Nazis right after January 1933 was to purge public and school libraries of "Jewish and un-German elements," leaving empty spaces on the shelves, since new "literature" wasn't written yet and new schoolbooks, adapted to the Nazis' standards, weren't printed until 1936. That same year they initiated compulsory membership in the Hitler Youth, starting at the age of ten with boys organized into Jungvolk and Hitler Jungen and girls and young women into the Bund Deutscher Mädel (League of German Girls). What the Reich of the future needed were fearless, proud men of steel and yielding, fertile women—preferably blond—not effete intellectuals.

"The children can't be blamed for having been enthusiastic members of the Hitler Youth," Cäsar Hagener points out. "They grew up with that ideology and couldn't be expected to protect themselves from National Socialism; to do so, children would have had to be unaffected by all outside influences. It was their world, and the Hitler Youth programs were very attractive, with sports, contests, and decorations. It was possible for the son of a Communist or a Social Democrat to become a highly decorated Hitler Youth leader. I accuse the teachers who didn't perceive what was going on, and who taught Nazi ideology and glorified war, of having failed their profession."

In the last years of the war there was not much academic activity in Germany. The Nazi state was concerned with other problems besides education. Many schools were destroyed by bombs and virtually all Germans between fifteen and sixty years of age—Cäsar Hagener was drafted in 1940—were mobilized for the *Endkampf* (the final struggle) by the end of 1944. Hunger, death, and the will to survive prevailed over culture and education. Who needs to know algebra when the world is falling apart?

In 1945 denazification fever broke out in the defeated nation and re- 35
versed the roles of master and servant. For over a decade the country had been straining to purge itself of "un-German elements," and now the occupying powers were trying to purge it of all Nazi elements. Yet their efforts only exposed the unfeasibility of such a gargantuan task, since it involved much more than just the Nazi Party and the SS. Twelve years under the swastika had produced all kinds of "literature," art, music, film—indeed, a whole society had to be taken apart and its guiding principles destroyed. Naturally, reforming the educational system was a high priority, and millions of schoolbooks were thrown out, but some had to be preserved. The specially assigned Allied education officers decided which schoolbooks could still be used (after tearing out a Nazi-contaminated page or censoring a suspicious chapter or two). The approved books were stamped, and were circulated until new ones could be printed, which wasn't until the early fifties.

"The British, our occupiers, did everything wrong, because nothing could be worked out intellectually. They came over here with certain expectations and this incredibly bad image of the enemy, and they were very surprised to find their task not as easy as they had thought. They tried to control the situation by being very strict."

Reforming the faculty was even more problematic, since many teachers had been forced to join the Nazi Party and it wasn't always easy to tell who was a "real" Nazi and who wasn't. As a rule of thumb, those who appeared to have cooperated unwillingly were permitted to continue teaching, younger teachers who had been educated under the Nazi regime were retrained in special seminars, while those who had been active supporters were barred from teaching for as long as two years.

Cäsar Hagener still gets angry over how easily former colleagues were rehired. "After 1945, nobody seemed to remember what a Nazi was, and people who I knew were definitely Nazis by nature landed on top again. I was one of a group of young teachers who protested violently against this tendency—and I felt like a McCarthy witch-hunter. I saw these people as criminals who did a lot of harm to us teachers."

Still, the main consideration was that teachers were badly needed. The war had wiped out a whole generation of young men, and keeping professionals from their profession in Germany after 1945 was as uneconomical as it was impractical: what was left was what Germany's children got. It's safe to say that by 1950 almost all teachers were back in schools and universities regardless of their past.

In the years immediately following the war, the few schools that were 40
not badly damaged were overcrowded with children of all ages and several grades gathered together in one room. There was cardboard in place of windows, and opening umbrellas inside the school on rainy days was as natural as being sent home for a "cold-weather holiday" because there was no heat. The teacher had to be a good-humored ringmaster, innovative and full of stories; because of the book shortage, he had to know his lessons by heart. The students also needed good memories, because there wasn't any

paper. Arithmetic and grammar assignments were often written down on the margins of newspapers.

It might have been the only time in Germany when school lessons were extemporaneous, personal, and an accurate reflection of real life. School was suddenly a popular place where humanity prevailed over theory. Teachers were not merely authority figures but people who had been harmed by the war just like the students and their families, and much of the time was spent discussing how to steal potatoes and coal and other survival tactics, which were more pressing than Pythagoras.

How did a teacher in those years explain history while it was happening? The change from "Nazis are good" to "Nazis are bad" must have been a confusing experience for the uprooted, disillusioned children of the Third Reich. Children weren't denazified. They had to adapt to "democracy" without shedding a brown skin. All the values they had learned to defend so passionately crumbled before their eyes and the reality they once trusted was rearranged silently, without their consent. The glorious, thunderous Third Reich was a gyp. The Jews weren't "*Volks* enemy number one" anymore. And as for the Führer, he wasn't a superhuman hero, but a vicious little coward, a maniac who wanted to exterminate a whole people and almost succeeded. What irreparable mistrust must have become lodged in the minds of all these young Germans whose youth was trampled flat by goose-stepping jackboots.

But teachers didn't explain history at all. "I'm afraid to say that it didn't occur to the students to bring up Adolf in any form. We had all survived and dealt mostly with the effects of the war in a practical sense. I tried to do nice, positive things with the children, who had it bad enough as it was," Cäsar Hagener explains, and adds, almost surprised, "It is amazing how extremely apolitical we were. Any reflection was impossible under the circumstances, because everything was defined in terms of the struggle of daily life, which had a dynamic all by itself."

He also knows why the adolescents of the fifties and sixties were as uninquisitive as their teachers and parents were silent. "There was strong resentment toward the grown-ups. The teenagers had a fine sense for the things that didn't quite fit together with the Nazis. I didn't have any luck with my own three sons; they frustrated my desire to talk about the past by calling it lecturing, so I ended up talking about it mostly in foreign countries, where the people seemed to be more interested in it."

Things have changed radically during the last twenty years. There has 45
been a small revolution in the German classroom. While teachers after the war were much younger and more outspoken than their predecessors, students became rebellious and undisciplined.

Cäsar Hagener remembers his school days. "My own generation and my students lived in a very strict and conformist structure which existed much earlier than 1933. Sure, there were provocative and rebellious personalities, but this phenomenon of developing an independent mind is new. Today it wouldn't be possible to stand in front of a class in uniform and in all seriousness talk about racial theory. The students would die laughing."

German students today often know more facts about the Third Reich than both their parents and the immediate postwar generation and are not afraid to ask questions. Yet their interest in Nazism is strictly intellectual, and they generally succeed in remaining emotionally detached. They don't know yet that they can't escape the past. Tragically, almost all of Cäsar Hagener's contemporaries have managed to escape their Nazi past. In his opinion: "You can't put a whole nation on the couch. I find my own contemporaries just plain terrible and I don't have much contact with many old friends anymore. In their eyes I'm too critical, a guy who fouls his own nest and who can't see the good sides of the Nazi era—which infuriates and bores me at the same time. They reject the radical examination of the past. But it's necessary, since we know better than most that terrible things can and did happen."

Analyzing the Text

1. From the narrator's perspective, what was odd about the way in which the Holocaust was taught? How did her search for a satisfactory explanation about this event change her relationship with her family and school authorities?
2. In what way did accounts in history books of the post-war reconstruction not correspond with her own childhood memories?

Understanding Reichel's Techniques

1. How did her interview with Herr Hagener provide insights into the pressures to which teachers were subjected and give her some of the answers she sought?
2. What features of this essay allow the reader to share the narrator's struggle to clarify an issue that is of great importance to her?

Arguing for an Interpretation

1. Does the way in which the narrator presents her quest suggest that she was doing it for her own self-aggrandizement or was she really sincere? Explain your answer.
2. You might rent the subtitled acclaimed German film *The Nasty Girl* (1990), which is based on Reichel's account, and compare it with her essay. How does each genre treat the same events differently?

MARK SALZMAN

Mark Salzman was born in 1959 and graduated Phi Beta Kappa, summa cum laude, from Yale in 1982 with a degree in Chinese language and literature. From 1982 to 1984, he lived in Chang-sha, Hunan, in the People's Republic of China, where he taught English at Hunan Medical College. There he studied with Pan Qingfu, one of China's greatest traditional boxers. Iron and Silk *(1986) recounts his adventures and provides a fascinating behind-the-scenes glimpse into the workings of Chinese society. "Lessons," drawn from this book, describes the extraordinary opportunity that studying martial arts with Pan Qingfu offered, along with the comic misunderstanding produced by their being from such different cultures. His recent work includes* The Soloist *(1994),* Lost in

Place: Growing Up Absurd in Suburbia *(1995), and* Lying Awake *(2000).*

Lessons

I was to meet Pan at the training hall four nights a week, to receive private instruction after the athletes finished their evening workout. Waving and wishing me good night, they politely filed out and closed the wooden doors, leaving Pan and me alone in the room. First he explained that I must start from scratch. He meant it, too, for beginning that night, and for many nights thereafter, I learned how to stand at attention. He stood inches away from me and screamed, "Stand straight!" then bored into me with his terrifying gaze. He insisted that I maintain eye contact for as long as he stood in front of me, and that I meet his gaze with one of equal intensity. After as long as a minute of this silent torture, he would shout "At ease!" and I could relax a bit, but not smile or take my eyes away from his. We repeated this exercise countless times, and I was expected to practice it four to six hours a day. At the time, I wondered what those staring contests had to do with wushu,[1] but I came to realize that everything he was to teach me later was really contained in those first few weeks when we stared at each other. His art drew strength from his eyes; this was his way of passing it on.

After several weeks I came to enjoy staring at him. I would break into a sweat and feel a kind of heat rushing up through the floor into my legs and up into my brain. He told me that when standing like that, I must at all times be prepared to duel, that at any moment he might attack, and I should be ready to defend myself. It exhilarated me to face off with him, to feel his power and taste the fear and anticipation of the blow. Days and weeks passed, but the blow did not come.

One night he broke the lesson off early, telling me that tonight was special. I followed him out of the training hall, and we bicycled a short distance to his apartment. He lived with his wife and two sons on the fifth floor of a large, anonymous cement building. Like all the urban housing going up in China today, the building was indistinguishable from its neighbors, mercilessly practical and depressing in appearance. Pan's apartment had three rooms and a small kitchen. A private bathroom and painted, as opposed to raw, cement walls in all the rooms identified it as the home of an important family. The only decoration in the apartment consisted of some silk banners, awards and photographs from Pan's years as the national wushu champion and from the set of *Shaolin Temple.* Pan's wife, a doctor, greeted me with all sorts of homemade snacks and sat me down at a table set for two. Pan sat across from me and poured two glasses of baijiu. He called to his sons, both in their teens, and they appeared from the bedroom instantly. They stood in complete silence until Pan asked them to greet me, which they did, very politely, but so softly I could barely hear them. They were handsome boys, and the elder, at about fourteen, was taller than me and had a moustache. I tried asking them questions to put them at ease, but they answered only by nodding. They apparently had no

[1]wushu, or kung fu.

idea how to behave toward something like me and did not want to make any mistakes in front of their father. Pan told them to say good night, and they, along with his wife, disappeared into the bedroom. Pan raised his glass and proposed that the evening begin.

He told me stories that made my hair stand on end, with such gusto that I thought the building would shake apart. When he came to the parts where he vanquished his enemies, he brought his terrible hand down on the table or against the wall with a crash, sending our snacks jumping out of their serving bowls. His imitations of cowards and bullies were so funny I could hardly breathe for laughing. He had me spellbound for three solid hours; then his wife came in to see if we needed any more food or baijiu. I took the opportunity to ask her if she had ever been afraid for her husband's safety when, for example, he went off alone to bust up a gang of hoodlums in Shenyang. She laughed and touched his right hand. "Sometimes I figured he'd be late for dinner." A look of tremendous satisfaction came over Pan's face, and he got up to use the bathroom. She sat down in his chair and looked at me. "Every day he receives tens of letters from all over China, all from people asking to become his student. Since he made the movie, it's been almost impossible for him to go out during the day." She refilled our cups, then looked at me again. "He has trained professionals for more than twenty-five years now, but in all that time he has accepted only one private student." After a long pause, she gestured at me with her chin. "You." Just then Pan came back into the room, returned to his seat and started a new story. This one was about a spear:

While still a young man training for the national wushu competition, 5
Pan overheard a debate among some of his fellow athletes about the credibility of an old story. The story described a famous warrior as being able to execute a thousand spear-thrusts without stopping to rest. Some of the athletes felt this to be impossible: after fifty, one's shoulders ache, and by one hundred the skin on the left hand, which guides the spear as the right hand thrusts, twists and returns it, begins to blister. Pan had argued that surely this particular warrior would not have been intimidated by aching shoulders and blisters, and soon a challenge was raised. The next day Pan went out into a field with a spear, and as the other athletes watched, executed one thousand and seven thrusts without stopping to rest. Certain details of the story as Pan told it—that the bones of his left hand were exposed, and so forth—might be called into question, but the number of thrusts I am sure is accurate, and the scar tissue on his left palm indicates that it was not easy for him.

One evening later in the year, when I felt discouraged with my progress in a form of Northern Shaolin boxing called "Changquan," or "Long Fist," I asked Pan if he thought I should discontinue the training. He frowned, the only time he ever seemed genuinely angry with me, and said quietly, "When I say I will do something, I do it, exactly as I said I would. In my whole life, I have never started something without finishing it. I said that in the time we have, I would make your wushu better than you could imagine, and I will. Your only responsibility to me is to practice and to learn. My responsibility to you is much greater! Every time you think your task is great, think how much greater mine is. Just keep this in mind: if you fail"—here he paused to make sure I understood—"I will lose face."

Though my responsibility to him was merely to practice and to learn, he had one request that he vigorously encouraged me to fulfill—to teach him English. I felt relieved to have something to offer him, so I quickly prepared some beginning materials and rode over to his house for the first lesson. When I got there, he had a tape recorder set up on a small table, along with a pile of oversized paper and a few felt-tip pens from a coloring set. He showed no interest at all in my books, but sat me down next to the recorder and pointed at the pile of paper. On each sheet he had written out in Chinese dozens of phrases, such as "We'll need a spotlight over there," "These mats aren't springy enough," and "Don't worry—it's just a shoulder dislocation." He asked me to write down the English translation next to each phrase, which took a little over two and a half hours. When I was finished, I asked him if he could read my handwriting, and he smiled, saying that he was sure my handwriting was fine. After a series of delicate questions, I determined that he was as yet unfamiliar with the alphabet, so I encouraged him to have a look at my beginning materials. "That's too slow for me," he said. He asked me to repeat each of the phrases I'd written down five times into the recorder, leaving enough time after each repetition for him to say it aloud after me. "The first time should be very slow—one word at a time, with a pause after each word so I can repeat it. The second time should be the same. The third time you should pause after every other word. The fourth time read it through slowly. The fifth time you can read it fast." I looked at the pile of phrase sheets, calculated how much time this would take, and asked if we could do half today and half tomorrow, as dinner was only three hours away. "Don't worry!" he said, beaming. "I've prepared some food for you here. Just tell me when you get hungry." He sat next to me, turned on the machine, then turned it off again. "How do you say, 'And now, Mark will teach me English'?" I told him how and he repeated it, at first slowly, then more quickly, twenty or twenty-one times. He turned the machine on. "And now, Mark will teach me English." I read the first phrase, five times as he had requested, and he pushed a little note across the table. "Better read it six times," it read, "and a little slower."

After several weeks during which we nearly exhausted the phrasal possibilities of our two languages, Pan announced that the time had come to do something new. "Now I want to learn routines." I didn't understand. "Routines?" "Yes. Everything, including language, is like wushu. First you learn the basic moves, or words, then you string them together into routines." He produced from his bedroom a huge sheet of paper made up of smaller pieces taped together. He wanted me to write a story on it. The story he had in mind was a famous Chinese folk tale, "How Yu Gong Moved the Mountain." The story tells of an old man who realized that, if he only had fields where a mountain stood instead, he would have enough arable land to support his family comfortably. So he went out to the mountain with a shovel and a bucket and started to take the mountain down. All his neighbors made fun of him, calling it an impossible task, but Yu Gong disagreed; it would just take a long time, and after several tens of generations had passed, the mountain would at last become a field and his family would live comfortably. Pan had me write this story in big letters, so that he could paste it up on his bedroom wall, listen to the tape I was to make and read along as he lay in bed.

Not only did I repeat this story into the tape recorder several dozen times—at first one word at a time, and so on—but Pan invited Bill, Bob and Marcy over for dinner one night and had them read it a few times for variety. After they had finished, Pan said that he would like to recite a few phrases for them to evaluate and correct. He chose some of his favorite sentences and repeated each seven or eight times without a pause. He belted them out with such fierce concentration we were all afraid to move lest it disturb him. At last he finished and looked at me, asking quietly if it was all right. I nodded and he seemed overcome with relief. He smiled, pointed at me and said to my friends, "I was very nervous just then. I didn't want him to lose face."

While Pan struggled to recite English routines from memory, he began 10
teaching me how to use traditional weapons. He would teach me a single move, then have me practice it in front of him until I could do it ten times in a row without a mistake. He always stood about five feet away from me, with his arms folded, grinding his teeth, and the only time he took his eyes off me was to blink. One night in the late spring I was having a particularly hard time learning a move with the staff. I was sweating heavily and my right hand was bleeding, so the staff had become slippery and hard to control. Several of the athletes stayed on after their workout to watch and to enjoy the breeze that sometimes passed through the training hall. Pan stopped me and indicated that I wasn't working hard enough. "Imagine," he said, "that you are participating in the national competition, and those athletes are your competitors. Look as if you know what you are doing! Frighten them with your strength and confidence." I mustered all the confidence I could, under the circumstances, and flung myself into the move. I lost control of the staff, and it whirled straight into my forehead. As if in a dream, the floor raised up several feet to support my behind, and I sat staring up at Pan while blood ran down across my nose and a fleshy knob grew between my eyebrows. The athletes sprang forward to help me up. They seemed nervous, never having had a foreigner knock himself out in their training hall before, but Pan, after asking if I felt all right, seemed positively inspired. "Sweating and bleeding. Good."

Every once in a while, Pan felt it necessary to give his students something to think about, to spur them on to greater efforts. During one morning workout two women practiced a combat routine, one armed with a spear, the other with a *dadao,* or halberd. The dadao stands about six feet high and consists of a broadsword attached to a thick wooden pole, with an angry-looking spike at the far end. It is heavy and difficult to wield even for a strong man, so it surprised me to see this young woman, who could not weigh more than one hundred pounds, using it so effectively. At one point in their battle the woman with the dadao swept it toward the other woman's feet, as if to cut them off, but the other woman jumped up in time to avoid the blow. The first woman, without letting the blade of the dadao stop, brought it around in another sweep, as if to cut the other woman in half at the waist. The other woman, without an instant to spare, bent straight from the hips so that the dadao slashed over her back and head, barely an inch away. This combination was to be repeated three times in rapid succession before moving on to the next exchange. The women practiced this move several times, none of which satisfied Pan. "Too slow, and the weapon is too far away from her. It should graze her back as it goes by." They tried again, but still Pan growled angrily. Suddenly he got up and took the dadao from the first woman. The entire training hall went silent and still. Without warming up at all, Pan ordered the woman with the spear to get ready, and to move fast when the time came. His body looked as though electricity had suddenly passed through it, and the huge blade flashed toward her. Once, twice the dadao flew beneath her feet, then swung around in a terrible arc and rode her back with flawless precision. The third time he added a little twist at the end, so that the blade grazed up her neck and sent a little decoration stuck in her pigtails flying across the room.

I had to sit down for a moment to ponder the difficulty of sending an object roughly the shape of an oversized shovel, only heavier, across a girl's back and through her pigtails, without guide ropes or even a safety helmet. Not long before, I had spoken with a former troupe member who, when practicing with this instrument, had suddenly found himself on his knees. The blade, unsharpened, had twirled a bit too close to him and passed through his Achilles' tendon without a sound. Pan handed the dadao back to the woman and walked over to me. "What if you had made a mistake?" I asked. "I never make mistakes," he said, without looking at me.

Analyzing the Text

1. What factors might explain why Pan chooses Mark to be the only private student (American or Chinese) he ever had?
2. What aspects of Chinese culture has Mark come to appreciate when he trades English lessons for martial arts instruction?

Understanding Salzman's Techniques

1. What is the relevance of the Chinese folktale "How Yu Gong Moved the Mountain" to Salzman's apprenticeship?
2. What similarities can you discover between Pan's approach to learning English and his methods of teaching Chinese martial arts?

Arguing for an Interpretation

1. What part does the concept of not "losing face" play in Chinese culture, and what evidence can you cite to show that Pan lives according to this value?
2. In your opinion, who learns more from the other, Pan from Mark or Mark from Pan, and why?

Short Fiction

JAMES JOYCE

James Joyce (1882–1941) was born in Dublin and received a rigorous classical education at Jesuit schools, including University College, Dublin. He left Ireland in 1902 and spent the rest of his life in Switzerland and France. Although he first studied medicine, he dropped out to write poetry, which was eventually published in 1907 as Chamber Music. *Joyce earned a living by teaching in a Berlitz Language School and developed a unique literary style first evident in* Dubliners, *a collec-*

tion of short stories (1914) that included "Araby," reprinted below. Many of these stories are drawn from Joyce's experiences, as is his first novel, A Portrait of the Artist as a Young Man *(1916).* Ulysses *(1922) is one of the most innovative literary works of the century and interweaves an account of a modern-day Dubliner, Leopold Bloom, with stories drawn from Homer's* Odyssey *and the ancient Greek world. Joyce's use of the stream-of-consciousness technique makes the reader feel part of the character's thoughts in a way traditional narrative usually does not. Joyce's last work was* Finnegan's Wake *(1939), a monumental perplexing work involving all of human history and language. In "Araby," we can see Joyce's careful preparation for the moment of revelation, or epiphany, through which his characters gain sudden insight into their own lives.*

Araby

North Richmond Street, being blind, was a quiet street except at the hour when the Christian Brothers' School set the boys free. An uninhabited house of two storeys stood at the blind end, detached from its neighbours in a square ground. The other houses of the street, conscious of decent lives within them, gazed at one another with brown imperturbable faces.

The former tenant of our house, a priest, had died in the back drawing-room. Air, musty from having been long enclosed, hung in all the rooms, and the waste room behind the kitchen was littered with old useless papers. Among these I found a few paper-covered books, the pages of which were curled and damp: *The Abbot,* by Walter Scott, *The Devout Communicant,* and *The Memoirs of Vidocq.* I liked the last best because its leaves were yellow. The wild garden behind the house contained a central apple-tree and a few straggling bushes under one of which I found the late tenant's rusty bicycle-pump. He had been a very charitable priest; in his will he had left all his money to institutions and the furniture of his house to his sister.

When the short days of winter came dusk fell before we had well eaten our dinners. When we met in the street the houses had grown sombre. The space of sky above us was the colour of ever-changing violet and towards it the lamps of the street lifted their feeble lanterns. The cold air stung us and we played till our bodies glowed. Our shouts echoed in the silent street. The career of our play brought us through the dark muddy lanes behind the houses where we ran the gauntlet of the rough tribes from the cottages, to the back doors of the dark dripping gardens where odours arose from the ashpits, to the dark odorous stables where a coachman smoothed and combed the horse or shook music from the buckled harness. When we returned to the street light from the kitchen windows had filled the areas. If my uncle was seen turning the corner we hid in the shadow until we had seen him safely housed. Or if Mangan's sister came out on the doorstep to call her brother in to his tea we watched her from our shadow peer up and down the street. We waited to see whether she would remain or go in and, if she remained, we left our shadow and walked up to Mangan's steps resignedly. She was waiting for us, her figure defined by the light from the half-opened door. Her brother always teased her before he obeyed and I stood by the railings looking at her. Her dress swung as she moved her body and the soft rope of her hair tossed from side to side.

Every morning I lay on the floor in the front parlour watching her door. The blind was pulled down to within an inch of the sash so that I could not be seen. When she came out on the doorstep my heart leaped. I ran to the hall, seized my books, and followed her. I kept her brown figure always in my eye and, when we came near the point at which our ways diverged, I quickened my pace and passed her. This happened morning after morning. I had never spoken to her, except for a few casual words, and yet her name was like a summons to all my foolish blood.

5 Her image accompanied me even in places the most hostile to romance. On Saturday evenings when my aunt went marketing I had to go to carry some of the parcels. We walked through the flaring streets, jostled by drunken men and bargaining women, amid the curses of labourers, the shrill litanies of shop-boys who stood on guard by the barrel of pigs' cheeks, the nasal chanting of street-singers, who sang a *come-all-you* about O'Donovan Rossa,[1] or a ballad about the troubles in our native land. These noises converged in a single sensation of life for me: I imagined that I bore my chalice safely through a throng of foes. Her name sprang to my lips at moments in strange prayers and praises which I myself did not understand. My eyes were often full of tears (I could not tell why) and at times a flood from my heart seemed to pour itself out into my bosom. I thought little of the future. I did not know whether I would ever speak to her or not or, if I spoke to her, how I could tell her of my confused adoration. But my body was like a harp and her words and gestures were like fingers running upon the wires.

One evening I went into the back drawing-room in which the priest had died. It was a dark rainy evening and there was no sound in the house. Through one of the broken panes I heard the rain impinge upon the earth, the fine incessant needles of water playing in the sodden beds. Some distant lamp or lighted window gleamed below me. I was thankful that I could see so little. All my senses seemed to desire to veil themselves and, feeling that I was about to slip from them, I pressed the palms of my hands together until they trembled, murmuring: *"O love! O love!"* many times.

At last she spoke to me. When she addressed the first words to me I was so confused that I did not know what to answer. She asked me was I going to *Araby.* I forgot whether I answered yes or no. It would be a splendid bazaar, she said she would love to go.

"And why can't you?" I asked.

While she spoke she turned a silver bracelet round and round her wrist. She could not go, she said, because there would be a retreat that week in her convent. Her brother and two other boys were fighting for their caps and I was alone at the railings. She held one of the spikes, bowing her head towards me. The light from the lamp opposite our door caught the white curve of her neck, lit up her hair that rested there and,

---

[1]Jeremiah O'Donovan (1831–1915), born in County Cork, was nicknamed "Dynamite Rossa" for espousing any and all means to achieve Irish independence.

falling, lit up the hand upon the railing. It fell over one side of her dress and caught the white border of a petticoat, just visible as she stood at ease.

"It's well for you," she said. 10

"If I go," I said, "I will bring you something."

What innumerable follies laid waste my waking and sleeping thoughts after that evening! I wished to annihilate the tedious intervening days. I chafed against the work of school. At night in my bedroom and by day in the classroom her image came between me and the page I strove to read. The syllables of the word *Araby* were called to me through the silence in which my soul luxuriated and cast an Eastern enchantment over me. I asked for leave to go to the bazaar on Saturday night. My aunt was surprised and hoped it was not some Freemason affair. I answered few questions in class. I watched my master's face pass from amiability to sternness; he hoped I was not beginning to idle. I could not call my wandering thoughts together. I had hardly any patience with the serious work of life which, now that it stood between me and my desire, seemed to me child's play, ugly monotonous child's play.

On Saturday morning I reminded my uncle that I wished to go to the bazaar in the evening. He was fussing at the hallstand, looking for the hat-brush, and answered me curtly:

"Yes, boy, I know."

As he was in the hall I could not go into the front parlour and lie at the 15
window. I left the house in bad humour and walked slowly towards the school. The air was pitilessly raw and already my heart misgave me.

When I came home to dinner my uncle had not yet been home. Still it was early. I sat staring at the clock for some time and, when its ticking began to irritate me, I left the room. I mounted the staircase and gained the upper part of the house. The high cold empty gloomy rooms liberated me and I went from room to room singing. From the front window I saw my companions playing below in the street. Their cries reached me weakened and indistinct and, leaning my forehead against the cool glass, I looked over at the dark house where she lived. I may have stood there for an hour, seeing nothing but the brown-clad figure cast by my imagination, touched discreetly by the lamplight at the curved neck, at the hand upon the railings and at the border below the dress.

When I came downstairs again I found Mrs. Mercer sitting at the fire. She was an old garrulous woman, a pawnbroker's widow, who collected used stamps for some pious purpose. I had to endure the gossip of the tea-table. The meal was prolonged beyond an hour and still my uncle did not come. Mrs. Mercer stood up to go: she was sorry she couldn't wait any longer, but it was after eight o'clock and she did not like to be out late, as the night air was bad for her. When she had gone I began to walk up and down the room, clenching my fists. My aunt said:

"I'm afraid you may put off your bazaar for this night of Our Lord."

At nine o'clock I heard my uncle's latchkey in the halldoor. I heard him talking to himself and heard the hallstand rocking when it had received the weight of his overcoat. I could interpret these signs. When he was midway through his dinner I asked him to give me the money to go to the bazaar. He had forgotten.

"The people are in bed and after their first sleep now," he said. 20

I did not smile. My aunt said to him energetically:

"Can't you give him the money and let him go? You've kept him late enough as it is."

My uncle said he was very sorry he had forgotten. He said he believed in the old saying: "All work and no play makes Jack a dull boy." He asked me where I was going and, when I had told him a second time he asked me did I know *The Arab's Farewell to his Steed*. When I left the kitchen he was about to recite the opening lines of the piece to my aunt.

I held a florin[2] tightly in my hand as I strode down Buckingham Street towards the station. The sight of the streets thronged with buyers and glaring with gas recalled to me the purpose of my journey. I took my seat in a third-class carriage of a deserted train. After an intolerable delay the train moved out of the station slowly. It crept onward among ruinous houses and over the twinkling river. At Westland Row Station a crowd of people pressed to the carriage doors; but the porters moved them back, saying that it was a special train for the bazaar. I remained alone in the bare carriage. In a few minutes the train drew up beside an improvised wooden platform. I passed out on to the road and saw by the lighted dial of a clock that it was ten minutes to ten. In front of me was a large building which displayed the magical name.

I could not find any sixpenny entrance and, fearing that the bazaar would be closed, I passed in quickly through a turnstile, handing a shilling to a weary-looking man. I found myself in a big hall girdled at half its height by a gallery. Nearly all the stalls were closed and the greater part of the hall was in darkness. I recognised a silence like that which pervades a church after a service. I walked into the centre of the bazaar timidly. A few people were gathered about the stalls which were still open. Before a curtain, over which the words *Café Chantant* were written in coloured lamps, two men were counting money on a salver. I listened to the fall of the coins.

Remembering with difficulty why I had come I went over to one of the stalls and examined porcelain vases and flowered tea-sets. At the door of the stall a young lady was talking and laughing with two young gentlemen. I remarked their English accents and listened vaguely to their conversation.

"O, I never said such a thing!"

"O, but you did!"

"O, but I didn't!"

"Didn't she say that?"

"Yes. I heard her."

"O, there's a . . . fib!"

Observing me the young lady came over and asked me did I wish to buy anything. The tone of her voice was not encouraging; she seemed to have spoken to me out of a sense of duty. I looked humbly at the great jars that stood like eastern guards at either side of the dark entrance to the stall and murmured:

"No, thank you."

The young lady changed the position of one of the vases and went back to the two young men. They began to talk of the same subject. Once or twice the young lady glanced at me over her shoulder.

I lingered before her stall, though I knew my stay was useless, to make my interest in her wares seem the more real. Then I turned away slowly and walked down the middle of the bazaar. I allowed the two pennies to fall against the sixpence in my pocket. I heard a voice call from one end of

[2] A silver coin worth two shillings.

the gallery that the light was out. The upper part of the hall was now completely dark.

Gazing up into the darkness I saw myself as a creature driven and derided by vanity; and my eyes burned with anguish and anger.

Analyzing the Text

1. How old would you say the boy is in the story, and why do you think Joyce has him live with an aunt and uncle instead of with parents?
2. How does the boy's late arrival at the bazaar and the conversation he overhears cause him to question the basis for his romantic fantasy?

Understanding Joyce's Techniques

1. How does the older narrator who tells the story about his experiences as a boy feel about them?
2. What role do images of darkness and blindness play in communicating the mood of the boy's fall from innocence?

Arguing for an Interpretation

1. What exactly is the boy infatuated with—romance, Mangan's sister, the chance to find excitement in a confining environment?
2. To what extent does the title and the bazaar to which it refers function symbolically? How does it convey a set of associations that raises it beyond the literal?

KATHERINE MANSFIELD

Katherine Mansfield (1888–1923) was born in New Zealand, the daughter of a wealthy banker who was knighted. A talented cellist, she first studied at the Royal Academy of Music in London before turning to writing short stories. In 1911 she became friends with the celebrated literary critic and editor, John Middleton Murray, whom she married in 1918. Her first collection was published under the title In a German Pension ***(1911). Mansfield's work is in large part autobiographical and her preferred themes are family relationships, young people at turning points in their lives, and the elderly. Her chronic invalidism endowed her with a great sensitivity and sympathy for the lonely and the rejected. Mansfield also had suffered the loss of her brother in World War I and increasingly returned to incidents in their childhood for material for her stories. She was part of the literary circle that included Leonard and Virginia Woolf and D. H. Lawrence, and was greatly influenced not only by Woolf, but also by Chekhov and James Joyce. She was diagnosed with tuberculosis and spent her last days at the Gurdjieff Institute for the Harmonic Development of Man at Fontainebleau, France, where she died at thirty-five. Her highly acclaimed collections include*** The Garden Party and Other Stories *(1922), in which the following story first appeared, and* The Dove's Nest and Other Stories *(1923).*

Her First Ball

Exactly when the ball began Leila would have found it hard to say. Perhaps her first real partner was the cab. It did not matter that she shared the cab with the Sheridan girls and their brother. She sat back in her own little corner of it, and the bolster on which her hand rested felt like the sleeve of an unknown young man's dress suit; and away they bowled, past waltzing lampposts and houses and fences and trees.

"Have you really never been to a ball before, Leila? But, my child, how too weird—" cried the Sheridan girls.

"Our nearest neighbor was fifteen miles," said Leila softly, gently opening and shutting her fan.

Oh, dear, how hard it was to be indifferent like the others! She tried not to smile too much; she tried not to care. But every single thing was so new and exciting . . . Meg's tuberoses, Jose's long loop of amber, Laura's little dark head, pushing above her white fur like a flower through snow. She would remember for ever. It even gave her a pang to see her cousin Laurie throw away the wisps of tissue paper he pulled from the fastenings of his new gloves. She would like to have kept those wisps as a keepsake, as a remembrance. Laurie leaned forward and put his hand on Laura's knee.

"Look here, darling," he said. "The third and the ninth as usual. Twig?" 5

Oh, how marvellous to have a brother! In her excitement Leila felt that if there had been time, if it hadn't been impossible, she couldn't have helped crying because she was an only child, and no brother had ever said "Twig?" to her; no sister would ever say, as Meg said to Jose that moment, "I've never known your hair go up more successfully than it has tonight!"

But, of course, there was no time. They were at the drill hall already; there were cabs in front of them and cabs behind. The road was bright on either side with moving fan-like lights, and on the pavement gay couples seemed to float through the air; little satin shoes chased each other like birds.

"Hold on to me, Leila; you'll get lost," said Laura.

"Come on, girls, let's make a dash for it," said Laurie.

Leila put two fingers on Laura's pink velvet cloak, and they were 10
somehow lifted past the big golden lantern, carried along the passage, and pushed into the little room marked "Ladies." Here the crowd was so great there was hardly space to take off their things; the noise was deafening. Two benches on either side were stacked high with wraps. Two old women in white aprons ran up and down tossing fresh armfuls. And everybody was pressing forward trying to get at the little dressing table and mirror at the far end.

A great quivering jet of gas lighted the ladies' room. It couldn't wait; it was dancing already. When the door opened again and there came a burst of tuning from the drill hall, it leaped almost to the ceiling.

Dark girls, fair girls were patting their hair, tying ribbons again, tucking handkerchiefs down the fronts of their bodices, smoothing marble-white gloves. And because they were all laughing it seemed to Leila that they were all lovely.

"Aren't there any invisible hairpins?" cried a voice. "How most extraordinary! I can't see a single invisible hairpin."

"Powder my back, there's a darling," cried some one else.

"But I must have a needle and cotton. I've torn simply miles and miles of the frill," wailed a third.

Then, "Pass them along, pass them along!" The straw basket of programs was tossed from arm to arm. Darling little pink-and-silver programs, with pink pencils and fluffy tassels. Leila's fingers shook as she took one out of the basket. She wanted to ask someone, "Am I meant to have one too?" but she had just time to read: "Waltz 3. *Two, Two in a Canoe.* Polka 4. *Making the Feathers Fly,*" when Meg cried, "Ready, Leila?" and they pressed their way through the crush in the passage towards the big double doors of the drill hall.

Dancing had not begun yet, but the band had stopped tuning, and the noise was so great it seemed that when it did begin to play it would never be heard. Leila, pressing close to Meg, looking over Meg's shoulder, felt that even the little quivering colored flags strung across the ceiling were talking. She quite forgot to be shy; she forgot how in the middle of dressing she had sat down on the bed with one shoe off and one shoe on and begged her mother to ring up her cousins and say she couldn't go after all. And the rush of longing she had had to be sitting on the veranda of their forsaken upcountry home, listening to the baby owls crying "More pork" in the moonlight, was changed to a rush of joy so sweet that it was hard to bear alone. She clutched her fan, and, gazing at the gleaming, golden floor, the azaleas, the lanterns, the stage at one end with its red carpet and gilt chairs and the band in a corner, she thought breathlessly, "How heavenly; how simply heavenly!"

All the girls stood grouped together at one side of the doors, the men at the other, and the chaperones in dark dresses, smiling rather foolishly, walked with little careful steps over the polished floor towards the stage.

"This is my little country cousin Leila. Be nice to her. Find her partners; she's under my wing," said Meg, going up to one girl after another.

Strange faces smiled at Leila—sweetly, vaguely. Strange voices answered, "Of course, my dear." But Leila felt the girls didn't really see her. They were looking towards the men. Why didn't the men begin? What were they waiting for? There they stood, smoothing their gloves, patting their glossy hair and smiling among themselves. Then, quite suddenly, as if they had only just made up their minds that that was what they had to do, the men came gliding over the parquet. There was a joyful flutter among the girls. A tall, fair man flew up to Meg, seized her program, scribbled something; Meg passed him on to Leila. "May I have the pleasure?" He ducked and smiled. There came a dark man wearing an eyeglass, then cousin Laurie with a friend, and Laura with a little freckled fellow whose tie was crooked. Then quite an old man—fat, with a big bald patch on his head—took her program and murmured, "Let me see, let me see!" And he was a long time comparing his program, which looked black with names, with hers. It seemed to give him so much trouble that Leila was ashamed. "Oh, please don't bother," she said eagerly. But instead of replying the fat man wrote something, glanced at her again. "Do I remember this bright little face?" he said softly. "Is it known to me of yore?" At that moment the band began playing; the fat man disappeared. He was tossed away on a great wave of music that came flying over the gleaming floor, breaking the groups up into couples, scattering them, sending them spinning. . . .

Leila had learned to dance at boarding school. Every Saturday afternoon the boarders were hurried off to a little corrugated iron mission hall where Miss Eccles (of London) held her "select" classes. But the difference between that dusty-smelling hall—with calico texts on the walls, the poor terrified little woman in a brown velvet toque with rabbit's ears thumping the cold piano, Miss Eccles poking the girls' feet with her long white wand—and this was so tremendous that Leila was sure if her partner didn't come and she had to listen to that marvelous music and to watch the others sliding, gliding over the golden floor, she would die at least, or faint, or lift her arms and fly out of one of those dark windows that showed the stars.

"Ours, I think—" Some one bowed, smiled, and offered her his arm; she hadn't to die after all. Some one's hand pressed her waist, and she floated away like a flower that is tossed into a pool.

"Quite a good floor, isn't it?" drawled a faint voice close to her ear.

"I think it's most beautifully slippery," said Leila.

"Pardon!" The faint voice sounded surprised. Leila said it again. And 25
there was a tiny pause before the voice echoed, "Oh, quite!" and she was swung round again.

He steered so beautifully. That was the great difference between dancing with girls and men, Leila decided. Girls banged into each other, and stamped on each other's feet; the girl who was gentleman always clutched you so.

The azaleas were separate flowers no longer; they were pink and white flags streaming by.

"Were you at the Bells' last week," the voice came again. It sounded tired. Leila wondered whether she ought to ask him if he would like to stop.

"No, this is my first dance," said she.

Her partner gave a little gasping laugh. "Oh, I say," he protested. 30

"Yes, it is really the first dance I've ever been to." Leila was most fervent. It was such a relief to be able to tell somebody. "You see, I've lived in the country all my life up until now. . . ."

At that moment the music stopped, and they went to sit on two chairs against the wall. Leila tucked her pink satin feet under and fanned herself, while she blissfully watched the other couples passing and disappearing through the swing doors.

"Enjoying yourself, Leila?" asked Jose, nodding her golden head.

Laura passed and gave her the faintest little wink; it made Leila wonder for a moment whether she was quite grown up after all. Certainly her partner did not say very much. He coughed, tucked his handkerchief away, pulled down his waistcoat, took a minute thread off his sleeve. But it didn't matter. Almost immediately the band started, and her second partner seemed to spring from the ceiling.

"Floor's not bad," said the new voice. Did one always begin with the 35
floor? And then, "Were you at the Neaves' on Tuesday?" And again Leila explained. Perhaps it was a little strange that her partners were not more interested. For it was thrilling. Her first ball! She was only at the beginning of everything. It seemed to her that she had never known what the night was like before. Up till now it had been dark, silent, beautiful very often—oh, yes—but mournful somehow. Solemn. And now it would never be like that again—it had opened dazzling bright.

"Care for an ice?" said her partner. And they went through the swing doors, down the passage, to the supper room. Her cheeks burned, she was fearfully thirsty. How sweet the ices looked on little glass plates, and how cold the frosted spoon was, iced too! And when they came back to the hall there was the fat man waiting for her by the door. It gave her quite a shock again to see how old he was; he ought to have been on the stage with the fathers and mothers. And when Leila compared him with her other partners he looked shabby. His waistcoat was creased, there was a button off his glove, his coat looked as if it was dusty with French chalk.

"Come along, little lady," said the fat man. He scarcely troubled to clasp her, and they moved away so gently, it was more like walking than dancing. But he said not a word about the floor. "Your first dance, isn't it?" he murmured.

"How *did* you know?"

"Ah," said the fat man, "that's what it is to be old!" He wheezed faintly as he steered her past an awkward couple. "You see, I've been doing this kind of thing for the last thirty years."

"Thirty years?" cried Leila. Twelve years before she was born! 40

"It hardly bears thinking about, does it?" said the fat man gloomily. Leila looked at his bald head, and she felt quite sorry for him.

"I think it's marvelous to be still going on," she said kindly.

"Kind little lady," said the fat man, and he pressed her a little closer, and hummed a bar of the waltz. "Of course," he said, "you can't hope to last anything like as long as that. No-o," said the fat man, "long before that you'll be sitting up there on the stage, looking on, in your nice black velvet. And these pretty arms will have turned into little short fat ones, and you'll beat time with such a different kind of fan—a black bony one." The fat man seemed to shudder. "And you'll smile away like the poor old dears up there, and point to your daughter, and tell the elderly lady next to you how some dreadful man tried to kiss her at the club ball. And your heart will ache, ache"—the fat man squeezed her closer still, as if he really was sorry for that poor heart—"because no one wants to kiss you now. And you'll say how unpleasant these polished floors are to walk on, how dangerous they are. Eh, Mademoiselle Twinkletoes?" said the fat man softly.

Leila gave a light little laugh, but she did not feel like laughing. Was it—could it all be true? It sounded terribly true. Was this first ball only the beginning of her last ball after all? At that the music seemed to change; it sounded sad, sad it rose upon a great sigh. Oh, how quickly things changed! Why didn't happiness last for ever? For ever wasn't a bit too long.

"I want to stop," she said in a breathless voice. The fat man led her to the door. 45

"No," she said, "I won't go outside. I won't sit down. I'll just stand here, thank you." She leaned against the wall, tapping with her foot, pulling up her gloves and trying to smile. But deep inside her a little girl threw her pinafore over her head and sobbed. Why had he spoiled it all?

"I say, you know," said the fat man, "you mustn't take me seriously, little lady."

"As if I should" said Leila, tossing her small dark head and sucking her underlip. . . .

Again the couples paraded. The swing doors opened and shut. Now new music was given out by the bandmaster. But Leila didn't want to dance any more. She wanted to be home, or sitting on the veranda listening to those baby owls. When she looked through the dark windows at the stars, they had long beams like wings. . . .

But presently a soft, melting, ravishing tune began, and a young man with curly hair bowed before her. She would have to dance, out of politeness, until she could find Meg. Very stiffly she walked into the middle; very haughtily she put her hand on his sleeve. But in one minute, in one turn, her feet glided, glided. The lights, the azaleas, the dresses, the pink faces, the velvet chairs, all became one beautiful flying wheel. And when her next partner bumped her into the fat man and he said, "Par*don*," she smiled at him more radiantly than ever. She didn't even recognize him again.

Analyzing the Text

1. How does the information Mansfield provides about Leila's background help the reader understand why her first ball means so much to her?
2. How does Leila react, over the course of the story, to her dancing partner's prognostications about the future that awaits her?

Understanding Mansfield's Techniques

1. How does Mansfield use certain images and references to the music being played to underscore Leila's change in mood?
2. Why is it significant that Leila's dancing partner is described as simply "the fat man" and appears on close inspection to be "shabby"?

Arguing for an Interpretation

1. In your opinion, what does the mysterious "fat man" symbolize: the disillusionment of growing up, a representation of her real future, or a killjoy? Explain your answer.
2. Does the fact that Leila represses what the "fat man" has to say make it more or less likely she will live out the future he has described for her?

HANAN AL-SHAYKH

Hanan al-Shaykh was born in 1945 in Lebanon and was raised in a traditional Shiite Moslem family. She began her studies at the American College for Girls in Cairo in 1963 and four years later returned to Beirut where she worked as a journalist and began writing short stories and novels. Originally written in Arabic, al-Shaykh's works have been published in Lebanon and have been acclaimed for her capacity to realistically create situations in which her protagonists, often women, gain a new perspective despite the cultural pressures forced upon them. Two of her novels, The Story of Zahra ***(1986) and*** Women of Sand and Myrrh ***(1989), have been translated into English as well as her short story collection*** I Sweep the Sun off Rooftops ***(1998). Her latest work is*** Only in London ***(2001). "The Persian Carpet," translated***

by Denys Johnson-Davies (1983) from Arabic Short Stories, *closely observes the behavior and emotions of a girl who is forced to realize that the circumstances leading to her parents getting divorced were very different from what she had believed as a child.*

The Persian Carpet

When Maryam had finished plaiting my hair into two pigtails, she put her finger to her mouth and licked it, then passed it over my eyebrows, moaning: "Ah, what eyebrows you have—they're all over the place!" She turned quickly to my sister and said: "Go and see if your father's still praying." Before I knew it my sister had returned and was whispering "He's still at it," and she stretched out her hands and raised them skywards in imitation of him. I didn't laugh as usual, nor did Maryam; instead, she took up the scarf from the chair, put it over her hair and tied it hurriedly at the neck. Then, opening the wardrobe carefully, she took out her handbag, placed it under her arm and stretched out her hands to us. I grasped one and my sister the other. We understood that we should, like her, proceed on tiptoe, holding our breath as we made our way out through the open front door. As we went down the steps, we turned back towards the door, then towards the window. Reaching the last step, we began to run, only stopping when the lane had disappeared out of sight and we had crossed the road and Maryam had stopped a taxi.

Our behaviour was induced by fear, for today we would be seeing my mother for the first time since her separation by divorce from my father. He had sworn he would not let her see us, for, only hours after the divorce, the news had spread that she was going to marry a man she had been in love with before her family had forced her into marrying my father.

My heart was pounding. This was not from fear or from running but was due to anxiety and a feeling of embarrassment about the meeting that lay ahead. Though in control of myself and my shyness, I knew that I would be incapable—however much I tried—of showing my emotions, even to my mother; I would be unable to throw myself into her arms and smother her with kisses and clasp her head as my sister would do with such spontaneity. I had thought long and hard about this ever since Maryam had whispered in my ear—and in my sister's—that my mother had come from the south and that we were to visit her secretly the following day. I began to imagine that I would make myself act exactly as my sister did, that I would stand behind her and imitate her blindly. Yet I know myself: I have committed myself to myself by heart. However much I tried to force myself, however much I thought in advance about what I should and shouldn't do, once I was actually faced by the situation and was standing looking down at the floor, my forehead puckered into an even deeper frown, I would find I had forgotten what I had resolved to do. Even then, though, I would not give up hope but would implore my mouth to break into a smile; it would none the less be to no avail.

When the taxi came to a stop at the entrance to a house, where two lions stood on columns of red sandstone, I was filled with delight and immediately forgot my apprehension. I was overcome with happiness at the thought that my mother was living in a house where two lions stood at the entrance. I heard my sister imitate the roar of a lion and I turned to her in envy. I saw her stretching up her hands in an attempt to clutch the lions. I thought to myself: She's always uncomplicated and jolly, her gaiety never leaves her, even at the most critical moments—and here she was, not a bit worried about this meeting.

5 But when my mother opened the door and I saw her, I found myself unable to wait and rushed forward in front of my sister and threw myself into her arms. I had closed my eyes and all the joints of my body had grown numb after having been unable to be at rest for so long. I took in the unchanged smell of her hair, and I discovered for the first time how much I had missed her and wished that she would come back and live with us, despite the tender care shown to us by my father and Maryam. I couldn't rid my mind of that smile of hers when my father agreed to divorce her, after the religious sheikh had intervened following her threats to pour kerosene over her body and set fire to herself if my father wouldn't divorce her. All my senses were numbed by that smell of her, so well preserved in my memory. I realized how much I had missed her, despite the fact that after she'd hurried off behind her brother to get into the car, having kissed us and started to cry, we had continued with the games we were playing in the lane outside our house. As night came, and for the first time in a long while we did not hear her squabbling with my father, peace and quiet descended upon the house—except that is for the weeping of Maryam, who was related to my father and had been living with us in the house ever since I was born.

Smiling, my mother moved me away from her so that she could hug and kiss my sister, and hug Maryam again, who had begun to cry. I heard my mother, who was in tears, say to her "Thank you," and she wiped her tears with her sleeve and looked me and my sister up and down, saying: "God keep them safe, how they've sprung up!" She put both arms round me, while my sister buried her head in my mother's waist, and we all began to laugh when we found that it was difficult for us to walk like that. Reaching the inner room, I was convinced her new husband was inside because my mother said, smiling: "Mahmoud loves you very much and he would like it if your father would give you to me so that you can live with us and become his children too." My sister laughed and answered: "Like that we'd have two fathers." I was still in a benumbed state, my hand placed over my mother's arm, proud at the way I was behaving, at having been able without any effort to be liberated from myself, from my shackled hands, from the prison of my shyness, as I recalled to mind the picture of my meeting with my mother, how I had spontaneously thrown myself at her, something I had thought wholly impossible, and my kissing her so hard I had closed my eyes.

Her husband was not there. As I stared down at the floor I froze. In confusion I looked at the Persian carpet spread on the floor, then gave my mother a long look. Not understanding the significance of my look, she turned and opened a cupboard from which she threw me an embroidered blouse, and moving across to a drawer in the dressing-table, she took out an ivory comb with red hearts painted on it and gave it to my sister. I stared down at the Persian carpet, trembling with burning rage. Again I looked at my mother and she interpreted my gaze as being one of tender longing, so she put her arms round me, saying: "You must come every other day, you must spend the whole of Friday at my place." I remained motionless, wishing that I could remove her arms from around me and sink my teeth into that white forearm. I wished that the moment of meeting could be undone and re-enacted, that she could again open the door and I could stand there—as I should have done—with my eyes staring down at the floor and my forehead in a frown.

The lines and colours of the Persian carpet were imprinted on my memory. I used to lie on it as I did my lessons; I'd be so close to it that I'd gaze at its pattern and find it looking like slices of red water-melon repeated over and over again. But when I sat down on the couch, I would see that each slice of melon had changed into a comb with thin teeth. The cluster of flowers surrounding its four sides were purple-coloured. At the beginning of summer my mother would put mothballs on it and on the other ordinary carpets and would roll them up and place them on top of the cupboard. The room would look stark and depressing until autumn came, when she would take them up to the roof and spread them out. She would gather up the mothballs, most of which had dissolved from the summer's heat and humidity, then, having brushed them with a small broom, she'd leave them there. In the evening she'd bring them down and lay them out where they belonged. I would be filled with happiness as their bright colours once again brought the room back to life. This particular carpet, though, had disappeared several months before my mother was divorced. It had been spread out on the roof in the sun and in the afternoon my mother had gone up to get it and hadn't found it. She had called my father and for the first time I had seen his face flushed with anger. When they came down from the roof, my mother was in a state of fury and bewilderment. She got in touch with the neighbours, all of whom swore they hadn't seen it. Suddenly my mother exclaimed: "Ilya!" Everyone stood speechless: not a word from my father or from my sister or from our neighbours Umm Fouad and Abu Salman. I found myself crying out: "Ilya? Don't say such a thing, it's not possible."

Ilya was an almost blind man who used to go round the houses of the quarter repairing cane chairs. When it came to our turn, I would see him, on my arrival back from school, seated on the stone bench outside the house with piles of straw in front of him and his red hair glinting in the sunlight. He would deftly take up the strands of straw and, like fishes, they'd slip through the mesh. I would watch him as he coiled them round with great dexterity, then bring them out again until he had formed a circle of straw for the seat of the chair, just like the one that had been there before. Everything was so even and precise: it was as though his hands were a machine and I would be amazed at the speed and nimbleness of his fingers. Sitting as he did with his head lowered, it looked as though he were using his eyes. I once doubted that he could see more than vague shapes in front of him, so I squatted down and looked into his rosy-red face and was able to see his half-closed eyes behind his glasses. They had in them a white line that pricked at my heart and sent me hurrying off to the kitchen, where I found a bag of dates on the table, and I heaped some on a plate and gave them to Ilya.

10 I continued to stare at the carpet as the picture of Ilya, red of face and hair, appeared to me. I was made aware of his hand as he walked up the stairs on his own; of him sitting on his chair, of his bargaining over the price for his work, of how he ate and knew that he had finished everything on the plate, of his drinking from the pitcher, with the water flowing

easily down his throat. Once at midday, having been taught by my father that before entering a Muslim house he should say "Allah" before knocking at the door and entering, as a warning to my mother in case she were unveiled, my mother rushed at him and asked him about the carpet. He made no reply, merely making a sort of sobbing noise. As he walked off, he almost bumped into the table and, for the first time, tripped. I went up to him and took him by the hand. He knew me by the touch of my hand, because he said to me in a half-whisper: "Never mind, child." Then he turned round to leave. As he bent over to put on his shoes, I thought I saw tears on his cheeks. My father didn't let him leave before saying to him: "Ilya, God will forgive you if you tell the truth." But Ilya walked off, steadying himself against the railings. He took an unusually long time as he felt his way down the stairs. Then he disappeared from sight and we never saw him again.

Analyzing the Text

1. What circumstances have made it necessary for the narrator and her sister to visit their mother in secret? What details suggest how much it means to her to see her mother again?
2. Why does the girl experience such a dramatic change in her feelings towards her mother?

Understanding al-Shaykh's Techniques

1. How does al-Shaykh's characterization of Ilya add to the pathos of the story?
2. In what way does the "Persian carpet" almost become another character in the story whose silent testimony carries great weight?

Arguing for an Interpretation

1. How does al-Shaykh's choice of a first person point of view make the story more dramatic than if it were related by an omniscient narrator?
2. Do you think the girl's rage is warranted, or is it a consequence of her extraordinary excitement at seeing her mother again and then being so disappointed?

JOYCE CAROL OATES

Joyce Carol Oates was born in Lockport, New York, in 1938 and raised on her grandparents' farm in Erie County, New York. She graduated from Syracuse University in 1960 and earned an M.A. at the University of Wisconsin. She has taught writing and literature at Princeton University since 1978. Oates received the O. Henry Special Award for Continuing Achievement and the National Book Award in 1970 for her novel them. *Oates is a prolific author who has published (on average) two books a year and has written countless essays and reviews. Her work covers the spectrum from novels and short fiction, poetry, plays, and criticism to nonfic-*

tion works on topics ranging from the poetry of D. H. Lawrence to boxing. "Where Are You Going, Where Have You Been?" first appeared in The Wheel of Love *(1965). This story was inspired by an article in* Life *magazine titled "The Pied Piper of Tucson," about a 23-year-old man who frequented teenage hangouts, picked up girls, took them for rides in his gold convertible, and ultimately was convicted for murdering three of them. Her recent works include* Faithless: Tales of Transgression *(2001),* Middle Age: A Romance *(2001),* Beasts *(2002), and* The Tatooed Girl, a novel *(2003).*

Where Are You Going, Where Have You Been?

For Bob Dylan[1]

Her name was Connie. She was fifteen and she had a quick nervous giggling habit of craning her neck to glance into mirrors, or checking other people's faces to make sure her own was all right. Her mother, who noticed everything and knew everything and who hadn't much reason any longer to look at her own face, always scolded Connie about it. "Stop gawking at yourself, who are you? You think you're so pretty?" she would say. Connie would raise her eyebrows at these familiar complaints and look right through her mother, into a shadowy vision of herself as she was right at that moment: she knew she was pretty and that was everything. Her mother had been pretty once too, if you could believe those old snapshots in the album, but now her looks were gone and that was why she was always after Connie.

"Why don't you keep your room clean like your sister? How've you got your hair fixed—what the hell stinks? Hair spray? You don't see your sister using that junk."

Her sister June was twenty-four and still lived at home. She was a secretary in the high school Connie attended, and if that wasn't bad enough—with her in the same building—she was so plain and chunky and steady that Connie had to hear her praised all the time by her mother and her mother's sisters. June did this, June did that, she saved money and helped clean the house and cooked and Connie couldn't do a thing, her mind was all filled with trashy daydreams. Their father was away at work most of the time and when he came home he wanted supper and he read the newspaper at supper and after supper he went to bed. He didn't bother talking much to them, but around his bent head Connie's mother kept picking at her until Connie wished her mother was dead and she herself was dead and it was all over. "She makes me want to throw up sometimes," she complained to her friends. She had a high, breathless, amused voice which made everything she said a little forced, whether it was sincere or not.

[1]Bob Dylan (1941–) is a composer, author and singer who created and popularized folk rock during the 1960s.

There was one good thing: June went places with girl friends of hers, girls who were just as plain and steady as she, and so when Connie wanted to do that her mother had no objections. The father of Connie's best girl friend drove the girls the three miles to town and left them off at a shopping plaza, so that they could walk through the stores or go to a movie, and when he came to pick them up again at eleven he never bothered to ask what they had done.

5 They must have been familiar sights, walking around that shopping plaza in their shorts and flat ballerina slippers that always scuffed the sidewalk, with charm bracelets jingling on their thin wrists; they would lean together to whisper and laugh secretly if someone passed by who amused or interested them. Connie had long dark blond hair that drew anyone's eye to it, and she wore part of it pulled up on her head and puffed out and the rest of it she let fall down her back. She wore a pullover jersey blouse that looked one way when she was at home and another way when she was away from home. Everything about her had two sides to it, one for home and one for anywhere that was not home: her walk that could be childlike and bobbing, or languid enough to make anyone think she was hearing music in her head, her mouth which was pale and smirking most of the time, but bright and pink on these evenings out, her laugh which was cynical and drawling at home—"Ha, ha, very funny"—but high-pitched and nervous anywhere else, like the jingling of the charms on her bracelet.

Sometimes they did go shopping or to a movie, but sometimes they went across the highway, ducking fast across the busy road, to a drive-in restaurant where older kids hung out. The restaurant was shaped like a big bottle, though squatter than a real bottle, and on its cap was a revolving figure of a grinning boy who held a hamburger aloft. One night in midsummer they ran across, breathless with daring, and right away someone leaned out a car window and invited them over, but it was just a boy from high school they didn't like. It made them feel good to be able to ignore him. They went up through the maze of parked and cruising cars to the bright-lit, fly-infested restaurant, their faces pleased and expectant as if they were entering a sacred building that loomed out of the night to give them what haven and what blessing they yearned for. They sat at the counter and crossed their legs at the ankles, their thin shoulders rigid with excitement and listened to the music that made everything so good: the music was always in the background like music at a church service, it was something to depend upon.

A boy named Eddie came in to talk with them. He sat backwards on his stool, turning himself jerkily around in semi-circles and then stopping and turning again, and after a while he asked Connie if she would like something to eat. She said she did and so she tapped her friend's arm on her way out—her friend pulled her face up into a brave droll look—and Connie said she would meet her at eleven, across the way. "I just hate to leave her like that," Connie said earnestly, but the boy said that she wouldn't be alone for long. So they went out to his car and on the way Connie couldn't help but let her eyes wander over the windshields and faces all around her, her face gleaming with the joy that had nothing to do with Eddie or even this place; it might have been the music. She drew her shoulders up and sucked in her breath with the pure pleasure of being alive, and just at that moment she happened to glance at a face just a few feet from hers. It was a boy with shaggy black hair, in a convertible jalopy painted gold. He stared at her and then his lips widened into a grin. Connie slit her eyes at him and turned away, but she couldn't help glancing back and there he was still watching her. He wagged a finger and laughed and said, "Gonna get you, baby," and Connie turned away again without Eddie noticing anything.

She spent three hours with him, at the restaurant where they ate hamburgers and drank Cokes in wax cups that were always sweating, and then down an alley a mile or so away, and when he left her off at five to eleven only the movie house was still open at the plaza. Her girl friend was there, talking with a boy. When Connie came up the two girls smiled at each other and Connie said, "How was the movie?" and the girl said, "*You* should know." They rode off with the girl's father, sleepy and pleased, and Connie couldn't help but look at the darkened shopping plaza with its big empty parking lot and its signs that were faded and ghostly now, and over at the drive-in restaurant where cars were still circling tirelessly. She couldn't hear the music at this distance.

Next morning June asked her how the movie was and Connie said, "So-so."

She and that girl and occasionally another girl went out several times a 10
week that way, and the rest of the time Connie spent around the house—it was summer vacation—getting in her mother's way and thinking, dreaming, about the boys she met. But all the boys fell back and dissolved into a single face that was not even a face, but an idea, a feeling, mixed up with the urgent insistent pounding of the music and the humid night air of July. Connie's mother kept dragging her back to the daylight by finding things for her to do or saying suddenly, "What's this about the Pettinger girl?"

And Connie would say nervously, "Oh, her. That dope." She always drew thick clear lines between herself and such girls, and her mother was simple and kindly enough to believe her. Her mother was so simple, Connie thought, that it was maybe cruel to fool her so much. Her mother went scuffling around the house in old bedroom slippers and complained over the telephone to one sister about the other, then the other called up and the two of them complained about the third one. If June's name was mentioned her mother's tone was approving, and if Connie's name was mentioned it was disapproving. This did not really mean she disliked Connie and actually Connie thought that her mother preferred her to June because she was prettier, but the two of them kept up a pretense of exasperation, a sense that they were tugging and struggling over something of little value to either of them. Sometimes, over coffee, they were almost friends, but something would come up—some vexation that was like a fly buzzing suddenly around their heads—and their faces went hard with contempt.

One Sunday Connie got up at eleven—none of them bothered with church—and washed her hair so that it could dry all day long, in the sun. Her parents and sister were going to a barbecue at an aunt's house and Connie said no, she wasn't interested, rolling her eyes, to let mother know just what she thought of it. "Stay home alone then," her mother said sharply. Connie sat out back in a lawn chair and watched them drive away, her father quiet and bald, hunched around so that he could back the car out, her mother with a look that was still angry and not at all softened through the windshield, and in the back seat poor old June all dressed up as if she didn't know what a barbecue was, with all the running yelling kids and the flies. Connie sat with her eyes closed in the sun, dreaming and dazed with the warmth about her as if this were a kind of love, the caresses of love, and her mind slipped over onto thoughts of the boy she had been with the night before and how nice he had been, how sweet it always was, not the way someone like June would suppose but sweet, gentle, the way it was in movies and promised in songs; and when she opened her eyes she hardly knew where she was, the back yard ran off into weeds and a fenceline of trees and behind it the sky was perfectly blue and still. The asbestos "ranch house" that was now three years old startled her—it looked small. She shook her head as if to get awake.

It was too hot. She went inside the house and turned on the radio to drown out the quiet. She sat on the edge of her bed, barefoot, and listened for an hour and a half to a program called XYZ Sunday Jamboree, record after record of hard, fast, shrieking songs she sang along with, interspersed by exclamations from "Bobby King": "An' look here you girls at Napoleon's—Son and Charley want you to pay real close attention to this song coming up!"

And Connie paid close attention herself, bathed in a glow of slow-pulsed joy that seemed to rise mysteriously out of the music itself and lay languidly about the airless little room, breathed in and breathed out with each gentle rise and fall of her chest.

After a while she heard a car coming up the drive. She sat up at once, 15
startled, because it couldn't be her father so soon. The gravel kept crunching all the way in from the road—the driveway was long—and Connie ran to the window. It was a car she didn't know. It was an open jalopy, painted a bright gold that caught the sun opaquely. Her heart began to pound and her fingers snatched at her hair, checking it, and she whispered "Christ. Christ," wondering how bad she looked. The car came to a stop at the side door and the horn sounded four short taps as if this were a signal Connie knew.

She went into the kitchen and approaching the door slowly, then hung out the screen door, her bare toes curling down off the step. There were two boys in the car and now she recognized the driver: he had shaggy, shabby black hair that looked crazy as a wig and he was grinning at her.

"I ain't late, am I?" he said.

"Who the hell do you think you are?" Connie said.

"Toldja I'd be out, didn't I?"

"I don't even know who you are." 20

She spoke sullenly, careful to show no interest or pleasure, and he spoke in a fast bright monotone. Connie looked past him to the other boy, taking her time. He had fair brown hair, with a lock that fell onto his forehead. His sideburns gave him a fierce, embarrassed look, but so far he hadn't even bothered to glance at her. Both boys wore sunglasses. The driver's glasses were metallic and mirrored everything in miniature.

"You wanta come for a ride?" he said.

Connie smirked and let her hair fall loose over one shoulder.

"Don'tcha like my car? New paint job," he said. "Hey."

"What?" 25

"You're cute."

She pretended to fidget, chasing flies away from the door.

"Don'tcha believe me, or what?" he said.

"Look, I don't even know who you are," Connie said in disgust.

"Hey, Ellie's got a radio, see. Mine's broke down." He lifted his friend's 30 arm and showed her the little transistor the boy was holding, and now Connie began to hear the music. It was the same program that was playing inside the house.

"Bobby King?" she said.

"I listen to him all the time. I think he's great."

"He's kind of great," Connie said reluctantly.

"Listen, that guy's *great*. He knows where the action is."

Connie blushed a little, because the glasses made it impossible for her 35 to see just what this boy was looking at. She couldn't decide if she liked him or if he was just a jerk, and so she dawdled in the doorway and wouldn't come down or go back inside. She said, "What's all that stuff painted on your car?"

"Can'tcha read it?" He opened the door very carefully, as if he was afraid it might fall off. He slid out just as carefully, planting his feet firmly on the ground, the tiny metallic world in his glasses slowing down like gelatine hardening and in the midst of it Connie's bright green blouse. "This here is my name, to begin with," he said. ARNOLD FRIEND was written in tar-like black letters on the side, with a drawing of a round grinning face that reminded Connie of a pumpkin, except it wore sunglasses. "I wanta introduce myself, I'm Arnold Friend and that's my real name and I'm gonna be your friend, honey, and inside the car's Ellie Oscar, he's kinda shy." Ellie brought his transistor up to his shoulder and balanced it there. "Now these numbers are a secret code, honey," Arnold Friend explained. He read off the numbers 33, 19, 17 and raised his eyebrows at her to see what she thought of that, but she didn't think much of it. The left rear fender had been smashed and around it was written, on the gleaming gold background: DONE BY CRAZY WOMAN DRIVER. Connie had to laugh at that. Arnold Friend was pleased at her laughter and looked up at her. "Around the other side's a lot more—you wanta come and see them?"

"No."

"Why not?"

"Why should I?"

"Don'tcha wanta see what's on the car? Don'tcha wanta go for a ride?" 40

"I don't know."

"Why not?"

"I got things to do."

"Like what?"

"Things." 45

He laughed as if she had said something funny. He slapped his thighs. He was standing in a strange way, leaning back against the car as if he were balancing himself. He wasn't tall, only an inch or so taller than she would be if she came down to him. Connie liked the way he was dressed, which was the way all of them dressed: tight faded jeans stuffed into black, scuffed boots, a belt that pulled his waist in and showed how lean he was, and a white pull-over shirt that was a little soiled and showed the hard small muscles of his arms and shoulders. He looked as if he probably did hard work, lifting and carrying things. Even his neck looked muscular. And his face was a familiar face, somehow: the jaw and chin and cheeks slightly darkened, because he hadn't shaved for a day or two, and the nose long and hawk-like, sniffing as if she were a treat he was going to gobble up and it was all a joke.

"Connie, you ain't telling the truth. This is your day set aside for a ride with me and you know it," he said, still laughing. The way he straightened and recovered from his fit of laughing showed that it had been all fake.

"How do you know what my name is?" she said suspiciously.

"It's Connie."

50 "Maybe and maybe not."

"I know my Connie," he said, wagging his finger. Now she remembered him even better, back at the restaurant, and her cheeks warmed at the thought of how she sucked in her breath just at the moment she passed him—how she must have looked to him. And he had remembered her. "Ellie and I come out here especially for you," he said. "Ellie can sit in back. How about it?"

"Where?"

"Where what?"

"Where're we going?"

55 He looked at her. He took off the sunglasses and she saw how pale the skin around his eyes was, like holes that were not in shadow but instead in light. His eyes were like chips of broken glass that catch the light in an amiable way. He smiled. It was as if the idea of going for a ride somewhere, to some place, was a new idea to him.

"Just for a ride, Connie sweetheart."

"I never said my name was Connie," she said.

"But I know what it is. I know your name and all about you, lots of things," Arnold Friend said. He had not moved yet but stood still leaning back against the side of his jalopy. "I took a special interest in you, such a pretty girl, and found out all about you like I know your parents and sister are gone somewheres and I know where and how long they're going to be gone, and I know who you were with last night, and your best friend's name is Betty. Right?"

He spoke in a simple lilting voice, exactly as if he were reciting the words to a song. His smile assured her that everything was fine. In the car Ellie turned up the volume on his radio and did not bother to look around at them.

60 "Ellie can sit in the back seat," Arnold Friend said. He indicated his friend with a casual jerk of his chin, as if Ellie did not count and she could not bother with him.

"How'd you find out all that stuff?" Connie said.

"Listen? Betty Schultz and Tony Fitch and Jimmy Pettinger and Nancy Pettinger," he said, in a chant. "Raymond Stanley and Bob Hutter—"

"Do you know all those kids?"

"I know everybody."

65 "Look, you're kidding. You're not from around here."

"Sure."

"But—how come we never saw you before?"

"Sure you saw me before," he said. He looked down at his boots, as if he were a little offended. "You just don't remember."

"I guess I'd remember you," Connie said.

70 "Yeah?" He looked up at this, beaming. He was pleased. He began to mark time with the music from Ellie's radio, tapping his fists lightly to-

gether. Connie looked away from his smile to the car, which was painted so bright it almost hurt her eyes to look at it. She looked at that name, ARNOLD FRIEND. And up at the front fender was an expression that was familiar—MAN THE FLYING SAUCERS. It was an expression kids had used the year before, but didn't use this year. She looked at it for a while as if the words meant something to her that she did not yet know.

"What're you thinking about? Huh?" Arnold Friend demanded. "Not worried about your hair blowing around in the car, are you?"

"No."

"Think I maybe can't drive good?"

"How do I know?"

75 "You're a hard girl to handle. How come?" he said. "Don't you know I'm your friend? Didn't you see me put my sign in the air when you walked by?"

"What sign?"

"My sign." And he drew an X in the air, leaning out toward her. They were maybe ten feet apart. After his hand fell back to his side the X was still in the air, almost visible. Connie let the screen door close and stood perfectly still inside it, listening to the music from her radio and the boy's blend together. She stared at Arnold Friend. He stood there so stiffly relaxed, pretending to be relaxed, with one hand idly on the door handle as if he were keeping himself up that way and had no intention of ever moving again. She recognized most things about him, the tight jeans that showed his thighs and buttocks and the greasy leather boots and the tight shirt, and even that slippery friendly smile of his, that sleepy dreamy smile that all the boys used to get across ideas they didn't want to put into words. She recognized all this and also the singsong way he talked, slightly mocking, kidding, but serious and a little melancholy, and she recognized the way he tapped one fist against the other in homage to the perpetual music behind him. But all these things did not come together.

She said suddenly, "Hey, how old are you?"

His smile faded. She could see then that he wasn't a kid, he was much older—thirty, maybe more. At this knowledge her heart began to pound faster.

80 "That's a crazy thing to ask. Can'tcha see I'm your own age?"

"Like hell you are."

"Or maybe a coupla years older, I'm eighteen."

"Eighteen?" she said doubtfully.

He grinned to reassure her and lines appeared at the corners of his mouth. His teeth were big and white. He grinned so broadly his eyes became slits and she saw how thick the lashes were, thick and black as if painted with a black tar-like material. Then he seemed to become embarrassed, abruptly, and looked over his shoulder at Ellie. "*Him,* he's crazy," he said. "Ain't he a riot, he's a nut, a real character." Ellie was still listening to the music. His sunglasses told nothing about what he was thinking. He wore a bright orange shirt unbuttoned halfway to show his chest, which was a pale, bluish chest and not muscular like Arnold Friend's. His shirt collar was turned up all around and the very tips of the collar pointed out past his chin as if they were protecting him. He was pressing the transistor radio up against his ear and sat there in a kind of daze, right in the sun.

85 "He's kinda strange," Connie said.

"Hey, she says you're kinda strange! Kinda strange!" Arnold Friend cried. He pounded on the car to get Ellie's attention. Ellie turned for the first time and Connie saw with shock that he wasn't a kid either—he had a fair, hairless face, cheeks reddened slightly as if the veins grew too close to the surface of his skin, the face of a forty-year-old baby. Connie felt a wave of dizziness rise in her at this sight and she stared at him as if waiting for something to change the shock of the moment, make it all right again. Ellie's lips kept shaping words, mumbling along with the words blasting his ear.

"Maybe you two better go away," Connie said faintly.

"What? How come?" Arnold Friend cried. "We come out here to take you for a ride. It's Sunday." He had the voice of the man on the radio now. It was the same voice, Connie thought. "Don'tcha know it's Sunday all day and honey, no matter who you were with last night today you're with Arnold Friend and don't you forget it!—Maybe you better step out here," he said, and this last was in a different voice. It was a little flatter, as if the heat was finally getting to him.

"No. I got things to do."

"Hey." 90

"You two better leave."

"We ain't leaving until you come with us."

"Like hell I am—"

"Connie, don't fool around with me. I mean, I mean, don't fool *around*," he said, shaking his head. He laughed incredulously. He placed his sunglasses on top of his head, carefully, as if he were indeed wearing a wig, and brought the stems down behind his ears. Connie stared at him, another wave of dizziness and fear rising in her so that for a moment he wasn't even in focus but was just a blur, standing there against his gold car, and she had the idea that he had driven up the driveway all right but had come from nowhere before that and belonged nowhere and that everything about him and even the music that was so familiar to her was only half real.

"If my father comes and sees you—" 95

"He ain't coming. He's at a barbecue."

"How do you know that?"

"Aunt Tillie's. Right now they're—uh—they're drinking. Sitting around," he said vaguely, squinting as if he were staring all the way to town and over to Aunt Tillie's back yard. Then the vision seemed to clear and he nodded energetically. "Yeah. Sitting around. There's your sister in a blue dress, huh? And high heels, the poor sad bitch—nothing like you, sweetheart! And your mother's helping some fat woman with the corn, they're cleaning the corn—husking the corn—"

"What fat woman?" Connie cried.

"How do I know what fat woman. I don't know every goddamn fat 100
woman in the world!" Arnold Friend laughed.

"Oh, that's Mrs. Hornby. . . . Who invited her?" Connie said. She felt a little light-headed. Her breath was coming quickly.

"She's too fat. I don't like them fat. I like them the way you are, honey," he said, smiling sleepily at her. They stared at each other for a while, through the screen door. He said softly, "Now what you're going to do is this: you're going to come out that door. You're going to sit up front with me and Ellie's going to sit in the back, the hell with Ellie, right? This isn't Ellie's date. You're my date. I'm your lover, honey."

"What? You're crazy—"

"Yes, I'm your lover. You don't know what that is but you will," he said. "I know that too. I know all about you. But look: it's real nice and you couldn't ask for nobody better than me, or more polite. I always keep my word. I'll tell you how it is, I'm always nice at first, the first time. I'll hold you so tight you won't think you have to try to get away or pretend anything because you'll know you can't. And I'll come inside you where it's all secret and you'll give in to me and you'll love me—"

"Shut up! You're crazy!" Connie said. She backed away from the door. 105
She put her hands against her ears as if she'd heard something terrible, something not meant for her. "People don't talk like that, you're crazy," she muttered. Her heart was almost too big now for her chest and its pumping made sweat break out all over her. She looked out to see Arnold Friend pause and then take a step toward the porch lurching. He almost fell. But, like a clever drunken man, he managed to catch his balance. He wobbled in his high boots and grabbed hold of one of the porch posts.

"Honey?" he said. "You still listening?"

"Get the hell out of here!"

"Be nice, honey. Listen."

"I'm going to call the police—"

He wobbled again and out of the side of his mouth came a fast spat 110
curse, an aside not meant for her to hear. But even this "Christ!" sounded forced. Then he began to smile again. She watched this smile come, awkward as if he were smiling from inside a mask. His whole face was a mask, she thought wildly, tanned down onto his throat but then running out as if he had plastered make-up on his face but had forgotten about his throat.

"Honey—? Listen, here's how it is. I always tell the truth and I promise you this: I ain't coming in that house after you."

"You better not! I'm going to call the police if you—if you don't—"

"Honey," he said, talking right through her voice, "honey, I'm not coming in there but you are coming out here. You know why?"

She was panting. The kitchen looked like a place she had never seen before, some room she had run inside but which wasn't good enough, wasn't going to help her. The kitchen window had never had a curtain, after three years, and there were dishes in the sink for her to do—probably—and if you ran your hand across the table you'd probably feel something sticky there.

"You listening, honey? Hey?" 115

"—going to call the police—"

"Soon as you touch the phone I don't need to keep my promise and can come inside. You won't want that."

She rushed forward and tried to lock the door. Her fingers were shaking. "But why lock it," Arnold Friend said gently, talking right into her face. "It's just a screen door. It's just nothing." One of his boots was at a strange angle, as if his foot wasn't in it. It pointed out to the left, bent at the ankle. "I mean, anybody can break through a screen door and glass and wood and iron or anything else if he needs to, anybody at all and specially Arnold Friend. If the place got lit up with a fire, honey, you'd come running out into my arms, right into my arms and safe at home—like you knew I was your lover and'd stopped fooling around, I don't mind a nice shy girl but I don't like no fooling around." Part of those words were spoken with a slightly rhythmic lilt, and Connie somehow recognized them—the echo of a song from last year, about a girl rushing into her boy friend's arms and coming home again—

Connie stood barefoot on the linoleum floor, staring at him. "What do you want?" she whispered.

"I want you," he said. 120

"What?"

"Seen you that night and thought, that's the one, yes sir. I never needed to look any more."

"But my father's coming back. He's coming to get me. I had to wash my hair first—" She spoke in a dry, rapid voice, hardly raising it for him to hear.

"No, your daddy is not coming and yes, you had to wash your hair and you washed it for me. It's nice and shining and all for me, I thank you, sweetheart," he said, with a mock bow, but again he almost lost his balance. He had to bend and adjust his boots. Evidently his feet did not go all the way down; the boots must have been stuffed with something so that he would seem taller. Connie stared out at him and behind him Ellie in the car, who seemed to be looking off toward Connie's right, into nothing. This Ellie said, pulling the words out of the air one after another as if he were just discovering them, "You want me to pull out the phone?"

"Shut your mouth and keep it shut," Arnold Friend said, his face red 125
from bending over or maybe from embarrassment because Connie had seen his boots. "This ain't none of your business."

"What—what are you doing? What do you want?" Connie said. "If I call the police they'll get you, they'll arrest you—"

"Promise was not to come in unless you touch that phone, and I'll keep that promise," he said. He resumed his erect position and tried to force his shoulders back. He sounded like a hero in a movie, declaring something important. He spoke too loudly and it was as if he were speaking to someone behind Connie. "I ain't made plans for coming in that house where I don't belong but just for you to come out to me, the way you should. Don't you know who I am?"

"You're crazy," she whispered. She backed away from the door but did not want to go into another part of the house, as if this would give him permission to come through the door. "What do you. . . . You're crazy, you. . . ."

"Huh? What're you saying, honey?"

Her eyes darted everywhere in the kitchen. She could not remember 130
what it was, this room.

"This is how it is, honey: you come out and we'll drive away, have a nice ride. But if you don't come out we're gonna wait till your people come home and then they're all going to get it."

"You want that telephone pulled out?" Ellie said. He held the radio away from his ear and grimaced, as if without the radio the air was too much for him.

"I toldja shut up, Ellie." Arnold Friend said, "You're deaf, get a hearing aid, right? Fix yourself up. This little girl's no trouble and's gonna be nice to me, so Ellie keep to yourself, this ain't your date—right? Don't hem in on me. Don't hog. Don't crush. Don't bird dog. Don't trail me," he said in a rapid meaningless voice, as if he were running through all the expressions he'd learned but was no longer sure which one of them was in style, then rushing on to new ones, making them up with his eyes closed, "Don't crawl under my fence, don't squeeze in my chipmunk hole, don't sniff my glue, suck my popsicle, keep your own greasy fingers on yourself!" He shaded his eyes and peered in at Connie, who was backed against the kitchen table. "Don't mind him, honey, he's just a creep. He's a dope. Right? I'm the boy for you and like I said you come out here nice like a lady and give me your hand, and nobody else gets hurt, I mean, your nice old bald-headed daddy and your mummy and your sister in her high heels. Because listen: why bring them in this?"

"Leave me alone," Connie whispered.

"Hey, you know that old woman down the road, the one with the 135
chickens and stuff—you know her?"

"She's dead!"

"Dead? What? You know her?" Arnold Friend said.

"She's dead—"

"Don't you like her?"

"She's dead—she's—she isn't here any more—" 140

"But don't you like her, I mean, you got something against her? Some grudge or something?" Then his voice dipped as if he were conscious of rudeness. He touched the sunglasses on top of his head as if to make sure they were still there. "Now you be a good girl."

"What are you going to do?"

"Just two things, or maybe three," Arnold Friend said. "But I promise it won't last long and you'll like me that way you get to like people you're close to. You will. It's all over for you here, so come on out. You don't want your people in any trouble, do you?"

She turned and bumped against a chair or something, hurting her leg, but she ran into the back room and picked up the telephone. Something roared in her ear, a tiny roaring, and she was so sick with fear that she could do nothing but listen to it—the telephone was clammy and very heavy and her fingers groped down to the dial but were too weak to touch it. She began to scream into the phone, into the roaring. She cried out, she cried for her mother, she felt her breath start jerking back and forth in her lungs as if it were something Arnold Friend were stabbing her with again and again with no tenderness. A noisy sorrowful wailing rose all about her and she was locked inside it the way she was locked inside this house.

After a while she could hear again. She was sitting on the floor, with 145
her wet back against the wall.

Arnold Friend was saying from the door, "That's a good girl. Put the phone back."

She kicked the phone away from her.

"No, honey. Pick it up. Put it back right."

She picked it up and put it back. The dial tone stopped.

"That's a good girl. Now you come outside." 150

She was hollow with what had been fear, but what was now just an emptiness. All that screaming had blasted it out of her. She sat, one leg cramped under her, and deep inside her brain was something like a pinpoint of light that kept going and would not let her relax. She thought, I'm not going to see my mother again. She thought, I'm not going to sleep in my bed again. Her bright green blouse was all wet.

Arnold Friend said, in a gentle-loud voice that was like a stage voice. "The place where you came from ain't there any more, and where you had in mind to go is cancelled out. This place you are now—inside your daddy's house—is nothing but a cardboard box I can knock down any time. You know that and always did know it. You hear me?"

She thought, I have got to think. I have to know what to do.

"We'll go out to a nice field, out in the country here where it smells so nice and it's sunny," Arnold Friend said. "I'll have my arms tight around you so you won't need to try to get away and I'll show you what love is like, what it does. The hell with this house! It looks solid all right," he said. He ran a fingernail down the screen and the noise did not make Connie shiver, as it would have the day before. "Now put your hand on your heart, honey. Feel that? That feels solid too but we know better, be nice to me, be sweet like you can because what else is there for a girl like you but to be sweet and pretty and give in?—and get away before her people come back?"

She felt her pounding heart. Her hands seemed to enclose it. She 155
thought for the first time in her life that it was nothing that was hers, that belonged to her, but just a pounding, living thing inside this body that wasn't hers either.

"You don't want them to get hurt," Arnold Friend went on. "Now get up, honey. Get up all by yourself."

She stood.

"Now turn this way. That's right. Come over to me—Ellie, put that away, didn't I tell you? You dope. You miserable creep dope," Arnold Friend said. His words were not angry but only part of an incantation. The incantation was kindly. "Now come out through the kitchen to me honey and let's see a smile, try it, you're a brave sweet little girl and now they're eating corn and hotdogs cooked to bursting over an outdoor fire, and they don't know one thing about you and never did and honey you're better than them because not one of them would have done this for you."

Connie felt the linoleum under her feet; it was cool. She brushed her hair back out of her eyes. Arnold Friend let go of the post tentatively and opened his arms for her, his elbows pointing up toward each other and his wrist limp, to show that this was an embarrassed embrace and a little mocking, he didn't want to make her self-conscious.

She put out her hand against the screen. She watched herself push the 160
door slowly open as if she were safe back somewhere in the other doorway, watching this body and this head of long hair moving out into the sunlight where Arnold Friend waited.

"My sweet little blue-eyed girl," he said, in a half-sung sigh that had nothing to do with her brown eyes but was taken up just the same by the vast sunlit reaches of the land behind him and on all sides of him, so much land that Connie had ever seen before and did not recognize except to know that she was going to it.

Analyzing the Text

1. Why is it significant that everything about Connie "had two sides to it"? In what ways does Connie see herself as being different from both her mother and sister?
2. How does the description of Arnold Friend—his unusual hair, pale skin, awkward way of walking in his boots, out-of-date expressions, and car—suggest he is not what he appears to be? Who do you think he really is, or what do you think he represents?

Understanding Oates's Techniques

1. What is the significance of the inverted question in the title as it relates to Connie's aspirations?

2. In what way is Connie's growing alarm about who Arnold Friend really is made more acute when he describes events across town at her family's barbecue?

Arguing for an Interpretation

1. What do you think Arnold Friend means when he says at the end "not one of them would have done this for you"? In your opinion, does Connie really have a choice, and if so, what is it?
2. Is Arnold Friend a force for good or evil? Is he going to end Connie's life or give her a new beginning? Make a case for either interpretation.

KATE CHOPIN

Kate Chopin (1851–1904) was born Katherine O'Flaherty, the daughter of a successful St. Louis businessman and his French Creole wife. After her father died in 1855, Kate was raised by her mother and great-grandmother. When she was nineteen, she married Oscar Chopin and accompanied him to New Orleans where he established himself as a cotton broker. After his business failed, they moved to his family plantation in Louisiana where he opened a general store. After his sudden death in 1883, Chopin managed the plantation for a year, but then decided to return to St. Louis with her six children. She began to submit stories patterned on the realistic fiction of Guy de Maupassant to local papers and national magazines, including the Saturday Evening Post *and* Atlantic Monthly. *Her stories of Creole life were widely praised for their realistic delineation of Creole manners and customs and were later collected in* Bayou Folk *(1894) and* A Night in Acadie *(1897). Her novel* The Awakening *(1899), although widely praised as a masterpiece for its frank depiction of its heroine's sexual awakening and need for self-fulfillment, created a public controversy. Chopin's sensitivity to the stifling social pressures on women in a patriarchal society, and her skillful use of foreshadowing, are evident in "The Story of an Hour" (1894).*

The Story of an Hour

Knowing that Mrs. Mallard was afflicted with a heart trouble, great care was taken to break to her as gently as possible the news of her husband's death.

It was her sister Josephine who told her, in broken sentences; veiled hints that revealed in half concealing. Her husband's friend Richards was there, too, near her. It was he who had been in the newspaper office when intelligence of the railroad disaster was received, with Brently Mallard's name leading the list of "killed." He had only taken the time to assure himself of its truth by a second telegram, and had hastened to forestall any less careful, less tender friend in bearing the sad message.

She did not hear the story as many women have heard the same, with a paralyzed inability to accept its significance. She wept at once, with sudden, wild abandonment, in her sister's arms. When the storm of grief had spent itself she went away to her room alone. She would have no one follow her.

There stood, facing the open window, a comfortable, roomy armchair. Into this she sank, pressed down by a physical exhaustion that haunted her body and seemed to reach into her soul.

5 She could see in the open square before her house the tops of trees that were all aquiver with the new spring life. The delicious breath of rain was in the air. In the street below a peddler was crying his wares. The notes of a distant song which some one was singing reached her faintly, and countless sparrows were twittering in the eaves.

There were patches of blue sky showing here and there through the clouds that had met and piled one above the other in the west facing her window.

She sat with her head thrown back upon the cushion of the chair, quite motionless, except when a sob came up into her throat and shook her, as a child who had cried itself to sleep continues to sob in its dreams.

She was young, with a fair, calm face, whose lines bespoke repression and even a certain strength. But now there was a dull stare in her eyes, whose gaze was fixed away off yonder on one of those patches of blue sky. It was not a glance of reflection, but rather indicated a suspension of intelligent thought.

There was something coming to her and she was waiting for it, fearfully. What was it? She did not know; it was too subtle and elusive to name. But she felt it, creeping out of the sky, reaching toward her through the sounds, the scents, the color that filled the air.

10 Now her bosom rose and fell tumultuously. She was beginning to recognize this thing that was approaching to possess her, and she was striving to beat it back with her will—as powerless as her two white slender hands would have been.

When she abandoned herself a little whispered word escaped her slightly parted lips. She said it over and over under her breath: "free, free, free!" The vacant stare and the look of terror that had followed it went from her eyes. They stayed keen and bright. Her pulses beat fast, and the coursing blood warmed and relaxed every inch of her body.

She did not stop to ask if it were or were not a monstrous joy that held her. A clear and exalted perception enabled her to dismiss the suggestion as trivial.

She knew that she would weep again when she saw the kind, tender hands folded in death; the face that had never looked save with love upon her, fixed and gray and dead. But she saw beyond that bitter moment a long procession of years to come that would belong to her absolutely. And she opened and spread her arms out to them in welcome.

There would be no one to live for her during those coming years: she would live for herself. There would be no powerful will bending hers in that blind persistence with which men and women believe they have a right to impose a private will upon a fellow-creature. A kind intention or a cruel intention made the act seem no less a crime as she looked upon it in that brief moment of illumination.

15 And yet she had loved him—sometimes. Often she had not. What did it matter! What could love, the unsolved mystery, count for in face of this possession of self-assertion which she suddenly recognized as the strongest impulse of her being!

"Free! Body and soul free!" she kept whispering.

Josephine was kneeling before the closed door with her lips to the keyhole, imploring for admission. "Louise, open the door! I beg; open the door—you will make yourself ill. What are you doing, Louise? For heaven's sake open the door."

"Go away. I am not making myself ill." No; she was drinking in a very elixir of life through that open window.

Her fancy was running riot along those days ahead of her. Spring days, and summer days, and all sorts of days that would be her own. She breathed a quick prayer that life might be long. It was only yesterday she had thought with a shudder that life might be long.

20 She arose at length and opened the door to her sister's importunities. There was a feverish triumph in her eyes, and she carried herself unwittingly like a goddess of Victory. She clasped her sister's waist, and together they descended the stairs. Richards stood waiting for them at the bottom.

Some one was opening the front door with a latchkey. It was Brently Mallard who entered, a little travel-stained, composedly carrying his grip-sack and umbrella. He had been far from the scene of accident, and did not even know there had been one. He stood amazed at Josephine's piercing cry; at Richards' quick motion to screen him from the view of his wife.

But Richards was too late.

When the doctors came they said she had died of heart disease—of joy that kills.

Analyzing the Text

1. What details suggest that until this moment Mrs. Mallard led a sheltered life and has lived a vicarious existence through her husband?
2. What actually kills Mrs. Mallard, and how do her true emotions contrast with what others believe she feels?

Understanding Chopin's Techniques

1. How does Chopin's descriptions of the landscape foreshadow Mrs. Mallard's true feelings before she herself is aware of them?
2. How does Mrs. Mallard's heart trouble play a role in both a figurative and literal sense in explaining her fate?

Arguing for an Interpretation

1. In what ways does this story express Kate Chopin's critique of contemporary social relationships during her era?
2. What elements in the story explain why Mrs. Mallard could not continue to live, now knowing what her true needs were that she had previously repressed?

Jerzy Kosinski

Jerzy Kosinski (1933–1991) was born in Lodz, Poland. When the Nazis occupied Poland in 1939, he was sent by his parents to live in the countryside where his nightmarish experiences later formed the basis for his classic of Holocaust fiction, The Painted Bird *(1965). After receiving degrees in sociology and history, he emigrated to the United States and published two nonfiction books:* The Future is Ours, Comrade *(1960) and* No Third Path *(1962) under the pseudonym Joseph Novak. In 1973 he was elected president of the American Center of P.E.N., an international writer's association. A prolific writer, Kosinski's second novel,* Steps *(1968) received the National Book Award. In 1970 he received the American Academy of Arts and Letters Award for Literature. Other novels include* The Devil Tree *(1973),* Cockpit *(1975),* Pinball *(1982), and* The Hermit of 69th Street *(1988). His 1971 novel* Being There *was made into the Academy Award-winning 1979 film. Burdened by an increasingly serious heart condition, Kosinski committed suicide in 1991. Chapter 4 of* The Painted Bird, *"The Miller's Tale," depicts how a boy known only as "the gypsy" reacts to his first experience of seeing the effects of jealousy and revenge in the lives of the East European peasants with whom he has found temporary shelter.*

The Miller's Tale

I was now living at the miller's, whom the villagers had nicknamed Jealous. He was more taciturn than was usual in the area. Even when neighbors came to pay him a visit, he would just sit, taking an occasional sip of vodka, and drawling out a word once in a while, lost in thought or staring at a dried-up fly stuck to the wall.

He abandoned his reverie only when his wife entered the room. Equally quiet and reticent, she would always sit down behind her husband, modestly dropping her gaze when men entered the room and furtively glanced at her.

I slept in the attic directly above their bedroom. At night I was awakened by their quarrels. The miller suspected his wife of flirting and lasciviously displaying her body in the fields and in the mill before a young plowboy. His wife did not deny this, but sat passive and still. Sometimes the quarrel did not end. The enraged miller lit candles in the room, put on his boots, and beat his wife. I would cling to a crack in the floorboards and watch the miller lashing his naked wife with a horsewhip. The woman cowered behind a feather quilt tugged off the bed, but the man pulled it away, flung it on the floor, and standing over her with his legs spread wide continued to lash her plump body with the whip. After every stroke, red blood-swollen lines would appear on her tender skin.

The miller was merciless. With a grand sweep of the arm he looped the leather thong of the whip over her buttocks and thighs, slashed her breasts and neck, scourged her shoulders and shins. The woman weakened and lay whining like a puppy. Then she crawled toward her husband's legs, begging forgiveness.

Finally the miller threw down the whip and, after blowing out the can- 5
dle, went to bed. The woman remained groaning. The following day she would cover her wounds, move with difficulty, and wipe away her tears with bruised, cut palms.

There was another inhabitant of the hut: a well-fed tabby cat. One day she was seized by a frenzy. Instead of mewing she emitted half-smothered squeals. She slid along the walls as sinuously as a snake, swung her pulsating flanks, and clawed at the skirts of the miller's wife. She growled in a strange voice and moaned, her raucous shrieks making everyone restless. At dusk the tabby whined insanely, her tail beating her flanks, her nose thrusting.

The miller locked the inflamed female in the cellar and went to his mill, telling his wife that he would bring the plowboy home for supper. Without a word the woman set about preparing the food and table.

The plowboy was an orphan. It was his first season of work at the miller's farm. He was a tall, placid youth with flaxen hair which he habitually pushed back from his sweating brow. The miller knew that the villagers gossiped about his wife and the boy. It was said that she changed when she gazed into the boy's blue eyes. Heedless of the risk of being noticed by her husband, she impulsively hiked her skirt high above her knees with one hand, and with the other pushed down the bodice of her dress to display her breasts, all the time staring into the boy's eyes.

The miller returned with the young man, carrying in a sack slung over his shoulder, a tomcat borrowed from a neighbor. The tomcat had a head as large as a turnip and a long, strong tail. The tabby was howling lustingly in the cellar. When the miller released her, she sprang to the center of the room. The two cats began to circle one another mistrustfully, panting, coming nearer and nearer.

The miller's wife served supper. They ate silently. The miller sat at the 10
middle of the table, his wife on one side and the plowboy on the other. I ate my portion squatting by the oven. I admired the appetites of the two men: huge chunks of meat and bread, washed down with gulps of vodka, disappeared in their throats like hazelnuts.

The woman was the only one who chewed her food slowly. When she bowed her head low over the bowl the plowboy would dart a glance faster than lightning at her bulging bodice.

In the center of the room the tabby suddenly arched her body, bared her teeth and claws, and pounced on the tomcat. He halted, stretched his back, and sputtered saliva straight into her inflamed eyes. The female circled him, leaped toward him, recoiled, and then struck him in the muzzle. Now the tomcat stalked around her cautiously, sniffing her intoxicating odor. He arched his tail and tried to come at her from the rear. But the female would not let him; she flattened her body on the floor and turned like a millstone, striking his nose with her stiff, outstretched paws.

Fascinated, the miller and the other two stared silently while eating. The woman sat with a flushed face; even her neck was reddening. The plowboy raised his eyes, only to drop them at once. Sweat ran down through his short hair and he continually pushed it away from his hot brow. Only the miller sat calmly eating, watching the cats, and glancing casually at his wife and guest.

The tomcat suddenly came to a decision. His movements became lighter. He advanced. She moved playfully as if to draw back, but the male leapt high and flopped onto her with all fours. He sank his teeth in her neck and intently, tautly, plunged directly into her without any squirming. When satiated and exhausted, he relaxed. The tabby, nailed to the floor, screamed shrilly and sprang out from under him. She jumped onto the cooled oven and tossed about on it like a fish, looping her paws over her neck, rubbing her head against the warm wall.

15 The miller's wife and the plowboy ceased eating. They stared at each other, gaping over their food-filled mouths. The woman breathed heavily, placed her hands under her breasts and squeezed them, clearly unaware of herself. The plowboy looked alternately at the cats and at her, licked his dry lips, and got down his food with difficulty.

The miller swallowed the last of his meal, leaned his head back, and abruptly gulped down his glass of vodka. Though drunk, he got up, and grasping his iron spoon and tapping it, he approached the plowboy. The youth sat bewildered. The woman hitched up her skirt and began puttering at the fire.

The miller bent over the plowboy and whispered something in his reddened ear. The youth jumped up as if pricked with a knife and began to deny something. The miller asked loudly now whether the boy lusted after his wife. The plowboy blushed but did not answer. The miller's wife turned away and continued to clean the pots.

The miller pointed at the strolling tomcat and again whispered something to the youth. The latter, with an effort, rose from the table, intending to leave the room. The miller came forward overturning his stool and, before the youth realized it, suddenly pushed him against the wall, pressed one arm against his throat, and drove a knee into his stomach. The boy could not move. Terror stricken, panting loudly, he babbled something.

The woman dashed toward her husband, imploring and wailing. The awakened tabby cat lying on the oven looked down on the spectacle, while the frightened tomcat leapt onto the table.

20 With a single kick the miller got the woman out of his way. And with a rapid movement such as women use to gouge out the rotten spots while peeling potatoes, he plunged the spoon into one of the boy's eyes and twisted it.

The eye sprang out of his face like a yolk from a broken egg and rolled down the miller's hand onto the floor. The plowboy howled and shrieked, but the miller's hold kept him pinned against the wall. Then the blood-covered spoon plunged into the other eye, which sprang out even faster. For a moment the eye rested on the boy's cheek as if uncertain what to do next; then it finally tumbled down his shirt onto the floor.

It all had happened in a moment. I could not believe what I had seen. Something like a glimmer of hope crossed my mind that the gouged eyes could be put back where they belonged. The miller's wife was screaming wildly. She rushed to the adjoining room and woke up her children, who also started crying in terror. The plowboy screamed and then grew silent covering his face with his hands. Rivulets of blood seeped through his fingers down his arms, dripping slowly on his shirt and trousers.

The miller, still enraged, pushed him toward the window as though unaware that the youth was blind. The boy stumbled, cried out, and nearly knocked over a table. The miller grabbed him by the shoulders, opened the door with his foot, and kicked him out. The boy yelled again, stumbled through the doorway, and fell down in the yard. The dogs started barking, though they did not know what had happened.

The eyeballs lay on the floor. I walked around them, catching their steady stare. The cats timidly moved out into the middle of the room and began to play with the eyes as if they were balls of thread. Their own pupils narrowed to slits from the light of the oil lamp. The cats rolled the eyes around, sniffed them, licked them, and passed them to one another gently with their padded paws. Now it seemed that the eyes were staring at me from every corner of the room, as though they had acquired a new life and motion of their own.

I watched them with fascination. If the miller had not been there I my- 25
self would have taken them. Surely they could still see. I would keep them in my pocket and take them out when needed, placing them over my own. Then I would see twice as much, maybe even more. Perhaps I could attach them to the back of my head and they would tell me, though I was not quite certain how, what went on behind me. Better still, I could leave the eyes somewhere and they would tell me later what happened during my absence.

Maybe the eyes had no intention of serving anyone. They could easily escape from the cats and roll out of the door. They could wander over the fields, lakes, and woods, viewing everything about them, free as birds released from a trap. They would no longer die, since they were free, and being small they could easily hide in various places and watch people in secret. Excited, I decided to close the door quietly and capture the eyes.

The miller, evidently annoyed by the cats' play, kicked the animals away and squashed the eyeballs with his heavy boots. Something popped under his thick sole. A marvelous mirror, which could reflect the whole world, was broken. There remained on the floor only a crushed bit of jelly. I felt a terrible sense of loss.

The miller, paying no attention to me, seated himself on the bench and swayed slowly as he fell asleep. I stood up cautiously, lifted the bloodied spoon from the floor and began to gather the dishes. It was my duty to keep the room neat and the floor swept. As I cleaned I kept away from the crushed eyes, uncertain what to do with them. Finally I looked away and quickly swept the ooze into the pail and threw it in the oven.

In the morning I awoke early. Underneath me I heard the miller and his wife snoring. Carefully I packed a sack of food, loaded the comet with hot embers and, bribing the dog in the yard with a piece of sausage, fled from the hut.

At the mill wall, next to the barn, lay the plowboy. At first I meant to 30
pass him by quickly, but I stopped when I realized that he was sightless. He was still stunned. He covered his face with his hands, he moaned and sobbed. There was caked blood on his face, hands, and shirt. I wanted to say something, but I was afraid that he would ask me about his eyes and then I would have to tell him to forget about them, since the miller had stamped them into pulp. I was terribly sorry for him.

I wondered whether the loss of one's sight would deprive a person also of the memory of everything that he had seen before. If so, the man would no longer be able to see even in his dreams. If not, if only the eyeless could still see through their memory, it would not be too bad. The world seemed to be pretty much the same everywhere, and even though people differed from one another, just as animals and trees did, one should know fairly well what they looked like after seeing them for years. I had lived only seven years, but I remembered a lot of things. When I closed my eyes, many details came back still more vividly. Who knows, perhaps without his eyes the plowboy would start seeing an entirely new, more fascinating world.

I heard some sound from the village. Afraid that the miller might wake up, I went on my way, touching my eyes from time to time. I walked more cautiously now, for I knew that eyeballs did not have strong roots. When one bent down they hung like apples from a tree and could easily drop out. I resolved to jump across fences with my head held up; but on my first try I stumbled and fell down. I lifted my fingers fearfully to my eyes to see whether they were still there. After carefully checking that they opened and closed properly, I noticed with delight the partridges and thrushes in flight. They flew very fast but my sight could follow them and even overtake them as they soared under the clouds, becoming smaller than raindrops. I made a promise to myself to remember everything I saw; if someone should pluck out my eyes, then I would retain the memory of all that I had seen for as long as I lived.

Analyzing the Text

1. What is the effect of witnessing the bizarre consequences of jealousy and revenge on the young boy?
2. How does seeing the detached eyes of the plowboy lead the narrator to conclude that the ability to remember events and experiences are all-important?

Understanding Kosinski's Techniques

1. Kosinski's narrative is curiously matter-of-fact, given the bizarre nature of the events being described. How is this approach designed to stimulate the reader's emotional reactions?
2. What role do the tomcat and his mate play in foreshadowing and paralleling the actions of the human characters?

Arguing for an Interpretation

1. Would the events in this story have the same impact if related from the perspective of one of the other characters? Explain your answer. Try your hand at rewriting this narrative as seen through the eyes of one of the other characters.
2. The boy in this episode is only 7 years old. Are his perceptions, observations, and conclusions credible, given this fact? If so, what do they imply about his loss of innocence as a child?

Natsume Soseki

Natsume Soseki (1867–1916) was one of Japan's most distinguished writers. He taught English at Tokyo University and was literary editor of the Asahi Newspaper. *Considered to be a milestone in Japanese literature,* I Am a Cat *(1905) brought Soseki instant recognition as an in-*

cisive observer of Japanese bourgeois life. This work was translated into English by Katsue Shibata and Motomari Kai in 1961. Soseki's work, like that of other twentieth-century Japanese writers, reveals the influence of the West on Japanese life and culture. The first chapter from I Am a Cat *introduces a professor of English and his family as they appear through the eyes of a cat who has taken up residence in their home.*

I Am a Cat

I am a cat but as yet I have no name.

I haven't the faintest idea of where I was born. The first thing I do remember is that I was crying "meow, meow," somewhere in a gloomy damp place. It was there that I met a human being for the first time in my life. Though I found this all out at a later date, I learned that this human being was called a Student, one of the most ferocious of the human race. I also understand that these Students sometimes catch us, cook us and then take to eating us. But at that time, I did not have the slightest idea of all this so I wasn't frightened a bit. When this Student placed me on the palm of his hand and lifted me up lightly, I only had the feeling of floating around. After a while, I got used to this position and looked around. This was probably the first time I had a good look at a so-called human being. What impressed me as being most strange still remains deeply imbedded in my mind: the face which should have been covered with hair was a slippery thing similar to what I now know to be a teakettle. I have since come across many other cats but none of them are such freaks. Moreover, the center of the Student's face protruded to a great extent, and from the two holes located there, he would often emit smoke. I was extremely annoyed by being choked by this. That this was what they term as tobacco, I came to know only recently.

I was snuggled up comfortably in the palm of this Student's hand when, after a while, I started to travel around at a terrific speed. I was unable to find out if the Student was moving or if it was just myself that was in motion, but in any case I became terribly dizzy and a little sick. Just as I was thinking that I couldn't last much longer at this rate, I heard a thud and saw sparks. I remember everything up till that moment but think as hard as I can, I can't recall what took place immediately after this.

When I came to, I could not find the Student anywhere. Nor could I find the many cats that had been with me either. Moreover, my dear mother had also disappeared. And the extraordinary thing was that this place, when compared to where I had been before, was extremely bright—ever so bright. I could hardly keep my eyes open. This was because I had been removed from my straw bed and thrown into a bamboo bush.

Finally, mustering up my strength, I crawled out from this bamboo 5
grove and found myself before a large pond. I sat on my haunches and tried to take in the situation. I didn't know what to do but suddenly I had an idea. If I could attract some attention by meowing, the Student might come back to me. I commenced but this was to no avail; nobody came.

By this time, the wind had picked up and came blowing across the pond. Night was falling. I sensed terrible pangs of hunger. Try as I would, my voice failed me and I felt as if all hope were lost. In any case, I resolved to get myself to a place where there was food and so, with this decision in mind, I commenced to circle the water by going around to the left.

This was very difficult but at any rate, I forced myself along and eventually came to a locality where I sensed Man. Finding a hole in a broken bamboo fence, I crawled through, having confidence that it was worth the try, and lo! I found myself within somebody's estate. Fate is strange; if that hole had not been there, I might have starved to death by the roadside. It is well said that every tree may offer shelter. For a long time afterwards, I often used this hole for my trips to call on Mi-ke, the tomcat living next door.

Having sneaked into the estate, I was at a loss as to what the next step should be. Darkness had come and my belly cried for food. The cold was bitter and it started to rain. I had no time to fool around any longer so I went in to a room that looked bright and cozy. Coming to think of it now, I had entered somebody's home for the first time. It was there that I was to confront other humans.

The first person I met was the maid Osan. This was a human much worse than the Student. As soon as she saw me, she grabbed me by the neck and threw me outdoors. I sensed I had no chance against her sudden action so I shut my eyes and let things take their course. But I couldn't endure the hunger and the cold any longer. I don't know how many times I was thrown out but because of this, I came to dislike Osan all through. That's one reason why I stole the fish the other day and why I felt so proud of myself.

When the maid was about to throw me out for the last time, the mas- 10
ter of the house made his appearance and asked what all the row was about. The maid turned to him with me hanging limp from her hand, and told him that she had repeatedly tried throwing this stray cat out but that it always kept sneaking into the kitchen again—and that she didn't like it at all. The master, twisting his moustache, looked at me for a while and then told the maid to let me in. He then left the room. I took it that the master was a man of few words. The maid, still mad at me, threw me down on the kitchen floor. In such a way, I was able to establish this place as my home.

At first it was very seldom that I got to see my master. He seemed to be a schoolteacher. Coming home from school he'd shut himself up in his study and would hardly come out for the rest of the day. His family thought him to be very studious and my master also made out as if he were. But actually, he wasn't as hard working as they all believed him to be. I'd often sneak up and look into his study only to find him taking a nap. Sometimes I would find him drivelling on the book he had been reading before dozing off.

He was a man with a weak stomach so his skin was somewhat yellowish. He looked parched and inactive, yet he was a great consumer of food. After eating as much as he possibly could, he'd take a dose of Taka-diastase and then open a book. After reading a couple of pages, however, he'd become drowsy and again commence drooling. This was his daily routine. Though I am a cat myself, at times I think that schoolteachers are very fortunate. If I were to be reborn a man, I would, without doubt, become a teacher. If you can keep a job and still sleep as much as my master did, even cats could manage such a profession. But according to my master—and he makes it plain—there's nothing so hard as teaching. Especially when his friends come to visit him, he does a lot of complaining.

When I first came to this home, nobody but the master was nice to me. Wherever I went, they would kick me around and I was given no other consideration. The fact that they haven't given me a name even as of today goes to show how much they care for me. That's why I try to stay close to my master.

In the morning, when my master reads the papers, I always sit on his lap; and when he takes his nap, I perch on his back. This doesn't mean that he likes it, but then, on the other hand, it doesn't mean that he dislikes it—it has simply become a custom.

Experience taught me that it is best for me to sleep on the container for boiled rice in the mornings as it is warm, and on a charcoal-burning foot warmer in the evenings. I generally sleep on the veranda on fine days. But most of all, I like to crawl into the same bed with the children of the house at night. By children, I mean the girls who are five and three years old respectively. They sleep together in the same bed in their own room. In some way or other, I try to slip into their bed and crawl in between them. But if one of them wakes up, then it is terrible. The girls—especially the smaller one—raise an awful cry in the middle of the night and holler, "There's that cat in here again!" At this, my weak-stomached master wakes up and comes in to help them. It was only the other day that he gave me a terrible whipping with a ruler for indulging in this otherwise pleasant custom.

In coming to live with human beings, I have had the chance to observe them and the more I do the more I come to the conclusion that they are terribly spoiled, especially the children. When they feel like it, they hold you upside down or cover your head with a bag; and at times, they throw you around or try squeezing you into the cooking range. And on top of that, should you so much as bare a claw to try to stop them, the whole family is after you. The other day, for instance, I tried sharpening my claws just for a second on the straw mat of the living room when the Mrs. noticed me. She got furious and from then on, she won't let me in the sitting room. I can be cold and shivering in the kitchen but they never take the trouble to bother about me. When I met Shiro across the street whom I respected, she kept telling me there was nothing as inconsiderate as humans.

Only the other day, four cute little kittens were born to Shiro. But the Student who lives with the family threw all four of them into a pond behind the house on the third day. Shiro told me all this in tears and said that in order for us cats to fulfil parental affection and to have a happy life, we will have to overthrow the human race. Yes, what she said was all very logical. Mi-ke, next door, was extremely furious when I told him about Shiro. He said that humans did not understand the right of possession of others. With us cats, however, the first one that finds the head of a dried sardine or the navel of a gray mullet gets the right to eat it. Should anyone try to violate this rule, we are allowed to use force in order to keep our find. But humans depend on their great strength to take what is legally ours away from us and think it right.

Shiro lives in the home of a soldier and Mi-ke in the home of a lawyer. I live in the home of a schoolteacher and, in comparison, I am far more optimistic about such affairs than either of them. I am satisfied only in trying to live peacefully day after day. I don't believe that the human race will prosper forever so all I have to do is to relax and wait for the time when cats will reign.

Coming to think of the way they act according to their whims—another word for selfishness—I'm going to tell you more about my master. To tell the truth, my master can't do anything well but he likes to stick his nose into everything. Going in for composing *haiku,*[1] he contributes his poems to the *Hototogisu* magazine, or writes some modern poetry for the *Myojo* magazine; or at times, he composes a piece in English, but all grammatically wrong. Then again, he finds himself engrossed in archery or tries singing lyrical plays; or maybe he tries a hand at playing discordant tunes on the violin. What is most disheartening is the fact that he cannot manage any of them well. Though he has a weak stomach, he does his best.

When he enters the toilet, he commences chanting so he is nicknamed "Mr. Mensroom" by his neighbors. Yet, he doesn't mind such things and continues his chanting: "This is Taira-no-Munemori. . . ." Everybody says, "There goes Munemori again," and then bursts out laughing. I don't know exactly what had come over him about a month after I first established myself at his place, but one pay day he came home all excited carrying with him a great big bundle. I couldn't help feeling curious about the contents.

The package happened to contain a set of water colors, brushes and drawing paper. It seems that he had given up lyrical plays and writing verses and was going in for painting. The following day, he shut himself up in his study and without even taking his daily nap, he drew pictures. This continued day after day. But what he drew remained a mystery because others could not even guess what they were. My master finally came to the conclusion that he wasn't as good a painter as he had thought himself to be. One day he came home with a man who considers himself an aesthetic and I heard them talking to each other.

"It's funny but it's difficult to draw as well as you want. When a painting is done by others, it looks so simple. But when you do a work with a brush yourself, it's quite a different thing," said my master. Coming to think of it, he did have plenty of proof to back up his statement.

His friend, looking over his gold-rimmed glasses, said, "You can't expect to draw well right from the beginning. In the first place, you can't expect to draw anything just from imagination, and by shutting yourself up in a room at that. Once the famous Italian painter Andrea del Sarto[2] said that to draw, you have to interpret nature in its original form. The stars in the sky, the earth with flowers shining with dew, the flight of birds and the running animals, the ponds with their goldfish, and the black crow in a withered tree—nature is the one great panorama of the living world. How about it? If you want to draw something recognizable, why not do some sketching?"

"Did del Sarto really say all those things? I didn't know that. All right, just as you say," said my master with admiration. The eyes behind the gold-rimmed glasses shone, but with scorn.

The following day, as I was peacefully enjoying my daily nap on the veranda, my master came out from his study, something quite out of the ordi-

[1]Haiku: a major form of Japanese verse written in 17 syllables, divided into three lines of 5, 7, and 5 syllables, employing evocative allusions and comparisons.
[2]Andrea del Sarto (1486–1531).

nary, and sat down beside me. Wondering what he was up to, I slit my eyes open just a wee bit and took a look. I found him trying out Andrea del Sarto's theory on me. I could not suppress a smile. Having been encouraged by his friend, my master was using me as a model.

I tried to be patient and pretended to continue my nap. I wanted to yawn like anything but when I thought of my master trying his best to sketch me, I felt sorry for him, and so I killed it. He first drew my face in outline and then began to add colors. I'd like to make a confession here: as far as cats are concerned, I have to admit that I'm not one of those you'd call perfect or beautiful; my back, my fur or even my face cannot be considered superior in any way to those of other cats. Yet, even though I may be uncomely, I am hardly as ugly as what my master was painting. In the first place, he shaded my color all wrong. I am really somewhat like a Persian cat, a light gray with a shade of yellow with lacquer-like spots—as can be vouched by anyone. But according to my master's painting, my color was not yellow nor was it black. It wasn't gray or brown. It wasn't even a combination of these colors but something more like a smearing together of many tones. What was most strange about the drawing was that I had no eyes. Of course, I was being sketched while taking a nap so I won't complain too much, but you couldn't even find the location of where they should have been. You couldn't tell if I was a sleeping cat or a blind cat. I thought, way down inside me, that if this is what they called the Andrea del Sarto way of drawing pictures, it wasn't worth a sen.

But as to the enthusiasm of my master, I had to bow my head humbly. I couldn't disappoint him by moving but, if you'll excuse my saying so, I had wanted to go outside to relieve myself from a long while back. The muscles of my body commenced fidgeting and I felt that I couldn't hold out much longer. So, trying to excuse myself, I stretched out my forelegs, gave my neck a little twist and indulged in a long slow yawn. Going this far, there was no need for me to stay still any longer because I had changed my pose. I then stepped outside to accomplish my object.

But my master, in disappointment and rage, shouted from within the room, "You fool!" My master, in abusing others, has the habit of using this expression. "You fool!" This is the best he can manage as he doesn't know any other way to swear. Even though he had not known how long I had endured the urgent call of nature, I still consider him uncivilized for this. If he had ever given me a smile or some other encouragement when I climbed onto his back, I could have forgiven him this time, but the fact is that he never considers my convenience. That he should holler, "You fool!" only because I was about to go and relieve myself was more than I could stand. In the first place, humans take too much for granted. If some power doesn't appear to control them better, there's no telling how far they will go in their excesses.

I could endure their being so self-willed but I've heard many other complaints regarding mankind's lack of virtue, and they are much worse.

Right in back of the house, there is a patch of tea plants. It isn't large 30
but it is nice and sunny. When the children of the house are so noisy that I can't enjoy my naps peacefully or when, because of idleness, my digestion is bad, I usually go out to the tea patch to enjoy the magnanimous surroundings. One lovely autumn day about two o'clock in the afternoon, after taking my after-lunch nap, I took a stroll through this patch. I walked along, smelling each tea plant as I went, until I reached a cryptomeria hedge at the west end.

There I found a large cat sleeping soundly, using a withered chrysanthemum in lieu of a mat. It seemed as if he didn't notice me coming, for he kept snoring loudly. I was overwhelmed at his boldness;—after sneaking into somebody else's yard. He was a big black cat.

The sun, now past midday, cast its brilliant rays upon his body and reflected themselves to give the impression of flames bursting from his soft fur. He had such a big frame that he seemed fit to be called a king of the feline family. He was more than twice my size. Admiration and a feeling of curiosity made me forget the past and the future, and I could only stare at him.

The soft autumn breeze made the branches of the paulawnia above quiver lightly and a couple of leaves came fluttering down upon the thicket of dead chrysanthemums. Then the great "king" opened his eyes. I can still feel the thrill of that moment. The amber light in his eyes shone much brighter than the jewels man holds as precious. He did not move at all. The glance he shot at me concentrated on my small forehead, and he abruptly asked me who I was. The great king's directness betrayed his rudeness. Yet, there was a power in his voice that would have terrified dogs, and I found myself shaking with fear. But thinking it inadvisable not to pay my respects, I said, "I am a cat though, as yet, I don't have any name." I said this while pretending to be at ease but actually my heart was beating away at a terrific speed. Despite my courteous reply, he said, "A cat? You don't say so! Where do you live?" He was extremely audacious.

"I live here in the schoolteacher's house."

"I thought so. You sure are skinny." Gathering from his rudeness I couldn't imagine him coming from a very good family. But, judging from his plump body, he seemed to be well fed and able to enjoy an easy life. As for myself, I couldn't refrain from asking, "And who are you?"

"Me? Huh—I'm Kuro, living at the rickshawman's place."

So this was the cat living at the rickshawman's house! He was known in the vicinity as being awfully unruly. Actually he was admired within the home of the rickshawman but, having no education, nobody else befriended him. He was a hoodlum from whom others shied. When I heard him tell me who he was, I felt somewhat uneasy and, at the same time, I felt slightly superior. With the intention of finding out how much learning he had, I asked him some more questions.

"I was just wondering which of the two is the greater—the rickshawman or the schoolteacher."

"What a question! The rickshawman, naturally. Just take a look at your teacher—he's all skin and bones," he snorted.

"You look extremely strong. Most probably, living at the rickshawman's house, you get plenty to eat."

"What? I don't go unfed anywhere! Stick with me for a while instead of going around in circles in the tea patch and you'll look better yourself in less than a month."

"Sure, some day, maybe. But to me, it seems as though the schoolteacher lives in a bigger house than the rickshawman," I purred.

"Huh! What if the house is big? That doesn't mean you get your belly full there, does it?"

He seemed extremely irritated and, twitching his pointed ears, he walked away without saying another word. This was my first encounter with Kuro of the house of the rickshawman, but not the last.

Since then, we've often talked together. Whenever we do, Kuro always 45
commences bragging, as one living with a rickshawman would.

One day, we were lying in the tea patch and indulging in some small talk. As usual, he kept bragging about the adventures he had had, and then he got around to asking me, "By the way, how many rats have you killed?"

Intellectually I am much more developed than Kuro but when it comes to using strength and showing bravado, there is no comparison. I was prepared for something like this but when he actually asked me the question, I felt extremely embarrassed. But facts are facts; I could not lie to him: "To tell the truth, I have been wanting to catch one for a long time but the opportunity has never come."

Kuro twitched the whiskers which stood out straight from his muzzle and laughed hard. Kuro is conceited, as those who brag usually are, so when I find him being sarcastic I try to say something to appease him. In this way, I am able to manage him pretty well. Having learned this during our first meeting, I stayed calm when he laughed. I realized that it would be foolish to commit myself now by giving unasked-for reasons. I figured it best, at this stage, to let him brag about his own adventures and so I purred quietly, "Being as old as you are, you've probably caught a lot of rats yourself." I was trying to get him to talk about himself. And, as I had expected, he took the bait.

"Well, can't say a lot—maybe about thirty or forty." He was very proud of this and continued, "I could handle one or two hundred rats alone but when it comes to weasels, they're not to my liking. A weasel once gave me a terrible time."

"So? And what happened?" I chimed in. Kuro blinked several times be- 50
fore he continued. "It was at the time of our annual housecleaning last summer. The master crawled under the veranda to put away a sack of lime, and—what do you think? He surprised a big weasel which came bouncing out."

"Oh?" I pretended to admire him.

"As you know, a weasel is only a little bigger than a rat. Thinking him to be just another big mouse, I cornered him in a ditch."

"You did?"

"Yeah. Just as I was going in for the *coup de grace*—can you imagine what he did? Well, it raised its tail and—ooph! You ought to have taken a whiff. Even now when I see a weasel I get giddy." So saying, he rubbed his nose with one of his paws as if he were still trying to stop the smell. I felt somewhat sorry for him so, with the thought of trying to liven him up a little, I said, "But when it comes to rats, I hardly believe they would have a chance against you. Being such a famous rat catcher, you probably eat nothing else and that's why you're so plump and glossy, I'm sure."

I had said this to get him into a better mood but actually it had the 55
contrary effect. He let a big sigh escape and replied, "When you come to think of it, it's not all fun. Rats are interesting but, you know, there's nobody as crafty as humans in this world. They take all the rats I catch over to the police box. The policeman there doesn't know who actually catches them so he hands my master five sen per head. Because of me, my master has made a near profit of one yen and fifty sen, but yet he doesn't give me any decent food. Do you know what humans are? Well, I'll tell you. They're men, yes, but thieves at heart."

Even Kuro, who was not any too bright, understood such logic and he bristled his back in anger. I felt somewhat uneasy so I murmured some excuse and went home. It was because of this conversation that I made up my mind never to catch rats. But, on the other hand, neither do I go around hunting for other food. Instead of eating an extravagant dinner, I simply go to sleep. A cat living with a schoolteacher gets to become, in nature, just like a teacher himself. If I'm not careful I might still become just as weak in the stomach as my master.

Speaking of my master the schoolteacher, it finally dawned upon him that he could not ever hope to get anywhere with water-color painting. He wrote the following entry in his diary, dated December 1:

> Met a man today at a party. It's said that he's a debauchee and he looked like one. Such individuals are liked by women, so it may be quite proper to say that such people cannot help becoming dissipated. His wife was formerly a geisha girl and I envy him. Most of the people who criticize debauchees generally have no chance to become one themselves. Still, others who claim to be debauchees have no qualifications to become so worldly. They simply force themselves into that position. Just as in the case of my water-color painting, there was absolutely no fear of my making good. But indifferent to others, I might think that I was good at it. If some men are considered worldly only because they drink *sake* at restaurants, frequent geisha houses and stop over for the night, and go through all the necessary motions, then it stands to reason that I should be able to call myself a remarkable painter. But my water-color paintings will never be a success.

In regard to this theory, I cannot agree. That a schoolteacher should envy a man who has a wife who was once a geisha shows how foolish and inferior my master is. But his criticism of himself as a water-color painter is unquestionably true. Though my master understands many of his own shortcomings, he cannot get over being terribly conceited. On December 4, he wrote:

> Last night, I attempted another painting but I have finally come to understand that I have no talent. I dreamed that somebody had framed the pictures I have lying around, and had hung them on the wall. Upon seeing them framed, I suddenly thought that I was an excellent painter. I felt happy and kept looking but, when the day dawned, I awoke and again clearly realized that I am still a painter of no talent.

Even in his dreams, my master seemed to regret his having given up painting. This is characteristic of a learned man, a frustrated water-color painter and one who can never become a man of the world.

The day after my master had had his dream, his friend, the man of arts, 60
came to see him again. The first question he asked my master was "How are the pictures getting along?"

My master calmly answered, "According to your advice I'm working hard at sketching. Just as you said, I am finding interesting shapes and detailed changes of colors which I had never noticed before. Due to the fact that artists in Western countries have persisted in sketching, they have reached the development we see today. Yes, all this must be due to Andrea del Sarto." He did not mention what he had written in his diary, but only continued to show his admiration for del Sarto.

The artist scratched his head and commenced to laugh, "That was all a joke, my friend."

"What's that?" My master didn't seem to understand.

"Andrea del Sarto is only a person of my own highly imaginative creation. I didn't think you'd take it so seriously. Ha, ha, ha." The artist was greatly enjoying himself.

Listening to all this from the veranda, I couldn't help wondering what 65
my master would write in his diary about that conversation. This artist was a person who took great pleasure in fooling others. As if he did not realize how his joke about Andrea del Sarto hurt my master, he boasted more: "When playing jokes, some people take them so seriously that they reveal great comic beauty, and it's a lot of fun. The other day I told a student that Nicholas Nickleby had advised Gibbon to translate his great story of the French Revolution from a French textbook and to have it published under his own name. This student has an extremely good memory and made a speech at the Japanese Literature Circle quoting everything I had told him. There were about a hundred people in the audience and they all listened very attentively. Then there's another time. One evening, at a gathering of writers, the conversation turned to Harrison's historical novel *Theophano*. I said that it was one of the best historical novels ever written, especially the part where the heroine dies. 'That really gives you the creeps'—that's what I said. An author who was sitting opposite me was one of those types who cannot and will not say no to anything. He immediately voiced the opinion that that was a most famous passage. I knew right away that he had never read any more of the story than I had."

With wide eyes, my nervous and weak-stomached master asked, "What would you have done if the other man had really read the story?"

The artist did not show any excitement. He thought nothing of fooling other people. The only thing that counted was not to be caught in the act.

"All I would have had to do is to say that I had made a mistake in the title or something to that effect." He kept on laughing. Though this artist wore a pair of gold-rimmed glasses, he looked somewhat like Kuro of the rickshawman's.

My master blew a few smoke rings but he had an expression on his face that showed he wouldn't have the nerve to do such a thing. The artist, with a look in his eyes as if saying, "That's why you can't paint pictures," only continued. "Jokes are jokes but, getting down to facts, it's not easy to draw. They say that Leonardo da Vinci once told his pupils to copy a smear on a wall. That's good advice. Sometimes when you're gazing at water leaking along the wall in a privy, you see some good patterns. Copy them carefully and you're bound to get some good designs."

"You're only trying to fool me again." 70

"No, not this time. Don't you think it's a wonderful idea? Just what da Vinci himself would have suggested."

"Just as you say," replied my master, half surrendering. But he still hasn't made any sketches in the privy—at least not yet.

Kuro of the rickshawman's wasn't looking well. His glossy fur began to fade and fall out. His eyes, which I formerly compared to amber, began to collect mucus. What was especially noticeable was his lack of energy. When I met him in the tea patch, I asked him how he felt.

"I'm still disgusted with the weasel's stink and with the fisherman. The fish seller hit me with a pole again the other day."

The red leaves of the maple tree were beginning to show contrast to the green of the pines here and there. The maples shed their foliage like dreams of the past. The fluttering petals of red and white fell from the tea plants one after another until there were none remaining. The sun slanted its rays deeper and deeper into the southern veranda and seldom did a day pass that the late autumn wind didn't blow. I felt as though my napping hours were being shortened.

My master still went to school every day and, coming home, he'd still bottle himself up in his study. When he had visitors he'd continue to complain about his job. He hardly ever touched his water colors again. He had discontinued taking Taka-diastase for his indigestion, saying that it didn't do him any good. It was wonderful now that the little girls were attending kindergarten every day but returning home, they'd sing loudly and bounce balls and, at times, they'd still pick me up by the tail.

I still had nothing much to eat so I did not become very fat but I was healthy enough. I didn't become sick like Kuro and, as always, I took things as they came. I still didn't try to catch rats, and I still hated Osan, the maid. I still didn't have a name but you can't always have what you want. I resigned myself to continue living here at the home of this schoolteacher as a cat without a name.

Analyzing the Text

1. How does the cat's view of the schoolteacher show him as he really is, as compared with the way he sees himself?
2. What subtle or overt resemblances link each of the cats mentioned with its owner? For example, how is the narrator like the schoolmaster, Mi-ke similar to the lawyer, and Kuro like the rickshawman?

Understanding Soseki's Techniques

1. What features display Soseki's ingenuity in creating such a lifelike human personality for a cat? Which details make real the ingenious choice of a cat's point of view in terms of the cat's relationship with others of his species? Why is it significant that he doesn't have a name?
2. In what way is the cat's viewpoint effective in providing a vantage point on life in a Japanese household?

Arguing for an Interpretation

1. In what way might this be considered a satire on self-delusion based on the difference between the way the professor sees himself and the way the cat sees him?
2. What could your pet say about you that no one else knows? What character traits does the name you gave this pet reveal about you? What name would you give the cat in this story, and why?

Tayeb Salih

Tayeb Salih was born in the northern province of the Sudan in 1929. He was head of drama in the BBC's Arabic Service and worked for UNESCO in Paris. His writings include Season of Migration to the North *(1969), and the collection of a short novel and stories titled* The Wedding of Zein *(1978), from which "A Handful of Dates" (translated by Denys Johnson-Davies) was taken. This book was made into a film that won an award at the Cannes Film Festival in 1976. This story describes a boy's reaction to the discovery that his grandfather's business practices conflict with the teachings of the Koran, the sacred book of Islam, which Muslims believe express the divine teachings revealed to the prophet Muhammed. Ironically, despite the enlightened perspective that Salih brings to all his writing, he was found to be too secular and was the subject of a* fatwa *(religious decree) to ban his works in 1997 in the Sudan. He lives in the United States and has served as an important official with UNESCO in Europe and the Middle East.*

A Handful of Dates

I must have been very young at the time. While I don't remember exactly how old I was, I do remember that when people saw me with my grandfather they would pat me on the head and give my cheek a pinch—things they didn't do to my grandfather. The strange thing was that I never used to go out with my father, rather it was my grandfather who would take me with him wherever he went, except for the mornings when I would go to the mosque to learn the Koran. The mosque, the river and the fields—these were the landmarks in our life. While most of the children of my age grumbled at having to go to the mosque to learn the Koran, I used to love it. The reason was, no doubt, that I was quick at learning by heart and the Sheikh always asked me to stand up and recite the *Chapter of the Merciful* whenever we had visitors, who would pat me on my head and cheek just as people did when they saw me with my grandfather.

Yes, I used to love the mosque, and I loved the river too. Directly we finished our Koran reading in the morning I would throw down my wooden slate and dart off, quick as a genie, to my mother, hurriedly swallow down my breakfast, and run off for a plunge in the river. When tired of swimming about I would sit on the bank and gaze at the strip of water that wound away eastwards and hid behind a thick wood of acacia trees. I loved to give rein to my imagination and picture to myself a tribe of giants living behind that wood, a people tall and thin with white beards and sharp noses, like my grandfather. Before my grandfather ever replied to my many questions he would rub the tip of his nose with his forefinger; as for his beard, it was soft and luxuriant and as white as cotton-wool—never in my life have I seen anything of a purer whiteness or greater beauty. My grandfather must also have been extremely tall, for I never saw anyone in the whole area address him without having to look up at him, nor did I see him enter a house without having to bend so low that I was put in mind of the way the river wound round behind the wood of acacia trees. I loved him and would imagine myself, when I grew to be a man, tall and slender like him, walking along with great strides.

I believe I was his favourite grandchild: no wonder, for my cousins were a stupid bunch and I—so they say—was an intelligent child. I used to know when my grandfather wanted me to laugh, when to be silent; also I would remember the times for his prayers and would bring him his prayer-rug and fill the ewer for his ablutions without his having to ask me. When he had nothing else to do he enjoyed listening to me reciting to him from the Koran in a lilting voice, and I could tell from his face that he was moved.

One day I asked him about our neighbour Masood. I said to my grandfather: 'I fancy you don't like our neighbour Masood?'

To which he answered, having rubbed the tip of his nose: 'He's an indolent man and I don't like such people.'

I said to him: 'What's an indolent man?'

My grandfather lowered his head for a moment, then looking across at the wide expanse of field, he said: 'Do you see it stretching out from the edge of the desert up to the Nile bank? A hundred feddans. Do you see all those date palms? And those trees—sant, acacia, and sayal? All this fell into Masood's lap, was inherited by him from his father.'

Taking advantage of the silence that had descended upon my grandfather, I turned my gaze from him to the vast area defined by his words. 'I don't care,' I told myself, 'who owns those date palms, those trees or this black, cracked earth—all I know is that it's the arena for my dreams and my playground.'

My grandfather then continued: 'Yes, my boy, forty years ago all this belonged to Masood—two-thirds of it is now mine.'

This was news to me for I had imagined that the land had belonged to my grandfather ever since God's Creation.

'I didn't own a single feddan when I first set foot in this village. Masood was then the owner of all these riches. The position has changed now, though, and I think that before Allah calls to Him I shall have bought the remaining third as well.'

I do not know why it was I felt fear at my grandfather's words—and pity for our neighbour Masood. How I wished my grandfather wouldn't do what he'd said! I remembered Masood's singing, his beautiful voice and powerful laugh that resembled the gurgling of water. My grandfather never used to laugh.

I asked my grandfather why Masood had sold his land.

'Women,' and from the way my grandfather pronounced the word I felt that 'women' was something terrible. 'Masood, my boy, was a much-married man. Each time he married he sold me a feddan or two.' I made the quick calculation that Masood must have married some ninety women. Then I remembered his three wives, his shabby appearance, his lame donkey and its dilapidated saddle, his djellaba with the torn sleeves. I had all but rid my mind of the thoughts that jostled in it when I saw the man approaching us, and my grandfather and I exchanged glances.

'We'll be harvesting the dates today,' said Masood. 'Don't you want to 15
be there?'

I felt, though, that he did not really want my grandfather to attend. My grandfather, however, jumped to his feet and I saw that his eyes sparkled momentarily with an intense brightness. He pulled me by the hand and we went off to the harvesting of Masood's dates.

Someone brought my grandfather a stool covered with an ox-hide, while I remained standing. There was a vast number of people there, but though I knew them all, I found myself for some reason, watching Masood: aloof from the great gathering of people he stood as though it were no concern of his, despite the fact that the date palms to be harvested were his own. Sometimes his attention would be caught by the sound of a huge clump of dates crashing down from on high. Once he shouted up at the boy perched on the very summit of the date palm who had begun hacking at a clump with his long, sharp sickle: 'Be careful you don't cut the heart of the palm.'

No one paid any attention to what he said and the boy seated at the very summit of the date palm continued, quickly and energetically, to work away at the branch with his sickle till the clump of dates began to drop like something descending from the heavens.

I, however, had begun to think about Masood's phrase 'the heart of the palm'. I pictured the palm tree as something with feeling, something possessed of a heart that throbbed. I remembered Masood's remark to me when he had once seen me playing about with the branch of a young palm tree: 'Palm trees, my boy, like humans, experience joy and suffering.' And I had felt an inward and unreasoned embarrassment.

When I again looked at the expanse of ground stretching before me I saw 20
my young companions swarming like ants around the trunks of the palm trees, gathering up dates and eating most of them. The dates were collected into high mounds. I saw people coming along and weighing them into measuring bins and pouring them into sacks, of which I counted thirty. The crowd of people broke up, except for Hussein the merchant, Mousa the owner of the field next to ours on the east, and two men I'd never seen before.

I heard a low whistling sound and saw that my grandfather had fallen asleep. Then I noticed that Masood had not changed his stance, except that he had placed a stalk in his mouth and was munching at it like someone surfeited with food who doesn't know what to do with the mouthful he still has.

Suddenly my grandfather woke up, jumped to his feet and walked towards the sacks of dates. He was followed by Hussein the merchant, Mousa the owner of the field next to ours, and the two strangers. I glanced at Masood and saw that he was making his way towards us with extreme slowness, like a man who wants to retreat but whose feet insist on going forward. They formed a circle round the sacks of dates and began examining them, some taking a date or two to eat. My grandfather gave me a fistful, which I began munching. I saw Masood filling the palms of both hands with dates and bringing them up close to his nose, then returning them.

Then I saw them dividing up the sacks between them. Hussein the merchant took ten; each of the strangers took five. Mousa the owner of the field next to ours on the eastern side took five, and my grandfather took five. Understanding nothing, I looked at Masood and saw that his eyes were darting about to left and right like two mice that have lost their way home.

'You're still fifty pounds in debt to me,' said my grandfather to Masood. 'We'll talk about it later.'

Hussein called his assistants and they brought along donkeys, the two 25
strangers produced camels, and the sacks of dates were loaded on to them. One of the donkeys let out a braying which set the camels frothing at the mouth and complaining noisily. I felt myself drawing close to Masood, felt my hand stretch out towards him as though I wanted to touch the hem of his garment. I heard him make a noise in his throat like the rasping of a lamb being slaughtered. For some unknown reason, I experienced a sharp sensation of pain in my chest.

I ran off into the distance. Hearing my grandfather call after me. I hesitated a little, then continued on my way. I felt at that moment that I hated him. Quickening my pace, it was as though I carried within me a secret I wanted to rid myself of. I reached the river bank near the bend it made behind the wood of acacia trees. Then, without knowing why, I put my finger into my throat and spewed up the dates I'd eaten.

Analyzing the Text

1. In what way do the grandfather's actions involving Masood come into conflict with the teachings of the Koran that the boy has learned? Why is this all the more ironic since the grandfather has derived so much pleasure from hearing the boy recite from the Koran?
2. In what way does this story represent a turning point in the boy's perspective toward the grandfather whom he had previously idolized and unquestionably loved?

Understanding Salih's Techniques

1. In what way does the boy's reaction illustrate (although he doesn't why) his reluctance to become the kind of person he now perceives his grandfather to be?
2. How does Salih use the boy's sensitivity to the date palms and what he imagines they feel to foreshadow the boy's later reaction to his grandfather's failure to follow the dictates of the Koran?

Arguing for an Interpretation

1. Why is it ironic that the grandfather views himself as a much better person than Masood?
2. In what way does Salih present a complex, rather than a simplistic, picture of what constitutes goodness? What role does the "Chapter of the Merciful" in the Koran play in providing a standard for judging actions and behavior?

Poems

Linda Pastan

Linda Pastan was born in 1932 in New York and was educated at Radcliffe (B.A., 1954), Simmons College (M.L.S.,

1955) and Brandeis University (M.A., 1957). Her poetry explores the metaphysical implications of ordinary life and the mystery of what we take for granted. Her collected poems include Carnival Evening: New and Selected Poems—1968–1998 *(1998) and* PM/AM: New and Selected Poems *(1981) in which "Ethics" first appeared. A recent collection is* The Last Uncle: Poems *(2002).*

Ethics

In ethics class so many years ago
our teacher asked this question every fall:
if there were a fire in a museum
which would you save, a Rembrandt painting
or an old woman who hadn't many
years left anyhow? Restless on hard chairs
caring little for pictures or old age
we'd opt one year for life, the next for art
and always half-heartedly. Sometimes
the woman borrowed my grandmother's face
leaving her usual kitchen to wander
some drafty, half-imagined museum.
One year, feeling clever, I replied
why not let the woman decide herself?
Linda, the teacher would report, eschews
the burdens of responsibility.
This fall in a real museum I stand
before a real Rembrandt, old woman,
or nearly so, myself. The colors
within this frame are darker than autumn,
darker even than winter—the browns of earth,
though earth's most radiant elements burn
through the canvas. I know now that woman
and painting and season are almost one
and all beyond saving by children.

Analyzing the Text

1. How would you characterize the voice you hear in this poem and the emotional attitude of the speaker?
2. How has the speaker's understanding of the hypothetical dilemma proposed to her by her teacher altered with the passage of time?

Understanding Pastan's Techniques

1. How does the contrast between the two situations and time periods make the underlying theme more apparent?
2. How is the impact of the poem strengthened by the associations with fall and winter?

Arguing for an Interpretation

1. Do you agree with the speaker's rejection of the hypothetical question posed by her teacher in the ethics class? Why or why not?
2. In your opinion, is the speaker's problem a failure to take responsibility when she was young, and even now that she is the "old woman"? Why or why not? You might visit a Rembrandt Web site and compare your reactions to hers.

ROBERT FROST

Robert Frost (1874-1963) was born in San Francisco and lived there until the age of 11, although most people think of him as having grown up in New England. He spent his high school years in a Massachusetts mill town and studied at Harvard for two years. He worked a farm in New Hampshire that he had acquired in 1900, took a teaching job at the Pinkerton Academy, and wrote poetry that he had no luck in getting published. In 1912 he moved with his wife and five children to England, rented a farm, and met with success in publishing A Boy's Will *(1913) and* North of Boston *(1914). After the outbreak of World War I, he returned to the United States, where he was increasingly accorded recognition. He taught at Amherst College sporadically for many years. Frost won the Pulitzer Prize for poetry four times. He was a friend of John F. Kennedy, who invited him to read a poem at the presidential inauguration in 1961. Many of the qualities that made Frost's poetry so popular can be seen in "The Road Not Taken" (1916).*

The Road Not Taken

Two roads diverged in a yellow wood,
And sorry I could not travel both
And be one traveler, long I stood
And looked down one as far as I could
To where it bent in the undergrowth;

Then took the other, as just as fair,
And having perhaps the better claim,
Because it was grassy and wanted wear;
Though as for that the passing there
Had worn them really about the same,

And both that morning equally lay
In leaves no step had trodden black.
Oh, I kept the first for another day!

Yet knowing how way leads on to way,
I doubted if I should ever come back.

I shall be telling this with a sigh
Somewhere ages and ages hence:
Two roads diverged in a wood, and I—
I took the one less traveled by,
And that has made all the difference.

Analyzing the Text

1. How does the speaker rationalize his choice of the road he does take, and how does he now feel about having made this choice?
2. How does Frost use the speaker's decision to take the less traveled road as a jumping-off point to explore the important life choices he faced as a young man? How do you understand "less-traveled" in this context?

Understanding Frost's Techniques

1. In what sense is the psychological sensibility of the speaker more sophisticated than the anecdotal manner in which the poem is written?
2. Take a close look at Frost's use of tenses. In what time periods is the speaker located: exclusively in the past, in the present, or some combination of both?

Arguing for an Interpretation

1. Why do you think the poem is titled "The Road Not Taken" in view of the speaker's choice? Does the line "I shall be telling this with a sigh" imply regret?
2. Translate Frost's poem into your own words. Why is he happy about the choices he has made? What would be the less-traveled road for you? Would you consider taking it? Why or why not?

FADWA TUQAN

Fadwa Tuqan, one of ten children, was born in 1917 to an influential land-owning family in Nablus, which is now the west bank of the Jordan where she still lives. Her brother was the nationalist poet, Ibrahim Tuqan, whose work influenced her greatly. Born into a very conservative society where women were kept in isolation and away from opportunities for intellectual endeavor, Tuqan succeeded despite extraordinary difficulties and today is one of the most widely recognized poets in the Arab world. She has met with world leaders, including President Jamal Abd al-Nasser of Egypt and Moshe Dayan of Israel. Tuqan has been publishing her poetry since 1952, including the highly acclaimed collections In Front of the Locked Door *(1973) and* Give Us Love *(1979). She received the Honorary Palestine Prize for Poetry in 1996 and was the subject of a documentary film in 1999. Her poetry is characterized by an unusual candor about her emotional life, as in "I Found It" from her autobiography,* A Mountainous Journey, *translated by Naomi Shibab Nye and Salma Khadra Jayyusi (1990). "I Found It" conveys the excitement of bringing one's talent and individuality to flower against incredible cultural odds. The joyful voice of this poem made it a rallying cry for many Arabic women authors.*

I Found It

I found it on a radiant day
after a long drifting.
It was green and blossoming
as the sun over palm trees
scattered golden bouquets;
April was generous that season
with loving and sun.

I found it
after a long wandering.
It was a tender evergreen bough
where birds took shelter,
a bough bending gently under storms
which later was straight again,
rich with sap,
never snapping in the wind's hand.
It stayed supple
as if there were no bad weather,
echoing the brightness of stars,
the gentle breeze,
the dew and the clouds.

I found it
on a vivid summer day
after a long straying,
a tedious search.
It was a quiet lake
where thirsty human wolves
and swirling winds could only briefly
disturb the waters.
then they would clear again like crystal
to be the moon's mirror,
swimming place of light and blue,
bathing pool for the guardian stars.

I found it!
And now when the storms wail
and the face of the sun is masked in clouds,

when my shining fate revolves to dark,
my light will never be extinguished!
Everything that shadowed my life
wrapping it with night after night
has disappeared, laid down
in memory's grave,
since the day
my soul found
my soul.

Analyzing the Text

1. How does the poem describe the speaker's search for inner peace and equilibrium?
2. In what different environments has the speaker pursued her quest? From the metaphors Tuqan uses, what can you infer about the "it" she finds?

Understanding Tuqan's Techniques

1. In what way does the description of different settings represent different stages of the speaker's psychological journey?
2. What features of the poem enable us to understand how important her quest has become?

Arguing for an Interpretation

1. What can you infer about the nature of the obstacles that the speaker has had to overcome? Are these psychological, social, physical, or political?
2. Is Tuqan's tactic of presenting her quest in such an elliptical manner more effective than if she had explicitly described what she was searching for? Explain your answer.

XU GANG

Xu Gang was born in 1945 in Shanghai, and was drafted into the Army in 1962. He began publishing poetry in 1963, and initially became well known for his poems that supported the objectives of the Cultural Revolution. Disillusioned by the bloodshed it produced, Gang experienced the frustration and alienation felt by many intellectuals after the Revolution, a mood that is expressed in "Red Azalea on the Cliff." In 1974, he graduated from Beijing University and worked for The People's Daily, *China's most important newspaper, until 1987. Published collections of his poetry include* The Great River of Full Tide, The Flower of Rain, Dedicated to October, Songs for the Far Away, *and* One Hundred Lyrics. *He has received the National Prize for Poetry, the October Magazine Award, the Yu Hua Prize, and other awards. Since 1989 he has lived in Guangdong Province and in Paris. Lyrical and symbolic in the way that they invest common objects with metaphorical meanings, Xu Gang's poems characteristically infuse landscapes with sentiments and emotions as in "Red Azalea on the Cliff," translated by Fang Dai, Dennis Ding, and Edward Morin (1982).*

Red Azalea on the Cliff

Red azalea, smiling
From the cliffside at me,
You make my heart shudder with fear!
A body could smash and bones splinter in the canyon
Beauty, always looking on at disaster.

But red azalea on the cliff,
That you comb your twigs even in a mountain gale
Calms me down a bit.
Of course you're not wilfully courting danger,
Nor are you at ease with whatever happens to you.
You're merely telling me: beauty is nature.

Would anyone like to pick a flower
To give to his love
Or pin to his own lapel?
On the cliff there is no road
And no azalea grows where there is a road.
If someone actually reached that azalea,
Then an azalea would surely bloom in his heart.

Red azalea on the cliff,
You smile like the Yellow Mountains,
Whose sweetness encloses slyness,
Whose intimacy embraces distance.
You remind us all of our first love.
Sometimes the past years look
Just like the azalea on the cliff.

Analyzing the Text

1. What do the red azaleas that seem so fragile growing on the side of a cliff that would be dangerous to climb represent to the speaker?
2. How does the speaker's attitude toward the red azaleas change over the course of the poem? What would he like to achieve?

Understanding Gang's Techniques

1. How does the imagery in the poem use the contrast between fragility and beauty and a dangerous, hard-to-reach location to symbolize conflicting impulses in the speaker's psyche?

2. What elements in the poem suggest that the journey, rather than the goal, is more important?

Arguing for an Interpretation

1. How believable do you find the speaker's transition from the red azalea to a first love? Does the red azalea really stand for the speaker's reluctance to approach someone he loves? Explain your answer.
2. If you had to pick something in the natural environment to express these feelings, what would you choose and why?

Mariam Baruch

Mariam Baruch was born in Poland and came to Israel as a child. Her two books of poetry In the Midst *(1992) and* Yearning *(1999) were hailed by poets and critics. She is also known in Israel as a sculptor and artist. The following poem was translated by Rahel Chalfi in collaboration with Karen Alkalay-Gut.*

Sunflower

A sunflower turns after the sun
Its seed ripens
concealed

I turned
after your sculpted temples
where the coldness of your heart
shone out to me

My seed was not kindled

I am waiting

When your body stoops
I shall come to you
on tiptoe

And then perhaps you shall see me
and think
that I came to you
from afar

Analyzing the Text

1. What comparison does the speaker make between her unrequited devotion and a sunflower?
2. How does the speaker hope she will be perceived, once she is acknowledged?

Understanding Baruch's Techniques

1. What images does the poet use to contrast human emotions with processes in nature?
2. What details suggest that the speaker wishes to be perceived as a unique presence rather than as an ordinary person in this world?

Arguing for an Interpretation

1. Do you find the speaker's slavish devotion unseemly? Why or why not? What clues suggest a role reversal in the second half of the poem?
2. In your opinion, is the sunflower an appropriate choice or would another flower have served as well? If so, what would this flower be, and how would the poem change as a result? Who do you think her devotion is directed toward (a parent, a lover, God, a child)? Write a few paragraphs explaining your answer.

WILLIAM BLAKE

William Blake (1757–1827) is recognized as a painter, sculptor, spiritual visionary, and a poet of extraordinary talent. He was born in London to a working class family and was educated by his father at home by reading philosophy, the Bible, and poetry. At ten, he was enrolled in a drawing school, and at 14 became apprenticed to the well-known engraver, James Basire. By 1779, Blake was commissioned to illustrate the works of writers. In 1782, he married Catherine Boucher, whom he taught to read, write, and assist him with his engraving. Between 1783 and 1793 he wrote, illustrated, and printed his most famous lyrics, Songs of Innocence *and* Songs of Experience *(in which the following poem first appeared), which are hand-tinted and look somewhat like the illuminated manuscripts of medieval times. Blake's genius lay in his breaking away from the formalism of the eighteenth century. He fused his many talents in the service of mystical insights expressed in sublime lyrics that were worlds away from the classical allusions and formal language of his contemporaries.*

Ah! Sun-flower

AH! SUN-FLOWER, weary of time,
Who countest the steps of the Sun,
Seeking after that sweet golden clime
Where the traveller's journey is done;

Where the youth pined away with desire,
And the pale Virgin shrouded in snow,
Arise from their graves, and aspire
Where my Sun-flower wishes to go.

Analyzing the Text

1. How does Blake characterize the sunflower and what does the poem suggest about the nature of the realm where "my sunflower wishes to go"?
2. How does Blake enhance the symbolic power of the poem by omitting any specific references to a particular person, time, or place?

Understanding Blake's Techniques

1. What paradox does Blake create by contrasting the images of unfulfilled desire and icy renunciation with that of a sunflower basking in the sun? What attitude is suggested by the title?
2. How do the images in the poem imbue it with a tragic undertone that suggests something important about the nature of the speaker?

Arguing for an Interpretation

1. Although the sunflower has experienced fulfillment in the natural world, what does it lack? How is this desire equated with a resurrection for those who have experienced no comparable sense of fulfillment?
2. In your opinion, is this a religious poem? If so, what qualities make it such? What insight does the speaker gain into his own life that he uses the sunflower to symbolize?

MAURICE KENNY

Born in 1929 near the Saint Lawrence River in upstate New York, in the traditional lands of the "People of the Flint," his Mohawk Indian ancestors, Kenny was later taken south to Bayonne, New Jersey, to live with his mother. A year later, when he was in danger of being sent to reform school, his father came to New York to retrieve him and took him back to live with him in Watertown, New York. After high school, Kenny returned to Manhattan, worked in a bookstore, and studied with Louise Bogan, the distinguished American poet. He spent two years in Mexico and then opened a nightclub in

Puerto Rico. In 1967, he settled in Brooklyn where he continues to live. A near fatal heart attack in 1974 renewed his desire to focus on his Native American roots, and in the years immediately following some of his best-known works were published. Twenty-four of his books have been published and his poems have been translated into a dozen languages. He has been influential in shaping the course of Native American writing. He has coedited the poetry journal Contact/II, *is publisher of* Strawberry Press, *and through his associations with A. K. Wesasne Notes (named for the location of the Mohawk nation) and Studies in American Indian Literature, he has encouraged young Native American poets. Kenny has been nominated twice for the Pulitzer Prize. His novel* Black Robe: Isaac Jogues *(1987) was given the National Public Radio for Broadcasting Award and has been translated into French and Russian. Collections of his works include* Is Summer This Bare *(1985),* Rain and Other Fictions *(1985),* Greyhounding This America *(1987),* Roman Nose and Other Essays *(1987),* In the Time of the Present: New Poems *(2000), and a collection of short stories,* Tortured Skins, and Other Fictions *(2000). Kenny received the American Book Award in 1984 for* The Mama Poems *in which "Sometimes . . . Injustice" first appeared. As with other poems in this volume, Kenny projects a voice that, despite being dispossessed, finds strength in claiming his heritage against all odds.*

Sometimes . . . Injustice

The day I was born my father bought me a 22.
A year later my mother traded it for a violin.
Ten years later my big sister traded that
for a guitar, and gave it to her boy-friend . . .
who sold it.

Now you know why I never learned to hunt,
or learned how to play a musical instrument,
or became a Wall St. broker.

Analyzing the Text

1. How is the speaker's destiny determined by the actions of his family? What is the speaker's attitude toward this?
2. What can you infer about the story underlying each of the events the speaker describes and the relationship he has with members of his family?

Understanding Kenny's Techniques

1. What are the different hopes, aspirations, and necessary compromises that have shaped the speaker's life, as reflected in the 22-rifle, the violin, and the guitar?
2. How is each "injustice" mentioned in the poem related to a failure on the part of the speaker? Explain your answer.

Arguing for an Interpretation

1. In your opinion, what is the real nature of the injustice that confronts the speaker: racism, indifference of his family, or some other grievance?
2. Does the tone of the poem suggest that he is really angry and blames others for his "failure"? Why or why not?

OCTAVIO PAZ

Born in Mexico City in 1914, Octavio Paz has spent a good deal of his life traveling throughout the world. He lived in Spain during the Spanish Civil War and was influenced by the poetry of Quevedo and Gongora. In 1940, he resided in the United States when he received a Guggenheim Fellowship and came into contact with the poetry of Eliot, Pound, and Cummings. From 1946 to 1951 he lived in Paris, participated in the Surrealist movement and drew upon ancient Mexican mythology to produce Sun Stone, *a masterpiece of this period. From 1962 until 1968 he was Mexico's ambassador to India, whose culture, art, and philosophy influenced his writing. The concepts of detachment from the outside world, the illusory nature of reality, the illusion of the ego, and transcendence through the senses appear as themes in his poetry written during this period. Paz resigned as ambassador to protest the Mexican government's repressive actions taken against students before the 1968 Olympic games. He has held distinguished teaching positions at Cambridge University, the University of Texas at Austin, and Harvard. Paz's influence on contemporary Mexican writing has been extraordinary because of his ability to encompass the main intellectual currents of modern times in a bewildering number of fields, including art, aesthetics, philosophy, Oriental religion, anthropology, psychology, and political ideology, themes that appear in his twenty volumes of essays, short fiction, and poetry. His monumental achievement was recognized in 1990 when he was awarded the Nobel Prize for Literature. Paz died in 1998. Most of his poetry has appeared in English in the* Collected Poems, 1957–1987 *(1987). Volumes of his poetry include* Piedra de Sol *(1957) and* Configurations 1958–69 *(1973), and among his celebrated prose works are* Labyrinth of Solitude *(1961),* Convergences *(1987), and* Eagle or Sun *(1990). In "The Street," translated by Willis Knapp Jones (1963), Paz presents an eerie dream world from the perspective of a speaker who is both pursuer and pursued. In this work, Paz blends surrealism with symbolism to depict a fragmented consciousness searching for lost unity.*

The Street

The street is very long and filled with silence.
I walk in shadow and I trip and fall,
And then get up and walk with unseeing feet
Over the silent stones and the dry leaves,
And someone close behind, tramples them, too.
If I slow down and stop, he also stops,
If I run, so does he. I look. No one!
The whole street seems so dark, with no way out.
And though I turn and turn, I can't escape.
I always find myself on the same street.
Where no one waits for me and none pursues.
Where I pursue, a man who trips and falls
Gets up and seeing me, keeps saying: "No one!"

Analyzing the Text

1. In what ways does the speaker find himself in a situation very different from the one he expected?
2. What does the speaker realize at the end of the poem that he did not acknowledge at the beginning?

Understanding Paz's Techniques

1. What aspects of the poem suggest the surrealistic character of a dream? In what sense might the "street" have a larger meaning?
2. How does the shift in point of view in the last lines contrast ironically with preceding events?

Arguing for an Interpretation

1. How do you see the speaker in the poem: as someone destined to repeat his mistakes, as a paranoid personality, or as someone who is experiencing *déjà vu*?
2. At what point did you become aware that the pursuer had become the pursued? How does the atmosphere contribute to the sense of tension Paz creates? For example, what might be the significance of the fact that the man being watched trips and falls?

Emily Dickinson

Emily Dickinson (1830–1886) was born in Amherst, Massachusetts, and spent her entire life there. She attended the Mount Holyoke Female Seminary, where she quarreled frequently with the school's headmistress, who wanted her to accept Calvinist views. Dickinson became more reclusive in her mid-twenties, retired to the seclusion of her family, and in 1861 began writing poetry that was strongly influenced by the ideas of Ralph Waldo Emerson. She maintained a correspondence with Thomas Wentworth Higginson, an abolitionist editor who encouraged her to write poetry. During her life, she published only seven of the nearly 1,800 poems that she wrote. After her death, a selection of her work aroused public interest, and her stature as one of the great American poets is now unquestioned. "Tell All the Truth but Tell It Slant" expresses her artistic credo.

Tell All the Truth but Tell It Slant

Tell all the Truth but tell it slant—
Success in Circuit lies
Too bright for our infirm Delight
The Truth's superb surprise
As Lightning to the Children eased
With explanation kind
The Truth must dazzle gradually
Or every man be blind—

Analyzing the Text

1. In what way must poets reveal the truth gradually so as not to overwhelm the listener?
2. In what way can poetry blind, dazzle, or terrorize if the insights are not modulated?

Understanding Dickinson's Techniques

1. How does the metaphor that Dickinson uses to explain her reasons for telling the truth indirectly illuminate her choice?
2. What images underscore Dickinson's view that poetry can communicate truth just as if it were a force of nature?

Arguing for an Interpretation

1. How might the quality of Dickinson's personal reticence lead some readers to perceive her poetry as obscure? Did you find this poem obscure? Why or why not?
2. Dickinson compares readers who would be overwhelmed by direct statements of the truth with children who would be frightened were things

not explained carefully and kindly to them. In your opinion, does she include herself as well, or is she patronizing the reader?

Robert Desnos

Robert Desnos was born in 1900 in Paris into a bourgeois family who owned a café. As a young man he was strongly influenced by the writings of Victor Hugo and Arthur Rimbaud, and first published poems in a Dadaist magazine. He was part of a group of writers, including Louis Aragon, Paul Eluard, and André Breton, who were instrumental in creating a school of literary surrealism. Desnos published many books of poetry. When war broke out in 1939 he served in the French army. During the German occupation, he worked with the French resistance, and was arrested by the Nazis and sent to a concentration camp in Czechoslovakia, where he died in 1945. His work, Selected Poems, *translated into English, was published in 1991. "Midway," translated from the French by George Quasha, first appeared in* The Random House Book of Twentieth-Century French Poetry, *edited by Paul Auster, 1982.*

Midway

There is a precise instant in time
When a man reaches the exact center of his life,
A fraction of a second,
A fugitive particle of time quicker than a glance,
More fleeting than lovers' bliss,
Faster than light,
And a man is awake to this moment.

Long roads strain thru green wreathes
To reach the tower where a Lady drowses
Whose beauty defies all kisses, seasons,
As a star against wind, a stone against knives.

A shimmering boat sinks and shrieks.
At the top of a tree a flag flaps.
A woman—her hair stylish and stockings loose at the ankles—
Shows up at the corner
Impassioned, shimmering,
Her hand shielding an antiquated lamp billowing smoke.

And again a drunken dock-worker sings on a bridge,
And again a girl bites her lover's lips,

And again a rose-petal falls in an empty bed,
And again three clocks strike the same hour
A few minutes apart,
And again a man walking down the street turns back
Hearing his name called,
But it's not him she's calling,
And again a cabinet minister in full dress,
Irked by his shirt-tail caught between his trousers and his shorts,
Inaugurates an orphanage,
And again a truck barrelling flat-out
Thru empty streets at night
Drops a marvellous tomato that rolls in the gutter
To be swept away later,
And again a fire breaks out on the sixth floor of a building
Flaming in the heart of a silent, indifferent city,
And again a man hears a song—
Long forgotten—and soon to be forgotten all over,
And again many things,
Many other things that a man sees at the precise instant of the center of his life,
Many other things unfold at length in the shortest of earth's short instants.
He squeezes the mystery of this second, this fraction of a second,

But he says, "Get rid of these dark thoughts,"
And he gets rid of these dark thoughts.
And what could he say,
And what could be do
That's any better?

Analyzing the Text

1. What revelations await someone who is prepared to become fully conscious at the midpoint of his or her life?
2. How does the unnamed protagonist react to the kaleidoscopic flood of images?

Understanding Desnos's Techniques

1. Why does Desnos choose the midpoint of someone's life rather than any other moment for such intense revelations?
2. What is Desnos's attitude toward the protagonist's inability to withstand such intense, cacophonous perceptions?

Arguing for an Interpretation

1. How would it be possible to know when the midpoint of someone's life actually occurred? Is Desnos saying that these perceptions are available at every other moment as well? Explain your answer.
2. The unusual tone of this poem is both playful and serious. How do the images suggest the insufficiently appreciated revelation of everyday life?

Sara Teasdale

Sara Teasdale (1884–1933) was raised and educated in St. Louis and traveled to Europe and the Near East. After returning to the United States, she settled in New York and lived a life very similar to the independent "solitary" she describes in this poem. Her published works include* Rivers to the Sea *(1915) and* Love Songs *(1917).* Love Songs *went through five editions in one year and won Teasdale a special Pulitzer award, the first given for a book of poetry in this country.

The Solitary

My heart has grown rich with the passing of years,
I have less need now than when I was young

To share myself with every comer
Or shape my thoughts into words with my tongue.

It is one to me that they come or go
If I have myself and the drive of my will,
And strength to climb on a summer night
And watch the stars swarm over the hill.

Let them think I love them more than I do,
Let them think I care, though I go alone;
If it lifts their pride, what is it to me
Who am self-complete as a flower or a stone.

Analyzing the Text

1. In what way has the speaker changed from when she was young?
2. How does the speaker feel toward the way others perceived her?

Understanding Teasdale's Techniques

1. How often does the speaker use the word "my" or "I," and what significance does this have?
2. Why do you think the speaker has chosen metaphors drawn from nature to characterize her independence?

Arguing for an Interpretation

1. Do you believe it is possible or desirable for someone to become as "self-complete as a flower or a stone"? Why, or why not? Alternatively, you might consider whether one becomes more self-sufficient as one grows older.
2. Do you feel the speaker has gained more than she has lost? Explain your answer.

Drama

Tennessee Williams

Tennesse Williams (1911–1983), the preeminent American playwright, was born Thomas Lanier Williams in Columbus, Mississippi, to an Episcopalian minister's daughter and a traveling salesman. His family, including a brother and sister, moved to St. Louis in 1918, where he grew up and attended the University of Missouri until poverty forced him to drop out. He later received his B.A. from the University of Iowa. The 1945 production of The Glass Menagerie *brought Williams instant recognition, a judgment reconfirmed with the Broadway success two years later of* A Streetcar Named Desire. *His other major plays include* Summer and Smoke *(1948),* Rose Tattoo *(1951),* Cat on a Hot Tin Roof *(1955, Pulitzer Prize),* Suddenly Last Summer *(1958),* Sweet Bird of Youth *(1959), and* The Night of the Iguana *(1961) all of which were adapted as widely popular films.* The Glass Menagerie *is a sympathetic account of a dysfunctional Southern family and the fantasies and delusions that rule their lives.*

The Glass Menagerie

The Characters

AMANDA WINGFIELD (*the mother*)

A little woman of great but confused vitality clinging frantically to another time and place. Her characterization must be carefully created, not copied from type. She is not paranoiac, but her life is paranoia. There is much to admire in Amanda, and as much to love and pity as there is to laugh at. Certainly she has endurance and a kind of heroism, and though her foolishness makes her unwittingly cruel at times, there is tenderness in her slight person.

LAURA WINGFIELD (*her daughter*)

Amanda, having failed to establish contact with reality, continues to live vitally in her illusions, but Laura's situation is even graver. A childhood illness has left her crippled, one leg slightly shorter than the other, and held in a brace. This defect need not be more than suggested on the stage. Stemming from this, Laura's separation increases till she is like a piece of her own glass collection, too exquisitely fragile to move from the shelf.

TOM WINGFIELD (*her son*)

And the narrator of the play. A poet with a job in a warehouse. His nature is not remorseless, but to escape from a trap he has to act without pity.

JIM O'CONNOR (*the gentleman caller*)

A nice, ordinary, young man.

PRODUCTION NOTES

Being a "memory play," *The Glass Menagerie* can be presented with unusual freedom of convention. Because of its considerably delicate or tenuous material, atmospheric touches and subtleties of direction play a particularly important part. Expressionism and all other unconventional techniques in drama have only one valid aim, and that is a closer approach to truth. When a play employs unconventional techniques, it is not, or certainly shouldn't be, trying to escape its responsibility of dealing with reality, or interpreting experience, but is actually or should be attempting to find a closer approach, a more penetrating and vivid expression of things as they are. The straight realistic play with its genuine Frigidaire and authentic ice-cubes, its characters who speak exactly as its audience speaks, corresponds to the academic landscape and has the same virtue of a photographic likeness. Everyone should know nowadays the unimportance of the photographic in art: that truth, life, or reality is an organic thing which the poetic imagination can represent or suggest, in essence, only through transformation, through changing into other forms than those which were merely present in appearance.

These remarks are not meant as a preface only to this particular play. They have to do with a conception of a new, plastic theatre which must take the place of the exhausted theatre of realistic conventions if the theatre is to resume vitality as a part of our culture.

THE SCREEN DEVICE: There is *only one important difference between the original and the acting version of the play* and that is the *omission* in the latter of the device that I tentatively included in my *original* script. This device was the use of a screen on which were projected magic-lantern slides bearing images or titles. I do not regret the omission of this device from the original Broadway production. The extraordinary power of Miss Taylor's° performance made it suitable to have the utmost simplicity in the physical production. But I think it may be interesting to some readers to see how this device was conceived. So I am putting it into the published manuscript. These images and legends, projected from behind, were cast on a section of wall between the front-room and dining-room areas, which should be indistinguishable from the rest when not in use.

The purpose of this will probably be apparent. It is to give accent to certain values in each scene. Each scene contains a particular point (or several) which is structurally the most important. In an episodic play, such as this, the basic structure or narrative line may be obscured from the audience; the effect may seem fragmentary rather than architectural. This may not be the fault of the play so much as a lack of attention in the audience. The legend or image upon the screen will strengthen the effect of what is merely allusion in the writing and allow the primary point to be made more simply and lightly than if the entire responsibility were on the spoken lines. Aside from this structural value, I think the screen will have a definite emotional appeal, less definable but just as important. An imaginative producer or director may invent many other uses for this device than those indicated in the present script. In fact the possibilities of the device seem much larger to me than the instance of this play can possibly utilize.

Miss Taylor's: Williams is referring to the American actress Laurette Taylor (1884–1946) who first played the role of Amanda.

THE MUSIC: Another extra-literary accent in this play is provided by the use of music. A single recurring tune, "The Glass Menagerie,"° is used to give emotional emphasis to suitable passages. This tune is like circus music, not when you are on the grounds or in the immediate vicinity of the parade, but when you are at some distance and very likely thinking of something else. It seems under those circumstances to continue almost interminably and it weaves in and out of your preoccupied consciousness; then it is the lightest, most delicate music in the world and perhaps the saddest. It expresses the surface vivacity of life with the underlying strain of immutable and inexpressible sorrow. When you look at a piece of delicately spun glass you think of two things: how beautiful it is and how easily it can be broken. Both of those ideas should be woven into the recurring tune, which dips in and out of the play as if it were carried on a wind that changes. It serves as a thread of connection and allusion between the narrator with his separate point in time and space and the subject of his story. Between each episode it returns as reference to the emotion, nostalgia, which is the first condition of the play. It is primarily Laura's music and therefore comes out most clearly when the play focuses upon her and the lovely fragility of glass which is her image.

THE LIGHTING: The lighting in the play is not realistic. In keeping with the atmosphere of memory, the stage is dim. Shafts of light are focused on selected areas or actors, sometimes in contradistinction to what is the apparent center. For instance, in the quarrel scene between Tom and Amanda, in which Laura has no active part, the clearest pool of light is on her figure. This is also true of the supper scene, when her silent figure on the sofa should remain the visual center. The light upon Laura should be distinct from the others, having a peculiar pristine clarity such as light used in early religious portraits of female saints or madonnas. A certain correspondence to light in religious paintings, such as El Greco's,° where the figures are radiant in atmosphere that is relatively dusky, could be effectively used throughout the play. (It will also permit a more effective use of the screen.) A free, imaginative use of light can be of enormous value in giving a mobile, plastic quality to plays of a more or less static nature.

Tennessee Williams

Scene 1

The Wingfield apartment is in the rear of the building, one of those vast hive-like conglomerations of cellular living-units that flower as warty growths in overcrowded urban centers of lower middle-class population and are symptomatic of the impulse of this largest and fundamentally enslaved section of American society to avoid fluidity and differentiation and to exist and function as one interfused mass of automatism.

The apartment faces an alley and is entered by a fire escape, a structure whose name is a touch of accidental poetic truth, for all of these huge buildings are always burning with the slow and implacable

"The Glass Menagerie": Music for the play was composed by Paul Bowles. **El Greco:** A Greek painter (1541–1614) who lived in Spain; famous for his portraits of elongated and distorted figures in rapt religious ecstasy.

fires of human desperation. The fire escape is part of what we see—that is, the landing of it and steps descending from it.

The scene is memory and is therefore nonrealistic. Memory takes a lot of poetic license. It omits some details; others are exaggerated, according to the emotional value of the articles it touches, for memory is seated predominantly in the heart. The interior is therefore rather dim and poetic.

At the rise of the curtain, the audience is faced with the dark, grim rear wall of the Wingfield tenement. This building is flanked on both sides by dark, narrow alleys which run into murky canyons of tangled clotheslines, garbage cans, and the sinister latticework of neighboring fire escapes. It is up and down these side alleys that exterior entrances and exits are made during the play. At the end of Tom's opening commentary, the dark tenement wall slowly becomes transparent° and reveals the interior of the ground-floor Wingfield apartment.

Nearest the audience is the living room, which also serves as a sleeping room for Laura, the sofa unfolding to make her bed. Just beyond, separated from the living room by a wide arch or second proscenium with transparent faded portieres° (or second curtain), is the dining room. In an old-fashioned whatnot° in the living room are seen scores of transparent glass animals. A blown-up photograph of the father hangs on the wall of the living room, to the left of the archway. It is the face of a very handsome young man in a doughboy's° First World War cap. He is gallantly smiling, ineluctably smiling, as if to say "I will be smiling forever."

Also hanging on the wall, near the photograph, are a typewriter keyboard chart and a Gregg shorthand diagram. An upright typewriter on a small table stands beneath the charts.

The audience hears and sees the opening scene in the dining room through both the transparent fourth wall of the building and the transparent gauze portieres of the dining-room arch. It is during this revealing scene that the fourth wall slowly ascends, out of sight. This transparent exterior wall is not brought down again until the very end of the play, during Tom's final speech.

The narrator is an undisguised convention of the play. He takes whatever license with dramatic convention is convenient to his purposes.

Tom enters, dressed as a merchant sailor, and strolls across to the fire escape. There he stops and lights a cigarette. He addresses the audience.

TOM. Yes, I have tricks in my pocket, I have things up my sleeve. But I am the opposite of a stage magician. He gives you illusion that has the appearance of truth. I give you truth in the pleasant disguise of illusion.

To begin with, I turn back time. I reverse it to that quaint period, the thirties, when the huge middle class of America was matriculating in a school for the blind. Their eyes had failed them, or they had failed their eyes, and so they were having their fingers pressed forcibly down on the fiery Braille alphabet of a dissolving economy.

---

transparent: The wall has been painted on a piece of fabric to create the illusion of a solid backdrop that can be seen through when lit from behind. **portieres:** Curtains hung in a doorway either to replace the door or for decoration. **whatnot:** A stand with shelves for bric-a-brac and ornaments. **doughboy:** A nickname for American infantrymen in Europe during World War I so called because the buttons on their uniforms resembled dumplings.

In Spain there was revolution. Here there was only shouting and confusion. In Spain there was Guernica.° Here there were disturbances of labor, sometimes pretty violent, in otherwise peaceful cities such as Chicago, Cleveland, Saint Louis . . . This is the social background of the play.

(*Music begins to play.*)

The play is memory. Being a memory play, it is dimly lighted, it is sentimental, it is not realistic. In memory everything seems to happen to music. That explains the fiddle in the wings.

I am the narrator of the play, and also a character in it. The other characters are my mother, Amanda, my sister, Laura, and a gentleman caller who appears in the final scenes. He is the most realistic character in the play, being an emissary from a world of reality that we were somehow set apart from. But since I have a poet's weakness for symbols, I am using this character also as a symbol; he is the long-delayed but always expected something that we live for.

There is a fifth character in the play who doesn't appear except in this larger-than-life-size photograph over the mantel. This is our father who left us a long time ago. He was a telephone man who fell in love with long distances; he gave up his job with the telephone company and skipped the light fantastic out of town . . .

The last we heard of him was a picture postcard from Mazatlan, on the Pacific coast of Mexico, containing a message of two words: "Hello—Goodbye!" and no address.

I think the rest of the play will explain itself. . . .

(*Amanda's voice becomes audible through the portieres.*)

(*Legend on screen:* "Où sont les neiges."°)

(*Tom divides the portieres and enters the dining room. Amanda and Laura are seated at a drop-leaf table. Eating is indicated by gestures without food or utensils. Amanda faces the audience. Tom and Laura are seated profile. The interior has lit up softly and through the scrim we see Amanda and Laura seated at the table.*)

AMANDA. (*calling*) Tom?

TOM. Yes, Mother.

AMANDA. We can't say grace until you come to the table!

TOM. Coming, Mother. (*He bows slightly and withdraws, reappearing a few moments later in his place at the table.*)

AMANDA. (*to her son*) Honey, don't *push* with your *fingers.* If you have to push with something, the thing to push with is a crust of bread. And chew—chew! Animals have secretions in their stomachs which enable them to digest food without mastication, but human beings are supposed to chew their food before they swallow it down. Eat food leisurely, son, and really enjoy it. A well-cooked meal has lots of delicate

---

Guernica: a Basque town in northern Spain annihilated by the Germans who fought with forces supporting Francisco Franco's fascists during the Spanish Civil War in 1937.
"Où sont les neiges": "Where are the snows (of yesteryear)," refrain from "The Ballade of Dead Ladies" by the French medieval writer François Villon (1431–1463).

flavors that have to be held in the mouth for appreciation. So chew your food and give your salivary glands a chance to function!

(Tom deliberately lays his imaginary fork down and pushes his chair back from the table.)

TOM. I haven't enjoyed one bite of this dinner because of your constant directions on how to eat it. It's you that make me rush through meals with your hawklike attention to every bite I take. Sickening—spoils my appetite—all this discussion of—animals' secretion—salivary glands—mastication!

AMANDA. *(lightly)* Temperament like a Metropolitan star.°

(Tom rises and walks toward the living room.)

You're not excused from the table.

TOM. I'm getting a cigarette.

AMANDA. You smoke too much.

(Laura rises)

LAURA. I'll bring in the blanc mange.°

(Tom remains standing with his cigarette by the portieres.)

AMANDA. *(rising)* No, sister, no, sister°—you be the lady this time and I'll be the darky.

LAURA. I'm already up.

AMANDA. Resume your seat, little sister—I want you to stay fresh and pretty—for gentlemen callers!

LAURA. *(sitting down)* I'm not expecting any gentlemen callers.

AMANDA. *(crossing out to the kitchenette, airily)* Sometimes they come when they are least expected! Why, I remember one Sunday afternoon in Blue Mountain°—

(She enters the kitchenette.)

TOM. I know what's coming!

LAURA. Yes. But let her tell it.

TOM. Again?

LAURA. She loves to tell it.

(Amanda returns with a bowl of dessert.)

AMANDA. One Sunday afternoon in Blue Mountain—your mother received—*seventeen!*—gentlemen callers! Why, sometimes there weren't chairs enough to accommodate them all. We had to send the nigger over to bring in folding chairs from the parish house.

TOM. *(remaining at the portieres)* How did you entertain those gentlemen callers?

AMANDA. I understood the art of conversation!

TOM. I bet you could talk.

Metropolitan star: like a temperamental diva at the Metropolitan Opera in New York. **blanc mange:** a vanilla flavored sweet molded pudding or custard. **sister:** when Amanda was growing up in the South the oldest daughter was called "sister" by her parents and siblings. **Blue mountain:** refers to an imaginary version of Clarksville, Mississippi, where Williams grew up which bordered plantations and the genteel world of the Old South that Amanda recollects.

AMANDA. Girls in those days *knew* how to talk, I can tell you.

TOM. Yes?

(*Image on screen: Amanda as a girl on a porch, greeting callers.*)

AMANDA. They knew how to entertain their gentlemen callers. It wasn't enough for a girl to be possessed of a pretty face and a graceful figure—although I wasn't slighted in either respect. She also needed to have a nimble wit and a tongue to meet all occasions.

TOM. What did you talk about?

AMANDA. Things of importance going on in the world! Never anything coarse or common or vulgar.

She addresses Tom as though he were seated in the vacant chair at the table though he remains by the portieres. He plays this scene as though reading from a script.°

My callers were gentleman—all! Among my callers were some of the most prominent young planters of the Mississippi Delta—planters and sons of planters!

(*Tom motions for music and a spot of light on Amanda. Her eyes lift, her face glows, her voice becomes rich and elegiac.*)

(*Screen legend:* "Où sont les neiges d'antan?"°)

There was young Champ Laughlin who later became vice-president of the Delta Planters Bank. Hadley Stevenson who was drowned in Moon Lake and left his widow one hundred and fifty thousand in Government bonds. There were the Cutrere brothers, Wesley and Bates. Bates was one of my bright particular beaux! He got in a quarrel with that wild Wainwright boy. They shot it out on the floor of Moon Lake Casino. Bates was shot through the stomach. Died in the ambulance on his way to Memphis. His widow was also well provided-for, came into eight or ten thousand acres, that's all. She married him on the rebound—never loved her—carried my picture on him the night he died! And there was that boy that every girl in the Delta had set her cap for! That beautiful, brilliant young Fitzhugh boy from Greene County!

TOM. What did he leave his widow?

AMANDA. He never married! Gracious, you talk as though all of my old admirers had turned up their toes to the daisies!

TOM. Isn't this the first you've mentioned that still survives?

AMANDA. That Fitzhugh boy went North and made a fortune—came to be known as the Wolf of Wall Street! He had the Midas touch,° whatever he touched turned to gold! And I could have been Mrs. Duncan J. Fitzhugh, mind you! But—I picked your *father!*

LAURA. (*rising*) Mother, let me clear the table.

AMANDA. No, dear, you go in front and study your typewriter chart. Or practice your shorthand a little. Stay fresh and pretty!—It's almost time for our gentlemen callers to start arriving. (*She flounces girlishly toward*

---

script: At this point, Tom acts as a character within the play and as the stage manager. **"Où sont les neiges d'antan?":** "Where are the snows of yesteryear?" **Midas touch:** in classical mythology, a Phrygian king who had the power of turning whatever he touched into gold.

the kitchenette.) How many do you suppose we're going to entertain this afternoon?

(*Tom throws down the paper and jumps up with a groan.*)

LAURA. (*alone in the dining room*) I don't believe we're going to receive any, Mother.

AMANDA. (*reappearing airily*) What? No one?—not one? You must be joking!

(*Laura nervously echoes her laugh. She slips in a fugitive manner through the half-open portieres and draws them gently behind her. A shaft of very clear light is thrown on her face against the faded tapestry of the curtains. Faintly the music of "The Glass Menagerie" is heard as she continues lightly:*)

Not one gentleman caller? It can't be true! There must be a flood, there must have been a tornado!

LAURA. It isn't a flood, it's not a tornado, Mother. I'm just not popular like you were in Blue Mountain. . . .

(*Tom utters another groan. Laura glances at him with a faint, apologetic smile. Her voice catches a little:*)

Mother's afraid I'm going to be an old maid.

(*The scene dims out with the "Glass Menagerie" music.*)

Scene 2

On the dark stage the screen is lighted with the image of blue roses. Gradually Laura's figure becomes apparent and the screen goes out. The music subsides.

Laura is seated in the delicate ivory chair at the small clawfoot table. She wears a dress of soft violet material for a kimono—her hair is tied back from her forehead with a ribbon. She is washing and polishing her collection of glass. Amanda appears on the fire escape steps. At the sound of her ascent, Laura catches her breath, thrusts the bowl of ornaments away, and seats herself stiffly before the diagram of the typewriter keyboard as though it held her spellbound. Something has happened to Amanda. It is written in her face as she climbs to the landing: a look that is grim and hopeless and a little absurd. She has on one of those cheap or imitation velvety-looking cloth coats with imitation fur collar. Her hat is five or six years old, one of those dreadful cloche hats that were worn in the late Twenties, and she is clutching an enormous black patent-leather pocketbook with nickel clasps and initials. This is her full-dress outfit, the one she usually wears to the D.A.R.° Before entering she looks through the door. She purses her lips, opens her eyes very wide, rolls them upward and shakes her head. Then she slowly lets herself in the door. Seeing her mother's expression, Laura touches her lips with a nervous gesture.

D.A.R.: the national society of the Daughters of the American Revolution (founded in 1890), a patriotic organization of women whose ancestors aided the Revolutionary cause.

LAURA. Hello, Mother, I was— (*She makes a nervous gesture toward the chart on the wall. Amanda leans against the shut door and stares at Laura with a martyred look.*)

AMANDA. Deception? Deception? (*She slowly removes her hat and gloves, continuing the sweet suffering stare. She lets the hat and gloves fall on the floor—a bit of acting.*)

LAURA. (*shakily*) How was the D.A.R. meeting?

(*Amanda slowly opens her purse and removes a dainty white handkerchief which she shakes out delicately and delicately touches to her lips and nostrils.*)

Didn't you go to the D.A.R. meeting, Mother?

AMANDA. (*faintly, almost inaudibly*) —No.—No. (*then more forcibly:*) I did not have the strength—to go to the D.A.R. In fact, I did not have the courage! I wanted to find a hole in the ground and hide myself in it forever! (*She crosses slowly to the wall and removes the diagram of the typewriter keyboard. She holds it in front of her for a second, staring at it sweetly and sorrowfully—then bites her lips and tears it in two pieces.*)

LAURA. (*faintly*) Why did you do that, Mother?

(*Amanda repeats the same procedure with the chart of the Gregg Alphabet.*)

Why are you—

AMANDA. Why? Why? How old are you, Laura?

LAURA. Mother, you know my age.

AMANDA. I thought you were an adult; it seems that I was mistaken. (*She crosses slowly to the sofa and sinks down and stares at Laura.*)

LAURA. Please don't stare at me, Mother.

(*Amanda closes her eyes and lowers her head. There is a ten-second pause.*)

AMANDA. What are we going to do, what is going to become of us, what is the future?

(*There is another pause.*)

LAURA. Has something happened, Mother?

(*Amanda draws a long breath, takes out the handkerchief again, goes through the dabbing process.*)

Mother, has—something happened?

AMANDA. I'll be all right in a minute, I'm just bewildered— (*She hesitates.*) —by life....

LAURA. Mother, I wish that you would tell me what's happened!

AMANDA. As you know, I was supposed to be inducted into my office at the D.A.R. this afternoon.

(*Screen image: A swarm of typewriters.*)

But I stopped off at Rubicam's Business College to speak to your teachers about your having a cold and ask them what progress they thought you were making down there.

LAURA. Oh....

AMANDA. I went to the typing instructor and introduced myself as your mother. She didn't know who you were.

"Wingfield," she said, "We don't have any such student enrolled at the school!"

I assured her she did, that you had been going to classes since early in January.

"I wonder," she said, "if you could be talking about that terribly shy little girl who dropped out of school after only a few days' attendance?"

"No," I said, "Laura, my daughter, has been going to school every day for the past six weeks!"

"Excuse me," she said. She took the attendance book out and there was your name, unmistakably printed, and all the dates you were absent until they decided that you had dropped out of school.

I still said, "No, there must have been some mistake! There must have been some mix-up in the records!"

And she said, "No—I remember her perfectly now. Her hands shook so that she couldn't hit the right keys! The first time we gave a speed test, she broke down completely—was sick at the stomach and almost had to be carried into the wash room! After that morning she never showed up any more. We phoned the house but never got any answer"—While I was working at Famous-Barr,° I suppose, demonstrating those—

(*She indicates a brassiere with her hands.*)

Oh! I felt so weak I could barely keep on my feet! I had to sit down while they got me a glass of water! Fifty dollars' tuition, all of our plans—my hopes and ambitions for you—just gone up the spout, just gone up the spout like that.

(*Laura draws a long breath and gets awkwardly to her feet. She crosses to the Victrola and winds it up.*°)

What are you doing?

LAURA. Oh! (*She releases the handle and returns to her seat.*)

AMANDA. Laura, where have you been going when you've gone out pretending that you were going to business college?

LAURA. I've just been going out walking.

AMANDA. That's not true.

LAURA. It is. I just went walking.

AMANDA. Walking? Walking? In winter? Deliberately courting pneumonia in that light coat? Where did you walk to, Laura?

LAURA. All sorts of places—mostly in the park.

AMANDA. Even after you'd started catching that cold?

LAURA. It was the lesser of two evils, Mother.

(*Screen image: Winter scene in a park.*)

I couldn't go back there. I—threw up—on the floor!

AMANDA. From half past seven till after five every day you mean to tell me you walked around the park, because you wanted to make me think that you were still going to Rubicam's Business College?

Famous-Barr: an upscale department store in St. Louis, Missouri. **winds it up:** refers to a mechanically powered phonograph that Laura must rewind freqently.

LAURA. It wasn't as bad as it sounds. I went inside places to get warmed up.

AMANDA. Inside where?

LAURA. I went in the art museum and the bird houses at the Zoo. I visited the penguins every day! Sometimes I did without lunch and went to the movies. Lately I've been spending most of my afternoons in the Jewel Box, that big glass house where they raise the tropical flowers.

AMANDA. You did all this to deceive me, just for deception? (*Laura looks down.*) Why?

LAURA. Mother, when you're disappointed, you get that awful suffering look on your face, like the picture of Jesus' mother in the museum!

AMANDA. Hush!

LAURA. I couldn't face it.

(*There is a pause. A whisper of strings is heard. Legend on screen: "The Crust of Humility."*)

AMANDA. (*hopelessly fingering the huge pocketbook*) So what are we going to do the rest of our lives? Stay home and watch the parades go by? Amuse ourselves with the glass menagerie, darling? Eternally play those worn-out phonograph records your father left as a painful reminder of him? We won't have a business career—we've given that up because it gave us nervous indigestion! (*She laughs wearily.*) What is there left but dependency all our lives? I know so well what becomes of unmarried women who aren't prepared to occupy a position. I've seen such pitiful cases in the South—barely tolerated spinsters living upon the grudging patronage of sister's husband or brother's wife!—stuck away in some little mousetrap of a room—encouraged by one in-law to visit another—little birdlike women without any nest—eating the crust of humility all their life!

Is that the future that we've mapped out for ourselves? I swear it's the only alternative I can think of! (*She pauses.*) It isn't a very pleasant alternative, is it? (*She pauses again.*) Of course—some girls *do marry.*

(*Laura twists her hands nervously.*)

Haven't you ever liked some boy?

LAURA. Yes. I liked one once. (*She rises.*) I came across his picture a while ago.

AMANDA. (*with some interest*) He gave you his picture?

LAURA. No, it's in the yearbook.

AMANDA. (*disappointed*) Oh—a high school boy.

(*Screen image: Jim as the high school hero bearing a silver cup.*)

LAURA. Yes. His name was Jim. (*She lifts the heavy annual from the claw-foot table.*) Here he is in *The Pirates of Penzance.*°

AMANDA. (*absently*) The what?

LAURA. The operetta the senior class put on. He had a wonderful voice and we sat across the aisle from each other Mondays, Wednesdays and Fridays in the Aud. Here he is with the silver cup for debating! See his grin?

AMANDA. (*absently*) He must have had a jolly disposition.

LAURA. He used to call me—Blue Roses.

(*Screen image: Blue roses.*)

The Pirates of Penzance: light comic opera by W. S. Gilbert and Arthur Sullivan that had its premiere in 1879 in New York.

AMANDA. Why did he call you such a name as that?

LAURA. When I had that attack of pleurosis—he asked me what was the matter when I came back. I said pleurosis—he thought that I said Blue Roses! So that's what he always called me after that. Whenever he saw me, he'd holler, "Hello, Blue Roses!" I didn't care for the girl that he went out with. Emily Meisenbach. Emily was the best-dressed girl at Soldan. She never struck me, though, as being sincere . . . It says in the Personal Section—they're engaged. That's—six years ago! They must be married by now.

AMANDA. Girls that aren't cut out for business careers usually wind up married to some nice man. (*She gets up with a spark of revival.*) Sister, that's what you'll do!

(*Laura utters a startled, doubtful laugh. She reaches quickly for a piece of glass.*)

LAURA. But, Mother—

AMANDA. Yes? (*She goes over to the photograph.*)

LAURA. (*in a tone of frightened apology*) I'm—crippled!

AMANDA. Nonsense! Laura, I've told you never, never to use that word. Why, you're not crippled, you just have a little defect—hardly noticeable, even! When people have some slight disadvantage like that, they cultivate other things to make up for it—develop charm—and vivacity—and—*charm!* That's all you have to do! (*She turns again to the photograph.*) One thing your father had *plenty of*—was *charm!*

(*The scene fades out with music.*)

Scene 3

(*Legend on screen: "After the fiasco—"*

Tom speaks from the fire escape landing.)

TOM. After the fiasco at Rubicam's Business College, the idea of getting a gentleman caller for Laura began to play a more and more important part in Mother's calculations. It became an obsession. Like some archetype of the universal unconscious, the image of the gentleman caller haunted our small apartment. . . .

(*Screen image: A young man at the door of a house with flowers.*)

An evening at home rarely passed without some allusion to this image, this specter, this hope. . . . Even when he wasn't mentioned, his presence hung in Mother's preoccupied look and in my sister's frightened, apologetic manner—hung like a sentence passed upon the Wingfields!

Mother was a woman of action as well as words. She began to take logical steps in the planned direction. Late that winter and in the early spring—realizing that extra money would be needed to properly feather the nest and plume the bird—she conducted a vigorous campaign on the telephone, roping in subscribers to one of those magazines for matrons called *The Homemaker's Companion,* the type of journal that features the serialized sublimations of ladies of letters who think in terms of delicate cuplike breasts, slim, tapering waists, rich, creamy thighs, eyes like wood smoke in autumn, fingers that soothe and caress like strains of music, bodies as powerful as Etruscan sculpture.

(*Screen image: The cover of a glamor magazine.*

Amanda enters with the telephone on a long extension cord. She is spotlighted in the dim stage.)

AMANDA. Ida Scott? This is Amanda Wingfield! We *missed* you at the D.A.R. last Monday! I said to myself: She's probably suffering with that sinus condition! How is that sinus condition?

Horrors! Heaven have mercy!—You're a Christian martyr, yes, that's what you are, a Christian martyr!

Well, I just now happened to notice that your subscription to the *Companion's* about to expire! Yes, it expires with the next issue, honey!—just when that wonderful new serial by Bessie Mae Hopper is getting off to such an exciting start. Oh, honey, it's something that you can't miss! You remember how *Gone with the Wind*° took everybody by storm? You simply couldn't go out if you hadn't read it. All everybody *talked* was Scarlett O'Hara. Well, this is a book that critics already compare to *Gone with the Wind.* It's the *Gone with the Wind* of the post-World-War generation!—What?—Burning?—Oh, honey, don't let them burn, go take a look in the oven and I'll hold the wire! Heavens—I think she's hung up!

(*The scene dims out.*)

(*Legend on screen: "You think I'm in love with Continental Shoemakers?"*)

(*Before the lights come up again, the violent voices of Tom and Amanda are heard. They are quarreling behind the portieres. In front of them stands Laura with clenched hands and panicky expression. A clear pool of light is on her figure throughout this scene.*)

TOM. What in Christ's name am I—

AMANDA. (*shrilly*) Don't you use that—

TOM. —supposed to do!

AMANDA. —expression! Not in my—

TOM. Ohhh!

AMANDA. —presence! Have you gone out of your senses?

TOM. I have, that's true, *driven* out!

AMANDA. What is the matter with you, you—big—big—IDIOT!

TOM. Look!—I've got *no thing,* no single thing—

AMANDA. Lower your voice!

TOM. —in my life here that I can call my OWN! Everything is—

AMANDA. Stop that shouting!

TOM. Yesterday you confiscated my books! You had the nerve to—

AMANDA. I took that horrible novel back to the library—yes! That hideous book by that insane Mr. Lawrence.°

(*Tom laughs wildly.*)

Gone with the Wind: novel written by Margaret Mitchell (1900–1949) published in 1936 that is set in the South during the Civil War in which Scarlett O'Hara is the heroine. **Lawrence:** refers to the English poet and novelist, D. H. Lawrence (1885–1930), who advocated sexual freedom.

I cannot control the output of diseased minds or people who cater to them—

(*Tom laughs still more wildly.*)

BUT I WON'T ALLOW SUCH FILTH BROUGHT INTO MY HOUSE! No, no, no, no, no!

TOM. House, house! Who pays rent on it, who makes a slave of himself to—

AMANDA. (*fairly screeching*) Don't you DARE to—

TOM. No, no, *I* mustn't say things! *I've* got to just—

AMANDA. Let me tell you—

TOM. I don't want to hear any more!

(*He tears the portieres open. The dining-room area is lit with turgid smoky red glow. Now we see Amanda; her hair is in metal curlers and she is wearing a very old bathrobe, much too large for her slight figure, a relic of the faithless Mr. Wingfield. The upright typewriter now stands on the drop-leaf table, along with a wild disarray of manuscripts. The quarrel was probably precipitated by Amanda's interruption of Tom's creative labor. A chair lies overthrown on the floor. Their gesticulating shadows are cast on the ceiling by the fiery glow.*)

AMANDA. You *will* hear more, you—

TOM. No, I won't hear more, I'm going out!

AMANDA. You come right back in—

TOM. Out, out, out! Because I'm—

AMANDA. Come back here, Tom Wingfield! I'm not through talking to you!

TOM. Oh, go—

LAURA. (*desperately*) —Tom!

AMANDA. You're going to listen, and no more insolence from you! I'm at the end of my patience!

(*He comes back toward her.*)

TOM. What do you think I'm at? Aren't I supposed to have any patience to reach the end of, Mother? I know, I know. It seems unimportant to you, what I'm *doing*—what I *want* to do—having a little *difference* between them! You don't think that—

AMANDA. I think you've been doing things that you're ashamed of. That's why you act like this. I don't believe that you go every night to the movies. Nobody goes to the movies night after night. Nobody in their right minds goes to the movies as often as you pretend to. People don't go to the movies at nearly midnight, and movies don't let out at two A.M. Come in stumbling. Muttering to yourself like a maniac! You get three hours' sleep and then go to work. Oh, I can picture the way you're doing down there. Moping, doping, because you're in no condition.

TOM. (*wildly*) No, I'm in no condition!

AMANDA. What right have you got to jeopardize your job? Jeopardize the security of us all? How do you think we'd manage if you were—

TOM. Listen! You think I'm crazy about the *warehouse?* (*He bends fiercely toward her slight figure.*) You think I'm in love with the Continental Shoemakers? You think I want to spend fifty-five *years* down there in that—*celotex interior!* with—*fluorescent—tubes!* Look! I'd rather somebody picked up a crowbar and battered out my brains—than go back mornings! I *go!* Every time you come in yelling that God damn "*Rise and*

Shine!" "*Rise and Shine!*" I say to myself, "How *lucky dead* people are!" But I get up. I *go!* For sixty-five dollars a month I give up all that I dream of doing and being *ever!* And you say self—*self's* all I ever think of. Why, listen, if self is what I thought of, Mother, I'd be where he is—GONE! (*He points to his father's picture.*) As far as the system of transportation reaches! (*He starts past her. She grabs his arm.*) Don't grab at me, Mother!

AMANDA. Where are you going?

TOM. I'm going to the *movies!*

AMANDA. I don't believe that lie!

(*Tom crouches toward her, overtowering her tiny figure. She backs away, gasping.*)

TOM. I'm going to opium dens! Yes, opium dens, dens of vice and criminals' hangouts, Mother. I've joined the Hogan Gang,° I'm a hired assassin, I carry a tommy gun in a violin case! I run a string of cat houses in the Valley! They call me Killer, Killer Wingfield, I'm leading a double-life, a simple, honest warehouse worker by day, by night a dynamic *czar* of the *underworld, Mother.* I go to gambling casinos, I spin away fortunes on the roulette table! I wear a patch over one eye and a false mustache, sometimes I put on green whiskers. On those occasions they call me—*El Diablo!*° Oh, I could tell you many things to make you sleepless! My enemies plan to dynamite this place. They're going to blow us all sky-high some night! I'll be glad, very happy, and so will you! You'll go up, up on a broomstick, over Blue Mountain with seventeen gentlemen callers! You ugly—babbling old—*witch*. . . .

(*He goes through a series of violent, clumsy movements, seizing his overcoat, lunging to the door, pulling it fiercely open. The women watch him, aghast. His arm catches in the sleeve of the coat as he struggles to pull it on. For a moment he is pinioned by the bulky garment. With an outraged groan he tears the coat off again, splitting the shoulder of it, and hurls it across the room. It strikes against the shelf of Laura's glass collection, and there is a tinkle of shattering glass. Laura cries out as if wounded.*

Music.

Screen legend: "The Glass Menagerie."

LAURA. (*shrilly*) *My glass!*—menagerie. . . . (*She covers her face and turns away.*)

(*But Amanda is still stunned and stupefied by the "ugly witch" so that she barely notices this occurrence. Now she recovers her speech.*)

AMANDA. (*in an awful voice*) I won't speak to you—until you apologize!

(*She crosses through the portieres and draws them together behind her. Tom is left with Laura. Laura clings weakly to the mantel with her face averted. Tom stares at her stupidly for a moment. Then he*

Hogan gang: an infamous criminal organization of the 1930s in St. Louis, headed by Edward J. "Jellyroll" Hogan, Jr. and his brother, James, the sons of a police officer. ***El Diablo:*** refers to the devil (in Spanish).

crosses to the shelf. He drops awkwardly on his knees to collect the fallen glass, glancing at Laura as if he would speak but couldn't.

"The Glass Menagerie" music steals in as the scene dims out.)

Scene 4

The interior of the apartment is dark. There is a faint light in the alley. A deep-voiced bell in a church is tolling the hour of five.

Tom appears at the top of the alley. After each solemn boom of the bell in the tower, he shakes a little noisemaker or rattle as if to express the tiny spasm of man in contrast to the sustained power and dignity of the Almighty. This and the unsteadiness of his advance make it evident that he has been drinking. As he climbs the few steps to the fire escape landing light steals up inside. Laura appears in the front room in a nightdress. She notices that Tom's bed is empty. Tom fishes in his pockets for his door key, removing a motley assortment of articles in the search, including a shower of movie ticket stubs and an empty bottle. At last he finds the key, but just as he is about to insert it, it slips from his fingers. He strikes a match and crouches below the door.

TOM. (*bitterly*) One crack—and it falls through!

(*Laura opens the door.*)

LAURA. Tom! Tom, what are you doing?

TOM. Looking for a door key.

LAURA. Where have you been all this time?

TOM. I have been to the movies.

LAURA. All this time at the movies?

TOM. There was a very long program. There was a Garbo° picture and a Mickey Mouse and a travelogue and a newsreel and a preview of coming attractions. And there was an organ solo and a collection for the Milk Fund—simultaneously—which ended up in a terrible fight between a fat lady and an usher!

LAURA. (*innocently*) Did you have to stay through everything?

TOM. Of course! And, oh I forgot! There was a big stage show! The headliner on this stage show was Malvolio° the Magician. He performed wonderful tricks, many of them, such as pouring water back and forth between pitchers. First it turned to wine and then it turned to beer and then it turned to whisky. I know it was whisky it finally turned into because he needed somebody to come up out of the audience to help him, and I came up—both shows! It was Kentucky Straight Bourbon. A very generous fellow, he gave souvenirs. (*He pulls from his back pocket a shimmering rainbow-colored scarf.*) He gave me this. This is his magic scarf. You can have it, Laura. You wave it over a canary cage and you get a bowl of goldfish. You wave it over the goldfish bowl and they fly away canaries.... But the wonderfullest trick of all was the coffin trick. We nailed him into a coffin and he got out of the coffin without removing one nail. (*He has come inside.*)

Garbo: refers to Greta Garbo (1905–1990), a famous Swedish star who appeared in American silent and early sound films. **Malvolio:** a melancholic puritanical character in Shakespeare's play *Twelfth Night* whose name means "evil wishing" in Latin.

There is a trick that would come in handy for me—get me out of this two-by-four situation! (*He flops onto the bed and starts removing his shoes.*)

LAURA. Tom—shhh!

TOM. What're you shushing me for?

LAURA. You'll wake up Mother.

TOM. Goody, goody! Pay 'er back for all those "Rise an' Shines." (*He lies down, groaning.*) You know it don't take much intelligence to get yourself into a nailed-up coffin, Laura. But who in hell ever got himself out of one without removing one nail?

(*As if in answer, the father's grinning photograph lights up. The scene dims out.*)

(*Immediately following, the church bell is heard striking six. At the sixth stroke the alarm clock goes off in Amanda's room, and after a few moments we hear her calling: "Rise and Shine! Rise and Shine! Laura, go tell your brother to rise and shine!"*)

TOM. (*sitting up slowly*) I'll rise—but I won't shine.

(*The light increases.*)

AMANDA. Laura, tell your brother his coffee is ready.

(*Laura slips into the front room.*)

LAURA. Tom!—It's nearly seven. Don't make Mother nervous.

(*He stares at her stupidly.*)

(*Beseechingly.*) Tom, speak to Mother this morning. Make up with her, apologize, speak to her!

TOM. She won't to me. It's her that started not speaking.

LAURA. If you just say you're sorry she'll start speaking.

TOM. Her not speaking—is that such a tragedy?

LAURA. Please—please!

AMANDA. (*calling from the kitchenette*) Laura, are you going to do what I asked you to do, or do I have to get dressed and go out myself?

LAURA. Going, going—soon as I get on my coat!

(*She pulls on a shapeless felt hat with a nervous, jerky movement, pleadingly glancing at Tom. She rushes awkwardly for her coat. The coat is one of Amanda's, inaccurately made-over, the sleeves too short for Laura.*)

Butter and what else?

AMANDA. (*entering from the kitchenette*) Just butter. Tell them to charge it.

LAURA. Mother, they make such faces when I do that.

AMANDA. Sticks and stones can break our bones, but the expression on Mr. Garfinkel's face won't harm us! Tell your brother his coffee is getting cold.

LAURA. (*at the door*) Do what I asked you, will you, will you, Tom?

(*He looks sullenly away.*)

AMANDA. Laura, go now or just don't go at all!

LAURA. (*rushing out*) Going—going!

(*A second later she cries out. Tom springs up and crosses to the door. Tom opens the door.*)

TOM. Laura?

LAURA. I'm all right. I slipped, but I'm all right.

AMANDA. (*peering anxiously after her*) If anyone breaks a leg on those fire-escape steps, the landlord ought to be sued for every cent he possesses!

(*She shuts the door. Now she remembers she isn't speaking to Tom and returns to the other room.*)

(As Tom comes listlessly for his coffee, she turns her back to him and stands rigidly facing the window on the gloomy gray vault of the areaway. Its light on her face with its aged but childish features is cruelly sharp, satirical as a Daumier print.°

The music of "Ave Maria"° is heard softly.

Tom glances sheepishly but sullenly at her averted figure and slumps at the table. The coffee is scalding hot; he sips it and gasps and spits it back in the cup. At his gasp, Amanda catches her breath and half turns. Then she catches herself and turns back to the window. Tom blows on his coffee, glancing sidewise at his mother. She clears her throat. Tom clears his. He starts to rise, sinks back down again, scratches his head, clears his throat again. Amanda coughs. Tom raises his cup in both hands to blow on it, his eyes staring over the rim of it at his mother for several moments. Then he slowly sets the cup down and awkwardly and hesitantly rises from the chair.)

TOM. (*hoarsely*) Mother. I—I apologize, Mother.

(*Amanda draws a quick, shuddering breath. Her face works grotesquely. She breaks into childlike tears.*)

I'm sorry for what I said, for everything that I said, I didn't mean it.

AMANDA. (*sobbingly*) My devotion has made me a witch and so I make myself hateful to my children!

TOM. No, you don't.

AMANDA. I worry so much, don't sleep, it makes me nervous!

TOM. (*gently*) I understand that.

AMANDA. I've had to put up a solitary battle all these years. But you're my right-hand bower!° Don't fall down, don't fail!

TOM. (*gently*) I try, Mother.

AMANDA. (*with great enthusiasm*) Try and you will *succeed!* (*The notion makes her breathless.*) Why, you—you're just *full* of natural endowments! Both of my children—they're *unusual* children! Don't you think I know it? I'm so—*proud!* Happy and—feel I've—so much to be thankful for but—promise me one thing, son!

TOM. What, Mother?

AMANDA. Promise, son, you'll—never be a drunkard!

TOM. (*turns to her grinning*) I will never be a drunkard, Mother.

Daumier print: refers to Honoré Daumier (1808–1879), a French caricaturist, painter and sculptor whose prints satirized politics and the society of his time. **"Ave Maria":** refers to the Roman Catholic prayer to the Virgin Mary as set to music by Franz Schubert (1797–1828). **right-hand bower; or rightbower:** refers to the Jack of trump in a card game, that is, the second-highest card after the joker.

AMANDA. That's what frightened me so, that you'd be drinking! Eat a bowl of Purina!

TOM. Just coffee, Mother.

AMANDA. Shredded wheat biscuit?

TOM. No. No, Mother, just coffee.

AMANDA. You can't put in a day's work on an empty stomach. You've got ten minutes—don't gulp! Drinking too-hot liquids makes cancer of the stomach.... Put cream in.

TOM. No, thank you.

AMANDA. To cool it.

TOM. No! No, thank you, I want it black.

AMANDA. I know, but it's not good for you. We have to do all that we can to build ourselves up. In these trying times we live in, all that we have to cling to is—each other. . . . That's why it's so important to—Tom, I—I sent out your sister so I could discuss something with you. If you hadn't spoken I would have spoken to you. (*She sits down.*)

TOM. (*gently*) What is it, Mother, that you want to discuss?

AMANDA. *Laura!*

(*Tom puts his cup down slowly.*)

(*Legend on screen "Laura." Music: "The Glass Menagerie."*)

TOM. —Oh.—Laura . . .

AMANDA. (*touching his sleeve*) You know how Laura is. So quiet but—still water runs deep! She notices things and I think she—broods about them.

(*Tom looks up.*)

A few days ago I came in and she was crying.

TOM. What about?

AMANDA. You.

TOM. Me?

AMANDA. She has an idea that you're not happy here.

TOM. What gave her that idea?

AMANDA. What gives her any idea? However, you do act strangely. I—I'm not criticizing, understand *that!* I know your ambitions do not lie in the warehouse, that like everybody in the whole wide world—you've had to—make sacrifices, but—Tom—Tom—life's not easy, it calls for—Spartan endurance! There's so many things in my heart that I cannot describe to you! I've never told you but I—*loved* your father....

TOM. (*gently*) I know that, Mother.

AMANDA. And you—when I see you taking after his ways! Staying out late—and—well, you *had* been drinking the night you were in that—terrifying condition! Laura says that you hate the apartment and that you go out nights to get away from it! Is that true, Tom?

TOM. No. You say there's so much in your heart that you can't describe to me. That's true of me, too. There's so much in my heart that I can't describe to *you!* So let's respect each other's—

AMANDA. But, why—*why,* Tom—are you always so *restless?* Where do you *go* to, nights?

TOM. I—go to the movies.

AMANDA. Why do you go to the movies so much, Tom?

TOM. I go to the movies because—I like adventure. Adventure is something I don't have much of at work, so I go to the movies.

AMANDA. But, Tom, you go to the movies *entirely* too *much!*

TOM. I like a lot of adventure.

(Amanda looks baffled, then hurt. As the familiar inquisition resumes, Tom becomes hard and impatient again. Amanda slips back into her querulous attitude toward him.

Image on screen: A sailing vessel with Jolly Roger.°)

AMANDA. Most young men find adventure in their careers.

TOM. Then most young men are not employed in a warehouse.

AMANDA. The world is full of young men employed in warehouses and offices and factories.

TOM. Do all of them find adventure in their careers?

AMANDA. They do or they do without it! Not everybody has a craze for adventure.

TOM. Man is by instinct a lover, a hunter, a fighter, and none of those instincts are given much play at the warehouse!

AMANDA. Man is by instinct! Don't quote instinct to me! Instinct is something that people have got away from! It belongs to animals! Christian adults don't want it!

TOM. What do Christian adults want, then, Mother?

AMANDA. Superior things! Things of the mind and the spirit! Only animals have to satisfy instincts! Surely your aims are somewhat higher than theirs! Than monkeys—pigs—

TOM. I reckon they're not.

AMANDA. You're joking. However, that isn't what I wanted to discuss.

TOM. (*rising*) I haven't much time.

AMANDA. (*pushing his shoulders*) Sit down.

TOM. You want me to punch in red° at the warehouse, Mother?

AMANDA. You have five minutes. I want to talk about Laura.

(*Screen legend: "Plans and Provisions."*)

TOM. All right! What about Laura?

AMANDA. We have to be making some plans and provisions for her. She's older than you, two years, and nothing has happened. She just drifts along doing nothing. It frightens me terribly how she just drifts along.

TOM. I guess she's the type that people call home girls.

AMANDA. There's no such type, and if there is, it's a pity! That is unless the home is hers, with a husband!

TOM. What?

AMANDA. Oh, I can see the handwriting on the wall as plain as I see the nose in front of my face! It's terrifying! More and more you remind me of your father! He was out all hours without explanation!—Then *left! Goodbye!* And me with the bag to hold: I saw that letter you got from the Merchant Marine. I know what you're dreaming of. I'm not standing here blindfolded. (*She pauses.*) Very well, then. Then *do* it! But not till there's somebody to take your place.

Jolly Roger: the skull and crossbones pirate flag. **punch in red:** refers to the late arrival time stamped in red by a time clock.

TOM. What do you mean?

AMANDA. I mean that as soon as Laura has got somebody to take care of her, married, a home of her own, independent—why, then you'll be free to go wherever you please, on land, on sea, whichever way the wind blows you! But until that time you've got to look out for your sister. I don't say me because I'm old and don't matter! I say for your sister because she's young and dependent.

I put her in business college—a dismal failure! Frightened her so it made her sick at the stomach. I took her over to the Young People's League at the church. Another fiasco. She spoke to nobody, nobody spoke to her. Now all she does is fool with those pieces of glass and play those worn-out records. What kind of a life is that for a girl to lead?

TOM. What can I do about it?

AMANDA. Overcome selfishness! Self, self, self is all that you ever think of!

(*Tom springs up and crosses to get his coat. It is ugly and bulky. He pulls on a cap with earmuffs.*)

Where is your muffler? Put your wool muffler on!

(*He snatches it angrily from the closet, tosses it around his neck and pulls both ends tight.*)

Tom! I haven't said what I had in mind to ask you.

TOM. I'm too late to—

AMANDA. (*catching his arm—very importunately; then shyly*) Down at the warehouse, aren't there some—nice young men?

TOM. No!

AMANDA. There *must* be—*some* . . .

TOM. Mother— (*He gestures.*)

AMANDA. Find out one that's clean-living—doesn't drink and ask him out for sister!

TOM. What?

AMANDA. For *sister!* To *meet!* Get *acquainted!*

TOM. (*stamping to the door*) Oh, my *go-osh!*

AMANDA. Will you? (*He opens the door. She says, imploringly:*) Will you?

(*He starts down the fire escape.*)

Will you? *Will* you, dear?

TOM. (*calling back*) *Yes!*

(*Amanda closes the door hesitantly and with a troubled but faintly hopeful expression.*

Screen image: The cover of a glamor magazine.

The spotlight picks up Amanda on the phone.)

AMANDA. Ella Cartwright? This is Amanda Wingfield! How are you honey? How is that kidney condition?

(*There is a five-second pause.*)

Horrors!

(*There is another pause.*)

You're a Christian martyr, yes, honey, that's what you are, a Christian martyr! Well; I just now happened to notice in my little red book that your subscription to the *Companion* has just run out! I knew that you wouldn't want to miss out on the wonderful serial starting in this new issue. It's by Bessie Mae Hopper, the first thing she's written since *Honeymoon for Three.* Wasn't that a strange and interesting story? Well, this one is even lovelier, I believe. It has a sophisticated, society background. It's all about the horsey set on Long Island!

(*The light fades out.*)

Scene 5

(Legend on the screen: "Annunciation."

Music is heard as the light slowly comes on.

It is early dusk of a spring evening. Supper has just been finished in the Wingfield apartment. Amanda and Laura, in light-colored dresses, are removing dishes from the table in the dining room, which is shadowy, their movements formalized almost as a dance or ritual, their moving forms as pale and silent as moths. Tom, in white shirt and trousers, rises from the table and crosses toward the fire escape.)

AMANDA. (*as he passes her*) Son, will you do me a favor?

TOM. What?

AMANDA. Comb your hair! You look so pretty when your hair is combed!

(*Tom slouches on the sofa with the evening paper. Its enormous headline reads: "Franco Triumphs."*°)

There is only one respect in which I would like you to emulate your father.

TOM. What respect is that?

AMANDA. The care he always took of his appearance. He never allowed himself to look untidy.

(*He throws down the paper and crosses to the fire escape.*)

Where are you going?

TOM. I'm going out to smoke.

AMANDA. You smoke too much. A pack a day at fifteen cents a pack. How much would that amount to in a month? Thirty times fifteen is how much, Tom? Figure it out and you will be astounded at what you could save. Enough to give you a night-school course in accounting at Washington U.° Just think what a wonderful thing that would be for you, son!

(*Tom is unmoved by the thought.*)

TOM. I'd rather smoke. (*He steps out on the landing, letting the screen door slam.*)

"Franco Triumphs": in January, 1939, the Republican forces of Francisco Franco (1892–1975) defeated the Loyalists, ending the Spanish Civil War. Franco was the fascist dictator of Spain from 1939 until his death. **Washington U.:** a prestigious liberal arts university in St. Louis.

AMANDA. (*sharply*) I know! That's the tragedy of it. . . . (*Alone, she turns to look at her husband's picture.*)

(*Dance music: "The World Is Waiting for the Sunrise!"*°)

TOM. (*to the audience*) Across the alley from us was the Paradise Dance Hall. On evenings in spring the windows and doors were open and the music came outdoors. Sometimes the lights were turned out except for a large glass sphere that hung from the ceiling. It would turn slowly about and filter the dusk with delicate rainbow colors. Then the orchestra played a waltz or a tango, something that had a slow and sensuous rhythm. Couples would come outside, to the relative privacy of the alley. You could see them kissing behind ash pits and telephone poles. This was the compensation for lives that passed like mine, without any change or adventure. Adventure and change were imminent in this year. They were waiting around the corner for all these kids. Suspended in the mist over Berchtesgaden,° caught in the folds of Chamberlain's umbrella. In Spain there was Guernica! But here there was only hot swing music and liquor, dance halls, bars, and movies, and sex that hung in the gloom like a chandelier and flooded the world with brief, deceptive rainbows. . . . All the world was waiting for bombardments!

(*Amanda turns from the picture and comes outside.*)

AMANDA. (*sighing*) A fire escape landing's a poor excuse for a porch. (*She spreads a newspaper on a step and sits down, gracefully and demurely as if she were settling into a swing on a Mississippi veranda.*) What are you looking at?

TOM. The moon.

AMANDA. Is there a moon this evening?

TOM. It's rising over Garfinkel's Delicatessen.

AMANDA. So it is! A little silver slipper of a moon. Have you made a wish on it yet?

TOM. Um-hum.

AMANDA. What did you wish for?

TOM. That's a secret.

AMANDA. A secret, huh? Well, I won't tell mine either. I will be just as mysterious as you.

TOM. I bet I can guess what yours is.

AMANDA. Is my head so transparent?

TOM. You're not a sphinx.°

AMANDA. No, I don't have secrets. I'll tell you what I wished for on the moon. Success and happiness for my precious children! I wish for that whenever there's a moon, and when there isn't a moon, I wish for it, too.

"The World . . . Sunrise": refers to a popular song written in 1919 by Eugene Lockhart and Ernest Seitz. **Berchtesgaden . . . Chamberlain . . . Guernica:** three references that foreshadowed World War II. Berchtesgaden was Hitler's protected residence in the Bavarian Alps; Neville Chamberlain (1869–1940) was a British Prime Minister who always carried an umbrella and sought to avoid war by appeasing Hitler; Guernica is the town whose destruction symbolized the horrors of war, especially the killing of women and children. **sphinx:** in classical mythology, a monster represented as having the head and breast of a woman, the body of a lion, and the wings of an eagle, who proposed a riddle to Oedipus and killed herself when he answered correctly; a mysterious person.

TOM. I thought perhaps you wished for a gentleman caller.

AMANDA. Why do you say that?

TOM. Don't you remember asking me to fetch one?

AMANDA. I remember suggesting that it would be nice for your sister if you brought home some nice young man from the warehouse. I think that I've made that suggestion more than once.

TOM. Yes, you have made it repeatedly.

AMANDA. Well?

TOM. We are going to have one.

AMANDA. *What?*

TOM. A gentleman caller!

(*The annunciation is celebrated with music.*

Amanda rises.

Image on screen: A caller with a bouquet.)

AMANDA. You mean you have asked some nice young man to come over?

TOM. Yep. I've asked him to dinner.

AMANDA. You really did?

TOM. I did!

AMANDA. You did, and did he—*accept?*

TOM. He did!

AMANDA. Well, well—well, well! That's—lovely!

TOM. I thought that you would be pleased.

AMANDA. It's definite then?

TOM. Very definite.

AMANDA. Soon?

TOM. Very soon.

AMANDA. For heaven's sake, stop putting on and tell me some things, will you?

TOM. What things do you want me to tell you?

AMANDA. *Naturally* I would like to know when he's *coming!*

TOM. He's coming tomorrow.

AMANDA. *Tomorrow?*

TOM. Yep. Tomorrow.

AMANDA. But, Tom!

TOM. Yes, Mother?

AMANDA. Tomorrow gives me no time!

TOM. Time for what?

AMANDA. Preparations! Why didn't you phone me at once, as soon as you asked him, the minute that he accepted? Then, don't you see, I could have been getting ready!

TOM. You don't have to make any fuss.

AMANDA. Oh, Tom, Tom, Tom, of course I have to make a fuss! I want things nice, not sloppy! Not thrown together. I'll certainly have to do some fast thinking, won't I?

TOM. I don't see why you have to think at all.

AMANDA. You just don't know. We can't have a gentleman caller in a pigsty! All my wedding silver has to be polished, the monogrammed table linen ought to be laundered! The windows have to be washed and fresh curtains put up. And how about clothes? We have to *wear* something, don't we?

TOM. Mother, this boy is no one to make a fuss over!

AMANDA. Do you realize he's the first young man we've introduced to your sister? It's terrible, disgraceful that poor little sister has never received a single gentleman caller! Tom, come inside! (*She opens the screen door.*)

TOM. What for?

AMANDA. I want to ask you some things.

TOM. If you're going to make such a fuss, I'll call it off, I'll tell him not to come!

AMANDA. You certainly won't do anything of the kind. Nothing offends people worse than broken engagements. It simply means I'll have to work like a Turk! We won't be brilliant, but we will pass inspection. Come on inside.

(*Tom follows her inside, groaning.*)

Sit down.

TOM. Any particular place you would like me to sit?

AMANDA. Thank heavens I've got that new sofa! I'm also making payments on a floor lamp I'll have sent out! And put the chintz covers on, they'll brighten things up! Of course I'd hoped to have these walls re-papered.... What is the young man's name?

TOM. His name is O'Connor.

AMANDA. That, of course, means fish°—tomorrow is Friday! I'll have that salmon loaf—with Durkee's dressing! What does he do? He works at the warehouse?

TOM. Of course! How else would I—

AMANDA. Tom, he—doesn't drink?

TOM. Why do you ask me that?

AMANDA. Your father *did!*

TOM. Don't get started on that!

AMANDA. He *does* drink, then?

TOM. Not that I know of!

AMANDA. Make sure, be certain! The last thing I want for my daughter's a boy who drinks!

TOM. Aren't you being a little bit premature? Mr. O'Connor has not yet appeared on the scene!

AMANDA. But will tomorrow. To meet your sister, and what do I know about his character? Nothing! Old maids are better off than wives of drunkards!

TOM. Oh, my God!

AMANDA. Be still!

TOM. (*leaning forward to whisper*) Lots of fellows meet girls whom they don't marry!

AMANDA. Oh, talk sensibly, Tom—and don't be sarcastic! (*She has gotten a hairbrush*)

TOM. What are you doing?

AMANDA. I'm brushing that cowlick down! (*She attacks his hair with the brush.*) What is this young man's position at the warehouse?

TOM. (*submitting grimly to the brush and the interrogation*) This young man's position is that of a shipping clerk, Mother.

AMANDA. Sounds to me like a fairly responsible job, the sort of job *you* would be in if you just had more *get-up.* What is his salary? Have you any idea?

TOM. I would judge it to be approximately eighty-five dollars a month.

---

fish: Amanda assumes O'Connor is Catholic and thus is not allowed to eat meat on Fridays (a policy that was discontinued in the 1960s).

AMANDA. Well—not princely, but—

TOM. Twenty more than I make.

AMANDA. Yes, how well I know! But for a family man, eighty-five dollars a month is not much more than you can just get by on....

TOM. Yes, but Mr. O'Connor is not a family man.

AMANDA. He might be, mightn't he? Some time in the future?

TOM. I see. Plans and provisions.

AMANDA. You are the only young man that I know of who ignores the fact that the future becomes the present, the present the past, and the past turns into everlasting regret if you don't plan for it!

TOM. I will think that over and see what I can make of it.

AMANDA. Don't be supercilious with your mother! Tell me some more about this—what do you call him?

TOM. James D. O'Connor. The D. is for Delaney.

AMANDA. Irish on *both* sides! *Gracious!* And he doesn't drink?

TOM. Shall I call him up and ask him right this minute?

AMANDA. The only way to find out about those things is to make discreet inquiries at the proper moment. When I was a girl in Blue Mountain and it was suspected that a young man drank, the girl whose attentions he had been receiving, if any girl *was,* would sometimes speak to the minister of his church, or rather her father would if her father was living, and sort of feel him out on the young man's character. That is the way such things are discreetly handled to keep a young woman from making a tragic mistake!

TOM. Then how did you happen to make a tragic mistake?

AMANDA. That innocent look of your father's had everyone fooled! He *smiled*—the world was *enchanted!* No girl can do worse than put herself at the mercy of a handsome appearance! I hope that Mr. O'Connor is not too good-looking.

TOM. No, he's not too good-looking. He's covered with freckles and hasn't too much of a nose.

AMANDA. He's not right-down homely, though?

TOM. Not right-down homely. Just medium homely, I'd say.

AMANDA. Character's what to look for in a man.

TOM. That's what I've always said, Mother.

AMANDA. You've never said anything of the kind and I suspect you would never give it a thought.

TOM. Don't be so suspicious of me.

AMANDA. At least I hope he's the type that's up and coming.

TOM. I think he really goes in for self-improvement.

AMANDA. What reason have you to think so?

TOM. He goes to night school.

AMANDA. *(beaming)* Splendid! What does he do, I mean study?

TOM. Radio engineering and public speaking!

AMANDA. Then he has visions of being advanced in the world! Any young man who studies public speaking is aiming to have an executive job some day! And radio engineering? A thing for the future! Both of these facts are very illuminating. Those are the sort of things that a mother should know concerning any young man who comes to call on her daughter. Seriously or—not.

TOM. One little warning. He doesn't know about Laura. I didn't let on that we had dark ulterior motives. I just said, why don't you come and have dinner with us? He said okay and that was the whole conversation.

AMANDA. I bet it was! You're eloquent as an oyster. However, he'll know about Laura when he gets here. When he sees how lovely and sweet and pretty she is, he'll thank his lucky stars he was asked to dinner.

TOM. Mother, you mustn't expect too much of Laura.

AMANDA. What do you mean?

TOM. Laura seems all those things to you and me because she's ours and we love her. We don't even notice she's crippled any more.

AMANDA. Don't say crippled! You know that I never allow that word to be used!

TOM. But face facts, Mother. She is and—that's not all—

AMANDA. What do you mean "not all"?

TOM. Laura is very different from other girls.

AMANDA. I think the difference is all to her advantage.

TOM. Not quite all—in the eyes of others—strangers—she's terribly shy and lives in a world of her own and those things make her seem a little peculiar to people outside the house.

AMANDA. Don't say peculiar.

TOM. Face the facts. She is.

(The dance hall music changes to a tango that has a minor and somewhat ominous tone.)

AMANDA. In what way is she peculiar—may I ask?

TOM. *(gently)* She lives in a world of her own—a world of little glass ornaments, Mother. . . .

(He gets up. Amanda remains holding the brush, looking at him, troubled.)

She plays old phonograph records and—that's about all— *(He glances at himself in the mirror and crosses to the door.)*

AMANDA. *(sharply)* Where are you going?

TOM. I'm going to the movies. *(He goes out the screen door.)*

AMANDA. Not to the movies, every night to the movies! *(She follows quickly to the screen door.)* I don't believe you always go to the movies!

(He is gone. Amanda looks worriedly after him for a moment. Then vitality and optimism return and she turns from the door, crossing to the portieres.)

Laura! Laura!

(Laura answers from the kitchenette.)

LAURA. Yes, Mother.

AMANDA. Let those dishes go and come in front!

(Laura appears with a dish towel. Amanda speaks to her gaily.)

Laura, come here and make a wish on the moon!

(Screen image: The Moon.)

LAURA. *(entering)* Moon—moon?

AMANDA. A little silver slipper of a moon. Look over your left shoulder, Laura, and make a wish!

(Laura looks faintly puzzled as if called out of sleep. Amanda seizes her shoulders and turns her at an angle by the door.)

Now! Now, darling, *wish!*

LAURA. What shall I wish for, Mother?

AMANDA. (*her voice trembling and her eyes suddenly filling with tears*) Happiness! Good fortune!

(*The sound of the violin rises and the stage dims out.*)

Scene 6

(*The light comes up on the fire escape landing. Tom is leaning against the grill, smoking. Screen image: The high school hero.*)

TOM. And so the following evening I brought Jim home to dinner. I had known Jim slightly in high school. In high school Jim was a hero. He had tremendous Irish good nature and vitality with the scrubbed and polished look of white chinaware. He seemed to move in a continual spotlight. He was a star in basketball, captain of the debating club, president of the senior class and the glee club and he sang the male lead in the annual light operas. He was always running or bounding, never just walking. He seemed always at the point of defeating the law of gravity. He was shooting with such velocity through his adolescence that you would logically expect him to arrive at nothing short of the White House by the time he was thirty. But Jim apparently ran into more interference after his graduation from Soldan. His speed had definitely slowed. Six years after he left high school he was holding a job that wasn't much better than mine.

(*Screen image: The Clerk.*)

He was the only one at the warehouse with whom I was on friendly terms. I was valuable to him as someone who could remember his former glory, who had seen him win basketball games and the silver cup in debating. He knew of my secret practice of retiring to a cabinet of the washroom to work on poems when business was slack in the warehouse. He called me Shakespeare. And while the other boys in the warehouse regarded me with suspicious hostility, Jim took a humorous attitude toward me. Gradually his attitude affected the others, their hostility wore off and they also began to smile at me as people smile at an oddly fashioned dog who trots across their path at some distance.

I knew that Jim and Laura had known each other at Soldan, and I had heard Laura speak admiringly of his voice. I didn't know if Jim remembered her or not. In high school Laura had been as unobtrusive as Jim had been astonishing. If he did remember Laura, it was not as my sister, for when I asked him to dinner, he grinned and said, "You know, Shakespeare, I never thought of you as having folks!"

He was about to discover that I did....

(*Legend on screen: "The accent of a coming foot."*)

(*The light dims out on Tom and comes up in the Wingfield living room—a delicate lemony light. It is about five on a Friday evening of late spring which comes "scattering poems in the sky."*

Amanda has worked like a Turk in preparation for the gentleman caller. The results are astonishing. The new floor lamp with its rose silk shade is in place, a colored paper lantern conceals the broken light fixture in the ceiling, new billowing white curtains are at the windows, chintz covers are on the chairs and sofa, a pair of new sofa pillows make their initial appearance. Open boxes and tissue paper are scattered on the floor.

Laura stands in the middle of the room with lifted arms while Amanda crouches before her, adjusting the hem of a new dress, devout and ritualistic. The dress is colored and designed by memory. The arrangement of Laura's hair is changed; it is softer and more becoming. A fragile, unearthly prettiness has come out in Laura: she is like a piece of translucent glass touched by light, given a momentary radiance, not actual, not lasting.)

AMANDA. (*impatiently*) Why are you trembling?

LAURA. Mother, you've made me so nervous!

AMANDA. How have I made you nervous?

LAURA. By all this fuss! You make it seem so important!

AMANDA. I don't understand you, Laura. You couldn't be satisfied with just sitting home, and yet whenever I try to arrange something for you, you seem to resist it. (*She gets up.*) Now take a look at yourself. No, wait! Wait just a moment—I have an idea!

LAURA. What is it now?

(*Amanda produces two powder puffs which she wraps in handkerchiefs and stuffs in Laura's bosom.*)

LAURA. Mother, what are you doing?

AMANDA. They call them "Gay Deceivers"!

LAURA. I won't wear them!

AMANDA. You will!

LAURA. Why should I?

AMANDA. Because, to be painfully honest, your chest is flat.

LAURA. You make it seem like we were setting a trap.

AMANDA. All pretty girls are a trap, a pretty trap, and men expect them to be.

(*Legend on screen: "A pretty trap."*)

Now look at yourself, young lady. This is the prettiest you will ever be! (*She stands back to admire Laura.*) I've got to fix myself now! You're going to be surprised by your mother's appearance!

(*Amanda crosses through the portieres, humming gaily. Laura moves slowly to the long mirror and stares solemnly at herself. A wind blows the white curtains inward in a slow, graceful motion and with a faint, sorrowful sighing.*)

AMANDA. (*from somewhere behind the portieres*) It isn't dark enough yet.

(*Laura turns slowly before the mirror with a troubled look.*

Legend on screen: "This is my sister: Celebrate her with strings!" Music plays.)

AMANDA. (*laughing, still not visible*) I'm going to show you something. I'm going to make a spectacular appearance!

LAURA. What is it, Mother?

AMANDA. Possess your soul in patience—you will see! Something I've resurrected from that old trunk! Styles haven't changed so terribly much after all. . . . (*She parts the portieres.*) Now just look at your mother! (*She wears a girlish frock of yellowed voile with a blue silk sash. She carries a bunch of jonquils—the legend of her youth is nearly revived. Now she speaks feverishly:*) This is the dress in which I led the cotillion. Won the cakewalk twice at Sunset Hill, wore one Spring to the Governor's Ball in Jackson!° See how I sashayed around the ballroom, Laura? (*She raises her skirt and does a mincing step around the room.*) I wore it on Sundays for my gentlemen callers! I had it on the day I met your father. . . . I had malaria fever all that Spring. The change of climate from East Tennessee to the Delta—weakened resistance. I had a little temperature all the time—not enough to be serious—just enough to make me restless and giddy! Invitations poured in—parties all over the Delta! "Stay in bed," said Mother, "you have a fever!"—but I just wouldn't. I took quinine° but kept on going, going! Evenings, dances! Afternoons, long, long rides! Picnics—lovely! So lovely, that country in May—all lacy with dogwood, literally flooded with jonquils! That was the spring I had the craze for jonquils. Jonquils became an absolute obsession. Mother said, "Honey, there's no more room for jonquils." And still I kept on bringing in more jonquils. Whenever, wherever I saw them, I'd say, "Stop! Stop! I see jonquils!" I made the young men help me gather the jonquils! It was a joke, Amanda and her jonquils. Finally there were no more vases to hold them, every available space was filled with jonquils. No vases to hold them? All right, I'll hold them myself! And then I— (*She stops in front of the picture. Music plays.*) met your father! Malaria fever and jonquils and then—this—boy. . . . (*She switches on the rose-colored lamp.*) I hope they get here before it starts to rain. (*She crosses the room and places the jonquils in a bowl on the table.*) I gave your brother a little extra change so he and Mr. O'Connor could take the service car home.

LAURA. (*with an altered look*) What did you say his name was?

AMANDA. O'Connor.

LAURA. What is his first name?

AMANDA. I don't remember. Oh, yes, I do. It was—Jim.

(*Laura sways slightly and catches hold of a chair.*

Legend on screen: "Not Jim!")

LAURA. (*faintly*) Not—Jim!

AMANDA. Yes, that was it, it was Jim! I've never known a Jim that wasn't nice!

(*The music becomes ominous.*)

LAURA. Are you sure his name is Jim O'Connor?

AMANDA. Yes. Why?

LAURA. Is he the one that Tom used to know in high school?

AMANDA. He didn't say so. I think he just got to know him at the warehouse.

LAURA. There was a Jim O'Connor we both knew in high school— (*Then, with effort.*) If that is the one that Tom is bringing to dinner—you'll have to excuse me, I won't come to the table.

Jackson: the capital city of Mississippi where Amanda attended cotillions, or formal balls, given for debutantes. The cakewalk was a popular dance step in Amanda's youth.
quinine: a drug used to counter the effects of malaria.

AMANDA. What sort of nonsense is this?

LAURA. You asked me once if I'd ever liked a boy. Don't you remember I showed you this boy's picture?

AMANDA. You mean the boy you showed me in the yearbook?

LAURA. Yes, that boy.

AMANDA. Laura, Laura, were you in love with that boy?

LAURA. I don't know, Mother. All I know is I couldn't sit at the table if it was him!

AMANDA. It won't be him! It isn't the least bit likely. But whether it is or not, you will come to the table. You will not be excused.

LAURA. I'll have to be, Mother.

AMANDA. I don't intend to humor your silliness, Laura. I've had too much from you and your brother, both! So just sit down and compose yourself till they come. Tom has forgotten his key so you'll have to let them in, when they arrive.

LAURA. (*panicky*) Oh, Mother—*you* answer the door!

AMANDA. (*lightly*) I'll be in the kitchen—busy!

LAURA. Oh, Mother, please answer the door, don't make me do it!

AMANDA. (*crossing into the kitchenette*) I've got to fix the dressing for the salmon. Fuss, fuss—silliness!—over a gentleman caller!

(*The door swings shut, Laura is left alone.*

Legend on screen: "Terror!"

She utters a low moan and turns off the lamp—sits stiffly on the edge of the sofa, knotting her fingers together.

Legend on screen: "The Opening of a Door!"

Tom and Jim appear on the fire escape steps and climb to the landing. Hearing their approach, Laura rises with a panicky gesture. She retreats to the portieres. The doorbell rings. Laura catches her breath and touches her throat. Low drums sound.)

AMANDA. (*calling*) Laura, sweetheart! The door!

(*Laura stares at it without moving.*)

JIM. I think we just beat the rain.

TOM. Uh-huh. (*He rings again, nervously. Jim whistles and fishes for a cigarette.*)

AMANDA. (*very, very gaily*) Laura, that is your brother and Mr. O'Connor! Will you let them in, darling?

(*Laura crosses toward the kitchenette door.*)

LAURA. (*breathlessly*) Mother—you go to the door!

(*Amanda steps out of the kitchenette and stares furiously at Laura. She points imperiously at the door.*)

LAURA. Please, please!

AMANDA. (*in a fierce whisper*) What is the matter with you, you silly thing?

LAURA. (*desperately*) Please, you answer it, *please!*

AMANDA. I told you I wasn't going to humor you, Laura. Why have you chosen this moment to lose your mind?

LAURA. Please, please, please, you go!

AMANDA. You'll have to go to the door because I can't.

LAURA. (*despairingly*) I can't either!

AMANDA. *Why?*

LAURA. I'm *sick!*

AMANDA. I'm sick, too—of your nonsense! Why can't you and your brother be normal people? Fantastic whims and behavior!

(*Tom gives a long ring.*)

Preposterous goings on! Can you give me one reason— (*She calls out lyrically.*) *Coming!* Just one second!—why you should be afraid to open a door? Now you answer it, Laura!

LAURA. Oh, oh, oh . . . (*She returns through the portieres, darts to the Victoria, winds it frantically and turns it on.*)

AMANDA. Laura Wingfield, you march right to that door!

LAURA. *Yes—yes, Mother!*

(*A faraway, scratchy rendition of "Dardanella"° softens the air and gives her strength to move through it. She slips to the door and draws it cautiously open. Tom enters with the caller, Jim O'Connor.*)

TOM. Laura, this is Jim. Jim, this is my sister, Laura.

JIM. (*stepping inside*) I didn't know that Shakespeare had a sister!

LAURA. (*retreating, stiff and trembling, from the door*) How—how do you do?

JIM. (*heartily, extending his hand*) Okay!

(*Laura touches it hesitantly with hers.*)

JIM. Your hand's *cold,* Laura!

LAURA. Yes, well—I've been playing the Victrola. . . .

JIM. Must have been playing classical music on it! You ought to play a little hot swing music to warm you up!

LAURA. Excuse me—I haven't finished playing the Victrola. . . . (*She turns awkwardly and hurries into the front room. She pauses a second by the Victrola. Then she catches her breath and darts through the portieres like a frightened deer.*)

JIM. (*grinning*) What was the matter?

TOM. Oh—with Laura? Laura is—terribly shy.

JIM. Shy, huh? It's unusual to meet a shy girl nowadays. I don't believe you ever mentioned you had a sister.

TOM. Well, now you know. I have one. Here is the *Post Dispatch.*° You want a piece of it?

JIM. Uh-huh.

TOM. What piece? The comics?

JIM. Sports! (*He glances at it.*) Ole Dizzy Dean° is on his bad behavior.

TOM. (*uninterested*) Yeah? (*He lights a cigarette and goes over to the fire-escape door.*)

JIM. Where are *you* going?

TOM. I'm going out on the terrace.

"Dardanella": a popular tune written in 1919 by Fred Fisher, Felix Bernard and Johnny S. Black. **Post Dispatch:** *The St. Louis Post Dispatch,* a local newspaper. **Dizzy Dean:** the nickname of Jerome Herman Dean (1911–1974), a well-known pitcher with the St. Louis Cardinals from 1932 to 1938.

JIM. (*going after him*) You know, Shakespeare—I'm going to sell you a bill of goods!

TOM. What goods?

JIM. A course I'm taking.

TOM Huh?

JIM. In public speaking! You and me, we're not the warehouse type.

TOM. Thanks—that's good news. But what has public speaking got to do with it?

JIM. It fits you for—executive positions!

TOM. Awww.

JIM. I tell you it's done a helluva lot for me.

(*Image on screen: Executive at his desk.*)

TOM. In what respect?

JIM. In every! Ask yourself what is the difference between you an' me and men in the office down front? Brains?—No!—Ability?—No! Then what? Just one little thing—

TOM. What is that one little thing?

JIM. Primarily it amounts to—social poise! Being able to square up to people and hold your own on any social level!

AMANDA. (*from the kitchenette*) Tom?

TOM. Yes, Mother?

AMANDA. Is that you and Mr. O'Connor?

TOM. Yes, Mother.

AMANDA. Well, you just make yourselves comfortable in there.

TOM. Yes, Mother.

AMANDA. Ask Mr. O'Connor if he would like to wash his hands.

JIM. Aw, no—no—thank you—I took care of that at the warehouse. Tom—

TOM. Yes?

JIM. Mr. Mendoza was speaking to me about you.

TOM. Favorably?

JIM. What do you think?

TOM. Well—

JIM. You're going to be out of a job if you don't wake up.

TOM. I am waking up—

JIM. You show no signs.

TOM. The signs are interior.

(*Image on screen: The sailing vessel with the Jolly Roger again.*)

TOM. I'm planning to change. (*He leans over the fire escape rail, speaking with quiet exhilaration. The incandescent marquees and signs of the first-run movie houses light his face from across the alley. He looks like a voyager.*) I'm right at the point of committing myself to a future that doesn't include the warehouse and Mr. Mendoza or even a night-school course in public speaking.

JIM. What are you gassing about?

TOM. I'm tired of the movies.

JIM. Movies!

TOM. Yes, movies! Look at them—(*a wave toward the marvels of Grand Avenue*) All of those glamorous people—having adventures—hogging it all, gobbling the whole thing up! You know what happens? People go to the *movies* instead of *moving!* Hollywood characters are supposed to have all the adventures for everybody in America, while everybody in America sits in a dark room and watches them have them! Yes, until there's a war. That's when adventure becomes available to the masses! *Everyone's* dish, not only Gable's.° Then the people in the dark room come out of the dark room to have some adventures themselves—goody, goody! It's our turn now, to go to the South Sea Island—to make a safari—to be exotic, far-off! But I'm not patient. I don't want to wait till then. I'm tired of the *movies* and I am *about* to *move!*

JIM. (*incredulously*) Move?

TOM. Yes.

JIM. When?

TOM. Soon!

JIM. Where? Where?

(*The music seems to answer the question, while Tom thinks it over. He searches in his pockets.*)

TOM. I'm starting to boil inside. I know I seem dreamy, but inside—well, I'm boiling! Whenever I pick up a shoe, I shudder a little thinking how short life is and what I am doing! Whatever that means, I know it doesn't mean shoes—except as something to wear on a traveler's feet! (*He finds what he has been searching for in his pockets and holds out a paper to Jim.*) Look—

JIM. What?

TOM. I'm a member.

JIM. (*reading*) The Union of Merchant Seamen.

TOM. I paid my dues this month, instead of the light bill.

JIM. You will regret it when they turn off the lights.

TOM. I won't be here.

JIM. How about your mother?

TOM. I'm like my father. The bastard son of a bastard! Did you notice how he's grinning in his picture in there? And he's been absent going on sixteen years!

JIM. You're just talking, you drip. How does your mother feel about it?

TOM. Shhh! Here comes Mother! Mother is not acquainted with my plans!

AMANDA. (*coming through the portieres*) Where are you all?

TOM. On the terrace, Mother.

(*They start inside. She advances to them. Tom is distinctly shocked at her appearance. Even Jim blinks a little. He is making his first contact with the girlish Southern vivacity and in spite of the night-school course in public speaking is somewhat thrown off the beam by the unexpected outlay of social charm. Certain responses are attempted by Jim but are swept aside by Amanda's gay laughter and chatter. Tom is embarrassed but after the first shock Jim reacts very warmly. He grins and chuckles, is altogether won over.*

Image on screen: Amanda as a girl.)

AMANDA. (*coyly smiling, shaking her girlish ringlets*) Well, well, well, so this is Mr. O'Connor. Introductions entirely unnecessary. I've heard so much about you from my boy. I finally said to him, Tom—good gra-

---

Gable: refers to Clark Gable (1901–1960), an immensely popular American screen idol.

cious!—why don't you bring this paragon to supper? I'd like to meet this nice young man at the warehouse!—instead of just hearing him sing your praises so much! I don't know why my son is so stand-offish—that's not Southern behavior!

Let's sit down and—I think we could stand a little more air in here! Tom, leave the door open. I felt a nice fresh breeze a moment ago. Where has it gone to? Mmm, so warm already! And not quite summer, even. We're going to burn up when summer really gets started. However, we're having—we're having a very light supper. I think light things are better fo' this time of year. The same as light clothes are. Light clothes an' light food are what warm weather calls fo'. You know our blood gets so thick during th' winter—it takes a while fo' us to *adjust* ourselves!—when the season changes . . . It's come so quick this year. I wasn't prepared. All of sudden—heavens! Already summer! I ran to the trunk an' pulled out this light dress—terribly old! Historical almost! But feels so good—so good an' co-ol, y'know. . . .

TOM. Mother—

AMANDA. Yes, honey?

TOM. How about—supper?

AMANDA. Honey, you go ask Sister if supper is ready! You know that Sister is in full charge of supper! Tell her you hungry boys are waiting for it. (*To Jim.*) Have you met Laura?

JIM. She—

AMANDA. Let you in? Oh, good, you've met already! It's rare for a girl as sweet an' pretty as Laura to be domestic! But Laura is, thank heavens, not only pretty but also very domestic. I'm not at all. I never was a bit. I never could make a thing but angel-food cake. Well, in the South we had so many servants. Gone, gone, gone. All vestige of gracious living! Gone completely! I wasn't prepared for what the future brought me. All of my gentlemen callers were sons of planters and so of course I assumed that I would be married to one and raise my family on a large piece of land with plenty of servants. But man proposes—and woman accepts the proposal to vary that old, old saying a little but—I married no planter! I married a man who worked for the telephone company! That gallantly smiling gentleman over there! (*She points to the picture.*) A telephone man who—fell in love with long-distance! Now he travels and I don't even know where! But what am I going on for about my—tribulations? Tell me yours—I hope you don't have any! Tom?

TOM. (*returning*) Yes, Mother?

AMANDA. Is supper nearly ready?

TOM. It looks to me like supper is on the table.

AMANDA. Let me look— (*She rises prettily and looks through the portieres.*) Oh lovely! But where is Sister?

TOM. Laura is not feeling well and she says that she thinks she'd better not come to the table.

AMANDA. What? Nonsense! Laura? Oh, Laura!

LAURA. (*from the kitchenette, faintly*) Yes, Mother.

AMANDA. You really must come to the table. We won't be seated until you come to the table! Come in, Mr. O'Connor. You sit over there and I'll. . . . Laura? Laura Wingfield! You're keeping us waiting, honey! We can't say grace until you come to the table!

(The kitchenette door is pushed weakly open and Laura comes in. She is obviously quite faint, her lips trembling, her eyes wide and staring. She moves unsteadily toward the table.

Screen legend: "Terror!"

Outside a summer storm is coming on abruptly. The white curtains billow inward at the windows and there is a sorrowful murmur from the deep blue dusk.

Laura suddenly stumbles; she catches at a chair with a faint moan.)

TOM. Laura!

AMANDA. Laura!

(There is a clap of thunder.

Screen legend: "Ah!")

(despairingly) Why, Laura, you are ill, darling! Tom, help your sister into the living room, dear! Sit in the living room, Laura—rest on the sofa. Well! (To Jim as Tom helps his sister to the sofa in the living room.) Standing over the hot stove made her ill! I told her that it was just too warm this evening, but—

(Tom comes back to the table.)

Is Laura all right now?

TOM. Yes.

AMANDA. What is that? Rain? A nice cool rain has come up! *(She gives Jim a frightened look.)* I think we may—have grace—now . . . *(Tom looks at her stupidly.)* Tom, honey—you say grace!

TOM. Oh . . . "For these and all thy mercies—"

(They bow their heads, Amanda stealing a nervous glance at Jim. In the living room Laura, stretched on the sofa, clenches her hand to her lips, to hold back a shuddering sob.)

God's Holy Name be praised—

(The scene dims out.)

Scene 7

(It is half an hour later. Dinner is just being finished in the dining room, Laura is still huddled upon the sofa, her feet drawn under her, her head resting on a pale blue pillow, her eyes wide and mysteriously watchful. The new floor lamp with its shade of rose-colored silk gives a soft, becoming light to her face, bringing out the fragile, unearthly prettiness which usually escapes attention. From outside there is a steady murmur of rain, but it is slackening and soon stops; the air outside becomes pale and luminous as the moon breaks through the clouds. A moment after the curtain rises, the lights in both rooms flicker and go out.)

JIM. Hey, there, Mr. Light Bulb!

(Amanda laughs nervously.

Legend on screen: "Suspension of a public service.")

AMANDA. Where was Moses when the lights went out? Ha-ha. Do you know the answer to that one, Mr. O'Connor?

JIM. No, Ma'am, what's the answer?

AMANDA. In the dark!

(*Jim laughs appreciatively.*)

Everybody sit still. I'll light the candles. Isn't it lucky we have them on the table? Where's a match? Which of you gentlemen can provide a match?

JIM. Here.

AMANDA. Thank you, Sir.

JIM. Not at all, Ma'am!

AMANDA. (*as she lights the candles*) I guess the fuse has burnt out. Mr. O'Connor, can you tell a burnt-out fuse? I know I can't and Tom is a total loss when it comes to mechanics. (*They rise from the table and go into the kitchenette, from where their voices are heard.*) Oh, be careful you don't bump into something. We don't want our gentleman caller to break his neck. Now wouldn't that be a fine howdy-do?

JIM. Ha-ha! Where is the fuse-box?

AMANDA. Right here next to the stove. Can you see anything?

JIM. Just a minute.

AMANDA. Isn't electricity a mysterious thing? Wasn't it Benjamin Franklin who tied a key to a kite? We live in such a mysterious universe, don't we? Some people say that science clears up all the mysteries for us. In my opinion it only creates more! Have you found it yet?

JIM. No, Ma'am. All these fuses look okay to me.

AMANDA. Tom!

TOM. Yes, Mother?

AMANDA. That light bill I gave you several days ago. That one I told you we got the notices about?

(*Legend on screen: "Ha!"*)

TOM. Oh—yeah.

AMANDA. You didn't neglect to pay it by any chance?

TOM. Why, I—

AMANDA. Didn't! I might have known it!

JIM. Shakespeare probably wrote a poem on that light bill, Mrs. Wingfield.

AMANDA. I might have known better than to trust him with it! There's such a high price for negligence in this world!

JIM. Maybe the poem will win a ten-dollar prize.

AMANDA. We'll just have to spend the remainder of the evening in the nineteenth century, before Mr. Edison made the Mazda lamp!°

JIM. Candlelight is my favorite kind of light.

AMANDA. That shows you're romantic! But that's no excuse for Tom. Well, we got through dinner. Very considerate of them to let us get through dinner before they plunged us into everlasting darkness, wasn't it, Mr. O'Connor?

JIM. Ha-ha!

Mazda lamp: named for Ahura Mazda, the Persian god of light; refers to the first workable incandescent lamp developed in 1879 by Thomas A. Edison (1847–1931).

AMANDA. Tom, as a penalty for your carelessness you can help me with the dishes.

JIM. Let me give you a hand.

AMANDA. Indeed you will not!

JIM. I ought to be good for something.

AMANDA. Good for something? (*Her tone is rhapsodic.*) *You?* Why, Mr. O'Connor, nobody, *nobody's* given me this much entertainment in years—as you have!

JIM. Aw, now, Mrs. Wingfield!

AMANDA. I'm not exaggerating, not one bit! But Sister is all by her lonesome. You go keep her company in the parlor! I'll give you this lovely old candelabrum that used to be on the altar at the Church of the Heavenly Rest. It was melted a little out of shape when the church burnt down. Lightning struck it one spring. Gypsy Jones was holding a revival at the time and he intimated that the church was destroyed because the Episcopalians gave card parties.

JIM. Ha-ha.

AMANDA. And how about you coaxing Sister to drink a little wine? I think it would be good for her! Can you carry both at once?

JIM. Sure. I'm Superman!

AMANDA. Now, Thomas, get into this apron!

(*Jim comes into the dining room, carrying the candelabrum, its candles lighted, in one hand and a glass of wine in the other. The door of the kitchenette swings closed on Amanda's gay laughter; the flickering light approaches the portieres. Laura sits up nervously as Jim enters. She can hardly speak from the almost intolerable strain of being alone with a stranger.*

Screen legend: "I don't suppose you remember me at all!"

At first, before Jim's warmth overcomes her paralyzing shyness, Laura's voice is thin and breathless, as though she had just run up a steep flight of stairs. Jim's attitude is gently humorous. While the incident is apparently unimportant, it is to Laura the climax of her secret life.)

JIM. Hello there, Laura.

LAURA. [*faintly*] Hello.

(*She clears her throat.*)

JIM. How are you feeling now? Better?

LAURA. Yes. Yes, thank you.

JIM. This is for you. A little dandelion wine. (*He extends the glass toward her with extravagant gullantry.*)

LAURA. Thank you.

JIM. Drink it—but don't get drunk!

(*He laughs heartily. Laura takes the glass uncertainly; she laughs shyly.*)

Where shall I set the candles?

LAURA. Oh—oh, anywhere . . .

JIM. How about here on the floor? Any objections?

LAURA. No.

JIM. I'll spread a newspaper under to catch the drippings. I like to sit on the floor. Mind if I do?

LAURA. Oh, no.

JIM. Give me a pillow?

LAURA. What?

JIM. A pillow!

LAURA. Oh . . . (*She hands him one quickly.*)

JIM. How about you? Don't you like to sit on the floor?

LAURA. Oh—yes.

JIM. Why don't you, then?

LAURA. I—will.

JIM. Take a pillow!

(*Laura does. She sits on the floor on the other side of the candelabrum. Jim crosses his legs and smiles engagingly at her.*) I can't hardly see you sitting way over there.

LAURA. I can—see you.

JIM. I know, but that's not fair, I'm in the limelight.

(*Laura moves her pillow closer.*)

Good! Now I can see you! Comfortable?

LAURA. Yes.

JIM. So am I. Comfortable as a cow! Will you have some gum?

LAURA. No, thank you.

JIM. I think that I will indulge, with your permission. (*He musingly unwraps a stick of gum and holds it up.*) Think of the fortune made by the guy that invented the first piece of chewing gum. Amazing, huh? The Wrigley Building° is one of the sights of Chicago—I saw it when I went up to the Century of Progress.° Did you take in the Century of Progress?

LAURA. No, I didn't.

JIM. Well, it was quite a wonderful exposition. What impressed me most was the Hall of Science. Gives you an idea of what the future will be in America, even more wonderful than the present time is! (*There is a pause. Jim smiles at her.*) Your brother tells me you're shy. Is that right—Laura?

LAURA. I—don't know.

JIM. I judge you to be an old-fashioned type of girl. Well, I think that's a pretty good type to be. Hope you don't think I'm being too personal—do you?

LAURA. (*Hastily, out of embarrassment*) I believe I *will* take a piece of gum, if you—don't mind. (*clearing her throat*) Mr. O'Connor, have you—kept up with your singing?

JIM. Singing? Me?

LAURA. Yes. I remember what a beautiful voice you had.

JIM. When did you hear me sing?

(*Laura does not answer, and in the long pause which follows a man's voice is heard singing offstage.*)

Wrigley Building: one of the first skyscrapers in the United States, completed in 1924.
Century of Progress: the world's fair held in Chicago (1933–1934).

VOICE:

> O blow, ye winds, heigh-ho,
> A-roving I will go!
> I'm off to my love
> With a boxing glove—
> Ten thousand miles away!

JIM. You say you've heard me sing?

LAURA. Oh, Yes! Yes, very often . . . I—don't suppose—you remember me—at all?

JIM. (*smiling doubtfully*) You know I have an idea I've seen you before. I had that idea soon as you opened the door. It seemed almost like I was about to remember your name. But the name that I started to call you—wasn't a name! And so I stopped myself before I said it.

LAURA. Wasn't it—Blue Roses?

JIM. (*springing up, grinning*) Blue Roses! My gosh, yes—Blue Roses! That's what I had on my tongue when you opened the door! Isn't it funny what tricks your memory plays? I didn't connect you with high school somehow or other. But that's where it was; it was high school. I didn't even know you were Shakespeare's sister! Gosh, I'm sorry.

LAURA. I didn't expect you to. You—barely knew me!

JIM. But we did have a speaking acquaintance, huh?

LAURA. Yes, we—spoke to each other.

JIM. When did you recognize me?

LAURA. Oh, right away!

JIM. Soon as I came in the door?

LAURA. When I heard your name I thought it was probably you. I knew that Tom used to know you a little in high school. So when you came in the door—well, then I was—sure.

JIM. Why didn't you *say* something, then?

LAURA. (*breathlessly*) I didn't know what to say, I was—too surprised!

JIM. For goodness sakes! You know, this sure is funny!

LAURA. Yes! Yes, isn't it, though . . .

JIM. Didn't we have a class in something together?

LAURA. Yes, we did.

JIM. What class was that?

LAURA. It was—singing—chorus!

JIM. Aw!

LAURA. I sat across the aisle from you in the Aud.

JIM. Aw!

LAURA. Mondays, Wednesdays, and Fridays.

JIM. Now I remember—you always came in late.

LAURA. Yes, it was so hard for me, getting upstairs. I had that brace on my leg—it clumped so loud!

JIM. I never heard any clumping.

LAURA. (*wincing at the recollection*) To me it sounded like—thunder!

JIM. Well, well, well, I never even noticed.

LAURA. And everybody was seated before I came in. I had to walk in front of all those people. My seat was in the back row. I had to go clumping all the way up the aisle with everyone watching!

JIM. You shouldn't have been self-conscious.

LAURA. I know, but I was. It was always such a relief when the singing started.

JIM. Aw, yes, I've placed you now! I used to call you Blue Roses. How was it that I got started calling you that?

LAURA. I was out of school a little while with pleurosis. When I came back you asked me what was the matter. I said I had pleurosis—you thought that I said *Blue Roses.* That's what you always called me after that!

JIM. I hope you didn't mind.

LAURA. Oh, no—I liked it. You see, I wasn't acquainted with many—people. . . .

JIM. As I remember you sort of stuck by yourself.

LAURA. I—I—never have had much luck at—making friends.

JIM. I don't see why you wouldn't.

LAURA. Well, I—started out badly.

JIM. You mean being—

LAURA. Yes, it sort of—stood between me—

JIM. You shouldn't have let it!

LAURA. I know, but it did, and—

JIM. You were shy with people!

LAURA. I tried not to be but never could—

JIM. Overcome it?

LAURA. No, I—I never could!

JIM. I guess being shy is something you have to work out of kind of gradually.

LAURA. (*sorrowfully*) Yes—I guess it—

JIM. Takes time!

LAURA. Yes—

JIM. People are not so dreadful when you know them. That's what you have to remember! And everybody has problems, not just you, but practically everybody has got some problems. You think of yourself as having the only problems, as being the only one who is disappointed. But just look around you and you will see lots of people as disappointed as you are. For instance, I hoped when I was going to high school that I would be further along at this time, six years later, than I am now. You remember that wonderful write-up I had in *The Torch?*

LAURA. Yes! (*She rises and crosses to the table.*)

JIM. It said I was bound to succeed in anything I went into!

(*Laura returns with the high school yearbook.*)

Holy Jeez! *The Torch!*

(*He accepts it reverently. They smile across the book with mutual wonder. Laura crouches beside him and they begin to turn the pages. Laura's shyness is dissolving in his warmth.*)

LAURA. Here you are in *The Pirates of Penzance!*

JIM. (*wistfully*) I sang the baritone lead in that operetta.

LAURA. (*raptly*) So—*beautifully!*

JIM. (*protesting*) Aw—

LAURA. Yes, yes—beautifully—beautifully!

JIM. You heard me?

LAURA. All three times!

JIM. No!

LAURA. Yes!

JIM. All three performances?

LAURA. (*looking down*) Yes.

JIM. Why?

LAURA. I—wanted to ask you to—autograph my program. (*She takes the program from the back of the yearbook and shows it to him.*)

JIM. Why didn't you ask me to?

LAURA. You were always surrounded by your own friends so much that I never had a chance to.

JIM. You should have just—

LAURA. Well, I—thought you might think I was—

JIM. Thought I might think you was—what?

LAURA. Oh—

JIM. (*with reflective relish*) I was beleaguered by females in those days.

LAURA. You were terribly popular!

JIM. Yeah—

LAURA. You had such a—friendly way—

JIM. I was spoiled in high school.

LAURA. Everybody—liked you!

JIM. Including you?

LAURA. I—yes, I—did, too— (*She gently closes the book in her lap.*)

JIM. Well, well, well! Give me that program, Laura.

(*She hands it to him. He signs it with a flourish.*)

There you are—better late than never!

LAURA. Oh, I—what a—surprise!

JIM. My signature isn't worth very much right now. But some day—maybe—it will increase in value! Being disappointed is one thing and being discouraged is something else. I am disappointed but I am not discouraged. I'm twenty-three years old. How old are you?

LAURA. I'll be twenty-four in June.

JIM. That's not old age!

LAURA. No, but—

JIM. You finished high school?

LAURA. (*with difficulty.*) I didn't go back.

JIM. You mean you dropped out?

LAURA. I made bad grades in my final examinations. (*She rises and replaces the book and the program on the table. Her voice is strained.*) How is—Emily Meisenbach getting along?

JIM. Oh, that kraut-head!

LAURA. Why do you call her that?

JIM. That's what she was.

LAURA. You're not still—going with her?

JIM. I never see her.

LAURA. It was in the "Personal" section that you were—engaged!

JIM. I know, but I wasn't impressed by that—propaganda!

LAURA. It wasn't—the truth?

JIM. Only in Emily's optimistic opinion!

LAURA. Oh—

(*Legend: "What have you done since high school?"*

Jim lights a cigarette and leans indolently back on his elbows smiling at Laura with a warmth and charm which lights her inwardly with altar candles. She remains by the table, picks up a piece from the glass menagerie collection, and turns it in her hands to cover her tumult.)

JIM. (*after several reflective puffs on his cigarette.*) What have you done since high school?

(*She seems not to hear him.*)

Huh?

(*Laura looks up.*)

I said what have you done since high school, Laura?

LAURA. Nothing much.

JIM. You must have been doing something these six long years.

LAURA. Yes.

JIM. Well, then, such as what?

LAURA. I took a business course at business college—

JIM. How did that work out?

LAURA. Well, not very—well—I had to drop out, it gave me—indigestion—

(*Jim laughs gently.*)

JIM. What are you doing now?

LAURA. I don't do anything—much. Oh, please don't think I sit around doing nothing! My glass collection takes up a good deal of time. Glass is something you have to take good care of.

JIM. What did you say—about glass?

LAURA. Collection I said—I have one— (*She clears her throat and turns away again, acutely shy.*)

JIM. (*abruptly*) You know what I judge to be the trouble with you? Inferiority complex! Know what that is? That's what they call it when someone low-rates himself! I understand it because I had it too. Although my case was not so aggravated as yours seems to be. I had it until I took up public speaking, developed my voice, and learned that I had an aptitude for science. Before that time I never thought of myself as being outstanding in any way whatsoever! Now I've never made a regular study of it, but I have a friend who says I can analyze people better than doctors that make a profession of it. I don't claim that to be necessarily true, but I can sure guess a person's psychology. Laura! (*He takes out his gum.*) Excuse me, Laura. I always take it out when the flavor is gone. I'll use this scrap of paper to wrap it in. I know how it is to get it stuck on a shoe. (*He wraps the gum in paper and puts it in his pocket.*) Yep—that's what I judge to be your principal trouble. A lack of confidence in yourself as a person. You don't have the proper amount of faith in yourself. I'm basing that fact on a number of your remarks and also on certain observations I've made. For instance that clumping you thought was so awful in high school. You say that you even dreaded to walk into class. You see what you did? You dropped out of school, you gave up an education because of a clump, which as far as I know was practically nonexistent! A little physical defect is what you have. Hardly noticeable even! Magnified thousands of times by imagination! You know what my strong advice to you is? Think of yourself as *superior* in some way!

LAURA. In what way would I think?

JIM. Why, man alive, Laura! Just look about you a little. What do you see? A world full of common people! All of 'em born and all of 'em going to die! Which of them has one-tenth of your good points! Or mine! Or anyone else's, as far as that goes—gosh! Everybody excels in some one thing. Some in many! (*He unconsciously glances at himself in the mirror.*) All you've got to do is discover in *what!* Take me, for instance. (*He adjusts his tie at the mirror.*) My interest happens to lie in electrodynamics. I'm taking a course in radio engineering at night school, Laura, on top of a fairly responsible job at the warehouse. I'm taking that course and studying public speaking.

LAURA. Ohhhh.

JIM. Because I believe in the future of television! (*turning his back to her*) I wish to be ready to go up right along with it. Therefore I'm planning to get in on the ground floor. In fact I've already made the right connections and all that remains is for the industry itself to get under way! Full steam— (*His eyes are starry.*) *Knowledge*—Zzzzzp! *Money*—Zzzzzp!—Power! That's the cycle democracy is built on!

(*His attitude is convincingly dynamic. Laura stares at him, even her shyness eclipsed in her absolute wonder. He suddenly grins.*)

I guess you think I think a lot of myself!

LAURA. No—o-o-o, I—

JIM. Now how about you? Isn't there something you take more interest in than anything else?

LAURA. Well, I do—as I said—have my—glass collection—

(*A peal of girlish laughter rings from the kitchenette.*)

JIM. I'm not right sure I know what you're talking about. What kind of glass is it?

LAURA. Little articles of it, they're ornaments mostly! Most of them are little animals made out of glass, the tiniest little animals in the world. Mother calls them a glass menagerie! Here's an example of one, if you'd like to see it! This one is one of the oldest. It's nearly thirteen.

(*Music: "The Glass Menagerie."*

He stretches out his hand.)

Oh, be careful—if you breathe, it breaks!

JIM. I'd better not take it. I'm pretty clumsy with things.

LAURA. Go, on, I trust you with him! (*She places the piece in his palm.*) There now—you're holding him gently! Hold him over the light, he loves the light! You see how the light shines through him?

JIM. It sure does shine!

LAURA. I shouldn't be partial, but he is my favorite one.

JIM. What kind of a thing is this one supposed to be?

LAURA. Haven't you noticed the single horn on his forehead?

JIM. A unicorn, huh?

LAURA. Mmmm-hmmm!

JIM. Unicorns—aren't they extinct in the modern world?

LAURA. I know!

JIM. Poor little fellow, he must feel sort of lonesome.

LAURA. (*smiling*) Well, if he does, he doesn't complain about it. He stays on a shelf with some horses that don't have horns and all of them seem to get along nicely together.

JIM. How do you know?

LAURA. (*lightly*) I haven't heard any arguments among them!

JIM. (*grinning*) No arguments, huh? Well, that's a pretty good sign! Where shall I set him?

LAURA. Put him on the table. They all like a change of scenery once in a while!

JIM. Well, well, well, well— (*He places the glass piece on the table, then raises his arms and stretches.*) Look how big my shadow is when I stretch!

LAURA. Oh, oh, yes—it stretches across the ceiling!

JIM. (*crossing to the door*) I think it's stopped raining. (*He opens the fire-escape door and the background music changes to a dance tune.*) Where does the music come from?

LAURA. From the Paradise Dance Hall across the alley.

JIM. How about cutting the rug a little, Miss Wingfield?

LAURA. Oh, I—

JIM. Or is your program filled up? Let me have a look at it. (*He grasps an imaginary card.*) Why, every dance is taken! I'll just have to scratch some out.

(*Waltz music: "La Golondrina"*°)

Ahh, a waltz!

(*He executes some sweeping turns by himself, then holds his arms toward Laura.*)

LAURA. (*breathlessly*) I—can't dance.

JIM. There you go, that inferiority stuff!

LAURA. I've never danced in my life!

JIM. Come on, try!

LAURA. Oh, but I'd step on you!

JIM. I'm not made out of glass.

LAURA. How—how—how do we start?

JIM. Just leave it to me. You hold your arms out a little.

LAURA. Like this?

JIM. (*taking her in his arms*) A little bit higher. Right. Now don't tighten up, that's the main thing about it—relax.

LAURA. (*laughing breathlessly*) It's hard not to.

JIM. Okay.

LAURA. I'm afraid you can't budge me.

JIM. What do you bet I can't? (*He swings her into motion.*)

LAURA. Goodness, yes, you can!

JIM. Let yourself go, now, Laura, just let yourself go.

LAURA. I'm—

JIM. Come on!

LAURA. —trying!

JIM. Not so stiff—easy does it!

LAURA. I know but I'm—

JIM. Loosen th' backbone! There now, that's a lot better.

LAURA. Am I?

JIM. Lots, lots better! (*He moves her about the room in a clumsy waltz.*)

LAURA. Oh, my!

JIM. Ha-ha!

LAURA. Oh, my goodness!

"La Golondrina": a popular Mexican song written in 1883 by Narciso Seradell (1843–1910).

JIM. Ha-ha-ha!

(*They suddenly bump into the table, and the glass piece on it falls to the floor. Jim stops the dance.*)

What did we hit?

LAURA. Table.

JIM. Did something fall off it? I think—

LAURA. Yes.

JIM. I hope that it wasn't the little glass horse with the horn!

LAURA. Yes. (*She stoops to pick it up.*)

JIM. Aw, aw, aw. Is it broken?

LAURA. Now it is just like all the other horses.

JIM. It's lost its—

LAURA. Horn! It doesn't matter. Maybe it's a blessing in disguise.

JIM. You'll never forgive me. I bet that that was your favorite piece of glass.

LAURA. I don't have favorites much. It's no tragedy, Freckles. Glass breaks so easily. No matter how careful you are. The traffic jars the shelves and things fall off them.

JIM. Still I'm awfully sorry that I was the cause.

LAURA. (*smiling*) I'll just imagine he had an operation. The horn was removed to make him feel less—freakish!

(*They both laugh.*)

Now he will feel more at home with the other horses, the ones that don't have horns. . . .

JIM. Ha-ha, that's very funny! (*Suddenly he is serious.*) I'm glad to see that you have a sense of humor. You know—you're—well—very different! Surprisingly different from anyone else I know! (*His voice becomes soft and hesitant with a genuine feeling.*) Do you mind me telling you that?

(*Laura is abashed beyond speech.*)

I mean it in a nice way—

(*Laura nods shyly, looking away.*)

You make me feel sort of—I don't know how to put it! I'm usually pretty good at expressing things, but—this is something that I don't know how to say!

(*Laura touches her throat and clears it—turns the broken unicorn in her hands. His voice becomes softer.*)

Has anyone ever told you that you were pretty?

(*There is a pause, and the music rises slightly. Laura looks up slowly, with wonder, and shakes her head.*)

Well, you are! In a very different way from anyone else. And all the nicer because of the difference, too.

(*His voice becomes low and husky. Laura turns away, nearly faint with the novelty of her emotions.*)

I wish that you were my sister. I'd teach you to have some confidence in yourself. The different people are not like other people, but being different is nothing to be ashamed of. Because other people are not such wonderful people. They're one hundred times one thousand. You're one times one! They walk all over the earth. You just stay here. They're common as—weeds, but—you—well, you're—*Blue Roses*!

(*Image on screen: Blue Roses.*

The music changes.)

LAURA. But blue is wrong for—roses. . . .

JIM. It's right for you! You're—pretty!

LAURA. In what respect am I pretty?

JIM. In all respects—believe me! Your eyes—your hair—are pretty! Your hands are pretty! (*He catches hold of her hand.*) You think I'm making this up because I'm invited to dinner and have to be nice. Oh, I could do that! I could put on an act for you, Laura, and say lots of things without being very sincere. But this time I am. I'm talking to you sincerely. I happened to notice you had this inferiority complex that keeps you from feeling comfortable with people. Somebody needs to build your confidence up and make you proud instead of shy and turning away and—blushing. Somebody—ought to—*kiss* you, Laura!

(*His hand slips slowly up her arm to her shoulder as the music swells tumultuously. He suddenly turns about and kisses her on the lips. When he releases her, Laura sinks on the sofa with a bright, dazed look. Jim backs away and fishes in his pocket for a cigarette.*

Legend on screen: "A souvenir.")

Stumblejohn!

(*He lights the cigarette, avoiding her look. There is a peal of girlish laughter from Amanda in the kitchenette. Laura slowly raises and opens her hand. It still contains the little broken glass animal. She looks at it with a tender, bewildered expression.*)

Stumblejohn! I shouldn't have done that—that was way off the beam. You don't smoke, do you?

(*She looks up, smiling, not hearing the question. He sits beside her rather gingerly. She looks at him speechlessly—waiting. He coughs decorously and moves a little further aside as he considers the situation and senses her feelings, dimly, with perturbation. He speaks gently.*)

Would you—care for a mint?

(*She doesn't seem to hear him but her look grows brighter even.*)

Peppermint? Life Saver? My pocket's a regular drugstore—wherever I go. . . . (*He pops a mint in his mouth. Then he gulps and decides to make a clean breast of it. He speaks slowly and gingerly.*) Laura, you know, if I had a sister like you, I'd do the same thing as Tom. I'd bring out fellows and—introduce her to them. The right type of boys—of a type to—appreciate her. Only—well—he made a mistake about me. Maybe I've got no call to be saying this. That may not have been the idea in having me over. But what if it was? There's nothing wrong about that. The only trouble is that in my case—I'm not in a situation to—do the right thing. I can't take down your number and say I'll phone. I can't call up next week and—ask for a date. I thought I had better explain the situation in case you—misunderstood it and—I hurt your feelings. . . .

(*There is a pause. Slowly, very slowly, Laura's look changes, her eyes returning slowly from his to the glass figure in her palm. Amanda utters another gay laugh in the kitchenette.*)

LAURA. (*faintly*) You—won't—call again?

JIM. No, Laura, I can't. (*He rises from the sofa.*) As I was just explaining, I've—got strings on me, Laura, I've—been going steady! I go out all the time with a girl named Betty. She's a home-girl like you, and Catholic, and Irish, and in a great many ways we—get along fine. I met her last summer on a moonlight boat trip up the river to Alton,° on the *Majestic*. Well—right away from the start it was—love!

(*Legend: Love!*

Laura sways slightly forward and grips the arm of the sofa. He fails to notice, now enrapt in his own comfortable being.)

Being in love has made a new man of me!

(*Leaning stiffly forward, clutching the arm of the sofa, Laura struggles visibly with her storm. But Jim is oblivious; she is a long way off.*)

The power of love is really pretty tremendous! Love is something that—changes the whole world, Laura!

(*The storm abates a little and Laura leans back. He notices her again.*)

It happened that Betty's aunt took sick, she got a wire and had to go to Centralia.° So Tom—when he asked me to dinner—I naturally just accepted the invitation, not knowing that you—that he—that I— (*He stops awkwardly.*) Huh—I'm a stumblejohn!

(*He flops back on the sofa. The holy candles on the altar of Laura's face have been snuffed out. There is a look of almost infinite desolation. Jim glances at her uneasily.*)

I wish that you would—say something.

(*She bites her lip which was trembling and then bravely smiles. She opens her hand again on the broken glass figure. Then she gently takes his hand and raises it level with her own. She carefully places the unicorn in the palm of his hand, then pushes his fingers closed upon it.*)

What are you—doing that for? You want me to have him? Laura?

(*She nods.*)

What for?

LAURA. A—souvenir. . . .

Alton: a city in Illinois, on the Mississippi River, twenty miles north of St. Louis. **Centralia:** a city in Illinois sixty miles east of St. Louis.

(She rises unsteadily and crouches beside the Victrola to wind it up.

Legend on screen: "Things have a way of turning out so badly!" Or image: "Gentleman caller waving goodbye—gaily."

At this moment Amanda rushes brightly back into the living room. She bears a pitcher of fruit punch in an old-fashioned cut-glass pitcher, and a plate of macaroons. The plate has a gold border and poppies painted on it.)

AMANDA. Well, well, well! Isn't the air delightful after the shower? I've made you children a little liquid refreshment. (*She turns gaily to Jim.*) Jim, do you know that song about lemonade?

"Lemonade, lemonade
Made in the shade and stirred with a spade—
Good enough for any old maid!"

JIM. (*uneasily*) Ha-ha! No—I never heard it.

AMANDA. Why, Laura! You look so serious!

JIM. We were having a serious conversation.

AMANDA. Good! Now you're better acquainted!

JIM. (*uncertainly*) Ha-ha! Yes.

AMANDA. You modern young people are much more serious-minded than my generation. I was so gay as a girl!

JIM. You haven't changed, Mrs. Wingfield.

AMANDA. Tonight I'm rejuvenated! The gaiety of the occasion. Mr. O'Connor! (*She tosses her head with a peal of laughter, spilling some lemonade.*) Oooo! I'm baptizing myself!

JIM. Here—let me—

AMANDA. (*setting the pitcher down*) There now. I discovered we had some maraschino cherries. I dumped them in, juice and all!

JIM. You shouldn't have gone to that trouble, Mrs. Wingfield.

AMANDA. Trouble, trouble? Why, it was loads of fun! Didn't you hear me cutting up in the kitchen? I bet your ears were burning! I told Tom how outdone with him I was for keeping you to himself so long a time! He should have brought you over much, much sooner! Well, now that you've found your way, I want you to be a very frequent caller! Not just occasional but all the time. Oh, we're going to have a lot of gay times together! I see them coming! Mmm, just breathe that air! So fresh, and the moon's so pretty! I'll skip back out—I know where my place is when young folks are having a—serious conversation!

JIM. Oh, don't go out, Mrs. Wingfield. The fact of the matter is I've got to be going.

AMANDA. Going, now? You're joking! Why, it's only the shank of the evening,° Mr. O'Connor!

JIM. Well, you know how it is.

AMANDA. You mean you're a young workingman and have to keep workingmen's hours. We'll let you off early tonight. But only on the condition that next time you stay later. What's the best night for you? Isn't Saturday night the best night for you workingmen?

JIM. I have a couple of time-clocks to punch, Mrs. Wingfield. One at morning, another one at night!

---

shank of the evening: the early, best part of the evening.

AMANDA. My, but you *are* ambitious! You work at night, too?

JIM. No, Ma'am, not work but—Betty!

(*He crosses deliberately to pick up his hat. The band at the Paradise Dance Hall goes into a tender waltz.*)

AMANDA. Betty? Betty? Who's—Betty!

(*There is an ominous cracking sound in the sky.*)

JIM. Oh, just a girl. The girl I go steady with!

(*He smiles charmingly. The sky falls.*

Legend: "The Sky Falls.")

AMANDA. (*a long-drawn exhalation*) Ohhh . . . Is it a serious romance, Mr. O'Connor?

JIM. We're going to be married the second Sunday in June.

AMANDA. Ohhh—how nice! Tom didn't mention that you were engaged to be married.

JIM. The cat's not out of the bag at the warehouse yet. You know how they are. They call you Romeo and stuff like that. (*He stops at the oval mirror to put on his hat. He carefully shapes the brim and the crown to give a discreetly dashing effect.*) It's been a wonderful evening, Mrs. Wingfield. I guess this is what they mean by Southern hospitality.

AMANDA. It really wasn't anything at all.

JIM. I hope it don't seem like I'm rushing off. But I promised Betty I'd pick her up at the Wabash depot, an' by the time I get my jalopy down there her train'll be in. Some women are pretty upset if you keep 'em waiting.

AMANDA. Yes, I know—the tyranny of women! (*She extends her hand.*) Goodbye, Mr. O'Connor. I wish you luck—and happiness—and success! All three of them, and so does Laura! Don't you, Laura?

LAURA. Yes!

JIM. (*taking Laura's hand*) Goodbye, Laura. I'm certainly going to treasure that souvenir. And don't you forget the good advice I gave you. (*He raises his voice to a cheery shout.*) So long, Shakespeare! Thanks again, ladies. Good night!

(*He grins and ducks jauntily out. Still bravely grimacing, Amanda closes the door on the gentleman caller. Then she turns back to the room with a puzzled expression. She and Laura don't dare to face each other. Laura crouches beside the Victrola to wind it.*)

AMANDA. (*faintly*) Things have a way of turning out so badly. I don't believe that I would play the Victrola. Well, well—well! Our gentleman caller was engaged to be married? (*She raises her voice.*) Tom!

TOM. (*from the kitchenette*) Yes, Mother?

AMANDA. Come in here a minute. I want to tell you something awfully funny.

TOM. (*entering with a macaroon and a glass of the lemonade*) Has the gentleman caller gotten away already?

AMANDA. The gentleman caller has made an early departure. What a wonderful joke you played on us!

TOM. How do you mean?

AMANDA. You didn't mention that he was engaged to be married.

TOM. Jim? Engaged?

AMANDA. That's what he just informed us.

TOM. I'll be jiggered! I didn't know about that.

AMANDA. That seems very peculiar.

TOM. What's peculiar about it?

AMANDA. Didn't you call him your best friend down at the warehouse?

TOM. He is, but how did I know?

AMANDA. It seems extremely peculiar that you wouldn't know your best friend was going to be married!

TOM. The warehouse is where I work, not where I know things about people!

AMANDA. You don't know things anywhere! You live in a dream; you manufacture illusions!

(*He crosses to the door.*)

Where are you going?

TOM. I'm going to the movies.

AMANDA. That's right, now that you've had us make such fools of ourselves. The effort, the preparations, all the expense! The new floor lamp, the rug, the clothes for Laura! All for what? To entertain some other girl's fiancé! Go to the movies, go! Don't think about us, a mother deserted, an unmarried sister who's crippled and has no job! Don't let anything interfere with your selfish pleasure! Just go, go, go—to the movies!

TOM. All right, I will! The more you shout about my selfishness to me the quicker I'll go, and I won't go to the movies!

AMANDA. Go, then! Go to the moon—you selfish dreamer!

(*Tom smashes his glass on the floor. He plunges out on the fire escape, slamming the door. Laura screams in fright. The dance-hall music becomes louder. Tom stands on the fire escape, gripping the rail. The moon breaks through the storm clouds, illuminating his face.*

Legend on screen: "And so goodbye . . ."

Tom's closing speech is timed with what is happening inside the house. We see, as though through soundproof glass, that Amanda appears to be making a comforting speech to Laura, who is huddled upon the sofa. Now that we cannot hear the mother's speech, her silliness is gone and she has dignity and tragic beauty. Laura's hair hides her face until, at the end of the speech, she lifts her head to smile at her mother. Amanda's gestures are slow and graceful, almost dancelike, as she comforts her daughter. At the end of her speech she glances a moment at the father's picture—then withdraws through the portieres. At the close of Tom's speech, Laura blows out the candles, ending the play.)

TOM. I didn't go to the moon, I went much further—for time is the longest distance between two places. Not long after that I was fired for writing a poem on the lid of a shoe-box. I left Saint Louis. I descended the steps of this fire escape for a last time and followed, from then on, in my father's footsteps, attempting to find in motion what was lost in space. I traveled around a great deal. The cities swept about me like dead leaves, leaves that were brightly colored but torn away from the branches. I would have stopped, but I was pursued by something. It always came upon me unawares, taking me altogether by surprise. Perhaps it was a familiar bit of music. Perhaps it was only a piece of transparent glass. Perhaps I am walking along a street at night, in some strange city, before I have found companions. I pass the lighted window of a shop where perfume is sold. The window is filled with pieces of colored glass, tiny transparent bottles in delicate colors, like bits of a shattered rainbow. Then all at once my sister touches my shoulder. I turn around and look into her eyes. Oh, Laura, Laura, I tried to leave you behind me, but I am more faithful than I intended to be! I reach for a cigarette, I cross the street, I run into the movies or a bar, I buy a drink, I speak to the nearest stranger—anything that can blow your candles out!

(*Laura bends over the candles.*)

For nowadays the world is lit by lightning! Blow out your candles, Laura—and so goodbye. . . .

(*She blows the candles out.*)

Analyzing the Text

1. How do we know that Laura has removed herself from reality and prefers to live in her illusions?
2. What hopes does she attach to Jim O'Connor, her gentleman caller?

Understanding Williams's Techniques

1. What is Williams's attitude toward the characters and family he depicts? Is he sympathetic to their dreams and fantasies and aspirations? How do you know this?
2. In what way is the "glass menagerie" an apt symbol for the emotional underpinnings of the characters?

Arguing for an Interpretation

1. As the narrator, Tom Wingfield might be assumed to have greater insight into the family's delusions than do Amanda and Laura. How does Williams demonstrate that Tom is also caught up in these fantasies?
2. Is there such a thing as the mystique of the South, and if so, what are its characteristics as represented in Williams's play?

Christopher Durang

Christopher Durang was born in Montclair, New Jersey in 1949. He received a B. A. from Harvard and in his senior year wrote The Nature and Purpose of the Universe *(1971), a satire on middle-class life that helped secure his acceptance at the Yale School of Drama, where he earned an M.F.A. in 1974. At Yale, Durang wrote and acted in many plays that were produced on and off Broadway in the years that followed, including* The Marriage of Betty and Boo *(1973) and* 'dentity Crisis *(1975). Success came with* Sister Mary Ignatius Explains It All for You *(1979), a work that received an Obie award. Other works that display Durang at his most iconoclastic are* Beyond Therapy

(1981), The Actor's Nightmare *(1981), and* Baby with the Bathwater *(1984). A recent work is* Betty's Summer Vacation *(1999).* For Whom the Southern Belle Tolls, *Durang's parody of Tennessee Williams's* The Glass Menagerie, *was featured in* Durang, Durang, *a program of one-act plays that was premiered in New York City in 1994.*

For Whom the Southern Belle Tolls

Characters

AMANDA, *the mother*
LAWRENCE, *the son*
TOM, *the other son*
GINNY

Lights up on a fussy living room setting. Enter Amanda, the Southern belle mother.

AMANDA. Rise and shine! Rise and shine! (*Calls off.*) Lawrence, honey, come on out here and let me have a look at you!

(Enter Lawrence, who limps across the room. He is very sensitive, and is wearing what are clearly his dress clothes. Amanda fiddles with his bow tie and stands back to admire him.)

AMANDA. Lawrence, honey, you look lovely.

LAWRENCE. No, I don't mama. I have a pimple on the back of my neck.

AMANDA. Don't say the world "pimple," honey, it's common. Now your brother Tom is bringing home a girl from the warehouse for you to meet, and I want you to make a good impression, honey.

LAWRENCE. It upsets my stomach to meet people, mama.

AMANDA. Oh, Lawrence honey, you're so sensitive it makes me want to hit you.

LAWRENCE. I don't need to meet people, mama. I'm happy just by myself, playing with my collection of glass cocktail stirrers.

(Lawrence limps over to a table on top of which sits a glass jar filled with glass swizzle sticks.)

AMANDA. Lawrence, you are a caution. Only retarded people and alcoholics are interested in glass cocktail stirrers.

LAWRENCE (*picking up some of them*). Each one of them has a special name, mama. This one is called Stringbean because it's long and thin; and this one is called Stringbean because it's long and thin; and this one is called Blue because it's blue.

AMANDA. All my children have such imagination, why was I so blessed? Oh, Lawrence honey, how are you going to get on in the world if you just stay home all day, year after year, playing with your collection of glass cocktail stirrers?

LAWRENCE. I don't like the world, mama, I like it here in this room.

AMANDA. I know you do, Lawrence honey, that's part of your charm. Some days. But, honey, what about making a living?

LAWRENCE. I can't work, mama. I'm crippled. (*He limps over to the couch and sits.*)

AMANDA. There is nothing wrong with your leg, Lawrence honey, all the doctors have told you that. This limping thing is an affectation.

LAWRENCE. I only know how I feel, mama.

AMANDA. Oh if only I had connections in the Mafia, I'd have someone come and break both your legs.

LAWRENCE. Don't try to make me laugh, mama. You know I have asthma.

AMANDA. Your asthma, your leg, your eczema. You're just a mess, Lawrence.

LAWRENCE. I have scabs from the itching, mama.

AMANDA. That's lovely, Lawrence. You must tell us more over dinner.

LAWRENCE. Alright.

AMANDA. That was a joke, Lawrence.

LAWRENCE. Don't try to make me laugh, mama. My asthma.

AMANDA. Now, Lawrence, I don't want you talking about your ailments to the feminine caller your brother Tom is bringing home from the warehouse, honey. No nice-bred young lady likes to hear a young man discussing his eczema, Lawrence.

LAWRENCE. What else can I talk about, mama?

AMANDA. Talk about the weather. Or Red China.

LAWRENCE. Or my collection of glass cocktail stirrers?

AMANDA. I suppose so, honey, if the conversation comes to some godawful standstill. Otherwise, I'd shut up about it. Conversation is an art, Lawrence. Back at Blue Mountain, when I had seventeen gentlemen callers, I was able to converse with charm and vivacity for six hours without stop and never once mention eczema or bone cancer or vivisection. Try to emulate me, Lawrence, honey. Charm and vivacity. And charm. And vivacity. And charm.

LAWRENCE. Well, I'll try, but I doubt it.

AMANDA. Me too, honey. But we'll go through the motions anyway, won't we?

LAWRENCE. I don't know if I want to meet some girl who works in a warehouse, mama.

AMANDA. Your brother Tom says she's a lovely girl with a nice personality. And where else does he meet girls except the few who work at the warehouse? He only seems to meet men at the movies. Your brother goes to the movies entirely too much. I must speak to him about it.

LAWRENCE. It's unfeminine for a girl to work at a warehouse.

AMANDA. Lawrence, honey, if you can't go out the door without getting an upset stomach or an attack of vertigo, then we got to find some nice girl who's willing to support you. Otherwise, how am I ever going to get you out of this house and off my hands?

LAWRENCE. Why do you want to be rid of me, mama?

AMANDA. I suppose it's unmotherly of me, dear, but you really get on my nerves. Limping around the apartment, pretending to have asthma. If only some nice girl would marry you and I knew you were taken care of, then I'd feel free to start to live again. I'd join Parents Without Partners, I'd go to dinner dances, I'd have a life again. Rather than just watch you mope about this stupid apartment. I'm not bitter, dear, it's just that I hate my life.

LAWRENCE. I understand, mama.

AMANDA. Do you, dear? Oh, you're cute. Oh listen, I think I hear them.

TOM (*from offstage*). Mother, I forgot my key.

LAWRENCE. I'll be in the other room. (*Starts to limp away.*)

AMANDA. I want you to let them in, Lawrence.

LAWRENCE. Oh, I couldn't mama. She'd see I limp.

AMANDA. Then don't limp, damn it.

TOM (*from off*). Mother, are you there?

AMANDA. Just a minute, Tom, honey. Now, Lawrence, you march over to that door or I'm going to break all your swizzle sticks.

LAWRENCE. Mama, I can't.

AMANDA. Lawrence, you're a grown boy. Now you answer that door like any normal person.

LAWRENCE. I can't.

TOM. Mother, I'm going to break the door down in a minute.

AMANDA. Just be patient, Tom. Now you're causing a scene, Lawrence. I want you to answer that door.

LAWRENCE. My eczema itches.

AMANDA. I'll itch it for you in a second, Lawrence.

TOM. Alright, I'm breaking it down.

Sound of door breaking down. Enter Tom and Ginny Bennett, *a vivacious girl dressed in factory clothes.*

AMANDA. Oh, Tom, you got in.

TOM. Why must we go through this every night? You know the stupid fuck won't open the door, so why don't you let him alone about it? (*To Ginny.*) My kid brother has a thing about answering doors. He thinks people will notice his limp and his asthma and his eczema.

LAWRENCE. Excuse me. I think I hear someone calling me in the other room. (*Limps off, calls to imaginary person.*) Coming!

AMANDA. Now see what you've done. He's probably going to refuse to come to the table due to your insensitivity. Oh, was any woman as cursed as I? With one son who's too sensitive and another one who's this big ox. I'm sorry, how rude of me. I'm Amanda Wingvalley. You must be Virginia Bennett from the warehouse. Tom has spoken so much about you I feel you're almost one of the family, preferably a daughter-in-law. Welcome, Virginia.

GINNY. (*speaking very loudly*). Call me Ginny or Gin. But just don't call me late for dinner! (*Roars with laughter.*)

AMANDA. Oh, how amusing. (*Whispers to Tom.*) Why is she shouting? Is she deaf?

GINNY. You're asking why I am speaking loudly. It's so that I can be heard! I am taking a course in public speaking, and so far we've covered organizing your thoughts and speaking good and loud so the people in the back of the room can hear you.

AMANDA. Public speaking. How impressive. You must be interested in improving yourself.

GINNY (*truly not having heard*). What?

AMANDA (*loudly*). YOU MUST BE INTERESTED IN IMPROVING YOURSELF.

GINNY (*loudly and happily*). YES I AM!

TOM. When's dinner? I want to get this over with fast if everyone's going to shout all evening.

GINNY. What?

AMANDA (*to Ginny*). Dinner is almost ready, Ginny.

GINNY. Who's Freddy?

AMANDA. Oh, Lord. No, dear. DINNER IS READY.

GINNY. Oh good. I'm as hungry as a bear! (*Growls enthusiastically.*)

AMANDA. You must be very popular at the warehouse, Ginny.

GINNY. No popsicle for me, ma'am, although I will take you up on some gin.

AMANDA (*confused*). What?

GINNY (*loudly*). I WOULD LIKE SOME GIN.

AMANDA. Well, fine. I think I'd like to get drunk too. Tom, why don't you go and make two Southern ladies some nice summer gin and tonics? And see if your sister would like a lemonade.

TOM. Sister?

AMANDA. I'm sorry, did I say sister? I meant brother.

TOM (*calling as he exits*). Hey, four eyes, you wanna lemonade?

AMANDA. Tom's so amusing. He calls Lawrence four eyes even though he doesn't wear glasses.

GINNY. And does Lawrence wear glasses?

AMANDA (*confused*). What?

GINNY. You said Tom called Lawrence four eyes even though he doesn't wear glasses, and I wondered if Lawrence wore glasses. Because that would, you see, explain it.

AMANDA (*looks at her with despair*). Ah. I don't know. I'll have to ask Lawrence someday. Speaking of Lawrence, let me go check on the supper and see if I can convince him to come out here and make conversation with you.

GINNY. No, thank you, ma'am, I'll just have the gin.

AMANDA. What?

GINNY. What?

AMANDA. Never mind. I'll be back. Or with luck I won't.

(*Amanda exits. Ginny looks around uncomfortably, and crosses to the table with the collection of glass cocktail stirrers.*)

GINNY. They must drink a lot here.

(*Enter Tom with a glass of gin for Ginny.*)

TOM. Here's some gin for Ginny.

GINNY. What?

TOM. Here's your poison.

GINNY. No, thanks, I'll just wait here.

TOM. Have you ever thought all that loud machinery at the warehouse may be affecting your hearing?

GINNY. Scenery? You mean, like trees? Yeah, I like trees.

TOM. I like trees, too.

AMANDA (*from offstage*). Now you get out of that bed this minute, Lawrence Wingvalley, or I'm going to give that overbearing girl your entire collection of glass gobbledygook—is that clear?

(*Amanda pushes in Lawrence, who is wearing a nightshirt.*)

AMANDA. I believe Lawrence would like to visit with you, Ginny.

GINNY (*shows her drink*). Tom brought me my drink already, thank you, Mrs. Wingvalley.

AMANDA. You know a hearing aid isn't really all that expensive, dear, you might look into that.

GINNY. No, if I have the gin, I don't really want any Gatorade. Never liked the stuff anyway. But you feel free.

AMANDA. Thank you, dear. I will. Come, Tom, come to the kitchen and help me prepare the dinner. And we'll let the two young people converse. Remember, Lawrence. Charm and vivacity.

TOM. I hope this dinner won't take long, mother. I don't want to get to the movies too late.

AMANDA. Oh shut up about the movies.

(*Amanda and Tom exit. Lawrence stands still, uncomfortable. Ginny looks at him pleasantly. Silence for a while.*)

GINNY. Hi.

LAWRENCE. Hi. (*Pause.*) I'd gone to bed.

GINNY. I never eat bread. It's too fattening. I have to watch my figure if I want to get ahead in the world. Why are you wearing that nightshirt?

LAWRENCE. I'd gone to bed. I wasn't feeling well. My leg hurts and I have a headache, and I have palpitations of the heart.

GINNY. I don't know. Hum a few bars, and I'll see.

LAWRENCE. We've met before, you know.

GINNY. I've never seen snow. Is it exciting?

LAWRENCE. We were in high school together. You were voted Girl Most Likely To Succeed. We sat next to one another in glee club.

GINNY. I'm sorry, I really can't hear you. You're talking too softly.

LAWRENCE (*louder*). You used to call me BLUE ROSES.

GINNY. Blue Roses? Oh yes, I remember, sort of. Why did I do that?

LAWRENCE. I had been absent from school for several months, and when I came back, you asked me where I'd been, and I said I'd been sick with viral pneumonia, but you thought I said "blue roses."

GINNY. I didn't get much of that, but I remember you now. You used to make a spectacle of yourself every day in glee class, clumping up the aisle with this great big noisy leg brace on your leg. God, you made a racket.

LAWRENCE. I was always so afraid people were looking at me, and pointing. But then eventually mama wouldn't let me wear the leg brace anymore. She gave it to the Salvation Army.

GINNY. I've never been in the army. How long were you in for?

LAWRENCE. I've never been in the army. I have asthma.

GINNY. You do? May I see it?

LAWRENCE (*confused*). See it?

GINNY. Well, sure, unless you don't want to.

LAWRENCE. Maybe you want to see my collection of glass cocktail stirrers. (*He limps to the table, and limps back to her, holding his collection.*)

LAWRENCE (holds up a stick). I call this one Stringbean, because it's long and thin.

GINNY. Thank you. (*Puts it in her glass and stirs it.*)

LAWRENCE (*fairly appalled*). They're not for use. (*Takes it back from her.*) They're a collection.

GINNY. Well, I guess I stirred it enough.

LAWRENCE. They're my favorite thing in the world. (*Holds up another one.*) I call this one Q-tip, because I realized it looks like a Q-tip, except it's made out of glass and doesn't have little cotton swabs at the end of it. (*She looks blank.*) Q-TIPS.

GINNY. Really? (*She takes it and puts it in her ear.*)

LAWRENCE. No! Don't put it in your ear. (*Takes it back.*) Now it's disgusting.

GINNY. Well, I didn't think it was a Q-tip, but that's what you said it was.

LAWRENCE. I call it that. I think I'm going to throw it out now. (*Holds up another one.*) I call this one Pinocchio because if you hold it perpendicular to your nose it makes your nose look long. (*He holds it to his nose.*)

GINNY. Uh huh.

LAWRENCE. And I call this one Henry Kissinger, because he wears glasses and it's made of glass.

GINNY. Uh huh. (*Takes it and stirs her drink.*)

LAWRENCE. No! They're just for looking, not for stirring. Mama, she's making a mess with my collection.

AMANDA (*from off*). Oh shut up about your collection, honey, you're probably driving the poor girl bananas.

GINNY. No bananas, thank you! My nutritionist says I should avoid potassium. You know what I take your trouble to be, Lawrence?

LAWRENCE. Mama says I'm retarded.

GINNY. I know you're tired, I figured that's why you put on the nightshirt, but this won't take long. I judge you to be lacking in self-confidence. Am I right?

LAWRENCE. Well, I am afraid of people and things, and I have a lot of ailments.

GINNY. But that makes you special, Lawrence.

LAWRENCE. What does?

GINNY. I don't know. Whatever you said. And that's why you should present yourself with more confidence. Throw back your shoulders, and say, "HI! HOW YA DOIN'?" Now you try it.

LAWRENCE (*unenthusiastically, softly*). Hello, How are you?

GINNY (*looking at watch, in response to his supposed question*). I don't know, it's about 8:30, but this won't take long and then you can go to bed. Alright, now try it. (*Booming.*) "H! HOW YA DOIN'?"

LAWRENCE. Hi. How ya doin'?

GINNY. Now swagger a bit. (*Kinda butch.*) HI. HOW YA DOIN'?

LAWRENCE (*imitates her fairly successfully*). HI. HOW YA DOIN'?

GINNY. Good, Lawrence. That's much better, Again.

(*Amanda and Tom enter from behind them and watch this.*)

GINNY (*continued*). HI! HOW YA DOIN'?

LAWRENCE. HI! HOW YA DOIN'?

GINNY. THE BRAVES PLAYED A HELLUVA GAME, DON'TCHA THINK?

LAWRENCE. THE BRAVES PLAYED A HELLUVA GAME, DON'TCHA THINK?

AMANDA. Oh God I feel sorry for their children. Is this the only girl who works at the warehouse, Tom?

GINNY. HI, MRS. WINGVALLEY, YOUR SON LAWRENCE AND I ARE GETTING ON JUST FINE. AREN'T WE, LAWRENCE?

AMANDA. Please, no need to shout, I'm not deaf, even if you are.

GINNY. What?

AMANDA. I'm glad you like Lawrence.

GINNY. What?

AMANDA. I'M GLAD YOU LIKE LAWRENCE.

GINNY. What?

AMANDA. WHY DON'T YOU MARRY LAWRENCE?

GINNY (*looks shocked; has heard this*). Oh.

LAWRENCE. Oh, mama.

GINNY. Oh dear, I see. So that's why Shakespeare asked me here.

AMANDA (*to Tom*). Shakespeare?

TOM. The first day of work she asked my name, and I said Tom Wingvalley, and she thought I said Shakespeare.

GINNY. Oh dear, Mrs. Wingvalley, if I had a young brother as nice and as special as Lawrence is, I'd invite girls from the warehouse home to meet him too.

AMANDA. I'm sure I don't know what you mean.

GINNY. And you're probably hoping I'll say that I'll call again.

AMANDA. Really, we haven't even had dinner yet. Tom, shouldn't you be checkin' on the roast pigs feet?

TOM. I guess so. If anything interesting happens, call me. (*Exits.*)

GINNY. But I'm afraid I won't be calling on Lawrence again.

LAWRENCE. This is so embarrassing. I told you I wanted to stay in my room.

AMANDA. Hush up, Lawrence.

GINNY. But, Lawrence, I don't want you to think that I won't be calling because I don't like you. I do like you.

LAWRENCE. You do?

GINNY. Sure. I like everybody. But I got two time clocks to punch, Mrs. Wingvalley. One at the warehouse, and one at night.

AMANDA. At night? You have a second job? That is ambitious.

GINNY. Not a second job, ma'am. Betty.

AMANDA. Pardon?

GINNY. Now who's deaf, eh what? Betty. I'm involved with a girl named Betty. We've been going together for about a year. We're saving money so that we can buy a farmhouse and a tractor together. So you (*to Lawrence*) can see why I can't visit your son, though I wish I could. No hard feelings, Lawrence. You're a good kid.

LAWRENCE (*offers her another swizzle stick*). I want you to keep this. It's my very favorite one. I call it Thermometer because it looks like a thermometer.

GINNY. You want me to have this?

LAWRENCE. Yes, as a souvenir.

GINNY (*offended*). Well, there's no need to call me a queer. Fuck you and your stupid swizzle sticks. (*Throws the offered gift upstage.*)

LAWRENCE (*very upset*). You've broken it!

GINNY. What?

LAWRENCE. You've broken it. YOU'VE BROKEN IT.

GINNY. So I've broken it. Big fuckin' deal. You have twenty more of them here.

AMANDA. Well, I'm so sorry you have to be going.

GINNY. What?

AMANDA. Hadn't you better be going?

GINNY. What?

AMANDA. Go away!

GINNY. Well I guess I can tell when I'm not wanted. I guess I'll go now.

AMANDA. You and Betty must come over some evening. Preferably when we're out.

GINNY. I wasn't shouting. (*Calls off.*) So long, Shakespeare. See you at the warehouse. (*To Lawrence.*) So long, Lawrence. I hope your rash gets better.

LAWRENCE (*saddened, holding the broken swizzle stick*). You broke Thermometer.

GINNY. What?

LAWRENCE. YOU BROKE THERMOMETER!

GINNY. Well, what was a thermometer doing in with the swizzle sticks anyway?

LAWRENCE. Its name was Thermometer, you nitwit!

AMANDA. Let it go, Lawrence. There'll be other swizzle sticks. Good-bye, Virginia.

GINNY. I sure am hungry. Any chance I might be able to take a sandwich with me?

AMANDA. Certainly you can shake hands with me, if that will make you happy.

GINNY. I said I'm hungry.

AMANDA. Really, dear? What part of Hungary are you from?

GINNY. Oh never mind. I guess I'll go.

AMANDA. That's right. You have two time clocks. It must be getting near to when you punch in Betty.

GINNY. Well, so long, everybody. I had a nice time. (*Exits.*)

AMANDA. Tom, come in here please. Lawrence, I don't believe I would play the victrola right now.

LAWRENCE. What victrola?

AMANDA. Any victrola.

(*Enter Tom.*)

TOM. Yes, mother? Where's Ginny?

AMANDA. The feminine caller made a hasty departure.

TOM. Old four eyes bored her to death, huh?

LAWRENCE. Oh, drop dead.

TOM. We should have you institutionalized.

AMANDA. That's the first helpful thing you've said all evening, but first things first. You played a little joke on us, Tom.

TOM. What are you talking about?

AMANDA. You didn't mention that your friend is already spoken for.

TOM. Really? I didn't even think she liked men.

AMANDA. Yes, well. It seems odd that you know so little about a person you see everyday at the warehouse.

TOM. The warehouse is where I work, not where I know things about people.

AMANDA. The disgrace. The expense of the pigs feet, a new tie for Lawrence. And you—bringing a lesbian into this house. We haven't had a lesbian in this house since your grandmother died, and now you have the audacity to bring in that . . . that . . .

LAWRENCE. Dyke.

AMANDA. Thank you, Lawrence. That overbearing, booming-voiced bull dyke. Into a Christian home.

TOM. Oh look, who cares? No one in their right mind would marry four eyes here.

AMANDA. You have no Christian charity, or filial devotion, or fraternal affection.

TOM. I don't want to listen to this. I'm going to the movies.

AMANDA. You go to the movies to excess, Tom. It isn't healthy.

LAWRENCE. While you're out, could you stop at the liquor store and get me some more cocktail stirrers? She broke Thermometer, and she put Q-tip in her ear.

AMANDA. Listen to your brother, Tom. He's pathetic. How are we going to support ourselves once you go? And I know you want to leave. I've seen the brochure for the merchant marines in your underwear drawer. And the application to the Air Force. And your letter of inquiry to the Ballet Trockadero. So I'm not unaware of what you're thinking. But don't leave us until you fulfill your duties here, Tom. Help brother find a wife, or a job, or a doctor. Or consider euthanasia. But don't leave me here all alone, saddled with him.

LAWRENCE. Mama, don't you like me?

AMANDA. Of course, dear. I'm just making jokes.

LAWRENCE. Be careful of my asthma.

AMANDA. I'll try, dear. Now why don't you hold your breath in case you get a case of terminal hiccups?

LAWRENCE. Alright. (*Holds his breath.*)

TOM. I'm leaving.

AMANDA. Where are you going?

TOM. I'm going to the movies.

AMANDA. I don't believe you go to the movies. What did you see last night?

TOM. Hyapatia Lee in "Beaver City."

AMANDA. And the night before that?

TOM. I don't remember. "Humpy Busboys" or something.

AMANDA. Humpy what?

TOM. Nothing. Leave me alone.

AMANDA. These are not mainstream movies, Tom. Why can't you see a normal movie like "The Philadelphia Story." Or "The Bitter Tea of General Yen"?

TOM. Those movies were made in the 1930s.

AMANDA. They're still good today.

TOM. I don't want to have this conversation. I'm going to the movies.

AMANDA. That's right, go to the movies! Don't think about us, a mother alone, an unmarried brother who thinks he's crippled and has no job. Stop holding your breath, Lawrence, mama was kidding. (*Back to Tom.*) Don't let anything interfere with your selfish pleasure. Go see your pornographic trash that's worse than anything Mr. D. H. Lawrence ever envisioned. Just go, go, go—to the movies!

TOM. Alright, I will! And the more you shout about my selfishness and my taste in movies the quicker I'll go, and I won't just go to the movies!

AMANDA. Go then! Go to the moon—you selfish dreamer!

(*Tom exits.*)

AMANDA (*continued*). Oh Lawrence, honey, what's to become of us?

LAWRENCE. Tom forgot his newspaper, mama.

AMANDA. He forgot a lot more than that, Lawrence honey. He forgot his mama and brother.

(*Amanda and Lawrence stay in place. Tom enters down right and stands apart from them in a spot. He speaks to the audience.*)

TOM. I didn't go to the moon, I went to the movies. In Amsterdam. A long, lonely trip working my way on a freighter. They had good movies in

Amsterdam. They weren't in English, but I didn't really care. And as for my mother and brother—well, I was adopted anyway. So I didn't miss them.

Or at least so I thought. For something pursued me. It always came upon me unawares, it always caught me by surprise. Sometimes it would be a swizzle stick in someone's vodka glass, or sometimes it would just be a jar of pigs feet. But then all of a sudden my brother touches my shoulder, and my mother puts her hands around my neck, and everywhere I look I am reminded of them. And in all the bars I go to there are those damn swizzle sticks everywhere. I find myself thinking of my brother Lawrence. And of his collection of glass. And of my mother. I begin to think that their story would maybe make a good novel, or even a play. A mother's hopes, a brother's dreams. Pathos, humor, even tragedy. But then I lose interest. I really haven't the energy. So I'll leave them both, dimly lit, in my memory. For nowadays the world is lit by lightning, and when we get those colored lights going, it feels like I'm on LSD. Or some other drug. Or maybe it's the trick of memory, and the fact that life is very, very sad. Play with your cocktail stirrers, Lawrence. And so, good-bye.

AMANDA (*calling over in Tom's direction*). Tom, I hear you out on the porch talking. Who are you talking to?

TOM. No one, mother. I'm just on my way to the movies.

AMANDA. Well, try not to be too late, you have to work early at the warehouse tomorrow. And please don't bring home any visitors from the movies, I'm not up to it after that awful girl. Besides, if some sailor misses his boat, that's no reason you have to put him up in your room. You're too big-hearted, son.

TOM. Yes, mother. See you later. (*Exits.*)

LAWRENCE. Look at the light through the glass, mama. (*Looks through a swizzle stick.*) Isn't it amazin'?

AMANDA. Yes, I guess it is, Lawrence. Oh, but both my children are weird. What have I done, O Lord, to deserve them?

LAWRENCE. Just lucky, mama.

AMANDA. Don't make jokes, Lawrence. Your asthma. Your eczema. My life.

LAWRENCE. Don't be sad, mama. We have each other for company and amusement.

AMANDA. That's right. It's always darkest before the dawn. Or right before a typhoon sweeps up and kills everybody.

LAWRENCE. Oh, poor mama, let me try to cheer you up with my collection. Is that a good idea?

AMANDA. It's just great, Lawrence. Thank you.

LAWRENCE. I call this one Daffodil, because its yellow, and daffodils are yellow.

AMANDA. Uh huh.

LAWRENCE (*holds up another one*). And I call this one Curtain Rod because it reminds me of a curtain rod.

AMANDA. Uh huh.

LAWRENCE. And I call this one Ocean, because it's blue, and the ocean is . . .

AMANDA. I THOUGHT YOU CALLED THE BLUE ONE BLUE, YOU IDIOT CHILD! DO I HAVE TO LISTEN TO THIS PATHETIC PRATTLING THE REST OF MY LIFE??? CAN'T YOU AT LEAST BE CONSISTENT???

LAWRENCE (*pause, hurt*). No, I guess I can't.

AMANDA. Well, try, can't you?

(*Silence.*)

I'm sorry, Lawrence. I'm a little short-tempered today.

LAWRENCE. That's alright.

(Silence.)

AMANDA *(trying to make up)*. Do you have any other swizzle sticks with names, Lawrence?

LAWRENCE. Yes, I do. (*Holds one up.*) I call this one "Mama." (*He throws it over his shoulder onto the floor.*)

AMANDA. Well, that's lovely, Lawrence, thank you.

LAWRENCE. I guess I can be a little short-tempered too.

AMANDA. Yes, well, whatever. I think we won't kill each other this evening, alright?

LAWRENCE. Alright.

AMANDA. I'll just distract myself from my rage and despair, and read about other people's rage and despair in the newspaper, shall I? (*Picks up Tom's newspaper.*) Your brother has the worst reading and viewing taste of any living creature. This is just a piece of filth. (*Reads.*) Man Has Sex With Chicken, Then Makes Casserole. (*Closes the paper.*) Disgusting. Oh, Lawrence honey, look—it's the Evening Star. (*She holds the paper out in front of them.*) Let's make a wish on it, honey, shall we?

LAWRENCE. Alright, mama.

(Amanda holds up the newspaper, and she and Lawrence close their eyes and make a wish.)

AMANDA. What did you wish for, darlin'?

LAWRENCE. More swizzle sticks.

AMANDA. You're so predictable, Lawrence. It's part of your charm, I guess.

LAWRENCE. What did you wish for, mama?

AMANDA. The same thing, honey. Maybe just a little happiness, too, but mostly just some more swizzle sticks.

(*Sad music. Amanda and Lawrence look up at the Evening Star. Fade to black.*)

Analyzing the Text

1. Satire is not necessarily mean-spirited. What exactly is Durang satirizing: Williams's play, or the mythic qualities of the South?
2. How does Durang use gender role reversals for comic effect?

Understanding Durang's Techniques

1. How are Durang's comic variations on Williams's characters and their predicament meant to satirize the assumptions underlying Williams's play? Take a look at his transpositions; why is each variation funny?
2. How does Durang parody the ways in which Williams's characters express themselves?

Arguing for an Interpretation

1. In your opinion, which playwright is more creative, Tennessee Williams or Christopher Durang? Explain your answer.

2. If Williams had had the opportunity to read or watch Durang's spoof of his play, what might he have said?

Connections

1. How do Sabine Reichel's essay and Jerzy Kosinski's work of fiction depict children coming to terms with prejudice and violence?
2. Compare Mark Salzman's account with Xu Gang's poem to discover a distinctive Chinese way of looking at achievement.
3. Why would Emily Dickinson recommend her approach to Leila, the main character, in Katherine Mansfield's story "Her First Ball"?
4. Compare the presence or absence of the foreshadowing of a surprise ending in the stories by Hanan al-Shaykh ("The Persian Carpet"), Tayeb Salih ("A Handful of Dates"), and Kate Chopin ("The Story of an Hour").
5. How do both Jerzy Kosinski and Natsume Soseki make use of the unobtrusive observers who stand apart from the events described in their stories?
6. What similar satiric techniques underlie Natsume Soseki's portrait of a Japanese professor of English and Christopher Durang's spoof of the Wingfield family in Tennessee Williams's play?
7. Compare how Linda Pastan and Robert Frost develop the theme of a hypothetical choice that becomes real.
8. Contrast the very different perspectives on the view of life as a journey in Robert Frost's and Octavio Paz's poems.
9. Discuss the effect of growing up in a dysfunctional family in Maurice Kenny's poem and in the plays by Tennessee Williams and Christopher Durang.
10. Compare the ways in which children serve as a metaphor for innocence in Emily Dickinson's poem, and in the stories by Jerzy Kosinski and James Joyce.
11. In what ways do both Robert Desnos in his poem and Joyce Carol Oates in her story use the concept of a moment of truth that can prove to be either threatening or liberating?
12. Compare the metaphors used to describe a long sought-for state of self-sufficiency in the poems by Sara Teasdale and Fadwa Tuqan.
13. In what sense can the antagonist Arnold Friend in Joyce Carol Oates's story be considered a nightmare version of the gentleman caller in Tennessee Williams's play?
14. How do both Miriam Baruch and William Blake start from the same natural image (the sunflower), and then proceed in opposite directions and draw very different conclusions?

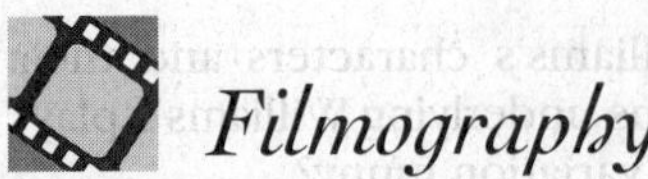

Filmography

The Wizard of Oz (1939) Director: Victor Fleming. Performers: Judy Garland, Ray Bolger, Burt Lahr, Margaret Hamilton.
In this classic, a dissatisfied young girl learns "there's no place like home" in her adventures over the rainbow.

The Graduate (1967) Director: Mike Nichols. Performers: Dustin Hoffman, Anne Bancroft, Katherine Ross.

A recent college graduate learns to maneuver the dangers of adulthood when he has an affair with the mother of the girl he loves.

Amarcord (1974) Director: Federico Fellini. Performers: Magali Noel.

A semi-autobiographical lush fantasy takes us into the director's childhood village in the 1930s. [Italy]

The Tin Drum (1979) Director: Volker Schlondorff. Performers: David Bennett, Mario Adorf.

In this magic realist film, the life of a young boy who refuses to grow up is seen as a metaphor for Nazi Germany. [Germany]

Diner (1982) Director: Barry Levinson. Performers: Steve Guttenberg, Kevin Bacon.

This film, set in 1959, is about a group of high school friends who meet at a Baltimore diner and philosophize about life's changes as they enter their twenties.

Diva (1982) Director: Jean-Jacques Beineix. Performers: Frederic Andrei.

At a concert, a young courier secretly tapes his operatic idol, who has never been recorded, and gets mixed up with the police and Japanese bootleggers who run a recording studio. [France]

Smooth Talk (1985) Director: Joyce Chopra. Performers: Laura Dern, Treat Williams.

Based On Joyce Carol Oates's story "Where Are You Going, Where Have You Been?" this movie dramatizes a disturbing encounter between a naive girl and a mysterious stranger.

Stand by Me (1986) Director: Rob Reiner. Performers: River Phoenix, Wil Wheaton.

Based on the Stephen King novella "The Body," this film tells the story of four 12-year-old boys who journey into the Oregon wilderness to discover the body of a missing boy, and learn much about themselves and the world.

The Glass Menagerie (1987) Director: Paul Newman. Performers: Joanne Woodward, John Malkovich.

Film adaptation of Tennesee Williams's story, written by the author, of an aging Southern belle, and her crippled daughter who covets her collection of glass animals.

Babette's Feast (1987) Director: Gabriel Axel. Performers: Stephane Audran.

A widowed French woman who prepares a lavish feast for her father's 100th birthday unnerves conservative villagers with unanticipated pleasure. [Denmark]

Cinema Paradiso (1988) Director: Giuseppe Tornatore. Performers: Philippe Noiret.

A captivating memoir of a young boy's experiences working in a movie theater in a small town in Italy just after World War II. [Italy]

Iron and Silk (1990) Director: Shirley Sun. Performers: Mark Salzman, Pan Qingfu.

In this semi-documentary based on his autobiography, we follow Salzman on his quest to learn martial arts from the Chinese master.

The Nasty Girl (1990) Director: Michael Verhoeven. Performers: Lena Stolze.

Based on Sabine Reichel's account, this film tells the story of a young German model, who, while doing research on the history of her hometown under the Third Reich, is harrassed but refuses to cease her quest for the truth.

Heavenly Creatures (1994) Director: Peter Jackson. Performers: Kate Winslet.

This haunting, surreal film is about two thirteen-year-old girls whose friendship ultimately leads them to commit a murder. [New Zealand]

Wild Reeds (1995) Director: Andre Techine. Performers: Gael Morel, Frederic Gormy.
A gay teenager in France experiences his first love—for a biracial boy—against the backdrop of the Algerian Revolution. [France]

Central Station (1998) Director: Walter Salles, Jr. Performers: Fernanda Montenegro, Vinicius de Oliveira.
A bitter elderly woman helps a young boy travel across country in search of his long-lost father after the boy's mother is killed by a hit-and-run driver. [Brazil]

Chapter 5

Gender

Women have served all these centuries as looking-glasses possessing the magic and delicious power of reflecting the figure of man at twice its natural size.

Virginia Woolf

Culture plays an enormous role in shaping expectations attached to sex roles. This process, sometimes called socialization, determines how each of us assimilates our culture's ideas of what it means to act as a male or female. We tend to acquire a sense of our own sexual identity in conjunction with societal expectations. Yet, these expectations differ strikingly from culture to culture. For example, in male-dominated Islamic Middle-Eastern societies, the sex roles and relationships between men and women are very different from those in modern industrial societies.

Gender stereotypes shape our perceptions in subtle and far-reaching ways. For example, sexist language not only reveals unconscious attitudes, but has the unfortunate effect of sanctioning these distorted perceptions. Powerful works of literature cause us to reconsider our assumptions about what we view as the natural assignment of gender roles and to consider whose interests are being served in terms of political power and economic opportunities.

The writers in this chapter address questions of how some societies give authority and value to the roles of men while treating women as if they were invisible. This attitude is most apparent in how a particular society greets the birth of a female infant. Gender is not only a question of difference but of power, and concepts of masculinity and femininity vary widely in societies and in historical periods.

This chapter presents many contemporary works by writers around the world that explore the complexities arising in relationships between the sexes. In "The Myth of the Latin Woman," Judith Ortiz Cofer describes how different cultural expectations in her native Puerto Rico and the United States cast her as a stereotyped "hot-blooded Latina." The attitude toward female sexuality in

Middle-Eastern culture is powerfully explored by an Egyptian physician and feminist, Nawal El Saadawi, in "The Mutilated Half."

"The Lady with the Pet Dog," by the nineteenth-century Russian writer Anton Chekhov, creates a wistful account of two lovers whose lives can never quite become the dream they imagined. In Kurt Vonnegut, Jr.'s "Who Am I This Time?" two innocents become their real selves while playing the leads in classic dramas and discover they love each other. From Mali, Sembene Ousmane's poignant story, "Her Three Days," depicts the plight of a third wife waiting for her husband's infrequent three-day visit. Margaret Atwood explores variations in the delicate balance of stability and surprise in fictionalized relationships between men and women in "Happy Endings."

James Joyce in "Eveline" tells the story of a girl who longs to escape her dreary Dublin existence and must decide whether to run away to Buenos Aires with her lover. Ernest Hemingway reveals an unsuspected depth of meaning in a deceptively simple story of a couple traveling in Spain who come to a crossroad in their relationship in "Hills Like White Elephants." Wishes do come true in Robert Fox's ultra-short, yet encompassing, "A Fable." Charlotte Perkins Gilman draws on personal experiences in "The Yellow Wallpaper" to describe how mental illness in women was misdiagnosed and mistreated in the late 1800s. A French-Canadian author, Monique Proulx, in "Feint of Heart," answers the question whether people can be too sophisticated for their own good. In "Jewellery," the Italian writer Alberto Moravia explores the themes of jealousy, love, and friendship gone wrong.

The perspectives of male and female poets provide interesting counterpoints from different eras on the themes of romantic love, nostalgia, rejection, chauvinism, and marriage. John Frederick Nims offers a witty update of Shakespeare's classic sonnet. Robert Browning and Elizabeth Barrett Browning offer complementary perspectives on love and marriage. Attraction and ambivalence toward commitment is explored by Gregory Corso and Jimmy Santiago Baca. The poems by Edna St. Vincent Millay, Muriel Rukeyser, and Grace Caroline Bridges project a wide spectrum of style and tone from the humorous and sarcastic to the serious and profound.

Susan Glaspell's *Trifles* and David Ives's *Sure Thing* offer a striking contrast of period, setting, and tone. Glaspell's play, written in 1916, takes us inside a murder investigation in Maine where the clues have different meanings for men and women. David Ives's contemporary comic work (1994) places us on the front lines of dating and courtship—with a most unusual twist.

Essays

Judith Ortiz Cofer

Judith Ortiz Cofer, a poet and novelist, was born in 1952 in Hormigueros, Puerto Rico. After her father, a career navy officer, retired, the family settled in Georgia where Cofer attended Augusta College. During college she married and, with her husband and daughter, moved to Florida where she finished a master's degree in English at Florida Atlantic University. A fellowship allowed her

to pursue graduate work at Oxford University, after which she returned to Florida and began teaching English and writing poetry. Her first volume of poetry, Peregrina *(1985), won the Riverstone International Poetry Competition and was followed by two more poetry collections,* Reaching for the Mainland *(1987) and* Terms of Survival *(1988). Her first novel,* The Line of the Sun *(1989), was listed as one of 1989's "twenty-five books to remember" by the New York City Public Library System. Her recent works include a collection of short stories,* An Island Like You: Stories of the Barrio *(1995),* The Year of Our Revolution *(1998), and* Woman in Front of the Sun: On Becoming a Writer *(2000). Cofer is a Professor of English and Creative Writing at the University of Georgia. In the following essay, drawn from her collection* The Latin Deli: Prose and Poetry *(1993), Cofer explores the destructive effects of the Latina stereotype.*

The Myth of the Latin Woman

I Just Met a Girl Named Maria

On a bus trip to London from Oxford University where I was earning some graduate credits one summer, a young man, obviously fresh from a pub, spotted me and as if struck by inspiration went down on his knees in the aisle. With both hands over his heart he broke into an Irish tenor's rendition of "Maria" from *West Side Story.* My politely amused fellow passengers gave his lovely voice the round of gentle applause it deserved. Though I was not quite as amused, I managed my version of an English smile: no show of teeth, no extreme contortions of the facial muscles—I was at this time of my life practicing reserve and cool. Oh, that British control, how I coveted it. But "Maria" had followed me to London, reminding me of a prime fact of my life: you can leave the island, master the English language, and travel as far as you can, but if you are a Latina, especially one like me who so obviously belongs to Rita Moreno's gene pool, the island travels with you.

This is sometimes a very good thing—it may win you that extra minute of someone's attention. But with some people, the same things can make *you* an island—not a tropical paradise but an Alcatraz, a place nobody wants to visit. As a Puerto Rican girl living in the United States and wanting like most children to "belong," I resented the stereotype that my Hispanic appearance called forth from many people I met.

Growing up in a large urban center in New Jersey during the 1960s, I suffered from what I think of as "cultural schizophrenia." Our life was designed by my parents as a microcosm of their *casas* on the island. We spoke in Spanish, ate Puerto Rican food bought at the *bodega,* and practiced strict Catholicism at a church that allotted us a one-hour slot each week for mass, performed in Spanish by a Chinese priest trained as a missionary for Latin America.

As a girl I was kept under strict surveillance by my parents, since my virtue and modesty were, by their cultural equation, the same as their honor. As a teenager I was lectured constantly on how to behave as a proper *senorita.* But it was a conflicting message I received, since the Puerto Rican mothers also encouraged their daughters to look and act like women and to dress in clothes our Anglo friends and their mothers found too "mature" and flashy. The difference was, and is, cultural; yet I often felt humiliated when I appeared at an American friend's party wearing a dress more suitable to a semi-formal than to a playroom birthday celebration. At Puerto Rican festivities, neither the music nor the colors we wore could be too loud.

5 I remember Career Day in our high school, when teachers told us to come dressed as if for a job interview. It quickly became obvious that to the Puerto Rican girls "dressing up" meant wearing their mothers' ornate jewelry and clothing, more appropriate (by mainstream standards) for the company Christmas party than as daily office attire. That morning I had agonized in front of my closet, trying to figure out what a "career girl" would wear. I knew how to dress for school (at the Catholic school I attended, we all wore uniforms), I knew how to dress for Sunday mass, and I knew what dresses to wear for parties at my relatives' homes. Though I do not recall the precise details of my Career Day outfit, it must have been a composite of these choices. But I remember a comment my friend (an Italian American) made in later years that coalesced my impressions of that day. She said that at the business school she was attending, the Puerto Rican girls always stood out for wearing "everything at once." She meant, of course, too much jewelry, too many accessories. On that day at school we were simply made the negative models by the nuns, who were themselves not credible fashion experts to any of us. But it was painfully obvious to me that to the others, in their tailored skirts and silk blouses, we must have seemed "hopeless" and "vulgar." Though I now know that most adolescents feel out of step much of the time, I also know that for the Puerto Rican girls of my generation that sense was intensified. The way our teachers and classmates looked at us that day in school was just a taste of the cultural clash that awaited us in the real world, where prospective employers and men on the street would often misinterpret our tight skirts and jingling bracelets as a "come-on."

Mixed cultural signals have perpetuated certain stereotypes—for example, that of the Hispanic woman as the "hot tamale" or sexual firebrand. It is a one-dimensional view that the media have found easy to promote. In their special vocabulary, advertisers have designated "sizzling" and "smoldering" as the adjectives of choice for describing not only the foods but also the women of Latin America. From conversations in my house I recall hearing about the harassment that Puerto Rican women endured in factories where the "boss-men" talked to them as if sexual innuendo was all they understood, and worse, often gave them the choice of submitting to their advances or being fired.

It is custom, however, not chromosomes, that leads us to choose scarlet over pale pink. As young girls, it was our mothers who influenced our decisions about clothes and colors—mothers who had grown up on a tropical island where the natural environment was a riot of primary colors, where showing your skin was one way to keep cool as well as to look sexy. Most important of all, on the island, women perhaps felt freer to dress and move more provocatively since, in most cases, they were protected by the traditions, mores, and laws of a Spanish/Catholic system of morality and machismo whose main rule was: *You may look at my sister, but if you touch her I will kill you.* The extended family and church structure could provide a young woman with a circle of safety in her small pueblo on the island; if a man "wronged" a girl, everyone would close in to save her family honor.

My mother has told me about dressing in her best party clothes on Saturday nights and going to the town's plaza to promenade with her girlfriends in front of the boys they liked. The males were thus given an opportunity to admire the women and to express their admiration in the form of *piropos:* erotically charged street poems they composed on the spot. (I have myself been subjected to a few *piropos* while visiting the island, and they can be outrageous, although custom dictates that they must never cross into obscenity.) This ritual, as I understand it, also entails a show of studied indifference on the woman's part; if she is "decent," she must not acknowledge the man's impassioned words. So I do understand how things can be lost in translation. When a Puerto Rican girl dressed in her idea of what is attractive meets a man from the mainstream culture who has been trained to react to certain types of clothing as a sexual signal, a clash is likely to take place. I remember the boy who took me to my first formal dance leaning over to plant a sloppy, over-eager kiss painfully on my mouth; when I didn't respond with sufficient passion, he remarked resentfully: "I thought you Latin girls were supposed to mature early," as if I were expected to *ripen* like a fruit or vegetable, not just grow into womanhood like other girls.

It is surprising to my professional friends that even today some people, including those who should know better, still put others "in their place." It happened to me most recently during a stay at a classy metropolitan hotel favored by young professional couples for weddings. Late one evening after the theater, as I walked toward my room with a colleague (a woman with whom I was coordinating an arts program), a middle-aged man in a tuxedo, with a young girl in satin and lace on his arm, stepped directly into our path. With his champagne glass extended toward me, he exclaimed "Evita!"[1]

10 Our way blocked, my companion and I listened as the man half-recited, half-bellowed "Don't Cry for Me, Argentina." When he finished, the young girl said: "How about a round of applause for my daddy?" We complied, hoping this would bring the silly spectacle to a close. I was becoming aware that our little group was attracting the attention of the other guests. "Daddy" must have perceived this too, and he once more barred the way as we tried to walk past him. He began to shout-sing a ditty to the tune of "La Bamba"—except the lyrics were about a girl named Maria whose exploits rhymed with her name and gonorrhea. The girl kept saying "Oh, Daddy" and looking at me with pleading eyes. She wanted me to laugh along with the others. My companion and I stood silently waiting for the man to end his offensive song. When he finished, I looked not at him but at his daughter. I advised her calmly never to ask her father what he had done in the army. Then I walked between them and to my room. My friend complimented me on my cool handling of the situation, but I confessed that I had really wanted to push the jerk into the swimming pool.

---

[1]A musical about Eva Duarte de Peron, the former first lady of Argentina.

This same man—probably a corporate executive, well-educated, even worldly by most standards—would not have been likely to regale an Anglo woman with a dirty song in public. He might have checked his impulse by assuming that she could be somebody's wife or mother, or at least *somebody* who might take offense. But, to him, I was just an Evita or a Maria: merely a character in his cartoon-populated universe.

Another facet of the myth of the Latin woman in the United States is the menial, the domestic—Maria the housemaid or countergirl. It's true that work as domestics, as waitresses, and in factories is all that's available to women with little English and few skills. But the myth of the Hispanic menial—the funny maid, mispronouncing words and cooking up a spicy storm in a shiny California kitchen—has been perpetuated by the media in the same way that "Mammy" from *Gone with the Wind* became America's idea of the black woman for generations. Since I do not wear my diplomas around my neck for all to see, I have on occasion been sent to that "kitchen" where some think I obviously belong.

One incident has stayed with me, though I recognize it as a minor offense. My first public poetry reading took place in Miami, at a restaurant where a luncheon was being held before the event. I was nervous and excited as I walked in with notebook in hand. An older woman motioned me to her table, and thinking (foolish me) that she wanted me to autograph a copy of my newly published slender volume of verse, I went over. She ordered a cup of coffee from me, assuming that I was the waitress. (Easy enough to mistake my poems for menus, I suppose.) I know it wasn't an intentional act of cruelty. Yet of all the good things that happened later, I remember that scene most clearly, because it reminded me of what I had to overcome before anyone would take me seriously. In retrospect I understand that my anger gave my reading fire. In fact, I have almost always taken any doubt in my abilities as a challenge, the result most often being the satisfaction of winning a convert, of seeing the cold, appraising eyes warm to my words, the body language change, the smile that indicates I have opened some avenue for communication. So that day as I read, I looked directly at that woman. Her lowered eyes told me she was embarrassed at her faux pas, and when I willed her to look up at me, she graciously allowed me to punish her with my full attention. We shook hands at the end of the reading and I never saw her again. She has probably forgotten the entire incident, but maybe not.

Yet I am one of the lucky ones. There are thousands of Latinas without the privilege of an education or the entrees into society that I have. For them life is a constant struggle against the misconceptions perpetuated by the myth of the Latina. My goal is to try to replace the old stereotypes with a much more interesting set of realities. Every time I give a reading, I hope the stories I tell, the dreams and fears I examine in my work, can achieve some universal truth that will get my audience past the particulars of my skin color, my accent, or my clothes.

I once wrote a poem in which I called all Latinas "God's brown daughters." This poem is really a prayer of sorts, offered upward, but also, through the human-to-human channel of art, outward. It is a prayer for communication and for respect. In it, Latin women pray "in Spanish to an Anglo God/ with a Jewish heritage," and they are "fervently hoping/ that if not omnipotent,/ at least He be bilingual."

Analyzing the Text

1. What characteristics define, from Cofer's perspective, the "Maria" stereotype in terms of style, clothes, and behavior? How has this stereotype been a source of harassment for Cofer?
2. In what sense is Cofer's desire to succeed as a writer a reaction to the repeated instances in which she was misperceived because of her ethnicity?

Understanding Cofer's Techniques

1. How do the instances of ethnic stereotyping described by Cofer illustrate her thesis and enable her readers to better understand what she condemns?
2. What aspects of Cofer's essay enable the reader to understand why behavior that is considered normal in one culture is considered sexually provocative in another?

Arguing for an Interpretation

1. To what extent does the skill with which Cofer uses language and her self-deprecating wit disprove the "myth of the Latin woman"? Explain your answer.
2. Does Cofer appear to be overly defensive in her reactions and transform herself into a victim for the purpose of this essay? Why or why not?

NAWAL EL SAADAWI

Nawal El Saadawi is an Egyptian physician and internationally acclaimed writer whose work publicizing the injustices and brutalities to which Arab women are subject is well known throughout the world. Born in the village of Kafrtahla on the banks of the Nile in 1931, she completed her secondary and college education in Egypt and later studied at Columbia University in New York. She has worked as a physician and psychiatrist in both Cairo and rural areas of Egypt. She lost her position as Egypt's director of education in the Ministry of Health because of the outspoken views expressed in her first nonfiction book, Women and Sex *(1972). In it, she openly challenged the restrictions placed on women in Arab society. She was later imprisoned by Anwar Sadat, and her many books, including seven novels, four collections of short stories, and five works of nonfiction, are still banned in Egypt, Saudi Arabia, and Libya. Since her release from prison in 1982, she has continued to write and is an activist for women's rights in the Arab world. "The Mutilated Half" is drawn from* The Hidden Face of Eve: Women in the Arab World, *translated and edited by El Saadawi's husband, Dr. Sherif Hetata, in 1980. In this work, El Saadawi investigates the cultural origins of the widely practiced but rarely discussed procedure of female circumcision, an operation she herself endured at the age of six. Most recently she has written* Walking Through Fire: A Life of Nawal El Saadawi *(2002), translated by Hetata.*

The Mutilated Half

The practice of circumcising girls is still a common procedure in a number of Arab countries such as Egypt, the Sudan, Yemen and some of the Gulf states.

The importance given to virginity and an intact hymen in these societies is the reason why female circumcision still remains a very widespread practice despite a growing tendency, especially in urban Egypt, to do away with it as something outdated and harmful. Behind circumcision lies the belief that, by removing parts of girls' external genital organs, sexual desire is minimized. This permits a female who has reached the "dangerous age" of puberty and adolescence to protect her virginity, and therefore her honour, with greater ease. Chastity was imposed on male attendants in the female harem by castration which turned them into inoffensive eunuchs. Similarly female circumcision is meant to preserve the chastity of young girls by reducing their desire for sexual intercourse.

Circumcision is most often performed on female children at the age of seven or eight (before the girl begins to get menstrual periods). On the scene appears the *daya* or local midwife. Two women members of the family grasp the child's thighs on either side and pull them apart to expose the external genital organs and to prevent her from struggling—like trussing a chicken before it is slain. A sharp razor in the hand of the *daya* cuts off the clitoris.

During my period of service as a rural physician, I was called upon many times to treat complications arising from this primitive operation, which very often jeopardized the life of young girls. The ignorant *daya* believed that effective circumcision necessitated a deep cut with the razor to ensure radical amputation of the clitoris, so that no part of the sexually sensitive organ would remain. Severe haemorrhage was therefore a common occurrence and sometimes led to loss of life. The *dayas* had not the slightest notion of asepsis, and inflammatory conditions as a result of the operation were common. Above all, the lifelong psychological shock of this cruel procedure left its imprint on the personality of the child and accompanied her into adolescence, youth and maturity. Sexual frigidity is one of the after-effects which is accentuated by other social and psychological factors that influence the personality and mental make-up of females in Arab societies. Girls are therefore exposed to a whole series of misfortunes as a result of outdated notions and values related to virginity, which still remains the fundamental criterion of a girl's honour. In recent years, however, educated families have begun to realize the harm that is done by the practice of female circumcision.

5 Nevertheless a majority of families still impose on young female children the barbaric and cruel operation of circumcision. The research that I carried out on a sample of 160 Egyptian girls and women showed that 97.5% of uneducated families still insisted on maintaining the custom, but this percentage dropped to 66.2% among educated families.[1]

When I discussed the matter with these girls and women it transpired that most of them had no idea of the harm done by circumcision, and some of them even thought that it was good for one's health and conducive to cleanliness and "purity." (The operation in the common language of the people is in fact called the cleansing or purifying operation.) Despite the fact that the percentage of educated women who have under-

[1]This research study was carried out in the years 1973 and 1974 in the School of Medicine, Ein Shams University, under the title: *Women and Neurosis.*

gone circumcision is only 66.2%, as compared with 97.5% among uneducated women, even the former did not realize the effect that this amputation of the clitoris could have on their psychological and sexual health. The dialogue that occurred between these women and myself would run more or less as follows:

"Have you undergone circumcision?"

"Yes."

"How old were you at the time?"

"I was a child, about seven or eight years old." 10

"Do you remember the details of the operation?"

"Of course. How could I possibly forget?"

"Were you afraid?"

"Very afraid. I hid on top of the cupboard [in other cases she would say under the bed, or in the neighbour's house], but they caught hold of me, and I felt my body tremble in their hands."

"Did you feel any pain?" 15

"Very much so. It was like a burning flame and I screamed. My mother held my head so that I could not move it, my aunt caught hold of my right arm and my grandmother took charge of my left. Two strange women whom I had not seen before tried to keep me from moving my thighs by pushing them as far apart as possible. The *daya* sat between these two women, holding a sharp razor in her hand which she used to cut off the clitoris. I was scared and suffered such great pain that I lost consciousness at the flame that seemed to sear me through and through."

"What happened after the operation?"

"I had severe bodily pains, and remained in bed for several days, unable to move. The pain in my external genital organs led to retention of urine. Every time I wanted to urinate the burning sensation was so unbearable that I could not bring myself to pass water. The wound continued to bleed for some time, and my mother used to change the dressing for me twice a day."

"What did you feel on discovering that a small organ in your body had been removed?"

"I did not know anything about the operation at the time, except that 20
it was very simple, and that it was done to all girls for purposes of cleanliness, purity and the preservation of a good reputation. It was said that a girl who did not undergo this operation was liable to be talked about by people, her behaviour would become bad, and she would start running after men, with the result that no one would agree to marry her when the time for marriage came. My grandmother told me that the operation had only consisted in the removal of a very small piece of flesh from between my thighs, and that the continued existence of this small piece of flesh in its place would have made me unclean and impure, and would have caused the man whom I would marry to be repelled by me."

"Did you believe what was said to you?"

"Of course I did. I was happy the day I recovered from the effects of the operation, and felt as though I was rid of something which had to be removed, and so had become clean and pure."

Those were more or less the answers that I obtained from all those interviewed, whether educated or uneducated. One of them was a medical student from Ein Shams School of Medicine. She was preparing for her final examinations and I expected her answers to be different, but in fact they were almost identical to the others. We had quite a long discussion which I reproduce here as I remember it.

"You are going to be a medical doctor after a few weeks, so how can you believe that cutting off the clitoris from the body of a girl is a healthy procedure, or at least not harmful?"

"This is what I was told by everybody. All the girls in my family have been circumcised. I have studied anatomy and medicine, yet I have never heard any of the professors who taught us explain that the clitoris had any function to fulfil in the body of a woman, neither have I read anything of the kind in the books which deal with the medical subjects I am studying."

"That is true. To this day medical books do not consider the science of sex as a subject which they should deal with. The organs of a woman worthy of attention are considered to be only those directly related to reproduction, namely the vagina, the uterus and the ovaries. The clitoris, however, is an organ neglected by medicine, just as it is ignored and disdained by society."

"I remember a student asking the professor one day about the clitoris. The professor went red in the face and answered him curtly, saying that no one was going to ask him about this part of the female body during examinations, since it was of no importance."

My studies led me to try and find out the effect of circumcision on the girls and women who had been made to undergo it, and to understand what results it had on the psychological and sexual life. The majority of the normal cases I interviewed answered that the operation had no effect on them. To me it was clear that in the face of such questions they were much more ashamed and intimidated than the neurotic cases were. But I did not allow myself to be satisfied with these answers, and would go on to question them closely about their sexual life both before and after the circumcision was done. Once again I will try to reproduce the dialogue that usually occurred.

"Did you experience any change of feeling or of sexual desire after the operation?"

"I was a child and therefore did not feel anything."

"Did you not experience any sexual desire when you were a child?"

"No, never. Do children experience sexual desire?"

"Children feel pleasure when they touch their sexual organs, and some form of sexual play occurs between them, for example, during the game of bride and bridegroom usually practised under the bed. Have you never played this game with your friends when still a child?"

At these words the young girl or woman would blush, and her eyes would probably refuse to meet mine, in an attempt to hide her confusion. But after the conversation had gone on for some time, and an atmosphere of mutual confidence and understanding had been established, she would begin to recount her childhood memories. She would often refer to the pleasure she had felt when a man of the family permitted himself certain sexual caresses. Sometimes these caresses would be proffered by the domestic servant, the house porter, the private teacher or the neighbour's son. A college student told me that her brother had been wont to caress her sexual organs and that she used to experience acute enjoyment. However after undergoing circumcision she no longer had the same sensation of pleasure. A married woman admitted that during intercourse with her husband she had never experienced the slightest sexual enjoyment, and that her last memories of any form of pleasurable sensation went back twenty years, to the age of six, before she had undergone circumcision. A young girl told me that she had been accustomed to practise masturbation, but had given it up completely after removal of the clitoris at the age of ten.

The further our conversations went, and the more I delved into their 35
lives, the more readily they opened themselves up to me and uncovered the secrets of childhood and adolescence, perhaps almost forgotten by them or only vaguely realized.

Being both a woman and a medical doctor I was able to obtain confessions from these women and girls which it would be almost impossible, except in very rare cases, for a man to obtain. For the Egyptian woman, accustomed as she is to a very rigid and severe upbringing built on a complete denial of any sexual life before marriage, adamantly refuses to admit that she has ever known, or experienced, anything related to sex before the first touches of her husband. She is therefore ashamed to speak about such things with any man, even the doctor who is treating her.

My discussions with some of the psychiatrists who had treated a number of the young girls and women in my sample, led me to conclude that there were many aspects of the life of these neurotic patients that remained unknown to them.This was due either to the fact that the psychiatrist himself had not made the necessary effort to penetrate deeply into the life of the woman he was treating, or to the tendency of the patient herself not to divulge those things which her upbringing made her consider matters not to be discussed freely, especially with a man.

In fact the long and varied interchanges I had over the years with the majority of practising psychiatrists in Egypt, my close association with a large number of my medical colleagues during the long periods I spent working in health centres and general or specialized hospitals and, finally, the four years I spent as a member of the National Board of the Syndicate of Medical Professions, have all led me to the firm conclusion that the medical profession in our society is still incapable of understanding the fundamental problems with which sick people are burdened, whether they be men or women, but especially if they are women. For the medical profession, like any other profession in society, is governed by the political, social and moral values which predominate, and like other professions is one of the institutions which is utilized more often than not to protect these values and perpetuate them.

Men represent the vast majority in the medical profession, as in most professions. But apart from this, the mentality of women doctors differs little, if at all, from that of the men, and I have known quite a number of them who were even more rigid and backward in outlook than their male colleagues.

A rigid and backward attitude towards most problems, and in particu- 40
lar towards women and sex, predominates in the medical profession, and particularly within the precincts of the medical colleges in the Universities.

Before undertaking my research study on "Women and Neurosis" at Ein Shams University, I had made a previous attempt to start it at the Kasr El Eini Medical College in the University of Cairo, but had been obliged to give up as a result of the numerous problems I was made to confront. The most important obstacle of all was the overpowering traditionalist mentality that characterized the professors responsible for my research work, and to whom the word "sex" could only be equated to the word "shame." "Respectable research" therefore could not possibly have sex as its subject, and should under no circumstances think of penetrating into areas even remotely related to it. One of my medical colleagues in the Research Committee advised me not to refer at all to the question of sex in the title of my research paper, when I found myself obliged to shift to Ein Shams University. He warned me that any such reference would most probably lead to fundamental objections which would jeopardize my chances of going ahead with it. I had initially chosen to define my subject as "Problems that confront the sexual life of modern Egyptian women," but after prolonged negotiations I was prevailed to delete the word "sexual" and replace it by "psychological." Only thus was it possible to circumvent the sensitivities of the professors at the Ein Shams Medical School and obtain their consent to go ahead with the research.

After I observed the very high percentages of women and girls who had been obliged to undergo circumcision, or who had been exposed to different forms of sexual violation or assault in their childhood, I started to look for research undertaken in these two areas, either in the medical colleges or in research institutes, but in vain. Hardly a single medical doctor or researcher had ventured to do any work on these subjects, in view of the sensitive nature of the issues involved. This can also be explained by the fact that most of the research carried out in such institutions is of a formal and superficial nature, since its sole aim is to obtain a degree or promotion. The path of safety is therefore the one to choose, and safety means to avoid carefully all subjects of controversy. No one is therefore prepared to face difficulties with the responsible academic and scientific authorities, or to engage in any form of struggle against them, or their ideas. Nor is anyone prepared to face up to those who lay down the norms of virtue, morals and religious behaviour in society. All the established leaderships in the area related to such matters suffer from a pronounced allergy to the word "sex," and any of its implications, especially if it happens to be linked to the word "woman."

Nevertheless I was fortunate enough to discover a small number of medical doctors who had the courage to be different, and therefore to examine some of the problems related to the sexual life of women. I would like to cite, as one of the rare examples, the only research study carried out on the question of female circumcision in Egypt and its harmful effects. This was the joint effort of Dr. Mahmoud Koraim and Dr. Rushdi Ammar, both from Ein Shams Medical College, and which was published in 1965. It is composed of two parts, the first of which was printed under the title *Female Circumcision and Sexual Desire,*[2] and the second, under the title *Complications of Female Circumcision.*[3] The conclusions arrived at as a result of this research study, which covered 651 women circumcised during childhood, may be summarized as follows:

(1) Circumcision is an operation with harmful effects on the health of women, and is the cause of sexual shock to young girls. It reduces the capacity of a woman to reach the peak of her sexual pleasure (i.e., orgasm) and has a definite though lesser effect in reducing sexual desire.

(2) Education helps to limit the extent to which female circumcision is practised, since educated parents have an increasing tendency to refuse the

[2]*Female Circumcision and Sexual Desire,* Mahmoud Koraim and Rushdi Ammar (Ein Shams University Press, Cairo, 1965).

[3]*Complications of Female Circumcision,* the same authors (Cairo, 1965).

operation for their daughters. On the other hand, uneducated families still go in for female circumcision in submission to prevailing traditions, or in the belief that removal of the clitoris reduces the sexual desire of the girl, and therefore helps to preserve her virginity and chastity after marriage.

(3) There is no truth whatsoever in the idea that female circumcision helps in reducing the incidence of cancerous disease of the external genital organs.

(4) Female circumcision in all its forms and degrees, and in particular the fourth degree known as Pharaonic or Sudanese excision, is accompanied by immediate or delayed complications such as inflammations, haemorrhage, disturbances in the urinary passages, cysts or swellings that can obstruct the urinary flow or the vaginal opening.

(5) Masturbation in circumcised girls is less frequent than was observed by Kinsey in girls who have not undergone this operation.

I was able to exchange views with Dr. Mahmoud Koraim during several meetings in Cairo. I learnt from him that he had faced numerous difficulties while undertaking his research, and was the target of bitter criticism from some of his colleagues and from religious leaders who considered themselves the divinely appointed protectors of morality, and therefore required to shield society from such impious undertakings, which constituted a threat to established values and moral codes.

The findings of my research study coincided with some of the conclusions arrived at by my two colleagues on a number of points. There is no longer any doubt that circumcision is the source of sexual and psychological shock in the life of the girl, and leads to a varying degree of sexual frigidity according to the woman and her circumstances. Education helps parents realize that this operation is not beneficial, and should be avoided, but I have found that the traditional education given in our schools and universities, whose aim is simply some certificate, or degree, rather than instilling useful knowledge and culture, is not very effective in combating the long-standing, and established traditions that govern Egyptian society, and in particular those related to sex, virginity in girls, and chastity in women. These areas are strongly linked to moral and religious values that have dominated and operated in our society for hundreds of years.

Since circumcision of females aims primarily at ensuring virginity before marriage, and chastity throughout, it is not to be expected that its practice will disappear easily from Egyptian society or within a short period of time. A growing number of educated families are, however, beginning to realize the harm that is done to females by this custom, and are therefore seeking to protect their daughters from being among its victims. Parallel to these changes, the operation itself is no longer performed in the old primitive way, and the more radical degrees approaching, or involving, excision are dying out more rapidly. Nowadays, even in Upper Egypt and the Sudan, the operation is limited to the total, or more commonly the partial, amputation of the clitoris. Nevertheless, while undertaking my research, I was surprised to discover, contrary to what I had previously thought, that even in educated urban families over 50% still consider circumcision as essential to ensure female virginity and chastity.

Many people think that female circumcision only started with the advent of Islam. But as a matter of fact it was well known and widespread in some areas of the world before the Islamic era, including in the Arab peninsula. Mahomet the Prophet tried to oppose this custom since he considered it harmful to the sexual health of the woman. In one of his sayings the advice reported as having been given by him to Om Attiah, a woman who did tattooings and circumcision, runs as follows: "If you circumcise, take only a small part and refrain from cutting most of the clitoris off . . . The woman will have a bright and happy face, and is more welcome to her husband, if her pleasure is complete."[4]

This means that the circumcision of girls was not originally an Islamic custom, and was not related to monotheistic religions, but was practised in societies with widely varying religious backgrounds, in countries of the East and the West, and among peoples who believed in Christianity, or in Islam, or were atheistic . . . Circumcision was known in Europe as late as the 19th century, as well as in countries like Egypt, the Sudan, Somaliland, Ethiopia, Kenya, Tanzania, Ghana, Guinea and Nigeria. It was also practised in many Asian countries such as Sri Lanka and Indonesia, and in parts of Latin America. It is recorded as going back far into the past under the Pharaonic Kingdoms of Ancient Egypt, and Herodotus mentioned the existence of female circumcision seven hundred years before Christ was born. This is why the operation as practised in the Sudan is called "Pharaonic excision."

For many years I tried in vain to find relevant sociological or anthropological studies that would throw some light on the reasons why such a brutal operation is practised on females. However I did discover other practices related to girls and female children which were even more savage. One of them was burying female children alive almost immediately after they were born, or even at a later stage. Other examples are the chastity belt, or closing the aperture of the external genital organs with steel pins and a special iron lock.[5] This last procedure is extremely primitive and very much akin to Sudanese circumcision where the clitoris, external lips and internal lips are completely excised, and the orifice of the genital organs closed with a flap of sheep's intestines leaving only a very small opening barely sufficient to let the tip of the finger in, so that the menstrual and urinary flows are not held back. This opening is slit at the time of marriage and widened to allow penetration of the male sexual organ. It is widened again when a child is born and then narrowed down once more. Complete closure of the aperture is also done on a woman who is divorced, so that she literally becomes a virgin once more and can have no sexual intercourse except in the eventuality of marriage, in which case the opening is restored.

55 In the face of all these strange and complicated procedures aimed at preventing sexual intercourse in women except if controlled by the husband, it is natural that we should ask ourselves why women, in particular, were subjected to such torture and cruel suppression. There seems to be no doubt that society, as represented by its dominant classes and male structure, realized at a very early stage that sexual desire in the female is very powerful, and that women, unless controlled and subjugated by all sorts of measures, will not submit themselves to the moral, social, legal and religious constraints with which they have been surrounded, and in particular the constraints related to monogamy. The patriarchal system, which came into being when society had reached a certain stage of development and which necessitated the imposition of one husband on the woman

---

[4]See *Dawlat El Nissa'a,* Abdel Rahman El Barkouky, first edition (Renaissance Bookshop, Cairo, 1945).

[5]Desmond Morris, *The Naked Ape* (Corgi, 1967), p. 76.

whereas a man was left free to have several wives, would never have been possible, or have been maintained to this day, without the whole range of cruel and ingenious devices that were used to keep her sexuality in check and limit her sexual relations to only one man, who had to be her husband. This is the reason for the implacable enmity shown by society towards female sexuality, and the weapons used to resist and subjugate the turbulent force inherent in it. The slightest leniency manifested in facing this "potential danger" meant that woman would break out of the prison bars to which marriage had confined her, and step over the steely limits of a monogamous relationship to a forbidden intimacy with another man, which would inevitably lead to confusion in succession and inheritance, since there was no guarantee that a strange man's child would not step into the waiting line of descendants. Confusion between the children of the legitimate husband and the outsider lover would mean the unavoidable collapse of the patriarchal family built around the name of the father alone.

History shows us clearly that the father was keen on knowing who his real children were, solely for the purpose of handing down his landed property to them. The patriarchal family, therefore, came into existence mainly for economic reasons. It was necessary for society simultaneously to build up a system of moral and religious values, as well as a legal system capable of protecting and maintaining these economic interests. In the final analysis we can safely say that female circumcision, the chastity belt and other savage practices applied to women are basically the result of the economic interests that govern society. The continued existence of such practices in our society today signifies that these economic interests are still operative. The thousands of *dayas,* nurses, paramedical staff and doctors, who make money out of female circumcision, naturally resist any change in these values and practices which are a source of gain to them. In the Sudan there is a veritable army of *dayas* who earn a livelihood out of the series of operations performed on women, either to excise their external genital organs, or to alternately narrow and widen the outer aperture according to whether the woman is marrying, divorcing, remarrying, having a child or recovering from labour.[6]

Economic factors and, concomitantly, political factors are the basis upon which such customs as female circumcision have grown up. It is important to understand the facts as they really are, the reasons that lie behind them. Many are the people who are not able to distinguish between political and religious factors, or who conceal economic and political motives behind religious arguments in an attempt to hide the real forces that lie at the basis of what happens in society and in history. It has very often been proclaimed that Islam is at the root of female circumcision, and is also responsible for the under-privileged and backward situation of women in Egypt and the Arab countries. Such a contention is not true. If we study Christianity it is easy to see that this religion is much more rigid and orthodox where women are concerned than Islam. Nevertheless, many countries were able to progress rapidly despite the preponderance of Christianity as a religion. This progress was social, economic, scientific and also affected the life and position of women in society.

[6]Rose Oldfield, "Female genital mutilation, fertility control, women's roles, and patrilineage in modern Sudan," *American Ethnologist,* Vol. II, No. 4, November 1975.

That is why I firmly believe that the reasons for the lower status of women in our societies, and the lack of opportunities for progress afforded to them, are not due to Islam, but rather to certain economic and political forces, namely those of foreign imperialism operating mainly from the outside, and of the reactionary classes operating from the inside. These two forces cooperate closely and are making a concerted attempt to misinterpret religion and to utilize it as an instrument of fear, oppression and exploitation.

Religion, if authentic in the principles it stands for, aims at truth, equality, justice, love and a healthy wholesome life for all people, whether men or women. There can be no true religion that aims at disease, mutilation of the bodies of female children, and amputation of an essential part of their reproductive organs.

If religion comes from God, how can it order man to cut off an organ 60
created by Him as long as that organ is not diseased or deformed? God does not create the organs of the body haphazardly without a plan. It is not possible that He should have created the clitoris in woman's body only in order that it be cut off at an early stage in life. This is a contradiction into which neither true religion nor the Creator could possibly fall. If God has created the clitoris as a sexually sensitive organ, whose sole function seems to be the procurement of sexual pleasure for women, it follows that He also considers such pleasure for women as normal and legitimate, and therefore as an integral part of mental health. The psychic and mental health of women cannot be complete if they do not experience sexual pleasure.

There are still a large number of fathers and mothers who are afraid of leaving the clitoris intact in the bodies of their daughters. Many a time they have said to me that circumcision is a safeguard against the mistakes and deviations into which a girl may be led. This way of thinking is wrong and even dangerous because what protects a boy or a girl from making mistakes is not the removal of a small piece of flesh from the body, but consciousness and understanding of the problems we face, and a worthwhile aim in life, an aim which gives it meaning and for whose attainment we exert our mind and energies. The higher the level of consciousness to which we attain, the closer our aims draw to human motives and values, and the greater our desire to improve life and its quality, rather than to indulge ourselves in the mere satisfaction of our senses and the experience of pleasure, even though these are an essential part of existence. The most liberated and free of girls, in the true sense of liberation, are the least preoccupied with sexual questions, since these no longer represent a problem. On the contrary, a free mind finds room for numerous interests and the many rich experiences of a cultured life. Girls that suffer sexual suppression, however, are greatly preoccupied with men and sex. And it is a common observation that an intelligent and cultured woman is much less engrossed in matters related to sex and to men than is the case with ordinary women, who have not got much with which to fill their lives. Yet at the same time such a woman takes much more initiative to ensure that she will enjoy sex and experience pleasure, and acts with a greater degree of boldness than others. Once sexual satisfaction is attained, she is able to turn herself fully to other important aspects of life.

In the life of liberated and intelligent women, sex does not occupy a disproportionate position, but rather tends to maintain itself within normal limits. In contrast, ignorance, suppression, fear and all sorts of limitations exaggerate the role of sex in the life of girls and women, and cause it to swell out of all proportion and to end up by occupying the whole, or almost the whole, of their lives.

Analyzing the Text

1. In what way did female circumcision change the author's relationship to her parents, husband, and colleagues and help explain her desire as a physician to investigate the reasons for its continued existence?
2. Why does a key element in El Saadawi's argument depend on showing that social and cultural forces rather than the dictates of Islam are responsible for the continuance of female circumcision? What are these social and cultural forces?

Understanding El Saadawi's Techniques

1. To what extent does El Saadawi strengthen her argument by citing case histories, conducting interviews, and adopting a straighforward objective tone?
2. How does El Saadawi's use of her personal experiences help support her argument?

Arguing for an Interpretation

1. In your opinion, does El Saadawi make a credible case in arguing that female circumcision is an outdated custom? Why or why not? How could she have made her argument stronger?
2. El Saadawi is clearly at odds with other female physicians who accept the practice as necessary. Does she present their side fairly enough in your opinion? Why or why not?

Short Fiction

ANTON CHEKHOV

Anton Chekhov (1860–1904) was born in a small town in Russia where his father was a proprietor of a grocery store. He entered Moscow University to study medicine, and during his studies also assumed the burden of supporting his family (by writing humorous sketches and stories for periodicals). After graduating in 1884, his health became impaired by tuberculosis and although he took up the practice of medicine, his true vocation was that of writing. In the next seven years, he wrote as many as 600 stories, which have had a profound influence on modern fiction. As a dramatist, he is best known for The Seagull *(1896),* Uncle Vanya *(1899),* The Three Sisters *(1901), and* The Cherry Orchard *(1904). In "The Lady with the Pet Dog" (1899), translated by Avrahm*

Yarmolinsky in 1947, we can see Chekhov's keen observation of human nature and the silent loneliness that afflicts his characters, who find it difficult to transform their lives in order to pursue their dreams.

The Lady with the Pet Dog

I

A new person, it was said, had appeared on the esplanade: a lady with a pet dog. Dmitry Dmitrich Gurov, who had spent a fortnight at Yalta and had got used to the place, had also begun to take an interest in new arrivals. As he sat in Vernet's confectionery shop, he saw, walking on the esplanade, a fair-haired young woman of medium height, wearing a beret; a white Pomeranian was trotting behind her.

And afterwards he met her in the public garden and in the square several times a day. She walked alone, always wearing the same beret and always with the white dog, no one knew who she was and everyone called her simply "the lady with the pet dog."

"If she is here alone without husband or friends," Gurov reflected, "it wouldn't be a bad thing to make her acquaintance."

He was under forty, but he already had a daughter twelve years old, and two sons at school. They had found a wife for him when he was very young, a student in his second year, and by now she seemed half as old again as he. She was a tall, erect woman with dark eyebrows, stately and dignified and, as she said of herself, intellectual. She read a great deal, used simplified spelling in her letters, called her husband, not Dmitry, but Dimitry, while he privately considered her of limited intelligence, narrow-minded, dowdy, was afraid of her, and did not like to be at home. He had begun being unfaithful to her long ago—had been unfaithful to her often and, probably for that reason, almost always spoke ill of women, and when they were talked of in his presence used to call them "the inferior race."

5 It seemed to him that he had been sufficiently tutored by bitter experience to call them what he pleased, and yet he could not have lived without "the inferior race" for two days together. In the company of men he was bored and ill at ease, he was chilly and uncommunicative with them, but when he was among women he felt free, and knew what to speak to them about and how to comport himself, and even to be silent with them was no strain on him. In his appearance, in his character, in his whole make-up there was something attractive and elusive that disposed women in his favor and allured them. He knew that, and some force seemed to draw him to them, too.

Oft-repeated and really bitter experience had taught him long ago that with decent people—particularly Moscow people—who are irresolute and slow to move, every affair which at first seems a light and charming adventure inevitably grows into a whole problem of extreme complexity, and in the end a painful situation is created. But at every new meeting with an interesting woman this lesson of experience seemed to slip from his memory, and he was eager for life, and everything seemed so simple and diverting.

One evening while he was dining in the public garden the lady in the beret walked up without haste to take the next table. Her expression, her gait, her dress, and the way she did her hair told him that she belonged to the upper class, that she was married, that she was in Yalta for the first time and alone, and that she was bored there. The stories told of the immorality in Yalta are to a great extent untrue; he despised them, and knew that such stories were made up for the most part by persons who would have been glad to sin themselves if they had had the chance, but when the lady sat down at the next table three paces from him, he recalled these stories of easy conquests, of trips to the mountains, and the tempting thought of a swift, fleeting liaison, a romance with an unknown woman of whose very name he was ignorant suddenly took hold of him.

He beckoned invitingly to the Pomeranian, and when the dog approached him, shook his finger at it. The Pomeranian growled; Gurov threatened it again.

The lady glanced at him and at once dropped her eyes.

"He doesn't bite," she said and blushed.

"May I give him a bone?" he asked; and when she nodded he inquired affably, "Have you been in Yalta long?"

"About five days."

"And I am dragging out the second week here."

There was a short silence.

"Time passes quickly, and yet it is so dull here!" she said, not looking at him.

"It's only the fashion to say it's dull here. A provincial will live in Belyov or Zhizdra and not be bored, but when he comes here it's 'Oh, the dullness! Oh, the dust!' One would think he came from Granada."

She laughed. Then both continued eating in silence, like strangers, but after dinner they walked together and there sprang up between them the light banter of people who are free and contented, to whom it does not matter where they go or what they talk about. They walked and talked of the strange light on the sea: the water was a soft, warm, lilac color, and there was a golden band of moonlight upon it. They talked of how sultry it was after a hot day. Gurov told her that he was a native of Moscow, that he had studied languages and literature at the university, but had a post in a bank, that at one time he had trained to become an opera singer but had given it up, that he owned two houses in Moscow. And he learned from her that she had grown up in Petersburg, but had lived in S1since her marriage two years previously, that she was going to stay in Yalta for about another month; and that her husband, who needed a rest, too, might perhaps come to fetch her. She was not certain whether her husband was a member of a Government Board or served on a Zemstvo Council,[1] and this amused her. And Gurov learned too that her name was Anna Sergeyevna.

Afterwards in his room at the hotel he thought about her—and was certain that he would meet her the next day. It was bound to happen. Getting into bed he recalled that she had been a schoolgirl only recently, doing lessons like his own daughter; he thought how much timidity and angularity there was still in her laugh and her manner of talking with a stranger. It must have been the first time in her life that she was alone in a setting in which she was followed, looked at, and spoken to for one secret

[1]*Zemstvo Council* County council.

purpose alone, which she could hardly fail to guess. He thought of her slim, delicate throat, her lovely gray eyes.

"There's something pathetic about her, though," he thought, and dropped off.

II

A week had passed since they had struck up an acquaintance. It was a holiday. It was close indoors, while in the street the wind whirled the dust about and blew people's hats off. One was thirsty all day, and Gurov often went into the restaurant and offered Anna Sergeyevna a soft drink or ice cream. One did not know what to do with oneself.

In the evening when the wind had abated they went out on the pier to watch the steamer come in. There were a great many people walking about the dock; they had come to welcome someone and they were carrying bunches of flowers. And two peculiarities of a festive Yalta crowd stood out: the elderly ladies were dressed like young ones and there were many generals.

Owing to the choppy sea, the steamer arrived late, after sunset, and it was a long time tacking about before it put in at the pier. Anna Sergeyevna peered at the steamer and the passengers through her lorgnette as though looking for acquaintances, and whenever she turned to Gurov her eyes were shining. She talked a great deal and asked questions jerkily, forgetting the next moment what she had asked; then she lost her lorgnette in the crush.

The festive crowd began to disperse; it was now too dark to see people's faces; there was no wind any more, but Gurov and Anna Sergeyevna still stood as though waiting to see someone else come off the steamer. Anna Sergeyevna was silent now, and sniffed her flowers without looking at Gurov.

"The weather has improved this evening," he said. "Where shall we go now? Shall we drive somewhere?"

She did not reply.

Then he looked at her intently, and suddenly embraced her and kissed her on the lips, and the moist fragrance of her flowers enveloped him; and at once he looked round him anxiously, wondering if anyone had seen them.

"Let us go to your place," he said softly. And they walked off together rapidly.

The air in her room was close and there was the smell of the perfume she had bought at the Japanese shop. Looking at her, Gurov thought: "What encounters life offers!" From the past he preserved the memory of carefree, good-natured women whom love made gay and who were grateful to him for the happiness he gave them, however brief it might be; and of women like his wife who loved without sincerity, with too many words, affectedly, hysterically, with an expression that it was not love or passion that engaged them but something more significant; and of two or three others, very beautiful, frigid women, across whose faces would suddenly flit a rapacious expression—an obstinate desire to take from life more than it could give, and these were women no longer young, capricious, unreflecting, domineering, unintelligent, and when Gurov grew cold to them their beauty aroused his hatred, and the lace on their lingerie seemed to him to resemble scales.

But here there was the timidity, the angularity of inexperienced youth, a feeling of awkwardness; and there was a sense of embarrassment, as though someone had suddenly knocked at the door. Anna Sergeyevna, "the lady with the pet dog," treated what had happened in a peculiar way, very seriously, as though it were her fall—so it seemed, and this was odd and inappropriate. Her features drooped and faded, and her long hair hung down sadly on either side of her face; she grew pensive and her dejected pose was that of a Magdalene in a picture by an old master.

"It's not right," she said. "You don't respect me now, you first of all." 30

There was a watermelon on the table. Gurov cut himself a slice and began eating it without haste. They were silent for at least half an hour.

There was something touching about Anna Sergeyevna; she had the purity of a well-bred, naive woman who has seen little of life. The single candle burning on the table barely illumined her face, yet it was clear that she was unhappy.

"Why should I stop respecting you, darling?" asked Gurov. "You don't know what you're saying."

"God forgive me," she said, and her eyes filled with tears. "It's terrible."

"It's as though you were trying to exonerate yourself." 35

"How can I exonerate myself? No. I am a bad, low woman; I despise myself and I have no thought of exonerating myself. It's not my husband but myself I have deceived. And not only just now; I have been deceiving myself for a long time. My husband may be a good, honest man, but he is a flunkey! I don't know what he does, what his work is, but I know he is a flunkey! I was twenty when I married him. I was tormented by curiosity; I wanted something better. 'There must be a different sort of life,' I said to myself. I wanted to live! To live, to live! Curiosity kept eating at me—you don't understand it, but I swear to God I could no longer control myself, something was going on in me, I could not be held back. I told my husband I was ill, and came here. And here I have been walking about as though in a daze, as though I were mad; and now I have become a vulgar, vile woman whom anyone may despise."

Gurov was already bored with her, he was irritated by her naive tone, by her repentance, so unexpected and so out of place, but for the tears in her eyes he might have thought she was joking or play-acting.

"I don't understand, my dear," he said softly. "What do you want?"

She hid her face on his breast and pressed close to him.

"Believe me, believe me, I beg you," she said. "I love honesty and purity, 40
and sin is loathsome to me, I don't know what I'm doing. Simple people say, 'The Evil One has led me astray.' And I may say of myself now that the Evil One has led me astray."

"Quiet, quiet," he murmured.

He looked into her fixed, frightened eyes, kissed her, spoke to her softly and affectionately, and by degrees she calmed down, and her gaiety returned, both began laughing.

Afterwards when they went out there was not a soul on the esplanade. The town with its cypresses looked quite dead, but the sea was still sounding as it broke upon the beach; a single launch was rocking on the waves and on it a lantern was blinking sleepily.

They found a cab and drove to Oreanda.

"I found out your surname in the hall just now: it was written on the 45
board—von Dideritz," said Gurov. "Is your husband German?"

"No; I believe his grandfather was German, but he is Greek Orthodox himself."

At Oreanda they sat on a bench not far from the church, looked down at the sea, and were silent. Yalta was barely visible through the morning mist; white clouds rested motionlessly on the mountaintops. The leaves did not stir on the trees, cicadas twanged, and the monotonous muffled sound of the sea that rose from below spoke of the peace, the eternal sleep awaiting us. So it rumbled below when there was no Yalta, no Oreanda here; so it rumbles now, and it will rumble as indifferently and as hollowly when we are no more. And in this constancy, in this complete indifference to the life and death of each of us, there lies, perhaps, a pledge of our eternal salvation, of the unceasing advance of life upon earth, of unceasing movement towards perfection. Sitting beside a young woman who in the dawn seemed so lovely, Gurov, soothed and spellbound by these magical surroundings—the sea, the mountains, the clouds, the wide sky—thought how everything is really beautiful in this world when one reflects: everything except what we think or do ourselves when we forget the higher aims of life and our own human dignity.

A man strolled up to them—probably a guard—looked at them, and walked away. And this detail, too, seemed so mysterious and beautiful. They saw a steamer arrive from Feodosia, its lights extinguished in the glow of dawn.

"There is dew on the grass," said Anna Sergeyevna, after a silence.

"Yes, it's time to go home."

They returned to the city.

Then they met every day at twelve o'clock on the esplanade, lunched and dined together, took walks, admired the sea. She complained that she slept badly, that she had palpitations, asked the same questions, troubled now by jealousy and now by the fear that he did not respect her sufficiently. And often in the square or the public garden, when there was no one near them, he suddenly drew her to him and kissed her passionately. Complete idleness, these kisses in broad daylight exchanged furtively in dread of someone's seeing them, the heat, the smell of the sea, and the continual flitting before his eyes of idle, well-dressed, well-fed people, worked a complete change in him; he kept telling Anna Sergeyevna how beautiful she was, how seductive, was urgently passionate; he would not move a step away from her, while she was often pensive and continually pressed him to confess that he did not respect her, did not love her in the least, and saw in her nothing but a common woman. Almost every evening rather late they drove somewhere out of town, to Oreanda or to the waterfall; and the excursion was always a success, the scenery invariably impressed them as beautiful and magnificent.

They were expecting her husband, but a letter came from him saying that he had eye-trouble, and begging his wife to return home as soon as possible. Anna Sergeyevna made haste to go.

"It's a good thing I am leaving," she said to Gurov. "It's the hand of Fate!"

She took a carriage to the railway station, and he went with her. They were driving the whole day. When she had taken her place in the express, and when the second bell had rung, she said, "Let me look at you once more—let me look at you again. Like this."

She was not crying but was so sad that she seemed ill and her face was quivering.

"I shall be thinking of you—remembering you," she said. "God bless you, be happy. Don't remember evil against me. We are parting forever—it has to be, for we ought never to have met. Well, God bless you."

The train moved off rapidly, its lights soon vanished, and a minute later there was no sound of it, as though everything had conspired to end as quickly as possible that sweet trance, that madness. Left alone on the platform, and gazing into the dark distance, Gurov listened to the twang of the grasshoppers and the hum of the telegraph wires, feeling as though he had just waked up. And he reflected, musing, that there had now been another episode or adventure in his life, and it, too, was at an end, and nothing was left of it but a memory. He was moved, sad, and slightly remorseful: this young woman whom he would never meet again had not been happy with him; he had been warm and affectionate with her, but yet in his manner, his tone, and his caresses there had been a shade of light irony, the slightly coarse arrogance of a happy male who was, besides, almost twice her age. She had constantly called him kind, exceptional, highminded; obviously he had seemed to her different from what he really was, so he had involuntarily deceived her.

Here at the station there was already a scent of autumn in the air; it was a chilly evening.

"It is time for me to go north, too," thought Gurov as he left the plat- 60
form. "High time!"

III

At home in Moscow the winter routine was already established, the stoves were heated, and in the morning it was still dark when the children were having breakfast and getting ready for school, and the nurse would light the lamp for a short time. There were frosts already. When the first snow falls, on the first day the sleighs are out, it is pleasant to see the white earth, the white roofs; one draws easy, delicious breaths, and the season brings back the days of one's youth. The old limes and birches, white with hoar-frost, have a good-natured look; they are closer to one's heart than cypresses and palms, and near them one no longer wants to think of mountains and the sea.

Gurov, a native of Moscow, arrived there on a fine frosty day, and when he put on his fur coat and warm gloves and took a walk along Petrovka, and when on Saturday night he heard the bells ringing, his recent trip and the places he had visited lost all charm for him. Little by little he became immersed in Moscow life, greedily read three newspapers a day, and declared that he did not read the Moscow papers on principle. He already felt a longing for restaurants, clubs, formal dinners, anniversary celebrations, and it flattered him to entertain distinguished lawyers and actors, and to play cards with a professor at the physicians' club. He could eat a whole portion of meat stewed with pickled cabbage and served in a pan, Moscow style.

A month or so would pass and the image of Anna Sergeyevna, it seemed to him, would become misty in his memory, and only from time to time he would dream of her with her touching smile as he dreamed of others. But more than a month went by, winter came into its own, and everything was still clear in his memory as though he had parted from Anna Sergeyevna only yesterday. And his memories glowed more and more vividly. When in the evening stillness the voices of his children preparing their lessons reached his study, or when he listened to a song or to an organ playing in a restaurant, or when the storm howled in the chimney, suddenly everything would rise up in his memory, what had happened on the pier and the early morning with the mist on the mountains, and the steamer coming from Feodosia, and the kisses. He would pace about his room a long time, remembering and smiling, then his memories passed into reveries, and in his imagination the past would mingle with what was to come. He did not dream of Anna Sergeyevna, but she followed him about everywhere and watched him. When he shut his eyes he saw her before him as though she were there in the flesh, and she seemed to him lovelier, younger, tenderer than she had been, and he imagined himself a finer man than he had been in Yalta. Of evenings she peered out at him from the bookcase, from the fireplace, from the corner—he heard her breathing, the caressing rustle of her clothes. In the street he followed the women with his eyes, looking for someone who resembled her.

Already he was tormented by a strong desire to share his memories with someone. But in his home it was impossible to talk of his love, and he had no one to talk to outside; certainly he could not confide in his tenants or in anyone at the bank. And what was there to talk about? He hadn't loved her then, had he? Had there been anything beautiful, poetical, edifying, or simply interesting in his relations with Anna Sergeyevna? And he was forced to talk vaguely of love, of women, and no one guessed what he meant; only his wife would twitch her black eyebrows and say, "The part of a philanderer does not suit you at all, Dimitry."

65 One evening, coming out of the physicians' club with an official with whom he had been playing cards, he could not resist saying:

"If you only knew what a fascinating woman I became acquainted with at Yalta!"

The official got into his sledge and was driving away, but turned suddenly and shouted:

"Dmitry Dmitrich!"

"What is it?"

70 "You were right this evening: the sturgeon was a bit high."

These words, so commonplace, for some reason moved Gurov to indignation, and struck him as degrading and unclean. What savage manners, what mugs! What stupid nights, what dull, humdrum days! Frenzied gambling, gluttony, drunkenness, continual talk always about the same thing! Futile pursuits and conversations always about the same topics take up the better part of one's time, the better part of one's strength, and in the end there is left a life clipped and wingless, an absurd mess, and there is no escaping or getting away from it—just as though one were in a madhouse or a prison.

Gurov, boiling with indignation, did not sleep all night. And he had a headache all the next day. And the following nights too he slept badly, he sat up in bed, thinking, or paced up and down his room. He was fed up with his children, fed up with the bank; he had no desire to go anywhere or to talk of anything.

In December during the holidays he prepared to take a trip and told his wife he was going to Petersburg to do what he could for a young friend—and he set off for S——. What for? He did not know, himself. He wanted to see Anna Sergeyevna and talk with her, to arrange a rendezvous if possible.

He arrived at S—— in the morning, and at the hotel took the best room, in which the floor was covered with gray army cloth, and on the table there was an inkstand, gray with dust and topped by a figure on horseback, its hat in its raised hand and its head broken off. The porter gave him the necessary information: von Dideritz lived in a house of his own on Staro-Goncharnaya Street, not far from the hotel: he was rich and lived well and kept his own horses; everyone in the town knew him. The porter pronounced the name: "Dridiritz."

Without haste Gurov made his way to Staro-Goncharnaya Street and 75
found the house. Directly opposite the house stretched a long gray fence studded with nails.

"A fence like that would make one run away," thought Gurov, looking now at the fence, now at the windows of the house.

He reflected: this was a holiday, and the husband was apt to be at home. And in any case, it would be tactless to go into the house and disturb her. If he were to send her a note, it might fall into her husband's hands, and that might spoil everything. The best thing was to rely on chance. And he kept walking up and down the street and along the fence, waiting for the chance. He saw a beggar go in at the gate and heard the dogs attack him; then an hour later he heard a piano, and the sound came to him faintly and indistinctly. Probably it was Anna Sergeyevna playing. The front door opened suddenly, and an old woman came out, followed by the familiar white Pomeranian. Gurov was on the point of calling to the dog, but his heart began beating violently, and in his excitement he could not remember the Pomeranian's name.

He kept walking up and down, and hated the gray fence more and more, and by now he thought irritably that Anna Sergeyevna had forgotten him, and was perhaps already diverting herself with another man, and that that was very natural in a young woman who from morning till night had to look at that damn fence. He went back to his hotel room and sat on the couch for a long while, not knowing what to do, then he had dinner and a long nap.

"How stupid and annoying all this is!" he thought when he woke and looked at the dark windows: it was already evening. "Here I've had a good sleep for some reason. What am I going to do at night?"

He sat on the bed, which was covered with a cheap gray blanket of 80
the kind seen in hospitals, and he twitted himself in his vexation:

"So there's your lady with the pet dog. There's your adventure. A nice place to cool your heels in."

That morning at the station a playbill in large letters had caught his eye. *The Geisha* was to be given for the first time. He thought of this and drove to the theater.

"It's quite possible that she goes to first nights," he thought.

The theater was full. As in all provincial theaters, there was a haze above the chandelier, the gallery was noisy and restless; in the front row, before the beginning of the performance the local dandies were standing with their hands clasped behind their backs; in the Governor's box the Governor's daughter, wearing a boa, occupied the front seat, while the Governor himself hid modestly behind the portiere and only his hands were visible; the curtain swayed, the orchestra was a long time tuning up. While the audience was coming in and taking their seats, Gurov scanned the faces eagerly.

Anna Sergeyevna, too, came in. She sat down in the third row, and 85
when Gurov looked at her his heart contracted, and he understood clearly that in the whole world there was no human being so near, so precious, and so important to him, she, this little, undistinguished woman, lost in a provincial crowd, with a vulgar lorgnette in her hand, filled his whole life now, was his sorrow and his joy, the only happiness that he now desired

for himself, and to the sounds of the bad orchestra, of the miserable local violins, he thought how lovely she was. He thought and dreamed.

A young man with small side-whiskers, very tall and stooped, came in with Anna Sergeyevna and sat down beside her; he nodded his head at every step and seemed to be bowing continually. Probably this was the husband whom at Yalta, in an access of bitter feeling, she had called a flunkey. And there really was in his lanky figure, his side-whiskers, his small bald patch, something of a flunkey's retiring manner; his smile was mawkish, and in his buttonhole there was an academic badge like a waiter's number.

During the first intermission the husband went out to have a smoke; she remained in her seat. Gurov, who was also sitting in the orchestra, went up to her and said in a shaky voice, with a forced smile:

"Good evening!"

She glanced at him and turned pale, then looked at him again in horror, unable to believe her eyes, and gripped the fan and the lorgnette tightly together in her hands, evidently trying to keep herself from fainting. Both were silent. She was sitting, he was standing, frightened by her distress and not daring to take a seat beside her. The violins and the flute that were being tuned up sang out. He suddenly felt frightened: it seemed as if all the people in the boxes were looking at them. She got up and went hurriedly to the exit; he followed her, and both of them walked blindly along the corridors and up and down stairs, and figures in the uniforms prescribed for magistrates, teachers, and officials of the Department of Crown Lands, all wearing badges, flitted before their eyes, as did also ladies, and fur coats on hangers; they were conscious of drafts and the smell of stale tobacco. And Gurov, whose heart was beating violently, thought:

"Oh, Lord! Why are these people here and this orchestra!" 90

And at that instant he suddenly recalled how when he had seen Anna Sergeyevna off at the station he had said to himself that all was over between them and that they would never meet again. But how distant the end still was!

On the narrow, gloomy staircase over which it said "To the Amphitheatre," she stopped.

"How you frightened me!" she said, breathing hard, still pale and stunned. "Oh, how you frightened me! I am barely alive. Why did you come? Why?"

"But do understand, Anna, do understand—" he said hurriedly, under his breath. "I implore you, do understand—"

She looked at him with fear, with entreaty, with love; she looked at him 95
intently, to keep his features more distinctly in her memory.

"I suffer so," she went on, not listening to him. "All this time I have been thinking of nothing but you, I live only by the thought of you. And I wanted to forget, to forget, but why, oh, why have you come?"

On the landing above them two high school boys were looking down and smoking, but it was all the same to Gurov; he drew Anna Sergeyevna to him and began kissing her face and hands.

"What are you doing, what are you doing!" she was saying in horror, pushing him away. "We have lost our senses. Go away today; go away at once—I conjure you by all that is sacred, I implore you—People are coming this way!"

Someone was walking up the stairs.

100 "You must leave," Anna Sergeyevna went on in a whisper. "Do you hear, Dmitry Dmitrich? I will come and see you in Moscow. I have never been happy, I am unhappy now, and I never, never shall be happy, never! So don't make me suffer still more! I swear I'll come to Moscow. But now let us part. My dear, good, precious one, let us part!"

She pressed his hand and walked rapidly downstairs, turning to look round at him, and from her eyes he could see that she really was unhappy. Gurov stood for a while, listening, then when all grew quiet, he found his coat and left the theater.

IV

And Anna Sergeyevna began coming to see him in Moscow. Once every two or three months she left S—— telling her husband that she was going to consult a doctor about a woman's ailment from which she was suffering—and her husband did and did not believe her. When she arrived in Moscow she would stop at the Slavyansky Bazar Hotel, and at once send a man in a red cap to Gurov. Gurov came to see her, and no one in Moscow knew of it.

Once he was going to see her in this way, on a winter morning (the messenger had come the evening before and not found him in). With him walked his daughter, whom he wanted to take to school; it was on the way. Snow was coming down in big wet flakes.

"It's three degrees above zero,[2] and yet it's snowing," Gurov was saying to his daughter. "But this temperature prevails only on the surface of the earth; in the upper layers of the atmosphere there is quite a different temperature."

105 "And why doesn't it thunder in winter, papa?"

He explained that, too. He talked, thinking all the while that he was on his way to a rendezvous, and no living soul knew of it, and probably no one would ever know. He had two lives, an open one, seen and known by all who needed to know it, full of conventional truth and conventional falsehood, exactly like the lives of his friends and acquaintances; and another life that went on in secret. And through some strange, perhaps accidental, combination of circumstances, everything that was of interest and importance to him, everything that was essential to him, everything about which he felt sincerely and did not deceive himself, everything that constituted the core of his life, was going on concealed from others; while all that was false, the shell in which he hid to cover the truth—his work at the bank, for instance, his discussions at the club, his references to the "inferior race," his appearances at anniversary celebrations with his wife—all that went on in the open. Judging others by himself, he did not believe what he saw, and always fancied that every man led his real, most interesting life under cover of secrecy as under cover of night. The personal life of every individual is based on secrecy, and perhaps it is partly for that reason that civilized man is so nervously anxious that personal privacy should be respected.

Having taken his daughter to school, Gurov went on to the Slavyansky Bazar Hotel. He took off his fur coat in the lobby, went upstairs, and knocked gently at the door. Anna Sergeyevna, wearing his favorite gray

---

[2]*three degrees above zero* On the Celsius scale—about thirty-seven degrees Fahrenheit.

dress, exhausted by the journey and by waiting, had been expecting him since the previous evening. She was pale, and looked at him without a smile, and he had hardly entered when she flung herself on his breast. That kiss was a long, lingering one, as though they had not seen one another for two years.

"Well, darling, how are you getting on there?" he asked. "What news?"

"Wait; I'll tell you in a moment—I can't speak."

She could not speak; she was crying. She turned away from him, and 110
pressed her handkerchief to her eyes.

"Let her have her cry; meanwhile I'll sit down," he thought, and he seated himself in an armchair.

Then he rang and ordered tea, and while he was having his tea she remained standing at the window with her back to him. She was crying out of sheer agitation, in the sorrowful consciousness that their life was so sad, that they could only see each other in secret and had to hide from people like thieves! Was it not a broken life?

"Come, stop now, dear!" he said.

It was plain to him that this love of theirs would not be over soon, that the end of it was not in sight. Anna Sergeyevna was growing more and more attached to him. She adored him, and it was unthinkable to tell her that their love was bound to come to an end some day; besides, she would not have believed it!

He went up to her and took her by the shoulders, to fondle her and 115
say something diverting, and at that moment he caught sight of himself in the mirror.

His hair was already beginning to turn gray. And it seemed odd to him that he had grown so much older in the last few years, and lost his looks. The shoulders on which his hands rested were warm and heaving. He felt compassion for this life, still so warm and lovely, but probably already about to begin to fade and wither like his own. Why did she love him so much? He always seemed to women different from what he was, and they loved in him not himself, but the man whom their imagination created and whom they had been eagerly seeking all their lives; and afterwards, when they saw their mistake, they loved him nevertheless. And not one of them had been happy with him. In the past he had met women, come together with them, parted from them, but he had never once loved; it was anything you please, but not love. And only now when his head was gray he had fallen in love, really, truly—for the first time in his life.

Anna Sergeyevna and he loved each other as people do who are very close and intimate, like man and wife, like tender friends; it seemed to them that Fate itself had meant them for one another, and they could not understand why he had a wife and she a husband; and it was as though they were a pair of migratory birds, male and female, caught and forced to live in different cages. They forgave each other what they were ashamed of in their past, they forgave everything in the present, and felt that this love of theirs had altered them both.

Formerly in moments of sadness he had soothed himself with whatever logical arguments came into his head, but now he no longer cared for logic, he felt profound compassion, he wanted to be sincere and tender.

"Give it up now, my darling," he said. "You've had your cry; that's enough. Let us have a talk now, we'll think up something."

Then they spent a long time taking counsel together, they talked of 120
how to avoid the necessity for secrecy, for deception, for living in different

cities, and not seeing one another for long stretches of time. How could they free themselves from these intolerable fetters?

"How? How?" he asked, clutching his head. "How?"

And it seemed as though in a little while the solution would be found, and then a new and glorious life would begin; and it was clear to both of them that the end was still far off, and that what was to be most complicated and difficult for them was only just beginning.

Analyzing the Text

1. How does Chekhov characterize Dmitry initially and how does he change as a result of his relationship with Anna?
2. How does knowing about Dmitry's wife and Anna's husband influence your attitude toward them?

Understanding Chekhov's Techniques

1. Why do you think Chekhov leaves the end of the story unresolved? Does the lack of a clear ending mar or enhance the story's effectiveness?
2. Why do you think Chekhov tells the story from Dmitry's perspective rather than Anna's? Speculate on how the same events appeared to her.

Arguing for an Interpretation

1. Is Chekhov sympathetic or critical of Dimitry and Anna and their predicament? Explain your answer.
2. If Anna and Dimitry were free to marry each other, would they be in love as deeply as they are or, in your opinion, does their love exist mainly because of the secrecy and excitement? Explain your answer.

KURT VONNEGUT, JR.

Kurt Vonnegut, Jr. (1922–) was born in Indianapolis and studied biochemistry and anthropology at Cornell University before being drafted in World War II. His experiences as a prisoner of the Germans in Dresden, when the city was firebombed by the Allied forces, served as the basis for Slaughterhouse Five *(1969), the work that brought him fame. He is also the author of such iconoclastic masterpieces as* Cat's Cradle *(1963),* Sirens of Titan *(1971),* Breakfast of Champions *(1973),* Timequake *(1993), and innumerable short stories written for magazines. The unique voice he creates in his fiction recalls Voltaire's delightful assaults on human folly and greed. His long and productive career reveals a satirist's gift for mixing a keen sense of the absurd with science fiction, always tempered by compassion. In 1999 he wrote a book with Lee Stringer about writing,* Like Shaking Hands with God: A Conversation About Writing. *A recent work is* God Bless You, Dr. Kevorkian *(2000), an ironic allusion to his 1965 novel* God Bless You, Mr. Rosewater. *The following story is from* Welcome to the Monkey House *(1961).*

Who Am I This Time?

The North Crawford Mask and Wig Club, an amateur theatrical society I belong to, voted to do Tennessee Williams's *A Streetcar Named Desire* for the spring play. Doris Sawyer, who always directs, said she couldn't direct this time because her mother was so sick. And she said the club ought to develop some other directors anyway, because she couldn't live forever, even though she'd made it safely to seventy-four.

So I got stuck with the directing job, even though the only thing I'd ever directed before was the installation of combination aluminum storm windows and screens I'd sold. That's what I am, a salesman of storm windows and doors, and here and there a bathtub enclosure. As far as acting goes, the highest rank I ever held on stage was either butler or policeman, whichever's higher.

I made a lot of conditions before I took the directing job, and the biggest one was that Harry Nash, the only real actor the club has, had to take the Marlon Brando part in the play. To give you an idea of how versatile Harry is, inside of one year he was Captain Queeg in *The Caine Mutiny Court Martial,* then Abe Lincoln in *Abe Lincoln in Illinois* and then the young architect in *The Moon is Blue.* The year after that, Harry Nash was Henry the Eighth in *Anne of the Thousand Days* and Doc in *Come Back Little Sheba,* and I was after him for Marlon Brando in *A Streetcar Named Desire.* Harry wasn't at the meeting to say whether he'd take the part or not. He never came to meetings. He was too shy. He didn't stay away from meetings because he had something else to do. He wasn't married, didn't go out with women—didn't have any close men friends either. He stayed away from all kinds of gatherings because he never could think of anything to say or do without a script.

So I had to go down to Miller's Hardware Store, where Harry was a clerk, the next day and ask him if he'd take the part. I stopped off at the telephone company to complain about a bill I'd gotten for a call to Honolulu, I'd never called Honolulu in my life.

And there was this beautiful girl I'd never seen before behind the 5
counter at the phone company, and she explained that the company had put in an automatic billing machine and that the machine didn't have all the bugs out of it yet. It made mistakes. "Not only did I not call Honolulu," I told her, "I don't think anybody in North Crawford ever has or will."

So she took the charge off the bill, and I asked her if she was from around North Crawford. She said no. She said she just came with the new billing machine to teach local girls how to take care of it. After that, she said, she would go with some other machine to someplace else. "Well," I said, "as long as people have to come along with the machines, I guess we're all right."

"What?" she said.

"When machines start delivering themselves," I said, "I guess that's when the people better start really worrying."

"Oh," she said. She didn't seem very interested in that subject, and I wondered if she was interested in anything. She seemed kind of numb, almost a machine herself, an automatic phone-company politeness machine.

10 "How long will you be in town here?" I asked her.

"I stay in each town eight weeks, sir," she said. She had pretty blue eyes, but there sure wasn't much hope or curiosity in them. She told me she had been going from town to town like that for two years, always a stranger.

And I got it in my head that she might make a good Stella for the play. Stella was the wife of the Marlon Brando character, the wife of the character I wanted Harry Nash to play. So I told her where and when we were going to hold tryouts, and said the club would be very happy if she'd come.

She looked surprised, and she warmed up a little. "You know," she said, "that's the first time anybody ever asked me to participate in any community thing."

"Well," I said, "there isn't any other way to get to know a lot of nice people faster than to be in a play with 'em."

15 She said her name was Helene Shaw. She said she might just surprise me—and herself. She said she just might come.

You would think that North Crawford would be fed up with Harry Nash in plays after all the plays he'd been in. But the fact was that North Crawford probably could have gone on enjoying Harry forever, because he was never Harry on stage. When the maroon curtain went up on the stage in the gymnasium of the Consolidated Junior-Senior High School, Harry, body and soul, was exactly what the script and the director told him to be.

Somebody said one time that Harry ought to go to a psychiatrist so he could be something important and colorful in real life, too—so he could get married anyway, and maybe get a better job than just clerking in Miller's Hardware Store for fifty dollars a week. But I don't know what a psychiatrist could have turned up about him that the town didn't already know. The trouble with Harry was he'd been left on the doorstep of the Unitarian Church when he was a baby, and he never did find out who his parents were.

When I told him there in Miller's that I'd been appointed director, that I wanted him in my play, he said what he always said to anybody who asked him to be in a play—and it was kind of sad, if you think about it.

"Who am I this time?" he said.

20 So I held the tryouts where they're always held—in the meeting room on the second floor of the North Crawford Public Library. Doris Sawyer, the woman who usually directs, came to give me the benefit of all her experience. The two of us sat in state upstairs, while the people who wanted parts waited below. We called them upstairs one by one.

Harry Nash came to the tryouts, even though it was a waste of time. I guess he wanted to get that little bit more acting in.

For Harry's pleasure, and our pleasure, too, we had him read from the scene where he beats up his wife. It was a play in itself, the way Harry did it, and Tennessee Williams hadn't written it all either. Tennessee Williams didn't write the part, for instance, where Harry, who weighs about one hundred forty-five, who's about five feet eight inches tall, added fifty pounds to his weight and four inches to his height by just picking up a playbook. He had a short little double-breasted bellows-back grade-school graduation suit coat on and a dinky little red tie with a horsehead on it. He took off the coat and tie, opened his collar, then turned his back to Doris and me, getting up steam for the part. There was a great big rip in the back of his shirt, and it looked like a fairly new shirt too. He'd ripped it on purpose, so he could be that much more like Marlon Brando, right from the first.

When he faced us again, he was huge and handsome and conceited and cruel. Doris read the part of Stella, the wife, and Harry bullied that old, old lady into believing that she was a sweet, pregnant girl married to a sexy gorilla who was going to beat her brains out. She had me believing it too. And I read the lines of Blanche, her sister in the play, and darned if Harry didn't scare me into feeling like a drunk and faded Southern belle.

And then, while Doris and I were getting over our emotional experiences, like people coming out from under ether, Harry put down the playbook, put on his coat and tie, and turned into the pale hardware-store clerk again.

25 "Was—was that all right?" he said, and he seemed pretty sure he wouldn't get the part.

"Well," I said, "for a first reading, that wasn't too bad."

"Is there a chance I'll get the part?" he said. I don't know why he always had to pretend there was some doubt about his getting a part, but he did.

"I think we can safely say we're leaning powerfully in your direction," I told him.

He was very pleased. "Thanks! Thanks a lot!" he said, and he shook my hand.

30 "Is there a pretty new girl downstairs?" I said, meaning Helene Shaw.

"I didn't notice," said Harry.

It turned out that Helene Shaw *had* come for the tryouts, and Doris and I had our hearts broken. We thought the North Crawford Mask and Wig Club was finally going to put a really good-looking, really young girl on stage, instead of one of the beat-up forty-year-old women we generally have to palm off as girls.

But Helene Shaw couldn't act for sour apples. No matter what we gave her to read, she was the same girl with the same smile for anybody who had a complaint about his phone bill.

Doris tried to coach her some, to make her understand that Stella in the play was a very passionate girl who loved a gorilla because she needed a gorilla. But Helene just read the lines the same way again. I don't think a volcano could have stirred her up enough to say, "Oo."

35 "Dear," said Doris, "I'm going to ask you a personal question."

"All right," said Helene.

"Have you ever been in love?" said Doris. "The reason I ask," she said, "remembering some old love might help you put more warmth in your acting."

Helene frowned and thought hard. "Well," she said, "I travel a lot, you know. And practically all the men in the different companies I visit are married and I never stay anyplace long enough to know many people who aren't."

"What about school?" said Doris. "What about puppy love and all the other kinds of love in school?"

40 So Helene thought hard about that, and then she said, "Even in school I was always moving around a lot. My father was a construction worker, following jobs around, so I was always saying hello or good-by to someplace, without anything in between."

"Um," said Doris.

"Would movie stars count?" said Helene. "I don't mean in real life. I never knew any. I just mean up on the screen."

Doris looked at me and rolled her eyes. "I guess that's love of a kind," she said.

And then Helene got a little enthusiastic. "I used to sit through movies over and over again," she said, "and pretend I was married to whoever the man movie star was. They were the only people who came with us. No matter where we moved, movie stars were there."

"Uh huh," said Doris. 45

"Well, thank you, Miss Shaw," I said. "You go downstairs and wait with the rest. We'll let you know."

So we tried to find another Stella. And there just wasn't one, not one woman in the club with the dew still on her. "All we've got are Blanches," I said, meaning all we had were faded women who could play the part of Blanche, Stella's faded sister. "That's life, I guess—twenty Blanches to one Stella."

"And when you find a Stella," said Doris, "it turns out she doesn't know what love is."

Doris and I decided there was one last thing we could try. We could get Harry Nash to play a scene along with Helene. "He just might make her bubble the least little bit," I said.

"That girl hasn't got a bubble in her," said Doris. 50

So we called down the stairs for Helene to come back on up, and we told somebody to go find Harry. Harry never sat with the rest of the people at tryouts—or at rehearsals either. The minute he didn't have a part to play, he'd disappear into some hiding place where he could hear people call him, but where he couldn't be seen. At tryouts in the library he generally hid in the reference room, passing the time looking at flags of different countries in the front of the dictionary.

Helene came back upstairs, and we were very sorry and surprised to see that she'd been crying.

"Oh, dear," said Doris. "Oh, my—now what on earth's the trouble, dear?"

"I was terrible, wasn't I?" said Helene, hanging her head.

Doris said the only thing anybody can say in an amateur theatrical society when somebody cries. She said, "Why, no dear—you were marvelous." 55

"No, I wasn't," said Helene. "I'm a walking icebox, and I know it."

"Nobody could look at you and say that," said Doris.

"When they get to know me, they can say it," said Helene. "When people get to know me, that's what they *do* say." Her tears got worse. "I don't want to be the way I am," she said. "I just can't help it, living the way I've lived all my life. The only experiences I've had have been in crazy dreams of movie stars. When I meet somebody nice in real life, I feel as though I were in some kind of big bottle, as though I couldn't touch that person, no matter how hard I tried." And Helene pushed on air as though it were a big bottle all around her.

"You ask me if I've ever been in love," she said to Doris. "No—but I want to be. I know what this play's about. I know what Stella's supposed to feel and why she feels it. I—I—I—" she said, and her tears wouldn't let her go on.

"You what, dear?" said Doris gently. 60

"I—" said Helene, and she pushed on the imaginary bottle again. "I just don't know how to begin," she said.

There was heavy clumping on the library stairs. It sounded like a deep-sea diver coming upstairs in his lead shoes. It was Harry Nash, turning himself into Marlon Brando. In he came, practically dragging his knuckles on the floor. And he was so much in character that the sight of a weeping woman made him sneer.

"Harry," I said, "I'd like you to meet Helene Shaw. Helene—this is Harry Nash. If you get the part of Stella, he'll be your husband in the play." Harry didn't offer to shake hands. He put his hands in his pockets, and he hunched over, and he looked her up and down, gave her looks that left her naked. Her tears stopped right then and there.

"I wonder if you two would play the fight scene," I said, "and then the reunion scene right after it."

"Sure," said Harry, his eyes still on her. Those eyes burned up clothes 65
faster than she could put them on. "Sure," he said, "if Stell's game."

"What?" said Helene. She'd turned the color of cranberry juice.

"Stell—Stella," said Harry. "That's you. Stell's my wife."

I handed the two of them playbooks. Harry snatched his from me without a word of thanks. Helene's hands weren't working very well, and I had to kind of mold them around the book.

"I'll want something I can throw," said Harry.

"What?" I said. 70

"There's one place where I throw a radio out a window," said Harry. "What can I throw?"

So I said an iron paperweight was the radio, and I opened the window wide. Helene Shaw looked scared to death.

"Where you want us to start?" said Harry, and he rolled his shoulders like a prizefighter warming up.

"Start a few lines back from where you throw the radio out the window," I said.

"O.K., O.K.," said Harry, warming up, warming up. He scanned the 75
stage directions. "Let's see," he said, "after I throw the radio, she runs off stage, and I chase her, and I sock her one."

"Right," I said.

"O.K., baby," Harry said to Helene, his eyelids drooping. What was about to happen was wilder than the chariot race in *Ben Hur.* "On your mark," said Harry. "Get ready, baby. Go!"

When the scene was over, Helene Shaw was as hot as a hod carrier, as limp as an eel. She sat down with her mouth open and her head hanging to one side. She wasn't in any bottle any more. There wasn't any bottle to hold her up and keep her safe and clean. The bottle was gone.

"Do I get the part or don't I?" Harry snarled at me.

"You'll do," I said. 80

"You said a mouthful!" he said. "I'll be going now. . . . See you around, Stella," he said to Helene, and he left. He slammed the door behind him.

"Helene?" I said. "Miss Shaw?"

"Mf?" she said.

"The part of Stella is yours," I said. "You were great!"

"I was?" she said. 85

"I had no idea you had that much fire in you, dear," Doris said to her.

"Fire?" said Helene. She didn't know if she was afoot or on horseback.

"Skyrockets! Pinwheels! Roman candles!" said Doris.

"Mf," said Helene. And that was all she said. She looked as though she were going to sit in the chair with her mouth open forever.

"Stella," I said.

"Huh?" she said.

"You have my permission to go."

So we started having rehearsals four nights a week on the stage of the Consolidated School. And Harry and Helene set such a pace that everybody in the production was half crazy with excitement and exhaustion before we'd rehearsed four times. Usually a director has to beg people to learn their lines, but I had no such trouble. Harry and Helene were working so well together that everybody else in the cast regarded it as a duty and an honor and a pleasure to support them.

I was certainly lucky—or thought I was. Things were going so well, so hot and heavy, so early in the game that I had to say to Harry and Helene after one love scene, "Hold a little something back for the actual performance, would you please? You'll burn yourselves out."

I said that at the fourth or fifth rehearsal, and Lydia Miller, who was playing Blanche, the faded sister, was sitting next to me in the audience. In real life, she's the wife of Verne Miller. Verne owns Miller's Hardware Store. Verne was Harry's boss.

"Lydia," I said to her, "have we got a play or have we got a play?"

"Yes," she said, "you've got a play, all right." She made it sound as though I'd committed some kind of crime, done something just terrible. "You should be very proud of yourself."

"What do you mean by that?" I said.

Before Lydia could answer, Harry yelled at me from the stage, asked if I was through with him, asked if he could go home. I told him he could and, still Marlon Brando, he left, kicking furniture out of his way and slamming doors. Helene was left all alone on the stage, sitting on a couch with the same gaga look she'd had after the tryouts. That girl was drained.

I turned to Lydia again and I said, "Well—until now, I thought I had every reason to be happy and proud. Is there something going on I don't know about?"

"Do you know that girl's in love with Harry?" said Lydia.

"In the play?" I said.

"What play?" said Lydia. "There isn't any play going on now, and look at her up there." She gave a sad cackle. "You aren't directing this play."

"Who is?" I said.

"Mother Nature at her worst," said Lydia. "And think what it's going to do to that girl when she discovers what Harry really is." She corrected herself. "What Harry really isn't," she said.

I didn't do anything about it, because I didn't figure it was any of my business. I heard Lydia try to do something about it, but she didn't get very far.

"You know," Lydia said to Helene one night, "I once played Ann Rutledge, and Harry was Abraham Lincoln."

Helene clapped her hands. "That must have been heaven!" she said.

"It was, in a way," said Lydia. "Sometimes I'd get so worked up, I'd love Harry the way I'd love Abraham Lincoln. I'd have to come back to earth and remind myself that he wasn't ever going to free the slaves, that he was just a clerk in my husband's hardware store."

"He's the most marvelous man I ever met," said Helene.

"Of course, one thing you have to get set for, when you're in a play with Harry," said Lydia, "is what happens after the last performance."

"What are you talking about?" said Helene.

"Once the show's over," said Lydia, "whatever you thought Harry was just evaporates into thin air."

"I don't believe it," said Helene.

"I admit it's hard to believe," said Lydia. 115

Then Helene got a little sore. "Anyway, why tell me about it?" she said. "Even if it is true, what do I care?"

"I—I don't know," said Lydia, backing away. "I—I just thought you might find it interesting."

"Well, I don't," said Helene.

And Lydia slunk away, feeling about as frowzy and unloved as she was supposed to feel in the play. After that nobody said anything more to Helene to warn her about Harry, not even when word got around that she'd told the telephone company that she didn't want to be moved around anymore, that she wanted to stay in North Crawford.

So the time finally came to put on the play. We ran it for three nights— 120
Thursday, Friday, and Saturday—and we murdered those audiences. They believed every word that was said on stage, and when the maroon curtain came down they were ready to go to the nut house along with Blanche, the faded sister.

On Thursday night the other girls at the telephone company sent Helene a dozen red roses. When Helene and Harry were taking a curtain call together, I passed the roses over the footlights to her. She came forward for them, took one rose from the bouquet to give to Harry. But when she turned to give Harry the rose in front of everybody, Harry was gone. The curtain came down on that extra little scene—that girl offering a rose to nothing and nobody.

I went backstage, and I found her still holding that one rose. She'd put the rest of the bouquet aside. There were tears in her eyes. "What did I do wrong?" she said to me. "Did I insult him some way?"

"No," I said. "He always does that after a performance. The minute it's over, he clears out as fast as he can."

"And tomorrow he'll disappear again?"

"Without even taking off his makeup." 125

"And Saturday?" she said. "He'll stay for the cast party on Saturday, won't he?"

"Harry never goes to parties," I said. "When the curtain comes down on Saturday, that's the last anybody will see of him till he goes to work on Monday."

"How sad," she said.

Helene's performance on Friday night wasn't nearly so good as Thursday's. She seemed to be thinking about other things. She watched Harry take off after curtain call. She didn't say a word.

On Saturday she put on the best performance yet. Ordinarily it was 130
Harry who set the pace. But on Saturday Harry had to work to keep up with Helene.

When the curtain came down on the final curtain call, Harry wanted to get away, but he couldn't. Helene wouldn't let go his hand. The rest of the cast and the stage crew and a lot of well-wishers from the audience were all standing around Harry and Helene, and Harry was trying to get his hand back.

"Well," he said, "I've got to go."

"Where?" she said.

"Oh," he said, "home."

"Won't you please take me to the cast party?" she said. 135

He got very red. "I'm afraid I'm not much on parties," he said. All the Marlon Brando in him was gone. He was tongue-tied, he was scared, he was shy—he was everything Harry was famous for being between plays.

"All right," she said. "I'll let you go—if you promise me one thing."

"What's that?" he said, and I thought he would jump out a window if she let go of him then.

"I want you to promise to stay here until I get you your present," she said.

"Present?" he said, getting even more panicky. 140

"Promise?" she said.

He promised. It was the only way he could get his hand back. And he stood there miserably while Helene went down to the ladies' dressing room for the present. While he waited, a lot of people congratulated him on being such a fine actor. But congratulations never made him happy. He just wanted to get away.

Helene came back with the present. It turned out to be a little blue book with a big red ribbon for a place marker. It was a copy of *Romeo and Juliet.* Harry was very embarrassed. It was all he could do to say "Thank you."

"The marker marks my favorite scene," said Helene.

"Um," said Harry. 145

"Don't you want to see what my favorite scene is?" she said.

So Harry had to open the book to the red ribbon.

Helene got close to him, and read a line of Juliet's. " 'How cam'st thou hither, tell me, and wherefore?' " she read. " 'The orchard walls are high and hard to climb, and the place death, considering who thou art, if any of my kinsmen find thee here.' " She pointed to the next line. "Now, look what Romeo says," she said.

"Um," said Harry.

"Read what Romeo says," said Helene. 150

Harry cleared his throat. He didn't want to read the line, but he had to. " 'With love's light wings did I o'erperch these walls,' " he read out loud in his everyday voice. But then a change came over him. " 'For stony limits cannot hold love out,' " he read, and he straightened up, and eight years dropped away from him, and he was brave and gay. " 'And what love can do, that dares love attempt,' " he read, " 'therefore thy kinsmen are no let to me.' "

" 'If they do see thee they will murther thee,' " said Helene, and she started him walking toward the wings.

" 'Alack!' " said Harry, " 'there lies more peril in thine eye than twenty of their swords.' " Helene led him toward the backstage exit. " 'Look thou but sweet,' " said Harry, " 'and I am proof against their enmity.' "

" 'I would not for the world they saw thee here,' " said Helene, and that was the last we heard. The two of them were out the door and gone.

They never did show up at the cast party. One week later they were 155
married.

They seem very happy, although they're kind of strange from time to time, depending on which play they're reading to each other at the time.

I dropped into the phone company office the other day, on account of the billing machine was making dumb mistakes again. I asked her what plays she and Harry'd been reading lately.

"In the past week," she said, "I've been married to Othello, been loved by Faust and been kidnaped by Paris. Wouldn't you say I was the luckiest girl in town?"

I said I thought so, and I told her most of the women in town thought so too.

"They had their chance," she said.

"Most of 'em couldn't stand the excitement," I said. And I told her I'd been asked to direct another play. I asked if she and Harry would be available for the cast. She gave me a big smile and said, "Who are we this time?"

Analyzing the Text

1. What circumstances bring Helene Shaw and Harry Nash together, and what effect does this have on each of their lives? What is different about Helene from any of the other women with whom Harry has acted on stage?
2. What might you conclude about the motives of the narrator (the stage manager) in getting Helene and Harry together, and what sense do you get of what these productions mean to the community?

Understanding Vonnegut's Techniques

1. What function does the play within a play have in allowing Harry to release a suppressed side of his personality?
2. What details does Vonnegut use to create the contrast between the everyday lives of Helene and Harry and who they become on stage?

Arguing for an Interpretation

1. In your opinion, why does Vonnegut use Tennesse Williams's play "A Streetcar Named Desire" as the catalyst that might transform Harry and Helene? Is the fact that they fall in love any less authentic because it has been set up and manipulated by the stage manager and Helene herself?
2. Discuss the paradox of being free to be yourself when you are being someone else. Would you say Helene and Harry are hiding behind the roles of Stella and Stanley, or that these roles permit them to be their real selves? Is Vonnegut making the case for the transforming power of great literature in the lives of ordinary people (in this case, a clerk at a hardware store and a telephone company employee)?

Sembene Ousmane

Sembene Ousmane was born in Senegal, North Africa, in 1923. Essentially self-educated, he became a fisherman like his father, then moved to Dakar until the outbreak of World War II when he was drafted into the French Army and saw action in Italy and Germany. After the war, he went to Marseille where he worked as a docker, joined the French Communist party, and became a union orga-

nizer. After his fourth novel, Ousmane studied at the Moscow Film School and wrote and directed several films including The Money Order, *which won a prize at the Venice Film Festival.* Zala, *based on his 1973 novel, went on to become one of a series of successful films that established his reputation as a director. Ousmane's novel, a massive two-volume work,* Le Dernier de l'empire, *was published in 1981. In 1992, he wrote* Niiwam and Taaw. *"Her Three Days," translated by Len Ortzen, is taken from Ousmane's 1974 collection of short stories,* Tribal Scars. *In this compassionate and realistic account of the plight of a third wife waiting for her husband to return, Ousmane dramatizes the customs governing Muslim life in Mali under which every wife of a Muslim is entitled to three days of her husband's company each month.*

Her Three Days

She raised her haggard face, and her far-away look ranged beyond the muddle of roofs, some tiled, others of thatch or galvanized-iron; the wide fronds of the twin coconut-palms were swaying slowly in the breeze, and in her mind she could hear their faint rustling. Noumbe was thinking of "her three days." Three days for her alone, when she would have her husband Mustapha to herself . . . It was a long time since she had felt such emotion. To have Mustapha! The thought comforted her. She had heart trouble and still felt some pain, but she had been dosing herself for the past two days, taking more medicine than was prescribed. It was a nice syrup that just slipped down, and she felt the beneficial effects at once. She blinked; her eyes were like two worn buttonholes, with lashes that were like frayed thread, in little clusters of fives and threes; the whites were the colour of old ivory.

"What's the matter, Noumbe?" asked Aida, her next-door neighbour, who was sitting at the door of her room.

"Nothing," she answered, and went on cutting up the slice of raw meat, helped by her youngest daughter.

"Ah, it's your three days," exclaimed Aida, whose words held a meaning that she could not elaborate on while the little girl was present. She went on: "You're looking fine enough to prevent a holy man from saying his prayers properly!"

"Aida, be careful what you say," she protested, a little annoyed. 5

But it was true; Noumbe had plaited her hair and put henna on her hands and feet. And that morning she had got the children up early to give her room a thorough clean. She was not old, but one pregnancy after another—and she had five children—and her heart trouble had aged her before her time.

"Go and ask Laity to give you five francs' worth of salt and twenty francs' worth of oil," Noumbe said to the girl. "Tell him I sent you. I'll pay for them as soon as your father is here, at midday." She looked disapprovingly at the cut-up meat in the bottom of the bowl.

The child went off with the empty bottle and Noumbe got to her feet. She was thin and of average height. She went into her one-room shack, which was sparsely furnished; there was a bed with a white cover, and in one corner stood a table with pieces of china on display. The walls were covered with enlargements and photos of friends and strangers framed in passe-partout.

When she came out again she took the Moorish stove and set about lighting it.

Her daughter had returned from her errand.

"He gave them to you?" asked Noumbe.

"Yes, mother."

A woman came across the compound to her. "Noumbe, I can see that you're preparing a delicious dish."

"Yes," she replied. "It's my three days. I want to revive the feasts of the old days, so that his palate will retain the taste of the dish for many moons, and he'll forget the cooking of his other wives."

"Ah-ha! So that his palate is eager for dishes to come," said the woman, who was having a good look at the ingredients.

"I'm feeling in good form," said Noumbe, with some pride in her voice. She grasped the woman's hand and passed it over her loins.

"*Thieh, souya dome!* I hope you can say the same tomorrow morning . . ."

The woman clapped her hands; as if it were a signal or an invitation, other women came across, one with a metal jar, another with a saucepan, which they beat while the woman sang:

> *Sope dousa rafetail,*
> *Sopa nala dousa rafetail*
> *Sa yahi n'diguela.*
> (Worship of you is not for your beauty,
> I worship you not for your beauty
> But for your backbone.)

In a few moments, they improvised a wild dance to this chorus. At the end, panting and perspiring, they burst out laughing. Then one of them stepped into Noumbe's room and called the others.

"Let's take away the bed! Because tonight they'll wreck it!"

"She's right. Tomorrow this room will be . . ."

Each woman contributed an earthy comment which set them all laughing hilariously. Then they remembered they had work to do, and brought their amusement to an end; each went back to her family occupations.

Noumbe had joined in the laughter; she knew this boisterous "ragging" was the custom in the compound. No one escaped it. Besides, she was an exceptional case, as they all knew. She had a heart condition and her husband had quite openly neglected her. Mustapha had not been to see her for a fortnight. All this time she had been hoping that he would come, if only for a moment. When she went to the clinic for mothers and children she compelled her youngest daughter to stay at home, so that—thus did her mind work—if her husband turned up the child could detain him until she returned. She ought to have gone to the clinic again this day, but she had spent what little money she possessed on preparing for Mustapha. She did not want her husband to esteem her less than his other wives, or to think her meaner. She did not neglect her duty as a mother, but her wifely duty came first—at certain times.

She imagined what the next three days would be like; already her "three days" filled her whole horizon. She forgot her illness and her baby's ailments. She had thought about these three days in a thousand different ways. Mustapha would not leave before the Monday morning. In her mind she could see Mustapha and his henchmen crowding into her room, and could hear their suggestive jokes. "If she had been a perfect wife . . ." She laughed to herself. "Why shouldn't it always be like that for every woman—to have a husband of one's own?" She wondered why not.

The morning passed at its usual pace, the shadows of the coconut-palms and the people growing steadily shorter. As midday approached, the housewives busied themselves with the meal. In the compound each one stood near her door, ready to welcome her man. The kids were playing around, and their mothers' calls to them crossed in the air. Noumbe gave her children a quick meal and sent them out again. She sat waiting for Mustapha to arrive at any moment . . . he wouldn't be much longer now.

An hour passed, and the men began going back to work. Soon the compound was empty of the male element; the women, after a long siesta, joined one another under the coconut-palms and the sounds of their gossiping gradually increased.

Noumbe, weary of waiting, had finally given up keeping a lookout. Dressed in her mauve velvet, she had been on the watch since before midday. She had eaten no solid food, consoling herself with the thought that Mustapha would appear at any moment. Now she fought back the pangs of hunger by telling herself that in the past Mustapha had a habit of arriving late. In those days, this lateness was pleasant. Without admitting it to herself, those moments (which had hung terribly heavy) had been very sweet; they prolonged the sensual pleasure of anticipation. Although those minutes had been sometimes shot through with doubts and fears (often, very often, the thought of her coming disgrace had assailed her; for Mustapha, who had taken two wives before her, had just married another), they had not been too hard to bear. She realized that those demanding minutes were the price she had to pay for Mustapha's presence. Then she began to reckon up the score, in small ways, against the *veudieux,* the other wives. One washed his *boubous*[1] when it was another wife's turn, or kept him long into the night; another sometimes held him in her embrace a whole day, knowing quite well that she was preventing Mustapha from carrying out his marital duty elsewhere.

She sulked as she waited; Mustapha had not been near her for a fortnight. All these bitter thoughts brought her up against reality: four months ago Mustapha had married a younger woman. This sudden realization of the facts sent a pain to her heart, a pain of anguish. The additional pain did not prevent her heart from functioning normally, rather was it like a sick person whose sleep banishes pain but who once awake again finds his suffering is as bad as ever, and pays for the relief by a redoubling of pain.

She took three spoonfuls of her medicine instead of the two prescribed, and felt a little better in herself.

She called her youngest daughter. "Tell Mactar I want him."

---

[1]*boubous*: a body-length embroidered gown.

The girl ran off and soon returned with her eldest brother.

"Go and fetch your father," Noumbe told him.

"Where, mother?"

"Where? Oh, on the main square or at one of your other mothers'."

"But I've been to the main square already, and he wasn't there." 35

"Well, go and have another look. Perhaps he's there now."

The boy looked up at his mother, then dropped his head again and reluctantly turned to go.

"When your father has finished eating, I'll give you what's left. It's meat. Now be quick, Mactar."

It was scorching hot and the clouds were riding high. Mactar was back after an hour. He had not found his father. Noumbe went and joined the group of women. They were chattering about this and that; one of them asked (just for the sake of asking), "Noumbe, has your uncle (darling) arrived?" "Not yet," she replied, then hastened to add, "Oh, he won't be long now. He knows it's my three days." She deliberately changed the conversation in order to avoid a long discussion about the other three wives. But all the time she was longing to go and find Mustapha. She was being robbed of her three days. And the other wives knew it. Her hours alone with Mustapha were being snatched from her. The thought of his being with one of the other wives, who was feeding him and opening his waistcloth when she ought to be doing all that, who was enjoying those hours which were hers by right, so numbed Noumbe that it was impossible for her to react. The idea that Mustapha might have been admitted to hospital or taken to a police station never entered her head.

40 She knew how to make tasty little dishes for Mustapha which cost him nothing. She never asked him for money. Indeed, hadn't she got herself into debt so that he would be more comfortable and have better meals at her place? And in the past, when Mustapha sometimes arrived unexpectedly—this was soon after he had married her—hadn't she hastened to make succulent dishes for him? All her friends knew this.

A comforting thought coursed through her and sent these aggressive and vindictive reflections to sleep. She told herself that Mustapha was bound to come to her this evening. The certainty of his presence stripped her mind of the too cruel thought that the time of her disfavour was approaching; this thought had been as much a burden to her as a heavy weight dragging a drowning man to the bottom. When all the bad, unfavourable thoughts besetting her had been dispersed, like piles of rubbish on waste land swept by a flood, the future seemed brighter, and she joined in the conversation of the women with childish enthusiasm, unable to hide her pleasure and her hopes. It was like something in a parcel; questioning eyes wondered what was inside, but she alone knew and enjoyed the secret, drawing an agreeable strength from it. She took an active part in the talking and brought her wit into play. All this vivacity sprang from the joyful conviction that Mustapha would arrive this evening very hungry and be hers alone.

In the far distance, high above the tree-tops, a long trail of dark-grey clouds tinged with red was hiding the sun. The time for the *tacousane,* the afternoon prayer, was drawing near. One by one, the women withdrew to their rooms, and the shadows of the trees grew longer, wider and darker.

Night fell; a dark, starry night.

Noumbe cooked some rice for the children. They clamoured in vain for some of the meat. Noumbe was stern and unyielding: "The meat is for your father. He didn't eat at midday." When she had fed the children, she washed herself again to get rid of the smell of cooking and touched up her toilette, rubbing oil on her hands, feet and legs to make the henna more brilliant. She intended to remain by her door, and sat down on the bench; the incense smelt strongly, filling the whole room. She was facing the entrance to the compound and could see the other women's husbands coming in.

But for her there was no one.

She began to feel tired again. Her heart was troubling her, and she had a fit of coughing. Her inside seemed to be on fire. Knowing that she would not be going to the dispensary during her "three days," in order to economize, she went and got some wood-ash which she mixed with water and drank. It did not taste very nice, but it would make the medicine last longer, and the drink checked and soothed the burning within her for a while. She was tormenting herself with the thoughts passing through her mind. Where can he be? With the first wife? No, she's quite old. The second then? Everyone knew that she was out of favour with Mustapha. The third wife was herself. So he must be with the fourth. There were puckers of uncertainty and doubt in the answers she gave herself. She kept putting back the time to go to bed, like a lover who does not give up waiting when the time of the rendezvous is long past, but with an absurd and stupid hope waits still longer, self-torture and the heavy minutes chaining him to the spot. At each step Noumbe took, she stopped and mentally explored the town, prying into each house inhabited by one of the other wives. Eventually she went indoors.

So that she would not be caught unawares by Mustapha nor lose the advantages which her make-up and good clothes gave her, she lay down on the bed fully dressed and alert. She had turned down the lamp as far as possible, so the room was dimly lit. But she fell asleep despite exerting great strength of mind to remain awake and saying repeatedly to herself, "I shall wait for him." To make sure that she would be standing there expectantly when he crossed the threshold, she had bolted the door. Thus she would be the devoted wife, always ready to serve her husband, having got up at once and appearing as elegant as if it were broad daylight. She had even thought of making a gesture as she stood there, of passing her hands casually over her hips so that Mustapha would hear the clinking of the beads she had strung round her waist and be incited to look at her from head to foot.

Morning came, but there was no Mustapha.

When the children awoke they asked if their father had come. The oldest of them, Mactar, a promising lad, was quick to spot that his mother had not made the bed, that the bowl containing the stew was still in the same place, by a dish of rice, and the loaf of bread on the table was untouched. The children got a taste of their mother's anger. The youngest, Amadou, took a long time over dressing. Noumbe hurried them up and sent the youngest girl to Laity's to buy five francs' worth of ground coffee. The children's breakfast was warmed-up rice with a meagre sprinkling of gravy from the previous day's stew. Then she gave them their wings, as the saying goes, letting them all out except the youngest daughter. Noumbe inspected the bottle of medicine and saw that she had taken a lot of it; there were only three spoonfuls left. She gave herself half a spoonful and made up for the rest with her mixture of ashes and water. After that she felt calmer.

"Why, Noumbe, you must have got up bright and early this morning, to 50
be so dressed up. Are you going off on a long journey?"

It was Aida, her next-door neighbour, who was surprised to see her dressed in such a manner, especially for a woman who was having "her three days." Then Aida realized what had happened and tried to rectify her mistake.

"Oh, I see he hasn't come yet. They're all the same, these men!"

"He'll be here this morning, Aida." Noumbe bridled, ready to defend her man. But it was rather her own worth she was defending, wanting to conceal what an awful time she had spent. It had been a broken night's sleep, listening to harmless sounds which she had taken for Mustapha's footsteps, and this had left its mark on her already haggard face.

"I'm sure he will! I'm sure he will!" exclaimed Aida, well aware of this comedy that all the women played in turn.

"Mustapha is such a kind man, and so noble in his attitude," added an- 55
other woman, rubbing it in.

"If he weren't, he wouldn't be my master," said Noumbe, feeling flattered by this description of Mustapha.

The news soon spread round the compound that Mustapha had slept elsewhere during Noumbe's three days. The other women pitied her. It was against all the rules for Mustapha to spend a night elsewhere. Polygamy had its laws, which should be respected. A sense of decency and common dignity restrained a wife from keeping the husband day and night when his whole person and everything connected with him belonged to another wife during "her three days." The game, however, was not without its underhand tricks that one wife played on another; for instance, to wear out the man and hand him over when he was incapable of performing his conjugal duties. When women criticized the practice of polygamy they always found that the wives were to blame, especially those who openly dared to play a dirty trick. The man was whitewashed. He was a weakling who always ended by falling into the enticing traps set for him by woman. Satisfied with this conclusion, Noumbe's neighbours made common cause with her and turned to abusing Mustapha's fourth wife.

Noumbe made some coffee—she never had any herself, because of her heart. She consoled herself with the thought that Mustapha would find more things at her place. The bread had gone stale; she would buy some more when he arrived.

The hours dragged by again, long hours of waiting which became harder to bear as the day progressed. She wished she knew where he was . . . The thought obsessed her, and her eyes became glazed and searching. Every time she heard a man's voice she straightened up quickly. Her heart was paining her more and more, but the physical pain was separate from the mental one; they never came together, alternating in a way that reminded her of the acrobatic feat of a man riding two speeding horses.

At about four o'clock Noumbe was surprised to see Mustapha's sec- 60
ond wife appear at the door. She had come to see if Mustapha was there, knowing that it was Noumbe's three days. She did not tell Noumbe the reason for her wishing to see Mustapha, despite being pressed. So Noumbe

concluded that it was largely due to jealousy, and was pleased that the other wife could see how clean and tidy her room was, and what a display of fine things she had, all of which could hardly fail to make the other think that Mustapha had been (and still was) very generous to her, Noumbe. During the rambling conversation her heart thumped ominously, but she bore up and held off taking any medicine.

Noumbe remembered only too well that when she was newly married she had usurped the second wife's three days. At that time she had been the youngest wife. Mustapha had not let a day pass without coming to see her. Although not completely certain, she believed she had conceived her third child during this wife's three days. The latter's presence now and remarks that she let drop made Noumbe realize that she was no longer the favourite. This revelation, and the polite, amiable tone and her visitor's eagerness to inquire after her children's health and her own, to praise her superior choice of household utensils, her taste in clothes, the cleanliness of the room and the lingering fragrance of the incense, all this was like a stab in cold blood, a cruel reminder of the perfidy of words and the hypocrisy of rivals; and all part of the world of women. This observation did not get her anywhere, except to arouse a desire to escape from the circle of polygamy and to cause her to ask herself—it was a moment of mental aberration really—"Why do we allow ourselves to be men's playthings?"

The other wife complimented her and insisted that Noumbe's children should go and spend a few days with her own children (in this she was sincere). By accepting in principle, Noumbe was weaving her own waist-cloth of hypocrisy. It was all to make the most of herself, to set tongues wagging so that she would lose none of her respectability and rank. The other wife casually added—before she forgot, as she said—that she wanted to see Mustapha, and if mischief-makers told Noumbe that "their" husband had been to see her during Noumbe's three days, Noumbe shouldn't think ill of her, and she would rather have seen him here to tell him what she had to say. To save face, Noumbe dared not ask her when she had last seen Mustapha. The other would have replied with a smile, "The last morning of my three days, of course. I've only come here because it's urgent." And Noumbe would have looked embarrassed and put on an air of innocence. "No, that isn't what I meant. I just wondered if you had happened to meet him by chance."

Neither of them would have lost face. It was all that remained to them. They were not lying, to their way of thinking. Each had been desired and spoilt for a time; then the man, like a gorged vulture, had left them on one side and the venom of chagrin at having been mere playthings had entered their hearts. They quite understood, it was all quite clear to them, that they could sink no lower; so they clung to what was left to them, that is to say, to saving what dignity remained to them by false words and gaining advantages at the expense of the other. They did not indulge in this game for the sake of it. This falseness contained all that remained of the flame of dignity. No one was taken in, certainly not themselves. Each knew that the other was lying, but neither could bring herself to further humiliation, for it would be the final crushing blow.

The other wife left. Noumbe almost propelled her to the door, then stood there thoughtful for a few moments. Noumbe understood the reason for the other's visit. She had come to get her own back. Noumbe felt absolutely sure that Mustapha was with his latest wife. The visit meant in fact: "You stole those days from me because I am older than you. Now a younger woman than you is avenging me. Try as you might to make everything nice and pleasant for him, you have to toe the line with the rest of us now, you old carcass. He's slept with someone else—and he will again."

The second day passed like the first, but was more dreadful. She ate no proper food, just enough to stave off the pangs of hunger.

It was Sunday morning and all the men were at home; they nosed about in one room and another, some of them cradling their youngest in their arms, others playing with the older children. The draught-players had gathered in one place, the card-players in another. There was a friendly atmosphere in the compound, with bursts of happy laughter and sounds of guttural voices, while the women busied themselves with the housework.

Aida went to see Noumbe to console her, and said without much conviction, "He'll probably come today. Men always seem to have something to do at the last minute. It's Sunday today, so he'll be here."

"Aida, Mustapha doesn't work," Noumbe pointed out, hard-eyed. She gave a cough. "I've been waiting for him now for two days and nights! When it's my three days I think the least he could do is to be here—at night, anyway. I might die . . ."

"Do you want me to go and look for him?"

"No."

She had thought "yes." It was the way in which Aida had made the offer that embarrassed her. Of course she would like her to! Last night, when everyone had gone to bed, she had started out and covered quite some distance before turning back. The flame of her dignity had been fanned on the way. She did not want to abase herself still further by going to claim a man who seemed to have no desire to see her. She had lain awake until dawn, thinking it all over and telling herself that her marriage to Mustapha was at an end, that she would divorce him. But this morning there was a tiny flicker of hope in her heart: "Mustapha will come, all the same. This is my last night."

She borrowed a thousand francs from Aida, who readily lent her the money. And she followed the advice to send the children off again, to Mustapha's fourth wife.

"Tell him that I must see him at once, I'm not well!"

She hurried off to the little market near by and bought a chicken and several other things. Her eyes were feverishly, joyfully bright as she carefully added seasoning to the dish she prepared. The appetizing smell of her cooking was wafted out to the compound and its Sunday atmosphere. She swept the room again, shut the door and windows, but the heady scent of the incense escaped through the cracks between the planks.

The children returned from their errand.

"Is he ill?" she asked them.

"No, mother. He's going to come. We found him with some of his friends at Voulimata's (the fourth wife). He asked about you."

"And that's all he said?"

"Yes, mother."

"Don't come indoors. Here's ten francs. Go and play somewhere else."

A delicious warm feeling spread over her. "He was going to come." Ever since Friday she had been harbouring spiteful words to throw in his face. He would beat her, of course . . . But never mind. Now she found it would be useless to utter those words. Instead she would do everything possible to make up for the lost days. She was happy, much too happy to bear a grudge against him, now that she knew he was coming—he might even be on the way with his henchmen. The only means of getting her own back was to cook a big meal . . . then he would stay in bed.

She finished preparing the meal, had a bath and went on to the rest of her toilette. She did her hair again, put antimony on her lower lip, eyebrows and lashes, then dressed in a white starched blouse and a hand-woven waist-cloth, and inspected her hands and feet. She was quite satisfied with her appearance.

But the waiting became prolonged.

No one in the compound spoke to her for fear of hurting her feelings. She had sat down outside the door, facing the entrance to the compound, and the other inhabitants avoided meeting her sorrowful gaze. Her tears overflowed the brim of her eyes like a swollen river its banks; she tried to hold them back, but in vain. She was eating her heart out.

The sound of a distant tom-tom was being carried on the wind. Time passed over her, like the seasons over monuments. Twilight came and darkness fell.

On the table were three plates in a row, one for each day.

"I've come to keep you company," declared Aida as she entered the room. Noumbe was sitting on the foot of the bed—she had fled from the silence of the others. "You mustn't get worked up about it," went on Aida. "Every woman goes through it. Of course it's not nice! But I don't think he'll be long now."

Noumbe raised a moist face and bit her lips nervously. Aida saw that she had made up her mind not to say anything.

Everything was shrouded in darkness; no light came from her room. After supper, the children had refrained from playing their noisy games.

Just when adults were beginning to feel sleepy and going to bed, into the compound walked Mustapha, escorted by two of his lieutenants. He was clad entirely in white. He greeted the people still about in an oily manner, then invited his companions into Noumbe's hut.

She had not stirred.

"Wife, where's the lamp?"

"Where you left it this morning when you went out."

"How are you?" inquired Mustapha when he had lit the lamp. He went and sat down on the bed, and motioned to the two men to take the bench.

"God be praised," Noumbe replied to his polite inquiry. Her thin face seemed relaxed and the angry lines had disappeared.

"And the children?"

"They're well, praise be to God."

"Our wife isn't very talkative this evening," put in one of the men.

"I'm quite well, though."

"Your heart isn't playing you up now?" asked Mustapha, not unkindly.

"No, it's quite steady," she answered.

"God be praised! Mustapha, we'll be off," said the man, uncomfortable at Noumbe's cold manner.

"Wait," said Mustapha, and turned to Noumbe. "Wife, are we eating tonight or tomorrow?"

"Did you leave me something when you went out this morning?"

"What? That's not the way to answer." 105

"No, uncle (darling). I'm just asking . . . Isn't it right?"

Mustapha realized that Noumbe was mocking him and trying to humiliate him in front of his men.

"You do like your little joke. Don't you know it's your three days?"

"Oh, uncle, I'm sorry, I'd quite forgotten. What an unworthy wife I am!" she exclaimed, looking straight at Mustapha.

"You're making fun of me!" 110

"Oh, uncle, I shouldn't dare! What, I? And who would help me into Paradise, if not my worthy husband? Oh, I would never poke fun at you, neither in this world nor the next."

"Anyone would think so."

"Who?" she asked.

"You might have stood up when I came in, to begin with . . ."

"Oh, uncle, forgive me. I'm out of my mind with joy at seeing you 115
again. But whose fault is that, uncle?"

"And just what are these three plates for?" said Mustapha with annoyance.

"These three plates?" She looked at him, a malicious smile on her lips. "Nothing. Or rather, my three days. Nothing that would interest you. Is there anything here that interests you . . . uncle?"

As if moved by a common impulse, the three men stood up.

Noumbe deliberately knocked over one of the plates. "Oh, uncle, forgive me . . ." Then she broke the other two plates. Her eyes had gone red; suddenly a pain stabbed at her heart, she bent double, and as she fell to the floor gave a loud groan which roused the whole compound.

Some women came hurrying in. "What's the matter with her?" 120

"Nothing . . . only her heart. Look what she's done, the silly woman. One of these days her jealousy will suffocate her. I haven't been to see her—only two days, and she cries her eyes out. Give her some ash and she'll be all right," gabbled Mustapha, and went off.

"Now these hussies have got their associations, they think they're going to run the country," said one of his men.

"Have you heard that at Bamako they passed a resolution condemning polygamy?" added the other. "Heaven preserve us from having only one wife."

"They can go out to work then," pronounced Mustapha as he left the compound.

Aida and some of the women lifted Noumbe on to the bed. She was 125
groaning. They got her to take some of her mixture of ash and water . . .

Analyzing the Text

1. How is the story shaped as an exploration of the importance that having "her three days" with her husband has for Noumbe?
2. What changes can you observe in Noumbe's character between the beginning of the story and its conclusion? What does she do or say that implies she is not the same person as she was at the beginning?

Understanding Ousmane's Techniques

1. How do Ousmane's descriptions of the preparations Noumbe makes provide important insights into what Mustapha's visit means to her?

2. How do the details Ousmane provides about Noumbe's memories of how she acted when she was the new wife add an ironic dimension to the story?

Arguing for an Interpretation

1. What elements in Ousmane's portrayal suggest that he wishes his audience to both pity and admire Noumbe in her role as third wife? Explain your answer.
2. What means does Ousmane use to make you sympathetic to the plight of the main character? In your opinion, is the story constructed as a vehicle for social criticism of polygamy in Mali? Explain your answer.

MARGARET ATWOOD

Margaret Atwood was born in Ottawa, Ontario, in 1939. She was educated at the University of Toronto, where she came under the influence of the critic Northrup Frye, whose theories of mythical modes in literature she has adapted to her own purposes in her prolific writing of poetry, novels, and short stories. She is the author of more than 20 volumes of poetry and fiction, including The Handmaid's Tale *(1986), which was made into a film in 1989. Her short story collections include* Bluebeard's Egg and Other Stories *(1986). She also edited the* Oxford Book of Canadian Short Stories in English *(1987). Her most recent works include* Alias Grace: A Novel *(1996),* A Quiet Game *(1997),* Two Solitudes *(1998),* Blind Assassin *(2001), and* Negotiating with the Dead: A Writer on Writing *(2002). "Happy Endings," a gleeful dissection of narrative mutations, first appeared in* Ms. *magazine, February 1983.*

Happy Endings

John and Mary meet.
What happens next?
If you want a happy ending, try A.

A. John and Mary fall in love and get married. They both have worthwhile and remunerative jobs which they find stimulating and challenging. They buy a charming house. Real estate values go up. Eventually, when they can afford live-in help, they have two children, to whom they are devoted. The children turn out well. John and Mary have a stimulating and challenging sex life and worthwhile friends. They go on fun vacations together. They retire. They both have hobbies which they find stimulating and challenging. Eventually they die. This is the end of the story.

B. Mary falls in love with John but John doesn't fall in love with Mary. He merely uses her body for selfish pleasure and ego gratification of a tepid kind. He comes to her apartment twice a week and she cooks him dinner, you'll notice that he doesn't even consider her worth the price of a dinner out, and after he's eaten the dinner he fucks her and after that he falls asleep, while she does the dishes so he won't think she's untidy, having all those dirty dishes lying around, and puts on fresh lipstick so she'll look good when he wakes up, but when he wakes up he doesn't even notice, he puts on his socks and his shorts and his pants and his shirt and his tie and his shoes, the reverse order from the one in which he took them off. He doesn't take off Mary's clothes, she takes them off herself, she acts as if she's dying for it every time, not because she likes sex exactly, she doesn't, but she wants John to think she does because if they do it often enough surely he'll get used to her, he'll come to depend on her and they will get married, but John goes out the door with hardly so much as a good-night and three days later he turns up at six o'clock and they do the whole thing over again.

Mary gets run-down. Crying is bad for your face, everyone knows that and so does Mary but she can't stop. People at work notice. Her friends tell her John is a rat, a pig, a dog, he isn't good enough for her, but she can't believe it. Inside John, she thinks, is another John, who is much nicer. This other John will emerge like a butterfly from a cocoon, a Jack from a box, a pit from a prune, if the first John is only squeezed enough.

One evening John complains about the food. He has never complained about the food before. Mary is hurt.

Her friends tell her they've seen him in a restaurant with another woman, whose name is Madge. It's not even Madge that finally gets to Mary: it's the restaurant. John has never taken Mary to a restaurant. Mary collects all the sleeping pills and aspirins she can find, and takes them and a half a bottle of sherry. You can see what kind of a woman she is by the fact that it's not even whiskey. She leaves a note for John. She hopes he'll discover her and get her to the hospital in time and repent and then they can get married, but this fails to happen and she dies.

John marries Madge and everything continues as in A.

C. John, who is an older man, falls in love with Mary, and Mary, who is only twenty-two, feels sorry for him because he's worried about his hair falling out. She sleeps with him even though she's not in love with him. She met him at work. She's in love with someone called James, who is twenty-two also and not yet ready to settle down.

John on the contrary settled down long ago: this is what is bothering him. John has a steady, respectable job and is getting ahead in his field, but Mary isn't impressed by him, she's impressed by James, who has a motorcycle and a fabulous record collection. But James is often away on his motorcycle, being free. Freedom isn't the same for girls, so in the meantime Mary spends Thursday evenings with John. Thursdays are the only days John can get away.

John is married to a woman called Madge and they have two children, a charming house which they bought just before the real estate values went up, and hobbies which they find stimulating and challenging, when they have the time. John tells Mary how important she is to him, but of course he can't leave his wife because a commitment is a commitment. He goes on about this more than is necessary and Mary finds it boring, but older men can keep it up longer so on the whole she has a fairly good time.

One day James breezes in on his motorcycle with some top-grade California hybrid and James and Mary get higher than you'd believe possible and they climb into bed. Everything becomes very underwater, but along comes John, who has a key to Mary's apartment. He finds them stoned and entwined. He's hardly in any position to be jealous, considering Madge, but nevertheless he's overcome with despair. Finally he's middle-aged, in two years he'll be bald as an egg and he can't stand it. He purchases a handgun, saying he needs it for target practice—this is the thin part of the plot, but it can be dealt with later—and shoots the two of them and himself.

Madge, after a suitable period of mourning, marries an understanding man called Fred and everything continues as in A, but under different names.

D. Fred and Madge have no problems. They get along exceptionally well and are good at working out any little difficulties that may arise. But their charming house is by the seashore and one day a giant tidal wave approaches. Real estate values go down. The rest of the story is about what caused the tidal wave and how they escape from it. They do, though thousands drown, but Fred and Madge are virtuous and lucky. Finally on high ground they clasp each other, wet and dripping and grateful, and continue as in A.

E. Yes, but Fred has a bad heart. The rest of the story is about how kind and understanding they both are until Fred dies. Then Madge devotes herself to charity work until the end of A. If you like, it can be "Madge," "cancer," "guilty and confused," and "bird watching."

F. If you think this is all too bourgeois, make John a revolutionary and Mary a counterespionage agent and see how far that gets you. Remember, this is Canada. You'll still end up with A, though in between you may get a lustful brawling saga of passionate involvement, a chronicle of our times, sort of.

You'll have to face it, the endings are the same however you slice it. Don't be deluded by any other endings, they're all fake, either deliberately fake, with malicious intent to deceive, or just motivated by excessive optimism if not by downright sentimentality.

The only authentic ending is the one provided here:

John and Mary die. John and Mary die. John and Mary die.

So much for endings. Beginnings are always more fun. True connoisseurs, however, are known to favor the stretch in between, since it's the hardest to do anything with.

That's about all that can be said for plots, which anyway are just one 5
thing after another, a what and a what and a what.

Now try How and Why.

Analyzing the Text

1. How does Choice A illustrate the conventional happy ending? What variations does Atwood describe, using characters with the same names, in Choice B and Choice C? What point does Atwood make when she gets to Choice D with Fred and Madge?
2. According to Atwood, in what way is showing the "why" and "how" of a story much more difficult and challenging for a writer than simply stating "what" happens?

Understanding Atwood's Techniques

1. How is John's behavior related to each woman's view of herself in the various scenarios in which he appears?
2. What elements in this story suggest that Atwood is satirizing the kind of literary talks given before book clubs in Canada? What ironic comments does Atwood make about the contrast between the kinds of books written about Canadian life and real life in Canada?
3. How does the language Atwood uses in describing Choice B differ from the language she uses in Choice A? What explains this difference?

Arguing for an Interpretation

1. What is it that people really want when they say they want a happy ending? What does Atwood say is important to her as a novelist, above and beyond simply providing a happy ending? How does she dramatize the shallowness of the conventional happy ending?
2. What is Atwood's point in using the same character names for all her different permutations? Was this confusing? Would it have been better if she had made up different names for each scenario? Why or why not?

James Joyce

James Joyce (1882–1941) was born in Dublin and received a rigorous classical education at Jesuit schools, including University College, Dublin. He left Ireland in 1902 and spent the rest of his life in Switzerland and France. Although he first studied medicine, he dropped out to write poetry, which was eventually published in 1907 as Chamber Music. *Joyce earned a living by teaching in a Berlitz Language School and developed a unique literary style first evident in* Dubliners, *a collection of short stories (1914) that included "Eveline," reprinted below. Many of these stories are drawn from Joyce's experiences, as is his first novel,* A Portrait of the Artist as a Young Man, *published in 1916.* Ulysses *(1922) is one of the most innovative literary works of the century, and interweaves an account of a modern-day*

Dubliner, Leopold Bloom, with stories drawn from Homer's Odyssey *and the ancient Greek world. Joyce's use of the stream-of-consciousness technique makes the reader feel part of the character's thoughts in a way traditional narrative usually does not. Joyce's last work was* Finnegan's Wake *(1939), a monumental, perplexing work involving all of human history and language. In "Eveline," we can see Joyce's careful preparation for the moment of revelation, or epiphany, through which his characters gain sudden insight into their own lives.*

Eveline

She sat at the window watching the evening invade the avenue. Her head was leaned against the window curtains and in her nostrils was the odor of dusty cretonne. She was tired.

Few people passed. The man out of the last house passed on his way home; she heard his footsteps clacking along the concrete pavement and afterwards crunching on the cinder path before the new red houses. One time there used to be a field there in which they used to play every evening with other people's children. Then a man from Belfast bought the field and built houses in it—not like their little brown houses but bright brick houses with shining roofs. The children of the avenue used to play together in that field—the Devines, the Waters, the Dunns, little Keogh the cripple, she and her brothers and sisters. Ernest, however, never played: he was too grown up. Her father used often to hunt them in out of the field with his blackthorn stick; but usually little Keogh used to keep *nix* and call out when he saw her father coming. Still they seemed to have been rather happy then. Her father was not so bad then; and besides, her mother was alive. That was a long time ago; she and her brothers and sisters were all grown up; her mother was dead. Tizzie Dunn was dead, too, and the Waters had gone back to England. Everything changes. Now she was going to go away like the others, to leave her home.

Home! She looked round the room, reviewing all its familiar objects which she had dusted once a week for so many years, wondering where on earth all the dust came from. Perhaps she would never see again those familiar objects from which she had never dreamed of being divided. And yet during all those years she had never found out the name of the priest whose yellowing photograph hung on the wall above the broken harmonium beside the colored print of the promises made to Blessed Margaret Mary Alacoque. He had been a school friend of her father. Whenever he showed the photograph to a visitor her father used to pass it with a casual word:

—He is in Melbourne now.

5 She had consented to go away, to leave her home. Was that wise? She tried to weigh each side of the question. In her home anyway she had shelter and food; she had those whom she had known all her life about her. Of course she had to work hard both in the house and at business. What would they say of her in the Stores when they found out that she had run away with a fellow? Say she was a fool, perhaps; and her place would be

filled up by advertisement. Miss Gavan would be glad. She had always had an edge on her, especially whenever there were people listening.

—Miss Hill, don't you see these ladies are waiting?

—Look lively, Miss Hill, please.

She would not cry many tears at leaving the Stores.

But in her new home, in a distant unknown country, it would not be like that. Then she would be married—she, Eveline. People would treat her with respect then. She would not be treated as her mother had been. Even now, though she was over nineteen, she sometimes felt herself in danger of her father's violence. She knew it was that that had given her the palpitations. When they were growing up he had never gone for her, like he used to go for Harry and Ernest, because she was a girl; but latterly he had begun to threaten her and say what he would do to her only for her dead mother's sake. And now she had nobody to protect her. Ernest was dead and Harry, who was in the church decorating business, was nearly always down somewhere in the country. Besides, the invariable squabble for money on Saturday nights had begun to weary her unspeakably. She always gave her entire wages—seven shillings—and Harry always sent up what he could but the trouble was to get any money from her father. He said she used to squander the money, that she had no head, that he wasn't going to give her his hard-earned money to throw about the streets, and much more, for he was usually fairly bad of a Saturday night. In the end he would give her the money and ask her had she any intention of buying Sunday's dinner. Then she had to rush out as quickly as she could and do her marketing, holding her black leather purse tightly in her hand as she elbowed her way through the crowds and returning home late under her load of provisions. She had hard work to keep the house together and to see that the two young children who had been left to her charge went to school regularly and got their meals regularly. It was hard work—a hard life—but now that she was about to leave it she did not find it a wholly undesirable life.

She was about to explore another life with Frank. Frank was very kind, 10
manly, open-hearted. She was to go away with him by the night-boat to be his wife and to live with him in Buenos Aires where he had a home waiting for her. How well she remembered the first time she had seen him; he was lodging in a house on the main road where she used to visit. It seemed a few weeks ago. He was standing at the gate, his peaked cap pushed back on his head and his hair tumbled forward over a face of bronze. Then they had come to know each other. He used to meet her outside the Stores every evening and see her home. He took her to see *The Bohemian Girl* and she felt elated as she sat in an unaccustomed part of the theater with him. He was awfully fond of music and sang a little. People knew that they were courting and, when he sang about the lass that loves a sailor, she always felt pleasantly confused. He used to call her Poppens out of fun. First of all it had been an excitement for her to have a fellow and then she had begun to like him. He had tales of distant countries. He had started as a deck boy at a pound a month on a ship of the Allan Line going out to Canada. He told her the names of the ships he had been on and the names of the different services. He had sailed through the Straits of Magellan and he told her stories of the terrible Patagonians. He had fallen on his feet in Buenos Aires, he said, and had come over to the old country just for a holi-

day. Of course, her father had found out the affair and had forbidden her to have anything to say to him.

—I know these sailor chaps, he said.

One day he had quarreled with Frank and after that she had to meet her lover secretly.

The evening deepened in the avenue. The white of two letters in her lap grew indistinct. One was to Harry; the other was to her father. Ernest had been her favorite but she liked Harry too. Her father was becoming old lately, she noticed; he would miss her. Sometimes he could be very nice. Not long before, when she had been laid up for a day, he had read her out a ghost story and made toast for her at the fire. Another day, when their mother was alive, they had all gone for a picnic to the Hill of Howth. She remembered her father putting on her mother's bonnet to make the children laugh.

Her time was running out but she continued to sit by the window, leaning her head against the window curtain, inhaling the odor of dusty cretonne. Down far in the avenue she could hear a street organ playing. She knew the air. Strange that it should come that very night to remind her of the promise to her mother, her promise to keep the home together as long as she could. She remembered the last night of her mother's illness; she was again in the close dark room at the other side of the hall and outside she heard a melancholy air of Italy. The organ-player had been ordered to go away and given sixpence. She remembered her father strutting back into the sickroom saying:

—Damned Italians! coming over here! 15

As she mused the pitiful vision of her mother's life laid its spell on the very quick of her being—that life of commonplace sacrifices closing in final craziness. She trembled as she heard again her mother's voice saying constantly with foolish insistence:

—Derevaun Seraun! Derevaun Seraun!°

She stood up in a sudden impulse of terror. Escape! She must escape! Frank would save her. He would give her life, perhaps love, too. But she wanted to live. Why should she be unhappy? She had a right to happiness. Frank would take her in his arms, fold her in his arms. He would save her.

She stood among the swaying crowd in the station at the North Wall. He held her hand and she knew that he was speaking to her, saying something about the passage over and over again. The station was full of soldiers with brown baggages. Through the wide doors of the sheds she caught a glimpse of the black mass of the boat, lying in beside the quay wall, with illumined portholes. She answered nothing. She felt her cheek pale and cold and, out of a maze of distress, she prayed to God to direct her, to show her what was her duty. The boat blew a long mournful whistle into the mist. If she went, tomorrow she would be on the sea with Frank, steaming toward Buenos Aires. Their passage had been booked. Could she still draw back after all he had done for her? Her distress awoke a nausea in her body and she kept moving her lips in silent fervent prayer.

A bell clanged upon her heart. She felt him seize her hand: 20

—Come!

All the seas of the world tumbled about her heart. He was drawing her into them: he would drown her. She gripped with both hands at the iron railing.

Derevaun Seraun!: "The end of pleasure is pain!" (Gaelic).

—Come!

No! No! No! It was impossible. Her hands clutched the iron in frenzy. Amid the seas she sent a cry of anguish!

—Eveline! Evvy!

He rushed beyond the barrier and called to her to follow. He was shouted at to go on but he still called to her. She set her white face to him, passive, like a helpless animal. Her eyes gave him no sign of love or farewell or recognition.

Analyzing the Text

1. Why is Eveline's father antagonistic to the idea of her seeing Frank? How does the thought of her mother make Eveline want to leave?
2. How would you characterize Eveline's expectations about Frank before she meets him at the dock?

Understanding Joyce's Techniques

1. Strangely enough, Joyce does not actually describe Eveline. Why do you think he does this, and how do you imagine she appears?
2. What role do the multiple water images play in the final paragraphs of this story in communicating Eveline's emotions? Did it lessen the shock of her choice? Why or why not?

Arguing for an Interpretation

1. Write two paragraphs explaining, in your opinion, why Eveline did not go with Frank to Buenos Aires. Why do you think Joyce chose this particular city instead of one in Europe?
2. How do you imagine Eveline's life would turn out many years after this event?

Ernest Hemingway

Ernest Hemingway (1899–1961) was born in Oak Park, Illinois, to a middle-class family. His father, a doctor, took him on hunting and fishing trips, which formed the basis for many of his short stories that appeared in **In Our Time** ***(1925). He worked for the*** **Kansas City Star** ***as a reporter and developed a distinct clipped, terse style, which became his hallmark. After graduating from high school in 1918, he volunteered as an ambulance driver in World War I, served with distinction, and was seriously wounded on the Italian Front. Over his lifetime, he covered many wars, including the Civil War in Spain in 1937, reflected in*** **For Whom the Bell Tolls** ***(1940). Hemingway lived in Paris and was considered part of the "Lost Generation" along with Gertrude Stein, Ezra Pound, Sherwood Anderson, and F. Scott Fitzgerald. The success of his novels*** **The Sun Also Rises** ***(reflecting his absorption with bull fighting, 1926) and*** **A Farewell to Arms** ***(1929) brought him fame and fortune. Throughout his***

life, he was an active sportsman (he was an amateur boxer in his youth) and his pursuit of big-game hunting and deep-sea fishing are reflected in his works The Green Hills of Africa *(1935) and* The Old Man and the Sea *(1952), which led to his winning both the Nobel Prize for Literature and the Pulitzer Prize in 1954. Many of his novels and stories have been made into popular films. Hemingway's literary style has had an inestimable influence on succeeding generations of writers. He suffered from cancer, and in 1961 took his own life with a shotgun at his Idaho hunting lodge. The story "Hills Like White Elephants" first appeared in his collection of short stories,* Men Without Women *(1927), and exhibits his spare ascetic style and uncanny gift for dialogue.*

Hills Like White Elephants

The hills across the valley of the Ebro were long and white. On this side there was no shade and no trees and the station was between two lines of rails in the sun. Close against the side of the station there was the warm shadow of the building and a curtain, made of strings of bamboo beads, hung across the open door into the bar, to keep out flies. The American and the girl with him sat at a table in the shade, outside the building. It was very hot and the express from Barcelona would come in forty minutes. It stopped at this junction for two minutes and went on to Madrid.

"What should we drink?" the girl asked. She had taken off her hat and put it on the table.

"It's pretty hot," the man said.

"Let's drink beer."

"Dos cervezas," the man said into the curtain. 5

"Big ones?" a woman asked from the doorway.

"Yes. Two big ones."

The woman brought two glasses of beer and two felt pads. She put the felt pads and the beer glasses on the table and looked at the man and the girl. The girl was looking off at the line of hills. They were white in the sun and the country was brown and dry.

"They look like white elephants," she said.

"I've never seen one," the man drank his beer. 10

"No, you wouldn't have."

"I might have," the man said. "Just because you say I wouldn't have doesn't prove anything."

The girl looked at the bead curtain. "They've painted something on it," she said. "What does it say?"

"Anis del Toro. It's a drink,"

"Could we try it?" 15

The man called "Listen" through the curtain. The woman came out from the bar.

"Four reales."

"We want two Anis del Toro."

"With water?"

"Do you want it with water?"

"I don't know," the girl said. "Is it good with water?"

"It's all right."

"You want them with water?" asked the woman.

"Yes, with water."

"It tastes like licorice," the girl said and put the glass down.

"That's the way with everything."

"Yes," said the girl. "Everything tastes of licorice. Especially all the things you've waited so long for, like absinthe."

"Oh, cut it out."

"You started it," the girl said. "I was being amused. I was having a fine time."

"Well, let's try and have a fine time."

"All right. I was trying. I said the mountains looked like white elephants. Wasn't that bright?"

"That was bright."

"I wanted to try this new drink: That's all we do, isn't it—look at things and try new drinks?"

"I guess so."

The girl looked across at the hills.

"They're lovely hills," she said. "They don't really look like white elephants. I just meant the coloring of their skin through the trees."

"Should we have another drink?"

"All right."

The warm wind blew the bead curtain against the table.

"The beer's nice and cool," the man said.

"It's lovely," the girl said.

"It's really an awfully simple operation, Jig," the man said. "It's not really an operation at all."

The girl looked at the ground the table legs rested on.

"I know you wouldn't mind it, Jig. It's really not anything. It's just to let the air in."

The girl did not say anything.

"I'll go with you and I'll stay with you all the time. They just let the air in and then it's all perfectly natural."

"Then what will we do afterward?"

"We'll be fine afterward. Just like we were before."

"What makes you think so?"

"That's the only thing that bothers us. It's the only thing that's made us unhappy."

The girl looked at the bead curtain, put her hand out, and took hold of two of the strings of beads.

"And you think then we'll be all right and be happy."

"I know we will. You don't have to be afraid. I've known lots of people that have done it."

"So have I," said the girl. "And afterward they were all so happy."

"Well," the man said, "if you don't want to you don't have to. I wouldn't have you do it if you didn't want to. But I know it's perfectly simple."

"And you really want to?"

"I think it's the best thing to do. But I don't want you to do it if you don't really want to."

"And if I do it you'll be happy and things will be like they were and you'll love me?"

"I love you now. You know I love you."

"I know. But if I do it, then it will be nice again if I say things are like white elephants, and you'll like it?"

"I'll love it. I love it now but I just can't think about it. You know how I get when I worry."

"If I do it you won't ever worry?"

"I won't worry about that because it's perfectly simple."

"Then I'll do it. Because I don't care about me."

"What do you mean?"

"I don't care about me."

"Well, I care about you."

"Oh, yes. But I don't care about me. And I'll do it and then everything will be fine."

"I don't want you to do it if you feel that way."

The girl stood up and walked to the end of the station. Across, on the other side, were fields of grain and trees along the banks of the Ebro. Far away, beyond the river, were mountains. The shadow of a cloud moved across the field of grain and she saw the river through the trees.

"And we could have all this," she said. "And we could have everything and every day we make it more impossible."

"What did you say?"

"I said we could have everything."

"We can have everything."

"No, we can't."

"We can have the whole world."

"No, we can't."

"We can go everywhere."

"No, we can't. It isn't ours any more."

"It's ours."

"No, it isn't. And once they take it away, you never get it back."

"But they haven't taken it away."

"We'll wait and see."

"Come on back in the shade," he said. "You mustn't feel that way."

"I don't feel any way," the girl said. "I just know things."

"I don't want you to do anything that you don't want to do—"

"Nor that isn't good for me," she said. "I know. Could we have another beer?"

"All right. But you've got to realize—"

"I realize," the girl said. "Can't we maybe stop talking?"

They sat down at the table and the girl looked across at the hills on the dry side of the valley and the man looked at her and at the table.

"You've got to realize," he said, "that I don't want you to do it if you don't want to. I'm perfectly willing to go through with it if it means anything to you."

"Doesn't it mean anything to you? We could get along."

"Of course it does. But I don't want anybody but you. I don't want any one else. And I know it's perfectly simple."

"Yes, you know it's perfectly simple."

"It's all right for you to say that, but I do know it."

"Would you do something for me now?"

"I'd do anything for you."

"Would you please please please please please please please stop talking?"

He did not say anything but looked at the bags against the wall of the station. There were labels on them from all the hotels where they had spent nights.

"But I don't want you to," he said, "I don't care anything about it."

"I'll scream," the girl said.

The woman came out through the curtains with two glasses of beer and put them down on the damp felt pads. "The train comes in five minutes," she said.

"What did she say?" asked the girl.

"That the train is coming in five minutes."

The girl smiled brightly at the woman, to thank her.

"I'd better take the bags over to the other side of the station," the man said. She smiled at him.

"All right. Then come back and we'll finish the beer."

He picked up the two heavy bags and carried them around the station to the other tracks. He looked up the tracks but could not see the train. Coming back, he walked through the barroom, where people waiting for the train were drinking. He drank an Anis at the bar and looked at the people. They were all waiting reasonably for the train. He went out through the bead curtain. She was sitting at the table and smiled at him.

"Do you feel better?" he asked.

"I feel fine," she said. "There's nothing wrong with me. I feel fine."

Analyzing the Text

1. What clues suggest that the characters whom Hemingway refers to as "the American and the girl" are at an important turning point in their relationship, that coincides with having to change trains on the way to Madrid?
2. The American and the girl have completely opposite views on the question whether or not the girl, whose name is Jig, should have the "operation." What might the "operation" be, and what does it mean to each of them?

Understanding Hemingway's Techniques

1. In common speech, the phrase "white elephant" connotes something not needed, a luxury; on the other hand, a "white elephant" would be a truly unique creature. How does Hemingway draw on these opposite connotations to underscore how each character reacts to the surrounding scenery? In what ways might the title also subtly suggest pregnancy?
2. How does Hemingway use the contrast between the common beverage, beer, and an uncommon drink ("Anis del Toro") to further define the preferences of the two characters and what each wants from life?

Arguing for an Interpretation

1. Nowhere in the story does Hemingway explicitly mention that the American and the girl might be discussing an abortion he wishes her to have. In an essay, make a case either for or against this interpretation, tak-

ing into account as many specific clues as possible. How does the couple's relationship change as a result of the conversation we hear? For example, what is the significance of the American stopping in the barroom to have an "Anis del Toro" when two beers are waiting for him back at the table? What might Hemingway mean to suggest by emphasizing the weight of the bags ("two heavy bags") that the man carries at the end of the story?

2. Choose any of the details in the story and follow them through from the beginning, such as the baggage and the meaning of the hills being compared to white elephants, or the fruitfulness and sterility of the landscape on different sides of the station, as linked with the choice to be made. Why does the girl want her companion to simply be quiet after she has agreed to his request, and why does he keep talking? Explain your answer.

Robert Fox

Robert Fox was born in 1943 in Brooklyn, New York. He received his B.A. from Brooklyn College in 1967 and an M.A. from Ohio University in 1970, where he also taught English. For the last 30 years, Fox has lived in Columbus, Ohio, where he has served on the Ohio Arts Council as the literature program coordinator, and as poet-in-residence. His works include two novels, TLAR *(1987) and* CODPOL *(1987), and a blues CD titled* Primary Blues *(1994). His unusual style of short fiction is modeled on the work of William Saroyan, Isaac Babel, and Jorge Luis Borges. "A Fable" originally appeared in the Midwestern University Quarterly (1966, No. 3) and was later published in* Sudden Fiction: American Short-Short Stories *(1986).*

In this story, Fox creates a simple, yet profound, parable about what makes people happy and what they expect from life.

A Fable

The young man was clean shaven and neatly dressed. It was early Monday morning and he got on the subway. It was the first day of his first job and he was slightly nervous; he didn't know exactly what his job would be. Otherwise he felt fine. He loved everybody he saw. He loved everybody on the street and everybody disappearing into the subway, and he loved the world because it was a fine clear day and he was starting his first job.

Without kicking anybody, the young man was able to find a seat on the Manhattan-bound train. The car filled quickly and he looked up at the people standing over him envying his seat. Among them were a mother and daughter who were going shopping. The daughter was a beautiful girl with blond hair and soft-looking skin, and he was immediately attracted to her.

"He's staring at you," the mother whispered to the daughter.

"Yes, Mother, I feel so uncomfortable. What shall I *do?*"

"He's in love with you." 5

"In love with me? How can you tell?"

"Because I'm your mother."

"But what shall I do?"

"Nothing. He'll try to talk to you. If he does, answer him. Be nice to him. He's only a boy."

The train reached the business district and many people got off. The girl and her mother found seats opposite the young man. He continued to look at the girl who occasionally looked to see if he was looking at her.

The young man found a good pretext for standing in giving his seat to an elderly man. He stood over the girl and her mother. They whispered back and forth and looked up at him. At another stop the seat next to the girl was vacated, and the young man blushed but quickly took it.

"I knew it," the mother said between her teeth. "I knew it, I *knew* it."

The young man cleared his throat and tapped the girl. She jumped.

"Pardon me," he said. "You're a very pretty girl."

"Thank you," she said.

"Don't talk to him," her mother said. "Don't answer him. I'm warning you. Believe me."

"I'm in love with you," he said to the girl.

"I don't believe you," the girl said.

"Don't answer him," the mother said.

"I really do," he said. "In fact, I'm so much in love with you that I want to marry you."

"Do you have a job?" she said.

"Yes, today is my first day. I'm going to Manhattan to start my first day of work."

"What kind of work will you do?" she asked.

"I don't know exactly," he said. "You see, I didn't start yet."

"It sounds exciting," she said.

"It's my first job, but I'll have my own desk and handle a lot of papers and carry them around in a briefcase, and it will pay well, and I'll work my way up."

"I love you," she said.

"Will you marry me?"

"I don't know. You'll have to ask my mother."

The young man rose from his seat and stood before the girl's mother. He cleared his throat very carefully for a long time. "May I have the honor of having your daughter's hand in marriage?" he said, but he was drowned out by the subway noise.

The mother looked up at him and said, "What?" He couldn't hear her either, but he could tell by the movement of her lips and by the way her face wrinkled up that she said, What.

The train pulled to a stop.

"May I have the honor of having your daughter's hand in marriage!" he shouted, not realizing there was no subway noise. Everybody on the train looked at him, smiled, and then they all applauded.

"Are you crazy?" the mother asked.

The train started again.

"What?" he said.

"Why do you want to marry her?" she asked.

"Well, she's pretty—I mean, I'm in love with her."

"Is that all?"

"I guess so," he said. "Is there supposed to be more?"

"No. Not usually," the mother said. "Are you working?"

"Yes. As a matter of fact, that's why I'm going into Manhattan so early. Today is the first day of my first job."

"Congratulations," the mother said.

"Thanks," he said. "Can I marry your daughter?"

"Do you have a car?" she asked.

"Not yet," he said. "But I should be able to get one pretty soon. And a house, too."

"A house?"

"With lots of rooms."

"Yes, that's what I expected you to say," she said. She turned to her daughter. "Do you love him?"

"Yes, Mother, I do."

"Why?"

"Because he's good, and gentle, and kind."

"Are you sure?"

"Yes."

"Then you really love him."

"Yes."

"Are you sure there isn't anyone else that you might love and might want to marry?"

"No, Mother," the girl said.

"Well, then," the mother said to the young man. "Looks like there's nothing I can do about it. Ask her again."

The train stopped.

"My dearest one," he said, "will you marry me?"

"Yes," she said.

Everybody in the car smiled and applauded.

"Isn't life wonderful?" the boy asked the mother.

"Beautiful," the mother said.

The conductor climbed down from between the cars as the train started up and, straightening his dark tie, approached them with a solemn black book in his hand.

Analyzing the Text

1. What elements in this story emphasize that it is structured as an encounter between what is real and what would be desirable if it were possible?
2. In what sense does the mother serve an important role as the foil or counterpoint to the young man's quest to marry the daughter?

Understanding Fox's Techniques

1. What elements of this short work of fiction make it a fable, as opposed to just a short-short story?
2. What role does the setting on a subway and the short period of time in which these life-altering events occur play in the overall effect of the story?

Arguing for an Interpretation

1. Did you find the story involving and compelling, or was it so unrealistic that you could not empathize with the characters? Explain your answer.

Which details make the characterizations of the young man, the girl, and her mother believable despite the surrealistic premise?

2. Do the values the story dramatizes involve a compromise between romance and pragmatism? What if this wasn't the first day of his job? Is it more about society's expectations and less about romance, and if so, why?

CHARLOTTE PERKINS GILMAN

Charlotte Perkins Gilman (1860–1935) was born in Hartford, Connecticut, into a family that, despite their poverty, made every attempt to give her the advantages of an education. She married an artist, Charles Stetson, in 1884, and after the birth of their daughter the following year, she suffered a nervous breakdown. Her struggle with depression brought her to the attention of an eminent neurologist, whose prescription for a "rest cure" had disastrous consequences (parallel to those experienced by the narrator in "The Yellow Wallpaper"). In later life, she became an advocate for social and political reform. Her book Women and Economics *(1898) anticipated the work of such feminists as Simone de Beauvoir, a half-century later. She promoted her views through public lectures and in her magazine,* The Forerunner, *which she edited from 1909 to 1916.*

The Yellow Wallpaper

It is very seldom that mere ordinary people like John and myself secure ancestral halls for the summer.

A colonial mansion, a hereditary estate, I would say a haunted house and reach the height of romantic felicity—but that would be asking too much of fate!

Still I will proudly declare that there is something queer about it.

Else, why should it be let so cheaply? And why have stood so long untenanted?

John laughs at me, of course, but one expects that. 5

John is practical in the extreme. He has no patience with faith, an intense horror of superstition, and he scoffs openly at any talk of things not to be felt and seen and put down in figures.

John is a physician, and *perhaps*—(I would not say it to a living soul, of course, but this is dead paper and a great relief to my mind)—*perhaps* that is one reason I do not get well faster.

You see, he does not believe I am sick! And what can one do?

If a physician of high standing, and one's own husband, assures friends and relatives that there is really nothing the matter with one but temporary nervous depression—a slight hysterical tendency—what is one to do?

My brother is also a physician, and also of high standing, and he says the same thing. 10

So I take phosphates or phosphites—whichever it is—and tonics, and air and exercise, and journeys, and am absolutely forbidden to "work" until I am well again.

Personally, I disagree with their ideas.

Personally, I believe that congenial work, with excitement and change, would do me good.

But what is one to do?

I did write for a while in spite of them; but it *does* exhaust me a good deal—having to be so sly about it, or else meet with heavy opposition. 15

I sometimes fancy that in my condition, if I had less opposition and more society and stimulus—but John says the very worst thing I can do is to think about my condition, and I confess it always makes me feel bad.

So I will let it alone and talk about the house.

The most beautiful place! It is quite alone, standing well back from the road, quite three miles from the village. It makes me think of English places that you read about, for there are hedges and walls and gates that lock, and lots of separate little houses for the gardeners and people.

There is a *delicious* garden! I never saw such a garden—large and shady, full of box-bordered paths, and lined with long grape-covered arbors with seats under them.

There were greenhouses, too, but they are all broken now. 20

There was some legal trouble, I believe, something about the heirs and co-heirs; anyhow, the place has been empty for years.

That spoils my ghostliness, I am afraid, but I don't care—there is something strange about the house—I can feel it.

I even said so to John one moonlight evening, but he said what I felt was a draught, and shut the window.

I get unreasonably angry with John sometimes. I'm sure I never used to be so sensitive. I think it is due to this nervous condition.

But John says if I feel so I shall neglect proper self-control; so I take pains to control myself—before him at least, and that makes me very tired. 25

I don't like our room a bit. I wanted one downstairs that opened on the piazza and had roses all over the window, and such pretty old-fashioned chintz hangings! But John would not hear of it.

He said there was only one window and not room for two beds, and no near room for him if he took another.

He is very careful and loving, and hardly lets me stir without special direction.

I have a schedule prescription for each hour in the day; he takes all care from me, and so I feel basely ungrateful not to value it more.

He said he came here solely on my account, that I was to have perfect rest and all the air I could get. "Your exercise depends on your strength, my dear," said he, "and your food somewhat on your appetite; but air you can absorb all the time." So we took the nursery at the top of the house. 30

It is a big, airy room, the whole floor nearly, with windows that look all ways, and air and sunshine galore. It was nursery first and then playroom and gymnasium, I should judge; for the windows are barred for little children, and there are rings and things in the walls.

The paint and paper look as if a boys' school had used it. It is stripped off—the paper—in great patches all around the head of my bed, about as far as I can reach, and in a great place on the other side of the room low down. I never saw a worse paper in my life. One of those sprawling flamboyant patterns committing every artistic sin.

It is dull enough to confuse the eye in following, pronounced enough to constantly irritate and provoke study, and when you follow the lame uncertain curves for a little distance they suddenly commit suicide—plunge off at outrageous angles, destroy themselves in unheard-of contradictions.

The color is repellent, almost revolting: a smouldering unclean yellow, strangely faded by the slow-turning sunlight. It is a dull yet lurid orange in some places, a sickly sulphur tint in others.

No wonder the children hated it! I should hate it myself if I had to live in this room long.

There comes John, and I must put this away—he hates to have me write a word.

We have been here two weeks, and I haven't felt like writing before, since that first day.

I am sitting by the window now, up in this atrocious nursery, and there is nothing to hinder my writing as much as I please, save lack of strength.

John is away all day, and even some nights when his cases are serious.

I am glad my case is not serious!

But these nervous troubles are dreadfully depressing.

John does not know how much I really suffer. He knows there is no reason to suffer, and that satisfies him.

Of course it is only nervousness. It does weigh on me so not to do my duty in any way!

I meant to be such a help to John, such a real rest and comfort, and here I am a comparative burden already!

Nobody would believe what an effort it is to do what little I am able—to dress and entertain, and order things.

It is fortunate Mary is so good with the baby. Such a dear baby!

And yet I *cannot* be with him, it makes me so nervous.

I suppose John never was nervous in his life. He laughs at me so about this wallpaper!

At first he meant to repaper the room, but afterward he said that I was letting it get the better of me, and that nothing was worse for a nervous patient than to give way to such fancies.

He said that after the wallpaper was changed it would be the heavy bedstead, and then the barred windows, and then that gate at the head of the stairs, and so on.

"You know the place is doing you good," he said, "and really, dear, I don't care to renovate the house just for a three months' rental."

"Then do let us go downstairs," I said. "There are such pretty rooms there."

Then he took me in his arms and called me a blessed little goose, and said he would go down cellar, if I wished, and have it whitewashed into the bargain.

But he is right enough about the beds and windows and things.

It is as airy and comfortable room as any one need wish, and, of course, I would not be so silly as to make him uncomfortable just for a whim.

I'm really getting quite fond of the big room, all but that horrid paper.

Out of one window I can see the garden—those mysterious deep-shaded arbors, the riotous old-fashioned flowers, and bushes and gnarly trees.

Out of another I get a lovely view of the bay and a little private wharf belonging to the estate. There is a beautiful shaded lane that runs down there from the house. I always fancy I see people walking in these numerous paths and arbors, but John has cautioned me not to give way to fancy in the least. He says that with my imaginative power and habit of story-making, a nervous weakness like mine is sure to lead to all manner of excited fancies, and that I ought to use my will and good sense to check the tendency. So I try.

I think sometimes that if I were only well enough to write a little it would relieve the press of ideas and rest me.

But I find I get pretty tired when I try. 60

It is so discouraging not to have any advice and companionship about my work. When I get really well, John says we will ask Cousin Henry and Julia down for a long visit; but he says he would as soon put fireworks in my pillow-case as to let me have those stimulating people about now.

I wish I could get well faster.

But I must not think about that. This paper looks to me as if it *knew* what a vicious influence it had!

There is a recurrent spot where the pattern lolls like a broken neck and two bulbous eyes stare at you upside down.

I get positively angry with the impertinence of it and the everlasting- 65
ness. Up and down and sideways they crawl, and those absurd unblinking eyes are everywhere. There is one place where two breadths didn't match, and the eyes go all up and down the line, one a little higher than the other.

I never saw so much expression in an inanimate thing before, and we all know how much expression they have! I used to lie awake as a child and get more entertainment and terror out of blank walls and plain furniture than most children could find in a toy-store.

I remember what a kindly wink the knobs of our big old bureau used to have, and there was one chair that always seemed like a strong friend.

I used to feel that if any of the other things looked too fierce I could always hop into that chair and be safe.

The furniture in this room is no worse than inharmonious, however, for we had to bring it all from downstairs. I suppose when this was used as a playroom they had to take the nursery things out, and no wonder! I never saw such ravages as the children have made here.

The wallpaper, as I said before, is torn off in spots, and it sticketh 70
closer than a brother—they must have had perseverance as well as hatred.

Then the floor is scratched and gouged and splintered, the plaster itself is dug out here and there, and this great heavy bed, which is all we found in the room, looks as if it had been through the wars.

But I don't mind it a bit—only the paper.

There comes John's sister. Such a dear girl as she is, and so careful of me! I must not let her find me writing.

She is a perfect and enthusiastic housekeeper, and hopes for no better profession. I verily believe she thinks it is the writing which made me sick!

But I can write when she is out, and see her a long way off from these 75
windows.

There is one that commands the road, a lovely shaded winding road, and one that just looks off over the country. A lovely country, too, full of great elms and velvet meadows.

This wallpaper has a kind of sub-pattern in a different shade, a particularly irritating one, for you can only see it in certain lights, and not clearly then.

But in the places where it isn't faded and where the sun is just so—I can see a strange, provoking, formless sort of figure that seems to skulk about behind that silly and conspicuous front design.

There's sister on the stairs!

Well, the Fourth of July is over! The people are all gone, and I am tired out. John thought it might do me good to see a little company, so we just had mother and Nellie and the children down for a week.

Of course I didn't do a thing. Jennie sees to everything now.

But it tired me all the same.

John says if I don't pick up faster he shall send me to Weir Mitchell[1] in the fall.

But I don't want to go there at all. I had a friend who was in his hands once, and she says he is just like John and my brother, only more so!

Besides, it is such an undertaking to go so far.

I don't feel as if it was worth while to turn my hand over for anything, and I'm getting dreadfully fretful and querulous.

I cry at nothing, and cry most of the time.

Of course I don't when John is here, or anybody else, but when I am alone.

And I am alone a good deal just now. John is kept in town very often by serious cases, and Jennie is good and lets me alone when I want her to.

So I walk a little in the garden or down that lovely lane, sit on the porch under the roses, and lie down up here a good deal.

I'm getting really fond of the room in spite of the wallpaper. Perhaps *because* of the wallpaper.

It dwells in my mind so!

I lie here on this great immovable bed—it is nailed down, I believe—and follow that pattern about by the hour. It is as good as gymnastics, I assure you. I start, we'll say, at the bottom, down in the corner over there where it has not been touched, and I determine for the thousandth time that I *will* follow that pointless pattern to some sort of a conclusion.

I know a little of the principle of design, and I know this thing was not arranged on any laws of radiation, or alternation, or repetition, or symmetry, or anything else that I ever heard of.

It is repeated, of course, by the breadths, but not otherwise.

Looked at in one way each breadth stands alone; the bloated curves and flourishes—a kind of "debased Romanesque"[2] with delirium tremens go waddling up and down in isolated columns of fatuity.

But, on the other hand, they connect diagonally, and the sprawling outlines run off in great slanting waves of optic horror, like a lot of wallowing sea-weeds in full chase.

The whole thing goes horizontally, too, at least it seems so, and I exhaust myself in trying to distinguish the order of its going in that direction.

---

[1]*Dr. Silas Weir Mitchell:* 19th-century physician known for his treatment of psychosomatic illnesses.

[2]*Romanesque:* a style of art and architecture that prevailed throughout Europe from the mid-11th to the mid-12th centuries and that made use of Roman architectural features such as the rounded arch and the barrel vault.

They have used a horizontal breadth for a frieze, and that adds wonderfully to the confusion.

There is one end of the room where it is almost intact, and there, when the crosslights fade and the low sun shines directly upon it, I can almost fancy radiation after all—the interminable grotesque seems to form around a common center and rush off in headlong plunges of equal distraction.

It makes me tired to follow it. I will take a nap, I guess.

I don't know why I should write this.

I don't want to.

I don't feel able.

And I know John would think it absurd. But I *must* say what I feel and think in some way—it is such a relief!

But the effort is getting to be greater than the relief.

Half the time now I am awfully lazy, and lie down ever so much. John says I mustn't lose my strength, and has me take cod liver oil and lots of tonics and things, to say nothing of ale and wine and rare meat.

Dear John! He loves me very dearly, and hates to have me sick. I tried to have a real earnest reasonable talk with him the other day, and tell him how I wish he would let me go and make a visit to Cousin Henry and Julia.

But he said I wasn't able to go, nor able to stand it after I got there; and I did not make out a very good case for myself, for I was crying before I had finished.

It is getting to be a great effort for me to think straight. Just this nervous weakness, I suppose.

And dear John gathered me up in his arms, and just carried me upstairs and laid me on the bed, and sat by me and read to me till it tired my head.

He said I was his darling and his comfort and all he had, and that I must take care of myself for his sake, and keep well.

He says no one but myself can help me out of it, that I must use my will and self-control and not let any silly fancies run away with me.

There's one comfort—the baby is well and happy, and does not have to occupy this nursery with the horried wallpaper.

If we had not used it, that blessed child would have! What a fortunate escape! Why, I wouldn't have a child of mine, an impressionable little thing, live in such a room for worlds.

I never thought of it before, but it is lucky that John kept me here after all; I can stand it so much easier than a baby, you see.

Of course I never mention it to them any more—I am too wise—but I keep watch for it all the same.

There are things in that paper that nobody knows but me, or ever will.

Behind that outside pattern the dim shapes get clearer every day.

It is always the same shape, only very numerous.

And it is like a woman stooping down and creeping about behind that pattern. I don't like it a bit. I wonder—I begin to think—I wish John would take me away from here!

It is so hard to talk with John about my case, because he is so wise, and because he loves me so.

But I tried it last night.

It was moonlight. The moon shines in all around just as the sun does.

I hate to see it sometimes, it creeps so slowly, and always comes in by one window or another.

John was asleep and I hated to waken him, so I kept still and watched the moonlight on that undulating wallpaper till I felt creepy.

The faint figure behind seemed to shake the pattern, just as if she wanted to get out.

I got up softly and went to feel and see if the paper *did* move, and when I came back John was awake.

"What is it, little girl?" he said. "Don't go walking about like that—you'll get cold."

I thought it was a good time to talk, so I told him that I really was not gaining here, and that I wished he would take me away.

"Why, darling!" said he, "our lease will be up in three weeks, and I can't see how to leave before.

"The repairs are not done at home, and I cannot possibly leave town just now. Of course if you were in any danger, I could and would, but you really are better, dear, whether you can see it or not. I am a doctor, dear, and I know. You are gaining flesh and color, your appetite is better, I feel really much easier about you."

"I don't weigh a bit more," said I, "nor as much; and my appetite may be better in the evening when you are here, but it is worse in the morning when you are away!"

"Bless her little heart!" said he with a big hug. "She shall be as sick as she pleases! But now let's improve the shining hours by going to sleep, and talk about it in the morning!"

"And you won't go away?" I asked gloomily.

"Why, how can I, dear? It is only three weeks more and then we will take a nice little trip of a few days while Jennie is getting the house ready. Really, dear, you are better!"

"Better in body perhaps—" I began, and stopped short, for he sat up straight and looked at me with such a stern, reproachful look that I could not say another word.

"My darling," said he, "I beg of you, for my sake and for our child's sake, as well as for your own, that you will never for one instant let that idea enter your mind! There is nothing so dangerous, so fascinating, to a temperament like yours. It is a false and foolish fancy. Can you not trust me as a physician when I tell you so?"

So of course I said no more on that score, and we went to sleep before long. He thought I was asleep first, but I wasn't, and lay there for hours trying to decide whether that front pattern and the back pattern really did move together or separately.

On a pattern like this, by daylight, there is a lack of sequence, a defiance of law, that is a constant irritant to a normal mind.

The color is hideous enough, and unreliable enough, and infuriating enough, but the pattern is torturing.

You think you have mastered it, but just as you get well under way in following, it turns a back-somersault and there you are. It slaps you in the face, knocks you down, and tramples upon you. It is like a bad dream.

The outside pattern is a florid arabesque, reminding one of a fungus. If you can imagine a toadstool in joints, an interminable string of toadstools, budding and sprouting in endless convolutions—why, that is something like it.

That is, sometimes!

There is one marked peculiarity about this paper, a thing nobody seems to notice but myself, and that is that it changes as the light changes.

When the sun shoots in through the east window—I always watch for that first long, straight ray—it changes so quickly that I never can quite believe it.

That is why I watch it always.

By moonlight—the moon shines in all night when there is a moon—I wouldn't know it was the same paper.

At night in any kind of light, in twilight, candlelight, lamplight, and worst of all by moonlight, it becomes bars! The outside pattern, I mean, and the woman behind it is as plain as can be.

I didn't realize for a long time what the thing was that showed behind, 150
that dim sub-pattern, but now I am quite sure it is a woman.

By daylight she is subdued, quiet. I fancy it is the pattern that keeps her so still. It is so puzzling. It keeps me quiet by the hour.

I lie down ever so much now. John says it is good for me, and to sleep all I can.

Indeed he started the habit by making me lie down for an hour after each meal.

It is a very bad habit I am convinced, for you see I don't sleep.

And that cultivates deceit, for I don't tell them I'm awake—oh, no! 155

The fact is I am getting a little afraid of John.

He seems very queer sometimes, and even Jennie has an inexplicable look.

It strikes me occasionally, just as a scientific hypothesis, that perhaps it is the paper!

I have watched John when he did not know I was looking, and come into the room suddenly on the most innocent excuses, and I've caught him several times *looking at the paper!* And Jennie too. I caught Jennie with her hand on it once.

She didn't know I was in the room, and when I asked her in a quiet, a 160
very quiet voice, with the most restrained manner possible, what she was doing with the paper, she turned around as if she had been caught stealing, and looked quite angry—asked me why I should frighten her so!

Then she said that the paper stained everything it touched, that she had found yellow smooches on all my clothes and John's and she wished we would be more careful!

Did not that sound innocent? But I know she was studying that pattern, and I am determined that nobody shall find it out but myself!

Life is very much more exciting now than it used to be. You see, I have something more to expect, to look forward to, to watch. I really do eat better, and am more quiet than I was.

John is so pleased to see me improve! He laughed a little the other day, and said I seemed to be flourishing in spite of my wallpaper.

I turned it off with a laugh. I had no intention of telling him it was 165
because of the wallpaper—he would make fun of me. He might even want to take me away.

I don't want to leave now until I have found it out. There is a week more, and I think that will be enough.

I'm feeling ever so much better?

I don't sleep much at night, for it is so interesting to watch developments; but I sleep a good deal in the daytime.

In the daytime it is tiresome and perplexing.

There are always new shoots on the fungus, and new shades of yellow all over it. I cannot keep count of them, though I have tried conscientiously.

It is the strangest yellow, that wallpaper! It makes me think of all the yellow things I ever saw—not beautiful ones like buttercups, but old, foul, bad yellow things.

But there is something else about that paper—the smell! I noticed it the moment we came into the room, but with so much air and sun it was not bad. Now we have had a week of fog and rain, and whether the windows are open or not, the smell is here.

It creeps all over the house.

I find it hovering in the dining-room, skulking in the parlor, hiding in the hall, lying in wait for me on the stairs.

It gets into my hair.

Even when I go to ride, if I turn my head suddenly and surprise it—there is that smell!

Such a peculiar odor, too! I have spent hours in trying to analyze it, to find what it smelled like.

It is not bad—at first—and very gentle, but quite the subtlest, most enduring odor I ever met.

In this damp weather it is awful, I wake up in the night and find it hanging over me.

It used to disturb me at first. I thought seriously of burning the house—to reach the smell.

But now I am used to it. The only thing I can thing of that it is like is the *color* of the paper! A yellow smell.

There is a very funny mark on this wall, low down, near the mopboard. A streak that runs round the room. It goes behind every piece of furniture, except the bed, a long, straight, even *smooch,* as if it had been rubbed over and over.

I wonder how it was done and who did it, and what they did it for. Round and round and round—round and round and round—it makes me dizzy!

I really have discovered something at last.

Through watching so much at night, when it changes so, I have finally found out.

The front pattern *does* move—and no wonder! The woman behind shakes it!

Sometimes I think there are a great many women behind, and sometimes only one, and she crawls around fast, and her crawling shakes it all over.

Then in the very bright spots she keeps still, and in the very shady spots she just takes hold of the bars and shakes them hard.

And she is all the time trying to climb through. But nobody could climb through that pattern—it strangles so; I think that is why it has so many heads.

They get through and then the pattern strangles them off and turns them upside down, and makes their eyes white!

If those heads were covered or taken off it would not be half so bad.

I think that woman gets out in the daytime!

And I'll tell you why—privately—I've seen her!

I can see her out of every one of my windows!

It is the same woman, I know, for she is always creeping, and most women do not creep by daylight.

I see her in that long shaded lane, creeping up and down. I see her in those dark grape arbors, creeping all around the garden.

I see her on that long road under the trees, creeping along, and when a carriage comes she hides under the blackberry vines.

I don't blame her a bit. It must be very humiliating to be caught creeping by daylight!

I always lock the door when I creep by daylight. I can't do it at night, for I know John would suspect something at once.

And John is so queer now that I don't want to irritate him. I wish he would take another room! Besides, I don't want anybody to get that woman out at night but myself.

I often wonder if I could see her out of all the windows at once.

But, turn as fast as I can, I can only see out of one at one time.

And though I always see her, she *may* be able to creep faster than I can turn! I have watched her sometimes away off in the open country, creeping as fast as a cloud shadow in a wind.

If only that top pattern could be gotten off from the under one! I mean to try it, little by little.

I have found out another funny thing, but I shan't tell it this time! It does not do to trust people too much.

There are only two more days to get this paper off, and I believe John is beginning to notice. I don't like the look in his eyes.

And I heard him ask Jennie a lot of professional questions about me. She had a very good report to give.

She said I slept a good deal in the daytime.

John knows I don't sleep very well at night, for all I'm so quiet!

He asked me all sorts of questions, too, and pretended to be very loving and kind.

As if I couldn't see through him!

Still, I don't wonder he acts so, sleeping under this paper for three months.

It only interests me, but I feel sure John and Jennie are affected by it.

Hurrah! This is the last day, but it is enough. John is to stay in town over night, and won't be out until this evening.

Jennie wanted to sleep with me—the sly thing; but I told her I should undoubtedly rest better for a night all alone.

That was clever, for really I wasn't alone a bit! As soon as it was moonlight and that poor thing began to crawl and shake the pattern, I got up and ran to help her.

I pulled and she shook. I shook and she pulled, and before morning we had peeled off yards of that paper.

A strip about as high as my head and half around the room.

And then when the sun came and that awful pattern began to laugh at me, I declared I would finish it today!

We go away tomorrow, and they are moving all my furniture down again to leave things as they were before.

Jennie looked at the wall in amazement, but I told her merrily that I did it out of pure spite at the vicious thing.

She laughed and said she wouldn't mind doing it herself, but I must not get tired.

How she betrayed herself that time!

But I am here, and no person touches this paper but Me—not *alive!*

She tried to get me out of the room—it was too patent! But I said it was so quiet and empty and clean now that I believed I would lie down again and sleep all I could, and not to wake me even for dinner—I would call when I woke.

So now she is gone, and the servants are gone, and the things are gone, and there is nothing left but that great bedstead nailed down, with the canvas mattress we found on it.

We shall sleep downstairs tonight, and take the boat home tomorrow.

I quite enjoy the room, now it is bare again.

How those children did tear about here!

This bedstead is fairly gnawed!

But I must get to work.

I have locked the door and thrown the key down into the front path.

I don't want to go out, and I don't want to have anybody come in, till John comes.

I want to astonish him.

I've got a rope up here that even Jennie did not find. If that woman does get out, and tries to get away, I can tie her!

But I forgot I could not reach far without anything to stand on!

This bed will *not* move!

I tried to lift and push it until I was lame, and then I got so angry I bit off a little piece at one corner—but it hurt my teeth.

Then I peeled off all the paper I could reach standing on the floor. It sticks horribly and the pattern just enjoys it! All those strangled heads and bulbous eyes and waddling fungus growths just shriek with derision!

I am getting angry enough to do something desperate. To jump out of the window would be admirable exercise, but the bars are too strong even to try.

Besides I wouldn't do it. Of course not. I know well enough that a step like that is improper and might be misconstrued.

I don't like to *look* out of the windows even—there are so many of those creeping women, and they creep so fast.

I wonder if they all come out of that wallpaper as I did?

But I am securely fastened now by my well-hidden rope—you don't get *me* out in the road there!

I suppose I shall have to get back behind the pattern when it comes night, and that is hard!

It is so pleasant to be out in this great room and creep around as I please!

I don't want to go outside. I won't, even if Jennie asks me to.

For outside you have to creep on the ground, and everything is green instead of yellow.

But here I can creep smoothly on the floor, and my shoulder just fits in that long smooch around the wall, so I cannot lose my way.

Why there's John at the door!

It is no use, young man, you can't open it!

How he does call and pound!

Now he's crying to Jennie for an axe.

It would be a shame to break down that beautiful door!

"John, dear!" said I in the gentlest voice. "The key is down by the front steps, under a plantain leaf!"

That silenced him for a few moments.

Then he said, very quietly indeed, "Open the door, my darling!"

"I can't," said I. "The key is down by the front door under a plantain leaf!" And then I said it again, several times, very gently and slowly, and said it so often that he had to go and see, and he got it of course, and came in. He stopped short by the door.

"What is the matter?" he cried. "For God's sake, what are you doing!"

I kept on creeping just the same, but I looked at him over my shoulder.

"I've got out at last," said I, "in spite of you and Jennie! And I've pulled off most of the paper, so you can't put me back!"

Now why should that man have fainted? But he did, and right across my path by the wall, so that I had to creep over him every time!

Analyzing the Text

1. In your opinion, is the narrator already insane at the beginning of the story, or does she become so at a later point?
2. What responsibility, if any, does the narrator's husband John (who is a physician) bear for her mental deterioration?

Understanding Gilman's Techniques

1. How does the narrator's perceptions of the yellow wallpaper mirror her disturbed mental state?
2. Why is it significant that we never hear the narrator's name, but know the names of all the other characters?

Arguing for an Interpretation

1. "The Yellow Wallpaper" ends with an unusual action, that of the narrator "creeping" or crawling. How do you understand this action in relationship to the preceding events in the story?
2. To what extent is the story intended as an indictment of the prevailing psychiatric and medical treatment of the mentally ill in the late nineteenth century? Why was it in the interests of the society at that time to believe that women were particularly susceptible to insanity and needed this kind of treatment?

Monique Proulx

Monique Proulx was born in Quebec City in 1952. She is best known for her short stories, including Feint of Heart, *the title story of her 1983 collection,* Sans coeur et sans reproche, *translated by Matt Cohen. This bittersweet story follows the relationship of two young people in Quebec City whose pose of world-weary sophistication interferes with their finding happiness. She has also written*

Invisible Man at the Window *(1995) which she adapted as a screenplay in 1999, and* Aurora Montrealis *(1997).*

Feint of Heart

Might as well come right out with it: love stories don't do much for me. They rarely loosen my tear ducts. Other people's love stories, that is, the ones Guy des Cars will be cranking out until Cupid himself, with heaving stomach, sticks him full of arrows to shut him up. Or the ones that limp across our movie and TV screens and fill our nights with sweet, gritty fantasies. Love stories are personal, if you want my opinion: either you have one or you don't, and if you don't have one life's disgusting enough without some honey-tongued sadist purring his into your ear. But a love story of your own: well, that's another matter altogether. Once you've known love in all its force and fragility, words just can't describe the dizzying eddies that sweep us to the heights—and who cares about other people's love stories when you're drifting in the regions of interstellar bliss, which is perhaps the only reality that matters after all. But enough of that. Whether you like it or not I'm going to tell you the story of Françoise and Benoît in love: because you're a bunch of hopeless romantics—yes, I can see it in your eyes that drip with emotion whenever you see a beautiful, banal young couple exchange a peck on the cheek, not to mention a cavernous kiss—because fresh-sliced heart served up with no matter what revolting sauce is your favourite gourmet treat, you sentimental anthropophagist creeps, and for a lot of other reasons that are none of your business.

But let's get one thing straight right away: this is a perfectly ordinary story, not at all rife with dramatic incident. The "heroes" are heroic in name only: there isn't a single case of creeping, insidious leukemia, and neither protagonist suffers from even the tiniest fatal cerebral lesion. They're normal, ordinary folks, as healthy as can be expected, given their propensity for alcohol, nicotine, animal fats and the various controlled substances they turn to for life's little pleasures. So you've been warned, and don't come whining to me if the conclusion isn't bloody enough for your liking.

Among today's young intelligentsia there's an impressive clique of misguided perfectionists who, in the name of Independence, complicate their lives beyond belief. I'll get back to that. For the moment, let's just say that Françoise and Benoît were members in good standing when they first met in a little bar on rue Saint-Jean, which will remain anonymous unless the owner offers me drinks on the house for at least ten days running.

It was a Monday night in winter—quiet, nothing out of the ordinary. As soon as Françoise walked into the bar with a suicidal-looking friend at her side, her sleep-walker's shuffle—was it chance or fate—took her to the very back, right next to the seat where Benoît was peacefully reading. On the chair beside him sat an ill-defined individual, considerably the worse for drink, the sort of quiet old bum you often see in bars, who occasionally turns out to be a PhD in mathematics or a former Nobel Peace Prize laureate. Françoise took a seat without looking at anyone, the friend flopped down beside her with a melodramatic whoosh, Benoît's eyes stayed glued to his book and the bum muttered something unintelligible. Time passed.

The friend—let's call her Marie, she's just a bit player here—had been 5
delivering an endless, monotonous litany of complaints about life, love, death and other profound matters for some time, to judge by Françoise's weary silence, when suddenly the bum made a sound like a death rattle—guttural and rather frightening. All heads turned his way, including those of a small group of individuals—the only other customers in the bar—sitting a few tables away. The septuagenarian dipsomaniac hadn't succumbed to a run-of-the-mill heart attack. On the contrary, his cheeks had suddenly gone purple and he was pointing, stupefied, at the walls of the bar, emitting lugubrious noises all the while. Finally he yelped something intelligible: "Horrible! Hideous! Horrible!"

Curious heads turned away from the bum and converged upon the apparent cause of this vast spill of emotion: the walls of the bar. There was nothing special about the aforesaid walls, aside from the fact that they were covered with paintings by a local artist. It's true that the artist in question was inordinately prone to formless, provocative dribbles and smears, but who, in these troubled, permissive and culturally undistinguished times, can boast of his or her ability to distinguish the beautiful from the ugly? So. The bum did *not* approve of the work of the artist in question; in fact, he clearly disapproved. The small group a few tables away from Françoise, Benoît and company resumed their discussion somewhat resentfully. Benoît gave the bum an approving snicker, Françoise gave the sorry-looking pictures an amused glance, friend Marie tried to resume her dreary soliloquy—in short, everything was just about back to normal. The old man wasn't impressed; he stood up and started shrieking insults at the pictures threatening to slice them to shreds if they weren't removed from his sight.

"Garbage!" he yelled. "Trash! Makes me puke!"

And so forth. Now, among the small group of individuals seated, as I mentioned, a few tables away, were some friends of the maligned artist, and they were beginning to think the joke had gone a bit far. A tall bearded man got up, almost knocking over his chair in the process, and waved his fist at the bum.

"If that old wreck doesn't shut up, I'll bust his jaw!"

The old wreck, delighted and encouraged by the attention, only 10
stepped up the abuse, producing new, even more eloquent epithets. The tall, bearded man stomped over to him.

Then Benoît stood and calmly laid his book on the table.

"I think they're ugly too," he said blandly. "In fact, I think they're hideous, repugnant and stercoraceous."

Which cleared the decks for action. The artist's fan club sent their table flying, Benoît and the bearded man prepared for battle, the panic-stricken waiter burst into the fray—and the little old man, with a snort, began to take the pictures off the wall.

Suddenly a firm, strident voice rose from the budding scuffle and, surprisingly, paralyzed the crowd.

"Monsieur Riopelle! That's enough! Sit down, Monsieur Riopelle." 15

Françoise was tugging gently at the old bum's arm, forcing him to leave the pictures be. She pushed him onto a chair, holding him in a firm yet respectful grip.

"Calm down, Monsieur Riopelle. Young artists deserve a break too—don't they, Monsieur Riopelle?"

After a long, stunned silence, the artist's fan club slowly took their seats again, and it's here that my story, or rather the story of Françoise and Benoît, really gets underway.

Now you weren't born yesterday and you're well aware that the bum was no more Jean-Paul Riopelle than I'm Simone de Beauvoir. Françoise and Benoît found themselves at the same table, doubled over—discreetly—in the same uncontrollable laughter. Friend Marie had finally gone, the group at the other table was gradually breaking up, the old bum—who was nothing more or less than a full-time rubby—sank into a comatose slumber. For our hero and heroine, though, their chattering, their mutual glee, and their delight in each other's wit were endless, and now Françoise's hand finds its way, as if by chance, onto Benoît's thigh, and in their eyes there dances an odd sort of shared glimmer that now and then reduces them to silence, and here they are, a little later, fused and confused in Françoise's big double bed, laughing harder and harder through all the blazing pores of their skin.

Now let's be frank. This nocturnal liaison was not, in itself, exceptional—not for Françoise, and not for Benoît. Both were happily bound for thirty and they were accustomed to light-hearted, effervescent flings, tossed off as voraciously as champagne, just for a few spins of the clock. They were familiar with sudden yearnings for passion that would draw them inexorably into the bed of a stranger with an ever-so-sensual voice encountered in some smoky bar.

At times the fling would have happy consequences: a one-night stand would turn into a regular lover, for a while at least, and the relationship would develop into one of affectionate complicity, free of hassles.

Other times, the fling would turn out to be a full-fledged disaster: after awakening to a vague anxiety bordering on disgust, one would be astonished to find oneself beside some pale, nondescript stranger with whom no communication was possible, but who, behind the veil of the previous night's alcoholic vapours, had seemed brilliant.

To get back to the case in question, everything had been proceeding as smooth as silk from the moment Françoise and Benoît first made contact until the next day when they parted. In fact, they hadn't slept very well. It was as if, in the course of their mutual explorations, their bodies had set off a series of flash fires they couldn't extinguish, and their consuming hilarity kept them awake all night. Hunger finally tugged them from bed the next morning, their eyes rimmed in black, aching all over, but in a splendid mood regardless, and they carried right on with their giggles and winks and confessions. The omelette was good. Benoît—surprise!—knew how to make filtered coffee, and Françoise—oh, joy!—wasn't a grow-your-own-granola type. In a word, they were enraptured as they parted at Françoise's door, repeating how enjoyable it had been and so on and so forth. Then came the last peck on the cheek, the final wink and giggle, and a nonchalant, "Be seeing you. Take care." And so it began.

Françoise devoted the rest of the week to her usual activities with a surplus of energy and zeal that she didn't, at the time, find suspect. Her "usual activities," it should be said, would normally have been enough to consume the vitality of half a dozen less dynamic souls. Françoise was a born activist, and the financial problems of one Philémon Tremblay, Third Avenue, unemployed—one-armed, asbestositic, tubercular—and the tribulations of one Roberte Roberge, rue Couillard, tenant—grappling with rent increases directly proportional to the size of her giant cockroaches—gave her serious difficulty in sleeping. Françoise could be found in any association that proposed direct action to improve the fate of the world in general, and the quality of her neighbours' lives in particular.

Benoît didn't sit still either, in the days that followed, but was active in 25
his own inward and reflective way, which often resembled mere daydreaming. He was a teaching assistant at Laval University, in the literature department actually, but what he did there was closer to revolutionary sociology than literary studies. There was a kind of serene, spontaneous authority in his most innocuous presentations ("Why are the poor not interested in reading?" "Is feminist literature authentically progressive?" "Who really stands to profit from the book-publishing industry?") that had the knack of stimulating passionate discussions among his students and even, at times—to his great astonishment—provoking outside the university stormy demonstrations and the distribution of frankly subversive tracts that claimed to be inspired by him.

Whatever, the week passed normally, or almost: it wasn't till Friday night that Philémon Tremblay's money problems and Roberte Roberge's bugs aroused in Françoise only a sort of irritable indifference, and she suddenly started thinking about Benoît and the night they'd spent together. In fact, she realized she'd been thinking about it nonstop, insidiously, despite the variety of tasks she had compelled herself to carry on with, and that wasn't normal for a why-not-round-off-the-evening sort of fling. She even caught herself glaring at her phone, which was silent—or might as well have been, if you know what I mean—and getting vaguely depressed and wondering if he'd call and telling herself he wouldn't and remembering his hands so soft and velvet and that adorable dimple in his chin and thinking maybe she ought to go back to the little bar 'cause you never know and then saying no, he probably has a wife and five kids—the interesting ones always do.

As there'd been a tacit agreement not to broach the subject of another meeting or any formal commitment, and as he himself hadn't dared to contravene it—out of pride or God knows what ridiculous principle—Benoît, for his part, was concocting, along with his lecture notes, some complex manoeuvres that would allow him to see Françoise again, without making it too obvious. There was the telephone, of course—because he'd made a note of her number without being too obvious—but wouldn't such a primitive mode of communication risk the displeasure of a woman who transcended, without effort, it seemed, such petty, practical details of everyday life? (I know . . .) There remained—of the measures that wouldn't seem too obvious—the chance encounter. Benoît had peeked several times inside the little bar on rue Saint-Jean—which will remain anonymous unless the owner, etc.—and he hadn't seen Françoise (she wasn't there, she was waiting, at home, by the telephone), and that was all it took to convince him that she didn't care if she ever saw him again, she was so beautiful, so free, so far above the petty, practical details of everyday life, and undoubtedly had her hands full coping with the earnest attentions of a dozen men more interesting than he was.

Right. A pair of idiots, I grant you. But be patient, there's worse to come.

As there's a limit to everything, even to the blackest streak of lousy luck and the crassest stupidity, they finally ran into one another at the newsstand near Françoise's apartment, where Benoît—oddly enough—had been buying his papers for two weeks. They recognized each other at once, obviously, but didn't even exchange a peck on the cheek, overwhelmed as they were by an all-consuming stupefaction that had them stammering nonsense about the snow that would or wouldn't fall and the weather past and future. But they did manage, with an unconvincing air of nonchalance, to make a date for that evening. "If you aren't tied up, that is. . . ." That night found them at his place or hers, it really doesn't matter, and this time Cupid's aim was right on target. He took their breath away, turned their legs to jelly, flung them together like molten lava. They saw each other the next day and the day after that and every night afterwards for weeks and weeks and always there was the same electrifying ardour, the same unalloyed delirium.

This might be the place to bring up independence again, with a capi- 30
tal "I"—no, my lambs, you haven't been forgotten—in the name of which we make so many sacrifices, especially once it's hardened into a virtue.

It pleased both Françoise and Benoît to consider themselves—eyes modestly lowered, though, as befitted their leftish convictions—part of a mature and highly developed élite, utterly dedicated to the examination and liberation of the self, which had learned how to function on its own (that's what Independence means after all, or something pretty close, with all due respect to my two-volume dictionary). On the subject of love, it follows that they both had airy theories (rather unlike those of John Paul II), which condemned both systematic lumping into couples and unhealthy possessiveness. I'm not telling you anything new when I point out that, when you profess to hold to certain theories with even a modicum of sincerity, the trouble starts when you have to make them conform with reality.

In the beginning, euphoria came easily. It was its own begetter. They were swept along by an incredibly powerful current they hardly dared believe in, that left them exhausted and fulfilled.

Every day as dusk began to fall, Françoise would pick Benoît up at the university or wait for him with a pretended nonchalance at the back of a café or throw herself into the preparation of a gargantuan dinner for two that she knew she'd only pick at, for the emotions of love paralyzed her stomach and her appetite as surely as a bout of nausea. Every day, Benoît would twitch with impatience until late afternoon when he'd see Françoise's indefinable smile, and he never wearied of swooping her up in a violent embrace, of feeling her reel with desire against him, of cooing spectacular trivia into her ear that would melt both their hearts and cause them, with sudden gravity, to exchange a look that left them all a-flutter.

Until . . . Right. Until they take fright as they realize to what extent the well-oiled gears of their lives have unquestionably been disturbed. They start to daydream, to find more and more suspect the peace of mind and security in which they've lately been submerged up to the neck. Françoise, who's always been a lyrical advocate of the need for creative independence and sanctifying solitude, glumly discovers that she NEEDS Benoît: she turns to him at night with undeniable eagerness and rapture that leave her awash with guilt; he turns up at any hour of the day, nesting at the very core of her thoughts, even though she was sure she was safe among her tenants and her jobless. . . . She seems to be in the process of succumbing to feminine atavism, getting caught in the time-worn role of the near-wife devoured by the Other.

As for Benoît, he finds himself overreacting to a friendly jibe by one of 35
his students who saw him with Françoise. He suddenly has the disagreeable impression that his image has betrayed him, that he's gradually lost control of his own emotions, that he's playing the bashful lover in a caricature of a melodrama that has nothing to do with him, that's totally at odds with his libertarian principles. . . . He begins to doubt the authenticity of his inexplicable, all-consuming feeling for Françoise. He thinks it's unhealthy, mawkish, restricting—in a word, conformist. The evidence is clear: he's well on the way to giving in to petit bourgeois happiness.

In short, it's Benoît who strikes the first blow. Boldly and manfully. He unplugs his phone and plays dead for several days. Françoise, concerned and saddened by his abrupt silence, finally runs into him one night as she's strolling, woebegone, through the Latin Quarter. Having spotted him through a café window, she unthinkingly heads inside and makes her way toward him. He greets her with torrents of affection, as if nothing has changed, enquires about her health and the well-being of the unemployed Philémon Tremblay. He gets lost in a woolly discourse on the latest Altman film which he's just seen at the Cartier with Manon or Sandra or Marie who, as it happens, is even now at his side and whose thigh he is almost absent-mindedly patting. Françoise plays along as if nothing was wrong, smiles pleasantly at Manon or Sandra or Marie, dazzlingly outdoes him on the subject of Altman's style—so peculiarly engaging and so unexpectedly American—then finally gets up, gives Benoît an excessively polite kiss, flashes a charming smile at Manon or Sandra or Marie, and leaves the café—distraught, knees quaking, and with an uncontrollable desire to throw up and scream. She drags herself home, upbraiding herself aloud and giving herself inward kicks to ward off the real pain. Oh, it was nothing to get worked up about, just a passing fancy she'd inflated like some prepubescent crush, that's all. . . . Françoise is almost relieved, despite the frightful ache that's spreading through her belly: now, at least, she can go on believing there's no such thing as love. She stretches out on her bed, flicks on the TV, forbids herself to cry and eventually falls into a dreamless sleep, as though nothing had happened: stoicism is a precondition for Independence.

First thing the next morning, though, who should phone but Benoît—all sweetness and light, and secretly ravaged by a nagging anxiety that kept him awake all night. What if Françoise was so hurt by his inexplicable behaviour that she refused to see him again. . . . But no—Françoise speaks in her usual voice, pleasant and warm, tells him she's fine, and they make a date for that night. Miraculously, they get together as if nothing had happened: with their usual passion and fire, laughing and embracing like old accomplices. Françoise asks no questions, Benoît offers no confession. They maintain a tacit silence about what *may* have happened the night before—and the days before that.

And so the tone is set. Benoît is convinced he was right to introduce those breathing spaces into their relationship—not only does Françoise not hold it against him, she seems to be welcoming the change with her unshakeable good humour; perhaps deep down she was even hoping for it. And so Benoît multiplies his meetings with Manon or Sandra or Marie, sets up others with Sylvie, Laura and Julie, and banishes guilt from both his vocabulary and his daily life. By behaving as if nothing has happened, Françoise finally convinces herself she's living through a healthy, normal situation, one that's even somehow privileged (traditional couples are so quick to give in to possessiveness and neurotic jealousy . . .) and that her relationship with Benoît is turning out to be, basically, completely satisfying, giving her exactly what she needs. After all, don't they see each other at least twice a week, and isn't it absolutely sensational, fantastically passionate, every time? What more could she ask? It's only the remnants of romantic culture, decadent vestiges she hasn't had time to shed, that still make her start painfully and feel an acute, inexplicable anguish whenever she sees Benoît exchange familiar, tender gestures with someone else. . . . And then she decides that a meaningful quickie or two would do her a world of good, so she goes back to cruising, a tried-and-true activity at which, I might add, she excelled before Benoît came into her life. So now it's Benoît's turn to feel something like an icy swell rising in him as he sees Françoise's indefinable smile reflected in someone else's eyes, as he sneaks a peek at her sensual hand brushing against a leg other than his. But there are new ground rules now, and there's nothing to do but carry on in the same offhand, swaggering manner, to nervously gulp down the rest of his beer and look around for a woman to go home with tonight, so he won't be outdone.

And then one night Françoise is sitting with a friend—sure, let's call her Marie. Why not?—in the little bar from the beginning of the story, and as a matter of fact she's just launched into a loud, clear discourse on the merits and advantages of her relationship with Benoît when who should walk in but . . . He spots Françoise and gives her a knowing wink. He sits at a table with a gorgeous blonde—yet another one—whom he clearly already knows, as he starts up a passionate conversation punctuated with furtive fondling and inconsequential little kisses—inconsequential, Françoise tells herself, recognizing at once the vague cramp that even now is clenching her guts, though it doesn't stop her from pursuing with increased fervour her discourse on the fidelity, yes, the sort of inner, visceral fidelity, that marks her relationship with Benoît, even though, from all appearances, even though . . . And then, suddenly, she stops talking. Breaks off in mid-sentence with no warning, just like that. She doesn't even pretend to be following the conversation, but slumps into an odd sort of torpor from which her friend Marie can't shake her. When the gorgeous blonde gets up to go to the can or straight to hell—who cares—Françoise glides over to Benoît and tells him in a hoarse little voice, without giving him time for a smile or a kiss, that she has just discovered that she doesn't have the knack for being super cool, so she's pulling out, giving up, she's tired of stomach aches, she's exhausted from making up stories for herself. Benoît is silent, she utters a definitive goodnight that sounds like a farewell, and now she's outside, encased in an Olympian calm, friend Marie hard on her heels.

We find them both much later, in another bar, needless to say, unwinding into strong drink the never-ending skein of female rancour—he was never capable of love, I should have known, when I think of what I invested in that relationship, God, women are crazy to love the way we do, so much for nothing, waiter, five more beers, five beers to help me forget that times are tough and men are wimps. . . . Françoise is awash in a sort of lyric intoxication. She's found herself even though she's lost Benoît; at least this pain is unequivocal, with no little tricks, it'll be easier to assuage, to cauterize it, starting tonight with that dish with the bedroom eyes who's been hovering around, whom she brutally decides to pick up—for her libido, only her libido, and also to warm up the left side of her big double bed—the nights are so chilly now.

When she eventually goes home on the arm of the stranger who may with a little luck turn out to be a good lover, Françoise finds Benoît—who else!—haggard and shivering on her landing, his eyes distorted by something wet that looks like tears. He tells her he loves her—what else!—that he doesn't want to lose her, all in a tone that cannot be mistaken, on the landing of an aging apartment, in the slanting pre-dawn light, with a stranger planted there like a coatrack, who finally takes off because nobody's paying any attention to him.

So there it is. I've reached the epilogue, dear hearts. But where's the ending, the real ending, how does it *really* end (a bang? a whimper? fireworks or cold shower?), you ask with the look of a lustful pterodactyl. All right. I can see right through your new-wave hairdo. I know what's on your mind. Maybe Françoise and Benoît get married—sure, why not—it's still done. It's been all the rage for the past few years, in fact, amazingly popular with the under-twenty-fives. Don't get your hopes up, my little badgers. After all, I did make it clear that Françoise and Benoît were intelligent youngsters, well aware of life or, at least, a few of the primary truths, starting with this one: the marital arts are inevitably, every single time, transformed into martial arts. Okay, fine, so you resign yourselves, sighing like a duck-billed platypus being stroked the wrong way. Whether they marry or not, whether they have children or not, Françoise and Benoît might well enjoy a long and flawless happiness, for all eternity. Sure. Don't get me wrong—I'd like that, too. But things don't turn out that way in real life, where love isn't organized by those chaps from Hollywood or Harlequin. So let me tell you what happens to Françoise and Benoît: after all the twists and turns and tortuous manoeuvres through which we've followed them, they finally reach a workable compromise between independence and commitment—which is rare, ultra-rare. In fact, their relationship is very special, a passionate, gripping love affair that lasts three years. Or five. Or eight. And then one day they decide to split up because it's time, because they'd only hurt each other if they tried to revive what's already dead between them, because nothing lasts forever, alas, and they have high standards and abhor pretense. I'm not saying they burned all their bridges. No. When you've achieved an intense, almost total communion with someone—which is rare, ultra-rare—when you've lived a real-life love story, in a word, you never really leave each other altogether: there's a neatly laid-out compartment in your heart that no one else can fill.

Listen: only last year, on the anniversary of the day they met, Françoise received from Benoît—special delivery—a big rectangular package. She was home with some friends and a passing lover—Max, let's call him, or Pierre or Victor-Hippolyte—when she opened the parcel. It was a print, a reproduction of a weird-looking hairy owl, pasted like a party favour onto a hazy landscape. When she recognized the picture that had got Monsieur Riopelle so worked up, Françoise laughed. Then, if you must know, she started to blubber, blubbered like a calf, like a Magdalene, blubbered hard enough to bust a gut, tirelessly, inconsolably, till we had to call Benoît to help us calm her down.

And that's why alcohol and Colombian gold and lovely lavender stories exist. That's why I've told you about Françoise and Benoît, and that's why I'm on my way to down a few little carafes of plonk.[1] There are truths that are difficult to digest, there are truths to be swallowed a spoonful at a time, slowly, slowly, so as not to upset the stomach. This one, for example.

If you're strong, you know that life's a road on which you're always alone, even with love, even if people have halted along the way to engage our emotions. We must carry on, carry on to the end, till we can touch the little light that's shining just for us, till we can embrace its light, a special little light for each of us, at the end, at the very end of the road.

Analyzing the Text

1. Initially, what attracts François and Benôit to each other? How would you characterize the world that they are part of and its values?
2. What elements in the story make the reader aware of the extent to which the characters's conceptions of themselves differ from their real feelings?

Understanding Proulx's Techniques

1. How does the choice of an omniscient narrator allow us to share every nuance of each character's thoughts, feelings, and motivations? How would you characterize the narrator's voice? Does the narrator make you feel greater sympathy for François and Benôit than you otherwise might have? Why or why not?
2. Why is it ironic that at the end Benôit sends François the same picture that began their relationship so many years before?

Arguing for an Interpretation

1. In your opinion, if François and Benôit had met in a different environment, would the outcome of their story have been different? Why or why not?
2. Does the voice of the narrator enhance or detract from the effectiveness of the story? You might try to rewrite a scene or two from the perspective of either François or Benôit.

ALBERTO MORAVIA

Have you ever wondered why jewelry becomes an object of desire for so many people? To what extent is its mystique based on cultural values? The Italian writer Alberto Moravia (1907–1990) addresses this issue in his short story "Jewellery" (the spelling is British), translated by Angus Davidson, which originally appeared in Roman Tales *(1956). Moravia focuses on the symbolic role that jewelry serves in enhancing self-worth in male-dominated Italian culture. He completed his first novel,* The Time of Indifference *(1929), before he was 20 and published it at his own expense. Ten of his novels and several collections of his short stories have been translated into English. His novel* Two Women *(1957) was made into the 1961 Academy-award winning film, starring*

[1] a not-so-fine local wine.

Sophia Loren. Moravia's last work was his autobiography, Life *(1990).*

Jewellery

You can be quite sure that, when a woman finds her way into a group of men friends, that group, without the slightest doubt, is bound to disintegrate and each member of it to go off on his own account. That year we formed a group of young men who were all in the closest sympathy with each other, always united, always in agreement, always together. We were all of us earning a very good living, Tore with his garage, the two Modesti brothers with their meat-broker's business, Pippo Morganti with his pork-butcher's shop, Rinaldo with his bar, and I with a varied assortment of things: at that moment I was dealing in resin and products allied to it. Although we were all under thirty, none of us weighed less than twelve or thirteen stone: we all knew how to wield a knife and fork. During the day we were at work; but from seven o'clock onwards we were always together, first at Rinaldo's bar in the Corso Vittorio, and then in a restaurant with a garden in the neighborhood of the Chiesa Nuova. We spent Sundays together, of course: either at the stadium watching football matches, or on expeditions to the Castelli Romani, or, in the warm weather, at Ostia or Ladispoli. There were six of us, yet it might be said that we were one single person. So, supposing that one of us was smitten by a caprice, the other five were soon smitten too. With regard to jewellery, it was Tore who started it: he came one evening to the restaurant wearing a wristwatch of massive gold, with a plaited gold strap nearly an inch wide. We asked him who had given it to him. "The Director of the Bank of Italy," he said, by which he meant that he had bought it with his own money. Then he slipped it off and showed it to us: it was a watch of a well-known make, double-cased and with a second hand, and, together with its stiff plaited strap, it weighed goodness knows how much. It made a great impression upon us. "An investment," said somebody. But Tore replied: "What d'you mean, an investment? I like wearing it on my wrist, that's all." When we met next day at the usual restaurant, Morganti already had a wristwatch of his own, with a gold strap too, but not such a heavy one. Then it was the turn of the Modesti brothers who each bought one—larger ones than Tore's and with plaited straps that were less solid but broader. As for Rinaldo and me, as we both liked Tore's watch, we asked him where he had got it and then went together to a good shop in the Corso and each bought one.

It was now May, and often in the evenings we used to go to Monte Mario, to the inn there, to drink wine and eat fresh beans and sheep's milk cheese. One evening Tore put out his hand to help himself to beans and we all saw a ring on his finger, a massive ring containing a diamond of no very great size but a fine one nevertheless. "My goodness!" we exclaimed. "Now look here," he said roughly, "you're not to imitate me, you pack of monkeys.... I bought this so as to be different." However, he took it off and we passed it round: it was really a very fine diamond, limpid, perfect. But Tore is a big, rather soft-looking chap, with a flat, flabby face, two little pig-like eyes, a nose that looks as if it were made of butter and a mouth like a purse with broken hinges. With that ring on his small, fat finger and that watch on his stumpy wrist, he looked almost like a woman. The diamond ring, as he wished, was not copied. However, we each of us bought a nice ring for ourselves. The Modesti brothers had two similar rings made both of red gold but with different stones in them, one green and one blue; Rinaldo bought himself a ring of a more or less antique style, pierced and carved, with a brown cameo containing a little white figure of a nude woman; Morganti, always anxious to cut a dash, acquired one actually made of platinum, with a black stone; while I myself, being more conventional, contented myself with a ring which had a square setting and a flat yellow stone upon which I had my initials cut, so that I could use it for sealing parcels. After the rings came cigarette-cases. It was Tore, as usual, who began it, by producing a long, flat case—made of gold, of course—with crossed lines incised on it, and snapping it open under our noses; and then everyone imitated him, some in one way and some in another. After the cigarette-cases, we all indulged our own whims: somebody bought a bracelet with a medal, to wear on his other wrist; somebody else a pressure-controlled fountain pen; somebody else a little chain with a cross and a medallion of the Madonna to hang round his neck; and somebody else a cigarette-lighter. Tore, vainest of all, acquired three more rings; and now he looked more like a woman than ever, especially when he took off his jacket and appeared in a short-sleeved shirt, displaying his big, soft arms and hands covered with rings.

We were all laden with jewellery now; and I don't know why, but it was just at that moment that things began to go wrong. It didn't amount to much—a little teasing, a few rather caustic remarks, a few sharp retorts. And then one evening Rinaldo, who owned the bar, arrived at our usual restaurant with a girl, his new cashier. Her name was Lucrezia and she was perhaps not yet even twenty, but she was as fully developed as a woman of thirty. Her skin was white as milk, her eyes black, large, steady and expressionless, her mouth red, her hair black. She looked indeed like a statue, especially as she always remained still and composed and hardly spoke at all. Rinaldo confided to us that he had found her by means of a commercial advertisement, and he said he knew nothing about her, not even whether she had a family or whom she lived with. She was just the right person, he added, for the cash-desk: a girl like that attracted clients by her good looks and then, by her serious demeanour, kept them at a distance; a plain girl fails to attract, and a pretty but forthcoming one does no work and creates disorder. The presence of Lucrezia that evening caused considerable constraint among us: we sat very upright the whole time, with our jackets on, talking in a reserved manner without any jokes or coarse words and eating very politely; even Tore tried to eat his fruit with a knife and fork, without much success however. Next day we all rushed to the bar to see her at her duties. She was sitting on a tiny stool, her hips—which were already too broad for her age—bulging over its sides: and her haughty bosom was almost pressing against the keys of the cash-register. We all stood there open-mouthed as we watched her calmly, precisely, unhurriedly distributing price-dockets, continually pressing down the keys of the machine without even looking at them, her eyes fixed straight ahead of her in the direction of the bar counter. She notified the barman, each time, in a quiet, impersonal voice: "Two coffees. . . . One bitter. . . . One orangeade. . . . One beer." She never smiled, she never looked at the customer; and certainly there were some who went up very close to her in the hope of being looked at. She was dressed with propriety, but like the poor girl that she was: in a simple, sleeveless white dress. But clean, fresh, well ironed. *She* wore no jewellery, not even ear-rings, although the lobes of her ears had been pierced. We, of course, when we saw how pretty she was, started making jokes, encouraged by Rinaldo, who was proud of her. But she, after the first few jokes, said: "We shall meet at the restaurant this evening, shan't we? So leave me in peace now. . . . I don't like being disturbed while I'm working." Tore, to whom these words were addressed because he was the most prying and ill-mannered, said with feigned surprise: "I say, I'm sorry . . . we're only poor people, and we didn't know we had to do with a princess. . . . I'm sorry . . . we didn't mean any offense." She replied, drily: "I'm not a princess but a poor girl who works for her living . . . and I'm not offended. . . . One coffee and one bitter." And so we went away feeling rather humiliated.

In the evening we all met, as usual, at the restaurant. Rinaldo and Lucrezia were the last to arrive; and we immediately ordered our dinner. For a short time, while we were waiting for our food, there was again a feeling of constraint; then the proprietor brought in a big dish of chicken *alla romana,* already cut up, with tomato sauce and red peppers. We all looked at each other, and Tore, interpreting our common feeling, exclaimed: "You know what I say? When I eat I like to feel free . . . do as I do and you'll feel better." As he spoke he seized hold of a leg of chicken and, lifting it to his mouth with his two ring-covered hands, started to devour it. This was the signal; after a moment of hesitation we all began eating with our hands—all except Rinaldo and, of course, Lucrezia who nibbled delicately at a little piece of breast. After the first moment we recovered ourselves and went back, in every possible respect, to our old noisy ways. We talked as we ate and ate as we talked; we gulped down brimming glasses of wine with our mouths full; we slouched back in our chairs; we told our usual racy stories. In fact, perhaps out of defiance, we behaved worse than usual; and I don't remember ever having eaten so much, and with so much enjoyment, as I did that evening. When we had finished dinner, Tore loosened the buckle of his trouser-band and uttered a profound belch, which would have shaken the ceiling if it hadn't happened that we were out of doors, under a pergola. "Ugh, I feel better," he declared. He took a toothpick and, as he always did, started prodding at his teeth, all of them, one by one, and then all over again; and finally, with the toothpick stuck into the corner of his mouth, he told us a really indecent story. At this, Lucrezia rose to her feet and said: "Rinaldo, I feel tired. . . . If you don't mind, will you take me home now?" We all exchanged meaningful glances: she had been Rinaldo's cashier for barely two days and already she was talking to him familiarly and calling him by his Christian name. A commercial advertisement in the paper, indeed! They went out and, the moment they had gone, Tore gave another belch and said: "About time too . . . I'd had enough. . . . Did you see the haughtiness of it? And him following behind as good as gold . . . as meek as a lamb! As for that commercial advertisement—matrimonial advertisement, I should say!"

For two or three days the same scenes were repeated: Lucrezia eating 5
composedly and silently; the rest of us trying to pretend she wasn't there; Rinaldo divided between Lucrezia and us and not knowing what line to take. But there was something brewing, we all felt that. The girl—still waters run deep—gave no sign, but all the time she was wanting Rinaldo to choose between herself and us. At last, one evening, for no precise reason—perhaps because it was hot and, as one knows, heat gets on people's nerves—Rinaldo, half-way through dinner, made an attack upon us, in this

way: "This is the last time I'm coming to eat with you." We were all astonished, and Tore asked: "Oh, is that really so? And may we ask why?" "Because I don't like you." "You don't like us? Well, I'm sure we're all very sorry for that—really terribly sorry." "You're a bunch of swine, that's what you are." "Now be careful what you say, but . . . are you crazy?" "Yes, you're a bunch of swine; I say it and I repeat it. . . . Eating with you makes me feel sick." By this time we were all red in the face with anger, and some of us had jumped up from the table. "It's you," said Tore, "who's the biggest swine of all. Who gave you the right to judge us? Haven't we always been all together? Haven't we always done the same things?" "You be quiet," Rinaldo said to him; "with all that jewellery on you, you look like one of those women—you know who I mean. . . . All you need is some scent. . . . I say, haven't you ever thought of putting on some scent?" This blow was aimed at all of us; and, realizing the source from which it came, we all looked at Lucrezia: but she, hypocritically, kept on pulling Rinaldo by the sleeve and urging him to stop and come away. Then Tore said: "You've got jewellery too . . . you've got a watch and a ring and a bracelet . . . just as much as anyone else." Rinaldo was beside himself now. "But you know what I'm going to do?" he cried. "I'm taking them all off and giving them to her. . . . Come on, take them, Lucrezia, I'm giving them to you." As he spoke, he slipped off his ring, his bracelet, his wristwatch, pulled his cigarette-case out of his pocket and threw the whole lot into the girl's lap. "None of the rest of you," he said insultingly, "would ever do that . . . you *couldn't* do it." "Go to hell," said Tore; but you could see, now, that he was ashamed of having all those rings on his fingers. "Rinaldo," said Lucrezia calmly, "take your things and let's go." She gathered all the things Rinaldo had given her into a heap and put them into his pocket. Rinaldo, however, owing to some kind of grudge that he had against us, continued to abuse us even while allowing Lucrezia to drag him away. "You're a bunch of swine, I tell you. . . . Why don't you learn how to eat; why don't you learn how to live. . . . Swine!" "Idiot!" shouted Tore, mad with rage. "Imbecile! . . . You've allowed yourself to be led away by that other idiot who's standing beside you!" If you could have seen Rinaldo! He jumped right over the table and seized hold of Tore by the collar of his shirt. We had to pull them apart.

That evening, after they had gone, we did not breathe a word and we all left after a few minutes. Next evening we met again, but now our old gaiety was gone. We noticed, on this occasion, that several of the rings had vanished and some of the watches too. After two evenings we none of us had any jewellery left, and we were duller than ever. A week went by and then, with one excuse and another, we ceased to meet at all. It was all finished, and, as one knows, when things are finished they don't begin again: no one likes warmed-up soup. Later on I heard that Rinaldo had married Lucrezia; I was told that, at the church, she was more thickly covered with jewellery than a statue of the Madonna. And Tore? I saw him at his garage a short time ago. He had a ring on his finger, but it was not of gold and it had no diamond in it; it was one of those silver rings that mechanics wear.

Analyzing the Text

1. How would you characterize the relationship among the six friends before Lucrezia arrives? What unites them and what role does jewelry play in their friendship?

2. What attracts Rinaldo to Lucrezia, and how does his relationship with his friends change after he meets her? Why is it significant that at first she has no jewelry, and then at the end of the story is "more thickly covered with jewelry than a statue of the Madonna"?

Understanding Moravia's Techniques

1. What details suggest that Lucrezia herself is the ultimate jewel?
2. How would you characterize the tone of the narrator and his attitude toward the events he describes? Is he sorry, puzzled, angry, jealous?

Arguing for an Interpretation

1. Is Lucrezia actually a surrogate for the jewelry Rinaldo used to wear? Does she raise his status so that he no longer has to wear jewelry? Why or why not?
2. Does Lucrezia actually cause the relationship between the men to disintegrate, or was it at the point of doing so anyway? Explain your answer.

Poems

Edna St. Vincent Millay

Edna St. Vincent Millay (1892–1950) was born in Rockland, Maine. She began writing poetry in adolescence, and won several prizes from St. Nicholas *magazine. An early poem, "Renascence" (1912) elicited praise from an admirer and fellow poet and began a romantic relationship that resulted in some of her best love sonnets. After she graduated from Vassar College, she wrote, produced, and acted in plays in New York and at the Provincetown Playhouse. She received a Pulitzer Prize for* The Ballad of the Harp-Weaver and Other Poems *(1923), the same year in which she married Eugen Jan Boissevaim. Under the pseudonym "Nancy Boyd," she issued a collection of essays,* Distressing Dialogues *(1924), that had previously appeared as individual articles in* Vanity Fair. *Her numerous books of poetry brought her literary fame and made her a symbol for the pursuit of personal freedom for many women. Millay's poems are always passionate, autobiographical, and in some cases, modeled on the hedonistic verse of the Roman poet Catullus (84–54 B.C.).*

What Lips My Lips Have Kissed

What lips my lips have kissed, and where, and why,
I have forgotten, and what arms have lain
Under my head till morning; but the rain
Is full of ghosts tonight, that tap and sigh

Upon the glass and listen for reply,
And in my heart there stirs a quiet pain
For unremembered lads that not again
Will turn to me at midnight with a cry.
Thus in the winter stands the lonely tree,
Nor knows what birds have vanished one by one,
Yet knows its boughs more silent than before:
I cannot say what loves have come and gone,
I only know that summer sang in me
A little while, that in me sings no more.

Analyzing the Text

1. What events in the speaker's life does this poem allude to, and what is the speaker's attitude toward them?
2. Would you characterize the speaker's life as a hedonistic one that she now regrets? Why or why not?

Understanding Millay's Techniques

1. How do the metaphors and images in this poem convey the speaker's feelings?
2. What aspects of this poem suggest that the speaker is remarkably objective about how she has lived her life?

Arguing for an Interpretation

1. Is Millay's choice of a "lonely tree" whose branches are no longer visited by birds an effective image in communicating the emotional state of the speaker? Why or why not?
2. What causes the speaker the most pain: a lost capacity for feeling, the passage of youth, an inability to sustain a relationship over time, or something else?

MURIEL RUKEYSER

Muriel Rukeyser (1913–1980) lived most of her life in New York and was educated at Vassar College and Columbia University. Although from an affluent background, most of Rukeyser's friends were socialists, labor organizers, or artists, and her poetry from the outset was directed against racial, political, and economic injustice of the kind that led to the execution of the immigrants Sacco and Vanzetti. She began publishing her work in the early 1930s and along with Elizabeth Bishop and Mary McCarthy founded a literary magazine. Her first book of poetry, Theory of Flight *(1935), renounced the artificially poetic in favor of lyrical articulation of personal experience. Her poetry gave voice to the victimized in such volumes as* The Soul and Body of John Brown *(1940) and* The Green Wave *(1948); books that deal directly with social injustice in America and with the atrocities of World War II. Her later volumes,* Body of Waking *(1958),* The Speed of Darkness *(1968),* Breaking Open *(1973), and* The Gates

(1976) oppose the imagery of giving birth to the violence she witnessed and protested against in Korea and in Vietnam. In "Myth" (1973), Rukeyser presents a witty update of the encounter between Oedipus and the Sphinx to point out the limitations of a male-centered perspective.

Myth

Long afterward, Oedipus, old and blinded, walked the
roads. He smelled a familiar smell. It was
the Sphinx. Oedipus said, "I want to ask one question.
Why didn't I recognize my mother?" "You gave the
wrong answer," said the Sphinx. "But that was what
made everything possible," said Oedipus. "No," she said.
"When I asked, What walks on four legs in the morning,
two at noon, and three in the evening, you answered,
Man. You didn't say anything about woman."
"When you say Man," said Oedipus, "you include women
too. Everyone knows that." She said, "That's what
you think."

Analyzing the Text

1. How is Oedipus characterized in this poem? How is his insensitivity made the subject of mockery rather than outright condemnation?
2. Why is it significant that Oedipus is unable to recognize his own mother, and how is this connected to the wrong answer he gives to the Sphinx's riddle?

Understanding Rukeyser's Techniques

1. In what way does the visual appearance of the poem reinforce the sense of an encounter or debate between Oedipus and the Sphinx?
2. How does the kind of language Rukeyser uses update this ancient story and make it seem quite contemporary?

Arguing for an Interpretation

1. Is this a poem about "political correctness," as such, or does it suggest a deeper obtuseness of men toward women? Explain your answer.
2. Discuss the different meanings the word "myth" (the title) might have, and how this illuminates different aspects of the poem.

GREGORY CORSO

(Nunzio) Gregory Corso (1930–2001) was born in New York and became a central figure in the Beat movement, along with Allen Ginsburg and Jack Kerouac. Corso had a checkered career including a three-year stint in prison

for petty theft as a teenager. He worked as a laborer on the New York docks, as a reporter for the Los Angeles Examiner, *and as a merchant seaman. He taught in the English Department at the State University of New York at Buffalo (1965–1970). His poems are strongly influenced by jazz, especially the music of Charlie Parker and Miles Davis, in their innovative offbeat style. A prolific writer, Corso's works include the extended poem* Bomb *(1958), and his collections,* Gasoline *(1958),* Long Live Man *(1962), and* Minefield: New and Selected Poems *(1991). The following poem, "Marriage," a comic riff on T. S. Eliot's 1917 "The Lovesong of J. Alfred Prufrock," first appeared in* Happy Birthday of Death *(1960). The personality we hear in this poem is, by turns, childish, insightful, irreverent, and sentimental. Corso's voice is unmistakable and authentic.*

Marriage

Should I get married? Should I be good?
Astound the girl next door
with my velvet suit and faustus hood?
Don't take her to movies but to cemeteries
tell all about werewolf bathtubs and forked clarinets
then desire her and kiss her and all the preliminaries
and she going just so far and I understanding why
not getting angry saying You must feel! It's beautiful to feel!
Instead take her in my arms
lean against an old crooked tombstone
and woo her the entire night the constellations in the
  sky—

When she introduces me to her parents
back straightened, hair finally combed, strangled by a tie,
should I sit knees together on their 3rd degree sofa
and not ask Where's the bathroom?
How else to feel other than I am,
often thinking Flash Gordon[1] soap—
O how terrible it must be for a young man
seated before a family and the family thinking
We never saw him before! He wants our Mary Lou!
After tea and homemade cookies they ask
What do you do for a living?
Should I tell them? Would they like me then?
Say All right get married, we're not losing a daughter

[1]Science fiction hero of comic strip and film.

we're gaining a son—
And should I then ask Where's the bathroom?

O God, and the wedding! All her family and her friends
and only a handful of mine all scroungy and bearded
just wait to get at the drinks and food—
And the priest! he looking at me as if I masturbated
asking me Do you take this woman
for your lawful wedded wife!
And I trembling what to say say Pie Glue!
I kiss the bride all those corny men slapping me on the back
She's all yours, boy! Ha-ha-ha!
And in their eyes you could see
some obscene honeymoon going on—
Then all that absurd rice and clanky cans and shoes
Niagara Falls! Hordes of us!
Husbands! Wives! Flowers! Chocolates!
All streaming into cosy hotels
All going to do the same thing tonight
The indifferent clerk he knowing what was going to happen
The lobby zombies they knowing what
The whistling elevator man he knowing
The winking bellboy knowing
Everybody knowing!
I'd be almost inclined not to do anything!
Stay up all night! Stare that hotel clerk in the eye!
Screaming: I deny honeymoon! I deny honeymoon!
running rampant into those almost climactic suites
yelling Radio belly! Cat shovel!
O I'd live in Niagara forever! in a dark cave beneath the Falls
I'd sit there the Mad Honeymooner
devising ways to break marriages, a scourge of bigamy
a saint of divorce—

But I should get married I should be good
How nice it'd be to come home to her
and sit by the fireplace and she in the kitchen
aproned young and lovely wanting my baby
and so happy about me she burns the roast beef
and comes crying to me and I get up from my big papa chair
saying Christmas teeth! Radiant brains! Apple deaf!
God what a husband I'd make! Yes, I should get married!
So much to do! like sneaking into Mr Jones' house late at night
and cover his golf clubs with 1920 Norwegian books
Like hanging a picture of Rimbaud on the lawnmower
Like pasting Tannu Tuva[2] postage stamps

[2]Region in Asia of former Soviet Union.

all over the picket fence
Like when Mrs Kindhead comes to collect
for the Community Chest
grab her and tell her There are unfavourable omens in the
    sky!
And when the mayor comes to get my vote tell him
When are you going to stop people killing whales!
And when the milkman comes leave him a note in the bottle
Penguin dust, bring me penguin dust, I want penguin dust—

Yet if I should get married and it's Connecticut and snow
and she gives birth to a child and I am sleepless, worn,
up for nights, head bowed against a quiet window
the past behind me,
finding myself in the most common of situations
a trembling man knowledged with responsibility
not twig-smear nor Roman coin soup—
O what would that be like!
Surely I'd give it for a nipple a rubber Tacitus
For a rattle a bag of broken Bach records
Tack Della Francesca all over its crib
Sew the Greek alphabet on its bib
And build for its playpen a roofless Parthenon

No, I doubt I'd be that kind of father
not rural not snow no quiet window
but hot smelly tight New York City
seven flights up, roaches and rats in the walls
a fat Reichian[3] wife screeching over potatoes Get a job!
And five nose running brats in love with Batman[4]
And the neighbours all toothless and dry haired
like those hag masses of the 18th century
all wanting to come in and watch TV
The landlord wants his rent
Grocery store Blue Cross Gas & Electric Knights of
    Columbus
Impossible to lie back and dream
Telephone snow, ghost parking—
No! I should not get married I should never get married!
But—imagine if I were married
to a beautiful sophisticated woman
tall and pale wearing an elegant black dress
and long black gloves
holding a cigarette holder in one hand
and a highball in the other
and we lived high up in a penthouse with a huge window
from which we could see all of New York
and even farther on clearer days
No, can't imagine myself married to that pleasant prison
    dream—

[3]Wilhelm Reich (1897–1957), psychoanalyst. [4]Comic book, TV, and film hero.

O but what about love? I forget love
not that I am incapable of love
it's just that I see love as odd as wearing shoes—
I never wanted to marry a girl who was like my mother
And Ingrid Bergman[5] was always impossible
And there's maybe a girl now but she's already married
And I don't like men and—
but there's got to be somebody!
Because what if I'm 60 years old and not married,
all alone in a furnished room with pee stains on my
    underwear
and everybody else is married!
All the universe married but me!

Ah, yet well I know that were a woman possible as I am
    possible
then marriage would be possible—
Like SHE[6] in her lonely alien gaud waiting her Egyptian lover
so I wait—bereft of 2,000 years and the bath of life.

Analyzing the Text

1. What does the speaker reveal about himself that explains his anxieties and ambivalence toward getting married?
2. What leads the speaker to conclude that there may actually be a girl out there for him?

Understanding Corso's Techniques

1. What images suggest that the speaker tries to extricate himself from the stereotypes he holds about marriage and fatherhood? Does he succeed?
2. In what way do the bizarre and unusual kaleidoscope of images Corso uses to characterize the speaker suggest a unique personality who would find it difficult to make the compromises necessary in marriage?

Arguing for an Interpretation

1. In your opinion, is the speaker a likely prospect for marriage? Why or why not?
2. Do you think the speaker is trying to talk himself out of ever getting married, or to talk himself into it? Explain your answer.

JIMMY SANTIAGO BACA

Jimmy Santiago Baca was born in New Mexico in 1952. He currently lives on a small farm outside Albuquerque. Baca wrote the poems in the collection Immigrants in Our Own Land *(1979) while he was in prison. Baca has written the screenplay for the 1993*

---

[5]Famous film star (1918–1982). [6]Refers to Ayesha, the sorceress heroine of H. Rider Haggard's (1856–1925) novel *She* (1887) who exemplifies the mystery of love.

film, Bound by Honor. *Baca's poetry often tells the story of mestizo outcasts who confront hurdles thrown up by American society that isolate those who do not fit in. Baca has established himself as an important force in Chicano literature. His poetry is a passionate exploration of life in the urban barrios and landscapes of New Mexico. Baca's recent works include* In the Way of the Sun *(1997) and* Set This Book on Fire *(1999). The following poem, "Spliced Wire," from* What's Happening *(1982), confronts the realities of love and betrayal.*

Spliced Wire

I filled your house with light.
There was warmth in all corners
of the house. My words I gave you
like soft warm toast in early morning.
I brewed your tongue
to a rich dark coffee, and drank
my fill. I turned on the music for you,
playing notes along the crest
of your heart, like birds,
eagles, ravens, owls on rim of red canyon.
I brought reception clear to you,
and made the phone ring at your request,
from Paris or South America,
you could talk to any of the people,
as my words gave them life,
from a child in a boat with his father,
to a prisoner in a concentration camp,
all at your bedside.

And then you turned away, wanted
a larger mansion. I said no. I left you.
The plug pulled out, the house blinked out,
Into a quiet darkness, swallowing wind,
collecting autumn leaves like stamps
between its old boards where they stick.

You say, or carry the thought with you
to comfort you, that faraway somewhere,
lightning knocked down all the power lines.
But no my love, it was I,
pulling the plug. Others will come, plug in,
but often the lights will dim weakly

in storms, the music stop to a drawl,
the warmth shredded by cold drafts.

Analyzing the Text

1. From the speaker's point of view, what went wrong in the relationship? Keep in mind you are only getting one side of the story.
2. Does the tone suggest the speaker is rationalizing to save his wounded ego?

Understanding Baca's Techniques

1. How does the phrase "spliced wire" serve as a controlling image that advances the speaker's claims?
2. How do the everyday objects (telephone, light bulbs, radio) serve as metaphors for the connections the speaker claims he brought to the relationship?

Arguing for an Interpretation

1. Are jealousy and possessiveness the real reasons why this relationship fell apart, or is it more likely that the speaker's inflated view of his contributions alienated his partner? Explain your answer.
2. Write a variation of "Spliced Wire" in which the events the speaker describes appear from the perspective of the other person.

GRACE CAROLINE BRIDGES

Grace Caroline Bridges's poetry has appeared in the Evergreen Chronicles, The Northland Review, *and* Great River Review. *"Lisa's Ritual, Age 10" was published in* Looking for Home: Women Writing About Exile *(1990). The distinctive effects of the following poem are due to Bridges's ability to communicate a child's experience of violation through words and images that re-create the shock of this trauma rather than merely describing it.*

Lisa's Ritual, Age 10

Afterwards when he is finished with her
lots of mouthwash helps
to get rid of her father's cigarette taste.
She runs a hot bath
        to soak away the pain
                like red dye leaking from her
                        school dress in the washtub.
She doesn't cry.

When the bathwater cools she adds more hot.
She brushes her teeth for a long time.

Then she finds the corner of her room,
curls against it. There the wall is
hard and smooth
as teacher's new chalk, white
as a clean bedsheet. Smells
fresh. Isn't sweaty, hairy, doesn't stick
to skin. Doesn't hurt much
when she presses her small backbone
into it. The wall is steady
while she falls away:
first the hands lost
arms dissolving feet gone
the legs dis- jointed
body cracking down
the center like a fault
she falls inside
slides down like
dust like kitchen dirt
slips off
the dustpan into
noplace

a place where
nothing happens,
nothing ever happened.

When she feels the cool
wall against her cheek
she doesn't want to
come back. Doesn't want to
think about it.
The wall is quiet, waiting.
It is tall like a promise
only better.

Analyzing the Text

1. How does the "ritual" in the title allow Lisa to psychologically distance herself from the horror to which she is subjected?
2. What features of the poem suggest that a child who has experienced this kind of abuse may well develop a dissociative identity disorder as a way of coping?

Understanding Bridges's Techniques

1. How does the spacing of the words on the page help draw the reader into Lisa's mind and communicate her sense of mental disintegration?
2. What images in the poem intensify the contrast between what is soiled and what is clean, and underscore the nature of the experience Lisa has endured and her reaction to it?

Arguing for an Interpretation

1. What insight does this poem offer into the psychological survival strategy of dissociation to which abused children resort? Do some research to discover how this differs from schizophrenia, with which it might be confused.
2. Do you feel this was an appropriate subject for a poem? Why or why not?

ROBERT FREDERICK NIMS

Robert Frederick Nims (1913–1999) was born in Muskegon, Michigan and received a Ph.D. from the University of Chicago in 1945. He taught at a wide variety of colleges and universities, including the University of Florida, Harvard University, and as visiting professor at the Universities of Florence, Milan, and Madrid. His many collections of poetry include The Iron Pastoral *(1947),* The Kiss: A Jambalaya *(1982), and in 1990,* The Six-Cornered Snowflake, *and* Zany in Denim. *Among his many honors and awards are the Harriet Monroe Memorial Prize (1942) and the Aiken Taylor Award (1991). "Love Poem" originally appeared in* Selected Poems *(1982) and reveals the same qualities of "sensuous responsiveness combined with an inquisitive intellect," that the critic M. L. Rosenthal praised in his review of Nims's first book of poetry.*

Love Poem

My clumsiest dear, whose hands shipwreck vases,
At whose quick touch all glasses chip and ring,
Whose palms are bulls in china, burs in linen,
And have no cunning with any soft thing

Except all ill-at-ease fidgeting people:
The refugee uncertain at the door,
You make at home; deftly you steady
The drunk clambering on his undulant floor.

Unpredictable dear, the taxi drivers' terror,
Shrinking from far headlights pale as a dime
Yet leaping before red apoplectic streetcars—
Misfit in any space. And never on time.

A wrench in clocks and the solar system. Only
With words and people and love you move at ease.
In traffic of wit expertly maneuver
And keep us, all devotion, at your knees.

Forgetting your coffee spreading on our flannel,
Your lipstick grinning on our coat,
So gaily in love's unbreakable heaven
Our souls on glory of spilt bourbon float.

Be with me, darling, early and late. Smash glasses—
I will study wry music for your sake.
For should your hands drop white and empty
All the toys of the world would break.

Analyzing the Text

1. The person about whom this poem was written has quite different qualities when dealing with things and with people. What are they?
2. What compels the speaker's admiration and love despite the maladroitness that is both unintentional and comic?

Understanding Nims's Techniques

1. How is the poem structured so that the qualifications and second thoughts become the dominant theme?
2. What images dramatize the qualities the speaker cherishes (that ironically are absent in relationship to objects and schedules) about the woman he loves?

Arguing for an Interpretation

1. Do you think that the speaker is really alluding to himself when he says that she is good at dealing with "ill-at-ease, fidgeting people, refugees, and unsteady drunks"?
2. Nims hints that others might not see the speaker's loved one as he does. In what ways might the poem be considered a defense of his loved one, and in what way does the speaker recast the traditional poem in praise of a woman's important qualities? Is this more effective than a conventional tribute? Why or why not?

William Shakespeare

William Shakespeare (1564–1616) was born in Stratford-upon-Avon, the son of a prosperous merchant, and received his early education at Stratford Grammar School. In 1582, he married Anne Hathaway and over the next 20 years established himself as a professional actor and playwright in London. Shakespeare's sonnets, of which there are 154, were probably written in the 1590s but were first published in 1609. The 14 lines of the Shakespearean sonnet fall into three quatrains and a couplet rhyming abab cdcd efef gg. *They hint at a story involving a young man, a "dark lady," and the poet himself, together with a "rival poet."* Sonnet 130 *expresses a witty variation on the typical courtly poem of praise and presents a realistic portrait of flawed attributes that, notwithstanding, still communicates great affection.*

130

My mistress' eyes are nothing like the sun;
Coral is far more red than her lips' red;
If snow be white, why then her breasts are dun;
If hairs be wires, black wires grow on her head;
I have seen roses damasked,[1] red and white,
But no such roses see I in her cheeks;
And in some perfumes is there more delight
Than in the breath that from my mistress reeks;
I love to hear her speak, yet well I know
That music hath a far more pleasing sound;
I grant I never saw a goddess go;[2]
My mistress, when she walks, treads on the ground.
And yet, by heaven, I think my love as rare
As any she[3] belied with false compare.

Analyzing the Text

1. In what way does the speaker challenge each of the conventional features that are traditional subjects of praise in courtly poetry?
2. After building a case against his mistress's appeal, how does the speaker reverse course and affirm the value of what he had seemed to disparage?

Understanding Shakespeare's Techniques

1. In what way does the exact double rhyme of the last two lines convey a sense of conviction and finality that contrasts with the alternating end-rhymes in the previous lines of the sonnet? How does this pattern of emphasis help the speaker make the case?
2. The speaker is at some pains to describe the utterly ordinary outer appearance of his beloved when compared with the love and devotion she elicits. How does this convey the speaker's ability to discriminate and make correct judgments, although in the form of a reverse compliment?

Arguing for an Interpretation

1. Is the poem directed more against the conventions governing love poems in Shakespeare's day than it is a heartfelt tribute? Does this poem seem sincere? Why or why not?
2. Write a short poem in which the person you praise is first realistically assessed against an ideal, and then defended for some quality that is not immediately obvious to others.

Robert Browning

Robert Browning (1812–1889) was born near London, into a family where he was educated largely at home browsing through his father's 6,000 book library. He attended school at the University of London, but quite

[1]*damasked:* mingled. [2]*go:* walk. [3]*any she:* any woman.

early turned to writing poetry (which initially proved to be too obscure to gain popular approval). A chance compliment by the invalid poetess, Elizabeth Barrett, began what proved to be an intense love affair and courtship. In 1846, they were secretly married and moved to Italy where they lived first in Pisa and then in Florence. Browning earned both critical acclaim and popular success with a collection of 50 dramatic monologues, Men and Women *(1855). In 1861, Elizabeth died and he returned to London. His later poetic works include* Dramatis Personae *(1864) and his most ambitious work,* The Ring and the Book *(1869), a 21,000 line poem offering the perspectives of nine different speakers on an archaic Roman murder trial. The* dramatic monologue *Browning perfected emphasizes how people deceive themselves in the act of trying to persuade others—features that can be observed in "My Last Duchess" (1842).*

My Last Duchess

FERRARA

THAT'S MY last Duchess painted on the wall,
Looking as if she were alive. I call
That piece a wonder, now: Frà Pandolf's hands
Worked busily a day, and there she stands.
Will't please you sit and look at her? I said
"Frà Pandolf" by design, for never read
Strangers like you that pictured countenance,
The depth and passion of its earnest glance,
But to myself they turned (since none puts by
The curtain I have drawn for you, but I)
And seemed as they would ask me, if they durst,
How such a glance came there; so, not the first
Are you to turn and ask thus. Sir, 'twas not
Her husband's presence only, called that spot
Of joy into the Duchess' cheek; perhaps
Frà Pandolf chanced to say, "Her mantle laps
Over my lady's wrist too much," or "Paint
Must never hope to reproduce the faint
Half-flush that dies along her throat": such stuff
Was courtesy, she thought, and cause enough
For calling up that spot of joy. She had
A heart—how shall I say?—too soon made glad,
Too easily impressed: she liked whate'er
She looked on, and her looks went everywhere.
Sir, 'twas all one! My favour at her breast,
The dropping of the daylight in the West,

The bough of cherries some officious fool
Broke in the orchard for her, the white mule
She rode with round the terrace—all and each
Would draw from her alike the approving speech,
Or blush, at least. She thanked men,—good! but thanked
Somehow—I know not how—as if she ranked
My gift of a nine-hundred-years-old name
With anybody's gift. Who'd stoop to blame
This sort of trifling? Even had you skill
In speech—(which I have not)—to make your will
Quite clear to such an one, and say, "Just this
Or that in you disgusts me; here you miss,
Or there exceed the mark"—and if she let
Herself be lessoned so, nor plainly set
Her wits to yours, forsooth, and made excuse,
—E'en then would be some stooping; and I choose
Never to stoop. Oh sir, she smiled, no doubt,
Whene'er I passed her; but who passed without
Much the same smile? This grew; I gave commands;
Then all smiles stopped together. There she stands
As if alive. Will't please you rise? We'll meet
The company below, then. I repeat,
The Count your master's known munificence
Is ample warrant that no just pretence
Of mine for dowry will be disallowed;
Though his fair daughter's self, as I avowed
At starting, is my object. Nay, we'll go
Together down, sir. Notice Neptune, though,
Taming a sea-horse, thought a rarity,
Which Claus of Innsbruck cast in bronze for me!

Analyzing the Text

1. With whom is the duke speaking about his previous wife, and why? Given the events in the poem, why is this situation ironic?
2. What kinds of things are most important to the duke, and why was he displeased with his former wife?

Understanding Browning's Techniques

1. What does the duke's attitude toward expensive possessions such as a commissioned painting suggest about his view of women?
2. What details tell us how the visitor appears to respond to the duke's story? What is the visitor's objective?

Arguing for an Interpretation

1. How does the dramatic monologue, as Browning developed it, allow characters to reveal much about themselves indirectly? In your opinion, is this a superior technique to direct narrative commentary? Explain your answer.

2. To what extent are the duke and the prospective father-in-law's agent meant to represent the aristocracy of sixteenth-century Italy? What function did marriages serve in this society?

ELIZABETH BARRETT BROWNING

Elizabeth Barrett Browning (1806-1861) was given a thorough education in Greek, Latin, French, Italian, German, and Spanish from tutors. She began writing poetry at the age of eight. Plagued by ill health, she settled in the family home in London in 1841 and devoted what energy she had to writing. A two-volume collection of her poems elicited a letter from Robert Browning that initated their celebrated correspondence. In the Sonnets from the Portuguese,[1] *written during 1846, Elizabeth charts her growing love for him. Her father was violently opposed to their marrying, and so they eloped to Italy in 1846. Her poetry is not only about love but political change and social justice.*

How Do I Love Thee?

43

How do I love thee? Let me count the ways.
I love thee to the depth and breadth and height
My soul can reach, when feeling out of sight
For the ends of Being and ideal Grace.
I love thee to the level of everyday's
Most quiet need, by sun and candlelight.
I love thee freely, as men strive for Right;
I love thee purely, as they turn from Praise.
I love thee with the passion put to use
In my old griefs, and with my childhood's faith,
I love thee with a love I seemed to lose
With my lost saints—I love thee with the breadth,
Smiles, tears, of all my life—and, if God choose,
I shall but love thee better after death.

Analyzing the Text

1. In what ways does the speaker blend an idealized romantic love with hopes for political and social justice?
2. Has the speaker's love taken on a quality of almost quasi-religious devotion? Explain your answer.

[1]From *Sonnets from the Portuguese,* No. 43. These love poems addressed to Browning are lightly disguised as translations from a fictitious Portuguese source.

Understanding Browning's Techniques

1. How does this sonnet develop the spatial metaphor expressed in line 2?
2. Beginning at line 10, the sonnet shifts to the temporal dimension, referring to "old griefs," "childhood's faith," and "lost saints" (line 12). How does this shift in focus amend the catalog listing "the ways of love"?

Arguing for an Interpretation

1. In your opinion, has the speaker drawn into her personal love feelings usually associated with social idealism and religion by displacing lofty sentiments and emotions onto the object of her affection?
2. Do you believe this kind of idealized love is capable of being sustained in the real world? Why or why not?

Drama

SUSAN GLASPELL

Susan Glaspell (1882-1948) was born and raised in Davenport, Iowa, and graduated from Drake University in 1899. She worked as a reporter and wrote short stories that were published in Harper's *and* Ladies' Home Journal. *Glaspell won a Pulitzer Prize for drama in 1931 for* Alison's House, *which was based on Emily Dickinson's life. She wrote* Trifles *in 1916 for the Provincetown Players on Cape Cod, in Massachusetts. This play was based on a murder trial she had covered while working as a reporter for the* Des Moines News. Trifles *(1916) offers an instructive example of the ways in which men and women perceive events and their own roles in life in a traditional society.*

Trifles

Cast of Characters

GEORGE HENDERSON, *county attorney*

HENRY PETERS, *sheriff*

LEWIS HALE, *a neighboring farmer*

MRS. PETERS

MRS. HALE

SCENE. *The kitchen in the now abandoned farmhouse of John Wright, a gloomy kitchen, and left without having been put in order—unwashed pans under the sink, a loaf of bread outside the bread-box, a dish-towel on the table—other signs of incompleted work. At the rear the outer door opens and the Sheriff comes in followed by the County Attorney and Hale. The Sheriff and Hale are men in middle life, the County Attorney is a young man; all are much bundled up and go at once to the stove. They are followed by the two women—the Sheriff's wife first; she is a slight wiry woman, a thin nervous face. Mrs. Hale is larger and would ordinarily be called more comfortable looking, but she is disturbed now and looks fearfully about as she enters. The women have come in slowly, and stand close together near the door.*

COUNTY ATTORNEY. (*Rubbing his hands.*) This feels good. Come up to the fire, ladies.

MRS. PETERS. (*After taking a step forward.*) I'm not—cold.

SHERIFF. (*Unbuttoning his overcoat and stepping away from the stove as if to mark the beginning of official business.*) Now, Mr. Hale, before we move things about, you explain to Mr. Henderson just what you saw when you came here yesterday morning.

COUNTY ATTORNEY. By the way, has anything been moved? Are things just as you left them yesterday?

SHERIFF. (*Looking about.*) It's just the same. When it dropped below zero last night I thought I'd better send Frank out this morning to make a fire for us—no use getting pneumonia with a big case on, but I told him not to touch anything except the stove—and you know Frank.

COUNTY ATTORNEY. Somebody should have been left here yesterday.

SHERIFF. Oh—yesterday. When I had to send Frank to Morris Center for that man who went crazy—I want you to know I had my hands full yesterday. I knew you could get back from Omaha by today and as long as I went over everything here myself—

COUNTY ATTORNEY. Well, Mr. Hale, tell just what happened when you came here yesterday morning.

HALE. Harry and I had started to town with a load of potatoes. We came along the road from my place and as I got here I said, "I'm going to see if I can't get John Wright to go in with me on a party telephone." I spoke to Wright about it once before and he put me off, saying folks talked too much anyway, and all he asked was peace and quiet—I guess you know about how much he talked himself; but I thought maybe if I went to the house and talked about it before his wife, though I said to Harry that I didn't know as what his wife wanted made much difference to John—

COUNTY ATTORNEY. Let's talk about that later, Mr. Hale. I do want to talk about that, but tell now just what happened when you got to the house.

HALE. I didn't hear or see anything; I knocked at the door, and still it was all quiet inside. I knew they must be up, it was past eight o'clock. So I knocked again, and I thought I heard somebody say, "Come in." I wasn't sure, I'm not sure yet, but I opened the door—this door (*Indicating the door by which the two women are still standing.*) and there in the rocker—(*Pointing to it.*) sat Mrs. Wright.

(They all look at the rocker.)

COUNTY ATTORNEY. What—was she doing?

HALE. She was rockin' back and forth. She had her apron in her hand and was kind of—pleating it.

COUNTY ATTORNEY. And how did she—look?

HALE. Well, she looked queer.

COUNTY ATTORNEY. How do you mean—queer?

HALE. Well, as if she didn't know what she was going to do next. And kind of done up.

COUNTY ATTORNEY. How did she seem to feel about your coming?

HALE. Why, I don't think she minded—one way or other. She didn't pay much attention. I said, "How do, Mrs. Wright, it's cold, ain't it?" And she said, "Is it?"—and went on kind of pleating at her apron. Well, I was surprised; she didn't ask me to come up to the stove, or to set down, but just sat there, not even looking at me, so I said, "I want to see John." And then she—laughed. I guess you would call it a laugh. I thought of Harry and the team outside, so I said a little sharp: "Can't I see John?" "No," she says, kind o' dull like. "Ain't he home?" says I. "Yes," says she, "he's home." Then why can't I see him?" I asked her, out of patience. "Cause he's dead," says she. "*Dead?*" says I. She just nodded her head, not getting a bit excited, but rockin' back and forth. "Why—where is he?" says I, not knowing what to say. She just pointed upstairs—like that. (*Himself pointing to the room above.*) I got up, with the idea of going up there. I walked from there to here—then I says, "Why, what did he die of?" "He died of a rope round his neck," says she, and just went on pleatin' at her apron. Well, I went out and called Harry. I thought I might—need help. We went upstairs and there he was lyin'—

COUNTY ATTORNEY. I think I'd rather have you go into that upstairs, where you can point it all out. Just go on now with the rest of the story.

HALE. Well, my first thought was to get that rope off. It looked . . . (*Stops, his face twitches.*) . . . but Harry, he went up to him, and he said, "No, he's dead all right, and we'd better not touch anything." So we went back downstairs. She was still sitting that same way. "Has anybody been notified?" I asked. "No," says she, unconcerned. "Who did this, Mrs. Wright?" said Harry. He said it businesslike—and she stopped pleatin' of her apron. "I don't know," she says. "You don't *know?*" says Harry. "No," says she. "Weren't you sleepin' in the bed with him?" says Harry. "Yes," says she, "but I was on the inside." "Somebody slipped a rope round his neck and strangled him and you didn't wake up?" says Harry. "I didn't wake up," she said after him. We must 'a looked as if we didn't see how that could be, for after a minute she said, "I sleep sound." Harry was going to ask her more questions but I said maybe we ought to let her tell her story first to the coroner, or the sheriff, so Harry went fast as he could to Rivers' place, where there's a telephone.

COUNTY ATTORNEY. And what did Mrs. Wright do when she knew that you had gone for the coroner?

HALE. She moved from that chair to this one over here (*Pointing to a small chair in the corner.*) and just sat there with her hands held together and looking down. I got a feeling that I ought to make some conversation, so I said I had come in to see if John wanted to put in a telephone, and at that she started to laugh, and then she stopped and looked at me—scared. (*The County Attorney, who has had his notebook out, makes a note.*) I dunno, maybe it wasn't scared. I wouldn't like to say it was. Soon Harry got back, and then Dr. Lloyd came, and you, Mr. Peters, and so I guess that's all I know that you don't.

COUNTY ATTORNEY. (*Looking around.*) I guess we'll go upstairs first—and then out to the barn and around there. (*To the Sheriff.*) You're convinced that there was nothing important here—nothing that would point to any motive.

SHERIFF. Nothing here but kitchen things.

(*The County Attorney, after again looking around the kitchen, opens the door of a cupboard closet. He gets up on a chair and looks on a shelf. Pulls his hand away.*)

COUNTY ATTORNEY. Here's a nice mess.

(*The women draw nearer.*)

MRS. PETERS. (*To the other woman.*) Oh, her fruit; it did freeze. (*To the Lawyer.*) She worried about that when it turned so cold. She said the fire'd go out and her jars would break.

SHERIFF. Well, can you beat the women! Held for murder and worryin' about her preserves.

COUNTY ATTORNEY. I guess before we're through she may have something more serious than preserves to worry about.

HALE. Well, women are used to worrying over trifles.

(*The two women move a little closer together.*)

COUNTY ATTORNEY. (*With the gallantry of a young politician.*) And yet, for all their worries, what would we do without the ladies? (*The women do not unbend. He goes to the sink, takes a dipperful of water from the pail and pouring it into a basin, washes his hands. Starts to wipe them on the roller-towel, turns it for a cleaner place.*) Dirty towels! (*Kicks his foot against the pans under the sink.*) Not much of a housekeeper, would you say, ladies?

MRS. HALE. (*Stiffly.*) There's a great deal of work to be done on a farm.

COUNTY ATTORNEY. To be sure. And yet (*With a little bow to her.*) I know there are some Dickson county farmhouses which do not have such roller towels.

(*He gives it a pull to expose its full length again.*)

MRS. HALE. Those towels get dirty awful quick. Men's hands aren't always as clean as they might be.

COUNTY ATTORNEY. Ah, loyal to your sex, I see. But you and Mrs. Wright were neighbors. I suppose you were friends, too.

MRS. HALE. (*Shaking her head.*) I've not seen much of her of late years. I've not been in this house—it's more than a year.

COUNTY ATTORNEY. And why was that? You didn't like her?

MRS. HALE. I liked her all well enough. Farmers' wives have their hands full, Mr. Henderson. And then—

COUNTY ATTORNEY. Yes—?

MRS. HALE. (*Looking about.*) It never seemed a very cheerful place.

COUNTY ATTORNEY. No—it's not cheerful. I shouldn't say she had the home-making instinct.

MRS. HALE. Well, I don't know as Wright had, either.

COUNTY ATTORNEY. You mean that they didn't get on very well?

MRS. HALE. No, I don't mean anything. But I don't think a place'd be any cheerfuller for John Wright's being in it.

COUNTY ATTORNEY. I'd like to talk more of that a little later. I want to get the lay of things upstairs now.

(*He goes to the left, where three steps lead to a stair door.*)

SHERIFF. I suppose anything Mrs. Peters does'll be all right. She was to take in some clothes for her, you know, and a few little things. We left in such a hurry yesterday.

COUNTY ATTORNEY. Yes, but I would like to see what you take, Mrs. Peters, and keep an eye out for anything that might be of use to *us.*

MRS. PETERS. Yes, Mr. Henderson.

(The women listen to the men's steps on the stairs, then look about the kitchen.)

MRS. HALE. I'd hate to have men coming into my kitchen, snooping around and criticising.

(She arranges the pans under the sink which the Lawyer had shoved out of place.)

MRS. PETERS. Of course it's no more than their duty.

MRS. HALE. Duty's all right, but I guess that deputy sheriff that came out to make the fire might have got a little of this on. (*Gives the roller towel a pull.*) Wish I'd thought of that sooner. Seems mean to talk about her for not having things slicked up when she had to come away in such a hurry.

MRS. PETERS. (*Who had gone to a small table in the left rear corner of the room, and lifted one end of a towel that covers a pan.*) She had bread set.

(Stands still.)

MRS. HALE. (*Eyes fixed on a loaf of bread beside the breadbox, which is on a low shelf at the other side of the room. Moves slowly toward it.*) She was going to put this in there. (*Picks up loaf, then abruptly drops it. In a manner of returning to familiar things.*) It's a shame about her fruit. I wonder if it's all gone. (*Gets up on the chair and looks.*) I think there's some here that's all right, Mrs. Peters. Yes—here; (*Holding it toward the window.*) this is cherries, too. (*Looking again.*) I declare I believe that's the only one. (*Gets down, bottle in her hand. Goes to the sink and wipes it off on the outside.*) She'll feel awful bad after all her hard work in the hot weather. I remember the afternoon I put up my cherries last summer.

(She puts the bottle on the big kitchen table, center of the room. With a sigh, is about to sit down in the rocking-chair. Before she is seated realizes what chair it is; with a slow look at it, steps back. The chair which she has touched rocks back and forth.)

MRS. PETERS. Well, I must get those things from the front room closet. (*She goes to the door at the right, but after looking into the other room, steps back.*) You coming with me, Mrs. Hale? You could help me carry them.

(They go in the other room; reappear, Mrs. Peters carrying a dress and skirt, Mrs. Hale following with a pair of shoes.)

MRS. PETERS. My, it's cold in there.

(She puts the clothes on the big table and hurries to the stove.)

MRS. HALE. (*Examining the skirt.*) Wright was close. I think maybe that's why she kept so much to herself. She didn't even belong to the Ladies

Aid. I suppose she felt she couldn't do her part, and then you don't enjoy things when you feel shabby. She used to wear pretty clothes and be lively, when she was Minnie Foster, one of the town girls singing in the choir. But that—oh, that was thirty years ago. This all you was to take in?

MRS. PETERS. She said she wanted an apron. Funny thing to want, for there isn't much to get you dirty in jail, goodness knows. But I suppose just to make her feel more natural. She said they was in the top drawer in this cupboard. Yes, here. And then her little shawl that always hung behind the door. (*Opens stair door and looks.*) Yes, here it is.

(*Quickly shuts door leading upstairs.*)

MRS. HALE. (*Abruptly moving toward her.*) Mrs. Peters?

MRS. PETERS. Yes, Mrs. Hale?

MRS. HALE. Do you think she did it?

MRS. PETERS. (*In a frightened voice.*) Oh, I don't know.

MRS. HALE. Well, I don't think she did. Asking for an apron and her little shawl. Worrying about her fruit.

MRS. PETERS. (*Starts to speak, glances up, where footsteps are heard in the room above. In a low voice.*) Mr. Peters says it looks bad for her. Mr. Henderson is awful sarcastic in a speech and he'll make fun of her sayin' she didn't wake up.

MRS. HALE. Well, I guess John Wright didn't wake when they was slipping that rope under his neck.

MRS. PETERS. No, it's strange. It must have been done awful crafty and still. They say it was such a—funny way to kill a man, rigging it all up like that.

MRS. HALE. That's just what Mr. Hale said. There was a gun in the house. He says that's what he can't understand.

MRS. PETERS. Mr. Henderson said coming out that what was needed for the case was a motive; something to show anger, or—sudden feeling.

MRS. HALE. (*Who is standing by the table.*) Well, I don't see any signs of anger around here. (*She puts her hand on the dish towel which lies on the table, stands looking down at table, one half of which is clean, the other half messy.*) It's wiped to here. (*Makes a move as if to finish work, then turns and looks at loaf of bread outside the breadbox. Drops towel. In that voice of coming back to familiar things.*) Wonder how they are finding things upstairs. I hope she had it a little more red-up° up there. You know, it seems kind of *sneaking*. Locking her up in town and then coming out here and trying to get her own house to turn against her!

MRS. PETERS. But Mrs. Hale, the law is the law.

MRS. HALE. I s'pose 'tis. (*Unbuttoning her coat.*) Better loosen up your things, Mrs. Peters. You won't feel them when you go out.

(*Mrs. Peters takes off her fur tippet,° goes to hang it on hook at back of room, stands looking at the under part of the small corner table.*)

MRS. PETERS. She was piecing a quilt.

(*She brings the large sewing basket and they look at the bright pieces.*)

---

red-up: neat, and orderly. **tippet:** a scarf which covers the neck and shoulders.

MRS. HALE. It's log cabin pattern. Pretty, isn't it? I wonder if she was goin' to quilt it or just knot it?

(Footsteps have been heard coming down the stairs. The Sheriff enters followed by Hale and the County Attorney.)

SHERIFF. They wonder if she was going to quilt it or just knot it!

(The men laugh; the women look abashed.)

COUNTY ATTORNEY. *(Rubbing his hands over the stove.)* Frank's fire didn't do much up there, did it? Well, let's go out to the barn and get that cleared up.

(The men go outside.)

MRS. HALE. *(Resentfully.)* I don't know as there's anything so strange, our takin' up our time with little things while we're waiting for them to get the evidence. *(She sits down at the big table smoothing out a block with decision.)* I don't see as it's anything to laugh about.

MRS. PETERS. *(Apologetically.)* Of course they've got awful important things on their minds.

(Pulls up a chair and joins Mrs. Hale at the table.)

MRS. HALE. *(Examining another block.)* Mrs. Peters, look at this one. Here, this is the one she was working on, and look at the sewing! All the rest of it has been so nice and even. And look at this! It's all over the place! Why, it looks as if she didn't know what she was about!

(After she has said this they look at each other, then start to glance back at the door. After an instant Mrs. Hale has pulled at a knot and ripped the sewing.)

MRS. PETERS. Oh, what are you doing, Mrs. Hale?

MRS. HALE. *(Mildly.)* Just pulling out a stitch or two that's not sewed very good. *(Threading a needle.)* Bad sewing always made me fidgety.

MRS. PETERS. *(Nervously.)* I don't think we ought to touch things.

MRS. HALE. I'll just finish up this end. *(Suddenly stopping and leaning forward.)* Mrs. Peters?

MRS. PETERS. Yes, Mrs. Hale?

MRS. HALE. What do you suppose she was so nervous about?

MRS. PETERS. Oh—I don't know. I don't know as she was nervous. I sometimes sew awful queer when I'm just tired. *(Mrs. Hale starts to say something, looks at Mrs. Peters, then goes on sewing.)* Well I must get these things wrapped up. They may be through sooner than we think. *(Putting apron and other things together.)* I wonder where I can find a piece of paper, and string.

MRS. HALE. In that cupboard, maybe.

MRS. PETERS. *(Looking in cupboard.)* Why, here's a bird-cage. *(Holds it up.)* Did she have a bird, Mrs. Hale?

MRS. HALE. Why, I don't know whether she did or not—I've not been here for so long. There was a man around last year selling canaries cheap, but I don't know as she took one; maybe she did. She used to sing real pretty herself.

MRS. PETERS. *(Glancing around.)* Seems funny to think of a bird here. But she must have had one, or why would she have a cage? I wonder what happened to it?

MRS. HALE. I s'pose maybe the cat got it.

MRS. PETERS. No, she didn't have a cat. She's got that feeling some people have about cats—being afraid of them. My cat got in her room and she was real upset and asked me to take it out.

MRS. HALE. My sister Bessie was like that. Queer, ain't it?

MRS. PETERS. (*Examining the cage.*) Why, look at this door. It's broke. One hinge is pulled apart.

MRS. HALE. (*Looking too.*) Looks as if someone must have been rough with it.

MRS. PETERS. Why, yes.

(*She brings the cage forward and puts it on the table.*)

MRS. HALE. I wish if they're going to find any evidence they'd be about it. I don't like this place.

MRS. PETERS. But I'm awful glad you came with me, Mrs. Hale. It would be lonesome for me sitting here alone.

MRS. HALE. It would, wouldn't it? (*Dropping her sewing.*) But I tell you what I do wish, Mrs. Peters. I wish I had come over sometimes when *she* was here. I—(*Looking around the room.*)—wish I had.

MRS. PETERS. But of course you were awful busy, Mrs. Hale—your house and your children.

MRS. HALE. I could've come. I stayed away because it weren't cheerful—and that's why I ought to have come. I—I've never liked this place. Maybe because it's down in a hollow and you don't see the road. I dunno what it is, but it's a lonesome place and always was. I wish I had come over to see Minnie Foster sometimes. I can see now—

(*Shakes her head.*)

MRS. PETERS. Well, you mustn't reproach yourself, Mrs. Hale. Somehow we just don't see how it is with other folks until—something comes up.

MRS. HALE. Not having children makes less work—but it makes a quiet house, and Wright out to work all day, and no company when he did come in. Did you know John Wright, Mrs. Peters?

MRS. PETERS. Not to know him; I've seen him in town. They say he was a good man.

MRS. HALE. Yes—good; he didn't drink, and kept his word as well as most, I guess, and paid his debts. But he was a hard man, Mrs. Peters. Just to pass the time of day with him—(*Shivers.*) Like a raw wind that gets to the bone. (*Pauses, her eye falling on the cage.*) I should think she would 'a wanted a bird. But what do you suppose went with it?

MRS. PETERS. I don't know, unless it got sick and died.

(*She reaches over and swings the broken door, swings it again, both women watch it.*)

MRS. HALE. You weren't raised round here, were you? (*Mrs. Peters shakes her head.*) You didn't know—her?

MRS. PETERS. Not till they brought her yesterday.

MRS. HALE. She—come to think of it, she was kind of like a bird herself—real sweet and pretty, but kind of timid and—fluttery. How—she—did—change. (*Silence; then as if struck by a happy thought and relieved to get back to everyday things.*) Tell you what, Mrs. Peters, why don't you take the quilt in with you? It might take up her mind.

MRS. PETERS. Why, I think that's a real nice idea, Mrs. Hale. There couldn't possibly be any objection to it, could there? Now, just what would I take? I wonder if her patches are in here—and her things.

(*They look in the sewing basket.*)

MRS. HALE. Here's some red. I expect this has got sewing things in it. (*Brings out a fancy box.*) What a pretty box. Looks like something somebody would give you. Maybe her scissors are in here. (*Opens box. Suddenly puts her hand to her nose.*) Why—(*Mrs. Peters bends nearer, then turns her face away.*) There's something wrapped up in this piece of silk.

MRS. PETERS. Why, this isn't her scissors.

MRS. HALE. (*Lifting the silk.*) Oh, Mrs. Peters—it's—

(*Mrs. Peters bends closer.*)

MRS. PETERS. It's the bird.

MRS. HALE. (*Jumping up.*) But, Mrs. Peters—look at it! Its neck! Look at its neck! It's all—other side *to.*

MRS. PETERS. Somebody—wrung—its—neck.

(*Their eyes meet. A look of growing comprehension, of horror. Steps are heard outside. Mrs. Hale slips box under quilt pieces, and sinks into her chair. Enter Sheriff and County Attorney. Mrs. Peters rises.*)

COUNTY ATTORNEY. (*As one turning from serious things to little pleasantries.*) Well, ladies, have you decided whether she was going to quilt it or knot it?

MRS. PETERS. We think she was going to—knot it.

COUNTY ATTORNEY. Well, that's interesting, I'm sure. (*Seeing the bird-cage.*) Has the bird flown?

MRS. HALE. (*Putting more quilt pieces over the box.*) We think the—cat got it.

COUNTY ATTORNEY. (*Preoccupied.*) Is there a cat?

(*Mrs. Hale glances in a quick covert way at Mrs. Peters.*)

MRS. PETERS. Well, not *now.* They're superstitious, you know. They leave.

COUNTY ATTORNEY. (*To Sheriff Peters, continuing an interrupted conversation.*) No sign at all of anyone having come from the outside. Their own rope. Now let's go up again and go over it piece by piece. (*They start upstairs.*) It would have to have been someone who knew just the—

(*Mrs. Peters sits down. The two women sit there not looking at one another, but as if peering into something and at the same time holding back. When they talk now it is in the manner of feeling their way over strange ground, as if afraid of what they are saying, but as if they cannot help saying it.*)

MRS. HALE. She liked the bird. She was going to bury it in that pretty box.

MRS. PETERS. (*In a whisper.*) When I was a girl—my kitten—there was a boy took a hatchet, and before my eyes—and before I could get there—(*Covers her face an instant.*) If they hadn't held me back I would have—(*Catches herself, looks upstairs where steps are heard, falters weakly.*)—hurt him.

MRS. HALE. (*With a slow look around her.*) I wonder how it would seem never to have had any children around. (*Pause.*) No, Wright wouldn't like the bird—a thing that sang. She used to sing. He killed that, too.

MRS. PETERS. (*Moving uneasily.*) We don't know who killed the bird.

MRS. HALE. I knew John Wright.

MRS. PETERS. It was an awful thing was done in this house that night, Mrs. Hale. Killing a man while he slept, slipping a rope around his neck that choked the life out of him.

MRS. HALE. His neck. Choked the life out of him.

(*Her hand goes out and rests on the bird-cage.*)

MRS. PETERS. (*With rising voice.*) We don't know who killed him. We don't know.

MRS. HALE. (*Her own feeling not interrupted.*) If there'd been years and years of nothing, then a bird to sing to you, it would be awful—still, after the bird was still.

MRS. PETERS. (*Something within her speaking.*) I know what stillness is. When we homesteaded in Dakota, and my first baby died—after he was two years old, and me with no other then—

MRS. HALE. (*Moving.*) How soon do you suppose they'll be through, looking for the evidence?

MRS. PETERS. I know what stillness is. (*Pulling herself back.*) The law has got to punish crime, Mrs. Hale.

MRS. HALE. (*Not as if answering that.*) I wish you'd seen Minnie Foster when she wore a white dress with blue ribbons and stood up there in the choir and sang. (*A look around the room.*) Oh, I *wish* I'd come over here once in a while! That was a crime! That was a crime! Who's going to punish that?

MRS. PETERS. (*Looking upstairs.*) We mustn't—take on.

MRS. HALE. I might have known she needed help! I know how things can be—for women. I tell you, it's queer, Mrs. Peters. We live close together and we live far apart. We all go through the same things—it's all just a different kind of the same thing. (*Brushes her eyes, noticing the bottle of fruit, reaches out for it.*) If I was you I wouldn't tell her her fruit was gone. Tell her it *ain't*. Tell her it's all right. Take this in to prove it to her. She—she may never know whether it was broke or not.

MRS. PETERS. (*Takes the bottle, looks about for something to wrap it in; takes petticoat from the clothes brought from the other room, very nervously begins winding this around the bottle. In a false voice.*) My, it's a good thing the men couldn't hear us. Wouldn't they just laugh! Getting all stirred up over a little thing like a—dead canary. As if that could have anything to do with—with—wouldn't they *laugh!*

(*The men are heard coming down stairs.*)

MRS. HALE. (*Under her breath.*) Maybe they would—maybe they wouldn't.

COUNTY ATTORNEY. No, Peters, it's all perfectly clear except a reason for doing it. But you know juries when it comes to women. If there was some definite thing. Something to show—something to make a story about—a thing that would connect up with this strange way of doing it—

(*The women's eyes meet for an instant. Enter Hale from outer door.*)

HALE. Well, I've got the team° around. Pretty cold out there.

COUNTY ATTORNEY. I'm going to stay here a while by myself. (*To the Sheriff.*) You can send Frank out for me, can't you? I want to go over everything. I'm not satisfied that we can't do better.

SHERIFF. Do you want to see what Mrs. Peters is going to take in?

(*The County Attorney goes to the table, picks up the apron, laughs.*)

COUNTY ATTORNEY. Oh, I guess they're not very dangerous things the ladies have picked out. (*Moves a few things about, disturbing the quilt pieces which cover the box. Steps back.*) No, Mrs. Peters doesn't need supervising. For that matter, a sheriff's wife is married to the law. Ever think of it that way, Mrs. Peters?

MRS. PETERS. Not—just that way.

SHERIFF. (*Chuckling.*) Married to the law. (*Moves toward the other room.*) I just want you to come in here a minute, George. We ought to take a look at these windows.

COUNTY ATTORNEY. (*Stoffingly.*) Oh, windows!

SHERIFF. We'll be right out, Mr. Hale.

(*Hale goes outside. The Sheriff follows the County Attorney into the other room. Then Mrs. Hale rises, hands tight together, looking intensely at Mrs. Peters, whose eyes make a slow turn, finally meeting Mrs. Hale's. A moment Mrs. Hale holds her, then her own eyes point the way to where the box is concealed. Suddenly Mrs. Peters throws back quilt pieces and tries to put the box in the bag she is wearing. It is too big. She opens box, starts to take bird out, cannot touch it, goes to pieces, stands there helpless. Sound of a knob turning in the other room. Mrs. Hale snatches the box and puts it in the pocket of her big coat. Enter County Attorney and Sheriff.*)

COUNTY ATTORNEY. (*Facetiously.*) Well, Henry, at least we found out that she was not going to quilt it. She was going to—what is it you call it, ladies?

MRS. HALE. (*Her hand against her pocket.*) We call it—knot it, Mr. Henderson.

CURTAIN

Analyzing the Text

1. In what dramatic ways do the men (the County Attorney and the Sheriff) look for clues and draw conclusions differently from the women (Mrs. Hale and Mrs. Peters)?
2. To what does the title of the play refer and why is it ironic?

Understanding Glaspell's Techniques

1. How does Glaspell use natural objects (for example, the bird cage and the dead canary) as symbols to establish and reinforce important ideas?
2. How does the characterization of John Wright help explain what happens to him and allow us to understand how marrying him changed Minnie Foster?

---

team: team of horses drawing a wagon.

Arguing for an Interpretation

1. In your opinion, would the play have been more effective if Minnie were a speaking character? Why or why not?
2. In what sense can this play be considered an early feminist work that comments on many issues in society?

DAVID IVES

David Ives (1943–) was born in Chicago and educated at Northwestern University and the Yale Drama School. Ives's work appears in diverse formats, including television, film, opera, and the theater. He has written several one-act plays for the annual comedy festival of Manhattan Punch Line, where* Sure Thing *was performed in 1988. Six of his one-act comedies have been collected in* All in the Timing *(1994). The following two-character play is a lighthearted inventive variation on the premise that if we could take back our verbal blunders on the spot relationships would never fail.

Sure Thing

Characters

BILL and BETTY, both in their late 20s

Setting

A café table, with a couple of chairs

Betty is reading at the table. An empty chair opposite her. Bill enters.

BILL. Excuse me. Is this chair taken?

BETTY. Excuse me?

BILL. Is this taken?

BETTY. Yes it is.

BILL. Oh. Sorry.

BETTY. Sure thing.

(*A bell rings softly.*)

BILL. Excuse me. Is this chair taken?

BETTY. Excuse me?

BILL. Is this taken?

BETTY. No, but I'm expecting somebody in a minute.

BILL. Oh. Thanks anyway.

BETTY. Sure thing.

(*A bell rings softly.*)

BILL. Excuse me. Is this chair taken?

BETTY. No, but I'm expecting somebody very shortly.

BILL. Would you mind if I sit here till he or she or it comes?

BETTY. (*Glances at her watch.*) They do seem to be pretty late . . .

BILL. You never know who you might be turning down.

BETTY. Sorry. Nice try, though.

BILL. Sure thing. (*Bell.*) Is this seat taken?

BETTY. No it's not.

BILL. Would you mind if I sit here?

BETTY. Yes I would.

BILL. Oh. (*Bell.*) Is this chair taken?

BETTY. No it's not.

BILL. Would you mind if I sit here?

BETTY. No. Go ahead.

BILL. Thanks. (*He sits. She continues reading.*) Every place else seems to be taken.

BETTY. Mm-hm.

BILL. Great place.

BETTY. Mm-hm.

BILL. What's the book?

BETTY. I just wanted to read in quiet, if you don't mind.

BILL. No. Sure thing. (*Bell.*) Every place else seems to be taken.

BETTY. Mm-hm.

BILL. Great place for reading.

BETTY. Yes, I like it.

BILL. What's the book?

BETTY. *The Sound and the Fury.*

BILL. Oh. Hemingway. (*Bell.*) What's the book?

BETTY. *The Sound and the Fury.*

BILL. Oh. Faulkner.

BETTY. Have you read it?

BILL. Not . . . actually. I've sure read *about* it, though. It's supposed to be great.

BETTY. It is great.

BILL. I hear it's great. (*Small pause.*) Waiter? (*Bell.*) What's the book?

BETTY. *The Sound and the Fury.*

BILL. Oh. Faulkner.

BETTY. Have you read it?

BILL. I'm a Mets fan, myself. (*Bell.*)

BETTY. Have you read it?

BILL. Yeah, I read it in college.

BETTY. Where was college?

BILL. I went to Oral Roberts University. (*Bell.*)

BETTY. Where was college?

BILL. I was lying. I never really went to college. I just like to party. (*Bell.*)

BETTY. Where was college?

BILL. Harvard.

BETTY. Do you like Faulkner?

BILL. I love Faulkner. I spent a whole winter reading him once.

BETTY. I've just started.

BILL. I was so excited after ten pages that I went out and bought everything else he wrote. One of the greatest reading experiences of my life. I mean, all that incredible psychological understanding. Page after page of gorgeous prose. His profound grasp of the mystery of time and human existence. The smells of the earth. . . . What do you think?

BETTY. I think it's pretty boring. (*Bell.*)

BILL. What's the book?

BETTY. *The Sound and the Fury.*

BILL. Oh! Faulkner!

BETTY. Do you like Faulkner?

BILL. I love Faulkner.

BETTY. He's incredible.

BILL. I spent a whole winter reading him once.

BETTY. I was so excited after ten pages that I went out and bought everything else he wrote.

BILL. All that incredible psychological understanding.

BETTY. And the prose is so gorgeous.

BILL. And the way he's grasped the mystery of time—

BETTY. —and human existence. I can't believe I've waited this long to read him.

BILL. You never know. You might not have liked him before.

BETTY. That's true.

BILL. You might not have been ready for him. You have to hit these things at the right moment or it's no good.

BETTY. That's happened to me.

BILL. It's all in the timing. (*Small pause.*) My name's Bill, by the way.

BETTY. I'm Betty.

BILL. Hi.

BETTY. Hi. (*Small pause.*)

BILL. Yes I thought reading Faulkner was . . . a great experience.

BETTY. Yes. (*Small pause.*)

BILL. *The Sound and the Fury . . .* (*Another small pause.*)

BETTY. Well. Onwards and upwards. (*She goes back to her book.*)

BILL. Waiter—? (*Bell.*) You have to hit these things at the right moment or it's no good.

BETTY. That's happened to me.

BILL. It's all in the timing. My name's Bill, by the way.

BETTY. I'm Betty.

BILL. Hi.

BETTY. Hi.

BILL. Do you come in here a lot?

BETTY. Actually I'm just in town for two days from Pakistan.

BILL. Oh. Pakistan. (*Bell.*) My name's Bill, by the way.

BETTY. I'm Betty.

BILL. Hi.

BETTY. Hi.

BILL. Do you come in here a lot?

BETTY. Every once in a while. Do you?

BILL. Not so much anymore. Not as much as I used to. Before my nervous breakdown. (*Bell.*) Do you come in here a lot?

BETTY. Why are you asking?

BILL. Just interested.

BETTY. Are you really interested, or do you just want to pick me up?

BILL. No, I'm really interested.

BETTY. Why would you be interested in whether I come in here a lot?

BILL. Just . . . getting acquainted.

BETTY. Maybe you're only interested for the sake of making small talk long enough to ask me back to your place to listen to some music, or because you've just rented some great tape for your VCR, or because you've got some terrific unknown Django Reinhardt record, only all you really want to do is fuck—which you won't do very well—after which you'll go into the bathroom and pee very loudly, then pad into the kitchen and get yourself a beer from the refrigerator without asking me whether I'd like anything, and then you'll proceed to lie back down beside me and confess that you've got a girlfriend named Stephanie who's away at medical school in Belgium for a year, and that you've been involved with her—*off and on*—in what you'll call a very "intricate" relationship, for about *seven YEARS.* None of which *interests* me, mister!

BILL. Okay. (*Bell.*) Do you come in here a lot?

BETTY. Every other day, I think.

BILL. I come in here quite a lot and I don't remember seeing you.

BETTY. I guess we must be on different schedules.

BILL. Missed connections.

BETTY. Yes. Different time zones.

BILL. Amazing how you can live right next door to somebody in this town and never even know it.

BETTY. I know.

BILL. City life.

BETTY. It's crazy.

BILL. We probably pass each other in the street every day. Right in front of this place, probably.

BETTY. Yep.

BILL. (*Looks around.*) Well the waiters here sure seem to be in some different time zone. I can't seem to locate one anywhere. . . . Waiter! (*He looks back.*) So what do you— (*He sees that she's gone back to her book.*)

BETTY. I beg pardon?

BILL. Nothing. Sorry. (*Bell.*)

BETTY. I guess we must be on different schedules.

BILL. Missed connections.

BETTY. Yes. Different time zones.

BILL. Amazing how you can live right next door to somebody in this town and never even know it.

BETTY. I know.

BILL. City life.

BETTY. It's crazy.

BILL. You weren't waiting for somebody when I came in, were you?

BETTY. Actually I was.

BILL. Oh. Boyfriend?

BETTY. Sort of.

BILL. What's a sort-of boyfriend?

BETTY. My husband.

BILL. Ah-ha. (*Bell.*) You weren't waiting for somebody when I came in, were you?

BETTY. Actually I was.

BILL. Oh. Boyfriend?

BETTY. Sort of.

BILL. What's a sort-of boyfriend?

BETTY. We were meeting here to break up.

BILL. Mm-hm ... (*Bell.*) What's a sort-of boyfriend?

BETTY. My lover. Here she comes right now! (*Bell.*)

BILL. You weren't waiting for somebody when I came in, were you?

BETTY. No, just reading.

BILL. Sort of a sad occupation for a Friday night, isn't it? Reading here, all by yourself?

BETTY. Do you think so?

BILL. Well sure. I mean, what's a good-looking woman like you doing out alone on a Friday night?

BETTY. Trying to keep away from lines like that.

BILL. No, listen— (*Bell.*) You weren't waiting for somebody when I came in, were you?

BETTY. No, just reading.

BILL. Sort of a sad occupation for a Friday night, isn't it? Reading here all by yourself?

BETTY. I guess it is, in a way.

BILL. What's a good-looking woman like you doing out alone on a Friday night anyway? No offense, but ...

BETTY. I'm out alone on a Friday night for the first time in a very long time.

BILL. Oh.

BETTY. You see, I just recently ended a relationship.

BILL. Oh.

BETTY. Of rather long standing.

BILL. I'm sorry. (*Small pause.*) Well listen, since reading by yourself *is* such a sad occupation for a Friday night, would you like to go elsewhere?

BETTY. No ...

BILL. Do something else?

BETTY. No thanks.

BILL. I was headed out to the movies in a while anyway.

BETTY. I don't think so.

BILL. Big chance to let Faulkner catch his breath. All those long sentences get him pretty tired.

BETTY. Thanks anyway.

BILL. Okay.

BETTY. I appreciate the invitation.

BILL. Sure thing. (*Bell.*) You weren't waiting for somebody when I came in, were you?

BETTY. No, just reading.

BILL. Sort of a sad occupation for a Friday night, isn't it? Reading here all by yourself?

BETTY. I guess I was trying to think of it as existentially romantic. You know—cappuccino, great literature, rainy night ...

BILL. That only works in Paris. We *could* hop the late plane to Paris. Get on a Concorde. Find a café ...

BETTY. I'm a little short on plane fare tonight.

BILL. Darn it, so am I.

BETTY. To tell you the truth, I was headed to the movies after I finished this section. Would you like to come along? Since you can't locate a waiter?

BILL. That's a very nice offer, but ...

BETTY. Uh-huh. Girlfriend?

BILL. Two, actually. One of them's pregnant, and Stephanie.— (*Bell.*)

BETTY. Girlfriend?

BILL. No, I don't have a girlfriend. Not if you mean the castrating bitch I dumped last night. (*Bell.*)

BETTY. Girlfriend?

BILL. Sort of. Sort of.

BETTY. What's a sort-of girlfriend?

BILL. My mother. (*Bell.*) I just ended a relationship, actually.

BETTY. Oh.

BILL. Of rather long standing.

BETTY. I'm sorry to hear it.

BILL. This is my first night out alone in a long time. I feel a little bit at sea, to tell you the truth.

BETTY. So you didn't stop to talk because you're a Moonie, or you have some weird political affiliation—?

BILL. Nope. Straight-down-the-ticket Republican. (*Bell.*) Straight-down-the-ticket Democrat. (*Bell.*) Can I tell you something about politics? (*Bell.*) I like to think of myself as a citizen of the universe. (*Bell.*) I'm unaffiliated.

BETTY. That's a relief. So am I.

BILL. I vote my beliefs.

BETTY. Labels are not important.

BILL. Labels are not important, exactly. Take me, for example. I mean, what does it matter if I had a two-point at—(*Bell.*)—three-point at—(*Bell.*)—four-point at college? Or if I did come from Pittsburgh—(*Bell.*)—Cleveland—(*Bell.*)—Westchester County?

BETTY. Sure.

BILL. I believe that a man is what he is. (*Bell.*) A person is what he is. (*Bell.*) A person is . . . what they are.

BETTY. I think so too.

BILL. So what if I admire Trotsky? (*Bell.*) So what if I once had a total-body liposuction? (*Bell.*) So what if I don't have a penis? (*Bell.*) So what if I once spent a year in the Peace Corps? I was acting on my convictions.

BETTY. Sure.

BILL. You can't just hang a sign on a person.

BETTY. Absolutely. I'll bet you're a Scorpio. (*Many bells ring.*) Listen, I was headed to the movies after I finished this section. Would you like to come along?

BILL. That sounds like fun. What's playing?

BETTY. A couple of the really early Woody Allen movies.

BILL. Oh.

BETTY. You don't like Woody Allen?

BILL. Sure. I like Woody Allen.

BETTY. But you're not crazy about Woody Allen.

BILL. Those early ones kind of get on my nerves.

BETTY. Uh-huh. (*Bell.*)

BILL. (*Simultaneously.*)	BETTY. (*Simultaneously.*)
Y'know I was headed to the—	I was thinking about—

BILL. I'm sorry.

BETTY. No, go ahead.

BILL. I was going to say that I was headed to the movies in a little while, and . . .

BETTY. So was I.

BILL. The Woody Allen festival?

BETTY. Just up the street.

BILL. Do you like the early ones?

BETTY. I think anybody who doesn't ought to be run off the planet.

BILL. How many times have you seen *Bananas?*

BETTY. Eight times.

BILL. Twelve. So are you still interested? (*Long pause.*)

BETTY. Do you like Entenmann's crumb cake . . .?

BILL. Last night I went out at two in the morning to get one. (*Small pause.*) Did you have an Etch-a-Sketch as a child?

BETTY. Yes! And do you like Brussels sprouts? (*Small pause.*)

BILL. No, I think they're disgusting.

BETTY. They *are* disgusting!

BILL. Do you still believe in marriage in spite of current sentiments against it?

BETTY. Yes.

BILL. And children?

BETTY. Three of them.

BILL. Two girls and a boy.

BETTY. Harvard, Vassar and Brown.

BILL. And will you love me?

BETTY. Yes.

BILL. And cherish me forever?

BETTY. Yes.

BILL. Do you still want to go to the movies?

BETTY. Sure thing.

BILL AND BETTY. (*Together.*) *Waiter!*

BLACKOUT

Analyzing the Text

1. What kinds of things are turn-offs for both Betty and Bill? What does this imply about how difficult it is for them to find someone compatible?
2. Despite the whimsical nature of the premise, what, in your opinion, are Betty and Bill really looking for in each other?

Understanding Ives's Techniques

1. How does Ives make the ringing bell almost into another character who will or won't permit the conversation to take place and thereby create suspense?
2. What details suggest that their relationship really begins when Bill and Betty move beyond the need for scripted responses?

Arguing for an Interpretation

1. Despite its witty premise, what serious contemporary social issues are addressed in *Sure Thing?*
2. What do you think Ives meant by the title? Explain your answer.

Connections

1. Discuss the expectations and limitations placed on women in Muslim societies referred to in Nawal El Saadawi's essay and in Sembene Ousmane's story.

2. How are the problems faced by the women in Charlotte Perkins Gilman's "The Yellow Wallpaper," Sembene Ousmane's "Her Three Days," and Ernest Hemingway's "Hills Like White Elephants" surprisingly similar although they take place in very different cultures and in different eras?
3. Compare the reasons why the relationships that initially look so promising ultimately fail in James Joyce's "Eveline" and in Monique Proulx's "Feint of Heart."
4. How are trains and journeys used as mythic equivalents for important life decisions in Ernest Hemingway's "Hills Like White Elephants" and in Robert Fox's "A Fable"?
5. Discuss how psychological power games can destroy relationships in stories by Monique Proulx ("Feint of Heart") and Alberto Moravia ("Jewellery").
6. Discuss how Muriel Rukeyser, in her poem, "Myth," and Judith Ortiz Cofer, in her essay, "Myth of the Latin Woman," assail sexual stereotyping.
7. Compare the works by Edna St. Vincent Millay, Elizabeth Barrett Browning, and Anton Chekhov in terms of the meaning that romantic love has in the lives of the protagonists.
8. Compare and contrast the speakers in Corso's poem "Marriage" and Jimmy Santiago Baca's "Spliced Wire" in terms of the contributions the speakers think they have made or could make in a relationship.
9. If Grace Caroline Bridges's "Lisa's Ritual, Age 10" was looked at as a crime, what gender-based assumptions would help or hinder the investigation, as in Susan Glaspell's drama *Trifles?*
10. In what way does John Frederick Nims's "Love Poem" represent a contemporary variation on Shakespeare's poem? How do both poets distinguish between what is personally important to them and what society values?
11. How do the themes of male chauvinism and murder intertwine in Robert Browning's poem and Susan Glaspell's play in very opposite ways?
12. Discuss David Ives's *Sure Thing* as a witty, possibly cynical variation on Kurt Vonnegut's "Who Am I This Time?" and Robert Fox's "A Fable."
13. To what extent does Monique Proulx's story "Feint of Heart" embody the variations Atwood describes in "Happy Endings"?

Filmography

Wuthering Heights (1939) Director: William Wyler. Performers: Lawrence Olivier, Merle Oberon.

This screen adaptation of Emily Brontë's romantic novel captures the tragic grandeur of a doomed love between Heathcliff and Cathy on the Yorkshire moors.

Casablanca (1942) Director: Michael Curtiz. Performers: Ingrid Bergman, Humphrey Bogart.

Classic romantic drama in which Bogart runs a gin joint in Morocco during the Nazi occupation and meets an old flame.

The Palm Beach Story (1942). Director: Preston Sturges. Performers: Joel McCrae, Claudette Colbert, Mary Astor.

A young wife tries to divorce the poor husband she loves in order to marry a millionaire who could fund her husband's business ventures in this classic screwball comedy.

The African Queen (1951) Director: John Huston. Performers: Humphrey Bogart, Katherine Hepburn.

Classic war of the sexes between a Bible-quoting spinster and a hard-drinking steamer captain set in Africa against the background of World War I.

A Streetcar Named Desire (1951) Director: Elia Kazan. Performers: Marlon Brando, Kim Hunter, Vivien Leigh.

Based on Tennessee Williams's play about a neurotic southern belle who visits her sister and is driven mad by her brutal brother-in-law.

Rear Window (1954) Director: Alfred Hitchcock. Performers: Grace Kelly, James Stewart.

A newspaper photographer who is trapped in his apartment while recuperating from a broken leg spies on the activities of his neighbors, aided by the beautiful girl he hesitates to marry in this Hitchcock classic.

Diabolique (1955) Director: Henri-Georges Clouzot. Performers: Simone Signoret, Vera Clouzot.

The wife and mistress of a sadistic schoolmaster kill him, get rid of the body, but soon become guilt-ridden and believe that he is still alive. [France]

Black Orpheus (1958) Director: Marcel Camus. Performer: Marpessa Dawn.

The legend of Orpheus and Eurydice are retold in modern-day Rio de Janiero during the carnival when a streetcar conductor tries to protect a girl who is followed by Death. [Brazil]

Some Like It Hot (1959) Director: Billy Wilder. Performers: Tony Curtis, Jack Lemmon, Marilyn Monroe.

A screamingly funny gender farce about musicians who witness the infamous St. Valentine's Day massacre and escape by dressing as women and joining an all-girl band.

Harold and Maude (1971) Director: Hal Ashby. Performer: Ruth Gordon.

A cult classic about an octogenarian and a twenty-year-old obsessed with suicide who meet at a funeral and develop a friendship that turns into a romantic relationship.

The Spirit of the Beehive (1973) Director: Victor Erice. Performer: Fernando Romez.

A haunting film about a young Spanish girl, who after seeing the 1931 movie, *Frankenstein,* begins a journey to find him. [Spain]

La Cage aux Folles (1978) Director: Edouard Molinaro. Performers: Ugo Tognazzi, Michel Serrault.

A gay St. Tropez nightclub owner and his lover pretend to be a married, straight middle-class couple when his son becomes engaged to a girl from a right-wing family in this hilarious and touching film. [France]

Tootsie (1982) Director: Sydney Pollack. Performers: Dustin Hoffman, Bill Murray, Jessica Lange.

A struggling actor disguises himself as a woman to get a part in a soap opera in this delightful and truthful comedy.

Pauline at the Beach (1983) Director: Eric Rohmer. Performers: Arielle Dombasie, Amanda Langlet.

Twelve-year-old Pauline and her recently divorced cousin spend the summer at their family's beach house, and each has a brief romance. [France]

Ju Dou (1990) Director: Zhang Yimou. Performer: Gong Li.

A tragic and compelling story set in rural China about the third wife of an old abusive factory owner who finds true love with his nephew. [China]

Dogfight (1991) Director: Nancy Savoca. Performers: Lili Taylor, River Phoenix.

A young soldier on his last night stateside before leaving for Vietnam falls in love with a girl he has just met to bring to a Marine "dogfight"—a contest to see who shows up at a bar with the ugliest date.

Thelma and Louise (1991) Director: Ridley Scott. Performers: Susan Sarandon, Geena Davis.

The first feminist "buddy" movie in which a housewife escaping her abusive husband and a world-weary waitress embark on a journey and discover themselves and the violence of the surrounding society.

Like Water for Chocolate (1993) Director: Alfonso Arau. Performer: Lumi Carazos.

A girl caring for her mother imparts all her fantasies of escape and longing for romance into the wonderful food she prepares and inspires all who consume it with erotic yearnings. [Mexico]

Welcome to the Dollhouse (1995) Director: Todd Solondz. Performers: Heather Matarazzo, Victoria Davis.

A socially awkward girl experiences the pain of rejection and the bittersweet reality of her first love.

Crouching Tiger, Hidden Dragon (2000) Director: Ang Lee. Performers: Chow Yun-Fat, Michelle Yeoh.

A martial arts love story set in nineteenth-century China that features exquisite battle scenes choreographed by Yuen Wo-Ping. [China]

Amelie (2001) Director: Jean-Pierre Jeunet. Performer: Audrey Tautou.

A Paris waitress discovers a box of hidden childhood treasures behind a wall in her apartment and begins a quest to return them to their rightful owners and finds herself intervening in their lives and, in the course of doing so, finds her own true love. [France]

L.I.E. (2001) Director: Michael Cuesta. Performers: Brian Cox, Paul Franklin Dano.

A middle-aged pedophile meets a troubled teenager and finds his feelings are more paternal than they are erotic.

Monsoon Wedding (2001) Director: Mira Nair. Performer: Vasundhara Das.

The story, set in modern-day New Delhi with an extended cast of characters and subplots, focuses on the predicament of a girl, who while promised to be married to an Indian computer programmer living in America, is carrying on a romance with a married man. [India]

Chapter 6

Class, Race, and Ethnicity

I used to think I was poor. Then they told me I wasn't poor, I was needy. Then they told me it was self-defeating to think of myself as needy, I was deprived. Then they told me deprived was a bad image, I was underprivileged. Then they told me underprivileged was overused, I was disadvantaged. I still don't have a dime. But I sure have a great vocabulary.

Jules Feiffer

Every society is capable of being characterized in terms of social class. Although principles by which class is identified vary widely from culture to culture—from the amount of money you earn in the United States, to what kind of accent you speak with in England, to what religious caste you are born into in India—class serves to set boundaries around individuals in terms of opportunities and possibilities. Conflicts based on inequalities of social class are often intertwined with those of race and ethnicity because minorities usually receive the least amount of education, have less political clout, earn the least income, and find work in occupations considered menial without the possibility of advancement. Class conditions our entire lives by setting limitations that determine, more than we might like to admit, who we can be friends with, what our goals are, and even who we can marry. For example, consider how class permeates the different connotations of phrases people use to describe (1) getting a *job,* (2) looking for *work,* (3) seeking *employment,* or (4) finding a *position.*

Questions of social class require us to consider the ways any society apportions power, as well as wealth. In many cultures, class status has been linked with assumed differences in individual worth that, on close inspection, have turned out to be socially constructed. The works in this chapter provide windows into the prevailing distribution of power and privilege and allow us to understand how hidden agendas shape attitudes toward various groups according to class, race, and ethnicity. These works offer insight into the actual everyday lives of men and women who have been categorized and, in many cases, marginalized, by these stereotypes. The experiences revealed here suggest that class differences are not natural, nor are they inevitable.

Selections in this chapter take up the crucial and often unrecognized relationships among race, sense of identity, and class, through works of fiction and nonfiction that explore positions of power and powerlessness. Margaret Sanger, who was an early advocate for the dissemination of birth control information, in her essay "The Turbid Ebb and Flow of Misery" describes the blighted lives of poor women caused by unwanted children. In "A Modest Proposal," Jonathan Swift creates an outrageous satire based on a plan to ameliorate the lives of the poverty-stricken in Ireland. An essay by Mary Crow Dog and Richard Erdoes, "Civilize Them with a Stick" describes the endemic racism experienced by Native Americans attending a government-run boarding school. James Baldwin, in "Letter to My Nephew," speaks from the heart about the importance of human dignity in a society that uses racial distinctions to diminish the self-esteem of blacks.

A timeless story, "Désirée's Baby" by Kate Chopin, explores conflicts of class and racism in turn-of-the-century Louisiana. F. Scott Fitzgerald in "Winter Dreams" creates a poignant story that parallels his own experiences as a young man who lacked the means to marry the girl he loved. A classic story, "The Necklace" by Guy de Maupassant, dramatizes the power of vanity and its ironic lifelong consequences in the lives of an impoverished young couple. In "The Button," Mahdokht Kashkuli takes us into the mind of a young boy in modern-day Iran whose family has placed him in an orphanage. Catherine Lim in "Paper" tells how the chance to build their dream house based on making a quick profit on the Singapore Stock Exchange destroys a couple's life. Dorothy Allison in "I'm Working on My Charm" reveals how diplomacy is an essential skill for an aspiring Southern waitress serving Northerners. Lastly, the Argentinian writer Liliana Heker, in "The Stolen Party," describes how class barriers form an impenetrable obstacle to those who try to rise above their station in life.

The poems continue this chapter's exploration of class, sense of identity, and self-esteem in various countries. The voices heard in these poems are those of men and women of different races and several nations.

The renowned playwright Bertolt Brecht, in his poem "A Worker Reads History," teaches a valuable, but often overlooked lesson, about who should be credited with the achievements ascribed to the great. From Germany, Mascha Kaléko, in "Mannequins," contrasts the meager backstage life of fashion models with their glamorous public image. Léon Damas, from French Guiana, in "Hiccup" recreates his mother's litany of complaints regarding his failings to mimic white social etiquette. In "The Nine of Cups," Marge Piercy "reads" the Tarot cards and discovers that contemporary American culture is caught in a vicious downward spiral of materialism and a quest for creature comforts. Linda Hogan, of the Chickasaw Indian tribe, explores in "Workday" the profound social gulf between the world of Native Americans and the dominant white values of the university community where she teaches. From the 19th century we encounter the story of a former slave, Francis E. W. Harper, who challenged preconceptions and became literate. The African American poet Nikki Giovanni describes in "Nikki-Rosa" the sense of love and security her family provided for her despite their poverty. Insight into the unexpected philosophical benefits of field work is offered by Gary Soto in "Dirt." Martín Espada, in "Jorge the Church Janitor Finally Quits," strikes a rueful note of exasperation.

Nobel prize-winning playwright Dario Fo's dark comedy, *We Won't Pay! We Won't Pay!* dramatizes what happens when a typical law-abiding worker in modern-day Italy has to face the fact that his wife has been stealing food to make ends meet and that those with power do not have his best interests at heart.

Essays

Margaret Sanger

Margaret Sanger (1883–1966) was an early advocate for the dissemination of birth control information in America. In "The Turbid Ebb and Flow of Misery" from Margaret Sanger: An Autobiography *(1938),*[1] *she describes the horrendous circumstances and ignorance of sexual matters that compelled her to fight for the rights of poor women. She organized the first conference on birth control in the United States and wrote numerous books and articles on the subject throughout her life.*

The Turbid Ebb and Flow of Misery

Every night and every morn
Some to misery are born.
Every morn and every night
Some are born to sweet delight.
Some are born to sweet delight,
Some are born to endless night.

WILLIAM BLAKE

During these years [about 1912] in New York trained nurses were in great demand. Few people wanted to enter hospitals; they were afraid they might be "practiced" upon, and consented to go only in desperate emergencies. Sentiment was especially vehement in the matter of having babies. A woman's own bedroom, no matter how inconveniently arranged, was the usual place for her lying-in. I was not sufficiently free from domestic duties to be a general nurse, but I could ordinarily manage obstetrical cases because I was notified far enough ahead to plan my schedule. And after serving my two weeks I could get home again.

Sometimes I was summoned to small apartments occupied by young clerks, insurance salesmen, or lawyers, just starting out, most of them un-

---

[1]Chapter 7 of *An Autobiography* (1938). Sanger has taken her chapter title from a line in Matthew Arnold's poem "Dover Beach."

der thirty and whose wives were having their first or second baby. They were always eager to know the best and latest method in infant care and feeding. In particular, Jewish patients, whose lives centered around the family, welcomed advice and followed it implicitly.

But more and more my calls began to come from the Lower East Side, as though I were being magnetically drawn there by some force outside my control. I hated the wretchedness and hopelessness of the poor, and never experienced that satisfaction in working among them that so many noble women have found. My concern for my patients was now quite different from my earlier hospital attitude. I could see that much was wrong with them which did not appear in the physiological or medical diagnosis. A woman in childbirth was not merely a woman in childbirth. My expanded outlook included a view of her background, her potentialities as a human being, the kind of children she was bearing, and what was going to happen to them.

The wives of small shopkeepers were my most frequent cases, but I had carpenters, truck drivers, dishwashers, and pushcart vendors. I admired intensely the consideration most of these people had for their own. Money to pay doctor and nurse had been carefully saved months in advance—parents-in-law, grandfathers, grandmothers, all contributing.

As soon as the neighbors learned that a nurse was in the building they 5
came in a friendly way to visit, often carrying fruit, jellies, or gefüllter fish made after a cherished recipe. It was infinitely pathetic to me that they, so poor themselves, should bring me food. Later they drifted in again with the excuse of getting the plate, and sat down for a nice talk; there was no hurry. Always back of the little gift was the question, "I am pregnant (or my daughter, or my sister is). Tell me something to keep from having another baby. We cannot afford another yet."

I tried to explain the only two methods I had ever heard of among the middle classes, both of which were invariably brushed aside as unacceptable. They were of no certain avail to the wife because they placed the burden of responsibility solely upon the husband—a burden which he seldom assumed. What she was seeking was self-protection she could herself use, and there was none.

Below this stratum of society was one in truly desperate circumstances. The men were sullen and unskilled, picking up odd jobs now and then, but more often unemployed, lounging in and out of the house at all hours of the day and night. The women seemed to slink on their way to market and were without neighborliness.

These submerged, untouched classes were beyond the scope of organized charity or religion. No labor union, no church, not even the Salvation Army reached them. They were apprehensive of everyone and rejected help of any kind, ordering all intruders to keep out; both birth and death they considered their own business. Social agents, who were just beginning to appear, were profoundly mistrusted because they pried into homes and lives, asking questions about wages, how many were in the family, had any of them ever been in jail. Often two or three had been there or were now under suspicion of prostitution, shoplifting, purse snatching, petty thievery, and, in consequence, passed furtively by the big blue uniforms on the corner.

The utmost depression came over me as I approached this surreptitious region. Below Fourteenth Street I seemed to be breathing a different air, to be in another world and country where the people had habits and customs alien to anything I had ever heard about.

There were then approximately ten thousand apartments in New York 10
into which no sun ray penetrated directly; such windows as they had opened only on a narrow court from which rose fetid odors. It was seldom cleaned, though garbage and refuse often went down into it. All these dwellings were pervaded by the foul breath of poverty, that moldy, indefinable, indescribable smell which cannot be fumigated out, sickening to me but apparently unnoticed by those who lived there. When I set to work with antiseptics, their pungent sting, at least temporarily, obscured the stench.

I remember one confinement case to which I was called by the doctor of an insurance company. I climbed up the five flights and entered the airless rooms, but the baby had come with too great speed. A boy of ten had been the only assistant. Five flights was a long way; he had wrapped the placenta in a piece of newspaper and dropped it out the window into the court.

Many families took in "boarders," as they were termed, whose small contributions paid the rent. These derelicts, wanderers, alternately working and drinking, were crowded in with the children; a single room sometimes held as many as six sleepers. Little girls were accustomed to dressing and undressing in front of the men, and were often violated, occasionally by their own fathers or brothers, before they reached the age of puberty.

Pregnancy was a chronic condition among the women of this class. Suggestions as to what to do for a girl who was "in trouble" or a married woman who was "caught" passed from mouth to mouth—herb teas, turpentine, steaming, rolling downstairs, inserting slippery elm, knitting needles, shoe-hooks. When they had word of a new remedy they hurried to the drugstore, and if the clerk were inclined to be friendly he might say, "Oh, that won't help you, but here's something that may." The younger druggists usually refused to give advice because, if it were to be known, they would come under the law; midwives were even more fearful. The doomed women implored me to reveal the "secret" rich people had, offering to pay me extra to tell them; many really believed I was holding back information for money. They asked everybody and tried anything, but nothing did them any good. On Saturday nights I have seen groups of from fifty to one hundred with their shawls over their heads waiting outside the office of a five-dollar abortionist.

Each time I returned to this district, which was becoming a recurrent nightmare, I used to hear that Mrs. Cohen "had been carried to a hospital, but had never come back," or that Mrs. Kelly "had sent the children to a neighbor and had put her head into the gas oven." Day after day such tales were poured into my ears—a baby born dead, great relief—the death of an older child, sorrow but again relief of a sort—the story told a thousand times of death from abortion and children going into institutions. I shuddered with horror as I listened to the details and studied the reasons back of them—destitution linked with excessive childbearing. The waste of life seemed utterly senseless. One by one worried, sad, pensive, and aging faces marshaled themselves before me in my dreams, sometimes appealingly, sometimes accusingly.

These were not merely "unfortunate conditions among the poor" such 15
as we read about. I knew the women personally. They were living, breathing, human beings, with hopes, fears, and aspirations like my own, yet their

weary, misshapen bodies, "always ailing, never failing," were destined to be thrown on the scrap heap before they were thirty-five. I could not escape from the facts of their wretchedness; neither was I able to see any way out. My own cozy and comfortable family existence was becoming a reproach to me.

Then one stifling mid-July day of 1912 I was summoned to a Grand Street tenement. My patient was a small, slight Russian Jewess, about twenty-eight years old, of the special cast of feature to which suffering lends a madonna-like expression. The cramped three-room apartment was in a sorry state of turmoil. Jake Sachs, a truck driver scarcely older than his wife, had come home to find the three children crying and her unconscious from the effects of a self-induced abortion. He had called the nearest doctor, who in turn had sent for me. Jake's earnings were trifling, and most of them had gone to keep the none-too-strong children clean and properly fed. But his wife's ingenuity had helped them to save a little, and this he was glad to spend on a nurse rather than have her go to a hospital.

The doctor and I settled ourselves to the task of fighting the septicemia. Never had I worked so fast, never so concentratedly. The sultry days and nights were melted into a torpid inferno. It did not seem possible there could be such heat, and every bit of food, ice, and drugs had to be carried up three flights of stairs.

Jake was more kind and thoughtful than many of the husbands I had encountered. He loved his children, and had always helped his wife wash and dress them. He had brought water up and carried garbage down before he left in the morning, and did as much as he could for me while he anxiously watched her progress.

After a fortnight Mrs. Sachs' recovery was in sight. Neighbors, ordinarily fatalistic as to the results of abortion, were genuinely pleased that she had survived. She smiled wanly at all who came to see her and thanked them gently, but she could not respond to their hearty congratulations. She appeared to be more despondent and anxious than she should have been, and spent too much time in meditation.

At the end of three weeks, as I was preparing to leave the fragile pa- 20
tient to take up her difficult life once more, she finally voiced her fears, "Another baby will finish me, I suppose?"

"It's too early to talk about that," I temporized.

But when the doctor came to make his last call, I drew him aside. "Mrs. Sachs is terribly worried about having another baby."

"She well may be," replied the doctor, and then he stood before her and said, "Any more such capers, young woman, and there'll be no need to send for me."

"I know, doctor," she replied timidly, "but," and she hesitated as though it took all her courage to say it, "what can I do to prevent it?"

The doctor was a kindly man, and he had worked hard to save her, but 25
such incidents had become so familiar to him that he had long since lost whatever delicacy he might once have had. He laughed good-naturedly. "You want to have your cake and eat it too, do you? Well, it can't be done."

Then picking up his hat and bag to depart he said, "Tell Jake to sleep on the roof."

I glanced quickly at Mrs. Sachs. Even through my sudden tears I could see stamped on her face an expression of absolute despair. We simply looked at each other, saying no word until the door had closed behind the doctor. Then she lifted her thin, blue-veined hands and clasped them beseechingly. "He can't understand. He's only a man. But you do, don't you? Please tell me the secret, and I'll never breathe it to a soul. *Please!*"

What was I to do? I could not speak the conventionally comforting phrases which would be of no comfort. Instead, I made her as physically easy as I could and promised to come back in a few days to talk with her again. A little later, when she slept, I tiptoed away.

Night after night the wistful image of Mrs. Sachs appeared before me. I made all sorts of excuses to myself for not going back. I was busy on other cases; I really did not know what to say to her or how to convince her of my own ignorance; I was helpless to avert such monstrous atrocities. Time rolled by and I did nothing.

The telephone rang one evening three months later, and Jake Sachs' agitated voice begged me to come at once; his wife was sick again and from the same cause. For a wild moment I thought of sending someone else, but actually, of course, I hurried into my uniform, caught up my bag, and started out. All the way I longed for a subway wreck, an explosion, anything to keep me from having to enter that home again. But nothing happened, even to delay me. I turned into the dingy doorway and climbed the familiar stairs once more. The children were there, young little things.

Mrs. Sachs was in a coma and died within ten minutes. I folded her still hands across her breast, remembering how they had pleaded with me, begging so humbly for the knowledge which was her right. I drew a sheet over her pallid face. Jake was sobbing, running his hands through his hair and pulling it out like an insane person. Over and over again he wailed, "My God! My God! My God!"

I left him pacing desperately back and forth, and for hours I myself walked and walked and walked through the hushed streets. When I finally arrived home and let myself quietly in, all the household was sleeping. I looked out my window and down upon the dimly lighted city. Its pains and griefs crowded in upon me, a moving picture rolled before my eyes with photographic clearness; women writhing in travail to bring forth little babies; the babies themselves naked and hungry, wrapped in newspapers to keep them from the cold; six-year-old children with pinched, pale, wrinkled faces, old in concentrated wretchedness, pushed into gray and fetid cellars, crouching on stone floors, their small scrawny hands scuttling through rags, making lamp shades, artificial flowers; white coffins, black coffins, coffins, coffins interminably passing in never-ending succession. The scenes piled one upon another on another. I could bear it no longer.

As I stood there the darkness faded. The sun came up and threw its reflection over the house tops. It was the dawn of a new day in my life also. The doubt and questioning, the experimenting and trying, were now to be put behind me. I knew I could not go back merely to keeping people alive.

I went to bed, knowing that no matter what it might cost, I was finished with palliatives and superficial cures; I was resolved to seek out the root of evil, to do something to change the destiny of mothers whose miseries were vast as the sky.

Analyzing the Text

1. In what way did the encounter with women in these circumstances, especially Mrs. Sachs, change the course of Sanger's own life?

2. Which details make especially clear the extent to which access to information on birth control was limited by social class? What insight does Sanger provide into the reasons why poor women on the Lower East Side of New York were totally ignorant of birth control methods?

Understanding Sanger's Techniques

1. To what extent do your personal assumptions and experiences differ from those of Sanger? What means does Sanger use to enlist the readers' sympathy for women who might have easily remained statistics?
2. A key element in creating an effective narrative is to make the reader wonder what will happen next. At what points did Sanger create the most suspense?

Arguing for an Interpretation

1. Sanger prefaces her essay with a quote drawn from William Blake and titles her essay with a line drawn from the Victorian poet Matthew Arnold's "Dover Beach." What dimension do these literary references add to her realistic narrative?
2. Should federally funded family planning agencies (which exist as a result of Sanger's efforts) be permitted to suggest abortion as an option for pregnant women? Why or why not? You might wish to consult relevant Web sites such as *The Women of the Hall—Margaret Sanger* at <http://www.greatwomen.org/sanger.htm>.

JONATHAN SWIFT

Jonathan Swift (1667–1745), certainly one of the keenest minds of his age, was born in Dublin, into an impoverished family who were originally from England. He was educated at Trinity College, Dublin, with the help of his wealthy uncle, and in 1688 left Ireland and became a Secretary to Sir William Temple in Moor Park, England. There he tutored Esther Johnson, Temple's ward, rumored to be Temple's illegimate daughter, who later became the "Stella" of Swift's letters and poems. He returned to Ireland in 1694, where he was ordained an Anglican priest, and spent a brief time in a parish in Belfast. Dissatisfied with this life, he returned to England and became active in the literary intellectual life of London, where he became friends with prominent figures such as Addison and Steele, and Alexander Pope. In 1713 he was named Dean of St. Patrick's Cathedral in Dublin. When his political ambitions in England were crushed with the defeat of the Tory party the following year, Swift returned to Ireland for good. A prolific writer of enormous brilliance, over the course of his life, Swift used his pen to champion various causes and to assail those in power. In 1724, he published a series of satirical letters against the projected English plan to debase the Irish coinage. He signed these letters M. B. Drapier, and the English government was so outraged they offered a reward of

300 pounds for the author's identity (which no one disclosed). From 1721 to 1725, he worked on his masterpiece, Gulliver's Travels, *a satire on human nature, which was published anonymously in 1726 and became an instant best-seller. The following essay, "A Modest Proposal," was published in 1729 and was written to protest repressive economic measures against the Irish by the Whig government in England. By 1740, Swift's mental condition seriously worsened; in 1742, guardians were appointed to care for him until his death three years later.*

A Modest Proposal

For Preventing the Children of Poor People in Ireland from Being a Burden to Their Parents or Country, and for Making Them Beneficial to the Public

It is a melancholy object to those who walk through this great town,[1] or travel in the country, when they see the streets, the roads, and cabin doors crowded with beggars of the female sex, followed by three, four, or six children, all in rags and importuning every passenger for an alms. These mothers, instead of being able to work for their honest livelihood, are forced to employ all their time in strolling to beg sustenance for their helpless infants; who as they grow up either turn thieves, for want of work, or leave their dear native country to fight for the Pretender[2] in Spain, or sell themselves to the Barbados.[3]

I think it is agreed by all parties that this prodigious number of children in the arms, or on the backs, or at the heels of their mothers, and frequently of their fathers, is, in the present deplorable state of the kingdom, a very great additional grievance; and therefore whoever could find out a fair, cheap, and easy method of making these children sound, useful members of the commonwealth would deserve so well of the public as to have his statue set up for a preserver of the nation.

But my intention is very far from being confined to provide only for the children of professed beggars: it is of a much greater extent and shall take in the whole number of infants at a certain age who are born of parents in effect as little able to support them as those who demand our charity in the streets.

As to my own part, having turned my thoughts for many years upon this important subject and maturely weighed the several schemes of other projectors, I have always found them grossly mistaken in their computa-

---

[1]*this great town*: Dublin.

[2]*the Pretender*: James Stuart (1688–1766), son of King James II, "pretender" or claimant to the throne which his father had lost in the Revolution of 1688. He was Catholic, and Ireland was loyal to him.

[3]*sell ... Barbados*: Because of extreme poverty, many of the Irish bound or sold themselves to obtain passage to the West Indies or other British possessions in North America. They agreed to work for their new masters, usually planters, for a specified number of years.

tion. It is true, a child just dropped from its dam may be supported by her milk for a solar year, with little other nourishment: at most not above the value of two shillings, which the mother may certainly get, or the value in scraps, by her lawful occupation of begging; and it is exactly at one year old that I propose to provide for them in such a manner, as, instead of being a charge upon their parents or the parish, or wanting food and raiment for the rest of their lives, they shall, on the contrary, contribute to the feeding and partly to the clothing of many thousands.

There is likewise another great advantage in my scheme, that it will 5
prevent those voluntary abortions and that horrid practice of women murdering their bastard children, alas! too frequent among us, sacrificing the poor innocent babes, I doubt more to avoid the expense than the shame, which would move tears and pity in the most savage and inhuman breast.

The number of souls in this kingdom being usually reckoned one million and a half, of these I calculate there may be about two hundred thousand couple whose wives are breeders; from which number I subtract thirty thousand couple, who are able to maintain their own children (although I apprehend there cannot be so many, under the present distresses of the kingdom), but this being granted, there will remain an hundred and seventy thousand breeders. I again subtract fifty thousand for those women who miscarry, or whose children die by accident or disease within the year. There only remain one hundred and twenty thousand children of poor parents annually born. The question therefore is, How this number shall be reared and provided for? which, as I have already said, under the present situation of affairs, is utterly impossible by all the methods hitherto proposed. For we can neither employ them in handicraft or agriculture; we neither build houses (I mean in the country) nor cultivate land: they can very seldom pick up a livelihood by stealing till they arrive at six years old, except where they are of towardly[4] parts; although I confess they learn the rudiments much earlier; during which time they can, however, be properly looked upon only as probationers; as I have been informed by a principal gentleman in the county of Cavan, who protested to me that he never knew above one or two instances under the age of six, even in a part of the kingdom so renowned for the quickest proficiency in that art.

I am assured by our merchants that a boy or a girl before twelve years old is no salable commodity; and even when they come to this age they will not yield above three pounds, or three pounds and half a crown at most, on the exchange; which cannot turn to account either to the parents or kingdom, the charge of nutriment and rags having been at least four times that value.

I shall now therefore humbly propose my own thoughts, which I hope will not be liable to the least objection.

I have been assured by a very knowing American of my acquaintance in London that a young healthy child well nursed is at a year old a most delicious, nourishing, and wholesome food, whether stewed, roasted, baked, or boiled; and I make no doubt that it will equally serve in a fricassee or a ragout.[5]

I do therefore humbly offer it to public consideration that of the hun- 10
dred and twenty thousand children already computed, twenty thousand

---

[4]*towardly*: dutiful; easily managed.

[5]*ragout*: (ra gü´), a highly seasoned meat stew.

may be reserved for breed, whereof only one-fourth part to be males; which is more than we allow to sheep, black cattle, or swine; and my reason is that these children are seldom the fruits of marriage, a circumstance not much regarded by our savages; therefore one male will be sufficient to serve four females. That the remaining hundred thousand may, at a year old, be offered in sale to the persons of quality and fortune through the kingdom; always advising the mother to let them suck plentifully in the last month, so as to render them plump and fat for a good table. A child will make two dishes at an entertainment for friends; and when the family dines alone, the fore or hind quarter will make a reasonable dish, and seasoned with a little pepper or salt will be very good boiled on the fourth day, especially in winter.

I have reckoned upon a medium that a child just born will weigh twelve pounds, and in a solar year, if tolerably nursed, will increase to twenty-eight pounds.

I grant this food will be somewhat dear, and therefore very proper for landlords, who, as they have already devoured most of the parents, seem to have the best title to the children.

Infant's flesh will be in season throughout the year, but more plentifully in March, and a little before and after: for we are told by a grave author, an eminent French physician,[6] that fish being a prolific diet, there are more children born in Roman Catholic countries about nine months after Lent than at any other season; therefore, reckoning a year after Lent, the markets will be more glutted than usual, because the number of popish infants is at least three to one in this kingdom: and therefore it will have one other collateral advantage, by lessening the number of papists among us.

I have already computed the charge of nursing a beggar's child (in which list I reckon all cottagers, laborers, and four-fifths of the farmers) to be about two shillings per annum, rags included; and I believe no gentleman would repine to give ten shillings for the carcass of a good fat child, which, as I have said, will make four dishes of excellent nutritive meat, when he has only some particular friend or his own family to dine with him. Thus the squire will learn to be a good landlord and grow popular among his tenants; the mother will have eight shillings net profit and be fit for work till she produces another child.

Those who are more thrifty (as I must confess the times require) may 15
flay the carcass; the skin of which artificially[7] dressed will make admirable gloves for ladies and summer boots for fine gentlemen.

As to our city of Dublin, shambles[8] may be appointed for this purpose in the most convenient parts of it, and butchers we may be assured will not be wanting; although I rather recommend buying the children alive and dressing them hot from the knife as we do roasting pigs.

A very worthy person, a true lover of his country, and whose virtues I highly esteem, was lately pleased, in discoursing on this matter, to offer a refinement upon my scheme. He said that many gentlemen of this kingdom, having of late destroyed their deer, he conceived that the want of venison might be well supplied by the bodies of young lads and maidens,

---

[6] *grave author . . . physician*: François Rabelais (c. 1494–1553), who was anything but a "grave author."

[7] *artificially*: artfully; skillfully.

[8] *shambles*: slaughterhouses.

not exceeding fourteen years of age nor under twelve; so great a number of both sexes in every country being now ready to starve for want of work and service; and these to be disposed of by their parents, if alive, or otherwise by their nearest relations. But with due deference to so excellent a friend and so deserving a patriot, I cannot be altogether in his sentiments; for as to the males, my American acquaintance assured me from frequent experience that their flesh was generally tough and lean, like that of our schoolboys, by continual exercise, and their taste disagreeable; and to fatten them would not answer the charge. Then as to the females, it would, I think, with humble submission be a loss to the public, because they soon would become breeders themselves: and besides, it is not improbable that some scrupulous people might be apt to censure such a practice (although indeed very unjustly), as a little bordering upon cruelty; which, I confess, has always been with me the strongest objection against any project, how well soever intended.

But in order to justify my friend, he confessed that this expedient was put into his head by the famous Psalmanazar,[9] a native of the island Formosa, who came from thence to London above twenty years ago: and in conversation told my friend that in his country when any young person happened to be put to death, the executioner sold the carcass to persons of quality as a prime dainty; and that in his time the body of a plump girl of fifteen, who was crucified for an attempt to poison the emperor, was sold to his imperial majesty's prime minister of state, and other great mandarins of the court, in joints from the gibbet, at four hundred crowns. Neither indeed can I deny that if the same use were made of several plump girls in this town, who, without one single groat to their fortunes, cannot stir abroad without a chair, and appear at a playhouse and assemblies in foreign fineries which they never will pay for, the kingdom would not be the worse.

Some persons of a desponding spirit are in great concern about that vast number of poor people who are aged, diseased, or maimed; and I have been desired to employ my thoughts, what course may be taken to ease the nation of so grievous an encumbrance. But I am not in the least pain upon that matter, because it is very well known that they are every day dying and rotting, by cold and famine, and filth and vermin, as fast as can be reasonably expected. And as to the young laborers, they are now in almost as hopeful a condition: they cannot get work, and consequently pine away for want of nourishment to a degree that if at any time they are accidentally hired to common labor, they have not strength to perform it; and thus the country and themselves are happily delivered from the evils to come.

I have too long digressed and therefore shall return to my subject. I 20
think the advantages, by the proposal which I have made, are obvious and many, as well as of the highest importance.

For first, as I have already observed, it would greatly lessen the number of papists, with whom we are yearly overrun, being the principal breeders of the nation, as well as our most dangerous enemies; and who stay at home on purpose to deliver the kingdom to the Pretender, hoping to take their advantage by the absence of so many good Protestants, who have

[9]*Psalmanazar*: the imposter George Psalmanazar (c. 1679–1763), a Frenchman who passed himself off in England as a Formosan, and wrote a totally fictional "true" account of Formosa, in which he described cannibalism.

chosen rather to leave their country than stay at home and pay tithes against their conscience to an Episcopal curate.[10]

Secondly, the poorer tenants will have something valuable of their own, which by law may be made liable to distress,[11] and help to pay their landlord's rent; their corn and cattle being already seized, and money a thing unknown.

Thirdly, whereas the maintenance of a hundred thousand children, from two years old and upwards, cannot be computed at less than ten shillings a piece per annum, the nation's stock will be thereby increased fifty thousand pounds per annum, beside the profit of a new dish introduced to the tables of all gentlemen of fortune in the kingdom who have any refinement in taste. And the money will circulate among ourselves, the goods being entirely of our own growth and manufacture.

Fourthly, the constant breeders, besides the gain of eight shillings sterling per annum by the sale of their children, will be rid of the charge of maintaining them after the first year.

Fifthly, this food would likewise bring great custom to taverns: where the vintners will certainly be so prudent as to procure the best receipts for dressing it to perfection, and consequently have their houses frequented by all the fine gentlemen, who justly value themselves upon their knowledge in good eating: and a skilful cook, who understands how to oblige his guests, will contrive to make it as expensive as they please.

Sixthly, this would be a great inducement to marriage, which all wise nations have either encouraged by rewards or enforced by laws and penalties. It would increase the care and tenderness of mothers toward their children, when they were sure of a settlement for life to the poor babes, provided in some sort by the public, to their annual profit instead of expense. We should see an honest emulation among the married women, which of them could bring the fattest child to the market. Men would become as fond of their wives during the time of their pregnancy as they are now of their mares in foal, their cows in calf, or sows when they are ready to farrow; nor offer to beat or kick them (as is too frequent a practice) for fear of a miscarriage.

Many other advantages might be enumerated. For instance, the addition of some thousand carcasses in our exportation of barreled beef, the propagation of swine's flesh, and improvement in the art of making good bacon, so much wanted among us by the great destruction of pigs, too frequent at our tables; which are no way comparable in taste or magnificence to a well-grown, fat, yearling child, which roasted whole will make a considerable figure at a lord mayor's feast, or any other public entertainment. But this and many others I omit, being studious of brevity.

Supposing that one thousand families in this city would be constant customers for infants' flesh, besides others who might have it at merry meetings, particularly weddings and christenings, I compute that Dublin would take off annually about twenty thousand carcasses; and the rest of the kingdom (where probably they will be sold somewhat cheaper) the remaining eighty thousand.

I can think of no one objection that will possibly be raised against this proposal, unless it should be urged that the number of people will be

[10]*Protestants . . . curate*: Swift is here attacking the absentee landlords.
[11]*distress*: distraint, the legal seizure of property for payment of debts.

thereby much lessened in the kingdom. This I freely own, and it was indeed one principal design in offering it to the world. I desire the reader will observe that I calculate my remedy for this one individual kingdom of Ireland, and for no other that ever was, is, or, I think, ever can be upon earth. Therefore let no man talk to me of other expedients: of taxing our absentees at five shillings a pound: of using neither clothes nor household furniture, except what is of our own growth and manufacture: of utterly rejecting the materials and instruments that promote foreign luxury: of curing the expensiveness of pride, vanity, idleness, and gaming in our women: of introducing a vein of parsimony, prudence, and temperance: of learning to love our country, in the want of which we differ even from Laplanders and the inhabitants of Topinamboo:[12] of quitting our animosities and factions, nor acting any longer like the Jews, who were murdering one another at the very moment their city was taken:[13] of being a little cautious not to sell our country and conscience for nothing: of teaching landlords to have at least one degree of mercy toward their tenants: lastly, of putting a spirit of honesty, industry, and skill into our shopkeepers; who, if a resolution could now be taken to buy only our native goods, would immediately unite to cheat and exact upon us in the price, the measure, and the goodness, nor could ever yet be brought to make one fair proposal of just dealing, though often and earnestly invited to it.[14]

Therefore, I repeat, let no man talk to me of these and the like expedi- 30
ents, till he has at least some glimpse of hope that there will ever be some hearty and sincere attempt to put them in practice.

But as to myself, having been wearied out for many years with offering vain, idle, visionary thoughts, and at length utterly despairing of success, I fortunately fell upon this proposal; which, as it is wholly new, so it has something solid and real, of no expense and little trouble, full in our own power, and whereby we can incur no danger in disobliging England. For this kind of commodity will not bear exportation, the flesh being of too tender a consistence to admit a long continuance in salt, although perhaps I could name a country which would be glad to eat up our whole nation without it.[15]

After all, I am not so violently bent upon my own opinion as to reject any offer proposed by wise men, which shall be found equally innocent, cheap, easy, and effectual. But before something of that kind shall be advanced in contradiction to my scheme, and offering a better, I desire the author or authors will be pleased maturely to consider two points. First, as things now stand, how they will be able to find food and raiment for an hundred thousand useless mouths and backs. And, secondly, there being a round million of creatures in human figure throughout this kingdom, whose whole subsistence put into a common stock would leave them in debt two millions of pounds sterling, adding those who are beggars by profession to the bulk of farmers, cottagers, and laborers, with their wives and children, who are beggars in effect; I desire those politicians, who dislike my overture, and may perhaps be so bold as to attempt an answer, that

---

[12]*Topinamboo*: a savage area of Brazil.

[13]*city was taken*: While the Roman Emperor Titus was besieging Jerusalem, which he took and destroyed in A.D. 70, within the city factions of fanatics were waging bloody warfare.

[14]*invited to it*: Swift had already made all these proposals in various pamphlets.

[15]*a country . . . without it*: England; this is another way of saying, "The English are devouring the Irish."

they will first ask the parents of these mortals, whether they would not at this day think it a great happiness to have been sold for food at a year old in the manner I prescribe, and thereby have avoided such a perpetual scene of misfortunes as they have since gone through by the oppression of landlords, the impossibility of paying rent without money or trade, the want of common sustenance, with neither house nor clothes to cover them from the inclemencies of the weather, and the most inevitable prospect of entailing the like or greater miseries upon their breed for ever.

I profess, in the sincerity of my heart, that I have not the least personal interest in endeavoring to promote this necessary work, having no other motive than the public good of my country, by advancing our trade, providing for infants, relieving the poor, and giving some pleasure to the rich. I have no children by which I can propose to get a single penny; the youngest being nine years old, and my wife past childbearing.

Analyzing the Text

1. How would you characterize the narrator? What is a "projector" and in what sense is his proposal "modest"?
2. What is the narrator's attitude toward the poor in Ireland? At what point did you realize the "proposal" Swift was making was intended to be viewed ironically and not literally?

Understanding Swift's Techniques

1. Paragraph 4 refers to a "child just dropped from its dam," and the essay contains other terms applied only to animals. What does Swift aim to accomplish by using these kinds of references?
2. What are some of the shocking details about life in Ireland that the narrator casually reveals, and how do these strengthen Swift's satire?

Arguing for an Interpretation

1. Who are the principal targets of this satire, and to what extent does Swift criticize the Irish for not doing enough to help themselves?
2. Write your own "modest proposal" offering a palpably offensive solution to a social problem (for example, corporate corruption, greed in sports, anti-smoking ordinances), and develop it using Swift's techniques of verbal irony and understatement. Keep in mind that Swift was parodying the pamphlets dealing with population and poverty written in the 18th century, and spoofing their proposals and the way they used statistics to make their points.

Mary Crow Dog and Richard Erdoes

Mary Crow Dog, who took the name Mary Brave Bird, was born in 1956 and grew up on a South Dakota reservation in a one-room cabin without running water or electricity. She joined the new movement of tribal pride sweeping Native American communities in the 1960s and 1970s and was at the siege of Wounded Knee, South Dakota, in 1973. She married the American

Indian Movement (AIM) leader Leonard Crow Dog, the movement's chief medicine man. Her powerful autobiography Lakota Woman, *written with Richard Erdoes, one of America's leading writers on Native American affairs and the author of eleven books, became a national best-seller and won the American Book Award for 1991. In it she describes what it was like to grow up a Sioux in a white-dominated society. Her second book,* Ohitka Woman *(1993), also written with Richard Erdoes, continues the story of a woman whose struggle for a sense of self and freedom is a testament to her will and spirit. In "Civilize Them with a Stick" from* Lakota Woman, *the author recounts her experiences as a young student at a boarding school run by the Bureau of Indian Affairs.*

Civilize Them with a Stick

Gathered from the cabin, the wickiup, and the tepee,
partly by cajolery and partly by threats,
partly by bribery and partly by force,
they are induced to leave their kindred
to enter these schools and take upon themselves
the outward appearance of civilized life.

Annual report of the Department of Interior, 1901

It is almost impossible to explain to a sympathetic white person what a typical old Indian boarding school was like; how it affected the Indian child suddenly dumped into it like a small creature from another world, helpless, defenseless, bewildered, trying desperately and instinctively to survive and sometimes not surviving at all. I think such children were like the victims of Nazi concentration camps trying to tell average, middle-class Americans what their experience had been like. Even now, when these schools are much improved, when the buildings are new, all gleaming steel and glass, the food tolerable, the teachers well trained and well intentioned, even trained in child psychology—unfortunately the psychology of white children, which is different from ours—the shock to the child upon arrival is still tremendous. Some just seem to shrivel up, don't speak for days on end, and have an empty look in their eyes. I know of an eleven-year-old on another reservation who hanged herself, and in our school, while I was there, a girl jumped out of the window, trying to kill herself to escape an unbearable situation. That first shock is always there. . . .

The mission school at St. Francis was a curse for our family for generations. My grandmother went there, then my mother, then my sisters and I. At one time or other every one of us tried to run away. Grandma told me once about the bad times she had experienced at St. Francis. In those days they let students go home only for one week every year. Two days were used up for transportation, which meant spending just five days out of three hundred and sixty-five with her family. And that was an improvement. Before grandma's time, on many reservations they did not let the students go home at all until they had finished school. Anybody who disobeyed the nuns was severely punished. The building in which my grandmother stayed had three floors, for girls only. Way up in the attic were little cells, about five by five by ten feet. One time she was in church and instead of praying she was playing jacks. As punishment they took her to one of those little cubicles where she stayed in darkness because the windows had been boarded up. They left her there for a whole week with only bread and water for nourishment. After she came out she promptly ran away, together with three other girls. They were found and brought back. The nuns stripped them naked and whipped them. They used a horse buggy whip on my grandmother. Then she was put back into the attic—for two weeks.

My mother had much the same experiences but never wanted to talk about them, and then there I was, in the same place. The school is now run by the BIA—the Bureau of Indian Affairs—but only since about fifteen years ago. When I was there, during the 1960s, it was still run by the Church. The Jesuit fathers ran the boys' wing and the Sisters of the Sacred Heart ran us—with the help of the strap. Nothing had changed since my grandmother's days. I have been told recently that even in the '70s they were still beating children at that school. All I got out of school was being taught how to pray. I learned quickly that I would be beaten if I failed in my devotions or, God forbid, prayed the wrong way, especially prayed in Indian to Wakan Tanka, the Indian Creator.

The girls' wing was built like an F and was run like a penal institution. Every morning at five o'clock the sisters would come into our large dormitory to wake us up, and immediately we had to kneel down at the sides of our beds and recite the prayers. At six o'clock we were herded into the church for more of the same. I did not take kindly to the discipline and to marching by the clock, left-right, left-right. I was never one to like being forced to do something. I do something because I feel like doing it. I felt this way always, as far as I can remember, and my sister Barbara felt the same way. An old medicine man once told me: "Us Lakotas are not like dogs who can be trained, who can be beaten and keep on wagging their tails, licking the hand that whipped them. We are like cats, little cats, big cats, wildcats, bobcats, mountain lions. It doesn't matter what kind, but cats who can't be tamed, who scratch if you step on their tails." But I was only a kitten and my claws were still small.

5 Barbara was still in the school when I arrived and during my first year or two she could still protect me a little bit. When Barb was a seventh-grader she ran away together with five other girls, early in the morning before sunrise. They brought them back in the evening. The girls had to wait for two hours in front of the mother superior's office. They were hungry and cold, frozen through. It was wintertime and they had been running the whole day without food, trying to make good their escape. The mother superior asked each girl, "Would you do this again?" She told them that as punishment they would not be allowed to visit home for a month and that she'd keep them busy on work details until the skin on their knees and elbows had worn off. At the end of her speech she told each girl, "Get up from this chair and lean over it." She then lifted the girls' skirts and pulled down their underpants. Not little girls either, but teenagers. She had a

leather strap about a foot long and four inches wide fastened to a stick, and beat the girls, one after another, until they cried. Barb did not give her that satisfaction but just clenched her teeth. There was one girl, Barb told me, the nun kept on beating and beating until her arm got tired.

I did not escape my share of the strap. Once, when I was thirteen years old, I refused to go to Mass. I did not want to go to church because I did not feel well. A nun grabbed me by the hair, dragged me upstairs, made me stoop over, pulled my dress up (we were not allowed at the time to wear jeans), pulled my panties down, and gave me what they called "swats"—twenty-five swats with a board around which Scotch tape had been wound. She hurt me badly.

My classroom was right next to the principal's office and almost every day I could hear him swatting the boys. Beating was the common punishment for not doing one's homework, or for being late to school. It had such a bad effect upon me that I hated and mistrusted every white person on sight, because I met only one kind. It was not until much later that I met sincere white people I could relate to and be friends with. Racism breeds racism in reverse.

The routine at St. Francis was dreary. Six A.M., kneeling in church for an hour or so; seven o'clock, breakfast, eight o'clock, scrub the floor, peel spuds, make classes. We had to mop the dining room twice every day and scrub the tables. If you were caught taking a rest, doodling on the bench with a fingernail or knife, or just rapping, the nun would come up with a dish towel and just slap it across your face, saying, "You're not supposed to be talking, you're supposed to be working!" Monday mornings we had cornmeal mush, Tuesday oatmeal, Wednesday rice and raisins, Thursday cornflakes, and Friday all the leftovers mixed together or sometimes fish. Frequently the food had bugs or rocks in it. We were eating hot dogs that were weeks old, while the nuns were dining on ham, whipped potatoes, sweet peas, and cranberry sauce. In winter our dorm was icy cold while the nuns' rooms were always warm.

I have seen little girls arrive at the school, first-graders, just fresh from home and totally unprepared for what awaited them, little girls with pretty braids, and the first thing the nuns did was chop their hair off and tie up what was left behind their ears. Next they would dump the children into tubs of alcohol, a sort of rubbing alcohol, "to get the germs off." Many of the nuns were German immigrants, some from Bavaria, so that we sometimes speculated whether Bavaria was some sort of Dracula country inhabited by monsters. For the sake of objectivity I ought to mention that two of the German fathers were great linguists and that the only Lakota-English dictionaries and grammars which are worth anything were put together by them.

At night some of the girls would huddle in bed together for comfort 10
and reassurance. Then the nun in charge of the dorm would come in and say, "What are the two of you doing in bed together? I smell evil in this room. You girls are evil incarnate. You are sinning. You are going to hell and burn forever. You can act that way in the devil's frying pan." She would get them out of bed in the middle of the night, making them kneel and pray until morning. We had not the slightest idea what it was all about. At home we slept two and three in a bed for animal warmth and a feeling of security.

The nuns and the girls in the two top grades were constantly battling it out physically with fists, nails, and hair-pulling. I myself was growing from a kitten into an undersized cat. My claws were getting bigger and were itching for action. About 1969 or 1970 a strange young white girl appeared on the reservation. She looked about eighteen or twenty years old. She was pretty and had long, blond hair down to her waist, patched jeans, boots, and a backpack. She was different from any other white person we had met before. I think her name was Wise. I do not know how she managed to overcome our reluctance and distrust, getting us into a corner, making us listen to her, asking us how we were treated. She told us that she was from New York. She was the first real hippie or Yippie we had come across. She told us of people called the Black Panthers, Young Lords, and Weathermen. She said, "Black people are getting it on. Indians are getting it on in St. Paul and California. How about you?" She also said, "Why don't you put out an underground paper, mimeograph it. It's easy. Tell it like it is. Let it all hang out." She spoke a strange lingo but we caught on fast.

Charlene Left Hand Bull and Gina One Star were two full-blood girls I used to hang out with. We did everything together. They were willing to join me in a Sioux uprising. We put together a newspaper which we called the *Red Panther.* In it we wrote how bad the school was, what kind of slop we had to eat—slimy, rotten, blackened potatoes for two weeks—the way we were beaten. I think I was the one who wrote the worst article about our principal of the moment, Father Keeler. I put all my anger and venom into it. I called him a goddam wasicun son of a bitch. I wrote that he knew nothing about Indians and should go back to where he came from, teaching white children whom he could relate to. I wrote that we knew which priests slept with which nuns and that all they ever could think about was filling their bellies and buying a new car. It was the kind of writing which foamed at the mouth, but which also lifted a great deal of weight from one's soul.

On Saint Patrick's Day, when everybody was at the big powwow, we distributed our newspapers. We put them on windshields and bulletin boards, in desks and pews, in dorms and toilets. But someone saw us and snitched on us. The shit hit the fan. The three of us were taken before a board meeting. Our parents, in my case my mother, had to come. They were told that ours was a most serious matter, the worst thing that had ever happened in the school's long history. One of the nuns told my mother, "Your daughter really needs to be talked to." "What's wrong with my daughter?" my mother asked. She was given one of our *Red Panther* newspapers. The nun pointed out its name to her and then my piece, waiting for mom's reaction. After a while she asked, "Well, what have you got to say to this? What do you think?"

My mother said, "Well, when I went to school here, some years back, I was treated a lot worse then these kids are. I really can't see how they can have any complaints, because we was treated a lot stricter. We could not even wear skirts halfway up our knees. These girls have it made. But you should forgive them because they are young. And it's supposed to be a free country, free speech and all that. I don't believe what they done is wrong." So all I got out of it was scrubbing six flights of stairs on my hands and knees, every day. And no boy-side privileges.

15 The boys and girls were still pretty much separated. The only time one could meet a member of the opposite sex was during free time, between four and five-thirty, in the study hall or on benches or the volleyball court

outside, and that was strictly supervised. One day Charlene and I went over to the boys' side. We were on the ball team and they had to let us practice. We played three extra minutes, only three minutes more than we were supposed to. Here was the nuns' opportunity for revenge. We got twenty-five swats. I told Charlene, "We are getting too old to have our bare asses whipped that way. We are old enough to have babies. Enough of this shit. Next time we fight back." Charlene only said, "Hoka-hay!"

We had to take showers every evening. One little girl did not want to take her panties off and one of the nuns told her, "You take those underpants off—or else!" But the child was ashamed to do it. The nun was getting her swat to threaten the girl. I went up to the sister, pushed her veil off, and knocked her down. I told her that if she wanted to hit a little girl she should pick on me, pick one her own size. She got herself transferred out of the dorm a week later.

In a school like this there is always a lot of favoritism. At St. Francis it was strongly tinged with racism. Girls who were near-white, who came from what the nuns called "nice families," got preferential treatment. They waited on the faculty and got to eat ham or eggs and bacon in the morning. They got the easy jobs while the skins, who did not have the right kind of background—myself among them—always wound up in the laundry room sorting out ten bushel baskets of dirty boys' socks every day. Or we wound up scrubbing the floors and doing all the dishes. The school therefore fostered fights and antagonism between whites and breeds, and between breeds and skins. At one time Charlene and I had to iron all the robes and vestments the priests wore when saying Mass. We had to fold them up and put them into a chest in the back of the church. In a corner, looking over our shoulders, was a statue of the crucified Savior, all bloody and beaten up. Charlene looked up and said, "Look at that poor Indian. The pigs sure worked him over." That was the closest I ever came to seeing Jesus.

I was held up as a bad example and didn't mind. I was old enough to have a boyfriend and promptly got one. At the school we had an hour and a half for ourselves. Between the boys' and the girls' wings were some benches where one could sit. My boyfriend and I used to go there just to hold hands and talk. The nuns were very uptight about any boy-girl stuff. They had an exaggerated fear of anything having even the faintest connection with sex. One day in religion class, an all-girl class, Sister Bernard singled me out for some remarks, pointing me out as a bad example, an example that should be shown. She said that I was too free with my body. That I was holding hands which meant that I was not a good example to follow. She also said that I wore unchaste dresses, skirts which were too short, too suggestive, shorter than regulations permitted, and for that I would be punished. She dressed me down before the whole class, carrying on and on about my unchastity.

I stood up and told her, "You shouldn't say any of those things, miss. You people are a lot worse than us Indians. I know all about you, because my grandmother and my aunt told me about you. Maybe twelve, thirteen years ago you had a water stoppage here in St. Francis. No water could get through the pipes. There are water lines right under the mission, underground tunnels and passages where in my grandmother's time only the nuns and priests could go, which were off-limits to everybody else. When the water backed up they had to go through all the water lines and clean them out. And in those huge pipes they found the bodies of new-born babies. And they were white babies. They weren't Indian babies. At least when our girls have babies, they don't do away with them that way, like flushing them down the toilet, almost.

20 "And that priest they sent here from Holy Rosary in Pine Ridge because he molested a little girl. You couldn't think of anything better than dump him on us. All he does is watch young women and girls with that funny smile on his face. Why don't you point him out for an example?"

Charlene and I worked on the school newspaper. After all we had some practice. Every day we went down to Publications. One of the priests acted as the photographer, doing the enlarging and developing. He smelled of chemicals which had stained his hands yellow. One day he invited Charlene into the darkroom. He was going to teach her developing. She was developed already. She was a big girl compared to him, taller too. Charlene was nicely built, not fat, just rounded. No sharp edges anywhere: All of a sudden she rushed out of the darkroom, yelling to me, "Let's get out of here! He's trying to feel me up. That priest is nasty." So there was this too to contend with—sexual harassment. We complained to the student body. The nuns said we just had a dirty mind.

We got a new priest in English. During one of his first classes he asked one of the boys a certain question. The boy was shy. He spoke poor English, but he had the right answer. The priest told him, "You did not say it right. Correct yourself. Say it over again." The boy got flustered and stammered. He could hardly get out a word. But the priest kept after him: "Didn't you hear? I told you to do the whole thing over. Get it right this time." He kept on and on.

I stood up and said, "Father, don't be doing that. If you go into an Indian's home and try to talk Indian, they might laugh at you and say. 'Do it over correctly. Get it right this time!'"

He shouted at me, "Mary, you stay after class. Sit down right now!"

25 I stayed after class, until after the bell. He told me, "Get over here!"

He grabbed me by the arm, pushing me against the blackboard, shouting. "Why are you always mocking us? You have no reason to do this."

I said, "Sure I do. You were making fun of him. You embarrassed him. He needs strengthening, not weakening. You hurt him. I did not hurt you."

He twisted my arm and pushed real hard. I turned around and hit him in the face, giving him a bloody nose. After that I ran out of the room, slamming the door behind me. He and I went to Sister Bernard's office. I told her, "Today I quit school. I'm not taking any more of this, none of this shit anymore. None of this treatment. Better give me my diploma. I can't waste any more time on you people."

Sister Bernard looked at me for a long, long time. She said, "All right, Mary Ellen, go home today. Come back in a few days and get your diploma." And that was that. Oddly enough, that priest turned out okay. He taught a class in grammar, orthography, composition, things like that. I think he wanted more respect in class. He was still young and unsure of himself. But I was in there too long. I didn't feel like hearing it. Later he became a good friend of the Indians, a personal friend of myself and my husband. He stood up for us during Wounded Knee[1] and after. He stood up to

[1] *Wounded Knee*: Originally, a battle that took place in 1890 between Sioux Indians and U.S. troops. The author refers to the 1973 uprising of the Lakota Indians against the Federal Bureau of Investigation in South Dakota at the same location.

his superiors, stuck his neck way out, became a real people's priest. He even learned our language. He died prematurely of cancer. It is not only the good Indians who die young, but the good whites, too. It is the timid ones who know how to take care of themselves who grow old. I am still grateful to that priest for what he did for us later and for the quarrel he picked with me—or did I pick it with him?—because it ended a situation which had become unendurable for me. The day of my fight with him was my last day in school.

Analyzing the Text

1. What aspects of life at the government-run boarding school illustrate the government's desire to not merely educate Native Americans, but to transform them? How did Mary Crow Dog react to the experiences to which she was subjected?
2. What historical insight do the experiences of Mary Crow Dog's mother and grandmother provide into those of Mary Crow Dog herself?

Understanding Crow Dog's Techniques

1. Why does Mary Crow Dog place such great emphasis on the underground newspaper? Why was this event so crucial at this stage in her life?
2. How does Mary Crow Dog's use of colloquial and nonstandard English enhance the realism of her account?

Arguing for an Interpretation

1. To what extent does Mary Crow Dog offset her account of the institutionalized racism at the boarding school with portraits of the teachers and priests who were unexpectedly helpful? Does this enhance her credibility?
2. What aspects of this essay gave you insight into the vast gulf that separated Native Americans from white mainstream society at the time these events took place?

James Baldwin

James Baldwin (1924-1987) was born and raised in Harlem where his stepfather was an evangelical minister. Alienated by racism in the United States, he moved to Paris in 1948. When he returned to America nine years later, he became involved in the civil rights movement and devoted himself to the exploration of the quest for personal identity in the lives of African Americans. His first novel, Go Tell It On the Mountain *(1953), explores the problems of racial and sexual identity, as do* Giovanni's Room *(1956) and* Another Country *(1962). Baldwin's most important essays and social commentaries appear in* Notes of a Native Son *(1955),* Nobody Knows My Name *(1961), and* The Fire Next Time *(1963), in which "Letter to My Nephew" was first published. His last works include a book of essays,* The Price of the

Ticket *(1985), a novel,* Harlem Quartet *(1987), and a play,* The Welcome Table *(1987).*

Letter to My Nephew

Dear James:

I have begun this letter five times and torn it up five times. I keep seeing your face, which is also the face of your father and my brother. Like him, you are tough, dark, vulnerable, moody—with a very definite tendency to sound truculent because you want no one to think you are soft. You may be like your grandfather in this. I don't know; but certainly both you and your father resemble him very much physically. Well, he is dead, he never saw you, and he had a terrible life; he was defeated long before he died because, at the bottom of his heart, he really believed what white people said about him. This is one of the reasons that he became so holy. I am sure that your father has told you something about all that. Neither you nor your father exhibit any tendency towards holiness: you really *are* of another era, part of what happened when the Negro left the land and came into what the late E. Franklin Frazier called "the cities of destruction." You can only be destroyed by believing that you really are what the white world calls a *nigger.* I tell you this because I love you, and please don't you ever forget it.

I have known both of you all your lives, have carried your Daddy in my arms and on my shoulders, kissed and spanked him and watched him learn to walk. I don't know if you've known anybody from that far back; if you've loved anybody that long, first as an infant, then as a child, then as a man, you gain a strange perspective on time and human pain and effort. Other people cannot see what I see whenever I look into your father's face as it is today are all those other faces which were his. Let him laugh and I see a cellar your father does not remember and a house he does not remember and I hear in his present laughter his laughter as a child. Let him curse and I remember him falling down the cellar steps, and howling, and I remember, with pain, his tears, which my hand or your grandmother's so easily wiped away. But no one's hand can wipe away those tears he sheds invisibly today, which one hears in his laughter and in his speech and in his songs. I know what the world has done to my brother and how narrowly he has survived it. And I know, which is much worse, and this is the crime of which I accuse my country and my countrymen, and for which neither I nor time nor history will ever forgive them, that they have destroyed and are destroying hundreds of thousands of lives and do not know it and do not want to know it. One can be, indeed one must strive to become, tough and philosophical concerning destruction and death, for this is what most of mankind has been best at since we have heard of man. (But remember: *most* of mankind is not *all* of mankind.) But it is not permissible that the authors of devastation should also be innocent. It is the innocence which constitutes the crime.

Now, my dear namesake, these innocent and well-meaning people, your countrymen, have caused you to be born under conditions not very far removed from those described for us by Charles Dickens in the London of more than a hundred years ago. (I hear the chorus of the innocents screaming, "No! This is not true! How *bitter* you are"—but I am writing this letter to *you,* to try to tell you something about how to handle *them,* for most of them do not yet really know that you exist. I *know* the conditions under which you were born, for I was there. Your countrymen were *not* there, and haven't made it yet. Your grandmother was also there, and no one has ever accused her of being bitter. I suggest that the innocents check with her. She isn't hard to find. Your countrymen don't know that *she* exists, either, though she has been working for them all their lives.)

Well, you were born, here you came, something like fifteen years ago; and though your father and mother and grandmother, looking about the streets through which they were carrying you, staring at the walls into which they brought you, had every reason to be heavyhearted, yet they were not. For here you were, Big James, named for me—you were a big baby, I was not—here you were: to be loved. To be loved, baby, hard, at once, and forever, to strengthen you against the loveless world. Remember that: I know how black it looks today, for you. It looked bad that day, too, yes, we were trembling. We have not stopped trembling yet, but if we had not loved each other none of us would have survived. And now you must survive because we love you, and for the sake of your children and your children's children.

This innocent country set you down in a ghetto in which, in fact, it in- 5
tended that you should perish. Let me spell out precisely what I mean by that, for the heart of the matter is here, and the root of my dispute with my country. You were born where you were born and faced the future that you faced because you were black and *for no other reason.* The limits of your ambition were, thus, expected to be set forever. You were born into a society which spelled out with brutal clarity, and in as many ways as possible, that you were a worthless human being. You were not expected to aspire to excellence: you were expected to make peace with mediocrity. Wherever you have turned, James, in your short time on this earth, you have been told where you could go and what you could do (and *how* you could do it) and where you could live and whom you could marry. I know your countrymen do not agree with me about this, and I hear them saying, "You exaggerate." They do not know Harlem, and I do. So do you. Take no one's word for anything, including mine—but trust your experience. Know whence you came. If you know whence you came, there is really no limit to where you can go. The details and symbols of your life have been deliberately constructed to make you believe what white people say about you. Please try to remember that what they believe, as well as what they do and cause you to endure, does not testify to your inferiority but to their inhumanity and fear. Please try to be clear, dear James, through the storm which rages about your youthful head today, about the reality which lies behind the words *acceptance* and *integration.* There is no reason for you to try to become like white people and there is no basis whatever for their impertinent assumption that *they* must accept *you.* The really terrible thing, old buddy, is that *you* must accept *them.* And I mean that very seriously. You must accept them and accept them with love. For these innocent people have no other hope. They are, in effect, still trapped in a history which they do not understand; and until they understand it, they cannot be released from it. They have had to believe for many years, and

for innumerable reasons, that black men are inferior to white men. Many of them, indeed, know better, but, as you will discover, people find it very difficult to act on what they know. To act is to be committed, and to be committed is to be in danger. In this case, the danger, in the minds of most white Americans, is the loss of their identity. Try to imagine how you would feel if you woke up one morning to find the sun shining and all the stars aflame. You would be frightened because it is out of the order of nature. Any upheaval in the universe is terrifying because it so profoundly attacks one's sense of one's own reality. Well, the black man has functioned in the white man's world as a fixed star, as an immovable pillar: and as he moves out of his place, heaven and earth are shaken to their foundations. You, don't be afraid. I said that it was intended that you should perish in the ghetto, perish by never being allowed to go behind the white man's definitions, by never being allowed to spell your proper name. You have, and many of us have, defeated this intention; and, by a terrible law, a terrible paradox, those innocents who believed that your imprisonment made them safe are losing their grasp of reality. But these men are your brothers—your lost, younger brothers. And if the word *integration* means anything, this is what it means: that we, with love, shall force our brothers to see themselves as they are, to cease fleeing from reality and begin to change it. For this is your home, my friend, do not be driven from it; great men have done great things here, and will again, and we can make America what America must become. It will be hard, James, but you come from sturdy, peasant stock, men who picked cotton and dammed rivers and built railroads, and, in the teeth of the most terrifying odds, achieved an unassailable and monumental dignity. You come from a long line of great poets, some of the greatest poets since Homer. One of them said, *The very time I thought I was lost, My dungeon shook and my chains fell off.*

You know, and I know, that the country is celebrating one hundred years of freedom one hundred years too soon. We cannot be free until they are free. God bless you, James, and Godspeed.

Your uncle,
James

Analyzing the Text

1. What attitude is vitally important for Baldwin to instill in his nephew, and why is he especially fearful of the tragic consequences of racism?
2. What does Baldwin mean by the "cities of destruction," and why is it important for him to make his nephew aware of the integral role that black people have played in the history of the nation?

Understanding Baldwin's Techniques

1. What stylistic qualities (diction, imagery, sentence structure) underscore that Baldwin has written a letter rather than a formal essay to express his concerns about racism in the United States?
2. What aspects of this letter evoke the phrasings and rhythm of a sermon, and how does Baldwin use imagery to reinforce his thesis?

Arguing for an Interpretation

1. As a grandson of slaves whose career as a writer began when segregation was still legal, Baldwin was most concerned with the destructive psycho-

logical effects of racism in the everyday lives of blacks. How well do you think his letter strikes a balance between solidifying a personal relationship and warning his nephew of the tragic consequences of racism while encouraging him to not become bitter?

2. What insight does this letter offer into Baldwin's fictional works, such as *Go Tell It On the Mountain* (1953) or his short story "Sonny's Blues" (1957)? In your opinion, are Baldwin's concerns as expressed in his nonfiction and fiction still relevant? Why or why not?

Short Fiction

Kate Chopin

Kate Chopin (1851–1904) was born Katherine O'Flaherty, the daughter of a successful St. Louis businessman and his French Creole wife. After her father died in 1855, Kate was raised by her mother and great-grandmother. When she was nineteen, she married Oscar Chopin and accompanied him to New Orleans where he established himself as a cotton broker. After his business failed, they moved to his family plantation in Louisiana where he opened a general store. After his sudden death in 1883, Chopin managed the plantation for a year, but then decided to return to St. Louis with her six children. She began to submit stories patterned on the realistic fiction of Guy de Maupassant to local papers and national magazines, including the Saturday Evening Post *and* Atlantic Monthly. *Her stories of Creole life were widely praised for their realistic delineation of Creole manners and customs and were later collected in* Bayou Folk *(1894) and* A Night in Acadie *(1897). Her novel* The Awakening *(1899), although widely praised as a masterpiece for its frank depiction of its heroine's sexual awakening and need for self-fulfillment, created a public controversy. Chopin's uncompromising delineation of the pressures of class and race in Louisiana at the time are clearly seen in the poignant story "Désirée's Baby" (1899).*

Désirée's Baby

As the day was pleasant, Madame Valmondé drove over to L'Abri to see Désirée and the baby.

It made her laugh to think of Désirée with a baby. Why, it seems but yesterday that Désirée was little more than a baby herself; when Monsieur in riding through the gateway of Valmondé had found her lying asleep in the shadow of the big stone pillar.

The little one awoke in his arms and began to cry for "Dada." That was as much as she could do or say. Some people thought she might have strayed there of her own accord, for she was of the toddling age. The prevailing belief was that she had been purposely left by a party of Texans, whose canvas-covered wagon, late in the day, had crossed the ferry that Coton Maïs kept, just below the plantation. In time Madame Valmondé abandoned every speculation but the one that Désirée had been sent to her by a beneficent Providence to be the child of her affection, seeing that she was without child of the flesh. For the girl grew to be beautiful and gentle, affectionate and sincere—the idol of Valmondé.

It was no wonder, when she stood one day against the stone pillar in whose shadow she had lain asleep, eighteen years before, that Armand Aubigny riding by and seeing her there, had fallen in love with her. That was the way all the Aubignys fell in love, as if struck by a pistol shot. The wonder was that he had not loved her before; for he had known her since his father brought him home from Paris, a boy of eight, after his mother died there. The passion that awoke in him that day, when he saw her at the gate, swept along like an avalanche, or like a prairie fire, or like anything that drives headlong over all obstacles.

Madame Valmondé bent her portly figure over Désirée and kissed her, 5
holding her an instant tenderly in her arms. Then she turned to the child.

"This is not the baby!" she exclaimed, in startled tones. French was the language spoken at Valmondé in those days.

"I knew you would be astonished," laughed Désirée, "at the way he has grown. The little *cochon de lait!*[1] Look at his legs, mamma, and his hands and fingernails,—real fingernails. Zandrine had to cut them this morning. Isn't it true, Zandrine?"

The woman bowed her turbaned head majestically, "Mais si, Madame."

"And the way he cries," went on Désirée, "is deafening. Armand heard him the other day as far away as La Blanche's cabin."

Madame Valmondé had never removed her eyes from the child. She 10
lifted it and walked with it over to the window that was lightest. She scanned the baby narrowly, then looked as searchingly at Zandrine, whose face was turned to gaze across the fields.

"Yes, the child has grown, has changed," said Madame Valmondé, slowly, as she replaced it beside its mother. "What does Armand say?"

Désirée's face became suffused with a glow that was happiness itself.

"Oh, Armand is the proudest father in the parish, I believe, chiefly because it is a boy, to bear his name; though he says not—that he would have loved a girl as well. But I know it isn't true. I know he says that to please me. And mamma," she added, drawing Madame Valmondé's head down to her, and speaking in a whisper, "he hasn't punished one of them—not one of them—since baby is born. Even Négrillon, who pretended to have burnt his leg that he might rest from work—he only laughed, and said Négrillon was a great scamp. Oh, mamma, I'm so happy; it frightens me."

What Désirée said was true. Marriage, and later the birth of his son, had softened Armand Aubigny's imperious and exacting nature greatly. This was what made the gentle Désirée so happy, for she loved him desperately. When he frowned she trembled, but loved him. When he smiled, she asked no greater blessing of God. But Armand's dark, handsome face

[1]Literally "pig of milk"—a big feeder.

had not often been disfigured by frowns since the day he fell in love with her.

When the baby was about three months old, Désirée awoke one day to the conviction that there was something in the air menacing her peace. It was at first too subtle to grasp. It had only been a disquieting suggestion; an air of mystery among the blacks; unexpected visits from far-off neighbors who could hardly account for their coming. Then a strange, an awful change in her husband's manner, which she dared not ask him to explain. When he spoke to her, it was with averted eyes, from which the old love light seemed to have gone out. He absented himself from home; and when there, avoided her presence and that of her child, without excuse. And the very spirit of Satan seemed suddenly to take hold of him in his dealings with the slaves. Désirée was miserable enough to die. 15

She sat in her room, one hot afternoon, in her *peignoir,* listlessly drawing through her fingers the strands of her long, silky brown hair that hung about her shoulders. The baby, half naked, lay asleep upon her own great mahogany bed, that was like a sumptuous throne, with its satin-lined half canopy. One of La Blanche's little quadroon boys—half naked too—stood fanning the child slowly with a fan of peacock feathers. Désirée's eyes had been fixed absently and sadly upon the baby, while she was striving to penetrate the threatening mist that she felt closing about her. She looked from her child to the boy who stood beside him; and back again, over and over. "Ah!" It was a cry that she could not help, which she was not conscious of having uttered. The blood turned like ice in her veins, and a clammy moisture gathered upon her face.

She tried to speak to the little quadroon boy; but no sound would come, at first. When he heard his name uttered, he looked up, and his mistress was pointing to the door. He laid aside the great, soft fan, and obediently stole away, over the polished floor, on his bare tiptoes.

She stayed motionless, with gaze riveted upon her child, and her face the picture of fright.

Presently her husband entered the room, and without noticing her, went to a table and began to search among some papers which covered it.

"Armand," she called to him, in a voice which must have stabbed him, if he was human. But he did not notice. "Armand," she said again. Then she rose and tottered towards him. "Armand," she panted once more, clutching his arm, "look at our child. What does it mean? Tell me." 20

He coldly but gently loosened her fingers from about his arm and thrust the hand away from him. "Tell me what it means!" she cried despairingly.

"It means," he answered lightly, "that the child is not white; it means that you are not white."

A quick conception of all that this accusation meant for her nerved her with unwonted courage to deny it. "It is a lie; it is not true, I am white! Look at my hair, it is brown; and my eyes are gray, Armand, you know they are gray. And my skin is fair," seizing his wrist. "Look at my hand, whiter than yours, Armand," she laughed hysterically.

"As white as La Blanche's," he returned cruelly, and went away leaving her alone with their child.

When she could hold a pen in her hand, she sent a despairing letter to Madame Valmondé. 25

"My mother, they tell me I am not white. Armand has told me I am not white. For God's sake tell them it is not true. You must know it is not true. I shall die. I must die. I cannot be so unhappy, and live."

The answer that came was as brief:

"My own Désirée: Come home to Valmondé; back to your mother who loves you. Come with your child."

When the letter reached Désirée she went with it to her husband's study, and laid it open upon the desk before which he sat. She was like a stone image: silent, white, motionless after she placed it there.

In silence he ran his cold eyes over the written words. He said nothing. "Shall I go, Armand?" she asked in tones sharp with agonized suspense.

"Yes, go."

"Do you want me to go?"

"Yes, I want you to go."

He thought Almighty God had dealt cruelly and unjustly with him; and felt, somehow, that he was paying Him back in kind when he stabbed thus into his wife's soul. Moreover he no longer loved her, because of the unconscious injury she had brought upon his home and his name.

She turned away like one stunned by a blow, and walked slowly towards the door, hoping he would call her back.

"Good-by, Armand," she moaned.

He did not answer her. That was his last blow at fate.

Désirée went in search of her child. Zandrine was pacing the sombre gallery with it. She took the little one from the nurse's arms with no word of explanation, and descending the steps, walked away, under the live-oak branches.

It was an October afternoon; the sun was just sinking. Out in the still fields the Negroes were picking cotton.

Désirée had not changed the thin white garment nor the slippers which she wore. Her hair was uncovered and the sun's rays brought a golden gleam from its brown meshes. She did not take the broad, beaten road which led to the far-off plantation of Valmondé. She walked across a deserted field, where the stubble bruised her tender feet, so delicately shod, and tore her thin gown to shreds.

She disappeared among the reeds and willows that grew thick along the banks of the deep, sluggish bayou; and she did not come back again.

• • • • • • • • •

Some weeks later there was a curious scene enacted at L'Abri. In the centre of the smoothly swept back yard was a great bonfire. Armand Aubigny sat in the wide hallway that commanded a view of the spectacle; and it was he who dealt out to a half dozen negroes the material which kept this fire ablaze.

A graceful cradle of willow, with all its dainty furbishings, was laid upon the pyre, which had already been fed with the richness of a priceless *layette*. Then there were silk gowns, and velvet and satin ones added to these; laces, too, and embroideries; bonnets and gloves; for the *corbeille*[2] had been of rare quality.

The last thing to go was a tiny bundle of letters; innocent little scribblings that Désirée had sent to him during the days of their espousal. There was the remnant of one back in the drawer from which he took them. But

---

[2]Basket; linens, clothing, and accessories collected in anticipation of a baby's birth.

it was not Désirée's; it was part of an old letter from his mother to his father. He read it. She was thanking God for the blessing of her husband's love:

"But, above all," she wrote, "night and day, I thank the good God for having so arranged our lives that our dear Armand will never know that his mother, who adores him, belongs to the race that is cursed with the brand of slavery."

Analyzing the Text

1. What can you infer about Armand's character and his past behavior from the fact that he has not punished one slave since his baby was born?
2. How does Armand's behavior toward Désirée change after the baby is 3 months old? What causes this change in his behavior?

Understanding Chopin's Techniques

1. In retrospect, what clues would have pointed you toward the truth disclosed at the end of the story?
2. How does Chopin develop the character of Armand in connection with the image of fire throughout the story?

Arguing for an Interpretation

1. In what sense might the story be considered as much a tragedy for Armand as it is for Désirée? Keep in mind that Armand's father reacted quite differently to the same circumstances.
2. In what way does the choice that faces Armand, between a wife that he had loved and fear of being shamed in the eyes of society, embody Chopin's judgment of the society of her era?

F. Scott Fitzgerald

F. Scott Fitzgerald (1896–1940) was born in St. Paul, Minnesota, and attended Princeton but left before graduating to join the army in World War I. While stationed in Alabama, he fell in love with Zelda Sayre but was unable to marry her because he could not support her in the style to which she was accustomed. This fact alone would suggest that his fiction is intensely autobiographical, since many of his novels, including the acclaimed The Great Gatsby *(1925), and his short stories such as "Winter Dreams" (1922) reprinted below, embody this theme. He is generally perceived as the voice of the "Jazz Age," one of the "lost generation" (as Gertrude Stein described those who had served in World War I and had become disillusioned), whose hopes and despair are expressed in his works. The success he gained at the age of*

24 from his first novel, This Side of Paradise *(1920), enabled him to marry Zelda, a decision that would ironically plunge him into a life of extravagance, debt, and alcoholism. Zelda's increasing mental illness is recounted in* Tender Is the Night *(1934).*

Winter Dreams

I

Some of the caddies were poor as sin and lived in one-room houses with a neurasthenic cow in the front yard, but Dexter Green's father owned the second best grocery-store in Black Bear—the best one was "The Hub," patronized by the wealthy people from Sherry Island—and Dexter caddied only for pocket-money.

In the fall when the days became crisp and gray, and the long Minnesota winter shut down like the white lid of a box, Dexter's skis moved over the snow that hid the fairways of the golf course. At these times the country gave him a feeling of profound melancholy—it offended him that the links should lie in enforced fallowness, haunted by ragged sparrows for the long season. It was dreary, too, that on the tees where the gay colors fluttered in summer there were now only the desolate sand-boxes knee-deep in crusted ice. When he crossed the hills the wind blew cold as misery, and if the sun was out he tramped with his eyes squinted up against the hard dimensionless glare.

In April the winter ceased abruptly. The snow ran down into Black Bear Lake scarcely tarrying for the early golfers to brave the season with red and black balls. Without elation, without an interval of moist glory, the cold was gone.

Dexter knew that there was something dismal about this Northern spring, just as he knew there was something gorgeous about the fall. Fall made him clinch his hands and tremble and repeat idiotic sentences to himself, and make brisk abrupt gestures of command to imaginary audiences and armies. October filled him with hope which November raised to a sort of ecstatic triumph, and in this mood the fleeting brilliant impressions of the summer at Sherry Island were ready grist to his mill. He became a golf champion and defeated Mr. T. A. Hedrick in a marvellous match played a hundred times over the fairways of his imagination, a match each detail of which he changed about untiringly—sometimes he won with almost laughable ease, sometimes he came up magnificently from behind. Again, stepping from a Pierce-Arrow automobile, like Mr. Mortimer Jones, he strolled frigidly into the lounge of the Sherry Island Golf Club—or perhaps, surrounded by an admiring crowd, he gave an exhibition of fancy diving from the spring-board of the club raft. . . . Among those who watched him in open-mouthed wonder was Mr. Mortimer Jones.

And one day it came to pass that Mr. Jones—himself and not his 5
ghost—came up to Dexter with tears in his eyes and said that Dexter was the —— best caddy in the club, and wouldn't he decide not to quit if Mr. Jones made it worth his while, because every other —— caddy in the club lost one ball a hole for him—regularly ——

"No, sir," said Dexter decisively,"I don't want to caddy any more."Then, after a pause:"I'm too old."

"You're not more than fourteen.Why the devil did you decide just this morning that you wanted to quit? You promised that next week you'd go over to the State tournament with me."

"I decided I was too old."

Dexter handed in his "A Class" badge, collected what money was due him from the caddy master, and walked home to Black Bear Village.

"The best —— caddy I ever saw," shouted Mr. Mortimer Jones over a drink that afternoon."Never lost a ball! Willing! Intelligent! Quiet! Honest! Grateful!"

The little girl who had done this was eleven—beautifully ugly as little girls are apt to be who are destined after a few years to be inexpressibly lovely and bring no end of misery to a great number of men. The spark, however, was perceptible.There was a general ungodliness in the way her lips twisted down at the corners when she smiled, and in the—Heaven help us!—in the almost passionate quality of her eyes.Vitality is born early in such women. It was utterly in evidence now, shining through her thin frame in a sort of glow.

She had come eagerly out on to the course at nine o'clock with a white linen nurse and five small new golf-clubs in a white canvas bag which the nurse was carrying.When Dexter first saw her she was standing by the caddy house, rather ill at ease and trying to conceal the fact by engaging her nurse in an obviously unnatural conversation graced by startling and irrelevant grimaces from herself.

"Well, it's certainly a nice day, Hilda," Dexter heard her say. She drew down the corners of her mouth, smiled, and glanced furtively around, her eyes in transit falling for an instant on Dexter.

Then to the nurse:

"Well, I guess there aren't very many people out here this morning, are there?"

The smile again—radiant, blatantly artificial—convincing.

"I don't know what we're supposed to do now," said the nurse, looking nowhere in particular.

"Oh, that's all right. I'll fix it up."

Dexter stood perfectly still, his mouth slightly ajar. He knew that if he moved forward a step his stare would be in her line of vision—if he moved backward he would lose his full view of her face. For a moment he had not realized how young she was. Now he remembered having seen her several times the year before—in bloomers.

Suddenly, involuntarily, he laughed, a short abrupt laugh—then, startled by himself, he turned and began to walk quickly away.

"Boy!"

Dexter stopped.

"Boy —— "

Beyond question he was addressed. Not only that, but he was treated to that absurd smile, that preposterous smile—the memory of which at least a dozen men were to carry into middle age.

"Boy, do you know where the golf teacher is?"

"He's giving a lesson."

"Well, do you know where the caddy-master is?"

"He isn't here yet this morning."

“Oh.” For a moment this baffled her. She stood alternately on her right and left foot.

“We'd like to get a caddy,” said the nurse. “Mrs. Mortimer Jones sent us 30
out to play golf, and we don't know how without we get a caddy.”

Here she was stopped by an ominous glance from Miss Jones, followed immediately by the smile.

“There aren't any caddies here except me,” said Dexter to the nurse, “and I got to stay here in charge until the caddy-master gets here.”

“Oh.”

Miss Jones and her retinue now withdrew, and at a proper distance from Dexter became involved in a heated conversation, which was concluded by Miss Jones taking one of the clubs and hitting it on the ground with violence. For further emphasis she raised it again and was about to bring it down smartly upon the nurse's bosom, when the nurse seized the club and twisted it from her hands.

“You damn little mean old *thing!*” cried Miss Jones wildly. 35

Another argument ensued. Realizing that the elements of the comedy were implied in the scene, Dexter several times began to laugh, but each time restrained the laugh before it reached audibility. He could not resist the monstrous conviction that the little girl was justified in beating the nurse.

The situation was resolved by the fortuitous appearance of the caddy-master, who was appealed to immediately by the nurse.

“Miss Jones is to have a little caddy, and this one says he can't go.”

“Mr. McKenna said I was to wait here till you came,” said Dexter quickly.

“Well, he's here now.” Miss Jones smiled cheerfully at the caddy-master. 40
Then she dropped her bag and set off at a haughty mince toward the first tee.

“Well?” The caddy-master turned to Dexter. “What you standing there like a dummy for? Go pick up the young lady's clubs.”

“I don't think I'll go out to-day,” said Dexter.

“You don't ———”

“I think I'll quit.”

The enormity of his decision frightened him. He was a favorite caddy, 45
and the thirty dollars a month he earned through the summer were not to be made elsewhere around the lake. But he had received a strong emotional shock, and his perturbation required a violent and immediate outlet.

It is not so simple as that, either. As so frequently would be the case in the future, Dexter was unconsciously dictated to by his winter dreams.

II

Now, of course, the quality and the seasonability of these winter dreams varied, but the stuff of them remained. They persuaded Dexter several years later to pass up a business course at the State university—his father, prospering now, would have paid his way—for the precarious advantage of attending an older and more famous university in the East, where he was bothered by his scanty funds. But do not get the impression, because his winter dreams happened to be concerned at first with musings on the rich, that there was anything merely snobbish in the boy. He wanted not association with glittering things and glittering people—he wanted the glittering things themselves. Often he reached out for the best without knowing why he wanted it—and sometimes he ran up against the mysterious denials and prohibitions in which life indulges. It is with one of those denials and not with his career as a whole that this story deals.

He made money. It was rather amazing. After college he went to the city from which Black Bear Lake draws its wealthy patrons. When he was only twenty-three and had been there not quite two years, there were already people who liked to say: "Now *there's* a boy—". All about him rich men's sons were peddling bonds precariously, or investing patrimonies precariously, or plodding through the two dozen volumes of the "George Washington Commercial Course," but Dexter borrowed a thousand dollars on his college degree and his confident mouth, and bought a partnership in a laundry.

It was a small laundry when he went into it but Dexter made a specialty of learning how the English washed fine woollen golf-stockings without shrinking them, and within a year he was catering to the trade that wore knickerbockers. Men were insisting that their Shetland hose and sweaters go to his laundry just as they had insisted on a caddy who could find golf-balls. A little later he was doing their wives' lingerie as well—and running five branches in different parts of the city. Before he was twenty-seven he owned the largest string of laundries in his section of the country. It was then that he sold out and went to New York. But the part of his story that concerns us goes back to the days when he was making his first big success.

When he was twenty-three Mr. Hart—one of the gray-haired men who 50
like to say "Now there's a boy"—gave him a guest card to the Sherry Island Golf Club for a week-end. So he signed his name one day on the register, and that afternoon played golf in a foursome with Mr. Hart and Mr. Sandwood and Mr. T. A. Hedrick. He did not consider it necessary to remark that he had once carried Mr. Hart's bag over this same links, and that he knew every trap and gully with his eyes shut—but he found himself glancing at the four caddies who trailed them, trying to catch a gleam or gesture that would remind him of himself, that would lessen the gap which lay between his present and his past.

It was a curious day, slashed abruptly with fleeting, familiar impressions. One minute he had the sense of being a trespasser—in the next he was impressed by the tremendous superiority he felt toward Mr. T. A. Hedrick, who was a bore and not even a good golfer any more.

Then, because of a ball Mr. Hart lost near the fifteenth green, an enormous thing happened. While they were searching the stiff grasses of the rough there was a clear call of "Fore!" from behind a hill in their rear. And as they all turned abruptly from their search a bright new ball sliced abruptly over the hill and caught Mr. T. A. Hedrick in the abdomen.

"By Gad!" cried Mr. T. A. Hedrick, "they ought to put some of these crazy women off the course. It's getting to be outrageous."

A head and a voice came up together over the hill:

"Do you mind if we go through?" 55

"You hit me in the stomach!" declared Mr. Hedrick wildly.

"Did I?" The girl approached the group of men. "I'm sorry. I yelled 'Fore!' "

Her glance fell casually on each of the men—then scanned the fairway for her ball.

"Did I bounce into the rough?"

It was impossible to determine whether this question was ingenuous 60
or malicious. In a moment, however, she left no doubt, for as her partner came up over the hill she called cheerfully:

"Here I am! I'd have gone on the green except that I hit something."

As she took her stance for a short mashie shot, Dexter looked at her closely. She wore a blue gingham dress, rimmed at throat and shoulders with a white edging that accentuated her tan. The quality of exaggeration, of thinness, which had made her passionate eyes and down-turning mouth absurd at eleven, was gone now. She was arrestingly beautiful. The color in her cheeks was centered like the color in a picture—it was not a "high" color, but a sort of fluctuating and feverish warmth, so shaded that it seemed at any moment it would recede and disappear. This color and the mobility of her mouth gave a continual impression of flux, of intense life, of passionate vitality—balanced only partially by the sad luxury of her eyes.

She swung her mashie impatiently and without interest, pitching the ball into a sand-pit on the other side of the green. With a quick, insincere smile and a careless "Thank you!" she went on after it.

"That Judy Jones!" remarked Mr. Hedrick on the next tee, as they waited—some moments—for her to play on ahead. "All she needs is to be turned up and spanked for six months and then to be married off to an old-fashioned cavalry captain."

"My God, she's good-looking!" said Mr. Sandwood, who was just over thirty.

"Good-looking!" cried Mr. Hedrick contemptuously, "she always looks as if she wanted to be kissed! Turning those big cow-eyes on every calf in town!"

It was doubtful if Mr. Hedrick intended a reference to the maternal instinct.

"She'd play pretty good golf if she'd try," said Mr. Sandwood.

"She has no form," said Mr. Hedrick solemnly.

"She has a nice figure," said Mr. Sandwood.

"Better thank the Lord she doesn't drive a swifter ball," said Mr. Hart, winking at Dexter.

Later in the afternoon the sun went down with a riotous swirl of gold and varying blues and scarlets, and left the dry, rustling night of Western summer. Dexter watched from the veranda of the Golf Club, watched the even overlap of the waters in the little wind, silver molasses under the harvest-moon. Then the moon held a finger to her lips and the lake became a clear pool, pale and quiet. Dexter put on his bathing-suit and swam out to the farthest raft, where he stretched dripping on the wet canvas of the springboard.

There was a fish jumping and a star shining and the lights around the lake were gleaming. Over on a dark peninsula a piano was playing the songs of last summer and of summers before that—songs from "Chin-Chin" and "The Count of Luxemburg" and "The Chocolate Soldier"—and because the sound of a piano over a stretch of water had always seemed beautiful to Dexter he lay perfectly quiet and listened.

The tune the piano was playing at that moment had been gay and new five years before when Dexter was a sophomore at college. They had played it at a prom once when he could not afford the luxury of proms, and he had stood outside the gymnasium and listened. The sound of the tune precipitated in him a sort of ecstasy and it was with that ecstasy he viewed what happened to him now. It was a mood of intense appreciation, a sense that, for once, he was magnificently attune to life and that everything about him was radiating a brightness and a glamour he might never know again.

A low, pale oblong detached itself suddenly from the darkness of the 75
Island, spitting forth the reverberate sound of a racing motor-boat. Two white streamers of cleft water rolled themselves out behind it and almost immediately the boat was beside him, drowning out the hot tinkle of the piano in the drone of its spray. Dexter raising himself on his arms was aware of a figure standing at the wheel, of two dark eyes regarding him over the lengthening space of water—then the boat had gone by and was sweeping in an immense and purposeless circle of spray round and round in the middle of the lake. With equal eccentricity one of the circles flattened out and headed back toward the raft.

"Who's that?" she called, shutting off her motor. She was so near now that Dexter could see her bathing-suit, which consisted apparently of pink rompers.

The nose of the boat bumped the raft, and as the latter tilted rakishly he was precipitated toward her. With different degrees of interest they recognized each other.

"Aren't you one of those men we played through this afternoon?" she demanded.

He was.

"Well, do you know how to drive a motor-boat? Because if you do I 80
wish you'd drive this one so I can ride on the surf-board behind. My name is Judy Jones"—she favored him with an absurd smirk—rather, what tried to be a smirk, for, twist her mouth as she might, it was not grotesque, it was merely beautiful—"and I live in a house over there on the Island, and in that house there is a man waiting for me. When he drove up at the door I drove out of the dock because he says I'm his ideal."

There was a fish jumping and a star shining and the lights around the lake were gleaming. Dexter sat beside Judy Jones and she explained how her boat was driven. Then she was in the water, swimming to the floating surfboard with a sinuous crawl. Watching her was without effort to the eye, watching a branch waving or a sea-gull flying. Her arms, burned to butternut, moved sinuously among the dull platinum ripples, elbow appearing first, casting the forearm back with a cadence of falling water, then reaching out and down, stabbing a path ahead.

They moved out into the lake; turning, Dexter saw that she was kneeling on the low rear of the now uptilted surf-board.

"Go faster," she called, "fast as it'll go."

Obediently he jammed the lever forward and the white spray mounted at the bow. When he looked around again the girl was standing up on the rushing board, her arms spread wide, her eyes lifted toward the moon.

"It's awful cold," she shouted. "What's your name?" 85

He told her.

"Well, why don't you come to dinner to-morrow night?"

His heart turned over like the fly-wheel of the boat, and, for the second time, her casual whim gave a new direction to his life.

III

Next evening while he waited for her to come down-stairs, Dexter peopled the soft deep summer room and the sun-porch that opened from it with the men who had already loved Judy Jones. He knew the sort of men they were—the men who when he first went to college had entered from the great prep schools with graceful clothes and the deep tan of healthy summers. He had seen that, in one sense, he was better than these men. He was newer and stronger. Yet in acknowledging to himself that he wished his children to be like them he was admitting that he was but the rough, strong stuff from which they eternally sprang.

When the time had come for him to wear good clothes, he had known 90
who were the best tailors in America, and the best tailors in America had made him the suit he wore this evening. He had acquired that particular reserve peculiar to his university, that set it off from other universities. He recognized the value to him of such a mannerism and he had adopted it; he knew that to be careless in dress and manner required more confidence than to be careful. But carelessness was for his children. His mother's name had been Krimslich. She was a Bohemian of the peasant class and she had talked broken English to the end of her days. Her son must keep to the set patterns.

At a little after seven Judy Jones came down-stairs. She wore a blue silk afternoon dress, and he was disappointed at first that she had not put on something more elaborate. This feeling was accentuated when, after a brief greeting, she went to the door of a butler's pantry and pushing it open called: "You can serve dinner, Martha." He had rather expected that a butler would announce dinner, that there would be a cocktail. Then he put these thoughts behind him as they sat down side by side on a lounge and looked at each other.

"Father and mother won't be here," she said thoughtfully.

He remembered the last time he had seen her father, and he was glad the parents were not to be here to-night—they might wonder who he was. He had been born in Keeble, a Minnesota village fifty miles farther north, and he always gave Keeble as his home instead of Black Bear Village. Country towns were well enough to come from if they weren't inconveniently in sight and used as footstools by fashionable lakes.

They talked of his university, which she had visited frequently during the past two years, and of the near-by city which supplied Sherry Island with its patrons, and whither Dexter would return next day to his prospering laundries.

During dinner she slipped into a moody depression which gave 95
Dexter a feeling of uneasiness. Whatever petulance she uttered in her throaty voice worried him. Whatever she smiled at—at him, at a chicken liver, at nothing—it disturbed him that her smile could have no root in mirth, or even in amusement. When the scarlet corners of her lips curved down, it was less a smile than an invitation to a kiss.

Then, after dinner, she led him out on the dark sun-porch and deliberately changed the atmosphere.

"Do you mind if I weep a little?" she said.

"I'm afraid I'm boring you," he responded quickly.

"You're not. I like you. But I've just had a terrible afternoon. There was a man I cared about, and this afternoon he told me out of a clear sky that he was poor as a church-mouse. He'd never even hinted it before. Does this sound horribly mundane?"

"Perhaps he was afraid to tell you." 100

"Suppose he was," she answered. "He didn't start right. You see, if I'd thought of him as poor—well, I've been mad about loads of poor men, and fully intended to marry them all. But in this case, I hadn't thought of him that way, and my interest in him wasn't strong enough to survive the shock. As if a girl calmly informed her fiancé that she was a widow. He might not object to widows, but ——"

"Let's start right," she interrupted herself suddenly. "Who are you, anyhow?"

For a moment Dexter hesitated. Then:

"I'm nobody," he announced. "My career is largely a matter of futures."

"Are you poor?" 105

"No," he said frankly, "I'm probably making more money than any man my age in the Northwest. I know that's an obnoxious remark, but you advised me to start right."

There was a pause. Then she smiled and the corners of her mouth drooped and an almost imperceptible sway brought her closer to him, looking up into his eyes. A lump rose in Dexter's throat, and he waited breathless for the experiment, facing the unpredictable compound that would form mysteriously from the elements of their lips. Then he saw—she communicated her excitement to him, lavishly, deeply, with kisses that were not a promise but a fulfillment. They aroused in him not hunger demanding renewal but surfeit that would demand more surfeit . . . kisses that were like charity, creating want by holding back nothing at all.

It did not take him many hours to decide that he had wanted Judy Jones ever since he was a proud, desirous little boy.

IV

It began like that—and continued, with varying shades of intensity, on such a note right up to the dénouement. Dexter surrendered a part of himself to the most direct and unprincipled personality with which he had ever come in contact. Whatever Judy wanted, she went after with the full pressure of her charm. There was no divergence of method, no jockeying for position or premeditation of effects—there was a very little mental side to any of her affairs. She simply made men conscious to the highest degree of her physical loveliness. Dexter had no desire to change her. Her deficiencies were knit up with a passionate energy that transcended and justified them.

110 When, as Judy's head lay against his shoulder that first night, she whispered, "I don't know what's the matter with me. Last night I thought I was in love with a man and to-night I think I'm in love with you ——"—it seemed to him a beautiful and romantic thing to say. It was the exquisite excitability that for the moment he controlled and owned. But a week later he was compelled to view this same quality in a different light. She took him in her roadster to a picnic supper, and after supper she disappeared, likewise in her roadster, with another man. Dexter became enormously upset and was scarcely able to be decently civil to the other people present. When she assured him that she had not kissed the other man, he knew she was lying—yet he was glad that she had taken the trouble to lie to him.

He was, as he found before the summer ended, one of a varying dozen who circulated about her. Each of them had at one time been favored above all others—about half of them still basked in the solace of occasional sentimental revivals. Whenever one showed signs of dropping out through long neglect, she granted him a brief honeyed hour, which encouraged him to tag along for a year or so longer. Judy made these forays upon the helpless and defeated without malice, indeed half unconscious that there was anything mischievous in what she did.

When a new man came to town every one dropped out—dates were automatically cancelled.

The helpless part of trying to do anything about it was that she did it all herself. She was not a girl who could be "won" in the kinetic sense—she was proof against cleverness, she was proof against charm; if any of these assailed her too strongly she would immediately resolve the affair to a physical basis, and under the magic of her physical splendor the strong as well as the brilliant played her game and not their own. She was entertained only by the gratification of her desires and by the direct exercise of her own charm. Perhaps from so much youthful love, so many youthful lovers, she had come, in self-defense, to nourish herself wholly from within.

Succeeding Dexter's first exhilaration came restlessness and dissatisfaction. The helpless ecstasy of losing himself in her was opiate rather than tonic. It was fortunate for his work during the winter that those moments of ecstasy came infrequently. Early in their acquaintance it had seemed for a while that there was a deep and spontaneous mutual attraction—that first August, for example—three days of long evenings on her dusky veranda, of strange wan kisses through the late afternoon, in shadowy alcoves or behind the protecting trellises of the garden arbors, of mornings when she was fresh as a dream and almost shy at meeting him in the clarity of the rising day. There was all the ecstasy of an engagement about it, sharpened by his realization that there was no engagement. It was during those three days that, for the first time, he had asked her to marry him. She said "maybe some day," she said "kiss me," she said "I'd like to marry you," she said "I love you"—she said—nothing.

The three days were interrupted by the arrival of a New York man 115
who visited at her house for half September. To Dexter's agony, rumor engaged them. The man was the son of the president of a great trust company. But at the end of a month it was reported that Judy was yawning. At a dance one night she sat all evening in a motor-boat with a local beau, while the New Yorker searched the club for her frantically. She told the local beau that she was bored with her visitor, and two days later he left. She was seen with him at the station, and it was reported that he looked very mournful indeed.

On this note the summer ended. Dexter was twenty-four, and he found himself increasingly in a position to do as he wished. He joined two clubs in the city and lived at one of them. Though he was by no means an integral part of the stag-lines at these clubs, he managed to be on hand at dances where Judy Jones was likely to appear. He could have gone out socially as much as he liked—he was an eligible young man, now, and popular with down-town fathers. His confessed devotion to Judy Jones had rather solidified his position. But he had no social aspirations and rather despised the dancing men who were always on tap for the Thursday or Saturday parties and who filled in at dinners with the younger married set. Already he was playing with the idea of going East to New York. He wanted to take Judy Jones with him. No disillusion as to the world in which she had grown up could cure his illusion as to her desirability.

Remember that—for only in the light of it can what he did for her be understood.

Eighteen months after he first met Judy Jones he became engaged to another girl. Her name was Irene Scheerer, and her father was one of the men who had always believed in Dexter. Irene was light-haired and sweet and honorable, and a little stout, and she had two suitors whom she pleasantly relinquished when Dexter formally asked her to marry him.

Summer, fall, winter, spring, another summer, another fall—so much he had given of his active life to the incorrigible lips of Judy Jones. She had treated him with interest, with encouragement, with malice, with indifference, with contempt. She had inflicted on him the innumerable little slights and indignities possible in such a case—as if in revenge for having ever cared for him at all. She had beckoned him and yawned at him and beckoned him again and he had responded often with bitterness and narrowed eyes. She had brought him ecstatic happiness and intolerable agony of spirit. She had caused him untold inconvenience and not a little trouble. She had insulted him, and she had ridden over him, and she had played his interest in her against his interest in his work—for fun. She had done everything to him except to criticize him—this she had not done—it seemed to him only because it might have sullied the utter indifference she manifested and sincerely felt toward him.

When autumn had come and gone again it occurred to him that he 120
could not have Judy Jones. He had to beat this into his mind but he convinced himself at last. He lay awake at night for a while and argued it over. He told himself the trouble and the pain she had caused him, he enumerated her glaring deficiencies as a wife. Then he said to himself that he loved her, and after a while he fell asleep. For a week, lest he imagined her husky voice over the telephone or her eyes opposite him at lunch, he worked hard and late, and at night he went to his office and plotted out his years.

At the end of a week he went to a dance and cut in on her once. For almost the first time since they had met he did not ask her to sit out with him or tell her that she was lovely. It hurt him that she did not miss these things—that was all. He was not jealous when he saw that there was a new man to-night. He had been hardened against jealousy long before.

He stayed late at the dance. He sat for an hour with Irene Scheerer and talked about books and about music. He knew very little about either. But he was beginning to be master of his own time now, and he had a rather priggish notion that he—the young and already fabulously successful Dexter Green—should know more about such things.

That was in October, when he was twenty-five. In January, Dexter and Irene became engaged. It was to be announced in June, and they were to be married three months later.

The Minnesota winter prolonged itself interminably, and it was almost May when the winds came soft and the snow ran down into Black Bear Lake at last. For the first time in over a year Dexter was enjoying a certain tranquility of spirit. Judy Jones had been in Florida, and afterward in Hot Springs, and somewhere she had been engaged, and somewhere she had broken it off. At first, when Dexter had definitely given her up, it had made him sad that people still linked them together and asked for news of her, but when he began to be placed at dinner next to Irene Scheerer people didn't ask him about her any more—they told him about her. He ceased to be an authority on her.

May at last. Dexter walked the streets at night when the darkness was 125
damp as rain, wondering that so soon, with so little done, so much of ecstasy had gone from him. May one year back had been marked by Judy's poignant, unforgivable, yet forgiven turbulence—it had been one of those rare times when he fancied she had grown to care for him. That old penny's worth of happiness he had spent for this bushel of content. He knew that Irene would be no more than a curtain spread behind him, a hand moving among gleaming tea-cups, a voice calling to children . . . fire and loveliness were gone, the magic of nights and the wonder of the varying hours and seasons . . . slender lips, down-turning, dropping to his lips and bearing him up into a heaven of eyes. . . . The thing was deep in him. He was too strong and alive for it to die lightly.

In the middle of May when the weather balanced for a few days on the thin bridge that led to deep summer he turned in one night at Irene's house. Their engagement was to be announced in a week now—no one would be surprised at it. And to-night they would sit together on the lounge at the University Club and look on for an hour at the dancers. It gave him a sense of solidity to go with her—she was so sturdily popular, so intensely "great."

He mounted the steps of the brownstone house and stepped inside.

"Irene," he called.

Mrs. Scheerer came out of the living-room to meet him.

"Dexter," she said, "Irene's gone up-stairs with a splitting headache. She 130
wanted to go with you but I made her go to bed."

"Nothing serious, I—"

"Oh, no. She's going to play golf with you in the morning. You can spare her for just one night, can't you, Dexter?"

Her smile was kind. She and Dexter liked each other. In the living-room he talked for a moment before he said good-night.

Returning to the University Club, where he had rooms, he stood in the doorway for a moment and watched the dancers. He leaned against the door-post, nodded at a man or two—yawned.

"Hello, darling." 135

The familiar voice at his elbow startled him. Judy Jones had left a man and crossed the room to him—Judy Jones, a slender enamelled doll in cloth of gold: gold in a band at her head, gold in two slipper points at her dress's hem. The fragile glow of her face seemed to blossom as she smiled at him. A breeze of warmth and light blew through the room. His hands in the pockets of his dinner-jacket tightened spasmodically. He was filled with a sudden excitement.

"When did you get back?" he asked casually.

"Come here and I'll tell you about it."

She turned and he followed her. She had been away—he could have wept at the wonder of her return. She had passed through enchanted streets, doing things that were like provocative music. All mysterious happenings, all fresh and quickening hopes, had gone away with her, come back with her now.

She turned in the doorway. 140

"Have you a car here? If you haven't, I have."

"I have a coupé."

In then, with a rustle of golden cloth. He slammed the door. Into so many cars she had stepped—like this—like that—her back against the leather, so—her elbow resting on the door—waiting. She would have been soiled long since had there been anything to soil her—except herself—but this was her own self outpouring.

With an effort he forced himself to start the car and back into the street. This was nothing, he must remember. She had done this before, and he had put her behind him, as he would have crossed a bad account from his books.

He drove slowly down-town and, affecting abstraction, traversed the 145
deserted streets of the business section, peopled here and there where a movie was giving out its crowd or where consumptive or pugilistic youth lounged in front of pool halls. The clink of glasses and the slap of hands on the bars issued from saloons, cloisters of glazed glass and dirty yellow light.

She was watching him closely and the silence was embarrassing, yet in this crisis he could find no casual word with which to profane the hour. At a convenient turning he began to zigzag back toward the University Club.

"Have you missed me?" she asked suddenly.

"Everybody missed you."

He wondered if she knew of Irene Scheerer. She had been back only a day—her absence had been almost contemporaneous with his engagement.

"What a remark!" Judy laughed sadly—without sadness. She looked at 150
him searchingly. He became absorbed in the dashboard.

"You're handsomer than you used to be," she said thoughtfully. "Dexter, you have the most rememberable eyes."

He could have laughed at this, but he did not laugh. It was the sort of thing that was said to sophomores. Yet it stabbed at him.

"I'm awfully tired of everything, darling." She called every one darling, endowing the endearment with careless, individual comraderie. "I wish you'd marry me."

The directness of this confused him. He should have told her now that he was going to marry another girl, but he could not tell her. He could as easily have sworn that he had never loved her.

"I think we'd get along," she continued, on the same note, "unless prob- 155
ably you've forgotten me and fallen in love with another girl."

Her confidence was obviously enormous. She had said, in effect, that she found such a thing impossible to believe, that if it were true he had merely committed a childish indiscretion—and probably to show off. She would forgive him, because it was not a matter of any moment but rather something to be brushed aside lightly.

"Of course you could never love anybody but me," she continued. "I like the way you love me. Oh, Dexter, have you forgotten last year?"

"No, I haven't forgotten."

"Neither have I!"

Was she sincerely moved—or was she carried along by the wave of 160
her own acting?

"I wish we could be like that again," she said, and he forced himself to answer:

"I don't think we can."

"I suppose not.... I hear you're giving Irene Scheerer a violent rush."

There was not the faintest emphasis on the name, yet Dexter was suddenly ashamed.

"Oh, take me home," cried Judy suddenly; "I don't want to go back to 165
the idiotic dance—with those children."

Then, as he turned up the street that led to the residence district, Judy began to cry quietly to herself. He had never seen her cry before.

The dark street lightened, the dwellings of the rich loomed up around them, he stopped his coupé in front of the great white bulk of the Mortimer Joneses house, somnolent, gorgeous, drenched with the splendor of the damp moonlight. Its solidity startled him. The strong walls, the steel of the girders, the breadth and beam and pomp of it were there only to bring out the contrast with the young beauty beside him. It was sturdy to accentuate her slightness—as if to show what a breeze could be generated by a butterfly's wing.

He sat perfectly quiet, his nerves in wild clamor, afraid that if he moved he would find her irresistibly in his arms. Two tears had rolled down her wet face and trembled on her upper lip.

"I'm more beautiful than anybody else," she said brokenly, "why can't I be happy?" Her moist eyes tore at his stability—her mouth turned slowly downward with an exquisite sadness: "I'd like to marry you if you'll have me, Dexter. I suppose you think I'm not worth having, but I'll be so beautiful for you, Dexter."

A million phrases of anger, pride, passion, hatred, tenderness fought on 170
his lips. Then a perfect wave of emotion washed over him, carrying off with it a sediment of wisdom, of convention, of doubt, of honor. This was his girl who was speaking, his own, his beautiful, his pride.

"Won't you come in?" He heard her draw in her breath sharply.

Waiting.

"All right," his voice was trembling, "I'll come in."

V

It was strange that neither when it was over nor a long time afterward did he regret that night. Looking at it from the perspective of ten years, the fact that Judy's flare for him endured just one month seemed of little importance. Nor did it matter that by his yielding he subjected himself to a deeper agony in the end and gave serious hurt to Irene Scheerer and to Irene's parents, who had befriended him. There was nothing sufficiently pictorial about Irene's grief to stamp itself on his mind.

Dexter was at bottom hard-minded. The attitude of the city on his ac- 175
tion was of no importance to him, not because he was going to leave the city, but because any outside attitude on the situation seemed superficial. He was completely indifferent to popular opinion. Nor, when he had seen that it was no use, that he did not possess in himself the power to move fundamentally or to hold Judy Jones, did he bear any malice toward her. He loved her, and he would love her until the day he was too old for loving—but he could not have her. So he tasted the deep pain that is reserved only for the strong, just as he had tasted for a little while the deep happiness.

Even the ultimate falsity of the grounds upon which Judy terminated the engagement that she did not want to "take him away" from Irene—Judy, who had wanted nothing else—did not revolt him. He was beyond any revulsion or any amusement.

He went East in February with the intention of selling out his laundries and settling in New York—but the war came to America in March and changed his plans. He returned to the West, handed over the management of the business to his partner, and went into the first officers' training-camp in late April. He was one of those young thousands who greeted the war with a certain amount of relief, welcoming the liberation from webs of tangled emotion.

VI

This story is not his biography, remember, although things creep into it which have nothing to do with those dreams he had when he was young. We are almost done with them and with him now. There is only one more incident to be related here, and it happens seven years farther on.

It took place in New York, where he had done well—so well that there were no barriers too high for him. He was thirty-two years old, and, except for one flying trip immediately after the war, he had not been West in seven years. A man named Devlin from Detroit came into his office to see him in a business way, and then and there this incident occurred, and closed out, so to speak, this particular side of his life.

"So you're from the Middle West," said the man Devlin with careless 180
curiosity. "That's funny—I thought men like you were probably born and raised on Wall Street. You know—wife of one of my best friends in Detroit came from your city. I was an usher at the wedding."

Dexter waited with no apprehension of what was coming.

"Judy Simms," said Devlin with no particular interest; "Judy Jones she was once."

"Yes, I knew her." A dull impatience spread over him. He had heard, of course, that she was married—perhaps deliberately he had heard no more.

"Awfully nice girl," brooded Devlin meaninglessly, "I'm sort of sorry for her."

"Why?" Something in Dexter was alert, receptive, at once. 185

"Oh, Lud Simms has gone to pieces in a way. I don't mean he ill-uses her, but he drinks and runs around——"

"Doesn't she run around?"

"No. Stays at home with her kids."

"Oh."

"She's a little too old for him," said Devlin. 190

"Too old!" cried Dexter. "Why, man, she's only twenty-seven."

He was possessed with a wild notion of rushing out into the streets and taking a train to Detroit. He rose to his feet spasmodically.

"I guess you're busy," Devlin apologized quickly. "I didn't realize——"

"No, I'm not busy," said Dexter, steadying his voice. "I'm not busy at all. Not busy at all. Did you say she was—twenty-seven? No, I said she was twenty-seven."

"Yes, you did," agreed Devlin dryly. 195

"Go on, then. Go on."

"What do you mean?"

"About Judy Jones."

Devlin looked at him helplessly.

"Well, that's—I told you all there is to it. He treats her like the devil. 200
Oh, they're not going to get divorced or anything. When he's particularly outrageous she forgives him. In fact, I'm inclined to think she loves him. She was a pretty girl when she first came to Detroit."

A pretty girl! The phrase struck Dexter as ludicrous.

"Isn't she—a pretty girl, any more?"

"Oh, she's all right."

"Look here," said Dexter, sitting down suddenly, "I don't understand. You say she was a 'pretty girl' and now you say she's 'all right.' I don't understand what you mean—Judy Jones wasn't a pretty girl, at all. She was a great beauty. Why, I knew her, I knew her. She was——"

Devlin laughed pleasantly.

"I'm not trying to start a row," he said. "I think Judy's a nice girl and I like her. I can't understand how a man like Lud Simms could fall madly in love with her, but he did." Then he added: "Most of the women like her."

Dexter looked closely at Devlin, thinking wildly that there must be a reason for this, some insensitivity in the man or some private malice.

"Lots of women fade just like *that,*" Devlin snapped his fingers. "You must have seen it happen. Perhaps I've forgotten how pretty she was at her wedding. I've seen her so much since then, you see. She has nice eyes."

A sort of dullness settled down upon Dexter. For the first time in his life he felt like getting very drunk. He knew that he was laughing loudly at something Devlin had said, but he did not know what it was or why it was funny. When, in a few minutes, Devlin went he lay down on his lounge and looked out the window at the New York sky-line into which the sun was sinking in dull lovely shades of pink and gold.

He had thought that having nothing else to lose he was invulnerable at last—but he knew that he had just lost something more, as surely as if he had married Judy Jones and seen her fade away before his eyes.

The dream was gone. Something had been taken from him. In a sort of panic he pushed the palms of his hands into his eyes and tried to bring up a picture of the waters lapping on Sherry Island and the moonlit veranda, and gingham on the golf-links and the dry sun and the gold color of her neck's soft down. And her mouth damp to his kisses and her eyes plaintive with melancholy and her freshness like new fine linen in the morning. Why, these things were no longer in the world! They had existed and they existed no longer.

For the first time in years the tears were streaming down his face. But they were for himself now. He did not care about mouth and eyes and moving hands. He wanted to care, and he could not care. For he had gone away and he could never go back any more. The gates were closed, the sun was gone down, and there was no beauty but the gray beauty of steel that withstands all time. Even the grief he could have borne was left behind in the country of illusion, of youth, of the richness of life, where his winter dreams had flourished.

"Long ago," he said, "long ago, there was something in me, but now that thing is gone. Now that thing is gone, that thing is gone. I cannot cry. I cannot care. That thing will come back no more."

Analyzing the Text

1. What new directions does Dexter's life take each time he encounters Judy Jones?
2. What does Dexter's choice of Judy over Irene reveal about him? What contrasting sets of values do the two girls represent?

Understanding Fitzgerald's Techniques

1. How are each of the six sections designed to draw the reader into identifying with Dexter in his pursuit of "winter dreams"? What causes his dream to disappear?

2. Surprise is an important element in this story. At what points were you genuinely shocked by what the characters said or did? What would you have expected the outcome of the story to be when you first began reading it?

Arguing for an Interpretation

1. How does hearing of Judy Jones's loss of beauty (and abusive marriage) terminate Dexter's "winter dreams" once and for all? Why do you think he reacts as he does? Explain your answer.
2. This story emphasizes a recurrent theme of the betrayed romantic ideal that figures prominently in many of Fitzgerald's novels, such as *The Great Gatsby* or *Tender Is the Night,* and many of his short stories that reflect events in Fitzgerald's life. An interesting research project would be to compare any of Fitzgerald's works in terms of this theme. A useful source is *The F. Scott Fitzgerald Centenary Home Page* at <http://www.sc.edu/fitzgerald/index.html>.

Guy de Maupassant

Guy de Maupassant (1850–1893), in his relatively brief life, wrote almost 300 short stories, six novels, and more than 200 sketches for newspapers and magazines, as well as essays on travel and dramatic adaptations. His best stories appear at first to be little more than brief anecdotes, but they reveal a wealth of psychological insight and an unusual balance of detachment and sympathy for the human condition. De Maupassant was born in Rouen, Normandy, near the seacoast town of Dieppe, in France. He received his early education from his literate and cultured mother before being enrolled at the age of thirteen in a seminary from which he was soon expelled for insubordination. He served as a soldier in the Franco-Prussian War of 1870–1871 and then settled in Paris as a clerk in the Naval Ministry. He became a protégé of Flaubert and was part of the famous literary circle in Paris that included Turgenev, Edmond Goncourt, Alphonse Daudet, and Émile Zola. His fame was assured with the publication of the short story "Boulle de Suif" (Ball of Fat) (1880) in an anthology edited by Zola. His novels include Une Vie *(1883),* Bel Ami *(1885), and* Pierre et Jean *(1888). Collections of his short stories include* La Maison Tellier *(1881),* Mademoiselle Fifi *(1882), and* Contes et Nouvelles *(1885), among others. A dissolute life led de Maupassant to contract syphilis, which led to an untimely death at the age of 42. "The Necklace," translated by Ernest Boyd and others, from* The Collected Novels and Stories of Guy de Maupassant *(1924), epitomizes de Maupassant's narrative technique. In its use of irony, precise detail, and the surprise ending, this story illustrates why de*

Maupassant is widely recognized as a master of the short story.

The Necklace

She was one of those pretty, charming young ladies, born, as if through an error of destiny, into a family of clerks. She had no dowry, no hopes, no means of becoming known, appreciated, loved, and married by a man either rich or distinguished; and she allowed herself to marry a petty clerk in the office of the Board of Education.

She was simple, not being able to adorn herself, but she was unhappy, as one out of her class; for women belong to no caste, no race; their grace, their beauty, and their charm serving them in the place of birth and family. Their inborn finesse, their instinctive elegance, their suppleness of wit are their only aristocracy, making some daughters of the people the equal of great ladies.

She suffered incessantly, feeling herself born for all delicacies and luxuries. She suffered from the poverty of her apartment, the shabby walls, the worn chairs, and the faded stuffs. All these things, which another woman of her station would not have noticed, tortured and angered her. The sight of the little Breton,[1] who made this humble home, awoke in her sad regrets and desperate dreams. She thought of quiet antechambers with their Oriental hangings lighted by high bronze torches, and of the two great footmen in short trousers who sleep in the large armchairs, made sleepy by the heavy air from the heating apparatus. She thought of large drawing rooms hung in old silks, of graceful pieces of furniture carrying bric-a-brac of inestimable value, and of the little perfumed coquettish apartments made for five o'clock chats with most intimate friends, men known and sought after, whose attention all women envied and desired.

When she seated herself for dinner before the round table, where the tablecloth had been used three days, opposite her husband who uncovered the tureen with a delighted air, saying: "Oh! the good potpie! I know nothing better than that," she would think of the elegant dinners, of the shining silver, of the tapestries peopling the walls with ancient personages and rare birds in the midst of fairy forests; she thought of the exquisite food served on marvelous dishes, of the whispered gallantries, listened to with the smile of the Sphinx while eating the rose-colored flesh of the trout or a chicken's wing.

She had neither frocks nor jewels, nothing. And she loved only those 5
things. She felt that she was made for them. She had such a desire to please, to be sought after, to be clever and courted.

She had a rich friend, a schoolmate at the convent, whom she did not like to visit; she suffered so much when she returned. And she wept for whole days from chagrin, from regret, from despair and disappointment.

One evening her husband returned, elated, bearing in his hand a large envelope.

---

[1]*Breton:* a native of Brittany, a coastal region in western France.

"Here," he said, "here is something for you."

She quickly tore open the wrapper and drew out a printed card on which were inscribed these words:

> The Minister of Public Instruction and Madame George Ramponneau ask the honor of M. and Mme. Loisel's[2] company Monday evening, January 18, at the Minister's residence.

Instead of being delighted, as her husband had hoped, she threw the invitation spitefully upon the table, murmuring:

"What do you suppose I want with that?"

"But, my dearie, I thought it would make you happy. You never go out, and this is an occasion, and a fine one! I had a great deal of trouble to get it. Everybody wishes one, and it is very select; not many are given to employees. You will see the whole official world there."

She looked at him with an irritated eye and declared impatiently:

"What do you suppose I have to wear to such a thing as that?"

He had not thought of that; he stammered:

"Why, the dress you wear when we go to the theater. It seems very pretty to me."

He was silent, stupefied, in dismay, at the sight of his wife weeping. Two great tears fell slowly from the corners of her eyes toward the corners of her mouth; he stammered:

"What is the matter? What is the matter?"

By a violent effort she had controlled her vexation and responded in a calm voice, wiping her moist cheeks:

"Nothing. Only I have no dress and consequently I cannot go to this affair. Give your card to some colleague whose wife is better fitted out than I."

He was grieved but answered:

"Let us see, Matilda. How much would a suitable costume cost, something that would serve for other occasions, something very simple?"

She reflected for some seconds, making estimates and thinking of a sum that she could ask for without bringing with it an immediate refusal and a frightened exclamation from the economical clerk.

Finally she said in a hesitating voice:

"I cannot tell exactly, but it seems to me that four hundred francs[3] ought to cover it."

He turned a little pale, for he had saved just this sum to buy a gun that he might be able to join some hunting parties the next summer, on the plains at Nanterre, with some friends who went to shoot larks up there on Sunday. Nevertheless, he answered:

"Very well. I will give you four hundred francs. But try to have a pretty dress."

The day of the ball approached, and *Mme.* Loisel seemed sad, disturbed, anxious. Nevertheless, her dress was nearly ready. Her husband said to her one evening:

---

[2]*Ramponneau ... M. and Mme. Loisel's: M.* and *Mme.* are the abbreviations for *Monsieur* and *Madame,* respectively.

[3]*four hundred francs:* about $240 in United States currency at the time of the story. The franc itself was worth about sixty cents.

"What is the matter with you? You have acted strangely for two or three days."

And she responded: "I am vexed not to have a jewel, not one stone, nothing to adorn myself with. I shall have such a poverty-laden look. I would prefer not to go to this party."

He replied: "You can wear some natural flowers. At this season they look very chic. For ten francs you can have two or three magnificent roses."

She was not convinced. "No," she replied, "there is nothing more humiliating than to have a shabby air in the midst of rich women."

Then her husband cried out: "How stupid we are! Go and find your friend *Madame* Forestier and ask her to lend you her jewels. You are well enough acquainted with her to do this."

She uttered a cry of joy. "It is true!" she said. "I had not thought of that."

The next day she took herself to her friend's house and related her story of distress. *Mme.* Forestier went to her closet with the glass doors, took out a large jewel case, brought it, opened it, and said: "Choose, my dear."

She saw at first some bracelets, then a collar of pearls, then a Venetian cross of gold and jewels and admirable workmanship. She tried the jewels before the glass, hesitated, but could neither decide to take them nor leave them. Then she asked:

"Have you nothing more?"

"Why, yes. Look for yourself. I do not know what will please you."

Suddenly she discovered in a black satin box a superb necklace of diamonds, and her heart beat fast with an immoderate desire. Her hands trembled as she took them up. She placed them about her throat, against her dress, and remained in ecstasy before them. Then she asked in a hesitating voice full of anxiety:

"Could you lend me this? Only this?"

"Why, yes, certainly."

She fell upon the neck of her friend, embraced her with passion, then went away with her treasure.

The day of the ball arrived. *Mme.* Loisel was a great success. She was the prettiest of all, elegant, gracious, smiling, and full of joy. All the men noticed her, asked her name, and wanted to be presented. All the members of the Cabinet wished to waltz with her. The Minister of Education paid her some attention.

She danced with enthusiasm, with passion, intoxicated with pleasure, thinking of nothing, in the triumph of her beauty, in the glory of her success, in a kind of cloud of happiness that came of all this homage and all this admiration, of all these awakened desires and this victory so complete and sweet to the heart of woman.

She went home toward four o'clock in the morning. Her husband had been half asleep in one of the little salons since midnight with three other gentlemen whose wives were enjoying themselves very much.

He threw around her shoulders the wraps they had carried for the coming home, modest garments of everyday wear, whose poverty clashed with the elegance of the ball costume. She felt this and wished to hurry away in order not to be noticed by the other women who were wrapping themselves in rich furs.

Loisel detained her. "Wait," said he. "You will catch cold out there. I am going to call a cab."

But she would not listen and descended the steps rapidly. When they were in the street they found no carriage, and they began to seek for one, hailing the coachmen whom they saw at a distance.

They walked along toward the Seine,[4] hopeless and shivering. Finally they found on the dock one of those old nocturnal coupés that one sees in Paris after nightfall, as if they were ashamed of their misery by day.

50 It took them as far as their door in Martyr Street, and they went wearily up to their apartment. It was all over for her. And on his part he remembered that he would have to be at the office by ten o'clock.

She removed the wraps from her shoulders before the glass for a final view of herself in her glory. Suddenly she uttered a cry. Her necklace was not around her neck.

Her husband, already half undressed, asked: "What is the matter?"

She turned toward him excitedly:

"I have—I have—I no longer have *Madame* Forestier's necklace."

55 He arose in dismay: "What! How is that? It is not possible."

And they looked in the folds of the dress, in the folds of the mantle, in the pockets, everywhere. They could not find it.

He asked: "You are sure you still had it when we left the house?"

"Yes, I felt it in the vestibule as we came out."

"But if you had lost it in the street we should have heard it fall. It must be in the cab."

60 "Yes. It is probable. Did you take the number?"

"No. And you, did you notice what it was?"

"No."

They looked at each other, utterly cast down. Finally Loisel dressed himself again.

"I am going," said he, "over the track where we went on foot, to see if I can find it."

65 And he went. She remained in her evening gown, not having the force to go to bed, stretched upon a chair, without ambition or thoughts.

Toward seven o'clock her husband returned. He had found nothing.

He went to the police and to the cab offices and put an advertisement in the newspapers, offering a reward; he did everything that afforded them a suspicion of hope.

She waited all day in a state of bewilderment before this frightful disaster. Loisel returned at evening, with his face harrowed and pale, and had discovered nothing.

"It will be necessary," said he, "to write to your friend that you have broken the clasp of the necklace and that you will have it repaired. That will give us time to turn around."

70 She wrote as he dictated.

At the end of a week they had lost all hope. And Loisel, older by five years, declared:

"We must take measures to replace this jewel."

The next day they took the box which had enclosed it to the jeweler whose name was on the inside. He consulted his books.

---

[4]*Seine:* river that flows through the center of Paris.

"It is not I, *Madame,*" said he, "who sold this necklace; I only furnished the casket."

Then they went from jeweler to jeweler, seeking a necklace like the 75
other one, consulting their memories, and ill, both of them, with chagrin and anxiety.

In a shop of the Palais-Royal[5] they found a chaplet of diamonds which seemed to them exactly like the one they had lost. It was valued at forty thousand francs. They could get it for thirty-six thousand.

They begged the jeweler not to sell it for three days. And they made an arrangement by which they might return it for thirty-four thousand francs if they found the other one before the end of February.

Loisel possessed eighteen thousand francs which his father had left him. He borrowed the rest.

He borrowed it, asking for a thousand francs of one, five hundred of another, five louis[6] of this one, and three louis of that one. He gave notes, made ruinous promises, took money of usurers and the whole race of lenders. He compromised his whole existence, in fact, risked his signature without even knowing whether he could make it good or not, and, harrassed by anxiety for the future, by the black misery which surrounded him, and by the prospect of all physical privations and moral torture, he went to get the new necklace, depositing on the merchant's counter thirty-six thousand francs.

When *Mme.* Loisel took back the jewels to *Mme.* Forestier the latter 80
said to her in a frigid tone:

"You should have returned them to me sooner, for I might have needed them."

She did open the jewel box as her friend feared she would. If she should perceive the substitution what would she think? What should she say? Would she take her for a robber?

Mme. Loisel now knew the horrible life of necessity. She did her part, however, completely, heroically. It was necessary to pay this frightful debt. She would pay it. They sent away the maid; they changed their lodgings; they rented some rooms under a mansard roof.

She learned the heavy cares of a household, the odious work of a kitchen. She washed the dishes, using her rosy nails upon the greasy pots and the bottoms of the stew pans. She washed the soiled linen, the chemises and dishcloths, which she hung on the line to dry; she took down the refuse to the street each morning and brought up the water, stopping at each landing to breathe. And, clothed like a woman of the people, she went to the grocer's, the butcher's, and the fruiterer's with her basket on her arm, shopping, haggling to the last sou[7] her miserable money.

Every month it was necessary to renew some notes, thus obtaining 85
time, and to pay others.

The husband worked evenings, putting the books of some merchants in order, and nights he often did copying at five sous a page.

And this life lasted for ten years.

At the end of ten years they had restored all, all, with interest of the usurer, and accumulated interest, besides.

---

[5] *Palais-Royal:* a Parisian shopping district.

[6] *Louis:* a French gold coin equal in value to twenty francs. At the time of the story, five louis were worth about sixty dollars.

[7] *sou:* a former French coin that was worth one-twentieth of a franc, or about a penny.

Mme. Loisel seemed old now. She had become a strong, hard woman, the crude woman of the poor household. Her hair badly dressed, her skirts awry, her hands red, she spoke in a loud tone and washed the floors in large pails of water. But sometimes, when her husband was at the office, she would seat herself before the window and think of that evening party of former times, of that ball where she was so beautiful and so flattered.

How would it have been if she had not lost that necklace? Who knows? Who knows? How singular is life and how full of changes! How small a thing will ruin or save one!

One Sunday, as she was taking a walk in the Champs Élysées[8] to rid herself of the cares of the week, she suddenly perceived a woman walking with a child. It was *Mme.* Forestier, still young, still pretty, still attractive. *Mme.* Loisel was affected. Should she speak to her? Yes, certainly. And now that she had paid, she would tell her all. Why not?

She approached her. "Good morning, Jeanne."

Her friend did not recognize her and was astonished to be so familiarly addressed by this common personage. She stammered:

"But, *Madame*—I do not know—You must be mistaken."

"No, I am Matilda Loisel."

Her friend uttered a cry of astonishment:

"Oh! My poor Matilda! How you have changed."

"Yes, I have had some hard days since I saw you, and some miserable ones—and all because of you."

"Because of me? How is that?"

"You recall the diamond necklace that you loaned me to wear to the Minister's ball?"

"Yes, very well."

"Well, I lost it."

"How is that, since you returned it to me?"

"I returned another to you exactly like it. And it has taken us ten years to pay for it. You can understand that it was not easy for us who have nothing. But it is finished, and I am decently content."

Mme. Forestier stopped short. She said:

"You say that you bought a diamond necklace to replace mine?"

"Yes. You did not perceive it then? They were just alike."

And she smiled with a proud and simple joy. *Mme.* Forestier was touched and took both her hands as she replied:

"Oh, my poor Matilda! Mine were false. They were not worth over five hundred francs!"

Analyzing the Text

1. What information does de Maupassant provide about Matilda Loisel's appearance and family background that help explain her aspirations? What makes her reluctant to go to the party, and what can we infer about her husband from his response?
2. What details suggest the extent to which Matilda has changed as a result of the self-imposed obligation of replacing the lost necklace? In your view,

[8]*Champs Élysées:* a famous avenue in Paris.

does the author think more highly of her at the end of the story than at the beginning? Explain your answer.

Understanding de Maupassant's Techniques

1. What clues does de Maupassant provide that foreshadow the surprise ending of the story? How does his use of the third-person point of view enable him to keep the ending a secret to the very last moment?
2. What small ironies throughout the story make the central irony of the ending even more poignant?

Arguing for an Interpretation

1. Would you describe the ending of the story as being happy or unhappy? In a few paragraphs, speculate on how Matilda and her husband reacted to the discovery that the original borrowed necklace was not real, and that they had returned a genuine one. Should Mme. Forestier keep the returned real necklace? Why or why not?
2. Irony is an elusive concept because it can take many forms: verbal, situational, and dramatic. What instances of these different forms of irony can you discover in "The Necklace" and what do they contribute to the overall effect of the story?

Mahdokht Kashkuli

Mahdokht Kashkuli was born in 1950 in Teheran, Iran. She was married at age fourteen and, unlike similar marriages, hers did not prevent her from pursuing her education. She succeeded in obtaining her bachelor of arts in performing literature from Teheran University. By 1982 she had completed two masters' degrees, one in library science and one in linguistics, and a doctorate in the language, culture, and religion of Ancient Iran from the same university. She started her career first as a researcher for Iranian Educational Television from 1975 to 1985 and then as a professor of performing literature at Teheran University. Her short stories, including "The Fable of Rain in Iran," "The Fable of Creation in Iran," "Our Customs, Our Share," "The Pearl and the Moon," and "Tears and Water" have won her national recognition. "The Button," translated by Soraya Sullivan, was first published in the summer of 1978 in the periodical Arash. *This short story explores the heartbreaking consequences of a family's poverty in contemporary Iran.*

The Button

My sister was perched in the doorway, sobbing bitterly; her curly, russet hair was stuck to her sweaty forehead. My mother was doing her wash by the pond, paying no attention to my sister's sobs or my father's shouts, "Hurry up Reza! Move it!" I was holding on to the edge of the mantle shelf tightly, wishing that my hand would remain glued there permanently. It was only a few nights ago that I had heard, with my own ears, my father's voice whispering to my mother, "Woman, stop grumbling! God knows that my heart is aching too, but we don't have a choice. I can't even provide them with bread. What else can I do? This way, we'll have one less mouth to feed." I had cocked my ears to hear who that "one less mouth to feed" was. I remained frozen, holding my breath for a few minutes; then I heard my father say, "Reza is the naughtiest of all; the most restless. Akbar and Asghar are more tame, and we can't send the girls away. It's not wise." Suddenly a dry cough erupted from my mouth. My father called out, "Reza! Reza! Are you awake?" I did not answer him. He fell silent, and then my mother's snorts followed the awkward silence. My father went on, "Woman, who said the orphanage is a bad place? They teach the kids, they feed them, they clothe them. At least this one will have a chance to live a good life." My mother's snorts stopped. She groaned, "I don't know. I don't know anything. Just do what you think is best." And then there was silence.

Why are they going to make me the "one less mouth to feed"? What is an orphanage? I wish I hadn't nibbled the bread on my way home from the bakery; I wish I hadn't quarreled with Asghar; I wish I hadn't messed around with my mother's yarn, as if it were a ball; I wish I hadn't pulled the bottle out of Kobra's mouth, and drunk her milk; I wish I could stay still, like the mannequin in the clothing store at the corner. Then they wouldn't make me the "one less mouth to feed." My pillow was soaked with tears.

I ran outside with puffy eyes the next morning. Ahmad was standing at the other end of the alley, keeping watch for Husain so he could pick a fight with him. I yelled, "Ahmad, Ahmad! What's an orphanage?" Keeping his eyes still on the door to Husain's house, Ahmad said, "It's a place where they put up poor people's children." "Have you been there?" I asked. He shouted indignantly, "Listen to this goddamn wretch! You can't be nice to anyone these days!" I ran back to the house, scared. If Ahmad hadn't been waiting for Husain, he surely would have beaten me up.

My father's screams shot up again, "Are you deaf? Hurry up, it's late!" I released my grip on the shelf and went down the stairs. The saltiness of my tears burned my face. My father said, "What's wrong? Why are you crying? Come, my boy! Come wash your face!" Then he took my hand and led me to the pond and splashed a handful of the murky water on my face. He wiped my face with his coat lining. I became uneasy. My father seldom showed signs of affection; I suspected that he was being affectionate because he had decided to make me the "one less mouth to feed." We walked towards the door. He pulled aside the old cotton rug hanging before the door with his bony hands. Then he said, in a tone as if he were talking to himself, "One thousand . . . God knows, I had to pull a thousand strings before they agreed to admit you."

5 I asked, while I kept my head down, "Why?" My father screamed angrily, "He asks why again! Because!" I lowered my head. My eyes met his shoes. They were strangely crooked and worn out; maybe he had them on wrong. . . . The lower part of his long underwear showed from beneath his pants. He was wearing a belt to hold his loose pants up, and they creased like my mother's skirt. "I'm telling you, Reza, a thousand strings," he repeated. "You must behave when you get there." I didn't look at him but said grudgingly, "I don't want to behave!"

He threw a darting glance at me and raved, his hand rising to cuff me on the back of the neck but he changed his mind and said instead, "They'll teach you how to behave yourself." Indignantly I said, "I don't want to go to an orphanage, and if you take me there, I'll run away." I pulled my hand out of his quickly and ran ahead, knowing that he'd hit me this time. But he didn't. He only said, "You think they admit everyone? I've been running around for a year, resorting to everyone I know." I said, "Dad, I don't want to go to the orphanage. They keep poor children there." "What, do you think you are, rich?" my father said. "Listen to him use words bigger than his mouth!" And he broke out laughing. When he laughed I saw his gold teeth. There were two of them. I thought to myself, "What does it take to be rich? My father has gold teeth, my mother has gold teeth, and my brother has a fountain pen." I looked at his face. He wasn't laughing anymore; his face had turned gray. I said spontaneously, "Dad, is the landlord rich?" He didn't hear me, or it seemed he didn't, and said absentmindedly, "What?" I said, "Nothing."

I thought about the landlord. He sends his oldest son or his young daughter to collect the rent two weeks before the rent is due. His oldest son enters my father's shop and stands in the front of the mirror, scrutinizing himself, resting one hand on his waist. My father rushes to him and says, "Do you want a haircut?" The landlord's son responds, "No. You just gave me one on Thursday." My father says politely, "What can I do for you, then?" The landlord's son says, "Is the rent ready?" My father answers, "Give me a few more days. Tell Haji Agha I'll pay before the due date." And the next day his young daughter shows up in the shop. She is so small that she can hardly see herself in the mirror. She holds her veil tightly under her chin with those tiny, delicate hands, and says, "Hello!" My father smiles and says, "Hello, cutie pie! What can I do for you?" The girl laughs cheerfully and says, "My father sent me after the rent. If it's ready, give it to me." My father picks a sugar cube out of the sugar bowl, puts it gently in her palm, and says, "Tell Haji Agha, fine!"

We reached the intersection. My father held my hand in his tightly and stopped to look around. We then crossed the street. He was mumbling to himself, "The damn thing is so far away. . . ."

I felt sick. I said, "Wait a minute!" He eyed me curiously and said, "Why, what's wrong?" I said, "I'm tired; I don't want to go to the orphanage." He mimicked me, pursing his lips, and said, "You don't understand! You were always dumb, dense!"

I remembered that my father was always unhappy with me, although I 10
swept the shop everyday and watered the China roses he had planted in front of the shop. I would take my shirt off on hot summer afternoons and jump in the brook with my underpants. The elastic of my pants was always loose and I always tried to tie it into a knot, never succeeding to make it tight enough to stay. In the brook, I held my pants with one hand while I watered the China roses with a small bowl. It felt nice and cool there. Flies would gather around my shoulders and arms. Grandmother used to say, "God made flies out of wax." But I didn't understand why they didn't melt in the hot sun; they flew off my body and landed on the China rose flowers and I shook the branches with my bowl to disperse them. The flowers were my father's and no fly was allowed to sit on them. In spite of all my efforts, my father was always unhappy with me; he was unhappy with my mother, with my sisters and brothers, with the landlord, and with the neighbors. But he was happy with one person: God. He would sigh, tap himself hard on the forehead, and say, "Thank God!"

I said to him one day, "Why are you thanking God, Dad?" Suddenly, he hit me in the mouth with the back of his hand. My upper lip swelled and my mouth tasted bloody. I was used to the taste of blood because whenever I bled in the nose, I tasted blood in my mouth. I covered my mouth, walked to the garden and spat in the dirt. I looked at the bubbles on my spittle, tapped myself on the forehead and said, "Thank God!" Then I picked up a piece of watermelon skin lying on the brook and smacked it on the head of a yellow dog that always used to nap by the electric post. The yellow dog only opened its eyes, looked at me indifferently, and shut its eyes again, thanking God, perhaps.

We passed another street before we got to the bus station. A few people were waiting in line; one of them was sitting at the edge of the brook. My father took my hand and led me to the front of the bus line. Someone said, "This is not the end of the line, old man!" I only looked at my father.

He said to me, "Ignore him. Just stay right here!" The bus came and my father pushed me towards it. I tore my feet off the ground and jumped on the coach-stop, feeling as if I were floating in the air. Someone said, "Old man, the end of the line is on the other side! Look how people give you a headache on a Monday morning!" My father didn't hear him; he pushed me forward. I was stuck between a seat and the handle bar. . . . So, today is Monday. . . . Every week on Monday my mother does her wash. The clothesline spread around the entire yard. I liked the smell of damp clothes. In spite of my mother's curses, I liked cupping my hands underneath the dripping clothes so that the water that dripped could tickle my palms. Every Monday we had yogurt soup for lunch. My brother and I would take a bowl to the neighborhood dairy store to buy yogurt. On the way back, we took turns licking the surface of the yogurt. When we handed the bowl to my mother, she would scream at us and beat the first one of us she could get her hands on. . . . I felt depressed. I wished I could jump out the window.

The bus stopped at a station and we got off. My father walked ahead of me while I dragged my feet along behind him.

He waited for me to catch up, then he said, "Move it! He walks like a corpse. Hurry up, it's late!" I stopped momentarily and said, "Dad, I don't want to go. I don't want to go to the orphanage." My father froze in his spot. He said incredulously, "What did you say? You think you know what's good for you? Don't you want to become a decent human being some day? They have rooms, there. They have food, and they'll teach you everything you need to learn to get a decent job." I sobbed, "To hell with anyone who has a decent job. To hell with decent jobs. I don't want one! I like staying home. I like playing with Asghar and Akbar. I want to sell roasted corn with the kids from the neighborhood in the summer. I want to help you out in the shop. I don't want to go."

My father sprang towards me, but suddenly retreated and became affectionate. He said, "Let's go, good boy! We're almost there." I felt sorry for him because every time he was kind he looked miserable. My father was walking ahead of me and I was following him, dragging my feet on the street like that yellow dog. On the next street, we stopped in front of a big metal door. A chair was placed inside the door to keep it ajar. A man was sitting on the chair, playing with a ring of prayer beads. He had on a navy blue coat with metal buttons. His eyes were half-closed and his mouth was open. His cheeks were puffy, as if he had a toothache. My father greeted him and said, "Mr. Guard!" The man opened his eyes. Strands of blood ran through the white of his eyes. He said with a gloomy voice, "What is it, what do you want?" My father thrust his hand in both his pockets, took out an envelope and extended it toward the guard with both hands. The man looked at my father, then threw a threatening glance at me. He yawned, stared at the envelope for a while (I didn't believe he could read), shook his head, coughed, and said, "They won't leave you alone; one leaves, another comes!" Then he pushed the door with the tip of his shoes. The door opened just enough to let me in.

After my father walked through the doorway behind me, the guard gave him the envelope and said, "The first door!" My father was walking fast, and when he opened the hallway door, my heart started beating violently and I started to cry. He said, "My boy, my sweet Reza, this is a nice place. The people here are nice, the kids are all your own age. . . ."

He didn't finish his sentence. He pushed on the door. The door opened and I saw a woman inside the room. I wished she were my mother, but she was heavier than my mother, with a deep vertical wrinkle between her eyebrows. She wore a blue uniform and her hair was a bleached blonde.

My father pushed me further in and said, "Greet her, Reza! Greet her!" I didn't feel like greeting anyone.

My father handed the woman the envelope. She opened it, pulled the letter out halfway, and started reading it. Then she turned to my father and said, "Go to the office so they can complete his file."

My father leaped and ran out the door. Then, as though he had remembered something, he returned and stood in front of the door, rubbing his hand on the wood frame of the door. He raised one hand to tap on his forehead and say, "Thank God," but stopped, rubbed his forehead gently and sighed. His eyes were as moist and shiny as the eyes of the yellow dog hanging around his shop. Her head still lowered on the letter, the woman said, "Go, old man! What are you waiting for? Go to the office!" Father took a few steps backwards, then tore himself from the door and disappeared into the corridor.

The woman looked at me, then turned her gaze toward the window and fixed it there. While she had her back to me, she said, "Don't cry, boy! Please don't, I'm not in the mood!" Then she turned around and put her hands on my shoulders. Her hands were as heavy as my mother's but not as warm. She took my hand and walked me toward the door. We passed one corridor, and entered another. Then we entered a room, then another corridor and another room. There were a few people in the room. One was sitting in the doorway, whistling; one was leaning against the desk; one was sitting in a chair writing something. Although the room was furnished with chairs and desks, it was not warm. The woman said, "Say hello to these people!" I looked at her but didn't say anything. I didn't feel like talking to them. I didn't hear what they said to each other, either. I only wanted to sit still and look at them. We left that room and went into another. There was another woman there. I wished she were my mother. She was wearing a blue uniform and had a red scarf around her neck. I think she had a cold because she sniffled constantly. As soon as she saw me, she checked me out thoroughly and spoke with a nasal voice, "Is he new here? I don't know where we're going to put him." She then opened a closet, took out a uniform and said to me, "Take your jacket off and wear this!" Then she continued, "Take your shirt off, too. How long has it been since your last shower?" I didn't answer. Her words hit my ears and bounced right off. She went toward the closet again and asked, "Are you done?" I looked around and then looked at myself, my eyes becoming fixed on my jacket. It had only one button. The button had belonged to my mother's jacket before she used it to replace my missing button. The woman's voice went on, "Quit stalling, boy! Hurry up, I have tons of work to do!"

I put my hand on the button and pulled it out, then hid it in my palm. The woman said, "Are you done?" I said, "Yes!"

I thrust the button in my uniform pocket and wiped my tears with the back of my hand.

Analyzing the Text

1. How would you characterize Reza's relationship with his father? Why does the father choose Reza, rather than one of the other three children, to send to an orphanage?
2. How does the button mentioned in the title reveal Reza's feelings and emotions in response to being separated from his family? How does the button come to symbolize what he has lost?

Understanding Kashkuli's Techniques

1. What means does Kashkuli use to enable the reader to understand how Reza feels about being sent to the orphanage? What role do Reza's imagined transgressions play in enhancing the reader's sympathy for him?
2. How does Kashkuli make it possible for the reader to draw inferences about the economic and social conditions in modern-day Iran? Why is this important given the action the father takes?

Arguing for an Interpretation

1. What aspects of the story suggest that Mahdokht Kashkuli is critical of the father's religious fatalism? In a few paragraphs, discuss the function of this key element in Kashkuli's characterization of the father.
2. Is Kashkuli's choice of viewpoint an effective one? How would the story have changed if it had been related from an objective point of view instead?

Catherine Lim

Catherine Lim (b. 1942-) is one of Singapore's foremost writers. She currently works for the Curriculum Development Institute of Singapore, writing English language instructional materials for use in the primary schools. Her widely praised collections of short stories include Little Ironies—Stories of Singapore *(1978), from which "Paper" is taken,* Or Else, The Lightning God and Other Stories *(1980), and* The Shadow of a Shadow of a Dream—Love Stories of Singapore *(1981). She is also the author of several novels including* The Bondmaid *(1995),* The Teardrop Story Woman *(1998), and* Following the Wrong God Home *(2001). Her short stories have been compared to those of Guy de Maupassant for their accuracy of observation, clarity in presentation of character, and precise detail. Lim's stories reveal a wealth of information about the forces, customs, and pressures that shape the lives of the Chinese community in Singapore, a densely populated metropolis in which Chinese, Malay, and Indian cultures coexist and thrive. "Paper" is set against the turbulent background of the Singapore Stock Exchange, a volatile financial market reflecting the seemingly limitless possibilities of one of the world's most productive financial, industrial, and commercial centers. This story dramatically explores how the lure of easy money leads a man and his wife to tragic consequences.*

Paper

He wanted it, he dreamed of it, he hankered after it, as an addict after his opiate. Once the notion of a big beautiful house had lodged itself in his imagination, Tay Soon nurtured it until it became the consuming passion of his life. A house. A dream house such as he had seen on his drives with his wife and children along the roads bordering the prestigious housing estates on the island, and in the glossy pages of *Homes* and *Modern Living*. Or rather, it was a house which was an amalgam of the best, the most beautiful aspects of the houses he had seen. He knew every detail of his dream house already, from the aluminum sliding doors to the actual shade of the dining room carpet to the shape of the swimming pool. Kidney. He rather liked the shape. He was not ashamed of the enthusiasm with which he spoke of the dream house, an enthusiasm that belonged to women only, he was told. Indeed, his enthusiasm was so great that it had infected his wife and even his children, small though they were. Soon his wife Yee Lian was describing to her sister Yee Yeng, the dream house in all its perfection of shape and decor, and the children were telling their cousins and friends, "My daddy says that when our house is ready . . ."

They talked of the dream house endlessly. It had become a reality stronger than the reality of the small terrace house which they were sharing with Tay Soon's mother, to whom it belonged. Tay Soon's mother, whose little business of selling bottled curries and vegetable preserves which she made herself, left her little time for dreams, clucked her tongue and shook her head and made sarcastic remarks about the ambitiousness of young people nowadays.

"What's wrong with this house we're staying in?" she asked petulantly. "Aren't we all comfortable in it?"

Not as long as you have your horrid ancestral altars all over the place, and your grotesque sense of colour—imagine painting the kitchen wall bright pink. But Yee Lian was tactful enough to keep the remarks to herself, or to make them only to her sister Yee Yeng, otherwise they were sure to reach the old lady, and there would be no end to her sharp tongue.

The house—the dream house—it would be a far cry from the little ter- 5
race house in which they were all staying now, and Tay Soon and Yee Lian talked endlessly about it, and it grew magnificently in their imaginations,

this dream house of theirs with its timbered ceiling and panelled walls and sunken circular sitting room which was to be carpeted in rich amber. It was no empty dream, for there was much money in the bank already. Forty thousand dollars had been saved. The house would cost many times that, but Tay Soon and Yee Lian with their good salaries would be able to manage very well. Once they took care of the down payment, they would be able to pay back monthly over a period of ten years—fifteen, twenty—what did it matter how long it took as long as the dream house was theirs? It had become the symbol of the peak of earthly achievement, and all of Tay Soon's energies and devotion were directed towards its realisation. His mother said, "You're a show-off; what's so grand about marble flooring and a swimming pool? Why don't you put your money to better use?" But the forty thousand grew steadily, and after Tay Soon and Yee Lian had put in every cent of their annual bonuses, it grew to forty eight thousand, and husband and wife smiled at the smooth way their plans were going.

It was a time of growing interest in the stock market. The quotations for stocks and shares were climbing the charts, and the crowds in the rooms of the broking houses were growing perceptibly. Might we not do something about this? Yee Lian said to her husband. Do you know that Dr. Soo bought Rustan Banking for four dollars and today the shares are worth seven dollars each? The temptation was great. The rewards were almost immediate. Thirty thousand dollars' worth of NBE became fifty-five thousand almost overnight. Tay Soon and Yee Lian whooped. They put their remaining eighteen thousand in Far East Mart. Three days later the shares were worth twice that much. It was not to be imagined that things could stop here. Tay Soon secured a loan from his bank and put twenty thousand in OHTE. This was a particularly lucky share; it shot up to four times its value in three days.

"Oh, this is too much, too much," cried Yee Lian in her ecstasy, and she sat down with pencil and paper, and found after a few minutes' calculation that they had made a cool one hundred thousand in a matter of days.

And now there was to be no stopping. The newspapers were full of it, everybody was talking about it, it was in the very air. There was plenty of money to be made in the stock exchange by those who had guts—money to be made by the hour, by the minute, for the prices of stocks and shares were rising faster than anyone could keep track of them! Dr. Soo was said—he laughingly dismissed it as a silly rumour—Dr. Soo was said to have made two million dollars already. If he sold all his shares now, he would be a millionaire twice over. And Yee Yeng, Yee Lian's sister, who had been urged with sisterly goodwill to come join the others make money, laughed happily to find that the shares she had bought for four twenty on Tuesday had risen to seven ninety-five on Friday—she laughed and thanked Yee Lian who advised her not to sell yet, it was going further, it would hit the ten dollar mark by next week. And Tay Soon both laughed and cursed—cursed that he had failed to buy a share at nine dollars which a few days later had hit seventeen dollars! Yee Lian said reproachfully, "I thought I told you to buy it, darling," and Tay Soon had beaten his forehead in despair and said, "I know, I know, why didn't I! Big fool that I am!" And he had another reason to curse himself—he sold five thousand West Parkes at sixteen twenty-three per share, and saw, to his horror, West Parkes climb to eighteen ninety the very next day!

"I'll never sell now," he vowed. "I'll hold on. I won't be so foolish." And the frenzy continued. Husband and wife couldn't talk or think of anything else. They thought fondly of their shares—going to be worth a million altogether soon. A million! In the peak of good humour, Yee Lian went to her mother-in-law, forgetting the past insults, and advised her to join the others by buying some shares; she would get her broker to buy them immediately for her, there was sure money in it. The old lady refused curtly, and to her son later, she showed great annoyance, scolding him for being so foolish as to put all his money in those worthless shares. "Worthless!" exploded Tay Soon. "Do you know, Mother, if I sold all my shares today, I would have the money to buy fifty terrace houses like the one you have?"

His wife said, "Oh, we'll just leave her alone. I was kind enough to offer 10
to help her make money. But since she's so nasty and ungrateful, we'll leave her alone." The comforting, triumphant thought was that soon, very soon, they would be able to purchase their dream house; it would be even more magnificent than the one they had dreamt of, since they had made almost a—Yee Lian preferred not to say the sum. There was the old superstitious fear of losing something when it is too often or too directly referred to, and Yee Lian had cautioned her husband not to make mention of their gains.

"Not to worry, not to worry," he said jovially, not superstitious like his wife. "After all, it's just paper gains so far."

The downward slide, or the bursting of the bubble as the newspapers dramatically called it, did not initially cause much alarm. For the speculators all expected the shares to bounce back to their original strength and thence continue the phenomenal growth. But that did not happen. The slide continued.

Tay Soon said nervously, "Shall we sell? Do you think we should sell?" but Yee Lian said stoutly, "There is talk that this decline is a technical thing only—it will be over soon, and then the rise will continue. After all, see what is happening in Hong Kong and London and New York. Things are as good as ever."

"We're still making, so not to worry," said Yee Lian after a few days. Their gains were pared by half. A few days later, their gains were pared to marginal.

There is talk of a recovery, insisted Yee Lian. Do you know, Tay Soon, 15
Dr. Soo's wife is buying up some OHTE and West Parkes now? She says these two are sure to rise. She has some inside information that these two are going to climb past the forty-dollar mark—

Tay Soon sold all his shares and put the money in OHTE and West Parkes. OHTE and West Parkes crashed shortly afterwards. Some began to say the shares were not worth the paper of the certificates.

"Oh, I can't believe, I can't believe it," gasped Yee Lian, pale and sick. Tay Soon looked in mute horror at her.

"All our money was in OHTE and West Parkes," he said, his lips dry.

"That stupid Soo woman!" shrieked Yee Lian. "I think she deliberately led me astray with her advice! She's always been jealous of me—ever since she knew we were going to build a house grander than hers!"

"How are we going to get our house now?" asked Tay Soon in deep 20
distress, and for the first time he wept. He wept like a child, for the loss of all his money, for the loss of the dream house that he had never stopped loving and worshipping.

The pain bit into his very mind and soul, so that he was like a madman, unable to go to his office to work, unable to do anything but haunt the broking houses, watching with frenzied anxiety for OHTE and West Parkes to show him hope. But there was no hope. The decline continued with gleeful rapidity. His broker advised him to sell, before it was too late, but he shrieked angrily, "What! Sell at a fraction at which I bought them! How can this be tolerated!"

And he went on hoping against hope.

He began to have wild dreams in which he sometimes laughed and sometimes screamed. His wife Yee Lian was afraid and she ran sobbing to her sister who never failed to remind her curtly that all her savings were gone, simply because when she had wanted to sell, Yee Lian had advised her not to.

"But what is your sorrow compared to mine," wept Yee Lian, "see what's happening to my husband. He's cracking up! He talks to himself, he doesn't eat, he has nightmares, he beats the children. Oh, he's finished!"

Her mother-in-law took charge of the situation, while Yee Lian, wide- 25
eyed in mute horror at the terrible change that had come over her husband, shrank away and looked to her two small children for comfort. Tight-lipped and grim, the elderly woman made herbal medicines for Tay Soon, brewing and straining for hours, and got a Chinese medicine man to come to have a look at him.

"There is a devil in him," said the medicine man, and he proceeded to make him a drink which he mixed with the ashes of a piece of prayer paper. But Tay Soon grew worse. He lay in bed, white, haggard and delirious, seeming to be beyond the touch of healing. In the end, Yee Lian, on the advice of her sister and friends, put him in hospital.

"I have money left for the funeral," whimpered the frightened Yee Lian only a week later, but her mother-in-law sharply retorted, "You leave everything to me! I have the money for his funeral, and I shall give him the best! He wanted a beautiful house all his life; I shall give him a beautiful house now!"

She went to the man who was well-known on the island for his beautiful houses, and she ordered the best. It would come to nearly a thousand dollars, said the man, a thin, wizened fellow whose funeral gauntness and pallor seemed to be a concession to his calling.

That doesn't matter, she said, I want the best. The house is to be made of superior paper, she instructed, and he was to make it to her specifications. She recollected that he, Tay Soon, had often spoken of marble flooring, a timbered ceiling and a kidney-shaped swimming pool. Could he simulate all these in paper?

The thin, wizened man said, "I've never done anything like that before. 30
All my paper houses for the dead have been the usual kind—I can put in paper furniture and paper cars, paper utensils for the kitchen and paper servants, all that the dead will need in the other world. But I shall try to put in what you've asked for. Only it will cost more."

The house when it was ready, was most beautiful to see. It stood seven feet tall, a delicate framework of wire and thin bamboo strips covered with finely worked paper of a myriad colours. Little silver flowers, scattered liberally throughout the entire structure, gave a carnival atmosphere. There was a paper swimming pool (round, as the man had not understood "kidney") which had to be fitted inside the house itself, as there was no provision for a garden or surrounding grounds. Inside the house were paper figures; there were at least four servants to attend to the needs of the master who was posed beside two cars, one distinctly a Chevrolet and the other a Mercedes.

At the appointed time, the paper house was brought to Tay Soon's grave and set on fire there. It burned brilliantly, and in three minutes was a heap of ashes on the grave.

Analyzing the Text

1. What details suggest the extent to which Tay Soon has identified himself with the magnificent dream house he wishes to buy? What does it represent to him? Why is he unwilling to settle for a lesser house that he could afford?
2. What roles do Tay Soon's wife and mother play in the story? To what extent do his mother's values differ from those of Tay Soon and his wife?

Understanding Lim's Techniques

1. How does the recurrent use of the word "paper" focus your attention on the story's central theme? In how many contexts does it occur? Why is the final image ironic?
2. Lim has constructed the story as a series of four scenes. What did you think would happen next at the end of each of these? To what extent were you surprised at what actually happened?

Arguing for an Interpretation

1. Analyze the way Lim portrays the very different attitudes toward material possessions in the views of the mother or Tay Soon and his wife. To discover what you really value, consider the hypothetical scenario of having to save only one thing (not a person or pet) from your house if there was a fire, flood, or other catastrophe. What does the significance of this item imply about your attitude toward material goods?
2. In what way does the miniature paper house in the story's final scene ironically symbolize what happened to Tay Soon's and Yee Lian's pursuit of their dream home?

DOROTHY ALLISON

Dorothy Allison was born in 1949 in Greenville, South Carolina, into an impoverished family and was abused by her stepfather, traumatic experiences that she later incorporated into her fiction. She won a National Merit scholarship to Florida Presbyterian College and received an M.A. in anthropology at the New School for Social Research, New York. She received national recognition for her autobiographical novel, Bastard out of Carolina *(1992), which was filmed for television (1996). Her second novel is* Cavedweller *(1998). Allison's book of essays is* Skin: Talking About Sex, Class and Literature *(1994). Her autobiography "Two or Three Things I Know for Sure" was produced as a short documentary for the PBS series* POV *in 1998. Her fiction has been widely reprinted in collections, including* The Vintage Book of International Lesbian Fiction: An Anthology *(1999). I'm Working on My Charm" is drawn from* Trash, *a collection of short stories (1988) which originally won two Lambda Literary Awards.*

I'm Working on My Charm

I'm working on my charm.

It was one of those parties where everyone pretends to know everyone else. My borrowed silk blouse kept pulling out of my skirt, so I tried to stay with my back to the buffet and ignore the bartender who had a clear view of my problem. The woman who brushed my arm was a friend of the director of the organization where I worked, a woman who was known for her wardrobe and sudden acts of well-publicized generosity. She tossed her hair back when she saw me and laughed like an old familiar friend. "Southerners are so charming, I always say, giving their children such clever names."

She had a wine glass in one hand and a cherry tomato in the other, and she gestured with that tomato—a wide, witty, "charmed" gesture I do not remember ever seeing in the South. "I just love yours. There was a girl at school had a name like yours, two names said as one actually. Barbara-Jean, I think, or Ruth-Anne. I can't remember anymore, but she was the sweetest, most soft-spoken girl. I just loved her."

She smiled again, her eyes looking over my head at someone else. She leaned in close to me, "It's so wonderful that you can be with us, you know. Some of the people who have worked here, well . . . you know, well, we have so much to learn from you—gentility, you know, courtesy, manners, charm, all of that."

For a moment I was dizzy, overcome with the curious sensation of 5
floating out of the top of my head. It was as if I looked down on all the other people in that crowded room, all of them sipping their wine and half of them eating cherry tomatoes. I watched the woman beside me click her teeth against the beveled edge of her wine glass and heard the sound of my mother's voice hissing in my left ear, *Yankeeeeeees!* It was all I could do not to nod.

When I was sixteen I worked counter with my mama back of a Moses Drug-store planted in the middle of a Highway 50 shopping mall. I was trying to save money to go to college, and ritually, every night, I'd pour my tips into a can on the back of my dresser. Sometimes my mama'd throw in a share of hers to encourage me, but mostly hers was spent even before we got home—at the Winn Dixie at the far end of the mall or the Maryland Fried Chicken right next to it.

Mama taught me the real skills of being a waitress—how to get an order right, get the drinks there first and the food as fast as possible so it would still be hot, and to do it all with an expression of relaxed good humor. "You don't have to smile," she explained, "but it does help." "Of course," she had to add, "don't go 'round like a grinning fool. Just smile like you know what you're doing, and never *look* like you're in a hurry." I found it difficult to keep from looking like I was in a hurry, especially when I got out of breath running from steam table to counter. Worse, moving at the speed I did, I tended to sway a little and occasionally lost control of a plate.

"Never," my mama told me, "serve food someone has seen fall to the floor. It's not only bad manners, it'll get us all in trouble. Take it in the back, clean it off, and return it to the steam table." After awhile I decided I could just run to the back, count to ten, and take it back out to the customer with an apology. Since I usually just dropped biscuits, cornbread, and baked potatoes—the kind of stuff that would roll on a plate—I figured brushing it off was sufficient. But once, in a real rush to an impatient customer, I watched a ten-ounce T-bone slip right off the plate, flip in the air, and smack the rubber floor mat. The customer's mouth flew open, and I saw my mama's eyes shoot fire. Hurriedly I picked it up by the bone and ran to the back with it. I was running water on it when Mama came in the back room.

"All right," she snapped, "you are not to run, you are not even to walk fast. And," she added, taking the meat out of my fingers and dropping it into the open waste can, "you are not, not ever to drop anything as expensive as that again." I watched smoky frost from the leaky cooler float up toward her blonde curls, and I promised her tearfully that I wouldn't.

10 The greater skills Mama taught me were less tangible than rules about speed and smiling. What I needed most from her had a lot to do with being as young as I was, as naive, and quick to believe the stories put across the counter by all those travelers heading North. Mama always said I was the smartest of her daughters and the most foolish. I believed everything I read in books, and most of the stuff I heard on the TV, and all of Mama's carefully framed warnings never seemed to quite slow down my capacity to take people as who they wanted me to think they were. I tried hard to be like my mama but, as she kept complaining, I was just too quick to trust—badly in need of a little practical experience.

My practical education began the day I started work. The first comment by the manager was cryptic but to the point. "Well, sixteen." Harriet smiled, looking me up and down, "At least you'll up the ante." Mama's friend, Mabel, came over and squeezed my arm. "Don't get nervous, young one. We'll keep moving you around. You'll never be left alone."

Mabel's voice was reassuring even if her words weren't, and I worked her station first. A family of four children, parents, and a grandmother took her biggest table. She took their order with a wide smile, but as she passed me going down to the ice drawer, her teeth were point on point. "Fifty cents," she snapped, and went on. Helping her clean the table thirty-five minutes later I watched her pick up two lone quarters and repeat "fifty cents," this time in a mournfully conclusive tone.

It was a game all the waitresses played. There was a butter bowl on the back counter where the difference was kept, the difference between what you guessed and what you got. No one had to play, but most of the women did. The rules were simple. You had to make your guess at the tip *before* the order was taken. Some of the women would cheat a little, bringing the menus with the water glasses and saying, "I want ya'll to just look this over carefully. We're serving one fine lunch today." Two lines of conversation and most of them could walk away with a guess within five cents.

However much the guess was off went into the bowl. If you said fifty cents and got seventy-five cents, then twenty-five cents went to the bowl. Even if you said seventy-five cents and got fifty cents instead, you had to throw in that quarter—guessing high was as bad as guessing short. "We used to just count the short guesses," Mabel explained, "but this makes it more interesting."

Once Mabel was sure she'd get a dollar and got stiffed instead. She was 15
so mad she counted out that dollar in nickels and pennies, and poured it into the bowl from a foot in the air. It made a very satisfying angry noise, and when those people came back a few weeks later no one wanted to serve them. Mama stood back by the pharmacy sign smoking her Pall Mall cigarette and whispered in my direction, "Yankees." I was sure I knew just what she meant.

At the end of each week, the women playing split the butter bowl evenly.

Mama said I wasn't that good a waitress, but I made up for it in eagerness. Mabel said I made up for it in "tail." "Those salesmen sure do like how you run back to that steam table," she said with a laugh, but she didn't say it where Mama could hear. Mama said it was how I smiled.

"You got a heartbreaker's smile," she told me. "You make them think of when they were young." Behind her back, Mabel gave me her own smile, and a long slow shake of her head.

Whatever it was, by the end of the first week I'd earned four dollars more in tips than my mama. It was almost embarrassing. But then they turned over the butter bowl and divided it evenly between everyone but me. I stared and Mama explained. "Another week and you can start adding to the pot. Then you'll get a share. For now just write down two dollars on Mr. Aubrey's form."

"But I made a lot more than that," I told her. 20

"Honey, the tax people don't need to know that." Her voice was patient. "Then when you're in the pot, just report your share. That way we all report the same amount. They expect that."

"Yeah, they don't know nothing about initiative," Mabel added, rolling her hips in illustration of her point. It made her heavy bosom move dramatically, and I remembered times I'd seen her do that at the counter. It made me feel even more embarrassed and angry.

When we were alone I asked Mama if she didn't think Mr. Aubrey knew that everyone's reports on their tips were faked.

"He doesn't say what he knows," she replied, "and I don't imagine he's got a reason to care."

I dropped the subject and started the next week guessing on my tips. 25

Salesmen and truckers were always a high guess. Women who came with a group were low, while women alone were usually a fair twenty-five cents on a light lunch—if you were polite and brought them their coffee first. It was 1966, after all, and a hamburger cost sixty-five cents. Tourists were more difficult. I learned that noisy kids meant a small tip, which seemed the highest injustice. Maybe it was a kind of defensive arrogance that made the parents of those kids leave so little, as if they were saying, "Just because little Kevin gave you a headache and poured ketchup on the floor doesn't mean I owe you anything."

Early morning tourists who asked first for tomato juice, lemon, and coffee were a bonus. They were almost surely leaving the Jamaica Inn just up the road, which had a terrible restaurant but served the strongest drinks in the country. If you talked softly you never got less than a dollar, and sometimes for nothing more than juice, coffee, and aspirin.

I picked it up. In three weeks I started to really catch on and started making sucker bets like the old man who ordered egg salad. Before I even carried the water glass over, I snapped out my counter rag, turned all the way around, and said, "five." Then as I turned to the stove and the rack of menus, I mouthed, "dollars."

Mama frowned while Mabel rolled her shoulders and said, "An't we growing up fast!"

I just smiled my heartbreaker's smile and got the man his sandwich. 30
When he left I snapped that five dollar bill loudly five times before I put it in my apron pocket. "My mama didn't raise no fool," I told the other women, who laughed and slapped my behind like they were glad to see me cutting up.

But Mama took me with her on her break. We walked up toward the Winn Dixie where she could get her cigarettes cheaper than in the drugstore.

"How'd you know?" she asked.

"'Cause that's what he always leaves," I told her.

"What do you mean *always?*"

"Every Thursday evening when I close up." I said it knowing she was 35
going to be angry.

"He leaves you a five dollar bill every Thursday night!" Her voice sounded strange, not angry exactly but not at all pleased either.

"Always," I said, and I added, "and he pretty much always has egg salad."

Mama stopped to light her last cigarette. Then she just stood there for a moment, breathing deeply around the Pall Mall and watching me while my face got redder and redder.

"You think you can get along without it?" she asked finally.

"Why?" I asked her. "I don't think he's going to stop." 40

"Because," she said, dropping the cigarette and walking on, "you're not working any more Thursday nights."

On Sundays the counter didn't open until after church at one o'clock. But at one sharp, we started serving those big gravy lunches and went right on till four. People would come in prepared to sit and eat big—coffee, salad, country fried steak with potatoes and gravy, or ham with red-eye gravy and carrots and peas. You'd also get a side of hog's head biscuits and a choice of three pies for dessert.

Tips were as choice as the pies, but Sunday had its trials. Too often, some tight-browed couple would come in at two o'clock and order breakfast—fried eggs and hash browns. When you told them we didn't serve breakfast on Sundays, they'd get angry.

"Look girl," they might say, "just bring me some of that ham you're serving those people, only bring me eggs with it. You can do that," and the contempt in their voices clearly added, "even you."

It would make me mad as sin. "Sir, we don't cook on the grill on 45
Sundays. We only have what's on the Sunday menu. When you make up your mind, let me know."

"Tourists," I'd mutter to Mama.

"No, *Yankees,*" she'd say, and Mabel would nod.

Then she might go over with an offer of boiled eggs, that ham, and a biscuit. She'd talk nice, drawling like she never did with me or friends, while she moved slower than you'd think a wide-awake person could. "Uh huh," she'd say, and "shore-nuf," and offer them honey for their biscuits or tell them how red-eye gravy is made, or talk about how sorry it is that we don't serve grits on Sunday. That couple would grin wide and start slowing their words down, while the regulars would choke on their coffee. Mama never bet on the tip, just put it all into the pot, and it was usually enough to provoke a round of applause after the couple was safely out the door.

Mama said nothing about it except the first time when she told me, "Yankees eat boiled eggs for breakfast," which may not sound like much, but had the force of a powerful insult. It was a fact that the only people we knew who ate boiled eggs in the morning were those stray tourists and people on the TV set who we therefore assumed had to be Yankees.

Yankees ate boiled eggs, laughed at grits but ate them in big helpings, 50
and had plenty of money to leave outrageous tips but might leave nothing for no reason that I could figure out. It wasn't the accent that marked Yankees. They talked different, but all kinds of different. There seemed to be a great many varieties of them, not just Northerners, but Westerners, Canadians, Black people who talked oddly enough to show they were foreign, and occasionally strangers who didn't even speak English. Some were friendly, some deliberately nasty. All of them were Yankees, strangers, unpredictable people with an enraging attitude of superiority who would say the rudest things as if they didn't know what an insult was.

"They're the ones the world was made for," Harriet told me late one night. "You and me, your mama, all of us, we just hold a place in the landscape for them. Far as they're concerned, once we're out of sight we just disappear."

Mabel plain hated them. Yankees didn't even look when she rolled her soft wide hips. "Son of a bitch," she'd say when some fish-eyed, clipped-tongue stranger would look right through her and leave her less than fifteen cents. "He must think we get fat on the honey of his smile." Which was even funnier when you'd seen that the man hadn't smiled at all.

"But give me an inch of edge and I can handle them," she'd tell me. "Sweets, you just stretch that drawl. Talk like you're from Mississippi, and they'll eat it up. For some reason, Yankees got strange sentimental notions about Mississippi."

"They're strange about other things too," Mama would throw in. "They think they can ask you personal questions just 'cause you served them a cup of coffee." Some salesman once asked her where she got her hose with the black thread sewed up the back and Mama hadn't forgiven him yet.

But the thing everyone told me and told me again was that you just 55
couldn't trust yourself with them. Nobody bet on Yankee tips, they might leave anything. Once someone even left a New York City subway token. Mama thought it a curiosity but not the equivalent of real money. Another one ordered one cup of coffee to go and twenty packs of sugar.

"They made 'road-liquor' out of it," Mabel said. "Just add an ounce of vodka and set it down by the engine exhaust for a month or so. It'll cook up into a bitter poison that'll knock you cross-eyed."

It sounded dangerous to me, but Mabel didn't think so. "Not that I would drink it," she'd say, "but I wouldn't fault a man who did."

They stole napkins, not one or two but a boxful at a time. Before we switched to sugar packets, they'd come in, unfold two or three napkins, open them like diapers, and fill them up with sugar before they left. Then they might take the knife and spoon to go with it. Once I watched a man take out a stack of napkins I was sure he was going to walk off with. But instead he sat there for thirty minutes making notes on them, then balled them all up and threw them away when he left.

My mama was scandalized by that. "And right over there on the shelf is a notebook selling for ten cents. What's wrong with these people?"

"They're living in the movies," Mabel whispered, looking back toward 60
the counter.

"Yeah, Bette Davis[1] movies," I added.

"I don't know about the movies." Harriet put her hand on Mama's shoulder. "But they don't live in the real world with the rest of us."

"No," Mama said, "they don't."

I take a bite of cherry tomato and hear Mama's voice again. *No,* she says.

"No," I say. I tuck my blouse into my skirt and shift in my shoes. If I 65
close my eyes, I can see Mabel's brightly rouged cheekbones, Harriet's pitted skin, and my mama's shadowed brown eyes. When I go home tonight I'll write her about this party and imagine how she'll laugh about it all. The woman who was talking to me has gone off across the room to the other bar. People are giving up nibbling and going on to more serious eating. One of the men I work with every day comes over with a full plate and a wide grin.

"Boy," he drawls around a bite of the cornbread I contributed to the buffet, "I bet you sure can cook."

"Bet on it," I say, with my Mississippi accent. I swallow the rest of a cherry tomato and give him my heartbreaker's smile.

Analyzing the Text

1. What upsets the narrator's mother about the five-dollar tip her daughter has received every Thursday night?
2. How would you characterize the "charm" the narrator says she has been working on? What has she learned from being a waitress in terms of how she now treats people?

Understanding Allison's Techniques

1. Over the course of the story, Allison includes many words that reveal the narrator's disdain for her customers, especially tourists from the North. What are some of these words and phrases and how do they add to the story's realism?

[1]Bette Davis (1908–1989), American film star.

2. What details suggest how naive the narrator was, and what she had learned after working as a waitress?

Arguing for an Interpretation

1. What elements in the story suggest that the characters are uncomfortable with being sexually stereotyped?
2. From the point of view of the narrator, her mother, and coworkers, what is so offensive about the Yankees? Is it a North-South issue, or a class issue? Explain your answer.

Liliana Heker

Liliana Heker (1943-) was born in Buenos Aires, Argentina and achieved fame with her first volume of short stories, Those Who Beheld the Burning Bush *(1966), when she was in her early 20s. Between 1977 and 1986, she was the editor of a literary magazine* El Ornitorrinco *("The Platypus"), which served as a forum for writers during the period when Argentina was under a military dictatorship. She is also the author of a novel* Zona de Clivage *(1988) and many short stories. "The Stolen Party," reprinted below, first appeared in translation in* Other Fires: Short Fiction by Latin American Women *(1985), translated by Alberto Manguel. She has also written the as yet untranslated* Fin de la Historia *(1996) and* Hermanas de Shakespeare *(1999).*

The Stolen Party

As soon as she arrived she went straight to the kitchen to see if the monkey was there. It was: what a relief! She wouldn't have liked to admit that her mother had been right. *Monkeys at a birthday?* her mother had sneered. *Get away with you, believing any nonsense you're told!* She was cross, but not because of the monkey, the girl thought; it's just because of the party.

"I don't like you going," she told her. "It's a rich people's party."

"Rich people go to Heaven too," said the girl, who studied religion at school.

"Get away with Heaven," said the mother. "The problem with you, young lady, is that you like to fart higher than your ass."

The girl didn't approve of the way her mother spoke. She was barely 5
nine, and one of the best in her class.

"I'm going because I've been invited," she said. "And I've been invited because Luciana is my friend. So there."

"Ah yes, your friend," her mother grumbled. She paused. "Listen, Rosaura," she said at last. "That one's not your friend. You know what you are to them? The maid's daughter, that's what."

Rosaura blinked hard: she wasn't going to cry. Then she yelled: "Shut up! You know nothing about being friends!"

Every afternoon she used to go to Luciana's house and they would both finish their homework while Rosaura's mother did the cleaning. They had their tea in the kitchen and they told each other secrets. Rosaura loved everything in the big house, and she also loved the people who lived there.

"I'm going because it will be the most lovely party in the whole world, Luciana told me it would. There will be a magician, and he will bring a monkey and everything."

The mother swung around to take a good look at her child, and pompously put her hands on her hips.

"Monkeys at a birthday?" she said. "Get away with you, believing any nonsense you're told!"

Rosaura was deeply offended. She thought it unfair of her mother to accuse other people of being liars simply because they were rich. Rosaura too wanted to be rich, of course. If one day she managed to live in a beautiful palace, would her mother stop loving her? She felt very sad. She wanted to go to that party more than anything else in the world.

"I'll die if I don't go," she whispered, almost without moving her lips.

And she wasn't sure whether she had been heard, but on the morning of the party she discovered that her mother had starched her Christmas dress. And in the afternoon, after washing her hair, her mother rinsed it in apple vinegar so that it would be all nice and shiny. Before going out, Rosaura admired herself in the mirror, with her white dress and glossy hair, and thought she looked terribly pretty.

Señora Ines also seemed to notice. As soon as she saw her, she said:

"How lovely you look today, Rosaura."

Rosaura gave her starched skirt a slight toss with her hands and walked into the party with a firm step. She said hello to Luciana and asked about the monkey. Luciana put on a secretive look and whispered into Rosaura's ear: "He's in the kitchen. But don't tell anyone, because it's a surprise."

Rosaura wanted to make sure. Carefully she entered the kitchen and there she saw it: deep in thought, inside its cage. It looked so funny that the girl stood there for a while, watching it, and later, every so often, she would slip out of the party unseen and go and admire it. Rosaura was the only one allowed into the kitchen. Señora Ines had said: "You yes, but not the others, they're much too boisterous, they might break something." Rosaura had never broken anything. She even managed the jug of orange juice, carrying it from the kitchen into the dining-room. She held it carefully and didn't spill a single drop. And Señora Ines had said: "Are you sure you can manage a jug as big as that?" Of course she could manage. She wasn't a butterfingers, like the others. Like that blonde girl with the bow in her hair. As soon as she saw Rosaura, the girl with the bow had said:

"And you? Who are you?"

"I'm a friend of Luciana," said Rosaura.

"No," said the girl with the bow, "you are not a friend of Luciana because I'm her cousin and I know all her friends. And I don't know you."

"So what," said Rosaura. "I come here every afternoon with my mother and we do our homework together."

"You and your mother do your homework together?" asked the girl, laughing.

"I and Luciana do our homework together," said Rosaura, very seriously.

The girl with the bow shrugged her shoulders.

"That's not being friends," she said. "Do you go to school together?"

"No."

"So where do you know her from?" said the girl, getting impatient.

Rosaura remembered her mother's words perfectly. She took a deep 30
breath.

"I'm the daughter of the employee," she said.

Her mother had said very clearly: "If someone asks, you say you're the daughter of the employee; that's all." She also told her to add: "And proud of it." But Rosaura thought that never in her life would she dare say something of the sort.

"What employee?" said the girl with the bow. "Employee in a shop?"

"No," said Rosaura angrily. "My mother doesn't sell anything in any shop, so there."

"So how come she's an employee?" said the girl with the bow. 35

Just then Señora Ines arrived saying *shh shh,* and asked Rosaura if she wouldn't mind helping serve out the hot-dogs, as she knew the house so much better than the others.

"See?" said Rosaura to the girl with the bow, and when no one was looking she kicked her in the shin.

Apart from the girl with the bow, all the others were delightful. The one she liked best was Luciana, with her golden birthday crown; and then the boys. Rosaura won the sack race, and nobody managed to catch her when they played tag. When they split into two teams to play charades, all the boys wanted her for their side. Rosaura felt she had never been so happy in all her life.

But the best was still to come. The best came after Luciana blew out the candles. First the cake. Señora Ines had asked her to help pass the cake around, and Rosaura had enjoyed the task immensely, because everyone called out to her, shouting "Me, me!" Rosaura remembered a story in which there was a queen who had the power of life or death over her subjects. She had always loved that, having the power of life or death. To Luciana and the boys she gave the largest pieces, and to the girl with the bow she gave a slice so thin one could see through it.

After the cake came the magician, tall and bony, with a fine red cape. A 40
true magician: he could untie handkerchiefs by blowing on them and make a chain with links that had no openings. He could guess what cards were pulled out from a pack, and the monkey was his assistant. He called the monkey "partner." "Let's see here, partner," he would say, "Turn over a card." And, "Don't run away, partner: time to work now."

The final trick was wonderful. One of the children had to hold the monkey in his arms and the magician said he would make him disappear.

"What, the boy?" they all shouted.

"No, the monkey!" shouted back the magician.

Rosaura thought that this was truly the most amusing party in the whole world.

The magician asked a small fat boy to come and help, but the small fat 45
boy got frightened almost at once and dropped the monkey on the floor. The magician picked him up carefully, whispered something in his ear, and the monkey nodded almost as if he understood.

"You mustn't be so unmanly, my friend," the magician said to the fat boy.

"What's unmanly?" said the fat boy.

The magician turned around as if to look for spies.

"A sissy," said the magician. "Go sit down."

Then he stared at all the faces, one by one. Rosaura felt her heart tremble. "You, with the Spanish eyes," said the magician. And everyone saw that he was pointing at her.

She wasn't afraid. Neither holding the monkey, nor when the magician made him vanish; not even when, at the end, the magician flung his red cape over Rosaura's head and uttered a few magic words . . . and the monkey reappeared, chattering happily, in her arms. The children clapped furiously. And before Rosaura returned to her seat, the magician said:

"Thank you very much, my little countess."

She was so pleased with the compliment that a while later, when her mother came to fetch her, that was the first thing she told her.

"I helped the magician and he said to me, 'Thank you very much, my little countess.' "

It was strange because up to then Rosaura had thought that she was angry with her mother. All along Rosaura had imagined that she would say to her: "See that the monkey wasn't a lie?" But instead she was so thrilled that she told her mother all about the wonderful magician.

Her mother tapped her on the head and said: "So now we're a countess!" But one could see that she was beaming.

And now they both stood in the entrance, because a moment ago Señora Ines, smiling, had said: "Please wait here a second."

Her mother suddenly seemed worried.

"What is it?" she asked Rosaura.

"What is what?" said Rosaura. "It's nothing; she just wants to get the presents for those who are leaving, see?"

She pointed at the fat boy and at a girl with pigtails who were also waiting there, next to their mothers. And she explained about the presents. She knew, because she had been watching those who left before her. When one of the girls was about to leave, Señora Ines would give her a bracelet. When a boy left, Señora Ines gave him a yo-yo. Rosaura preferred the yo-yo because it sparkled, but she didn't mention that to her mother. Her mother might have said: "So why don't you ask for one, you blockhead?" That's what her mother was like. Rosaura didn't feel like explaining that she'd be horribly ashamed to be the odd one out. Instead she said:

"I was the best-behaved at the party."

And she said no more because Señora Ines came out into the hall with two bags, one pink and one blue.

First she went up to the fat boy, gave him a yo-yo out of the blue bag, and the fat boy left with his mother. Then she went up to the girl and gave her a bracelet out of the pink bag, and the girl with the pigtails left as well.

Finally she came up to Rosaura and her mother. She had a big smile on her face and Rosaura liked that. Señora Ines looked down at her, then looked up at her mother, and then said something that made Rosaura proud:

"What a marvellous daughter you have, Herminia."

For an instant, Rosaura thought that she'd give her two presents: the bracelet and the yo-yo. Señora Ines bent down as if about to look for something. Rosaura also leaned forward, stretching out her arm. But she never completed the movement.

Señora Ines didn't look in the pink bag. Nor did she look in the blue bag. Instead she rummaged in her purse. In her hand appeared two bills.

"You really and truly earned this," she said handing them over. "Thank you for all your help, my pet."

Rosaura felt her arms stiffen, stick close to her body, and then she noticed her mother's hand on her shoulder. Instinctively she pressed herself against her mother's body. That was all. Except her eyes. Rosaura's eyes had a cold, clear look that fixed itself on Señora Ines's face.

Señora Ines, motionless, stood there with her hand outstretched. As if she didn't dare draw it back. As if the slightest change might shatter an infinitely delicate balance.

Analyzing the Text

1. How does Rosaura's view of herself change between the beginning and the end of the story? What does she do or say that helps you to understand the impact of the events at the party?
2. In what sense might the birthday party be thought of as "stolen," especially in terms of social class? In what other ways can you understand the title of this story?

Understanding Heker's Techniques

1. What means does Heker use to enable the reader to understand the unusual interpretations that Rosaura attaches to key events? Which of these events most vividly foreshadows the outcome?
2. How does Rosaura's mother serve as a foil for Rosaura's aspirations? How would the same events at the party appear from her mother's perspective?

Arguing for an Interpretation

1. In what ways do the mothers and the daughters in this story see themselves as making decisions that control their lives? What factors influence their views of themselves?
2. Does Rosaura's mother want to protect her from being disillusioned, or does she wish her to know and accept her true status? Explain your answer.

Poems

BERTOLT BRECHT

Bertolt Brecht (1898–1956) was born in Augsburg, Germany and studied medicine at Munich University before turning to a career in theater. Because of his criticism of Hitler and the Nazi regime, he was forced into exile in 1933 and sought asylum in many countries—Russia, France, Norway—before coming to the United States in 1941. His plays and radio scripts use expressionism, often to the point of exaggeration, to communicate his ironic social critique. His best known plays are The Three Penny Opera *(1928) written with Kurt Weill,* The Life of Galileo *(1939),* Mother Courage and Her Children

(1941), The Good Woman of Setzuan *(1943), and* The Caucasian Chalk Circle *(1947). Although he was famous as a playwright and director, Brecht was also a poet who aimed to instruct his readers, as we can see in "A Worker Reads History" (1936) translated by H. R. Hays, which first appeared in* Selected Poems *(1947).*

A Worker Reads History

Who built the seven gates of Thebes?
The books are filled with names of kings.
Was it kings who hauled the craggy blocks of stone?
And Babylon, so many times destroyed,
Who built the city up each time? In which of Lima's
houses,
That city glittering with gold, lived those who built it?
In the evening when the Chinese wall was finished
Where did the masons go? Imperial Rome
Is full of arcs of triumph. Who reared them up? Over whom
Did the Caesars triumph? Byzantium lives in song,
Were all her dwellings palaces? And even in Atlantis of the
legend
The night the sea rushed in,
The drowning men still bellowed for their slaves.

Young Alexander conquered India.
He alone?
Caesar beat the Gauls.
Was there not even a cook in his army?
Philip of Spain wept as his fleet
Was sunk and destroyed. Were there no other tears?
Frederick the Great triumphed in the Seven Years War. Who
Triumphed with him?

Each page a victory,

At whose expense the victory ball?
Every ten years a great man,
Who paid the piper?

So many particulars.
So many questions.

Analyzing the Text

1. According to Brecht, what different roles (unmentioned in history books) have workers played in past civilizations? In what sense might the phrase "Each page a victory" be construed as ironic?

2. How does the phrase "Every ten years a great man, /Who paid the piper?" express Brecht's ironic view of the way historians customarily treat important events and leaders?

Understanding Brecht's Technique

1. How does the title of the poem suggest that Brecht wishes his readers to view historical events from an unusual and atypical perspective? How does the way the poem is written, as a series of questions, support this viewpoint?
2. Although Brecht draws attention to the role of those normally invisible in history books, he doesn't mention working women. Would the poem have been as effective if he had included women? Why or why not?

Arguing for an Interpretation

1. At the time Brecht wrote this poem, history texts omitted accounts of the working class and other marginalized groups. When you studied history in school, to what extent were the books you read similar to those Brecht satirizes? In your opinion, is Brecht's point still valid? Why or why not?
2. In his poetry as in his plays, Brecht aimed at reaching the audience's intellect rather than their emotions. How does this concept operate in this poem, and how is it different from other poems?

Mascha Kaléko

Mascha Kaléko (1912–1975) began contributing poems to local Berlin newspapers while studying there. She soon became famous throughout Germany for her ironic depiction of urban life and her satiric wit, tempered by an essentially romantic and melodic style. Kaléko's work provides witty, ironic descriptions of petit-bourgeois life in Berlin during the Weimar Republic. In her Das lyrische Stenogrammheft (The Lyrical Stenographer's Notebook) *(1933), love can be expressed only in shorthand on one's afternoon off. In 1938, she was forced to emigrate and lived in New York City and Jerusalem until her death 37 years later. Other works include* Kleines Lesebuch für Grosse *(1934; reprinted in 1956), and* Verse für Zeitgenossen *(1945; reprinted in 1980). The appeal of her poetry to contemporary audiences continues to grow, something we can easily appreciate from reading "Mannequins," a sardonic backstage glimpse of the less than glamorous private life of fashion models, translated by Susan L. Cocalis (1986).*

Mannequins

Wanted: Model, with a size 6 figure.
Easy, pleasant work . . .

Just smiling and flattering the whole day through . . .
It gets you down.

—Whatever they promise to do:
We remain sound.
We show off in silks the *dernier cri,*
Knowing: they will never belong to me.
That door is closed to us.
We wear the rags from the stockroom,
And say to the damsels with figures "in bloom":
"Madam, . . . it's marvelous!"

We live from day to day on bread, butter, and tea.
We have to make do.
And sometimes a gentleman takes us to eat . . .
. . . If we want to.
What good is this wrapping of crèpe satin—
You are what you are: just a mannequin.
That's nothing to laugh at.
We worry about every cent at night,
Yet we must, like toy dolls, appear bright
Lest the customers complain about that.

Our legs are our working capital,
And our references.
Salary: as high as our hips are small.
Logical consequences . . .
Condition: well-proportioned, discreet, and—lovely,
(For that's the store's policy.)
And if men have something off-color to say,
Don't cry "No!" and don't show your shame.
It's all part of the company's name
And part of your pay.

Analyzing the Text

1. In what way do the lines in the want-ad that precede the poem contrast with the reality the speaker describes?
2. Which details most effectively describe how little control the models have over their own lives?

Understanding Kaléko's Techniques

1. How is the poem designed to undercut assumptions and illusions about the kind of lives models lead? In what sense does the title express the author's thesis about the way models reflect society's fantasies about women?
2. What aspects of the poem enable the reader to empathize with the extent to which models must encourage their clients' dreams (while simultaneously suppressing their own feelings)?

Arguing for an Interpretation

1. In what ways does this poem satirize the expectations of bourgeois society? What other professions also require women to reshape themselves to conform to society's expectations? Do you think Kaléko's poem makes a persuasive case for her point of view? Why or why not?
2. Why is the title an apt description of the speaker's life?

Léon Gontran Damas

Léon Damas (1912–1978) was born in the capital city of Cayenne, French Guiana—in the shadow of Devil's Island—the son of a middle-class mulatto family conscious of its intellectual and social position. His childhood was dominated by a mother imbued with ultra-white values. Chronic asthma kept Damas virtually bedridden until the age of 6. Eventually, he was well enough to be sent to Fort-de-France, Martinique, to attend Lycée Schoelcher where he first met the poet Aime Cesarie. From there, he went to Paris to continue his education, devoting himself at first to law and Oriental languages. He gained considerable prestige with his collection of poetry, Pigments *(1936), which appeared as the first substantial artistic work in the movement known as* negritude, *an international literary movement promoting the awareness of black culture. This volume of poetry was seized and banned by the government that, on the eve of World War I, found the inflammatory verse dangerous to French security in the colonies. Ironically, Damas served with the French Armed Forces in World War II, earning several decorations for meritorious conduct. After the war he was elected a deputy to the National Assembly from French Guiana and has since served in a variety of positions with the Ministry of Foreign Affairs. Volumes of his work include poetry in* Graffiti *(1952) and* Black-Label *(1956), a collection of essays,* Return to Guiana *(1938), and a volume of short stories,* Veillées noires *(1943). "Hiccup," translated by Norman R. Shapiro (1970), is an amusing portrait of the extent to which Damas as a boy was never able to fulfill his mother's expectations.*

Hiccup

And it doesn't help to swallow seven gulps of water
three or four times every twenty-four hours
back comes my childhood
in a hiccup that jolts
my instinct
like the cop shaking the tramp

Disaster
tell me about the disaster
tell me about it

My mother hoping for a very table-manners son
    Hands on the table
    bread is not cut
    bread is broken

bread is not wasted
bread the gift of God
bread of the sweat of your Father's brow
bread of the bread

A bone is eaten with restraint and discretion
a stomach should be polite
and every polite stomach
learns not to belch
a fork is not a tooth-pick
you must not blow your nose
so everyone can see
and hear
and besides sit up straight
a well-bred nose
does not mop up the plate

And besides this besides that
and besides in the name of the Father
the Son
the Holy Ghost
at the end of every meal

And besides this besides that
and then disaster
tell me about the disaster
tell me about it

My mother hoping for a syllabus son

Unless you learn your history lesson
you shall not go to mass
on Sunday
in all your Sunday best

This child will bring disgrace upon our name
this child will be for Heaven's sake

Be still
How often have I told you that you must speak French
the French of France
the Frenchman's French
French French

Disaster
tell me about the disaster
tell me about it

My Mother hoping for a son
just like his mother

You didn't say hello to Madame next door
and your shoes all dirty again

just let me catch you playing in the street
or on the grass or the Savane
under the War Memorial
playing games
running around with little So-and-so
with So-and-so who wasn't even baptised

Disaster
tell me about the disaster
tell me about it

My Mother hoping for a son who was very do
very re
very mi
very fa
very sol
very la
very si
very do
re-mi-fa
sol-la-si
do

I understand that once again you missed
your vi-o-lin lesson
A banjo
you said a banjo
is that what you said
a banjo
you really said
a banjo
Oh no young man
you must learn that our kind of people frown
on ban
and jo
and gui
and tar
that's not for us *mulattos*
that kind of thing is only for the *blacks*

Analyzing the Text

1. In what ways do the values and social expectations of the speaker's mother lead her to find fault with her son's table manners, language, choice of playmates, and musical preferences?
2. Why is the speaker's mother so upset that her son prefers the banjo to the violin? What social criticism does Damas express through this incident?

Understanding Damas's Techniques

1. How is the poem's structure designed to simulate an argument between two people? Why is this form particularly effective in dramatizing the speaker's problem with his mother?

2. The title might at first appear odd. Why would a hiccup, that is, an involuntary response, be an appropriate image for the speaker's inability to suppress the memories of his mother's complaints?

Arguing for an Interpretation

1. How does Damas use humor to satirize prevailing social values including the definition of what it is to be mulatto, black, or white?
2. Were you subjected to attempts to improve your table manners or diction or to play a musical instrument as a way of raising your social status? Discuss your experiences and your attitude toward the implied values such projects embody.

Marge Piercy

Marge Piercy was born in 1936. She received a B.A. in 1957 from the University of Michigan and an M.A. in 1958 from Northwestern University. She is a prolific novelist and poet. Piercy's novels include Woman on the Edge of Time *(1976) and* Vida *(1979). Collections of her poetry are* Circles of the Water *(1982) in which the following poem appeared, and* The Art of Blessing the Day: Poems with a Jewish Theme *(1999). A recent work is* Sleeping with Cats: A Memoir *(2002). "The Nine of Cups" is typical of Piercy's satiric meditations on economic, racial, and sexual inequality in contemporary American life.*

The Nine of Cups[1]

Not fat, not gross, just well fed and hefty he sits before what's his,
the owner, the ultimate consumer, the overlord.
No human kidneys can pump nine cups of wine through
but that's missing the point of having: possession is power
whether he owns apartment houses or herds of prime beef
or women's soft hands or the phone lines or the right to kill
or pieces of paper that channel men's working hours.

He is not malcontent. He has the huge high-colored
healthy face you see on executives just massaged.
He eats lobster, he drinks aged scotch, he buys pretty women.
He buys men who write about how he is a servant of circumstance.

[1]A tarot card signifying good fortune.

He buys armies to shoot peasants squatting on his oil.

He is your landlord: he shuts off the heat and the light and the water,
he shuts off air, he shuts off growth, he shuts off your sex.
He buys men who know geology for him, he buys men who count stars,
he buys women who paint their best dreams all over his ceiling.
He buys giants who grow for him and dwarfs who shrink
and he eats them all, he eats, he eats well,
he eats and twenty Bolivians starve, a division of labor.

You are in his cup, you float like an icecube, you sink like an onion.
Guilt is the training of his servants that we may serve harder.
His priests sell us penance for his guilt,
his psychiatrists whip our parents through our cold bowels,
his explainers drone of human nature and the human condition.

He is squatting on our heads laughing. He belches with health.
He feels so very good he rewards us with TV sets
which depict each one of us his servants sitting
just as fat and proud and ready to stomp
in front of the pile of tin cans we call our castle.

On the six o'clock news the Enemy attacks.
Then our landlord spares no expense to defend us,
for the hungry out there want to steal our TV sets.
He raises our taxes one hundred per cent
and sells us weapons and sends us out to fight.
We fight and we die, for god, country and the dollar
and then we come back home
and he raises the rent.

Analyzing the Text

1. What attributes define the "he" referred to in the poem? Which details communicate the kind of control this individual exercises over everyone else?
2. What economic and social values does Piercy assail in this poem?

Understanding Piercy's Techniques

1. Why does Piercy choose a card from the tarot deck ("the nine of cups") that traditionally signifies material good fortune to symbolize all that she finds worthy of condemnation?
2. Why is the last stanza particularly ironic in view of the cumulative indictment Piercy levels against the establishment?

Arguing for an Interpretation

1. According to Piercy, in what ways do capitalism and consumerism reinforce each other?
2. What official aspects of society's institutions brainwash us to accept this unjust and grotesque reality as normal? Is her criticism well founded? Why or why not?

LINDA HOGAN

Linda Hogan, Chickasaw poet, novelist, and essayist, was born in 1947 in Denver, Colorado, and grew up in Oklahoma. She taught American Indian Studies at the University of Minnesota from 1984 to 1991 and is currently professor of American Studies and American Indian Studies at the University of Colorado. Her poetry has been collected in Seeing Through the Sun *(1985) which received an American Book Award from the Before Columbus Foundation,* The Book of Medicines *(1993), and* Solar Storms *(1996). She has also published short stories, one of which, "Aunt Moon's Young Man" was featured in* Best American Short Stories *(1989). Her novel* Mean Spirit *was nominated for a Pulitzer Prize (1990). Hogan's latest work is* The Woman Who Watches Over the World: A Native Memoir *(2001). In "Workday," she uses the occasion of a bus ride she took when returning from working at the University of Colorado to explore the gap between Native Americans and her middle-class white coworkers.*

Workday

I go to work
though there are those who were missing today
from their homes.
I ride the bus
and I do not think of children without food
or how my sisters are chained to prison beds.

I go to the university
and out for lunch
and listen to the higher-ups
tell me all they have read
about Indians
and how to analyze this poem.
They know us
better than we know ourselves.

I ride the bus home
and sit behind the driver.
We talk about the weather
and not enough exercise.
I don't mention Victor Jara's mutilated hands
or men next door
in exile
or my own family's grief over the lost child.

When I get off the bus
I look back at the light in the windows
and the heads bent
and how the women are all alone
in each seat
framed in the windows
and the men are coming home,
then I see them walking on the Avenue,
the beautiful feet,
the perfect legs
even with their spider veins,
the broken knees
with pins in them,
the thighs with their cravings,
the pelvis
and small back
with its soft down,
the shoulders which bend forward
and forward and forward
to protect the heart from pain.

Analyzing the Text

1. Through what details does Hogan raise the question as to whether the speaker has lost touch with her own Native American people?
2. What images suggest that the speaker feels that she is little more than a token Native American at the university where she teaches?

Understanding Hogan's Techniques

1. What sense do you get of the speaker's feelings about the psychological and physical costs for Native Americans who are trying to survive in mainstream society?
2. How does the bus ride itself serve as a microcosm of the journey between the two different worlds the speaker traverses?

Arguing for an Interpretation

1. Why is the speaker in "Workday" alienated from the educated community in which she works? Conversely, what connects her with the workers on the bus?
2. Have you ever experienced a sense of alienation at a workplace because of differences in race, class, or gender? Describe what happened.

Francis E. W. Harper

Francis Ellen Watkins Harper (1824–1911) was born in Baltimore, the daughter of free blacks. She attended a school run by her uncle and worked as a seamstress and as a teacher. In the 1850s she began actively working and lecturing for the abolitionist cause. Her writing includes Poems on Miscellaneous Subjects *(1854), a volume of antislavery verse that sold 12,000 copies by 1858 and went through some 20 editions;* Sketches of Southern Life *(1872); and a novel,* Iola Leroy *(1892), recognized as the first novel by a black author to describe Reconstruction.*

Learning to Read

Very soon the Yankee teachers
Came down and set up school;
But, oh! how the Rebs did hate it,—
It was agin' their rule.

Our masters always tried to hide
Book learning from our eyes;
Knowledge didn't agree with slavery—
'Twould make us all too wise.

But some of us would try to steal
A little from the book,
And put the words together,
And learn by hook or crook.

I remember Uncle Caldwell,
Who took pot liquor[1] fat
And greased the pages of his book,
And hid it in his hat

And had his master ever seen
The leaves upon his head,
He'd have thought them greasy papers,
But nothing to be read.

And there was Mr. Turner's Ben,
Who heard the children spell,
And picked the words right up by heart,
And learned to read 'em well.

Well, the Northern folks kept sending
The Yankee teachers down;

[1] *Pot liquor:* broth in which meat and/or vegetables have cooked.

And they stood right up and helped us,
Though Rebs did sneer and frown.

And, I longed to read my Bible,
For precious words it said;
But when I begun to learn it,
Folks just shook their heads,

And said there is no use trying,
Oh! Chloe, you're too late;
But as I was rising sixty,
I had no time to wait.

So I got a pair of glasses,
And straight to work I went,
And never stopped till I could read
The hymns and Testament.

Then I got a little cabin
A place to call my own—
And I felt as independent
As the queen upon her throne.

Analyzing the Text

1. In the society Harper describes, why would learning to read pose a danger?
2. What motivates Harper to learn to read and in what way does reading change her life?

Understanding Harper's Techniques

1. How do the examples of slaves who learned to read illustrate their ingenuity in overcoming obstacles in order to become literate?
2. How does Harper show the interrelationship between literacy, self-reliance, and owning property?

Arguing for an Interpretation

1. How does the fact that Chloe is not only a former slave, but is 60 years old, make her accomplishment all the more remarkable?
2. What would be a comparable achievement for you that learning to read was for Chloe? What would motivate you to undertake it?

NIKKI GIOVANNI

Nikki Giovanni was born in 1943 in Knoxville, Tennessee, the daughter of a probation officer and a social worker. She graduated with honors from Fisk University in 1967 and did postgraduate work at the University of Pennsylvania School of Social Work and Columbia University School of Fine Arts. She has taught

black studies at Queens College, City University of New York, and English at Rutgers University (1968–1970). She is currently a professor of creative writing at Virginia Tech University. Giovanni attained prominence in the late 1960s and early 1970s with her poetry on the themes of racial pride and family values. Collections of her poetry include Black Judgement *(1968) in which Giovanni's reminiscences of her childhood, "Nikki-Rosa," first appeared. Her recent works include* Love Poems *(1997) and* Blues: For All the Changes: New Poems *(1999).*

Nikki-Rosa

childhood remembrances are always a drag
if you're Black
you always remember things like living in Woodlawn°
with no inside toilet
and if you become famous or something
they never talk about how happy you were to have your
mother
all to yourself and
how good the water felt when you got your bath from one
of those
big tubs that folk in chicago barbecue in
and somehow when you talk about home
it never gets across how much you
understood their feelings
as the whole family attended meetings about Hollydale
and even though you remember
your biographers never understand
your father's pain as he sells his stock
and another dream goes
and though you're poor it isn't poverty that
concerns you
and though they fought a lot
it isn't your father's drinking that makes any difference
but only that everybody is together and you
and your sister have happy birthdays and very good
christmasses
and I really hope no white person ever has cause to write
about me
because they never understand Black love is Black wealth
and they'll

Woodlawn: a predominantly black suburb of Cincinnati, Ohio.

probably talk about my hard childhood and never understand that
all the while I was quite happy

Analyzing the Text

1. In what way did the speaker's childhood differ from how her biographers understand it?
2. What racial preconceptions does Giovanni refute in this poem?

Understanding Giovanni's Techniques

1. In what way does the appearance of the lines and the rhythms and pauses that they create underscore the point Giovanni makes?
2. What details in the poem explore the question of what constitutes "true" wealth?

Arguing for an Interpretation

1. To what extent is Giovanni's poem stronger because she is uncompromisingly honest in describing the material deprivations and psychological despair that most people could not overcome?
2. In what way does this poem dramatize what artists do as compared with academics (such as sociologists or historians) who chronicle the facts about social conditions?

GARY SOTO

Gary Soto (1952-) was born and raised in Fresno, California, and is the author of ten poetry collections, most notably New and Selected Poems, *a 1995 finalist for both the Los Angeles Times Book Award and the National Book Award. His recollections* Living Up the Street *received the Before Columbus Foundation 1985 American Book Award. His poems have appeared in many literary magazines, including* The Nation, Ploughshares, *and* Poetry *where "Dirt" originally appeared in 2002. He received the U.S. Award of the International Poetry Forum and was awarded fellowships from the Guggenheim Foundation and from the National Endowment for the Arts. His film* The Pool Party *received the 1993 Andrew Carnegie Medal. He wrote the libretto for an opera,* Nerd-landia *for The Los Angeles Opera. In 1999, he received the Literature Award from the Hispanic Heritage Foundation, and the PEN Center West Book Award for* Petty Crimes *(1998). He presently serves as Young People's Ambassador for the California Rural Legal Assistance (CRLA) and the United Farm Workers (UFW). His recent works include* Poetry Lover *(2001) and* Amnesia in a Republican county *(2003).*

Dirt

apologies to Wallace Stevens

The philosopher says, The soil is man's intelligence,
And if so, then we are smarter than any tweedy Prof.,
We with the hoes, the horizon flat wherever we turn.
The sun comes up angry. The wind bullies us from behind,
And as we space beet plants with tiny golf swings
I say to my brother in the next row,
We're smarter than you think.
He looks up with his dirty face—
What are you talking about?
And I answer with a laugh,
Say, as I slaughter two more plants,
I got me two sandwiches to eat. How 'bout you?
My brother pleats his brow, tells me to shut up—
I do. The wind pushes,
The sun's half wafer of light reddens.
A dog's bark echoes from the canal.
Where workers will later wash their feet at the day's end.
I'm glad to be by my brother,
Glad for this education in the Big Bosses' skinny rows.
I chop my beets, keep my mouth closed.
I think to myself, I'm in college,
I'm in this field where crows follow me like guards.
I'm thinking of the philosopher dead thirty years
And covered smartly in the same ancient dirt
Lifted and falling from my hoe.

Analyzing the Text

1. In what way does working in the beet fields provide an education for the speaker comparable, or even superior, to that which he might obtain in college?
2. What emotional bond exists between the speaker and his brother, and how does Soto place the work they do in the context of what all laborers do?

Understanding Soto's Techniques

1. How does Soto frame the poem using references to the philosophical meaning of physical labor in the fields and how is this ironically contrasted with big business and higher education?
2. How does Soto capture the rhythm and gestures of planting in the phrasing of the lines?

Arguing for an Interpretation

1. In what sense might the poem be seen as an ironic tribute to the philosophical truths one learns through physical labor as compared with the abstractions one learns in college?

2. Wallace Stevens was an American poet (1879–1955) who wrote elegant philosophical verse while pursuing a career as an insurance executive. How might Soto be drawing an analogy to the speaker's experiences of being in the working world and being an artist and philosopher? You might wish to read some of Stevens's poems (such as "The Emperor of Ice Cream" [1922] or "The Man with the Blue Guitar" [1937]).

MARTÍN ESPADA

Martín Espada was born in 1957 in Brooklyn, New York into a politically active family (his father was a leader in the Puerto Rican community during the civil rights movement). He graduated from the University of Wisconsin and earned a degree in law from Northeastern University. He is currently a professor of English at the University of Massachusetts, Amherst. Espada's committment (whether as an attorney, educator, or poet) is as a spokesman for the underclass of Hispanic immigrants, and he gives voice to their sense of powerlessness, as can be seen in the following poem that first appeared in Rebellion Is the Circle of a Lover's Hands *(1990). Recent collections of his work include* A Mayan Astronomer in Hell's Kitchen: Poems *(2000) and* Alabanza: New and Selected Poems, 1982–2002 *(2003).*

Jorge the Church Janitor Finally Quits

No one asks
where I am from,
I must be
from the country of janitors,

I have always mopped this floor.
Honduras, you are a squatter's camp
outside the city
of their understanding.

No one can speak
my name,
I host the fiesta
of the bathroom,
stirring the toilet
like a punchbowl.
The Spanish music of my name
is lost
when the guests complain

about toilet paper.

What they say
must be true:
I am smart,
but I have a bad attitude.

No one knows
that I quit tonight,
maybe the mop
will push on without me,
sniffing along the floor
like a crazy squid
with stringy gray tentacles.
They will call it Jorge.

Analyzing the Text

1. What ironic point does Espada make about the extent to which Jorge's white employers identify him with his mop?
2. What further irony comes from the fact that he is a church janitor?

Understanding Espada's Techniques

1. How do allusions to fiestas and the "Spanish music of my name" emphasize the otherness of Jorge's position in relationship to white mainstream culture?
2. How does the image of the three-way connection between the mop, a squid, and Jorge underscore the dehumanizing way immigrants are viewed and treated?

Arguing for an Interpretation

1. How does Jorge's understandable "bad attitude" and his decision to quit offer insights into how Espada uses poetry as a vehicle for social protest?
2. Do you agree with Espada that the United States is not a very friendly home for immigrants? In your opinion, is Jorge a victim of social oppression or simply a disgruntled worker? Explain your answer.

Drama

DARIO FO

Dario Fo was born in San Giano, Italy, in 1926. In 1940, Fo moved to Milan to study art at the Brera Art College and started improvising stories and sketches. In 1942, Fo helped his father in the Resistance, and deserted from the army. From 1945 to 1951, Fo studied set design and architecture at Milan Polytechnic. After several years of staging and performing in variety shows and satirical reviews, he and his wife, Franca Rame, created their own company, La Compagnia Dario Fo-Franca Rame. They gained celebrity status in Italy, beginning in the early 1960s, from their appearances on a nationally televised variety show. In 1968, Fo formed the company Nuova Scena, performing for workers in labor halls and nontraditional locations throughout Italy in plays that address the Italian sociopolitical scene. Fo is the author of some 32 plays and has had his works produced in 14 countries. The Accidental Death of an Anarchist *(1984) and* We Won't Pay! We Won't Pay! *(1974) are among the greatest comic hits of both the experimental and commercial theater during the past 20 years. More recent plays include* The Pope and the Witch *(1993),* The Open Couple *(1994), and* An Ordinary Day *(1994). Fo won the Nobel Prize for Literature in 1997.*

Ron Jenkins in Clowns, Politics, and Miracles *(1986) wrote that "Fo's politics are skillfully embedded into the comic structure of his material. Instead of blatantly proclaiming his opposition to economic injustices, Fo creates stories that center on the tension between freedom and oppression. He then orchestrates comic climaxes so that they coincide with the victim's liberation from servitude, so that laughter and the defeat of tyranny are simultaneously linked in the audience's mind."*

In We Won't Pay! We Won't Pay!, *translated by Ron Jenkins (2001), Fo creates a hilarious farce set against the background of the Milan food riots in which a working-class wife goes to absurd extremes to conceal from her law-abiding husband the fact that she and her best friend have stolen food from their local supermarket after a protest against rising prices developed into a riot.*

We Won't Pay! We Won't Pay!

Edited by Franca Rame
Translated by Ron Jenkins

Five Characters

ANTONIA

GIOVANNI

MARGHERITA

LUIGI

STATE TROOPER

POLICE SERGEANT

GRAVEDIGGER

GRANDFATHER

SEVERAL TROOPERS AND POLICEMEN

NOTE: The role of the State Trooper, the Police Sergeant, the Gravedigger and the Grandfather are played by the same actor.

Act One

Antonia's apartment: a modest working-class home. On the right side of the stage is a dresser and a bed. On the left side is a hat rack and a wardrobe. Center stage is a table. Upstage is a set of glass-doored shelves for dishes. There is a refrigerator, a gas stove and two gas tanks hooked together for welding.

The lights go up on the entrance to the apartment. Antonia and her younger friend, Margherita, enter. They are loaded down with numerous plastic bags overflowing with merchandise. They set the bags down on the table.

ANTONIA. It's a good thing I ran into you, or I don't know how I ever could have carried all this stuff.

MARGHERITA. Can I ask where you found the money to pay for it all.

ANTONIA. I won it . . . in a lottery . . . the church was raffling off scratch tickets . . . mine had a portrait of the pope, in silhouette, in the pope mobile.

MARGHERITA. The pope mobile . . . come on!

ANTONIA. Why, you don't believe it?

MARGHERITA. No!

ANTONIA. Okay, then I'll tell you the truth.

MARGHERITA (*Sitting*). Go on. Tell me.

ANTONIA. This morning I had to go grocery shopping, but I didn't know how I could buy anything, because I didn't have any money. So I walked into the supermarket, and I see a crowd of women. They're all raising hell because the prices are higher than they were just the day before. (*She looks into the sacks and goes back and forth putting things into the kitchen shelves*). The manager's trying to calm them down. "Well, there's nothing I can do about it," he said. "The distributors set the prices, and they've decided to raise them." "They decided? With whose permission?" "With nobody's permission. It's the free market. Free competition." "Free competition against who? Against us? And we're supposed to give in? . . . While they fire our husbands . . . and keep raising prices . . ." So I yelled, "You're the thieves!" . . . And then I hid, because I was really scared.

MARGHERITA. Good for you!

ANTONIA. Then one of the women said, "We've had enough! This time, we're setting the prices. We'll pay what we paid last month. And if you don't like it, we won't pay nothing. Understand?" You should have seen the manager. He turned white as a sheet. "You're out of your minds. I'm calling the police." He runs for the telephone behind the cash register, but the phone doesn't work. Somebody cut the line. "Excuse me. I've got to get to my office. Excuse me . . ." But he can't get through . . . not with all the women around him . . . so he pushes them . . . they push him . . . and while we were pushing, a woman pretended he'd punched her in the belly, and fell down on the ground as if she'd fainted.

MARGHERITA. Ah . . . nice move!

ANTONIA. You should have seen what an artist she was! Just like the real thing . . . And there was a fat old woman there, she was huge, waving her finger like it was a machine gun . . . she pointed it at the manager and said, "Coward! Picking a fight with a defenseless woman, and she's pregnant. And now if she loses her baby, what's going to happen to you! They'll throw you in jail. Murderer." And then we all started chanting together: "BABY KILLER! BABY KILLER! BABY KILLER!" (*Bursts out laughing*) It was great.

MARGHERITA. And then . . . what happened?

ANTONIA. Well, that prick of a manager was so scared he caved in completely . . . we paid whatever we wanted to pay.

MARGHERITA. (*Laughing*). Ah! Ah!

ANTONIA. "The cops are coming," someone shouts. We all start running. We're dropping our bags on the ground. We're crying with fear. It's a false alarm. Some truckers came to help when they heard us shouting: "Hey. Calm down. What's there to be afraid of. Don't get your panties in a wad worrying about the police. You're within your rights to pay a fair price. Let 'em have it!" So this is the payback for all the money they've stolen from us in all the years we've been shopping there. And then a woman yelled, "We won't pay anything! We won't pay. We won't pay. We won't pay. We won't pay!" We went back and started shopping all over again. We shopped and we shopped and we shopped. You don't know how good it feels to shop without spending money.

MARGHERITA. Ah, how beautiful! What a shame I wasn't there!

ANTONIA. But in the meantime, the police actually did show up, for real . . . in riot gear . . . I can't tell you how scared I was! I was shaking, we were all shaking, our bags were shaking . . . the noise from the plastic was deafening! But this time, none of the women ran away. We walked calmly out of the supermarket with decisive faces . . . so firm, so honest . . . we looked like Hillary Clinton defending her man . . . and we said to the cops, "Oh, thank God you're here. Finally! Go in there and arrest those thieves!"

MARGHERITA. How beautiful!

ANTONIA. It was thrilling! It was a shopping spree to end all shopping sprees! Not because we didn't pay for the stuff, but because suddenly we were all there together with the courage to stand up for ourselves. And we caught the bastards off balance. Now they're the ones who are afraid. Soon supermarkets will have to put those plastic theft protection devices on every onion.

MARGHERITA. But what are you going to tell your husband? You're not going to try to sell him the story about the pope mobile.

ANTONIA. Why, you don't think he'll buy it?

MARGHERITA. Not a chance.

ANTONIA. Yeah . . . maybe it's a bit much. The problem is, he's a man. You know how men are. They can't see the big picture. He's a law-and-order freak. Who knows what kind of tantrum he'll throw! "How could you do such a thing?" he'll say. "My father built a good life for his children by following the rules. I follow the rules. We're poor, but we're honest!" He doesn't know that I've spent everything, that there's nothing left to pay the gas, the electric or the rent ... I don't even know how many months behind we are ...

MARGHERITA. I haven't paid the rent for five months! And I didn't manage to get in on the shopping spree like you did ...

ANTONIA. There's enough stuff here to feed a day-care center. Take some home.

MARGHERITA. No, no, please. Thanks, but I don't have any money to pay for it.

ANTONIA (*Serious*). Well, if you can't pay for it ... (*Changes tone*) Are you crazy! I donated this stuff to myself ... Go on, take it home. Take it!

MARGHERITA. Sure, and then what am I going to tell my husband? He'd murder me!

ANTONIA (*Taking cans out of the bag*). Mine would just lock himself in the closet.

MARGHERITA (*Astonished*). In the closet?

ANTONIA (*Points at wardrobe*). Yeah! For ten years ... every time we have an argument ... he locks himself in that wardrobe. He's very organized about it! He has his little flashlight, his little chair. And he reads Dante's *Inferno*. He's trying to memorize it. (*Looks at can in her hand*) What's this? (*Reads*) "Meat compost for cats and dogs"?

MARGHERITA (*Reads*). "Homogenized for the beefy flavor your pet can't resist"! But why did you take this?

ANTONIA. In the confusion ... I just grabbed what was there ... (*Takes another can*) Look at this one!!

MARGHERITA (*Reads*). "Bird seed for canaries"!!

ANTONIA Well, it's a good thing I didn't pay for this stuff, or I'd be eating ... (*Reads*) "Frozen rabbit heads"!

MARGHERITA. Frozen heads?

ANTONIA. That's what it says: "To enrich the meals of your chickens ... five rabbit heads for twenty cents." At least it's cheap. (*Disappointed*) But I can't return this stuff ... they'll just arrest me.

MARGHERITA (*Laughing*). And you wanted me to bring this junk home to my Luigi?

ANTONIA. Oh, no! I'm much too attached to my rabbit heads ... You take home the bad stuff: the oil, the pasta ... go on, get moving. Your husband's on the night shift, so you'll have time to hide it all.

MARGHERITA.. Yeah ... and what if the police start searching house to house?

ANTONIA. Don't be silly! The whole neighborhood was at the supermarket ... you think the police are going to come and search every house ... (*Opens a window*) Oh dammit, my husband! He's coming up. Quick, get this stuff out of here ...

MARGHERITA (*Frightened*). Where should I put it?

ANTONIA. Under your coat! (*Margherita stuffs some of the bags under her coat*) Help me get it under the bed ... (*Takes all the bags on the table and stuffs them under the bed. She puts the animal food on the counter behind her*) If Giovanni finds out, he'll call the police. "Officer, arrest my wife. She's an enemy of the people!" Come on, run ... and keep it quiet! Tell him some fairy tale.

(*Margherita goes to the door and bumps into Antonia's husband, Giovanni, entering the house.*)

MARGHERITA (*In a hurry, very embarrassed*). Good morning, Giovanni.

GIOVANNI. Oh, good morning, Margherita ... how are you?

MARGHERITA. Fine, thank you . . . 'Bye, Antonia, see you later . . . (*She leaves*)

(*Giovanni remains perplexed and looks at Margherita's belly as she leaves.*)

ANTONIA. So, Giovanni, why are you standing there? It's about time you came home. Where have you been?

(*Antonia prepares the table for dinner, plastic plates, napkins, etc.*)

GIOVANNI. What's up with Margherita?

ANTONIA. Why, what should be up?

GIOVANNI. Well . . . she's all fat up front: there's a belly!

ANTONIA. So? Is that the first time you ever saw a married woman with a belly?

GIOVANNI. You mean she's pregnant?

ANTONIA. Well, it's one of those things that can happen when you make love.

GIOVANNI. But, how many months is it? I just saw her last Sunday and it didn't seem like . . .

ANTONIA. What do you know about these things? It's already been a week since last Sunday . . . and in a week, who knows what could happen!

GIOVANNI. Listen, I'm not that stupid . . . Luigi works next to me on the assembly line. He tells me everything . . . and he never said anything about having a baby . . .

ANTONIA. Well . . . there are some things . . . people don't bother to talk about.

GIOVANNI. What are you talking about? Is it too embarrassing? "Oh, God, I made my wife pregnant!"

ANTONIA (*Searching*). Maybe . . . he hasn't said anything . . . because he doesn't know yet. (*Giovanni looks at her dumbfounded. She continues unperturbed*) And if he doesn't know, how could he tell you?

GIOVANNI. What do you mean he doesn't know?

ANTONIA. Eh, yes. It's obvious. She doesn't want to tell him.

GIOVANNI. What do you mean she doesn't want to tell him?

ANTONIA. Eh, yes, because she . . . that girl . . . is very shy. And he, Luigi . . . is always saying it's too soon, it's not the right time, they have to get organized first . . . and if she gets pregnant the company where she works will fire her. He's so worried about it that he makes her take the pill.

GIOVANNI. And if he makes her take the pill, how come she's pregnant?

ANTONIA. Well, obviously, it had no effect. It happens, you know!

GIOVANNI. And if it happens, then why does she have to hide it from her husband. It's not her fault, is it?

ANTONIA. Well, maybe the pill had no effect, because of the fact . . . that she didn't take it . . . if you don't take the pill . . . (*Doesn't know what to say*) . . . it can happen that the pill . . . has no effect.

GIOVANNI. But what are you saying?!

ANTONIA. Eh . . . yes . . . she's very Catholic. And since the pope has declared the pill to be a mortal sin . . .

GIOVANNI. You're crazy! The pope! Her with a nine-month belly and her husband hasn't noticed?

ANTONIA (*Getting in deeper difficulty*). Maybe Luigi hasn't noticed . . . because Margherita . . . binds herself up!

GIOVANNI. Binds herself up!?

ANTONIA. Yes, yes. She ties it all in tight . . . very tight . . . so no one can see! It got to the point where today I just had to say, "You're crazy. Do you want to lose the baby? Unbind yourself immediately, and who cares if they fire you! The baby's more important!" Was I right?

GIOVANNI. Of course you were right. You were right, yes!

ANTONIA. Did I do the right thing?

GIOVANNI. Yes, yes . . . the right thing.

ANTONIA. And so she . . . Margherita . . . decided to unbind herself and: ploff!!! A big belly!! You should have seen it, Giovanni!

GIOVANNI. I saw it!

ANTONIA. And I also said, "If your husband gives you any trouble, tell him to come to my house, and my Giovanni will teach him a thing or two." Was I right?

GIOVANNI. Of course you were right?

ANTONIA. Did I do the right thing?

GIOVANNI. Yes, yes . . .

ANTONIA. Listen to you: "Yes, yes . . ." Is that any way to answer? Are you holding something against me? Tell me, what have I done now? (*Takes a broom and starts sweeping the house*)

GIOVANNI. No, I'm not holding anything against you. If I'm upset it's because of what happened at work today.

ANTONIA. Why, what happened?

GIOVANNI. There's all this tension in the air . . . All this talk about downsizing . . . yesterday the company fired four dead men . . . Yes, four dead men! Died two months ago . . . four welders . . . and they fired them . . . for absenteeism. There's so much mistrust floating around that you can never relax. And then today in the cafeteria some guys . . . five of them, started raising hell about the food: "It's disgusting. Pig slop. Right out of the dumpster!"

ANTONIA. When it was really fine cuisine cooked with farm fresh ingredients?

GIOVANNI. No, no . . . it was absolutely disgusting . . . but that's no reason to whip everyone up into a mass frenzy.

ANTONIA. A mass frenzy? You said there were only five of them.

GIOVANNI. At first! But then everyone got into it . . . they all ate and left without paying!

ANTONIA. Them, too?

GIOVANNI. What do you mean, "Them, too?"

ANTONIA. I mean, not only those five, but all the others, too . . .

GIOVANNI. Yes, everybody got into the act.

ANTONIA (*Feigning indignation*). How shocking!

GIOVANNI. But that's not all: I passed by a bunch of women at the supermarket, the one near work . . . and they were all shouting . . . maybe three hundred of them . . . loaded down with bags of stuff. So I asked what was going on . . . and they told me that they had only paid what they decided they wanted to pay!

ANTONIA (*Still more indignant*). Oh, what a thing to do!

GIOVANNI. And what's worse, they stormed the checkout counter, and most of them left without paying anything at all.

ANTONIA. Them, too?!

GIOVANNI. What do you mean, "Them, too?!"

ANTONIA. Eh, I mean . . . like those bums from your factory who didn't pay for their lunches.

GIOVANNI. Eh, yes, them, too!

ANTONIA. Oh, what a thing to do! Look at me, I'm standing here in shock.

GIOVANNI. I don't know what kind of husbands those women have, but if my wife ever did anything like that I'd make her eat every tin can she stole . . . and the can opener too! And I hope you don't get it into your head to pull a stunt like that, because if I find out you've been ripping off supermarkets, or even paying one penny less than what is marked on those little stickers, I'll . . . I'll . . .

ANTONIA. I know . . . you'll make me eat every tin can I stole and the can opener too.

GIOVANNI. No, worse! . . . I'd pack my bags and you'd never see me again. And what's more, I'd murder you first, and divorce you later!

ANTONIA (*Furious*). Listen, with that attitude you can leave now . . . without a divorce. How dare you even insinuate that I . . .? Look, before I'd bring home anything that was not bought at a legal price, I'd . . . I'd . . . I'd let you starve to death!

GIOVANNI. That's more like it. And speaking of starving, what's for dinner? (*Sits at the table*)

ANTONIA. This! (*Angrily, she throws on the table a can of meat for cats and dogs*)

GIOVANNI. What's this?

ANTONIA. Can't you read? It's meat compost[1] for cats and dogs.

GIOVANNI. Meat compost for cats and dogs?

ANTONIA. It's delicious!

GIOVANNI. Delicious for dogs maybe!

ANTONIA. That's all I could afford. Besides, it's cheap, and nutritious . . . and full of protein . . . estrogen-free . . . so it won't make you fat! It's exquisite! Look, it says so right here!

GIOVANNI. Are you kidding?

ANTONIA. Who's kidding? You don't know what it's like to go grocery shopping without any money.

GIOVANNI. Come on, I'm not a dog. You eat it!

ANTONIA. Oh, yes. I'll eat it, yes! (*Starts barking*)

GIOVANNI. Isn't there anything else?

ANTONIA. Yes, I can make you a little soup.

GIOVANNI. What kind?

ANTONIA (*Pulling out the package from the shelf*). Bird seed for canaries.

GIOVANNI. Bird seed!

ANTONIA. Yes, it's delicious . . . and you know it helps fight diabetes!

GIOVANNI. But I don't have diabetes!

ANTONIA. Well, it's not my fault you don't have it yet . . . and besides, it's half the price of rice.

GIOVANNI. Listen, you've got to make up your mind. Am I a dog or a canary?

ANTONIA. Oh, don't be silly . . . Angela next door makes it every morning for her husband . . . and he loves it . . .

GIOVANNI. Yeah, I noticed he's been growing a few feathers lately! And this morning when we were waiting for the bus his foot started going like this. (*Makes chicken movement*) Then his neck went like this. (*Mimes chicken walk*) And when the bus came he . . . (*Imitates rooster*) "Cockadoodledoo" (*Mimes a rooster flapping wings*) "I think I'll be getting to work on my own today."

ANTONIA. Stop joking around. This bird seed is a blessing! The secret is in the broth . . . see, I also got some frozen rabbit heads. (*Puts the package with the rabbit heads under his nose*)

[1] *compost:* by products

GIOVANNI. Rabbit heads?

ANTONIA. Sure! Bird seed soup is always made with rabbit! Only the heads, though . . . frozen.

GIOVANNI (*Puts on his jacket and goes toward the door*). Okay, okay . . . I get it . . . see you later!

ANTONIA. Where are you going?

GIOVANNI. Where do you want me to go? I'm going out for dinner.

ANTONIA. And what are you going to do for money?

GIOVANNI. Right, give me some money.

ANTONIA. From where?

GIOVANNI. What do you mean, from where? Don't tell me there's none left . . .

ANTONIA. No, but maybe you forgot that tomorrow we have to pay the gas, electricity and rent. Or do you want them to evict us, and cut off the gas and lights.

GIOVANNI. Dammit! We'll starve to death, but at least we'll be illuminated.

(*Antonia puts on her coat*)

Where are you going?

ANTONIA. To Margherita's. She did a lot of shopping today, and I'm going to borrow a few things. I'll be right back.

GIOVANNI. Don't come back with any rabbit heads.

ANTONIA. No, I'll just bring the feet. (*She leaves*)

GIOVANNI. Yeah, very funny . . . while I'm here hungry as a . . . I could even eat a . . . (*Takes a can in his hand, turning it as he reads the label*) "A gourmet treat for your dogs and cats! Homogenized, tasty . . ." Well, maybe I'll just see what it smells like. How do you open it? Look at that. Typical. They forget to give you the key. Oh, look, it's self-opening. For dogs and cats who are self-starters. (*Opens the can and sniffs it*) Ah, doesn't smell too bad . . . kind of like ground kidney with pickled marmalade and a dash of cod-liver oil. (*Puts the can next to his ear and laughs*) You can hear the ocean! (*Laughs in disgust; changes tone*) Who knows, maybe I'll try just a taste! (*From outside there are the sounds of police sirens, shouting crowds and military orders*) What's going on out there? (*Goes to an imaginary window in the middle of the proscenium and makes signs to a neighbor across the street*) Aldo! Hey, Aldo! What's happening? Yes, I can see it's the police . . . but what do they want? Oh, stolen merchandise! From where? What, the supermarket? Which supermarket? Oh, . . . here too? The one in the neighborhood? But when did it happen? Today? Who did it? What do you mean, everyone? Stop exaggerating! A thousand women! No, my wife wasn't there, I'm sure. She's so set against that kind of stuff that she'd rather eat frozen rabbit heads! No, just the heads . . . you throw the rest away. They're delicious. You crack them in half with a few drops of lemon and . . . (*Mimes eating one*) . . . like an oyster! No, no. No way . . . My wife didn't even leave the house today. She had to unbind her best friend's belly. No, no, it doesn't hurt . . . she just took off the wrapping that she tied herself up with so her husband, Luigi, wouldn't know she was pregnant . . . because he was making her take the pill . . . but she had orders from the pope, so the pill had no effect, and it only took a week for her belly to blow up like a beach ball . . . what!! What do you mean, you don't understand? (*Looks down on the street, hears the shouts and orders*) What's that? A house to house search? Well if they try to come in here, I'll teach them a thing or two! Because that's an out and out provocation!

(*There's a knock at the door.*)

VOICE FROM OUTSIDE. Can I come in?

GIOVANNI. Who is it?

VOICE FROM OUTSIDE. Open up. Police!

GIOVANNI (*Opening the door*). Police? What do you want?

(*A Police Sergeant enters. A local cop on the beat.*)

SERGEANT. This is a search. Here's the warrant. We're searching the whole building.

GIOVANNI. For what?

SERGEANT. There was an assault on the supermarket today. A thousand women, and men too, removed a large quantity of merchandise at reduced prices . . . and some of them didn't pay anything at all. We're looking for the stolen goods or, if you prefer, the merchandise acquired at deep discount.

GIOVANNI. So you come looking for it at my house. That's like calling me a thief, a looter, a hooligan!

SERGEANT. Listen. This is not my choice. I get my orders and I have to carry them out.

GIOVANNI. Just following orders, eh . . . but I'm warning you . . . this is a provocation . . . You come here insulting people dying of hunger . . . Look at what we're reduced to eating: homogenized meat compost for cats and dogs! (*Thrusts the can toward the officer*)

SERGEANT. What?!

GIOVANNI. Yeah! We can't afford decent food . . . We've got to be creative. Use our heads . . . rabbit heads! (*Puts the bag of frozen rabbit heads under the officer's nose*)

SERGEANT. You really eat this stuff?

GIOVANNI. It's not bad, you know! Do you want to try some? No kidding . . . a few drops of lemon and it goes down like cat shit! Taste it. It's good for the nerves.

SERGEANT. No thanks . . . I never vomit before dinner.

GIOVANNI. I understand . . . Maybe you'd prefer me to fix you a nice soup made from bird seed for canaries?

SERGEANT. Bird seed?

GIOVANNI. Yeah! Look it's right here: costs only ten cents a pound . . . eat a little bit . . . and before you know it . . . a few feathers . . . and then . . . then your wings start to flutter . . . (*Imitates a rooster*) and you become a chicken. Or maybe you'd prefer another barnyard animal. A pig perhaps. (*He snorts*) After all you are a cop. (*Snorts again*)

SERGEANT. I can see you've been reduced to hard times here. And to tell you the truth, on a policeman's salary, my family's not doing much better. My wife has to perform miracles in the kitchen too! Listen, I understand what you're going through . . . and, I shouldn't say this, but I understand why the neighborhood women had to do what they did today. Personally I sympathize with them completely: the only defense against thieves is confiscation.

GIOVANNI (*Astonished, looks at the officer incredulously*). You mean, you mean . . . you think they were right.

SERGEANT. Sure they were . . . they couldn't put up with all this for much longer. You might not believe me, but sometimes it disgusts me to be a policeman . . . to have to rob people of their dignity. And for who . . . for the politicians and slumlords who steal them blind and leave them homeless and hungry . . . Those bastards are the real thieves. (*Takes off his hat*)

GIOVANNI. Are you really a cop?

SERGEANT. Yes, I'm a cop.

GIOVANNI. You've got some pretty strange ideas for a policeman.

SERGEANT. I'm just a guy who thinks things out, and gets pissed off about them! You've got to stop looking at us policemen as a bunch of idiots who salivate when we hear a whistle and follow orders—jump, bark, bite—like a bunch of guard dogs! As if we didn't have minds of our own.

GIOVANNI. If that's how you feel, may I ask why you chose to join the police force?

SERGEANT. Did you choose to eat that dog food or those rabbit heads?

GIOVANNI. No! It was my nutritionist's idea. (*Becomes serious*) No, of course not.

SERGEANT. See. I didn't make this choice on my own either. It was sign up or die hungry. And *inter nos*, I've got a college degree, dear sir.

GIOVANNI. Oh, college? Is that where you learned to say *"inter nos"*?

MALE VOICE (*From outside*). Sergeant . . . we've finished out here . . . what should we do . . . keep looking?

SERGEANT (*Toward the door, to the man outside*). Don't stand around busting my balls . . . . Search the other goddamn floors you scumbag. (*Continues his discussion with Giovanni*) Anyway, I was saying that I've got a degree. My father tightened his belt for years so I could go to college . . . and in the end what did it get me? Nothing: I had no choice . . . dear sir! "Join the police force and see the world." I've seen the world. It's a world of bastards, thieves and con men!

GIOVANNI. But not all policemen think like you. Some of them like being police.

SERGEANT. Sure, some guys buy into it. They get off on giving orders. They need to oppress somebody else to feel good about themselves.

GIOVANNI. This is amazing! Excuse me, but are you really a cop? Because now I feel it's my turn to defend the police. We need police, don't we? Without them, we'd have chaos . . . someone has to lay down the law!

SERGEANT. And what if the law is wrong? What if it's just a cover-up for robbery?

GIOVANNI. Well, uh, then there's the political parties . . . the democratic system . . . laws can be reformed.

SERGEANT. But who's going to do the reforming? Where are the reforms? What is reform! Lies, that's what reforms are! They've been promising us reforms for umpteen years, but has that gotten us better health care, or less homeless people on the streets. Believe me, the only real reform will come when people start thinking for themselves and reforming things on their own. Because until the day that people have faith in each other, with trust, patience, a sense of responsibility, and self-discipline . . . and move on . . . nothing is going to change! And now, if you'll excuse me, I have to do my job. (*Puts his hat on and goes toward the door*)

GIOVANNI (*Snickering*). I was waiting for that. The utopian subversive puts his hat back on and turns into a policeman again.

SERGEANT. You're right. I'm all words . . . I vent and I'm gone.

GIOVANNI. Without even conducting a little search? Come on! You're insulting me! Do a little snooping just to humor me . . . anywhere, under the bed, in the cupboard . . .

SERGEANT. Thanks, but I'll pass. Good-bye and good eating! (*He leaves*)

GIOVANNI. That guy was an undercover agent. He was trying to trick me into talking, and if I had agreed with him he'd be: "Stop right there! You're under arrest."

(Antonia comes in out of breath.)

ANTONIA. Have they been here too?

GIOVANNI. Who?

ANTONIA. They're searching the neighborhood, house to house.

GIOVANNI. Yes, I know.

ANTONIA. They've already arrested the Mambettis and the Fossanis . . . they've found groceries in lots of houses, and confiscated everything!

GIOVANNI. It serves them right. That's what they get for breaking the law.

ANTONIA. But they've also taken away things people paid for legitimately.

GIOVANNI. Of course, it always happens that way. When looters go wild, people who have nothing to do with it always end up suffering. For example when they came here—

ANTONIA. They came here?

GIOVANNI. Of course.

ANTONIA. And what did they find?

GIOVANNI (*Surprised*). Why, what should they find?

ANTONIA (*Trying to divert him, changes tone*). Nothing. No, I was just saying . . . you never know . . . sometimes you're convinced that you don't have anything in the house, and then out of nowhere . . .

GIOVANNI. And then out of nowhere?

ANTONIA. And then out of nowhere the police plant stuff in your house . . . to trap you! It wouldn't be the first time . . .

GIOVANNI. You mean you think they'd actually put bags of pasta and sugar under the bed? I'd better take a look.

ANTONIA (*Grabs him from behind, stopping him with a violent jerk*). No!

GIOVANNI. What are you doing? Are you crazy? You displaced a vertebra!

ANTONIA. I forbid you to touch my bedcover! I just washed it . . . I'll give a look myself . . . meanwhile, you go and let in Margherita.

GIOVANNI. Margherita? Where is she?

ANTONIA. She's there, behind the door. (*Pretends to look under the bed*) No, there's nothing's there.

GIOVANNI (*Goes to the door*). Are you losing your mind, letting a poor pregnant woman stand out in the hall? Oh, my God, Margherita, what are you doing there. Come inside, come in. (*Margherita enters trying to stop herself from laughing*) What's wrong. Why are you crying?

ANTONIA (*Goes to Margherita and sits her down on the bed*). Come here, Margherita . . . (*To her husband*) Oh, the poor girl was home all alone . . . and with all those police sniffing around, she was terrified! Can you believe that one of the officers wanted to squeeze her belly?

GIOVANNI. What for?

ANTONIA. Because he got it in his head that instead of a baby, she had bags of pasta and fine herbs in there.

GIOVANNI. The son of a bitch!

ANTONIA. Yeah, you said it . . . And so I told her to come over here to our house. Did I do the right thing?

GIOVANNI. Of course you did the right thing! (*Approaches Margherita and tries to help her take off her coat*) Stay here and relax, Margherita . . . take off your coat . . .

MARGHERITA (*Frightened*). No!

GIOVANNI. Make yourself comfortable . . .
MARGHERITA. No!

(Antonia intercepts Giovanni and grabs him by the shoulder.)

GIOVANNI (*Lets out a scream, then turns toward Antonia, furiously*). If you keep smacking around my vertebra every five minutes, I'm going to go into the wardrobe and never come out again.
ANTONIA. She told you she'd rather keep her coat on! She's cold!
GIOVANNI. But it's hot in here!
ANTONIA. It's hot for you, but pregnant women are always cold! Maybe she's got a fever!
GIOVANNI. A fever! Is she sick!
ANTONIA. She's in labor!
GIOVANNI. Already?
ANTONIA. What do you mean, "Already?" What do you know about it? A half hour ago you didn't even know she was pregnant and now you're amazed that she's in labor!
GIOVANNI. Well, it seems to me, you might say . . . maybe it's a little premature!
ANTONIA. You think you know better than her?
GIOVANNI. But if she's in labor, maybe we should call the doctor, or an ambulance.

(Antonia goes to the cupboard and takes out two pillows. She places them on the bed so that Margherita can lie down comfortably.)

ANTONIA. Oh sure, an ambulance. There's not a chance in hell we'd find a vacant bed! You have no idea what it's like in those hospitals. You have to make reservations a month in advance!
GIOVANNI. So why didn't she reserve a place?
ANTONIA. That's right, we run the errands, we make the babies, and you want us to make the reservations too! And why didn't her husband do it?
GIOVANNI. But her husband didn't know about it. How could he think of it?
ANTONIA. Very convenient! Just give us the paychecks and then it's, "Pay the bills!" You make us pregnant and then, "Take care of it yourself! Take the pill." And who cares if the poor wife, who's a strict Catholic, dreams all night of the pope saying, "It's a sin, you must procreate!"
GIOVANNI. Apart from the pope . . . how long has Margherita been pregnant?
ANTONIA. What do you care?
GIOVANNI. No, I was just saying . . . because she hasn't even been married five months yet . . .
ANTONIA. So what? Isn't it possible that they might have made love before they got married . . . or are you turning moralistic on us . . . you're worse than the pope!
GIOVANNI. Luigi told me that they only made love after they were married.
MARGHERITA. My Luigi talks to you about those things?!!
GIOVANNI (*Embarrassed*). We were playing pool . . .
ANTONIA. Jesus, Mary and Joseph!!! What a bum! Margherita, that's grounds for divorce!
GIOVANNI. Let's not get carried away . . .
ANTONIA. What do you mean? Going around talking about private, personal moments . . . to just anyone out on the street.

GIOVANNI (*Insulted*). I'm not "just anyone out on the street." I'm his friend! His best friend! He tells me everything. He asks my advice . . . because I'm older, and I've got more experience!

ANTONIA (*Shoots him a look full of irony*). Oh, oh, he's got more experience! (*Giovanni is about to respond, but there is a knock at the door*) Who's there?

VOICE FROM OUTSIDE. Police. Open up!

GIOVANNI: Again?

MARGHERITA: Oh, God!

(*Giovanni opens the door. The same actor who played the Police Sergeant is now wearing the uniform of a State Trooper and has a mustache. Two other troopers enter behind him.*)

GIOVANNI. Well, hello . . . you again?

TROOPER. What do you mean, "you again?"

GIOVANNI. Sorry, I thought you were the one from before.

TROOPER. Which one from before?

GIOVANNI. The police sergeant.

TROOPER. But I'm a state trooper.

GIOVANNI. I see. And you've got a mustache too. So you must be someone else. What can I do for you?

TROOPER. We have to conduct a search.

GIOVANNI. Your colleague from the police force just did that a little while ago.

TROOPER. That doesn't matter. We'll do it again ourselves.

GIOVANNI. So you don't trust them . . . You've come to make sure they haven't botched things up! Then I guess the National Guard will come to check up on you. Next it'll be the CIA . . . and then frogmen from the Marines will show up in our bathtub . . . (*Mimes a grotesque frogman*)

TROOPER (*Angry*). Listen, cut the comedy. Just show us around and let us do our job.

ANTONIA (*Bursts out*). Sure, your job is to make sure we comply with orders. (*Troopers open the wardrobe and cupboards*) Why don't you ever check to make sure that management is honoring our contracts, that the air in our workplaces is breathable, that they're not downsizing our jobs so that they can exploit child workers in third world countries, that they're not evicting us from our homes, and starving us to death! (*Giovanni tries to calm his wife*)

GIOVANNI. No, no. You shouldn't talk like that, because they're disgusted by all those things themselves. Isn't that true, officer, that you're fed up with robbing people in the name of authority. Tell my wife how you police officers are sick and tired of salivating when the whistle blows: "Follow orders! Jump. Bark! Bite like a bunch of guard dogs . . ." (*Howls like a guard dog on a chain*)

TROOPER. Could you say that again, please? (*Giovanni barks*) No, the part about the guard dogs?

GIOVANNI. Yes, I was just saying that you're just bought and sold by the politicians to help them get reelected!

TROOPER. Is that right?

GIOVANNI. Yes, I was just . . .

TROOPER (*Turns to the two Troopers*). Cuff him!

(*The two Troopers move to put handcuffs on Giovanni.*)

GIOVANNI. Handcuffs? Excuse me, but why?

TROOPER. For insulting a public official.

GIOVANNI. What insult? I'm just saying what your colleague, the police sergeant, told me a few minutes ago . . . he's the one who told me that you feel like servants of the politicians, slaves of the system.

TROOPER. Who's "you"? . . . us state troopers?

GIOVANNI. No, he was talking about them . . . the city cops on the street.

TROOPER. Oh, the city cops. (*Laughs derisively at the insult to city cops*) Okay, take off the handcuffs. But watch what you say about us state troopers.

GIOVANNI. Okay, okay, I'm watching, I'm watching.

(*The Troopers continue their search. One of them begins searching near the bed.*)

ANTONIA (*To Margherita*). Moan, go on, cry!

MARGHERITA. Aihoooaooo!

ANTONIA. Louder.

MARGHERITA (*Agonizing cries*). Ahiouua! Ahiaaooioo!

TROOPER. What is it? What's wrong with her?

ANTONIA. Pain, a lot of pain . . . she's in labor.

GIOVANNI. She's five months premature!

ANTONIA. She was traumatized a little while ago . . . the police tried to squeeze her belly . . .

TROOPER. Squeeze her belly?

GIOVANNI. Yeah, to see if, maybe, instead of a baby, she had rice or pasta in there. Go on, why don't you help yourselves while you're here: squeeze her to make sure! Go ahead, squeeze away!

(*Margherita continues screaming hysterically.*)

TROOPER. Have you called an ambulance?

ANTONIA. An ambulance? Why?

TROOPER. Do you want her to die right here? Besides, if she's premature like you say, she might lose the baby.

GIOVANNI. He's right! I told you we should have called an ambulance.

ANTONIA. And I told you already that without a reservation, the hospital won't admit her. They'll send her driving around to every hospital in town. She'll die in the car!

(*From outside there is the sound of a siren.*)

TROOPER (*Looking out the window*). Look, it's the ambulance that we called for the sick woman downstairs. (*Turns to the two Troopers*) Come on, give me a hand. We can take her too.

ANTONIA (*Stopping them*). No, for God's sake . . . don't disturb her.

MARGHERITA (*Crying in fear*). No, I don't want to go to the hospital.

ANTONIA. See, she doesn't want to go.

MARGHERITA. I want my husband, my husband . . . Ahio! Ahiuaaoo!

ANTONIA. Hear that? She wants her husband . . . and he's not around because he works the night shift. I'm sorry, but without her husband's consent, we can't take this responsibility.

GIOVANNI. Eh, no, we can't take it.

TROOPER. Oh, you can't take it, can you. You'd rather take responsibility for having her die right here?

ANTONIA. What difference does it make?

TROOPER. In the hospital they might be able to save her, and maybe the baby too!

GIOVANNI. But it's premature. I already told you!

ANTONIA. Yes, it's premature! And with all those potholes in the road, the baby will pop out right in the car. How could a five-month baby survive that?

TROOPER. Obviously, you have no idea of the progress that modern medicine has made in our times. Haven't you ever heard about test-tube babies?

ANTONIA. Yes, I've heard about them, but what's this got to do with test tubes? The baby's five months old. You can't stuff it in a test tube . . . you can't even put it in an oxygen tent.

GIOVANNI. Of course not, such a little baby under a tent . . . what's he going to do, go camping?

TROOPER. You people are completely ignorant! Haven't you ever seen the hospital equipment they're using these days . . . at the gynecological centers? I worked a shift there five months ago, and I actually saw the doctors perform a transplant.

GIOVANNI AND ANTONIA. What kind of transplant?

TROOPER. A premature baby transplant. They took a four-and-a-half-month-old fetus from a woman who couldn't hold it any longer and put it in the belly of another woman.

GIOVANNI. In her belly?!

TROOPER. Yes, a cesarean. They put it in there with the placenta and everything . . . and four months later . . . just last month, it was born again, healthy as a fish!

GIOVANNI (*Incredulous*). A fish? . . .

TROOPER. Yes!

GIOVANNI. I think it was some kind of a trick.

TROOPER. What do you mean trick? I saw it myself. Sure it's hard to believe: a baby that's born twice . . . a baby with two mothers!

MARGHERITA. I don't want to do it. I don't want to do it. I won't give my consent.

ANTONIA. See . . . she won't give her consent . . . so we can't make her go.

TROOPER. I'll give the consent. I'll take responsibility.

ANTONIA. That is complete and utter arrogance! You come into our home, you search everywhere, put us in handcuffs . . . and now you want to drag us into an ambulance! We know you won't leave us alone to live our lives, but at least you can let us die in peace wherever we want to.

TROOPER. No, you can't die in peace wherever you want to.

GIOVANNI. Of course not, we have to die according to the law! (*Goes toward the wardrobe*)

TROOPER. And you, enough with the jokes. I already told you once . . . Where's he going?

GIOVANNI (*Opens the wardrobe door, enters, and sticks his head out*). I'll be in my office . . .

ANTONIA. Come out. Stop it! Now's not the time. Come on, let's bring her downstairs.

TROOPER. Should we get a stretcher?

ANTONIA. No, she'll go down on her own . . . You can walk, can't you?

MARGHERITA. Yes, yes . . . (*She gets up. She suddenly puts her hands on her belly to arrange the stolen goods*) Oh, no, no, it's slipping out! . . .

ANTONIA. Dammit! Could you please step outside a moment . . .

TROOPER. Why?

ANTONIA. It's a woman's thing! (*The men leave. To Margherita, angrily*) Idiot! (*Imitates her*) "It's slipping out! . . ." (*Changes tone*) This trooper's going to hang us!

MARGHERITA. If it's slipping out, it's slipping out!

ANTONIA. Oh, shut up! And another thing, is that any way to walk? Haven't you ever seen the way pregnant women walk? Do they walk like this? (*Grotesquely imitates Margherita*) Who are you kidding! When a pregnant woman walks . . . think of the Virgin Mary! (*Advances majestically*)

MARGHERITA. I knew it would end up like this! What's going to happen at the hospital when they realize I'm pregnant with rice and tin cans?

ANTONIA. Nothing's going to happen, because we're never going to get to the hospital.

MARGHERITA. Sure, because they're going to arrest us first.

ANTONIA. Stop whining! As soon as we get into the ambulance, we'll tell the driver where things stand . . . I'm sure he'll help us.

MARGHERITA. What if he turns us in instead?

ANTONIA. Stop it, he's not going to turn us in! And pull up your belly! (*She helps her*)

MARGHERITA. Another bag's slipping out. I'm falling apart!

ANTONIA. Hold onto it! Oh what a mess!

MARGHERITA. No, don't press there . . . Oh, my God, you ripped the packet of olives in pickle juice. Ahhhhhh!!!!

(*Giovanni and the Troopers return, alarmed by her shouting.*)

GIOVANNI. Now what happened?

MARGHERITA. It's coming out! It's all coming out!

GIOVANNI. The baby's coming out! The baby's coming out! Quick, officers, help me grab her arms!

(*They follow his lead.*)

TROOPER (*Supporting Margherita's back with his arm*). She's all wet! What is it?

ANTONIA. She's breaking her water!

GIOVANNI. Ohhh! Look at that water! . . . (*Mimes being in a swamp*) Quick, or she'll have the baby right here!

MARGHERITA. It's coming out! It's coming out!

(*Margherita is carried offstage. Giovanni returns immediately.*)

GIOVANNI. Wait for me. I'll get my jacket and be right there.

ANTONIA. Where are you going?

GIOVANNI. To see the premature baby get born . . .

ANTONIA. No, you stay home! This is a woman's thing. I'll go! (*Puts on her coat*) Get a rag and clean all that water off the floor. (*She leaves*)

GIOVANNI. I see, okay . . . I'll get a rag and start cleaning . . . because that's a man's thing! (*Grabs a rag and leans against the window*) What a mess! Who knows how Luigi will take it when he comes home tomorrow and all of a sudden finds out he's a father . . . he'll have a stroke! And then what if he finds his kid transplanted into the belly of another woman . . . he'll have a double stroke . . . and drop dead on the spot! I've got to talk to him first. Prepare him for it, little by little . . . give him the big picture . . . yeah, that's it . . . I'll start with the pope . . . (*Down on his hands and *knees wiping up the floor*) Ohhh! All that water! But what a funny odor . . . it smells like vinegar . . . (*Sniffs the rag*) It's pickle juice. (*Taken aback*) Pickle juice? I never knew! Before we're born, we spend nine months floating in pickle juice? (*Continues to wash the pavement*) Oh, look at that . . . what's that? An olive? We float in pickle juice with olives? Oh, that's how it . . . No! No! Olives have nothing to do with it. (*Hears another siren and gets up to go to the window*) Well, they're on their way. I hope it all turns out okay. But where did this olive come from? Oh, look, another one! Two olives? If I wasn't so unsure about where they came from I'd eat 'em . . . I'm starving! (*Puts the two olives on a plate on the table*) Maybe I'll try cooking up a little of that bird seed soup. At least it's organic. The water's already boiling. I'll put in a bouillon cube, some onion . . . (*Opens the refrigerator*) Look at that. I knew it . . . there's no bouillon . . . not even an onion . . . All I've got to put in is this rabbit head! Goddammit! (*Without thinking he leans against the welding canister*) How many times do I have to tell that dopey Antonia that this is a welding gun, not a lighter for the gas stove. It's dangerous! One day it'll blow up the house!

(*Luigi, Margherita's husband, opens the door.*)

LUIGI. Can I come in? Anybody home?

GIOVANNI. Oh, Luigi! But what are you doing here at this hour? You don't get off work until tomorrow morning.

LUIGI. Something happened. I'll explain later . . . but what I want to know is, where's my wife? I went home and the doors were open, but nobody was there.

GIOVANNI. Oh yeah, your wife was just here a few minutes ago. She went out with Antonia.

LUIGI. Where'd she go? What for?

GIOVANNI. Well, you know, it's a woman's thing.

LUIGI. And what would that be, that woman's thing.

GIOVANNI. It would be a thing that we wouldn't be interested in. We should only be interested in men's things.

LUIGI. What do you mean I shouldn't be interested? I'm very interested!

GIOVANNI. Ah, now you're interested, are you? And how come you weren't interested last month when you were supposed to reserve a bed like everyone else does?

LUIGI. A bed? For what?

GIOVANNI. Oh sure, that's woman's work, huh? It's the same old story! We give them our paychecks, and then we say, "Pay the bills." We make love to 'em and say, "Take the pill." We make them pregnant and it's, "You take care of it." They're the ones who nurse the babies.

LUIGI. What are you saying?

GIOVANNI. I'm saying that they're right. We're just a bunch of good-for-nothing loafers.

LUIGI. But what does all this have to do with the fact that my Margherita went off with the doors open and didn't even leave me a note, just disappeared like . . .

GIOVANNI. And why should she leave you a note? Weren't you supposed to be working the night shift? Which reminds me, how come you're home so early?

LUIGI. Work stoppage.

GIOVANNI. What do you mean?

LUIGI. We were protesting because they wanted to raise the price of our commuter passes thirty percent!

GIOVANNI. Christ! With all the tension there already, why would you want to screw things up even more?

LUIGI. Sure, sure, I agree it was a screwed-up thing to do. I even told the other guys, "Guys! It's useless trying to get them to bring down the price of our commuter passes."

GIOVANNI. Good for you!

LUIGI. "We should get our commuter passes for free!"

GIOVANNI. Are you out of your mind? We shouldn't pay anything?

LUIGI. Sure, the company should pay for our commute. And they should also pay us for the time we're on the train. Because we lose those hours, and believe you me, it ain't no vacation . . .

GIOVANNI. Who put this stuff in your head? Have you been talking to that police sergeant without the mustache who looks like the state trooper with the mustache?

LUIGI (*Tastes the contents of the open can*). Hey, this pâté is great . . . what kind is it?

GIOVANNI. Did you eat the stuff in that can?

LUIGI. Yeah, it's not bad. Sorry, I was hungry.

GIOVANNI. Without any lemon?

LUIGI. Why? Are you supposed to eat it with lemon?

GIOVANNI. Uh . . . I don't know . . . but are you sure it tastes all right?

LUIGI. Yeah, it's delicious.

GIOVANNI. Let me taste. Oh, that's not bad! Go open that other can on the sink.

(*They feast on the pet food at the table, making appreciative sounds of satisfaction.*)

LUIGI. Hey, what is this stuff?

GIOVANNI. It's a kind of pâté . . . for rich cats and dogs.

LUIGI. Pâté for cats and dogs? Come on, are you crazy?

GIOVANNI. No, I'm a gourmet! And while you're at it, taste this. (*Pours him some of the soup*) Taste it. Taste it!

LUIGI. Hey, this isn't bad! What's in it?

GIOVANNI. It's one of my specialties: bird seed soup . . . with broth from frozen rabbit heads!

(*Shocked, Luigi spits soup in Giovanni's face.*)

LUIGI. Bird seed soup with rabbit heads?

GIOVANNI. Yeah, it's a Chinese delicacy. Over there they call it "consommé du Won Ton Dim Sum Hang Yan Lo." When Nixon went to China, he was nuts about it. "I'll never go back to America. I'm gonna stay here and eat this soup forever." It's in the tapes.

LUIGI. But the bird seed's a little crunchy . . .

GIOVANNI. That's because it's bird seed pilaf . . . you've got to serve it *al dente.* The bird seed is always *al dente* and the rabbit heads are medium rare . . . (*Alarmed*) Did you eat those olives?

LUIGI. Yeah. Why. Shouldn't I have?

GIOVANNI (*Almost hysterical*). Eh, no, no, you shouldn't have! They were your wife's olives, you boob! You'd even stoop to eating fetus!

LUIGI. My wife's olives ... fetus? ...

GIOVANNI. Yeah. Don't you know that when a baby's born ... the woman loses her pickle juice? First there's the slipping part ... well, we'll leave that out for now ... then there's the problem of the pill that has no effect ... and that's because the pope never stays put ... he's always running all over the place ... he doesn't even know what day it is anymore ... night ... day ... now he's in Africa ... then he's in Brazil ... next stop India ... kisses the ground ... then a little dip in the papal pool, filled with holy water! Some skiing! Always the steep slopes ... SCVUM! SCVUM! And that's without the ski poles ... so his arms are free to bless people on the way down. (*Mimes ski-borne benedictions*) Dominus Pacem. Dominus Pacem. Dominus Pacem. (*Mimes high-speed blessings*)

LUIGI. Giovanni, what kind of talk is that? The pope ... olives ... fetus?

GIOVANNI. Yeah, you're the voice of reason, aren't you? The company should pay our train fare and give us wages for commuting time. Next you'll want them to pay a bonus to our wives when they make love with us ... because sex regenerates us, and makes us more productive!

LUIGI. That's right. You said it! We need some relief from this life of shit we're forced to live.

GIOVANNI. Well, let's not get carried away. It's not exactly a life of shit, is it ... we're better off than we used to be. We've got a house, maybe a little run-down, but it has what we need ... of course some of us have to work overtime ...

LUIGI. So what if I've got a stove and a refrigerator, if I'm disgusted by my life ... goddammit ... with a job that could be done by a trained monkey (*Mimes the assembly line*) Weld! Hammer! Drill! Weld! Hammer! One piece finished, here comes the next. Weld! (*Mechanically, Giovanni joins the movement without thinking*) Hammer! Faster! Weld ...

GIOVANNI. Hammer, drill, weld ... weld (*Stops himself suddenly*) For God's sake, what have you got me doing. You're making me crazy, too!

LUIGI. No, I'm not the one making you crazy. It's the way we live. Everything's going down the drain ... look at all the factories closing, toxic dumping, ethnic cleansing all over the world. Earthquakes. Hurricanes. The pope.

GIOVANNI. Yeah, scaring all the women in the world to make sure they get pregnant!

LUIGI. What were you saying about the pope getting pregnant? (*Laughs*)

GIOVANNI. No, he's not pregnant. I was talking about your wife.

LUIGI. What's my wife got to do with the pope?

GIOVANNI. Ah, you're pretending you don't know about it?

LUIGI. No. It's just that I don't know! What's this story about the pope?

GIOVANNI. Look, if you spent less time stirring up trouble at work and paid more attention to your wife, you'd know what she was dreaming about at night when the pope comes to her and says, "Don't take the pill for Christ's sake!"

LUIGI. Actually ... Margherita doesn't take the pill.

GIOVANNI. Oh, so you know. Who told you?

LUIGI. Who do you think told me? She doesn't have to take the pill because she can't have babies. She's got a malformation down there in the whatayacallit ...

GIOVANNI. You're the one with the malformation! In your head! Your wife is very healthy, and has no problem with having babies ... in fact she's having one.

LUIGI. Having a baby? When?

GIOVANNI. Now. In fact she could be giving birth this minute: five months premature!

LUIGI. Don't be silly. Five months. She doesn't even have a belly.

GIOVANNI. She doesn't have one because she tied it up . . . and then Antonia untied it and . . . PLAFF . . . a belly big enough to be nine months . . . maybe even eleven!

LUIGI. Come on, are you kidding me?

GIOVANNI. My wife, if you must know, took her in an ambulance to the hospital . . . because she just about gave birth to the kid here on the floor.

LUIGI. Here on the floor?

GIOVANNI. She broke her water here . . . I cleaned it up myself!

LUIGI. You cleaned up her water?

GIOVANNI. Well, it wasn't exactly water . . . pickle juice . . . with a few olives. The ones you just ate.

LUIGI. Listen, stop joking around. Where's my wife?

GIOVANNI. I told you. At the hospital.

LUIGI. Which hospital?

GIOVANNI. Who knows. If you'd have reserved a room a month ago like you're supposed to, we'd know. But no . . . now the baby's going to be born in the car . . . poor kid, in the middle of all those olives!

LUIGI. Come on, stop this nonsense! Tell me what hospital she's in or I'll punch you out.

GIOVANNI. Hey, calm down. I already told you that I don't know . . . No, wait, maybe they went to that Gyne . . . Gyneco . . . that Gynecological Place.

LUIGI. The Gynecological Place?

GIOVANNI. Yeah, the place where they do the premature baby transplants.

LUIGI. The premature baby transplants?

GIOVANNI. Where have you been living? At the Gynecological Place there's a machine with a tent full of oxygen . . . they take the woman with the baby that's premature by four-and-a-half, or even five months . . . then they take another woman to be the second mother . . . they do a cesarean . . . put the baby in the new belly, stuff in the placenta and everything . . . and then four months later . . . (*Pause*) . . . a fish!

LUIGI. Cut it out. I don't give a damn about your transplant machines, and cesareans . . . I want to know where the hell is this Gynecological Place. Get the telephone book and we can look it up.

GIOVANNI. I don't have a phone. What would I do with a phone book: read up on who lives in the neighborhood?

LUIGI. Come on, we can go to the bar downstairs. They've got a phone?

GIOVANNI. I just remembered. It's next to the new mall.

LUIGI. The new mall? Why would they go so far away?

GIOVANNI. I told you! It's the only place where they do the transplants! They'd find another woman. A healthy woman who happens to be near by. (*Stops; he has an idea*) Another woman? (*He screams*) Antonia! (*Luigi screams*) She's going to be right there . . . She'll be the first one they ask . . . and she's crazy enough to do it! She's going to have a transplant, and come home pregnant. Quick! Let's go!

(They exit, running.)

Act Two

Antonia and Margherita return. Margherita still has a big belly; she is sniffling.

ANTONIA (*Calling*). Giovanni. Giovanni! He's not here. He went to work. What time is it? (*Looks at the alarm clock on the shelves*) Five-thirty. Can you believe it? We've been out playing this charade for more than four hours. (*Peeks into the other room*)

MARGHERITA. I should never have listened to you! Look at the mess we're in now!

ANTONIA. You're such a complainer. It all worked out, didn't it? All we had to say to the ambulance team was, "Careful, this girl's not pregnant . . . but she's got a gut full of stolen goods," and they couldn't wait to give us a hand. They wanted to throw a party for us! And you were so worried . . . for nothing . . . you have to have faith in people! Me, I have faith in people! (*Looks into the refrigerator*) Where's the butter. Who stole my butter? Ah, no, there it is. Now I'll make you some soup. Ah, the rice. Give me a packet of rice. (*Margherita pulls a packet of rice out from the bag hidden under her coat. Antonia goes to the stove. She sees the pot*) But what's this stuff? The bird seed? Don't tell me that dopey Giovanni really cooked up a bird seed soup with rabbit heads! All you have to do is feed him a story and he swallows the whole thing. Let's see what I can whip up for you.

MARGHERITA. If you're making the soup just for me, don't bother. I'm not hungry. My stomach's all blocked up.

ANTONIA (*Margherita unpacks her "belly"*). What are you doing?

MARGHERITA. Did you think I was going to carry this stuff around the rest of my life?

ANTONIA. I don't want any stolen goods in my house! Is that clear? And while you're at it, could you help me get rid of the stuff under the bed. I'll make myself a little belly, too.

(*Takes some pillowcases from a drawer*)

MARGHERITA. And where will we put it all?

ANTONIA. We'll carry it out to my father-in-law's little shed behind the railroad tracks. He grows vegetables there. It will be a great hiding place.

MARGHERITA. That's enough, I can't take this anymore . . . I've had it to here with your harebrained schemes. I'm going home.

ANTONIA. You're a loser.

MARGHERITA. Well, if you're so smart, tell me what I say to my husband when he sees me without a belly . . . or a baby?

ANTONIA. Oh, I thought of that already. We'll tell him that you had a hysterical pregnancy.

MARGHERITA. Hysterical?

ANTONIA. Yes, it happens all the time . . . a woman thinks she's pregnant, her belly blows up, and then, when she's ready to give birth, all that comes out is air. Just air!

MARGHERITA. And how would I have gotten this hysterical pregnancy?

ANTONIA. From the pope. He kept coming to you in your dreams and saying, "Make a baby! Make a baby!" So you obeyed him: you made a baby . . . of air. Just the soul of a baby!

MARGHERITA. Now we drag the pope into the story.

ANTONIA. Look at all the times he's dragged us into his stories. (*Margherita has removed her bundles, while Antonia has re-stuffed her coat*) I'll be back in ten minutes . . .

MARGHERITA. But why don't you just get a cart and carry it all over there at once, instead of playing this pregnant mother game?

ANTONIA. Because we'd be caught right away. See those police wagons down there. They're waiting to catch you in the act! (*Brings the welding tanks to the stove*)

MARGHERITA. What are you doing? Won't you ruin it?

ANTONIA. No. It's Giovanni's welding canister. It's made of iron . . . it's special stuff called animonio . . . it can heat up to two thousand degrees without even turning red . . . (*Lights the gas stove with it*)

MARGHERITA (*Standing by the window, peeking out*). Look, it's Maria from the third floor. She's pregnant, too.

ANTONIA. Stealing all my ideas. Before you know it there'll be pregnant dogs walking by . . . pregnant men . . .

MARGHERITA. Listen, I thought it over. I'm coming with you. (*Starts reinserting the bags in her "belly" under her coat*)

ANTONIA. Brava! I knew you'd change your mind. Let's go. Today is the day of the mammas!

(*Scene change. A half-curtain runs the length of the proscenium. Giovanni and Luigi enter as if walking on the street. Luigi pulls out a beret and puts it on his head. Giovanni does the same.*)

LUIGI. Listen. I want to tell you something.

GIOVANNI. What.

LUIGI (*Can't bring himself to say it*). Look, it's raining. Like the saying goes, "When it rains, the government is stealing something."

GIOVANNI. Well, that's just to remind you that when it's sunny, the government is murdering somebody.

LUIGI. Goddammit, do you still have the energy to make jokes and keep laughing?

GIOVANNI. Me, no! But my feet, yes. They're dying for a good laugh! You and your bright idea of checking every hospital in town on foot. I've had enough. I'm going back to the station and get a train to work. I'll already be docked an hour's pay as it is.

(*Two stagehands walk by as the sound effect of a truck plays on the loudspeaker. The stagehands/truck drop several sacks in front of Luigi and Giovanni as they pass by, then exit.*)

Look! Those sacks must have fallen off that . . . truck. They're filled with coffee.

LUIGI. Yeah. Ethiopian. Kenyan. French vanilla. Let's take some home.

GIOVANNI. Are you crazy? Do you want to lower yourself to the level of thieves and looters? I don't take stuff that's not mine. I work for what I have.

LUIGI. Listen. What I was trying to tell you before is . . . starting tomorrow we're all being downsized.

GIOVANNI. Downsized?

LUIGI. Yeah. I heard it on the train. Six thousand out of twenty-six thousand employees are being downsized now. And the rest of the plant closes in the next few months.

GIOVANNI. They're closing the plant?

LUIGI. Not only that. We won't get paid for our last two weeks.

GIOVANNI. Come on. Help me load up this stuff. Let's take it all.

(*As they leave the State Trooper enters.*)

TROOPER. Drop those sacks or I'll shoot.

LUIGI. Look. He's got a gun.

TROOPER. Stop or I'll shoot.

GIOVANNI. Go ahead and shoot.

TROOPER (*Chases them offstage*). Those bastards.

(*Change of scene. The curtain stays down; only the lights change to indicate another street. It's dark. From stage left, Giovanni and Luigi reenter with their sacks.*)

GIOVANNI. You can do it. We're almost there. Wait. There's a police van . . . in front of my house . . .

LUIGI. Look at those two women crossing the street. Aren't they our wives?

GIOVANNI. No, it can't be them.

LUIGI. Sure, they're standing there in front of the building you live in. And one of them's pregnant.

GIOVANNI. No, take a better look . . . they're both pregnant.

LUIGI. Oh, I guess it's not them.

GIOVANNI (*Grabbing his shoulder*). Goddammit, we're trapped. Look across the street. It's the state trooper who was chasing us!

LUIGI. Why not? He knows where you live . . . he'll head straight to your house to find us!

GIOVANNI. So we'll go to your house!

LUIGI. Right. Keep moving. Let's go this way and shake him off. (*They exit through the curtain*)

(*The Trooper crosses the entire stage and exits to the left. He returns again, still looking for Luigi and Giovanni.*)

TROOPER. You can't get away . . . I know where you live! I know the streets! . . . I know how to read too!

(*In the dark the curtain rises and we find ourselves again in the house of Giovanni and Antonia. The two women are entering with big bellies. They are overwhelmed and exhausted.*)

ANTONIA. I want to die . . . I want to die . . .

MARGHERITA. Load, unload, I feel like I'm turning into a truck!

ANTONIA (*Goes to sit on the bed*). I want to die . . . Oh, God, the exhaustion of pregnancy.

MARGHERITA (*Loosens her coat and removes some lettuce leaves and a few cabbages*). Look, look at all the vegetables we have here from your father's farm. There's enough to make salads for a year!

ANTONIA. At this rate we'll never get the stuff out of here . . . With the cops down there we can't go out with big bellies, and come home with no bellies . . . and go out again with big bellies . . . no bellies . . . big bellies . . . no bellies. The soup! (*Runs to the oven*) I forgot about the soup . . . it'll be all burned up! My God, the hunger's gone to my brain . . . (*Lifts pot cover*) That's a relief. It didn't even boil . . . but why? It's been on four hours? The gas! Those bastards cut off the gas! Disgusting creeps, murderers, thieves . . . just because I didn't pay the gas bill. And they cut off the electricity too . . .

MARGHERITA. They cut off the gas?

ANTONIA. Yes. The man was here yesterday to check up on it . . . (*There's a knock at the door*) Who is it?

VOICE (*From outside*). Friends.

ANTONIA. What friends?

VOICE. I'm a friend of your husband's from work. He asked me to come and tell you something.

ANTONIA. Oh, my God! What could it be? (*Goes to open the door*)

MARGHERITA. Wait a second. Let me hide the lettuce. (*Puts it under her coat*)

ANTONIA. Just a moment please . . . I'm not dressed. (*Opens the door and sees the State Trooper*) You again? What kind of joke is this?

TROOPER. Stop right there, where you are! This time I've got you! Look at that. Now you're both pregnant! My how those bellies grow! I knew all along it was a trick!

ANTONIA. What kind of trick are you talking about?

MARGHERITA (*Letting herself flop on the bed in exhaustion*). Now we're in for it. I knew it. I knew it.

TROOPER (*To Margherita*). Glad to see you haven't lost your little bundle of joy. And you, madam . . . congratulations! In five hours you've made love, become a mommy, and arrived at your ninth month!

ANTONIA. Look, officer, you're making a mistake . . .

TROOPER. No, I made a mistake last time . . . when I fell for your little act with the labor pains and premature birth! But I'm not going to fall for it again. Out with the stolen goods!

ANTONIA. But what stolen goods are you talking about?

TROOPER. Let's stop playing games. Your scam's an open book: the husbands go out to commit the robberies, pass the bags to the wives, and all day long I see nothing but pregnant women! Now why is it that all the women in this neighborhood got buns in their ovens at the same time! Mature women, teenagers, little girls . . . Today I even saw an eighty-year-old woman who was pregnant . . . with twins!

ANTONIA. That's because . . . because of the Festival . . . the Festival of the Patron Saint . . . Santa Eulalia.

TROOPER. The Patron Saint?

ANTONIA. You don't know about her? What a saint! The holiest of saints! A good woman . . . who . . . who wanted to have children . . . she was obsessed . . . she wanted to get pregnant . . . but she couldn't do it . . . she just couldn't do it! Poor saint. Hard as she tried, she never succeeded . . . up to the point where the Heavenly Father Above took pity on her and: pscium! She was pregnant! . . . at sixty years old! A miracle!

TROOPER. Sixty years old?

ANTONIA. Yes, you can imagine, and her husband was over eighty!

TROOPER. But . . .

ANTONIA. The power of faith! They say, though, that the husband died immediately. Anyway, in memory of this miracle all the women in the neighborhood go around for three days with false bellies.

TROOPER. Oh, what a wonderful tradition. And is that why they empty out the supermarkets, to put stuff in their bellies? Come on! Enough with the fairy tales! Let me see what you have under there, or I'll lose my patience!

ANTONIA. And do what? Rip off our clothes? I warn you, that if you lay even a finger on us . . . a . . . a . . . a curse . . . will befall you!

TROOPER. Don't make me laugh. What curse?

ANTONIA. The same thing that happened to the incredulous husband of Santa Eulalia! The old man was a skeptic and he didn't believe her: "Santa Eulalia, come here right away. Open your blouse and let me see what you have in your belly, and I warn you, if you really are pregnant, I'll strangle you, because that baby's not mine." And then she, Santa Eulalia, opened her blouse, and a second miracle: out of her stomach . . . out of her stomach . . . came roses . . . roses . . . a cascade of roses.

TROOPER. Roses?

ANTONIA. Yes, but that's not all . . . all of a sudden the old man's eyes went black: "I can't see anymore. I can't see anymore," he shouted. "I'm blind! God has punished me!" "Oh, skeptic, now you believe," said Santa Eulalia. "Yes, I believe!" And then, third miracle: out of the roses sprang a ten-month-old baby boy who could already speak, and he said, "Papa, Papa, the Lord forgives you. Now you can die in peace." The baby put his little hand on the old man's head, and he dropped dead just like that.

TROOPER. Okay, story time's over. Now show me the roses . . . I mean . . . the goods. Hurry up!

ANTONIA. So you don't believe in the miracle?

TROOPER. Not at all.

ANTONIA. You're not afraid of the curse?

TROOPER. No, I said so already!

ANTONIA. Okay. Have it your way! Don't say I didn't warn you. (*To Margherita*) Come on. Get up and we'll show him together.

Santa Eulalia of the big belly
On whomever does not believe in the miracle
Let fall the curse
To whomever does not believe the oracle
Let come the evil black bastard
To darken his sight
Santa Eulalia, Santa Pia,
Unleash your curse
And so be it!!!!!

(*The two women open their coats.*)

TROOPER. What's all that stuff in there?

ANTONIA. What stuff? (*The two women make sounds of amazement*) Oh, look at that! It's a salad!

TROOPER. Salad?

ANTONIA. Yes, an apparition of a salad: chicory, endive, fennel and even a cabbage!

MARGHERITA. Me too, me too—I have a cabbage!

TROOPER. What's going on here? Why are you hiding all these vegetables in your stomach?

ANTONIA. But we didn't hide anything. Can't you see? It's a miracle!?

TROOPER. Yeah, the miracle of Our Lady of the Cabbage!

ANTONIA. Well, these days you make a miracle with whatever vegetable you can get your hands on. But whether you believe or not, there's nothing wrong with it, is there? Is there some law that says a citizen is not allowed to carry chicory, endive, fennel and cabbage in her belly? Is it prohibited?

TROOPER. No.

ANTONIA. Is there a law against it?

TROOPER. No.

ANTONIA. Then good-bye! (*Begins to usher him out*)

TROOPER. What do you mean, "good-bye!" (*Grabs the cabbage and presses the nozzle of his gun against it, as if holding it hostage*) All right! That's it! Tell me why you put all this stuff under your clothes . . . or else!

ANTONIA. I told you already. To make a belly in honor of the miracle of Santa Eulalia! And anyone who doesn't believe in it is cursed!

(*The lights dim slowly.*)

ANTONIA AND MARGHERITA.

Santa Eulalia of the big belly
On whomever does not believe in the miracle
Let fall the curse . . .

(*The women repeat the "prayer to Santa Eulalia." They notice with anxiety the dimming of the lights.*)

TROOPER. What's happening now? The lights are going out.

ANTONIA (*Very calmly*). What are you talking about, officer?

TROOPER. Can't you see . . . (*Worried*) It's getting dark . . .

ANTONIA. No, you must be mistaken . . . I can see just fine. (*To Margherita*) Can you see?

MARGHERITA (*Antonia kicks her*). Yes, yes . . . I can see . . .

ANTONIA. We can see. Maybe your eyesight is fading.

MARGHERITA (*Moves close to Antonia and whispers*). They cut off the electricity.

ANTONIA. Quiet!

TROOPER. Come on, stop kidding around. The light switch. Where's the light switch?

ANTONIA (*Moving comfortably, in spite of the darkness*). It's right here. Can't you see it? Wait, I'll try it . . . (*Clicks the switch audibly*) There, you see. Now it's off. Now it's on. There's an awful lot of light in my house! Don't you see it?

TROOPER. No, I can't see.

ANTONIA. Oh, my God. He's gone blind! It's the curse!

TROOPER. Cut it out! Open the window . . . I want to see outside!

ANTONIA. But the window is open!

MARGHERITA. Yes, the window's open. Can't you see?

ANTONIA. Come on, come and look. (*Leads him to a chair*) Look, over here. Watch out for the chair!

TROOPER (*Bumps into the chair*). Ahhiaa . . . Owww. That hurt!

ANTONIA. Pay attention when you walk!

TROOPER. How can I, if I can't see?

ANTONIA. Oh, I forgot, you're blind.

TROOPER (*Scared and angry*). Blind!!!!!!!!!!

ANTONIA. Come on . . . there's the window. (*Takes him to the shelves and opens the two glass cabinet doors on top*) Careful now . . . look, we're opening the window . . . feel the glass? (*The Trooper touches the glass tentatively*) Look out there . . . what a panorama! Sometimes I forget myself how beautiful it is. Let's hope the landlord doesn't realize what a great view this is, or he'll raise the rent!

TROOPER (*Desperate*). No I don't see it. I can't see anything. Dammit, what happened to me? A match ... Light a match!

ANTONIA (*Worried*). A match? . . . I have something better than a match (*Goes and gets the welding tank*) Stay there. Don't move. You don't know the house, and you might hurt yourself ... I'll bring it over ... it's a welding torch . . . (*She lights it*) Look, look . . what a beautiful red flame!

TROOPER. I don't see any flame ... let me touch it.

ANTONIA. No, no, can't you see it's red hot ...

TROOPER (*Arrogant*). I said let me touch it. That's an order! (*Antonia obeys*) Ah, ahiiaaoohoooo! My hand! I burned my hand! Oh God, that hurts! What a burn!

ANTONIA. I tried to warn you.

TROOPER (*Cries desperately*). I'm blind!

ANTONIA. Don't cry ... it's going to be all right ... come on ... at the end of the day what happened ... it's nothing ... so you've gone a little blind ...

TROOPER. I want to get out of here ... I've got to get out! (*Becoming more desperate*) I want to get out of this house ... to my superiors ...

ANTONIA. Wait, wait, I'll help you to the door ... Here it is ... there's the door ... (*Opens door to wardrobe*)

(*The State Trooper rushes into it like a madman, smashes his head on the interior, falls back staggering, and collapses on the floor.*)

MARGHERITA. He hit his head!

TROOPER. Ahhii! Who punched me?

ANTONIA (*Searching*). The baby . . . It's Santa Eulalia's baby. He's touched your forehead with his little hand!

TROOPER. That's some little hand! (*Collapses on the floor*)

ANTONIA. Officer . . . Officer! Dammit, he fainted. (*She gets down on her knees by the Trooper*)

MARGHERITA. Maybe he's dead!

ANTONIA. Always the optimist! What do you mean, dead ... get a pillow ... (*Margherita obeys*) No, he's not dead. He's just having some faintness ... a slight case of faintness ... he's fine ... he's breathing ...

MARGHERITA. He's dead, he's dead ... he's not breathing anymore!

ANTONIA. He's breathing ... he's breathing ... no ... he's not breathing! And his heart's not beating either!

MARGHERITA. Oh God! We killed a cop!

ANTONIA. Oh, yeah! Maybe I got a little carried away. What do we do now?

MARGHERITA. Ah, you're asking me? What do I have to do with it? It was all your idea ... I'm sorry but I'm going home ... The keys! Where did I put the keys to my house?

ANTONIA. Some friend you are. Walking out on me just like that.

MARGHERITA (*Finds keys on the shelf*). Ah, here they are! But I have another pair in my pocket. Two sets of keys! These are my husband's! So he was here ... he came looking for me ... and he forgot them!

ANTONIA. What do I care about that! I'm here with a dead cop and you're talking to me about keys!

MARGHERITA. That means that Luigi met Giovanni and he must have told him that I was pregnant, and now what am I supposed to say? You've got to think up something to get me out of this mess ...

ANTONIA. I'm desperate. (*Crying, she speaks to the unconscious Trooper*) Officer ... don't be that way ... let's make up ... It was just a little bump on the head ... officer ... wake up (*Lifts the officer's arm and lets it go. The arm falls heavily without life*) He's dead! He's really dead!

MARGHERITA. See what happens when you make fun of miracles?

ANTONIA. No, he was the one making fun of them . . . I even warned him: watch out for the curse, because Santa Eulalia is an awesome saint! (*She grabs him by the shoulders, lifts him up and drops him*)

MARGHERITA. And now what are you doing?

ANTONIA. Artificial respiration.

MARGHERITA. No. You have to use mouth-to-mouth resuscitation like they do when people drown.

ANTONIA. Now you want me to kiss a cop! With my political background! No ... you kiss him ...

MARGHERITA. No. I can't do it! Maybe we should get him an oxygen tank.

ANTONIA (*Thinks a moment*). I've got one. It's with Giovanni's welding equipment. One valve's for hydrogen, and the other's for oxygen. Come here and help me ... close the hydrogen valve ... like that ... and open the one for oxygen. Stay calm ... you'll see. As soon as he gets the oxygen, he'll come around! He'll even feel better than before! Like he spent a month in the mountains!

MARGHERITA. Are you sure it's going to work?

ANTONIA. No problem. You'll see ... (*Puts the welding canister tube into the officer's mouth*) The oxygen's going to his stomach . . . you see, his chest is rising . . . and then it falls . . . look . . . he's waking up . . . he's breathing ... see how nicely that chest rises ... and how it falls.

MARGHERITA. It looks to me like it's only rising . . . and his stomach too . . . stop ... you're going to blow him up.

(*The two women frantically try to turn off the infernal machine.*)

ANTONIA (*Lifts the tube up to the officer's mouth*). Oh, no. I gave him hydrogen instead of oxygen . . . Oh God, what a belly . . . what a belly! I made a policeman pregnant!

(*Blackout. Curtain falls. Giovanni and Luigi enter. The area in front of the curtain is understood to be the street outside Luigi's apartment. Giovanni and Luigi stand outside.*)

GIOVANNI. Well, we can't keep on sitting outside your place like a couple of bums. I'm going to see if I can break down the door with my shoulder.

LUIGI. No, you saw what happened when I tried. I couldn't get past the two locks.

GIOVANNI. Why do you have all that hardware?

LUIGI. My wife made me install it. She's terrified of thieves.

GIOVANNI. We're screwed.

LUIGI. Son of a bitch! Now I remember where I left the keys. At your house ...yeah ... on the table.

GIOVANNI. Are you sure?

LUIGI. Absolutely. Come on. Give me the keys to your house and I'll go get them.

GIOVANNI. Yeah, with that state trooper waiting outside my place! TRAC ... You're under arrest!

LUIGI. No, after all this time, he must be gone.

GIOVANNI. Don't kid yourself. That guy's a bloodhound. We can't even think of going back there.

(*They hear noises.*)

Dammit, someone's coming ...

LUIGI. Calm down, it's probably just a neighbor.

GIOVANNI. What do you mean, neighbor. It's that cop ... (*Tries to hide the bags*)

VOICE (*Offstage*). Excuse me, I need some information.

GIOVANNI. Dammit, we're screwed.

(*Gravedigger enters. It is the same actor who plays the Trooper.*)

LUIGI. No, it's not him. It looks like him, but it's not him.

GIOVANNI. You're right. It's not him.

GRAVEDIGGER. What were you saying? Who do I look like?

GIOVANNI. Damn, he looks just like him. Ah, I'm sorry for laughing, but you are the spitting image of the sergeant without the mustache who looks like the state trooper with the mustache. I feel like I'm in a play that I saw when I was a kid ... you know, one of those theatre companies where they can't afford to pay more than a few actors, so one of them has to play the parts of all the cops.

GRAVEDIGGER. But, really, I'm not a policeman.

GIOVANNI. Ah no, and what do you do?

GRAVEDIGGER. I'm an undertaker.

GIOVANNI AND LUIGI. Oh, Mother of God! (*With rapid gestures, the two of them touch their testicles*)

GIOVANNI (*Explains to the audience*). This is an Italian gesture expressing the fear of death. (*Demonstrates the gesture again and then turns to the Gravedigger*) Sorry, it was just an instinct.

GRAVEDIGGER. Oh, don't worry ... I understand ... everyone does that when they meet me ... I do it myself whenever I look in the mirror.

GIOVANNI. How nice.

GRAVEDIGGER. Can you tell me if a certain Sergio Prampolini lives around here.

LUIGI. Sure, he's upstairs on the third floor. But I'm sure he's not home. He's in the hospital. The poor guy is always sick! ...

GRAVEDIGGER. He's dead. But do you know if anyone in his family is coming home today? I've got to get someone to sign for the casket I've got out there.

GIOVANNI. Oh well, just leave it in the hall ... with a little note on it ... and when the son comes home: "Oh, it's Dad!" (*Mimes the action of carrying the casket on his shoulder*)

GRAVEDIGGER. A casket in the hallway? Abandoned? ... With all the people passing by ... little kids jumping in to play Indians paddling their canoe? No, I can't do that. I have to have the papers signed by someone who's responsible. You live here, don't you?

LUIGI. Yes, I live right there.

GRAVEDIGGER. Good, then it's all set. I'll leave the casket with you, you keep it in your house ... and this evening when the son of the deceased ...

GIOVANNI (*Shocked*). A dead man's coffin in my house?

GRAVEDIGGER. It doesn't take up much space, you know ... and if you overlook its macabre function, it's actually quite decorative.

GIOVANNI. Sure, put a little doily on top, and it's a portable bar!

GRAVEDIGGER. Be serious.

GIOVANNI. I'm dead serious.

LUIGI. The fact is, you see . . . we locked ourselves out.

GRAVEDIGGER. Oh, what a shame! Then, I'll have to return it to the warehouse.

GIOVANNI. No . . . maybe we can take it to my house. I live just down the street . . . I'll take care of everything. But you'd have to let us load these sacks into the casket . . . so our stuff won't get wet in the rain. The casket has a lid I hope?

GRAVEDIGGER. Yes, yes, it's a regulation casket. It's cheap, but even so we never make them without the lid.

GIOVANNI. What a great country we live in! Every coffin has a lid!

GRAVEDIGGER. OK. I'll leave the casket with you. (*He leaves*)

(*Giovanni and Luigi gather the bags.*)

GIOVANNI. I'd like to see a cop who's got the guts to stick his nose into a dead man's casket. I'll be the corpse, and you can be the undertaker making a delivery to the house. Come on. Let's get the sacks and go. (*They leave*)

(*Blackout. The curtain rises on the women in the house. The Trooper is still stretched out on the floor. Antonia is filling up a bag with the food from under the bed. Margherita is furious.*)

MARGHERITA. You're crazy. We're here with a dead man in the house and you're still worried about smuggling out rice and pasta.

ANTONIA. Well, it's the last trip. And besides, if he's dead, he's dead. Just come over here and help me lift the guy up . . . so we can get rid of him.

MARGHERITA. Where are we going to put him?

ANTONIA. In the wardrobe.

MARGHERITA. In the wardrobe?

ANTONIA. Where else? Haven't you ever seen a detective movie? They always put the body in the wardrobe.

(*They lift the officer to his feet. Antonia lifts him over her shoulders.*)

MARGHERITA (*Struggling*). He's heavy.

ANTONIA. What do you expect? He's a cop! (*Manipulates him as if he were a puppet and stows him away in the wardrobe*) There, he's in. Now let's put a coat hanger under his jacket so we can suspend him from this hook . . . (*They do it*) Perfect! Dammit, the door won't close. Let's push . . . come on. (*They push hard*) There! Look how nicely he fits in now! Just like Baby Jesus in the manger! (*Closes wardrobe door*)

MARGHERITA. Well, that's that. (*Mimes opening the window*) The rain's coming down by the bucketful.

ANTONIA. I'll be right back . . . I'm going in there for a minute . . . load up your belly . . . just one more trip and we're done . . . so exhausting! (*Goes out to the bathroom*)

(*The door opens. Luigi is there. He's wearing the cap of the Gravedigger.*)

LUIGI (*Barely peeking in, whispers*). Hey, is anybody home?

MARGHERITA. Who's there? . . . (*Frightened*) Luigi, is that you? What are you doing dressed up like that?

LUIGI. Margherita, my sweetie pie, finally . . . How are you? . . . Let me look at you! But don't you have a belly? The baby? Where's the baby? Did you lose it?

MARGHERITA. No, no . . . don't worry . . . everything's fine . . .

LUIGI. Really, everything's fine? And you're okay? Tell me . . .

MARGHERITA. Later, later . . . it's better if Antonia tells you . . .

LUIGI. Why Antonia?

GRAVEDIGGER (*From outside the door*). Hey this casket's heavy, are we coming in or not?

LUIGI. Yes, yes, come on in . . .

(*At that moment the door of the wardrobe opens so that the Trooper can be seen hanging inside. Margherita closes it quickly and runs into the other room.*)

Come on, Giovanni, get out of the casket . . .

GIOVANNI (*From outside the door*). Too bad, I was just getting comfortable in here . . .

(*The wardrobe door opens again. Without seeing what's inside, Giovanni closes the door. They put the coffin on the table.*)

MARGHERITA (*From the other room*). Antonia, Antonia, come here . . . hurry.

ANTONIA (*From offstage*): What is it . . . can't I even pee in peace?

GIOVANNI. They're both back?

LUIGI. Yes, yes, and everything's fine . . . they're all doing fine.

GIOVANNI. That's good . . . Close it, close the lid . . . (*To the Gravedigger*) Thank you. Thanks for everything.

GRAVEDIGGER. Don't mention it. (*He leaves*)

LUIGI. Listen, I have an idea. Let's close the door and lock ourselves in here until we unload everything. Then we can hide the stuff under the bed, and stand up the casket in the closet.

GIOVANNI. All right, go lock the door. (*Luigi does. They take the bags out of the casket and put them under the bed*)

MARGHERITA (*From the other room*). Hurry up, Antonia. I have to tell you something.

ANTONIA. I'm coming. I'm fixing my clothes. Everything's falling out.

GIOVANNI. There, it's done . . . the bags are all out of sight. Push, push them further under.

LUIGI. Look at that! We push the bags in on one side and they come out on the other . . . (*Bends over to look under the bed*) It didn't seem like that much in the casket! It looks like twice as much!

GIOVANNI. Of course it does, if you look at it with your head upside down . . . everything seems exaggerated that way . . . they call it the yoga effect . . . Come on, help me lift up the casket . . . No, wait, first let's take off the lid so it won't be too thick.

(*Giovanni and Luigi lift the casket and insert it into the wardrobe, after resting the lid up against the wall.*)

LUIGI. You're right . . . But what was that yoga effect you were talking about?

GIOVANNI. Oh, that was discovered in India . . . people there are so poor that when their hunger gets too much to bear . . . they stand on their heads . . . and while they're upside down they imagine whatever they want . . . all kinds of things to eat and drink . . .

LUIGI. And that makes the hunger go away?

GIOVANNI. No, but it keeps people off the streets. Come on, we've almost got it in—push.

(They manage to squeeze in the coffin so that the Trooper fits within it. They close the door without seeing the Trooper.)

LUIGI. Ah, so the illusion is enough to satisfy them . . . is that it?

GIOVANNI. Yeah, that's it . . . (*Tries to close the door of the wardrobe*)

LUIGI. You know I had an illusion, too.

GIOVANNI. Yeah, you told me.

LUIGI. No, no, another one . . . I thought I saw the state trooper in the closet.

GIOVANNI. State trooper? (*Opens the wardrobe door*) Good thing it was an illusion . . . Don't let me catch you standing on your head again, okay . . . Dammit, it won't close. (*Pushes, but door stays open*)

MARGHERITA (*From the other room*). Listen, Antonia, I'm getting tired of this . . . I'll just wait in there . . .

GIOVANNI. Go open the door. I can't move . . .

(Luigi runs to open the door. Margherita enters and sees Giovanni leaning against the wardrobe door.)

MARGHERITA. Oh, thanks, that's better . . . (*Sees Giovanni*) Oh, Giovanni, hello.

GIOVANNI. Hello. Your husband told me that everything went well . . . So did you have the baby or not?

ANTONIA (*Enters suddenly; to Margherita*). So what did you have to tell me that was so urgent?

(Antonia tries to hide her belly as much as possible, and slowly, bent over double, she goes toward the front door.)

GIOVANNI (*Blocks her with a shout*). Antonia! Your belly! You had the transplant?!

LUIGI. The transplant?!

ANTONIA. Well . . .

GIOVANNI (*Starts to walk into the wardrobe, but turns suddenly to block her*). Did you get the cesarean?

ANTONIA. A little.

GIOVANNI. What do you mean, a little?

ANTONIA. Well, in the end . . . it was the right thing.

LUIGI (*To Margherita*). Did you have a cesarean, too?

MARGHERITA. Uh, yes, well, I don't know . . . Antonia, did I have one?

LUIGI. Why are you asking her . . . don't you know?

ANTONIA. Uh, no, poor thing. They put her to sleep. And since she was asleep, how could she know?

GIOVANNI. You mean they operated on you while you were awake?

ANTONIA. What's with this interrogation? Why the third degree. I take the fifth. (*Almost out of sympathy, the cupboard's glass shelf doors and the front door of the house start opening, setting off an absurd merry-go-round of activity*) You could have asked how our health is, if we're living or dying. What do you care that we dragged ourselves out of bed like idiots against the doctors orders so that you wouldn't worry about us. And what do you think I should have done . . . she was going to lose her baby . . . I was in a position to save it . . . how could I say no . . . Aren't you always telling me that we have to help one another . . .

GIOVANNI. Yes, yes, you're right . . . I'm sorry . . . maybe you did the right thing . . . yes, of course you did.

LUIGI. Thank you, Antonia. Thank you, Antonia, for all you did. You are truly a remarkable woman.

GIOVANNI. Yes, truly a remarkable woman.

LUIGI (*To Margherita*). You tell her, too. Come on.

MARGHERITA. Yes, Antonia. You are a remarkable woman.

GIOVANNI. Come ... come here ... you shouldn't be standing up ... (*Sits her on the bed*) not with that cesarean, you know ... maybe it would have been better for you to stay there at the hospital.

ANTONIA. Don't be silly ... I'm fine ... didn't even notice it!

GIOVANNI. Yes, you look absolutely great ... And look at that great big belly! (*Caresses her stomach*) It's moving already!

LUIGI. It's moving? Excuse me, Antonia, can I touch it, too?

MARGHERITA. No, you're not touching a damn thing!

LUIGI. Eh, but it's my son, too, you know?

GIOVANNI. Yeah ... we're all related now.

MARGHERITA. What about me. All this cheering for Antonia ...

ANTONIA. Yeah. Do some cheering for Margherita. Go lift her up on your shoulders. I have to go. (*Gets up and rushes toward the door*)

GIOVANNI (*Blocking her way*). Go? Are you crazy? You're not going anywhere ... except to bed ... to stay warm ... in fact we'll move the bed next to the heater. (*Begins to move the bed*)

LUIGI. Stop, what are you doing!?

(*All look at him.*)

GIOVANNI. You're right ... it's too dangerous to move it, too dangerous ... the gas tanks are there ... (*Tries to put Antonia back on the bed*)

(*Antonia stops him; she's seen the cover of the coffin inside the wardrobe.*)

ANTONIA. Giovanni ... what's that?

GIOVANNI (*Distracting her while he tries to come up with a plausible response*). The gas tanks ... are there ... But you could at least have warned me ... instead of letting me worry ... all it would have taken was a phone call ...

ANTONIA. Giovanni, what's that?

GIOVANNI. All it takes is a dime ... a quarter ... you could have asked a nurse ... you could have said: "Look, call my house ... no, call the bar downstairs from my house ... and say ... listen, tell my husband?"

ANTONIA (*Interrupting him*). Excuse me, Giovanni, what is that thing ...

GIOVANNI (*Desperate, doesn't know what to say*). "Hello, could you tell my husband that everything's fine ..."

ANTONIA. Giovanni, what is that brown wooden object?!

GIOVANNI. Don't change the subject! How come, instead of calling me ... about the baby ... you keep talking to me about that disgusting piece of wood ... I'll burn it ... I don't know why I ever bought the thing ... it's ... it's ...

ANTONIA (*Exasperated*). Giovanni, what is it?

GIOVANNI. You still don't get it do you? Don't you ever watch TV? A child ... would understand right away, even a child ... watching TV ... the commercials ... especially when you see the foam ... the waves ...

ANTONIA. But what is it, Giovanni?

GIOVANNI. It's a surf board! They sell them at the factory . . . in front of the gate . . .

LUIGI. The gate.

GIOVANNI. Yeah. We're going to be laid off until January . . . so what are we going to do in December? Surf the Atlantic. I know. I know . . . you don't believe it . . . in fact it's something else entirely . . .

ANTONIA. What is it? . . .

GIOVANNI. You have such a limited imagination! It's a cradle! When I said to Luigi, "Look, Luigi, your wife's expecting a baby," right away he said, "A cradle, a cradle!"

LUIGI. A cradle.

GIOVANNI. So I went into the first cradle store I could find. And got the most modern cradle on the market. From Japan. It's a Toyota. (*Luigi and Giovanni grab the cover and rock it*) You see, it's got four holes here, two on each side . . . so you can suspend it from the ceiling with two steel cables . . . you put the baby in . . . you barely have to touch it and look how the cradle swings for hours . . . then, when the baby cries, just give it a slap and—ZAC! The spin of death! And the baby (*Mimes baby's terror*) frozen stiff. Doesn't make a peep for a week!

ANTONIA (*Noticing the size of the lid*). It looks a little big to me . . .

GIOVANNI. But babies are always growing!

(*Antonia stretches out on the bed, unconvinced. An Old Man comes to the door. It's the same actor who played the Sergeant, etc., with a white wig, his face covered in a cobweb of wrinkles.*)

OLD MAN. Excuse me. Am I disturbing you?

GIOVANNI. Oh, Papa, what a pleasure. Come in. Come in.

ANTONIA. Hi, Papa!

GIOVANNI. Do you know my friends? This is my father.

OLD MAN. My pleasure.

LUIGI. Giovanni, have you noticed that your father . . . looks a lot like the state trooper and the police sergeant?

GIOVANNI. Don't tell him, because he's already getting a little senile . . .

OLD MAN. I am not senile . . . (*Turns to Margherita*) How is my Antonia . . . oh, how beautiful you look . . . you're getting so much younger all the time.

GIOVANNI. No, Papa, she's not Antonia. That's Antonia.

OLD MAN. Is that so?

ANTONIA. Yes, Papa, it's me.

OLD MAN. What are you doing in bed? Are you sick?

GIOVANNI. No, she's expecting a baby.

OLD MAN. Oh, is that so? And where has he gone? Don't worry . . . you'll see, he'll come back. (*Looks at Luigi and confuses him for his grandson*) Oh, look, he's come back already. And he's all grown-up . . . You shouldn't keep your mamma waiting like that . . .

GIOVANNI. Dad, this is a friend.

OLD MAN. That's good! You should always be friends with your children. But I came here to tell you that they're throwing you out of your house.

GIOVANNI. Who?

OLD MAN. Your landlord. He sent the eviction letter to my house by mistake. Look here. It says that you haven't paid the rent for four months.

GIOVANNI. Don't be silly. It must be a mistake. Let me see that. Antonia always pays the rent on time, isn't that true Antonia?

ANTONIA. Yes, of course.

OLD MAN. In any case, they're going to clear out the whole building, because for months hardly anybody has been paying—

GIOVANNI. Who told you that?

OLD MAN. The sheriff . . . who's clearing people out apartment by apartment . . . a nice man!

(*Almost imperceptibly, voices shouting orders are heard outside.*)

LUIGI (*Goes to the window*). Take a look out there on the street. There's a whole squadron of police cars . . .

GIOVANNI. Yeah . . . look at that formation. It's like a war out there. And look at all those trucks.

OLD MAN. Sure, to carry away the furniture and everything else. All for free.

(*The noise outside increases: voices of women and children mixed with the shouting of orders.*)

VOICE OF A POLICEMAN (*From outside*). Come on . . . keep it moving . . . carry that stuff out . . . don't leave anything behind!

GIOVANNI. So I guess this eviction letter really is for us. Antonia, for God's sake! How did this happen?

ANTONIA. Don't shout. You'll scare the baby!

GIOVANNI. Okay, I'll speak softly. Antonia, is this true? Answer me.

ANTONIA. Okay: yes, it's true. I haven't paid the rent for four months, and I haven't paid the gas or electricity either . . . that's why they cut our service.

GIOVANNI. They cut off our gas and electric? Because you didn't pay the bill?

ANTONIA. Because with everything we earn between the two of us, there's barely enough to eat.

MARGHERITA. Luigi, I have something to tell you: I haven't paid the rent either.

LUIGI. No!

ANTONIA. See, see, we all have the same problem . . . everyone else who lives in our building, and the people across the street, too . . . and over there . . . everybody.

GIOVANNI. For God's sake, why didn't you tell me that you were short of money?

ANTONIA. But what could you have done . . . go out and commit a robbery?

GIOVANNI. Ah, no, of course not . . . but in the end . . .

ANTONIA. In the end, you would have had a fit and cursed the day you married me. (*Sniffles*)

LUIGI (*To Margherita*). And you, did you at least pay the gas and electricity?

MARGHERITA. Yes, yes, the gas and the electric, yes!

LUIGI. That's a relief.

GIOVANNI. Come on, don't cry. It's not good for the baby.

OLD MAN. That's right, that's right, everything will be all right. Oh, I just remembered. I came by to bring you something. Wait, I left it outside in the hall. (*Gets a bag and puts it on the table*) Sometimes I'm just not all here. There, look at this. I found this in my shed. It must be yours.

LUIGI (*Goes to the bag and looks inside*). What's this? Butter, flour, tomatoes?

ANTONIA. I've got nothing to do with it.

GIOVANNI. No, Papa, this isn't our stuff.

OLD MAN. Sure it is. I saw Antonia come out of my shed this morning?

ANTONIA. All right, yes, its the stuff I bought yesterday at reduced prices.

GIOVANNI. At the supermarket?

ANTONIA. Yes, but I only paid for half of it, the rest I stole . . .

GIOVANNI. Stole? You've become a robber?

ANTONIA. Yes!

LUIGI (*To Margherita*). You, too?

MARGHERITA. Yes, me, too . . .

ANTONIA. No, it's not true . . . she had nothing to do with it! She was just helping me out.

(*The two policemen from earlier enter.*)

POLICEMAN. Excuse me? The Bardi family . . . is that you?

GIOVANNI. Yes . . .

POLICEMAN. I've got an eviction notice here. You've got a half-hour to get ready. We'll be back in a few minutes to give you a hand . . . (*They leave*)

GIOVANNI. This is really unbelievable . . . I'm losing my mind!

LUIGI. Calm down, Giovanni . . . when it comes to talking about stealing, we should keep our mouths shut.

GIOVANNI. What do you mean "keep our mouths shut"! What's that got to do with it? We were in the middle of the street, don't you understand the difference . . . she's a disgrace, a dishonest criminal.

ANTONIA. Sure, you're right . . . I'm nothing but a criminal who throws mud on your poor but honorable name . . . and who also toys with your delicate sentiments of fatherhood . . . because you should know . . . (*Removes packages from belly*) all I've got in my belly is sugar, rice and pasta.

LUIGI. The baby, the transplant . . . (*To his wife*) Margherita?

GIOVANNI. I'm going to murder her . . . I'll murder her! (*Goes toward Antonia; Luigi blocks him*)

OLD MAN. Well, now that I've done what I came for . . . I'll bid you children good-bye. Have a nice day. (*He leaves*)

(*The noises outside get louder: women and men yelling, people shouting orders, sirens.*)

GIOVANNI. You dirty liar. How dare you joke about the story of our son! (*To Luigi*) Let me go.

ANTONIA. Let him kill me! Go ahead. I'm sick of this lousy life! And I'm fed up with your sermonizing . . . about law and order, and how you follow the rules, rules, rules . . . with such pride. Bullshit! You swallow your pride every day. And then when other people try to find a little dignity by breaking free of the rules you call them looters, bums, terrorists. Terrorism . . . Terrorism is being held hostage by a minimum-wage job. But you don't want to know how things really are.

GIOVANNI. I know how things are. And I can see. I'm mad as hell and I'm frustrated and I'm not the only one. Nobody can make ends meet. There's Aldo across the street whose wife left him when he lost his job. And how about our neighbors next door. They sleep four to a bed. People are hungry. And when they ask for help nobody listens. And the rage I feel isn't at you . . . it's at myself, and at the impotence I feel . . . when I'm being screwed over every day . . . because I don't see a way out. And it seems there's nobody out there who gives a shit about the people who end up on the street with no place to live. And you know what. I'm starting to take it personally. Because in just a few minutes the homeless are us.

ANTONIA. What happened, Giovanni, is that really you talking? Is your head screwed on straight?

GIOVANNI. I've felt like this for a long time . . . I just never had the courage to say it before. And there's something else you should know about me. I'm a thief too. Look under here. Luigi and I stole these: bags of coffee!

ANTONIA (*Truly astonished*). You stole!

LUIGI (*Going to the rescue*). Yes, but he only did it after he got mad about us getting laid off our jobs.

GIOVANNI. No, that was just the last straw . . . because for a long time I'd already been mad enough to scream . . . (*To Antonia*) And one more thing, Antonia . . . This is not a cradle. It's the lid to a dead man's coffin! (*Antonia reaches for her crotch, making the sign that expresses the fear of death*) Look in here. (*Goes to the wardrobe, Antonia and Margherita try to stop him*)

ANTONIA. No, stop, what are you doing?

GIOVANNI. I'm doing what I have to do . . . you should know everything . . .

(*Luigi helps Giovanni pull out the casket. The State Trooper is revealed.*)

STATE TROOPER. I can see! (*Comes out of wardrobe*) I can see! Santa Eulalia forgave me . . . she blessed me! (*Notices his belly*) I'm pregnant! God bless Santa Eulalia! . . . I'm a mother . . . I'm a mother! (*Exits running*) I'm a mother.

GIOVANNI. What day is it today? (*Hears shots and shouts from outside and runs to the window*) Look, the women are pulling their stuff off of the trucks. The police are shooting!

(*The others go to the window.*)

LUIGI. Yeah, and look at those kids on the rooftops . . . they're throwing things . . . tiles . . . bricks!

GIOVANNI. The police are shooting to kill. One kid's already down.

MARGHERITA. They're firing for keeps!

(*The four of them shout insults out the window.*)

ALL. Murderers . . . bastards . . . cowards . . .

LUIGI. They're running away . . . the police are running away!

ANTONIA. And over there, look! That woman has a hunting rifle. There in that window. She's shooting.

LUIGI. It's happening.

GIOVANNI. Of course it's happening. People have been putting up with things out of fear. But fear can turn into rage when you can't see any way out, and you watch your bills piling up and up and up, and you've got nothing in the bank. And you keep getting downsized and downsized and downsized until no one can even see you anymore.

MARGHERITA. There's a limit to what people can take.

ANTONIA. People are hungry. They're not just hungry for food. They're hungry for dignity. They're hungry for justice, for a chance.

GIOVANNI (*To the audience*). Desperation's funny, isn't it? Especially when it's somebody else's. Then it's really funny. It's a scream. It's a riot.

Remember the Los Angeles riots. Nobody expected them. You're smiling, aren't you? Sure, we all know that the poor people just burned down their own neighborhoods, and left themselves flat on their asses with nothing to show for all their rage. But just wait, because it might turn out that, little by little, they're going to get up off their asses onto their knees. And then they just might drag themselves up off the ground and onto their feet. And that's when we better start paying attention, because when people stand up for themselves, they can always find a way to make things happen.

(During this last speech, the lights dim until darkness is complete. Blackout.)

THE END

Analyzing the Text

1. Why can't Antonia tell her husband Giovanni the truth about how she obtained groceries she has brought home from the supermarket? What does Giovanni's response to Antonia's various stories tell you about him?
2. How do each of the following issues become a source of humor in the play: the masculine self-image in Italian society; the role of the pope and the Catholic Church; corruption in government, unions, and big business; fantasy values promoted by the media and films; mystique and authority of science?

Understanding Fo's Techniques

1. How do props (for example, the gas starter, cupboard, bed, casket, and packet of olives) play a particularly important role at crucial moments in the play?
2. How does the effect of any given scene depend on having the audience (or reader) anticipate how a character will respond to a surprising turn of events or unbelievable situation (for example, baby transplants, or the "miracle" of Saint Eulalia)?

Arguing for an Interpretation

1. What point is Fo trying to make by showing how Giovanni's experiences change him from the law-abiding citizen he was at the beginning of the play?
2. How does the play explore political, cultural, and religious aspects of Italian life in terms of class conflicts?

Connections

1. In what ways do the essays by Jonathan Swift (written in 1729 in Ireland) and Margaret Sanger (written at the beginning of the 20th century) offer different perspectives on the plight of the poor?
2. How do Mary Crow Dog and Linda Hogan, as Native Americans, express the estrangement they have experienced in very different social contexts in terms of education?
3. In what way is Dexter's pursuit of his "winter dreams" similar to the aspirations of Mme. Loisel in Guy de Maupassant's story and Tay Soon and his

wife in Catherine Lim's story? In a short essay, discuss each author's attitude toward social striving and its effect on human nature. Take into account that each story reflects a different cultural context and time period. Your essay should address the issue of how sympathetic each author is to the main character(s). Are they depicted as foolish, tragic, self-deluded, or pathetic?

4. What different insights do Jonathan Swift and Mahdokht Kashkuli offer on the fate of unwanted children? In your opinion, is Swift's approach more effective? Why or why not?
5. In a short essay, discuss how Guy de Maupassant in "The Necklace," Dorothy Allison in "I'm Working on My Charm," and Liliana Heker in "The Stolen Party" use lavish parties as a springboard for probing the issue of class boundaries.
6. In what different ways do the poems by Martín Espada and Mascha Kaléko illustrate Bertolt Brecht's thesis in "A Worker Reads History"?
7. In what different ways do Léon Damas in his poem, and Dario Fo in his play, use humor to satirize prevailing social values in their two very different cultures?
8. What similarities can you discover in Piercy's critique of capitalism and Brecht's analysis of how history is reported to serve vested interests?
9. What different strategies do Brecht and Linda Hogan (in "Workday") use to draw attention to groups that are normally invisible and to assert the social and historical importance of these groups? Which approach did you find more compelling and why?
10. In what sense do Francis E.W. Harper and Nikki Giovanni in their poems, Kate Chopin in her story, and James Baldwin in his essay explore the personal effects of race and class prejudices?
11. How do the speakers draw strength from their ethnic and racial communities to affirm their sense of self in the poems by Nikki Giovanni and Gary Soto?
12. To what extent do you agree with Marge Piercy's "The Nine of Cups" and Dario Fo's (see *We Won't Pay! We Won't Pay!*) criticism of capitalism and the forces that shape contemporary society (in America and in Italy)? Write a short essay expressing your views.

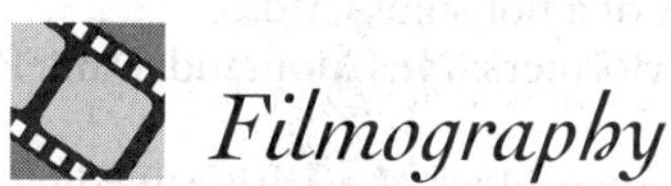

Filmography

Citizen Kane (1941) Director: Orson Welles. Performers: Orson Welles, Joseph Cotton.
A tour-de-force story of the success of a newspaper tycoon, based on the life of William Randolph Hearst.

Mildred Pierce (1945) Director: Michael Curtiz. Performers: Joan Crawford, Zachary Scott, Ann Blyth.
An adaptation of James M. Cain's novel about a hard-working divorcée who competes with her spoiled daughter for a playboy.

Oliver Twist (1948) Director: David Lean. Performers: Alec Guiness, Anthony Newley.
Based on Charles Dickens's story of a workhouse orphan who is forced into a life of crime with a gang of pickpockets.

No Way Out (1950) Director: Joseph L. Mankiewicz. Performers: Richard Widmark, Sidney Poitier.

A film that was before its time in its depiction of racial issues deals with a white gangster who blames a black doctor for his brother's death.

A Place in the Sun (1951) Director: George Stevens. Performers: Montgomery Clift, Elizabeth Taylor, Shelley Winters.

Based on Theodore Dreiser's novel *An American Tragedy* about a social-climbing laborer whose aspirations to join the upper class lead to tragedy.

Nights of Cabiria (1956) Director: Federico Fellini. Performers: Guilietta Massina, Amadeo Nazzari.

A poor prostitute prays for the Virgin Mary to change her life, with surprising results. [Italy]

High and Low (1962) Director: Ikira Kurosawa. Performer: Toshiro Mifune.

Based on an Ed McBain novel about a business tycoon whose son is abducted by kidnappers and must decide whether to pay the huge ransom that will ruin him after finding out the kidnappers have mistakenly taken his chauffeur's son. [Japan]

Diary of a Chambermaid (1964) Director: Luis Bunuel. Performers: Jeanne Moreau, Michel Piccoli.

A sensitive, educated young woman takes a job as a maid to a bourgeois family with plenty of material goods, but no real culture. [France]

Keetje Tippel (1975) Director: Paul Verhoeven. Performer: Monique Van De Ven.

This film based on the life of Neel Doff (who was nominated for the Nobel Prize in literature) provides insight into the exploitative social conditions from which a young Dutch prostitute rises from unbearable poverty to fortune and fame as a writer. [The Netherlands]

Educating Rita (1983) Director: Lewis Gilbert. Performers: Julie Walters, Michael Caine.

A working-class hairdresser tries to improve her life through education.

Trading Places (1983) Director: John Landis. Performers: Dan Aykroyd, Eddie Murphy, Jamie Lee Curtis.

Two elderly Wall Street brokers use an unemployed street hustler and a wealthy nephew to settle a wager as to whether heredity or environment is more important in producing success.

Do the Right Thing (1984) Director: Spike Lee. Performers: Danny Aiello, Ossie Davis.

Racial tensions erupt in Brooklyn over the course of a hot summer day.

Jean de Florette (1987) Director: Claude Berri. Performers: Yves Montand, Daniel Auteuil, Gerard Depardieu.

Two scheming farmers in drought-stricken Provence block the spring feeding the water to a nearby farm, hoping for their neighbor's failure so as to purchase the farm for next to nothing. [France]

Café au Lait (1994) Director: Mathieu Kassovitz. Performers: Julie Manduech, Mathieu Kassovitz, Hubert Kounde.

A pregnant young woman refuses to divulge which of her lovers—one white, one black—is the father of her child. [France]

Lakota Woman: Siege at Wounded Knee (1994) Director: Frank Pierson. Performers: Irene Bedard, Joseph Runningfox.

Based on Mary Crow Dog's autobiography that tells of her coming of age during the American Indian Movement's 1973 occupation of Wounded Knee.

Ridicule (1996) Director: Patrice Leconte. Performer: Charles Berling.

A country aristocrat comes to the court at Versailles where his success depends on mastering the arts of intrigue and ridicule. [France]

Secrets and Lies (1996) Director: Mike Leigh. Performers: Brenda Blethyn, Marianne Jean-Baptiste.
After the deaths of her adoptive parents, a beautiful, successful black woman who is an eye doctor goes in search of her birth mother only to find a drunken, illiterate white woman.

Character (1997) Director: Mike van Diem. Performer: Jan Decleir.
This film charts the relationship between a young lawyer and his all-powerful father, a bailiff, who tries to control his son's life but only succeeds in ruining his own. [The Netherlands]

Chapter 7

Politics and Power

You only have power over people so long as you don't take everything away from them. But when you've robbed a man of everything he's no longer in your power—he's free again.

Alexander Solzhenitsyn

In no area are the conflicts between different points of view more dramatic than between individual citizens and the nation-states to which they relinquish a degree of freedom in order to gain the benefits available only through the nation-state's collective political and social institutions (such as the military, the legal system, or health care). The allegiance individuals owe their governments, and the protection of individual rights that citizens expect in return, are the subject of intense analysis.

A politicized environment within a state has an intensely corrosive and debilitating effect on personal relationships when individual loyalties, values, and honor come into conflict with officially decreed allegiances. Authors in many countries and cultures describe the seductive and persuasive powers the state can mobilize through the threat of force and propaganda to manipulate the perceptions of the citizens under its control. Regimes also remain in power by channeling existing resentments of one group against another. Governments can control citizens by encouraging people to hate themselves and see themselves as helpless. This psychological dimension has been the basis of stories, poems, and plays that explore the predicaments of ordinary citizens trying to survive in repressive military and political regimes.

In the first essay, the conflict between individual conscience and the state is clearly illustrated in George Orwell's "Shooting an Elephant," where his disillusionment with British colonialism reaches a crisis point. The Chilean author Luis Sepulveda in "Daisy" displays an unusual ironic detachment in his account of coping with the literary pretensions of the guard when he was imprisoned. In Tim O'Brien's essay, "If I Die in a Combat Zone," we experience his intense inner conflict as he must decide whether to serve in Vietnam.

The short works of fiction in this chapter begin with Ambrose Bierce's classic "An Occurrence at Owl Creek Bridge," in which we empathize with the moment-to-moment perceptions of a Southern landowner who has been apprehended during the Civil War and is about to be hanged. Tadeusz Borowski's story "Silence" uses an unusual shift in perspective to bring home the impact of the dehumanizing effects of war on both the victims and oppressors. In "Home Soil," Irene Zabytko tells the story of a father and son claimed by the inhumanity of war during World War II and Vietnam. "Gregory," by Panos Ioannides, explores the conflict between personal loyalty and military duty during the Cypriot rebellion. In "The Censors," Luisa Valenzuela dramatizes the corrupting effect of power on an idealistic young man in Argentina. In "Cervicide," Gloria Anzaldúa tells the poignant story of a Mexican-American girl who has to kill her pet deer to save her father from going to jail. From Nicaragua, Ernesto Cardenal in "The Swede" relates how a Swedish traveler, inexplicably imprisoned in Central America, acts as an unwilling go-between and translator for the president of the country and his lady-love in Sweden. In the heartfelt tale "A Pair of Socks with Love," the Taiwanese author P'an Jen-mu portrays the struggle between personal loyalty and ideological fervor during the Cultural Revolution in China.

Poetry by writers of conscience, who in many cases have survived oppressive regimes, imprisonment, and physical and psychological torture in Armenia, Central America, Greece, Israel, and the United States, provides a unique insight into the human consquences of political turmoil and oppression. We hear the voices of Diana Der Hovanessian, writing of coming to terms with the genocide of her Armenian relatives by the Turks so many years before; Wilfred Owen, who creates an eerie meeting between a soldier and a man he had killed in battle; W. H. Auden, who parodies the conformist ideology of the modern political state; Carolyn Forché, who presents a terrifying and surreal encounter with a Central American dictator; Eleni Fourtouni, whose work portrays the Greek resistance against the Nazis; Ira Sadoff's discovery of old animosities in a new environment; Yehuda Amichai's thoughtful reflection on relationships between Jews and Arabs; and Margaret Atwood's catalogue of the effects of wars on soldiers and the women they leave behind.

The dramatic work in this chapter, *Protest,* a one-act play by Václav Havel, the former president of the Czech Republic, offers a theatrical realization of the meeting between a dissident writer (based on Havel's own experiences before being sentenced to four and a half years in prison for his political activities) and a successful hack who has compromised his political ideals and has put his talent at the service of those in power.

Essays

George Orwell

George Orwell was the pen name taken by Erich Blair (1903–1950), who was born in Bengal, India. Educated on a scholarship at Eton, he served as a British official in the police in Burma (1922–1927), and became disillusioned with the aims and methods of colonialism. He describes his struggle with poverty in his first book Down and Out in Paris and London *(1933), a gripping account of life on the fringe. In 1936, Orwell went to Spain to report on the Civil War and joined the Communist P.O.U.M. militia to fight against the Fascists. His account of this experience, in which he was severely wounded, titled* Homage to Catalonia *(1938), is an unflinching account of the bleak and comic aspects of trench warfare. In* Animal Farm *(1945), he satirized the Russian Revolution and the machinations of the Soviet bureaucracy. In his acclaimed novel,* Nineteen Eighty-Four *(1949), his distrust of totalitarianism emerged as a grim prophecy of a bureaucratic, regimented England of the future whose citizens are constantly watched by "big brother." Five collections of his essays have been published, including* Shooting an Elephant and Other Essays *(1946) where this selection first appeared.*

Shooting an Elephant

In Moulmein, in Lower Burma, I was hated by large numbers of people—the only time in my life that I have been important enough for this to happen to me. I was sub-divisional police officer of the town, and in an aimless, petty kind of way anti-European feeling was very bitter. No one had the guts to raise a riot, but if a European woman went through the bazaars alone somebody would probably spit betel juice over her dress. As a police officer I was an obvious target and was baited whenever it seemed safe to do so. When a nimble Burman tripped me up on the football field and the referee (another Burman) looked the other way, the crowd yelled with hideous laughter. This happened more than once. In the end the sneering yellow faces of young men that met me everywhere, the insults hooted after me when I was at a safe distance, got badly on my nerves. The young Buddhist priests were the worst of all. There were several thousands of them in the town and none of them seemed to have anything to do except stand on street corners and jeer at Europeans.

All this was perplexing and upsetting. For at that time I had already made up my mind that imperialism was an evil thing and the sooner I chucked up my job and got out of it the better. Theoretically—and secretly, of course—I was all for the Burmese and all against their oppressors, the British. As for the job I was doing, I hated it more bitterly than I can perhaps make clear. In a job like that you see the dirty work of Empire at close quarters. The wretched prisoners huddling in the stinking cages of the lock-ups, the grey, cowed faces of the long-term convicts, the scarred buttocks of the men who had been flogged with bamboos—all these oppressed me with an intolerable sense of guilt. But I could get nothing into perspective. I was young and ill-educated and I had had to think out my problems in the utter silence that is imposed on every Englishman in the East. I did not even know that the British Empire is dying, still less did I know that it is a great deal better than the younger empires that are going to supplant it. All I knew was that I was stuck between my hatred of the empire I served and my rage against the evil-spirited little beasts who tried to make my job impossible. With one part of my mind I thought of the

British Raj[1] as an unbreakable tyranny, as something clamped down, in *saecula saeculorum,*[2] upon the will of prostrate peoples; with another part I thought that the greatest joy in the world would be to drive a bayonet into a Buddhist priest's guts. Feelings like these are the normal by-products of imperialism; ask any Anglo-Indian official, if you can catch him off duty.

One day something happened which in a roundabout way was enlightening. It was a tiny incident in itself, but it gave me a better glimpse than I had had before of the real nature of imperialism—the real motives for which despotic governments act. Early one morning the sub-inspector at a police station the other end of the town rang me up on the 'phone and said that an elephant was ravaging the bazaar. Would I please come and do something about it? I did not know what I could do, but I wanted to see what was happening and I got on to a pony and started out. I took my rifle, an old .44 Winchester and much too small to kill an elephant, but I thought the noise might be useful *in terrorem.* Various Burmans stopped me on the way and told me about the elephant's doings. It was not, of course, a wild elephant, but a tame one which had gone "must."[3] It had been chained up, as tame elephants always are when their attack of "must" is due, but on the previous night it had broken its chain and escaped. Its mahout, the only person who could manage it when it was in that state, had set out in pursuit, but had taken the wrong direction and was now twelve hours' journey away, and in the morning the elephant had suddenly reappeared in the town. The Burmese population had no weapons and were quite helpless against it. It had already destroyed somebody's bamboo hut, killed a cow and raided some fruit-stalls and devoured the stock; also it had met the municipal rubbish van and, when the driver jumped out and took to his heels, had turned the van over and inflicted violences upon it.

The Burmese sub-inspector and some Indian constables were waiting for me in the quarter where the elephant had been seen. It was a very poor quarter, a labyrinth of squalid bamboo huts, thatched with palm-leaf, winding all over a steep hillside. I remember that it was a cloudy, stuffy morning at the beginning of the rains. We began questioning the people as to where the elephant had gone and, as usual, failed to get any definite information. That is invariably the case in the East; a story always sounds clear enough at a distance, but the nearer you get to the scene of events the vaguer it becomes. Some of the people said that the elephant had gone in one direction, some said that he had gone in another, some professed not even to have heard of any elephant. I had almost made up my mind that the whole story was a pack of lies, when we heard yells a little distance away. There was a loud, scandalized cry of "Go away, child! Go away this instant!" and an old woman with a switch in her hand came round the corner of a hut, violently shooting away a crowd of naked children. Some more women followed, clicking their tongues and exclaiming; evidently there was something that the children ought not to have seen. I rounded the hut and saw a man's dead body sprawling in the mud. He was an Indian, a black Dravidian coolie, almost naked, and he could not have been dead many minutes. The people said that the elephant had come suddenly

---

[1]The imperial government of British India and Burma.
[2]Forever and ever.
[3]Gone into sexual heat.

upon him round the corner of the hut, caught him with its trunk, put its foot on his back and ground him into the earth. This was the rainy season and the ground was soft, and his face had scored a trench a foot deep and a couple of yards long. He was lying on his belly with arms crucified and head sharply twisted to one side. His face was coated with mud, the eyes wide open, the teeth bared and grinning with an expression of unendurable agony. (Never tell me, by the way, that the dead look peaceful. Most of the corpses I have seen looked devilish.) The friction of the great beast's foot had stripped the skin from his back as neatly as one skins a rabbit. As soon as I saw the dead man I sent an orderly to a friend's house nearby to borrow an elephant rifle. I had already sent back the pony, not wanting it to go mad with fright and throw me if it smelt the elephant.

5 The orderly came back in a few minutes with a rifle and five cartridges, and meanwhile some Burmans had arrived and told us that the elephant was in the paddy fields below, only a few hundred yards away. As I started forward practically the whole population of the quarter flocked out of the houses and followed me. They had seen the rifle and were all shouting excitedly that I was going to shoot the elephant. They had not shown much interest in the elephant when he was merely ravaging their homes, but it was different now that he was going to be shot. It was a bit of fun to them, as it would be to an English crowd; besides they wanted the meat. It made me vaguely uneasy. I had no intention of shooting the elephant—I had merely sent for the rifle to defend myself if necessary—and it is always unnerving to have a crowd following you. I marched down the hill, looking and feeling a fool, with the rifle over my shoulder and an ever-growing army of people jostling at my heels. At the bottom, when you got away from the huts, there was a metalled road and beyond that a miry waste of paddy fields a thousand yards across, not yet ploughed but soggy from the first rains and dotted with coarse grass. The elephant was standing eight yards from the road, his left side towards us. He took not the slightest notice of the crowd's approach. He was tearing up bunches of grass, beating them against his knees to clean them and stuffing them into his mouth.

I had halted on the road. As soon as I saw the elephant I knew with perfect certainty that I ought not to shoot him. It is a serious matter to shoot a working elephant—it is comparable to destroying a huge and costly piece of machinery—and obviously one ought not to do it if it can possibly be avoided. And at that distance, peacefully eating, the elephant looked no more dangerous than a cow. I thought then and I think now that his attack of "must" was already passing off; in which case he would merely wander harmlessly about until the mahout came back and caught him. Moreover, I did not in the least want to shoot him. I decided that I would watch him for a little while to make sure that he did not turn savage again, and then go home.

But at that moment I glanced round at the crowd that had followed me. It was an immense crowd, two thousand at the least and growing every minute. It blocked the road for a long distance on either side. I looked at the sea of yellow faces above the garish clothes—faces all happy and excited over this bit of fun, all certain that the elephant was going to be shot. They were watching me as they would watch a conjurer about to perform a trick. They did not like me, but with the magical rifle in my hands I was momentarily worth watching. And suddenly I realized that I should have to shoot the elephant after all. The people expected it of me and I had got to do it; I could feel their two thousand wills pressing me forward, irresistibly. And it was at this moment, as I stood there with the rifle in my hands, that I first grasped the hollowness, the futility of the white man's dominion in the East. Here was I, the white man with his gun, standing in front of the unarmed native crowd—seemingly the leading actor of the piece; but in reality I was only an absurd puppet pushed to and fro by the will of those yellow faces behind. I perceived in this moment that when the white man turns tyrant it is his own freedom that he destroys. He becomes a sort of hollow, posing dummy, the conventionalized figure of a sahib. For it is the condition of his rule that he shall spend his life in trying to impress the "natives," and so in every crisis he has got to do what the "natives" expect of him. He wears a mask, and his face grows to fit it. I had got to shoot the elephant. I had committed myself to doing it when I sent for the rifle. A sahib has got to act like a sahib; he has got to appear resolute, to know his own mind and do definite things. To come all that way, rifle in hand, with two thousand people marching at my heels, and then to trail feebly away, having done nothing—no, that was impossible. The crowd would laugh at me. And my whole life, every white man's life in the East, was one long struggle not to be laughed at.

But I did not want to shoot the elephant. I watched him beating his bunch of grass against his knees, with that preoccupied grandmotherly air that elephants have. It seemed to me that it would be murder to shoot him. At that age I was not squeamish about killing animals, but I had never shot an elephant and never wanted to. (Somehow it always seems worse to kill a *large* animal.) Besides, there was the beast's owner to be considered. Alive, the elephant was worth at least a hundred pounds; dead, he would only be worth the value of his tusks, five pounds, possibly. But I had got to act quickly. I turned to some experienced-looking Burmans who had been there when we arrived, and asked them how the elephant had been behaving. They all said the same thing. He took no notice of you if you left him alone, but he might charge if you went too close to him.

It was perfectly clear to me what I ought to do. I ought to walk up to within, say, twenty-five yards of the elephant and test his behavior. If he charged, I could shoot; if he took no notice of me, it would be safe to leave him until the mahout came back. But also I knew that I was going to do no such thing. I was a poor shot with a rifle and the ground was soft mud into which one would sink at every step. If the elephant charged and I missed him, I should have about as much chance as a toad under a steam-roller. But even then I was not thinking particularly of my own skin, only of the watchful yellow faces behind. For at that moment, with the crowd watching me, I was not afraid in the ordinary sense, as I would have been if I had been alone. A white man mustn't be frightened in front of "natives"; and so, in general, he isn't frightened. The sole thought in my mind was that if anything went wrong those two thousand Burmans would see me pursued, caught, trampled on and reduced to a grinning corpse like that Indian up the hill. And if that happened it was quite probable that some of them would laugh. That would never do. There was only one alternative. I shoved the cartridges into the magazine and lay down on the road to get a better aim.

The crowd grew very still, and a deep, low, happy sigh, as of people 10
who see the theatre curtain go up at last, breathed from innumerable

throats. They were going to have their bit of fun after all. The rifle was a beautiful German thing with cross-hair sights. I did not then know that in shooting an elephant one would shoot to cut an imaginary bar running from ear-hole to ear-hole. I ought, therefore, as the elephant was sideways on, to have aimed straight at his ear-hole; actually I aimed several inches in front of this, thinking the brain would be further forward.

When I pulled the trigger I did not hear the bang or feel the kick—one never does when a shot goes home—but I heard the devilish roar of glee that went up from the crowd. In that instant, in too short a time, one would have thought, even for the bullet to get there, a mysterious, terrible change had come over the elephant. He neither stirred nor fell, but every line of his body had altered. He looked suddenly stricken, shrunken, immensely old, as though the frightful impact of the bullet had paralysed him without knocking him down. At last, after what seemed a long time—it might have been five seconds, I dare say—he sagged flabbily to his knees. His mouth slobbered. An enormous senility seemed to have settled upon him. One could have imagined him thousands of years old. I fired again into the same spot. At the second shot he did not collapse but climbed with desperate slowness to his feet and stood weakly upright, with legs sagging and head drooping. I fired a third time. That was the shot that did for him. You could see the agony of it jolt his whole body and knock the last remnant of strength from his legs. But in falling he seemed for a moment to rise, for as his hind legs collapsed beneath him he seemed to tower upward like a huge rock toppling, his trunk reaching skywards like a tree. He trumpeted, for the first and only time. And then down he came, his belly towards me, with a crash that seemed to shake the ground even where I lay.

I got up. The Burmans were already racing past me across the mud. It was obvious that the elephant would never rise again, but he was not dead. He was breathing very rhythmically with long rattling gasps, his great mound of a side painfully rising and falling. His mouth was wide open—I could see far down into caverns of pale pink throat. I waited a long time for him to die, but his breathing did not weaken. Finally I fired my two remaining shots into the spot where I thought his heart must be. The thick blood welled out of him like red velvet, but still he did not die. His body did not even jerk when the shots hit him, the tortured breathing continued without a pause. He was dying, very slowly and in great agony, but in some world remote from me where not even a bullet could damage him further. I felt that I had got to put an end to that dreadful noise. It seemed dreadful to see the great beast lying there, powerless to move and yet powerless to die, and not even to be able to finish him. I sent back for my small rifle and poured shot after shot into his heart and down his throat. They seemed to make no impression. The tortured gasps continued as steadily as the ticking of a clock.

In the end I could not stand it any longer and went away. I heard later that it took him half an hour to die. Burmans were bringing dahs[4] and baskets even before I left, and I was told they had stripped his body almost to the bones by the afternoon.

Afterwards, of course, there were endless discussions about the shooting of the elephant. The owner was furious, but he was only an Indian and could do nothing. Besides, legally I had done the right thing, for a mad ele-

[4]Butcher knives.

phant has to be killed, like a mad dog, if its owner fails to control it. Among the Europeans opinion was divided. The older men said I was right, the younger men said it was a damn shame to shoot an elephant for killing a coolie, because an elephant was worth more than any damn Coringhee coolie. And afterwards I was very glad that the coolie had been killed; it put me legally in the right and it gave me a sufficient pretext for shooting the elephant. I often wondered whether any of the others grasped that I had done it solely to avoid looking a fool.

Analyzing the Text

1. In what untenable position does Orwell find himself as a British official in Burma? How does he react to the task he is required to perform?
2. What different kinds of motivations—personal, political, circumstantial—prompted Orwell to shoot the elephant? In your view, which of these played the most decisive role?

Understanding Orwell's Techniques

1. How does Orwell frame his account so that his readers can feel what he felt and can understand why he became so disillusioned with the aims and methods of colonialism?
2. How does Orwell's completely objective analysis of his own motives and reactions serve to illustrate his conclusion that "when the white man turns tyrant it is his own freedom that he destroys"?

Arguing for an Interpretation

1. How does Orwell use the incident of being placed in the position of having to kill an elephant that had run wild and trampled a villager to examine the insidious effects of social pressure? Was he disillusioned with the political system he served, as such, or simply embarrassed by the specific incident? Explain your answer.
2. Orwell is quite famous for his exposition in his 1946 essay "Politics and the English Language" of the need for candor, plain speech, and freedom from self-deception in public rhetoric. To what extent does he display these qualities in "Shooting an Elephant"?

LUIS SEPULVEDA

The Chilean expatriot novelist Luis Sepulveda (b. 1949–) takes us inside the prison where he was confined and reveals, with surprising good humor, one of his experiences. This chapter, translated by Chris Andrews and drawn from Full Circle: A South American Journey, ***(1996), reveals Sepulveda's ironic sensibility as he tries to evade torture and remain an honest critic of his jailor's literary efforts. His works include his acclaimed detective novel*** The Old Man Who Read Love Stories

(1992), The Name of the Bullfighter *(1996),* Patagonia Express *(2001), and* Hot Line *(2002).*

Daisy

The military had rather inflated ideas of our destructive capacity. They questioned us about plans to assassinate all the officers in American military history, to blow up bridges and seal off tunnels, and to prepare for the landing of a terrible foreign enemy whom they could not identify.

Temuco is a sad, grey, rainy city. No-one would call it a tourist attraction, and yet the barracks of the Tucapel regiment came to house a sort of permanent international convention of sadists. The Chileans, who were the hosts, after all, were assisted in the interrogations by primates from Brazilian military intelligence—they were the worst—North Americans from the State Department, Argentinian paramilitary personnel, Italian neo-fascists and even some agents of Mossad.

I remember Rudi Weismann, a Chilean with a passion for the South and sailing, who was tortured and interrogated in the gentle language of the synagogues. This infamy was too much for Rudi, who had thrown in his lot with Israel: he had worked on a kibbutz, but in the end his nostalgia for Tierra del Fuego had brought him back to Chile. He simply could not understand how Israel could support such a gang of criminals, and though till then he had always been a model of good humour, he dried up like a neglected plant. One morning we found him dead in his sleeping bag. No need for an autopsy, his face made it clear: Rudi Weismann had died of sadness.

The commander of the Tucapel regiment—a basic respect for paper prevents me from writing his name—was a fanatical admirer of Field Marshal Rommel. When he found a prisoner he liked, he would invite him to recover from the interrogations in his office. After assuring the prisoner that everything that happened in the barracks was in the best interests of our great nation, the commander would offer him a glass of Korn—somebody used to send him this insipid, wheat-based liquor from Germany—and make him sit through a lecture on the Afrika Korps. The guy's parents or grandparents were German, but he couldn't have looked more Chilean: chubby, short-legged, dark untidy hair. You could have mistaken him for a truck driver or a fruit vendor, but when he talked about Rommel he became the caricature of a Nazi guard.

At the end of the lecture he would dramatise Rommel's suicide, click- 5
ing his heels, raising his right hand to his forehead to salute an invisible flag, muttering "Adieu geliebtes Vaterland," and pretending to shoot himself in the mouth. We all hoped that one day he would do it for real.

There was another curious officer in the regiment: a lieutenant struggling to contain a homosexuality that kept popping out all over the place. The soldiers had nicknamed him Daisy, and he knew it.

We could all tell that it was a torment for Daisy not to be able to adorn his body with truly beautiful objects, and the poor guy had to make do with the regulation paraphernalia. He wore a .45 pistol, two cartridge clips, a commando's curved dagger, two hand grenades, a torch, a walkie-talkie, the insignia of his rank and the silver wings of the parachute corps. The prisoners and the soldiers thought he looked like a Christmas tree.

This individual sometimes surprised us with generous and apparently disinterested acts—we didn't know that the Stockholm syndrome could be a military perversion. For example, after the interrogations he would suddenly fill our pockets with cigarettes or the highly prized aspirin tablets with vitamin C. One afternoon he invited me to his room.

"So you're a man of letters," he said, offering me a can of Coca-Cola.

"I've written a couple of stories. That's all," I replied.

"You're not here for an interrogation. I'm very sorry about what's happening, but that's what war is like. I want us to talk as one writer to another. Are you surprised? The army has produced some great men of letters. Think of Don Alonso de Ercilla y Zúñiga, for example."

"Or Cervantes," I added.

Daisy included himself among the greats. That was his problem. If he wanted adulation, he could have it. I drank the Coca-Cola and thought about Garcés, or rather, about his chicken, because, incredible as it seems, the cook had a chicken called Dulcinea, the name of Don Quixote's mistress.

One morning it jumped the wall which separated the common-law prisoners from the POWs, and it must have been a chicken with deep political convictions, because it decided to stay with us. Garcés caressed it and sighed, saying: "If I had a pinch of pepper and a pinch of cumin, I'd make you a chicken marinade like you've never tasted."

"I want you to read my poems and give me your opinion, your honest opinion," said Daisy, handing me a notebook.

I left that room with my pockets full of cigarettes, caramel sweets, tea bags and a tin of US Army marmalade. That afternoon I started to believe in the brotherhood of writers.

They transported us from the prison to the barracks and back in a cattle truck. The soldiers made sure there was plenty of cow shit on the floor of the truck before ordering us to lie face down with our hands behind our necks. We were guarded by four of them, with North American machine guns, one in each corner of the truck. They were almost all young guys brought down from northern garrisons, and the harsh climate of the South kept them flu-ridden and in a perpetually filthy mood. They had orders to fire on the bundles—us—at the slightest suspect movement, or on any civilian who tried to approach the truck. But as time wore on, the discipline gradually relaxed and they turned a blind eye to the packet of cigarettes or piece of fruit thrown from a window, or the pretty and daring girl who ran beside the truck blowing us kisses and shouting: "Don't give up, comrades! We'll win!"

Back in prison, as always, we were met by the welcoming committee organised by Doctor "Skinny" Pragnan, now an eminent psychiatrist in Belgium. First he examined those who couldn't walk and those who had heart problems, then those who had come back with a dislocation or with ribs out of place. Pragnan was expert at estimating how much electricity had been put into us on the grill, and patiently determined who would be able to absorb liquids in the next few hours. Then finally it was time to take communion: we were given the aspirin with vitamin C and an anticoagulant to prevent internal haematomas.

"Dulcinea's days are numbered," I said to Garcés, and looked for a corner in which to read Daisy's notebook.

The elegantly inscribed pages were redolent of love, honey, sublime 20
suffering and forgotten flowers. By the third page I knew that Daisy hadn't even gone to the trouble of reusing the ideas of the Mexican poet Amado Nervo—he'd simply copied out his poems word for word.

I called out to Peyuco Gálvez, a Spanish teacher, and read him a couple of lines.

"What do you think, Peyuco?"

"Amado Nervo. The book is called *The Interior Gardens.*"

I had got myself into a real jam. If Daisy found out that I knew the work of this sugary poet Nervo, then it wasn't Garcés's chicken whose days were numbered, but mine. It was a serious problem, so that night I presented it to the Council of Elders.

"Now, Daisy, would he be the passive or the active type?" enquired 25
Iriarte.

"Stop it, will you. My skin's at risk here," I replied.

"I'm serious. Maybe our friend wants to have an affair with you, and giving you the notebook was like dropping a silk handkerchief. And like a fool you picked it up. Perhaps he copied out the poems for you to find a message in them. I've known queens who seduced boys by lending them *Demian* by Hermann Hesse. If Daisy is the passive type, this business with Amado Nervo means he wants to test your nerve, so to speak. And if he's the active type, well, it would have to hurt less than a kick in the balls."

"Message my arse. He gave you the poems as his own, and you should say you liked them a lot. If he was trying to send a message, he should have given the notebook to Garcés; he's the only one who has an interior garden. Or maybe Daisy doesn't know about the pot plant," remarked Andrés Müller.

"Let's be serious about this. You have to say something to him, and Daisy mustn't even suspect that you know Nervo's poems," declared Pragnan.

"Tell him you liked the poems, but that the adjectives strike you as a 30
bit excessive. Quote Huidobro: when an adjective doesn't give life, it kills. That way you'll show him that you read his poems carefully and that you are criticising his work as a colleague," suggested Gálvez.

The Council of Elders approved of Gálvez's idea, but I spent two weeks on tenterhooks. I couldn't sleep. I wished they would come and take me to be kicked and electrocuted so I could give the damned notebook back. In those two weeks I came to hate good old Garcés:

"Listen, mate, if everything goes well, and you get a little jar of capers as well as the cumin and the pepper, we'll have such a feast with that chicken."

After a fortnight, I found myself at last stretched out face down on the mattress of cowpats with my hands behind my neck. I thought I was going mad: I was happy to be heading towards a session of the activity known as torture.

Tucapel barracks. Service Corps. In the background, the perpetual green of Cerro Ñielol, sacred to the Mapuche Indians. There was a waiting room outside the interrogation cell, like at the doctor's. There they made us sit on a bench with our hands tied behind our backs and black hoods over our heads. I never understood what the hoods were for, because once we got inside they took them off, and we could see the interrogators—the toy soldiers who, with panic-stricken faces, turned the handle of the generator, and the health officers who attached the electrodes to our anuses, testicles, gums and tongue, and then listened with stethoscopes to see who was faking and who had really passed out on the grill.

Lagos, a deacon of the Emmaus International ragmen, was the first to 35
be interrogated that day. For a year they had been working him over to find out how the organisation had come by a couple of dozen old military uniforms which had been found in their warehouses. A trader who sold army surplus gear had donated them. Lagos screamed in pain and repeated over and over what the soldiers wanted to hear: the uniforms belonged to an invading army which was preparing to land on the Chilean coast.

I was waiting for my turn when someone took off the hood. It was Lieutenant Daisy.

"Follow me," he ordered.

We went into an office. On the desk I saw a tin of cocoa and a carton of cigarettes which were obviously there to reward my comments on his literary work.

"Did you read my poesy?" he asked, offering me a seat.

Poesy. Daisy said poesy, not poetry. A man covered with pistols and 40
grenades can't say "poesy" without sounding ridiculous and effete. At that moment he revolted me, and I decided that even if it meant pissing blood, hissing when I spoke and being able to charge batteries just by touching them, I wasn't going to lower myself to flattering a plagiarising faggot in uniform.

"You have pretty handwriting, Lieutenant. But you know these poems aren't yours," I said, giving him back the notebook.

I saw him begin to shake. He was carrying enough arms to kill me several times over, and if he didn't want to stain his uniform, he could order someone else to do it. Trembling with anger he stood up, threw what was on the desk onto the floor and shouted:

"Three weeks in the cube. But first, you're going to visit the chiropodist, you piece of subversive shit!"

The chiropodist was a civilian, a landholder who had lost several thousand hectares in the land reform, and who was getting his revenge by participating in the interrogations as a volunteer. His speciality was peeling back toenails, which led to terrible infections.

I knew the cube. I had spent my first six months of prison there in 45
solitary confinement: it was an underground cell, one and a half metres wide by one and a half metres long by one and a half metres high. In the old days there had been a tannery in the Temuco jail, and the cube was used to store fat. The walls still stank of fat, but after a week your excrement fixed that, making the cube very much a place of your own.

You could only stretch out across the diagonal, but the low temperatures of southern Chile, the rainwater and the soldiers' urine made you want to curl up hugging your legs and stay like that wishing yourself smaller and smaller, so that eventually you could live on one of the islands of floating shit, which conjured up images of dream holidays. I was there for three weeks, running through Laurel and Hardy films, remembering the books of Salgari, Stevenson and London word by word, playing long games of chess, licking my toes to protect them from infection. In the cube I swore over and over again never to become a literary critic.

Analyzing the Text

1. To what paradoxical aspects of prison life does Sepulveda have to adapt in order to survive?
2. What unusual mixture of character traits and aspirations does "Daisy" display, and what kind of a relationship does Sepulveda have with him?

Understanding Sepulveda's Techniques

1. What elements in this autobiographical narrative suggest a work of fiction?
2. Sepulveda's attitude toward his predicament is unusual, as is his use of humor and irony. How do these qualities enable him to cope with the dangerous circumstances that confronted him?

Arguing for an Interpretation

1. If you were in the same situation as Sepulveda, would you have been as honest about Daisy's plagiarism? Why or why not?
2. Discuss the insights this account provides into the forms resistance can take for a political prisoner under a repressive military regime.

TIM O'BRIEN

Tim O'Brien was born in 1946 in Austin, Minnesota, and was educated at Macalester College and Harvard University. Drafted into the army during the Vietnam War, he attained the rank of sergeant and received the Purple Heart. His first published work, If I Die in a Combat Zone, Box Me Up and Ship Me Home *(1973), relates his experiences in Vietnam. This book is an innovative mixture of alternating chapters of fiction and autobiography in which the following nonfiction account first appeared.*

O'Brien's novel Northern Lights *(1974) was followed by the acclaimed work* Going After Cacciato *(1978), which won the National Book Award. Other works include* The Nuclear Age *(1985), a collection of stories entitled* The Things They Carried *(1990), and most recently,* Tomcat in Love *(1998), and* July, July *(2002).*

If I Die in a Combat Zone

The summer of 1968, the summer I turned into a soldier, was a good time for talking about war and peace. Eugene McCarthy was bringing quiet thought to the subject. He was winning votes in the primaries. College students were listening to him, and some of us tried to help out. Lyndon

Johnson was almost forgotten, no longer forbidding or feared; Robert Kennedy was dead but not quite forgotten; Richard Nixon looked like a loser. With all the tragedy and change that summer, it was fine weather for discussion.

And, with all of this, there was an induction notice tucked into a corner of my billfold.

So with friends and acquaintances and townspeople, I spent the summer in Fred's antiseptic cafe, drinking coffee and mapping out arguments on Fred's napkins. Or I sat in Chic's tavern, drinking beer with kids from the farms. I played some golf and tore up the pool table down at the bowling alley, keeping an eye open for likely-looking high school girls.

Late at night, the town deserted, two or three of us would drive a car around and around the town's lake, talking about the war, very seriously, moving with care from one argument to the next, trying to make it a dialogue and not a debate. We covered all the big questions: justice, tyranny, self-determination, conscience and the state, God and war and love.

College friends came to visit: "Too bad, I hear you're drafted. What will 5
you do?"

I said I didn't know, that I'd let time decide. Maybe something would change, maybe the war would end. Then we'd turn to discuss the matter, talking long, trying out the questions, sleeping late in the mornings.

The summer conversations, spiked with plenty of references to the philosophers and academicians of war, were thoughtful and long and complex and careful. But, in the end, careful and precise argumentation hurt me. It was painful to tread deliberately over all the axioms and assumptions and corollaries when the people on the town's draft board were calling me to duty, smiling so nicely.

"It won't be bad at all," they said. "Stop in and see us when it's over."

So to bring the conversations to a focus and also to try out in real words my secret fears, I argued for running away.

I was persuaded then, and I remain persuaded now, that the war was 10
wrong. And since it was wrong and since people were dying as a result of it, it was evil. Doubts, of course, hedged all this: I had neither the expertise nor the wisdom to synthesize answers; most of the facts were clouded, and there was no certainty as to the kind of government that would follow a North Vietnamese victory or, for that matter, an American victory, and the specifics of the conflict were hidden away—partly in men's minds, partly in the archives of government, and partly in buried, irretrievable history. The war, I thought, was wrongly conceived and poorly justified. But perhaps I was mistaken, and who really knew, anyway?

Piled on top of this was the town, my family, my teachers, a whole history of the prairie. Like magnets, these things pulled in one direction or the other, almost physical forces weighting the problem, so that, in the end, it was less reason and more gravity that was the final influence.

My family was careful that summer. The decision was mine and it was not talked about. The town lay there, spread out in the corn and watching me, the mouths of old women and Country Club men poised in a kind of eternal readiness to find fault. It was not a town, not a Minneapolis or New York, where the son of a father can sometimes escape scrutiny. More, I owed the prairie something. For twenty-one years I'd lived under its laws, accepted its education, eaten its food, wasted and guzzled its water, slept well at night, driven across its highways, dirtied and breathed its air, wallowed in its luxuries. I'd played on its Little League teams. I remembered Plato's *Crito,* when Socrates, facing certain death—execution, not war—had the chance to escape. But he reminded himself that he had seventy years in which he could have left the country, if he were not satisfied or felt the agreements he'd made with it were unfair. He had not chosen Sparta or Crete. And, I reminded myself, I hadn't thought much about Canada until that summer.

The summer passed this way. Gold afternoons on the golf course, a comforting feeling that the matter of war would never touch me, nights in the pool hall or drug store, talking with towns-folk, turning the questions over and over, being a philosopher.

Near the end of that summer the time came to go to the war. The family indulged in a cautious sort of Last Supper together, and afterward my father, who is brave, said it was time to report at the bus depot. I moped down to my bedroom and looked the place over, feeling quite stupid, thinking that my mother would come in there in a day or two and probably cry a little. I trudged back up to the kitchen and put my satchel down. Everyone gathered around, saying so long and good health and write and let us know if you want anything. My father took up the induction papers, checking on times and dates and all the last-minute things, and when I pecked my mother's face and grabbed the satchel for comfort, he told me to put it down, that I wasn't supposed to report until tomorrow.

After laughing about the mistake, after a flush of red color and a flood 15
of ribbing and a wave of relief had come and gone, I took a long drive around the lake, looking again at the place. Sunset Park, with its picnic table and little beach and a brown wood shelter and some families swimming. The Crippled Children's School. Slater Park, more kids. A long string of split level houses, painted every color.

The war and my person seemed like twins as I went around the town's lake. Twins grafted together and forever together, as if a separation would kill them both.

The thought made me angry.

In the basement of my house I found some scraps of cardboard and paper. With devilish flair, I printed obscene words on them, declaring my intention to have no part of Vietnam. With delightful viciousness, a secret will, I declared the war evil, the draft board evil, the town evil in its lethargic acceptance of it all. For many minutes, making up the signs, making up my mind, I was outside the town. I was outside the law, all my old ties to my loves and family broken by the old crayon in my hand. I imagined strutting up and down the sidewalks outside the depot, the bus waiting and the driver blaring his horn, the *Daily Globe* photographer trying to push me into line with the other draftees, the frantic telephone calls, my head buzzing at the deed.

On the cardboard, my strokes of bright red were big and ferocious looking. The language was clear and certain and burned with a hard, defiant, criminal, blasphemous sound. I tried reading it aloud.

Later in the evening I tore the signs into pieces and put the shreds in 20
the garbage can outside, clanging the gray cover down and trapping the messages inside. I went back into the basement. I slipped the crayons into their box, the same stubs of color I'd used a long time before to chalk in reds and greens on Roy Rogers' cowboy boots.

I'd never been a demonstrator, except in the loose sense. True, I'd taken a stand in the school newspaper on the war, trying to show why it seemed wrong. But, mostly, I'd just listened.

"No war is worth losing your life for," a college acquiantance used to argue. "The issue isn't a moral one. It's a matter of efficiency: what's the most efficient way to stay alive when your nation is at war? That's the issue."

But others argued that no war is worth losing your country for, and when asked about the case when a country fights a wrong war, those people just shrugged.

Most of my college friends found easy paths away from the problem, all to their credit. Deferments for this and that. Letters from doctors or chaplains. It was hard to find people who had to think much about the problem. Counsel came from two main quarters, pacifists and veterans of foreign wars.

But neither camp had much to offer. It wasn't a matter of peace, as the 25 pacifists argued, but rather a matter of when and when not to join others in making war. And it wasn't a matter of listening to an ex-lieutenant colonel talk about serving in a right war, when the question was whether to serve in what seemed a wrong one.

On August 13, I went to the bus depot. A Worthington *Daily Globe* photographer took my picture standing by a rail fence with four other draftees.

Then the bus took us through corn fields, to little towns along the way—Lismore and Rushmore and Adrian—where other recruits came aboard. With some of the tough guys drinking beer and howling in the back seats, brandishing their empty cans and calling one another "scum" and "trainee" and "GI Joe," with all this noise and hearty farewelling, we went to Sioux Falls. We spent the night in a YMCA. I went out alone for a beer, drank it in a corner booth, then I bought a book and read it in my room.

By noon the next day our hands were in the air, even the tough guys. We recited the proper words, some of us loudly and daringly and others in bewilderment. It was a brightly lighted room, wood paneled. A flag gave the place the right colors, there was some smoke in the air. We said the words, and we were soldiers.

I'd never been much of a fighter. I was afraid of bullies. Their ripe muscles made me angry: a frustrated anger. Still, I deferred to no one. Positively lorded myself over inferiors. And on top of that was the matter of conscience and conviction, uncertain and surface-deep but pure nonetheless: I was a confirmed liberal, not a pacifist; but I would have cast my ballot to end the Vietnam war immediately, I would have voted for Eugene McCarthy, hoping he would make peace. I was not soldier material, that was certain.

But I submitted. All the personal history, all the midnight conversa- 30 tions and books and beliefs and learning, were crumpled by abstention, extinguished by forfeiture, for lack of oxygen, by a sort of sleepwalking default. It was no decision, no chain of ideas or reasons, that steered me into the war.

It was an intellectual and physical stand-off, and I did not have the energy to see it to an end. I did not want to be a soldier, not even an observer to war. But neither did I want to upset a peculiar balance between the order I knew, the people I knew, and my own private world. It was not that I valued that order. But I feared its opposite, inevitable chaos, censure, embarrassment, the end of everything that had happened in my life, the end of it all.

And the stand-off is still there. I would wish this book could take the form of a plea for everlasting peace, a plea from one who knows; from one who's been there and come back, an old soldier looking back at a dying war.

That would be good. It would be fine to integrate it all to persuade my younger brother and perhaps some others to say no to wars and other battles.

Or it would be fine to confirm the odd beliefs about war: it's horrible, but it's a crucible of men and events and, in the end, it makes more of a man out of you.

35 But, still, none of these notions seems right. Men are killed, dead human beings are heavy and awkward to carry, things smell different in Vietnam, soldiers are afraid and often brave, drill sergeants are boors, some men think the war is proper and just and others don't and most don't care. Is that the stuff for a morality lesson, even for a theme?

Do dreams offer lessons? Do nightmares have themes, do we awaken and analyze them and live our lives and advise others as a result? Can the foot soldier teach anything important about war, merely for having been there? I think not. He can tell war stories.

Analyzing the Text

1. What conflicting sets of values weighed on O'Brien when he learned he was drafted? Of these, which was the most significant in determining his ultimate decision?
2. In what ways is the O'Brien who emerges from this account a very different person from the one the townspeople think they know?

Understanding O'Brien's Techniques

1. How would you characterize the tone O'Brien displays—regret, remorse, self-pity, dissatisfaction with himself? What details most effectively communicate this?
2. How does the fact that O'Brien presents himself as unsparingly honest, and even in an entirely unsympathetic light, enhance our ability to understand what he was feeling?

Arguing for an Interpretation

1. Although anyone reading O'Brien's account might speculate on what they would have done in his position, do you feel that his essay conveys the full complexity, ambiguity, and stress of the historical moment in which he was living?
2. How effectively does O'Brien communicate the contrast between the ordinary and pleasant life he lived and the shock of realizing that he was going off to a war he did not support and could very well be killed?

Short Fiction

Ambrose Bierce

Ambrose Bierce (1842–1914?) was born in rural Ohio, the youngest of a large devout poverty-stricken family. He enlisted in the Union Army at the outbreak of the Civil

War as a drummer boy, fought bravely in some of the most important battles, and rose from the rank of private to major. After the war, he became a journalist in San Francisco and wrote satiric pieces for a news weekly, of which he was soon made editor. The biting wit for which Bierce is so distinguished became his hallmark. He worked briefly in London as a journalist; after returning to the United States he wrote his famous "Prattler" column for the Argonaut *magazine. In 1887, William Randolph Hearst bought the column and placed it on the editorial page of the* Sunday Examiner. *He published tales of soldiers and civilians in 1891 and later followed them with* Can Such Things Be? *(1893) and his acerbic* The Devil's Dictionary *(1906). In 1913 he left for Mexico to cover the revolution and vanished without a trace. With characteristic aplomb, his last letter to a friend stated, "Goodbye, if you hear of my being stood up against a Mexican stone wall and shot to rags, please know that I think it a pretty good way to depart this life. It beats old age, disease, or falling down the cellar stairs." "An Occurrence at Owl Creek Bridge" (1890) has emerged as a classic. This haunting story reconstructs an experience so that impressions, colors, sounds, sensations, and time itself are thoroughly subordinated to the psychological state of the narrator.*

An Occurrence at Owl Creek Bridge

I

A man stood upon a railroad bridge in Northern Alabama, looking down into the swift waters twenty feet below. The man's hands were behind his back, the wrists bound with a cord. A rope loosely encircled his neck. It was attached to a stout cross-timber above his head, and the slack fell to the level of his knees. Some loose boards laid upon the sleepers supporting the metals of the railway supplied a footing for him and his executioners—two private soldiers of the Federal army, directed by a sergeant, who in civil life may have been a deputy sheriff. At a short remove upon the same temporary platform was an officer in the uniform of his rank, armed. He was a captain. A sentinel at each end of the bridge stood with his rifle in the position known as "support," that is to say, vertical in front of the left shoulder, the hammer resting on the forearm thrown straight across the chest—a normal and unnatural position, enforcing an erect carriage of the body. It did not appear to be the duty of these two men to know what was occurring at the centre of the bridge; they merely blockaded the two ends of the foot plank which traversed it.

Beyond one of the sentinels nobody was in sight; the railroad ran straight away into a forest for a hundred yards, then, curving, was lost to view. Doubtless there was an outpost further along. The other bank of the stream was open ground—a gentle acclivity crowned with a stockade of vertical tree trunks, loop-holed for rifles, with a single embrasure through which protruded the muzzle of a brass cannon commanding the bridge. Midway of the slope between bridge and fort were the spectators—a single company of infantry in line, at "parade rest," the butts of the rifles on the ground, the barrels inclining slightly backward against the right shoulder, the hands crossed upon the stock. A lieutenant stood at the right of the line, the point of his sword upon the ground, his left hand resting upon his right. Excepting the group of four at the centre of the bridge not a man moved. The company faced the bridge, staring stonily, motionless. The sentinels, facing the banks of the stream, might have been statues to adorn the bridge. The captain stood with folded arms, silent, observing the work of his subordinates but making no sign. Death is a dignitary who, when he comes announced, is to be received with formal manifestations of respect, even by those most familiar with him. In the code of military etiquette silence and fixity are forms of deference.

The man who was engaged in being hanged was apparently about thirty-five years of age. He was a civilian, if one might judge from his dress, which was that of a planter. His features were good—a straight nose, firm mouth, broad forehead, from which his long, dark hair was combed straight back, falling behind his ears to the collar of his well-fitted frock coat. He wore a moustache and pointed beard, but no whiskers; his eyes were large and dark grey and had a kindly expression which one would hardly have expected in one whose neck was in the hemp. Evidently this was no vulgar assassin. The liberal military code makes provision for hanging many kinds of people, and gentlemen are not excluded.

The preparations being complete, the two private soldiers stepped aside and each drew away the plank upon which he had been standing. The sergeant turned to the captain, saluted and placed himself immediately behind that officer, who in turn moved apart one pace. These movements left the condemned man and the sergeant standing on the two ends of the same plank, which spanned three of the cross-ties of the bridge. The end upon which the civilian stood almost, but not quite, reached a fourth. This plank had been held in place by the weight of the captain; it was now held by that of the sergeant. At a signal from the former, the latter would step aside, the plank would tilt and the condemned man go down between two ties. The arrangement commended itself to his judgment as simple and effective. His face had not been covered nor his eyes bandaged. He looked a moment at his "unsteadfast footing," then let his gaze wander to the swirling water of the stream racing madly beneath his feet. A piece of dancing driftwood caught his attention and his eyes followed it down the current. How slowly it appeared to move! What a sluggish stream!

He closed his eyes in order to fix his last thoughts upon his wife and 5
children. The water, touched to gold by the early sun, the brooding mists under the banks at some distance down the stream, the fort, the soldiers, the piece of drift—all had distracted him. And now he became conscious of a new disturbance. Striking through the thought of his dear ones was a sound which he could neither ignore nor understand, a sharp, distinct, metallic percussion like the stroke of a blacksmith's hammer upon the anvil; it had the same ringing quality. He wondered what it was, and whether immeasurably distant or near by—it seemed both. Its recurrence was regular, but as slow as the tolling of a death knell. He awaited each stroke with impatience and—he knew not why—apprehension. The inter-

vals of silence grew progressively longer; the delays became maddening. With their greater infrequency the sounds increased in strength and sharpness. They hurt his ear like the thrust of a knife; he feared he would shriek. What he heard was the ticking of his watch.

He unclosed his eyes and saw again the water below him. "If I could free my hands," he thought, "I might throw off the noose and spring into the stream. By diving I could evade the bullets, and, swimming, vigorously, reach the bank, take to the woods, and get away home. My home, thank God, is as yet outside their lines; my wife and little ones are still beyond the invader's farthest advance."

As these thoughts, which have here to be set down in words, were flashed into the doomed man's brain rather than evolved from it, the captain nodded to the sergeant. The sergeant stepped aside.

II

Peyton Farquhar was a well-to-do planter, of an old and highly-respected Alabama family. Being a slave owner, and, like other slave owners, a politician, he was naturally an original secessionist and ardently devoted to the Southern cause. Circumstances of an imperious nature which it is unnecessary to relate here, had prevented him from taking service with the gallant army which had fought the disastrous campaigns ending with the fall of Corinth, and he chafed under the inglorious restraint, longing for the release of his energies, the larger life of the soldier, the opportunity for distinction. That opportunity, he felt, would come, as it comes to all in war time. Meanwhile he did what he could. No service was too humble for him to perform in aid of the South, no adventure too perilous for him to undertake if consistent with the character of a civilian who was at heart a soldier, and who in good faith and without too much qualification assented to at least a part of the frankly villainous dictum that all is fair in love and war.

One evening while Farquhar and his wife were sitting on a rustic bench near the entrance to his ground, a grey-clad soldier rode up to the gate and asked for a drink of water.[1] Mrs. Farquhar was only too happy to serve him with her own white hands. While she was gone to fetch the water, her husband approached the dusty horseman and inquired eagerly for news from the front.

"The Yanks are repairing the railroads," said the man, "and are getting ready for another advance. They have reached the Owl Creek bridge, put it in order, and built a stockade on the other bank. The commandant has issued an order, which is posted everywhere, declaring that any civilian caught interfering with the railroad, its bridges, tunnels, or trains, will be summarily hanged. I saw the order."

"How far is it to the Owl Creek bridge?" Farquhar asked.

"About thirty miles."

"Is there no force on this side the creek?"

"Only a picket post half a mile out, on the railroad, and a single sentinel at this end of the bridge."

"Suppose a man—a civilian and student of hanging—should elude the picket post and perhaps get the better of the sentinel," said Farquhar, smiling, "what could he accomplish?"

---

[1] "A grey-clad soldier" refers to the gray uniforms worn by Confederate soldiers.

The soldier reflected. "I was there a month ago," he replied. "I observed that the flood of last winter had lodged a great quantity of driftwood against the wooden pier at this end of the bridge. It is now dry and would burn like tow."

The lady had now brought the water, which the soldier drank. He thanked her ceremoniously, bowed to her husband, and rode away. An hour later, after nightfall, he repassed the plantation, going northward in the direction from which he had come. He was a Federal scout.

III

As Peyton Farquhar fell straight downward through the bridge, he lost consciousness and was as one already dead. From this state he was awakened—ages later, it seemed to him—by the pain of a sharp pressure upon his throat, followed by a sense of suffocation. Keen, poignant agonies seemed to shoot from his neck downward through every fibre of his body and limbs. These pains appeared to flash along well-defined lines of ramification, and to beat with an inconceivably rapid periodicity. They seemed like streams of pulsating fire heating him to an intolerable temperature. As to his head, he was conscious of nothing but a feeling of fullness—of congestion. These sensations were unaccompanied by thought. The intellectual part of his nature was already effaced; he had power only to feel, and feeling was torment. He was conscious of motion. Encompassed in a luminous cloud, of which he was now merely the fiery heart, without material substance, he swung through unthinkable arcs of oscillation, like a vast pendulum. Then all at once, with terrible suddenness, the light about him shot upward with the noise of a loud plash; a frightful roaring was in his ears, and all was cold and dark. The power of thought was restored; he knew that the rope had broken and he had fallen into the stream. There was no additional strangulation; the noose about his neck was already suffocating him, and kept the water from his lungs. To die of hanging at the bottom of a river—the idea seemed to him ludicrous. He opened his eyes in the blackness and saw above him a gleam of light, but how distant, how inaccessible! He was still sinking, for the light became fainter and fainter until it was a mere glimmer. Then it began to grow and brighten, and he knew that he was rising toward the surface—knew it with reluctance, for he was now very comfortable. "To be hanged and drowned," he thought, "that is not so bad; but I do not wish to be shot. No: I will not be shot; that is not fair."

He was not conscious of an effort, but a sharp pain in his wrist apprised him that he was trying to free his hands. He gave the struggle his attention, as an idler might observe the feat of a juggler, without interest in the outcome. What splendid effort!—what magnificent, what superhuman strength! Ah, that was a fine endeavor! Bravo! The cord fell away; his arms parted and floated upward, the hands dimly seen on each side in the growing light. He watched them with a new interest as first one and then the other pounced upon the noose at his neck. They tore it away and thrust it fiercely aside, its undulations resembling those of a water-snake. "Put it back, put it back!" He thought he shouted these words to his hands, for the undoing of the noose had been succeeded by the direst pang which he had yet experienced. His neck arched horribly; his brain was on fire; his heart, which had been fluttering faintly, gave a great leap, trying to force itself out at his mouth. His whole body was racked and wrenched with an insupportable anguish! But his disobedient hands gave no heed to the command. They beat the water vigorously with quick, downward strokes, forcing him to the surface. He felt his head emerge; his eyes were blinded by the sunlight; his chest expanded convulsively, and with a supreme and crowning agony his lungs engulfed a great draught of air, which instantly he expelled in a shriek!

He was now in full possession of his physical senses. They were, in- 20
deed, preternaturally keen and alert. Something in the awful disturbance of his organic system had so exalted and refined them that they made record of things never before perceived. He felt the ripples upon his face and heard their separate sounds as they struck. He looked at the forest on the bank of the stream, saw the individual trees, the leaves and the veining of each leaf—saw the very insects upon them, the locusts, the brilliant-bodied flies, the grey spiders stretching their webs from twig to twig. He noted the prismatic colors in all the dewdrops upon a million blades of grass. The humming of the gnats that danced above the eddies of the stream, the beating of the dragon flies' wings, the strokes of the water spiders' legs, like oars which had lifted their boat—all these made audible music. A fish slid along beneath his eyes and he heard the rush of its body parting the water.

He had come to the surface facing down the stream; in a moment the visible world seemed to wheel slowly round, himself the pivotal point, and he saw the bridge, the fort, the soldiers upon the bridge, the captain, the sergeant, the two privates, his executioners. They were in silhouette against the blue sky. They shouted and gesticulated, pointing at him; the captain had drawn his pistol, but did not fire; the others were unarmed. Their movements were grotesque and horrible, their forms gigantic.

Suddenly he heard a sharp report and something struck the water smartly within a few inches of his head, spattering his face with spray. He heard a second report, and saw one of the sentinels with his rifle at his shoulder, a light cloud of blue smoke rising from the muzzle. The man in the water saw the eye of the man on the bridge gazing into his own through the sights of the rifle. He observed that it was a grey eye, and remembered having read that grey eyes were keenest and that all famous marksmen had them. Nevertheless, this one had missed.

A counter swirl had caught Farquhar and turned him half round; he was again looking into the forest on the bank opposite the fort. The sound of a clear, high voice in a monotonous singsong now rang out behind him and came across the water with a distinctness that pierced and subdued all other sounds, even the beating of the ripples in his ears. Although no soldier, he had frequented camps enough to know the dread significance of that deliberate, drawling, aspirated chant; the lieutenant on shore was taking a part in the morning's work. How coldly and pitilessly—with what an even, calm intonation, presaging and enforcing tranquility in the men—with what accurately-measured intervals fell those cruel words:

"Attention, company. . . . Shoulder arms. . . . Ready. . . . Aim. . . . Fire."

Farquhar dived—dived as deeply as he could. The water roared in his 25
ears like the voice of Niagara, yet he heard the dulled thunder of the volley, and rising again toward the surface, met shining bits of metal, singularly flattened, oscillating slowly downward. Some of them touched him on the face and hands, then fell away, continuing their descent. One lodged between his collar and neck; it was uncomfortably warm, and he snatched it out.

As he rose to the surface, gasping for breath, he saw that he had been a long time under water; he was perceptibly farther down stream—nearer to safety. The soldiers had almost finished reloading; the metal ramrods flashed all at one in the sunshine as they were drawn from the barrels, turned in the air, and thrust into their sockets. The two sentinels fired again, independently and ineffectually.

The hunted man saw all this over his shoulder; he was now swimming vigorously with the current. His brain was as energetic as his arms and legs; he thought with the rapidity of lightning.

"The officer," he reasoned, "will not make the martinet's error a second time. It is as easy to dodge a volley as a single shot. He has probably already given the command to fire at will. God help me, I cannot dodge them all!"

An appalling plash within two yards of him, followed by a loud rushing sound, *diminuendo,* which seemed to travel back through the air to the fort and died in an explosion which stirred the very river to its deeps![2] A rising sheet of water, which curved over him, fell down upon him, blinded him, strangled him! The cannon had taken a hand in the game. As he shook his head free from the commotion of the smitten water, he heard the deflected shot humming through the air ahead, and in an instant it was cracking and smashing the branches in the forest beyond.

"They will not do that again," he thought; "the next time they will use a charge of grape. I must keep my eye upon the gun; the smoke will apprise me—the report arrives too late; it lags behind the missile. It is a good gun."

Suddenly he felt himself whirled round and round—spinning like a top. The water, the banks, the forest, the now distant bridge, fort, and men—all were commingled and blurred. Objects were represented by their colors only; circular horizontal streaks of color—that was all he saw. He had been caught in a vortex and was being whirled on with a velocity of advance and gyration which made him giddy and sick. In a few moments he was flung upon the gravel at the foot of the left bank of the stream—the southern bank—and behind a projecting point which concealed him from his enemies. The sudden arrest of his motion, the abrasion of one of his hands on the gravel, restored him and he wept with delight. He dug his fingers into the sand, threw it over himself in handfuls and audibly blessed it. It looked like gold, like diamonds, rubies, emeralds; he could think of nothing beautiful which it did not resemble. The trees upon the bank were giant garden plants; he noted a definite order in their arrangement, inhaled the fragrance of their blooms. A strange, roseate light shone through the spaces among their trunks, and the wind made in their branches the music of æolian harps.[3] He had no wish to perfect his escape, was content to remain in that enchanting spot until retaken.

A whizz and rattle of grapeshot among the branches high above his head roused him from his dream. The baffled cannoneer had fired him a random farewell. He sprang to his feet, rushed up the sloping bank, and plunged into the forest.

All that day he travelled, laying his course by the rounding sun. The forest seemed interminable; nowhere did he discover a break in it, not even a

---

[2]*Diminuendo:* a gradually diminishing volume, a term used in music.

[3]æolian harp: a musical instrument consisting of a box equipped with strings of equal length that are tuned in unison. Such harps were placed in windows to produce harmonious tones sounded by the wind.

woodman's road. He had not known that he lived in so wild a region. There was something uncanny in the revelation.

By nightfall he was fatigued, footsore, famishing. The thought of his wife and children urged him on. At last he found a road which led him in what he knew to be the right direction. It was as wide and straight as a city street, yet it seemed untravelled. No fields bordered it, no dwelling anywhere. Not so much as the barking of a dog suggested human habitation. The black bodies of the great trees formed a straight wall on both sides, terminating on the horizon in a point, like a diagram in a lesson in perspective. Overhead, as he looked up through this rift in the wood, shone great golden stars looking unfamiliar and grouped in strange constellations. He was sure they were arranged in some order which had a secret and malign significance. The wood on either side was full of singular noises, among which—once, twice, and again—he distinctly heard whispers in an unknown tongue.

His neck was in pain, and, lifting his hand to it, he found it horribly 35
swollen. He knew that it had a circle of black where the rope had bruised it. His eyes felt congested; he could no longer close them. His tongue was swollen with thirst; he relieved its fever by thrusting it forward from between his teeth into the cool air. How softly the turf had carpeted the untravelled avenue! He could no longer feel the roadway beneath his feet!

Doubtless, despite his suffering, he fell asleep while walking, for now he sees another scene—perhaps he has merely recovered from a delirium. He stands at the gate of his own home. All is as he left it, and all bright and beautiful in the morning sunshine. He must have travelled the entire night. As he pushes open the gate and passes up the wide white walk, he sees a flutter of female garments; his wife, looking fresh and cool and sweet, steps down from the verandah to meet him. At the bottom of the steps she stands waiting, with a smile of ineffable joy, an attitude of matchless grace and dignity. Ah, how beautiful she is! He springs forward with extended arms. As he is about to clasp her, he feels a stunning blow upon the back of the neck; a blinding white light blazes all about him, with a sound like a shock of a cannon—then all is darkness and silence!

Peyton Farquhar was dead; his body, with a broken neck, swung gently from side to side beneath the timbers of the Owl Creek bridge.

Analyzing the Text

1. What do we know about Peyton Farquhar that might explain why he volunteers for the mission that results in his capture?
2. How has Bierce handled the passage of time as the story unfolds, so that we enter Farquhar's mind and perceive events as they appear to him?

Understanding Bierce's Techniques

1. How has Bierce depicted Farquhar as a sympathetic figure so that the reader will want to believe that he has managed to escape?
2. What different vantage points does Bierce take in each of the three sections of the story, and taken together, how do they lead to the final image?

Arguing for an Interpretation

1. Considering the many clues Bierce has inserted into the narrative through foreshadowing, why would the ending be a shock to many readers? Was it for you? Why or why not?

2. If the story is viewed as a deep psychological conflict in Farquhar's mind between the need to accept death and the desire to deny what is happening, how effectively does Bierce project both sides of this struggle? You might wish to rent the 1990 film *Jacob's Ladder*, and compare its use of the same premise to tell the story of a soldier in Vietnam.

TADEUSZ BOROWSKI

Tadeusz Borowski (1922–1951) was born in the Soviet Ukraine of Polish parents and was educated by attending secret lectures at Warsaw University during the Nazi occupation of Poland. He published his first volume of verse, Whenever the Earth, *in 1942. The following year he was arrested by the Gestapo and was ultimately sent to Auschwitz, where he survived by working as a hospital orderly. After the war, Borowski returned to Warsaw, where he lectured at the University. In 1946, the first of three collections based on his concentration camp experiences was published in Munich.* Farewell to Maria *and* A World of Stone *were published in Poland in 1948. The experience of his own dehumanization in the brutalizing conditions of Auschwitz formed the basis for his most significant work on the Holocaust, ironically titled,* This Way for the Gas, Ladies and Gentlemen *(1967), in which "Silence" first appeared. Borowski's searing, unsentimental portrayal of life in the concentration camps is told from the viewpoint of Vorabeiter ("foreman") Tadeusz, a narrator with whom Borowski himself is identified. Tragically, Borowski, who had survived the gas chambers and was seen as the bright hope of Polish literature, took his own life in July of 1951 at the age of 29 by turning on the gas.*

Silence

At last they seized him inside the German barracks, just as he was about to climb over the window ledge. In absolute silence they pulled him down to the floor and panting with hate dragged him into a dark alley. Here, closely surrounded by a silent mob, they began tearing at him with greedy hands.

Suddenly from the camp gate a whispered warning was passed from one mouth to another. A company of soldiers, their bodies leaning forward, their rifles on the ready, came running down the camp's main road, weaving between the clusters of men in stripes standing in the way. The crowd scattered and vanished inside the blocks. In the packed, noisy barracks the prisoners were cooking food pilfered during the night from neighbouring farmers. In the bunks and in the passageways between them, they were grinding grain in small flour-mills, slicing meat on heavy slabs of wood, peeling potatoes and throwing the peels on to the floor.

They were playing cards for stolen cigars, stirring batter for pancakes, gulping down hot soup, and lazily killing fleas. A stifling odour of sweat hung in the air, mingled with the smell of food, with smoke and with steam that liquefied along the ceiling beams and fell on the men, the bunks and the food in large, heavy drops, like autumn rain.

There was a stir at the door. A young American officer with a tin helmet on his head entered the block and looked with curiosity at the bunks and the tables. He wore a freshly pressed uniform; his revolver was hanging down, strapped in an open holster that dangled against his thigh. He was assisted by the translator who wore a yellow band reading "interpreter" on the sleeve of his civilian coat, and by the chairman of the Prisoners' Committee, dressed in a white summer coat, a pair of tuxedo trousers and tennis shoes. The men in the barracks fell silent. Leaning out of their bunks and lifting their eyes from the kettles, bowls and cups, they gazed attentively into the officer's face.

"Gentlemen," said the officer with a friendly smile, taking off his helmet—and the interpreter proceeded at once to translate sentence after sentence—"I know, of course, that after what you have gone through and after what you have seen, you must feel a deep hate for your tormentors. But we, the soldiers of America, and you, the people of Europe, have fought so that law should prevail over lawlessness. We must show our respect for the law. I assure you that the guilty will be punished, in this camp as well as in all the others. You have already seen, for example, that the S.S. men were made to bury the dead."

". . . right, we could use the lot at the back of the hospital. A few of them are still around," whispered one of the men in a bottom bunk.

". . . or one of the pits," whispered another. He sat straddling the bunk, his fingers firmly clutching the blanket.

"Shut up! Can't you wait a little longer? Now listen to what the American has to say," a third man, stretched across the foot of the same bunk, spoke in an angry whisper. The American officer was now hidden from their view behind the thick crowd gathered at the other end of the block.

"Comrades, our new Kommandant gives you his word of honour that all the criminals of the S.S. as well as among the prisoners will be punished," said the translator. The men in the bunks broke into applause and shouts. In smiles and gestures they tried to convey their friendly approval of the young man from across the ocean.

"And so the Kommandant requests," went on the translator, his voice turning somewhat hoarse, "that you try to be patient and do not commit lawless deeds, which may only lead to trouble, and please pass the sons of bitches over to the camp guards. How about it, men?"

The block answered with a prolonged shout. The American thanked the translator and wished the prisoners a good rest and an early reunion with their dear ones. Accompanied by a friendly hum of voices, he left the block and proceeded to the next.

Not until after he had visited all the blocks and returned with the soldiers to his headquarters did we pull our man off the bunk—where covered with blankets and half-smothered with the weight of our bodies he lay gagged, his face buried in the straw mattress—and dragged him on to the cement floor under the stove, where the entire block, grunting and growling with hatred, trampled him to death.

Analyzing the Text

1. How do the objectives of the American soldiers who liberate the concentration camp survivors differ from those of the prisoners?
2. What insight into the world of the concentration camp does Borowski provide that explains the choice of the title?

Understanding Borowski's Techniques

1. How do the details Borowski uses to describe the prisoners in the concentration camp reinforce the enormous gulf that separates them from their rescuers?
2. How do the comments of the prisoners reveal that they are simply biding their time before they take their revenge?

Arguing for an Interpretation

1. If you were one of the prisoners, do you think you would have acted as they did? Why or why not?
2. Why couldn't the young American officer, or others who had not endured what the prisoners had, ever really understand their feelings and actions? What insight does this story offer into the dehumanizing effects of warfare? Explain your answer.

IRENE ZABYTKO

Irene Zabytko was born in 1954 to a Ukrainian family in Chicago. Her fiction has won the PEN Syndicated Fiction Project, and she is the founder and publisher of Odessa Pressa *Productions. Her recent works are* The Sky Unwashed *(2000), a novel based on the nuclear accident in Chernobyl, Russia and* When Luba Leaves Home: A Profile in Stories *(2003). The following story originally appeared in* The Perimeter of Light: Writing about the Vietnam War, *edited by Vivian Vie Balfour (1992).*

Home Soil

I watch my son crack his knuckles, oblivious to the somber sounds of the Old Slavonic hymns the choir behind us is singing.

We are in the church where Bohdan, my son, was baptized nineteen years ago. It is Sunday. The pungent smell of frankincense permeates the darkened atmosphere of this cathedral. Soft sun rays illuminate the stained-glass windows. I sit near the one that shows Jesus on the cross looking down on some unidentifiable Apostles who are kneeling beneath His nailed feet. In the background, a tiny desperate Judas swings from a rope, the thirty pieces of silver thrown on the ground.

There is plenty of room in my pew, but my son chooses not to sit with me. I see him staring at the round carapace of a ceiling, stoic icons staring directly back at him. For the remainder of the Mass, he lightly drums his nervous fingers on top of the cover of *My Divine Friend,* the Americanized prayer book of the Ukrainian service. He took bongo lessons before he graduated high school, and learned the basic rolls from off a record, "Let's Swing with Bongos." I think it was supposed to make him popular with the girls at parties. I also think he joined the army because he wanted the virile image men in uniforms have that the bongos never delivered. When he returned from Nam, he mentioned after one of our many conversational silences that he lost the bongos, and the record is cracked, with the pieces buried somewhere deep inside the duffel bag he still hasn't unpacked.

Bohdan, my son, who calls himself Bob, has been back for three weeks. He looks so "American" in his green tailored uniform: his spit-shined vinyl dress shoes tap against the red-cushioned kneelers. It was his idea to go to church with me. He has not been anywhere since he came home. He won't even visit my garden.

Luba, my daughter, warned me he would be moody. She works for the 5
Voice of America and saw him when he landed from Nam in San Francisco. "Just don't worry, *tato*,"[1] she said to me on the telephone. "He's acting weird. Culture shock."

"Explain what you mean."

"Just, you know, strange." For a disc jockey, and a bilingual one at that, she is so inarticulate. She plays American jazz and tapes concerts for broadcasts for her anonymous compatriots in Ukraine. That's what she was doing when she was in San Francisco, taping some jazz concert. Pure American music for the huddled gold-toothed youths who risk their *komsomol* privileges and maybe their lives listening to these clandestine broadcasts and to my daughter's sweet voice. She will never be able to visit our relatives back there because American security won't allow it, and she would lose her job. But it doesn't matter. After my wife died, I have not bothered to keep up with anyone there, and I don't care if they have forgotten all about me. It's just as well.

I noticed how much my son resembled my wife when I first saw him again at the airport. He was alone, near the baggage claim ramp. He was taller than ever, and his golden hair was bleached white from the jungle sun. He inherited his mother's high cheekbones, but he lost his baby fat, causing his cheeks to jut out from his lean face as sharp as the arrowheads he used to scavenge for when he was a kid.

We hugged briefly. I felt his medals pinch through my thin shirt. "You look good, son," I tied. I avoided his eyes and concentrated on a pin shaped like an open parachute that he wore over his heart.

"Hi, *tato*," he murmured. We spoke briefly about his flight home from 10
San Francisco, how he'd seen Luba. We stood apart, unlike the other soldiers with their families who were hugging and crying on each other's shoulders in a euphoric delirium.

He grabbed his duffle bag from the revolving ramp and I walked behind him to see if he limped or showed any signs of pain. He showed nothing.

"Want to drive?" I asked, handing him the keys to my new Plymouth.

"Nah," he said. He looked around at the cars crowding the parking lot, and I thought he seemed afraid. "I don't remember how the streets go anymore."

An usher in his best borscht-red polyester suit waits for me to drop some money into the basket. It is old Pan[2] Medved, toothless except

---

[1]*tato:* "Father" or "Dad."

[2]*Pan:* a term of respect for adult males, the equivalent of *Mr.*

for the prominent gold ones he flashes at me as he pokes me with his basket.

15 "*Nu,* give," he whispers hoarsely, but loud enough for a well-dressed woman with lacquered hair who sits in front of me to turn around and stare in mute accusation.

I take out the gray and white snakeskin wallet Bohdan brought back for me, and transfer out a ten dollar bill. I want the woman to see it before it disappears into the basket. She smiles at me and nods.

Women always smile at me like that. Especially after they see my money and find out that I own a restaurant in the neighborhood. None of the Ukies[3] go there; they don't eat fries and burgers much. But the "jackees"—the Americans—do when they're sick of eating in the cafeteria at the plastics factory. My English is pretty good for a D.P., and no one has threatened to bomb my business because they accuse me of being a no-god bohunk commie. Not yet anyway.

But the women are always impressed. I usually end up with the emigrés—some of them Ukrainians. The Polish women are the greediest for gawdy trinkets and for a man to give them money so that they can return to their husbands and children in Warsaw. I like them the best anyway because they laugh more than the other women I see, and they know how to have a good time.

Bohdan knows nothing about my lecherous life. I told the women to stay clear after my son arrived. He is so lost with women. I think he was a virgin when he joined the army, but I'm sure he isn't now. I can't ask him.

20 After mass ends, I lose Bohdan in the tight clusters of people leaving their pews and genuflecting toward the iconostasis. He waits for me by the holy water font. It looks like a regular porcelain water fountain but without a spout. There is a sponge in the basin that is moistened with the holy water blessed by the priests here. Bohdan stands towering over the font, dabs his fingers into the sponge, but doesn't cross himself the way he was taught to do as a boy.

"What's the matter?" I ask in English. I hope he will talk to me if I speak to him in his language.

But Bohdan ignores me and watches an elderly woman gingerly entering the door of the confessional. "What she got to say? Why is she going in there?"

"Everyone has sins."

"Yeah, but who forgives?"

25 "God forgives," I say. I regret it because it makes me feel like a hypocrite whenever I parrot words I still find difficult to believe.

We walk together in the neighborhood; graffiti visible in the alley-ways despite the well-trimmed lawns with flowers and "bathtub" statues of the Blessed Mary smiling benevolently at us as we pass by the small bungalows. I could afford to move out of here, out of Chicago and into some nearby cushy suburb, Skokie or something. But what for? Some smart Jewish lawyer or doctor would be my next door neighbor and find out that I'm a Ukie and complain to me about how his grandmother was raped by Petliura.[4] I've heard it before. Anyway, I like where I am. I bought a

---

[3]*Ukies:* Ukrainian Americans.

[4]*Petliura:* Simeon Petliura (1879–1926), an anti-Bolshevik Ukrainian leader who was accused of responsibility for Jewish pogroms during World War I. When his forces were defeated by the Russians he went into exile in Paris, where he was ultimately assassinated by a Jewish nationalist.

three-flat apartment building after my wife died and I live in one of the apartments rent-free. I can walk to my business, and see the past—old women in babushkas sweeping the sidewalks in front of their cherished gardens; men in Italian-made venetian-slat sandals and woolen socks rushing to a chess match at the Soyuiez, a local meeting place where the D.P.s sit for hours rehashing the war over beers and chess.

Bohdan walks like a soldier. Not exactly a march, but a stiff gait that a good posture in a rigid uniform demands. He looks masculine, but tired and worn. Two pimples are sprouting above his lip where a faint moustache is starting.

"Want a cigarette?" I ask. Soldiers like to smoke. During the forties, I smoked that horrible cheap tobacco, *mahorka.* I watch my son puff heavily on the cigarette I've given him, with his eyes partially closed, delicately cupping his hands to protect it from the wind. In my life, I have seen so many soldiers in that exact pose; they all look the same. When their faces are contorted from sucking the cigarette, there is an unmistakable shadow of vulnerability and fear of living. That gesture and stance are more eloquent than the blood and guts war stories men spew over their beers.

Pan Medved, the battered gold-toothed relic in the church, has that look. Pan Holewski, one of my tenants, has it too. I would have known it even if he never openly displayed his old underground soldier's cap that sits on a bookshelf in the living room between small Ukrainian and American flags. I see it every time I collect the rent.

I wish Bohdan could tell me what happened to him in Vietnam. What 30
did he do? What was done to him? Maybe now isn't the time to tell me. He may never tell me. I never told anyone either.

I was exactly his age when I became a soldier. At nineteen, I was a student at the university in L'vov, which the Poles occupied. I was going to be a poet, to study poetry and write it, but the war broke out, and my family could not live on the romantic epics I tried to publish, so I was paid very well by the Nazis to write propaganda pamphlets. "Freedom for Ukrainians" I wrote—"Freedom for our people. Fight the Poles and Russians alongside our German brothers" and other such dreck. I even wrote light verse that glorified Hitler as the protector of the free Ukrainian nation that the Germans promised us. My writing was as naïve as my political ideas.

My new career began in a butcher shop, commandeered after the Polish owner was arrested and shot. I set my battered Underwood typewriter atop an oily wooden table where crescents of chicken feathers still clung between the cracks. Meat hooks that once held huge sides of pork hung naked in a back room, and creaked ominously like a deserted gallows whenever anyone slammed the front door. Every shred of meat had been stolen by looters after the Germans came into the city. Even the little bell that shopkeepers kept at the entrance was taken. But I was very comfortable in my surroundings. I thought only about how I was to play a part in a historical destiny that my valiant words would help bring about. That delusion lasted only about a week or so until three burly Nazis came in. "*Schnell!*" they said to me, pushing me out of my chair and pointing to the windows where I saw crowds chaotically swarming about. Before I could question the soldiers, one of them shoved a gun into my hands and pushed me out into the streets. I felt so bewildered until the moment I pointed my rifle at a man who was about—I thought—to hit me with a club of some sort. Suddenly, I felt such an intense charge of power, more so than I had ever felt writing some of my best poems. I was no longer dealing with abstract words and ideas for a mythological cause; I was responsible for life and death.

I enjoyed that power, until it seeped into my veins and poisoned my soul. It was only an instant, a brief interlude, a matter of hours until that transformation occurred. I still replay that scene in my mind almost forty years after it happened, no matter what I am doing, or who I am with.

I think she was a village girl. Probably a Jew, because on that particular day, the Jews were the ones chosen to be rounded up and sent away in cattle cars. Her hair was golden red, short and wavy as was the style, and her neck was awash in freckles. It was a crowded station in the center of the town, not far from the butcher shop. There were Germans shouting and women crying and church bells ringing. I stood with that German regulation rifle I hardly knew how to handle, frozen because I was too lightheaded and excited. I too began to yell at people and held the rifle against my chest, and I was very much aware of how everyone responded to my authority.

Then, this girl appeared in my direct line of vision. Her back was 35
straight, her shoulders tensed; she stopped in the middle of all the chaos. Simply stopped. I ran up and pushed her. I pushed her hard, she almost fell. I kept pushing her, feeling the thin material of her cheap wool jacket against my chapped eager hand; her thin muscles forced forward by my shoves. Once, twice, until she toppled into the open door of a train and fell toward a heap of other people moving deeper into the tiny confines of the stinking cattle car. She never turned around.

I should have shot her. I should have spared her from whatever she had to go through. I doubt she survived. I should have tried to find out what her name was, so I could track down her relatives and confess to them. At least in that way, they could have spat at me injustice and I would have finally received the absolution I will probably never find in this life.

I don't die. Instead, I go to the garden. It is Sunday evening. I am weeding the crop of beets and cabbages I planted in the patch in my backyard. The sun is lower, a breeze kicks up around me, but my forehead sweats. I breathe in the thick deep earth smells as the dirt crumbles and rotates against the blade of my hoe. I should destroy the honeysuckle vine that is slowly choking my plants, but the scent is so sweet, and its intoxicating perfume reminds me of a woman's gentleness.

I hoe for a while, but not for long, because out of the corner of my eye, I see Bohdan sitting on the grass tearing the firm green blades with his clenched hands. He is still wearing his uniform, all except the jacket, tie, and cap. He sits with his legs apart, his head down, ignoring the black flies that nip at his ears.

I wipe my face with a bright red bandana, which I brought with me to tie up the stalks of my drooping sunflowers. "Bohdan," I say to my son. "Why don't we go into the house and have a beer. I can finish this another time." I look at the orange sun. "It's humid and there's too many flies—means rain will be coming."

My son is quietly crying to myself. 40

"*Tato,* I didn't know anything," he cries out. "You know, I just wanted to jump out from planes with my parachute. I just wanted to fly . . ."

"I should have stopped you," I say more to myself than to him. Bohdan lets me stroke the thin spikes of his army regulation crew-cut which is soft and warm and I am afraid of how easily my hand can crush his skull.

I rock him in my arms the way I saw his mother embrace him when he was afraid to sleep alone.

There is not much more I can do right now except to hold him. I will hold him until he pulls away.

Analzying the Text

1. What did the narrator discover about himself during World War II that has since tormented him?
2. What is the relationship between the past event that the narrator obsessively remembers and his current concerns for his son who just returned from Vietnam?

Understanding Zabytko's Techniques

1. What ideas and phrases make clear that Zabytko intends for the reader to parallel the son's experiences with those of the narrator?
2. To what extent is the power of life and death given to the narrator during his wartime experiences ominously echoed in the statement "I'm afraid of how easily my hand can crush his skull"?

Arguing for an Interpretation

1. To what extent does the narrator wish to spare his son the lifelong torment he himself has suffered? How do we know this?
2. Why is it ironic that religion plays such an important role in the background of the story when the narrator speaks of "the absolution I will probably never find in this life"?

PANOS IOANNIDES

Panos Ioannides was born in Cyprus in 1935 and was educated in Cyprus, the United States, and Canada. He has been the head of television programs at Cyprus Broadcasting Corporation and is the author of many plays that have been staged or telecast internationally; he has also written novels, short stories, and radio scripts. Ioannides has won many awards for his prose works, such as his novel Census *(1968) and his short story collections* Epics of Cyprus *(1971) and* The Unseen View *(1973). "Gregory" was written in 1963 and first appeared in* The Charioteer, a Review of Modern Greek Literature *(1965). The English translation is by Marion Byron Raizis and Catherine Raizis. This compelling story is based on a true incident that took place during the Cypriot liberation struggle against the British in the late 1950s. Ioannides takes the unusual approach of letting the reader experience the torments of a soldier ordered to shoot a prisoner, Gregory, who had saved his life and had become his friend.*

Gregory

My hand was sweating as I held the pistol. The curve of the trigger was biting against my finger.

Facing me, Gregory trembled.

His whole being was beseeching me, "Don't!"

Only his mouth did not make a sound. His lips were squeezed tight. If it had been me, I would have screamed, shouted, cursed.

The soldiers were watching . . .

The day before, during a brief meeting, they had each given their opinions: "It's tough luck, but it has to be done. We've got no choice."

The order from Headquarters was clear: "As soon as Lieutenant Rafel's execution is announced, the hostage Gregory is to be shot and his body must be hanged from a telegraph pole in the main street as an exemplary punishment."

It was not the first time that I had to execute a hostage in this war. I had acquired experience, thanks to Headquarters which had kept entrusting me with these delicate assignments. Gregory's case was precisely the sixth.

The first time, I remember, I vomited. The second time I got sick and had a headache for days. The third time I drank a bottle of rum. The fourth, just two glasses of beer. The fifth time I joked about it, "This little guy, with the big pop-eyes, won't be much of a ghost!"

But why, dammit, when the day came did I have to start thinking that I'm not so tough, after all? The thought had come at exactly the wrong time and spoiled all my disposition to do my duty.

You see, this Gregory was such a miserable little creature, such a puny thing, such a nobody, damn him.

That very morning, although he had heard over the loudspeakers that Rafel had been executed, he believed that we would spare his life because we had been eating together so long.

"Those who eat from the same mess tins and drink from the same water canteen," he said, "remain good friends no matter what."

And a lot more of the same sort of nonsense.

He was a silly fool—we had smelled that out the very first day Headquarters gave him to us. The sentry guarding him had got dead drunk and had dozed off. The rest of us with exit permits had gone from the barracks. When we came back, there was Gregory sitting by the sleeping sentry and thumbing through a magazine.

"Why didn't you run away, Gregory?" we asked, laughing at him, several days later.

And he answered, "Where would I go in this freezing weather? I'm O.K. here."

So we started teasing him.

"You're dead right. The accommodations here are splendid . . ."

"It's not bad here," he replied. "The barracks where I used to be are like a sieve. The wind blows in from every side . . ."

We asked him about his girl. He smiled.

"Maria is a wonderful person," he told us. "Before I met her she was engaged to a no-good fellow, a pig. He gave her up for another girl. Then nobody in the village wanted to marry Maria. I didn't miss my chance. So what if she is second-hand. Nonsense. Peasant ideas, my friend. She's beautiful and good-hearted. What more could I want? And didn't she load me with watermelons and cucumbers every time I passed by her vegetable garden? Well, one day I stole some cucumbers and melons and watermelons and I took them to her. 'Maria,' I said, 'from now on I'm going to take care of you.' She started crying and then me, too. But ever since that day she has given me lots of trouble—jealousy. She wouldn't let me go even to my mother's. Until the day I was recruited, she wouldn't let me go far from her apron strings. But that was just what I wanted . . ."

He used to tell this story over and over, always with the same words, the same commonplace gestures. At the end he would have a good laugh and start gulping from his water jug.

His tongue was always wagging! When he started talking, nothing could stop him. We used to listen and nod our heads, not saying a word. But sometimes, as he was telling us about his mother and family problems, we couldn't help wondering, "Eh, well, these people have the same headaches in their country as we've got."

Strange, isn't it!

Except for his talking too much, Gregory wasn't a bad fellow. He was a marvelous cook. Once he made us some apple tarts, so delicious we licked the platter clean. And he could sew, too. He used to sew on all our buttons, patch our clothes, darn our socks, iron our ties, wash our clothes . . .

How the devil could you kill such a friend?

Even though his name was Gregory and some people on his side had killed one of ours, even though we had left wives and children to go to war against him and his kind—but how can I explain? He was our friend. He actually liked us! A few days before, hadn't he killed with his own bare hands a scorpion that was climbing up my leg? He could have let it send me to hell!

"Thanks, Gregory!" I said then, "Thank God who made you . . ."

When the order came, it was like a thunderbolt. Gregory was to be shot, it said, and hanged from a telegraph pole as an exemplary punishment.

We got together inside the barracks. We sent Gregory to wash some underwear for us.

"It ain't right."

"What is right?"

"Our duty!"

"Shit!"

"If you dare, don't do it! They'll drag you to court-martial and then bang-bang . . ."

Well, of course. The right thing is to save your skin. That's only logical. It's either your skin or his. His, of course, even if it was Gregory, the fellow you've been sharing the same plate with, eating with your fingers, and who was washing your clothes that very minute.

What could I do? That's war. We had seen worse things.

So we set the hour.

We didn't tell him anything when he came back from the washing. He slept peacefully. He snored for the last time. In the morning, he heard the news over the loudspeaker and he saw that we looked gloomy and he began to suspect that something was up. He tried talking to us, but he got no answers and then he stopped talking.

He just stood there and looked at us, stunned and lost . . .

Now, I'll squeeze the trigger. A tiny bullet will rip through his chest. Maybe I'll lose my sleep tonight but in the morning I'll wake up alive.

Gregory seems to guess my thoughts. He puts out his hand and asks, "You're kidding, friend! Aren't you kidding?"

What a jackass! Doesn't he deserve to be cut to pieces? What a thing to ask at such a time. Your heart is about to burst and he's asking if you're kidding. How can a body be kidding about such a thing? Idiot! This is no time for jokes. And you, if you're such a fine friend, why don't you make things easier for us? Help us kill you with fewer qualms? If you would get angry—curse our Virgin, our God—if you'd try to escape it would be much easier for us and for you.

So it is now.

Now, Mr. Gregory, you are going to pay for your stupidities wholesale. Because you didn't escape the day the sentry fell asleep; because you didn't escape yesterday when we sent you all alone to the laundry—we did it on purpose, you idiot! Why didn't you let me die from the sting of the scorpion?

So now don't complain. It's all your fault, nitwit.

Eh? What's happening to him now?

Gregory is crying. Tears flood his eyes and trickle down over his clean-shaven cheeks. He is turning his face and pressing his forehead against the wall. His back is shaking as he sobs. His hands cling, rigid and helpless, to the wall.

Now is my best chance, now that he knows there is no other solution and turns his face from us.

I squeeze the trigger.

Gregory jerks. His back stops shaking up and down.

I think I've finished him! How easy it is . . . But suddenly he starts crying out loud, his hands claw at the wall and try to pull it down. He screams, "No, no . . ."

I turn to the others. I expect them to nod, "That's enough."

They nod, "What are you waiting for?"

I squeeze the trigger again.

The bullet smashes into his neck. A thick spray of blood spurts out.

Gregory turns. His eyes are all red. He lunges at me and starts punching me with his fists.

"I hate you, hate you . . ." he screams.

I emptied the barrel. He fell and grabbed my leg as if he wanted to hold on.

He died with a terrible spasm. His mouth was full of blood and so were my boots and socks.

We stood quietly, looking at him.

When we came to, we stooped and picked him up. His hands were frozen and wouldn't let my legs go.

I still have their imprints, red and deep, as if made by a hot knife.

"We will hang him tonight," the men said.

"Tonight or now?" they said.

I turned and looked at them one by one.

"Is that what you all want?" I asked.

They gave me no answer.

"Dig a grave," I said. 70

Headquarters did not ask for a report the next day or the day after. The top brass were sure that we had obeyed them and had left him swinging from a pole.

They didn't care to know what happened to that Gregory, alive or dead.

Analyzing the Text

1. Why is Gregory's innocence a source of both admiration and irritation? What details illustrate that Gregory has become a friend to the narrator and the other soldiers?
2. Why is it ironic that the narrator's superiors never inquire whether their orders have been carried out?

Understanding Ioannides's Techniques

1. What function do flashbacks serve in generating and sustaining suspense? In your opinion, would the story have been more effective if told from Gregory's point of view rather than that of the executioner's?
2. How is the structure of the story designed to bring the psychological conflict experienced by the narrator to the crisis point? What details reveal that the narrator must make himself hate Gregory in order to kill him?

Arguing for an Interpretation

1. What does the narrator's order not to hang Gregory's body up reveal about his reactions after he shoots Gregory? To what extent does Gregory embody the qualities of humanity, decency, and tranquil domestic life that the soldiers have come to appreciate?
2. If you were in the narrator's shoes, what would you have done? Why do you think Gregory does not try to escape when he is given the opportunity to do so? Does that make Gregory a fool who deserves to be killed?

Luisa Valenzuela

Luisa Valenzuela was born in Buenos Aires, Argentina, in 1938 and grew up in a literary atmosphere. Jorge Luis Borges often visited her home and coauthored stories with her mother, the well-known novelist Luisa Mercedes Levinson. After attending the University of Buenos Aires, Valenzuela began her career writing for magazines and working on the editorial staff of La Nación. *She traveled widely in the United States, Europe, and Latin America and lived for three years in France. Her first book,* Clara: Thirteen Stories and a Novel *(1966), explores themes re-*

lating to the subjugation of women in Argentina. Her next publication was a collection of stories, Strange Things Happen Here *(1976), reflecting the horrors perpetrated by the Argentine military regime in the late 1970s. As civil liberties disappeared with the imposition of censorship, the bombing of publishers' offices, and individuals—known as the "disappeared"—were removed without a trace by the military police, Valenzuela fled Argentina to live in New York City. During her years in the United States, she taught creative writing at Columbia University and wrote a novel,* The Lizard's Tale *(1983). A more recent novel is* Bedside Manners *(1995).*

Valenzuela's short story, "The Censors," translated by David Unger, first appeared in The Open Door *(1988), a collection of stories whose title she chose because "The Open Door is the name of the most traditional, least threatening lunatic asylum in Argentina." In this ironic fable, Valenzuela explores how a treacherous political atmosphere and the corrupting lure of power can seduce even the most idealistic individual into collusion with the state.*

The Censors

Poor Juan! One day they caught him with his guard down before he could even realize that what he had taken as a stroke of luck was really one of fate's dirty tricks. These things happen the minute you're careless, as one often is. Juancito let happiness—a feeling you can't trust—get the better of him when he received from a confidential source Mariana's new address in Paris and knew that she hadn't forgotten him. Without thinking twice, he sat down at his table and wrote her a letter. *The* letter that now keeps his mind off his job during the day and won't let him sleep at night (what had he scrawled, what had he put on that sheet of paper he sent to Mariana?).

Juan knows there won't be a problem with the letter's contents, that it's irreproachable, harmless. But what about the rest? He knows that they examine, sniff, feel, and read between the lines of each and every letter, and check its tiniest comma and most accidental stain. He knows that all letters pass from hand to hand and go through all sorts of tests in the huge censorship offices and that, in the end, very few continue on their way. Usually it takes months, even years, if there aren't any snags; all this time the freedom, maybe even the life, of both sender and receiver is in jeopardy. And that's why Juan's so troubled: thinking that something might happen to Mariana because of his letters. Of all people, Mariana, who must finally feel safe there where she always dreamt she'd live. But he knows that the *Censor's Secret Command* operates all over the world and cashes in on the discount in air fares; there's nothing to stop them from going as far as that hidden Paris neighborhood, kidnapping Mariana, and returning to their cozy homes, certain of having fulfilled their noble mission.

Well, you've got to beat them to the punch, do what everyone tries to do: sabotage the machinery, throw sand in its gears, get to the bottom of the problem so as to stop it.

This was Juan's sound plan when he, like many others, applied for a censor's job—not because he had a calling or needed a job: no, he applied simply to intercept his own letter, a consoling albeit unoriginal idea. He was hired immediately, for each day more and more censors are needed and no one would bother to check on his references.

Ulterior motives couldn't be overlooked by the *Censorship Division,* 5
but they needn't be too strict with those who applied. They knew how hard it would be for the poor guys to find the letter they wanted and even if they did, what's a letter or two when the new censor would snap up so many others? That's how Juan managed to join the *Post Office's Censorship Division,* with a certain goal in mind.

The building had a festive air on the outside that contrasted with its inner staidness. Little by little, Juan was absorbed by his job, and he felt at peace since he was doing everything he could to get his letter for Mariana. He didn't even worry when, in his first month, he was sent to *Section K* where envelopes are very carefully screened for explosives.

It's true that on the third day, a fellow worker had his right hand blown off by a letter, but the division chief claimed it was sheer negligence on the victim's part. Juan and the other employees were allowed to go back to their work, though feeling less secure. After work, one of them tried to organize a strike to demand higher wages for unhealthy work, but Juan didn't join in; after thinking it over, he reported the man to his superiors and thus got promoted.

You don't form a habit by doing something once, he told himself as he left his boss's office. And when he was transferred to *Section J,* where letters are carefully checked for poison dust, he felt he had climbed a rung in the ladder.

By working hard, he quickly reached *Section E* where the job became more interesting, for he could now read and analyze the letters' contents. Here he could even hope to get hold of his letter, which, judging by the time that had elapsed, had gone through the other sections and was probably floating around in this one.

Soon his work became so absorbing that his noble mission blurred in 10
his mind. Day after day he crossed out whole paragraphs in red ink, pitilessly chucking many letters into the censored basket. These were horrible days when he was shocked by the subtle and conniving ways employed by people to pass on subversive messages; his instincts were so sharp that he found behind a simple "the weather's unsettled" or "prices continue to soar" the wavering hand of someone secretly scheming to overthrow the Government.

His zeal brought him swift promotion. We don't know if this made him happy. Very few letters reached him in *Section B*—only a handful passed the other hurdles—so he read them over and over again, passed them under a magnifying glass, searched for microprint with an electronic microscope, and tuned his sense of smell so that he was beat by the time he made it home. He'd barely manage to warm up his soup, eat some fruit, and fall into bed, satisfied with having done his duty. Only his darling mother worried, but she couldn't get him back on the right track. She'd say, though it wasn't always true: Lola called, she's at the bar with the girls, they miss you, they're waiting for you. Or else she'd leave a bottle of red wine on the table. But Juan wouldn't overdo it: any distraction could make him lose his edge and the perfect censor had to be alert, keen, attentive, and sharp to nab cheats. He had a truly patriotic task, both self-denying and uplifting.

His basket for censored letters became the best fed as well as the most cunning basket in the whole *Censorship Division.* He was about to congratulate himself for having finally discovered his true mission, when his letter to Mariana reached his hands. Naturally, he censored it without regret. And just as naturally, he couldn't stop them from executing him the following morning, another victim of his devotion to his work.

Analyzing the Text

1. How does Juan's initial motivation in applying for the job as a censor become sidetracked by his growing enthusiasm and skill in discerning censorable contents?
2. In what way does the choice of what to do with his own letter bring the conflict to a crisis?

Understanding Valenzuela's Techniques

1. How does Valenzuela arrange the offices within the censorship division so as to emphasize how the process goes from overt threats to barely discernable imaginary ones?
2. In what way does Juan's mother represent the values of a traditional normal life that Juan has cast aside?

Arguing for an Interpretation

1. Did you find the surprise ending to be contrived or adequately foreshadowed? Explain your answer.
2. In your opinion, has Valenzuela done an effective job in dramatizing how the average citizen, when given the opportunity to wield power, will buy into the system and how power corrupts even idealistic individuals? Why or why not?

GLORIA ANZALDÚA

Gloria Anzaldúa (b. 1942–) is a Chicana poet and fiction writer who grew up in south Texas. She has edited several highly praised anthologies. This Bridge Called My Back: Writings by Radical Women of Color *won the 1986 Before Columbus Foundation American Book Award.* Borderlands—La Frontera, the New Mestiza *was selected as one of the best books of 1987 by* Library Journal. *She has also written* Making Face, Making Soul *(1990). She has been a contributing editor for* Sinister Wisdom *since 1984 and has taught Chicano studies, feminist studies, and creative writing at the University of Texas at Austin, San Francisco State University, and the University of California, Santa Cruz. "Cervicide" first appeared in* Labyris *(vol. 4, no. 11, Winter 1983). In it, Anzaldúa tells the poignant story of a Mexican-American family living on the Texas border who are forced to kill a pet deer whose detection by the game warden would result in an unaffordable fine or the father's imprisonment. She has also written a novel,* La Prieta *(the title means "The Dark One") in 1997.*

Cervicide

La venadita. The small fawn. They had to kill their pet, the fawn. The game warden was on the way with his hounds. The penalty for being caught in possession of a deer was $250 or jail. The game warden would put *su papí en la cárcel.*

How could they get rid of the fawn? Hide it? No, *la guardia*'s hounds would sniff Venadita out. Let Venadita loose in the *monte?* They had tried that before. The fawn would leap away and seconds later return. Should they kill Venadita? The mother and Prieta looked toward *las carabinas* propped against the wall behind the kitchen door—the shiny barrel of the .22, the heavy metal steel of the 40-40. No, if *they* could hear his pickup a mile and a half down the road, he would hear the shot.

Quick, they had to do something. Cut Venadita's throat? Club her to death? The mother couldn't do it. She, Prieta, would have to be the one. The game warden and his *perros* were a mile down the road. Prieta loved her *papí.*

In the shed behind the corral, where they'd hidden the fawn, Prieta found the hammer. She had to grasp it with both hands. She swung it up. The weight folded her body backwards. A thud reverberated on Venadita's skull, a wave undulated down her back. Again, a blow behind the ear. Though Venadita's long lashes quivered, her eyes never left Prieta's face. Another thud, another tremor. *La guardia* and his hounds were driving up the front yard. The *venadita* looked up at her, the hammer rose and fell. Neither made a sound. The tawny, spotted fur was the most beautiful thing Prieta had ever seen. She remembered when they had found the fawn. She had been a few hours old. A hunter had shot her mother. The fawn had been shaking so hard, her long thin legs were on the edge of buckling. Prieta and her sister and brothers had bottle-fed Venadita, with a damp cloth had wiped her skin, had watched her tiny, perfectly formed hooves
harden and grow. 5

Prieta dug a hole in the shed, a makeshift hole. She could hear the warden talking to her mother. Her mother's English had suddenly gotten bad—she was trying to stall *la guardia!* Prieta rolled the fawn into the hole, threw in the empty bottle. With her fingers raked in the dirt. Dust caked on her arms and face where tears had fallen. She patted the ground flat with her hands and swept it with a dead branch. The game warden was strutting toward her. His hounds sniffing, sniffing, sniffing the ground in

---

Cervicide: the killing of a deer. In archetypal symbology the Self appears as a deer for women. *su papí en la cárcel:* her father in jail *monte:* the woods *Prieta:* literally one who is dark-skinned, a nickname

the shed. The hounds pawing pawing the ground. The game warden, straining on the leashes *les dio un tirón, sacó los perros.* He inspected the corrals, the edge of the woods, then drove away in his pickup.

Analyzing the Text

1. How does Prieta's being forced to choose between the life of her pet deer and her father's freedom illustrate the lack of power that illegal immigrants endure?
2. In what sense might the deer symbolize Prieta's innocence that can no longer exist?

Understanding Anzaldúa's Techniques

1. How does the beginning of the story provide necessary background information that frames the dramatic situation in which the conflict occurs?
2. How does Anzaldúa's characterization of the protagonist and the antagonists sharpen the dilemma leading to the moment of crisis?

Arguing for an Interpretation

1. In your view, what would be the psychological consequences for Prieta having to make such a choice and having to perform such an action?
2. To what extent do you think this story could serve as a political agenda in dramatizing the plight of illegal immigrants from Mexico? Explain your answer.

Ernesto Cardenal

Ernesto Cardenal was born in 1925 in Granada, Nicaragua. He attended the University of Mexico and Columbia University. After his conversion to Christianity in 1956, he studied to become a priest in Gethsemani, Kentucky, with Thomas Merton, the scholar, poet, and Trappist monk. The poetry Cardenal wrote during this period expresses feelings of love, social criticism, political passion, and the quest for a transcendent spiritual life, themes that continue throughout his life, as in The Gospel in Solentinamo *(1976). Cardenal is well known in the United States as a spokesman for justice and self-determination for Latin America. His poetry frequently touches on events in the history of Nicaragua, as in the volume* With Walker in Nicaragua and Other Early Poems, 1949–1954 *(1985). He was ordained a Roman Catholic priest in 1965 and became a prominent voice of "liberation theology" in Central America, a stance that brought him into conflict in the 1980s with Pope John Paul II. He served as the Minister of Culture in Nicaragua in the government of Daniel Ortega, following the overthrow of Somoza in 1979. In addition to many collections of po-*

---

les dio un tirón, sacó los perros: jerked the dogs out

etry, including, most recently, From Nicaragua With Love: Poems 1979–1986 *(1986), Cardenal's writing includes short stories and religious meditations. He has also written* Abide in Love *(1995). "The Swede," translated by John Lyons (1992), depicts an unusual triangle involving a Swede inexplicably imprisoned while traveling in Central America, the dictatorial president of the country, and a beautiful girl in Sweden with whom both men are in love.*

The Swede

I'm Swedish. And I begin by declaring that I am Swedish because this simple fact is the cause of all the strange things that have happened to me (which some will judge to be beyond belief) which I now propose to relate. So, as I was saying, I'm Swedish, and many years ago, I came, for a short visit, to this small and wretched Central American republic—where I still find myself—in search of an example of a curious species of the *Iguanidae* family not catalogued by my fellow countryman, Linnaeus, and which I consider to be a descendant of the dinosaur (although in the scientific community its existence is still the subject of controversy).

I had the ill-fortune that hardly had I crossed the border when I was arrested. Why I was arrested don't expect me to explain; for I've never managed to explain it to myself satisfactorily, however much I've tried to explain it to myself over the years, and there's no one in the world who can explain it. It's true that the country was in the throes of a revolution at the time and my Nordic appearance may have aroused suspicions, in addition to which I had committed the imprudence of coming to this country without knowing the language. You will say to me that none of these reasons sufficiently justifies being arrested; but I've already said that there was no satisfactory reason. Quite simply: I was arrested.

Trying to make them understand, in an unintelligible language, that I was Swedish did not help me in the least. My firm conviction that my country's representative would arrive to rescue me later vanished, when I discovered that this representative not only could not communicate with me, since he knew no Swedish and had never had the slightest relationship with my country, but also that he was a deaf old man and in poor health, and also he himself, frequently, was arrested.

In prison I met a great number of important people in the republic, who were also accustomed to being frequently arrested: ex-presidents, senators, army officers, respectable ladies and bishops, and even including on one occasion the chief of police himself. The arrival of these people, which occurred generally in large groups, upset the prison routine with all sorts of visitors, messages, food parcels, bribes to jailers, riots, and even on occasions escapes. These great floods of prisoners around the time of conspiracies always modified the situation of those of us who enjoyed, so to speak, a more permanent character in the prison, and from a single—relatively comfortable—cell you could be transferred to an immense cell crammed with people and where scarcely another would fit, or to an individual hole in which a person could scarcely fit, or even to the torture chamber—if the rest of the prison being full—this place was not in use.

But I'm not being accurate when I say the prison, since it wasn't one prison but many, and many times we were moved from one to another for no apparent reason: I believe I've been through almost all of them. Although a prominent member of the opposition who was in prison—and previously he'd been a prominent figure in the Government—once told me that there was one single prison; that the entire country was a prison, and that some were in "the prison" within that prison, others were under house arrest, but everyone was imprisoned in the country.

In these prisons one frequently comes across old trusted prisoners, who are serving a very long sentence for some crime, turned jailers, as also former jailers turned prisoners; and just as important men in the Government are sometimes arrested, equally there have been important Opposition prisoners who afterwards have gone on to occupy high Government positions (I can testify to one, who was held in this prison and who, so other prison companions have told me, even participated in an assassination attempt, yet is presently Minister of State), but the confusion grows even further with the secret agents and the prison spies, about whom one cannot be certain whether they are false Government spies in prison for having dealings with the Opposition or false prisoners put in prison by the Government to spy on the Opposition.

With regard to the Opposition, I should relate here what one of the most influential members of the Opposition once told me in confidence: "The Opposition—he told me—in reality does not exist; it's a fiction maintained by the Government, just as the Government Party likewise is another fiction. It ceased to exist long ago, but it suits us too to maintain this fiction of Opposition, although we are sometimes arrested on account of it." And whether this is true or not, I can't be sure. But a much more extraordinary—and more incredible—revelation was that made to me, in the greatest of secrecy, by one of the President's closest friends who—converted now into one of his most bitter enemies—found himself in prison. "The President—he told me—doesn't exist! He's a double! He ceased to exist a long time ago!" According to him, the President had had a double whom he used to foil attempts on his life, which frequently were false and hatched by the President himself, in order to see which of his friends fell into the trap with a view to getting rid of them (although this game also proved dangerous to him, as well as complicated, because it lent itself to the possibility that real conspirators might devise a false plot with his assistance with the intention of really getting rid of him) and it seems to be the case that one day either some plan of the President's failed or some plot of his enemies had succeeded (perhaps with the complicity of the double himself—whether out of personal ambition to replace the President or self-defence seeing his life threatened in the cruel role of double—although my informant didn't know the details or didn't wish to tell me them) but the fact had been that the double assumed the President's place; and whether all this is pure invention, or lies, or the truth, or a joke, or the ravings of a mind unbalanced by confinement, I cannot say, neither did I discover whether my informant's friendship, or his betrayal, related to the first President or to his supposed double, or both.

As you will appreciate, I had by now come to grips with the language, and acquired, in prison, a perfect knowledge of the entire country, and had had close dealings with the most influential figures of the Opposition (and even the Government as I've mentioned) who in prison confided in me matters which outside are not confided to a wife, nor even to fellow conspirators. It may be said then that the only important person in the country with whom I was not acquainted was the President. And here's where the most extraordinary part of my story begins: not only did I get to know the President, but furthermore I got to know him in a much more intimate way than any other individual from the Opposition or from the Government with whom to date I had had dealings. But let's not run ahead of the events.

At the beginning, when I was arrested, I repeated tirelessly that I was Swedish, but finally I stopped doing so, convinced that just as to me it was absurd that they should imprison me for being Swedish, to them it was equally absurd to release me for the simple reason of being Swedish. I'd been in this situation which I have related for many years, and lost hope that at the end of the President's term of office I'd see myself released (because he had re-elected himself), when some Government agents called at the prison to ask me—much to my astonishment—whether I was Swedish. Not without stammering for a moment, owing to the unexpectedness of the question and the interest which they displayed in asking it, I told them I was, and immediately they made me bathe, they shaved me and cut my hair (things they'd never done) and gave me a dress suit to wear. At first I thought that relations with my country had improved remarkably, although on the other hand so many preparations and ceremony—especially the dress suit—induced a deep fear in me, thinking that perhaps they were taking me to be killed. To some extent this fear faded when I discovered that they were taking me to the President.

Immediately I arrived all the doors were thrown open until I entered 10
the office of the President, who appeared to be waiting for me. The moment he saw me he greeted me politely: "Hello. How's it going?" Although I believe his question was rather insincere. Before I could respond he asked me whether I was Swedish. With a crisp "yes" I answered him, and again he asked: "Then you can speak Swedish?" I told him that this was so too, and I could see my reply pleased him. He then handed me a letter written in delicate female script in the language of my country, ordering me to translate it. (I later learned that when this letter arrived they had scoured the country high and low, to no avail, for someone who could read it, until somebody, fortunately, recalled having heard a prisoner cry out that he was Swedish.) The letter was from a girl who requested the President to send her a few of those beautiful gold coins which, so she'd heard, were in circulation here, expressing at the same time her admiration for the President of this exotic country, to whom she was also sending her picture: the photograph of the most beautiful girl that I have ever seen in my life!

After listening to my translation, the President, delighted by the letter and above all the girl's picture, dictated a reply to me not without romantic insinuations, in which he gladly acceded to the sending of the gold coins, a generous amount, while explaining nevertheless that this was expressly forbidden by the Law. I faithfully translated his thoughts into the Swedish language, firmly convinced that my unexpected usefulness might earn me not only my freedom, but perhaps even a modest position, or at least official backing for the tracking down of the desired *Iguanidae.* But as a measure of prudence for whatever might happen, I took the precaution of adding a few lines to the letter the President dictated to me, explaining my situation and imploring my beautiful compatriot to take steps to secure my freedom.

I was soon congratulating myself for this initiative, because the moment my work was over, to my great disappointment I was taken back to the prison, where the dress suit was removed, restoring me to my previous miserable state. Nonetheless the days from then on were now full of hope: the image of my beautiful saviour never left my mind, and not long after, a fresh bath and shave and the reappearance of the dress suit announced to me that the desired reply had arrived.

And so it proved to be. Just as I had foreseen, this letter referred almost exclusively to myself, imploring the President to release me, but (and this too I had already foreseen) I couldn't read that letter to the President, because, either he'd think that I was making it all up, or he would discover that I had previously inserted words of my own into his letter, punishing my boldness perhaps to the point of death.

So I found myself obliged to skip all references to my freedom, replacing them sadly with words of adulation for the President. But on the other hand in the chivalrous reply which he dictated to me, I had the opportunity to give a more detailed account of my story, dismissing at the same time the romantic idea she had of the President and revealing to her what in truth he was like.

From then on the beautiful girl began to write frequently, showing an 15
ever-increasing interest in my affair, so that shaves and baths and wearing of the dress suit increased, as at the same time did my hopes of freedom.

I gradually acquired ever more intimacy with her through the replies which the President dictated to me, which I took advantage of in order to unburden my own feelings. I must confess that during the long and monotonous intervals that occurred between one letter and another, the thought of my freedom (linked to the thought of the wonderful girl who might obtain it for me) never left my mind, and both thoughts frequently coalesced into a single thought, to the point that I no longer knew whether it was on account of my desire for freedom that I thought of her, or whether on account of desire for her that I thought of my freedom (she and my freedom were the same thing for me, as I told her so many times while the President was dictating). To put it more clearly: I'd fallen in love. It will appear improbable to those who read this narrative (being on the outside) that someone can fall in love, within the confines of a prison, with a woman far away, known to him only by her photograph. But I can assure you that I fell in love in this prison and with an intensity that those who are free cannot even imagine. Yet, to my misfortune, the President, that most cruel, misanthropic, solitary, extravagant man, had also fallen in love, or pretended to have done so, and, what was worse, I had been the instigator and promoter of that love, making him believe, with the aim of sustaining the correspondence, that the letters were for him.

In my long and anxious periods of confinement, I passed the time thoroughly preparing the next letter that I would read to the President, which was indispensable to me, since he never permitted me to read it through first to myself before proceeding to translate it, insisting rather that I should translate at the same time as I was reading, and furthermore (whether out of distrust of me or for the pleasure that it afforded him) he made me read the same letter three and even four times on the trot. And equally I prepared the fresh reply that I would write, polishing each sentence and striving to put into them all the poetry and traditional beauty of the Swedish language and even including from time to time my own brief compositions in verse.

In order to prolong my letters even further I made up for the President all sorts of questions about the history, customs and the political situation in the country, to which he always responded with great gusto. Thus, he then dictated to me long epistles, speaking of his Government and the Opposition and the affairs of State and consulting and asking his girlfriend's advice. So it transpired that, from a prison, I was giving advice to the Government and held in my hands the destiny of the country, without anyone, not even the President himself, being aware of this, and I secured the return of those in exile. I commuted sentences and set many of my prison companions free, although none of them was able to thank me for it. Yet the only person on whose behalf I could not intercede was myself.

One of the greatest pleasures of those days of dictation was to be able to look again at her picture, which the President brought out of hiding, so he said "to inspire himself." I asked her to send us more pictures and she did so, although as you will appreciate, they all ended up in the President's hands. My revenge consisted in the presents he sent her, which were numerous and of considerable value, which she received more as though they came from me.

Yet at the same time as my love had been growing so too had a dread 20
within me, and it was that huge collection of letters which were piling up on the President's desk, and in which finally, we did not even mention him except from time to time, and then so as to insult him. In a manner of speaking, each of those letters bore my death warrant.

The theme of freedom as you'd expect is the one that dominated our correspondence. We were forever dreaming up all sorts of plans or imagining possible stratagems. My first plan had been to go on strike, to refuse to translate further letters, unless I was granted my freedom; but then I was condemned to bread and water, and this, together with the even greater agony of not reading any more of her letters (which by now had become indispensable to me) broke my will. I then proposed as a condition that at least the shave and the bath and the decent clothes could be accorded to me on a regular basis and not merely on letter days (which was not only impracticable but also humiliating) but not even this was conceded, and then I had to submit unconditionally.

Later she proposed to travel out here so as to call on the President and make arrangements for my release (a plan which had the advantage of counting on the resolute support of the President, who for some time had been urging her to do so with some impatience) but I was utterly opposed to it, because without doubt it would mean losing her (and losing myself as well possibly). My proposal, on the other hand, that some other woman should come in her place, she rejected as something dangerous, besides being impossible. Another of her plans which really was on the point of being put into practice, was to obtain a forceful protest on the part of my Government and even a breaking off of relations, but I made her see in time that such a measure not only would not improve my situation, but rather would considerably worsen it and I'd never be heard of again. I was much more in favour of trying to improve relations between the two countries, then in such a lamentable state, but as she pointed out quite rightly: how to convince the Swedish Government to improve its relations on the basis that one of its citizens should have been unjustly imprisoned? But the most preposterous idea, suggested by a lawyer friend of hers, was that of demanding my extradition as a wanted criminal (to which I objected) failing to realise that if I was already being held for no reason, there being a charge against me, the President would have me put to death there and then.

But do not think that we were the only ones who were making plans, for all the prisoners (and even the whole country) lived all the time elaborating the most diverse and contradictory plans: the general strike or attempts on his life, civic action, revolution, alliance with the Government, rebellion, palace plot, violence and terrorism, passive resistance, poisoning, bombs, guerilla warfare, whispering campaigns, prayer, psychic powers. There was even a prisoner (a professor of mathematics) who was working on a very abstruse plan to overthrow the Government by means of mathematical laws (he conceived of an almost cosmic clandestine organisation which would continue to grow in geometric proportion and within a few weeks would be as large as the number of inhabitants in the whole country, and a few days later, having continued to grow, the inhabitants of the entire globe would not be sufficient, yet he failed to take into account that those who did not join the organisation would also increase in geometric proportion).

As for me, a fresh worry had come to join the others, and it was that of seeing how day by day I was becoming more dangerous in the President's eyes on account of the tremendous secret (together with the innumerable lesser confidences) of which I was the depository; although it is true that his love, real or feigned, constituted my greatest security, because he would not kill me while he required my services (but this security brought me anguish on another count, because needing my services it was more improbable that he would let me go). And the same hope I had at the beginning that one of my fellow countrymen might happen to pass through, had been transformed into the main fear, because the President might proudly show him a letter, and my deception would be uncovered.

There we were she and I, busy in the elaboration of a new plan which might prove to be more effective, when suddenly, that which most anxiously terrified me and with all the strength of my mind I had tried to avoid, came about: the President stopped being in love. His was not, to my misfortune, a gradual falling out of love, but sudden, without giving me time to prepare myself. Quite simply, the letters which arrived were no longer answered but thrown into the basket, and I was not called upon, except on the odd afternoon so as to read something or other, more out of curiosity and boredom, dictating to me afterwards cold, laconic replies with the aim of putting a stop to the affair. All the desperation and mortal anguish of my soul were poured into those lines and in the few letters that I still had the good fortune to read to the President. I in turn put the tenderest, the most affectionate and passionate entreaties of love that any woman has ever expressed, but with so little success he cut short the reading in the middle of a letter. To cap it all, the letters she wrote were above all reproachful of me, for not replying to her, raising doubts that I was still a prisoner and even coming to insinuate that I had never been a prisoner. The last occasion, when I was not even brought in dress suit to the

Presidential Residence but rather in the prison itself, an utterly definitive break was dictated to me by a guard, I understood that she, my freedom and everything, had come to an end, and my final, heart-rending words of farewell had been written.

The remaining sheets of paper and the pen were left for me in the cell, in case some other letter from me was again required, I presume. And whether the President did not have me killed because he remained grateful to me, or in case some other person writes from Sweden, or simply because he forgot about me, I don't know (and I still think of the possibility that they might have killed him—although this is unlikely—and that he who exists is another double). Neither do I know whether she has continued to write to me or if she now no longer remembers me, and the terrible absurd idea has even occurred to me that perhaps she never existed, but rather it was all hatched by someone from the Opposition in exile, in order to make fun of the President or to make fun of me (or by the President himself who is a cruel maniac) owing to a custom of thinking absurd ideas which lately I have developed in prison. Did you love me too, Selma Borjesson, as I loved you madly in this prison?

Much time has passed since then, and now once again I have lost hope of seeing myself released at the end of the President's term of office, because once again he has re-elected himself. The paper which was left over, and now serves no purpose, I have used to tell my story. I write in Swedish so the President will not understand it, should this fall into his hands. I end here because the paper is running out and perhaps it may be years before I have paper again (and perhaps I have only a few days left to live). In the remote case that some fellow countryman of mine should happen to read these pages, I implore him to remember Erik Hjalmar Ossiannilsson, if I am still not yet dead.

NOTE: *A friend of mine who was arrested found this manuscript in the prison, almost destroyed by damp, under a brick. It would appear to have been written many years ago. And years later an employee of the Ericksonn Telephone Company translated it for us. We have been unable to trace any data referring to the person who wrote it. I have published the text as it was given to me, making obvious corrections to the style and grammar.*

Analyzing the Text

1. What circumstances have led the narrator to correspond with the Swedish woman on behalf of the president? What complications ensue as a result?
2. What is ironic about the narrator's predicament both in terms of the power he acquires and how his actions are ultimately understood by the Swedish woman?

Understanding Cardenal's Techniques

1. What details suggest that the characterization of the president of the country and life under his regime is intended to be satiric?

2. To what extent does the note at the end change how the readers can understand the story?

Arguing for an Interpretation

1. The narrator's wish to get his story down on paper conflicts with his fear of being discovered. In your opinion, is this an inconsistent characterization on Cardenal's part? Why or why not?
2. In what way does the story suggest that there is an equivalence between being imprisoned by a dictator in a Central American country and being subject to the whims of the one with whom you are in love?

P'an Jen-mu

P'an Jen-mu was born in 1920 in Liaoning Province, Manchuria, grew up in Beijing, and graduated from the National Central University in Nanking with a B.A. in English. She spent three years teaching in Sinkiang, in western China, between Mongolia and Tibet, an experience that provided her with material for a number of her short stories. After moving to Taiwan, she served as editor in chief of the Children's Reading Program, sponsored by the Ministry of Education. Her publications include two prize-winning novels, My Cousin Lien-yi *(1951) and* Nightmare *(1953), as well as a collection of short stories,* Sorrow and Happiness in a Small World *(1981). Translated by Chen I-djen, "A Pair of Socks with Love" was first published in 1985 in the* Central Daily News *in Taiwan. The story presents an image of the prerevolutionary Chinese family and society, told from the perspective of a little girl in an upper-class family. The relationships between her parents, and between them and their servant, are presented in positive human terms. At the same time, the story exposes the oppression of the poor through a sensitive portrayal of the family's servant and the impoverished living conditions of beggars outside the village. "A Pair of Socks with Love" relates how the child's request that her servant be given real store-bought socks comes full circle, many years later, during the Cultural Revolution.*

A Pair of Socks with Love

I left home many decades ago and feel as if I have just been drifting along all these years. I often dream of home, but the one happy dream that I cherished the most was about my mother coming into my room, a smile on her face, to prepare and warm my bedding for me. It was a wintery night, and I was only seven or eight years old. The oil lamp cast a weak shadow as she folded my mauve-colored comforter into a Chinese style envelope, our version of a sleeping bag, and watched me take off my felt shoes and get into bed, which we called a *k'ang.*[1] I slid my legs into the folded comforter slowly; I took off my cotton wool padded maroon-colored raw silk gown, my fur vest, my blue cotton wool padded pants that were bound at the ankles. I would then be wearing only a white undergarment, an old pair of underpants, a red band around my stomach and was ready to ease myself into my comforter. The garments I shed would be placed on top of my bedding in the order they were taken off, one on top of the other, to make it easier to put them back on the next morning without having to search for them.

The last item to be taken off would be my cotton socks, which I handed to my mother. The next morning there would be a pair of clean socks in my felt shoes, one in each shoe.

I loved this moment when my mother prepared my bedding for me; still more, I loved the way she looked at me. She would gaze at me all the while I was undressing. I felt that she loved me, really loved me. After I left home, whenever I remembered that look in her eyes, I would begin to cry. Even when I dreamt about it, I would wake up crying.

After I slid all the way into my folded quilt she would then put a blanket on top of my feet, a threadbare Russian blanket. And she always added, "Don't kick it off." Always.

5 In our home we had the kind of bed known as a "fire *k'ang,*" which was always built against a window. One slept with one's feet facing the window and head towards the room. The window was papered on the outside and smeared with tung oil to prevent the rain and snow from dampening the window. It also protected it from gale winds. Cracks along the window were sealed with some coarse paper but still the cold wind would find its way in. The glass pane in the middle of the window would be frosted by the cold air outside, so it was always colder where one's feet were. I remembered very clearly one night when it was time to take off my socks, I said hesitantly, folding my hands, "Ma, may I sleep with my socks on tonight?"

"Sleep with your socks on? That won't do. What're you up to now? Figuring on getting into our *k'ang,* isn't that it?"

"No!"

"What is it then? If you sleep with your socks on your feet will feel like those of the hairy legged chicks. Try it if you don't believe me. It'll really make you feel awkward."

"How do you know, Ma?"

10 "I wore them to sleep on my wedding night. Just that once and it was awkward beyond words."

"I would also do it only once."

"Not even once. If you sleep with them on you may tend to kick your bedding off. If that happened you would find yourself frozen stiff in the wee hours of the morning. Have you forgotten that last year on the eighth day of the twelfth lunar month you caught a bad cold because you kicked off your bedding? You were feverish and sneezing like mad. Chung Jen had to get Chang the Lama to treat you. All that because you kicked off your bedding. Have you forgotten already? Now take them off right away."

"I won't do it this time, won't kick them off. If I do, may the skin around my eyes rot."

---

[1]A brick bed which can be kept warm by a fire fed from an adjoining room, usually the kitchen.

"So, you have learned to swear! Whom did you learn it from? Rotting of the skin around the eyes is harder to cure than colds and fever. The old monk from the temple would have to be fetched, and he would stick you with a needle."

"But, Ma, the old monk from the temple only knows how to grow cucumbers. He won't know what to do with a needle. That much I know."

"Nonetheless he knows how to look for a spike of sorghum to prop open the eyelids of little children with rotting skin around the eyes. Would you like that?"

"I won't kick, Ma! Then nothing would happen."

"I merely urge you to take off your socks. I really cannot figure out why it should cause so much difficulty. I heard you mention to Erh-niu in the south court only the day before yesterday, 'Don't you ever sleep in your socks! If you do your toes will stack up one against the other like your mother's. Notice how ugly they look in shoes?' Weren't those your very words?"

"The day before yesterday? The day before yesterday I had on a pair of cotton socks. Of course I had to say it was better to sleep without them. And what do I have on today? Don't you remember? A pair of imported knitted Dark Chrysanthemum brand socks! Look!"

As I argued with her I felt that reason was on my side and I began to sob.

Ma could only let me have my way; she probably agreed with me.

To this day I cherish a special feeling for this Dark Chrysanthemum brand of imported socks. It was the first article which served in my "modernization." Some fifty or sixty years ago everything I wore was homemade, everything except the string for my hair, the binding strips for my leggings, and the felt shoes I wore in the winter. Of all these homemade items the socks were the most uncomfortable things to wear. As one tried to pull them up beyond the heels one had to pull really hard. Children couldn't do it, and they often ended up on their backs with all four limbs kicking in the air.

At first, only Papa wore imported socks. Everyone in the household from Mama down treated them as something special. They were laundered in a separate basin, and the brand name was etched in everyone's memory. The paper that bore the trademark of this Dark Chrysanthemum brand of imported socks had only two colors: black and white, a black chrysanthemum on white, very striking. I was not entitled to wear imported socks, but the privilege of peeling off the trademark label was solely mine. If he should overlook having it pass through my hands before putting on a new pair of socks, I would stand outside in the snow if it were winter, and in the summer I would walk out and stand under the sun. I would not even come in to eat. Let them suffer!

I called the label I collected calico paper, and I saved it as I did cards from packages of cigarettes. I left my mark on all of them, a tiny little black fish. I issued them to those schoolmates of mine who were my friends. It was very useful in organizing a gang or a following.

Once when Papa took a trip to the provincial seat, for some unknown reason he went all out and bought Dark Chrysanthemum brand imported socks for every member of the family. He bought several dozens of them, some were made of cotton thread, some woolen or lisle. The ones for Mama were natural color lisle socks and over the knee. Since the word for knee sounded the same in our language as the word for a feast, I thought it stood to reason that the longer socks were meant for such occasions.

After I was settled in bed, Mama would turn down the wick and tiptoe out. But I wasn't sleeping; how could I? The cozy feeling I experienced this morning when I put on my socks was still circulating all through my body. They fit so well and felt so soft that it was like stepping on a cloud. In school I stuck my feet out to show my schoolmates. They all wanted to feel them and asked if they were expensive.

The peddler hawking peanuts, watermelon seeds and candied crab apples went by, and shortly after, I heard Papa returning. I knew he would come in to see me soon, so I pretended to be asleep.

At first Papa and Ma talked in whispers, then they talked louder, and Ma said, "Don't! The child may see us."

"Isn't she asleep?"

"Oh, you're cold."

"It's very cold outside, dry and cold, the way it is toward the end of the year."

"What's keeping you so busy? You're very late!"

"The detention room was rebuilt. It was made into living quarters. I went to inspect it."

"So that was what kept you busy! Where did you eat supper?"

"At the training factory; I ate with them. I got workers from the training factory to install glass panes on the windows for us. All the windows are Western style. This is the best room in the whole office compound. Yet no one dares to move in. Have to ask Chung Jen to move in."

"Did anybody ever die in that room?"

"Very likely, it was already there during the Ch'ing Dynasty."

"They say there used to be huge sticks, torture bars, and water torture benches there. Where are they now?"

"They have been moved to the hall."

"How come? They used to do it secretively, and now you want to punish openly?"

"Can't let the criminals think that I am not going to punish them at all."

"A little beating, and a little threat should be enough. Even criminals have parents and are the darlings of their fathers and mothers. I have often thought that if ever our own family or our children commit any offence, I wish they would be treated with mercy . . ."

"My goodness, how you let your thoughts wander! We won't commit any crime, and the first thing we teach our children would be not to commit any crime. The law of the land is improving day by day, and law-abiding citizens will not be wrongfully accused."

"Our ancestors were kind and merciful, thereby earning merit points with the gods and laying the foundation to build your future on. We should do the same for future generations; earn some merit points for them. Law is law, mercy is mercy, temper law with mercy."

I loved it when they talked about such official business. I knew where the torture chamber was. Whenever I had to pass that way, I always walked around it. I was afraid that the hand of a ghost would grab me and pull me into it. Now it would be all right; the torture chamber had been eliminated, and our houseboy Chung Jen was to move in.

Mama and Papa talked some more, still very softly. Then I sensed that they had walked around the screen, lifted the curtain and come into my room. I could smell the cold air brought in by Papa's blue silk fur robe. I opened my eyes ever so slightly and stole a look at him by dint of the light that came in with them. Today Papa was wearing a pair of copper-colored woolen Dark Chrysanthemum brand socks and black woolen shoes. I had taken off the trademark label before he put them on and it made me feel exceedingly filial to him.

Both of them bent down to look at me. Ma's breath was sweet and soft, and she tucked me in. I liked the feeling of her gold bracelet brushing against my cheeks. I also liked the smell of Papa, the smell of a mixture of paper and ink from the tip of his sleeves, the smell of the cold air and the smell of his black brocade vest. It was the smell of Papa and there was nothing that could take its place.

"Don't touch her; your hands are cold," Mama said very softly.

"I just touched her hair; no harm done."

"Still, it could have wakened her." 50

"Those tiny feet are sticking out from the bedding. How come this child is sleeping with her socks on?"

"Today is the first time she is wearing imported socks; no amount of arguing could make her take them off. She promised, and even swore that she would not kick off her bedding. Now as soon as she falls asleep, she has kicked them off." Ma stuck my feet back in and patted them.

"Take them off while she is sleeping."

"You know what would happen then. She would raise a ruckus tomorrow early in the morning."

"Where did she get that temper? Tell me." 55

"Don't! The child may see us. Don't."

They walked out quietly. Don't! Don't what? I stole a look. They walked out hand in hand. I had long suspected that they did something behind my back and now I had caught them at it. So that's what they do, hold hands!

I slept soundly, totally relaxed.

Sure enough, I woke up early, frozen. Mama was right; sleeping with socks on really made me feel like a hairy-legged chick. Not only had I kicked off my bedding, what was thrown over my feet now became cushions for them. My tummy was icy cold. Frost had formed on the window pane like feathers, very thick feathers. I quietly took my comb and went to look for Chun-hsi in the kitchen. She always got up early to cook sorghum gruel, the watery part of which was to be used to cook eggs for Papa.

"Chun-hsi, braid my hair for me. Hurry! And don't make it too tight." 60

Whenever Chun-hsi did my hair she always hurt me as if she were taking it out on me. She said it was because I had too much hair and it tended to knot. After a bout with typhoid I almost lost all my hair. My new head of hair was thicker than ever, but very short. My braid was very thick at the root and tapered off to a thin end. It looked very strange. When she finished braiding me she laughed and said, "I have never seen such a funny-looking broomlike braid as yours."

I, however, felt that it was more like a slippery black fish, very shiny and fresh out of water. "Chun-hsi, look at my imported socks!"

"Didn't you show them to me eight times already yesterday? Do I have to look at them again? Find Chung Jen and show them to him."

Of course I wanted to look for Chung Jen; I did not need her to arrange my itinerary for me. I had to find him to take me to school for the morning review session before breakfast, not to show off. He too had seen them eight times. I needed him to take me because on the way to school I had to pass a few homes that had dogs, also the grotto of the local god on a big stone tablet, which was put there to ward off evil spirits, the residence of a divorcee, also several huts out in the field where the beggars congregated. All these places looked especially scary early in the morning before the sun was up and there were few pedestrians around.

That torture chamber looked really different now with all new Western style windows. Nonetheless I felt intimidated as I approached it. I could only bring myself to call out for him in a small voice, "Chung Jen! Chung Jen!" I had to knock on the window pane a few times before waking him up. He yawned and muttered, "Here!"

Ma told me that little girls may not enter a man's bedroom, even if the man is a work hand or a servant from your own household. This room, however, had glass windows all over, unlike the one he had before, which had papered windows. I tried not to look, but even from the outside, with a slight turn of my head I saw clearly the procedure he followed rising from his bed.

He, too, had piled layer after layer of clothing on top of his bedding. He too put them on in the order they were laid out. Except, when it came to the last item, the socks, he did it very differently. In addition to his socks he put an extra layer of something on his feet.

First he laid out a piece of cloth measuring about two feet square. It was homespun and a dirty gray color. Then he stuck out his big foot on top of the cloth, and using both hands he started wrapping, his thick lips tightly pursed as three deep furrows appeared on his forehead as if they were assisting him in his task. After his foot was thus wrapped up he brought out a cotton sock from under the bedding, which was already adjusted to the shape of his foot from previous wear. Very carefully and with his lips still tightly pursed he stuffed his foot into it. He then proceeded to wrap the other foot.

How many years did I have to wait? No wonder it took him so long every day! I was both cold and anxious. If it dragged on like this the sun would be up and I would be late getting to school.

"Hurry up! Hurry up! This is really unbelievable, taking so long to put on socks!"

At long last his feet wrapped, socks on, he stuffed them into his old cotton padded shoes and got off the bed. Now, with me walking in front and him following behind we were on our way to the county primary school for girls. It was Mama's ruling that he should follow behind within a distance of five to ten paces.

This, however, was easier said than done. Chung Jen was like a grasshopper, tall and skinny. He had legs long and wide apart like the crane's and could overtake me in two or three steps. Ma said he wasn't like this when he first came to work for us at fifteen. He was a mere child, shortish and withered looking. He didn't even have a name; when asked he said it was Second Pillar. His pa was a criminal; he was sued for not paying his debts and was also otherwise involved and had to be sent to the provincial capital. He and his ma were left behind. They were very poor and had no way of making a living. Papa felt sorry for him and told him to come to work for us. Even then Ma had said, "This Second Pillar may look like a caterpillar, but how he can eat nonstop. He is no help at all, but he is honest and can be trusted." Later, when he was seventeen Papa found a wife for him and sent the wife to the countryside to wait on her mother-in-law while waiting for the return of her father-in-law. As for himself, he was promoted to office boy and was given the name Chung Jen. Ever since Papa had given him his name he liked to test people to see if they were literate. "Do you know how to read? Can you write my name?" Now he had surely come up in this world. He sent money home every month, and he learned to say, "I serve in the Pan's residence." (Even I did not know the meaning of the word "serve," but I pretended I did.) The only thing was that he would turn red all the way down to his neck at the mention of his wife. Mama let him go home once a month. And he was always given a basket full of food such as cakes and cookies to take back.

The county primary school was not far from home. It could be reached in less time than it took to finish a pipe. But he always had a lot to say on the way, to help slow him down and to show off what he knew, I guessed. He told me the names of all the dogs along the way, that Lao Wang's woman lent money out at high interest rates, the age of Lao Li's calf, and how many soybean cakes Lao Liu had made that year, and so forth. Incidentally, the first step toward making bean paste was to cook the soybeans and make them into cakes for fermentation.

I was in no mood to listen to that. There were no other children on the road; most likely I was late. It was all his fault.

"Chung Jen, you walk in front of me." 75

"That will never do. Mistress's order, I have to walk behind you."

"You walk fast. If I follow you, I would be walking faster too. Otherwise I'll be late and the teacher will make me stand in the corner."

"We are here at this time every day; why should we be late today? What are you up to? Don't try to take advantage of me. I won't listen to you, only to Mistress."

"If you walk in front of me then I can see if you walk funny with your feet wrapped in cloth, and if you look like a hairy-legged chick when you walk."

"Have you ever seen a hairy-legged chick my size?" 80

"Don't you feel uncomfortable wearing a piece of cloth inside your sock?"

"No more than having sand or pebbles in them."

"Does the cloth remain flat, or does it narrow into strips or become knotted?"

"They are wrapped around my feet."

"Don't they come loose? You did not tie them or fasten them in any manner." 85

"Should they become loose, there're always my socks to keep them in place."

"Do your socks fit that tightly? You must be very uncomfortable. Do your second and third toes double up one on top of another?"

He did not answer but followed quietly behind.

"You have to tell me why you wrap your feet in cloth." He pretended not to have heard.

I unexpectedly dashed up an earthen mound and ran around at the top against the wind, the black fish flying behind me and knocking against my neck. It scared Chung Jen and he screamed at me, "Come down quickly, please. You may find people urinating on the other side of the mound." 90

Sure enough there were people doing that on the other side, so I came down.

"You have to tell me why you must wrap them up; otherwise I'm going up there again."

"To save wear and tear of the socks."

"What's the sense of saving the wear and tear of such ragged old cotton socks? Don't you always bring back new ones every time you return from your home visit? Why are you so stingy? Why are you so careful? Your wife can make you more." I had turned around, stopped short, and asked with my arms akimbo.

"She . . . she doesn't know how." 95

"She doesn't know how to make socks? How can she be your wife when she doesn't even know how to make socks? What good is she anyway?"

Chung Jen found no answer, but he blushed all the way down his neck.

"Who made your socks for you?" We were on our way again.

"My ma made them."

I saw a beggar push open the door of the beggars' house, and I was 100
scared into total silence. Funny that I should be so afraid of a beggar. What was so scary about a beggar?

I was really late that day. It was my fault. Teacher had told us at the end of school the day before that the morning review session was to be held half an hour earlier, because he had to prepare for the arrival of an inspector. I was so happy with my imported Dark Chrysanthemum socks that I had forgotten about it. I was not punished for being late, but it was unsettling to be the last one to walk into the room and to have all eyes trained on me.

After the review session was over, all the other children went home for breakfast, but Chung Jen was not there yet to fetch me. I figured the others might be having a second helping of their sorghum gruel already when a tall figure with two long cranelike legs hopped in through the front door.

"You're late. If I should be late returning to school you have to make it up to me. Today the Inspector is coming. Whoever is late bringing his charge back to school will be beaten. Just watch out."

"I did not do it on purpose. The mistress wanted me to deliver bean rolls to the beggars."

On my way home I took an extra look at the beggars' house. It was by 105
then completely under the morning sun. If it were a huge piece of candy, it would have been halfway melted already. The reason I thought of it as such was because our teacher once told us a story about a witch who built a candy house to tempt little children.

It seemed to me that since Ma gave them all those bean rolls, all the beggars should be squatting on their heels along the wall and wolfing them down now, yet there was not a single one in sight.

"Why give them bean rolls? They're not hungry."

"The bean rolls were frozen hard as rock."

"I was asking why should they be given the rolls."

"It's close to the New Year. Mistress sends them these things on all 110
three festivals of the year. This is to earn merit points with the gods. You mustn't talk about it."

"What's she trying to earn? Merit points with the gods? What kind of a card is that? What can you exchange them for? Dark Chrysanthemum imported socks?"

"Child, sometimes you're very smart, and sometimes really dumb. How do I know what one can get in exchange for merit points? Maybe longevity or something of the sort."

"Is giving bean rolls to the beggars the only way to earn merit points?"

"All good deeds count. Your papa's abolishing torture and sending minor criminal offenders to the training factory to learn a trade is also a way of earning points."

"But to find you a wife who cannot make socks is not. For you now have to be very careful about wearing them out and have to wrap your feet in cloth."

"How you do ramble on."

"In the spring when hot air comes up from the earth do you still have to wrap them?" I remembered seeing hot air bubbling up from the waste land where the beggars' low and dilapidated house was. It always happened in the spring, and it was like the earth was making steamed rolls. This hot air could only be seen from a distance; it rippled like the waves bending the dried weeds and small trees in its way.

"Have to. Socks wear out faster when hot air rises from the earth. If I don't wrap my feet my ma would die of exhaustion."

"Ma! Chung Jen's ma is going to die from exhaustion." I couldn't wait to get home to make the pronouncement.

"What?"

"This morning he caused me to be late all because he had to wrap those smelly feet of his; took him an awful long time to do that."

"What about his mother?"

"He said if he did not wrap his feet in cloth he would be wearing out his socks too soon and his mother would die of exhaustion from making more socks."

"Ah."

"Ma, I have a solution."

"What is it?"

"Didn't Papa buy a whole lot of those Dark Chrysanthemum socks? I beg you to give him a few pairs; won't that take care of it?"

"Why? They're expensive."

"If he had imported socks to wear, he wouldn't need cotton socks; if he need not wear cotton socks, he would not have to wrap his feet in cloth. This way his mother would not die of exhaustion and I would not be late for school. Right?"

The following day Ma brought out two pairs of Papa's old imported socks and a brand new pair, which was white, a color Papa did not much care for.

"Give them to Chung Jen. You must not tear off the calico paper since it is a present. No itchy fingers!" Ma was talking about the trademark label. I was not going to let it go at that. What right had Chung Jen to be special? I could do that even with Papa's socks. I drew a black fish on the paper as always; my way of saying, "This too belongs to me."

Although Chung Jen now had three pairs of imported socks, some old, some new, he could not bring himself to wear them. He continued to wrap his feet in cloth and wear the cotton socks his ma made for him. When he reached twenty-five, he had saved enough money to buy a piece of land and went home to work his own land.

After I grew up, I left home and traveled to a distant land, but whenever I thought of home I always remembered Chung Jen. I remembered reading a story book for children. In it there was a picture of long-legged John, the idiot carrying his donkey home on his back. He reminded me of Chung Jen.

It has been more than thirty years since I left home and I never received any word from my family. In 1980 after the iron curtain of mainland China was opened slightly, I received this letter from my nephew:

> . . . In the Spring of 1967 Grandma had a stroke, and she became quite confused. The Red Guards came and they confiscated everything. Grandpa was accused of being a rightist; they accused him for serving as the provincial governor of an illegal regime. He was badly beaten and was dragged along and paraded on the streets, and was sent back to his native province. Eventually he was beaten to death at a mass rally. Grandpa never said a single word in defence of himself. It would have been useless any way. All he said was: I did nothing against the law! My conscience is clear. He died with his clothes totally shredded. After he died they dragged him off the stage. He was completely covered with blood, his two bare feet twitching as if they wanted to linger a little longer. My sister and I were forced to witness this violent act, but none of us dared to come forward. We had to draw a clear line of demarcation. Just then a white-haired old fellow with very long legs staggered up and blocked their way. He produced a brand new pair of white socks, tore the brand name paper off in haste and put the socks on Grandpa's feet. He muttered something unintelligible. The socks were instantly covered with blood, but Grandpa would not be going to the other world barefoot.
>
> I picked up the badly trodden paper with the trade name and kept it as a souvenir. It was a piece of white paper with the picture of a black chrysanthemum. The words "Dark Chrysanthemum brand" were printed on it, and there was also the picture of a small black fish. The paper had yellowed with age. It must have been an old relic. I wonder who was that old fellow and how was he connected with our family? I wanted to catch him and find out, but he disappeared in the crowd. Aunt, can you figure out who it could have been . . .

I could not finish the letter. Tears were running down my cheeks. I tried to wipe them away with my hands, but they kept coming. I had a blurred vision, through my tears, of a seven- or eight-year-old little girl walking in the front and followed by a long-legged servant of the family. A young and beautiful mother, her eyes full of love and tenderness holding the hand of the father as they watch a daughter walk toward the county primary school for girls. Suddenly the girl turned around and held on to the long legs of the servant and began to sob, as the shadows of Father and Mother shattered into pieces and faded away.

Analyzing the Text

1. How would you characterize the narrator's relationship with the servant Chung Jen? To what extent is the child ignorant of the impoverished circumstances under which most people live?

2. What is the significance of Chung Jen's final gesture—putting the socks he had been given as a gift on his former master's feet?

Understanding Jen-mu's Techniques

1. How does the structure of the story depend on flashbacks to provide necessary background information and to set up the central conflict?
2. How do the perceptions of the little girl as a naive narrator create possibilities for the reader to understand the significance of events that the child cannot? For example, what inference does the child draw from the fact that her parents hold hands at night?

Arguing for an Interpretation

1. In your opinion, is P'an Jen-mu's strategy in immersing the reader in the naive awareness of the little girl/narrator before revealing the fate of all the characters through a letter received thirty years later more effective than if she had told the story as a straight narrative? Explain your answer.
2. How does the characterization of the religious and ethical assumptions that guide the behavior of the mother and father and their treatment of Chung Jen provide the motivation that might explain the servant's last gesture?

Poems

DIANA DER HOVANESSIAN

Diana Der Hovanessian, born in New England, is an accomplished Armenian-American poet and translator. She is the author of ten books of poetry and translations and has won international and national awards and fellowships, including prizes from the Poetry Society of America, the Columbia/P.E.N. Translation Center, and the Massachusetts Arts Council. She is president of the New England Poetry Club and serves on the governing board of the Poetry Society of America. She has been writer in residence and guest lecturer at various universities. Her first book, How to Choose Your Past, *was published in 1978 and a recent volume of poetry is called* About Time *(1987). She won the Barcelona Peace Prize in 1985 for the poem "Songs of Bread," the title poem of a group entitled* Songs of Bread, Songs of Salt *(1990), in which she takes on the persona of the martyred Armenian poet Daniel Varoujan who was executed in 1915. Recent books of her poetry include* The Circle *(1996) and* Any Day Now *(2000). In "Looking at Cambodian News Photos," from* Songs of Bread, Songs of Salt, *seeing the photos of massacred Cambodians evokes the speaker's pent-up grief and forces her to confront the psychological effects of the Armenian massacre by the Turks that took place over half a century before.*

Looking at Cambodian News Photos

My sack of tiny
bones, bird
bones, my baby
with head so large
your thin neck bends,
my flimsy bag of breath,
all my lost cousins
unfed
wearing your pink flesh
like cloth
my pink rag doll
with head that grows
no hair,
eyes that cannot close,
my unborn past,
heaving your dry tears.

Analyzing the Text

1. In what way have the photographs the speaker witnesses triggered a long-suppressed awareness of an event that happened generations before?
2. To what extent does the psychological turmoil the speaker experiences lead to a sense of resolution?

Understanding Hovanessian's Techniques

1. How does the repetition of key terms (such as "my" and "your") bridge the gap between past and present?
2. To what extent do the short clipped phrases and brief images that comprise the poem suggest the enormous difficulty the speaker has in confronting her emotions?

Arguing for an Interpretation

1. Do you think writing this poem has been cathartic in allowing the speaker to accept what had happened to her relatives in Armenia? Why or why not?
2. Although unrelated, news photos of the collapse of the World Trade Center towers on September 11, 2001, could very well bring about the same kinds of emotional realizations for future generations. How might writing a poem upon seeing some of these photographs help someone in the future?

WILFRED OWEN

Wilfred Owen (1893–1918) was an Englishman who died on the French front in World War I. His work on the tragic horror and pity of war brought him public acclaim as a major writer of the century. He formed a friendship with Siegfried Sassoon, who published 24 of Owen's poems posthumously in 1920. Owen's poetry is stylistically distinctive, and in the following poem "Strange Meeting" (which was not completed before he was killed) he envisages an eerie encounter between a soldier and a man he has killed in combat.

Strange Meeting

It seemed that out of battle I escaped
Down some profound dull tunnel, long since scooped
Through granites which titanic wars had groined.
Yet also there encumbered sleepers groaned,
Too fast in thought or death to be bestirred.
Then, as I probed them, one sprang up, and stared
With piteous recognition in fixed eyes,
Lifting distressful hands as if to bless.
And by his smile I knew that sullen hall,
By his dead smile I knew we stood in Hell.
With a thousand pains that vision's face was grained;
Yet no blood reached there from the upper ground,
And no guns thumped, or down the flues made moan.
"Strange friend," I said, "here is no cause to mourn."
"None," said the other, "save the undone years,
The hopelessness. Whatever hope is yours,
Was my life also; I went hunting wild
After the wildest beauty in the world,
Which lies not calm in eyes, or braided hair,
But mocks the steady running of the hour,
And if it grieves, grieves richlier than here.
For by my glee might many men have laughed,
And of my weeping something had been left,
Which must die now. I mean the truth untold,
The pity of war, the pity war distilled.
Now men will go content with what we spoiled,
Or, discontent, boil bloody and be spilled.
They will be swift with swiftness of the tigress,
None will break ranks, though nations trek from progress.
Courage was mine, and I had mystery,
Wisdom was mine, and I had mastery;
To miss the march of this retreating world
Into vain citadels that are not walled.
Then, when much blood had clogged their chariot wheels
I would go up and wash them from sweet wells,
Even with truths that lie too deep for taint.
I would have poured my spirit without stint
But not through wounds; not on the cess of war.

Foreheads of men have bled where no wounds were.
I am the enemy you killed, my friend.
I knew you in this dark; for so you frowned
Yesterday, through me as you jabbed and killed.
I parried, but my hands were loath and cold.
Let us sleep now. . . ."

Analyzing the Text

1. In what respects is the man the speaker has killed in battle someone who is quite similar to himself with aspirations to serve humanity?
2. What does the speaker learn about the ways in which war has not only destroyed other men's hopes and ideals, but also has corrupted his own?

Understanding Owen's Techniques

1. How do the patterns of speech of the "strange friend," with its unusual consonantal rhyme scheme, enhance the poem's theme about the destructive effects of war on the human spirit?
2. What aspects of the poem make it an amalgam of didactic verse, allegory, and parable?

Arguing for an Interpretation

1. To what extent does the poem suggest that the "strange friend" is not merely another soldier, but a nobler alter ego of the speaker himself that has been destroyed by war?
2. What aspects of the poem suggest that Owen is using the framework of Dante's *Inferno* to bring Hell into the modern world?

W. H. Auden

W. H. Auden (1907–1973) was born in York, England, the son of a distinguished physician. He was educated at Oxford where he was part of a group of poets, including Louis MacNiece, Stephen Spender, and C. Day Lewis, who shared the goal of creating new poetic techniques to express heightened social consciousness. After graduating from Oxford in 1928, Auden spent a year in Berlin, where he was influenced by Marxist poet and playwright Bertolt Brecht. After teaching school in England and Scotland in the 1930s, he went to Spain in 1937, where he drove an ambulance for the Republicans in the war against the Fascists. He moved to the United States in 1939 and became an American citizen in 1946, dividing his time between New York and Europe. He was elected professor of poetry at Oxford in 1956. The most complete edition of his poetry is the posthumously published **Collected Poems** ***(1978). In "The Unknown Citizen" (1940) Auden satirizes a dehumanized materialistic society that requires absolute conformity of its citizens.***

The Unknown Citizen

(To JS/07/M/378
This Marble Monument
Is Erected by the State)

He was found by the Bureau of Statistics to be
One against whom there was no official complaint,
And all the reports on his conduct agree
That, in the modern sense of an old-fashioned word, he
was a saint,
For in everything he did he served the Greater Community.
Except for the War till the day he retired
He worked in a factory and never got fired,
But satisfied his employers, Fudge Motors Inc.
Yet he wasn't a scab or odd in his views,[1]
For his Union reports that he paid his dues,
(Our report on his Union shows it was sound)
And our Social Psychology workers found
That he was popular with his mates and liked a drink.
The Press are convinced that he bought a paper every day
And that his reactions to advertisements were normal in
every way.
Policies taken out in his name prove that he was fully
insured,
And his Health-card shows he was once in hospital but
left it cured.
Both Producers Research and High-Grade Living declare
He was fully sensible to the advantages of the
Installment Plan
And had everything necessary to the Modern Man,
A phonograph, radio, a car and a frigidaire.
Our researchers into Public Opinion are content
That he held the proper opinions for the time of year;
When there was peace, he was for peace; when there
was war, he went.
He was married and added five children to the population,
Which our Eugenist says was the right number for a parent
of his generation,[2]
And our teachers report that he never interfered with their
education.
Was he free? Was he happy? The question is absurd:
Had anything been wrong, we should certainly have heard.

[1] *Scab:* A worker who won't join the union or who takes a striker's job.
[2] *Eugenist:* An expert in eugenics, the science of improving the human race by careful selection of parents to breed healthier, more intelligent children.

Analyzing the Text

1. Why is it significant that no official complaint was ever brought against the unknown citizen? Why is it ironic that the poem is dedicated to the government-allocated numbers "JS/07/M/378" rather than a name?
2. What kind of society does the unknown citizen inhabit? Based on the evidence in the poem, how might you answer the question "Was he free? Was he happy?" (in line 28)?

Understanding Auden's Techniques

1. What effect does Auden achieve by capitalizing the impersonal institutions in this society, and how does he parody the language of bureaucracy to satirize the state?
2. Why is the word "unknown" in the title so important, especially in view of the questions asked about him and the statistical answers given?

Arguing for an Interpretation

1. To what extent is this poem a satire on personal passivity in a society where deviation from the statistical norm is considered a crime?
2. How does Auden use literary devices such as overstatement, understatement, and ironic ridicule to satirize the pomposity of bureaucratic language? How effective are these methods in getting his point across? What do you think Auden would say about our society, which has so many numbers allocated to its citizens in ways he never could have dreamt?

CAROLYN FORCHÉ

Carolyn Forché was born in Detroit in 1950. She was educated at Michigan State University and Bowling Green University and has taught at a number of colleges. While a journalist in El Salvador from 1978 to 1980, she reported on human rights conditions for Amnesty International. Her experiences there had a profound influence on her poetry and nonfiction writings. Her poetry collections include Gathering the Tribes *(1976) and* The Country Between Us *(1981). She is also the editor of* Against Forgetting: Twentieth-Century Poetry of Witness *(1993). "The Colonel" (1978) offers a surreal portrait of the hidden terrors lurking underneath the civilized veneer of normalcy in an unnamed Central American country. She has also written* The Angel of History *(1995) and* Blue Hour *(2003).*

The Colonel

What you have heard is true. I was in his house. His wife carried a tray of coffee and sugar. His daughter filed her nails, his son went out for the night. There were daily papers, pet dogs, a pistol on the cushion behind him. The moon swung bare on its black cord over the house. On the television was a cop show. It was in English. Broken bottles were embedded in the walls around the house to scoop the kneecaps from a man's legs or cut his hands to lace. On the windows there were gratings like those in liquor stores. We had dinner, rack of lamb, good wine, a gold bell was on the table for calling the maid. The maid brought green mangoes, salt, a type of bread. I was asked how I enjoyed the country. There was a brief commercial in Spanish. His wife took everything away. There was some talk then of how difficult it had become to govern. The parrot said hello on the terrace. The colonel told it to shut up, and pushed himself from the table. My friend said to me with his eyes: say nothing. The colonel returned with a sack used to bring groceries home. He spilled many human ears on the table. They were like dried peach halves. There is no other way to say this. He took one of them in his hands, shook it in our faces, dropped it into a water glass. It came alive there, I am tired of fooling around he said. As for the rights of anyone, tell your people they can go fuck themselves. He swept the ears to the floor with his arm and held the last of his wine in the air. Something for your poetry, no? he said. Some of the ears on the floor caught this scrap of his voice. Some of the ears on the floor were pressed to the ground.

Analyzing the Text

1. When the Colonel of this unnamed Central American country becomes irritated by the turn the dinner conversation has taken, what does he return to the dinner with and how does this display contrast with the trappings of a normal life that first greets the visitor?
2. What attitude toward human rights is implied by the trophies the Colonel presents to the visitor?

Understanding Forché's Techniques

1. How does this poem, although written in prose, use vivid imagery based on commonplace details to heighten the shock of the underlying brutality represented by the Colonel's trophies?
2. In what way is the display of hidden terrors underneath a civilized veneer of normalcy made more effective through the surreal contrast the poem develops?

Arguing for an Interpretation

1. The guest confronts an ethical dilemma during the meal at which human rights is discussed. How does the ending of the poem, with dismembered ears being described as pressing to the ground in terror at the sound of the Colonel's voice, reflect the speaker's predicament?
2. There are many details that might go unobserved (such as the reference to the "cop show" in English on the television, or the parrot on the terrace that says hello and is told to shut up). Choose a few of these and discuss how they contribute to the surreal irony of the poem.

Eleni Fourtouni

Eleni Fourtouni was born in Sparta, Greece, in 1933. Fourtouni's poetry springs from her translations of nine journals kept by Greek women political prisoners during the war in Greece. These journals were edited and compiled by Victoria Theodorou, herself an inmate of the prison and writer of one of the journals. These compilations and oral histories are called Greek Women of the Resistance. *Fourtouni's work includes a collection of poetry,* Monovassia *(1976) and an anthology she edited and translated,* Contemporary Greek Women Poets *(1978), in which "Child's Memory" first appeared. The act of cutting off the head of a fish her young son has just caught releases submerged childhood memories of brutalities committed during the Nazi occupation. She also wrote* Watch the Flame: Poems *(1983).*

Child's Memory

Every time I think of it
there's a peculiar tickle
at my throat
especially when I clean fish—
the fish my blond son brings me
proud of his catch—
and I must cut off the heads

my hand holding the knife hesitates—
that peculiar tickle again—
I set the knife aside
furtively I scratch my throat

then I bring the knife down
on the thick scaly neck—
not much of a neck really—
just below the gills
I hack at the slippery
hulk of bass
my throat itches
my hands stink fish
they drip blood
my knife cuts through

the great head is off
I breathe

Once again the old image comes
into focus—
the proud blond soldier

his polished black boots
his spotless green uniform
his smile
the sack he lugs
into the schoolyards

the children gather
the soldier dips his hand inside the sack
the children hold their breath
what is it what?
their ink-smudged hands fly to their eyes

but we're full of curiosity
between our spread fingers we see . . .

the soldier's laughter is loud
as he pulls out
the heads of two Greek partisans.

quickly I rinse the blood off my knife

Analyzing the Text

1. Describe the event from the past that has cast a shadow over the speaker's life in the present.
2. How has the speaker's relationship with her young son been changed by the spontaneous flashback to her own childhood during World War II?

Understanding Fourtouni's Techniques

1. In what way is the poem constructed to create suspense as to exactly what the event from the past was that has traumatized the speaker?
2. What images suggest how deeply rooted the feelings of repulsion and suffocation have become in the speaker's psyche because of the past trauma?

Arguing for an Interpretation

1. To what extent does the horror of the poem stem from the contrast between the clean-cut pleasant exterior of the German soldier and what he shows the Greek children?
2. Discuss the speaker's lost innocence because of this past event as it contrasts with the kind of life she has created for her young son.

IRA SADOFF

Ira Sadoff was born in 1945 in Brooklyn, New York, the son of Russian Jewish immigrants. He was educated at Cornell University (B.A., 1966) and the University of Oregon (M.F.A., 1968). He is currently Dana Professor of Poetry at Colby College in Waterville, Maine. Collections of his poetry include Emotional Traffic *(1989), in which "Nazis" first appeared, and* Grazing: Poems *(1998).*

Sadoff's poems deal with the way individuals are contained and controlled by larger patterns of history and attempt to bridge the gap between public events and private experiences.

Nazis

Thank God they're all gone
except for one or two in Clinton Maine
who come home from work
at Scott Paper or Diamond Match
to make a few crank calls
to the only Jew in New England
they can find

These make-shift students of history
whose catalogue of facts include
every Jew who gave a dollar
to elect the current governor
every Jew who'd sell this country out
to the insatiable Israeli state

I know exactly how they feel
when they say they want to smash my face

Someone's cheated them
they want to know who it is
they want to know who makes them beg
It's true Let's Be Fair
it's tough for almost everyone
I exaggerate the facts
to make a point

Just when I thought I could walk to the market
just when Jean the check-out girl
asks me how many cords of wood I chopped
and wishes me a Happy Easter
as if I've lived here all my life

Just when I can walk into the bank
and nod at the tellers who know my name
where I work who lived in my house in 1832
who know to the penny the amount
of my tiny Jewish bank account

Just when I'm sure we can all live together
and I can dine in their saltbox dining rooms
with the melancholy painting of Christ
on the wall their only consolation

just when I can borrow my neighbor's ladder
to repair one of the holes in my roof

I pick up the phone
and listen to my instructions

I see the town now from the right perspective
the gunner in the glass bubble
of his fighter plane shadowing the tiny man
with the shopping bag and pointy nose
his overcoat two sizes too large for him
skulking from one doorway to the next
trying to make his own way home

I can see he's not one of us

Analyzing the Text

1. How would you characterize the speaker's predicament until lines 39–40?
2. How does the seeming change in point of view add another dimension to the poem? Who is the "gunner"? Who is the "tiny man"?

Understanding Sadoff's Techniques

1. What details in the poem suggest the extent to which the speaker is isolated from his surrounding community? What stereotyped perceptions prevail?
2. What effect does Sadoff create by juxtaposing images that refer to Nazis in Europe during World War II with the supposed security in a small New England town?

Arguing for an Interpretation

1. In your opinion, what was Sadoff's purpose in writing a poem whose perspectives alternate in ways that make it difficult to establish who is speaking at the end? Who do you think it is, and why?
2. Does the poem suggest that the speaker would become a Nazi himself if he were given the opportunity? Explain your answer.

YEHUDA AMICHAI

Yehuda Amichai (1924–2000), one of the finest poets writing in modern Hebrew, was born in Wurzburg, Germany, of German-Jewish parents who emigrated to Jerusalem in 1936. During World War II, he fought in the British army's Jewish Brigade and served with distinction in the 1948 Israeli War of Independence and in subsequent conflicts in 1956 and 1973. Amichai has published six volumes of poetry, including Songs of Jerusalem and Myself *(1973),* Time *(1979), and* Great Tranquility: Questions and Answers *(1983); a collection of short stories,* The World Is a Room *(1984); and two novels, only one of which,* Not of This Time, Not of This Place *(1968), has been translated into English. Amichai has an unusual gift for transforming personal situations into universal ones, often by setting the present moment against the background of biblical places and religious legends. Many of his poems are set in Jerusalem and draw on its history and landscape to affirm the importance of human connections in a divided country and a troubled region. The tragic overtones of the Palestinian-Israeli conflict are apparent in "An Arab Shepherd Is Searching for His Goat on Mount Zion," translated by Chana Bloch. Recent collections of his works include* The Selected Poetry of Yehuda Amichai *(1996) and* Open Closed Open: Poems *(2000).*

An Arab Shepherd Is Searching for His Goat on Mount Zion

An Arab shepherd is searching for his goat on Mount Zion
and on the opposite mountain I am searching
for my little boy.
An Arab shepherd and a Jewish father
both in their temporary failure.
Our voices meet
above the Sultan's Pool in the valley between us.
neither of us wants
the child or the goat to get caught in the wheels
of the terrible *Had Gadya*[1] machine.

Afterward we found them among the bushes
and our voices came back inside us, laughing and crying.

Searching for a goat or a son
has always been the beginning
of a new religion in these mountains.

Analyzing the Text

1. How does the action of the poem refer to an age-old historical antagonism going back to biblical times?
2. In what way does the poem create a story that explores whether individuals can give up automatic responses and time-worn animosities in order to avoid losing something they both value?

---

[1]*Had Gadya:* literally, "one little goat"; a story first published in a Passover Seder book in 1590 in Prague, and intended to entertain children. Amichai uses it to symbolize a cycle of violence if thoughts of revenge are not put aside.

Understanding Amichai's Techniques

1. How does the structure of the poem sharply define the conflict between the opposing parties and increase suspense as to whether they can transcend their differences to act in their own best interests?
2. How does the reference to the "*Had Gadya* machine" introduce a sense that both sides are caught in a cycle of hate that can destroy them?

Arguing for an Interpretation

1. To what extent does Amichai suggest that hatred is learned and not innate, something that only becomes obvious when both parties need each other to avoid losing something that is precious?
2. Is the organization of the poem an effective one in that the initial lines set the mood for the events to come? Why or why not? What do you think Amichai meant by the last three lines? Could the "goat" refer to a scapegoat and could the "son" refer to the incident in the Hebrew Bible where Abraham was willing to sacrifice his son Isaac, until Jehovah relented and his son was replaced by a goat? Explain your answer.

Margaret Atwood

Margaret Atwood was born in Ottawa, Ontario, in 1939. She was educated at the University of Toronto, where she came under the influence of the critic Northrup Frye, whose theories of mythical modes in literature she has adapted to her own purposes in her prolific writing of poetry, novels, and short stories. She is the author of more than 20 volumes of poetry and fiction, including The Handmaid's Tale *(1986), which was subsequently made into a film in 1989. Her short story collections include* Bluebeard's Egg and Other Stories *(1986). She also edited the* Oxford Book of Canadian Short Stories in English *(1987). Her most recent works include* Alias Grace: A Novel *(1996),* A Quiet Game *(1997),* Two Solitudes *(1998),* Blind Assassin *(2001) and* Negotiating with the Dead: A Writer on Writing *(2002). In the following poem from* Power Politics *(1971), Atwood depicts how the women whom soldiers leave at home must adjust as wars change but always find themselves in the same predicament.*

At First I Was Given Centuries

At first I was given centuries
to wait in caves, in leather
tents, knowing you would never come back

Then it speeded up: only
several years between

the day you jangled off
into the mountains, and the day (it was
spring again) I rose from the embroidery
frame at the messenger's entrance.

That happened twice, or was it
more; and there was once, not so
long ago, you failed,
and came back in a wheelchair
with a mustache and a sunburn
and were insufferable.

Time before last though, I remember
I had a good eight months between
running alongside the train, skirts hitched, handing
you violets in at the window
and opening the letter; I watched
your snapshot fade for twenty years.

And last time (I drove to the airport
still dressed in my factory
overalls, the wrench
I had forgotten sticking out of the back
pocket; there you were,
zippered and helmeted, it was zero
hour, you said Be
Brave) it was at least three weeks before
I got the telegram and could start regretting.

But recently, the bad evenings
there are only seconds
between the warning on the radio and the
explosion; my hands
don't reach you

and on quieter nights
you jump up from
your chair without even touching your dinner
and I can scarcely kiss you goodbye
before you run out into the street and they shoot

Analyzing the Text

1. What recurrent predicament do women find themselves in during wars, according to the speaker?
2. As the poem progresses, we learn about the history of warfare solely as it affects the women left behind. How have the circumstances of war changed over the course of centuries, although the consequences remain the same?

Understanding Atwood's Techniques

1. How would you describe the voice you hear in the poem and what does it tell you about the suffering of women, as well as men, during wartime?

2. How does the poem create the sensation of time speeding up, and the always lessening interval between the soldiers' departure and women's grief? Is the title an apt expression of this theme? Why or why not?

Arguing for an Interpretation

1. To what extent is the effectiveness of the poem due to the skill with which Atwood evokes the circumstances of specific wars and the role of women during these times?
2. Although known as a feminist writer, has Atwood stereotyped women as invariably passive on the world stage? Why or why not?

Drama

VÁCLAV HAVEL

Václav Havel was born in Prague, Czechoslovakia, in 1936. Prevented from attending high school, he earned a diploma by attending night class and working as a laboratory assistant during the day. By age 20, Havel was publishing his first articles in literary and theatrical magazines. He worked as a stagehand at several theaters in Prague and rose to the position of resident playwright at the Ballustrade Theater.

His first play, Autostop *(1961), cowritten with Ivan Vyskocil, is a satire on society's preoccupation with automobiles. Havel's first full-length play,* The Garden Party *(1963), is widely regarded as the play that began the theater of the absurd in Czechoslovakia. A second full-length play,* The Memorandum *(1965), continued to articulate Havel's exploration of conflict between citizens and the political system. The play earned an OBIE Award when it was produced at the 1968 New York Shakespeare Festival. Months after Havel's third play,* The Increased Difficulty of Concentration *(1968), appeared, Havel discovered he was under government surveillance and was being watched 24 hours a day. Government censorship prevented him from finding a publisher or having his plays produced, and he resorted to circulating his works privately—even as foreign productions of his plays won him an international reputation.*

*His best-known works of the 1970s are his three one-act plays, often called The Vaněk Trilogy after the main character. All three plays—*Audience, Private View, *and* Protest*—focus on how the system intrudes into the lives of common citizens who are not dissidents. Throughout this period, Havel was repeatedly interrogated, held for detention, and imprisoned. He managed to write* Protest, *translated by Vera Blackwell, in 1979 while under surveillance and house arrest before being sentenced to* *prison for four and a half years. The accounts of his imprisonment, from which he was released in 1983 when he became violently ill, are in his nonfiction works,* Living in Truth *(1989),* Disturbing the Peace *(1990), and* Letters to Olga *(1990), a volume of letters written to his wife. The "Velvet Revolution" brought down the communist government in 1989.*

Havel became the first freely elected president of Czechoslovakia. In 1993 he was reelected as the president of the newly formed Czech Republic. He stepped down in February 2003 and was replaced by Václav Klaus. In Protest, *the dissident writer Vaněk, a semiautobiographical figure, is confronted by Staněk, a successful author who has made his peace with the system. Staněk's attempt to justify his own behavior is perhaps the most brilliant theatrical realization of pseudoreasoning and rationalization of political cowardice ever presented on a stage. Havel's reflections and thoughts have been published as* Spontaneous Mind: Selected Interviews, 1958–1996 *(2001).*

Protest

Characters

VANĚK

STANĚK

Place

Staněk's study, Prague.

Staněk's study. On the left, a massive writing desk, on it a typewriter, a telephone, reading glasses, and many books and papers; behind it, a large window with a view into the garden. On the right, two comfortable arm chairs and between them a small table. The whole back wall is covered by bookcases, filled with books and with a built-in bar. In one of the niches there is a tape recorder. In the right back corner, a door; on the right wall, a large surrealist painting. When the curtain rises, Staněk and Vaněk are on stage: Staněk, standing behind his desk, is emotionally looking at Vaněk, who is standing at the door holding a briefcase and looking at Staněk with signs of embarrassment. A short, tense pause. Then Staněk suddenly walks excitedly over to Vaněk, takes him by the shoulders with both arms, shakes him in a friendly way, calling out.)

STANĚK. Vaněk!—Hello!
(*Vaněk smiles timidly. Staněk lets go, trying to conceal his agitation.*)
Did you have trouble finding it?

VANĚK. Not really—

STANĚK. Forgot to mention the flowering magnolias. That's how you know it's my house. Superb, aren't they?

VANĚK. Yes—

STANĚK. I managed to double their blossoms in less than three years, compared to the previous owner. Have you magnolias at your cottage?

VANĚK. No—

STANĚK. You must have them! I'm going to find you two quality saplings and I'll come and plant them for you personally. *(Crosses to the bar and opens it.)* How about some brandy?

VANĚK. I'd rather not—

STANĚK. Just a token one. Eh?
(*He pours brandy into two glasses, hands one glass to Vaněk, and raises the other for a toast.*) Well—here's to our reunion!

VANĚK. Cheers—

(*Both drink; Vaněk shudders slightly.*)

STANĚK. I was afraid you weren't going to come.

VANĚK. Why?

STANĚK. Well, I mean, things got mixed up in an odd sort of way—What?—Won't you sit down?

VANĚK (*Sits down in an armchair, placing his briefcase on the floor beside him.*). Thanks—

STANĚK (*Sinks into an armchair opposite Vaněk with a sigh.*). That's more like it! Peanuts?

VANĚK. No, thanks—

STANĚK (*Helps himself. Munching.*). You haven't changed much in all these years, you know?

VANĚK. Neither have you—

STANĚK. Me? Come on! Getting on for fifty, going gray, aches and pains setting in—Not as we used to be, eh? And the present times don't make one feel any better either, what? When did we see each other last, actually?

VANĚK. I don't know—

STANĚK. Wasn't it at your last opening night?

VANĚK. Could be—

STANĚK. Seems like another age! We had a bit of an argument—

VANĚK. Did we?

STANĚK. You took me to task for my illusions and my over-optimism. Good Lord! How often since then I've had to admit to myself you were right! Of course, in those days I still believed that in spite of everything some of the ideals of my youth could be salvaged and I took you for an incorrigible pessimist.

VANĚK. But I'm not a pessimist—

STANĚK. You see, everything's turned around! (*Short pause.*) Are you—alone?

VANĚK. How do you mean, alone?

STANĚK. Well, isn't there somebody—you know—

VANĚK. Following me?

STANĚK. Not that I care! After all, it was me who called you up, right?

VANĚK. I haven't noticed anybody—

STANĚK. By the way, suppose you want to shake them off one of these days, you know the best place to do it?

VANĚK. No—

STANĚK. A department store. You mingle with the crowd, then at a moment when they aren't looking you sneak into the washroom and wait there for about two hours. They become convinced you managed to slip out through a side entrance and they give up. You must try it out sometime! (*Pause.*)

VANĚK. Seems very peaceful here—

STANĚK. That's why we moved here. It was simply impossible to go on writing near that railway station! We've been here three years, you know. Of course, my greatest joy is the garden. I'll show you around later—I'm afraid I'm going to boast a little—

VANĚK. You do the gardening yourself?

STANĚK. It's become my greatest private passion these days. Keep puttering about out there almost every day. Just now I've been rejuvenating the apricots. Developed my own method, you see, based on a mixture of natural and artificial fertilizers plus a special way of waxless grafting. You won't believe the results I get! I'll find some cuttings for you later on—

(*Staněk walks over to the desk, takes a package of foreign cigarettes out of a drawer, brings matches and an ashtray, and puts it all on the table in front of Vaněk.*) Ferdinand, do have a cigarette.

VANĚK. Thanks—

(*Vaněk takes a cigarette and lights it; Staněk sits in the other chair; both drink.*)

STANĚK. Well now, Ferdinand, tell me—How are you?

VANĚK. All right, thanks—

STANĚK. Do they leave you alone—at least now and then?

VANĚK. It depends—

(*Short pause.*)

STANĚK. And how was it in there?

VANĚK. Where?

STANĚK. Can our sort bear it at all?

VANĚK. You mean prison? What else can one do?

STANĚK. As far as I recall, you used to be bothered by hemorrhoids. Must have been terrible, considering the hygiene in there.

VANĚK. They gave me suppositories—

STANĚK. You ought to have them operated on, you know. It so happens a friend of mine is our greatest hemorrhoid specialist. Works real miracles. I'll arrange it for you.

VANĚK. Thanks—

(*Short pause.*)

STANĚK. You know, sometimes it all seems like a beautiful dream—all the exciting opening nights, private views, lectures, meetings—the endless discussions about literature and art! All the energy, the hopes, plans, activities, ideas—the wine-bars crowded with friends, the wild booze-ups, the madcap affrays in the small hours, the jolly girls dancing attendance on us! And the mountains of work we managed to get done, regardless!—That's all over now. It'll never come back!

VANĚK. Mmn—

(*Pause. Both drink.*)

STANĚK. Did they beat you?

VANĚK. No—

STANĚK. Do they beat people up in there?

VANĚK. Sometimes. But not the politicals—

STANĚK. I thought about you a great deal!

VANĚK. Thank you—

(*Short pause.*)

STANĚK. I bet in those days it never even occurred to you—

VANĚK. What?

STANĚK. How it'll all end up! I bet not even you had guessed that!

VANĚK. Mmn—

STANĚK. It's disgusting, Ferdinand, disgusting! The nation is governed by scum! And the people? Can this really be the same nation which not very long ago behaved so magnificently? All that horrible cringing, bowing and scraping! The selfishness, corruption and fear wherever you turn! What have they made of us, old pal? Can this really be us?

VANĚK. I don't believe things are as black as all that—

STANĚK. Forgive me, Ferdinand, but you don't happen to live in a normal environment. All you know are people who manage to resist this rot. You just keep on supporting and encouraging each other. You've no idea the sort of environment I've got to put up with! You're lucky you no longer have anything to do with it. Makes you sick at your stomach!

(*Pause. Both drink.*)

VANĚK. You mean television?

STANĚK. In television, in film studios—you name it.

VANĚK. There was a piece by you on the T.V. the other day—

STANĚK. You can't imagine what an ordeal that was! First they kept blocking it for over a year, then they started changing it around—changed my whole opening and the entire closing sequence! You wouldn't believe the trifles they find objectionable these days! Nothing but sterility and intrigues, intrigues and sterility! How often I tell myself—wrap it up, chum, forget it, go hide somewhere—grow apricots—

VANĚK. I know what you mean—

STANĚK. The thing is though, one can't help wondering whether one's got the right to this sort of escape. Supposing even the little one might be able to accomplish today can, in spite of everything, help someone in some way, at least give him a bit of encouragement, uplift him a little.—Let me bring you a pair of slippers.

VANĚK. Slippers? Why?

STANĚK. You can't be comfortable in those boots.

VANĚK. I'm all right—

STANĚK. Are you sure?

VANĚK. Yes. Really—

(*Both drink.*)

STANĚK. (*Pause.*) How about drugs? Did they give you any?

VANĚK. No—

STANĚK. No dubious injections?

VANĚK. Only some vitamin ones—

STANĚK. I bet there's some funny stuff in the food!

VANĚK. Just bromine against sex—

STANĚK. But surely they tried to break you down somehow!

VANĚK. Well—

STANĚK. If you'd rather not talk about it, it's all right with me.

VANĚK. Well, in a way, that's the whole point of pre-trial interrogations, isn't it? To take one down a peg or two—

STANĚK. And to make one talk!

VANĚK. Mmn—

STANĚK. If they should haul me in for questioning—which sooner or later is bound to happen—you know what I'm going to do?

VANĚK. What?

STANĚK. Simply not answer any of their questions! Refuse to talk to them at all! That's by far the best way. Least one can be quite sure one didn't say anything one ought not to have said!

VANĚK. Mmn—

STANĚK. Anyway, you must have steel nerves to be able to bear it all and in addition to keep doing the things you do.

VANĚK. Like what?

STANĚK. Well, I mean all the protests, petitions, letters—the whole fight for human rights! I mean the things you and your friends keep on doing—

VANĚK. I'm not doing so much—

STANĚK. Now don't be too modest, Ferdinand! I follow everything that's going on! I know! If everybody did what you do, the situation would be quite different! And that's a fact. It's extremely important there should be at least a few people here who aren't afraid to speak the truth aloud, to defend others, to call a spade a spade! What I'm going to say might sound a bit solemn perhaps, but frankly, the way I see it, you and your friends have taken on an almost superhuman task: to preserve and to carry the remains, the remnant of moral conscience through the present quagmire! The thread you're spinning may be thin, but—who knows—perhaps the hope of a moral rebirth of the nation hangs on it.

VANĚK. You exaggerate—

STANĚK. Well, that's how I see it, anyway.

VANĚK. Surely our hope lies in all the decent people—

STANĚK. But how many are there still around? How many?

VANĚK. Enough—

STANĚK. Are there? Even so, it's you and your friends who are the most exposed to view.

VANĚK. And isn't that precisely what makes it easier for us?

STANĚK. I wouldn't say so. The more you're exposed, the more responsibility you have towards all those who know about you, trust you, rely on you and look up to you, because to some extent you keep upholding their honour, too! (*Gets up.*) I'll get you those slippers!

VANĚK. Please don't bother—

STANĚK. I insist. I feel uncomfortable just looking at your boots. (*Pause. Staněk returns with slippers.*)

VANĚK. (*Sighs.*)

STANĚK. Here you are. Do take those ugly things off, I beg you. Let me—

(*Tries to take off Vaněk's boots.*) Won't you let me—Hold still—

VANĚK. (*Embarrassed.*) No—please don't—no—I'll do it— (*Struggles out of his boots, slips on slippers.*) There—Nice, aren't they? Thank you very much.

STANĚK. Good gracious, Ferdinand, what for?—(*Hovering over Vaněk.*) Some more brandy?

VANĚK. No more for me, thanks—

STANĚK. Oh, come on. Give me your glass!

VANĚK. I'm sorry, I'm not feeling too well—

STANĚK. Lost the habit inside, is that it?

VANĚK. Could be—But the point is—last night, you see—

STANĚK. Ah, that's what it is. Had a drop too many, eh?

VANĚK. Mmn—

STANĚK. I understand. (*Returns to his chair.*) By the way, you know the new wine-bar, "The Shaggy Dog"?

VANĚK. No—

STANĚK. You don't? Listen, the wine there comes straight from the cask, it's not expensive and usually it isn't crowded. Really charming spot, you know, thanks to a handful of fairly good artists who were permitted—believe it or not—to do the interior decoration. I can warmly recommend it to you. Lovely place. Where did you go, then?

VANĚK. Well, we did a little pub-crawling, my friend Landovský and I—

STANĚK. Oh, I see! You were with Landovský, were you? Well! In that case, I'm not at all surprised you came to a sticky end! He's a first class actor, but once he starts drinking—that's it! Surely you can take one more brandy! Right?

VANĚK. (*Sighs.*)

(*Drinks are poured. They both drink. Vaněk shudders.*)

STANĚK. (*Back in his armchair. Short pause.*) Well, how are things otherwise? You do any writing?

VANĚK. Trying to—

STANĬK. A play?

VANĚK. A one-act play—

STANĚK. Another autobiographical one?

VANĚK. More or less—

STANĚK. My wife and I read the one about the brewery[1] the other day. We thought it was very amusing.

VANĚK. I'm glad—

STANĚK. Unfortunately we were given a rather bad copy.[2] Very hard to read.

VANĚK. I'm sorry—

STANĚK. It's a really brilliant little piece! I mean it! Only the ending seemed to me a bit muddy. The whole thing wants to be brought to a more straightforward conclusion, that's all. No problem. You can do it.

(*Pause. Both drink. Vaněk shudders.*)

STANĚK. Well, how are things? How about Pavel?[3] Do you see him?

VANĚK. Yes—

---

[1]Staněk is referring to *Audience.*

[2]Literary works circulating as *samizdat* texts in typescript are understandably often of poor quality. If one gets to read the, say, sixth carbon copy on onion skin, the readability of the script leaves much to be desired.

[3]Staněk means Pavel Kohout.

STANĚK. Does he do any writing?

VANĚK. Just now he's finishing a one-act, as well. It's supposed to be performed together with mine—

STANĚK. Wait a minute. You don't mean to tell me you two have teamed up also as authors!

VANĚK. More or less—

STANĚK. Well, well!—Frankly, Ferdinand, try as I may, I don't get it. I don't. I simply can't understand this alliance of yours. Is it quite genuine on your part? Is it?—Good heavens! Pavel! I don't know! Just remember the way he started! We both belong to the same generation, Pavel and I, we've both—so to speak—spanned a similar arc of development, but I don't mind telling you that what he did in those days—Well! It was a bit too strong even for me!—Still, I suppose it's your business. You know best what you're doing.

VANĚK. That's right—

(*Pause. Both drink.*)

STANĚK. Is your wife fond of gladioli?

VANĚK. I don't know. I think so—

STANĚK. You won't find many places with such a large selection as mine. I've got thirty-two shades, whereas at a common or garden nursery you'll be lucky to find six. Do you think your wife would like me to send her some bulbs?

VANĚK. I'm sure she would—

STANĚK. There's still time to plant them you know. (*Pause.*) Ferdinand—

VANĚK. Yes?

STANĚK. Weren't you surprised when I suddenly called you up?

VANĚK. A bit—

STANĚK. I thought so. After all, I happen to be among those who've still managed to keep their heads above water and I quite understand that—because of this—you might want to keep a certain distance from me.

VANĚK. No, not I—

STANĚK. Perhaps not you yourself, but I realize that some of your friends believe that anyone who's still got some chance today has either abdicated morally, or is unforgivably fooling himself.

VANĚK. I don't think so—

STANĚK. I wouldn't blame you if you did, because I know only too well the grounds from which such prejudice could grow. (*An embarrassed pause.*) Ferdinand—

VANĚK. Yes?

STANĚK. I realize what a high price you have to pay for what you're doing. But please don't think it's all that easy for a man who's either so lucky, or so unfortunate as to be still tolerated by the official apparatus, and who—at the same time—wishes to live at peace with his conscience.

VANĚK. I know what you mean—

STANĚK. In some respects it may be even harder for him.

VANĚK. I understand.

STANĚK. Naturally, I didn't call you in order to justify myself! I don't really think there's any need. I called you because I like you and I'd be sorry to see you sharing the prejudice which I assume exists among your friends.

VANĚK. As far as I know nobody has ever said a bad word about you—

STANĚK. Not even Pavel?

VANĚK. No—

STANĚK. (*Embarrassed pause.*) Ferdinand—

VANĚK. Yes?

STANĚK. Excuse me— (*Gets up. Crosses to the tape recorder. Switches it on: Soft, nondescript background music. Staněk returns to his chair.*) Ferdinand, does the name Javurek mean anything to you?

VANĚK. The pop singer? I know him very well—

STANĚK. So I expect you know what happened to him.

VANĚK. Of course. They locked him up for telling a story during one of his performances. The story about the cop who meets a penguin in the street—

STANĚK. Of course. It was just an excuse. The fact is, they hate his guts because he sings the way he does. The whole thing is so cruel, so ludicrous, so base!

VANĚK. And cowardly—

STANĚK. Right! And cowardly! Look, I've been trying to do something for the boy. I mean, I know a few guys at the town council and at the prosecutor's office, but you know how it is. Promises, promises! They all say they're going to look into it, but the moment your back is turned they drop it like a hot potato, so they don't get their fingers burnt! Sickening, the way everybody looks out for number one!

VANĚK. Still, I think it's nice of you to have tried to do something—

STANĚK. My dear Ferdinand, I'm really not the sort of man your friends obviously take me for! Peanuts?

VANĚK. No, thanks—

STANĚK (*Short pause.*). About Javurek—

VANĚK. Yes?

STANĚK. Since I didn't manage to accomplish anything through private intervention, it occurred to me perhaps it ought to be handled in a somewhat different way. You know what I mean. Simply write something—a protest or a petition? In fact, this is the main thing I wanted to discuss with you. Naturally, you're far more experienced in these matters than I. If this document contains a few fairly well-known signatures—like yours, for example—it's bound to be published somewhere abroad which might create some political pressure. Right? I mean, these things don't seem to impress them all that much, actually—but honestly, I don't see any other way to help the boy. Not to mention Annie—

VANĚK. Annie?

STANĚK. My daughter.

VANĬK. Oh? Is that your daughter?

STANĚK. That's right.

VANĚK. Well, what about her?

STANĚK. I thought you knew.

VANĚK. Knew what?

STANĚK. She's expecting. By Javurek—

VANĚK. Oh, I see. That's why—

STANĚK. Wait a minute! If you mean the case interests me merely because of family matters—

VANĚK. I didn't mean that—

STANĚK. But you just said—

VANĚK. I only wanted to say, that's how you know about the case at all; you were explaining to me how you got to know about it. Frankly, I wouldn't have expected you to be familiar with the present pop scene. I'm sorry if it sounded as though I meant—

STANĚK. I'd get involved in this case even if it was someone else expecting his child! No matter who—

VANĚK. I know—

(Embarrassed pause.)

STANĚK. Well, what do you think about my idea of writing some sort of protest?

(Vaněk begins to look for something in his briefcase, finally finds a paper, and hands it to Staněk.)

VANĚK. I guess this is the sort of thing you had in mind—

STANĚK. What?

VANĚK. Here—

STANĚK. (*Grabs the document.*). What is it?

VANĚK. Have a look—

(Staněk takes the paper from Vaněk, goes quickly to the writing desk, picks up his glasses, puts them on, and begins to read attentively. Lengthy pause. Staněk shows signs of surprise. When he finishes reading, he puts aside his glasses and begins to pace around in agitation.)

STANĚK. Now isn't it fantastic! That's a laugh, isn't it? Eh? Here I was cudgeling my brains how to go about it, finally I take the plunge and consult you—and all this time you've had the whole thing wrapped up and ready! Isn't it marvellous? I knew I was doing the right thing when I turned to you! (*Staněk returns to the table, sits down, puts on his glasses again, and rereads the text.*) There! Precisely what I had in mind! Brief, to the point, fair, and yet emphatic. Manifestly the work of a professional! I'd be sweating over it for a whole day and I'd never come up with anything remotely like this!

VANĚK. (*Embarrassed.*)

STANĚK. Listen, just a small point—here at the end—do you think "willfulness" is the right word to use? Couldn't one find a milder synonym, perhaps? Somehow seems a bit misplaced, you know. I mean, the whole text is composed in very measured, factual terms—and this word here suddenly sticks out, sounds much too emotional, wouldn't you agree? Otherwise it's absolutely perfect. Maybe the second paragraph is somewhat superfluous; in fact, it's just a rehash of the first one. Except for the reference here to Javurek's impact on nonconformist youth. This is excellent and must stay in! How about putting it at the end instead of your "willfulness"? Wouldn't that do the trick?—But these are just my personal impressions. Good heavens! Why should you listen to what I have to say! On the whole the text is excellent, and no doubt it's going to hit the mark. Let me say again, Ferdinand, how much I admire you. Your knack for expressing the fundamental points of an issue, while avoiding all needless abuse, is indeed rare among our kind!

VANĚK. Come on—you don't really mean that—

(*Staněk takes off his glasses, goes over to Vaněk, puts the paper in front of him, sits again in the easy chair, and sips his drink. Short pause.*)

STANĚK. Anyway, it's good to know there's somebody around whom one can always turn to and rely on in a case like this.

VANĚK. But it's only natural, isn't it?

STANĚK. It may seem so to you. But in the circles where I've to move such things aren't in the least natural! The natural response is much more likely to be the exact opposite. When a man gets into trouble everybody drops him as soon as possible, the lot of them. And out of fear for their own positions they try to convince all and sundry they've never had anything to do with him; on the contrary, they sized him up right away, they had his number! But why am I telling you all this, you know best the sort of thing that happens! Right? When you were in prison your long-time theatre pals held forth against you on television. It was revolting—

VANĚK. I'm not angry with them—

STANĚK. But I am! And what's more I told them so. In no uncertain terms! You know, a man in my position learns to put up with a lot of things, but—if you'll forgive me—there are limits! I appreciate it might be awkward for you to blame them, as you happen to be the injured party. But listen to me, you've got to distance yourself from the affair! Just think: Once we, too, begin to tolerate this sort of muck—we're *de facto* assuming co-responsibility for the entire moral morass and indirectly contributing to its deeper penetration. Am I right?

VANĚK. Mmn—

STANĚK (*Short pause.*). Have you sent it off yet?

VANĚK. We're still collecting signatures—

STANĚK. How many have you got so far?

VANĚK. About fifty—

STANĚK. Fifty? Not bad! (*Short pause.*) Well, never mind, I've just missed the boat, that's all.

VANĚK. You haven't—

STANĚK. But the thing's already in hand, isn't it?

VANĚK. Yes, but it's still open—I mean—

STANĚK. All right, but now it's sure to be sent off and published, right? By the way, I wouldn't give it to any of the agencies, if I were you. They'll only print a measly little news item which is bound to be overlooked. Better hand it over directly to one of the big European papers, so the whole text gets published, including all the signatures!

VANĚK. I know—

STANĚK (*Short pause.*). Do they already know about it?

VANĚK. You mean the police?

STANĚK. Yes.

VANĚK. I don't think so. I suppose not—

STANĚK. Look here, I don't want to give you any advice, but it seems to me you ought to wrap it up as soon as possible, else they'll get wind of what's going on and they'll find a way to stop it. Fifty signatures should be enough! Besides, what counts is not the number of signatures, but their significance.

VANĚK. Each signature has its own significance!

STANĚK. Absolutely, but as far as publicity abroad is concerned, it is essential that some well-known names are represented, right? Has Pavel signed?

VANĚK. Yes—

STANĚK. Good. His name—no matter what one may think of him personally—does mean something in the world today!

VANĚK. No question—

STANĚK. (*Short pause.*). Listen, Ferdinand—

VANĚK. Yes?

STANĚK. There's one more thing I wanted to discuss with you. It's a bit delicate, though—

VANĚK. Oh?

STANĚK. Look here, I'm no millionaire, you know, but so far I've been able to manage—

VANĚK. Good for you—

STANĚK. Well, I was thinking—I mean—I'd like to—Look, a lot of your friends have lost their jobs. I was thinking—would you be prepared to accept from me a certain sum of money?

VANĚK. That's very nice of you! Some of my friends indeed find themselves in a bit of a spot. But there are problems, you know. I mean, one is never quite sure how to go about it. Those who most need help are often the most reluctant to accept—

STANĚK. You won't be able to work miracles with what I can afford, but I expect there are situations when every penny counts.

(***Takes out his wallet, removes two banknotes, hesitates, adds a third, hands them to Vaněk.***) Here—please—a small offering.

VANĚK. Thank you very much. Let me thank you for all my friends—

STANĚK. Gracious, we've got to help each other out, don't we? (*Pause.*) Incidentally, there's no need for you to mention this little contribution comes from me. I don't wish to erect a monument to myself. I'm sure you've gathered that much by now, eh?

VANĚK. Yes, Again many thanks—

STANĚK. Well now, how about having a look at the garden?

VANĚK. Mr. Staněk—

STANĚK. Yes?

VANĚK. We'd like to send it off tomorrow—

STANĚK. What?

VANĚK. The protest—

STANĚK. Excellent! The sooner the better!

VANĚK. So that today there's still—

STANĚK. Today you should think about getting some sleep! That's the main thing! Don't forget you've a bit of a hangover after last night and tomorrow is going to be a hard day for you!

VANĚK. I know. All I was going to say—

STANĚK. Better go straight home and unplug the phone. Else Ladovský rings you up again and heaven knows how you'll end up!

VANĚK. Yes, I know. There're only a few signatures I've still got to collect—it won't take long. All I was going to say—I mean, don't you think it would be helpful—as a matter of fact, it would, of course, be sensational! After all, practically everybody's read your *Crash!*

STANĚK. Oh, come on, Ferdinand! That was fifteen years ago!

VANĚK. But it's never been forgotten!

STANĚK. What do you mean—sensational?

VANĚK. I'm sorry, I had the impression you'd actually like to—

STANĚK. What?

VANĚK. Participate—

STANĚK. Participate? Wait a minute. Are you talking about (*points to the paper*) this? Is that what you're talking about?

VANĚK. Yes—

STANĚK. You mean I—

VANĚK. I'm sorry, but I had the impression—

(*Staněk finishes his drink, crosses to the bar, pours himself a drink, walks over to the window, looks out for a while, whereupon he suddenly turns to Vaněk with a smile.*)

STANĚK. Now that's a laugh, isn't it?

VANĚK. What's a laugh?

STANĚK. Come on, can't you see how absurd it is? Eh? I ask you over hoping you might write something about Javurek's case—you produce a finished text and what's more, one furnished with fifty signatures! I'm bowled over like a little child, can't believe my eyes and ears, I worry about ways to stop them from ruining your project—and all this time it hasn't occurred to me to do the one simple, natural thing which I should have done in the first place! I mean, at once sign the document myself! Well, you must admit it's absurd, isn't it?

VANĚK. Mmn—

STANĚK. Now, listen Ferdinand, isn't this a really terrifying testimony to the situation into which we've been brought? Isn't it? Just think: even I, though I know it's rubbish, even I've got used to the idea that the signing of protests is the business of local specialists, professionals in solidarity, dissidents! While the rest of us—when we want to do something for the sake of ordinary human decency—automatically turn to you, as though you were a sort of service establishment for moral matters. In other words, we're here simply to keep our mouths shut and to be rewarded by relative peace and quiet, whereas you're here to speak up for us and to be rewarded by blows on earth and glory in the heavens! Perverse, isn't it?

VANĚK. Mmn—

STANĚK. Of course it is! And they've managed to bring things to such a point that even a fairly intelligent and decent fellow—which, with your permission, I still think I am—is more or less ready to take this situation for granted! As though it was quite normal, perfectly natural! Sickening, isn't it? Sickening the depths we've reached! What do you say? Makes one puke, eh?

VANĚK. Well—

STANĚK. You think the nation can ever recover from all this?

VANĚK. Hard to say—

STANĚK. What can one do? What can one do? Well, seems clear, doesn't it? In theory, that is. Everybody should start with himself. What? However! Is this country inhabited only by Vaněks? It really doesn't seem that everybody can become a fighter for human rights.

VANĚK. Not everybody, no—

STANĚK. Where is it?

VANĚK. What?

STANĚK. The list of signatures, of course.

VANĚK. (*Embarrassed pause.*). Mr. Staněk—

STANĚK. Yes?

VANĚK. Forgive me, but—I'm sorry, I've suddenly a funny feeling that perhaps—

STANĚK. What funny feeling?

VANĚK. I don't know—I feel very embarrassed—Well, it seems to me perhaps I wasn't being quite fair—

STANĚK. In what way?

VANĚK. Well, what I did—was a bit of a con trick—in a way—

STANĚK. What are you talking about?

VANĚK. I mean, first I let you talk, and only then I ask for your signature—I mean, after you're already sort of committed by what you've said before, you see—

STANĚK. Are you suggesting that if I'd known you were collecting signatures for Javurek, I would never have started talking about him?

VANĚK. No, that's not what I mean—

STANĚK. Well, what do you mean?

VANĚK. How shall I put it—

STANĚK. Oh, come on! You mind I didn't organize the whole thing myself, is that it?

VANĚK. No, that's not it—

STANĚK. What is it then?

VANĚK. Well, it seems to me it would've been a quite different matter if I'd come to you right away and asked for your signature. That way you would've had an option—

STANĚK. And why didn't you come to me right away, actually? Was it because you'd simply written me off in advance?

VANĚK. Well, I was thinking that in your position—

STANĚK. Ah! There you are! You see? Now it's becoming clear what you really think of me, isn't it? You think that because now and then one of my pieces happens to be shown on television, I'm no longer capable of the simplest act of solidarity!

VANĚK. You misunderstand me.—What I meant was—

STANĚK. Let me tell you something, Ferdinand. (*Drinks. Short pause.*) Look here, if I've—willy-nilly—got used to the perverse idea that common decency and morality are the exclusive domain of the dissidents—then you've—willy-nilly—got used to the idea as well! That's why it never crossed your mind that certain values might be more important to me than my present position. But suppose even I wanted to be finally a free man, suppose even I wished to renew my inner integrity and shake off the yoke of humiliation and shame? It never entered your head that I might've been actually waiting for this very moment for years, what? You simply placed me once and for all among those hopeless cases, among those whom it would be pointless to count on in any way. Right? And now that you found I'm not entirely indifferent to the fate of others—you made that slip about my signature! But you saw at once what happened, and so you began to apologize to me. Good God! Don't you realize how you humiliate me? What if all this time I'd been hoping for an opportunity to act, to do something that would again make a man of me, help me to be once more at peace with myself, help me to find again the free play of my imagination and my lost sense of humour, rid me of the need to escape my traumas by minding the apricots and the blooming magnolias! Suppose even I prefer to live in truth! What if I want to return from the world of custom-made literature and the proto-culture of television to the world of art which isn't geared to serve anyone at all?

VANĚK. I'm sorry—forgive me! I didn't mean to hurt your feelings—. Wait a minute, I'll—just a moment—

(Vaněk opens his briefcase, rummages in it for a while, finally extracts the sheets with the signatures and hands them to Staněk. Staněk gets up slowly and crosses with the papers to the desk, where he sits down, puts on his glasses, and carefully studies the sheets nodding his head here and there. After a lengthy while, he takes off his glasses, slowly rises, thoughtfully paces around, finally turning to Vaněk.)

STANĚK. Let me think aloud. May I?

VANĚK. By all means—

STANĚK. (*Halts, drinks, begins to pace again as he talks.*). I believe I've already covered the main points concerning the subjective side of the matter. If I sign the document, I'm going to regain—after years of being continually sick to my stomach—my self-esteem, my lost freedom, my honour, and perhaps even some regard among those close to me. I'll leave behind the insoluble dilemmas, forced on me by the conflict between my concern for my position and my conscience. I'll be able to face with equanimity Annie, myself, and even that young man when he comes back. It'll cost me my job, though my job brings me no satisfaction—on the contrary, it brings me shame—nevertheless, it does support me and my family a great deal better than if I were to become a night watchman. It's more than likely that my son won't be permitted to continue his studies. On the other hand, I'm sure he's going to have more respect for me that way, than if his permission to study was bought by my refusal to sign the protest for Javurek, whom he happens to worship.—Well then. This is the subjective side of the matter. Now how about the objective side? What happens when—among the signatures of a few well-known dissidents and a handful of Javurek's teenage friends—there suddenly crops up—to everybody's surprise and against all expectation—my signature? The signature of a man who hasn't been heard from regarding civic affairs for years! Well? My co-signatories—as well as many of those who don't sign documents of this sort, but who nonetheless deep down side with those who do—are naturally going to welcome my signature with pleasure. The closed circle of habitual signers—whose signatures, by the way, are already beginning to lose their clout, because they cost practically nothing. I mean, the people in question have long since lost all ways and means by which they could actually pay for their signatures. Right? Well, this circle will be broken. A new name will appear, a name the value of which depends precisely on its previous absence. And of course, I may add, on the high price paid for its appearance! So much for the objective "plus" of my prospective signature. Now what about the authorities? My signature is going to surprise, annoy, and upset them for the very reasons which will bring joy to the other signatories. I mean, because it'll make a breach in the barrier the authorities have been building around your lot for so long and with such effort. All right. Let's see about Javurek. Concerning his case, I very much doubt my participation would significantly influence its outcome. And if so, I'm afraid it's more than likely going to have a negative effect. The authorities will be anxious to prove they haven't been panicked. They'll want to show that a surprise of this sort can't make them lose their cool. Which brings us to the consideration of what they're going to do to me. Surely, my signature is bound to have a much more significant influence on what happens in my case. No doubt, they're going to punish me far more cruelly than you'd expect. The point being that my punishment will serve them as a warning signal to all those who might be tempted to follow my example in the future, choose freedom, and thus swell the ranks of the dissidents. You may be sure they'll want to show them what the score is! Right? The thing is—well, let's face it—they're no longer worried all that much about dissident activities within the confines of the established ghetto. In some respects they even seem to prod them on here and there. But! What they're really afraid of is any semblance of a crack in the fence around the ghetto! So they'll want to exorcize the bogey of a prospective epidemic of dissent by an exemplary punishment of myself. They'll want to nip it in the bud, that's all. (*Drinks. Pause.*) The last question I've got to ask myself is this: what sort of reaction to my signature can one expect among those who, in one way or another, have followed what you might call "the path of accommodation." I mean people who are, or ought to be, our main concern, because—I'm sure you'll agree—our hope for the future depends above all on whether or not it will be possible to awake them from their slumbers and to enlist them to take an active part in civic affairs. Well, I'm afraid that my signature is going to be received with absolute resentment by this crucial section of the populace. You know why? Because, as a matter of fact, these people secretly hate the dissidents. They've become their bad conscience, their living reproach! That's how they see the dissidents. And at the same time, they envy them their honour and their inner freedom, values which they themselves were denied by fate. This is why they never miss an opportunity to smear the dissidents. And precisely this opportunity is going to be offered to them by my signature. They're going to spread nasty rumours about you and your friends. They're going to say that you who have nothing more to lose—you who have long since landed at the bottom of the heap and, what's more, managed to make yourselves quite at home in there—are now trying to drag down to your own level an unfortunate man, a man who's so far been able to stay above the salt line. You're dragging him down—irresponsible as you are—without the slightest compunction, just for your own whim, just because you wish to irritate the authorities by creating a false impression that your ranks are being swelled! What do you care about losing him his job! Doesn't matter, does it? Or do you mean to suggest you'll find him a job down in the dump in which you yourselves exist? What? No—Ferdinand! I'm sorry. I'm afraid I'm much too familiar with the way these people think! After all, I've got to live among them, day in day out. I know precisely what they're going to say. They'll say I'm your victim, shamelessly abused, misguided, led astray by your cynical appeal to my humanity! They'll say that in your ruthlessness you didn't shrink even from making use of my personal relationship to Javurek! And you know what? They're going to say that all the humane ideals you're constantly proclaiming have been tarnished by your treatment of me. That's the sort of reasoning one can expect from them! And I'm sure I don't have to tell you that the authorities are bound to support this interpretation, and to fan the coals as hard as they can! There are others, of course, somewhat more intelligent perhaps. These people might say that the extraordinary appearance of my signature among yours is actually counterproductive, in that it concentrates everybody's attention on my signature and away from the main issue concerning Javurek. They'll say it puts the whole protest in jeopardy, because one can't help asking oneself what was the purpose of the exercise: was it to help Javurek, or to parade a newborn dissident? I wouldn't be at all surprised if someone were to say that, as a matter of fact, Javurek was victimized by you and your friends. It might be suggested his personal tragedy only served you to further your ends—which are far removed from the fate of the unfortunate man. Furthermore, it'll be pointed out that by getting my signature you managed to dislodge me from the one area of operation—namely, backstage diplomacy, private intervention—where I've been so far able to manoeuvre and where I might have proved infinitely more helpful to Javurek in the end! I do hope you understand me, Ferdinand. I don't wish to exaggerate the importance of these opinions, nor am I prepared to become their slave. On the other hand, it seems to be in the interests of our case for me to take them into account. After all, it's a matter of a political decision and a good politician must consider all the issues which are likely to influence the end result of his action. Right? In these circumstances the question one must resolve is as follows: what do I prefer? Do I prefer the inner liberation which my signature is going to bring me, a liberation paid for—as it now turns out—by a basically negative objective impact—or do I choose the other alternative. I mean, the more beneficial effect which the protest would have without my signature, yet paid for by my bitter awareness that I've again—who knows, perhaps for the last time—missed a chance to shake off the bonds of shameful compromises in which I've been choking for years? In other words, if I'm to act indeed ethically—and I hope by now you've no doubt I want to do just that—which course should I take? Should I be guided by ruthless objective considerations, or by subjective inner feelings?

VANĚK. Seems perfectly clear to me—

STANĚK. And to me—

VANĚK. So that you're going to—

STANĚK. Unfortunately—

VANĚK. Unfortunately?

STANĚK. You thought I was—

VANĚK. Forgive me, perhaps I didn't quite understand—

STANĚK. I'm sorry if I've—

VANĚK. Never mind—

STANĚK. But I really believe—

VANĚK. I know—

(Both drink. Vaněk shudders. Lengthy embarrassed pause. Staněk takes the sheets and hands them with a smile to Vaněk who puts them, together with the text of the letter of protest, into his briefcase. He shows signs of embarrassment. Staněk crosses to the tape recorder, unplugs it, comes back and sits down.)

STANĚK. Are you angry?

VANĚK. No—

STANĚK. You don't agree, though—

VANĚK. I respect your reasoning—

STANĚK. But what do you think?

VANĚK. What should I think?

STANĚK. That's obvious, isn't it?

VANĚK. Is it?

STANĚK. You think that when I saw all the signatures, I did, after all, get the wind up!

VANĚK. I don't—

STANĚK. I can see you do!

VANĚK. I assure you—

STANĚK. Why don't you level with me?! Don't you realize that your benevolent hypocrisy is actually far more insulting than if you gave it to me straight?! Or do you mean I'm not even worthy of your comment?!

VANĚK. But I told you, didn't I, I respect your reasoning—

STANĚK. I'm not an idiot, Vaněk!

VANĚK. Of course not—

STANĚK. I know precisely what's behind your "respect"!

VANĚK. What is?

STANĚK. A feeling of moral superiority!

VANĚK. You're wrong—

STANĚK. Only, I'm not quite sure if you—you of all people—have any right to feel so superior!

VANĚK. What do you mean?

STANĚK. You know very well what I mean!

VANĚK. I don't—

STANĚK. Shall I tell you?

VANĚK. Please do—

STANĚK. Well! As far as I know, in prison you talked more than you should have!

(Vaněk jumps up, wildly staring at Staněk, who smiles triumphantly. Short tense pause. The phone rings. Vaněk, broken, sinks back into his chair. Staněk crosses to the telephone and lifts the receiver.)

STANĚK. Hello—yes—what? You mean—Wait a minute—I see—I see—Where are you? Yes, yes, of course—absolutely!—good—You bet!—Sure—I'll be here waiting for you! Bye bye. (*Staněk puts the receiver down and absent-mindedly stares into space. Lengthy pause. Vaněk gets up in embarrassment. Only now Staněk seems to realize that Vaněk is still there. He turns to him abruptly.*) You can go and burn it downstairs in the furnace!

VANĚK. What?

STANĚK. He's just walked into the canteen! To see Annie.

VANĚK. Who did?

STANĚK. Javurek! Who else?

VANĚK (*Jumps up.*). Javurek? You mean he was released? But that's wonderful! So your private intervention did work, after all! Just as well we didn't send off the protest a few days earlier! I'm sure they would've got their backs up and kept him inside!

(Staněk searchingly stares at Vaněk, then suddenly smiles, decisively steps up to him, and with both hands takes him by the shoulders.)

STANĚK. My dear fellow, you mustn't fret! There's always the risk that you can do more harm than good by your activities! Right? Heavens, if you should worry about this sort of thing, you'd never be able to do anything at all! Come, let me get you those saplings—

Analyzing the Text

1. What is the nature of the relationship between Vaněk and Staněk? What can you infer about their past relationship from what they reveal about themselves during their meeting?
2. How does Havel use the incident of drawing up and signing the petition to reveal the kind of person Staněk has become? How do we know that he has prospered while Vaněk has not?

Understanding Havel's Techniques

1. In what way is Staněk's long final monologue the turning point or climax of the play? How did this monologue change your perception of him from what it was at the beginning?
2. What details reveal that Vaněk is content to give Staněk enough rope to hang himself with rather than serve as prosecutor?

Arguing for an Interpretation

1. How does knowing that Václav Havel served as president of the Czech Republic and his experiences are probably the basis for the character of Vaněk influence your reaction to the play? Would the play have had the same effect on you without knowing anything about the playwright?
2. Drawing on your own experiences, evaluate Havel's success in dramatizing the effects of differences in political ideology and its effect on personal relationships.

Connections

1. In what ways do George Orwell and the narrator in "Home Soil" suffer because they are placed in untenable situations by virtue of being in unsought for positions of power?
2. In what way does Tim O'Brien's essay dramatize his anxiety about becoming an "unknown citizen" of the kind described in W. H. Auden's poem?
3. Compare how Ambrose Bierce in his story and Margaret Atwood in her poem manipulate the sense of time passing.
4. How do both Tadeusz Borowski in his story and Wilfred Owen in his poem present complementary perspectives on the relationship between soldiers and their victims?
5. In what ways do both Panos Ioannides and Irene Zabytko reveal how the narrators are dehumanized during wartime?
6. Discuss the use of satire and irony by Luisa Valenzuela in her story and W. H. Auden in his poem to point up the dangers of acquiescence to bureaucratic power.
7. How is the theme of lost childhood innocence dramatized in the stories by Gloria Anzaldúa and P'an Jen-mu, and in Eleni Fourtouni's poem?
8. Compare the use of letters (and what they do or do not contain) as a narrative device in Ernest Cardenal's "The Swede" and Luisa Valenzuela's "The Censors."

9. How does an event in the present trigger repressed memories and feelings in the poems by Diana Der Hovanessian and Eleni Fourtouni?
10. In what ways are the attitudes and actions of the Colonel in Carolyn Forché's poem comparable to Luis Sepulveda's jailor in "Daisy"?
11. How do both Ira Sadoff and Ambrose Bierce use unusual displacements of time and perspective to create their surprise endings?
12. Compare the depiction of sacrificial victims in Yehuda Amichai's poem and in Gloria Anzaldúa's story.
13. Discuss how being corrupted by the system is developed as a theme in both Luisa Valenzuela's "The Censors" and in Václav Havel's play *Protest*.

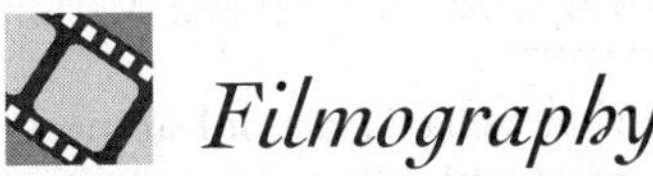

Filmography

Napoleon (1927) Director: Abel Gance. Performer: Albert Dieudonne.
A masterful recreation of the conqueror's early years was remade in 1955. [France]

Gone with the Wind (1939) Director: Victor Fleming. Performers: Clark Gable, Vivien Leigh.
Epic film traces the life of a Southern belle, Scarlett O'Hara, in the South during the Civil War and Reconstruction.

Fort Apache (1948) Director: John Ford. Performers: John Wayne, Henry Fonda, Shirley Temple.
One of the first westerns to present a somewhat critical view of the actions of the United States military in Indian territory.

The Third Man (1949) Director: Carol Reed. Performers: Orson Welles, Joseph Cotton.
A great score adds to the suspense when an American writer tries to determine whether an old friend, reputed to be a crime boss in post-war Vienna, has been murdered.

The Seven Samurai (1954) Director: Akira Kurosawa. Performers: Toshiro Mifune, Takashi Shimura.
In medieval Japan riven by civil war, a defenseless town hires seven ronin (masterless samurai) to defend them against marauding bandits who are themselves ronin. [Japan]

The Burmese Harp (1956) Director: Kon Ichikawa. Performer: Shoji Yasui.
This film, remade in 1985, is about a Japanese soldier at the end of World War II who is so repulsed by what he has seen and what he has become that he takes on the task of burying war casualties. [Japan]

Paths of Glory (1957) Director: Stanley Kubrick. Performers: Kirk Douglas, Ralph Meeker, Adolphe Menjou.
A commanding officer in the French army in World War I is ordered by superiors to undertake a suicidal attack, and his men face a court martial when the attack fails.

The Manchurian Candidate (1961) Director: John Frankenheimer. Performers: Frank Sinatra, Laurence Harvey, Angela Lansbury.
Political thriller about a Korean war officer who is convinced that he and his platoon were part of a secret communist plot designed to produce assassins through brainwashing techniques.

Doctor Zhivago (1965) Director: David Lean. Performers: Julie Christie, Omar Sharif, Rod Steiger.

A panoramic adaptation of Boris Pasternak's novel tells a poignant love story in the midst of the turbulent Bolshevik Revolution in Russia.

The Battle of Algiers (1966) Director: Gillo Pontecorvo. Performer: Yacef Saadi.
A landmark authentic account shot in documentary style of uprisings against French Colonial rule in 1954, Algiers. [Algeria/Italy]

Z (1969) Director: Constantin Costa-Gavras. Performers: Yves Montand, Irene Papas.
One of the best political thrillers ever made was based on the assassination of a Greek nationalist in the 1960s. [France/Algeria]

Man of Marble (1976) Director: Andrzej Wajda. Performers: Krystyna Janda, Herzy Radziwilowicz.
A female films school student researches a documentary on a man who had been a famous "heroic worker" years before but whose name has seemingly been erased from the pages of history. [Poland]

Apocalypse Now (1979) Director: Francis Ford Coppola. Performers: Marlon Brando, Martin Sheen.
Epic of the Vietnam war inspired by Joseph Conrad's novella "Heart of Darkness" about a disenchanted army captain on a mission into Cambodia to assassinate a renegade colonel.

Breaker Morant (1980) Director: Bruce Beresford. Performer: Edward Woodward.
Based on a true story, this anti-war film dramatizes the plight of three Australian soldiers put on trial in 1901 in South Africa for avenging the murder of several prisoners. [Australia]

Das Boot (1981) Director: Wolfgang Peterson. Performer: Juergen Prochnow.
Life in a German U-boat during World War II is recreated with realistic panache. [Germany]

The Official Story (1985) Director: Luis Puenzo. Performer: Norma Aleandro.
A family disintegrates when the mother suspects that her adopted young daughter may be a child stolen from one of the thousands of citizens taken as political prisoners by the repressive government. [Argentina]

Ran (1985) Director: Ikira Kurosawa. Performer: Tatsuya Nakadai.
The director's masterful adaptation of Shakespeare's *King Lear,* blended with plot elements from *MacBeth,* transposes the action into medieval Japan where ambition and greed devour family relationships when an aging warlord gives control of his empire to his oldest son. [Japan]

The Mahabharata (1989) Director: Peter Brook. Performer: Bruce Myers.
This internationally acclaimed glorious and compelling adaption of the ancient Indian epic about a cosmic battle between two ancient clans dramatizes every important theme in human experience. [Great Britain]

Europa, Europa (1991) Director: Agnieszka Holland. Performers: Marco Hofschneider, Julie Delphy.
Based on a true story, a young Jewish boy in World War II pretends to be a German in order to survive the Holocaust. [France, Germany, Russia]

Schindler's List (1993) Director: Steven Spielberg. Performers: Liam Neeson, Ralph Fiennes.
Based on the true story of Oscar Schindler, a womanizing war profiteer, who saved thousands of Jews from the Nazis by employing them in his factories.

Burnt by the Sun (1994) Director: Nikita Mikhalkov. Performer: Nikita Mikhalkov.
Set in Stalinist Russia in the 1930s, a Soviet revolutionary hero enjoys a day in the country until party officials show up and arrest him. [Russia]

Prisoner of the Mountains (1996) Director: Sergei Bodrov. Performer: Sergei Bodrov, Jr.

Adapted from Leo Tolstoy's novella, but updated in a modern political context, two Russian prisoners taken hostage in a remote Muslim village bond not only with each other but with their captors. [Russia]

L.A. Confidential (1997) Director: Curtis Hanson. Performers: Russell Crowe, Guy Pearce, Kevin Spacey, Kim Basinger.

Evocative and complex crime drama set in Hollywood in the 1950s that delves into corruption at every level.

Life Is Beautiful (1998) Director: Roberto Benigni. Performers: Roberto Benigni, Nicoletta Braschi.

A father fabricates an elaborate game designed to conceal from his young son their desperate situation in a concentration camp. [Italy]

Divided We Fall (2000) Director: Jan Malir. Performer: Boleslav Polivka.

Set in 1943, a couple hide a young Jewish man, who escaped the concentration camps, in their home, under the nose of a Nazi collaborator. [The Czech Republic]

No Man's Land (2001) Director: Danis Tanovic. Performer: Branko Djuric.

The U.N. peacekeepers are overwhelmed by the predicament of two soldiers, one Croatian, the other Serbian, who wind up in the same trench, one of whom is laying on a booby trapped land mine. [Bosnia]

Windtalkers (2002) Director: John Woo. Performers: Nicolas Cage, Christian Slater.

A World War II drama concerns a Marine assigned to protect a Navaho recruited to fool the Japanese with codes drawn from his native language.

Chapter 8

Outcasts, Scapegoats, and Exiles

America is not like a blanket—one piece of unbroken cloth, the same color, the same texture, the same size. America is more like a quilt—many patches, many pieces, many colors, many sizes, all woven and held together by a common thread.

Jesse Jackson

In some ways, our age—the age of the refugee, the displaced person, and mass immigration—is defined by the condition of exile. As communications, immigration, and travel make the world grow smaller, the potential for cross-cultural misunderstanding accelerates. Customs and rituals that may seem bizarre or strange to an outsider appear entirely normal and natural to those within the culture. Unfortunately, the potential for conflict exists as soon as cultures whose "natural" ways do not coincide make contact. Correspondingly, the need to become aware of the extent to which our and other people's conclusions about the world are guided by different cultural presuppositions grows.

For some exiles, ironically, the condition of *not* belonging, of being caught between two cultures, provides the chance to see things from outside the controlling frame of reference of their particular culture. For most, however, the jarring, intense, and often painful emotional experience produced by having to redefine oneself in a strange land, and trying to reconcile conflicting cultural values, forces a surrender of all ideas of safety and the comfort of familar surroundings and a common language.

The short stories, essays, and poems in this chapter explore the condition of exiles, whether refugees, immigrants, or travelers who are caught between two cultures and at home in neither, or those who are psychologically estranged because of being stereotyped as deviant or as the "other." An essay by Paul Monette, "Borrowed Time: An AIDS Memoir," retraces the origin of AIDS and describes its devastating effect on his own life. The survival of the human spirit in the harrowing conditions in Tijuana, on the United States–Mexico border, is graphically portrayed by Luis Alberto Urrea in "Border Story."

In the first story, "Neighbors," by Raymond Carver, a couple vicariously enter the lives of their friends who are out of town. The need of those who left their home in India, to adjust to life in the United States, underlies Jhumpa Lahiri's short story "This Blessed House." The classic tale "The Guest," by Albert Camus, explores the existential implications of exile in the story of a Frenchman torn by divided loyalties in Algeria. H. G. Wells, a pioneer of the science-fiction genre, creates in his story "The Country of the Blind" a profound parable that probes assumptions about cultural superiority. In Mahasweta Devi's "Giribala," set in Bengal, India, a mother chooses to leave her husband and village in order to save her youngest daughter from being sold into prostitution as were her sisters. "The Wedgwood Tea Set," whose form may remind you of an allegory or parable, by the Serbian writer Milorad Pavić, gives scapegoating a political dimension. In "And the Soul Shall Dance," Wakako Yamauchi dramatizes the conflicts between generations and cultures and the hardships an immigrant family faces in the Imperial Valley in California. Alice Walker, in "The Flowers," tells of a young girl's uneasy discovery about a past injustice.

Like the short stories, the poems in this chapter offer many perspectives—by writers from Sweden, Hawaii, Poland, and Israel—on what it is to be an outcast, scapegoat, or exile.

We share the experience of the rejection of people with AIDS (Bruce Springsteen, "Streets of Philadelphia"), of the void created by a failure to communicate (Lennart Sjögren, "The Roses"), and of the intolerance of the dominant Anglo culture toward minorities (in Wing Tek Lum's "Minority Poem"). Rahel Chalfi, in "Porcupine Fish," describes the feelings of vulnerability and bravado of a besieged minority. The state of exile is seen as an opportunity to dismantle barriers and celebrate new landscapes and visions (Diane Wakoski, "The Orange") and to maintain contact with one's native culture (Czeslaw Milosz, "My Faithful Mother Tongue"). The devastating psychological effects of rape, as expressed in Barbara Kingsolver's "This House I Cannot Leave," and mental deterioration described in Kelly Cherry's "Alzheimer's," add another perspective to our understanding of alienation.

The Arab world's leading playwright, Tewfik al-Hakim, adapts a centuries-old folktale in his hilarious one-act play, *The Donkey Market,* about the ingenuity of two unemployed laborers, to satirize the lack of progressive reform in modern Egyptian society.

Essays

PAUL MONETTE

Paul Monette was a distinguished writer of poetry, novels, and autobiographical volumes. He was born in 1945, attended Yale University, and first received critical attention in 1975 with the publication of his poetry collection The Carpenter at the Asylum. *His novels include* Taking Care of Mrs. Carroll *(1978),* The Gold Diggers *(1979),* The Long Shot *(1981),* Lightfall *(1982),* Afterlife *(1990), and* Halfway Home *(1991). Following the death from AIDS of his longtime lover Roger Horwitz, Monette addressed the tragedy in a collection of poems,* Love Alone: Eighteen Elegies for Rog *(1988), and wrote an acclaimed prose ac-*

count, Borrowed Time: An AIDS Memoir *(from which the following selection is taken) for which he received a National Book Critics Circle Award nomination for the best autobiography in 1988. Monette also wrote* Becoming a Man: Half a Life Story *(1992), in which he recounted the difficulties he experienced in coming to terms with his homosexuality.*

Monette was diagnosed as being HIV-positive in 1988 and died in 1995.

Borrowed Time: An AIDS Memoir

I don't know if I will live to finish this. Doubtless there's a streak of self-importance in such an assertion, but who's counting? Maybe it's just that I've watched too many sicken in a month and die by Christmas, so that a fatal sort of realism comforts me more than magic. All I know is this: The virus ticks in me. And it doesn't care a whit about our categories—when is full-blown, what's AIDS-related, what is just sick and tired? No one has solved the puzzle of its timing. I take my drug from Tijuana twice a day. The very friends who tell me how vigorous I look, how well I seem, are the first to assure me of the imminent medical breakthrough. What they don't seem to understand is, I used up all my optimism keeping my friend alive. Now that he's gone, the cup of my own health is neither half full nor half empty. Just half.

Equally difficult, of course, is knowing where to start. The world around me is defined now by its endings and its closures—the date on the grave that follows the hyphen. Roger Horwitz, my beloved friend, died of complications of AIDS on October 22, 1986, nineteen months and ten days after his diagnosis. That is the only real date anymore, casting its ice shadow over all the secular holidays lovers mark their calendars by. Until that long night in October, it didn't seem possible that any day could supplant the brute equinox of March 12—the day of Roger's diagnosis in 1985, the day we began to live on the moon.

The fact is, no one knows where to start with AIDS. Now, in the seventh year of the calamity, my friends in L.A. can hardly recall what it felt like any longer, the time before the sickness. Yet we all watched the toll mount in New York, then in San Francisco, for years before it ever touched us here. It comes like a slowly dawning horror. At first you are equipped with a hundred different amulets to keep it far away. Then someone you know goes into the hospital, and suddenly you are at high noon in full battle gear. They have neglected to tell you that you will be issued no weapons of any sort. So you cobble together a weapon out of anything that lies at hand, like a prisoner honing a spoon handle into a stiletto. You fight tough, you fight dirty, but you cannot fight dirtier than it.

I remember a Saturday in February 1982, driving Route 10 to Palm Springs with Roger to visit his parents for the weekend. While Roger drove, I read aloud an article from *The Advocate.* "Is Sex Making Us Sick?" There was the slightest edge of irony in the query, an urban cool that seems almost bucolic now in its innocence. But the article didn't mince words. It was the first in-depth reporting I'd read that laid out the shadowy nonfacts of what till then had been the most fragmented of rumors. The first cases were reported to the Centers for Disease Control (CDC) only six months before, but they weren't in the newspapers, not in L.A. I note in my diary in December '81 ambiguous reports of a "gay cancer," but I know I didn't have the slightest picture of the thing. Cancer of the *what?* I would have asked, if anyone had known anything.

5 I remember exactly what was going through my mind while I was reading, though I can't now recall the details of the piece. I was thinking: How is this not me? Trying to find a pattern I was exempt from. It was a brand of denial I would watch grow exponentially during the next few years, but at the time I was simply relieved. Because the article appeared to be saying that there was a grim progression toward this undefined catastrophe, a set of preconditions—chronic hepatitis, repeated bouts of syphilis, exotic parasites. No wonder my first baseline response was to feel safe. It was *them*—by which I meant the fast-lane Fire Island crowd, the Sutro Baths, the world of High Eros.

Not us.

I grabbed for that relief because we'd been through a rough patch the previous autumn. Till then Roger had always enjoyed a sort of no-nonsense good health: not an abuser of anything, with a constitutional aversion to hypochondria, and not wed to his mirror save for a minor alarm as to the growing dimensions of his bald spot. In the seven years we'd been together I scarcely remember him having a cold or taking an aspirin. Yet in October '81 he had struggled with a peculiar bout of intestinal flu. Nothing special showed up in any of the blood tests, but over a period of weeks he experienced persistent symptoms that didn't neatly connect: pains in his legs, diarrhea, general malaise. I hadn't been feeling notably bad myself, but on the other hand I was a textbook hypochondriac, and I figured if Rog was harboring some kind of bug, so was I.

The two of us finally went to a gay doctor in the Valley for a further set of blood tests. It's a curious phenomenon among gay middle-class men that anything faintly venereal had better be taken to a doctor who's "on the bus." Is it a sense of fellow feeling perhaps, or a way of avoiding embarrassment? Do we really believe that only a doctor who's *our* kind can heal us of the afflictions that attach somehow to our secret hearts? There is so much magic to medicine. Of course we didn't know then that those few physicians with a large gay clientele were about to be swamped beyond all capacity to cope.

The tests came back positive for amoebiasis. Roger and I began the highly toxic treatment to kill the amoeba, involving two separate drugs and what seems in memory thirty pills a day for six weeks, till the middle of January. It was the first time I'd ever experienced the phenomenon of the cure making you sicker. By the end of treatment we were both weak and had lost weight, and for a couple of months afterward were susceptible to colds and minor infections.

10 It was only after the treatment was over that a friend of ours, diagnosed with amoebas by the same doctor, took his slide to the lab at UCLA for a second opinion. And that was my first encounter with lab error. The doctor at UCLA explained that the slide had been misread; the squiggles that looked like amoebas were in fact benign. The doctor shook his head

and grumbled about "these guys who do their own lab work." Roger then retrieved his slide, took it over to UCLA and was told the same: no amoebas. We had just spent six weeks methodically ingesting poison for no reason at all.

So it wasn't the *Advocate* story that sent up the red flag for us. We'd been shaken by the amoeba business, and from that point on we operated at a new level of sexual caution. What is now called safe sex did not use to be so clearly defined. The concept didn't exist. But it was quickly becoming apparent, even then, that we couldn't wait for somebody else to define the parameters. Thus every gay man I know has had to come to a point of personal definition by way of avoiding the chaos of sexually transmitted diseases, or STD as we call them in the trade. There was obviously no one moment of conscious decision, a bolt of clarity on the shimmering freeway west of San Bernardino, but I think of that day when I think of the sea change. The party was going to have to stop. The evidence was too ominous: *We were making ourselves sick.*

Not that Roger and I were the life of the party. Roger especially didn't march to the different drum of *so many men, so little time,* the motto and anthem of the sunstruck summers of the mid-to-late seventies. He'd managed not to carry away from his adolescence the mark of too much repression, or indeed the yearning to make up for lost time. In ten years he had perhaps half a dozen contacts outside the main frame of our relationship, mostly when he was out of town on business. He was comfortable with relative monogamy, even at a time when certain quarters of the gay world found the whole idea trivial and bourgeois. I realize that in the world of the heterosexual there is a generalized lip service paid to exclusive monogamy, a notion most vividly honored in the breach. I leave the matter of morality to those with the gift of tongues; it was difficult enough for us to fashion a sexual ethics just for us. In any case, I was the one in the relationship who suffered from lost time. I was the one who would go after a sexual encounter as if it were an ice cream cone—casual, quick, good-bye.

But as I say, who's counting? I only want to make it plain to start with that we got very alert and very careful as far back as the winter of '82. That gut need for safety took hold and lingered, even as we got better again and strong. Thus I'm not entirely sure what I thought on another afternoon a year and a half later, when a friend of ours back from New York reported a conversation he'd had with a research man from Sloan-Kettering.

"He thinks all it takes is one exposure," Charlie said, this after months of articles about the significance of repeated exposure. More tenaciously than ever, we all wanted to believe the whole deepening tragedy was centered on those at the sexual frontiers who were fucking their brains out. The rest of us were fashioning our own little Puritan forts, as we struggled to convince ourselves that a clean slate would hold the nightmare at bay.

15 Yet with caution as our watchword starting in February of '82, Roger was diagnosed with AIDS three years later. So the turning over of new leaves was not to be on everybody's side. A lot of us were already ticking and didn't even know. The magic circle my generation is trying to stay within the borders of is only as real as the random past. Perhaps the young can live in the magic circle, but only if those of us who are ticking will tell our story. Otherwise it goes on being *us* and *them* forever, built like a wall

higher and higher, till you no longer think to wonder if you are walling it out or in.

Analyzing the Text

1. How did coming to terms with the reality of AIDS compel Monette to reassess many of the assumptions taken for granted about the homosexual lifestyle?
2. To what extent does Monette's personal chronicle reflect the changes that were simultanously taking place in the nation?

Understanding Monette's Techniques

1. How would you characterize the tone Monette projects in this account, and is it different from what you might have expected?
2. A central element in Monette's account is the story of his life with Roger. What relationship does this personal story have with society's growing awareness of AIDS?

Arguing for an Interpretation

1. The first sentence in this account ("I don't know if I will live to finish this") sets up a link between generations and might help explain why Monette wrote this. Do you think his narrative is intended as a memorial to Roger, as an attempt to deconstruct the mythologies associated with AIDS, or in some other way? Explain your answer.
2. In what way does Monette's account differ from the depiction of AIDS in popular movies such as *And the Band Played On* (1993), *Philadelphia* (1994), and *Love, Compassion and Valor* (1998)?

LUIS ALBERTO URREA

Luis Alberto Urrea was born in Tijuana in 1955 to an American mother and a Mexican father. He was raised in San Diego and graduated from the University of California in 1977. After working as a film extra, he worked as a volunteer from 1978 to 1982 with Spectrum Ministries, a Protestant organization with headquarters in San Diego that provided food, clothing, and medicine to the poor on the Mexican side of the border. In 1982, he went to Massachusetts, where he taught expository writing at Harvard. Among Urrea's many published works are By the Lake of Sleeping Children: The Secret Life of the Mexican Border *(1996),* Ghost Sickness *(1997),* Nobody's Son: Notes from an American Life *(1998),* Wandering Time: Western Notebooks *(1999), and* Six Kinds of Sky: A Collection of Short Fiction *(2002).* Across the Wire: Life and Hard Times on the Mexican Border *(1993), from which "Border Story" is taken, offers a compassionate and unprecedented account of what life is like for those refugees living on the Mexican side of the border.*

Border Story

When I was younger, I went to war. The Mexican border was the battlefield. There are many Mexicos; there are also many Mexican borders, any one of which could fill its own book. I, and the people with me, fought on a specific front. We sustained injuries and witnessed deaths. There were machine guns pointed at us, knives, pistols, clubs, even skyrockets. I caught a street-gang member trying to stuff a lit cherry bomb into our gas tank. On the same night, a drunk mariachi opened fire on the missionaries through the wall of his house.

We drove five beat-up vans. We were armed with water, medicine, shampoo, food, clothes, milk, and doughnuts. At the end of a day, like returning veterans from other battles, we carried secrets in our hearts that kept some of us awake at night, gave others dreams and fits of crying. Our faith sustained us—if not in God or "good," then in our work.

Others of us had no room for or interest in such drama, and came away unscathed—and unmoved. Some of us sank into the mindless joy of fundamentalism, some of us drank, some of us married impoverished Mexicans. Most of us took it personally. Poverty *is* personal: it smells and it shocks and it invades your space. You come home dirty when you get too close to the poor. Sometimes you bring back vermin: they hide in your hair, in your underpants, in your intestines. These unpleasant possibilities are a given. They are the price you occasionally have to pay.

In Tijuana and environs, we met the many ambassadors of poverty: lice, scabies, tapeworm, pinworm, ringworm, fleas, crab lice. We met diphtheria, meningitis, typhoid, polio, *turista* (diarrhea), tuberculosis, hepatitis, VD, impetigo, measles, chronic hernia, malaria, whooping cough. We met madness and "demon possession."

These were the products of dirt and disregard—bad things afflicting 5
good people. Their world was far from our world. Still, it would take you only about twenty minutes to get there from the center of San Diego.

For me, the worst part was the lack of a specific enemy. We were fighting a nebulous, all-pervasive *It*. Call it hunger. Call it despair. Call it the Devil, the System, Capitalism, the Cycle of Poverty, the Fruits of the Mexican Malaise. It was a seemingly endless circle of disasters. Long after I'd left, the wheel kept on grinding.

At night, the Border Patrol helicopters swoop and churn in the air all along the line. You can sit in the Mexican hills and watch them herd humans on the dusty slopes across the valley. They look like science fiction crafts, their hard-focused lights raking the ground as they fly.

Borderlands locals are so jaded by the sight of nightly people-hunting that it doesn't even register in their minds. But take a stranger to the border, and she will *see* the spectacle: monstrous Dodge trucks speeding into and out of the landscape; uniformed men patrolling with flashlights, guns, and dogs; spotlights; running figures; lines of people hurried onto buses by armed guards; and the endless clatter of the helicopters with their harsh white beams. A Dutch woman once told me it seemed altogether "un-American."

But the Mexicans keep on coming—and the Guatemalans, the Salvadorans, the Panamanians, the Colombians. The seven-mile stretch of

Interstate 5 nearest the Mexican border is, at times, so congested with Latin American pedestrians that it resembles a town square.

They stick to the center island. Running down the length of the island 10
is a cement wall. If the "illegals" (currently, "undocumented workers"; formerly, "wetbacks") are walking north and a Border Patrol vehicle happens along, they simply hop over the wall and trot south. The officer will have to drive up to the 805 interchange, or Dairy Mart Road, swing over the overpasses, then drive south. Depending on where this pursuit begins, his detour could entail five to ten miles of driving. When the officer finally reaches the group, they hop over the wall and trot north. Furthermore, because freeway arrests would endanger traffic, the Border Patrol has effectively thrown up its hands in surrender.

It seems jolly on the page. But imagine poverty, violence, natural disasters, or political fear driving you away from everything you know. Imagine how bad things get to make you leave behind your family, your friends, your lovers; your home, as humble as it might be; your church, say. Let's take it further—you've said good-bye to the graveyard, the dog, the goat, the mountains where you first hunted, your grade school, your state, your favorite spot on the river where you fished and took time to think.

Then you come hundreds—or thousands—of miles across territory utterly unknown to you. (Chances are, you have never traveled farther than a hundred miles in your life.) You have walked, run, hidden in the backs of trucks, spent part of your precious money on bus fare. There is no AAA or Travelers Aid Society available to you. Various features of your journey north might include police corruption; violence in the forms of beatings, rape, murder, torture, road accidents; theft; incarceration. Additionally, you might experience loneliness, fear, exhaustion, sorrow, cold, heat, diarrhea, thirst, hunger. There is no medical attention available to you. There isn't even Kotex.

Weeks or months later, you arrive in Tijuana. Along with other immigrants, you gravitate to the bad parts of town because there is nowhere for you to go in the glittery sections where the *gringos* flock. You stay in a run-down little hotel in the red-light district, or behind the bus terminal. Or you find your way to the garbage dumps, where you throw together a small cardboard nest and claim a few feet of dirt for yourself. The garbage-pickers working this dump might allow you to squat, or they might come and rob you or burn you out for breaking some local rule you cannot possibly know beforehand. Sometimes the dump is controlled by a syndicate, and goon squads might come to you within a day. They want money, and if you can't pay, you must leave or suffer the consequences.

In town, you face endless victimization if you aren't streetwise. The police come after you, street thugs come after you, petty criminals come after you; strangers try your door at night as you sleep. Many shady men offer to guide you across the border, and each one wants all your money now, and promises to meet you at a prearranged spot. Some of your fellow travelers end their journeys right here—relieved of their savings and left to wait on a dark corner until they realize they are going nowhere.

If you are not Mexican, and can't pass as *tijuanense,* a local, the tough 15
guys find you out. Salvadorans and Guatemalans are routinely beaten up and robbed. Sometimes they are disfigured. Indian—Chinantecas, Mixtecas,

Guasaves, Zapotecas, Mayas—are insulted and pushed around; often they are lucky—they are merely ignored. They use this to their advantage. Often they don't dream of crossing into the United States: a Mexican tribal person would never be able to blend in, and they know it. To them, the garbage dumps and street vending and begging in Tijuana are a vast improvement over their former lives. As Doña Paula, a Chinanteca friend of mine who lives at the Tijuana garbage dump, told me, "This is the garbage dump. Take all you need. There's plenty here for *everyone!*"

If you are a woman, the men come after you. You lock yourself in your room, and when you must leave it to use the pestilential public bathroom at the end of your floor, you hurry, and you check every corner. Sometimes the lights are out in the toilet room. Sometimes men listen at the door. They call you "good-looking" and "bitch" and "*mamacita,*" and they make kissing sounds at you when you pass.

You're in the worst part of town, but you can comfort yourself—at least there are no death squads here. There are no torturers here, or bandit land barons riding into your house. This is the last barrier, you think, between you and the United States—*los Yunaites Estaites.*

You still face police corruption, violence, jail. You now also have a wide variety of new options available to you: drugs, prostitution, white slavery, crime. Tijuana is not easy on newcomers. It is a city that has always thrived on taking advantage of a sucker. And the innocent are the ultimate suckers in the Borderlands.

If you have saved up enough money, you go to one of the *coyotes* (people-smugglers), who guide travelers through the violent canyons immediately north of the border. Lately, these men are also called *polleros,* or "chicken-wranglers." Some of them are straight, some are land pirates. Negotiations are tense and strange: *polleros* speak a Spanish you don't quite understand—like the word *polleros.* Linguists call the new borderspeak "Spanglish," but in Tijuana, Spanglish is mixed with slang and *pochismos* (the polyglot hip talk of Mexicans infected with *gringoismo;* the *cholos* in Mexico, or Chicanos on the American side).

Suddenly, the word for "yes," *si,* can be *simón* or *siról.* "No" is *chale.* 20
"Bike" (*bicicleta*) is *baica.* "Wife" (*esposà*) is *wafia.* "The police" (*la policía*) are *la chota.* "Women" are *rucas* or *morras.* You don't know what they're talking about.

You pay them all your money—sometimes it's your family's lifelong savings. Five hundred dollars should do it. "*Oralé,*" the dude tells you, which means "right on." You must wait in Colonia Libertad, the most notorious *barrio* in town, ironically named "Liberty."

The scene here is baffling. Music blares from radios. Jolly women at smoky taco stands cook food for the journeys, sell jugs of water. You can see the Border Patrol agents cruising the other side of the fence; they trade insults with the locals.

When the appointed hour comes, you join a group of *pollos* (chickens) who scuttle along behind the *coyote.* You crawl under the wires, or, if you go a mile east, you might be amazed to find that the famous American Border Fence simply stops. To enter the United States, you merely step around the end of it. And you follow your guide into the canyons. You might be startled to find groups of individuals crossing the line without *coyotes* leading them at all. You might wonder how they have mastered the canyons, and you might begin to regret the loss of your money.

If you have your daughters or mothers or wives with you—or if you are a woman—you become watchful and tense, because rape and gang rape are so common in this darkness as to be utterly unremarkable. If you have any valuables left after your various negotiations, you try to find a sly place to hide them in case you meet *pandilleros* (gang members) or *rateros* (thieves—ratmen). But, really, where can you put anything? Thousands have come before you, and the hiding places are pathetically obvious to robbers: in shoulder bags or clothing rolls, pinned inside clothes, hidden in underwear, inserted in body orifices.

If the *coyote* does not turn on you suddenly with a gun and take 25
everything from you himself, you might still be attacked by the *rateros.* If the *rateros* don't get you, there are roving zombies that you can smell from fifty yards downwind—these are the junkies who hunt in shambling packs. If the junkies somehow miss you, there are the *pandilleros*—gangbangers from either side of the border who are looking for some bloody fun. They adore "taking off" illegals because it's the perfect crime: there is no way they can ever be caught. They are Tijuana *cholos,* or Chicano *vatos,* or Anglo head-bangers.

Their sense of fun relies heavily on violence. Gang beatings are their preferred sport, though rape in all its forms is common, as always. Often the *coyote* will turn tail and run at the first sight of *pandilleros.* What's another load of desperate chickens to him? He's just making a living, taking care of business.

If he doesn't run, there is a good chance he will be the first to be assaulted. The most basic punishment these young toughs mete out is a good beating, but they might kill him in front of the *pollos* if they feel the immigrants need a lesson in obedience. For good measure, these boys—they are mostly *boys,* aged twelve to nineteen, bored with Super Nintendo and MTV—beat people and slash people and thrash the women they have just finished raping.

Their most memorable tactic is to hamstring the *coyote* or anyone who dares speak out against them. This entails slicing the muscles in the victim's legs and leaving him to flop around in the dirt, crippled. If you are in a group of *pollos* that happens to be visited by these furies, you are learning border etiquette.

Now, say you are lucky enough to evade all these dangers on your journey. Hazards still await you and your family. You might meet white racists, complimenting themselves with the tag "Aryans"; they "patrol" the scrub in combat gear, carrying radios, high-powered flashlights, rifles, and bats. Rattlesnakes hide in bushes—you didn't count on that complication. Scorpions, tarantulas, black widows. And, of course, there is the Border Patrol (*la migra*).

They come over the hills on motorcycles, on horses, in huge Dodge 30
Ramcharger four-wheel drives. They yell, wear frightening goggles, have guns. Sometimes they are surprisingly decent; sometimes they are too tired or too bored to put much effort into dealing with you. They collect you in a large group of fellow *pollos,* and a guard (a Mexican Border Patrol agent!) jokes with your group in Spanish. Some cry, some sulk, most laugh.

Mexicans hate to be rude. You don't know what to think—some of your fellow travelers take their arrest with aplomb. Sometimes the officers know their names. But you have been told repeatedly that the Border Patrol sometimes beats or kills people. Everyone talks about the Mexican girl molested inside its building.

The Border Patrol puts you into trucks that take you to buses that take you to compounds that load you onto other buses that transport you back to Tijuana and put you out. Your *coyote* isn't bothered in the least. Some of the regulars who were with you go across and get brought back a couple of times a night. But for you, things are different. You have been brought back with no place to sleep. You have already spent all your money. You might have been robbed, so you have only your clothes—maybe not all of them. The robbers may have taken your shoes. You might be bloodied from a beating by *pandilleros,* or an "accident" in the Immigration and Naturalization Service compound. You can't get proper medical attention. You can't eat, or afford to feed your family. Some of your compatriots have been separated from their wives or their children. Now their loved ones are in the hands of strangers, in the vast and unknown United States. The Salvadorans are put on planes and flown back to the waiting arms of the military. As you walk through the cyclone fence, back into Tijuana, the locals taunt you and laugh at your misfortune.

If you were killed, you have nothing to worry about.

Now what?

Perhaps you'll join one of the other groups that break through the Tortilla Curtain every night. The road-runners. They amass at dusk along the cement canal that separates the United States from Mexico. This wide alley is supposedly the Tijuana River, but it's usually dry, or running with sewage that Tijuana pumps toward the U.S. with great gusto.

As soon as everybody feels like it—there are no *coyotes* needed 35
here—you join the groups passing through the gaping holes in the fence. Houses and alleys and cantinas back up against it, and in some spots, people have driven stolen cars into the poles to provide a wider passage. You rush across the canal and up the opposite slope, timing your dash between passing *migra* trucks and the overflights of helicopters. Following the others, you begin your jog toward the freeway. Here, there are mostly just Border Patrol officers to outrun—not that hard if you're in good shape. There are still some white-supremacist types bobbling around, but the cops will get them if they do anything serious. No, here the problem is the many lanes of I-5.

You stand at the edge of the road and wonder how you're going to cut across five lanes of traffic going sixty miles an hour. Then, there is the problem of the next five lanes. The freeway itself is constructed to run parallel to the border, then swing north. Its underpasses and stormdrain pipes offer another subterranean world, but you don't know about them. All you know is you have to get across at some point, and get far from the hunters who would take you back.

If you hang around the shoulder of I-5 long enough, you will find that many of your companions don't make it. So many have been killed and injured that the *gringos* have put up warning signs to motorists to watch for running people. The orange signs show a man, a woman, and a child charging across. Some *gringos* are so crazy with hate for you that they speed up, or aim for you as you run.

The vague blood of over a hundred slain runners shadows the concrete.

On either side of the border, clustered near the gates, there are dapper-looking men, dressed in nice cowboy clothes, and they speak without looking anyone in the eye. They are saying, "Los Angeles, San Bernardino, San Francisco."

They have a going concern: business is good. 40

Once you've gotten across the line, there will always be the question of *Where do I go now?* "Illegal aliens" have to eat, sleep, find work. Once across, you must begin another journey.

Not everyone has the energy to go on. Even faith—in Jesus, the Virgin Mary, or the Streets of Gold—breaks down sooner or later. Many of these immigrants founder at the border. There is a sad swirl of humanity in Tijuana. Outsiders eddy there who have simply run out of strength. If North America does not want them, Tijuana wants them even less. They become the outcasts of an outcast region. We could all see them if we looked hard enough: they sell chewing gum. Their children sing in traffic. In bars downtown, the women will show us a breast for a quarter. They wash our windshields at every stoplight. But mostly, they are invisible. To see them, we have to climb up the little canyons all around the city, where the cardboard shacks and mud and smoke look like a lost triptych by Hieronymous Bosch. We have to wade into the garbage dumps and the orphanages, sit in the little churches and the hospitals, or go out into the back country, where they raise their goats and bake red bricks and try to live decent lives.

They are not welcome in Tijuana. And, for the most part, Tijuana itself is not welcome in the Motherland. Tijuana is Mexico's cast-off child. She brings in money and *gringos,* but nobody would dare claim her. As a Mexican diplomat once confided to me, "We both know Tijuana is not Mexico. The border is nowhere. It's a no-man's-land."

I was born there.

My Story

I was born in Tijuana, to a Mexican father and an American mother. I 45
was registered with the U.S. government as an American Citizen, Born Abroad. Raised in San Diego, I crossed the border all through my boyhood with abandon, utterly bilingual and bicultural. In 1977, my father died on the border, violently. (The story is told in detail in a chapter entitled "Father's Day.")

In the Borderlands, anything can happen. And if you're in Tijuana long enough, anything *will* happen. Whole neighborhoods appear and disappear seemingly overnight. For example, when I was a boy, you got into Tijuana by driving through the Tijuana River itself. It was a muddy floodplain bustling with animals and belching old cars. A slum that spread across the riverbed was known as "Cartolandia." In border-speak, this meant "Land of Cardboard."

Suddenly, it was time for Tijuana to spruce up its image to attract more American dollars, and Cartolandia was swept away by a flash flood of tractors. The big machines swept down the length of the river, crushing shacks and toppling fences. It was like magic. One week, there were choked multitudes of sheds; the next, a clear, flat space awaiting the blank concrete of a flood channel. Town—no town.

The inhabitants of Cartolandia fled to the outskirts, where they were better suited to Tijuana's new image as Shopping Mecca. They had effectively vanished. Many of them homesteaded the Tijuana municipal garbage dump. The city's varied orphanages consumed many of their children.

Tijuana's characteristic buzz can be traced directly to a mixture of dread and expectation: there's always something coming.

I never intended to be a missionary. I didn't go to church, and I had no 50
reason to believe I'd be involved with a bunch of Baptists. But in 1978, I had occasion to meet a remarkable preacher known as Pastor Von (Erhardt George von Trutzschler III, no less): as well as being a minister, he was a veteran of the Korean War, a graphic artist, a puppeteer, a German baron, an adventurer, and a practical joker. Von got me involved in the hardships and discipline he calls "Christian Boot Camp."

After working as a youth pastor in San Diego for many years, he had discovered Mexico in the late sixties. His work there began with the typical church do-good activities that everyone has experienced at least once: a bag of blankets for the orphans, a few Christmas toys, alms for the poor. As Protestantism spread in Mexico, however, interest in Von's preaching grew. Small churches and Protestant orphanages and Protestant *barrios,* lacking ministers of their own, began asking Von to teach. Preaching and pastoring led to more work; work led to more needs; more needs pulled in more workers. On it went until Von had put in thirty or so years slogging through the Borderlands mud, and his little team of die-hard renegades and border rats had grown to a nonprofit corporation (Spectrum Ministries, Inc.), where you'll find him today.

Von's religious ethic is similar in scope to Teresa of Calcutta's. Von favors actual works over heavy evangelism. Spectrum is based on a belief Christians call "living the gospel." This doctrine is increasingly rare in America, since it involves little lip service, hard work, and no glory.

Von often reminds his workers that they are "ambassadors of Christ" and should comport themselves accordingly. Visitors are indelicately stripped of their misconceptions and prejudices when they discover that the crust on Von and his crew is a mile thick: the sight of teenybopper Bible School girls enduring Von's lurid pretrip briefing is priceless. Insouciantly, he offers up his litany: lice, worms, pus, blood; diarrhea, rattletrap outhouses, no toilet paper; dangerous water and food; diseased animals that will leave you with scabies; rats, maggots, flies; *odor.* Then he confuses them by demanding love and respect for the poor. He caps his talk with: "Remember—you are not going to the zoo. These are people. Don't run around snapping pictures of them like they're animals. Don't rush into their shacks saying, 'Ooh, gross!' They live there. Those are their homes."

Because border guards often "confiscate" chocolate milk, the cartons must be smuggled into Mexico under bags of clothes. Because the floors of the vans get so hot, the milk will curdle, so the crew must first freeze it.

The endless variations of challenge in the Borderlands keep Von constantly alert—problems come three at a time and must be solved on the run.

55 Like the time a shipment of tennis shoes was donated to Spectrum. They were new, white, handsome shoes. The only problem was that no two shoes in the entire shipment matched. Von knew there was no way the Mexican kids could use *one* shoe, and they—like teens everywhere—were fashion-conscious and wouldn't be caught dead in unmatching sneakers.

Von's solution was practical and witty. He donned unmatched shoes and made his crew members wear unmatched shoes. Then he announced that it was the latest California surfer rage; kids in California weren't considered hip unless they wore unmatched shoes. The shipment was distributed, and shoeless boys were shod in the *faux* fashion craze begun by Chez Von.

Von has suffered for his beliefs. In the ever more conservative atmosphere of American Christianity (read: Protestantism), the efforts of Spectrum have come under fire on several occasions. He was once denounced because he refused to use the King James Bible in his sermons—clearly the sign of a heretic.

Von's terse reply to criticism: "It's hard to 'save' people when they're dead."

Von has a Monday night ministerial run into Tijuana, and in his heyday, he was hitting three or four orphanages a night. I was curious, unaware of the severity of the poverty in Tijuana. I knew it was there, but it didn't really mean anything to me. One night, in late October 1978, my curiosity got the better of me. I didn't believe Von could show me anything about my hometown that I didn't know. I was wrong. I quickly began to learn just how little I really knew.

60 He managed to get me involved on the first night. Actually, it was Von and a little girl named América. América lived in one of the orphanages barely five miles from my grandmother's house in the hills above Tijuana.

She had light hair and blue eyes like mine—she could have been my cousin. When she realized I spoke Spanish, she clutched my fingers and chattered for an hour without a break. She hung on harder when Von announced it was time to go. She begged me not to leave. América resorted to a tactic many orphanage children master to keep visitors from leaving—she wrapped her legs around my calf and sat on my foot. As I peeled her off, I promised to return on Von's next trip.

He was waiting for me in the alley behind the orphanage.

"What did you say to that girl?" he asked.

"I told her I'd come back next week."

65 He glared at me. "Don't *ever* tell one of my kids you're coming back," he snapped. "Don't you know she'll wait all week for you? Then she'll wait for months. Don't say it if you don't mean it."

"I mean it!" I said.

I went back the next time to see her. Then again. And, of course, there were other places to go before we got to América's orphanage, and there were other people to talk to after we left. Each location had people waiting with messages and questions to translate. It didn't take long for Von to approach me with a proposition. It seemed he had managed the impressive feat of spending a lifetime in Mexico without picking up any Spanish at all. Within two months, I was Von's personal translator.

It is important to note that translation is often more delicate an art than people assume. For example, Mexicans are regularly amused to read *TV Guide* listings for Spanish-language TV stations. If one were to leave the tilde (~) off the word años, or "years," the word becomes the plural for "anus." Many cheap laughs are had when "The Lost Years" becomes "The Lost Butt Holes."

It was clear that Von needed reliable translating. Once, when he had arranged a summer camping trip for *barrio* children, he'd written a list of items the children needed to take. A well-meaning woman on the team translated the list for Von, and they Xeroxed fifty or sixty copies.

The word for "comb" in Spanish is *peine,* but leave out a letter, and the word takes on a whole new meaning. Von's note, distributed to every child and all their families, read:

You must bring CLEAN CLOTHES

TOOTHPASTE

SOAP

TOOTHBRUSH

SLEEPING BAG

and BOYS—You Must Remember

to BRING YOUR PENIS!

Von estimates that in a ten-year period his crew drove several *million* miles in Mexico without serious incident. Over five-hundred people came and went as crew members. They transported more than sixty thousand visitors across the border.

In my time with him, I saw floods and three hundred-mile-wide prairie fires, car wrecks and gang fights, monkeys and blood and shit. I saw human intestines and burned flesh. I saw human fat through deep red cuts. I saw people copulating. I saw animals tortured. I saw birthday parties in the saddest sagging shacks. I looked down throats and up wombs with flashlights. I saw lice, rats, dying dogs, rivers black with pollywogs, and a mound of maggots three feet wide and two feet high. One little boy in the back country cooked himself with an overturned pot of boiling *frijoles;* when I asked him if it hurt, he sneered like Pancho Villa and said, "Nah." A maddened Pentecostal tried to heal our broken-down van by laying hands on the engine block. One girl who lived in a brickyard accidentally soaked her dress in diesel fuel and lit herself on fire. When I went in the shed, she was standing there, naked, her entire front burned dark brown and red. The only part of her not burned was her vulva; it was a startling cleft, a triangular island of white in a sea of burns.

I saw miracles, too. A boy named Chispi, deep in a coma induced by spinal meningitis, suffered a complete shutdown of one lobe of his brain. The doctors in the intensive care unit, looking down at his naked little body hard-wired to banks of machinery and pumps, just shook their heads. He was doomed to be a vegetable, at best. His mother, fished out of the cantinas in Tijuana's red-light district, spent several nights sitting in the hospital cafeteria sipping vending-machine coffee and telling me she hoped there were miracles left for people like her.

Chispi woke up. The machines were blipping and pinging, and he sat up and asked for Von. His brain had regenerated itself. They unhitched him, pulled out the catheters, and pulled the steel shunt out of his skull. He went home. There was no way anybody could explain it. Sometimes there were happy endings, and you spent as much time wondering about them as grieving over the tragedies.

75 God help me—it was fun. It was exciting and nasty. I strode, fearless, through the Tijuana garbage dumps and the Barrio of Shallow Graves. I was doing good deeds, and the goodness thrilled me. But the squalor, too, thrilled me. Each stinking gray *barrio* gave me a wicked charge. I was arrested one night by Tijuana cops; I was so terrified that my knees wobbled like Jell-O. After they let me go, I was happy for a week. Mexican soldiers pointed machine guns at my testicles. I thought I was going to die. Later, I was so relieved, I laughed about it for days. Over the years, I was cut, punctured, sliced: I love my scars. I had girlfriends in every village, in every orphanage, at each garbage dump. For a time, I was a hero. And at night, when we returned, caked in dried mud, smelly, exhausted, and the good Baptists of Von's church looked askance at us, we felt dangerous. The housewives, grandmothers, fundamentalists, rock singers, bikers, former drug dealers, schoolgirls, leftists, republicans, jarheads, and I were all transformed into *The Wild Bunch.*

It added a certain flair to my dating life as well. It was not uncommon for a Mexican crisis to track me down in the most unlikely places. I am reminded of the night I was sitting down to a fancy supper at a woman's apartment when the phone rang. A busload of kids from one of our orphanages had flipped over, killing the American daughter of the youth minister in charge of the trip. All the *gringos* had been arrested. The next hour was spent calling Tijuana cops, Mexican lawyers, cousins in Tijuana, and Von. I had to leave early to get across the border.

Incredibly, in the wake of this tragedy, the orphanage kids were taken to the beach by yet another *gringo* church group, and one of the boys was hit by a car and killed.

My date was fascinated by all this, no doubt.

Slowly, it became obvious that nobody outside the experience understood it. Only among ourselves was hunting for lice in each other's hair considered a nice thing. Nobody but us found humor in the appalling things we saw. No one else wanted to discuss the particulars of our bowel movements. By firsthand experience, we had become diagnosticians in the area of gastrointestinal affliction. Color and content spoke volumes to us: pale, mucus-heavy ropes of diarrhea suggested amoebas. Etc.

80 One of Von's pep talks revolved around the unconscionable wealth in the United States. "Well," he'd say to some unsuspecting *gringo,* "you're probably not rich. You probably don't even have a television. Oh, you *do?* You have three televisions? One in each room? Wow. But surely you don't have furniture? You do? Living room furniture and beds in the bedrooms? Imagine that!

"But you don't have a floor, do you? Do you have carpets? Four walls? A roof! What do you use for light—candles? *Lamps!* No way. Lamps.

"How about your kitchen—do you have a stove?"

He'd pick his way through the kitchen: the food, the plates and pots and pans, the refrigerator, the ice. Ice cream. Soda. Booze. The closets, the clothes in the closets. Then to the bathroom and the miracle of indoor plumbing. Whoever lived in that house suddenly felt obscenely rich.

I was never able to reach Von's level of commitment. The time he caught scabies, he allowed it to flourish in order to grasp the suffering of those from whom it originated. He slept on the floor because the majority of the world's population could not afford a bed.

Analyzing the Text

1. What impression do you get of the narrator's involvement? Why was he there and what did he hope to accomplish?
2. What are some of the dangers illegal immigrants face when crossing the border between Tijuana and California? What future awaits those who turn back?

Understanding Urrea's Techniques

1. What details in Urrea's description are especially effective in allowing his readers to empathize with the experiences he relates?
2. How does Urrea use humor to attempt to cope with an unmanageable situation?

Arguing for an Interpretation

1. What elements in this account make it clear that Urrea understands the role that religion plays for others, but is quite honest about his own motives for being there?
2. In your opinion, would a fictionalized version of this account have been more effective than this autobiographical essay? Explain your answer.

Short Fiction

RAYMOND CARVER

Raymond Carver (1938–1988) grew up in a logging town in Oregon and was educated at Humboldt State College (B.A., 1963) and at the University of Iowa, where he studied creative writing. He first received recognition in the 1970s with the publication of stories in the New Yorker, Esquire, *and the* Atlantic Monthly. *His first collection of short stories,* Will You Please Be Quiet, Please? *(1976), was nominated for the National Book Award. Subsequent collections include* What We Talk About When We Talk About Love *(1981),* Cathedral *(1983) and* Where I'm Calling From *(1988), in which "Neighbors" first appeared. A posthumous book of Carver's poetry,* All of Us, *was published in 1998. "Neighbors" displays Carver's conversational style and unique gift for getting to the heart of human relationships.*

Neighbors

Bill and Arlene Miller were a happy couple. But now and then they felt they alone among their circle had been passed by somehow, leaving Bill to attend to his bookkeeping duties and Arlene occupied with secretarial chores. They talked about it sometimes, mostly in comparison with the lives of their neighbors, Harriet and Jim Stone. It seemed to the Millers that the Stones lived a fuller and brighter life. The Stones were always going out for dinner, or entertaining at home, or traveling about the country somewhere in connection with Jim's work.

The Stones lived across the hall from the Millers. Jim was a salesman for a machine-parts firm and often managed to combine business with pleasure trips, and on this occasion the Stones would be away for ten days, first to Cheyenne, then on to St. Louis to visit relatives. In their absence, the Millers would look after the Stones' apartment, feed Kitty, and water the plants.

Bill and Jim shook hands beside the car. Harriet and Arlene held each other by the elbows and kissed lightly on the lips.

"Have fun," Bill said to Harriet.

"We will," said Harriet. "You kids have fun too." 5

Arlene nodded.

Jim winked at her. "Bye, Arlene. Take good care of the old man."

"I will," Arlene said.

"Have fun," Bill said.

"You bet," Jim said, clipping Bill lightly on the arm. "And thanks again, 10
you guys."

The Stones waved as they drove away, and the Millers waved too.

"Well, I wish it was us," Bill said.

"God knows, we could use a vacation," Arlene said. She took his arm and put it around her waist as they climbed the stairs to their apartment.

After dinner Arlene said, "Don't forget. Kitty gets liver flavor the first night." She stood in the kitchen doorway folding the handmade tablecloth that Harriet had bought for her last year in Santa Fe.

Bill took a deep breath as he entered the Stones' apartment. The air was al- 15
ready heavy and it was vaguely sweet. The sunburst clock over the television said half past eight. He remembered when Harriet had come home with the clock, how she had crossed the hall to show it to Arlene, cradling the brass case in her arms and talking to it through the tissue paper as if it were an infant.

Kitty rubbed her face against his slippers and then turned onto her side, but jumped up quickly as Bill moved to the kitchen and selected one of the stacked cans from the gleaming drainboard. Leaving the cat to pick at her food, he headed for the bathroom. He looked at himself in the mirror and then closed his eyes and then looked again. He opened the medicine chest. He found a container of pills and read the label—*Harriet Stone. One each day as directed*—and slipped it into his pocket. He went back to the kitchen, drew a pitcher of water, and returned to the living room. He finished watering, set the pitcher on the rug, and opened the liquor cabinet. He reached in back for the bottle of Chivas Regal. He took two drinks from the bottle, wiped his lips on his sleeve, and replaced the bottle in the cabinet.

Kitty was on the couch sleeping. He switched off the lights, slowly closing and checking the door. He had the feeling he had left something.

"What kept you?" Arlene said. She sat with her legs turned under her, watching television.

"Nothing. Playing with Kitty," he said, and went over to her and touched her breasts.

"Let's go to bed, honey," he said.

The next day Bill took only ten minutes of the twenty-minute break allotted for the afternoon and left at fifteen minutes before five. He parked the car in the lot just as Arlene hopped down from the bus. He waited until she entered the building, then ran up the stairs to catch her as she stepped out of the elevator.

"Bill! God, you scared me. You're early," she said.

He shrugged. "Nothing to do at work," he said.

She let him use her key to open the door. He looked at the door across the hall before following her inside.

"Let's go to bed," he said.

"Now?" She laughed. "What's gotten into you?"

"Nothing. Take your dress off." He grabbed for her awkwardly, and she said, "Good God, Bill."

He unfastened his belt.

Later they sent out for Chinese food, and when it arrived they ate hungrily, without speaking, and listened to records.

"Let's not forget to feed Kitty," she said.

"I was just thinking about that," he said. "I'll go right over."

He selected a can of fish flavor for the cat, then filled the pitcher and went to water. When he returned to the kitchen, the cat was scratching in her box. She looked at him steadily before she turned back to the litter. He opened all the cupboards and examined the canned goods, the cereals, the packaged foods, the cocktail and wine glasses, the china, the pots and pans. He opened the refrigerator. He sniffed some celery, took two bites of cheddar cheese, and chewed on an apple as he walked into the bedroom. The bed seemed enormous, with a fluffy white bedspread draped to the floor. He pulled out a nightstand drawer, found a half-empty package of cigarettes and stuffed them into his pocket. Then he stepped to the closet and was opening it when the knock sounded at the front door.

He stopped by the bathroom and flushed the toilet on his way.

"What's been keeping you?" Arlene said. "You've been over here more than an hour."

"Have I really?" he said.

"Yes, you have," she said.

"I had to go to the toilet," he said.

"You have your own toilet," she said.

"I couldn't wait," he said.

That night they made love again.

In the morning he had Arlene call in for him. He showered, dressed, and made a light breakfast. He tried to start a book. He went out for a walk and felt better. But after a while, hands still in his pockets, he returned to the apartment. He stopped at the Stones' door on the chance he might hear the cat moving about. Then he let himself in at his own door and went to the kitchen for the key.

Inside it seemed cooler than his apartment, and darker too. He wondered if the plants had something to do with the temperature of the air. He looked out the window, and then he moved slowly through each room considering everything that fell under his gaze, carefully, one object at a time. He saw ashtrays, items of furniture, kitchen utensils, the clock. He saw everything. At last he entered the bedroom, and the cat appeared at his feet. He stroked her once, carried her into the bathroom, and shut the door.

He lay down on the bed and stared at the ceiling. He lay for a while with his eyes closed, and then he moved his hand under his belt. He tried to recall what day it was. He tried to remember when the Stones were due back, and then he wondered if they would ever return. He could not remember their faces or the way they talked and dressed. He sighed and with effort rolled off the bed to lean over the dresser and look at himself in the mirror.

He opened the closet and selected a Hawaiian shirt. He looked until he found Bermudas, neatly pressed and hanging over a pair of brown twill slacks. He shed his own clothes and slipped into the shorts and the shirt. He looked in the mirror again. He went to the living room and poured himself a drink and sipped it on his way back to the bedroom. He put on a blue shirt, a dark suit, a blue and white tie, black wing-tip shoes. The glass was empty and he went for another drink.

In the bedroom again, he sat on a chair, crossed his legs, and smiled, observing himself in the mirror. The telephone rang twice and fell silent. He finished the drink and took off the suit. He rummaged through the top drawers until he found a pair of panties and a brassiere. He stepped into the panties and fastened the brassiere, then looked through the closet for an outfit. He put on a black and white checkered skirt and tried to zip it up. He put on a burgundy blouse that buttoned up the front. He considered her shoes, but understood they would not fit. For a long time he looked out the living-room window from behind the curtain. Then he returned to the bedroom and put everything away.

He was not hungry. She did not eat much, either. They looked at each other shyly and smiled. She got up from the table and checked that the key was on the shelf and then she quickly cleared the dishes.

He stood in the kitchen doorway and smoked a cigarette and watched her pick up the key.

"Make yourself comfortable while I go across the hall," she said. "Read the paper or something." She closed her fingers over the key. He was, she said, looking tired.

He tried to concentrate on the news. He read the paper and turned on the television. Finally he went across the hall. The door was locked.

"It's me. Are you still there, honey?" he called.

After a time the lock released and Arlene stepped outside and shut the door. "Was I gone so long?" she said.

"Well, you were," he said.

"Was I?" she said. "I guess I must have been playing with Kitty."

He studied her, and she looked away, her hand still resting on the doorknob.

"It's funny," she said. "You know—to go in someone's place like that." 55

He nodded, took her hand from the knob, and guided her toward their own door. He let them into their apartment.

"It *is* funny," he said.

He noticed white lint clinging to the back of her sweater, and the color was high in her cheeks. He began kissing her on the neck and hair and she turned and kissed him back.

"Oh, damn," she said. "Damn, damn," she sang, girlishly clapping her hands. "I just remembered. I really and truly forgot to do what I went over there to do. I didn't feed Kitty or do any watering." She looked at him. "Isn't that stupid?"

"I don't think so," he said. "Just a minute. I'll get my cigarettes and go 60
back with you."

She waited until he had closed and locked their door, and then she took his arm at the muscle and said. "I guess I should tell you. I found some pictures."

He stopped in the middle of the hall. "What kind of pictures?"

"You can see for yourself," she said, and she watched him.

"No kidding." He grinned. "Where?"

"In a drawer," she said. 65

"No kidding," he said.

And then she said, "Maybe they won't come back," and was at once astonished at her words.

"It could happen," he said. "Anything could happen."

"Or maybe they'll come back and . . ." but she did not finish.

They held hands for the short walk across the hall, and when he spoke 70
she could barely hear his voice.

"The key," he said. "Give it to me."

"What?" she said. She gazed at the door.

"The key," he said. "You have the key."

"My God," she said, "I left the key inside."

He tried the knob. It was locked. Then she tried the knob. It would not 75
turn. Her lips were parted, and her breathing was hard, expectant. He opened his arms and she moved into them.

"Don't worry," he said into her ear. "For God's sake, don't worry."

They stayed there. They held each other. They leaned into the door as if against a wind, and braced themselves.

Analyzing the Text

1. How do Bill and Arlene Miller's experiences in their neighbor's house change their relationship?
2. Given that they forget to water the plants and feed the cat, why is the ending significant?

Understanding Carver's Techniques

1. How does the opening of the story define the neighbors (the Stones) as people to be envied?
2. What signals alert the reader that the Millers are getting carried away with stepping outside their lives?

Arguing for an Interpretation

1. Although Carver doesn't editorialize, what can you infer about what must be going on in the minds of the main characters?
2. Would you consider the Millers bad neighbors, and would you let them house-sit for you? Why or why not?

JHUMPA LAHIRI

Jhumpa Lahiri was born in 1967 in London, the daughter of Bengali parents. She grew up in Rhode Island but spent considerable time in Calcutta. Her experiences there provide the basis for much of her fiction. She received a Ph.D. in Renaissance studies from Boston University. The Interpreter of Maladies *(1999), in which the following story first appeared, won the Pulitzer Prize for fiction. The title story was selected for both the O'Henry Award and the Best American Short Stories. Her fiction has been published in the* New Yorker, *the* Harvard Review, *and* Story Quarterly. *Her latest novel is* The Namesake *(2003). "This Blessed House" tells a humorous story of Indian newlyweds who find themselves at odds over whether to keep Christian artifacts left by the previous owners of their new home.*

This Blessed House

They discovered the first one in a cupboard above the stove, beside an unopened bottle of malt vinegar.

"Guess what I found." Twinkle walked into the living room, lined from end to end with taped-up packing boxes, waving the vinegar in one hand and a white porcelain effigy of Christ, roughly the same size as the vinegar bottle, in the other.

Sanjeev looked up. He was kneeling on the floor, marking, with ripped bits of a Post-it, patches on the baseboard that needed to be retouched with paint. "Throw it away."

"Which?"

"Both." 5

"But I can cook something with the vinegar. It's brand-new."

"You've never cooked anything with vinegar."

"I'll look something up. In one of those books we got for our wedding."

Sanjeev turned back to the baseboard, to replace a Post-it scrap that had fallen to the floor. "Check the expiration. And at the very least get rid of that idiotic statue."

"But it could be worth something. Who knows?" She turned it upside 10
down, then stroked, with her index finger, the minuscule frozen folds of its robes. "It's pretty."

"We're not Christian," Sanjeev said. Lately he had begun noticing the need to state the obvious to Twinkle. The day before he had to tell her that if she dragged her end of the bureau instead of lifting it, the parquet floor would scratch.

She shrugged. "No, we're not Christian. We're good little Hindus." She planted a kiss on top of Christ's head, then placed the statue on top of the fireplace mantel, which needed, Sanjeev observed, to be dusted.

By the end of the week the mantel had still not been dusted; it had, however, come to serve as the display shelf for a sizable collection of Christian paraphernalia. There was a 3-D postcard of Saint Francis done in four colors, which Twinkle had found taped to the back of the medicine cabinet, and a wooden cross key chain, which Sanjeev had stepped on with bare feet as he was installing extra shelving in Twinkle's study. There was a framed paint-by-number of the three wise men, against a black velvet background, tucked in the linen closet. There was also a tile trivet depicting a blond, unbearded Jesus, delivering a sermon on a mountaintop, left in one of the drawers of the built-in china cabinet in the dining room.

"Do you think the previous owners were born-agains?" asked Twinkle, making room the next day for a small plastic snow-filled dome containing a miniature Nativity scene, found behind the pipes of the kitchen sink.

Sanjeev was organizing his engineering texts from MIT in alphabetical order on a bookshelf, though it had been several years since he had needed to consult any of them. After graduating, he moved from Boston to Connecticut, to work for a firm near Hartford, and he had recently learned that he was being considered for the position of vice president. At thirty-three he had a secretary of his own and a dozen people working under his supervision who gladly supplied him with any information he needed. Still, the presence of his college books in the room reminded him of a time in his life he recalled with fondness, when he would walk each evening across the Mass. Avenue bridge to order Mughlai chicken with spinach from his favorite Indian restaurant on the other side of the Charles, and return to his dorm to write out clean copies of his problem sets.

"Or perhaps it's an attempt to convert people," Twinkle mused.

"Clearly the scheme has succeeded in your case."

She disregarded him, shaking the little plastic dome so that the snow swirled over the manger.

He studied the items on the mantel. It puzzled him that each was in its own way so silly. Clearly they lacked a sense of sacredness. He was further puzzled that Twinkle, who normally displayed good taste, was so charmed. These objects meant something to Twinkle, but they meant nothing to him. They irritated him. "We should call the Realtor. Tell him there's all this nonsense left behind. Tell him to take it away."

"Oh, Sanj." Twinkle groaned. "Please. I would feel terrible throwing them away. Obviously they were important to the people who used to live here. It would feel, I don't know, sacrilegious or something."

"If they're so precious, then why are they hidden all over the house? Why didn't they take them with them?"

"There must be others," Twinkle said. Her eyes roamed the bare off-white walls of the room, as if there were other things concealed behind the plaster. "What else do you think we'll find?"

But as they unpacked their boxes and hung up their winter clothes and the silk paintings of elephant processions bought on their honeymoon in Jaipur, Twinkle, much to her dismay, could not find a thing. Nearly a week had passed before they discovered, one Saturday afternoon, a larger-than-life-sized watercolor poster of Christ, weeping translucent tears the size of peanut shells and sporting a crown of thorns, rolled up behind a radiator in the guest bedroom. Sanjeev had mistaken it for a window shade.

"Oh, we must, we simply must put it up. It's too spectacular." Twinkle lit a cigarette and began to smoke it with relish, waving it around Sanjeev's head as if it were a conductor's baton as Mahler's Fifth Symphony roared from the stereo downstairs.

"Now, look. I will tolerate, for now, your little biblical menagerie in the 25
living room. But I refuse to have this," he said, flicking at one of the painted peanut-tears, "displayed in our home."

Twinkle stared at him, placidly exhaling, the smoke emerging in two thin blue streams from her nostrils. She rolled up the poster slowly, securing it with one of the elastic bands she always wore around her wrist for tying back her thick, unruly hair, streaked here and there with henna. "I'm going to put it in my study," she informed him. "That way you don't have to look at it."

"What about the housewarming? They'll want to see all the rooms. I've invited people from the office."

She rolled her eyes. Sanjeev noted that the symphony, now in its third movement, had reached a crescendo, for it pulsed with the telltale clashing of cymbals.

"I'll put it behind the door," she offered. "That way, when they peek in, they won't see. Happy?"

He stood watching her as she left the room, with her poster and her 30
cigarette; a few ashes had fallen to the floor where she'd been standing. He bent down, pinched them between his fingers, and deposited them in his cupped palm. The tender fourth movement, the *adagietto,* began. During breakfast, Sanjeev had read in the liner notes that Mahler had proposed to his wife by sending her the manuscript of this portion of the score. Although there were elements of tragedy and struggle in the Fifth Symphony, he had read, it was principally music of love and happiness.

He heard the toilet flush. "By the way," Twinkle hollered, "if you want to impress people, I wouldn't play this music. It's putting me to sleep."

Sanjeev went to the bathroom to throw away the ashes. The cigarette butt still bobbed in the toilet bowl, but the tank was refilling, so he had to wait a moment before he could flush it again. In the mirror of the medicine cabinet he inspected his long eyelashes—like a girl's, Twinkle liked to tease. Though he was of average build, his cheeks had a plumpness to them; this, along with the eyelashes, detracted, he feared, from what he hoped was a distinguished profile. He was of average height as well, and had wished ever since he had stopped growing that he were just one inch taller. For this reason it irritated him when Twinkle insisted on wearing high heels, as she had done the other night when they ate dinner in Manhattan. This was the first weekend after they'd moved into the house; by then the mantel had already filled up considerably, and they had bickered about it in the car on the way down. But then Twinkle had drunk four glasses of whiskey in a nameless bar in Alphabet City, and forgot all about it. She dragged him to a tiny bookshop on St. Mark's Place, where she browsed for nearly an hour, and when they left she insisted that they dance a tango on the sidewalk in front of strangers.

Afterward, she tottered on his arm, rising faintly over his line of vision, in a pair of suede three-inch leopard-print pumps. In this manner they walked the endless blocks back to a parking garage on Washington Square, for Sanjeev had heard far too many stories about the terrible things that happened to cars in Manhattan. "But I do nothing all day except sit at my desk," she fretted when they were driving home, after he had mentioned that her shoes looked uncomfortable and suggested that perhaps she should not wear them. "I can't exactly wear heels when I'm typing." Though he abandoned the argument, he knew for a fact that she didn't spend all day at her desk; just that afternoon, when he got back from a run, he found her inexplicably in bed, reading. When he asked why she was in bed in the middle of the day she told him she was bored. He had wanted to say to her then, You could unpack some boxes. You could sweep the attic. You could retouch the paint on the bathroom windowsill, and after you do it you could warn me so that I don't put my watch on it. They didn't bother her, these scattered, unsettled matters. She seemed content with whatever clothes she found at the front of the closet, with whatever magazine was lying around, with whatever song was on the radio—content yet curious. And now all of her curiosity centered around discovering the next treasure.

A few days later when Sanjeev returned from the office, he found Twinkle on the telephone, smoking and talking to one of her girlfriends in California even though it was before five o'clock and the long-distance rates were at their peak. "Highly devout people," she was saying, pausing every now and then to exhale. "Each day is like a treasure hunt. I'm serious. This you won't believe. The switch plates in the bedrooms were decorated with scenes from the Bible. You know, Noah's Ark and all that. Three bedrooms, but one is my study. Sanjeev went to the hardware store right away and replaced them, can you imagine, he replaced every single one."

Now it was the friend's turn to talk. Twinkle nodded, slouched on the 35
floor in front of the fridge, wearing black stirrup pants and a yellow chenille sweater, groping for her lighter. Sanjeev could smell something aromatic on the stove, and he picked his way carefully across the extra-long phone cord tangled on the Mexican terra-cotta tiles. He opened the lid of a pot with some sort of reddish brown sauce dripping over the sides, boiling furiously.

"It's a stew made with fish. I put the vinegar in it," she said to him, interrupting her friend, crossing her fingers. "Sorry, you were saying?" She was like that, excited and delighted by little things, crossing her fingers before any remotely unpredictable event, like tasting a new flavor of ice cream, or dropping a letter in a mailbox. It was a quality he did not understand. It made him feel stupid, as if the world contained hidden wonders he could not anticipate, or see. He looked at her face, which, it occurred to him, had not grown out of its girlhood, the eyes untroubled, the pleasing features unfirm, as if they still had to settle into some sort of permanent expression. Nicknamed after a nursery rhyme, she had yet to shed a childhood endearment. Now, in the second month of their marriage, certain things nettled him—the way she sometimes spat a little when she spoke, or left her undergarments after removing them at night at the foot of their bed rather than depositing them in the laundry hamper.

They had met only four months before. Her parents, who lived in California, and his, who still lived in Calcutta, were old friends, and across continents they had arranged the occasion at which Twinkle and Sanjeev were introduced—a sixteenth birthday party for a daughter in their circle—when Sanjeev was in Palo Alto on business. At the restaurant they were seated side by side at a round table with a revolving platter of spareribs and egg rolls and chicken wings, which, they concurred, all tasted the same. They had concurred too on their adolescent but still persistent fondness for Wodehouse novels, and their dislike for the sitar, and later Twinkle confessed that she was charmed by the way Sanjeev had dutifully refilled her teacup during their conversation.

And so the phone calls began, and grew longer, and then the visits, first he to Stanford, then she to Connecticut, after which Sanjeev would save in an ashtray left on the balcony the crushed cigarettes she had smoked during the weekend—saved them, that is, until the next time she came to visit him, and then he vacuumed the apartment, washed the sheets, even dusted the plant leaves in her honor. She was twenty-seven and recently abandoned, he had gathered, by an American who had tried and failed to be an actor; Sanjeev was lonely, with an excessively generous income for a single man, and had never been in love. At the urging of their matchmakers, they married in India, amid hundreds of well-wishers whom he barely remembered from his childhood, in incessant August rains, under a red and orange tent strung with Christmas tree lights on Mandeville Road.

"Did you sweep the attic?" he asked Twinkle later as she was folding paper napkins and wedging them by their plates. The attic was the only part of the house they had not yet given an initial cleaning.

"Not yet. I will, I promise. I hope this tastes good," she said, planting the steaming pot on top of the Jesus trivet. There was a loaf of Italian bread in a little basket, and iceberg lettuce and grated carrots tossed with bottled dressing and croutons, and glasses of red wine. She was not terribly ambitious in the kitchen. She bought preroasted chickens from the supermarket and served them with potato salad prepared who knew when, sold in little plastic containers. Indian food, she complained, was a bother; she detested chopping garlic, and peeling ginger, and could not operate a blender, and so it was Sanjeev who, on weekends, seasoned mustard oil with cinnamon sticks and cloves in order to produce a proper curry.

He had to admit, though, that whatever it was that she had cooked today, it was unusually tasty, attractive even, with bright white cubes of fish, and flecks of parsley, and fresh tomatoes gleaming in the dark brown-red broth.

"How did you make it?"

"I made it up."

"What did you do?"

"I just put some things into the pot and added the malt vinegar at the end."

"How much vinegar?"

She shrugged, ripping off some bread and plunging it into her bowl.

"What do you mean you don't know? You should write it down. What if you need to make it again, for a party or something?"

"I'll remember," she said. She covered the bread basket with a dishtowel that had, he suddenly noticed, the Ten Commandments printed on it. She flashed him a smile, giving his knee a little squeeze under the table. "Face it. This house is blessed."

The housewarming party was scheduled for the last Saturday in October, 50
and they had invited about thirty people. All were Sanjeev's acquaintances, people from the office, and a number of Indian couples in the Connecticut area, many of whom he barely knew, but who had regularly invited him, in his bachelor days, to supper on Saturdays. He often wondered why they included him in their circle. He had little in common with any of them, but he always attended their gatherings, to eat spiced chickpeas and shrimp cutlets, and gossip and discuss politics, for he seldom had other plans. So far, no one had met Twinkle; back when they were still dating, Sanjeev didn't want to waste their brief weekends together with people he associated with being alone. Other than Sanjeev and an ex-boyfriend who she believed worked in a pottery studio in Brookfield, she knew no one in the state of Connecticut. She was completing her master's thesis at Stanford, a study of an Irish poet whom Sanjeev had never heard of.

Sanjeev had found the house on his own before leaving for the wedding, for a good price, in a neighborhood with a fine school system. He was impressed by the elegant curved staircase with its wrought-iron banister, and the dark wooden wainscoting, and the solarium overlooking rhododendron bushes, and the solid brass 22, which also happened to be the date of his birth, nailed impressively to the vaguely Tudor facade. There were two working fireplaces, a two-car garage, and an attic suitable for converting into extra bedrooms if, the Realtor mentioned, the need should arise. By then Sanjeev had already made up his mind, was determined that he and Twinkle should live there together, forever, and so he had not bothered to notice the switch plates covered with biblical stickers, or the transparent decal of the Virgin on the half shell, as Twinkle liked to call it, adhered to the window in the master bedroom. When, after moving in, he tried to scrape it off, he scratched the glass.

The weekend before the party they were raking the lawn when he heard Twinkle shriek. He ran to her, clutching his rake, worried that she had discovered a dead animal, or a snake. A brisk October breeze stung the tops of his ears as his sneakers crunched over brown and yellow leaves. When he reached her, she had collapsed on the grass, dissolved in nearly silent laughter. Behind an overgrown forsythia bush was a plaster Virgin Mary as tall as their waists, with a blue painted hood draped over her head in the manner of an Indian bride. Twinkle grabbed the hem of her T-shirt and began wiping away the dirt staining the statue's brow.

"I suppose you want to put her by the foot of our bed," Sanjeev said.

She looked at him, astonished. Her belly was exposed, and he saw that there were goose bumps around her navel. "What do you think? Of course we can't put this in our bedroom."

"We can't?" 55

"No, silly Sanj. This is meant for outside. For the lawn."

"Oh God, no. Twinkle, no."

"But we must. It would be bad luck not to."

"All the neighbors will see. They'll think we're insane."

"Why, for having a statue of the Virgin Mary on our lawn? Every other 60
person in this neighborhood has a statue of Mary on the lawn. We'll fit right in."

"We're not Christian."

"So you keep reminding me." She spat onto the tip of her finger and started to rub intently at a particularly stubborn stain on Mary's chin. "Do you think this is dirt, or some kind of fungus?"

He was getting nowhere with her, with this woman whom he had known for only four months and whom he had married, this woman with whom he now shared his life. He thought with a flicker of regret of the snapshots his mother used to send him from Calcutta, of prospective brides who could sing and sew and season lentils without consulting a cookbook. Sanjeev had considered these women, had even ranked them in order of preference, but then he had met Twinkle. "Twinkle, I can't have the people I work with see this statue on my lawn."

"They can't fire you for being a believer. It would be discrimination."

"That's not the point." 65

"Why does it matter to you so much what other people think?"

"Twinkle, please." He was tired. He let his weight rest against his rake as she began dragging the statue toward an oval bed of myrtle, beside the lamppost that flanked the brick pathway. "Look, Sanj. She's so lovely."

He returned to his pile of leaves and began to deposit them by handfuls into a plastic garbage bag. Over his head the blue sky was cloudless. One tree on the lawn was still full of leaves, red and orange, like the tent in which he had married Twinkle.

He did not know if he loved her. He said he did when she had first asked him, one afternoon in Palo Alto as they sat side by side in a darkened, nearly empty movie theater. Before the film, one of her favorites, something in German that he found extremely depressing, she had pressed the tip of her nose to his so that he could feel the flutter of her mascara-coated eyelashes. That afternoon he had replied, yes, he loved her, and she was delighted, and fed him a piece of popcorn, letting her finger linger an instant between his lips, as if it were his reward for coming up with the right answer.

Though she did not say it herself, he assumed then that she loved him 70
too, but now he was no longer sure. In truth, Sanjeev did not know what love was, only what he thought it was not. It was not, he had decided, returning to an empty carpeted condominium each night, and using only the top fork in his cutlery drawer, and turning away politely at those weekend dinner parties when the other men eventually put their arms around the waists of their wives and girlfriends, leaning over every now and again to kiss their shoulders or necks. It was not sending away for classical music CDs by mail, working his way methodically through the major composers that the catalogue recommended, and always sending his payments in on time. In the months before meeting Twinkle, Sanjeev had begun to realize this. "You have enough money in the bank to raise three families," his mother reminded him when they spoke at the start of each month on the phone. "You need a wife to look after and love." Now he had one, a pretty one, from a suitably high caste, who would soon have a master's degree. What was there not to love?

That evening Sanjeev poured himself a gin and tonic, drank it and most of another during one segment of the news, and then approached Twinkle, who was taking a bubble bath, for she announced that her limbs ached from raking the lawn, something she had never done before. He didn't knock. She had applied a bright blue mask to her face, was smoking and sipping some bourbon with ice and leafing through a fat paperback book whose pages had buckled and turned gray from the water. He glanced at the cover; the only thing written on it was the word "Sonnets" in dark red letters. He took a breath, and then he informed her very calmly that after finishing his drink he was going to put on his shoes and go outside and remove the Virgin from the front lawn.

"Where are you going to put it?" she asked him dreamily, her eyes closed. One of her legs emerged, unfolding gracefully, from the layer of suds. She flexed and pointed her toes.

"For now I am going to put it in the garage. Then tomorrow morning on my way to work I am going to take it to the dump."

"Don't you dare." She stood up, letting the book fall into the water, bubbles dripping down her thighs. "I hate you," she informed him, her eyes narrowing at the word "hate." She reached for her bathrobe, tied it tightly about her waist, and padded down the winding staircase, leaving sloppy wet footprints along the parquet floor. When she reached the foyer, Sanjeev said, "Are you planning on leaving the house that way?" He felt a throbbing in his temples, and his voice revealed an unfamiliar snarl when he spoke.

"Who cares? Who cares what way I leave this house?" 75

"Where are you planning on going at this hour?"

"You can't throw away that statue. I won't let you." Her mask, now dry, had assumed an ashen quality, and water from her hair dripped onto the caked contours of her face.

"Yes I can. I will."

"No," Twinkle said, her voice suddenly small. "This is our house. We own it together. The statue is a part of our property." She had begun to shiver. A small pool of bathwater had collected around her ankles. He went to shut a window, fearing that she would catch cold. Then he noticed that some of the water dripping down her hard blue face was tears.

"Oh God, Twinkle, please, I didn't mean it." He had never seen her cry 80
before, had never seen such sadness in her eyes. She didn't turn away or try to stop the tears; instead she looked strangely at peace. For a moment she closed her lids, pale and unprotected compared to the blue that caked the rest of her face. Sanjeev felt ill, as if he had eaten either too much or too little.

She went to him, placing her damp toweled arms about his neck, sobbing into his chest, soaking his shirt. The mask flaked onto his shoulders.

In the end they settled on a compromise: the statue would be placed in a recess at the side of the house, so that it wasn't obvious to passersby, but was still clearly visible to all who came.

The menu for the party was fairly simple: there would be a case of champagne, and samosas from an Indian restaurant in Hartford, and big trays of rice with chicken and almonds and orange peels, which Sanjeev had spent the greater part of the morning and afternoon preparing. He had never entertained on such a large scale before and, worried that there would not be enough to drink, ran out at one point to buy another case of champagne just in case. For this reason he burned one of the rice trays and had to start it over again. Twinkle swept the floors and volunteered to pick up the samosas; she had an appointment for a manicure and a pedicure in that direction, anyway. Sanjeev had planned to ask if she would consider clearing the menagerie off the mantel, if only for the party, but she left while he was in the shower. She was gone for a good three hours, and so it was Sanjeev who did the rest of the cleaning. By five-thirty the entire house sparkled, with scented candles that Twinkle had picked up in Hartford illuminating the items on the mantel, and slender stalks of burning incense planted into the soil of potted plants. Each time he passed the mantel he winced, dreading the raised eyebrows of his guests as they viewed the flickering ceramic saints, the salt and pepper shakers designed to resemble Mary and Joseph. Still, they would be impressed, he hoped, by the lovely bay windows, the shining parquet floors, the impressive winding staircase, the wooden wainscoting, as they sipped champagne and dipped samosas in chutney.

Douglas, one of the new consultants at the firm, and his girlfriend Nora were the first to arrive. Both were tall and blond, wearing matching wire-rimmed glasses and long black overcoats. Nora wore a black hat full of sharp thin feathers that corresponded to the sharp thin angles of her face. Her left hand was joined with Douglas's. In her right hand was a bottle of cognac with a red ribbon wrapped around its neck, which she gave to Twinkle.

"Great lawn, Sanjeev," Douglas remarked. "We've got to get that rake out ourselves, sweetie. And this must be . . ."

"My wife. Tanima."

"Call me Twinkle."

"What an unusual name," Nora remarked.

Twinkle shrugged. "Not really. There's an actress in Bombay named Dimple Kapadia. She even has a sister named Simple."

Douglas and Nora raised their eyebrows simultaneously, nodding slowly, as if to let the absurdity of the names settle in. "Pleased to meet you, Twinkle."

"Help yourself to champagne. There's gallons."

"I hope you don't mind my asking," Douglas said, "but I noticed the statue outside, and are you guys Christian? I thought you were Indian."

"There are Christians in India," Sanjeev replied, "but we're not."

"I love your outfit," Nora told Twinkle.

"And I adore your hat. Would you like the grand tour?"

The bell rang again, and again and again. Within minutes, it seemed, the house had filled with bodies and conversations and unfamiliar fragrances. The women wore heels and sheer stockings, and short black dresses made of crepe and chiffon. They handed their wraps and coats to Sanjeev, who draped them carefully on hangers in the spacious coat closet, though Twinkle told people to throw their things on the ottomans in the solarium. Some of the Indian women wore their finest saris, made with gold filigree that draped in elegant pleats over their shoulders. The men wore jackets and ties and citrus-scented aftershaves. As people filtered from one room to the next, presents piled onto the long cherry-wood table that ran from one end of the downstairs hall to the other.

It bewildered Sanjeev that it was for him, and his house, and his wife, that they had all gone to so much care. The only other time in his life that something similar had happened was his wedding day, but somehow this was different, for these were not his family, but people who knew him only casually, and in a sense owed him nothing. Everyone congratulated him. Lester, another coworker, predicted that Sanjeev would be promoted to vice president in two months maximum. People devoured the samosas, and dutifully admired the freshly painted ceilings and walls, the hanging plants, the bay windows, the silk paintings from Jaipur. But most of all they admired Twinkle, and her brocaded *salwar-kameez,* which was the shade of a persimmon with a low scoop in the back, and the little string of white rose petals she had coiled cleverly around her head, and the pearl choker with a sapphire at its center that adorned her throat. Over hectic jazz records, played under Twinkle's supervision, they laughed at her anecdotes and observations, forming a widening circle around her, while Sanjeev replenished the samosas that he kept warming evenly in the oven, and getting ice for people's drinks, and opening more bottles of champagne with some difficulty, and explaining for the fortieth time that he wasn't Christian. It was Twinkle who led them in separate groups up and down the winding stairs, to gaze at the back lawn, to peer down the cellar steps. "Your friends adore the poster in my study," she mentioned to him triumphantly, placing her hand on the small of his back as they, at one point, brushed past each other.

Sanjeev went to the kitchen, which was empty, and ate a piece of chicken out of the tray on the counter with his fingers because he thought no one was looking. He ate a second piece, then washed it down with a gulp of gin straight from the bottle.

"Great house. Great rice." Sunil, an anesthesiologist, walked in, spooning food from his paper plate into his mouth. "Do you have more champagne?"

100 "Your wife's wow," added Prabal, following behind. He was an unmarried professor of physics at Yale. For a moment Sanjeev stared at him blankly, then blushed; once at a dinner party Prabal had pronounced that Sophia Loren was wow, as was Audrey Hepburn. "Does she have a sister?"

Sunil picked a raisin out of the rice tray. "Is her last name Little Star?"

The two men laughed and started eating more rice from the tray, plowing through it with their plastic spoons. Sanjeev went down to the cellar for more liquor. For a few minutes he paused on the steps, in the damp, cool silence, hugging the second crate of champagne to his chest as the party drifted above the rafters. Then he set the reinforcements on the dining table.

"Yes, everything, we found them all in the house, in the most unusual places," he heard Twinkle saying in the living room. "In fact we keep finding them."

"No!"

105 "Yes! Every day is like a treasure hunt. It's too good. God only knows what else we'll find, no pun intended."

That was what started it. As if by some unspoken pact, the whole party joined forces and began combing through each of the rooms, opening closets on their own, peering under chairs and cushions, feeling behind curtains, removing books from bookcases. Groups scampered, giggling and swaying, up and down the winding staircase.

"We've never explored the attic," Twinkle announced suddenly, and so everybody followed.

"How do we get up there?"

"There's a ladder in the hallway, somewhere in the ceiling."

110 Wearily Sanjeev followed at the back of the crowd, to point out the location of the ladder, but Twinkle had already found it on her own. "Eureka!" she hollered.

Douglas pulled the chain that released the steps. His face was flushed and he was wearing Nora's feather hat on his head. One by one the guests disappeared, men helping women as they placed their strappy high heels on the narrow slats of the ladder, the Indian women wrapping the free ends of their expensive saris into their waistbands. The men followed behind, all quickly disappearing, until Sanjeev alone remained at the top of the winding staircase. Footsteps thundered over his head. He had no desire to join them. He wondered if the ceiling would collapse, imagined, for a split second, the sight of all the tumbling drunk perfumed bodies crashing, tangled, around him. He heard a shriek, and then rising, spreading waves of laughter in discordant tones. Something fell, something else shattered. He could hear them babbling about a trunk. They seemed to be struggling to get it open, banging feverishly on its surface.

He thought perhaps Twinkle would call for his assistance, but he was not summoned. He looked about the hallway and to the landing below, at the champagne glasses and half-eaten samosas and napkins smeared with lipstick abandoned in every corner, on every available surface. Then he noticed that Twinkle, in her haste, had discarded her shoes altogether, for they lay by the foot of the ladder, black patent-leather mules with heels like golf tees, open toes, and slightly soiled silk labels on the instep where her soles had rested. He placed them in the doorway of the master bedroom so that no one would trip when they descended.

He heard something creaking open slowly. The strident voices had subsided to an even murmur. It occurred to Sanjeev that he had the house all to himself. The music had ended and he could hear, if he concentrated, the hum of the refrigerator, and the rustle of the last leaves on the trees outside, and the tapping of their branches against the windowpanes. With one flick of his hand he could snap the ladder back on its spring into the ceiling, and they would have no way of getting down unless he were to pull the chain and let them. He thought of all the things he could do, undisturbed. He could sweep Twinkle's menagerie into a garbage bag and get in the car and drive it all to the dump, and tear down the poster of weeping Jesus, and take a hammer to the Virgin Mary while he was at it. Then he would return to the empty house; he could easily clear up the cups and plates in an hour's time, and pour himself a gin and tonic, and eat a plate of warmed rice and listen to his new Bach CD while reading the liner notes so as to understand it properly. He nudged the ladder slightly, but it was sturdily planted against the floor. Budging it would require some effort.

"My God, I need a cigarette," Twinkle exclaimed from above.

Sanjeev felt knots forming at the back of his neck. He felt dizzy. He 115
needed to lie down. He walked toward the bedroom, but stopped short when he saw Twinkle's shoes facing him in the doorway. He thought of her slipping them on her feet. But instead of feeling irritated, as he had ever since they'd moved into the house together, he felt a pang of anticipation at the thought of her rushing unsteadily down the winding staircase in them, scratching the floor a bit in her path. The pang intensified as he thought of her rushing to the bathroom to brighten her lipstick, and eventually rushing to get people their coats, and finally rushing to the cherry-wood table when the last guest had left, to begin opening their housewarming presents. It was the same pang he used to feel before they were married, when he would hang up the phone after one of their conversations, or when he would drive back from the airport, wondering which ascending plane in the sky was hers.

"Sanj, you won't believe this."

She emerged with her back to him, her hands over her head, the tops of her bare shoulder blades perspiring, supporting something still hidden from view.

"You got it, Twinkle?" someone asked.

"Yes, you can let go."

Now he saw that her hands were wrapped around it: a solid silver bust 120
of Christ, the head easily three times the size of his own. It had a patrician bump on its nose, magnificent curly hair that rested atop a pronounced collarbone, and a broad forehead that reflected in miniature the walls and doors and lampshades around them. Its expression was confident, as if assured of its devotees, the unyielding lips sensuous and full. It was also sporting Nora's feather hat. As Twinkle descended, Sanjeev put his hands around her waist to balance her, and he relieved her of the bust when she had reached the ground. It weighed a good thirty pounds. The others began lowering themselves slowly, exhausted from the hunt. Some trickled downstairs in search of a fresh drink.

She took a breath, raised her eyebrows, crossed her fingers. "Would you mind terribly if we displayed it on the mantel? Just for tonight? I know you hate it."

He did hate it. He hated its immensity, and its flawless, polished surface, and its undeniable value. He hated that it was in his house, and that he owned it. Unlike the other things they'd found, this contained dignity, solemnity, beauty even. But to his surprise these qualities made him hate it all the more. Most of all he hated it because he knew that Twinkle loved it.

"I'll keep it in my study from tomorrow," Twinkle added. "I promise."

She would never put it in her study, he knew. For the rest of their days together she would keep it on the center of the mantel, flanked on either side by the rest of the menagerie. Each time they had guests Twinkle would explain how she had found it, and they would admire her as they listened. He gazed at the crushed rose petals in her hair, at the pearl and sapphire choker at her throat, at the sparkly crimson polish on her toes. He decided these were among the things that made Prabal think she was wow. His head ached from gin and his arms ached from the weight of the statue. He said, "I put your shoes in the bedroom."

"Thanks. But my feet are killing me." Twinkle gave his elbow a little 125
squeeze and headed for the living room.

Sanjeev pressed the massive silver face to his ribs, careful not to let the feather hat slip, and followed her.

Analyzing the Text

1. How does the discovery of Christian artifacts bring to the surface long-simmering differences in personalities between Twinkle and Sanjeev?
2. Why in the end does Sanjeev decide to accept what he knows will be a lifetime of bemused perplexity?

Understanding Lahiri's Techniques

1. How does Lahiri's characterization of Sanjeev and Twinkle make us aware of how Sanjeev is a slave to society's expectations while Twinkle is a free spirit? In view of this, why are the artifacts they discover especially ironic?

2. How does Lahiri use the party as a focal point during which Sanjeev must come to terms with their differences? Why is it significant that the bust of Christ differs radically from the Christian kitsch they have previously unearthed?

Arguing for an Interpretation

1. In what sense might the house into which Sanjeev and Twinkle move be described as "blessed"?
2. Did you find this story sacrilegious or offensive? Why or why not?

ALBERT CAMUS

Albert Camus (1913–1960) was born in Mondavi, Algeria (then a colony of France), in 1913 to Breton and Spanish parents. Despite the hardships of poverty and his bouts with tuberculosis, Camus excelled as both an athlete and scholarship student at the University of Algiers. Camus lived and worked as a journalist in Algeria until 1940 when he traveled to France and became active in the Resistance, serving as editor of the clandestine paper Combat.

Internationally recognized for his essays and novels, Camus received the Nobel Prize for Literature in 1957, a few years before he was killed in an automobile accident. Camus was closely associated with Jean-Paul Sartre and the French existentialist movement, but broke with Sartre and developed his own concept of the absurd that asserts the importance of human solidarity as the only value capable of redeeming a world without meaning.

Although Camus began as a journalist, his work soon extended far beyond journalism to encompass novels, such as The Stranger *(1942), the play* Caligula *(1944), and a lengthy essay defining his concept of the "absurd" hero, in* The Myth of Sisyphus *(1942). Camus's second novel,* The Plague *(1947), uses the description of a plague in a quarantined city to depict the human struggle against physical and spiritual evil in all its forms, a position Camus outlined in great detail in his nonfiction work* The Rebel *(1951). "The Guest," translated by Justin O'Brien, is drawn from his last collection of short stories,* Exile and the Kingdom *(1957). In this story, Camus returns to the landscape of his native Algeria to depict the poignant dilemma of his protagonist, Daru, a rural schoolteacher who resists being forced into complicity with the French during the war between France and Algeria, which lasted from 1954 to 1962. Set against the background of the Algerian struggle for independence, the story masterfully explores all the important themes of the burdens of freedom, brotherhood, responsibility,*

moral ambiguity, and the inevitability of choice that Camus grappled with throughout his life.

The Guest

The schoolmaster was watching the two men climb toward him. One was on horseback, the other on foot. They had not yet tackled the abrupt rise leading to the schoolhouse built on the hillside. They were toiling onward, making slow progress in the snow, among the stones, on the vast expanse of the high, deserted plateau. From time to time the horse stumbled. Without hearing anything yet, he could see the breath issuing from the horse's nostrils. One of the men, at least, knew the region. They were following the trail although it had disappeared days ago under a layer of dirty white snow. The schoolmaster calculated that it would take them half an hour to get onto the hill. It was cold; he went back into the school to get a sweater.

He crossed the empty frigid classroom. On the blackboard the four rivers of France, drawn with four different colored chalks, had been flowing toward their estuaries for the past three days. Snow had suddenly fallen in mid-October after eight months of drought without the transition of rain, and the twenty pupils, more or less, who lived in the villages scattered over the plateau had stopped coming. With fair weather they would return. Daru now heated only the single room that was his lodging, adjoining the classroom and giving also onto the plateau to the east. Like the class windows, his window looked to the south too. On that side the school was a few kilometers from the point where the plateau began to slope toward the south. In clear weather could be seen the purple mass of the mountain range where the gap opened onto the desert.

Somewhat warmed, Daru returned to the window from which he had first seen the two men. They were no longer visible. Hence they must have tackled the rise. The sky was not so dark, for the snow had stopped falling during the night. The morning had opened with a dirty light which had scarcely become brighter as the ceiling of clouds lifted. At two in the afternoon it seemed as if the day were merely beginning. But still this was better than those three days when the thick snow was falling amidst unbroken darkness with little gusts of wind that rattled the double door of the classroom. Then Daru had spent long hours in his room, leaving it only to go to the shed and feed the chickens or get some coal. Fortunately the delivery truck from Tadjid, the nearest village to the north, had brought his supplies two days before the blizzard. It would return in forty-eight hours.

Besides, he had enough to resist a siege, for the little room was cluttered with bags of wheat that the administration left as a stock to distribute to those of his pupils whose families had suffered from the drought. Actually they had all been victims because they were all poor. Every day Daru would distribute a ration to the children. They had missed it, he knew, during these bad days. Possibly one of the fathers or big brothers would come this afternoon and he could supply them with grain. It was just a matter of carrying them over to the next harvest. Now shiploads of wheat were arriving from France and the worst was over. But it would be hard to forget that poverty, that army of ragged ghosts wandering in the sunlight, the plateaus burned to a cinder month after month, the earth shriveled up little by little, literally scorched, every stone bursting into dust under one's foot. The sheep had died then by thousands and even a few men, here and there, sometimes without anyone's knowing.

5 In contrast with such poverty, he who lived almost like a monk in his remote schoolhouse, nonetheless satisfied with the little he had and with the rough life, had felt like a lord with his whitewashed walls, his narrow couch, his unpainted shelves, his well, and his weekly provision of water and food. And suddenly this snow, without warning, without the foretaste of rain. This is the way the region was, cruel to live in, even without men—who didn't help matters either. But Daru had been born here. Everywhere else, he felt exiled.

He stepped out onto the terrace in front of the schoolhouse. The two men were now halfway up the slope. He recognized the horseman as Balducci, the old gendarme he had known for a long time. Balducci was holding on the end of a rope an Arab who was walking behind him with hands bound and head lowered. The gendarme waved a greeting to which Daru did not reply, lost as he was in contemplation of the Arab dressed in a faded blue jellaba, his feet in sandals but covered with socks of heavy raw wool, his head surmounted by a narrow, short *chèche*. They were approaching. Balducci was holding back his horse in order not to hurt the Arab, and the group was advancing slowly.

Within earshot, Balducci shouted: "One hour to do the three kilometers from El Ameur!" Daru did not answer. Short and square in his thick sweater, he watched them climb. Not once had the Arab raised his head. "Hello" said Daru when they got up onto the terrace. "Come in and warm up." Balducci painfully got down from his horse without letting go the rope. From under his bristling mustache he smiled at the schoolmaster. His little dark eyes, deep-set under a tanned forehead, and his mouth surrounded with wrinkles made him look attentive and studious. Daru took the bridle, led the horse to the shed, and came back to the two men, who were now waiting for him in the school. He led them into his room. "I am going to heat up the classroom," he said. "We'll be more comfortable there." When he entered the room again, Balducci was on the couch. He had undone the rope tying him to the Arab, who had squatted near the stove. His hands still bound, the *chèche* pushed back on his head, he was looking toward the window. At first Daru noticed only his huge lips, fat, smooth, almost Negroid; yet his nose was straight, his eyes were dark and full of fever. The *chèche* revealed an obstinate forehead and, under the weathered skin now rather discolored by the cold, the whole face had a restless and rebellious look that struck Daru when the Arab, turning his face toward him, looked him straight in the eyes. "Go into the other room," said the schoolmaster, "and I'll make you some mint tea." "Thanks," Balducci said. "What a chore! How I long for retirement." And addressing his prisoner in Arabic: "Come on, you." The Arab got up and, slowly, holding his bound wrists in front of him, went into the classroom.

With the tea, Daru brought a chair. But Balducci was already enthroned on the nearest pupil's desk and the Arab had squatted against the teacher's platform facing the stove, which stood between the desk and the window. When he held out the glass of tea to the prisoner, Daru hesitated at the sight of his bound hands. "He might perhaps be untied." "Sure," said

Balducci, "that was for the trip." He started to get to his feet. But Daru, setting the glass on the floor, had knelt beside the Arab. Without saying anything, the Arab watched him with his feverish eyes. Once his hands were free, he rubbed his swollen wrists against each other, took the glass of tea, and sucked up the burning liquid in swift little sips.

"Good," said Daru. "And where are you headed?"

Balducci withdrew his mustache from the tea. "Here, son."

"Odd pupils! And you're spending the night?"

"No. I'm going back to El Ameur. And you will deliver this fellow to Tinguit. He is expected at police headquarters."

Balducci was looking at Daru with a friendly little smile.

"What's this story?" asked the schoolmaster. "Are you pulling my leg?"

"No, son. Those are the orders."

"The orders? I'm not . . ." Daru hesitated, not wanting to hurt the old Corsican. "I mean, that's not my job."

"What! What's the meaning of that? In wartime people do all kinds of jobs."

"Then I'll wait for the declaration of war!"

Balducci nodded.

"O.K. But the orders exist and they concern you too. Things are brewing, it appears. There is talk of a forthcoming revolt. We are mobilized, in a way."

Daru still had his obstinate look.

"Listen, son," Balducci said. "I like you and you must understand. There's only a dozen of us at El Ameur to patrol throughout the whole territory of a small department and I must get back in a hurry. I was told to hand this guy over to you and return without delay. He couldn't be kept there. His village was beginning to stir; they wanted to take him back. You must take him to Tinguit tomorrow before the day is over. Twenty kilometers shouldn't faze a husky fellow like you. After that, all will be over. You'll come back to your pupils and your comfortable life."

Behind the wall the horse could be heard snorting and pawing the earth. Daru was looking out the window. Decidedly, the weather was clearing and the light was increasing over the snowy plateau. When all the snow was melted, the sun would take over again and once more would burn the fields of stone. For days, still, the unchanging sky would shed its dry light on the solitary expanse where nothing had any connection with man.

"After all," he said, turning around toward Balducci, "what did he do?" And, before the gendarme had opened his mouth, he asked: "Does he speak French?"

"No, not a word. We had been looking for him for a month, but they were hiding him. He killed his cousin."

"Is he against us?"

"I don't think so. But you can never be sure."

"Why did he kill?"

"A family squabble, I think. One owed the other grain, it seems. It's not at all clear. In short, he killed his cousin with a billhook. You know, like a sheep, *kreezk!*"

Balducci made the gesture of drawing a blade across his throat and the Arab, his attention attracted, watched him with a sort of anxiety. Daru felt a sudden wrath against the man, against all men with their rotten spite, their tireless hates, their blood lust.

"And you?" he asked.

"After you. I'll eat too."

The thick lips opened slightly. The Arab hesitated, then bit into the cake determinedly.

The meal over, the Arab looked at the schoolmaster. "Are you the judge?"

"No, I'm simply keeping you until tomorrow."

"Why do you eat with me?"

"I'm hungry."

The Arab fell silent. Daru got up and went out. He brought back a folding bed from the shed, set it up between the table and the stove, perpendicular to his own bed. From a large suitcase which, upright in a corner, served as a shelf for papers, he took two blankets and arranged them on the camp bed. Then he stopped, felt useless, and sat down on his bed. There was nothing more to do or to get ready. He had to look at this man. He looked at him, therefore, trying to imagine his face bursting with rage. He couldn't do so. He could see nothing but the dark yet shining eyes and the animal mouth.

"Why did you kill him?" he asked in a voice whose hostile tone surprised him.

The Arab looked away.

"He ran away. I ran after him."

He raised his eyes to Daru again and they were full of a sort of woeful interrogation. "Now what will they do to me?"

"Are you afraid?"

He stiffened, turning his eyes away.

"Are you sorry?"

The Arab stared at him openmouthed. Obviously he did not understand. Daru's annoyance was growing. At the same time he felt awkward and self-conscious with his big body wedged between the two beds.

"Lie down there," he said impatiently. "That's your bed."

The Arab didn't move. He called to Daru:

"Tell me!"

The schoolmaster looked at him.

"Is the gendarme coming back tomorrow?"

"I don't know."

"Are you coming with us?"

"I don't know. Why?"

The prisoner got up and stretched out on top of the blankets, his feet toward the window. The light from the electric bulb shone straight into his eyes and he closed them at once.

"Why?" Daru repeated, standing beside the bed.

The Arab opened his eyes under the blinding light and looked at him, trying not to blink.

"Come with us," he said.

In the middle of the night, Daru was still not asleep. He had gone to bed after undressing completely; he generally slept naked. But when he suddenly realized that he had nothing on, he hesitated. He felt vulnerable and the temptation came to him to put his clothes back on. Then he shrugged his shoulders; after all, he wasn't a child and, if need be, he could break his adversary in two. From his bed he could observe him, lying on his back, still motionless with his eyes closed under the harsh light. When Daru turned out the light, the darkness seemed to coagulate all of a sudden. Little by little, the night came back to life in the window where the starless sky was stirring gently. The schoolmaster soon made out the body laying at his feet. The Arab still did not move, but his eyes seemed open. A faint wind was prowling around the schoolhouse. Perhaps it would drive away the clouds and the sun would reappear.

During the night the wind increased. The hens fluttered a little and then were silent. The Arab turned over on his side with his back to Daru, who thought he heard him moan. Then he listened for his guest's breathing, become heavier and more regular. He listened to that breath so close to him and mused without being able to go to sleep. In this room where he had been sleeping alone for a year, this presence bothered him. But it bothered him also by imposing on him a sort of brotherhood he knew well but refused to accept in the present circumstances. Men who share the same rooms, soldiers or prisoners, develop a strange alliance as if, having cast off their armor with their clothing, they fraternized every evening, over and above their differences, in the ancient community of dream and fatigue. But Daru shook himself; he didn't like such musings, and it was essential to sleep.

A little later, however, when the Arab stirred slightly, the schoolmaster was still not asleep. When the prisoner made a second move, he stiffened, on the alert. The Arab was lifting himself slowly on his arms with almost the motion of a sleepwalker. Seated upright in bed, he waited motionless without turning his head toward Daru, as if he were listening attentively. Daru did not stir, it had just occurred to him that the revolver was still in the drawer of his desk. It was better to act at once. Yet he continued to observe the prisoner, who, with the same slithery motion, put his feet on the ground, waited again, then began to stand up slowly. Daru was about to call out to him when the Arab began to walk, in a quite natural but extraordinarily silent way. He was heading toward the door at the end of the room that opened into the shed. He lifted the latch with precaution and went out, pushing the door behind him but without shutting it. Daru had not stirred. "He is running away," he merely thought. "Good riddance!" Yet he listened attentively. The hens were not fluttering; the guest must be on the plateau. A faint sound of water reached him, and he didn't know what it was until the Arab again stood framed in the doorway, closed the door carefully, and came back to bed without a sound. Then Daru turned his back on him and fell asleep. Still later he seemed, from the depths of his sleep, to hear furtive steps around the schoolhouse. "I'm dreaming! I'm dreaming!" he repeated to himself. And he went on sleeping.

When he awoke, the sky was clear; the loose window let in a cold, pure air. The Arab was asleep, hunched up under the blankets now, his mouth open, utterly relaxed. But when Daru shook him, he started dreadfully, staring at Daru with wild eyes as if he had never seem him and such a frightened expression that the schoolmaster stepped back. "Don't be afraid. It's me. You must eat." The Arab nodded his head and said yes. Calm had returned to his face, but his expression was vacant and listless.

The coffee was ready. They drank it seated together on the folding bed as they munched their pieces of the cake. Then Daru led the Arab under the shed and showed him the faucet where he washed. He went back into the room, folded the blankets and the bed, made his own bed and put the room in order. Then he went through the classroom and out onto the terrace. The sun was already rising in the blue sky; a soft, bright light was bathing the deserted plateau. On the ridge the snow was melting in spots. The stones were about to reappear. Crouched on the edge of the plateau, the schoolmaster looked at the deserted expanse. He thought of Balducci. He had hurt him, for he had sent him off in a way as if he didn't want to be associated with him. He could still hear the gendarme's farewell and, without knowing why, he felt strangely empty and vulnerable. At that moment, from the other side of the schoolhouse, the prisoner coughed. Daru listened to him almost despite himself and then, furious, threw a pebble that whistled through the air before sinking into the snow. That man's stupid crime revolted him, but to hand him over was contrary to honor. Merely thinking of it made him smart with humiliation. And he cursed at one and the same time his own people who had sent him this Arab and the Arab too who had dared to kill and not managed to get away. Daru got up, walked in a circle of the terrace, waited motionless, and then went back into the schoolhouse.

The Arab, leaning over the cement floor of the shed, was washing his teeth with two fingers. Daru looked at him and said: "Come." He went back into the room ahead of the prisoner. He slipped a hunting-jacket on over his sweater and put on walking-shoes. Standing, he waited until the Arab had put on his *chèche* and sandals. They went into the classroom and the schoolmaster pointed to the exit, saying: "Go ahead." The fellow didn't budge. "I'm coming," said Daru. The Arab went out. Daru went back into the room and made a package of pieces of rusk, dates, and sugar. In the classroom, before going out, he hesitated a second in front of his desk, then crossed the threshold and locked the door. "That's the way," he said. He started toward the east, followed by the prisoner. But, a short distance from the schoolhouse, he thought he heard a slight sound behind them. He retraced his steps and examined the surroundings of the house; there was no one there. The Arab watched him without seeming to understand. "Come on," said Daru.

They walked for an hour and rested beside a sharp peak of limestone. The snow was melting faster and faster and the sun was drinking up the puddles at once, rapidly cleaning the plateau, which gradually dried and vibrated like the air itself. When they resumed walking, the ground rang under their feet. From time to time a bird rent the space in front of them with a joyful cry. Daru breathed in deeply the fresh morning light. He felt a sort of rapture before the vast familiar expanse, now almost entirely yellow under its domes of blue sky. They walked an hour more, descending toward the south. They reached a level height made up of crumbly rocks. From there on, the plateau sloped down, eastward, toward a low plain where there were a few spindly trees and to the south, toward outcroppings of rock that gave the landscape a chaotic look.

Daru surveyed the two directions. There was nothing but the sky on the horizon. Not a man could be seen. He turned toward the Arab, who was looking at him blankly. Daru held out the package to him. "Take it," he said. "There are dates, bread, and sugar. You can hold out for two days. Here are a thousand francs too." The Arab took the package and the money but kept his full hands at chest level as if he didn't know what to do with what was being given him. "Now look," the schoolmaster said as he pointed in the direction of the east, "there's the way to Tinguit. You have a two-hour walk. At Tinguit you'll find the administration and the police. They are expecting you." The Arab looked toward the east, still holding the package and the money against his chest. Daru took his elbow and turned him rather roughly toward the south. At the foot of the height on which they stood could be seen a faint path. "That's the trail across the plateau. In a day's walk from here you'll find pasturelands and the first nomads. They'll take you in and shelter you according to their law." The Arab had now turned toward Daru and a sort of panic was visible in his expression. "Listen," he said. Daru shook his head: "No, be quiet. Now I'm leaving you." He turned his back on him, took two long steps in the direction of the school, looked hesitantly at the motionless Arab, and started off again. For a few minutes he heard nothing but his own step resounding on the cold ground and did not turn his head. A moment later, however, he turned around. The Arab was still there on the edge of the hill, his arms hanging now, and he was looking at the schoolmaster. Daru felt something rise in his throat. But he swore with impatience, waved vaguely, and started off again. He had already gone some distance when he again stopped and looked. There was no longer anyone on the hill.

Daru hesitated. The sun was now rather high in the sky and was begin- 105
ning to beat down on his head. The schoolmaster retraced his steps, at first somewhat uncertainly, then with decision. When he reached the little hill, he was bathed in sweat. He climbed it as fast as he could and stopped, out of breath, at the top. The rock-fields to the south stood out sharply against the blue sky, but on the plain to the west a steamy heat was already rising. And in that slight haze, Daru, with heavy heart, made out the Arab walking slowly on the road to prison.

A little later, standing before the window of the classroom, the schoolmaster was watching the clear light bathing the whole surface of the plateau, but he hardly saw it. Behind him on the blackboard, among the winding French rivers, sprawled the clumsily chalked-up words he had just read: "You handed over our brother. You will pay for this." Daru looked at the sky, the plateau, and, beyond, the invisible lands stretching all the way to the sea. In this vast landscape he had loved so much, he was alone.

Analyzing the Text

1. What do we know about Daru's background that would explain why he does not wish to step outside his role as teacher to enforce the rulings of the authorities? Between what conflicting loyalties is Daru torn?
2. How does Daru's feeling of common humanity make it increasingly difficult for him to turn the Arab over to the authorities? How does Daru try to avoid the responsibility of turning in the Arab?

Understanding Camus's Techniques

1. How do the descriptions of the physical environment (the stony landscape, the snow that suddenly falls, and the thaw that follows) underscore the human drama?
2. What is the significance of the message written on the blackboard? How are Daru's actions toward the Arab misunderstood by the local populace?

Arguing for an Interpretation

1. Why does the Arab, although free to choose, continue on the path leading to the town where he will be caught and imprisoned, and possibly even executed?
2. How does the story express Camus's existentialist philosophy about the unavoidability of making choices and the burdens of freedom?

H. G. Wells

H. G. (Herbert George) Wells (1866–1946) is generally acknowledged to have originated the genre of literature we now call science fiction with his novel The Time Machine *(1895). Born into a poor family and afflicted with tuberculosis, Wells was a student of the biologist Thomas Henry Huxley (whose grandson Aldous Huxley wrote* Brave New World *in 1932), who opened his mind to Charles Darwin's theories and the concept that humanity was an evolving species. Wells joined the Fabian Society of Sociologists in 1903 and was strongly influenced by their concept of a utopian political state. His brilliant novels include* The Island of Dr. Moreau *(1896),* The Invisible Man *(1897), and* The War of the Worlds *(1898), which was the basis of Orson Welles's famous 1938 radio play (which caused a panic throughout the United States). "The Country of the Blind" (1911) is perhaps Wells's finest short story and will evoke for many, Plato's "The Allegory of the Cave."*

The Country of the Blind

Three hundred miles and more from Chimborazo, one hundred from the snows of Cotopaxi, in the wildest wastes of Ecuador's Andes, there lies that mysterious mountain valley, cut off from the world of men, the Country of the Blind. Long years ago that valley lay so far open to the world that men might come at last through frightful gorges and over an icy pass into its equable meadows; and thither indeed men came, a family or so of Peruvian half-breeds fleeing from the lust and tyranny of an evil Spanish ruler. Then came the stupendous outbreak of Mindobamba, when it was night in Quito for seventeen days, and the water was boiling at Yaguachi and all the fish floating dying even as far as Guayaquil; everywhere along the Pacific slopes there were landslips and swift thawings and sudden floods, and one whole side of the Arauca crest slipped and came down in thunder, and cut off the Country of the Blind for ever from the exploring feet of men. But one of these early settlers had chanced to be on the hither side of the gorges when the world had so terribly shaken itself, and he perforce had to forget his wife and his child and all the friends and possessions he had left up there, and start life over again in the lower world. He started it again but ill, blindness overtook him, and he died of punishment in the mines; but the story he told begot a legend that lingers along the length of the Cordilleras of the Andes to this day.

He told of his reason for venturing back from that fastness, into which he had first been carried lashed to a llama, beside a vast bale of gear, when he was a child. The valley, he said, had in it all that the heart of man could desire—sweet water, pasture, and even climate, slopes of rich brown soil with tangles of a shrub that bore an excellent fruit, and on one side great hanging forests of pine that held the avalanches high. Far overhead, on three sides, vast cliffs of grey-green rock were capped by cliffs of ice; but the glacier stream came not to them but flowed away by the farther slopes, and only now and then huge ice masses fell on the valley side. In this valley it neither rained nor snowed, but the abundant springs gave a rich green pasture, that irrigation would spread over all the valley space. The settlers did well indeed there. Their beasts did well and multiplied, and but one thing marred their happiness. Yet it was enough to mar it greatly. A strange disease had come upon them, and had made all the children born to them there—and indeed, several older children also—blind. It was to seek some charm or antidote against this plague of blindness that he had with fatigue and danger and difficulty returned down the gorge. In those days, in such cases, men did not think of germs and infections but of sins; and it seemed to him that the reason of this affliction must lie in the negligence of these priestless immigrants to set up a shrine so soon as they entered the valley. He wanted a shrine—a handsome, cheap, effectual shrine—to be erected in the valley; he wanted relics and such-like potent things of faith, blessed objects and mysterious medals and prayers. In his wallet he had a bar of native silver for which he would not account; he insisted there was none in the valley with something of the insistence of an inexpert liar. They had all clubbed their money and ornaments together, having little need for such treasure up there, he said, to buy them holy help against their ill. I figure this dim-eyed young mountaineer, sunburnt, gaunt, and anxious, hat-brim clutched feverishly, a man all unused to the ways of the lower world, telling this story to some keen-eyed, attentive priest before the great convulsion; I can picture him presently seeking to return with pious and infallible remedies against that trouble, and the infinite dismay with which he must have faced the tumbled vastness where the gorge had once come out. But the rest of his story of mischances is lost to me, save that I know of his evil death after several years. Poor stray from that remoteness! The stream that had once made the gorge now bursts from the mouth of a rocky cave, and the legend his poor, ill-told story set going developed into the legend of a race of blind men somewhere "over there" one may still hear to-day.

And amidst the little population of that now isolated and forgotten valley the disease ran its course. The old became groping and purblind, the young saw but dimly, and the children that were born to them saw never at all. But life was very easy in that snow-rimmed basin, lost to all the world, with neither thorns nor briars, with no evil insects nor any beasts save the gentle breed of llamas they had lugged and thrust and followed up the beds of the shrunken rivers in the gorges up which they had come. The seeing had become purblind so gradually that they scarcely noted their loss. They guided the sightless youngsters hither and thither until they knew the whole valley marvellously, and when at last sight died out among them the race lived on. They had even time to adapt themselves to the blind control of fire, which they made carefully in stoves of stone. They were a simple strain of people at the first, unlettered, only slightly touched with the Spanish civilisation, but with something of a tradition of the arts of old Peru and of its lost philosophy. Generation followed generation. They forgot many things; they devised many things. Their tradition of the greater world they came from became mythical in colour and uncertain. In all things save sight they were strong and able; and presently the chance of birth and heredity sent one who had an original mind and who could talk and persuade among them, and then afterwards another. These two passed, leaving their effects, and the little community grew in numbers and in understanding, and met and settled social and economic problems that arose. Generation followed generation. Generation followed generation. There came a time when a child was born who was fifteen generations from that ancestor who went out of the valley with a bar of silver to seek God's aid, and who never returned. Thereabouts it chanced that a man came into this community from the outer world. And this is the story of that man.

He was a mountaineer from the country near Quito, a man who had been down to the sea and had seen the world, a reader of books in an original way, an acute and enterprising man, and he was taken on by a party of Englishmen who had come out to Ecuador to climb mountains, to replace one of their three Swiss guides who had fallen ill. He climbed here and he climbed there, and then came the attempt on Parascotopetl, the Matterhorn of the Andes, in which he was lost to the outer world. The story of the accident has been written a dozen times. Pointer's narrative is the best. He tells how the party worked their difficult and almost vertical way up to the very foot of the last and greatest precipice, and how they built a night shelter amidst the snow upon a little shelf of rock, and, with a touch of real dramatic power, how presently they found Nunez had gone from them. They shouted, and there was no reply, shouted and whistled, and for the rest of that night they slept no more.

5 As the morning broke they saw the traces of his fall. It seems impossible he could have uttered a sound. He had slipped eastward towards the unknown side of the mountain; far below he had struck a steep slope of snow, and ploughed his way down it in the midst of a snow avalanche. His track went straight to the edge of a frightful precipice, and beyond that everything was hidden. Far, far below, and hazy with distance, they could see trees rising out of a narrow, shut-in valley—the lost Country of the Blind. But they did not know it was the lost Country of the Blind, nor distinguish it in any way from any other narrow streak of upland valley. Unnerved by this disaster, they abandoned their attempt in the afternoon, and Pointer was called away to the war before he could make another attack. To this day Parascotopetl lifts an unconquered crest, and Pointer's shelter crumbles unvisited amidst the snows.

And the man who fell survived.

At the end of the slope he fell a thousand feet, and came down in the midst of a cloud of snow upon a snow slope even steeper than the one above. Down this he was whirled, stunned and insensible, but without a bone broken in his body; and then at last came to gentler slopes, and at last rolled out and lay still, buried amidst a softening heap of the white masses that had accompanied and saved him. He came to himself with a dim fancy that he was ill in bed; then realised his position with a mountaineer's intelligence, and worked himself loose and, after a rest or so, out until he saw the stars. He rested flat upon his chest for a space, wondering where he was and what had happened to him. He explored his limbs, and discovered that several of his buttons were gone and his coat turned over his head. His knife had gone from his pocket and his hat was lost, though he had tied it under his chin. He recalled that he had been looking for loose stones to raise his piece of the shelter wall. His ice-axe had disappeared.

He decided he must have fallen, and looked up to see, exaggerated by the ghastly light of the rising moon, the tremendous flight he had taken. For a while he lay, gazing blankly at that vast pale cliff towering above, rising moment by moment out of a subsiding tide of darkness. Its phantasmal, mysterious beauty held him for a space, and then he was seized with a paroxysm of sobbing laughter. . . .

After a great interval of time he became aware that he was near the lower edge of the snow. Below, down what was now a moonlit and practicable slope, he saw the dark and broken appearance of rock-strewn turf. He struggled to his feet, aching in every joint and limb, got down painfully from the heaped loose snow about him, went downward until he was on the turf, and there dropped rather than lay beside a boulder, drank deep from the flask in his inner pocket, and instantly fell asleep.

He was awakened by the singing of birds in the trees far below. 10

He sat up and perceived he was on a little alp at the foot of a vast precipice, that was grooved by the gully down which he and his snow had come. Over against him another wall of rock reared itself against the sky. The gorge between these precipices ran east and west and was full of the morning sunlight, which lit to the westward the mass of fallen mountain that closed the descending gorge. Below him it seemed there was a precipice equally steep, but behind the snow in the gully he found a sort of chimney-cleft dripping with snow-water down which a desperate man might venture. He found it easier than it seemed, and came at last to another desolate alp, and then after a rock climb of no particular difficulty to a steep slope of trees. He took his bearings and turned his face up the gorge, for he saw it opened out above upon green meadows, among which he now glimpsed quite distinctly a cluster of stone huts of unfamiliar fashion. At times his progress was like clambering along the face of a wall, and after a time the rising sun ceased to strike along the gorge, the voices of the singing birds died away, and the air grew cold and dark about him. But the distant valley with its houses was all the brighter for that. He came presently to talus, and among the rocks he noted—for he was an observant man—an unfamiliar fern that seemed to clutch out of the crevices with intense green hands. He picked a frond or so and gnawed its stalk and found it helpful.

About midday he came at last out of the throat of the gorge into the plain and the sunlight. He was stiff and weary; he sat down in the shadow of a rock, filled up his flask with water from a spring and drank it down, and remained for a time resting before he went on to the houses.

They were very strange to his eyes, and indeed the whole aspect of that valley became, as he regarded it, queerer and more unfamiliar. The greater part of its surface was lush green meadow, starred with many beautiful flowers, irrigated with extraordinary care, and bearing evidence of systematic cropping piece by piece. High up and ringing the valley about was a wall, and what appeared to be a circumferential water-channel, from which the little trickles of water that fed the meadow plants came, and on the higher slopes above this flocks of llamas cropped the scanty herbage. Sheds, apparently shelters or feeding-places for the llamas, stood against the boundary wall here and there. The irrigation streams ran together into a main channel down the centre of the valley, and this was enclosed on either side by a wall breast high. This gave a singularly urban quality to this secluded place, a quality that was greatly enhanced by the fact that a number of paths paved with black and white stones, and each with a curious little kerb at the side, ran hither and thither in an orderly manner. The houses of the central village were quite unlike the casual and higgledy-piggledy agglomeration of the mountain villages he knew; they stood in a continuous row on either side of a central street of astonishing cleanness; here and there their parti-coloured façade was pierced by a door, and not a solitary window broke their even frontage. They were parti-coloured with extraordinary irregularity; smeared with a sort of plaster that was sometimes grey, sometimes drab, sometimes slate-coloured or dark brown; and it was the sight of this wild plastering first brought the word "blind" into the thoughts of the explorer. "The good man who did that," he thought, "must have been as blind as a bat."

He descended a steep place, and so came to the wall and channel that ran about the valley, near where the latter spouted out its surplus contents into the deeps of the gorge in a thin and wavering thread of cascade. He could now see a number of men and women resting on piled heaps of grass, as if taking a siesta, in the remoter part of the meadow, and nearer the village a number of recumbent children, and then nearer at hand three men carrying pails on yokes along a little path that ran from the encircling wall towards the houses. These latter were clad in garments of llama cloth and boots and belts of leather, and they wore caps of cloth with back and ear flaps. They followed one another in single file, walking slowly and yawning as they walked, like men who have been up all night. There was something so reassuringly prosperous and respectable in their bearing that after a moment's hesitation Nunez stood forward as conspicuously as possible upon his rock, and gave vent to a mighty shout that echoed round the valley.

The three men stopped, and moved their heads as though they were 15
looking about them. They turned their faces this way and that, and Nunez gesticulated with freedom. But they did not appear to see him for all his gestures, and after a time, directing themselves towards the mountains far away to the right, they shouted as if in answer. Nunez bawled again, and then once more, and as he gestured ineffectually the word "blind" came up to the top of his thoughts. "The fools must be blind," he said.

When at last, after much shouting and wrath, Nunez crossed the stream by a little bridge, came through a gate in the wall, and approached them, he was sure that they were blind. He was sure that this was the Country of the Blind of which the legends told. Conviction had sprung upon him, and a sense of great and rather enviable adventure. The three stood side by side, not looking at him, but with their ears directed towards him, judging him by his unfamiliar steps. They stood close together like men a little afraid, and he could see their eyelids closed and sunken, as though the very balls beneath had shrunk away. There was an expression near awe on their faces.

"A man," one said, in hardly recognisable Spanish—"a man it is—a man or a spirit—coming down from the rocks."

But Nunez advanced with the confident steps of a youth who enters upon life. All the old stories of the lost valley and the Country of the Blind had come back to his mind, and through his thoughts ran this old proverb, as if it were a refrain—

"In the Country of the Blind the One-eyed Man is King."

"In the Country of the Blind the One-eyed Man is King."

And very civilly he gave them greeting. He talked to them and used his eyes.

"Where does he come from, brother Pedro?" asked one.

"Down out of the rocks."

"Over the mountains I come," said Nunez, "out of the country beyond there—where men can see. From near Bogota, where there are a hundred thousands of people, and where the city passes out of sight."

"Sight?" muttered Pedro. "Sight?"

"He comes," said the second blind man, "out of the rocks."

The cloth of their coats Nunez saw was curiously fashioned, each with a different sort of stitching.

They startled him by a simultaneous movement towards him, each with a hand outstretched. He stepped back from the advance of these spread fingers.

"Come hither," said the third blind man, following his motion and clutching him neatly.

And they held Nunez and felt him over, saying no word further until they had done so.

"Carefully," he cried, with a finger in his eye, and found they thought that organ, with its fluttering lids, a queer thing in him. They went over it again.

"A strange creature, Correa," said the one called Pedro. "Feel the coarseness of his hair. Like a llama's hair."

"Rough he is as the rocks that begot him," said Correa, investigating Nunez's unshaven chin with a soft and slightly moist hand. "Perhaps he will grow finer." Nunez struggled a little under their examination, but they gripped him firm.

"Carefully," he said again.

"He speaks," said the third man. "Certainly he is a man."

"Ugh!" said Pedro, at the roughness of his coat.

"And you have come into the world?" asked Pedro.

"Out of the world. Over mountains and glaciers; right over above there, half-way to the sun. Out of the great big world that goes down, twelve days' journey to the sea."

They scarcely seemed to heed him. "Our fathers have told us men may be made by the forces of Nature," said Correa. "It is the warmth of things and moisture, and rottenness—rottenness."

"Let us lead him to the elders," said Pedro.

"Shout first," said Correa, "lest the children be afraid. This is a marvelous occasion."

So they shouted, and Pedro went first and took Nunez by the hand to lead him to the houses.

He drew his hand away. "I can see," he said.

"See?" said Correa.

"Yes, see," said Nunez, turning towards him, and stumbled against Pedro's pail.

"His senses are still imperfect," said the third blind man. "He stumbles, and talks unmeaning words. Lead him by the hand."

"As you will," said Nunez, and was led along, laughing.

It seemed they knew nothing of sight.

Well, all in good time, he would teach them.

He heard people shouting, and saw a number of figures gathering together in the middle roadway of the village.

He found it taxed his nerve and patience more than he had anticipated, that first encounter with the population of the Country of the Blind. The place seemed larger as he drew near to it, and the smeared plasterings queerer, and a crowd of children and men and women (the women and girls, he was pleased to note, had some of them quite sweet faces, for all that their eyes were shut and sunken) came about him, holding on to him, touching him with soft, sensitive hands, smelling at him, and listening at every word he spoke. Some of the maidens and children, however, kept aloof as if afraid, and indeed his voice seemed coarse and rude beside their softer notes. They mobbed him. His three guides kept close to him with an effect of proprietorship, and said again and again, "A wild man out of the rocks."

"Bogota," he said. "Bogota. Over the mountain crests."

"A wild man—using wild words," said Pedro. "Did you hear that—*Bogota?* His mind is hardly formed yet. He has only the beginnings of speech."

A little boy nipped his hand. "Bogota!" he said mockingly.

"Ay! A city to your village. I come from the great world—where men have eyes and see."

"His name's Bogota," they said.

"He stumbled," said Correa, "stumbled twice as we came hither."

"Bring him to the elders."

And they thrust him suddenly through a doorway into a room as black as pitch, save at the end there faintly glowed a fire. The crowd closed in behind him and shut out all but the faintest glimmer of day, and before he could arrest himself he had fallen headlong over the feet of a seated man. His arm, outflung, struck the face of someone else as he went down; he felt the soft impact of features and heard a cry of anger, and for a moment he struggled against a number of hands that clutched him. It was a one-sided fight. An inkling of the situation came to him, and he lay quiet.

"I fell down," he said; "I couldn't see in this pitchy darkness."

There was a pause as if the unseen persons about him tried to understand his words. Then the voice of Correa said: "He is but newly formed. He stumbles as he walks and mingles words that mean nothing with his speech."

Others also said things about him that he heard or understood imperfectly.

"May I sit up?" he asked, in a pause. "I will not struggle against you again."

They consulted and let him rise.

The voice of an older man began to question him, and Nunez found himself trying to explain the great world out of which he had fallen, and the sky and mountains and sight and such-like marvels, to these elders who sat in darkness in the Country of the Blind. And they would believe and understand nothing whatever he told them, a thing quite outside his expectation. They would not even understand many of his words. For fourteen generations these people had been blind and cut off from all the seeing world; the names for all the things of sight had faded and changed; the story of the outer world was faded and changed to a child's story; and they had ceased to concern themselves with anything beyond the rocky slopes above their circling wall. Blind men of genius had arisen among them and questioned the shreds of belief and tradition they had brought with them from their seeing days, and had dismissed all these things as idle fancies, and replaced them with new and saner explanations. Much of their imagination had shrivelled with their eyes, and they had made for themselves new imaginations with their ever more sensitive ears and finger-tips. Slowly Nunez realised this; that his expectation of wonder and reverence at his origin and his gifts was not to be borne out; and after his poor attempt to explain sight to them had been set aside as the confused version of a new-made being describing the marvels of his incoherent sensations, he subsided, a little dashed, into listening to their instruction. And the eldest of the blind men explained to him life and philosophy and religion, how that the world (meaning their valley) had been first an empty hollow in the rocks, and then had come, first, inanimate things without the gift of touch, and llamas and a few other creatures that had little sense, and then men, and at last angels, whom one could hear singing and making fluttering sounds, but whom no one could touch at all, which puzzled Nunez greatly until he thought of the birds.

He went on to tell Nunez how this time had been divided into the warm and the cold, which are the blind equivalents of day and night, and how it was good to sleep in the warm and work during the cold, so that now, but for his advent, the whole town of the blind would have been asleep. He said Nunez must have been specially created to learn and serve the wisdom they had acquired, and for that all his mental incoherency and stumbling behavior he must have courage, and do his best to learn, and at that all the people in the doorway murmured encouragingly. He said the night—for the blind call their day night—was now far gone, and it behooved every one to go back to sleep. He asked Nunez if he knew how to sleep, and Nunez said he did, but that before sleep he wanted food.

They brought him food—llama's milk in a bowl, and rough salted bread—and led him into a lonely place to eat out of their hearing, and afterwards to slumber until the chill of the mountain evening roused them to begin their day again. But Nunez slumbered not at all.

Instead, he sat up in the place where they had left him, resting his limbs and turning the unanticipated circumstances of his arrival over and over in his mind.

Every now and then he laughed, sometimes with amusement, and 70
sometimes with indignation.

"Unformed mind!" he said. "Got no senses yet! They little know they've been insulting their heaven-sent king and master. I see I must bring them to reason. Let me think—let me think."

He was still thinking when the sun set.

Nunez had an eye for all beautiful things, and it seemed to him that the glow upon the snowfields and glaciers that rose about the valley on every side was the most beautiful thing he had ever seen. His eyes went from that inaccessible glory to the village and irrigated fields, fast sinking into the twilight, and suddenly a wave of emotion took him, and he thanked God from the bottom of his heart that the power of sight had been given him.

He heard a voice calling to him from out of the village.

"Ya ho there, Bogota! Come hither!"

At that he stood up smiling. He would show these people once and for all what sight would do for a man. They would seek him, but not find him.

"You move not, Bogota," said the voice.

He laughed noiselessly, and made two stealthy steps aside from the path.

"Trample not on the grass, Bogota; that is not allowed."

Nunez had scarcely heard the sound he made himself. He stopped amazed.

The owner of the voice came running up the piebald path towards him.

He stepped back into the pathway. "Here I am," he said.

"Why did you not come when I called you?" said the blind man. "Must you be led like a child? Cannot you hear the path as you walk?"

Nunez laughed. "I can see it," he said.

"There is no such word as *see,*" said the blind man, after a pause. "Cease this folly, and follow the sound of my feet."

Nunez followed, a little annoyed.

"My time will come," he said.

"You'll learn," the blind man answered. "There is much to learn in the world."

"Has no one told you, 'In the Country of the Blind the One-eyed Man is King'?"

"What is blind?" asked the blind man carelessly over his shoulder.

Four days passed, and the fifth found the King of the Blind still incognito, as a clumsy and useless stranger among his subjects.

It was, he found, much more difficult to proclaim himself than he had supposed, and in the meantime, while he meditated his *coup d'état,* he did what he was told and learned the manners and customs of the Country of the Blind. He found working and going about at night a particularly irksome thing, and he decided that that should be the first thing he would change.

They led a simple, laborious life, these people, with all the elements of virtue and happiness, as these things can be understood by men. They toiled, but not oppressively; they had food and clothing sufficient for their needs; they had days and seasons of rest; they made much of music and singing, and there was love among them, and little children.

It was marvellous with what confidence and precision they went about their ordered world. Everything, you see, had been made to fit their needs; each of the radiating paths of the valley area had a constant angle to the others, and was distinguished by a special notch upon its kerbing; all obstacles and irregularities of path or meadow had long since been cleared away; all their methods and procedure arose naturally from their special needs. Their senses had become marvellously acute; they could hear and judge the slightest gesture of a man a dozen paces away—could hear the very beating of his heart. Intonation had long replaced expression with them, and touches gesture, and their work with hoe and spade and fork was as free and confident as garden work can be. Their sensc of smell was extraordinarily fine; they could distinguish individual differences as readily as a dog can, and they went about the tending of the llamas, who lived among the rocks above and came to the wall for food and shelter, with ease and confidence. It was only when at last Nunez sought to assert himself that he found how easy and confident their movements could be.

He rebelled only after he had tried persuasion. 95

He tried at first on several occasions to tell them of sight. "Look you here, you people," he said. "There are things you do not understand in me."

Once or twice one or two of them attended to him; they sat with faces downcast and ears turned intelligently towards him, and he did his best to tell them what it was to see. Among his hearers was a girl, with eyelids less red and sunken than the others, so that one could almost fancy she was hiding eyes, whom especially he hoped to persuade. He spoke of the beauties of sight, of watching the mountains, of the sky and the sunrise, and they heard him with amused incredulity that presently became condemnatory. They told him there were indeed no mountains at all, but that the end of the rocks where the llamas grazed was indeed the end of the world; thence sprang a cavernous roof of the universe, from which the dew and the avalanches fell; and when he maintained stoutly the world had neither end nor roof such as they supposed, they said his thoughts were wicked. So far as he could describe sky and clouds and stars to them it seemed to them a hideous void, a terrible blankness in the place of the smooth roof to things in which they believed—it was an article of faith with them that the cavern roof was exquisitely smooth to the touch. He saw that in some manner he shocked them, and gave up that aspect of the matter altogether, and tried to show them the practical value of sight. One morning he saw Pedro in the path called Seventeen and coming towards the central houses, but still too far off for hearing or scent, and he told them as much. "In a little while," he prophesied, "Pedro will be here." An old man remarked that Pedro had no business on Path Seventeen, and then, as if in confirmation, that individual as he drew near turned and went transversely into Path Ten, and so back with nimble paces towards the outer wall. They mocked Nunez when Pedro did not arrive, and afterwards, when he asked Pedro questions to clear his character, Pedro denied and outfaced him, and was afterwards hostile to him.

Then he induced them to let him go a long way up the sloping meadows towards the wall with one complacent individual, and to him he promised to describe all that happened among the houses. He noted certain goings and comings, but the things that really seemed to signify to these people happened inside of or behind the windowless houses—the only things they took note of to test him by—and of these he could see or tell nothing; and it was after the failure of this attempt, and the ridicule they could not repress, that he resorted to force. He thought of seizing a spade and suddenly smiting one or two of them to earth, and so in fair combat showing the advantage of eyes. He went so far with that resolution as to seize his spade, and then he discovered a new thing about himself, and that was that it was impossible for him to hit a blind man in cold blood.

He hesitated, and found them all aware that he snatched up the spade. They stood alert, with their heads on one side, and bent ears towards him for what he would do next.

"Put that spade down," said one, and he felt a sort of helpless horror. 100
He came near obedience.

Then he thrust one backwards against a house wall, and fled past him and out of the village.

He went athwart one of their meadows, leaving a track of trampled grass behind his feet, and presently sat down by the side of one of their ways. He felt something of the buoyancy that comes to all men in the beginning of a fight, but more perplexity. He began to realise that you cannot even fight happily with creatures who stand upon a different mental basis to yourself. Far away he saw a number of men carrying spades and sticks come out of the street of houses, and advance in a spreading line along the several paths towards him. They advanced slowly, speaking frequently to one another, and ever and again the whole cordon would halt and sniff the air and listen.

The first time they did this Nunez laughed. But afterwards he did not laugh.

One struck his trail in the meadow grass, and came stooping and feeling his way along it.

For five minutes he watched the slow extension of the cordon, and 105
then his vague disposition to do something forthwith became frantic. He stood up, went a pace or so towards the circumferential wall, turned, and went back a little way. There they all stood in a crescent, still and listening.

He also stood still, gripping his spade very tightly in both hands. Should he charge them?

The pulse in his ears ran into the rhythm of "In the Country of the Blind the One-eyed Man is King!"

Should he charge them?

He looked back at the high and unclimbable wall behind—unclimbable because of its smooth plastering, but withal pierced with many little doors, and at the approaching line of seekers. Behind these, others were now coming out of the street of houses.

Should he charge them? 110

"Bogota!" called one. "Bogota! where are you?"

He gripped his spade still tighter, and advanced down the meadows towards the place of habitations, and directly he moved they converged upon him. "I'll hit them if they touch me," he swore; "by Heaven, I will. I'll hit." He called aloud, "Look here, I'm going to do what I like in this valley. Do you hear? I'm going to do what I like and go where I like!"

They were moving in upon him quickly, groping, yet moving rapidly. It was like playing blind man's buff, with everyone blindfolded except one. "Get hold of him!" cried one. He found himself in the arc of a loose curve of pursuers. He felt suddenly he must be active and resolute.

"You don't understand," he cried in a voice that was meant to be great and resolute, and which broke. "You are blind, and I can see. Leave me alone!"

"Bogota! Put down that spade, and come off the grass!" 115

The last order, grotesque in its urban familiarity, produced a gust of anger.

"I'll hurt you," he said, sobbing with emotion. "By Heaven, I'll hurt you. Leave me alone!"

He began to run, not knowing clearly where to run. He ran from the nearest blind man, because it was a horror to hit him. He stopped, and then made a dash to escape from their closing ranks. He made for where a gap was wide, and the men on either side, with a quick perception of the approach of his paces, rushed in on one another. He sprang forward, and then saw he must be caught, and *swish!* the spade had struck. He felt the soft thud of hand and arm, and the man was down with a yell of pain, and he was through.

Through! And then he was close to the street of houses again, and blind men, whirling spades and stakes, were running with a sort of reasoned swiftness hither and thither.

He heard steps behind him just in time, and found a tall man rushing 120
forward and swiping at the sound of him. He lost his nerve, hurled his spade a yard wide at his antagonist, and whirled about and fled, fairly yelling as he dodged another.

He was panic-stricken. He ran furiously to and fro, dodging when there was no need to dodge, and in his anxiety to see on every side of him at once, stumbling. For a moment he was down and they heard his fall. Far away in the circumferential wall a little doorway looked like heaven, and he set off in a wild rush for it. He did not even look round at his pursuers until it was gained, and he had stumbled across the bridge, clambered a little way among the rocks, to the surprise and dismay of a young llama, who went leaping out of sight, and lay down sobbing for breath.

And so his *coup d'état* came to an end.

He stayed outside the wall of the valley of the Blind for two nights and days without food or shelter, and meditated upon the unexpected. During these meditations he repeated very frequently and always with a profounder note of derision the exploded proverb: "In the Country of the Blind the One-eyed Man is King." He thought chiefly of ways of fighting and conquering these people, and it grew clear that for him no practicable way was possible. He had no weapons, and now it would be hard to get one.

The canker of civilisation had got to him even in Bogota, and he could not find it in himself to go down and assassinate a blind man. Of course, if he did that, he might then dictate terms on the threat of assassinating them all. But—sooner or later he must sleep! . . .

He tried also to find food among the pine trees, to be comfortable un- 125
der pine boughs while the frost fell at night, and—with less confidence—to catch a llama by artifice in order to try to kill it—perhaps by hammering it with a stone—and so finally, perhaps, to eat some of it. But the llamas had a doubt of him and regarded him with distrustful brown eyes, and spat when he drew near. Fear came on him the second day and fits of shivering. Finally he crawled down to the wall of the Country of the Blind and tried to make terms. He crawled along by the stream, shouting, until two blind men came out to the gate and talked to him.

"I was mad," he said. "But I was only newly made."

They said that was better.

He told them he was wiser now, and repented of all he had done.

Then he wept without intention, for he was very weak and ill now, and they took that as a favourable sign.

They asked him if he still thought he could "*see.*" 130

"No," he said. "That was folly. The word means nothing—less than nothing!"

They asked him what was overhead.

"About ten times ten the height of a man there is a roof above the world of—of rock—and very, very smooth." . . . He burst again into hysterical tears. "Before you ask me any more, give me some food or I shall die."

He expected dire punishments, but these blind people were capable of toleration. They regarded his rebellion as but one more proof of his general idiocy and inferiority; and after they had whipped him they appointed him to do the simplest and heaviest work they had for anyone to do, and he, seeing no other way of living, did submissively what he was told.

He was ill for some days, and they nursed him kindly. That refined his 135
submission. But they insisted on his lying in the dark, and that was a great misery. And blind philosophers came and talked to him of the wicked levity of his mind, and reproved him so impressively for his doubts about the lid of rock that covered their cosmic casserole that he almost doubted whether indeed he was not the victim of hallucination in not seeing it overhead.

So Nunez became a citizen of the Country of the Blind, and these people ceased to be a generalised people and became individualities and familiar to him, while the world beyond the mountains became more and more remote and unreal. There was Yacob, his master, a kindly man when not annoyed; there was Pedro, Yacob's nephew; and there was Medina-saroté, who was the youngest daughter of Yacob. She was little esteemed in the world of the blind, because she had a clear-cut face, and lacked that satisfying, glossy smoothness that is the blind man's ideal of feminine beauty; but Nunez thought her beautiful at first, and presently the most beautiful thing in the whole creation. Her closed eyelids were not sunken and red after the common way of the valley, but lay as though they might open again at any moment; and she had long eyelashes, which were considered a grave disfigurement. And her voice was strong, and did not satisfy the acute hearing of the valley swains. So that she had no lover.

There came a time when Nunez thought that, could he win her, he would be resigned to live in the valley for all the rest of his days.

He watched her; he sought opportunities of doing her little services, and presently he found that she observed him. Once at a rest-day gathering they sat side by side in the dim starlight, and the music was sweet. His hand came upon hers and he dared to clasp it. Then very tenderly she returned his pressure. And one day, as they were at their meal in the darkness, he felt her hand very softly seeking him, and as it chanced the fire leaped then and he saw the tenderness of her face.

He sought to speak to her.

He went to her one day when she was sitting in the summer moon- 140
light spinning. The light made her a thing of silver and mystery. He sat down at her feet and told her he loved her, and told her how beautiful she seemed to him. He had a lover's voice, he spoke with a tender reverence that came near to awe, and she had never before been touched by adoration. She made him no definite answer, but it was clear his words pleased her.

After that he talked to her whenever he could make an opportunity. The valley became the world for him, and the world beyond the mountains where men lived in sunlight seemed no more than a fairy tale he would some day pour into her ears. Very tentatively and timidly he spoke to her of sight.

Sight seemed to her the most poetical of fancies, and she listened to his description of the stars and the mountains and her own sweet white-lit beauty as though it was a guilty indulgence. She did not believe, she could only half understand, but she was mysteriously delighted, and it seemed to him that she completely understood.

His love lost its awe and took courage. Presently he was for demanding her of Yacob and the elders in marriage, but she became fearful and delayed. And it was one of her elder sisters who first told Yacob that Medina-saroté and Nunez were in love.

There was from the first very great opposition to the marriage of Nunez and Medina-saroté; not so much because they valued her as because they held him as a being apart, an idiot, an incompetent thing below the permissible level of a man. Her sisters opposed it bitterly as bringing discredit on them all; and old Yacob, though he had formed a sort of liking for his clumsy, obedient serf, shook his head and said the thing could not be. The young men were all angry at the idea of corrupting the race, and one went so far as to revile and strike Nunez. He struck back. Then for the first time he found an advantage in seeing, even by twilight, and after that fight was over no one was disposed to raise a hand against him. But they still found his marriage impossible.

Old Yacob had a tenderness for his last little daughter, and was grieved 145
to have her weep upon his shoulder.

"You see, my dear, he's an idiot. He has delusions; he can't do anything right."

"I know," wept Medina-saroté. "But he's better than he was. He's getting better. And he's strong, dear father, and kind—stronger and kinder than any other man in the world. And he loves me—and, father, I love him."

Old Yacob was greatly distressed to find her inconsolable, and, besides—what made it more distressing—he liked Nunez for many things. So he went and sat in the windowless council-chamber with the other elders and watched the trend of the talk, and said, at the proper time, "He's better than he was. Very likely, some day, we shall find him as sane as ourselves."

Then afterwards one of the elders, who thought deeply, had an idea. He was the great doctor among these people, their medicine-man, and he had a very philosophical and inventive mind, and the idea of curing Nunez of his peculiarities appealed to him. One day when Yacob was present he returned to the topic of Nunez.

"I have examined Bogota," he said, "and the case is clearer to me. I 150
think very probably he might be cured."

"That is what I have always hoped," said old Yacob.

"His brain is affected," said the blind doctor.

The elder murmured assent.

"Now, *what* affects it?"

"Ah!" said old Yacob. 155

"This," said the doctor, answering his own question. "Those queer things that are called the eyes, and which exist to make an agreeable soft depression in the face, are diseased, in the case of Bogota, in such a way as to affect his brain. They are greatly distended, he has eyelashes, and his eyelids move, and consequently his brain is in a state of constant irritation and distraction."

"Yes?" said old Yacob. "Yes?"

"And I think I may say with reasonable certainty that, in order to cure him completely, all that we need do is a simple and easy surgical operation—namely, to remove these irritant bodies."

"And then he will be sane?"

"Then he will be perfectly sane, and a quite admirable citizen." 160

"Thank Heaven for science!" said old Yacob, and went forth at once to tell Nunez of his happy hopes.

But Nunez's manner of receiving the good news struck him as being cold and disappointing.

"One might think," he said, "from the tone you take, that you did not care for my daughter."

It was Medina-saroté who persuaded Nunez to face the blind surgeons.

"*You* do not want me," he said, "to lose my gift of sight?" 165

She shook her head.

"My world is sight."

Her head drooped lower.

"There are the beautiful things, the beautiful little things—the flowers, the lichens among the rocks, the lightness and softness on a piece of fur, the far sky with its drifting down of clouds, the sunsets and the stars. And there is *you*. For you alone it is good to have sight, to see your sweet, serene face, your kindly lips, your dear, beautiful hands folded together.... It is these eyes of mine you won, these eyes that hold me to you, that these idiots seek. Instead, I must touch you, hear you, and never see you again. I must come under that roof of rock and stone and darkness, that horrible roof under which your imagination stoops.... No; you would not have me do that?"

A disagreeable doubt had risen in him. He stopped, and left the thing a 170
question.

"I wish," she said, "sometimes—" She paused.

"Yes?" said he, a little apprehensively.

"I wish sometimes—you would not talk like that."

"Like what?"

"I know it's pretty—it's your imagination. I love it, but *now*—" 175

He felt cold. *"Now?"* he said faintly.

She sat quite still.

"You mean—you think—I should be better, better perhaps—"

He was realising things very swiftly. He felt anger, indeed, anger at the dull course of fate, but also sympathy for her lack of understanding—a sympathy near akin to pity.

"Dear," he said, and he could see by her whiteness how intensely her 180
spirit pressed against the things she could not say. He put his arms about her, he kissed her ear, and they sat for a time in silence.

"If I were to consent to this?" he said at last, in a voice that was very gentle.

She flung her arms about him, weeping wildly. "Oh, if you would," she sobbed, "if only you would!"

For a week before the operation that was to raise him from the servitude and inferiority to the level of a blind citizen, Nunez knew nothing of sleep, and all through the warm sunlit hours, while the others slumbered happily, he sat brooding or wandered aimlessly, trying to bring his mind to bear on his dilemma. He had given his answer, he had given his consent, and still he was not sure. And at last work-time was over, the sun rose in splendour over the golden crests, and his last day of vision began for him. He had a few minutes with Medina-saroté before she went apart to sleep.

"To-morrow," he said, "I shall see no more."

185 "Dear heart!" she answered, and pressed his hands with all her strength.

"They will hurt you but little," she said; "and you are going through this pain—you are going through it, dear lover, for *me*. . . . Dear, if a woman's heart and life can do it, I will repay you. My dearest one, my dearest with the tender voice, I will repay."

He was drenched in pity for himself and her.

He held her in his arms, and pressed his lips to hers, and looked on her sweet face for the last time. "Good-bye!" he whispered at that dear sight, "good-bye!"

And then in silence he turned away from her.

190 She could hear his slow retreating footsteps, and something in the rhythm of them threw her into a passion of weeping.

He had fully meant to go to a lonely place where the meadows were beautiful with white narcissus, and there remain until the hour of his sacrifice should come, but as he went he lifted up his eyes and saw the morning, the morning like an angel in golden armour, marching down the steeps. . . .

It seemed to him that before this splendour he, and this blind world in the valley, and his love, and all, were no more than a pit of sin.

He did not turn aside as he had meant to do, but went on, and passed through the wall of the circumference and out upon the rocks, and his eyes were always upon the sunlit ice and snow.

He saw their infinite beauty, and his imagination soared over them to the things beyond he was now to resign for ever.

195 He thought of that great free world he was parted from, the world that was his own, and he had a vision of those further slopes, distance beyond distance, with Bogota, a place of multitudinous stirring beauty, a glory by day, a luminous mystery by night, a place of palaces and fountains and statues and white houses, lying beautifully in the middle distance. He thought how for a day or so one might come down through passes, drawing ever nearer and nearer to its busy streets and ways. He thought of the river journey, day by day, from great Bogota to the still vaster world beyond, through towns and villages, forest and desert places, the rushing river day by day, until its banks receded and the big steamers came splashing by, and one had reached the sea—the limitless sea, with its thousand islands, its thousands of islands, and its ships seen dimly far away in their incessant journeyings round and about that greater world. And there, unpent by mountains, one saw the sky—the sky, not such a disc as one saw it here, but an arch of immeasurable blue, a deep of deeps in which the circling stars were floating. . . .

His eyes scrutinised the great curtain of the mountains with a keener inquiry.

For example, if one went so, up that gully and to that chimney there, then one might come out high among those stunted pines that ran round in a sort of shelf and rose still higher and higher as it passed above the gorge. And then? That talus might be managed. Thence perhaps a climb might be found to take him up to the precipice that came below the snow; and if that chimney failed, then another farther to the east might serve his purpose better. And then? Then one would be out upon the amber-lit snow there, and halfway up to the crest of those beautiful desolations.

He glanced back at the village, then turned right round and regarded it steadfastly.

He thought of Medina-saroté, and she had become small and remote.

He turned again towards the mountain wall, down which the day had 200
come to him.

Then very circumspectly he began to climb.

When sunset came he was no longer climbing, but he was far and high. He had been higher, but he was still very high. His clothes were torn, his limbs were blood-stained, he was bruised in many places, but he lay as if he were at his ease, and there was a smile on his face.

From where he rested the valley seemed as if it were in a pit and nearly a mile below. Already it was dim with haze and shadow, though the mountain summits around him were things of light and fire. The little details of the rocks near at hand were drenched with subtle beauty—a vein of green mineral piercing the grey, the flash of crystal faces here and there, a minute, minutely beautiful orange lichen close beside his face. There were deep mysterious shadows in the gorge, blue deepening into purple, and purple into a luminous darkness, and overhead was the illimitable vastness of the sky. But he heeded these things no longer, but lay quite inactive there, smiling as if he were satisfied merely to have escaped from the valley of the Blind in which he had thought to be King.

The glow of the sunset passed, and the night came, and still he lay peacefully contented under the cold stars.

Analyzing the Text

1. Why does Nunez expect to become the ruler of the community of people who are born blind that he has stumbled upon? How, in turn, do they perceive Nunez?
2. The choice Nunez ultimately confronts is one that requires him to decide what is most important to him. In your opinion, what explains his final decision?

Understanding Wells's Techniques

1. In which specific details can you observe Wells's ingenuity in not only imagining the physical terrain, but in creating a coherent value system for the inhabitants of "the country of the blind"?
2. What details emphasize the psychological transformation Nunez goes through as he has to rethink his assumptions about what is normal?

Arguing for an Interpretation

1. How effectively does Wells dramatize the choice Nunez confronts? In his position, what would you have done?
2. In what sense might this story be understood as a parable somewhat like Plato's classic "The Allegory of the Cave" about the predicament confronting those who try to escape from cultural conditioning or coersive political or social environments? Analyze Wells's story in this way.

MAHASWETA DEVI

Mahasweta Devi was born in East Bengal in 1926, moved to West Bengal as an adolescent, and studied at Visva-Bharati and Calcutta universities where she received a master's degree in English. From a family with widespread literary and political influence, Devi joined the Gananatya, a group of highly accomplished, keenly political actors and writers who took the revolutionary step of bringing theater, on themes of burning interest in rural Bengal, to villages. Subsequently, she became a writer and journalist while holding a job as a college teacher in Calcutta. Over a period of years she has studied and lived among the tribal and outcast communities in southwest Bengal and southeast Bihar. Her stories, collected in Agnigarbha *(Womb of fire) (1978), focus on the semi-landless tribals and untouchables who are effectively denied rights guaranteed by the constitution, including a legal minimum wage. Her unique style of narrative realism reflects this emphasis on observations drawn from actual situations, persons, dialects, and idioms. "Giribala," translated into English from Bengali by Bardhan Kalpana, was first published in the magazine* Prasad *(Autumn 1982), a journal Devi created as a kind of people's magazine, which she still edits. Like her other stories, "Giribala" reflects carefully researched information Devi gathered directly from the lives of the rural underclass. This story tells the shocking tale of a woman whose husband sells their young daughters into prostitution.*

Giribala

Giribala[1] was born in a village called Talsana, in the Kandi subdivision of Murshidabad district.[2] Nobody ever imagined that she could think on her own, let alone act on her own thought. This Giribala, like so many others, was neither beautiful nor ugly, just an average-looking girl. But she had lovely eyes, eyes that somehow made her appearance striking.

In their caste, it was still customary to pay a bride-price. Aulchand gave Giri's father eighty rupees[3] and a heifer before he married her. Giri's father, in turn, gave his daughter four tolas[4] of silver, pots and pans, sleeping mats, and a cartload of mature bamboo that came from the bamboo clumps that formed the main wealth of Giri's father. Aulchand had told him that only because his hut had burned down did he need the bamboo to rebuild it. This was also the reason he gave for having to leave her with them for a few days—so that he could go to build a home for them.

[1]Literally, "mountain girl."
[2]In the United Province, near New Delhi.
[3]Approximately $20.
[4]One tola = .40 ounce.

Aulchand thus married Giri, and left. He did not come back soon.

Shortly after the marriage, Bangshi Dhamali,[5] who worked at the sub-post office in Nishinda, happened to visit the village. Bangshi enjoyed much prestige in the seven villages in the Nishinda area, largely due to his side business of procuring patients for the private practice of the doctor who was posted at the only hospital in the area. That way, the doctor supplemented his hospital salary by getting paid by the patients thus diverted from the hospital, and Bangshi supplemented his salary of 145 rupees from the sub-post office with the commission he got for procuring those patients. Bangshi's prestige went up further after he started using the medical terms he had picked up from being around the doctor.

For some reason that nobody quite recalled, Bangshi addressed Giri's 5
father as uncle. When Bangshi showed up on one of his patient-procuring trips, he looked up Giri's father and remarked disapprovingly about what he had just learned from his trip to another village, that he had given his only daughter in marriage to Aulchand, of all people.

"Yes. The proposal came along, and I thought he was all right."

"Obviously, you thought so. How much did he pay?"

"Four times twenty and one."

"I hope you're ready to face the consequences of what you've done."

"What consequences?" 10

"What can I say? You know that I'm a government servant myself and the right-hand man of the government doctor. Don't you think you should have consulted me first? I'm not saying that he's a bad sort, and I will not deny there was a time when I smoked *ganja*[6] with him. But I know what you don't know—the money he gave you as bride-price was not his. It's Channan's. You see, Channan's marriage had been arranged in Kalhat village. And Aulchand, as Channan's uncle, was trusted with the money to deliver as bride-price on behalf of Channan. He didn't deliver it there."

"What?"

"Channan's mother sat crying when she learned that Aulchand, who had been living under their roof for so long, could cheat them like that. Finally, Channan managed to get married by borrowing from several acquaintances who were moved by his plight."

"He has no place of his own? No land for a home to stand on?"

"Nothing of the sort." 15

"But he took a cartload of my bamboo to rebuild the hut on his land!"

"I was going to tell you about that too. He sold that bamboo to Channan's aunt for a hundred rupees and hurried off to the Banpur fair."

Giri's father was stunned. He sat with his head buried in his hands. Bangshi went on telling him about other similar tricks Aulchand had been pulling. Before taking leave, he finally said, perhaps out of mercy for the overwhelmed man, "He's not a bad one really. Just doesn't have any land, any place to live. Keeps traveling from one fair to another, with some singing party or other. That's all. Otherwise, he's not a bad sort."

Giri's father wondered aloud, "But Mohan never told me any of these things! He's the one who brought the proposal to me!"

"How could he, when he's Aulchand's right hand in these matters?" 20

---

[5]Literally, mischievious.

[6]Marijuana cigarettes, also known as "pip."

When Giri's mother heard all this from Giri's father, she was livid. She vowed to have her daughter married again and never to send her to live with the cheat, the thief.

But when after almost a year Aulchand came back, he came prepared to stop their mouths from saying what they wanted to say. He brought a large taro root, a new sari for his bride, a squat stool of jackfruit wood for his mother-in-law, and four new jute sacks for his father-in-law. Giri's mother still managed to tell him the things they had found out from Bangshi. Aulchand calmly smiled a generous, forgiving smile, saying, "One couldn't get through life if one believed everything that Bangshi-*dada* said.[7] Your daughter is now going to live in a brick house, not a mere mud hut. That's true, not false."

So, Giri's mother started to dress her only daughter to go to live with her husband. She took time to comb her hair into a nice bun, while weeping and lamenting, partly to herself and partly to her daughter, "This man is like a hundred-rooted weed in the yard. Bound to come back every time it's been pulled out. What he just told us are all lies, I know that. But with what smooth confidence he said those lies!"

Giri listened silently. She knew that although the groom had to pay a bride-price in their community, still a girl was only a girl. She had heard so many times the old saying: "A daughter born, To husband or death, She's already gone." She realized that her life in her own home and village was over, and her life of suffering was going to begin. Silently she wept for a while, as her mother tended to grooming her. Then she blew her nose, wiped her eyes, and asked her mother to remember to bring her home at the time of Durga puja[8] and to feed the red-brown cow that was her charge, adding that she had chopped some hay for the cow, and to water her young *jaba* tree that was going to flower someday.

Giribala, at the age of fourteen, then started off to make her home with her husband. Her mother put into a bundle the pots and pans that she would be needing. Watching her doing that, Aulchand remarked, "Put in some rice and lentils too. I've got a job at the house of the *babu.* Must report to work the moment I get back. There'll be no time to buy provisions until after a few days."

Giribala picked up the bundle of rice, lentils, and cooking oil and left her village, walking a few steps behind him. He walked ahead, and from time to time asked her to walk faster, as the afternoon was starting to fade. He took her to another village in Nishinda, to a large brick house with a large garden of fruit trees of all kinds. In the far corner of the garden was a crumbling hovel meant for the watchman. He took her to it. There was no door in the door opening. As if answering her thought, Aulchand said, "I'll fix the door soon. But you must admit the room is nice. And the pond is quite near. Now go on, pick up some twigs and start the rice."

"It's dark out there! Do you have a kerosene lamp?"

"Don't ask me for a kerosene lamp, or this and that. Just do what you can."

A maid from the babu's household turned up and saved Giri. She brought a kerosene lamp from the house and showed Giri to the pond,

---

[7]*Dada,* meaning elder brother, is also used to refer politely to or to address a friend or acquaintance older than oneself, but not old enough to be referred to or addressed as uncle. [Author's note.]

[8]Rituals designed to worship a household goddess of good fortune.

complaining about Aulchand and cautioning her about him. "What kind of heartless parents would give a tender young girl to a no-good ganja addict? How can he feed you? He has nothing. Gets a pittance taking care of the babu's cattle and doing odd jobs. Who knows how he manages to feed himself, doing whatever else he does! If you've been brought up on rice, my dear, you'd be wise enough to go back home tomorrow to leave behind the bits of silver that you have got on you."

But Giri did not go back home the next day for safekeeping her silver ornaments. Instead, in the morning she was found busy plastering with mud paste the exposed, uneven bricks of the wall of the crumbling room. Aulchand managed to get an old sheet of tin from the babu and nailed it to a few pieces of wood to make it stand; then he propped it up as a door for the room. Giri promptly got herself employed in the babu household for meals as her wage. After a few months, Aulchand remarked about how she had managed to domesticate a vagabond like him, who grew up without parents, never stayed home, and always floated around.

Giri replied, "Go, beg the babus for a bit of the land. Build your own home."

"Why will they give me land?"

"They will if you plead for the new life that's on its way. Ask them if a baby doesn't deserve to be born under a roof of its own. Even beggars and roving street singers have some kind of home."

"You're right. I too feel sad about not having a home of my own. Never felt that way before, though."

The only dream they shared was a home of their own.

However, their firstborn, a daughter they named Belarani,[9] was born in the crumbling hovel with the tin door. Before the baby was even a month old, Giri returned to her work in the babu household, and, as if to make up for her short absence from work, she took the heavy sheets, the flatweave rugs, and the mosquito nets to the pond to wash them clean. The lady of the house remarked on how she put her heart into the work and how clean her work was!

Feeling very magnanimous, the lady then gave Giri some of her children's old clothes, and once in a while she asked Giri to take a few minutes' break from work to feed the baby.

Belarani was followed by another daughter, Poribala, and a son, Rajib, all born in the watchman's hovel at the interval of a year and a half to two years. After the birth of her fourth child, a daughter she named Maruni,[10] she asked the doctor at the hospital, where she went for this birth, to sterilize her.

By then Aulchand had finally managed to get the babu's permission to use a little area of his estate to build a home for his family. He had even raised a makeshift shack on it. Now he was periodically going away for other kinds of work assigned to him.

He was furious to learn that Giri had herself sterilized, so furious that he beat her up for the first time. "Why did you do it? Tell me, why?"

Giri kept silent and took the beating. Aulchand grabbed her by the hair and punched her a good many times. Silently she took it all. After he

[9]Literally, "pretty queen."

[10]Literally meaning a girl likely to die; the name is perhaps intended to repel death, following the belief that death takes first the lives people want to cling to most. [Author's note.]

had stopped beating because he was tired and his anger temporarily spent, she calmly informed him that the Panchayat[11] was going to hire people for the road building and pay the wages in wheat.

"Why don't you see your father and get some bamboo instead?"

"What for?"

"Because you're the one who has been wanting a home. I could build a good one with some bamboo from your father."

"We'll both work on the Panchayat road and have our home. We'll save some money by working harder."

"If only we could mortgage or sell your silver trinkets, . . ."

Giribala did not say anything to his sly remark; she just stared at him. Aulchand had to lower his eyes before her silent stare. Giri had put her silver jewelry inside the hollow of a piece of bamboo, stuffed it up and kept it in the custody of the lady of the house she worked for. Belarani too started working there, when she was seven years old, doing a thousand odd errands to earn her meals. Bela was now ten, and growing like a weed in the rainy season. Giri would need the silver to get her married someday soon. All she had for that purpose was the bit of silver from her parents and the twenty-two rupees she managed to save from her years of hard work, secretly deposited with the mistress of the house, away from Aulchand's reach.

"I'm not going to sell my silver for a home. My father gave all he could for that, a whole cartload of bamboo, one hundred and sixty-two full stems, worth a thousand rupees at that time even in the markets of Nishinda."

"The same old story comes up again!" Aulchand was exasperated.

"Don't you want to see your own daughter married someday?"

"Having a daughter only means having to raise a slave for others. Mohan had read my palm and predicted a son in the fifth pregnancy. But, no, you had to make yourself sterile, so you could turn into a whore."

Giri grabbed the curved kitchen knife and hissed at him, "If ever I hear you say those evil things about me, I'll cut off the heads of the children and then my own head with this."

Aulchand quickly stopped himself, "Forget I said it. I won't, ever again."

For a few days after that he seemed to behave himself. He was sort of timid, chastised. But soon, probably in some way connected with the grudge of being chastised by her, the vile worm inside his brain started to stir again; once again Mohan, his trick master, was his prompter.

Mohan had turned up in the midst of the busy days they were spending in the construction of a bus road that was going to connect Nishinda with Krishnachawk.[12] Giri and Aulchand were both working there and getting as wages the wheat for their daily meals. Mohan too joined them to work there, and he sold his wheat to buy some rice, a pumpkin, and occasionally some fish to go with the wheat bread. He had remained the same vagabond that he always was, only his talking had become more sophisticated with a bohemian style picked up from his wanderings to cities and distant villages. He slept in the little porch facing the room occupied by Giri and her family.

[11]Governing body of the local village, usually made up of five officials ("pancha" means "five").

[12]A major junction.

Sitting there in the evenings, he expressed pity for Aulchand, "Tch! Tch! You seem to have got your boat stuck in the mud, my friend. Have you forgotten all about the life we used to have?"

Giri snapped at him, "You can't sit here doing your smart talking, which can only bring us ruin."

"My friend had such a good singing voice!"

"Perhaps he had that. Maybe there was money in it too. But that money would never have reached his home and fed his children."

Mohan started another topic one evening. He said that there was a great shortage of marriage-age girls in Bihar,[13] so that the Biharis with money were coming down for Bengali brides and paying a bundle for that! He mentioned that Sahadeb Bauri, a fellow he knew, a low-caste fellow like themselves, received five hundred rupees for having his daughter married to one of those bride-searching Biharis.

"Where is that place?" Aulchand's curiosity was roused.

"You wouldn't know, my friend, even if I explained where it is. Let me just say that it's very far and the people there don't speak Bengali."

"They paid him five hundred rupees?" Aulchand was hooked in.

"Yes, they did."

The topic was interrupted at that point by the noise that rose when people suddenly noticed that the cowshed of Kali-babu,[14] the Panchayat big shot, was on fire. Everybody ran in that direction to throw bucketfuls of water at it.

Giri forgot about the topic thus interrupted. But Aulchand did not.

Something must have blocked Giri's usual astuteness because she suspected nothing from the subsequent changes in her husband's tone.

For example, one day he said, "Who wants your silver? I'll get my daughter married and also my shack replaced with bricks and tin. My daughter looks lovelier every day from the meals in the babu home!"

Giri's mind sensed nothing at all to be alerted to. She only asked, "Are you looking for a groom for her?"

"I don't have to look. My daughter's marriage will just happen."

Giri did not give much thought to this strange answer either. She merely remarked that the sagging roof needed to be propped up soon.

Perhaps too preoccupied with the thought of how to get the roof propped up, Giri decided to seek her father's help and also to see her parents for just a couple of days. Holding Maruni to her chest and Rajib and Pori by the hand, she took leave of Belarani, who cried and cried because she was not being taken along to visit her grandparents. Giri, also crying, gave her eight annas to buy sweets to eat, telling her that she could go another time because both of them could not take off at the same time from their work at the babu's place, even if for only four days, including the two days in walking to and from there.

She had no idea that she was never to see Bela again. If she had, she would not only have taken her along, but she would also have held her tied to her bosom, she would not have let her out of her sight for a minute. She was Giri's beloved firstborn, even though Giri had to put her to work at the babu household ever since she was only seven; that was the only

---

[13]A state near Bengal.

[14]Kali means dark complexion; literally, "black."

way she could have her fed and clothed. Giri had no idea when she started for her parents' village, leaving Bela with a kiss on her forehead.

"A daughter born, To husband or death, She's already gone." That must be why seeing the daughter makes the mother's heart sing! Her father had been very busy trying to sell his bamboo and acquiring two *bighas*[15] of land meanwhile. He was apologetic about not being able in all this time to bring her over for a visit, and he asked her to stay on a few more days once she had made the effort to come on her own. Her mother started making puffed rice and digging up the taro root she had been saving for just such a special occasion. While her hands worked making things for them to eat, she lamented about what the marriage had done to her daughter, how it had tarnished her bright complexion, ruined her abundant hair, and made her collarbones stick out. She kept asking her to stay a few more days, resting and eating to repair the years of damage. Giri's little brother begged her to stay for a month.

For a few days, after many years, Giri found rest and care and heaping 75
servings of food. Her father readily agreed to give her the bamboo, saying how much he wanted his daughter to live well, in a manner he could be proud of. Giri could easily have used a few tears and got some other things from her father. Her mother asked her to weep and get a maund[16] of rice too while he was in the giving mood. But Giri did not do that. Giri was not going to ask for anything from her loved ones unless she absolutely had to. She walked over to the corner of the yard, to look at the hibiscus she had planted when she was a child. She watched with admiration its crimson flowers and the clean mud-plastered yard and the new tiles on the roof. She also wondered if her son Rajib could stay there and go to the school her brother went to. But she mentioned nothing to her parents about this sudden idea that felt like a dream.

She just took her children to the pond, and, with the bar of soap she had bought on the way, she scrubbed them and herself clean. She washed her hair too. Then she went to visit the neighbors. She was feeling lighthearted, as if she were in heaven, without the worries of her life. Her mother sent her brother to catch a fish from the canal, the new irrigation canal that had changed the face of the area since she last saw it. It helped to raise crops and catch fish throughout the year. Giri felt an unfamiliar wind of fulfillment and pleasure blowing in her mind. There was not the slightest hint of foreboding.

Bangshi Dhamali happened to be in the village that day, and he too remarked on how Giri's health and appearance had deteriorated since she went to live with that no-good husband of hers. He said that if only Aulchand were a responsible father and could look after the older kids, she could have gone to work in the house of the doctor who was now living in Bahrampur town, and after some time she could take all the children over there and have them all working for food and clothing.

Giri regarded his suggestion with a smile, and asked him instead, "Tell me, dad, how is it that when so many destitute people are getting little plots of land from the government, Rajib's father can't?"

---

[15]One *bigha* is roughly one-third of an acre. [Author's note.]
[16]Equal to approximately 85 pounds.

"Has he ever come to see me about it? Ever sought my advice on anything? I'm in government service myself, and the right-hand man of the hospital doctor as well. I could easily have gotten him a plot of land."

"I'm going to send him to you as soon as I get back." 80

It felt like a pleasant dream to Giri, that they could have a piece of land of their own for a home of their own. She knew that her husband was a pathetic vagabond. Still, she felt a rush of compassion for him. A man without his own home, his own land. How could such a man help being diffident and demoralized?

"Are you sure, Bangshi-dada? Shall I send him to you then?"

"Look at your own father. See how well he's managed things. He's now almost a part of the Panchayat. I don't know what's the matter with uncle, though. He could have seen to it that Aulchand got a bit of the land being distributed. I once told him as much, and he insulted me in the marketplace, snapped at me that Aulchand should be learning to use his own initiative."

Giri decided to ignore the tendentious remark and keep on pressing Bangshi instead, "Please, Bangshi-dada, you tell me what to do. You know how impractical that man is. The room he's put up in all these years doesn't even have a good thatch roof. The moon shines into it all night and the sun all day. I'm hoping to get Bela married someday soon. Where am I going to seat the groom's party? And, dada, would you look for a good boy for my daughter?"

"There is a good boy available. Obviously, you don't know that. He's 85
the son of my own cousin. Just started a grocery store of his own."

Giri was excited to learn that, and even Rajib's face lit up as he said that he could then go to work as a helper in his brother-in-law's shop and could bring home salt and oil on credit. Giri scolded him for taking after his father, wanting to live on credit rather than by work.

Giri ended up staying six days with her parents instead of two. She was about to take leave, wearing a sari without holes that her mother gave her, a bundle of rice on her head, and cheap new shirts and pants on her children. Just then, like the straw suddenly blown in, indicating the still unseen storm, Bangshi Dhamali came in a rush to see her father.

"I don't want to say if it is bad news or good news, uncle, but what I just heard is incredible. Aulchand had told Bela that he was going to take her to see her grandparents. Then with the help of Mohan, he took her to Kandi town, and there he got the scared twelve-year-old, the timid girl who had known only her mother, married to some strange man from Bihar. There were five girls like Bela taken there to be married to five unknown blokes. The addresses they left are all false. This kind of business is on the rise. Aulchand got four hundred rupees in cash. The last thing he was seen doing was, back from drinking with Mohan, crying and slobbering, 'Bela! Bela!' while Kali-babu of the village Panchayat was shouting at him."

The sky seemed to come crashing down on Giribala's head. She howled with pain and terror. Her father got some people together and went along with her, vowing to get the girl back, to break the hands of the girl's father, making him a cripple, and to finish Mohan for good.

They could not find Mohan. Just Aulchand. On seeing them, he kept 90
doing several things in quick succession. He vigorously twisted his own ears and nose to show repentance, he wept, perhaps with real grief, and from time to time he sat up straight, asserting that because Bela was his daughter it was nobody else's business how he got her married off.

They searched the surrounding villages as far as they could. Giri took out the silver she had deposited with the mistress of the house and went to the master, crying and begging him to inform the police and get a paid announcement made over the radio about the lost girl. She also accused them, as mildly as she could in her state of mind, for letting the girl go with her father, knowing as they did the lout that he was.

The master of the house persuaded Giri's father not to seek police help because that would only mean a lot of trouble and expense. The terrible thing had happened after all; Bela had become one more victim of this new business of procuring girls on the pretext of marriage. The police were not going to do much for this single case; they would most probably say that the father did it after all. Poor Bela had this written on her forehead!

Finally, that was the line everybody used to console Giri. The master of the house in which she and Bela worked day and night, the neighbors gathered there, even Giri's father ended up saying that—about the writing on the forehead that nobody could change. If the daughter was to remain hers, that would have been nice, they said in consolation, but she was only a daughter, not a son. And they repeated the age-old saying: "A daughter born, To husband or death, She's already gone."

Her father sighed and said with philosophical resignation, "It's as if the girl sacrificed her life to provide her father with money for a house."

Giri, crazed with grief, still brought herself to respond in the implied 95
context of trivial bickering, "Don't send him any bamboo, father. Let the demon do whatever he can on his own."

"It's useless going to the police in such matters," everybody said.

Giri sat silently with her eyes closed, leaning against the wall. Even in her bitter grief, the realization flashed through her mind that nobody was willing to worry about a girl child for very long. Perhaps she should not either. She too was a small girl once, and her father too gave her away to a subhuman husband without making sufficient inquiries.

Aulchand sensed that the temperature in the environment was dropping. He started talking defiantly and defending himself to her father by blaming Giri and answering her remark about him. "Don't overlook your daughter's fault. How promptly she brought out her silver chain to get her daughter back! If she had brought it out earlier, then there would have been a home for us and no need to sell my daughter. Besides, embarrassed as I am to tell you this, she had the operation to get cleaned out, saying, 'What good was it having more children when we can't feed the ones we've got?' Well, I've shown what good it can be, even if we got more daughters. So much money for a daughter!"

At this, Giri started hitting her own head against the wall so violently that she seemed to have suddenly gone insane with grief and anger. They had to grapple with her to restrain her from breaking her head.

Slowly the agitation died down. The babu's aunt gave Giri a choice 100
nugget of her wisdom to comfort her. "A daughter, until she is married, is her father's property. It's useless for a mother to think she has any say."

Giri did not cry any more after that night.

Grimly, she took Pori to the babu's house, to stay there and work in place of Bela, and told her that she would kill her if she ever went anywhere with her father. In grim silence, she went through her days of work and even more work. When Aulchand tried to say anything to her, she did not answer; she just stared at him. It scared Aulchand. The only time she spoke to him was to ask, "Did you really do it only because you wanted to build your home?"

"Yes. Believe me."

"Ask Mohan to find out where they give the children they buy full meals to eat. Then go and sell the other three there. You can have a brick and concrete house. Mohan must know it."

"How can you say such a dreadful thing, you merciless woman? Asking 105
me to sell the children. Is that why you got sterilized? And why didn't you take the bamboo that your father offered?"

Giri left the room and lay down in the porch to spend the night there. Aulchand whined and complained for a while. Soon he fell asleep.

Time did the ultimate, imperceptible talking! Slowly Giri seemed to accept it. Aulchand bought some panels of woven split-bamboo for the walls. The roof still remained covered with leaves. Rajib took the work of tending the babu's cattle. Maruni, the baby, grew into a child, playing by herself in the yard. The hardest thing for Giri now was to look at Pori because she looked so much like Bela, with Bela's smile, Bela's way of watching things with her head tilted to one side. The mistress of the house was full of similar praise for her work and her gentle manners.

Little Pori poured her heart into the work at the babu household as if it were far more than a means to the meals her parents couldn't provide, as if it were her vocation, her escape. Perhaps the work was the disguise for her silent engagement in constant, troubling thoughts. Why else would she sweep all the rooms and corridors ten times a day, when nobody had asked her to? Why did she carry those jute sacks for paddy storage to the pond to wash them diligently? Why else would she spend endless hours coating the huge unpaved yard with a rag dipped in mud-dung paste until it looked absolutely smooth from end to end?

When Pori came home in the evening, worn out from the day's constant work, Giri, herself drained from daylong work, would feed her some puffed rice or chickpea flour that she might happen to have at home. Then she would go and spend most of the evening roaming alone through the huge garden of the babus, absently picking up dry twigs and leaves for the stove and listening to the rustle of leaves, the scurrying of squirrels in the dark. The night wind soothed her raging despair, as it blew her matted hair, uncombed for how long she did not remember.

The gentle face of her firstborn would then appear before her eyes, 110
and she would hear the sound of her small voice, making some little plea on some little occasion. "Ma, let me stay home today and watch you make the puffed rice. If they send for me, you can tell them that Bela would do all the work tomorrow, but she can't go today. Would you, Ma, please?"

Even when grown up, with three younger ones after her, she loved to sleep nestled next to her mother. Once her foot was badly cut and bruised. The squat stool that the babu's aunt sat on for her oil massage had slipped and hit her foot. She bore the pain for days, until applying the warm oil from a lamp healed it. Whenever Giri had a fever, Bela somehow found some time in between her endless chores at the babu household to come to cook the rice and run back to work.

Bela, Belarani, Beli—
Her I won't abandon.

Yet my daughter named Beli,
To husband or death she's gone!

Where could she be now? How far from here? In which strange land? Giri roamed the nights through the trees, and she muttered absently, "Wherever you are, my daughter, stay alive! Don't be dead! If only I knew where you were, I'd go there somehow, even if I had to learn to fly like birds or insects. But I don't know where you were taken. I wrote you a letter, with the babu's help, to the address they left. You couldn't have got it, daughter, because it's a false address."

Absently Giri would come back with the twigs, cook the rice, feed Maruni, eat herself, and lie down with her children, leaving Aulchand's rice in the pot.

The days without work she stayed home, just sitting in the porch. The days she found work, she went far—by the bus that now plied along the road they had worked on a few years ago, the bus that now took only an hour and a half to reach Kandi town. There, daily-wage work was going on, digging feeder channels from the main canal. The babu's son was a labor contractor there. He also had the permit for running a bus. Giri took that bus to work.

There, one day she came across Bangshi Dhamali. He was sincere 115
when he said that he had difficulty recognizing her. "You've ruined your health and appearance. Must be the grief for that daughter. But what good is grieving going to do after all?"

"Not just that. I'm now worried about Pori. She's almost ten."

"Really! She was born only the other day, the year the doctor built his house, and electricity came to Nishinda. Pori was born in that year."

"Yes! If only I had listened to what you said to me about going to work at the doctor's house and taken the children to town! My son now tends the babu's cattle. If I had gone then, they could all be in school now!"

"Don't know about your children being able to go to school. But I do know that the town is now flooded with jobs. You could put all your children to work at least for daily meals."

Giri was aware that her thinking of sending her children to school an- 120
noyed Bangshi. She yielded, "Anyway, Bangshi-dada. What good is it being able to read a few pages if they've to live on manual labor anyway? What I was really going to ask you is to look for a boy for my Pori."

"I'll tell Aulchand when I come to know of one."

"No. No. Make sure that you tell me."

"Why are you still so angry with him? He certainly made a mistake. Can't it be forgiven? Negotiating a daughter's wedding can't be done with the mother. It makes the groom's side think there's something wrong in the family. When it comes to your son's wedding, the bride's side would talk to you. It's different with the daughter."

"At least let me know about it all, before making a commitment."

"I'll see what I can do. I happen to know a rickshaw plier in 125
Krishnachawk. Not very young, though. About twenty-five, I think."

"That's all right. After what happened to Bela, the groom's age is not my main concern."

"Your girl will be able to live in Krishnachawk. But the boy has no land, he lives by plying a rented rickshaw, which leaves him with barely five rupees a day. Makes a little extra by rolling bidis[17] at night. Doesn't have a home yet. He wants to get married because there's nobody to cook for him and look after him at the end of the day."

"You try for him. If it works out, I'd have her wedding this winter."

The total despondency in her mind since losing Bela suddenly moved a little to let in a glimmer of hope for Pori. She went on hopefully, saying, "I'll give her everything I've got. After that, I'll have just Maruni to worry about. But she's still a baby. I'll have time to think. Let me tell you Bangshi-dada, and I'm saying this not because she's my daughter, my Pori looks so lovely at ten. Perhaps the meals at the babu house did it. Come dada, have some tea inside the shop."

Bangshi sipped the tea Giri bought him and informed her that her fa- 130
ther was doing very well for himself, adding to his land and his stores of paddy, and remarked what a pity it was that he didn't help her much!

"It may not sound nice, sister. But the truth is that blood relation is no longer the main thing these days. Uncle now mixes with his equals, those who are getting ahead like himself, not with those gone to the dogs, like your man, even if you happen to be his daughter."

Giri just sighed, and quietly paid for the tea with most of the few coins tied in one end of the sari and tucked in her waist. Before taking leave, she earnestly reminded Bangshi about her request for finding a good husband for Pori.

Bangshi did remember. When he happened to see Aulchand shortly after that, he mentioned the rickshaw plier. Aulchand perked up, saying that he too was after a boy who plied a rickshaw, though his did it in Bahrampur, a bit further away but a much bigger place than Krishnachawk. The boy had a fancy beard, mustache, and hair, and he talked so smart and looked so impressive in some dead Englishman's pants and jacket he had bought for himself at the second-hand market. Aulchand asked Bangshi not to bother himself anymore about the rickshaw plier he had in mind.

Next time Giri saw Bangshi, she asked him if he had made contact with the rickshaw plier in Krishnachawk. He said that he had talked with Aulchand about it meanwhile and that she need not worry about it.

Aulchand then went looking for Mohan, his guide in worldly matters. 135
And why not? There was not a place Mohan hadn't been to, all the nearby small towns in West Bengal that Aulchand had only heard of: Lalbagh, Dhulian, Jangipur, Jiaganj, Farakka. In fact, Aulchand didn't even know that Mohan was now in a business flung much further, procuring girls for whorehouses in the big cities, where the newly rich businessmen and contractors went to satisfy their newfound appetite for the childlike, underdeveloped bodies of Bengali pubescent girls. Fed well for a few months, they bloomed so deliciously that they yielded back within a couple of years the price paid to procure them.

But it was very important to put up a show of marriage to procure them. It was no longer possible to get away with just paying some money for the girl. Any such straight procurer was now sure to get a mass beating from the Bengali villagers. Hence, the need for stories about a shortage of

[17]Tobacco cigarettes rolled with leaves.

marriage-age girls in Bihar and now the need for something even more clever. The weddings now had to look real, with a priest and all that. Then there would have to be some talk about the rituals that must be performed at the groom's place according to their local customs to complete the marriage, and so with the family's permission they must get back right away.

The "grooms from Bihar looking for brides in Bengal" story had circulated long enough. Newer tactics became necessary. The local matchmakers, who got a cut in each deal, were no longer informed enough about what was going on, but they sensed that it held some kind of trouble for their occupation. They decided not to worry too much about exactly how the cheating was done. They just took the position that they were doing what the girl's parents asked them to do—to make contact with potential grooms. They played down their traditional role as the source of information about the groom's family and background.

The girls' families too decided to go ahead despite the nonperformance of their usual source of information. Their reason for not talking and investigating enough was that the high bride-price they were offered and the little dowry they were asked to pay might then be revealed, and, because there was no dearth of envious people, someone might undo the arrangement. In some cases, they thought that they had no choice but an out-of-state groom because even in their low-caste communities, in which bride-price was customary, the Bengali grooms wanted several thousands of rupees in watches, radios, bicycles, and so on.

Since the incident of Bela, Kali-babu of the Panchayat refused to hire Aulchand on the road project or any other construction under the Panchayat. Aulchand found himself a bit out of touch, but, with plenty of free time, he went away for a few days trying to locate Mohan.

Mohan, meanwhile, was doing exceedingly well considering that he never got past the fourth grade in school. He had set up another business like a net around the block development office of Nishinda, to catch the peasants who came there for subsidized fertilizers and loans, part of which they somehow managed to lose to Mohan before they could get back to their village. Mohan was an extremely busy man these days.

He firmly shook his head at Aulchand's request, saying, "Count me out. Mohan Mandal has done enough of helping others. To help a father get his daughter married is supposed to be a virtue. You got the money. What did I get? The other side at least paid me forty rupees in broker's fee. And you? You used your money all on bamboo wall-panels. Besides, I'm afraid of your wife."

"She's the one who wants a rickshaw plier in a nearby town."

"Really?"

"Yes. But listen. You stay out of the thing and just put me in touch with a rickshaw plier boy in a big town like Bahrampur. My daughter will be able to live there; we'll go there to visit them. I'd like nothing better. Bela's mother too might be pleased with me."

"You want to make up with your wife this way, right?"

"I'd like to. The woman doesn't think of me as a human being. I want to show her that I can get my daughter married well without anyone's help. Only you can supply me that invisible help."

Mohan laughed and said, "All right. But I'll not get involved. I'll just make the contact, that's all. What if the big-town son-in-law has a long list of demands?"

"I'll have to borrow."

"I see. Go home now. I'll see what I can do."

Mohan gave it some thought. He must be more careful this time. He must keep the "groom from Bihar" setup hidden one step away and have a rickshaw plier boy in front, the one who will do the marrying and then pass her on. Aulchand's plea thus gave birth to a new idea in Mohan's head, but first he had to find a rickshaw plier boy. Who could play the part? He must go to town and check with some of his contacts.

Talking about Pori's marriage did reduce the distance between Giribala and Aulchand. Finally, one day Mohan informed Aulchand that he had the right match. "How much does he want?" Aulchand asked.

"He's already got a watch and a radio. He plies a cycle-rickshaw, so he wants no bicycle. Just the clothes for bride and groom, bed, shoes, umbrella, stuff like that. Quite a bargain, really."

"How much will he pay in bride-price?"

"One hundred rupees."

"Does he have a home for my daughter to live in?"

"He has a rented room. But he owns the cycle-rickshaw."

Aulchand and Giri were happy. When the future groom came to see the bride, Giri peeked from behind the door, studying him intently. Big, well-built body, well-developed beard and mustache. He said that his name was Manohar Dhamali. In Bahrampur, there was indeed a rickshaw plier named Manohar Dhamali. But this man's real name was Panu. He had just been acquitted from a robbery charge, due to insufficient evidence. Aulchand didn't know about this part. After getting out of jail, Panu had just married a girl like Poribala in Jalangi, another in Farakka, and delivered them to the "groom from Bihar" gang. He was commissioned to do five for five hundred rupees. Not much for his efforts, he thought, but not bad with his options at the moment. Panu had plans to move further away, to Shiliguri, to try new pastures as soon as this batch was over and he had some money in hand.

At the time of Bela's marriage, no relative was there, not even Giribala. This time, Giri's parents came. Women blew conch shells and ululated happily to solemnize each ritual. Giri, her face shining with sweat and excited oil glands, cooked rice and meat curry for the guests. She brought her silver ornaments from the housemistress and put them on Pori, who was dressed in a new sari that Giri's mother had brought. Her father had brought a sackful of rice for the feast. The babu family contributed fifty rupees. The groom came by bus in the company of five others. Pori looked even more like Bela. She was so lovely in the glow on her skin left from the turmeric rub and in the red *alta*[18] edging her small feet.

Next day, with the groom she took the bus and left for the town.

That was the last time Giri saw Pori's face. The day after, Aulchand went to the town with Rajib and Giri's young brother to visit the newly married couple, as the custom required. The night advanced, but they did not return. Very, very late in the night, Giri heard the sound of footsteps of people coming in, but silently. Giri knew at once. She opened the door, and saw Bangshi Dhamali holding Rajib's hand. Rajib cried out, "Ma!" Giri knew the terrible thing had happened again. Silently she looked on them. Giri's brother told her. There wasn't much to tell. They did find a Manohar

[18]Colored design traditionally worn before a marriage.

Dhamali in the town, but he was a middle-aged man. They asked the people around and were told that it must be another of Panu's acts. He was going around doing a lot of marrying. He seemed to be linked with some kind of gang.

Giri interrupted to ask Bangshi, "And Mohan is not behind this?"

"He's the mastermind behind this new play."

"And where's Rajib's father? Why isn't he with you?"

"He ran to catch Mohan when he heard that Mohan got five to seven hundred rupees from it. He left shouting incoherently, 'I want my daughter. I want my money.'"

Giri's little porch was again crowded with sympathetic, agitated peo- 165
ple, some of them suggesting that they find Mohan and beat him up, others wanting to go to the police station, but all of them doing just a lot of talking. "Are we living in a lawless land?" Lots of words, lots of noise.

Close to dawn, Aulchand came home. Overwhelmed by the events, he had finally gone to get drunk and he was talking and bragging, "I found out where he got the money from. Mohan can't escape Aulchand-sardar.[19] I twisted his neck until he coughed up my share of the money. Why shouldn't I get the money? The daughter is mine, and he'll be the one to take the money from putting her in a phony marriage? Where's Pori's mother? Foolish woman, you shouldn't have done that operation. The more daughters we have, the more money we can have. Now I'm going to have that home of ours done. Oh-ho-ho, my little Pori!"

Aulchand cried and wept and very soon he fell asleep on the porch. Giribala called up all her strength to quietly ask the crowd to go home. After they left, Giri sat by herself for a long time, trying to think what she should do now. She wanted to be dead. Should she jump into the canal? Last night, she heard some people talking, correctly perhaps, that the same fate may be waiting for Maruni too.

"Making business out of people's need to see their daughters married. Giri, this time you must take it to the police with the help of the babu. Don't let them get away with it. Go to the police, go to court."

Giri had looked on, placing her strikingly large eyes on their faces, then shaking her head. She would try nothing! Aulchand got his money at his daughter's expense. Let him try. Giri firmly shook her head.

Bangshi had remarked before leaving, "God must have willed that the 170
walls come from one daughter and the roof from the other."

Giri had silently gazed at his face too with her striking eyes.

After some time, Aulchand was crying and doing the straw roof at the same time. The more tears he shed, the more dry-eyed Giri became.

The babu's elderly aunt tried to console her with her philosophy of cliches, "Not easy to be a daughter's mother. They say that a daughter born is already gone, either to husband or to death. That's what happened to you. Don't I know why you aren't crying? They say that one cries from a little loss, but turns into stone with too much loss. Start working again. One gets used to everything except hunger."

Giri silently gazed at her too, as she heard the familiar words coming out of her mouth. Then she requested her to go and tell the babu's wife that Giri wanted to withdraw her deposited money immediately. She went

---

[19]Literally, "chief"; in the context, a form of self-praise.

to collect the money. She put it in a knot in her sari and tucked the knot in her waist.

She came back and stood by the porch, looking at the home Aulchand was building. Nice room. The split-bamboo woven panels of the wall were neatly plastered with mud and were now being topped with a new straw roof. She had always dreamed of a room like this. Perhaps that was wanting too much. That was why Beli and Pori had to become prostitutes—yes, prostitutes. No matter what euphemism is used, nobody ever sets up home for a girl bought with money. 175

Nice room. Giri thought she caught a flitting glimpse of Aulchand eyeing little Maruni while tying up the ends of the straw he had laid on the roof. Giri silently held those striking eyes of hers steadily on Aulchand's face for some time, longer than she had ever done before. And Aulchand thought that no matter how great her grief was, she must be impressed with the way their home was turning out after all.

The next morning brought the biggest surprise to all. Before sunrise, Giribala had left home, with Maruni on her hip and Rajib's hand held in hers. She had walked down to the big road and caught the early morning bus to the town. Later on, it also became known that at the Nishinda stop she had left a message for Pori's father with Bangshi Dhamali. The message was that Giri wanted Aulchand to live in his new room happily forever. But Giri was going away from his home to work in other people's homes in order to feed and raise her remaining children. And if he ever came to the town looking for her, she would put her neck on the rail line before a speeding train.

People were so amazed, even stunned by this that they were left speechless. What happened to Bela and Pori was happening to many others these days. But leaving one's husband was quite another matter. What kind of woman would leave her husband of many years just like that? Now, they all felt certain that the really bad one was not Aulchand, but Giribala. And arriving at this conclusion seemed to produce some kind of relief for their troubled minds.

And Giribala? Walking down the unfamiliar roads and holding Maruni on her hip and Rajib by the hand, Giribala only regretted that she had not done this before. If she had left earlier, then Bela would not have been lost, then Pori would not have been lost. If only she had had this courage earlier, her two daughters might have been saved.

As this thought grew insistent and hammered inside her brain, hot tears flooded her face and blurred her vision. But she did not stop even to wipe her tears. She just kept walking. 180

Analyzing the Text

1. Under what circumstances had Aulchand married Giribala? How does the reality of Giribala's married life contrast with the promises Aulchand had made to her and her parents?
2. Why is it ironic that the villagers blame Giribala at the end of the story and what does this reveal about the prevailing social views?

Understanding Devi's Techniques

1. How does Devi create suspense by dramatizing the unsuccessful measures Giribala takes to prevent her daughters from being sold into prostitution?

2. What details reveal the powerlessness of women in rural Bengal, especially those who are at the bottom of the caste system?

Arguing for an Interpretation

1. Who, in your opinion, is more to blame for what happens: Aulchand, his right-hand man, Mohan, Giribala's father, or Giribala herself? Explain your answer.
2. Is the matter-of-fact tone Devi adopts effective in making her story a vehicle for social reform? Why or why not?

Milorad Pavić

Milorad Pavić, one of the best known contemporary Serbian prose writers, was born in 1929 in Belgrade. He has been credited with the invention of a kind of fiction that gives the impression of an inexhaustible text through the blending of the fantastic into realistic narratives. This "hyperfiction," as it is known, is well illustrated by the following story, "The Wedgwood Tea Set," translated by Darka Topali, which originally appeared in The Prince of Fire: An Anthology of Contemporary Serbian Short Stories, *edited by Radmilla J. Gorup and Madezda Obradovic (1998). Notable among Pavić's works are* Landscape Painted with Tea *(1988),* Dictionary of the Khazars *(1988), and* The Inner Side of the Wind *(1993).*

The Wedgwood Tea Set

In the story you are about to read, the protagonists' names will be given at the end instead of the beginning.

At the capital's mathematics faculty, my younger brother, who was a student of philology and military science, introduced us to each other. Since she was searching for a companion with whom to prepare for Mathematics I, we began studying together, and as she did not come from another town as I did, we studied in her parents' big house. Quite early each morning, I passed by the shining Layland-Buffalo car, which belonged to her. In front of the door I would stoop down and look for a stone, put it in my pocket, ring the doorbell, and go upstairs. I carried no books, notebooks, or instruments; everything stayed at her place and was always ready for work. We studied from seven to nine, then we were served breakfast and would continue till ten; from ten to eleven we would usually go over the material already covered. All that time, I would be holding the stone in my hand. In case I should doze off, it would fall on the floor and wake me up before anyone noticed. After eleven she would continue to study, but not I. So we prepared for the mathematics exam every day except Sunday, when she studied alone. She very quickly realized that I could not keep up with her and that my knowledge lagged more and more behind hers. She thought that I went home to catch up on the lessons I had missed, but she never said a thing. "Let everyone like an earthworm eat his own way through," she thought, aware that by teaching another she wasn't teaching herself.

When the September term came, we agreed to meet on the day of the examination and take the exam together. Excited as she was, she didn't have time to be especially surprised that I didn't show up and that I did not take the exam, either. Only after she had passed the exam did she ask herself what had happened to me. But I didn't appear till winter. "Why should every bee gather honey, anyway?" she concluded, but still asked herself sometimes, "What's he up to? He is probably one of those smile-carriers, who buys his merchandise in the East, and sells it in the West, or vice versa. . . ."

When Mathematics II was on the agenda, she suddenly met me one morning, noticing with interest the new patches on my elbows and the newly grown hair, which she had not seen before. It was again the same. Each morning I would come at a certain hour, and she would descend through the green and layered air, as if through water full of cool and warm currents, open the door for me, sleepy, but with that mirror-breaking look of hers. She would watch for one moment how I squeezed out my beard into the cap and how I took off my gloves. Bringing together the middle finger and the thumb, with a decisive gesture I would simultaneously turn them inside out, thus taking them both off with the same movement. When that was over, she would immediately go to work. She made up her mind to study with all her strength, which happened daily. With untiring will and regularity, she delved into all details of the subject, no matter if it was morning, when we started out fresh, after breakfast, or toward the end, when she worked a bit more slowly but not skipping a single thing. I would still quit at eleven, and she would soon notice again that I couldn't concentrate on what I was doing, that my looks grew old in an hour, and that I was behind her again. She would look at my feet, one of which was always ready to step out, while the other was completely still. Then they would change positions.

5 When the January term arrived, she had the feeling that I could not pass the exam, but she was silent, feeling a trifle guilty herself. "Anyway," she concluded, "should I kiss his elbow to make him learn? If he cuts bread on his head, that's his own affair. . . ."

When I didn't show up then either, she was nevertheless surprised, and after finishing the exam looked for the list of candidates to check whether I was perhaps scheduled for the afternoon or some other day. To her great surprise, my name wasn't on the list for that day at all—or any other day, for that matter. It was quite obvious: I hadn't even signed up for that term.

When we saw each other again in May, she was preparing Concrete. When she asked me if I was studying for the exams I had not taken before, I told her that I, too, was preparing Concrete, and we continued to study together as in the old times, as if nothing had happened. We spent the whole spring studying, and when the June term came, she had already realized that I would not appear this time, either, and that she wouldn't be seeing me till fall. She watched me pensively with beautiful eyes so far apart that there was space between them for an entire mouth. And naturally, things were the same once again. She took and passed the Concrete exam, and I didn't even bother to come. Returning home satisfied with her success, but totally puzzled as far as my position was concerned, she noticed that, in the hurry of the previous day, I had forgotten my notebooks. Among them she caught sight of my student's booklet. She opened it and discovered with astonishment that I was not a student of mathematics at all, but of something else, and that I had been passing my exams regularly. She recalled the interminable hours of our joint study, which for me must have been a great strain without purpose, a big waste of time, and she asked the inevitable question: what for? Why did I spend all that time with her studying subjects that had nothing to do with my interests and the exams that I had to pass? She started thinking and came to one conclusion: one should always be aware of what is passed over in silence. The reason for all that was not the exam but she herself. Who would have thought that I would be so shy and unable to express my feelings for her? She immediately went to the rented room where I lived with a couple of people my age from Asia and Africa, was surprised by the poverty she saw, and received the information that I had gone home. When they also gave her the address of a small town near Salonica, she took her Buffalo without hesitation and started off toward the Aegean coast in search of me, having made up her mind to act as if she had discovered nothing unusual. So it was.

She arrived at sunset and found the house she had been told about wide open, with a great white bull tied to a nail, upon which fresh bread was impaled. Inside she noticed a bed, on the wall an icon, below the icon a red tassel, a pierced stone tied to a string, a top, a mirror, and an apple. A young naked person with long hair was lying on the bed, tanned by the sun, back turned to the window and resting on one elbow. The long ridge of the spine, which went all the way down the back and ended between the hips, curving slightly, vanished beneath a rough army blanket. She had the impression that the girl would turn any moment and that she would also see her breasts, deep, strong, and glowing in the warm evening. When that really took place, she saw that it was not a woman at all lying on the bed. Leaning on one arm I was chewing my moustache full of honey, which substituted for dinner. When she was noticed and brought into the house, she could still not help thinking of that first impression of finding a female person in my bed. But that impression, as well as the fatigue from a long drive, were soon forgotten. From a mirror-bottomed plate she received a double dinner: for herself and her soul in the mirror: some beans, a nut, and fish, and before the meal a small silver coin, which she held, as did I, under the tongue while eating. So one supper fed all four of us: the two of us and our two souls in the mirrors. After dinner she approached the icon and asked me what it represented.

"A television set," I told her. In other words, it is the window to another world which uses mathematics quite different from yours.

"How so?" she asked. 10

"Quite simple," I answered. "Machines, space crafts, and vehicles built on the basis of your quantitative mathematical evaluations are founded upon three elements, which are completely lacking in quantity. These are: singularity, the point, and the present moment. Only a sum of singularities constitutes a quantity; singularity itself is deprived of any quantitative measurement. As far as the point is concerned, since it doesn't have a single dimension, not width or height or length or depth, it can undergo neither measurement nor computation. The smallest components of time, however, always have one common denominator: that is the present moment, and it, too, is devoid of quantity and is immeasureable. Thus, the basic elements of your quantitative science represent something to whose very nature every quantitative approach is alien. How then should I believe in such a science? Why are machines made according to these quantitative misconceptions of such a short lifespan, three, four or more times shorter than the human ones? Look, I also have a white 'buffalo' like you. Only, he is made differently from yours, which was manufactured at Layland. Try him out and you will see that in a way he is better than the one you own."

"Is he tame?" she asked, smiling.

"Certainly," I answered. "Go ahead and try."

In front of the door she stroked the big white bull and slowly climbed onto his back. When I also mounted him, turning my back to the horns and facing her, I drove him by the sea, so that he had two feet in the water and the other two feet on the sand. She was surprised at first when I started to undress her. Piece by piece of her clothing fell into the water; then she started unbuttoning me. At one moment she stopped riding on the bull and started riding on me, feeling that I was growing heavier and heavier inside her. The bull beneath us did everything that we would otherwise have had to do ourselves, and she could tell no longer who was driving her pleasure, the bull or I. Sitting upon the double lover, she saw through the night how we passed by a forest of white cypresses, by people who were gathering dew and pierced stones on the seashore, by people who were building fires inside their own shadows and burning them up, by two women bleeding light, by a garden two hours long, where birds sang in the first hour and evening came in the second, where fruit bloomed in the first and there was a blizzard behind the winds. Then she felt that all the weight from me had passed into her and that the spurred bull had suddenly turned and taken her into the sea, leaving us finally to the waves that would separate us. . . .

However, she never told me a word about her discovery. In the fall, 15
when she was getting ready to graduate and when I offered to study with her again, she was not the least bit surprised. As before, we studied every day from seven until breakfast and then until half past ten; only now she did not try to help me master the subject I was doing and also stayed after ten-thirty for half an hour, which separated us from the books. When she graduated in September, she wasn't surprised at all when I didn't take the examination with her.

She was really surprised when she did not see me any more after that. Not that day, nor the following days, weeks, or examination terms. Never again. Astonished, she came to the conclusion that her assessment of my feelings for her was obviously wrong. Confused at not being able to tell what it was all about, she sat one morning in the same room in which we had studied together for years; then she caught sight of the Wedgwood tea set, which had been on the table since breakfast. Then she realized. For months, day after day, with tremendous effort and an immeasurable loss of time and energy, I had worked with her only in order to get a warm breakfast every morning, the only meal I was able to eat during those years. Having realized that, she asked herself another thing. Was it possible that in fact I hated her?

At the end, there is one more obligation left: to name the protagonists of this story. If the reader has not thought of it already, here is the answer. My name is the Balkans. Hers, Europe.

Analyzing the Text

1. How is the narrator, a university student, characterized at the beginning of the story and what ostensibly motivates him to spend so much time studying for exams with the girl? What clues begin to surface that suggest alternative explanations for his behavior?
2. What is the significance of the title insofar as it explains the mystery why the narrator spends so much time studying with the girl?

Understanding Pavić's Techniques

1. How does Pavić use the contrast between the way the girl lives and the narrator's circumstances as a theme of growing importance?
2. How do the details related to the narrator's poverty and lack of food begin to intrude in ways that suggest the real theme of the story?

Arguing for an Interpretation

1. Why is it ironic that the girl at one point believes the narrator is romantically interested in her? How is this element designed to make the reader assume this is a conventional love story?
2. After discovering what the characters really represent, what new perspective did you gain on the events in the story? You might wish to reread the story after you know it is a political allegory to appreciate Pavić's ingenuity in creating a kind of narrative called "hyperfiction," in which many different story lines are possible before they converge.

WAKAKO YAMAUCHI

Wakako Yamauchi was born in Westmoreland, California, in 1924, to parents who had immigrated from Japan. During World War II the family was sent to an internment camp in Arizona, where Yamauchi worked on the camp newspaper, the Poston Chronicle. *After the war, she took courses in design, drawing, and painting in Los Angeles, and from 1960 to 1974 submitted short stories and drawings to the* Los Angeles Rafu Shimpo, *a Japanese-American daily publication. The following short story was first published in 1974; in 1976 she expanded it into a play that was nominated by the Los Angeles Drama Critics Circle as outstanding new play of the year. Her published stories include "Marapoo Bay" (1989) and "Maybe" (1990). "And the Soul Shall Dance" reveals the intergenerational conflicts and tensions in an immigrant family and paints a complex and subtle portrait of a second wife and teenage stepdaughter struggling to survive in a new country.*

And the Soul Shall Dance

It's all right to talk about it now. Most of the principals are dead, except, of course, me and my younger brother, and possibly Kiyoko Oka, who might be near forty-five now, because, yes, I'm sure of it, she was fourteen then. I was nine, and my brother about four, so he hardly counts at all. Kiyoko's mother is dead, my father is dead, my mother is dead, and her father could not have lasted all these years with his tremendous appetite for alcohol and pickled chilies—those little yellow ones, so hot they could make your mouth hurt; he'd eat them like peanuts and tears would surge from his bulging thyroid eyes in great waves and stream down the dark coarse terrain of his face.

My father farmed then in the desert basin resolutely named Imperial Valley, in the township called Westmoreland; twenty acres of tomatoes, ten of summer squash, or vice versa, and the Okas lived maybe a mile, mile and a half, across an alkaline road, a stretch of greasewood, tumbleweed and white sand, to the south of us. We didn't hobnob much with them, because you see, they were a childless couple and we were a family: father, mother, daughter, and son, and we went to the Buddhist church on Sundays where my mother taught Japanese, and the Okas kept pretty much to themselves. I don't mean they were unfriendly; Mr. Oka would sometimes walk over (he rarely drove) on rainy days, all dripping wet, short and squat under a soggy newspaper, pretending to need a plow-blade or a file, and he would spend the afternoon in our kitchen drinking sake and eating chilies with my father. As he got progressively drunker, his large mouth would draw down and with the stream of tears, he looked like a kindly weeping bullfrog.

Not only were they childless, impractical in an area where large families were looked upon as labor potentials, but there was a certain strangeness about them. I became aware of it the summer our bathhouse burned down, and my father didn't get right down to building another, and a Japanese without a bathhouse . . . well, Mr. Oka offered us the use of his. So every night that summer we drove to the Okas for our bath, and we came in frequent contact with Mrs. Oka, and this is where I found the strangeness.

Mrs. Oka was small and spare. Her clothes hung on her like loose skin and when she walked, the skirt about her legs gave her a sort of webbed look. She was pretty in spite of the boniness and the dull calico and the barren look; I know now that she couldn't have been over thirty. Her eyes were large and a little vacant, although once I saw them fill with tears; the time I insisted we take the old Victrola over and we played our Japanese records for her. Some of the songs were sad, and I imagined the nostalgia she felt, but my mother said the tears were probably from yawning or from the smoke of her cigarettes. I thought my mother resented her for not being more hospitable; indeed, never a cup of tea appeared before us, and between them the conversation of women was totally absent: the rise and fall of gentle voices, the arched eyebrows, the croon of polite surprise. But more than this, Mrs. Oka was *different.*

Obviously she was shy, but some nights she disappeared altogether. She would see us drive into her yard and then lurch from sight. She was gone all evening. Where could she have hidden in that two-roomed house—where in that silent desert? Some nights she would wait out our visit with enormous forbearance, quietly pushing wisps of stray hair be-

hind her ears and waving gnats away from her great moist eyes, and some 5
nights she moved about with nervous agitation, her khaki canvas shoes slapping loudly as she walked. And sometimes there appeared to be welts and bruises on her usually smooth brown face, and she would sit solemnly, hands on lap, eyes large and intent on us. My mother hurried us home then: "Hurry, Masako, no need to wash well; hurry."

You see, being so poky, I was always last to bathe. I think the Okas bathed after we left because my mother often reminded me to keep the water clean. The routine was to lather outside the tub (there were buckets and pans and a small wooden stool), rinse off the soil and soap, and then soak in the tub of hot hot water and contemplate. Rivulets of perspiration would run down the scalp.

When my mother pushed me like this, I dispensed with ritual, rushed a bar of soap around me and splashed about a pan of water. So hastily toweled, my wet skin strapped the clothes to me, impeding my already clumsy progress. Outside, my mother would be murmuring her many apologies and my father, I knew, would be carrying my brother whose feet were already sandy. We would hurry home.

I thought Mrs. Oka might be insane and I asked my mother about it, but she shook her head and smiled with her mouth drawn down and said that Mrs. Oka loved her sake. This was unusual, yes, but there were other unusual women we knew. Mrs. Nagai was brought by her husband from a geisha house; Mrs. Tani was a militant Christian Scientist; Mrs. Abe, the midwife, was occult. My mother's statement explained much: sometimes Mrs. Oka was drunk and sometimes not. Her taste for liquor and cigarettes was a step in the realm of men; unusual for a Japanese wife, but at that time, in that place, and to me, Mrs. Oka loved her sake in the way my father loved his, in the way of Mr. Oka, and the way I loved my candy. That her psychology may have demanded this anesthetic, that she lived with something unendurable, did not occur to me. Nor did I perceive the violence of emotions that the purple welts indicated—or the masochism that permitted her to display these wounds to us.

In spite of her masculine habits, Mrs. Oka was never less than a woman. She was no lady in the area of social amenities; but the feminine in her was innate and never left her. Even in her disgrace, she was a small broken sparrow, slightly floppy, too slowly enunciating her few words, too carefully rolling her Bull Durham, cocking her small head and moistening the ocher tissue. Her aberration was a protest of the life assigned her; it was obstinate, but unobserved, alas, unheeded. "Strange" was the only concession we granted her.

Toward the end of summer, my mother said we couldn't continue bathing at the Okas'; when winter set in we'd all catch our death from the commuting and she'd always felt dreadful about our imposition on Mrs. Oka. So my father took the corrugated tin sheets he'd found on the highway and had been saving for some other use and built up our bathhouse
again. Mr. Oka came to help. 10

While they raised the quivering tin walls, Mr. Oka began to talk. His voice was sharp and clear above the low thunder of the metal sheets.

He told my father he had been married in Japan previously to the present Mrs. Oka's older sister. He had a child by the marriage, Kiyoko, a girl. He had left the two to come to America intending to send for them soon, but shortly after his departure, his wife passed away from an obscure stomach ailment. At the time, the present Mrs. Oka was young and had foolishly become involved with a man of poor reputation. The family was anxious to part the lovers and conveniently arranged a marriage by proxy and sent him his dead wife's sister. Well that was all right, after all, they were kin, and it would be good for the child when she came to join them. But things didn't work out that way, year after year he postponed calling for his daughter, couldn't get the price of fare together, and the wife—ahhh, the wife, Mr. Oka's groan was lost in the rumble of his hammering.

He cleared his throat. The girl was now fourteen, he said, and begged to come to America to be with her own real family. Those relatives had forgotten the favor he'd done in accepting a slightly used bride, and now tormented his daughter for being forsaken. True, he'd not sent much money, but if they knew, if they only knew how it was here.

"Well," he sighed, "who could be blamed? It's only right she be with me anyway."

"That's right," my father said.

"Well, I sold the horse and some other things and managed to buy a third-class ticket on the Taiyo-Maru. Kiyoko will get here the first week of September." Mr. Oka glanced toward my father, but my father was peering into a bag of nails. "I'd be much obliged to you if your wife and little girl," he rolled his eyes toward me, "would take kindly to her. She'll be lonely."

Kiyoko-san came in September. I was surprised to see so very nearly a woman; short, robust, buxom: the female counterpart of her father; thyroid eyes and protruding teeth, straight black hair banded impudently into two bristly shucks, Cuban heels and white socks. Mr. Oka brought her proudly to us.

"Little Masako here," for the first time to my recollection, he touched me; he put his rough fat hand on the top of my head, "is very smart in school. She will help you with your school work, Kiyoko," he said.

I had so looked forward to Kiyoko-san's arrival. She would be my soul mate; in my mind I had conjured a girl of my own proportion: thin and tall, but with the refinement and beauty I didn't yet possess that would surely someday come to the fore. My disappointment was keen and apparent. Kiyoko-san stepped forward shyly, then retreated with a short bow and small giggle, her fingers pressed to her mouth.

My mother took her away. They talked for a long time—about Japan, about enrollment in American school, the clothes Kiyoko-san would need, and where to look for the best values. As I watched them, it occurred to me that I had been deceived: this was not a child, this was a woman. The smile pressed behind her fingers, the way of her nod, so brief, like my mother when father scolded her: the face was inscrutable, but something—maybe spirit—shrank visibly, like a piece of silk in water. I was disappointed; Kiyoko-san's soul was barricaded in her unenchanting appearance and the smile she fenced behind her fingers.

She started school from third grade, one below me, and as it turned out, she quickly passed me by. There wasn't much I could help her with except to drill her on pronunciation—the "L" and "R" sounds. Every morning walking to our rural school: land, leg, library, loan, lot; every afternoon returning home: ran, rabbit, rim, rinse, roll. That was the extent of our communication; friendly but uninteresting.

One particularly cold November night—the wind outside was icy; I was sitting on my bed, my brother's and mine, oiling the cracks in my chapped hands by lamplight—someone rapped urgently at our door. It was Kiyoko-san; she was hysterical, she wore no wrap, her teeth were chattering, and except for the thin straw zori, her feet were bare. My mother led her to the kitchen, started a pot of tea, and gestured to my brother and me to retire. I lay very still but because of my brother's restless tossing and my father's snoring, was unable to hear much. I was aware, though, that drunken and savage brawling had brought Kiyoko-san to us. Presently they came to the bedroom. I feigned sleep. My mother gave Kiyoko-san a gown and pushed me over to make room for her. My mother spoke firmly: "Tomorrow you will return to them; you must not leave them again. They are your people." I could almost feel Kiyoko-san's short nod.

All night long I lay cramped and still, afraid to intrude into her hulking back. Two or three times her icy feet jabbed into mine and quickly retreated. In the morning I found my mother's gown neatly folded on the spare pillow. Kiyoko-san's place in bed was cold.

She never came to weep at our house again but I know she cried: her eyes were often swollen and red. She stopped much of her giggling and routinely pressed her fingers to her mouth. Our daily pronunciation drill petered off from lack of interest. She walked silently with her shoulders hunched, grasping her books with both arms, and when I spoke to her in my halting Japanese, she absently corrected my prepositions.

Spring comes early in the Valley; in February the skies are clear though the air is still cold. By March, winds are vigorous and warm and wild flowers dot the desert floor, cockleburs are green and not yet tenacious, the sand is crusty underfoot, everywhere there is a smell of things growing and the first tomatoes are showing green and bald.

25 As the weather changed, Kiyoko-san became noticeably more cheerful. Mr. Oka, who hated so to drive, could often be seen steering his dusty old Ford over the road that passes our house, and Kiyoko-san sitting in front would sometimes wave gaily to us. Mrs. Oka was never with them. I thought of these trips as the westernizing of Kiyoko-san: with a permanent wave, her straight black hair became tangles of tiny frantic curls; between her textbooks she carried copies of *Modern Screen* and *Photoplay*, her clothes were gay with print and piping, and she bought a pair of brown suede shoes with alligator trim. I can see her now picking her way gingerly over the deceptive white peaks of alkaline crust.

At first my mother watched their coming and going with vicarious pleasure. "Probably off to a picture show; the stores are all closed at this hour," she might say. Later her eyes would get distant and she would muse. "They've left her home again; Mrs. Oka is alone again, the poor woman."

Now when Kiyoko-san passed by or came in with me on her way home, my mother would ask about Mrs. Oka—how is she, how does she occupy herself these rainy days, or these windy or warm or cool days. Often the answers were polite: "Thank you, we are fine," but sometimes Kiyoko-san's upper lip would pull over her teeth, and her voice would become very soft and she would say, "Drink, always drinking and fighting." And those times my mother would invariably say, "Endure, soon you will be marrying and going away."

Once a young truck driver delivered crates at the Oka farm and he dropped back to our place to tell my father that Mrs. Oka had lurched behind his truck while he was backing up, and very nearly let him kill her. Only the daughter pulling her away saved her, he said. Thoroughly unnerved, he stopped by to rest himself and talk about it. Never, never, he said in wide-eyed wonder, had he seen a drunken Japanese woman. My father nodded gravely, "Yes, it's unusual," he said and drummed his knee with his fingers.

Evenings were longer now, and when my mother's migraines drove me from the house in unbearable self-pity, I would take walks in the desert. One night with the warm wind against me, the dune primrose and yellow poppies closed and fluttering, the greasewood swaying in languid orbit, I lay on the white sand beneath a shrub and tried to disappear.

A voice sweet and clear cut through the half-dark of the evening: 30

Red lips press against a glass
Drink the purple wine
        And the soul shall dance

Mrs. Oka appeared to be gathering flowers. Bending, plucking, standing, searching, she added to a small bouquet she clasped. She held them away; looked at them slyly, lids lowered, demure, then in a sudden and sinuous movement, she broke into a stately dance. She stopped, gathered more flowers, and breathed deeply into them. Tossing her head, she laughed—softly, beautifully, from her dark throat. The picture of her imagined grandeur was lost to me, but the delusion that transformed the bouquet of tattered petals and sandy leaves, and the aloneness of a desert twilight into a fantasy that brought such joy and abandon made me stir with discomfort. The sound broke Mrs. Oka's dance. Her eyes grew large and her neck tense—like a cat on the prowl. She spied me in the bushes. A peculiar chill ran through me. Then abruptly and with childlike delight, she scattered the flowers around her and walked away singing:

Falling, falling, petals on a wind . . .

That was the last time I saw Mrs. Oka. She died before the spring harvest. It was pneumonia. I didn't attend the funeral, but my mother said it was sad. Mrs. Oka looked peaceful, and the minister expressed the irony of the long separation of Mother and Child and the short-lived reunion; hardly a year together, she said. We went to help Kiyoko-san address and stamp those black-bordered acknowledgments.

When harvest was over, Mr. Oka and Kiyoko-san moved out of the Valley. We never heard from them or saw them again and I suppose in a large city, Mr. Oka found some sort of work, perhaps as a janitor or a dishwasher and Kiyoko-san grew up and found someone to marry.

Analyzing the Text

1. Under what circumstances did Mrs. Oka come to marry her husband, and how might these explain her actions?
2. In what ways does the narrator change as a result of knowing Mr. Oka's daughter, Kiyoko? How does the narrator's interpretation of Mrs. Oka's predicament differ from that of her mother?

Understanding Yamauchi's Techniques

1. How do the images used to describe Mrs. Oka's dance symbolize all that her life could have been?

2. To what extent do the elements of setting, such as the isolated, harsh agricultural environment, play in helping the reader understand Mrs. Oka's despair?

Arguing for an Interpretation

1. Could you make a case that Kiyoko is actually more of a victim than her stepmother, Mrs. Oka? Explain your answer. Do you agree with the narrator's final prediction about Kiyoko? Why or why not?
2. In a few paragraphs, complete the portrait started by Yamauchi about the narrator, her relationship to her parents, the Okas, and especially Kiyoko, and how she sees herself as a Japanese-American.

Alice Walker

Alice Walker was born in 1944 in Eatonton, Georgia, the eighth child of sharecroppers. She graduated from Sarah Lawrence College in 1965 and has taught at Yale, Wellesley, and other colleges. She has published three volumes of poetry and a book of essays. Her numerous works of fiction include **Meridian** ***(1982),*** **The Color Purple** ***(1982), which was made into a widely acclaimed motion picture and for which she won the Pulitzer Prize,*** **Possessing the Secret of Joy** ***(1992),*** **By the Light of My Father's Smile** ***(1998), and*** **The Way Forward Is with a Broken Heart** ***(2000). Walker currently operates Wild Trees Press, based in San Francisco. In "The Flowers," from*** **In Love and Trouble: Stories of Black Women** ***(1973), a girl on an innocent jaunt stumbles across a reminder of the region's past horrors.***

The Flowers

It seemed to Myop as she skipped lightly from hen house to pigpen to smokehouse that the days had never been as beautiful as these. The air held a keenness that made her nose twitch. The harvesting of the corn and cotton, peanuts and squash, made each day a golden surprise that caused excited little tremors to run up her jaws.

Myop carried a short, knobby stick. She struck out at random at chickens she liked, and worked out the beat of a song on the fence around the pigpen. She felt light and good in the warm sun. She was ten, and nothing existed for her but her song, the stick clutched in her dark brown hand, and the tat-de-ta-ta-ta of accompaniment.

Turning her back on the rusty boards of her family's sharecropper cabin, Myop walked along the fence till it ran into the stream made by the spring. Around the spring, where the family got drinking water, silver ferns and wildflowers grew. Along the shallow banks pigs rooted. Myop watched the tiny white bubbles disrupt the thin black scale of soil and the water that silently rose and slid away down the stream.

She had explored the woods behind the house many times. Often, in late autumn, her mother took her to gather nuts among the fallen leaves. Today she made her own path, bouncing this way and that way, vaguely keeping an eye out for snakes. She found, in addition to various common but pretty ferns and leaves, an armful of strange blue flowers with velvety ridges and a sweetsuds bush full of the brown, fragrant buds.

By twelve o'clock, her arms laden with sprigs of her findings, she was a mile or more from home. She had often been as far before, but the strangeness of the land made it not as pleasant as her usual haunts. It 5
seemed gloomy in the little cove in which she found herself. The air was damp, the silence close and deep.

Myop began to circle back to the house, back to the peacefulness of the morning. It was then she stepped smack into his eyes. Her heel became lodged in the broken ridge between brow and nose, and she reached down quickly, unafraid, to free herself. It was only when she saw his naked grin that she gave a little yelp of surprise.

He had been a tall man. From feet to neck covered a long space. His head lay beside him. When she pushed back the leaves and layers of earth and debris Myop saw that he'd had large white teeth, all of them cracked or broken, long fingers, and very big bones. All his clothes had rotted away except some threads of blue denim from his overalls. The buckles of the overalls had turned green.

Myop gazed around the spot with interest. Very near where she'd stepped into the head was a wild pink rose. As she picked it to add to her bundle she noticed a raised mound, a ring, around the rose's root. It was the rotted remains of a noose, a bit of shredding plowline, now blending benignly into the soil. Around an overhanging limb of a great spreading oak clung another piece. Frayed, rotted, bleached, and frazzled—barely there—but spinning restlessly in the breeze. Myop laid down her flowers.

And the summer was over.

Analyzing the Text

1. How would you characterize Myop at the beginning of the story?
2. What effect does the unexpected sight have on her?

Understanding Walker's Techniques

1. How does Walker structure the narrative to heighten suspense about the circumstances that have led to the remains Myop stumbles upon?
2. What details emphasize the contrast between her customary walks and the events of this day? What role do the images Walker uses to describe the remains play in communicating the underlying horror of events that took place in the past?

Arguing for an Interpretation

1. In what sense can the story be read as an allegory of short-sightedness (Myop as a shortened form of myopia) in unearthing historical realities that have been present, but ignored for many years?
2. What does Myop's decision to leave the flowers she had picked suggest about how this event has changed her life?

Poems

Bruce Springsteen

Bruce Springsteen was born 1949 in Freehold, New Jersey. He began performing in New York and New Jersey night clubs and signed with Columbia Records in 1972. He has given numerous nationwide and international concert tours with the E-Street Band. He received the Grammy Award for best male rock vocalist in 1984, 1987, 1994, and 2003. The Academy Award and the Golden Globe Award for best original song in a film were given to him for "Streets of Philadelphia" from the film Philadelphia *(1994). His albums include* Greetings from Asbury Park, N.J. *(1973),* Born to Run *(1975),* Darkness on the Edge of Town *(1978),* Born in the USA *(1984),* Tunnel of Love *(1987),* Bruce Springsteen's Greatest Hits *(1995), and* The Rising, *a tribute to the victims of September 11, 2001 which won the 2003 Grammy Award for best album.*

Streets of Philadelphia

I was bruised and battered: I couldn't tell what I felt.
I was unrecognizable to myself.
Saw my reflection in a window and didn't know my own face.
Oh, brother are you gonna leave me wastin' away on the streets of Philadelphia.
Ain't no angel gonna greet me: it's just you and I, my friend.
And my clothes don't fit me no more: I walked a thousand miles just to slip this skin.

I walked the avenue till my legs felt like stone.
I heard the voices of friends vanished and gone.
At night I could hear the blood in my veins
Just as black and whispering as the rain
On the streets of Philadelphia.
Ain't no angel gonna greet me: it's just you and I, my friend.
And my clothes don't fit me no more: I walked a thousand miles just to slip this skin.

The night has fallen. I'm lying awake.
I can feel myself fading away.
So, receive me, brother, with your faithless kiss.
Or will we leave each other alone like this
On the streets of Philadelphia?

Ain't no angel gonna greet me: it's just you and I, my friend.
And my clothes don't fit me no more: I walked a thousand
miles just to slip this skin.

Analyzing the Text

1. How would you characterize the voice you hear? What images convey the speaker's sense of losing himself because of having AIDS?
2. How does being recognized and acknowledged become a central theme in the song? At what point in the lyrics does the speaker appeal for this recognition?

Understanding Springsteen's Techniques

1. Which key phrases dramatize the theme of rejection?
2. How does the refrain function to underscore the psychological and emotional distance the speaker has traveled to reach this point?

Arguing for an Interpretation

1. Springsteen's song differs from a classic blues song in one important respect: blues generally mourn the loss of a lover, while this song is about the sorrow of losing one's self. How has Springsteen incorporated elements of blues and traditional gospel songs to create these lyrics?
2. To what extent has Springsteen managed to avoid being overly sentimental or reducing people with AIDS to stereotyped clichés? What effect did this song have on you?

LENNART SJÖGREN

Lennart Sjögren (b. 1930) lives in Oland, Sweden, in an agricultural community where he was born and grew up. He studied art in Gothenberg in the 1950s, and although he still paints, he is best known for his poetry. He has produced nearly twenty books, chiefly of poems, but also short stories, lyrical prose, and essays. His most recent collection of poems is Selected Poems *(1980). Sjögren's writing has the qualities of classic still-life paintings that present a self-contained world that conveys a paradoxical sense of life standing still. His work creates a sense of mystery, partly because the reader has to infer so much from a minimum of details. "The Roses," translated by Robin Fulton (1990), is a short prose piece (a genre practiced by many Swedish poets) in which a fragment of a total situation is subtly suggested through carefully chosen details.*

The Roses

The phones ring in the empty house, both upstairs and down. The carpets hear them ringing, so do the windows, and the faces inside the picture-frames. But these are all fixed in their places. They trust in Silence to hurry to the phone. The wallpaper roses are imprisoned in the walls and the cutlery is lying, in spite of its sheen, piled together in their compartments like life-time prisoners.

Silence leaps up from his chair, reaches the phone at the third ring, lifts the receiver and replies. But whoever is ringing hears nothing and calls hello in vain.

"It's about someone who's bleeding to death. Answer, for God's sake! Answer, and prevent a tragedy!"

"It's about the sharing out of an inheritance, it's a family matter. You must answer, your silence could have unforseeable legal consequences."

"It's about someone who's just been born. About the umbilical cord, you must realize!"

"It's about an impending accident which only your voice can prevent. A fateful mistake. Aren't you listening, you must listen!"

Again and again Silence calls out his reply into the receiver. But his voice cannot be transmitted through such wires.

"It's about some flowers that were ordered. Can the roses be delivered?"

But no matter how often the phone rings, nothing helps. The pictures persist with their wailing, and the window-panes still dream of being able to burst free. Silence sits in his chair paralyzed.

The unstopped bleeding proves fatal. The misunderstandings multiply. The umbilical cord is not cut. The inheritance goes to the wrong person. And the roses are left without a recipient.

Analyzing the Text

1. What psychological state does the poem evoke by describing different situations where a response is required?
2. How do the undelivered real roses symbolize the qualities that would have enabled the unseen occupants to break out of their isolation?

Understanding Sjögren's Techniques

1. Although we normally expect a writer to achieve a sense of dramatic conflict with human characters, how does Sjögren use household objects and furnishings to suggest an inability to communicate?
2. It is rather unusual to read a poem written in prose. How does the prose form of the poem suit its subject?

Arguing for an Interpretation

1. Speculate on the behind-the-scenes story that might explain the alienation dramatized in this poem.
2. In your opinion, has Sjögren done an effective job of allowing readers to infer the identity of the unseen occupants of the house? Why or why not?

To what extent does he suggest that the family members are more concerned about their social status than the well-being of each other?

WING TEK LUM

Wing Tek Lum was born in 1946 in Honolulu, Hawaii. Lum was educated at Brown University and the Union Theological Seminary in New York City, and worked in New York's Chinatown for four years. During his stay in New York, he received the Poetry Center's Discovery Award in 1970. He lived in Hong Kong for three years employed as a social worker before returning to Honolulu, where he helps operate the family real estate business. His first collection of poems, Expounding the Doubtful Points *(1987), reprinted 1995, won the Creative Literature Award from the Association for Asian American Studies in 1988 and The Before Columbus Foundation American Book Award in 1989. Most of Lum's poems deal with familial and domestic experiences in the context of Chinese-American-Hawaiian associations and cultural constructs. "Minority Poem" counters the myth of a pluralistic United States with an acerbic look at the underlying intolerance of the dominant Anglo culture that pays lip service to the ideals of multiculturalism.*

Minority Poem

Why
we're just as American
as apple pie—
that is, if you count
the leftover peelings
lying on the kitchen counter
which the cook has forgotten about
or doesn't know
quite what to do with
except hope that the maid
when she cleans off the chopping block
will chuck them away
into a garbage can she'll take out
on leaving for the night.

Analyzing the Text

1. In what way does the poem assail conventional assumptions about who is mainstream and who is marginal within American culture?

2. What kinds of unacknowledged labor does the author allude to by using the image of making an apple pie?

Understanding Tek Lum's Techniques

1. How would you characterize the voice of the speaker you hear in this poem?
2. In what way does the poem create a scenario that uses dramatic irony to satirize the traditional view of American mainstream culture?

Arguing for an Interpretation

1. In what ways does the poem argue for broadening the concept of what being an American means?
2. Is the poem an effective attack on the myth of a pluralistic United States? Why or why not?

Rahel Chalfi

Born in Israel, but reared in Mexico, Rahel Chalfi has been acclaimed as one of the most talented writers of Hebrew poetry. She is also a well-known playwright who has received a number of awards in both Israel and abroad, including best original play award in 1967 from Israel's Committee for Culture and Literature. Her play Felicidad *was published in English in 1974. She has also received the 1971 Shubert Playwriting Award from the University of California, Berkeley, the 1983 Film Award by the Israeli Film Institute, and the 1989 Prime Minister's Award for Literature. She has published five volumes of poetry, including* Submarine and Other Poems *(1976),* Free Fall *(1979),* Chameleon, or the Principle of Uncertainty *(1987),* Underwater and Other Poems *(1989), and* Matter *(1990). Chalfi's gifts as a poet reflect her remarkable sensitivity to a spectrum of minute feelings, sensations, and states of consciousness that have no corresponding words. The experience that is of special interest to her is the ineffable multifaceted quality of the single moment. "Porcupine Fish," translated by Robert Friend (1977), explores the tension between the need to show bravado and feelings of vulnerability.*

Porcupine Fish

Apparently a fish like you and me.
But there is something nail-like about him.

Slowly he glides,
examining himself in that great mirror called water
and asking why,
why these nails planted in his flesh,

why this need for endless wariness
that sharpens him, keeps him from being one
with the blue enfolding softness.

And then
the waters breathe,
something moves,
something alien perhaps,
certainly malign.
His spines bristle.
He turns into something else—
a swollen ball,
a small mountain of fear—
all roar, if one could hear.
His mouth—small, tight, rectangular—
distorts into a smile.
And his eyes, tiny pools in a suddenly vast forehead,
whirl violent images in his brain.

This time, however,
it was nothing really.

And he subsides
into the rigid destiny
of his nail-like self.

Analyzing the Text

1. What unusual features does the porcupine fish possess to scare off predators, and what details suggest a sense of a menacing environment?
2. What features of the poem suggest that Chalfi is drawing an analogy between the porcupine fish and the geopolitical situation in Israel?

Understanding Chalfi's Techniques

1. How does Chalfi use figurative language and personification to enhance a sense of psychological realism in the poem?
2. How does the form of the poem reflect the transformation of the porcupine fish and its return to a state of wariness?

Arguing for an Interpretation

1. How effective is Chalfi's portrait in communicating a sense of the porcupine fish's appearance, movements, and feelings?
2. Describe an object, animal, or natural force using metaphors or similes, but in the form of a riddle without telling the reader what the answer is. Your description should use active verbs that help your readers imagine the answer.

Diane Wakoski

Diane Wakoski was born in Whittier, California, in 1927. She was educated at the University of California, Berkeley, and settled in New York City in the early 1960s where she worked in a bookstore and taught English in a junior high school until 1969. During this period she wrote and published such volumes as Coins and Coffins *(1962),* The George Washington Poems *(1967), and* Inside the Blood Factory *(1968). She has taught at various universities, given poetry readings, and conducted verse-writing workshops. Volumes of her poetry include* Waiting for the King of Spain *(1976) and* The Man Who Shook Hands *(1978). Her collections include* Emerald Ice: Selected Poems 1962–1987 *(1988), which won the Poetry Society of America's William Carlos Williams Award and* Medea the Sorceress *(1990), in which "The Orange" appears. A recent work is* The Butcher's Apron: New and Selected Poems *(2000). She is currently writer in residence at Michigan State University. Taken as a whole, Wakoski's poetry projects an imaginary autobiography in which fantastic leaps of the imagination and surrealistic images allow her to reinvent her identity in ways that are typically American. As is typical of poetry of self-transformation, "The Orange" relies on digressions and tangential wanderings through imagery and fantasy to explore the speaker's sensation of freedom from emotional entanglements while driving from Los Angeles to Las Vegas.*

The Orange

Driving through the desert at night in summer
can be
like peeling an orange,
the windows rolled down, the prickly scent
of mesquite and sage
blowing through the car, the
perfume
of the twilight shadowed earth lingering,
as if the sticky juice
of the orange
were shading and matting your hands,
the acrid spray of the peel;
with its meaty white pillow
nestles into your fingers.

You are driving from Los Angeles to Las Vegas,
running from your loneliness, an empty house,
an ocean which brings neither father nor lover.

For one hour, the wind streams through
your car, a
three-year-old Pontiac you have named Green Greed;

for one hour, the scent of all the desert
plants makes you feel
loved, makes you
forget you have no one
to talk to. You do not care about the
myth of the West, about
the City of Angels and its beaches.

You are not yet even slightly
interested in
gambling.
You are 32
and feel you have a destiny. Somehow
in that car,
on that night, alone on the wind-cooled highway between
California
and Nevada, for one hour,
the fragrance of sage, especially,
made you complete,
moving swiftly over your face, through
nostrils, the car, you warm,
from desert day fire.

You were not even looking
yet, for Beethoven in Las Vegas,
Snake Mother in the desert.
Your life was over, or
had not yet begun. Did you see
a map of Michigan filling your hand
as you peeled the big navel orange,
the one which glowed like fireflies
that wink
in Michigan summer nights?
The white membrane, the orange raindrop
textured meat of the fruit
saturating your hands with sugar
as you drive, as you drove,
as you remembered one
beginning?

Analyzing the Text

1. How does the trip through the desert and the peeling of an orange coincide with the speaker's sense of sudden liberation from the obligations and responsibilities of her life?
2. Why is it significant that the poem seems to have been written from the vantage point of someone who is older, describing the feelings of an earlier self?

Understanding Wakoski's Techniques

1. How does Wakoski allude to the as yet unlived experiences that will become important to a former "you"?

2. What role do tactile and sensory images and the free-form nature of the stanzas play in creating a sense of freedom and emergence in the moment?

Arguing for an Interpretation

1. How effectively does Wakoski convey the sense of momentary release from responsibilites?
2. Is the orange a fortuitous choice or would some other natural object, such as an onion or a banana, served just as well? Explain your answer.

CZESLAW MILOSZ

One of the greatest twentieth-century Polish poets and essayists, and arguably one of the most important figures in world literature, Czeslaw Milosz was born in 1911 in Seteiniai, Lithuania (then part of the Russian empire). Milosz spent a good part of his youth in the city of Vilnius where he attended high school, and in 1929 he entered King Stefan Batory University. In 1930, he made his writing debut in a student journal and together with several other poets and critics founded a literary group, Zagary. In 1931, on a trip to Paris, Milosz met his distant relative, the French symbolist poet Oscar V. de L. Milosz, who influenced the evolution of his work. His first books of poetry, published when he was twenty-one, were greeted with critical acclaim. During World War II he worked with the underground Resistance movement against the Nazis and after the war he held posts in the Polish diplomatic service. While in Paris, in 1951, he sought political asylum and later moved to the United States where he still lives.

In addition to numerous volumes of poetry, Milosz, during this period, wrote The Captive Mind *(1953), a study of the capitulation of Eastern European intellectuals to Stalinism; a political novel,* The Seizure of Power *(1953); and* Native Realm, *a long treatise in verse on poetry's relation to nature and history (1957). In 1961, he took a position as professor of Slavic languages at the University of California, Berkeley, where he currently resides.*

Most of the poetry he has written since the 1960s is available in English translation in Selected Poems *(1973),* Bells in Winter *(1978),* The Witness of Poetry *(1983),* The Separate Notebooks *(1984), and* Unattainable Earth *(1986). He also began the extraordinarily ambitious project of translating the Bible into modern Polish, and to date has translated a number of books from both the Old and New Testaments. Recognition of his incomparable influence in areas as diverse as politics, poetics, history, and metaphysics came in the form of the Neustadt International Literary Prize in 1978 and the Nobel Prize for literature in 1980. Milosz's poetry is characterized by a strong historical sense and a constant awareness of per-*

sonal transience; the speaker seems to oscillate between his private concerns and contemplations of social and global problems. This predicament is eloquently presented in "My Faithful Mother Tongue" (1968), from The Collected Poems, 1931–1987 *(1988). His latest works include* New and Collected Poems, 1931–2001 *(2001) and* Milosz's ABC's *(2001).*

My Faithful Mother Tongue

Faithful mother tongue
I have been serving you.
Every night, I used to set before you little bowls of colors
so you could have your birch, your cricket, your finch
as preserved in my memory.

This lasted many years.
You were my native land; I lacked any other.
I believed that you would also be a messenger
between me and some good people
even if they were few, twenty, ten
or not born, as yet.

Now, I confess my doubt.
There are moments when it seems to me I have squandered my life.
For you are a tongue of the debased,
of the unreasonable, hating themselves
even more than they hate other nations,
a tongue of informers,
a tongue of the confused,
ill with their own innocence.

But without you, who am I?
Only a scholar in a distant country,
a success, without fears and humiliations.
Yes, who am I without you?
Just a philosopher, like everyone else.

I understand, this is meant as my education:
the glory of individuality is taken away,
Fortune spreads a red carpet
before the sinner in a morality play
while on the linen backdrop a magic lantern throws
images of human and divine torture.

Faithful mother tongue,
perhaps after all it's I who must try to save you.

So I will continue to set before you little bowls of colors
bright and pure if possible,
for what is needed in misfortune is a little order and
beauty.

Analyzing the Text

1. What motivates the speaker to continue writing in Polish when he could reach a much wider audience if he wrote in English?
2. In what different ways do the language and culture of Poland provide the ultimate key to Milosz's identity, both as a writer and as a person, despite the betrayals he condemns?

Understanding Milosz's Techniques

1. How does the image of "little bowls of color" express the unique contributions that he feels he is only able to make by using his "mother tongue"?
2. Which phrases demonstrate how profoundly his own sense of identity is connected with his native language?

Arguing for an Interpretation

1. In what sense is the speaker upholding an idealized view of his mother country despite changes in his own circumstances and a worsening political situation in Poland?
2. Milosz is not atypical in his fear that by losing contact with his native language, he will become a rootless exile. Create a counterargument urging Milosz to redefine himself in his new adopted country and to write in English.

BARBARA KINGSOLVER

Barbara Kingsolver was born in 1955 in Annapolis, Maryland, and was raised in rural Kentucky. She received her B.A. from DePauw University (1977) and a Master's degree in biology from the University of Arizona (1981). She had a career as a journalist and technical writer before turning to fiction and poetry in the 1980s. Her novels include The Poisonwood Bible *(1998) and* Prodigal Summer *(2000). Kingsolver's collections of poetry include* Another America *(1991), in which the following poem first appeared. She has also written nonfiction works, including* Holding the Line *(1989) and* High Tide in Tucson *(1995) and a collection of short stories,* Homeland *(1989). Her poetry is passionate and blends personal commentary with insight into contemporary patterns of family relationships. Her most recent work is a volume of essays,* Small Wonder *(2002).*

This House I Cannot Leave

My friend describes the burglar:
how he touched her clothes, passed through rooms
leaving himself there,
staining the space
between walls, a thing she can see.
She doesn't care what he took, only
that he has driven her out, she can't
stay in this house
she loved, scraped the colors of four families
from the walls and painted with her own,
and planted things.
She is leaving fruit trees behind.

She will sell, get out, maybe
another neighborhood.
People say
Get over it. The market isn't good. They advise
that she think about cash to mortgage
and the fruit trees

but the trees have stopped growing for her.

I offer no advice.
I tell her I know, she will leave. I am thinking
of the man who broke and entered

me.

Of the years it took to be home again
in this house I cannot leave.

Analyzing the Text

1. How does the speaker apply the problem confronting her friend to her own life? What important differences make the speaker's situation more poignant?
2. How do the poem's last lines suggest an uneasy coming to terms with a previous trauma the speaker experienced?

Understanding Kingsolver's Techniques

1. Why is the metaphor of a house that has been burglarized particularly apt to describe the speaker's predicament?
2. How do the references to the advice of other people make it clear that only those who have experienced a trauma of this kind can understand what it means?

Arguing for an Interpretation

1. In your opinion, why doesn't the speaker offer the same sensible advice of the other friends? What advice would you have given?

2. What insights does the poem offer into the psychology of defilement and what people need to feel whole again?

Kelly Cherry

Kelly Cherry was born in 1940 in Baton Rouge, Louisiana. She received a B.A. from Mary Washington College in 1961 and an M.F.A. from the University of North Carolina at Greensboro in 1967. She is currently professor of English at the University of Wisconsin at Madison. Her works of fiction include Augusta Played: A Novel *(1998) and* The Society of Friends: Stories *(1999). Her collections of poetry are* Death and Transfiguration *(1997), in which "Alzheimer's" first appeared, and* Rising Venus *(2002).*

Alzheimer's

He stands at the door, a crazy old man
Back from the hospital, his mind rattling
Like the suitcase, swinging from his hand,
That contains shaving cream, a piggy bank,
A book he sometimes pretends to read,
His clothes. On the brick wall beside him
Roses and columbine slug it out for space, claw the mortar.
The sun is shining, as it does late in the afternoon
In England, after rain.
Sun hardens the house, reifies it,
Strikes the iron grillwork like a smithy
And sparks fly off, burning in the bushes—
The rosebushes—
While the white wood trim defines solidity in space.
This is his house. He remembers it as his,
Remembers the walkway he built between the front room
And the garage, the rhododendron he planted in back,
The car he used to drive. He remembers himself,
A younger man, in a tweed hat, a man who loved
Music. There is no time for that now. No time for music,
The peculiar screeching of strings, the luxurious
Fiddling with emotion.
Other things have become more urgent.
Other matters are now of greater import, have more
Consequence, must be attended to. The first
Thing he must do, now that he is home, is decide who
This woman is, this old, white-haired woman
Standing here in the doorway,
Welcoming him in.

Analyzing the Text

1. What can you infer about the differences in the self-awareness of the "old man" in the poem before and after the onset of Alzheimer's?
2. Why is the final image in the last three lines especially effective in communicating how much of the "old man's" identity and memory have been lost?

Understanding Cherry's Techniques

1. In what way is the punctuation in the first six lines effective in communicating the physical and mental predicament of the subject of the poem?
2. How do the repeated words and pauses in the last seven lines enact the sense of urgency the subject experiences in trying to focus his thoughts?

Arguing for an Interpretation

1. To what extent does this poem lessen the tendency to dismiss the subject as merely a "crazy old man"?
2. How do the images in lines 15 through 20 serve as a flashback that makes the subject's present situation all the more tragic?

Drama

TEWFIK AL-HAKIM

Widely recognized as the Arab world's leading playwright, Tewfik al-Hakim (1898–1987) was born in Alexandria, Egypt. He studied law at the University of Cairo and at the Sorbonne in Paris. After serving as a public prosecutor in Alexandria, he held a variety of positions with the Egyptian government. He was appointed director general of the Egyptian National Library and served as Egyptian representative to UNESCO, based in Paris, in 1959–1960. He was awarded the State Literature Prize in 1961. Al-Hakim has made major pioneering contributions to the development of modern literary Arabic in his over one hundred plays, several novels, essays, and memoirs. His unique ability to seamlessly blend the theater of the absurd with satire and social criticism can be seen in plays such as Food for the Millions *(1963),* The Tree Climber *(1966), and* Fate of a Cockroach and Other Plays *(1973). In* The Donkey Market *(1975), translated by Denys Johnson-Davies, al-Hakim adapts a well-known story about the wise fool that has been part of Egyptian folklore for centuries. Desperate for food and longing for a place to sleep, two unemployed laborers hatch an ingenious scheme to delude a gullible farmer into believing that his newly purchased donkey has been transformed into a human being. Under its hilarious surface, this play grapples with the centuries-old cultural intransigence that makes it difficult to introduce constructive social changes into contemporary Egyptian society.*

The Donkey Market

Cast

TWO UNEMPLOYED MEN

FARMER

FARMER'S WIFE

Scene One

Near the donkey market. From afar is heard the braying of donkeys. Outside the market sit two men whose ragged clothes and filthy appearance indicate that they are out-of-work loafers.

FIRST UNEMPLOYED (*To his companion*). Are you able to tell me what the difference is between us and donkeys?

SECOND UNEMPLOYED. You can hear the difference with your own ears.

FIRST UNEMPLOYED. The braying?

SECOND UNEMPLOYED. Just so, the braying.

FIRST UNEMPLOYED. Couldn't this braying be donkey talk?

SECOND UNEMPLOYED. That's what it must be.

FIRST UNEMPLOYED. So they're talking now.

SECOND UNEMPLOYED. Maybe they're also shouting.

FIRST UNEMPLOYED. I wonder what they're saying?

SECOND UNEMPLOYED. You'd have to be a donkey to know that.

FIRST UNEMPLOYED. They talk to each other so loudly.

SECOND UNEMPLOYED. Naturally, don't they have to hear each other?

FIRST UNEMPLOYED. I thought donkeys whispered together.

SECOND UNEMPLOYED. Why? Why should they?

FIRST UNEMPLOYED. Just like us.

SECOND UNEMPLOYED. Don't worry . . . donkeys aren't like us.

FIRST UNEMPLOYED. You're quite right, donkeys are a civilised species.

SECOND UNEMPLOYED. What are you saying? Civilised?

FIRST UNEMPLOYED. Have you ever seen wild donkeys? There are wild horses and wild buffaloes and wild pigeons and wild cats, but ever since donkeys have been going around amongst us they've been working peacefully and talking freely.

SECOND UNEMPLOYED. Freely?

FIRST UNEMPLOYED. I mean aloud.

SECOND UNEMPLOYED. Talking about aloud, can you tell me why we aren't able to live decently, your goodself and my goodself?

FIRST UNEMPLOYED. Because your goodself and my goodself are broke.

SECOND UNEMPLOYED. And why are we broke?

FIRST UNEMPLOYED. Because no one gives a damn about us. If only we had a market like this donkey market, someone would buy us.

SECOND UNEMPLOYED. And why doesn't anybody buy us?

FIRST UNEMPLOYED. Because we're local merchandise.

SECOND UNEMPLOYED. What's wrong with that?

FIRST UNEMPLOYED. There's only money for foreign merchandise.

SECOND UNEMPLOYED. Why don't we go off and advertise ourselves?

FIRST UNEMPLOYED. How?

SECOND UNEMPLOYED. With our voices.

FIRST UNEMPLOYED. They wouldn't come out loud enough.

SECOND UNEMPLOYED. How is it that a donkey's voice comes out all right?

FIRST UNEMPLOYED. Because, as I told you, they're a civilised species.

SECOND UNEMPLOYED. You've got me interested. Oh, if only I were a donkey, like this one coming along? Look over there . . . the donkey being led along by the man who's taking it out from the market. I wonder how much he paid for it! Look how proud and cock-a-hoop he is as he takes it away!

FIRST UNEMPLOYED. I've had an idea.

SECOND UNEMPLOYED. What is it?

FIRST UNEMPLOYED. Would you like to become a donkey?

SECOND UNEMPLOYED. Me? How?

FIRST UNEMPLOYED. Don't ask questions. Would you like to or wouldn't you?

SECOND UNEMPLOYED. I'd like to, but how?

FIRST UNEMPLOYED. I'll tell you. You see the donkey that's coming towards us, being led by the man who bought it. Well, I'll go up to the man and distract him by chatting him up. At the same time you undo the rope round the donkey's neck without its owner noticing and tie it round your own neck.

SECOND UNEMPLOYED. That's all? And then what?

FIRST UNEMPLOYED. And then he'll lead you off and I'll lead off the donkey.

SECOND UNEMPLOYED. And where will he lead me off to?

FIRST UNEMPLOYED. I wouldn't be knowing, that's in the lap of the gods.

SECOND UNEMPLOYED. Are you talking seriously?

FIRST UNEMPLOYED. Isn't it you who want it this way?

SECOND UNEMPLOYED. I tie a rope round my neck and he leads me away?

FIRST UNEMPLOYED. And what's wrong with that? At least you'll have found yourself someone to guarantee that you get a bite to eat.

SECOND UNEMPLOYED. It won't be what you call a bite . . . more like a munch.

FIRST UNEMPLOYED. It's all the same . . . just something to eat.

SECOND UNEMPLOYED. As you say, it'll be a change from being hungry and without a roof over one's head. But how am I going to put myself over to the man?

FIRST UNEMPLOYED. That depends on how smart you are.

SECOND UNEMPLOYED. We'll have a go.

FIRST UNEMPLOYED. Hide yourself . . . the man mustn't catch sight of us together.

The two men part and the stage is empty. A man—he looks like a farmer—appears. He holds a rope with which he is leading a donkey. The First Unemployed approaches him.

FIRST UNEMPLOYED. Peace be upon you!

FARMER. And upon you be peace!

FIRST UNEMPLOYED. Good God, man, is it that you don't know me or what?

FARMER. You . . . who would you be?

FIRST UNEMPLOYED. Who would I be? Didn't we break bread together?

FARMER. I don't understand. You mean to say we once broke bread together?

FIRST UNEMPLOYED. You mean you've forgotten all that quickly? No one but a bastard forgets a good turn.

FARMER. Are you calling me a bastard?

FIRST UNEMPLOYED. May God strike dead anyone who said such a thing about you. What I meant was that anyone who forgets his friends . . . but then, thank God, you're really a decent and civil person, it's merely that it's just slipped your mind what I look like. The point is that we met at night, over dinner, and it just happened the moon wasn't out that night.

FARMER. The moon? When? Where?

FIRST UNEMPLOYED. I'll remind you. Just be patient till the knot's untied.

He looks furtively at his companion who has slipped by unnoticed and is engrossed in undoing the knot of the rope.

FARMER. What's untied?

FIRST UNEMPLOYED. I'm tongue-tied. You've embarrassed me, you've made me forget what I was saying. Give me some help. (*Stealing a glance at his companion and urging him to hurry up*) Get the knot untied and do me the favour of getting me out of this.

FARMER. I can't understand a thing you're saying.

FIRST UNEMPLOYED. You'll understand soon enough . . . once the knot's untied, which it must be . . . things have gone on for a long time . . . far too long. Man, get it untied quickly.

FARMER. But what shall I untie?

FIRST UNEMPLOYED (*Seeing that his companion has finished undoing the rope and has tied it round his neck and let the donkey loose*). Well, it's finally got untied all right. It's the Almighty God Himself who unties and solves things. Everything is untied and solved in its own good time. Everything has its time, and seeing as how you don't remember me now I'll leave you time in which to think it over at your leisure. God willing, we'll be meeting up soon and you'll remember me and you'll give me a real warm welcome. Peace be upon you.

He leaves the Farmer in a state of confusion. He goes behind the donkey, takes it and moves off without being noticed.

FARMER (*To himself*). Where did I meet him? Where did we have dinner? The moon wasn't out? Could be . . . these days one's mind wanders a bit.

He pulls at the donkey's halter so as to lead it away, not knowing that the Second Unemployed has taken the donkey's place.

FARMER (*Calling out*). C'mon, donkey.

The Second Unemployed imitates the braying of a donkey.

FARMER (*Looking round and being startled*). Hey, what's this? Who are you?

SECOND UNEMPLOYED. I'm the donkey.

FARMER. Donkey?

SECOND UNEMPLOYED. Yes, the donkey you've just bought at the market.

FARMER. It's impossible!

SECOND UNEMPLOYED. Why are you so surprised? Didn't you just buy me at the market?

FARMER. Yes, but . . .

SECOND UNEMPLOYED. But what?

FARMER. In the name of God the Merciful, the Compassionate!

SECOND UNEMPLOYED. Don't be frightened, I'm your donkey all right.

FARMER. How? ... you're human.

SECOND UNEMPLOYED. It's your destiny, your good luck.

FARMER. Are you really human or are you ... ?

SECOND UNEMPLOYED. Yes, human, not a genie. Don't worry, it can all be explained. Just calm down a bit.

FARMER. I ... I've calmed down.

SECOND UNEMPLOYED. Listen, then, my dear sir ... the explanation is that my father ... a nice fellow like your goodself ... was, however, real stubborn and got it into his head to marry me off to a girl I'd never seen and who'd never seen me. I refused but he still insisted. I suggested to him that we talk it over and come to some sort of understanding, that it had to be discussed in a spirit of freedom. He got angry and said, "I won't have sons of mine arguing with me." I said to him, "I refuse to accept what you're saying." So he said to me, "You're an ass." I said to him "I'm not an ass." He said, "I said you're an ass and you've got to be an ass," and he called upon God to turn me into an ass. It seems that at that moment the doors of Heaven were open and the prayer was answered and I was actually turned into a donkey. My father died and they found me in the livestock fold, having become part of his estate. They sold me at the market and you came along and bought me.

FARMER. Extraordinary! Then you are the donkey I bought?

SECOND UNEMPLOYED. The very same.

FARMER. And how is that you're now back again as a human being?

SECOND UNEMPLOYED. I told you, it's your destiny, your good luck. It seems you're one of those godly people and the good Lord, may He be praised and exalted, decided to honour you ...

FARMER. Really! But what's to be done now?

SECOND UNEMPLOYED. What's happened?

FARMER. What's happened is that you ... is that I ... I don't know how to go about things. What I mean to say is that I've lost my money, I'm ruined.

SECOND UNEMPLOYED. You haven't lost a thing.

FARMER. How's that?

SECOND UNEMPLOYED. Didn't you buy yourself a donkey? The donkey's right here.

FARMER. Where is he?

SECOND UNEMPLOYED. And where have I gone to?

FARMER. You?

SECOND UNEMPLOYED. Yes, me.

FARMER. You want to tell me that you're ...

SECOND UNEMPLOYED. Wholly your property. You bought me with your money on the understanding I'm a donkey. The deal was concluded. Let's suppose that after that I turn into something else, that's no fault of yours. You've made a purchase and that's the end of it.

FARMER. Yes, I bought ...

SECOND UNEMPLOYED. That's it ... relax.

FARMER. You mean to say you're my property now?

SECOND UNEMPLOYED. In accordance with the law. I'm yours by right. Right's right ... and yours is guaranteed.

FARMER. Fair enough. Good, so let's get going.

SECOND UNEMPLOYED. At your disposal.

FARMER. Turn here, O . . . Hey, what shall I call you?

SECOND UNEMPLOYED. Call me by any name. For instance, there's . . . there's Hassawi.[1] What d'you think of that for a name? Hassawi . . . come, Hassawi . . . go Hassawi!

FARMER. Hassawi?

SECOND UNEMPLOYED. It's relevant!

FARMER. May it have God's blessings. Let's go then . . . Mr Hassawi! Wait a moment, I think this business of the rope round your neck isn't really necessary.

SECOND UNEMPLOYED. As you think best.

FARMER. Better do without the rope . . . after all where would you go to? Wait while I undo it from round your neck.

SECOND UNEMPLOYED (*Undoing the rope himself*). Allow me. Allow me . . . if you'd be so good.

FARMER. Yes, that's right. Come along, let's go home, Mr . . . Hassawi.

Scene Two

Inside the farmer's house his Wife is occupied with various household jobs. She hears knocking at the door.

WIFE. Who is it?

FARMER (*From outside*). Me, woman. Open up.

WIFE (*Opens the door and her husband enters*). You were all this time at the market?

FARMER. I've only just got back.

WIFE. You bought the donkey?

FARMER. I bought . . .

WIFE. You put it into the fold?

FARMER. What fold are you talking about, woman? Come along in, Mr Hassawi.

WIFE. You've got a guest with you?

FARMER. Not a guest. He's what you might . . . I'll tell you later.

WIFE. Please come in.

FARMER. Off you go and make me a glass of tea.

(*The Wife goes off.*)

HASSAWI (*Looking around him*). It seems I . . .

FARMER. And what shall I say to my wife?

HASSAWI. Tell her the truth.

FARMER. The truth?

HASSAWI. Exactly . . . not a word more and not a word less. There's nothing better than plain-speaking.

FARMER. And where will you be sleeping in that case?

HASSAWI. In the fold.

FARMER. What do you mean "the fold"? Do you think that's right?

HASSAWI. That's where I belong. Don't change the order of things. The only thing is that if you've a mattress and a pillow you could put them down for me there.

---

[1]Hassawi is a well-known breed of riding donkey in Egypt.

FARMER. Fine, but what about food? It's not reasonable for you to eat straw, clover and beans.

HASSAWI. I'll eat beans . . . just as long as they're broad beans.

FARMER. With a little oil over them?

HASSAWI. And a slice of lemon.

FARMER. And you'll go on eating beans forever?

HASSAWI. It's all a blessing from God!

FARMER. Just as you say. Donkeys have just the one food. They don't know the difference between breakfast, lunch and dinner. It's straw and clover and beans and that's all.

HASSAWI. I know that.

FARMER. Fine, we've settled your sleeping and your food. Tell me now, what work are you going to do?

HASSAWI. All work donkeys do . . . except being ridden.

FARMER. Ridden?

HASSAWI. You can't ride me because you'd only fall off.

FARMER. And carrying things? For example I was intending taking a load of radishes and leeks on the donkey to the vegetable merchant.

HASSAWI. I'll do that job.

FARMER. You'll carry the vegetables on your shoulders?

HASSAWI. That's my business. I'll manage. I may be a donkey but I've got a brain.

FARMER. Brain? I was forgetting this question of a brain.

HASSAWI. Don't worry, this brain of mine's at your service. You can always rely on me. Just give me confidence and the right to talk things over with you freely.

FARMER. Meaning you can go on your own to the merchant with the produce?

HASSAWI. And agree for you the best price with him.

FARMER. We'll see.

WIFE (*From outside*). Tea!

HASSAWI. If you'll excuse me.

FARMER. Where are you going?

HASSAWI. I'm going to inspect the fold I'm sleeping in.

FARMER. You'll find it on your right as you go out.

(*Hassawi goes out. The Wife enters with the glass of tea.*)

WIFE (*Giving the tea to her husband*). Your guest has gone out?

FARMER. He's not a guest, woman. He's . . .

WIFE. What?

FARMER. He'd be a . . . a . . .

WIFE. Be a what?

FARMER. He's a . . . a . . .

WIFE. Who is he?

FARMER. You won't believe it.

WIFE. What won't I believe?

FARMER. What I'll tell you now.

WIFE. All right then, just tell me.

FARMER. He's . . . the donkey I bought.

WIFE. The donkey?

FARMER. Yes, didn't I go to the donkey market today to buy a donkey? He's the donkey I bought at the market.

WIFE. Man, do you want to make an utter fool of me?

FARMER. Didn't I tell you that you wouldn't believe me?

WIFE. But what shall I believe . . . that the market's selling human donkeys?

FARMER. He wasn't a human at the time I bought him . . . he was a donkey like the rest . . . and he was braying.

WIFE. He brays as well?

FARMER. Yes, by God, I swear by the Holy Book he was braying.

WIFE. And then?

FARMER. And then on the way home . . . I was leading him by the rope . . . I turned round and found that he'd changed into a human.

WIFE. God save us! . . . an afreet![2]

FARMER. No, woman, he's no *afreet* . . . he was transformed. Originally he was a human being, the son of decent folk like ourselves. He was then transformed into a donkey and they sold him off at the market. I bought him and God, may He be praised and exalted, decided to honour me so He turned him back into a human.

WIFE. Your omnipotence, O Lord!

FARMER. Well, that's what happened.

WIFE. But after all . . .

FARMER. What? What do you want to say?

WIFE. Nothing.

FARMER. No, there's something you want to say.

WIFE. I want to say . . . what I mean is . . . is . . . what are we going to do with him now, with him being a . . . a human being?

FARMER. Do what with him? Exactly as with any other donkey . . . and in addition to that he's got a brain as well.

WIFE. I suppose we won't be able to ride him?

FARMER. Let's forget about the question of riding for the moment.

WIFE. And we'll talk to him as with other human beings?

FARMER. Yes, talk to him and call him by his name.

WIFE. He's got a name?

FARMER. Of course, what do you think? His name's Hassawi. We'll call him and say to him, "Come here, Hassawi; go there, Hassawi."

WIFE. And where will he sleep?

FARMER. In the fold. You can put a mattress out for him there.

WIFE. And what will he eat?

FARMER. Beans . . . but with oil.

WIFE. With oil?

FARMER. And lemon.

WIFE. And he drinks tea?

FARMER. Let's not get him used to that.

WIFE. How lovely! . . . we've got a human donkey!

FARMER. Be careful, woman not to say such things to the neighbours or they'll be saying we've gone off our heads!

WIFE. And what shall I say to them?

FARMER. Say . . . say for example that he's a relative of ours from far away who's come to help us with the work during these few days just as we're coming into the month of Ramadan.

(*A knock at the door.*)

WIFE. Who is it?

---

[2]afreet: a powerful evil demon or monster.

HASSAWI (*From outside*). Me ... Hassawi.
WIFE (*To her husband*). It's him!
FARMER. Open the door for him.
WIFE (*Opens the door*). Come in ... and wipe your feet on the doorstep.
HASSAWI (*Entering*). I've cleaned myself a corner in the fold and spread it out with straw.
FARMER. There you are, my dear lady; he cleans up and makes his own bed ... yet another advantage.
WIFE. Yes, let him get used to doing that.
HASSAWI. I was coming about an important matter.
FARMER. To do with what?
HASSAWI. To do with the vegetable merchant.
FARMER. The vegetable merchant? What about him?
HASSAWI. A man came on his behalf ... I just met him at the door and he said the merchant was in a hurry to take delivery. I got him talking and understood that the prices of radishes and leeks would go up in Ramadan. I told him that you were still giving the matter your consideration because there's a new buyer who's offered you a better price. The man was shaken and immediately said that he was prepared to raise the price he was offering.
FARMER. He said so?
HASSAWI (*Producing some money*). I took a higher price from him. Here you are!
FARMER. God bless you!
HASSAWI. But I have a request to make of you.
FARMER. What is it?
HASSAWI. Would you allow me, before you decide definitely about something, to talk the matter over with you freely and frankly?
FARMER. I'm listening.
HASSAWI. Were you intending to hand over the whole crop to the merchant?
FARMER. Yes, the whole of it.
HASSAWI. Why?
FARMER. Because we need the money.
HASSAWI. Is it absolutely necessary at the present time?
FARMER. Yes it is. We're in dire need of money as we come up to Ramadan. Have you forgotten the dried fruits, the mixed nuts and the dried apricot paste we need to buy?
HASSAWI. I've had an idea.
FARMER. Let's have it.
HASSAWI. We set apart a portion of the crop and have it for seed for the new sowing instead of buying seed at a high price during the sowing season.
FARMER. It's a long long time until the new sowing.
WIFE. The Lord will look after the new sowing ... we're living in today.
HASSAWI. As you say. In any event I've given you my opinion ... I'm just afraid the time for the new sowing will come and you won't have the money to pay for the seeds and you'll have to borrow at interest or go off to a money-lender, and perhaps you'll be forced to sell me in the market.
FARMER. Let God look after such things.
WIFE. What's he talk so much for?
FARMER (*To Hassawi*). Have you got anything else to say?
HASSAWI. Yes, I'm frightened ...
FARMER. What are you frightened about? Tell us and let happen what may!
HASSAWI. Yes, I must say what I have in my mind and clear my conscience. As I was passing by your field just now I noticed that the feddans sown

under radishes and leeks had at lcast ten kerats lying fallow because the irrigation water isn't reaching there.

FARMER. And what can we do about that?

HASSAWI. It needs one or two shadoofs.

FARMER. We thought about it.

HASSAWI. And what stopped you?

FARMER. Money . . . where's the money?

HASSAWI (*Looking at the Wife's wrist*). Just one of the lady's bracelets . . .

WIFE (*Shouting*). Ruination!

HASSAWI. By putting ten kerats under irrigation you'll get the price of the bracelet back from the first sowing.

FARMER. You think so?

WIFE (*Beating her chest*). What disaster! Man, are you thinking of listening to what that animal has to say? Are you seriously thinking of selling my bracelets?

FARMER. We haven't yet bought or sold anything . . . we're just talking things over.

WIFE. Talking things over with your donkey, you sheep of a man?

FARMER. What's wrong with that? Let me hear what he has to say . . . you too.

WIFE. Me listen? Listen to that? Listen to that nonsensical talk that gives you an ache in the belly? He's been nothing but an ache in the belly from the moment he came.

FARMER. He's entitled to his opinion.

WIFE. His opinion? What opinion would that be? That thing has an opinion? Are we to be dictated to by the opinion of a donkey in the fold?

FARMER. He's not like other donkeys.

WIFE. So what! I swear by Him who created and fashioned you that if that donkey of yours doesn't take himself off and keep his hands away from my bracelets I'll not stay on under this roof!

FARMER. Be sensible and calm down. After all, have we agreed to go along with his opinion?

WIFE. That was all that was missing . . . for you to go along with his opinion! All your life you've been master in your own house and your word has been law. Then off you go to the market and come back dragging along behind you your dear friend Mr Hassawi, whose every opinion you listen to.

FARMER. His opinions and help have gained for us an increase in price from the merchant.

WIFE. An increase? He won't allow us to enjoy it. He wants to waste it all on his crazy ideas, just as we're about to have all the expenses of Ramadan . . . and then don't forget there's the Feast directly after Ramadan and for which we'll need cake . . .

FARMER. And after the cake for the Feast we'll have to face up to the Big Feast for which we'll need a sheep.

WIFE. Knowing this as you do, why do you listen to his talk?

FARMER. Listening doesn't do any harm.

WIFE. Who said so? A lot of buzzing in the ears is worse than magic.

FARMER. What you're saying is that we should tell him to keep his mouth shut?

WIFE. With lock and bolt . . . and put a sock in it! He's a donkey and must remain a donkey and you're the master of the house and must remain master of the house. You're not some tassel on a saddlebag at this time of life. Have some pride man . . . you, with your grey hairs!

FARMER. So I'm a tassel on a saddlebag?

WIFE. You're getting that way, I swear it. Your dear friend Hassawi is almost all-powerful here.

FARMER. How all-powerful, woman? I still have the reins in my hand.

HASSAWI (*To himself*). The reins?

WIFE. All right, what are you waiting for? Why don't you put the bridle on him as from now?

FARMER. And what does it matter if we let him ramble on as he wants?

HASSAWI (*To himself*). Ramble on?

WIFE. I'm frightened of all this rambling and rumbling of his.

FARMER. What are you frightened of?

WIFE. That he'll try to fool you and you'll believe him.

FARMER. Believe him? Why should I? Who said I was a donkey?

WIFE. The donkey's there in front of you and he's had his say.

FARMER. Talking's one thing and action's another.

WIFE. What action are you talking about . . . you've let the rope go.

FARMER. You're saying I should tie him by the neck?

WIFE. Like every other donkey.

FARMER. But he's human, woman.

WIFE. Originally he was a donkey. When you bought him from the donkey market, when you paid good money for him, he was a donkey, and so his place is out there in the fold and he mustn't enter the house or have a say in things. That's how it should be. If you don't like it I'll go out and call upon the neighbours to bear witness. I'll say to them: "Come to my rescue, folk . . . my man's gone crazy in the head and has bought a donkey from the market which he's made into a human and whose opinions he's listening to."

FARMER. Don't be mad, woman!

WIFE. By the Prophet, I'll do it . . .

FARMER. All right, keep quiet . . . that's it!

WIFE. What d'you mean, "That's it?" Explain!

FARMER. We'll go back to how we were and relax. Hey, you, Hassawi, listen here!

HASSAWI. Sir!

FARMER. See, this business of my asking your opinion and your asking mine doesn't work. I'm the man with the say-so round here, and all you've got to do is obey. What I mean is that that mouth of yours mustn't utter a word . . . understand? Go off to the fold while I arrange about your work.

HASSAWI. Certainly, but would you just allow me to say something . . . one last word?

WIFE. What cheek! He's told you that you shouldn't talk, that you should keep your mouth closed and shut up. You really are a cheeky fellow!

HASSAWI. That's it then . . . I've closed my mouth and shut up. With your permission. (*He goes out*)

Scene Three

Outside the door of the Farmer's house Hassawi suddenly sees his companion, the First Unemployed, approaching and leading the original donkey. The two friends embrace.

HASSAWI (*To his companion*). Tell me . . . what did you do?

FIRST UNEMPLOYED. And you? How did you get on?

HASSAWI. I'll tell you right now. How, though, did you know I was here?

FIRST UNEMPLOYED. I walked along far behind you without your noticing. Tell me . . . what happened with our friend the owner of the donkey?

HASSAWI. You're well rid of him. He's an idiotic man who doesn't know where his own good lies. And why have you now come back with the donkey?

FIRST UNEMPLOYED. We don't need it. Things are settled . . . the good Lord's settled them.

HASSAWI. How's that?

FIRST UNEMPLOYED. We've found work.

HASSAWI. You've found work?

FIRST UNEMPLOYED. For you and me.

HASSAWI. Where? Tell me quickly!

FIRST UNEMPLOYED. After I left you and went off, I and the donkey, I found a large field, where there were people sowing. I said them: "Have you got any work?" "Lots," they said . . . "for you and ten like you." I said to them: "I've got someone with me." "You're welcome," they said to me, "Go and bring him along immediately and start working." So I came to you right away.

HASSAWI. Extraordinary! There we were absolutely dying to get work, remember? People used to look at us and say "Off with you, you down-and-out tramps, off with the two of you . . . we've got no work for down-and-outs!"

FIRST UNEMPLOYED. It seems that having the donkey alongside me improved my reputation!

HASSAWI. You're right. Don't people always say "He works like a donkey"? A donkey means work just as a horse means honour. Don't people say that the riding of horses brings honour, that dogs are good guards, and that cats are thieves?

FIRST UNEMPLOYED. Yes, by God, that's right. They saw me with the donkey and said to themselves, "He can't be a down-and-out tramp . . . he must be one for hard work," so they took me on my face value and you sight unseen . . . on the basis of my recommendation!

HASSAWI. Your recommendation or the donkey's?

FIRST UNEMPLOYED. The donkey's. It actually got the work for both you and me. Isn't it only fair that we should return it to its owner?

HASSAWI. That's only fair.

FIRST UNEMPLOYED. What shall we say to him?

HASSAWI. We'll tell him to take back his donkey.

FIRST UNEMPLOYED. And you . . . didn't you pretend to be his donkey and tie the halter round your neck?

HASSAWI. He'll now prefer the real donkey.

FIRST UNEMPLOYED. Look, instead of handing over the donkey to him and getting into all sorts of arguments, with him asking us where the donkey was and where we were, we'll tie the donkey up for him in front of his house and clear off. What d'you think?

HASSAWI. Much the best idea . . . let's get going.

(They tie the donkey to the door of the house, then knock at the door and disappear from view. The door opens and the Farmer appears.)

FARMER (*Sees the donkey and is astonished and shouts*). Come along, woman!

WIFE (*Appearing at the door*). What's up?

FARMER. Look and see!

WIFE. What?

FARMER. He's been transformed again . . . Hassawi's become a donkey like he was at the market. He's exactly the same as he was when I bought him.

WIFE. Thanks be to God . . . how generous you are, O Lord!

FARMER. Yes, but . . .

WIFE. But what? What else do you want to say?

FARMER. But we're the cause.

WIFE. Why, though? What did we do to him?

FARMER. We did the same as his father did to him . . . he silenced him and turned him into a donkey!

WIFE. And what's wrong with him being a donkey? At least we can ride him.

FARMER. You're right. When he was a human with a brain he was useless for riding.

WIFE. And what did we need his brain for? What we want is something to ride, something that's going to bear our weight and take us from one place to another. Give thanks to the Lord, man, for returning your useful donkey to you.

FARMER (*Gently stroking the donkey's head*). Don't hold it against us, Hassawi! Fate's like that. I hope you're not annoyed. For us, though, you're still as you were . . . Mr Hassawi.

WIFE. Are you still at it, man? Are you still murmuring sweet nothings to that donkey? Mind . . . he'll go back to speaking again!

(*The Farmer leads his donkey away in silence towards the fold, while the wife lets out shrill cries of joy.*)

Analyzing the Text

1. How does the opening conversation between the two unemployed laborers create sympathy for their plight and help set up the premise of the play?
2. How would you characterize the farmer on whom they play their trick and the way he and his wife initially react to Mr. Hassawi's presence?

Understanding al-Hakim's Techniques

1. How do the descriptions of the characters and the references in the play provide the audience with enough information about the time period, setting, and social circumstances necessary to understand the action in the play?
2. What details does al-Hakim use to suggest the importance that religion plays in Egyptian society?

Arguing for an Interpretation

1. In your opinion, what is al-Hakim satirizing about Egyptian society when the farmer and his wife reject Mr. Hassawi's good suggestions?
2. What features of the play suggest that al-Hakim adapted it from a well-known Egyptian folktale, and how does he use a broad range of humor (from slapstick through subtle psychological and verbal details) to transform it into a poignant and thoughtful drama?

Connections

1. What complementary perspectives on the social effects of AIDS emerge from Paul Monette's essay and Bruce Springsteen's song lyrics?
2. Compare the motivations for Sanjeev's decision to stay with Twinkle in Jhumpa Lahiri's story with those of Nunez to leave the woman he loves in H. G. Wells's "The Country of the Blind."
3. Discuss the similarities between the stories by Albert Camus and H. G. Wells in terms of the illusions of the main characters (Daru and Nunez) that they can remain outside the social customs and loyalties that apply to everyone else.
4. How do Raymond Carver in his story "Neighbors" and Barbara Kingsolver and Lennart Sjögren in their poems use the metaphor of a home to express alienation?
5. Compare Luis Alberto Urrea's essay with H. G. Wells's story "The Country of the Blind" in terms of the narrators' loss of illusions.
6. In what way are the class and gender inequities dramatized by Mahasweta Devi in "Giribala" treated comically, in Jhumpa Lahiri's "This Blessed House"?
7. How is the theme of the journey used as a metaphor in Bruce Springsteen's "Streets of Philadelphia," in Diane Wakoski's poem "The Orange," and in Alice Walker's story "The Flowers"?
8. In what sense can the poems by Wing Tek Lum ("Minority Poem") and Rahel Chalfi ("Porcupine Fish") and Milorad Pavić's story "The Wedgwood Tea Set" be understood as allegories about those who are seen as outsiders?
9. Compare and contrast the ways in which Czeslaw Milosz in his poem ("My Faithful Mother Tongue") and Albert Camus in his story ("The Guest") explore the existential implications of exile.
10. How do Bruce Springsteen in his song lyrics and Kelly Cherry in her poem dramatize the theme of alienation from oneself and society?
11. How do both Raymond Carver and Wakako Yamauchi in their respective short stories use the concept of "neighbors" to impel the protagonists to discover themselves?
12. In what sense can Tewfik al-Hakim's play *The Donkey Market* and H. G. Wells's story "The Country of the Blind" be considered fables about how cultural traditions blind one to reality?

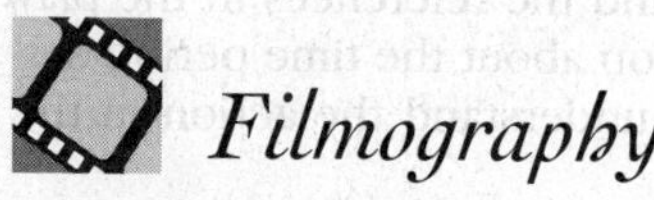

Filmography

The Garden of the Finzi-Continis (1971) Director: Vittorio De Sica. Performers: Dominique Sanda, Lino Capoliccio.
Rich Jewish adolescents in Italy come of age during the Holocaust. [Italy]

One Flew Over the Cuckoo's Nest (1975) Director: Milos Forman. Performers: Jack Nicholson, Louise Fletcher.
A tragicomic adaptation of Ken Kesey's classic novel about a hustler facing a jail sentence who feigns insanity and is put in a mental hospital instead.

The Elephant Man (1980) Director: David Lynch. Performers: John Hurt, Anthony Hopkins, Anne Bancroft.

Based on the life of John Merrick, a severely deformed man is helped by a sympathetic doctor to leave the world of freak shows.

El Norte (1983) Director: Gregory Nava. Performers: David Villalpando, Zaide Silvia Gutierrez.

In this gripping and poignant film, a Guatemalan brother and sister, persecuted in their homeland, make the arduous journey north ("El Norte") to America where they continue to struggle against overwhelming odds. [Guatemala]

My Beautiful Laundrette (1986) Director: Stephen Frears. Performers: Daniel Day Lewis, Gordon Warnekce.

Tensions between the white and Pakistani communities in working class London are exacerbated by a homosexual interracial couple.

Rain Man (1988) Director: Barry Levinson. Performers: Dustin Hoffman, Tom Cruise.

A con man whose wealthy father has left his fortune to an autistic brother he never knew existed takes his brother (who is a genius at games of chance) on a cross-country road trip.

Mississippi Masala (1992) Director: Mira Nair. Performers: Denzel Washington, Sarita Choudhury.

Trouble arises in a small Southern town when a young black man starts dating a woman whose parents have emigrated from India by way of Africa. [US/India]

Longtime Companion (1990) Director: Norman Rene. Performers: Campbell Scott, Bruce Davison, Mary-Louise Parker, Dermot Mulroney.

In this experimental film, a group of friends face the onslaught of the AIDS epidemic through the 1990s.

Iris (2001) Director: Richard Eyre. Performers: Judi Dench, Jim Broadbent, Kate Winslet.

A love story between novelist Iris Murdoch and her husband, from their days at Oxford to her affliction with Alzheimer's disease.

Rabbit-Proof Fence (2002) Director: Phillip Noyce. Performers: Kenneth Branagh, Everlyn Sampi.

Based on a true story of a young Aboriginal girl who leads her younger sister and cousin in an escape from a government camp, where Aboriginal half-caste children were removed from their homes in 1931, to be trained as domestic workers in order to be integrated into white society. [Australia].

Chapter 9

Nature and the Spirit

I'm astounded by people who want to 'know' the universe when it's hard enough to find your way around Chinatown.

Woody Allen

At some time in their lives, most people reflect on their relationship to a higher order of existence, whether one perceives it as an eternal force; the universe around us; a defined spiritual entity; or a concept that answers to a basic human need for a sense of order behind the turbulent appearance of everyday life. Some people are content to continue within the religious traditions in which they were raised; others are drawn to systems of belief that they find match their needs and perceptions of this spiritual dimension. If literature from around the world illustrates anything, it is this extraordinary multiplicity of different responses to the universal or cosmic.

This chapter presents works that reflect how people in many different cultures and societies look at themselves in relationship to the absolute, the eternal, the supernatural, or the concept of an ultimate truth. For some writers, the profound sense of being at one with nature offers the most meaningful connection to the world we share and sensitizes them to the encroachments of civilization and the threat posed to the Earth by excessive consumption, overpopulation, and the squandering of natural resources.

A pioneer of the wildlife conservation movement, Aldo Leopold, in "Thinking Like a Mountain," adopts an unusual perspective to convince us not to exterminate predators such as wolves lest we destabilize the ecosystem. Ursula K. Le Guin's "A Very Warm Mountain" communicates the disruptive force of a natural disaster while raising basic questions about the uneasy alliance between humanity and the natural world. In "Salvation," Langston Hughes recalls a moment of personal choice when he confronted the issue of hypocrisy and religious faith.

In the first of the chapter's short stories, Premchand (Bengal, India) dramatizes in "Deliverance" the fateful encounter between a village tanner and a Brahman priest. Naguib Mahfouz (Egypt) challenges the usual perceptions of time in his intriguing parable "Half a Day." A decree by the village elders sets off a chain of tragic consequences in Chinua Achebe's "Things Fall Apart"

(Nigeria). Edgar Allan Poe, the master of the macabre narrative, projects us into the terrifying realm of disease and inescapable fate in "The Masque of the Red Death." William Faulkner's classic story "A Rose for Emily" touches on the universal themes of unrequited love and retribution. An encounter between an ornithologist and an egotistical talking canary raises basic questions about how we perceive the world in "A Canary's Ideas," by Joaquim María Machado de Assis (Brazil). Carmen Naranjo (Costa Rica), in "And We Sold the Rain," creates a surrealistic fable in which economic, social, and environmental crises reflect the latest news. In the epilogue from Olaf Stapledon's "Star Maker," we accompany the narrator as he returns from a journey to the stars to confront the perilous events on Earth that threaten to destroy civilization.

The poems in this chapter present a vividly realized range of works exploring the relationships of individuals to their perception of a higher power, the universe, the natural world, or a cosmic dimension. In "The Sound of the Sea," Henry Wadsworth Longfellow evokes a wondrous sense of communion. Walt Whitman finds the night sky more inspiring than a lecture on astronomy in "When I Heard the Learn'd Astronomer." Anna Kamieńska (Poland) offers a wryly provocative view of the human condition in "Funny." Vasko Popa (Serbia), in the "The Lost Red Boot," invokes the image of his irrepressible great-grandmother to inspire his poetry. Next, Gerard Manley Hopkins extends the resources of language to its limits in order to capture the mystery and majesty of a kestral as Christ in "The Windhover." The surrealist Alfred Jarry (France) creates an ingenious spoof on pedantic commentary in "The Passion of Jesus Considered as An Uphill Race." In Dylan Thomas's (Wales) poem "Do Not Go Gentle into That Good Night," we share the poet's deeply felt response to his father's mortality. Bella Akhmadulina (Russia), in "The Garden," voices her belief that if imagination houses reality, then real time is time remembered. Jorge Luis Borges (Argentina), in "Afterglow," explores how the encroaching darkness after sunset and his own growing blindness make his quest for a spiritual meaning to existence more urgent. The personal costs of lifelong devotion become painfully clear in John Milton's sonnet, "When I consider how my light is spent." A life lived without regret is the theme of Mary Oliver's "When Death Comes." A quiet sense of certainty pervades William Wordsworth's classic lyric "Ode: Intimations of Immortality." In "Poetry and Religion," Les A. Murray (Australia) makes the case that poetry offers sublime truths comparable to that of religion. A vision of the return of Christ prophesied in the *New Testament* gives way to a terrifying embodiment of inhuman barbarism in "The Second Coming" by William Butler Yeats (Ireland).

Lastly, Shakespeare's classic drama *Hamlet, Prince of Denmark* presents a complex, multileveled examination of a young man who is ill-equipped by temperament to confront the political intrigues and murderous ambition of his uncle that engulf him in a tragic downward spiral.

Essays

ALDO LEOPOLD

Aldo Leopold (1887-1948), who is widely acknowledged as a pioneer of the wildlife conservation movement in the United States, was born in Burlington, Iowa. He attended the graduate program at the School of Forestry at Yale University. After graduation, he worked in the U.S. Forestry Service and became supervisor of the Carson National Forest in the Southwest. During this time, he evolved ideas about land management and the importance of maintaining healthy ecological systems. Through his efforts, the first protected wilderness area, located in Gila National Forest in New Mexico, was established. Leopold was instrumental in founding the Wilderness Society in 1934. He served as an advisor to the United Nations on conservation issues, and was posthumously honored in 1978 with the John Burroughs Medal in tribute to a lifetime of work in conservation. Leopold was an important forerunner in the tradition of nature writing. "Thinking Like a Mountain," drawn from his classic work A Sand County Almanac *(1949), reveals an exceptionally subtle appreciation of the interplay between animals and the environment.*

Thinking Like a Mountain

A deep chesty bawl echoes from rimrock to rimrock, rolls down the mountain, and fades into the far blackness of the night. It is an outburst of wild defiant sorrow, and of contempt for all the adversities of the world.

Every living thing (and perhaps many a dead one as well) pays heed to that call. To the deer it is a reminder of the way of all flesh, to the pine a forecast of midnight scuffles and of blood upon the snow, to the coyote a promise of gleanings to come, to the cowman a threat of red ink at the bank, to the hunter a challenge of fang against bullet. Yet behind these obvious and immediate hopes and fears there lies a deeper meaning, known only to the mountain itself. Only the mountain has lived long enough to listen objectively to the howl of a wolf.

Those unable to decipher the hidden meaning know nevertheless that it is there, for it is felt in all wolf country, and distinguishes that country from all other land. It tingles in the spine of all who hear wolves by night, or who scan their tracks by day. Even without sight or sound of wolf, it is implicit in a hundred small events: the midnight whinny of a pack horse, the rattle of rolling rocks, the bound of a fleeing deer, the way shadows lie under the spruces. Only the ineducable tyro can fail to sense the presence or absence of wolves, or the fact that mountains have a secret opinion about them.

My own conviction on this score dates from the day I saw a wolf die. We were eating lunch on a high rimrock, at the foot of which a turbulent river elbowed its way. We saw what we thought was a doe fording the torrent, her breast awash in white water. When she climbed the bank toward us and shook out her tail, we realized our error: it was a wolf. A half-dozen others, evidently grown pups, sprang from the willows and all joined in a welcoming mêlée of wagging tails and playful maulings. What was literally a pile of wolves writhed and tumbled in the center of an open flat at the foot of our rimrock.

In those days we had never heard of passing up a chance to kill a wolf. 5
In a second we were pumping lead into the pack, but with more excitement than accuracy: how to aim a steep downhill shot is always confusing. When our rifles were empty, the old wolf was down, and a pup was dragging a leg into impassable slide-rocks.

We reached the old wolf in time to watch a fierce green fire dying in her eyes. I realized then, and have known ever since, that there was something new to me in those eyes—something known only to her and to the mountain. I was young then, and full of trigger-itch; I thought that because fewer wolves meant more deer, that no wolves would mean hunters' paradise. But after seeing the green fire die, I sensed that neither the wolf nor the mountain agreed with such a view.

Since then I have lived to see state after state extirpate its wolves. I have watched the face of many a newly wolfless mountain, and seen the south-facing slopes wrinkle with a maze of new deer trails. I have seen every edible bush and seedling browsed, first to anaemic desuetude,[1] and then to death. I have seen every edible tree defoliated to the height of a saddlehorn. Such a mountain looks as if someone had given God a new pruning shears, and forbidden Him all other exercise. In the end the starved bones of the hoped-for deer herd, dead of its own too-much, bleach with the bones of the dead sage, or molder under the high-lined junipers.

I now suspect that just as a deer herd lives in mortal fear of its wolves, so does a mountain live in mortal fear of its deer. And perhaps with better cause, for while a buck pulled down by wolves can be replaced in two or three years, a range pulled down by too many deer may fail of replacement in as many decades.

So also with cows. The cowman who cleans his range of wolves does not realize that he is taking over the wolf's job of trimming the herd to fit the range. He has not learned to think like a mountain. Hence we have dustbowls, and rivers washing the future into the sea.

We all strive for safety, prosperity, comfort, long life, and dullness. The deer 10
strives with his supple legs, the cowman with trap and poison, the statesman with pen, the most of us with machines, votes, and dollars, but it all comes to the same thing: peace in our time. A measure of success in this is all well enough, and perhaps is a requisite to objective thinking, but too much safety seems to yield only danger in the long run. Perhaps this is behind Thoreau's dictum: In wildness is the salvation of the world. Perhaps this is the hidden meaning in the howl of the wolf, long known among mountains, but seldom perceived among men.

Analyzing the Text

1. In what way does the experience of shooting a wolf change Leopold's attitude?
2. According to Leopold, what consequences would follow from the extermination of wolves?

---

[1]*desuetude:* underused or abandoned; drained of sustenance.

Understanding Leopold's Techniques

1. How does Leopold's style help his readers understand his new awareness of "thinking like a mountain" and strengthen his thesis?
2. For what audience do you think Leopold wrote this—farmers, land or wildlife management specialists, the general public? What parts of his essay are explanatory and what parts are persuasive?

Arguing for an Interpretation

1. What assumptions about the value of wilderness emerge from Leopold's essay? How does his essay provide insight into how the idea of preserving wilderness areas has assumed symbolic importance in American culture?
2. To what extent did Leopold persuade you to adopt the perspective of "thinking like a mountain"? Write a few paragraphs either agreeing with Leopold, or from the perspective of a sportsman or hunter who disagreed with his argument.

URSULA K. LE GUIN

Ursula K. Le Guin, the popular author of many acclaimed science fiction works, was born in 1929, in Berkeley, California. She was educated at Radcliffe College, where she was elected to Phi Beta Kappa. She received an M.A. in romance literature from Columbia University in 1952. Le Guin has taught at Mercer University and at the University of Idaho and has conducted writing workshops at Pacific University, the University of Washington, Portland State University, and the University of Reading in England. Besides essays and children's books, Le Guin's significant contributions to science fiction and fantasy literature include The Left Hand of Darkness *(1969), winner of both a Hugo Award and a Science Fiction and Fantasy Writers of America Nebula Award;* The Farthest Shore *(1972), winner of a National Book Award and a Hugo Award; and* The Dispossessed: An Ambiguous Utopia *(1974), winner of the Nebula Award.* The Lathe of Heaven *(1971) was made into a PBS television movie shown in 1980. Her later works, including* Orsinian Tales *(1976),* Malfrena *(1979),* The Language of Night: Essays on Fantasy and Science Fiction *(1979),* The Compass Rose *(1982), and* Tehanu *(1990), envision utopian and magical worlds (Orsinia, the imagined archipelago of Earthsea, the far-flung planets of the Hainish Cycle) that offer alternatives to the usual male-dominated, autocratic, and technological vistas of traditional American science fiction. Her most recent works are* The Telling *(2000),* The Other Wind *(2001), and* The Birthday of the World and Other Stories *(2002). In "A Very Warm Mountain," Le Guin describes her reactions to witnessing the eruption of Mount St. Helens in 1980, 45 miles away from her home in Portland, Oregon.*

A Very Warm Mountain

An enormous region extending from north-central Washington to northeastern California and including most of Oregon east of the Cascades is covered by basalt lava flows. . . . The unending cliffs of basalt along the Columbia River . . . 74 volcanoes in the Portland area . . . A blanket of pumice that averages about 50 feet thick. . . .

—*Roadside Geology of Oregon*
Alt and Hyndman, 1978

Everybody takes it personally. Some get mad. Damn stupid mountain went and dumped all that dirty gritty glassy gray ash that flies like flour and lies like cement all over their roofs, roads, and rhododendrons. Now they have to clean it up. And the scientists are a real big help, all they'll say is we don't know; we can't tell, she might dump another load of ash on you just when you've got it all cleaned up. It's an outrage.

Some take it ethically. She lay and watched her forests being cut and her elk being hunted and her lakes being fished and fouled and her ecology being tampered with and the smoky, snarling suburbs creeping closer to her skirts, until she saw it was time to teach the White Man's Children a lesson. And she did. In the process of the lesson, she blew her forests to matchsticks, fried her elk, boiled her fish, wrecked her ecosystem, and did very little damage to the cities: so that the lesson taught to the White Man's Children would seem, at best, equivocal.

But everybody takes it personally. We try to reduce it to human scale. To make a molehill out of the mountain.

Some got very anxious, especially during the dreary white weather that hung around the area after May 18 (the first great eruption, when she blew 1300 feet of her summit all over Washington, Idaho, and points east) and May 25 (the first considerable ashfall in the thickly populated Portland area west of the mountain). Farmers in Washington State who had the real fallout, six inches of ash smothering their crops, answered the reporters' questions with polite stoicism; but in town a lot of people were cross and dull and jumpy. Some erratic behavior, some really weird driving. "Everybody on my bus coming to work these days talks to everybody else, they never used to." "Everybody on my bus coming to work sits there like a stone instead of talking to each other like they used to." Some welcomed the mild sense of urgency and emergency as bringing people together in mutual support. Some—the old, the ill—were terrified beyond reassurance. Psychologists reported that psychotics had promptly incorporated the volcano into their private systems; some thought they were controlling her, and some thought she was controlling them. Businessmen, whom we know from the Dow Jones Reports to be an almost ethereally timid and emotional breed, read the scare stories in Eastern newspapers and cancelled all their conventions here; Portland hotels are having a long cool summer. A Chinese Cultural Attaché, evidently preferring earthquakes, wouldn't come farther north than San Francisco. But many natives were irrationally exhilarated, secretly, heartlessly welcoming every steam-blast and earth-tremor: Go it, mountain!

5 Everybody read in the newspapers everywhere that the May 18 eruption was "five hundred times greater than the bomb dropped on Hiroshima." Some reflected that we have bombs much more than five hundred times more powerful than the 1945 bombs. But these are never mentioned in the comparisons. Perhaps it would upset people in Moscow, Idaho or Missoula, Montana, who got a lot of volcanic ash dumped on them, and don't want to have to think, what if that stuff had been radioactive? It really isn't nice to talk about it, is it. I mean, what if something went off in New Jersey, say, and *was* radioactive—Oh, stop it. That volcano's way out west there somewhere anyhow.

Everybody takes it personally.

I had to go into hospital for some surgery in April, while the mountain was in her early phase—she jumped and rumbled, like the Uncles in *A Child's Christmas in Wales,* but she hadn't done anything spectacular.[1] I was hoping she wouldn't perform while I couldn't watch. She obliged and held off for a month. On May 18 I was home, lying around with the cats, with a ringside view: bedroom and study look straight north about forty-five miles to the mountain.

I kept the radio tuned to a good country western station and listened to the reports as they came in, and wrote down some of the things they said. For the first couple of hours there was a lot of confusion and contradiction, but no panic, then or later. Late in the morning a man who had been about twenty miles from the blast described it: "Pumice-balls and mud-balls began falling for about a quarter of an hour, then the stuff got smaller, and by nine it was completely and totally black dark. You couldn't see ten feet in front of you!" He spoke with energy and admiration. Falling mud-balls, what next? The main West Coast artery, I-5, was soon closed because of the mud and wreckage rushing down the Toutle River towards the highway bridges. Walla Walla, 160 miles east, reported in to say their street lights had come on automatically at about ten in the morning. The Spokane-Seattle highway, far to the north, was closed, said an official expressionless voice, "on account of darkness."

At one-thirty that afternoon, I wrote:

> It has been warm with a white high haze all morning, since six A.M., when I saw the top of the mountain floating dark against yellow-rose sunrise sky above the haze.

10 That was, of course, the last time I saw or will ever see that peak.

> Now we can see the mountain from the base to near the summit. The mountain itself is whitish in the haze. All morning there has been this long, cobalt-bluish drift to the east from where the summit would be. And about ten o'clock there began to be visible clots, like cottage cheese curds, above the summit. Now the eruption cloud is visible from the summit of the mountain till obscured by a cloud layer at about twice the height of the mountain,

---

[1] *"A Child's Christmas in Wales"*: radio drama by the Welsh poet Dylan Thomas (1914–1953).

> i.e., 25–30,000 feet. The eruption cloud is very solid-looking, like sculptured marble, a beautiful blue in the deep relief of baroque curls, sworls, curled-cloud-shapes—darkening towards the top—a wonderful color. One is aware of motion, but (being shaky, and looking through shaky binoculars) I don't actually see the carven-blue-sworl-shapes move. Like the shadow on a sundial. It is *enormous.* Forty-five miles away. It is so much bigger than the mountain itself. It is silent, from this distance. Enormous, silent. It looks not like anything earthy, from the earth, but it does not look like anything atmospheric, a natural cloud, either. The blue of it is stormcloud blue but the shapes are far more delicate, complex, and immense than stormcloud shapes, and it has this solid look; a weightiness, like the capital of some unimaginable column—which in a way indeed it is, the pillar of fire being underground.

At four in the afternoon a reporter said cautiously, "Earthquakes are being felt in the metropolitan area," to which I added, with feeling, "I'll say they are!" I had decided not to panic unless the cats did. Animals are supposed to know about earthquakes, aren't they? I don't know what our cats know; they lay asleep in various restful and decorative poses on the swaying floor and the jiggling bed, and paid no attention to anything except dinner time. I was not allowed to panic.

At four-thirty a meteorologist, explaining the height of that massive, storm-blue pillar of cloud, said charmingly, "You must understand that the mountain is very warm. Warm enough to lift the air over it to 75,000 feet."

And a reporter: "Heavy mud flow on Shoestring Glacier, with continuous lightning." I tried to imagine that scene. I went to the television, and there it was. The radio and television coverage, right through, was splendid. One forgets the joyful courage of reporters and cameramen when there is something worth reporting, a real Watergate, a real volcano.

On the 19th, I wrote down from the radio, "A helicopter picked the logger up while he was sitting on a log surrounded by a mud flow." This rescue was filmed and shown on television: the tiny figure crouching hopeless in the huge abomination of ash and mud. I don't know if this man was one of the loggers who later died in the Emanuel Hospital burn center, or if he survived. They were already beginning to talk about the "killer eruption," as if the mountain had murdered with intent. Taking it personally . . . Of course she killed. Or did they kill themselves? Old Harry who wouldn't leave his lodge and his whiskey and his eighteen cats at Spirit Lake, and quite right too, at eighty-three; and the young cameraman and the young geologist, both up there on the north side on the job of their lives; and the loggers who went back to work because logging was their living; and the tourists who thought a volcano is like Channel Six, if you don't like the show you turn it off, and took their RVs and their kids up past the roadblocks and the reasonable warnings and the weary country sheriffs sick of arguing: they were all there to keep the appointment. Who made the appointment?

A firefighter pilot that day said to the radio interviewer, "We do what 15
the mountain says. It's not ready for us to go in."

On the 21st I wrote:

> Last night a long, strange, glowing twilight; but no ash has yet fallen west of the mountain. Today, fine, gray, mild, dense Oregon rain. Yesterday afternoon we could see her vaguely through the

> glasses. Looking appallingly lessened—short, flat—That is painful. She was so beautiful. She hurled her beauty in dust clear to the Atlantic shore, she made sunsets and sunrises of it, she gave it to the western wind. I hope she erupts magma and begins to build herself again. But I guess she is still unbuilding. The Pres. of the U.S. came today to see her. I wonder if he thinks he is on her level. Of course he could destroy much more than she has destroyed if he took a mind to.

On June 4 I wrote:

> Could see her through the glasses for the first time in two weeks or so. It's been dreary white weather with a couple of hours sun in the afternoons.—Not the new summit, yet; that's always in the roil of cloud/plume. But both her long lovely flanks. A good deal of new snow has fallen on her (while we had rain), and her SW face is white, black, and gray, much seamed, in unfamiliar patterns.
>
> "As changeless as the hills—"
>
> Part of the glory of it is being included in an event on the geologic scale. Being enlarged. "I shall lift up mine eyes unto the hills," yes: "whence cometh my help."

In all the Indian legends dug out by newspaper writers for the occasion, the mountain is female. Told in the Dick-and-Jane style considered appropriate for popular reportage of Indian myth, with all the syllables hyphenated, the stories seem even more naive and trivial than myths out of context generally do. But the theme of the mountain as woman—first ugly, then beautiful, but always a woman—is consistent. The mapmaking whites of course named the peak after a man, an Englishman who took his title, Baron St. Helens, from a town in the North Country: but the name is obstinately feminine. The Baron is forgotten, Helen remains. The whites who lived on and near the mountain called it The Lady. Called her The Lady. It seems impossible not to take her personally. In twenty years of living through a window from her I guess I have never really thought of her as "it."

She made weather, like all single peaks. She put on hats of cloud, and took them off again, and tried a different shape, and sent them all skimming off across the sky. She wore veils: around the neck, across the breast: white, silver, silver-gray, gray-blue. Her taste was impeccable. She knew the weathers that became her, and how to wear the snow.

Dr. William Hamilton of Portland State University wrote a lovely piece 20
for the college paper about "volcano anxiety," suggesting that the silver cone of St. Helens had been in human eyes a breast, and saying:

> St. Helens' real damage to us is not . . . that we have witnessed a denial of the trustworthiness of God (such denials are our familiar friends). It is the perfection of the mother that has been spoiled, for part of her breast has been removed. Our metaphor has had a mastectomy.
>
> At some deep level, the eruption of Mt. St. Helens has become a new metaphor for the very opposite of stability—for that greatest of twentieth-century fears—cancer. Our uneasiness may well rest on more elusive levels than dirty windshields.

This comes far closer to home than anything else I've read about the "meaning" of the eruption, and yet for me it doesn't work. Maybe it would work better for men. The trouble is, I never saw St. Helens as a breast. Some mountains, yes: Twin Peaks in San Francisco, of course, and other round, sweet California hills—breasts, bellies, eggs, anything maternal, bounteous, yielding. But St. Helens in my eyes was never part of a woman; she is a woman. And not a mother but a sister.

These emotional perceptions and responses sound quite foolish when written out in rational prose, but the fact is that, to me, the eruption was all mixed up with the women's movement. It may be silly but there it is; along the same lines, do you know any woman who wasn't rooting for Genuine Risk to take the Triple Crown? Part of my satisfaction and exultation at each eruption was unmistakably feminist solidarity. You men think you're the only ones can make a really nasty mess? You think you got all the firepower, and God's on your side? You think you run things? Watch this, gents. Watch the Lady act like a woman.

For that's what she did. The well-behaved, quiet, pretty, serene, domestic creature peaceably yielding herself to the uses of man all of sudden said NO. And she spat dirt and smoke and steam. She blackened half her face, in those first March days, like an angry brat. She fouled herself like a mad old harridan. She swore and belched and farted, threatened and shook and swelled, and then she spoke. They heard her voice two hundred miles away. Here I go, she said. I'm doing my thing now. Old Nobodaddy you better JUMP!

Her thing turns out to be more like childbirth than anything else, to my way of thinking. But not on our scale, not in our terms. Why should she speak in our terms or stoop to our scale? Why should she bear any birth that we can recognize? To us it is cataclysm and destruction and deformity. To her—well, for the language for it one must go to the scientists or to the poets. To the geologists. St. Helens is doing exactly what she "ought" to do—playing her part in the great pattern of events perceived by that noble discipline. Geology provides the only time-scale large enough to include the behavior of a volcano without deforming it. Geology, or poetry, which can see a mountain and a cloud as, after all, very similar phenomena. Shelley's cloud can speak for St. Helens:

> I silently laugh
> At my own cenotaph...
> And arise, and unbuild it again.

So many mornings waking I have seen her from the window before 25
any other thing: dark against red daybreak, silvery in summer light, faint above river-valley fog. So many times I have watched her at evening, the faintest outline in mist, immense, remote, serene: the center, the central stone. A self across the air, a sister self, a stone. "The stone is at the center," I wrote in a poem about her years ago. But the poem is impertinent. All I can say is impertinent.

When I was writing the first draft of this essay in California, on July 23, she erupted again, sending her plume to 60,000 feet. Yesterday, August 7, as I was typing the words "the 'meaning' of the eruption," I checked out the study window and there it was, the towering blue cloud against the quiet northern sky—the fifth major eruption. How long may her labor be? A year, ten years, ten thousand? We cannot predict what she may or might or will do, now, or next, or for the rest of our lives, or ever. A threat: a terror: a fulfillment. This is what serenity is built on. This unmakes the metapors. This is beyond us, and we must take it personally. This is the ground we walk on.

Analyzing the Text

1. In what respects does Mount St. Helens represent for Le Guin a personification of nature in feminist, not simply feminine, terms? What features of her account support this perception?
2. How did Le Guin's reaction to the eruption differ from others in the area and the way it was commented on by geologists and reported by the newspapers?

Understanding Le Guin's Techniques

1. How does the unusual style and structure of Le Guin's essay capture the unique nature of the event and the alternating periods of quiet and violent activity?
2. What images does Le Guin use that anthropomorphize Mount St. Helens and communicate the strong personal connection she has with it?

Arguing for an Interpretation

1. Le Guin does not mention that 22,000 people lost their lives in the eruption. In your opinion, would this fact have changed her perception or have made her portrayal appear to be in poor taste? Explain your answer.
2. Read Le Guin's novel *The Lathe of Heaven* (1971), and write a short paper arguing that scenes in it foreshadow the eruption of Mount St. Helens.

LANGSTON HUGHES

Langston Hughes (1902–1967) was born in Joplin, Missouri, and started writing poetry as a student in Central High School in Cleveland. After graduation he worked his way through Africa and Europe on cargo ships. In 1925, while he was working as a busboy in Washington, D.C., he encountered the poet Vachel Lindsay, who after reading Hughes's poems helped him publish his works. After the publication of his first book, The Weary Blues *(1926), Hughes toured the country giving poetry readings and became a leading figure in the Harlem Renaissance. He graduated from Lincoln University in Pennsylvania in 1929, returned to Harlem, and provided invaluable guidance to young writers. In "Salvation," which first appeared in his autobiography* The Big Sea *(1940), Hughes reveals his uncanny gift for dialogue and irony, as he re-creates a revival meeting that played a crucial role in his life.*

Salvation

I was saved from sin when I was going on thirteen. But not really saved. It happened like this. There was a big revival at my Auntie Reed's church. Every night for weeks there had been much preaching, singing, praying, and shouting, and some very hardened sinners had been brought to Christ, and the membership of the church had grown by leaps and bounds. Then just before the revival ended, they held a special meeting for children, "to bring the young lambs to the fold." My aunt spoke of it for days ahead. That night I was escorted to the front row and placed on the mourners' bench with all the other young sinners, who had not yet been brought to Jesus.

My aunt told me that when you were saved you saw a light, and something happened to you inside! And Jesus came into your life! And God was with you from then on! She said you could see and hear and feel Jesus in your soul. I believed her. I had heard a great many old people say that same thing and it seemed to me they ought to know. So I sat there calmly in the hot, crowded church, waiting for Jesus to come to me.

The preacher preached a wonderful rhythmical sermon, all moans and shouts and lonely cries and dire pictures of hell, and then he sang a song about the ninety and nine safe in the fold, but one little lamb was left out in the cold. Then he said: "Won't you come? Won't you come to Jesus? Young lambs, won't you come?" And he held out his arms to all us young sinners there on the mourners' bench. And the little girls cried. And some of them jumped up and went to Jesus right away. But most of us just sat there.

A great many old people came and knelt around us and prayed, old women with jet-black faces and braided hair, old men with work-gnarled hands. And the church sang a song about the lower lights are burning, some poor sinners to be saved. And the whole building rocked with prayer and song.

Still I kept waiting to *see* Jesus. 5

Finally all the young people had gone to the altar and were saved, but one boy and me. He was a rounder's son named Westley. Westley and I were surrounded by sisters and deacons praying. It was very hot in the church, and getting late now. Finally Westley said to me in a whisper: "God damn! I'm tired o' sitting here. Let's get up and be saved." So he got up and was saved.

Then I was left all alone on the mourners' bench. My aunt came and knelt at my knees and cried, while prayers and song swirled all around me in the little church. The whole congregation prayed for me alone in a mighty wail of moans and voices. And I kept waiting serenely for Jesus, waiting, waiting—but he didn't come. I wanted to see him, but nothing happened to me. Nothing! I wanted something to happen to me, but nothing happened.

I heard the songs and the minister saying: "Why don't you come? My dear child, why don't you come to Jesus? Jesus is waiting for you. He wants you. Why don't you come? Sister Reed, what is this child's name?"

"Langston," my aunt sobbed.

"Langston, why don't you come? Why don't you come and be saved? 10
Oh, Lamb of God! Why don't you come?"

Now it was really getting late. I began to be ashamed of myself, holding everything up so long. I began to wonder what God thought about

Westley, who certainly hadn't seen Jesus either, but who was now sitting proudly on the platform, swinging his knickerbockered legs and grinning down at me, surrounded by deacons and old women on their knees praying. God had not struck Westley dead for taking his name in vain or for lying in the temple. So I decided that maybe to save further trouble, I'd better lie, too, and say that Jesus had come, and get up and be saved.

So I got up.

Suddenly the whole room broke into a sea of shouting, as they saw me rise. Waves of rejoicing swept the place. Women leaped in the air. My aunt threw her arms around me. The minister took me by the hand and led me to the platform.

When things quieted down, in a hushed silence, punctuated by a few ecstatic "Amens," all the new young lambs were blessed in the name of God. Then joyous singing filled the room.

15 That night, for the last time in my life but one—for I was a big boy twelve years old—I cried. I cried, in bed alone, and couldn't stop. I buried my head under the quilts, but my aunt heard me. She woke up and told my uncle I was crying because the Holy Ghost had come into my life, and because I had seen Jesus. But I was really crying because I couldn't bear to tell her that I had lied, that I had deceived everybody in the church, that I hadn't seen Jesus, and that now I didn't believe there was a Jesus any more, since he didn't come to help me.

Analyzing the Text

1. Who are some of the people who have an interest in "saving" the young Langston Hughes? In each case, how would his salvation serve their interests?
2. What ultimately tips the balance and impels him to declare himself "saved"?

Understanding Hughes's Techniques

1. How does Hughes use imagery and figurative language to intensify a sense of drama?
2. In what way is the account shaped to build up suspense as to whether or not Hughes will succumb to pressure from the congregation?

Arguing for an Interpretation

1. Although Hughes behaves in an insincere manner, he does not seem hypocritical. What might account for this?
2. To what extent might Hughes be superimposing his adult awareness onto his childhood experience? Is it plausible that he would have been as fully conscious of all the nuances and expectations directed toward him as a boy? Explain your answer.

Short Fiction

PREMCHAND

Premchand (a pseudonym for Dhanpat Rai, 1880–1936), who is arguably the greatest writer in Hindi, was born

near Benares (present-day Varanasi), India. Although not from a wealthy family, he received a good education in Persian and Urdu. His earliest fiction was influenced by Dickens, Tolstoy, and Gandhi and from the outset was directed toward social reform. He produced an astonishing amount of work of the highest caliber, including 14 novels, 300 short stories, and several hundred essays in addition to numerous plays, screenplays, and translations. His short story "Deliverance," translated in 1988 by David Rubin, was made into a film by the great Indian film director Satyajit Ray.

Deliverance

Dukhi the tanner was sweeping in front of his door while Jhuriya, his wife, plastered the floor with cow-dung. When they both found a moment to rest from their work Jhuriya said, 'Aren't you going to the Brahman to ask him to come? If you don't he's likely to go off somewhere.'

'Yes, I'm going,' Dukhi said, 'But we have to think about what he's going to sit on.'

'Can't we find a cot somewhere? You could borrow one from the village headman's wife.'

'Sometimes the things you say are really aggravating! The people in the headman's house give me a cot? They won't even let a coal out of their house to light your fire with, so are they going to give me a cot? Even when they're where I can go and talk to them if I ask for a pot of water I won't get it, so who'll give me a cot? A cot isn't like the things we've got—cow-dung fuel or chaff or wood that anybody who wants can pick up and carry off. You'd better wash our own cot and set it out—in this hot weather it ought to be dry by the time he comes.'

'He won't sit on our cot,' Jhuriya said. 'You know what a stickler he is 5
about religion and doing things according to the rule.'

A little worried, Dukhi said, 'Yes, that's true. I'll break off some *mohwa*[1] leaves and make a mat for him, that will be the thing. Great gentlemen eat off *mohwa* leaves, they're holy. Hand me my stick and I'll break some off.'

'I'll make the mat, you go to him. But we'll have to offer him some food he can take home and cook, won't we? I'll put it in my dish—'

'Don't commit any such sacrilege!' Dukhi said. 'If you do, the offering will be wasted and the dish broken. *Baba*[2] will just pick up the dish and dump it. He flies off the handle very fast, and when he's in a rage he doesn't even spare his wife, and he beat his son so badly that even now the boy goes around with a broken hand. So we'll put the offering on a leaf too. Just don't touch it. Take Jhuri the *Gond*'s[3] daughter to the village merchant and bring back all the things we need. Let it be a complete offering—a full

---

[1]*mohwa:* a large branchy forest tree whose flowers are also used as food.
[2]*Baba:* father, a title of respect.
[3]*Gond:* one of the tribes belonging to the Madhya Pradesh region famous for their music, dance, paintings and sculpture.

two pounds of flour, a half of rice, a quarter of gram, an eighth of *ghee,*[4] salt, turmeric, and four *annas*[5] at the edge of the leaf. If you don't find the *Gond* girl then get the woman who runs the parching oven, beg her to go if you have to. Just don't touch anything because that will be a great wrong.'

After these instructions Dukhi picked up his stick, took a big bundle of grass and went to make his request to the Pandit. He couldn't go empty-handed to ask a favour of the Pandit; he had nothing except the grass for a present. If Panditji ever saw him coming without an offering, he'd shout abuse at him from far away.

Pandit Ghasiram was completely devoted to God. As soon as he awoke he would busy himself with his rituals. After washing his hands and feet at eight o'clock, he would begin the real ceremony of worship, the first part of which consisted of the preparation of *bhang.*[6] After that he would grind sandalwood paste for half-an-hour, then with a straw he would apply it to his forehead before the mirror. Between two lines of sandalwood paste he would draw a red dot. Then on his chest and arms he would draw designs of perfect circles. After this he would take out the image of the Lord, bathe it, apply the sandalwood to it, deck it with flowers, perform the ceremony of lighting the lamp before it and ringing a little bell. At ten o'clock he'd rise from his devotions and after a drink of the *bhang* go outside where a few clients would have gathered: such was the reward for his piety; this was his crop to harvest.

Today when he came from the shrine in his house he saw Dukhi the Untouchable tanner sitting there with a bundle of grass. As soon as he caught sight of him Dukhi stood up, prostrated himself on the ground, stood up again and folded his hands. Seeing the Pandit's glorious figure his heart was filled with reverence. How godly a sight!—a rather short, roly-poly fellow with a bald, shiny skull, chubby cheeks and eyes aglow with brahmanical energy. The sandalwood markings bestowed on him the aspect of the gods. At the sight of Dukhi he intoned, 'What brings you here today, little Dukhi?'

Bowing his head, Dukhi said, 'I'm arranging Bitiya's betrothal. Will your worship help us to fix an auspicious date? When can you find the time?'

'I have no time today,' Panditji said. 'But still, I'll manage to come toward evening.'

'No, maharaj, please come soon. I've arranged everything for you. Where shall I set this grass down?'

'Put it down in front of the cow and if you'll just pick up that broom sweep it clean in front of the door,' Panditji said. 'Then the floor of the sitting room hasn't been plastered for several days so plaster it with cow-dung. While you're doing that I'll be having my lunch, then I'll rest a bit and after that I'll come. Oh yes, you can split that wood too, and in the store-room there's a little pile of hay—just take it out and put it into the fodder bin.'

Dukhi began at once to carry out the orders. He swept the doorstep, he plastered the floor. This took until noon. Panditji went off to have his

---

[4]*ghee:* clarified butter that has the milk solids and water removed.
[5]*annas:* Indian currency. 16 annas = one rupee.
[6]*bhang:* a beverage made from the leaves and flowers of the cannabis plant that is mixed with spices and milk.

lunch. Dukhi, who had eaten nothing since morning, was terribly hungry. But there was no way he could eat here. His house was a mile away—if he went to eat there Panditji would be angry. The poor fellow suppressed his hunger and began to split the wood. It was a fairly thick tree trunk on which a great many devotees had previously tried their strength and it was ready to match iron with iron in any fight. Dukhi, who was used to cutting grass and bringing it to the market, had no experience with cutting wood. The grass would bow its head before his sickle but now even when he bought the axe down with all his strength it didn't make a mark on the trunk. The axe just glanced off. He was drenched in sweat, panting, he sat down exhausted and got up again. He could scarcely lift his hands, his legs were unsteady, he couldn't straighten out his back. Then his vision blurred, he saw spots, he felt dizzy, but still he went on trying. He thought that if he could get a pipeful of tobacco to smoke then perhaps he might feel refreshed. This was a Brahman village, and Brahmans didn't smoke tobacco at all like the low castes and Untouchables. Suddenly he remembered that there was a *Gond* living in the village too, surely he would have a pipeful. He set off at a run for the man's house at once, and he was in luck. The *Gond* gave him both pipe and tobacco, but he had no fire to light it with. Dukhi said, 'Don't worry about the fire, brother, I'll go to Panditji's house and ask him for a light, they're still cooking there.'

With this he took the pipe and came back and stood on the verandah of the Brahman's house, and he said, 'Master, if I could get just a little bit of light I'll smoke this pipeful.'

Panditji was eating and his wife said, 'Who's that man asking for a light?'

'It's only that damned little Dukhi the tanner. I told him to cut some wood. The fire's lit, so go give him his light.'

Frowning, the Panditayin said, 'You've become so wrapped up in your books and astrological charts that you've forgotten all about caste rules. If there's a tanner or a washerman or a birdcatcher why he can just come walking right into the house as though he owned it. You'd think it was an inn and not a decent Hindu's house. Tell that good-for-nothing to get out or I'll scorch his face with a firebrand.'

Trying to calm her down, Panditji said, 'He's come inside—so what? Nothing that belongs to you has been stolen. The floor is clean, it hasn't been desecrated. Why not just let him have his light—he's doing our work, isn't he? You'd have to pay at least four *annas* if you hired some labourer to split it.'

Losing her temper, the Panditayin said, 'What does he mean coming into this house!'

'It was the son of a bitch's bad luck, what else?' the Pandit said.

'It's all right,' she said, 'This time I'll give him his fire but if he ever comes into the house again like that I'll give him the coals in his face.'

Fragments of this conversation reached Dukhi's ears. He repented: it was a mistake to come. She was speaking the truth—how could a tanner ever come into a Brahman's house? These people were clean and holy, that was why the whole world worshipped and respected them. A mere tanner was absolutely nothing. He had lived all his life in the village without understanding this before.

Therefore when the Pandit's wife came out bringing coals it was like a miracle from heaven. Folding his hands and touching his forehead to the ground he said, 'Panditayin, Mother, it was very wrong of me to come inside your house. Tanners don't have much sense—if we weren't such fools why would we get kicked so much?'

The Panditayin had brought the coals in a pair of tongs. From a few feet away, with her veil drawn over her face, she flung the coals toward Dukhi. Big sparks fell on his head and drawing back hastily he shook them out of his hair. To himself he said, 'This is what comes of dirtying a clean Brahman's house. How quickly God pays you back for it! That's why everybody's afraid of Pandits. Everybody else gives up his money and never gets it back but who ever got any money out of a Brahman? Anybody who tried would have his whole family destroyed and his legs would turn leprous.' He went outside and smoked his pipe, then took up the axe and started to work again.

Because the sparks had fallen on him the Pandit's wife felt some pity for him. When the Pandit got up from his meal she said to him, 'Give this tanner something to eat, the poor fellow's been working for a long time, he must be hungry.'

Panditji considered this proposal entirely outside of the behavior ex- 30
pected of him. He asked, 'Is there any bread?'

'There are a couple of pieces left over.'

'What's the good of two or three pieces for a tanner? Those people need at least a good two pounds.'

His wife put her hands over her ears. 'My, my, a good two pounds! Then let's forget about it.'

Majestically Panditji said, 'If there's some bran and husks mix them in flour and make a couple of pancakes. That'll fill the bastard's belly up. You can never fill up these low-caste people with good bread. Plain millet is what they need.'

'Let's forget the whole thing,' the Panditayin said, 'I'm not going to kill 35
myself cooking in weather like this.'

When he took up the axe again after smoking his pipe, Dukhi found that with his rest the strength had to some extent come back into his arms. He swung the axe for about half-an-hour, then out of breath he sat down right there with his head in his hands.

In the meantime the *Gond* came. He said, 'Why are you wearing yourself out, old friend? You can whack it all you like but you won't split this trunk. You're killing yourself for nothing.'

Wiping the sweat from his forehead Dukhi said, 'I've still got to cart off a whole wagon-load of hay, brother.'

'Have you had anything to eat? Or are they just making you work without feeding you? Why don't you ask them for something?'

'How can you expect me to digest a Brahman's food, Chikhuri?' 40

'Digesting it is no problem, you have to get it first. He sits in there and eats like a king and then has a nice little nap after he tells you you have to split his wood. The government officials may force you to work for them but they pay you something for it, no matter how little. This fellow's gone one better, calling himself a holy man.'

'Speak softly, brother, if they hear you we'll be in trouble.'

With that Dukhi went back to work and began to swing the axe. Chikhuri felt so sorry for him that he came and took the axe out of Dukhi's hands and worked with it for a good half hour. But there was not even a crack in the wood. Then he threw the axe down and said, 'Whack it all you like but you won't split it, you're just killing yourself,' and he went away.

Dukhi began to think, 'Where did the *Baba* get hold of this trunk that can't be split? There's not even a crack in it so far. How long can I keep smashing into it? I've got a hundred things to do at home by now. In a house like mine there's no end to the work, something's always left over. But he doesn't worry about that. I'll just bring him his hay and tell him, '*Baba,* the wood didn't split. I'll come and finish it tomorrow.'

45 He lifted up the basket and began to bring the hay. From the storeroom to the fodder bin was no less than a quarter of a mile. If he'd really filled up the basket the work would have been quickly finished, but then who could have hoisted up the basket on his head? He couldn't raise a fully loaded basket, so he took just a little each time. It was four o'clock by the time he'd finished with the hay. At this time Pandit Ghasiram woke up, washed his hands and face, took some *paan*[7] and came outside. He saw Dukhi asleep with the basket still on his head. He shouted, '*Arrey*[8] Dukhiya, sleeping? The wood's lying there just the way it was. What's taken you so long? You've used up the whole day just to bring in a little fistful of hay and then gone and fallen asleep! Pick up the axe and split that wood. You haven't even made a dent in it. So if you don't find an auspicious day for your daughter's marriage, don't blame me. This is why they say that as soon as an Untouchable gets a little food in his house he can't be bothered with you any more.'

Dukhi picked up the axe again. He completely forgot what he'd been thinking about before. His stomach was pasted against his backbone—he hadn't so much as eaten breakfast that morning, there wasn't any time. Just to stand up seemed an impossible task. His spirit flagged, but only for a moment. This was the Pandit, if he didn't fix an auspicious day the marriage would be a total failure. And that was why everybody respected the Pandits—everything depended on getting the right day set. He could ruin anybody he wanted to. Panditji came close to the log and standing there began to goad him. 'That's right, give it a real hard stroke, a real hard one. Come on now, really hit it! Don't you have any strength in your arm? Smash it, what's the point of standing there thinking about it? That's it, it's going to split, there's a crack in it.'

Dukhi was in a delirium; some kind of hidden power seemed to have come into his hands. It was as though fatigue, hunger, weakness, all had left him. He was astonished at his own strength. The axe-strokes descended one after another like lightning. He went on driving the axe in this state of intoxication until finally the log split down the middle. And Dukhi's hands let the axe drop. At the same moment, overcome with dizziness, he fell, the hungry, thirsty, exhausted body gave up.

Panditji called, 'Get up, just two or three more strokes. I want it in small bits.' Dukhi did not get up. It didn't seem proper to Pandit Ghasiram to insist now. He went inside, drank some *bhang,* emptied his bowels, bathed and came forth attired in full Pandit regalia. Dukhi was still lying on the ground. Panditji shouted, 'Well, Dukhi, are you going to just stay lying here? Let's go, I'm on my way to your house! Everything's set, isn't it?' But still Dukhi did not get up.

A little alarmed, Panditji drew closer and saw that Dukhi was absolutely stiff. Startled half out of his wits he ran into the house and said to his wife, 'Little Dukhi looks as though he's dead.'

50 Thrown into confusion Panditayin said, 'But hasn't he just been chopping wood?'

[7]*paan:* betel leaf, used for digestion.
[8]*arrey:* an exclamation to get another's attention.

'He died right while he was splitting it. What's going to happen?'

Calmer, the Panditayin said, 'What do you mean what's going to happen? Send word to the tanners settlement so they can come and take the corpse away.'

In a moment the whole village knew about it. It happened that except for the *Gond* house everyone who lived there was Brahman. People stayed off the road that went there. The only path to the well passed that way—how were they to get water? Who would come to draw water with a tanner's corpse nearby? One old woman said to Panditji, 'Why don't you have this body thrown away? Is anybody in the village going to be able to drink water or not?'

The *Gond* went from the village to the tanners' settlement and told everyone the story. 'Careful now!' he said. 'Don't go to get the body. There'll be a police investigation yet. It's no joke that somebody killed this poor fellow. The somebody may be a pandit, but just in his own house. If you move the body you'll get arrested too.'

Right after this Panditji arrived. But there was nobody in the settlement ready to carry the corpse away. To be sure, Dukhi's wife and daughter both went moaning to Panditji's door and tore their hair and wept. About a dozen other women went with them, and they wept too and they consoled them, but there was no man with them to bear up the body. Panditji threatened the tanners, he tried to wheedle them, but they were very mindful of the police and not one of them stirred. Finally Panditji went home disappointed.

At midnight the weeping and lamentation were still going on. It was hard for the Brahmans to fall asleep. But no tanner came to get the corpse, and how could a Brahman lift up an Untouchable's body? It was expressly forbidden in the scriptures and no one could deny it.

Angrily the Panditayin said, 'Those witches are driving me out of my mind. And they're not even hoarse yet!'

'Let the hags cry as long as they want. When he was alive nobody cared a straw about him. Now that he's dead everybody in the village is making a fuss about him.'

'The wailing of tanners is bad luck,' the Panditayin said.

'Yes, very bad luck.'

'And it's beginning to stink already.'

'Wasn't that bastard a tanner? Those people eat anything, clean or not, without worrying about it.'

'No sort of food disgusts them!'

'They're all polluted!'

Somehow or other they got through the night. But even in the morning no tanner came. They could still hear the wailing of the women. The stench was beginning to spread quite a bit.

Panditji got out a rope. He made a noose and managed to get it over the dead man's feet and drew it tight. Morning mist still clouded the air. Panditji grabbed the rope and began to drag it, and he dragged it until it was out of the village. When he got back home he bathed immediately, read out prayers to Durga for purification, and sprinkled Ganges water around the house.

Out there in the field the jackals and kites, dogs and crows were picking at Dukhi's body. This was the reward of a whole life of devotion, service and faith.

Analyzing the Text

1. In what ways do the lives of Dukhi, the tanner, and Pandit, the Brahman, differ, and how? What insight does Premchand give into the role caste plays in Indian society?
2. In view of what happens to Dukhi, how might the title be interpreted?

Understanding Premchand's Techniques

1. How would you characterize Premchand's attitude toward his characters? What phrases make it obvious that he is sympathetic to Dukhi and critical of Pandit?
2. How does the episode of trying to split the impenetrable tree trunk come to symbolize Dukhi's futile struggle to break free from the caste system?

Arguing for an Interpretation

1. How would the story change if it were told from a third person omniscient point of view, where the reader could be privy to the thoughts and feelings of all the characters?
2. Is Premchand using the story as a platform to argue for the abolishment of the caste system, or at least for the lifting of the taboos against the untouchables? Why or why not?

NAGUIB MAHFOUZ

Naguib Mahfouz was born in 1911 in Ganaliyya—an old quarter of Cairo that served as a setting for several of his novels—to a family that earned its living from trade. In 1930 he entered the Secular University in Cairo where he studied philosophy. Mahfouz developed a narrative technique through which he could criticize the government without running the risk of antagonizing the authorities. In this way, Mahfouz veiled his criticism of the ruling powers through the framework of historical novels set in ancient Egypt, most notably in The Mockery of Fate *(1939),* Radobais *(1943), and* The Struggle of Thebes *(1944). In the late 1940s and 1950s he turned to a more realistic style, setting his stories in modern Egypt. Between 1956 and 1957 he produced his famous* Cairo Trilogy, *a sequence of novels that chronicles the changes in three generations of a middle-class Cairo family.*

Widely regarded as Egypt's leading literary figure, Naguib Mahfouz is the first Arabic-language author awarded the Nobel Prize in literature (1988) and only the second from the African continent (Wole Soyinka, a Nigerian, had won two years earlier). Generations of Arabs have read his works and sixteen of his novels have been adapted for films in Egypt. He brought enormous changes to Arab prose by synthesizing traditional literary style and modern speech to create a language understood by Arabs everywhere.

Mahfouz's prose works have been compared in spirit and tone to the social realism of Balzac and Dickens because of both the extent to which they reflect Egypt's volatile political history, and their accurate depiction of the distressing conditions under which the poor live. He has held a variety of government posts and has served as director of the Foundation for Support of the Cinema. In 1989, when Mahfouz spoke out against the Ayatollah Khomeini's death sentence on Salman Rushdie (for his novel The Satanic Verses*), Mahfouz was himself subject to death threats by Muslim fundamentalists. In English, his most recent works include* The Time and the Place and Other Stories *(1991), in which "Half a Day," translated by Davies Denys-Johnson, first appeared. This story is typical of Mahfouz's later works in its extensive use of allegory, symbolism, and experimental narrative techniques to explore spiritual themes. He has also written* Akhenaten, Dweller in Truth *(2000),* Respected Sir; Wedding Song; and The Search *(2001).*

Half a Day

I proceeded alongside my father, clutching his right hand, running to keep up with the long strides he was taking. All my clothes were new: the black shoes, the green school uniform, and the red tarboosh. My delight in my new clothes, however, was not altogether unmarred, for this was no feast day but the day on which I was to be cast into school for the first time.

My mother stood at the window watching our progress, and I would turn toward her from time to time, as though appealing for help. We walked along a street lined with gardens; on both sides were extensive fields planted with crops, prickly pears, henna trees, and a few date palms.

"Why school?" I challenged my father openly. "I shall never do anything to annoy you."

"I'm not punishing you," he said, laughing. "School's not a punishment. It's the factory that makes useful men out of boys. Don't you want to be like your father and brothers?"

I was not convinced. I did not believe there was really any good to be 5
had in tearing me away from the intimacy of my home and throwing me into this building that stood at the end of the road like some huge, high-walled fortress, exceedingly stern and grim.

When we arrived at the gate we could see the courtyard, vast and crammed full of boys and girls. "Go in by yourself," said my father, "and join them. Put a smile on your face and be a good example to others."

I hesitated and clung to his hand, but he gently pushed me from him. "Be a man," he said. "Today you truly begin life. You will find me waiting for you when it's time to leave."

I took a few steps, then stopped and looked but saw nothing. Then the faces of boys and girls came into view. I did not know a single one of them, and none of them knew me. I felt I was a stranger who had lost his way. But glances of curiosity were directed toward me, and one boy approached and asked, "Who brought you?"

"My father," I whispered.

"My father's dead," he said quite simply. 10

I did not know what to say. The gate was closed, letting out a pitiable screech. Some of the children burst into tears. The bell rang. A lady came along, followed by a group of men. The men began sorting us into ranks. We were formed into an intricate pattern in the great courtyard surrounded on three sides by high buildings of several floors; from each floor we were overlooked by a long balcony roofed in wood.

"This is your new home," said the woman. "Here too there are mothers and fathers. Here there is everything that is enjoyable and beneficial to knowledge and religion. Dry your tears and face life joyfully."

We submitted to the facts, and this submission brought a sort of contentment. Living beings were drawn to other living beings, and from the first moments my heart made friends with such boys as were to be my friends and fell in love with such girls as I was to be in love with, so that it seemed my misgivings had had no basis. I had never imagined school would have this rich variety. We played all sorts of different games: swings, the vaulting horse, ball games. In the music room we chanted our first songs. We also had our first introduction to language. We saw a globe of the Earth, which revolved and showed the various continents and countries. We started learning the numbers. The story of the Creator of the universe was read to us, we were told of His present world and of His Hereafter, and we heard examples of what He said. We ate delicious food, took a little nap, and woke up to go on with friendship and love, play and learning.

As our path revealed itself to us, however, we did not find it as totally sweet and unclouded as we had presumed. Dust-laden winds and unexpected accidents came about suddenly, so we had to be watchful, at the ready, and very patient. It was not all a matter of playing and fooling around. Rivalries could bring about pain and hatred or give rise to fighting. And while the lady would sometimes smile, she would often scowl and scold. Even more frequently she would resort to physical punishment.

In addition, the time for changing one's mind was over and gone and 15
there was no question of ever returning to the paradise of home. Nothing lay ahead of us but exertion, struggle, and perseverance. Those who were able took advantage of the opportunities for success and happiness that presented themselves amid the worries.

The bell rang announcing the passing of the day and the end of work. The throngs of children rushed toward the gate, which was opened again. I bade farewell to friends and sweethearts and passed through the gate. I peered around but found no trace of my father, who had promised to be there. I stepped aside to wait. When I had waited for a long time without avail, I decided to return home on my own. After I had taken a few steps, a middle-aged man passed by, and I realized at once that I knew him. He came toward me, smiling, and shook me by the hand, saying, "It's a long time since we last met—how are you?"

With a nod of my head, I agreed with him and in turn asked, "And you, how are you?"

"As you can see, not all that good, the Almighty be praised!"

Again he shook me by the hand and went off. I proceeded a few steps, then came to a startled halt. Good Lord! Where was the street lined with gardens? Where had it disappeared to? When did all these vehicles invade it? And when did all these hordes of humanity come to rest upon its surface? How did these hills of refuse come to cover its sides? And where were the fields that bordered it? High buildings had taken over, the street surged with children, and disturbing noises shook the air. At various points stood conjurers showing off their tricks and making snakes appear from baskets. Then there was a band announcing the opening of a circus, with clowns and weight lifters walking in front. A line of trucks carrying central security troops crawled majestically by. The siren of a fire engine shrieked, and it was not clear how the vehicle would cleave its way to reach the blazing fire. A battle raged between a taxi driver and his passenger, while the passenger's wife called out for help and no one answered. Good God! I was in a daze. My head spun. I almost went crazy. How could all this have happened in half a day, between early morning and sunset? I would find the answer at home with my father. But where was my home? I could see only tall buildings and hordes of people. I hastened on to the crossroads between the gardens and Abu Khoda. I had to cross Abu Khoda to reach my house, but the stream of cars would not let up. The fire engine's siren was shrieking at full pitch as it moved at a snail's pace, and I said to myself, "Let the fire take its pleasure in what it consumes." Extremely irritated, I wondered when I would be able to cross. I stood there a long time, until the young lad employed at the ironing shop on the corner came up to me. He stretched out his arm and said gallantly, "Grandpa, let me take you across."

Analyzing the Text

1. How would you characterize the boy's relationship with his father and when did you first suspect that the story covered more than the narrator's first day at school?
2. What changes take place in the boy's life and how does he begin to comprehend the many experiences that befall him?

Understanding Mahfouz's Techniques

1. In what way does the image of fire symbolize the cumulative effects of time on people and places and the boy himself?
2. What unusual compression does "half a day" signify in relationship to what actually happens?

Arguing for an Interpretation

1. Is the story simply about the sudden impact of the unrealized passage of time, or is it about the transformation of the boy's personality and his loss of innocence? Explain your answer.
2. Along with the psychological journey the story describes, what details suggest that Mahfouz is critical of the way Egyptian society has changed since the boy was young?

Chinua Achebe

Chinua Achebe was born in Ogidi, a village in eastern Nigeria, in 1930, the son of one of the first Igbo mission teachers. Igbo (previously spelled Ibo) is his native tongue, but he learned English—the language in which he writes—at a young age. After taking a degree in English literature from University College, Ibadan in 1953, he worked as a producer and director of the Nigerian Broadcasting Service until the outbreak of the Nigerian civil war in 1967. Achebe actively supported the Biafran struggle for independence, but with the defeat of the Republic of Biafra he joined the University of Nigeria, Nsukka, as a senior research fellow and served as the editor of Okike, *a journal devoted to African literature. Although Achebe has written essays, poetry, children's literature, and short stories collected in* The Sacrificial Egg and Other Stories *(1962),* Girls at War *(1972), and* African Short Stories *(1985), it is as a novelist that he is best known. His first novel,* Things Fall Apart *(1958), from which the following chapter is drawn, is widely acclaimed as a classic of African literature. This work describes how a stable and traditional Nigerian society disintegrates as a result of contact with western Europeans who destroy its political, economic, and religious institutions. In it and succeeding works—*No Longer at Ease *(1960),* Arrow of God *(1964),* A Man of the People *(1966), and* Anthills of the Savannah *(1988)—Achebe continues to counteract European distortions of traditional African culture in his unique style, characterized by subtle irony and compassion. His most recent work is* Home and Exile *(2000). Much of Achebe's work explores the tragic consequences for tribal cultures and the individuals in them when they lose touch with the traditional values that have sustained them. When the protagonist of* Things Fall Apart, *Okonkwo, needlessly participates in slaughtering his adopted son rather than risk being perceived as unmanly, he sets in motion terrible consequences that destroy both him and his clan.*

Things Fall Apart

For three years Ikemefuna lived in Okonkwo's household and the elders of Umuofia seemed to have forgotten about him. He grew rapidly like a yam tendril in the rainy season, and was full of the sap of life. He had become wholly absorbed into his new family. He was like an elder brother to Nwoye, and from the very first seemed to have kindled a new fire in the younger boy. He made him feel grown-up; and they no longer spent the evenings in mother's hut while she cooked, but now sat with Okonkwo in his *obi,*[1] or watched him as he tapped his palm tree for the evening wine. Nothing pleased Nwoye now more than to be sent for by his mother or another of his father's wives to do one of those difficult and masculine tasks in the home, like splitting wood, or pounding food. On receiving such a message through a younger brother or sister, Nwoye would feign annoyance and grumble aloud about women and their troubles.

Okonkwo was inwardly pleased at his son's development, and he knew it was due to Ikemefuna. He wanted Nwoye to grow into a tough young man capable of ruling his father's household when he was dead and gone to join the ancestors. He wanted him to be a prosperous man, having enough in his barn to feed the ancestors with regular sacrifices. And so he was always happy when he heard him grumbling about women. That showed that in time he would be able to control his women-folk. No matter how prosperous a man was, if he was unable to rule his women and his children (and especially his women) he was not really a man. He was like the man in the song who had ten and one wives and not enough soup for his foo-foo.[2]

So Okonkwo encouraged the boys to sit with him in his *obi,* and he told them stories of the land—masculine stories of violence and bloodshed. Nwoye knew that it was right to be masculine and to be violent, but somehow he still preferred the stories that his mother used to tell, and which she no doubt still told to her younger children—stories of the tortoise and his wily ways, and of the bird *encke-nti-oba*[3] who challenged the whole world to a wrestling contest and was finally thrown by the cat. He remembered the story she often told of the quarrel between Earth and Sky long ago, and how Sky withheld rain for seven years, until crops withered and the dead could not be buried because the hoes broke on the stony Earth. At last Vulture was sent to plead with Sky, and to soften his heart with a song of the suffering of the sons of men. Whenever Nwoye's mother sang this song he felt carried away to the distant scene in the sky where Vulture, Earth's emissary, sang for mercy. At last Sky was moved to pity, and he gave to Vulture rain wrapped in leaves of coco-yam. But as he flew home his long talon pierced the leaves and the rain fell as it had never fallen before. And so heavily did it rain on Vulture that he did not return to deliver his message but flew to a distant land, from where he had espied a fire. And when he got there he found it was a man making a sacrifice. He warmed himself in the fire and ate the entrails.

That was the kind of story that Nwoye loved. But he now knew that they were for foolish women and children, and he knew that his father wanted him to be a man. And so he feigned that he no longer cared for women's stories. And when he did this he saw that his father was pleased, and no longer rebuked him or beat him. So Nwoye and Ikemefuna would listen to Okonkwo's stories about tribal wars, or how, years ago, he had stalked his victim, overpowered him and obtained his first human head. And as he told them of the past they sat in darkness or the dim glow of logs, waiting for the women to finish their cooking. When they finished, each brought her bowl of foo-foo and bowl of soup to her husband. An oil

[1] *obi,* the large living quarters of the head of the family.
[2] *foo-foo,* a mashed form of a starchy, edible root, also known as the coco-yam.
[3] *encke-nti-oba,* a kind of bird.

lamp was lit and Okonkwo tasted from each bowl, and then passed two shares to Nwoye and Ikemefuna.

5 In this way the moons and the seasons passed. And then the locusts came. It had not happened for many a long year. The elders said locusts came once in a generation, reappeared every year for seven years and then disappeared for another lifetime. They went back to their caves in a distant land, where they were guarded by a race of stunted men. And then after another lifetime these men opened the caves again and the locusts came to Umuofia.

They came in the cold harmattan[4] season after the harvests had been gathered, and ate up all the wild grass in the fields.

Okonkwo and the two boys were working on the red outer walls of the compound. This was one of the lighter tasks of the after-harvest season. A new cover of thick palm branches and palm leaves was set on the walls to protect them from the next rainy season. Okonkwo worked on the outside of the wall and the boys worked from within. There were little holes from one side to the other in the upper levels of the wall, and through these Okonkwo passed the rope, or *tie-tie,*[5] to the boys and they passed it round the wooden stays and then back to him; and in this way the cover was strengthened on the wall.

The women had gone to the bush to collect firewood, and the little children to visit their playmates in the neighboring compounds. The harmattan was in the air and seemed to distill a hazy feeling of sleep on the world. Okonkwo and the boys worked in complete silence, which was only broken when a new palm frond was lifted on to the wall or when a busy hen moved dry leaves about in her ceaseless search for food.

And then quite suddenly a shadow fell on the world, and the sun seemed hidden behind a thick cloud. Okonkwo looked up from his work and wondered if it was going to rain at such an unlikely time of the year. But almost immediately a shout of joy broke out in all directions, and Umuofia, which had dozed in the noon-day haze, broke into life and activity.

10 "Locusts are descending," was joyfully chanted everywhere, and men, women and children left their work or their play and ran into the open to see the unfamiliar sight. The locusts had not come for many, many years, and only the old people had seen them before.

At first, a fairly small swarm came. They were the harbingers sent to survey the land. And then appeared on the horizon a slowly-moving mass like a boundless sheet of black cloud drifting towards Umuofia. Soon it covered half the sky, and the solid mass was now broken by tiny eyes of light like shining star dust. It was a tremendous sight, full of power and beauty.

Everyone was now about, talking excitedly and praying that the locusts should camp in Umuofia for the night. For although locusts had not visited Umuofia for many years, everybody knew by instinct that they were very good to eat. And at last the locusts did descend. They settled on every tree and on every blade of grass; they settled on the roofs and covered the bare ground. Mighty tree branches broke away under them, and the whole country became the brown-earth color of the vast, hungry swarm.

---

[4]*harmattan,* a dry parching land-breeze charged with dust.
[5]*tie-tie,* a creeping vine used as rope.

Many people went out with baskets trying to catch them, but the elders counseled patience till nightfall. And they were right. The locusts settled in the bushes for the night and their wings became wet with dew. Then all Umuofia turned out in spite of the cold harmattan, and everyone filled his bags and pots with locusts. The next morning they were roasted in clay pots and then spread in the sun until they became dry and brittle. And for many days this rare food was eaten with solid palm-oil.

Okonkwo sat in his *obi* crunching happily with Ikemefuna and Nwoye, and drinking palm-wine[6] copiously, when Ogbuefi Ezeudu came in. Ezeudu was the oldest man in this quarter of Umuofia. He had been a great and fearless warrior in his time, and was now accorded great respect in all the clan. He refused to join in the meal, and asked Okonkwo to have a word with him outside. And so they walked out together, the old man supporting himself with his stick. When they were out of earshot, he said to Okonkwo:

"That boy calls you father. Do not bear a hand in his death." Okonkwo 15
was surprised, and was about to say something when the old man continued: "Yes, Umuofia has decided to kill him. The Oracle of the Hills and the Caves has pronounced it. They will take him outside Umuofia as is the custom, and kill him there. But I want you to have nothing to do with it. He calls you his father."

The next day a group of elders from all the nine villages of Umuofia came to Okonkwo's house early in the morning, and before they began to speak in low tones Nwoye and Ikemefuna were sent out. They did not stay very long, but when they went away Okonkwo sat still for a very long time supporting his chin in his palms. Later in the day he called Ikemefuna and told him that he was to be taken home the next day. Nwoye overheard it and burst into tears, whereupon his father beat him heavily. As for Ikemefuna, he was at a loss. His own home had gradually become very faint and distant. He still missed his mother and his sister and would be very glad to see them. But somehow he knew he was not going to see them. He remembered once when men had talked in low tones with his father; and it seemed now as if it was happening all over again.

Later, Nwoye went to his mother's hut and told her that Ikemefuna was going home. She immediately dropped her pestle with which she was grinding pepper, folded her arms across her breast and sighed, "Poor child."

The next day, the men returned with a pot of wine. They were all fully dressed as if they were going to a big clan meeting or to pay a visit to a neighboring village. They passed their cloths under the right armpit, and hung their goatskin bags and sheathed machetes over their left shoulders. Okonkwo got ready quickly and the party set out with Ikemefuna carrying the pot of wine. A deathly silence descended on Okonkwo's compound. Even the very little children seemed to know. Throughout that day Nwoye sat in his mother's hut and tears stood in his eyes.

At the beginning of their journey the men of Umuofia talked and 20
laughed about the locusts, about their women, and about some effeminate men who had refused to come with them. But as they drew near to the outskirts of Umuofia silence fell upon them too.

The sun rose slowly to the center of the sky, and the dry, sandy footway began to throw up the heat that lay buried in it. Some birds chirruped

[6]*palm-wine,* wine made with distilled, fermented palm-tree sap.

in the forests around. The men trod dry leaves on the sand. All else was silent. Then from the distance came the faint beating of the *ekwe.*[7] It rose and faded with the wind—a peaceful dance from a distant clan.

"It is an *ozo*[8] dance," the men said among themselves. But no one was sure where it was coming from. Some said Ezimili, others Abame or Aninta. They argued for a short while and fell into silence again, and the elusive dance rose and fell with the wind. Somewhere a man was taking one of the titles of his clan, with music and dancing and a great feast.

The footway had now become a narrow line in the heart of the forest. The short trees and sparse undergrowth which surrounded the men's village began to give way to giant trees and climbers which perhaps had stood from the beginning of things, untouched by the ax and the bush-fire. The sun breaking through their leaves and branches threw a pattern of light and shade on the sandy footway.

Ikemefuna heard a whisper close behind him and turned round sharply. The man who had whispered now called out aloud, urging the others to hurry up.

"We still have a long way to go," he said. Then he and another man went before Ikemefuna and set a faster pace.

Thus the men of Umuofia pursued their way, armed with sheathed machetes, and Ikemefuna, carrying a pot of palm-wine on his head, walked in their midst. Although he had felt uneasy at first, he was not afraid now. Okonkwo walked behind him. He could hardly imagine that Okonkwo was not his real father. He had never been fond of his real father, and at the end of three years he had become very distant indeed. But his mother and his three-year-old sister . . . of course she would not be three now, but six. Would he recognize her now? She must have grown quite big. How his mother would weep for joy, and thank Okonkwo for having looked after him so well and for bringing him back. She would want to hear everything that had happened to him in all these years. Could he remember them all? He would tell her about Nwoye and his mother, and about the locusts. . . . Then quite suddenly a thought came upon him. His mother might be dead. He tried in vain to force the thought out of his mind. Then he tried to settle the matter the way he used to settle such matters when he was a little boy. He still remembered the song:

> Eze elina, elina!
> Sala
> Eze ilikwa ya
> Ikwaba akwa oligholi
> Ebe Danda nechi eze
> Ebe Uzuzu nete egwu
> Sala[9]

He sang it in his mind, and walked to its beat. If the song ended on his right foot, his mother was alive. If it ended on his left, she was dead. No,

---

[7]*ekwe,* a musical instrument; a type of drum made from wood.

[8]*ozo,* the name of one of the titles or rank men in the tribe sought to achieve.

[9]A song Ikemefuna recites to allay his fears; the lyrics tell of a king whose uncontrolled hunger leads to his overthrow and to starvation for his people.

not dead, but ill. It ended on the right. She was alive and well. He sang the song again, and it ended on the left. But the second time did not count. The first voice gets to Chukwu, or God's house. That was a favorite saying of children. Ikemefuna felt like a child once more. It must be the thought of going home to his mother.

One of the men behind him cleared his throat. Ikemefuna looked back, and the man growled at him to go on and not stand looking back. The way he said it sent cold fear down Ikemefuna's back. His hands trembled vaguely on the black pot he carried. Why had Okonkwo withdrawn to the rear? Ikemefuna felt his legs melting under him. And he was afraid to look back.

As the man who had cleared his throat drew up and raised his machete, Okonkwo looked away. He heard the blow. The pot fell and broke in the sand. He heard Ikemefuna cry, "My father, they have killed me!" as he ran towards him. Dazed with fear, Okonkwo drew his machete and cut him down. He was afraid of being thought weak.

As soon as his father walked in, that night, Nwoye knew that 30
Ikemefuna had been killed, and something seemed to give way inside him, like the snapping of a tightened bow. He did not cry. He just hung limp. He had had the same kind of feeling not long ago, during the last harvest season. Every child loved the harvest season. Those who were big enough to carry even a few yams in a tiny basket went with grown-ups to the farm. And if they could not help in digging up the yams, they could gather firewood together for roasting the ones that would be eaten there on the farm. This roasted yam soaked in red palm-oil and eaten in the open farm was sweeter than any meal at home. It was after such a day at the farm during the last harvest that Nwoye had felt for the first time a snapping inside him like the one he now felt. They were returning home with baskets of yams from a distant farm across the stream when they heard the voice of an infant crying in the thick forest. A sudden hush had fallen on the women, who had been talking, and they had quickened their steps. Nwoye had heard that twins were put in earthenware pots and thrown away in the forest, but he had never yet come across them.[10] A vague chill had descended on him and his head had seemed to swell, like a solitary walker at night who passes an evil spirit on the way. Then something had given way inside him. It descended on him again, this feeling, when his father walked in, that night after killing Ikemefuna.

Analyzing the Text

1. How does hearing Ikemefuna call him "father" precipitate Okonkwo's participation in the murder, something he has been explicitly warned against by the elders of the tribe? How at this moment is his "tragic flaw" triggered?
2. How does Nwoye react when he learns of his step-brother's death and of his father's participation in it?

[10]For the Igbo, the birth of twins was perceived as splitting one soul between two bodies, and was considered to be an evil omen.

Understanding Achebe's Techniques

1. How might the vulture story, in which unexpected gifts from the gods must be paid for, explain why the elders require the sacrifice of the young boy, Ikemefuna, after the unexpected bounty of locusts?
2. How does Achebe accentuate the pathos of the murder by allowing the reader to enter Ikemefuna's thoughts just before it occurs?

Arguing for an Interpretation

1. In what way do Okonkwo's actions transform him into a tragic figure and irrevocably change how others see him?
2. Okonkwo's aspirations for his son, Nwoye, are reflected in the stories that he tells him (which differ from the stories women tell their children). Do you get the impression that this emphasis on masculinity is Okonkwo's obsession rather than a value in Igbo society? Why or why not?

EDGAR ALLAN POE

Edgar Allan Poe (1809–1849) was born in Boston, Massachusetts. He was orphaned before he was three, and taken into the home of John Allan, a wealthy Richmond, Virginia merchant. Allan later disowned Poe when he chose a literary rather than a commercial career. Poe served 2 years in the Army and in 1830 received an appointment to West Point, from which he was dismissed within a year for a "gross neglect of duty." He served as the editor for a series of magazines, including the Southern Literary Messenger, Burton's Gentleman's Magazine, Graham's Magazine, *and later the* Broadway Journal. *In 1835, Poe married his cousin, Virginia Clemm, whose fragile health was a source of concern. They moved to Philadelphia, and Poe began to be recognized for his stories, literary essays, and poems (such as "The Raven," which appeared in 1845). Virginia died of tuberculosis in 1847 and was memorialized in Poe's poem "Annabel Lee." His last years were not happy ones and he died under mysterious circumstances at 40 in Baltimore, Maryland. Poe's influence on literature has been extraordinary. He incorporated symbolism and technical devices such as assonance, rhythm, and rhyme in poetry. He invented the modern detective story in tales such as "Murders in the Rue Morgue" and "The Purloined Letter," and created many psychological short stories such as "The Tell-Tale Heart," "The Black Cat," and "The Cask of Amontillado," which communicate a sense of guilt and terror. In "The Masque of the Red Death" (1842), Poe blends a folktale with reminiscences of the devasting plagues that swept Europe in the Middle Ages, and recent memories of a cholera outbreak in Baltimore, to create this somber and elegant tale.*

The Masque of the Red Death

The "Red Death" had long devastated the country. No pestilence had ever been so fatal, or so hideous. Blood was its Avatar[1] and its seal—the redness and the horror of blood. There were sharp pains, and sudden dizziness, and then profuse bleeding at the pores, with dissolution. The scarlet stains upon the body and especially upon the face of the victim, were the pest ban which shut him out from the aid and from the sympathy of his fellow-men. And the whole seizure, progress, and termination of the disease, were the incidents of half an hour.

But the Prince Prospero[2] was happy and dauntless and sagacious. When his dominions were half depopulated, he summoned to his presence a thousand hale and light-hearted friends from among the knights and dames of his court, and with these retired to the deep seclusion of one of his castellated abbeys. This was an extensive and magnificent structure, the creation of the prince's own eccentric yet august taste. A strong and lofty wall girdled it in. This wall had gates of iron. The courtiers, having entered, brought furnaces and massy hammers and welded the bolts. They resolved to leave means neither of ingress nor egress to the sudden impulses of despair or of frenzy from within. The abbey was amply provisioned. With such precautions the courtiers might bid defiance to contagion. The external world could take care of itself. In the meantime it was folly to grieve, or to think. The prince had provided all the appliances of pleasure. There were buffoons, there were improvisatori, there were ballet-dancers, there were musicians, there was Beauty, there was wine. All these and security were within. Without was the "Red Death."

It was toward the close of the fifth or sixth month of his seclusion, and while the pestilence raged most furiously abroad, that the Prince Prospero entertained his thousand friends at a masked ball of the most unusual magnificence.

It was a voluptuous scene, that masquerade. But first let me tell of the rooms in which it was held. There were seven—an imperial suite. In many palaces, however, such suites form a long and straight vista, while the folding doors slide back nearly to the walls on either hand, so that the view of the whole extent is scarcely impeded. Here the case was very different; as might have been expected from the duke's love of the *bizarre.* The apartments were so irregularly disposed that the vision embraced but little more than one at a time. There was a sharp turn at every twenty or thirty yards, and at each turn a novel effect. To the right and left, in the middle of each wall, a tall and narrow Gothic window looked out upon a closed corridor which pursued the windings of the suite. These windows were of stained glass whose color varied in accordance with the prevailing hue of the decorations of the chamber into which it opened. That at the eastern extremity was hung, for example, in blue—and vividly blue were its windows. The second chamber was purple in its ornaments and tapestries, and here the panes were purple. The third was green throughout, and so were the case-

---

[1]*Avatar:* an embodiment or concrete manifestation.

[2]*Prospero:* Refers to the principal character in Shakespeare's *The Tempest;* someone who is fortunate.

ments. The fourth was furnished and lighted with orange—the fifth with white—the sixth with violet. The seventh apartment was closely shrouded in black velvet tapestries that hung all over the ceiling and down the walls, falling in heavy folds upon a carpet of the same material and hue. But in this chamber only, the color of the windows failed to correspond with the decorations. The panes here were scarlet—a deep blood color. Now in no one of the seven apartments was there any lamp or candelabrum, amid the profusion of golden ornaments that lay scattered to and fro or depended from the roof. There was no light of any kind emanating from lamp or candle within the suite of chambers. But in the corridors that followed the suite, there stood, opposite to each window, a heavy tripod, bearing a brazier of fire, that projected its rays through the tinted glass and so glaringly illumined the room. And thus were produced a multitude of gaudy and fantastic appearances. But in the western or black chamber the effect of the firelight that streamed upon the dark hangings through the blood-tinted panes was ghastly in the extreme, and produced so wild a look upon the countenances of those who entered, that there were few of the company bold enough to set foot within its precincts at all.

It was in this apartment, also, that there stood against the western 5
wall, a gigantic clock of ebony. Its pendulum swung to and fro with a dull, heavy, monotonous clang; and when the minute-hand made the circuit of the face, and the hour was to be stricken, there came from the brazen lungs of the clock a sound which was clear and loud and deep and exceedingly musical, but of so peculiar a note and emphasis that, at each lapse of an hour, the musicians of the orchestra were constrained to pause, momentarily, in their performance, to hearken to the sound; and thus the waltzers perforce ceased their evolutions; and there was a brief disconcert of the whole gay company; and, while the chimes of the clock yet rang, it was observed that the giddiest grew pale, and the more aged and sedate passed their hands over their brows as if in confused revery or meditation. But when the echoes had fully ceased, a light laughter at once pervaded the assembly; the musicians looked at each other and smiled as if at their own nervousness and folly, and made whispering vows, each to the other, that the next chiming of the clock should produce in them no similar emotion; and then, after the lapse of sixty minutes (which embrace three thousand and six hundred seconds of the Time that flies), there came yet another chiming of the clock, and then were the same disconcert and tremulousness and meditation as before.

But, in spite of all these things, it was a gay and magnificent revel. The tastes of the duke were peculiar. He had a fine eye for colors and effects. He disregarded the *decora*[3] of mere fashion. His plans were bold and fiery, and his conceptions glowed with barbaric lustre. There are some who would have thought him mad. His followers felt that he was not. It was necessary to hear and see and touch him to be *sure* that he was not.

He had directed, in great part, the movable embellishments of the seven chambers, upon occasion of this great fête,[4] and it was his own guiding taste which had given character to the masqueraders. Be sure they were grotesque. There were much glare and glitter and piquancy and

---

[3]*decora:* current styles of adornment.
[4]*fête:* festive celebration.

phantasm—much of what has been since seen in "Hernani."[5] There were arabesque figures with unsuited limbs and appointments. There were delirious fancies such as the madman fashions. There were much of the beautiful, much of the wanton, much of the *bizarre,* something of the terrible, and not a little of that which might have excited disgust. To and fro in the seven chambers there stalked, in fact, a multitude of dreams. And these—the dreams—writhed in and about, taking hue from the rooms, and causing the wild music of the orchestra to seem as the echo of their steps. And, anon, there strikes the ebony clock which stands in the hall of the velvet. And then, for a moment, all is still, and all is silent save the voice of the clock. The dreams are stiff-frozen as they stand. But the echoes of the chime die away—they have endured but an instant—and a light, half-subdued laughter floats after them as they depart. And now again the music swells, and the dreams live, and writhe to and fro more merrily than ever, taking hue from the many-tinted windows through which stream the rays from the tripods. But to the chamber which lies most westwardly of the seven there are now none of the maskers who venture; for the night is waning away; and there flows a ruddier light through the blood-colored panes; and the blackness of the sable drapery appalls; and to him whose foot falls upon the sable carpet, there comes from the near clock of ebony a muffled peal more solemnly emphatic than any which reaches *their* ears who indulge in the more remote gaieties of the other apartments.

But these other apartments were densely crowded, and in them beat feverishly the heart of life. And the revel went whirlingly on, until at length there commenced the sounding of midnight upon the clock. And then the music ceased, as I have told; and the evolutions of the waltzers were quieted; and there was an uneasy cessation of all things as before. But now there were twelve strokes to be sounded by the bell of the clock; and thus it happened, perhaps that more of thought crept, with more of time, into the meditations of the thoughtful among those who revelled. And thus, too, it happened, perhaps that before the last echoes of the last chime had utterly sunk into silence, there were many individuals in the crowd who had found leisure to become aware of the presence of a masked figure, which had arrested the attention of no single individual before. And the rumor of this new presence having spread itself whisperingly around, there arose at length from the whole company a buzz, or murmur, expressive of disapprobation and surprise—then, finally, of terror, of horror, and of disgust.

In an assembly of phantasms such as I have painted, it may well be supposed that no ordinary appearance could have excited such sensation. In truth the masquerade license of the night was nearly unlimited; but the figure in question had out-Heroded Herod,[6] and gone beyond the bounds of even the prince's indefinite decorum. There are chords in the hearts of the most reckless which cannot be touched without emotion. Even with the utterly lost, to whom life and death are equally jests, there are matters of which no jest can be made. The whole company, indeed, seemed now deeply to feel that in the costume and bearing of the stranger neither wit nor propriety existed. The figure was tall and gaunt, and shrouded from head to foot in the habiliments of the grave. The mask which concealed

[5]*Hernani:* a tragedy (1830) by Victor Hugo (1802–1885), with spectacular scenes and costumes.

[6]*Herod:* quoted from Shakespeare's *Hamlet,* Act 3, scene 2, line 11; refers to unnecessary theatrics.

the visage was made so nearly to resemble the countenance of a stiffened corpse that the closest scrutiny must have had difficulty in detecting the cheat. And yet all this might have been endured, if not approved, by the mad revellers around. But the mummer had gone so far as to assume the type of the Red Death. His vesture was dabbled in *blood*—and his broad brow, with all the features of the face, was besprinkled with the scarlet horror.

When the eyes of Prince Prospero fell upon this spectral image 10
(which, with a slow and solemn movement, as if more fully to sustain its rôle, stalked to and fro among the waltzers) he was seen to be convulsed, in the first moment with a strong shudder either of terror or distaste; but, in the next, his brow reddened with rage.

"Who dares"—he demanded hoarsely of the courtiers who stood near him—"who dares insult us with this blasphemous mockery? Seize him and unmask him—that we may know whom we have to hang, at sunrise, from the battlements!"

It was in the eastern or blue chamber in which stood the Prince Prospero as he uttered these words. They rang throughout the seven rooms loudly and clearly, for the prince was a bold and robust man, and the music had become hushed at the waving of his hand.

It was in the blue room where stood the prince, with a group of pale courtiers by his side. At first, as he spoke, there was a slight rushing movement of this group in the direction of the intruder, who, at the moment was also near at hand, and now, with deliberate and stately step, made closer approach to the speaker. But from a certain nameless awe with which the mad assumptions of the mummer had inspired the whole party, there were found none who put forth hand to seize him; so that, unimpeded, he passed within a yard of the prince's person; and, while the vast assembly, as if with one impulse, shrank from the centres of the rooms to the walls, he made his way uninterruptedly, but with the same solemn and measured step which had distinguished him from the first, through the blue chamber to the purple—through the purple to the green—through the green to the orange—through this again to the white—and even thence to the violet, ere a decided movement had been made to arrest him. It was then, however, that the Prince Prospero, maddening with rage and the shame of his own momentary cowardice, rushed hurriedly through the six chambers, while none followed him on account of a deadly terror that had seized upon all. He bore aloft a drawn dagger, and had approached, in rapid impetuosity, to within three or four feet of the retreating figure, when the latter, having attained the extremity of the velvet apartment, turned suddenly and confronted his pursuer. There was a sharp cry—and the dagger dropped gleaming upon the sable carpet, upon which, instantly afterward, fell prostrate in death the Prince Prospero. Then, summoning the wild courage of despair, a throng of the revellers at once threw themselves into the black apartment, and, seizing the mummer, whose tall figure stood erect and motionless within the shadow of the ebony clock, gasped in unutterable horror at finding the grave cerements and corpse-like mask, which they handled with so violent a rudeness, untenanted by any tangible form.

And now was acknowledged the presence of the Red Death. He had come like a thief in the night,[7] And one by one dropped the revellers in

---

[7] ***Thief in the night:*** In 2 Peter 3:10: "But the day of the Lord will come as a thief in the night." Refers to an apocalypse or judgment.

the blood-bedewed halls of their revel, and died each in the despairing posture of his fall. And the life of the ebony clock went out with that of the last of the gay. And the flames of the tripods expired. And Darkness and Decay and the Red Death held illimitable dominion over all.

Analyzing the Text

1. What crisis confronts the country in which the story is set, and what does Prince Prospero's reaction to this crisis and to the "masked" figure tell us about him?
2. What role does the huge ebony clock play, and how does this object and its sound foreshadow the outcome of the story?

Understanding Poe's Techniques

1. How does the imagery used to characterize the last room reflect the nature of the epidemic (modelled on the "black death" or bubonic plague of the Middle Ages) from which the revelers have tried to escape?
2. How does Poe use a progression of colors as well as details of lighting and numerical symbolism to create the distinctive atmosphere of the story?

Arguing for an Interpretation

1. What elements in the story suggest that Poe is depicting either a mad genius or a heroic personality, or are they one and the same?
2. Compare the reactions of world governments to SARS (Severe Acute Repiratory Syndrome) with those of Prospero.

William Faulkner

William Faulkner (1897–1962) was born near Oxford, Mississippi, where Faulkner spent most of his life. During World War I he enlisted in the Royal Canadian Air Force. He intermittently lived in New Orleans and in Hollywood, where he met Sherwood Anderson, who encouraged him to write fiction. His first novel, Soldier's Pay, *was published in 1926. It was not until he wrote* Sartoris *(1929) that Faulkner discovered what was to become his characteristic style and setting. He transformed his hometown in rural Mississippi into the mythic Yoknapatawpha County and populated it with memorable characters of the old and new South. His novels include* The Sound and the Fury *(1929),* As I Lay Dying *(1930),* Light in August *(1932), and* Absalom, Absalom! *(1936). Faulkner's innovations with form and the stream-of-consciousness technique that scrambles chronology, but gives great insight into his characters' motivation, led to popular and critical acclaim. In 1950, he was awarded the Nobel Prize for Literature. His collection of short stories also won the National Book Award in the same year. In "A Rose for Emily" (1931), Faulkner creates an eerie and evocative*

tale—part gothic mystery and part romance—that draws us, along with the townspeople, into speculating about the life of the protagonist.

A Rose for Emily

1

When Miss Emily Grierson died, our whole town went to her funeral: the men through a sort of respectful affection for a fallen monument, the women mostly out of curiosity to see the inside of her house, which no one save an old manservant—a combined gardener and cook—had seen in at least ten years.

It was a big, squarish frame house that had once been white, decorated with cupolas and spires and scrolled balconies in the heavily lightsome style of the seventies, set on what had once been our most select street. But garages and cotton gins had encroached and obliterated even the august names of that neighborhood; only Miss Emily's house was left, lifting its stubborn and coquettish decay above the cotton wagons and the gasoline pumps—an eyesore among eyesores. And now Miss Emily had gone to join the representatives of those august names where they lay in the cedar-bemused cemetery among the ranked and anonymous graves of Union and Confederate soldiers who fell at the battle of Jefferson.

Alive, Miss Emily had been a tradition, a duty, and a care; a sort of hereditary obligation upon the town, dating from that day in 1894 when Colonel Sartoris, the mayor—he who fathered the edict that no Negro woman should appear on the streets without an apron—remitted her taxes, the dispensation dating from the death of her father on into perpetuity. Not that Miss Emily would have accepted charity. Colonel Sartoris invented an involved tale to the effect that Miss Emily's father had loaned money to the town, which the town, as a matter of business, preferred this way of repaying. Only a man of Colonel Sartoris' generation and thought could have invented it, and only a woman could have believed it.

When the next generation, with its more modern ideas, became mayors and aldermen, this arrangement created some little dissatisfaction. On the first of the year they mailed her a tax notice. February came, and there was no reply. They wrote her a formal letter, asking her to call at the sheriff's office at her convenience. A week later the mayor wrote her himself, offering to call or to send his car for her, and received in reply a note on paper of an archaic shape, in a thin, flowing calligraphy in faded ink, to the effect that she no longer went out at all. The tax notice was also enclosed, without comment.

They called a special meeting of the Board of Aldermen. A deputation 5
waited upon her, knocked at the door through which no visitor had passed since she ceased giving china-painting lessons eight or ten years earlier. They were admitted by the old Negro into a dim hall from which a stairway mounted into still more shadow. It smelled of dust and disuse—a close, dank smell. The Negro led them into the parlor. It was furnished in heavy, leather-covered furniture. When the Negro opened the blinds of one window, they could see that the leather was cracked; and when they sat

down, a faint dust rose sluggishly about their thighs, spinning with slow motions in the single sun-ray. On a tarnished gilt easel before the fireplace stood a crayon portrait of Miss Emily's father.

They rose when she entered—a small, fat woman in black, with a thin gold chain descending to her waist and vanishing into her belt, leaning on an ebony cane with a tarnished gold head. Her skeleton was small and spare; perhaps that was why what would have been merely plumpness in another was obesity in her. She looked bloated, like a body long submerged in motionless water, and of that pallid hue. Her eyes, lost in the fatty ridges of her face, looked like two small pieces of coal pressed into a lump of dough as they moved from one face to another while the visitors stated their errand.

She did not ask them to sit. She just stood in the door and listened quietly until the spokesman came to a stumbling halt. Then they could hear the invisible watch ticking at the end of the gold chain.

Her voice was dry and cold. "I have no taxes in Jefferson. Colonel Sartoris explained it to me. Perhaps one of you can gain access to the city records and satisfy yourselves."

"But we have. We are the city authorities, Miss Emily. Didn't you get a notice from the sheriff, signed by him?"

"I received a paper, yes," Miss Emily said. "Perhaps he considers himself 10
the sheriff . . . I have no taxes in Jefferson."

"But there is nothing on the books to show that, you see. We must go by the—"

"See Colonel Sartoris." (Colonel Sartoris had been dead almost ten years.) "I have no taxes in Jefferson. Tobe!" The Negro appeared. "Show these gentlemen out."

2

So she vanquished them, horse and foot, just as she had vanquished their fathers thirty years before about the smell. That was two years after her father's death and a short time after her sweetheart—the one we believed would marry her—had deserted her. After her father's death she went out very little; after her sweetheart went away, people hardly saw her at all. A few of the ladies had the temerity to call, but were not received, and the only sign of life about the place was the Negro man—a young man then—going in and out with a market basket.

"Just as if a man—any man—could keep a kitchen properly," the ladies said; so they were not surprised when the smell developed. It was another link between the gross, teeming world and the high and mighty Griersons.

A neighbor, a woman, complained to the mayor, Judge Stevens, eighty 15
years old.

"But what will you have me do about it, madam?" he said.

"Why, send her word to stop it," the woman said. "Isn't there a law?"

"I'm sure that won't be necessary," Judge Stevens said. "It's probably just a snake or a rat that nigger of hers killed in the yard. I'll speak to him about it."

The next day he received two more complaints, one from a man who came in diffident deprecation. "We really must do something about it, Judge. I'd be the last one in the world to bother Miss Emily, but we've got to do something." That night the Board of Aldermen met—three graybeards and one younger man, a member of the rising generation.

“It’s simple enough,” he said. “Send her word to have her place cleaned up. Give her a certain time to do it in, and if she don’t . . .” 20

“Dammit, sir,” Judge Stevens said, “will you accuse a lady to her face of smelling bad?”

So the next night, after midnight, four men crossed Miss Emily’s lawn and slunk about the house like burglars, sniffing along the base of the brickwork and at the cellar openings while one of them performed a regular sowing motion with his hand out of a sack slung from his shoulder. They broke open the cellar door and sprinkled lime there, and in all the outbuildings. As they recrossed the lawn, a window that had been dark was lighted and Miss Emily sat in it, the light behind her, and her upright torso motionless as that of an idol. They crept quietly across the lawn and into the shadow of the locusts that lined the street. After a week or two the smell went away.

That was when people had begun to feel sorry for her. People in our town, remembering how old lady Wyatt, her great-aunt, had gone completely crazy at last, believed that the Griersons held themselves a little too high for what they really were. None of the young men were quite good enough for Miss Emily and such. We had long thought of them as a tableau, Miss Emily a slender figure in white in the background, her father a spraddled silhouette in the foreground, his back to her and clutching a horsewhip, the two of them framed by the back-flung front door. So when she got to be thirty and was still single, we were not pleased exactly, but vindicated; even with insanity in the family she wouldn’t have turned down all of her chances if they had really materialized.

When her father died, it got about that the house was all that was left to her; and in a way, people were glad. At last they could pity Miss Emily. Being left alone, and a pauper, she had become humanized. Now she too would know the old thrill and the old despair of a penny more or less.

The day after his death all the ladies prepared to call at the house and offer condolence and aid, as is our custom. Miss Emily met them at the door, dressed as usual and with no trace of grief on her face. She told them that her father was not dead. She did that for three days, with the ministers calling on her, and the doctors, trying to persuade her to let them dispose of the body. Just as they were about to resort to law and force, she broke down, and they buried her father quickly. 25

We did not say she was crazy then. We believed she had to do that. We remembered all the young men her father had driven away, and we knew that with nothing left, she would have to cling to that which had robbed her, as people will.

3

She was sick for a long time. When we saw her again, her hair was cut short, making her look like a girl, with a vague resemblance to those angels in colored church windows—sort of tragic and serene.

The town had just let the contracts for paving the sidewalks, and in the summer after her father’s death they began the work. The construction company came with niggers and mules and machinery, and a foreman named Homer Barron, a Yankee—a big, dark, ready man, with a big voice and eyes lighter than his face. The little boys would follow in groups to hear him cuss the niggers, and the niggers singing in time to the rise and fall of picks. Pretty soon he knew everybody in town. Whenever you heard a lot of laughing anywhere about the square, Homer Barron would be in the center of the group. Presently we began to see him and Miss Emily on Sunday afternoons driving in the yellow-wheeled buggy and the matched team of bays from the livery stable.

At first we were glad that Miss Emily would have an interest, because the ladies all said, "Of course a Grierson would not think seriously of a Northerner, a day laborer." But there were still others, older people, who said that even grief could not cause a real lady to forget *noblesse oblige*—without calling it *noblesse oblige*. They just said, "Poor Emily. Her kinsfolk should come to her." She had some kin in Alabama; but years ago her father had fallen out with them over the estate of old lady Wyatt, the crazy woman, and there was no communication between the two families. They had not even been represented at the funeral.

And as soon as the old people said, "Poor Emily," the whispering began. "Do you suppose it's really so?" they said to one another. "Of course it is. What else could . . ." This behind their hands; rustling of craned silk and satin behind jalousies closed upon the sun of Sunday afternoon as the thin, swift clop-clop-clop of the matched team passed: "Poor Emily."

She carried her head high enough—even when we believed that she was fallen. It was as if she demanded more than ever the recognition of her dignity as the last Grierson; as if it had wanted that touch of earthiness to reaffirm her imperviousness. Like when she bought the rat poison, the arsenic. That was over a year after they had begun to say "Poor Emily," and while the two female cousins were visiting her.

"I want some poison," she said to the druggist. She was over thirty then, still a slight woman, though thinner than usual, with cold, haughty black eyes in a face the flesh of which was stained across the temples and about the eye-sockets as you imagine a lighthouse-keeper's face ought to look. "I want some poison," she said.

"Yes, Miss Emily. What kind? For rats and such? I'd recom—"

"I want the best you have. I don't care what kind."

The druggist named several. "They'll kill anything up to an elephant. But what you want is—"

"Arsenic," Miss Emily said. "Is that a good one?"

"Is . . . arsenic? Yes, ma'am. But what you want—"

"I want arsenic."

The druggist looked down at her. She looked back at him, erect, her face like a strained flag. "Why, of course," the druggist said. "If that's what you want. But the law requires you to tell what you are going to use it for."

Miss Emily just stared at him, her head tilted back in order to look him eye for eye, until he looked away and went and got the arsenic and wrapped it up. The Negro delivery boy brought her the package; the druggist didn't come back. When she opened the package at home there was written on the box, under the skull and bones: "For rats."

4

So the next day we all said, "She will kill herself"; and we said it would be the best thing. When she had first begun to be seen with Homer Barron, we had said, "She will marry him." Then we said, "She will persuade him yet," because Homer himself had remarked—he liked men, and it was known that he drank with the younger men in the Elks' Club—that he was not a marrying man. Later we said, "Poor Emily" behind the jalousies as they passed on Sunday afternoon in the glittering buggy, Miss Emily with her head high and Homer Barron with his hat cocked and a cigar in his teeth, reins and whip in a yellow glove.

Then some of the ladies began to say that it was a disgrace to the town and a bad example to the young people. The men did not want to interfere, but at last the ladies forced the Baptist minister—Miss Emily's people were Episcopal—to call upon her. He would never divulge what happened during that interview, but he refused to go back again. The next Sunday they again drove about the streets, and the following day the minister's wife wrote to Miss Emily's relations in Alabama.

So she had blood-kin under her roof again and we sat back to watch developments. At first nothing happened. Then we were sure that they were to be married. We learned that Miss Emily had been to the jeweler's and ordered a man's toilet set in silver, with the letters H.B. on each piece. Two days later we learned that she had bought a complete outfit of men's clothing, including a nightshirt, and we said, "They are married." We were really glad. We were glad because the two female cousins were even more Grierson than Miss Emily had ever been.

So we were not surprised when Homer Barron—the streets had been finished some time since—was gone. We were a little disappointed that there was not a public blowing-off, but we believed that he had gone on to prepare for Miss Emily's coming, or to give her a chance to get rid of the cousins. (By that time it was a cabal, and we were all Miss Emily's allies to help circumvent the cousins.) Sure enough, after another week they departed. And, as we had expected all along, within three days Homer Barron was back in town. A neighbor saw the Negro man admit him at the kitchen door at dusk one evening.

And that was the last we saw of Homer Barron. And of Miss Emily for 45
some time. The Negro man went in and out with the market basket, but the front door remained closed. Now and then we would see her at a window for a moment, as the men did that night when they sprinkled the lime, but for almost six months she did not appear on the streets. Then we knew that this was to be expected too; as if that quality of her father which had thwarted her woman's life so many times had been too virulent and too furious to die.

When we next saw Miss Emily, she had grown fat and her hair was turning gray. During the next few years it grew grayer and grayer until it attained an even pepper-and-salt iron-gray, when it ceased turning. Up to the day of her death at seventy-four it was still that vigorous iron-gray, like the hair of an active man.

From that time on her front door remained closed, save for a period of six or seven years, when she was about forty, during which she gave lessons in china-painting. She fitted up a studio in one of the downstairs rooms, where the daughters and granddaughters of Colonel Sartoris' contemporaries were sent to her with the same regularity and in the same spirit that they were sent to church on Sundays with a twenty-five-cent piece for the collection plate. Meanwhile her taxes had been remitted.

Then the newer generation became the backbone and the spirit of the town, and the painting pupils grew up and fell away and did not send their children to her with boxes of color and tedious brushes and pictures cut from the ladies' magazines. The front door closed upon the last one and remained closed for good. When the town got free postal delivery, Miss Emily alone refused to let them fasten the metal numbers above her door and attach a mailbox to it. She would not listen to them.

Daily, monthly, yearly we watched the Negro grow grayer and more stooped, going in and out with the market basket. Each December, we sent her a tax notice, which would be returned by the post office a week later, unclaimed. Now and then we would see her in one of the downstairs windows—she had evidently shut up the top floor of the house—like the carven torso of an idol in a niche, looking or not looking at us, we could never tell which. Thus she passed from generation to generation—dear, inescapable, impervious, tranquil, and perverse.

And so she died. Fell ill in the house filled with dust and shadows, with only a doddering Negro man to wait on her. We did not even know she was sick; we had long since given up trying to get any information from the Negro. He talked to no one, probably not even to her, for his voice had grown harsh and rusty, as if from disuse.

She died in one of the downstairs rooms, in a heavy walnut bed with a curtain, her gray head propped on a pillow yellow and moldy with age and lack of sunlight.

5

The Negro met the first of the ladies at the front door and let them in, with their husbands, sibilant voices and their quick, curious glances, and then he disappeared. He walked right through the house and out the back and was not seen again.

The two female cousins came at once. They held the funeral on the second day, with the town coming to look at Miss Emily beneath a mass of bought flowers, with the crayon face of her father musing profoundly above the bier and the ladies sibilant and macabre; and the very old men—some in their brushed Confederate uniforms—on the porch and the lawn, talking of Miss Emily as if she had been a contemporary of theirs, believing that they had danced with her and courted her perhaps, confusing time with its mathematical progression, as the old do, to whom all the past is not a diminishing road but, instead, a huge meadow which no winter ever quite touches, divided from them now by the narrow bottle-neck of the most recent decade of years.

Already we knew that there was one room in that region above stairs which no one had seen in forty years, and which would have to be forced. They waited until Miss Emily was decently in the ground before they opened it.

The violence of breaking down the door seemed to fill this room with pervading dust. A thin, acrid pall as of the tomb seemed to lie everywhere upon this room decked and furnished as for a bridal: upon the valance curtains of faded rose color, upon the rose-shaded lights, upon the dressing table, upon the delicate array of crystal and the man's toilet things backed with tarnished silver, silver so tarnished that the monogram was obscured. Among them lay a collar and tie, as if they had just been removed, which, lifted, left upon the surface a pale crescent in the dust. Upon a chair hung the suit, carefully folded; beneath it the two mute shoes and the discarded socks.

The man himself lay in the bed.

For a long while we just stood there, looking down at the profound and fleshless grin. The body had apparently once lain in the attitude of an embrace, but now the long sleep that outlasts love, that conquers even the grimace of love, had cuckolded him. What was left of him, rotted beneath what was left of the nightshirt, had become inextricable from the bed in which he lay; and upon him and upon the pillow beside him lay that even coating of the patient and biding dust.

Then we noticed that in the second pillow was the indentation of a head. One of us lifted something from it, and leaning forward, that faint and invisible dust dry and acrid in the nostrils, we saw a long strand of iron-gray hair.

Analyzing the Text

1. How does the characterization of Miss Emily's father help explain why she might have taken up with someone who was a Northerner and of a lower social class? How does the attitude of the townspeople toward Miss Emily change over the course of the narrative?
2. How does the final image ("a long strand of iron-gray hair" lying on the pillow) serve as the ultimate key that allows the reader to pull the story together?

Understanding Faulkner's Techniques

1. What elements in the story foreshadow its conclusion? What effects does Faulkner gain by rearranging the order in which events are told when compared with the order in which they happened?
2. What images or details in the story seem to suggest symbolic overtones, and how do they function?

Arguing for an Interpretation

1. Faulkner once referred to this as a ghost story and said that he saw it more as a young girl's repressed desire for a normal life taking a tragic turn rather than as a representation of the struggle between North and South. How do you interpret this story?
2. In your opinion, was Miss Emily expiating her crime by subjecting herself to the nightly vigil? Why or why not? Can you explain her behavior in another way?
3. What if the body of Homer had been discovered while Miss Emily was alive, and she had been tried for murder in that community? Would she have been acquitted or not? Explain your answer.

JOAQUIM MARÍA MACHADO DE ASSIS

Joaquim María Machado de Assis (1839–1908) was born in Rio de Janiero where he lived most of his life. His father, a house painter, was a mulatto Brazilian, the son of former slaves; his mother was a white Portuguese immigrant from the Azores. Machado attended only five years of elementary school. Beyond that, he educated himself and became fluent in several languages, including French, Spanish, and English. He began supporting himself at age fifteen, working at a variety of jobs, including typesetting, proofreading, and editing. In 1874 he entered the civil service in the Ministry of Agriculture and for the last 34 years of his life led the quiet, unturbulent life of a happily married, but childless, government bureaucrat. He used the financial security of his civil service position to carry on an astonishingly prolific career as a writer. Machado's early love was the theater, and by the time he was 30 he had written 19 plays and opera librettos, most of them produced by theater companies in the city. He was also a skilled poet and regular newspaper columnist. After 1870, he turned his attention primarily to short stories and novels. His first great success was Epitaph of a Small Winner *(1881), written from a startlingly original point of view, namely the posthumous memoirs of the narrator, Braz Cubas—a tongue-in-cheek account of his life.*

Machado's second novel, Philosopher or Dog? *(1891), and his acknowledged masterpiece,* Dom Casmurro *(1900), both feature protagonists who are reflective skeptics tinged with madness. These unreliable narrators are a feature of his work. His close attention to the protagonist's stream of consciousness, his cool irony, unexpected juxtaposition of times, characters, and value systems conveyed in a forceful, unique style anticipate many features of the 20th-century novel. He is now acknowledged by critics to be a master of the early modern novel, equal to Gustave Flaubert and Henry James. His complete works fill 31 volumes, and he is the author of over 100 short stories, of which "A Canary's Ideas," translated by Jack Schmitt and Lorie Ishimatsu (1976), is typical. In this story, an egocentric, reasoning canary forms his impression of the universe by what surrounds him at the moment.*

A Canary's Ideas

A man by the name of Macedo, who had a fancy for ornithology, related to some friends an incident so extraordinary that no one took him seriously. Some came to believe he had lost his mind. Here is a summary of his narration.

At the beginning of last month, as I was walking down the street, a carriage darted past me and nearly knocked me to the ground. I escaped by quickly side-stepping into a secondhand shop. Neither the racket of the horse and carriage nor my entrance stirred the proprietor, dozing in a folding chair at the back of the shop. He was a man of shabby appearance: his beard was the color of dirty straw, and his head was covered by a tattered cap which probably had not found a buyer. One could not guess that there was any story behind him, as there could have been behind some of the objects he sold, nor could one sense in him that austere, disillusioned sadness inherent in the objects which were remnants of past lives.

The shop was dark and crowded with the sort of old, bent, broken, tarnished, rusted articles ordinarily found in secondhand shops, and everything was in that state of semidisorder befitting such an establishment. This assortment of articles, though banal, was interesting. Pots without lids, lids without pots, buttons, shoes, locks, a black shirt, straw hats, fur hats, picture frames, binoculars, dress coats, a fencing foil, a stuffed dog, a pair of slippers, gloves, nondescript vases, epaulets, a velvet satchel, two hatracks, a slingshot, a thermometer, chairs, a lithographed portrait by the late Sisson, a backgammon board, two wire masks for some future Carnival—all this and more, which I either did not see or do not remember, filled the shop in the area around the door, propped up, hung, or displayed in glass cases as old as the objects inside them. Further inside the shop were many objects of similar appearance. Predominant were the large objects—chests of drawers, chairs, and beds—some of which were stacked on top of others which were lost in the darkness.

I was about to leave, when I saw a cage hanging in the doorway. It was as old as everything else in the shop, and I expected it to be empty so it would fit in with the general appearance of desolation. However, it wasn't empty. Inside, a canary was hopping about. The bird's color, liveliness, and charm added a note of life and youth to that heap of wreckage. It was the last passenger of some wrecked ship, who had arrived in the shop as complete and happy as it had originally been. As soon as I looked at the bird, it began to hop up and down, from perch to perch, as if it meant to tell me that a ray of sunshine was frolicking in the midst of that cemetery. I'm using this image to describe the canary only because I'm speaking to rhetorical people, but the truth is that the canary thought about neither cemetery nor sun, according to what it told me later. Along with the pleasure the sight of the bird brought me I felt indignation regarding its destiny and softly murmured these bitter words.

"What detestable owner had the nerve to rid himself of this bird for a 5
few cents? Or what indifferent soul, not wishing to keep his late master's pet, gave it away to some child, who sold it so he could make a bet on a soccer game?"

The canary, sitting on top of its perch, trilled this reply.

"Whoever you may be, you're certainly not in your right mind. I had no detestable owner, nor was I given to any child to sell. Those are the delusions of a sick person. Go and get yourself cured, my friend . . ."

"What?" I interrupted, not having had time to become astonished. "So your master didn't sell you to this shop? It wasn't misery or laziness that brought you, like a ray of sunshine, to this cemetery?"

"I don't know what you mean by 'sunshine' or 'cemetery.' If the canaries you've seen use the first of those names, so much the better, because it sounds pretty, but really, I'm sure you're confused."

"Excuse me, but you couldn't have come here by chance, all alone. Has 10
your master always been that man sitting over there?"

"What master? That man over there is my servant. He gives me food and water every day, so regularly that if I were to pay him for his services, it would be no small sum, but canaries don't pay their servants. In fact, since the world belongs to canaries, it would be extravagant for them to pay for what is already in the world."

Astonished by these answers, I didn't know what to marvel at more—the language or the ideas. The language, even though it entered my ears as human speech, was uttered by the bird in the form of charming trills. I looked all around me so I could determine if I were awake and saw that the street was the same, and the shop was the same dark, sad, musty place. The canary, moving from side, was waiting for me to speak. I then asked if it were lonely for the infinite blue space . . .

"But, my dear man," trilled the canary, "what does 'infinite blue space' mean?"

"But, pardon me, what do you think of this world? What is the world to you?"

"The world," retorted the canary, with a certain professional air, "is a secondhand shop with a small rectangular bamboo cage hanging from a nail. The canary is lord of the cage it lives in and the shop that surrounds it. Beyond that, everything is illusion and deception."

With this, the old man woke up and approached me, dragging his feet. He asked me if I wanted to buy the canary. I asked if he had acquired it in the same way he had acquired the rest of the objects he sold and learned that he had bought it from a barber, along with a set of razors.

"The razors are in very good condition." he said.

"I only want the canary."

I paid for it, ordered a huge, circular cage of wood and wire, and had it placed on the veranda of my house so the bird could see the garden, the fountain, and a bit of blue sky.

It was my intention to do a lengthy study of this phenomenon, without saying anything to anyone until I could astound the world with my extraordinary discovery. I began by alphabetizing the canary's language in order to study its structure, its relation to music, the bird's appreciation of aesthetics; its ideas and recollections. When this philological and psychological analysis was done, I entered specifically into the study of canaries: their origin, their early history, the geology and flora of the Canary Islands, the bird's knowledge of navigation, and so forth. We conversed for hours while I took notes, and it waited, hopped about, and trilled.

As I have no family other than two servants, I ordered them not to interrupt me, even to deliver a letter or an urgent telegram or to inform me of an important visitor. Since they both knew about my scientific pursuits, they found my orders perfectly natural and did not suspect that the canary and I understood each other.

Needless to say, I slept little, woke up two or three times each night, wandered about aimlessly, and felt feverish. Finally, I returned to my work in order to reread, add, and emend. I corrected more than one observation, either because I had misunderstood something or because the bird had not expressed it clearly. The definition of the world was one of these. Three weeks after the canary's entrance into my home, I asked it to repeat to me its definition of the world.

"The world," it answered, "is a sufficiently broad garden with a fountain in the middle, flowers, shrubbery, some grass, clear air, and a bit of blue up above. The canary, lord of the world, lives in a spacious cage, white and circular, from which it looks out on the rest of the world. Everything else is illusion and deception."

The language of my treatise also suffered some modifications, and I saw that certain conclusions which had seemed simple were actually presumptuous. I still could not write the paper I was to send to the National Museum, the Historical Institute, and the German universities, not due to a lack of material but because I first had to put together all my observations and test their validity. During the last few days, I neither left the house, answered letters, nor wanted to hear from friends or relatives. The canary was everything to me. One of the servants had the job of cleaning the bird's cage and giving it food and water every morning. The bird said nothing to him, as if it knew the man was completely lacking in scientific background. Besides, the service was no more than cursory, as the servant was not a bird lover.

One Saturday I awoke ill, my head and back aching. The doctor or- 25
dered complete rest. I was suffering from an excess of studying and was not to read or even think; nor was I even to know what was going on in the city or the rest of the outside world. I remained in this condition for five days. On the sixth day I got up, and only then did I find out that the canary, while under the servant's care, had flown out of its cage. My first impulse was to strangle the servant—I was choking with indignation and collapsed into my chair, speechless and bewildered. The guilty man defended himself, swearing he had been careful, but the wily bird had nevertheless managed to escape.

"But didn't you search for it?"

"Yes, I did, sir. First it flew up to the roof, and I followed it. It flew to a tree, and then who knows where it hid itself? I've been asking around since yesterday. I asked the neighbors and the local farmers, but no one has seen the bird."

I suffered immensely. Fortunately, the fatigue left me within a few hours, and I was soon able to go out to the veranda and the garden. There was no sign of the canary. I ran everywhere, making inquiries and posting announcements, all to no avail. I had already gathered my notes together to write my paper, even though it would be disjointed and incomplete, when I happened to visit a friend who had one of the largest and most beautiful estates on the outskirts of town. We were taking a stroll before dinner when this question was trilled to me:

"Greetings, Senhor Macedo, where have you been since you disappeared?"

It was the canary, perched on the branch of a tree. You can imagine 30
how I reacted and what I said to the bird. My friend presumed I was mad, but the opinions of friends are of no importance to me. I spoke tenderly to the canary and asked it to come home and continue our conversations in that world of ours, composed of a garden, a fountain, a veranda, and a white circular cage.

"What garden? What fountain?"

"The world, my dear bird."

"What world? I see you haven't lost any of your annoying professorial habits. The world," it solemnly concluded, "is an infinite blue space, with the sun up above."

Indignant, I replied that if I were to believe what it said, the world could be anything—it had even been a secondhand shop . . .

"A secondhand shop?" it trilled to its heart's content. "But is there 35
really such a thing as a secondhand shop?"

Analyzing the Text

1. In what different circumstances does the narrator encounter the canary? How does the canary redefine its conception of the world to suit each new environment in which it finds itself?
2. In what ways does the narrator become obsessed with every aspect of the canary's behavior?

Understanding Assis's Techniques

1. How does Assis characterize the canary (from Macedo's perspective) so as to suggest it might symbolize traits within his personality?
2. What details in the description of Macedo suggest that he sees the canary as a vehicle for self-aggrandizement?

Arguing for an Interpretation

1. What details in the story might suggest that it can be understood as a fable about egocentrism? Is Macedo actually insane? Explain your answer.
2. In what sense might the canary be perceived of as possessing a view of life and those character traits that Macedo lacks?

Carmen Naranjo

Born in Cartago, Costa Rica, in 1931, Carmen Naranjo has been an outstanding figure in Costa Rican cultural and political life, having served as ambassador to Israel. She is a prolific writer whose works include six novels, the most recent of which, Sobrepunto, *was published in 1985, three volumes of short stories, and several volumes of poetry, plays, and essays. She has twice received Costa Rica's National Prize for Literature and was awarded the Magon Prize, the highest honor conferred by the government on an individual, in recognition of her work on the behalf of culture. Naranjo served as secretary of culture and directs the most important publishing organization in Central America, the Editorial Universitaria Centro America. Naranjo's fiction blends realism with fantasy as a way of exploring important social issues through innovative narrative perspectives. "And We Sold the Rain," translated by Jo Anne Engelbert (1988), is a funny, yet grim satire of the economic agonies of a small Third World country in Central America that decides to raise cash by selling their most precious natural resource, rain, to Saudi Arabia.*

And We Sold the Rain

"This is a royal fuck-up," was all the treasury minister could say a few days ago as he got out of the jeep after seventy kilometers of jouncing over dusty rutted roads and muddy trails. His advisor agreed: there wasn't a cent in the treasury, the line for foreign exchange wound four times around the capital, and the IMF was stubbornly insisting that the country could expect no more loans until the interest had been paid up, public spending curtailed, salaries frozen, domestic production increased, imports reduced, and social programs cut.

The poor were complaining, "We can't even buy beans—they've got us living on radish tops, bananas and garbage; they raise our water bills but don't give us any water even though it rains every day, and on top of that they add on a charge for excess consumption for last year, even though there wasn't any water in the pipes then either."

"Doesn't anyone in this whole goddamned country have an idea that could get us out of this?" asked the president of the republic, who shortly before the elections, surrounded by a toothily smiling, impeccably tailored meritocracy, had boasted that by virtue of his university-trained mind (Ph.D. in developmental economics) he was the best candidate. Someone proposed to him that he pray to La Negrita; he did and nothing happened. Somebody else suggested that he reinstate the Virgin of Ujarrás. But after so many years of neglect, the pretty little virgin had gone deaf and ignored the pleas for help, even though the entire cabinet implored her, at the top of their lungs, to light the way to a better future and a happier tomorrow.

The hunger and poverty could no longer be concealed: the homeless, pockets empty, were squatting in the Parque Central, the Parque Nacional, and the Plaza de la Cultura. They were camping along Central and Second Avenues and in a shantytown springing up on the plains outside the city. Gangs were threatening to invade the national theater, the Banco Central, and all nationalized banking headquarters. The Public Welfare Agency was rationing rice and beans as if they were medicine. In the marketplace, robberies increased to one per second, and homes were burgled at the rate of one per half hour. Business and government were sinking in sleaze; drug lords operated uncontrolled, and gambling was institutionalized in order to launder dollars and attract tourists. Strangely enough, the prices of a few items went down: whiskey, caviar and other such articles of conspicuous consumption.

The sea of poverty that was engulfing cities and villages contrasted 5
with the growing number of Mercedes Benzes, BMWs and a whole alphabet of trade names of gleaming new cars.

The minister announced to the press that the country was on the verge of bankruptcy. The airlines were no longer issuing tickets because so much money was owed them, and travel became impossible; even official junkets were eliminated. There was untold suffering of civil servants suddenly unable to travel even once a month to the great cities of the world! A special budget might be the solution, but tax revenues were nowhere to be found, unless a compliant public were to go along with the president's brilliant idea of levying a tax on air—a minimal tax, to be sure, but, after all, the air was a part of the government's patrimony. Ten *colones* per breath would be a small price to pay.

July arrived, and one afternoon a minister without portfolio and without umbrella, noticing that it had started to rain, stood watching people run for cover. "Yes," he thought, "here it rains like it rains in Comala, like it rains in Macondo. It rains day and night, rain after rain, like a theater with the same movie, sheets of water. Poor people without umbrellas, without a change of clothes, they get drenched, people living in leaky houses, without a change of shoes for when they're shipwrecked. And here, all my poor colleagues with colds, all the poor deputies with laryngitis, the president with that worrisome cough, all this on top of the catastrophe itself. No TV station is broadcasting; all of them are flooded, along with the newspaper plants and the radio stations. A people without news is a lost people, because they don't know that everywhere else, or almost everywhere else, things are even worse. If we could only export the rain," thought the minister.

Meanwhile, the people, depressed by the heavy rains, the dampness, the lack of news, the cold, and their hunger and despair without their sitcoms and soap operas, began to rain inside and to increase the baby population—that is, to try to increase the odds that one of their progeny might survive. A mass of hungry, naked babies began to cry in concert every time it rained.

When one of the radio transmitters was finally repaired, the president was able to broadcast a message: He had inherited a country so deeply in debt that it could no longer obtain credit and could no longer afford to pay either the interest or the amortization on loans. He had to dismiss civil servants, suspend public works, cut off services, close offices, and spread his legs somewhat to transnationals. Now even these lean cows were dying; the fat ones were on the way, encouraged by the International Monetary Fund, the AID and the IDB, not to mention the EEC. The great danger was that the fat cows had to cross over the neighboring country on their way, and it was possible that they would be eaten up—even though they came by air, at nine thousand feet above the ground, in a first class stable in a pressurized, air-conditioned cabin. Those neighbors were simply not to be trusted.

The fact was that the government had faded in the people's memory. 10
By now no one remembered the names of the president or his ministers; people remembered them as "the one with glasses who thinks he's Tarzan's mother," or "the one who looks like the baby hog someone gave me when times were good, maybe a little uglier."

The solution came from the most unexpected source. The country had organized the Third World contest to choose "Miss Underdeveloped," to be elected, naturally, from the multitudes of skinny, dusky, round-shouldered, short-legged, half-bald girls with cavity-pocked smiles, girls suffering from parasites and God knows what else. The prosperous Emirate of the Emirs sent its designée, who in sheer amazement at how it rained and rained, widened her enormous eyes—fabulous eyes of harem and Koran delights—and was unanimously elected reigning Queen of Underdevelopment. Lacking neither eyeteeth nor molars, she was indeed the fairest of the fair. She returned in a rush to the Emirate of the Emirs, for she had acquired, with unusual speed, a number of fungal colonies that were taking over the territory under her toenails and fingernails, behind her ears, and on her left cheek.

"Oh, Father Sultan, my lord, lord of the moons and of the suns, if your Arabian highness could see how it rains and rains in that country, you would not believe it. It rains day and night. Everything is green, even the people; they are green people, innocent and trusting, who probably have never even thought about selling their most important resource, the rain. The poor fools think about coffee, rice, sugar, vegetables, and lumber, and they hold Ali Baba's treasure in their hands without even knowing it. What we would give to have such abundance!"

Sultan Abun dal Tol let her speak and made her repeat the part about the rain from dawn to dusk, dusk to dawn, for months on end. He wanted to hear over and over about that greenness that was forever turning greener. He loved to think of it raining and raining, of singing in the rain, of showers bringing forth flowers . . .

A long distance phone call was made to the office of the export minister from the Emirate of the Emirs, but the minister wasn't in. The trade minister grew radiant when Sultan Abun dal Tol, warming to his subject, instructed him to buy up rain and construct an aqueduct between their countries to fertilize the desert. Another call. Hello, am I speaking with the country of rain, not the rain of marijuana or cocaine, not that of laundered dollars, but the rain that falls naturally from the sky and makes the sandy desert green? Yes, yes, you are speaking with the export minister, and we are willing to sell you our rain. Of course, its production costs us nothing; it is a resource as natural to us as your petroleum. We will make you a fair and just agreement.

The news filled five columns during the dry season, when obstacles 15
like floods and dampness could be overcome. The president himself made the announcement: We will sell rain at ten dollars per cc. The price will be reviewed every ten years. Sales will be unlimited. With the earnings we will regain our independence and our self-respect.

The people smiled. A little less rain would be agreeable to everyone, and the best part was not having to deal with the six fat cows, who were more than a little oppressive. The IMF, the World Bank, the AID, the Embassy, the International Development Bank and perhaps the EEC would stop pushing the cows on them, given the danger that they might be stolen in the neighboring country, air-conditioned cabin, first class stable and all. Moreover, one couldn't count on those cows really being fat, since accepting them meant increasing all kinds of taxes, especially those on consumer goods, lifting import restrictions, spreading one's legs completely open to the transnationals, paying the interest, which was now a little higher, and amortizing the debt that was increasing at a rate only comparable to the spread of an epidemic. And as if this were not enough, it would be necessary to structure the cabinet a certain way, as some ministers were viewed by some legislators as potentially dangerous, as extremists.

The president added with demented glee, his face garlanded in sappy smiles, that French technicians, those guardians of European meritocracy, would build the rain funnels and the aqueduct, a guarantee of honesty, efficiency and effective transfer of technology.

By then we had already sold, to our great disadvantage, the tuna, the dolphins, and the thermal dome, along with the forests and all Indian artifacts. Also our talent, dignity, sovereignty, and the right to traffic in anything and everything illicit.

The first funnel was located on the Atlantic coast, which in a few months looked worse than the dry Pacific. The first payment from the emir arrived—in dollars!—and the country celebrated with a week's vacation. A little more effort was needed. Another funnel was added in the north and one more in the south. Both zones immediately dried up like raisins. The checks did not arrive. What happened? The IMF garnished them for interest payments. Another effort: a funnel was installed in the center of the country; where formerly it had rained and rained. It now stopped raining forever, which paralyzed brains, altered behavior, changed the climate, defoliated the corn, destroyed the coffee, poisoned aromas, devastated canefields, dessicated palm trees, ruined orchards, razed truck gardens, and narrowed faces, making people look and act like rats, ants, and cockroaches, the only animals left alive in large numbers.

To remember what we once had been, people circulated photographs 20
of an enormous oasis with great plantations, parks, and animal sanctuaries full of butterflies and flocks of birds, at the bottom of which was printed, "Come and visit us. The Emirate of Emirs is a paradise."

The first one to attempt it was a good swimmer who took the precaution of carrying food and medicine. Then a whole family left, then whole villages, large and small. The population dropped considerably. One fine day there was nobody left, with the exception of the president and his cabinet. Everyone else, even the deputies, followed the rest by opening the cover of the aqueduct and floating all the way to the cover at the other end, doorway to the Emirate of the Emirs.

In that country we were second-class citizens, something we were already accustomed to. We lived in a ghetto. We got work because we knew about coffee, sugar cane, cotton, fruit trees, and truck gardens. In a short time we were happy and felt as if these things too were ours, or at the very least, that the rain still belonged to us.

A few years passed; the price of oil began to plunge and plunge. The emir asked for a loan, then another, then many; eventually he had to beg and beg for money to service the loans. The story sounds all too familiar. Now the IMF has taken possession of the aqueducts. They have cut off the water because of a default in payments and because the sultan had the bright idea of receiving as a guest of honor a representative of that country that is a neighbor of ours.

Analyzing the Text

1. How would you characterize the attitude of the narrator toward the events in the story and toward the government officials?
2. What measures had the country taken in the past to raise currency? What desperate circumstances have led the country to sell its most precious resource? How is the plan implemented and with what effects?

Understanding Naranjo's Techniques

1. How do the detailed descriptions of sights, sounds, and settings make the bizarre premise of the story more credible?
2. What details suggest that the narrator serves as an alter ego or persona for Naranjo herself?

Arguing for an Interpretation

1. Although the premise of this story may seem far-fetched, in 2002, Turkey announced that it would sell its precious resource—water—to Israel (see

<http://news.bbc.co.uk/2/hi/europe/685812.stm>). What current policies that impact on natural resources deserve to be satirized? Address one of these in a 500-word satiric essay.

2. To what extent is the impact of this story due to the amazing torrent of words, images, concepts, and metaphors that engulf the reader? In your opinion, do these extravagant stylistic effects suit her theme? Explain your answer.

Olaf Stapledon

William Olaf Stapledon (1886–1950) was born near Liverpool, England. His middle name, "Olaf," does not reflect Scandinavian origin, but rather that his parents were reading a history of the kings of Norway when he was born. He was educated at Balliol College, Oxford, and briefly worked in the family shipping business in Port Said, Egypt, before serving with an ambulance unit in Flanders during World War I for which he was awarded the Croix de Guerre. He received a Ph.D. in philosophy from Liverpool University in 1925. Stapledon is credited with introducing concepts (such as genetic engineering and terraforming of other planets to make them suitable for human habitation) into science fiction that have become standard in the genre. His work has influenced writers as diverse as Jorge Luis Borges, C. S. Lewis, Stanislaw Lem, and Arthur C. Clarke (especially in his panoramic novel 2001*). Stapledon's works include* Last and First Men *(1930), which encompasses two billion years of evolution;* Sirius *(1944), a tale of a genetically enhanced intellectually superior dog, which many consider the best science fiction story with a nonhuman protagonist; and* Star Maker *(1937), from which the last chapter is reprinted here. This novel is told through the perspective of an English gentleman who takes an "astral" or out-of-body journey in which he observes the countless forms of civilizations that have appeared on planets in far-flung galaxies. The cumulative impact of this journey is conveyed with dazzling insight in the epilogue that follows.*

Star Maker

Epilogue: Back to Earth

I woke on the hill. The street lamps of our suburb outshone the stars. The reverberation of the clock's stroke was followed by eleven strokes more. I singled out our window. A surge of joy, of wild joy, swept me like a wave. Then peace.

The littleness, but the intensity, of earthly events! Gone, abolished in an instant, was the hypercosmical reality, the wild fountain of creations, and all the spray of worlds. Vanished, transmuted into fantasy, and into sublime irrelevance.

The littleness, but the intensity, of this whole grain of rock, with its film of ocean and of air, and its discontinuous, variegated, tremulous film of life; of the shadowy hills, of the sea, vague, horizonless; of the pulsating, cepheid, lighthouse; of the clanking railway trucks. My hand caressed the pleasant harshness of the heather.

Vanished, the hypercosmical apparition. Not such as I had dreamed must the real be, but infinitely more subtle, more dread, more excellent. And infinitely nearer home.

Yet, however false the vision in detail of structure, even perhaps in its 5
whole form, in temper surely it was relevant; in temper perhaps it was even true. The real itself, surely, had impelled me to conceive that image, false in every theme and facet, yet in spirit true.

The stars wanly trembled above the street lamps. Great suns? Or feeble sparks in the night sky? Suns, it was vaguely rumoured. Lights at least to steer by, and to beckon the mind from the terrestrial flurry; but piercing the heart with their cold spears.

Sitting there on the heather, on our planetary grain, I shrank from the abysses that opened up on every side, and in the future. The silent darkness, the featureless unknown, were more dread than all the terrors that imagination had mustered. Peering, the mind could see nothing sure, nothing in all human experience to be grasped as certain, except uncertainty itself; nothing but obscurity gendered by a thick haze of theories. Man's science was a mere mist of numbers; his philosophy but a fog of words. His very perception of this rocky grain and all its wonders was but a shifting and a lying apparition. Even oneself, that seeming-central fact, was a mere phantom, so deceptive, that the most honest of men must question his own honesty, so insubstantial that he must even doubt his very existence. And our loyalties! So self-deceiving, so misinformed and mis-conceived. So savagely pursued and hate-warped! Our very loves, and these in full and generous intimacy, must be condemned as unseeing, self-regarding, and self-gratulatory.

And yet? I singled out our window. We had been happy together! We had found, or we had created, our little treasure of community. This was the one rock in all the welter of experience. This, not the astronomical and hypercosmical immensity, nor even the planetary grain, this, this alone, was the solid ground of existence.

On every side was confusion, a rising storm, great waves already drenching our rock. And all around, in the dark welter, faces and appealing hands, half-seen and vanishing.

And the future? Black with the rising storm of this world's madness, 10
though shot through with flashes of a new and violent hope, the hope of a sane, a reasonable, a happier world. Between our time and that future, what horror lay in store? Oppressors would not meekly give way. And we two, accustomed only to security and mildness, were fit only for a kindly world; wherein, none being tormented, none turns desperate. We were adapted only to fair weather, for the practice of the friendly but not too difficult, not heroical virtues, in a society both secure and just. Instead, we found ourselves in an age of titanic conflict, when the relentless powers of

darkness and the ruthless because desperate powers of light were coming to grips for a death struggle in the world's torn heart, when grave choices must be made in crisis after crisis, and no simple or familiar principles were adequate.

Beyond our estuary a red growth of fire sprang from a foundry. At hand, the dark forms of the gorse lent mystery to the suburb's foot-worn moor.

In imagination I saw, behind our own hill's top, the farther and unseen hills. I saw the plains and woods and all the fields, each with its myriads of particular blades. I saw the whole land curving down from me, over the planet's shoulder. The villages were strung together on a mesh of roads, steel lines, and humming wires. Mist-drops on a cobweb. Here and there a town displayed itself as an expanse of light, a nebulous luminosity, sprinkled with stars.

Beyond the plains, London, neon-lit, seething, was a microscope-slide drawn from foul water, and crowded with nosing animalcules. Animalcules! In the stars' view, no doubt, these creatures were mere vermin; yet each to itself, and sometimes one to another, was more real than all the stars.

Gazing beyond London, imagination detected the dim stretch of the Channel, and then the whole of Europe, a patchwork of tillage and sleeping industrialism. Beyond poplared Normandy spread Paris, with the towers of Notre-Dame tipped slightly, by reason of Earth's curvature. Farther on, the Spanish night was ablaze with the murder of cities. Away to the left lay Germany, with its forests and factories, its music, its steel helmets. In cathedral squares I seemed to see the young men ranked together in thousands, exalted, possessed, saluting the flood-lit Führer. In Italy too, land of memories and illusions, the mob's idol spell-bound the young.

Far left-wards again, Russia, an appreciably convex segment of our globe, snow-pale in the darkness, spread out under the stars and cloud-tracts. Inevitably I saw the spires of the Kremlin, confronting the Red Square. There Lenin lay, victorious. Far off, at the foot of the Urals,[1] imagination detected the ruddy plumes and smoke-pall of Magnetostroy. Beyond the hills there gleamed a hint of dawn; for day, at my midnight, was already pouring westward across Asia, overtaking with its advancing front of gold and rose the tiny smoke-caterpillar of the Trans-Siberian Express. To the north, the iron-hard Arctic oppressed the exiles in their camps. Far southward lay the rich valleys and plains that once cradled our species. But there I now saw railway lines ruled across the snow. In every village Asiatic children were waking to another school-day, and to the legend of Lenin. South again the Himalayas, snow-clad from waist to crest, looked over the rabble of their foot-hills into crowded India. I saw the dancing cotton plants, and the wheat, and the sacred river that bore the waters of Kamet past rice-fields and crocodile-shallows, past Calcutta with its shipping and its offices, down to the sea. From my midnight I looked into China. The morning sun glanced from the flooded fields and gilded the ancestral graves. The Yang Tse, a gleaming, crumpled thread, rushed through its

[1] *Urals:* a 1,500 mile mountain chain in Russia that separates the continents of Europe and Asia.

gorge. Beyond the Korean ranges, and across the sea, stood Fujiyama, extinct and formal. Around it a volcanic population welled and seethed in that narrow land, like lava in a crater. Already it spilled over Asia a flood of armies and of trade.

Imagination withdrew and turned to Africa. I saw the manmade thread of water that joins West to East; then minarets, pyramids, the ever-waiting Sphinx. Ancient Memphis itself now echoed with the rumour of Magnetostroy. Far southward, black men slept beside the great lakes. Elephants trampled the crops. Farther still, where Dutch and English profit by the Negro millions, those hosts were stirred by vague dreams of freedom.

Peering beyond the whole bulge of Africa, beyond cloud-spread Table Mountain, I saw the Southern Ocean, black with storms, and then the ice-cliffs with their seals and penguins, and the high snow-fields of the one unpeopled continent. Imagination faced the midnight sun, crossed the Pole, and passed Erebus, vomiting hot lava down his ermine. Northward it sped over the summer sea, past New Zealand, that freer but less conscious Britain, to Australia, where clear-eyed horsemen collect their flocks.

Still peering eastward from my hill, I saw the Pacific, strewn with islands; and then the Americas, where the descendants of Europe long ago mastered the descendants of Asia, through priority in the use of guns, and the arrogance that guns breed. Beside the farther ocean, north and south, lay the old New World; the River Plate and Rio, the New England cities, radiating centre of the old new style of life and thought. New York, dark against the afternoon sun, was a cluster of tall crystals, a Stonehenge of modern megaliths. Round these, like fishes nibbling at the feet of waders, the great liners crowded. Out at sea also I saw them, and the plunging freighters, forging through the sunset, port holes and decks aglow. Stokers sweated at furnaces, look-out men in crow's-nests shivered, dance music, issuing from opened doors, was drowned by the wind.

The whole planet, the whole rock-grain, with its busy swarms, I now saw as an arena where two cosmical antagonists, two spirits, were already preparing for a critical struggle, already assuming terrestrial and local guise, and coming to grips in our half-awakened minds. In city upon city, in village after village, and in innumerable lonely farmsteads, cottages, hovels, shacks, huts, in all the crevices where human creatures were intent on their little comforts and triumphs and escapes, the great struggle of our age was brewing.

One antagonist appeared as the will to dare for the sake of the new, 20
the longed for, the reasonable and joyful world, in which every man and woman may have scope to live fully, and live in service of mankind. The other seemed essentially the myopic fear of the unknown; or was it more sinister? Was it the cunning will for private mastery, which fomented for its own ends the archaic, reason-hating, and vindictive, passion of the tribe.

It seemed that in the coming storm all the dearest things must be destroyed. All private happiness, all loving, all creative work in art, science, and philosophy, all intellectual scrutiny and speculative imagination, and all creative social building; all, indeed, that man should normally live for, seemed folly and mockery and mere self-indulgence in the presence of public calamity. But if we failed to preserve them, when would they live again?

How to face such an age? How to muster courage, being capable only of homely virtues? How to do this, yet preserve the mind's integrity, never to let the struggle destroy in one's own heart what one tried to serve in the world, the spirit's integrity.

Two lights for guidance. The first, our little glowing atom of community, with all that it signifies. The second, the cold light of the stars, symbol of the hypercosmical reality, with its crystal ecstasy. Strange that in this light, in which even the dearest love is frostily assessed, and even the possible defeat of our half-waking world is contemplated without remission of praise, the human crisis does not lose but gains significance. Strange, that it seems more, not less, urgent to play some part in this struggle, this brief effort of animalcules striving to win for their race some increase of lucidity before the ultimate darkness.

Analyzing the Text

1. How does Stapledon use the counterpoint between a grand cosmic scale and the finite human perspective of his narrator to put threatening historical trends into context?
2. How do we know that the narrator is now more concerned with the human world that he inhabits than with the cosmic journey from which he has returned?

Understanding Stapledon's Techniques

1. How is Stapledon's account organized to take his readers on a very accelerated but condensed tour of the planet? What role do images of water and light play in his characterization?
2. How does the language that Stapledon applies to humanity allow the reader to see both the inconsequential nature and simultaneously all-important significance of human life?

Arguing for an Interpretation

1. Is Stapledon's epilogue ultimately optimistic or pessimistic about the future of humanity? Explain your answer.
2. The prose Stapledon uses is so highly metaphorical that it might be considered a prose poem. In your view, can prose ever produce the same effects as poetry? Explain your answer, using this selection as an example.

Poems

Henry Wadsworth Longfellow

Henry Wadsworth Longfellow (1807–1882) was born in Portland, Maine, graduated from Bowdoin College in 1825, and mastered Spanish, French, Italian, German, and the Scandinavian languages. He became a professor of languages at Harvard in 1836. Longfellow could trace his ancestry to John and Priscilla Alden, who had come

over on the Mayflower *and whom the poet immortalized in his popular narrative,* The Courtship of Miles Standish *(1858). Along with James Russell Lowell, Oliver Wendell Holmes, and John Greenleaf Whittier, he was part of the group known as the Fireside Poets, who incorporated American legends and characters into poetry. He popularized figures in American folklore, as did Washington Irving. Longfellow's work was so widely read that he was one of the few poets able to live on the proceeds. Some of his best known works are* Evangeline *(1847) and* Paul Revere's Ride *(1863), which immortalized a figure unfamiliar to most Americans. In his later years, Longfellow undertook a translation of Dante's* Divine Comedy, *as a way of coming to terms with the death of his wife. The following poem presents a common experience, rendered with uncommon stylistic grace.*

The Sound of the Sea

The sea awoke at midnight from its sleep,
And round the pebbly beaches far and wide
I heard the first wave of the rising tide
Rush onward with uninterrupted sweep;
A voice out of the silence of the deep,
A sound mysteriously multiplied
As of a cataract from the mountain's side,
Or roar of winds upon a wooded steep.
So comes to us at times, from the unknown
And inaccessible solitudes of being,
The rushing of the sea-tides of the soul;
And inspirations, that we deem our own,
Are some divine foreshadowing and foreseeing
Of things beyond our reason or control.

Analyzing the Text

1. What signs are there that the speaker has made contact with a mystical or religious spirit in this vividly imagined poem?
2. What aspects of the poem suggest that the sense of revelation the speaker experiences is both an internal and external event?

Understanding Longfellow's Techniques

1. Where does Longfellow use alliteration and assonance to evoke the spirit of the ocean?
2. How do the first eight lines set the stage for an encounter between the speaker and a presence he associates with waves of the ocean? How does Longfellow use sound effects to intensify this sense of contact?

Arguing for an Interpretation

1. Do you find Longfellow's poem to be a bit otherworldly, or does it accurately communicate the experience people have when listening to the ocean? Explain your answer.
2. How effective do you find the visual appearance and indentations of lines along with the rhyme scheme in evoking the movement and sensation of ocean waves and "the sound of the sea"?

Walt Whitman

Walt Whitman (1819–1892) was born in then-rural Huntington, Long Island, into a family of Quakers. The family later moved to Brooklyn, then a city of fewer than 10,000, where he worked as a carpenter. He attended school briefly and in 1830 went to work as an office boy but soon turned to printing and journalism. Until the 1850s he worked as a newspaperman. He was the editor of the Brooklyn Eagle *from 1846 to 1848. In 1855, Whitman published the first of many editions of* Leaves of Grass, *a work that proved to be of unparalleled influence in establishing him as one of the most innovative figures of nineteenth-century poetry. In subsequent editions, he wrote long, intricately orchestrated poems that embrace the ideals of working-class democracy expressed in experimental free-verse rhythms and realistic imagery. When the Civil War broke out, Whitman was too old to enlist but went to the front in 1862 to be with his brother George, who had been reported wounded. During the remainder of the war, Whitman served as a nurse tending wounded soldiers, Union and Confederate alike. In "When I Heard the Learn'd Astronomer," Whitman contrasts the poet's disenchantment with the impersonal coldness of rational science with a mystical appreciation of nature.*

When I Heard the Learn'd Astronomer

When I heard the learn'd astronomer,
When the proofs, the figures, were ranged in columns
  before me,
When I was shown the charts and diagrams, to add, divide,
  and measure them,
When I sitting heard the astronomer where he lectured
  with much applause in the lecture-room,
How soon unaccountable I became tired and sick,

Till rising and gliding out I wander'd off by myself,
In the mystical moist night-air, and from time to time,
Look'd up in perfect silence at the stars.

Analyzing the Text

1. How does the speaker feel listening to the astronomer's lecture? In light of the speaker's response, why is the word "learn'd" in the title ironic?
2. How would you characterize the speaker's experience when he leaves the lecture and looks at the stars?

Understanding Whitman's Techniques

1. How does Whitman use two entirely different types of language to contrast science with nature?
2. How does Whitman use imagery, repetition, and alliteration in his free-verse stanza in a way that provides unity to the entire poem?

Arguing for an Interpretation

1. What argument is the poem making about the poet's intuitive empathetic rapport when contrasted with the rational methods of the scientist? Do you share Whitman's views? Why or why not?
2. To what extent has Whitman biased the outcome of the poem through the way in which he characterizes the astronomer? What insight does this give you into how a poem can be an argument?

ANNA KAMIEŃSKA

Anna Kamieńska (1920–1986), a poet, translator, critic, essayist, and editor, was the author of numerous collections of original and translated poetry (from Russian and other Slavic languages) as well as of anthologies, books for children, and collections of interpretations of poems. Initially a poet of peasant themes and moral concerns, she underwent a spiritual metamorphosis in the early 1970s, becoming an important poet of religious experience. "Funny," translated by Mieczyslaw Jastrun, offers a wryly thought-provoking view of the human condition.

Funny

What's it like to be a human
the bird asked

I myself don't know
it's being held prisoner by your skin
while reaching infinity
being a captive of your scrap of time

while touching eternity
being hopelessly uncertain
and helplessly hopeful
being a needle of frost
and a handful of heat
breathing in the air
and choking wordlessly
it's being on fire
with a nest made of ashes

eating bread
while filling up on hunger
it's dying without love
it's loving through death

That's funny said the bird
and flew effortlessly up into the air

Analyzing the Text

1. What details suggest the difficulties, uncertainties, and precariousness of the human condition, especially when seen from the bird's perspective?
2. How does the fact that the bird is described as flying "effortlessly" help to explain its response—"that's funny"—to the answer given to its question "what's it like to be a human"?

Understanding Kamieńska's Techniques

1. How do the metaphors and images used to characterize the human condition symbolize the gulf between the bird's perception and its human respondent?
2. In what sense might the poem be understood as an allegory for the gulf that makes it difficult for people in very different circumstances to understand each other?

Arguing for an Interpretation

1. Is a bird an appropriate choice as an archetypal figure of timelessness? Would another type of creature have worked as well? If so, what would it be, and why?
2. To understand what Kamieńska is trying to achieve, imagine the analogies you might use to describe what a particular color looks like to someone who is color blind. Alternatively, you might use metaphors or similes to describe an object, animal, or force in nature, phrased in the form of a riddle (for example, "I am shaky, cool, fruity, and lucid—what am I?")

Vasko Popa

Vasko Popa (1922–1991) was born in Grebenats, Banat, in northern Yugoslavia. He studied at the universities of Belgrade, Vienna, and Bucharest and lived in Belgrade where he was a member of the Serbian Academy of Sciences and an editor of the publishing house Nolit. Popa is one of a generation of east European poets, such as Zbigniew Herbert, whose poetry refuses to falsify experience through any hopeful efforts to change it. Popa's gift as a poet is to turn the most grisly confrontations into something playful. He draws on medieval literature, folk poetry, charms, riddles, games, and legends. He prefers older, native Slavonic words to terms drawn from international urban culture. Objects and beings in Popa's poetry are simultaneously earthy and spiritual. The image of the wolf that figures so prominently in Popa's work is both a four-footed beast and a metaphor that refers to St. Sava, the patron saint of Serbia. Popa is widely regarded as one of eastern Europe's foremost poets. Collections of his poetry include Bark *(1953),* Unrest-Field *(1956),* Secondary Heaven *(1968),* Earth Erect *(1972),* Wolf Salt *(1975),* Raw Flesh *(1975),* The House on the High Road *(1975),* Homage to the Lame Wolf: Selected Poems 1956–1975 *(1975), and* Collected Poems *(1978). "The Lost Red Boot," translated by Anne Pennington (1975), is typical of Popa's work in that it forces the reader to approach common things of everyday life with a new perspective. In this poem, he seeks to establish a new covenant between his family and himself as he begins a pilgrimage through his own Serbian past.*

The Lost Red Boot

My great-grandmother Sultana Uroshevitch
Used to sail the sky in a wooden trough
And catch rain-bearing clouds

With wolf-balms and others
She did many more
Great and small miracles

After her death
She went on meddling
In the business of the living

They dug her up
To teach her to behave
And to bury her better

She lay there rosy-cheeked
In her oaken coffin

On one foot she was wearing
A little red boot
With splashes of fresh mud

To the end of my life I'll search
For that other boot she lost

Analyzing the Text

1. What picture emerges of the speaker's great-grandmother? What details suggest that her free-spirited activities did not end with her death?
2. How did the opposition of the staid townspeople to the great-grandmother's nocturnal wanderings dramatize the choice facing the poet? What does he choose?

Understanding Popa's Techniques

1. How does the last image of "a little red boot/With splashes of fresh mud" symbolize the values to which the speaker now commits himself?
2. In what respects do the imagery and the story the poem tells reflect an older tradition of folk literature?

Arguing for an Interpretation

1. To what extent does the way the poem is constructed embody the values the speaker admires—does it take risks, make imaginative leaps?
2. In your opinion, is the speaker a worthy descendant of his great-grandmother? Why or why not?

Gerard Manley Hopkins

Gerard Manley Hopkins (1844–1889) attended High Gate School in London, where he won a poetry prize. He entered Balliol College, Oxford, in 1863 with the ambition of becoming a painter. He was drawn to Catholicism and despite the opposition of his parents became a Jesuit priest. After his ordination in 1877, he served as a parish priest in the industrial towns of Manchester and Liverpool. After 1881, he taught classical languages, first at a Jesuit seminary and then from 1884 onward at the Catholic University College in Dublin. After his untimely death from typhoid, his poetry was saved and later published by his friend and fellow writer Robert Bridges to great public acclaim. Hopkins's astounding originality consists in his rejection of the stanza forms, meter, and language of traditional 19th-century poetry. Instead, he weaves intricate patterns of sound and meaning together through alliteration, internal rhymes, and a variety of unusual sound effects. In "The Windhover" (published in 1918) Hopkins describes the soul-stirring effect of seeing a windhover (a small kestrel,[1] or falcon) flying into the wind.

The Windhover

To Christ our Lord

I caught this morning morning's minion,[2] kingdom of
daylight's dauphin,[3] dapple-dawn-drawn Falcon, in his riding
Of the rolling level underneath him steady air, and striding
High there, how he rung[4] upon the rein of a wimpling[5] wing
In his ecstasy! then, off, off forth on swing,
As a skate's heel sweeps smooth on a bow-bend; the hurl and gliding
Rebuffed the big wind. My heart in hiding
Stirred for a bird,—the achieve of, the mastery of the thing!

Brute beauty and valour and act, oh, air, pride, plume, here
Buckle![6] AND the fire that breaks from thee then, a billion
Times told lovelier, more dangerous, O my chevalier![7]

No wonder of it: shéer plód makes plough down sillion[8]
Shine, and blue-bleak embers, ah my dear,
Fall, gall themselves, and gash gold-vermillion.

Analyzing the Text

1. What features of the windhover's appearance and flight does the speaker notice?
2. How does the speaker apply elements of the windhover to his own life as a Jesuit priest?

Understanding Hopkins's Techniques

1. How do the unusual rhythms of the poem capture the sweeping motion of the kestrel's flight?
2. In the last stanza, how does the speaker apply the imagery of the crucifixion as an incentive to reapply himself to his chosen vocation?

[1]**kestrel** a small falcon that can hover facing the oncoming wind. [2]**minion** darling, favorite of a king. [3]**dauphin** eldest son of the king of France, hence, a princely figure, heir to something magnificent. [4]**rung** circled. [5]**wimpling** rippling. [6]**buckle** This word incorporates a range of meanings from "join together" to "crumple." The latter sense might describe a sudden swoop of the hovering falcon. [7]**chevalier** a French knight or noble champion. Cf. "dauphin" in 1.2. [8]**sillion** archaic word meaning "furrow" or "ridge between furrows."

Arguing for an Interpretation

1. Hopkins was reprimanded by his superiors in the Church for writing poetry that seemed to have an equal, if not greater, meaning for him than his need to subordinate his ego in the interests of his parish. Do you consider this poem as an effective defense that poetry and religion need not exclude each other? Why or why not?
2. Hopkins uses archaic medieval terms and phrases and obscure words. Does this enhance the poem's sense of mystery or simply make it inaccessible to modern readers? Explain your answer.

ALFRED JARRY

Alfred Jarry (1873–1907) was born and lived in France. He began writing in 1888 at the age of 15, a comic satire on his high school physics teacher, Monsieur Felix-Federic Hebert, that set the pattern for Jarry's checkered literary career. In 1902, he wrote a novel, The Supermale, *which conjectures the ways in which technology affects our minds, bodies, and all of society. The first and most famous of Jarry's plays is* Ubu Roi *(1896), a strange parody of Shakespeare's* Macbeth *in which a grotesque figure, Pere Ubu (based on a scandalous characterization of Monsieur Hebert), is set on conquering Poland. Jarry also invented his own science, called "Pataphysics" (based on an absurdist view of the world), that he applied to a variety of poems, dramas, and novels. Jarry was a dedicated cyclist and saw the bicycle as a liberator in which man could become one with a machine. He was not only eccentric in his writing but in his personal habits as well, and must have presented quite a spectacle at 5 feet tall riding around Paris on his bicycle (to which he had attached a large bell from a tram car) with two revolvers tucked into his belt. In the following prose poem (translated by Gary Fletcher), Jarry displays an unusual blend of intellectual brilliance, panache, his lifelong passion for cycling, and an absurdist philosophy that influenced later writers such as Eugene Ionesco and Samuel Beckett. He died at the age of 34 of poverty, overwork, and alcoholism.*

The Passion of Jesus Considered as an Uphill Race

Entered to race, Barabbas was scratched.

The starter was Pilate. He pulled out his waterclock (or clepsydra), which got his hands wet, unless he'd simply spat on them. And he dropped the flag.

Jesus broke loose at full speed.

According to that very good sports commentator, Saint Matthew, it was common practice in those days to flog bike sprinters at the start, the way a coachman does with his hippomotors. This whipping acts as a hygienic massage the same time as it stimulates. So Jesus started off in fine form, but immediately had a flat. A stretch of track seeded with thorns popped his front tire all the way around.

You can see an exact resemblance of this veritable 5
crown of thorns in bike shop windows today as part of an ad for puncture-proof tires. Jesus, however, didn't have any, racing only with ordinary single-tube tires.

The two thieves, obviously in the know and thus "thick as thieves," took the lead.

It isn't true that there were any nails. Those three things usually seen in the ads were actually a tire-changer, called a "Jiffy."

First of all, you should know about the spills. Before that, you have to picture the apparatus itself.

Today's bike frame is a relatively recent invention. It was first seen around 1890. Beforehand, the body was made out of two tubes welded together perpendicularly to each other. It was commonly referred to as "the right-angle" or "the cross" bike. Jesus, after his blow-out, trekked up on foot, shouldering his bike, or, if you like, his cross.

The scene is reproduced in contemporary etchings, from 10
snapshots. But, it seems, the sport of biking, as a result of the well-known accident—putting a thorny, troublesome end to the Passion, and even updated by a similar accident, almost on the anniversary, by Count Zborowski[1] on the Turbic slopes—was banned for a while by official state decree. That's why whenever glossy magazines reproduce the celebrated scene they imagine rather fanciful bikes. They confuse the cross of the machine's body with the cross made by its handlebar. Jesus is portrayed with his hands spread apart on the handlebar, and, by the way, Jesus rode lying flat on his back, in order to minimize air resistance.

Note too that the machine frame, or cross, just like bike wheels to be seen as of this writing, was made of wood.

A small number have wrongly insinuated that Jesus' machine was one of those two-wheeled bikes without pedals, fashionable at the beginning of the century. Hardly the way to win an uphill race. According to Saint Bridget,[2] Gregory of Tours,[3] and Irenaeus,[4] cyclophile hagiographers of yore,

---

[1]*Count Zborowski:* an amateur racing driver who was killed in 1903 when his cufflinks caught in the hand throttle of his car during a race in Monaco. His son, Louis, also a famous racer, invented the "Chitty Chitty Bang Bang" car, by putting an airplane engine in a Mercedes' chassis (which became the subject of a film).

[2]*St. Bridget:* the most celebrated saint of the Northern kingdoms (1303–1373).

[3]*Gregory of Tours:* French historian and Bishop of Tours (1538–1594) who wrote accounts of the miracles of saints.

[4]*Irenaeus:* Greek theologian and Bishop of Lyon, the earliest father of the Church (125–202).

the cross was furnished with a configuration which they called a "suppodaneum." You don't have to be a big scholar to translate this as a "pedal."

To the point, Lipsius,[5] Justinian,[6] Bosius,[7] and Erycius Puteanus[8] all describe another accessory which, according to Cornelius Curtius, circa 1643, can still be found on Japanese crosses: a jutting out on the shaft, made of leather or wood, which the rider straddles like a horse—evidently the saddle.

Moreover, such description wouldn't be too unfaithful to the definition the Chinese peoples give today for a bike: "A little mule, led along by its ears, and spurred on with a shower of foot blows."

15 We'll abridge our narration of the race itself, as it's been recited in detail by specialized works and exhibited as sculptures and paintings to be seen in ad hoc monuments.

There are fourteen curves to the very tough Golgotha course. Jesus took his first spill at the third curve. His mother, in the stands, started to fret.

His very good trainer, Simon the Cyrenian,[9] who but for the thorn accident would have "led" from in front, also cutting the wind factor, carried the machine.

Tho' not carrying anything, Jesus sweated profusely. It's uncertain whether or not a female spectator wiped his face. We do know for sure that Veronica, a lady reporter, snapped a shot of him with her Kodak.

The second spill came at the seventh curve, across slippery pavement. At the eleventh, he tripped a third time, on a rail.

20 Common Israelite Tom, Dick, and Harrys cheered him on, at the eighth curve, waving their handkerchiefs.

The well-known, deplorable accident occurred at the twelfth curve. At the time, Jesus was in a dead heat with the two thieves. It's known, too, that he continued the race airborne—but that's another story.

Analyzing the Text

1. What key aspects of the passion of Jesus does Jarry transform or recast as a sporting event?

---

[5]*Lipsius:* A Belgian classical philologist and humanist (1547–1606) who advocated stoic ideals in a Christian context.

[6]*Justinian:* Byzantine emperor (483–565) who built the Church of Hagia Sophia in Constantinople (Istanbul) that still stands.

[7]*Bosius:* Jacobus Bosius published a work in 1617 in Antwerp that described various methods of crucifixion.

[8]*Erycius Puteanus:* student of Lipsius (1574–1646).

[9]*Simon the Cyrenian:* the bystander seized by Roman soldiers and made to bear the heavy cross of Christ on the way to Golgatha as described in Matthew 27:32; Mark 15:21; and Luke 23:26.

2. What effect does Jarry produce by translating sacred events into a secular and mundane context?

Understanding Jarry's Techniques

1. How does Jarry caricature or parody the language and style of ultra-serious biblical commentators?
2. In what respects does the paraphernalia involved in a bicycle race lend itself to the content of Jarry's poem?

Arguing for an Interpretation

1. What exactly is Jarry parodying in this poem: religion in general, Christianity in particular, or the reverential minutiae that usually attends the discussion and analysis of sacred scriptures?
2. How can real sporting events (such as the Tour de France victories of American cancer survivor Lance Armstrong) be invested with quasi-religious overtones?

DYLAN THOMAS

Dylan Thomas (1914–1953) was born in Swansea, Wales, a place that provided the setting for much of his work. He grew up hearing his father read Shakespeare, other poets, and the Bible, which began his fascination with the sound of words. He left school at 15, spent a brief time as a newspaper reporter, and published his first volume of poetry when he was 20. He went on to live in London that year, married Caitlin Macnamara with whom he had a turbulent relationship, and began publishing well-received books of poetry and short fiction. A collection of stories of his childhood, Portrait of the Artist as a Young Dog, *appeared in 1940. Thomas also wrote film scripts, the most successful of which was* Under Milkwood *(published posthumously in 1954) that depicted the residents of a small Welsh town over the period of one day. Thomas's poetry, especially the volume* Deaths and Entrances *(1946), moves from the obscurity of his early verse to a simple, direct, and passionate statement about all living things moving through cycles of death and birth. "Do Not Go Gentle into That Good Night" (1952) was written at a time when Thomas's father was gravely ill. This poem is written in an unusual form called the* villanelle, *consisting of 19 lines, written in five tercets and a final quatrain, rhyming* aba aba aba aba aba abaa. *The restrictions imposed by this form imbue words with double meanings that Thomas uses to great effect.*

Do Not Go Gentle into That Good Night

Do not go gentle into that good night,
Old age should burn and rave at close of day;
Rage, rage against the dying of the light.

Though wise men at their end know dark is right,
Because their words had forked no lightning they
Do not go gentle into that good night.

Good men, the last wave by, crying how bright
Their frail deeds might have danced in a green bay,
Rage, rage against the dying of the light.

Wild men who caught and sang the sun in flight,
And learn, too late, they grieved it on its way,
Do not go gentle into that good night.

Grave men, near death, who see with blinding sight
Blind eyes could blaze like meteors and be gay,
Rage, rage against the dying of the light.

And you, my father, there on the sad height,
Curse, bless, me now with your fierce tears, I pray.
Do not go gentle into that good night.
Rage, rage against the dying of the light.

Analyzing the Text

1. According to the speaker, death should be met with what kind of attitude? Why does he think it is important to have this kind of attitude?
2. The speaker is critical of the ways four types of men ("wise men," "good men," "wild men," and "grave men") react to death. What deficiencies does he find in each?

Understanding Thomas's Techniques

1. The phrase "do not go gentle" acts as a kind of refrain throughout the poem. What different meanings does it acquire?
2. Thomas's poem is meant to be read aloud, as he frequently did. How does he use internal echoes of sounds (for example, "old age" and "close of day") within the *villanelle* framework to enhance the poem's effect? How does this intricate form imbue words with double meanings?

Arguing for an Interpretation

1. What elements in the poem suggest that it was written for Thomas's own father? Does this make the poem more effective, and if so, in what way?

2. Critics have assailed the obscurity of much of Thomas's poetry, while acknowledging his passion. Did you find this poem difficult to understand and unnecessarily complex, or is that part of its appeal?

Bella Akhmadulina

Bella Akhmadulina was born in 1937 in Moscow. She attended the Gorky Institute of World Literature. Her first book of poetry, String *(1962), describes everyday sights and scenes with a whimsical perspective that transforms her descriptions into highly personal images that are celebrated for their originality, emotional intensity, and wit. Critics have called her poetry classical, pointing out that her use of rhyme and meter recalls the poetry of Pushkin. Her growing maturity as a poet can be seen in each new volume, including* Chills *(1968),* The Snowstorm *(1977),* Dreams of Georgia *(1977),* The Secret *(1983), and* Selected Poems *(1988). In recent poems she returns to familiar themes—such as evocation of the past—through visions of other Russian poets, including Pushkin, Akhmatova, and Pasternak. In 1989, she was awarded the then Soviet Union's highest prize—the State Prize in Literature. The growing reflective quality of her poems combined with her experimentation with form, complicated figures of speech, and always-present sense of wonder, can be seen in "The Garden," translated by F. D. Reeve (1988). For Akhmadulina, the world of the poem is an actual landscape in which she acts out the roles of naturalist, historian, and keeper of the language. She has also written* Bella Akhmadulina: Fotografii *(1997).*

The Garden

I went out to the garden—but in *garden,*
the word, lies lush luxuriance.
As gorgeous as a full-blown rose, it
enriches sound and scent and glance.

The word is wider than what surrounds me:
inside it all is well and free;
its rich black soil makes sons and daughters
or orphaned and transplanted seeds.

Seedlings of dark innovations,
O *garden,* word, you are the gardener,

who to the clippers' gleam and clatter
  increase and spread the fruits you bear.

Set within your free-and-easy
  space are an old estate and the fate
of a family long gone, and the faded
  whiteness of their garden bench.

You are more fertile than the earth:
  you feed the roots of others' crowns.
From oak to oakwood, Oakboy, you are
  hearts' mail, and words'—the love, the blood.

Your shady grove is always darkened,
  but why did a lovelorn parasol
of lace look down in embarrassment
  in the face of hot weather coming on?

Perhaps I, who quest for a limp hand,
  redden my own knees on the stones?
A casual and impoverished gardener,
  what do I seek? Where do I tend?

If I had gone out, where would I really
  have gone? It's May—and solid mud.
I went out to a ruined wasteland
  and in it read that life was dead.

Dead! Gone! Where had it hurried to?
  It merely tasted the dried-up agony
of speechless lips and then reported:
  all things forever; only a moment for me.

For a moment in which I could not manage
  to see either self or garden clearly.
"I went out to the garden" was what I wrote.
  I did? Well, then, there must be

something to it? There is—and amazing
  how going to the garden takes no move.
I did not go out at all. I simply wrote the way I usually do,
  "I went out to the garden . . ."

Analyzing the Text

1. How does the poem demonstrate that poetry, for the speaker, is capable of creating an imaginative reality more compelling than the reality of an actual garden?
2. What details in the poem suggest that the speaker sees herself as a historian and caretaker of the language? To what extent does she feel adequate to her self-assigned mission?

Understanding Akhmadulina's Techniques

1. At what points did you become aware that the speaker was referring to the poet's power of image-making, storytelling, and the ability to create symbols, rather than an actual garden?
2. How does stanza 5 use the image of the oak to illustrate how the imagination creates more fertile productive hybrids than can exist in nature?

Arguing for an Interpretation

1. In what respects is this poem designed to trigger the reader's associations and experiences? Did it work this way with you? Explain your answer.
2. This poem takes us into the mind of a highly creative literary artist. What insight does it offer into why she finds imagination more satisfying than the real world? Why is it ironic that the word "garden" contains greater significance and memories for her than does a real garden?

JORGE LUIS BORGES

Jorge Luis Borges (1899–1986), a master storyteller, poet, essayist, and man of letters, was born in Buenos Aires. His father, a professor of psychology, entertained him in childhood with intellectual and philosophical conundrums that remained a lifelong interest. Educated in Europe, at which time he learned French and German, he began to write as a member of the Spanish avant-garde literary movement called Ultraisme, a form of expressionism in which image and metaphor take precedence over plot, character, and theme. In later life, Borges remained an antirealist. When he returned to Buenos Aires in 1921, he worked in the National Library, and became its director before Juan Perón ousted him from his post because of political differences. In 1935 Borges had his collection of short narrative pieces published, under the title Universal History of Infamy. *His first major anthology of short stories,* The Garden of Forking Paths *(1941), introduced a collection whose imaginative world is an immense labyrinth of multidimensional reality; the stories are written in a playfully allusive literary and philosophical language in which the narrators seek to understand their own significance and that of the world. Borges developed these themes in a variety of styles in* Fictions *(1944),* The Aleph *(1949),* Labyrinths *(1962), and* Dr. Brody's Report *(1972). Borges lived in Buenos Aires and had an enormous influence on contemporary Latin American writing. His dazzling sense of paradox and mystery can be seen in "Afterglow"—translated by Norman Thomas Di Giovanni, from* Jorge Luis Borges's Selected Poems 1923–1967 *(1972)—a poem that may reflect his increasing blindness as a result of the same hereditary eye disease that had blinded his father. Forced to dictate his work, he nevertheless continued to travel, teach, and lecture until his death.*

Afterglow

Sunset is always disturbing
whether theatrical or muted,
but still more disturbing is that last desperate glow
that turns the plain to rust
when on the horizon nothing is left
of the pomp and clamor of the setting sun.
How hard holding on to that light, so tautly drawn and
different,
that hallucination which the human fear of the dark
imposes on space
and which ceases at once
the moment we realize its falsity,
the way a dream is broken
the moment the sleeper knows he is dreaming.

Analyzing the Text

1. What does the speaker's response to the fading sunset reveal about him?
2. How does the desire to hold on to the last light of the day produce the impression described in the title?

Understanding Borges's Techniques

1. What does the sunset and its afterglow seem to symbolize for the speaker?
2. How does Borges use a sense of resistance midway through the poem to let the reader experience the tension the speaker feels?

Arguing for an Interpretation

1. Does Borges manage the transition between the end of the day and all other endings (the end of sight, the end of life) in a way that universalizes what was a specific event?
2. In your own words, explain what Borges is saying about our need to believe in things for which we do not have proof.

JOHN MILTON

John Milton (1608–1674) was born and brought up in London. His father was a fairly prosperous notary (or scrivener). Milton went to St. Paul's School and by 1625 had mastered Greek, Latin, and Hebrew as well as several European languages. He continued his education at Christ College, Cambridge University, where he earned a B.A. and an M.A. Milton decided not to study divinity and spent the next six years in private study at his father's country house. The works he composed during this period include "L'Allegro," a poem that praises happiness; "Il Penseroso," a complementary piece; Comus, *a masque; and "Lycidas," a pastoral elegy honoring Edward King, a*

Cambridge classmate of Milton's who drowned in a shipwreck in the Irish Sea. Milton then traveled abroad to Italy, where he met Galileo in 1638. Milton's commitment to the anti-royalist faction against King Charles I led to his appointment in 1649 as Latin secretary to Oliver Cromwell. In this capacity, he wrote propaganda pamphlets justifying the execution of the King. Milton's sight, which had always been precarious, failed, leaving him blind at the age of 43. With the overthrow of Cromwell and the restoration of King Charles II (in 1660), Milton went into retirement and continued to work on his major poem, Paradise Lost, *a compendious allegory intended to "justify the ways of God to men." Because of his blindness, he dictated this religious epic in 12 books to his three daughters. In later life, he composed a sequel (*Paradise Regained*), and a drama (not intended for stage production),* Samson Agonistes, *with quasi-autobiographical overtones. The following poem alludes to a parable of Jesus (Matt. 25:14–30) in which a servant is condemned for burying his one talent, or coin, instead of spending it. Milton equates this with his own predicament, since doctors had warned him that continued writing would cost him his eyesight, a sacrifice he made for the causes (theological and political) to which he was committed.*

When I consider how my light is spent

When I consider how my light is spent,
Ere half my days, in this dark world and wide,
And that one Talent which is death to hide
Lodg'd with me useless, though my Soul more bent
To serve therewith my Maker, and present
My true account, lest he returning chide,
"Doth God exact day-labour, light deny'd?"
I fondly ask. But Patience, to prevent
That murmur, soon replies, "God doth not need
Either man's work or his own gifts. Who best
Bear his mild yoke, they serve him best. His state
Is kingly: thousands at his bidding speed
And post o'er land and ocean without rest;
They also serve who only stand and wait."

Analyzing the Text

1. What problem or question does the speaker raise in the first eight lines of this poem, and how is it resolved in the final six lines?

2. How does the meaning of the word "talent," which refers to both an innate skill and a monetary unit, mentioned in the parable in Matthew 25:14–30 tie together various themes in the poem?

Understanding Milton's Techniques

1. How does Milton use the octave-sestet division of the sonnet to organize his meditation? How does the sense of closure of the sonnet form strengthen his conclusion?
2. How does the iambic pentameter of the poem add emotional force to his argument according to which words are stressed in any particular line?

Arguing for an Interpretation

1. How does knowing that this poem was written in 1655 after Milton had gone completely blind (in 1651) after a period of lessening sight add to your appreciation of the poem?
2. Is there any task that you would consider so important as to risk losing your sight, hearing, or any other sense, in order to perform it? Explain your answer.

MARY OLIVER

Mary Oliver was born in 1935 in Cleveland, Ohio, and attended Ohio State University and Vassar College. She has taught and been poet-in-residence at several colleges. An early collection of her poems, American Primitive *(1983), won the Pulitzer Prize. Oliver, a prolific writer, has also published numerous collections, including* West Wind *(1997),* Winter Hours: Poetry, Prose, and Essays *(1999), and* The Leaf and the Cloud *(2000). Her* New and Selected Poems *(1992) in which the following poem first appeared won the National Book Award. She currently teaches at Bennington College in Vermont.*

When Death Comes

When death comes
like the hungry bear in autumn;
When death comes and takes all the bright coins from his
    purse

to buy me, and snaps the purse shut,
when death comes
like the measles-pox;

when death comes
like an iceberg between the shoulder blades,

I want to step through the door full of curiosity,
wondering:
what is it going to be like, that cottage of darkness?

And therefore I look upon everything
as a brotherhood and a sisterhood,
and I look upon time as no more than an idea,
and I consider eternity as another possibility,

and I think of each life as a flower, as common
as a field daisy, and as singular,

and each name a comfortable music in the mouth
tending as all music does, toward silence,

and each body a lion of courage, and something
precious to the earth.

When it's over, I want to say: all my life
I was a bride married to amazement.
I was the bridegroom, taking the world into my arms.

When it is over, I don't want to wonder
if I have made of my life something particular,
and real.
I don't want to find myself sighing and frightened,
or full of argument.

I don't want to end up simply having visited this world.

Analyzing the Text

1. How does the prospect of death compel the speaker to define the kind of life she wished to have lived up to that point?
2. How does the exuberant and mystical tone the speaker projects characterize what she thinks one's attitude toward life should be?

Understanding Oliver's Techniques

1. In what respects is the blank verse the poem is written in more suitable for her subject than more traditional closed forms, such as a sonnet, would have been?
2. How does the poem weave its effects through the contrasting images used to characterize the arrival of death and the life just lived by the speaker?

Arguing for an Interpretation

1. How does the poem develop the theme of truly being in the world as opposed to simply having passed through it? Do you find Oliver's treatment of this theme persuasive? Why or why not?
2. Oliver's language bears an uncanny similarity to the language used by religious mystics such as St. Theresa of Avila (1515–1582). You might investigate the relationship between this poem and St. Theresa's writings, no-

tably her *Life* and the *Way of Perfection.* Discuss the very different perspectives these works embody.

William Wordsworth

*William Wordsworth (1770–1850) was born in a village on the edge of the Lake District in England. He attended St. John's College, Cambridge, in 1787, and began a series of walking tours of Switzerland and France that fired his imagination and are reflected in his autobiographical poem "The Prelude" (1805). He lived in France from 1791 to 1792 at the height of the French Revolution. In 1797, he began a lifelong friendship with the younger poet Samuel Coleridge, a creative association that led in 1798 to the publication of a groundbreaking volume of poems—*Lyrical Ballads*—whose down-to-earth style and everyday subjects set English poetry on a new course. Wordsworth's ability to communicate heartfelt reactions to inspiring landscapes and to see spiritual depths in everyday scenes is well illustrated in the poem "Ode: Intimations of Immortality from Recollections of Early Childhood" (1807).*

Ode: Intimations of Immortality from Recollections of Early Childhood

The Child is father of the Man;
And I could wish my days to be
Bound each to each by natural piety.

I

There was a time when meadow, grove, and stream,
The earth, and every common sight,
To me did seem
Apparelled in celestial light,
The glory and the freshness of a dream.
It is not now as it hath been of yore;—
Turn whereso'er I may,
By night or day,
The things which I have seen I now can see no more.

II

The Rainbow comes and goes,
And lovely is the Rose,
The Moon doth with delight

Look round her when the heavens are bare;
Waters on a starry night
Are beautiful and fair;
The sunshine is a glorious birth;
But yet I know, where'er I go,
That there hath past away a glory from the earth.

III

Now, while the birds thus sing a joyous song,
And while the young lambs bound
As to the tabor's sound,[1]
To me alone there came a thought of grief:
A timely utterance gave that thought relief,
And I again am strong:
The cataracts blow their trumpets from the steep;
No more shall grief of mind the season wrong;
I hear the Echoes through the mountains throng,
The Winds come to me from the fields of sleep,
And all the earth is gay;
Land and sea
Give themselves up to jollity,
And with the heart of May
Doth every Beast keep holiday;—
Thou Child of Joy,
Shout round me, let me hear thy shouts, thou happy
Shepherd-boy!

IV

Ye blessèd Creatures, I have heard the call
Ye to each other make; I see
The heavens laugh with you in your jubilee;
My heart is at your festival,
My head hath its coronal,[2]
The fulness of your bliss, I feel—I feel it all.
Oh evil day! if I were sullen
While Earth herself is adorning,
This sweet May-morning,
And the Children are culling
On every side,
In a thousand valleys far and wide,
Fresh flowers; while the sun shines warm,
And the Babe leaps up on his Mother's arm:—
I hear, I hear, with joy I hear!
—But there's a Tree, of many, one,
A single Field which I have looked upon,
Both of them speak of something that is gone:
The Pansy at my feet

[1]**tabor's sound** drumbeat. [2]**coronal** crown of flowers.

Doth the same tale repeat:
Whither is fled the visionary gleam?
Where is it now, the glory and the dream?

V

Our birth is but a sleep and a forgetting:
The Soul that rises with us, our life's Star,[3]
Hath had elsewhere its setting,
And cometh from afar:
Not in entire forgetfulness,
And not in utter nakedness,
But trailing clouds of glory do we come
From God, who is our home:
Heaven lies about us in our infancy!
Shades of the prison-house begin to close
Upon the growing Boy,
But He beholds the light, and whence it flows,
He sees it in his joy;
The Youth, who daily farther from the east
Must travel, still is Nature's Priest,
And by the vision splendid
Is on his way attended;
At length the Man perceives it die away,
And fade into the light of common day.

VI

Earth fills her lap with pleasures of her own;
Yearnings she hath in her own natural kind,
And, even with something of a Mother's mind,
And no unworthy aim,
The homely[4] Nurse doth all she can
To make her Foster-child, her Inmate Man,
Forget the glories he hath known,
And that imperial palace whence he came.

VII

Behold the Child among his new-born blisses,
A six years' Darling of a pigmy size!
See, where 'mid work of his own hand he lies,
Fretted,[5] by sallies of his mother's kisses,
With light upon him from his father's eyes!
See, at his feet, some little plan or chart,
Some fragment from his dream of human life,
Shaped by himself with newly-learned art;
A wedding or a festival,

[3]**Star** the sun. [4]**homely** familiar, friendly, simple. [5]**Fretted** bothered.

A mourning or a funeral;
And this hath now his heart,
And unto this he frames his song:
Then will he fit his tongue
To dialogues of business, love, or strife;
But it will not be long
Ere this be thrown aside,
And with new joy and pride
The little Actor cons[6] another part;
Filling from time to time his "humorous stage"[7]
With all the Persons, down to palsied Age,
That Life brings with her in her equipage;
As if his whole vocation
Were endless imitation.

VIII

Thou, whose exterior semblance doth belie
Thy Soul's immensity;
Thou best Philosopher, who yet dost keep
Thy heritage, thou Eye among the blind,
That, deaf and silent, read'st the eternal deep,[8]
Haunted for ever by the eternal mind,—
Mighty Prophet! Seer blest!
On whom those truths do rest,
Which we are toiling all our lives to find,
In darkness lost, the darkness of the grave;
Thou, over whom thy Immortality
Broods like the Day, a Master o'er a Slave,
A Presence which is not to be put by;
Thou little Child, yet glorious in the might
Of heaven-born freedom on thy being's height,
Why with such earnest pains dost thou provoke
The years to bring the inevitable yoke,
Thus blindly with thy blessedness at strife?
Full soon thy Soul shall have her earthly freight,
And custom lie upon thee with a weight,
Heavy as frost, and deep almost as life!

IX

O joy! that in our embers
Is something that doth live,
That nature yet remembers
What was so fugitive!
The thought of our past years in me doth breed
Perpetual benediction: not indeed

---

[6]**cons** learns. [7]**"humorous stage"** from a sonnet by Samuel Daniel (1562–1619). *Humorous* means "changeable" or "moody" here. [8]**eternal deep** mysteries of eternity.

For that which is most worthy to be blest;
Delight and liberty, the simple creed
Of Childhood, whether busy or at rest,
With new-fledged hope still fluttering in his breast:—
Not for these I raise
The song of thanks and praise;
But for those obstinate questionings
Of sense and outward things,
Fallings from us, vanishings;
Blank misgivings of a Creature
Moving about in worlds not realised,[9]
High instincts before which our mortal Nature
Did tremble like a guilty Thing surprised:
But for those first affections,
Those shadowy recollections,
Which, be they what they may,
Are yet the fountain-light of all our day,
Are yet a master-light of all our seeing;
Uphold us, cherish, and have power to make
Our noisy years seem moments in the being
Of the eternal Silence: truths that wake,
To perish never:
Which neither listlessness, nor mad endeavour,
Nor Man nor Boy,
Nor all that is at enmity with joy,
Can utterly abolish or destroy!
Hence in a season of calm weather
Though inland far we be
Our Souls have sight of that immortal sea
Which brought us hither,
Can in a moment travel thither,
And see the Children sport upon the shore,
And hear the mighty waters rolling evermore.

X

Then sing, ye Birds, sing, sing a joyous song!
And let the young Lambs bound
As to the tabor's sound!
We in thought will join your throng,
Ye that pipe and ye that play,
Ye that through your hearts today
Feel the gladness of the May!
What though the radiance which was once so bright
Be now for ever taken from my sight,
Though nothing can bring back the hour
Of splendour in the grass, of glory in the flower;
We will grieve not, rather find
Strength in what remains behind;
In the primal sympathy

[9]**not realised** not yet truly understood.

Which having been must ever be;
In the soothing thoughts that spring
Out of human suffering;
In the faith that looks through death,
In years that bring the philosophic mind.

XI

And O, ye Fountains, Meadows, Hills and Groves,
Forebode not any severing of our loves!
Yet in my heart of hearts I feel your might;
I only have relinquished one delight
To live beneath your more habitual sway.
I love the Brooks which down their channels fret,
Even more than when I tripped lightly as they;
The innocent brightness of a new-born Day
Is lovely yet;
The Clouds that gather round the setting sun
Do take a sober colouring from an eye
That hath kept watch o'er man's mortality;
Another race hath been, and other palms are won.
Thanks to the human heart by which we live,
Thanks to its tenderness, its joys, and fears,
To me the meanest flower that blows can give
Thoughts that do often lie too deep for tears.

Analyzing the Text

1. How have the speaker's experiences with nature renewed his belief in immortality which he initially had felt in childhood?
2. When Wordsworth speaks of a child's immensity of soul (he is referring to Samuel Coleridge's 6-year-old son, Hartley) and addresses him as "thou best Philosopher," what is his justification?

Understanding Wordsworth's Techniques

1. How do metaphors in the poem (for example, see lines 67–8; 71–2; and 126–28) help readers visualize the ideas Wordsworth explores?
2. How do the first four stanzas express the sense of loss, the next four provide an explanation, and the final three offer a consolation and a reason for Wordsworth to rejoice?

Arguing for an Interpretation

1. Although the poetic language Wordsworth uses is from another era, do his sentiments still ring true today? Do you find his analysis of the human condition credible and do you agree with his conclusions? Why or why not?
2. In what way do key aspects of this poem—Wordsworth's use of his own feelings as the true subject and his reverence for nature—illustrate quali-

ties associated with the Romantic Age (1780–1830) in literature (which included Coleridge, Byron, Shelley, and Keats)?

Les A. Murray

Les A. Murray was born in 1938 and grew up on a dairy farm in New South Wales, Australia. After retiring from a career as a translator of scholarly and technical material, he began a prolific career as a poet and writer. His work has been published in American Poetry Review, The New Yorker, The Atlantic, *and elsewhere. Collections of his poetry include* The Daylight Moon *(1988), from which the following poem is reprinted. More recently, he has written* Subhuman Redneck Poems *(1997),* Fredy Neptune: A Novel in Verse *(1999), and* Learning Human: Selected Poems Conscious and Verbal *(2001). He is regarded as Australia's leading poet, and his quirky, imaginative, and profound insights are evident in "Poetry and Religion."*

Poetry and Religion

Religions are poems. They concert
our daylight and dreaming mind, our
emotions, instinct, breath and native gesture

into the only whole thinking: poetry.
Nothing's said till it's dreamed out in words
and nothing's true that figures in words only.

A poem, compared with an arrayed religion,
may be like a soldier's one short marriage night
to die and live by. But that is a small religion.

Full religion is the large poem in loving repetition;
like any poem, it must be inexhaustible and complete
with turns where we ask Now why did the poet do that?

You can't pray a lie, said Huckleberry Finn;
you can't poe one either. It is the same mirror:
mobile, glancing, we call it poetry,

fixed centrally, we call it a religion,
and God is the poetry caught in any religion,
caught, not imprisoned. Caught as in a mirror

that he attracted, being in the world as poetry
is in the poem, a law against its closure.
There'll always be religion around while there is poetry

or a lack of it. Both are given, and intermittent,
as the action of those birds—crested pigeon, rosella
parrot—
who fly with wings shut, then beating, and again shut.

Analyzing the Text

1. In what ways do religions draw out and distill sustaining impulses that we need to live? According to Murray, how does poetry accomplish the same objective?
2. How does Murray's definition of "full religion" emphasize aspects of ritual and ceremony that are also important in poetry?

Understanding Murray's Techniques

1. Murray transforms the noun "poetry" into a verb in line 14. How does this make us think about what poetry does in a new way?
2. How does Murray use a pattern of repetition in the last words of his tercets (three-line stanzas) to evoke the way both religions and poems reflect and condense reality?

Arguing for an Interpretation

1. Readers are accustomed to sweeping claims on behalf of religions, but it is unusual to make these kinds of claims for poetry. Does Murray make a good case? Explain your answer.
2. Would people who felt a need for religion ever find the same need totally satisfied by poetry? Why or why not?

William Butler Yeats

William Butler Yeats (1865–1939), the distinguished Irish poet and playwright, was the son of an artist, John Yeats. Although initially drawn toward painting, he soon turned to poetry and became fascinated by Irish sagas and folklore. The landscape of county Sligo, where he was born and lived as a child, and the exploits of Irish heroes such as Cuchulain frequently appear in his early poetry. An early long poem, The Wanderings of Oisin *(1889), shows an intense nationalism, a feeling strengthened by his hopeless passion for the Irish patriot Maude Gonne. In 1898, he helped found the Irish Literary Theatre and later the world-renowned Abbey Theatre. As he grew older, Yeats's poetry moved from transcendentalism to a more physical realism, and the tension between the physical and the spiritual are central to poems such as*

"Sailing to Byzantium" and the "Crazy Jane" sequence. Some of his best work came late in The Tower *(1928),* The Winding Stair *(1933), and the work that was published posthumously in* Last Poems and Plays *(1940). Yeats received the Nobel Prize for literature in 1923 and is widely considered to be the greatest poet of the 20th century. The prophetic quality of Yeats's poetry springs from his earlier interest in the occult, concerns that became tempered by his premonition that the political anarchy and materialism of the modern age would inevitably lead to its own destruction. This theme is most brilliantly realized in what is perhaps his signature poem, "The Second Coming" (1920). After September 11, 2001, this poem became more relevant than ever.*

The Second Coming

Turning and turning in the widening gyre
The falcon cannot hear the falconer;
Things fall apart; the centre cannot hold;
Mere anarchy is loosed upon the world,
The blood-dimmed tide is loosed, and everywhere
The ceremony of innocence is drowned;
The best lack all conviction, while the worst
Are full of passionate intensity.
Surely some revelation is at hand;
Surely the Second Coming is at hand.[1]
The Second Coming! Hardly are those words out
When a vast image out of *Spiritus Mundi*[2]
Troubles my sight: somewhere in sands of the desert
A shape with lion body and the head of a man,

A gaze blank and pitiless as the sun,
Is moving its slow thighs, while all about it
Reel shadows of the indignant desert birds.
The darkness drops again; but now I know
That twenty centuries of stony sleep
Were vexed to nightmare by a rocking cradle,
And what rough beast, its hour come round at last,
Slouches towards Bethlehem to be born?

[1]The return (**"Second Coming"**) of Christ is prophesied in the New Testament (Matthew 24). Here the return is not of Jesus but of a terrifying inhuman embodiment of pre-Christian and pre-Grecian barbarism. The poem is a sharply prophetic response to the turmoil of Europe following World War I. [2]***Spiritus Mundi* (Latin):** Spirits of the World, that is, archetypal images in the "Great Memory" of the human psyche.

Analyzing the Text

1. How does the inability of the falconer to communicate with the falcon symbolize the loss of cohesion that the speaker sees as a defining characteristic of the 20th century?
2. Why is it ironic that the landscape in which the "rough beast" appears is the same region with which Christ's birth and the Second Coming are associated?

Understanding Yeats's Technique

1. How is the poem shaped to contrast the speaker's expectations of the Second Coming of Christ with the hideous apparition that suggests inhuman cruelty?
2. How do hard-to-define phrases such as "the blood-dimmed tide is loosed" contribute to the sense of mystery and ominous atmosphere?

Arguing for an Interpretation

1. In what sense do you understand one of the speaker's statements, such as "The best lack all conviction, while the worst/Are full of passionate intensity"?
2. Considering when the poem was written in the early 20th century, how might it still be seen as relevant and applicable to today's news? What form has the "rough beast" assumed?

Drama

William Shakespeare

William Shakespeare (1564–1616) was born in Stratford-upon-Avon, the son of a merchant, and received his early education at Stratford Grammar School. In 1582, at the age of 18, he married Anne Hathaway, who was then 26. They had a daughter, and twins (a boy and a girl). Over the next 20 years he established himself as a professional actor and playwright in London. Facts about his life are scant, but insight into his personality can be gleaned from his sonnets (of which there are 154), which were probably written in the 1590s, but were first published in 1609. The 14 lines of the Shakesperian sonnet fall into three quatrains and a couplet, rhyming abab cdcd efef gg. They express variations on familiar themes: the encroachment of time, loss, and death, and the undying power of love and friendship to resist these devastations. They hint at a story involving a young man, "a dark lady," and the poet himself, together with a "rival poet." However, Shakespeare's major contribution to literature is through his dramatic works. He created 35 plays in 25 years, encompassing the major genres in works such as Twelfth Night, As You Like It, *and* Midsummer Night's Dream *(comedy);* Richard III, Henry IV, *and* Henry V *(historical drama);* Cymbeline *and* The Tempest *(romance); and* Macbeth, Romeo and Juliet, King Lear, Othello, Antony and Cleopatra, *and* Hamlet *(tragedy).* Hamlet *(composed around 1600) is considered one of Shakespeare's most enigmatic, yet compelling dramas. Although the action of the play is somewhat convoluted, the basic events of the plot (drawn from Francois de Belleforest's* histoires tragiques, *1576) can be quickly outlined: before the action of the play begins, the elder Hamlet, King of Denmark, has been slain by his brother Claudius, who becomes King and marries Gertrude, the dead King's widow. The ghost of the deceased King (a part Shakespeare is thought to have played) appears to his son, Prince Hamlet, and implores him to avenge his murder. Although initially he is quite determined to do so, Hamlet (who is a student of philosophy) wavers and seeks additional proof that he ought to murder his Uncle Claudius. The drama concludes with a duel between Hamlet and a courtier, Laertes (whose father Hamlet has inadvertently killed and whose sister, Ophelia, has committed suicide as a result of Hamlet's rejection) and the death by poison of all the major characters. Hamlet's elaborate conjectures throughout the play (especially in his soliloquies) have made him a symbol of one whose obsessive ruminations paralyze his ability to act.*

The play was performed in the Globe theater (built in 1599), where Shakespeare was part owner and member of the acting company called The Lord Chamberlain's Men (later The King's Men). Most of Shakespeare's plays were performed in this open-air octagonal wooden structure with its thatched roof projecting over the 25 by 40 foot stage, and its three tiers of galleries, that could accommodate scenes of many different kinds from the most intimate love scenes to battle scenes with scores of characters. The central portion of the floor could be removed, as it is in the gravedigger's scene in Hamlet, *to create the illusion of an underworld. Scenery was less important than it is on the modern stage and props were limited to what could be carried on stage. Because women were not allowed to act in the theater, their parts were played by men, and boys, attired in female dress. Elizabethans were fond of elaborate costumes and sound effects, and music in the form of trumpets, kettle drums, and small cannons helped underscore the dramatic action on the stage. The Globe, which could hold up to 2500 people, attracted the most diverse audiences imaginable. The open area or "yard" in front of the stage would fill with the "groundlings" or standing spectators (including shop apprentices and servants) who paid perhaps a penny; for another penny, you could sit in the gallery sections out of the elements (good seats in the lower galleries cost another twopence). Courtiers and aristocrats might sit on the edge of the stage and play cards, converse, or even watch the play. Decorum as we know it in the modern theater did not exist, and poor and rich alike would snack throughout the performances on oranges, hazelnuts, and other foods. The Globe took its name from a sign out front that showed the mythological figure of Hercules supporting the world. A flag flew when plays would be performed. With all the theaters in London, these flags indicating performances must have been quite a colorful sight. Such was the world of the theater in Shakespeare's time.*

Background on *Hamlet*

There are a number of considerations to keep in mind while reading *Hamlet.* Queen Elizabeth I (1533–1603) was in the latter stages of her reign and had not produced an heir. Thus, one dimension of the play might have functioned as a kind of worst case scenario parable in which the rulers of a kingdom become so obsessed with internal politics and questions of rightful succession that they lose sight of the greater threat posed from without. England had a collective memory of the calamitous effect of civil war during the War of the Roses (1455–1485), and the possibility of claimants to the English throne after the Queen's death was not out of the question.

Another point to remember is that Shakespeare was expected to produce commercially competitive plays of the kind that would appeal to wide audiences (he received 10 percent of the gate receipts from each performance). A particularly successful kind of play was the revenge drama in which the hero had to go under cover and might even pretend to be mad in order to effect his revenge. The picture of the lone individual, or avenger, thrown upon his own resources in a hostile political environment was the keynote of these plays. Shakespeare was accommodating a public appetite in writing his own "revenger's tragedy." Doubtless there are personal considerations underlying the composition of the play since Shakespeare's father John, and his son Hamnet, had both died in the years immediately preceding its creation. The theme of sons seeking justice for their fathers permeates the dramatic structure of the play at all levels.

Since Shakespeare wrote for what was essentially a repertory company comprised exclusively of men, he was quite careful to restrict how many lines were given to the female characters so that the illusion would not be broken. From a modern point of view, the lack of many elements in the theater to which we are accustomed, such as a proscenium arch and curtains that close to signal the end of a scene, and elaborate background scenery, might seem to have put Shakespeare at a disadvantage. Instead, he created the world of the play through details of time, place, and setting, conveyed in evocative imagery. He also indicated the changes of scenes through end-rhymes in the speeches of the characters (for example, at the end of Scene 2 in Act I, we hear Hamlet say "Foul deeds will rise,/Though all the earth o'erwhelm them, to men's eyes"). By the time Shakespeare wrote *Hamlet,* his handling of blank verse had progressed far beyond what it was in his earlier plays and is more lifelike and closer to the rhythms of natural speech.

Moreover, his method of scene construction was closer to what we now consider normal since he does not begin with a set of characters and follow them through the play to the end, but rather introduces the main conflict through glimpses that build up suspense. For example, in Act I, Scene 1, the mood is one of unease, disturbing omens, and anxiety as to what this portends for the state of Denmark. Then when we are introduced to the court proper in Scene 2, we do not see them as they see themselves, that is, content with the new king, Claudius. The audience's suspicions are alerted and we are already predisposed to be sympathetic to Hamlet. Shakespeare also achieves a sense of cohesion and unity in what otherwise might strike some as being a chaotic and sprawling play by replicating the main action of a son seeking to avenge his father into the subplots of Laertes and Polonius, and the young Fortinbras and his father. Thus, we never lose track of the main theme.

Shakespeare also works within a consistent framework of imagery that springs from the action of the play. Claudius's use of poison to kill his brother, Hamlet's father, is equated with a terrible disease that can ravage the body politic and destroy it from within. The imagery of things being rotten, and erupting to the surface, and of a garden taken over by weeds, tie the play together on a subconscious level. Poisoning is an apt metaphor for the corrosive effects on all the relationships between the characters. For example, Hamlet no longer looks upon his mother, Gertrude, as being loyal and loving to his father. He suspects Ophelia of conniving with her father Polonius and Claudius to betray him. His former friends, Rosencrantz and Guildenstern, are willing to sell him out to win the king's favor.

We can see this process first develop when Hamlet returns from his interview with the ghost and wants to tell his friends, Horatio and Marcellus, what has transpired. He does not, but swears them to secrecy about the ghost's appearance. His paranoia dramatically accelerates when Ophelia inexplicably rejects him and then seems to serve as a shill to get Hamlet to incriminate himself.

The question as to why Hamlet is unable to effectuate his revenge and kill Claudius has been the subject of speculation by critics. The best clue might be to look at the situation as it appears to Hamlet and see how he reacts to the ghost's commands. We know that even before he had any real information, he was profoundly distressed by the fact that his mother could have remarried so quickly and to someone who, in Hamlet's and the public's estimation, was a shoddy second-rate imitation of Hamlet's father. Hamlet's first soliloquy (I.ii.129) is about suicide and this is before he even meets the ghost. Then the ghost of his father describes how he was murdered by Claudius and tells Hamlet to avenge his murder, but to leave Gertrude to heaven and to her conscience. Hamlet promises to honor the ghost's requests, forget everything else and not get distracted, and promptly begins blaming his mother and recording observations about the nature of villainy in general. Thus, from the beginning, Hamlet gets off track. He also resents being placed in the role of the avenger (I.v.197). What Hamlet really wants to achieve is to reverse Gertrude's good opinion of Claudius and he could not do this were he to kill Claudius first. Hamlet's motives might be described as wanting to set the record straight even more than he wants to save his father, who is burning in purgatory while this act goes unavenged. Hamlet's obsession with the truth being known is evident in his last request, as he is dying, when he asks Horatio to stay alive and set the record straight by telling his story.

The "play within the play" (III.ii.) performed before the court is designed to get Hamlet out from under his obligation by getting Claudius to confess publicly and thus, either sanction Hamlet's revenge or pass the burden onto the court. It is only when Gertrude dies at the end of the play, that Hamlet is finally able to bring himself to kill Claudius.

Another element that makes the play produce the effects of "pity and terror" (as Aristotle discussed in *Poetics*) is in what happens to Hamlet and the kind of person he becomes as a result of his response to this burden. We might ask how Hamlet becomes part of the problem rather than the solution.

Hamlet's slaying of Polonius and Rosencrantz and Guildenstern is handled by Shakespeare in ways that still allow the audience to be sympathetic to him. However, the causes of Ophelia's madness and suicide are quite another matter. Hamlet's first visit to Ophelia (II.i.78) after being denied access to her, and after his conversation with the ghost, might be understood as revealing his urgent desire to confide in her. He then has second thoughts, and does not, and begins to act the part of someone who has gone mad. He also has written a letter to her affirming his love which she gives to her father, Polonius, who in turn brings it to Claudius (II.ii.109). From this point, Hamlet's behavior towards Ophelia becomes suspect. He accuses Polonius of being a fishmonger or pimp (II.ii.174), warns him about the dangers of letting Ophelia loose as she might become pregnant, and alludes to the biblical story of Jephthah (II.ii.358) who sent his daughter out to be ravaged by a mob rather than give them the angels he was harboring. Add to these, Hamlet's explicit sexual comments to Ophelia (III.ii.94) while sitting by her side during the performance of the play and we have the framework for looking more closely at the songs that Ophelia sings during her mad scene (IV.v.23-66). The story they tell is of a girl who offers herself to a young man who seduces her and then tortures her with this fact. We can understand why Ophelia might have offered herself to Hamlet to restore her relationship with him and prove her love. We can also understand why Hamlet castigates her for being no better than Gertrude. The final piece of evidence is implicit in Hamlet's overly defensive protestations, upon learning of her death, that he loved her more than her brother, Laertes, ever could. At this moment he might have linked his treatment of her with her suicide. The consummate irony concerning Ophelia is that both Polonius and Laertes had told her that Hamlet could never be free to marry her. In fact Gertrude says at Ophelia's funeral that she had hoped Ophelia would be Hamlet's bride.

Digression is an important theme in the play as are failures of memory and volition. These link Hamlet's anguish in not being able to accomplish the mission he has accepted with other numerous examples of these kinds of lapses. Polonius's inability to stick to the subject (when he starts to critique Hamlet's letter for style in II.ii.111), Pyrrhus's inability to strike Priam in the First Player's speech about the siege of Troy (II.ii.427), Claudius's inability to truly pray for forgiveness (III.iii.38), Laertes' inability to kill Hamlet when he has the chance to do so (V.ii.270), are but a few.

Most importantly, Hamlet's soliloquies are filled with self-accusations and recriminations. He becomes aware that he lacks some vital element in his nature since he cannot fulfill his vow. It is this knowledge about his own limitations that makes Hamlet a tragic figure. The universal appeal of this play is that we can all, to some degree, see ourselves in Hamlet.

Hamlet, Prince of Denmark

[Dramatis Personae

GHOST *of Hamlet, the former King of Denmark*
CLAUDIUS, *King of Denmark, the former King's brother*
GERTRUDE, *Queen of Denmark, widow of the former King and now wife of Claudius*
HAMLET, *Prince of Denmark, son of the late King and of Gertrude*

POLONIUS, *councillor to the King*
LAERTES, *his son*
OPHELIA, *his daughter*
REYNALDO, *his servant*

HORATIO, *Hamlet's friend and fellow student*

VOLTIMAND,
CORNELIUS,
ROSENCRANTZ,
GUILDENSTERN, } *members of the Danish court*
OSRIC,
A GENTLEMAN,
A LORD,

BERNARDO,
FRANCISCO, } officers and soldiers on watch
MARCELLUS,

FORTINBRAS, Prince of Norway
CAPTAIN in his army

Three or Four PLAYERS, *taking the roles of* PROLOGUE, PLAYER KING, PLAYER QUEEN, *and* LUCIANUS
Two MESSENGERS
FIRST SAILOR
Two CLOWNS, *a gravedigger and his companion*
PRIEST
FIRST AMBASSADOR *from England*

Lords, Soldiers, Attendants, Guards, other Players, Followers of Laertes, other Sailors, another Ambassador or Ambassadors from England

SCENE: *Denmark*]

1.1

Enter Bernardo and Francisco, two sentinels, [*meeting*].

BERNARDO. Who's there?
FRANCISCO.
Nay, answer me. Stand and unfold yourself. 2
BERNARDO. Long live the King!
FRANCISCO. Bernardo?
BERNARDO. He.
FRANCISCO.
You come most carefully upon your hour.
BERNARDO.
'Tis now struck twelve. Get thee to bed, Francisco.
FRANCISCO.
For this relief much thanks. 'Tis bitter cold,
And I am sick at heart.
BERNARDO. Have you had quiet guard?
FRANCISCO. Not a mouse stirring.
BERNARDO. Well, good night.
If you do meet Horatio and Marcellus,
The rivals of my watch, bid them make haste. 14

1.1 Location: Elsinore castle. A guard platform.
2 me (Francisco emphasizes that *he* is the sentry currently on watch.) **unfold yourself** reveal your identity. **14 rivals** partners

Enter Horatio and Marcellus.

FRANCISCO.
I think I hear them.—Stand, ho! Who is there?
HORATIO. Friends to this ground.
MARCELLUS. And liegemen to the Dane.
FRANCISCO. Give you good night.
MARCELLUS.
Oh, farewell, honest soldier. Who hath relieved you?
FRANCISCO.
Bernardo hath my place. Give you good night.

Exit Francisco.

MARCELLUS. Holla! Bernardo!
BERNARDO. Say, what, is Horatio there?
HORATIO. A piece of him.
BERNARDO.
Welcome, Horatio. Welcome, good Marcellus.
HORATIO.
What, has this thing appeared again tonight?
BERNARDO. I have seen nothing.
MARCELLUS.
Horatio says 'tis but our fantasy,
And will not let belief take hold of him
Touching this dreaded sight twice seen of us.
Therefore I have entreated him along
With us to watch the minutes of this night,
That if again this apparition come
He may approve our eyes and speak to it.
HORATIO.
Tush, tush, 'twill not appear.
BERNARDO. Sit down awhile,
And let us once again assail your ears,
That are so fortified against our story,
What we have two nights seen.
HORATIO. Well, sit we down,
And let us hear Bernardo speak of this.
BERNARDO. Last night of all,
When yond same star that's westward from the pole
Had made his course t'illume that part of heaven
Where now it burns, Marcellus and myself,
The bell then beating one—

Enter Ghost.

MARCELLUS.
Peace, break thee off! Look where it comes again!

---

16 ground country, land **17 liegemen to the Dane** men sworn to serve the Danish king **18 Give** May God give **27 fantasy** imagination **30 along** to come along **31 watch** keep watch during **33 approve** corroborate **39 Last . . . all** i.e., This *very* last night. (Emphatic.) **40 pole** polestar, north star **41 his** its. **t'illume** to illuminate

BERNARDO.
In the same figure like the King that's dead.
MARCELLUS.
Thou art a scholar. Speak to it, Horatio.
BERNARDO.
Looks 'a not like the King? Mark it, Horatio.
HORATIO.
Most like. It harrows me with fear and wonder.
BERNARDO.
It would be spoke to.
MARCELLUS. Speak to it, Horatio.
HORATIO.
What art thou that usurp'st this time of night,
Together with that fair and warlike form
In which the majesty of buried Denmark
Did sometime march? By heaven, I charge thee, speak!
MARCELLUS.
It is offended.
BERNARDO. See, it stalks away.
HORATIO.
Stay! Speak, speak! I charge thee, speak!

Exit Ghost.

MARCELLUS. 'Tis gone and will not answer.
BERNARDO.
How now, Horatio? You tremble and look pale.
Is not this something more than fantasy?
What think you on't?
HORATIO.
Before my God, I might not this believe
Without the sensible and true avouch
Of mine own eyes.
MARCELLUS. Is it not like the King?
HORATIO. As thou art to thyself.
Such was the very armor he had on
When he the ambitious Norway combated.
So frowned he once when, in an angry parle,
He smote the sledded Polacks on the ice.
'Tis strange.
MARCELLUS.
Thus twice before, and jump at this dead hour,
With martial stalk hath he gone by our watch.
HORATIO.
In what particular thought to work I know not,

---

46 scholar one learned enough to know how to question a ghost properly **47 'a** he **49 It . . . to** (It was commonly believed that a ghost could not speak until spoken to.) **50 usurp'st** wrongfully takes over **52 buried Denmark** the buried King of Denmark **53 sometime** formerly **59 on't** of it **61 sensible** confirmed by the senses. **avouch** warrant, evidence **65 Norway** King of Norway **66 parle** parley **67 sledded** traveling on sleds. **Polacks** Poles **69 jump** exactly **70 stalk** stride **71 to work** i.e., to collect my thoughts and try to understand this

But in the gross and scope of mine opinion
This bodes some strange eruption to our state.

MARCELLUS.
Good now, sit down, and tell me, he that knows,
Why this same strict and most observant watch
So nightly toils the subject of the land,
And why such daily cast of brazen cannon
And foreign mart for implements of war,
Why such impress of shipwrights, whose sore task
Does not divide the Sunday from the week.
What might be toward, that this sweaty haste
Doth make the night joint-laborer with the day?
Who is't that can inform me?

HORATIO. That can I;
At least, the whisper goes so. Our last king,
Whose image even but now appeared to us,
Was, as you know, by Fortinbras of Norway,
Thereto pricked on by a most emulate pride,
Dared to the combat; in which our valiant Hamlet—
For so this side of our known world esteemed him—
Did slay this Fortinbras; who by a sealed compact
Well ratified by law and heraldry
Did forfeit, with his life, all those his lands
Which he stood seized of, to the conqueror;
Against the which a moiety competent
Was gagèd by our king, which had returned
To the inheritance of Fortinbras
Had he been vanquisher, as, by the same cov'nant
And carriage of the article designed,
His fell to Hamlet. Now, sir, young Fortinbras,
Of unimprovèd mettle hot and full,
Hath in the skirts of Norway here and there
Sharked up a list of lawless resolutes
For food and diet to some enterprise
That hath a stomach in't, which is no other—
As it doth well appear unto our state—
But to recover of us, by strong hand
And terms compulsatory, those foresaid lands
So by his father lost. And this, I take it,

72 gross and scope general drift **74 Good now** (An expression denoting entreaty or expostulation.) **76 toils** causes to toil. **subject** subjects **77 cast** casting **78 mart** shopping **79 impress** impressment, conscription **81 toward** in preparation **87 Thereto . . . pride** (Refers to old Fortinbras, not the Danish King.) **pricked** on incited. **emulate** emulous, ambitious **89 this . . . world** i.e., all Europe, the Western world **90 sealed** certified, confirmed **91 heraldry** chivalry **93 seized** possessed **94 Against the** in return for. **moiety competent** corresponding portion **95 gagèd** engaged, pledged. **had returned** would have passed **96 inheritance** possession **97 cov'nant** i.e., the *sealed compact* of line 90 **98 carriage . . . designed** purport of the article referred to **100 unimprovèd mettle** untried, undisciplined spirits **101 skirts** outlying regions, outskirts **102–4 Sharked . . . in't** rounded up (as a shark scoops up fish) a troop of lawless desperadoes to feed and supply an enterprise of considerable daring

Is the main motive of our preparations,
The source of this our watch, and the chief head
Of this posthaste and rummage in the land.

BERNARDO.
I think it be no other but e'en so.
Well may it sort that this portentous figure
Comes armèd through our watch so like the King
That was and is the question of these wars.

HORATIO.
A mote it is to trouble the mind's eye.
In the most high and palmy state of Rome,
A little ere the mightiest Julius fell,
The graves stood tenantless, and the sheeted dead
Did squeak and gibber in the Roman streets;
As stars with trains of fire and dews of blood,
Disasters in the sun; and the moist star
Upon whose influence Neptune's empire stands
Was sick almost to doomsday with eclipse.
And even the like precurse of feared events,
As harbingers preceding still the fates
And prologue to the omen coming on,
Have heaven and earth together demonstrated
Unto our climatures and countrymen.

Enter Ghost.

But soft, behold! Lo, where it comes again!
I'll cross it, though it blast me. (*It spreads his arms.*) Stay, illusion!
If thou hast any sound or use of voice,
Speak to me!
If there be any good thing to be done
That may to thee do ease and grace to me,
Speak to me!
If thou art privy to thy country's fate,
Which, happily, foreknowing may avoid,
Oh, speak!
Or if thou hast uphoarded in thy life
Extorted treasure in the womb of earth,
For which, they say, you spirits oft walk in death,
Speak of it! (*The cock crows.*) Stay and speak!—Stop it, Marcellus.

---

110 head source **111 posthaste and rummage** frenetic activity and bustle **113 Well . . . sort** That would explain why **115 question** focus of contention **116 mote** speck of dust **117 palmy** flourishing **118 Julius** Julius Caesar **119 sheeted** shrouded **121 As** (This abrupt transition suggests that matter is possibly omitted between lines 120 and 121.) **trains** trails **122 Disasters** unfavorable signs or aspects. **moist star** i.e., moon, governing tides **123 Neptune's . . . stands** the sea depends **124 Was . . . eclipse** was eclipsed nearly to the cosmic darkness predicted for the second coming of Christ and the ending of the world (see Matthew 24:29 and Revelation 6.12). **125 precurse** heralding, foreshadowing **126 harbingers** forerunners. **still** always **127 omen** calamitous event **129 climatures** climes, regions **130 soft** i.e., enough, break off **131 cross** stand in its path, confront. **blast** wither, strike with a curse. **s.d.** ***his*** its **137 privy to** in on the secret of **138 happily** haply, perchance

MARCELLUS.
Shall I strike at it with my partisan? 144
HORATIO. Do, if it will not stand. [*They strike at it.*]
BERNARDO. 'Tis here! 146
HORATIO. 'Tis here! [*Exit Ghost.*] 147
MARCELLUS. 'Tis gone.
We do it wrong, being so majestical,
To offer it the show of violence,
For it is as the air invulnerable,
And our vain blows malicious mockery.
BERNARDO.
It was about to speak when the cock crew.
HORATIO.
And then it started like a guilty thing
Upon a fearful summons. I have heard
The cock, that is the trumpet to the morn, 156
Doth with his lofty and shrill-sounding throat
Awake the god of day, and at his warning,
Whether in sea or fire, in earth or air,
Th'extravagant and erring spirit hies 160
To his confine; and of the truth herein
This present object made probation. 162
MARCELLUS.
It faded on the crowing of the cock.
Some say that ever 'gainst that season comes 164
Wherein our Savior's birth is celebrated,
This bird of dawning singeth all night long,
And then, they say, no spirit dare stir abroad;
The nights are wholesome, then no planets strike, 168
No fairy takes, nor witch hath power to charm, 169
So hallowed and so gracious is that time. 170
HORATIO.
So have I heard and do in part believe it.
But, look, the morn in russet mantle clad 172
Walks o'er the dew of yon high eastward hill.
Break we our watch up, and by my advice
Let us impart what we have seen tonight
Unto young Hamlet; for upon my life,
This spirit, dumb to us, will speak to him.
Do you consent we shall acquaint him with it,
As needful in our loves, fitting our duty?
MARCELLUS.
Let's do't, I pray, and I this morning know
Where we shall find him most conveniently.

Exeunt.

---

144 partisan long-handled spear **146–7 'Tis Here! 'Tis here!** (Perhaps they attempt to strike at the Ghost, but are baffled by its seeming ability to be here and there and nowhere.) **156 trumpet** trumpeter **160 extravagant and erring** wandering beyond bounds. (The words have similar meaning.) **hies** hastens **162 probation** proof **164 'gainst** just before **168 strike** destroy by evil influence **169 takes** bewitches **charm** cast a spell, control by enchantment **170 gracious** full of grace **172 russet** reddish brown

1.2

Flourish. Enter Claudius, King of Denmark, Gertrude [*the*] *Queen, Council, as Polonius and his son Laertes, Hamlet, cum aliis* [*including Voltimand and Cornelius*].

KING.
Though yet of Hamlet our dear brother's death 1
The memory be green, and that it us befitted
To bear our hearts in grief and our whole kingdom
To be contracted in one brow of woe,
Yet so far hath discretion fought with nature
That we with wisest sorrow think on him
Together with remembrance of ourselves.
Therefore our sometime sister, now our queen, 8
Th'imperial jointress to this warlike state, 9
Have we, as 'twere with a defeated joy—
With an auspicious and a dropping eye, 11
With mirth in funeral and with dirge in marriage,
In equal scale weighing delight and dole— 13
Taken to wife. [*To the others*] Nor have we herein barred
Your better wisdoms, which have freely gone
With this affair along. For all, our thanks.
Now follows that you know young Fortinbras, 17
Holding a weak supposal of our worth, 18
Or thinking by our late dear brother's death
Our state to be disjoint and out of frame, 20
Co-leaguèd with this dream of his advantage, 21
He hath not failed to pester us with message
Importing the surrender of those lands 23
Lost by his father, with all bonds of law, 24
To our most valiant brother. So much for him.
Now for ourself and for this time of meeting.
Thus much the business is: we have here writ
To Norway, uncle of young Fortinbras—
Who, impotent and bed-rid, scarcely hears 29
Of this his nephew's purpose—to suppress
His further gait herein, in that the levies, 31
The lists, and full proportions are all made 32
Out of his subject; and we here dispatch 33
You, good Cornelius, and you, Voltimand,

1.2 Location: The castle.
0.2 ***as*** i.e., such as, including. ***cum aliis*** with others **1 our** my. (The royal "we"; also in the following lines.) **8 sometime** former **9 jointress** woman possessing property with her husband **11 With . . . eye** with one eye smiling and the other weeping **13 dole** grief **17 Now . . . know** Next, you need to be informed that **18 weak supposal** low estimate **20 disjoint . . . frame** in a state of total disorder **21 Co-leaguèd . . . advantage** joined to his illusory sense of having the advantage over us and to his vision of future success **23 Importing** having for its substance **24 with . . . law** (See 1.1.91, "Well ratified by law and heraldry.") **29 impotent** helpless **31 His** i.e., Fortinbras'. **gait** proceeding **31–3 in that . . . subject** since the levying of troops and supplies is drawn entirely from the King of Norway's own subjects

For bearers of this greeting to old Norway,
Giving to you no further personal power
To business with the King more than the scope
Of these dilated articles allow. [*He gives a paper.*]
Farewell, and let your haste commend your duty.

CORNELIUS, VOLTIMAND.
In that, and all things, will we show our duty.

KING.
We doubt it nothing. Heartily farewell.
[*Exeunt Voltimand and Cornelius.*]

And now, Laertes, what's the news with you?
You told us of some suit; what is 't, Laertes?
You cannot speak of reason to the Dane
And lose your voice. What wouldst thou beg, Laertes,
That shall not be my offer, not thy asking?
The head is not more native to the heart,
The hand more instrumental to the mouth,
Than is the throne of Denmark to thy father.
What wouldst thou have, Laertes?

LAERTES. My dread lord,
Your leave and favor to return to France,
From whence though willingly I came to Denmark
To show my duty in your coronation,
Yet now I must confess, that duty done,
My thoughts and wishes bend again toward France
And bow them to your gracious leave and pardon.

KING.
Have you your father's leave? What says Polonius?

POLONIUS.
H'ath, my lord, wrung from me my slow leave
By laborsome petition, and at last
Upon his will I sealed my hard consent.
I do beseech you, give him leave to go.

KING.
Take thy fair hour, Laertes. Time be thine,
And thy best graces spend it at thy will!
But now, my cousin Hamlet, and my son—

HAMLET.
A little more than kin, and less than kind.

38 dilated set out at length **39 let . . . duty** let your swift obeying of orders, rather than mere words, express your dutifulness. **41 nothing** not at all. **44 the Dane** the Danish king **45 lose your voice** waste your speech. **47 native** closely connected, related **48 instrumental** serviceable **51 leave and favor** kind permission **56 bow . . . pardon** entreatingly make a deep bow, asking your permission to depart **58 H'ath** He has **60 sealed** (as if sealing a legal document). **hard** reluctant **62 Take thy fair hour** Enjoy your time of youth **63 And . . . will** and may your time be spent in exercising your best qualities. **64 cousin** any kin not of the immediate family **65 A little . . . kind** Too close a blood relation, and yet we are less than kinsmen in that our relationship lacks affection and is indeed unnatural. (Hamlet plays on *kind* as [1] kindly [2] belonging to nature, suggesting that Claudius is not the same kind of being as the rest of humanity. The line is often delivered as an aside, though it need not be.)

KING.
How is it that the clouds still hang on you?
HAMLET.
Not so, my lord. I am too much in the sun. 67
QUEEN.
Good Hamlet, cast thy nighted color off, 68
And let thine eye look like a friend on Denmark. 69
Do not forever with thy vailèd lids 70
Seek for thy noble father in the dust.
Thou know'st 'tis common, all that lives must die, 72
Passing through nature to eternity.
HAMLET.
Ay, madam, it is common.
QUEEN. If it be,
Why seems it so particular with thee? 75
HAMLET.
Seems, madam? Nay, it is. I know not "seems."
'Tis not alone my inky cloak, good mother,
Nor customary suits of solemn black, 78
Nor windy suspiration of forced breath, 79
No, nor the fruitful river in the eye, 80
Nor the dejected havior of the visage, 81
Together with all forms, moods, shapes of grief, 82
That can denote me truly. These indeed seem,
For they are actions that a man might play.
But I have that within which passes show;
These but the trappings and the suits of woe.
KING.
'Tis sweet and commendable in your nature, Hamlet,
To give these mourning duties to your father.
But you must know your father lost a father,
That father lost, lost his, and the survivor bound
In filial obligation for some term
To do obsequious sorrow. But to persever 92
In obstinate condolement is a course 93
Of impious stubbornness. 'Tis unmanly grief.
It shows a will most incorrect to heaven,
A heart unfortified, a mind impatient, 96
An understanding simple and unschooled. 97
For what we know must be and is as common
As any the most vulgar thing to sense, 99
Why should we in our peevish opposition
Take it to heart? Fie, 'tis a fault to heaven,

---

67 the sun i.e., the sunshine of the King's royal favor (with pun on *son*) **68 nighted color** (1) mourning garments of black (2) dark melancholy **69 Denmark** the King of Denmark **70 vailèd lids** lowered eyes **72 common** of universal occurrence. (But Hamlet plays on the sense of "vulgar" in line 74.) **75 particular** personal **78 customary** customary to mourning **79 suspiration** sighing **80 fruitful** abundant **81 havior** expression **82 moods** outward expression of feeling **92 obsequious** suited to obsequies or funerals. **93 condolement** sorrowing **96 unfortified** i.e., against adversity **97 simple** ignorant **99 As . . . sense** as the most ordinary experience

A fault against the dead, a fault to nature,
To reason most absurd, whose common theme
Is death of fathers, and who still hath cried,
From the first corpse till he that died today,
"This must be so." We pray you, throw to earth
This unprevailing woe and think of us
As of a father; for let the world take note,
You are the most immediate to our throne,
And with no less nobility of love
Than that which dearest father bears his son
Do I impart toward you. For your intent
In going back to school in Wittenberg,
It is most retrograde to our desire,
And we beseech you bend you to remain
Here in the cheer and comfort of our eye,
Our chiefest courtier, cousin, and our son.

QUEEN.
Let not thy mother lose her prayers, Hamlet.
I pray thee, stay with us, go not to Wittenberg.

HAMLET.
I shall in all my best obey you, madam.

KING.
Why, 'tis a loving and a fair reply.
Be as ourself in Denmark. Madam, come.
This gentle and unforced accord of Hamlet
Sits smiling to my heart, in grace whereof
No jocund health that Denmark drinks today
But the great cannon to the clouds shall tell,
And the King's rouse the heaven shall bruit again,
Respeaking earthly thunder. Come away.

Flourish. Exeunt all but Hamlet.

HAMLET.
Oh, that this too too sullied flesh would melt,
Thaw, and resolve itself into a dew!
Or that the Everlasting had not fixed
His canon 'gainst self-slaughter! Oh God, God,
How weary, stale, flat, and unprofitable
Seem to me all the uses of this world!
Fie on't, ah fie! 'Tis an unweeded garden

---

104 still always **105 the first corpse** (Abel's) **107 unprevailing** unavailing, useless **109 most immediate** next in succession **112 impart toward** liberally bestow on. **For** As for **113 to school** i.e., to your studies. **Wittenberg** famous German university founded in 1502 **114 retrograde** contrary **115 bend you** incline yourself **120 in all my best** to the best of my ability **124 to** i.e., at. **grace** thanksgiving **125 jocund** merry **127 rouse** drinking of a draft of liquor. **bruit again** loudly echo. **128 thunder** i.e., of trumpet and kettledrum, sounded when the King drinks; see 1.4.8–12 **129 sullied** defiled. (The early quartos read "sallied"; the Folio, "solid.") **132 canon** law

That grows to seed. Things rank and gross in nature
Possess it merely. That it should come to this! 137
But two months dead—nay, not so much, not two.
So excellent a king, that was to this 139
Hyperion to a satyr, so loving to my mother 140
That he might not beteem the winds of heaven 141
Visit her face too roughly. Heaven and earth,
Must I remember? Why, she would hang on him
As if increase of appetite had grown
By what it fed on, and yet within a month—
Let me not think on't; frailty, thy name is woman!—
A little month, or ere those shoes were old 147
With which she followed my poor father's body,
Like Niobe, all tears, why she, even she— 149
Oh God, a beast, that wants discourse of reason, 150
Would have mourned longer—married with my uncle,
My father's brother, but no more like my father
Than I to Hercules. Within a month,
Ere yet the salt of most unrighteous tears
Had left the flushing in her gallèd eyes, 155
She married. Oh, most wicked speed, to post 156
With such dexterity to incestuous sheets! 157
It is not, nor it cannot come to good.
But break, my heart, for I must hold my tongue.

Enter Horatio, Marcellus, and Bernardo.

HORATIO.
Hail to Your Lordship!

HAMLET. I am glad to see you well.
HORATIO!—or I do forget myself.

HORATIO.
The same, my lord, and your poor servant ever.

HAMLET.
Sir, my good friend; I'll change that name with you. 163
And what make you from Wittenberg, Horatio?— 164
Marcellus.

MARCELLUS. My good lord.

HAMLET.
I am very glad to see you. [*To Bernardo.*] Good even, sir.—
But what in faith make you from Wittenberg?

---

137 merely completely **139 to** in comparison to **140 Hyperion** Titan sun-god, father of Helios. **satyr** a lecherous creature of classical mythology, half-human but with a goat's legs, tail, ears, and horns **141 beteem** allow **147 or ere** even before **149 Niobe** Tantalus' daughter, Queen of Thebes, who boasted that she had more sons and daughters than Leto; for this, Apollo and Artemis, children of Leto, slew her fourteen children. She was turned by Zeus into a stone that continually dropped tears. **150 wants . . . reason** lacks the faculty of reason **155 gallèd** irritated, inflamed **156 post** hasten **157 incestuous** (In Shakespeare's day, the marriage of a man like Claudius to his deceased brother's wife was considered incestuous.) **163 change that name** i.e., give and receive reciprocally the name of "friend" rather than talk of "servant." Or Hamlet may be saying, "No, I am *your* servant." **164 make you from** are you doing away from

HORATIO.
A truant disposition, good my lord.
HAMLET.
I would not hear your enemy say so,
Nor shall you do my ear that violence
To make it truster of your own report 171
Against yourself. I know you are no truant.
But what is your affair in Elsinore?
We'll teach you to drink deep ere you depart.
HORATIO.
My lord, I came to see your father's funeral.
HAMLET.
I prithee, do not mock me, fellow student;
I think it was to see my mother's wedding.
HORATIO.
Indeed, my lord, it followed hard upon. 178
HAMLET.
Thrift, thrift, Horatio! The funeral baked meats 179
Did coldly furnish forth the marriage tables. 180
Would I had met my dearest foe in heaven 181
Or ever I had seen that day, Horatio! 182
My father!—Methinks I see my father.
HORATIO.
Where, my lord?
HAMLET. In my mind's eye, Horatio.
HORATIO.
I saw him once. 'A was a goodly king. 185
HAMLET.
'A was a man. Take him for all in all,
I shall not look upon his like again.
HORATIO.
My lord, I think I saw him yesternight.
HAMLET. Saw? Who?
HORATIO. My lord, the King your father.
HAMLET. The King my father?
HORATIO.
Season your admiration for a while 192
With an attent ear till I may deliver, 193
Upon the witness of these gentlemen,
This marvel to you.
HAMLET. For God's love, let me hear!
HORATIO.
Two nights together had these gentlemen,
Marcellus and Bernardo, on their watch,
In the dead waste and middle of the night, 198
Been thus encountered. A figure like your father,

---

171 To . . . of to make it trust **178 hard** close **179 baked meats** meat pies **180 coldly** i.e., as cold leftovers **181 dearest** closest (and therefore deadliest) **182 Or ever** ere, before **185 'A** He **192 Season your admiration** Moderate your astonishment **193 attent** attentive **198 dead waste** desolate stillness

Armèd at point exactly, cap-à-pie, 200
Appears before them, and with solemn march
Goes slow and stately by them. Thrice he walked
By their oppressed and fear-surprisèd eyes
Within his truncheon's length, whilst they, distilled 204
Almost to jelly with the act of fear, 205
Stand dumb and speak not to him. This to me
In dreadful secrecy impart they did, 207
And I with them the third night kept the watch,
Where, as they had delivered, both in time,
Form of the thing, each word made true and good,
The apparition comes. I knew your father;
These hands are not more like.

HAMLET. But where was this?

MARCELLUS.
My lord, upon the platform where we watch.

HAMLET.
Did you not speak to it?

HORATIO. My lord, I did,
But answer made it none. Yet once methought
It lifted up it head and did address 216
Itself to motion, like as it would speak; 217
But even then the morning cock crew loud, 218
And at the sound it shrunk in haste away
And vanished from our sight.

HAMLET. 'Tis very strange.

HORATIO.
As I do live, my honored lord, 'tis true,
And we did think it writ down in our duty
To let you know of it.

HAMLET.
Indeed, indeed, sirs. But this troubles me.
Hold you the watch tonight?

ALL. We do, my lord.

HAMLET. Armed, say you?

ALL. Armed, my lord.

HAMLET. From top to toe?

ALL. My lord, from head to foot.

HAMLET. Then saw you not his face?

HORATIO.
Oh, yes, my lord, he wore his beaver up. 231

HAMLET. What looked he, frowningly? 232

HORATIO.
A countenance more in sorrow than in anger.

HAMLET. Pale or red?

HORATIO. Nay, very pale.

HAMLET. And fixed his eyes upon you?

---

200 at point correctly in every detail. **cap-à-pie** from head to foot **204 truncheon** officer's staff. **distilled** dissolved **205 act** action, operation **207 dreadful** full of dread **216 it** its **216–17 did . . . speak** acted as though it was about to speak **218 even then** at that very instant **231 beaver** visor on the helmet **232 What** how

HORATIO. Most constantly.
HAMLET. I would I had been there.
HORATIO. It would have much amazed you.
HAMLET. Very like, very like. Stayed it long?
HORATIO.
While one with moderate haste might tell a hundred. 241
MARCELLUS, BERNARDO. Longer, longer.
HORATIO. Not when I saw 't.
HAMLET. His beard was grizzled—no?
HORATIO.
It was, as I have seen it in his life,
A sable silvered.
HAMLET. I will watch tonight.
Perchance 'twill walk again.
HORATIO. I warrant it will.
HAMLET.
If it assume my noble father's person,
I'll speak to it though hell itself should gape
And bid me hold my peace. I pray you all,
If you have hitherto concealed this sight,
Let it be tenable in your silence still, 252
And whatsoever else shall hap tonight,
Give it an understanding but no tongue.
I will requite your loves. So, fare you well.
Upon the platform twixt eleven and twelve
I'll visit you.
ALL. Our duty to Your Honor.
HAMLET.
Your loves, as mine to you. Farewell. 258

Exeunt [*all but Hamlet*].

My father's spirit in arms! All is not well.
I doubt some foul play. Would the night were come! 260
Till then sit still, my soul. Foul deeds will rise,
Though all the earth o'erwhelm them, to men's eyes.

Exit.

1.3

Enter Laertes and Ophelia, his sister.

LAERTES.
My necessaries are embarked. Farewell.
And, sister, as the winds give benefit
And convoy is assistant, do not sleep 3
But let me hear from you.
OPHELIA. Do you doubt that?

241 tell count **252 tenable** held **258 Your loves** i.e., Say "Your loves" to me, not just your "duty." **260 doubt** suspect
1.3 Location: Polonius' chambers.
3 convoy is assistant means of conveyance are available

LAERTES.
For Hamlet, and the trifling of his favor, 5
Hold it a fashion and a toy in blood, 6
A violet in the youth of primy nature, 7
Forward, not permanent, sweet, not lasting, 8
The perfume and suppliance of a minute— 9
No more.

OPHELIA. No more but so?

LAERTES. Think it no more.
For nature crescent does not grow alone 11
In thews and bulk, but as this temple waxes 12
The inward service of the mind and soul 13
Grows wide withal. Perhaps he loves you now, 14
And now no soil nor cautel doth besmirch 15
The virtue of his will; but you must fear, 16
His greatness weighed, his will is not his own. 17
For he himself is subject to his birth.
He may not, as unvalued persons do,
Carve for himself, for on his choice depends 20
The safety and health of this whole state,
And therefore must his choice be circumscribed
Unto the voice and yielding of that body 23
Whereof he is the head. Then if he says he loves you,
It fits your wisdom so far to believe it
As he in his particular act and place 26
May give his saying deed, which is no further
Than the main voice of Denmark goes withal. 28
Then weigh what loss your honor may sustain
If with too credent ear you list his songs, 30
Or lose your heart, or your chaste treasure open
To his unmastered importunity. 32
Fear it, Ophelia, fear it, my dear sister,
And keep you in the rear of your affection, 34
Out of the shot and danger of desire.
The chariest maid is prodigal enough 36
If she unmask her beauty to the moon. 37
Virtue itself scapes not calumnious strokes.
The canker galls the infants of the spring 39

---

5 For As for **6 toy in blood** passing amorous fancy **7 primy** in its prime, springtime **8 Forward** precocious **9 suppliance** pastime, something to fill the time **11–14 For nature . . . withal** For nature, as it ripens, does not grow only in physical strength, but as the body matures the inner qualities of mind and soul grow along with it. (Laertes warns Ophelia that the mature Hamlet may not cling to his youthful interests.) **15 soil nor cautel** blemish nor deceit **16 The . . . will** the purity of his desire **17 His greatness weighed** taking into account his high fortune **20 Carve** i.e., choose **23 voice and yielding** assent, approval **26 in . . . place** in his particular restricted circumstances **28 main voice** general assent. **withal** along with **30 credent** credulous. **list** listen to **32 unmastered** uncontrolled **34 keep . . . affection** don't advance as far as your affection might lead you. (A military metaphor.) **36 chariest** most scrupulously modest **37 If she unmask** if she does no more than show her beauty. **moon** (Symbol of chastity.) **39 canker galls** cankerworm destroys

Too oft before their buttons be disclosed, 40
And in the morn and liquid dew of youth 41
Contagious blastments are most imminent. 42
Be wary then; best safety lies in fear.
Youth to itself rebels, though none else near. 44

OPHELIA.
I shall the effect of this good lesson keep
As watchman to my heart. But, good my brother,
Do not, as some ungracious pastors do, 47
Show me the steep and thorny way to heaven,
Whiles like a puffed and reckless libertine 49
Himself the primrose path of dalliance treads,
And recks not his own rede.

Enter Polonius.

LAERTES. Oh, fear me not. 51
I stay too long. But here my father comes.
A double blessing is a double grace; 53
Occasion smiles upon a second leave. 54

POLONIUS.
Yet here, Laertes? Aboard, aboard, for shame!
The wind sits in the shoulder of your sail,
And you are stayed for. There—my blessing with thee!
And these few precepts in thy memory
Look thou character. Give thy thoughts no tongue, 59
Nor any unproportioned thought his act. 60
Be thou familiar, but by no means vulgar. 61
Those friends thou hast, and their adoption tried, 62
Grapple them unto thy soul with hoops of steel,
But do not dull thy palm with entertainment 64
Of each new-hatched, unfledged courage. Beware 65
Of entrance to a quarrel, but being in,
Bear't that th'opposèd may beware of thee. 67
Give every man thy ear, but few thy voice;
Take each man's censure, but reserve thy judgment. 69
Costly thy habit as thy purse can buy, 70
But not expressed in fancy; rich, not gaudy, 71
For the apparel oft proclaims the man,
And they in France of the best rank and station
Are of a most select and generous chief in that. 74

---

40 buttons be disclosed buds be opened **41 liquid dew** i.e., time when dew is fresh and bright **42 blastments** blights **44 Youth . . . rebels** Youth yields to the rebellion of the flesh **47 ungracious** ungodly **49 puffed** bloated, or swollen with pride **51 recks** heeds. **rede** counsel. **fear me not** don't worry on my account. **53–4 A double . . . leave** The goddess Occasion or Opportunity smiles on the happy circumstance of being able to say good-bye twice and thus receive a second blessing. **59 Look thou character** see to it that you inscribe **60 unproportioned** badly calculated, intemperate. **his** its **61 familiar** sociable. **vulgar** common **62 and . . . tried** and their suitability to be your friends having been put to the test **64 dull thy palm** i.e., shake hands so often as to make the gesture meaningless **65 courage** swashbuckler **67 Bear't that** manage it so that **69 censure** opinion, judgment **70 habit** clothing **71 fancy** excessive ornament, decadent fashion **74 Are . . . that** are of a most refined and well-bred preeminence in choosing what to wear

Neither a borrower nor a lender be,
For loan oft loses both itself and friend,
And borrowing dulleth edge of husbandry. 77
This above all: to thine own self be true,
And it must follow, as the night the day,
Thou canst not then be false to any man.
Farewell. My blessing season this in thee! 81

LAERTES.
Most humbly do I take my leave, my lord.

POLONIUS.
The time invests you. Go, your servants tend. 83

LAERTES.
Farewell, Ophelia, and remember well
What I have said to you.

OPHELIA. 'Tis in my memory locked,
And you yourself shall keep the key of it.

LAERTES. Farewell. *Exit Laertes.*

POLONIUS.
What is't, Ophelia, he hath said to you?

OPHELIA.
So please you, something touching the Lord Hamlet.

POLONIUS. Marry, well bethought. 91
'Tis told me he hath very oft of late
Given private time to you, and you yourself
Have of your audience been most free and bounteous.
If it be so—as so 'tis put on me, 95
And that in way of caution—I must tell you
You do not understand yourself so clearly
As it behooves my daughter and your honor. 98
What is between you? Give me up the truth.

OPHELIA.
He hath, my lord, of late made many tenders 100
Of his affection to me.

POLONIUS.
Affection? Pooh! You speak like a green girl,
Unsifted in such perilous circumstance. 103
Do you believe his tenders, as you call them?

OPHELIA.
I do not know, my lord, what I should think.

POLONIUS.
Marry, I will teach you. Think yourself a baby
That you have ta'en these tenders for true pay
Which are not sterling. Tender yourself more dearly, 108
Or—not to crack the wind of the poor phrase, 109
Running it thus—you'll tender me a fool. 110

---

77 husbandry thrift **81 season** mature **83 invests** besieges, presses upon. **tend** attend, wait **91 Marry** i.e., by the Virgin Mary. (A mild oath.) **95 put on** impressed on, told to **98 behooves** befits **100 tenders** offers **103 Unsifted** i.e., untried **108 sterling** legal currency. **Tender . . . dearly** (1) Bargain for your favors at a higher rate—i.e., hold out for marriage (2) Show greater care of yourself. **109 crack the wind** i.e., run it until it is broken-winded **110 tender . . . fool** (1) make a fool of me (2) present me with a *fool* or baby.

OPHELIA.
My lord, he hath importuned me with love
In honorable fashion.

POLONIUS.
Ay, fashion you may call it. Go to, go to. 113

OPHELIA.
And hath given countenance to his speech, my lord, 114
With almost all the holy vows of heaven.

POLONIUS.
Ay, springes to catch woodcocks. I do know, 116
When the blood burns, how prodigal the soul 117
Lends the tongue vows. These blazes, daughter,
Giving more light than heat, extinct in both
Even in their promise as it is a-making, 120
You must not take for fire. From this time
Be something scanter of your maiden presence. 122
Set your entreatments at a higher rate 123
Than a command to parle. For Lord Hamlet, 124
Believe so much in him that he is young, 125
And with a larger tether may he walk
Than may be given you. In few, Ophelia, 127
Do not believe his vows, for they are brokers, 128
Not of that dye which their investments show, 129
But mere implorators of unholy suits, 130
Breathing like sanctified and pious bawds, 131
The better to beguile. This is for all: 132
I would not, in plain terms, from this time forth
Have you so slander any moment leisure 134
As to give words or talk with the Lord Hamlet.
Look to't, I charge you. Come your ways. 136

OPHELIA. I shall obey, my lord.

Exeunt.

1.4

Enter Hamlet, Horatio, and Marcellus.

HAMLET.
The air bites shrewdly; it is very cold. 1

---

113 fashion mere form, pretense. **Go to** (An expression of impatience.) **114 countenance** credit, confirmation **116 springes** snares. **woodcocks** birds easily caught; here used to connote gullibility **117 prodigal** prodigally **120 it** i.e., the promise **122 something** somewhat **123–4 Set . . . parle** i.e., As defender of your chastity, negotiate for something better than a surrender simply because the besieger requests an interview. **124 For** As for **125 so . . . him** this much concerning him **127 In few** Briefly **128 brokers** go-betweens, procurers **129 dye** color or sort. **investments** clothes. (The vows are not what they seem.) **130 mere implorators** out-and-out solicitors **131 Breathing** speaking **132 for all** once for all, in sum **134 slander** abuse, misuse. **moment** moment's **136 Come your ways** Come along.

1.4 Location: The guard platform.

1 shrewdly keenly, sharply

HORATIO.
It is a nipping and an eager air. 2
HAMLET.
What hour now?
HORATIO. I think it lacks of twelve. 3
MARCELLUS.
No, it is struck.
HORATIO. Indeed? I heard it not.
It then draws near the season 5
Wherein the spirit held his wont to walk. 6

A flourish of trumpets, and two pieces go off [*within*].

What does this mean, my lord?
HAMLET.
The King doth wake tonight and takes his rouse, 8
Keeps wassail, and the swaggering upspring reels; 9
And as he drains his drafts of Rhenish down, 10
The kettledrum and trumpet thus bray out
The triumph of his pledge.
HORATIO. Is it a custom? 12
HAMLET. Ay, marry, is't,
But to my mind, though I am native here
And to the manner born, it is a custom 15
More honored in the breach than the observance. 16
This heavy-headed revel east and west 17
Makes us traduced and taxed of other nations. 18
They clepe us drunkards, and with swinish phrase 19
Soil our addition; and indeed it takes 20
From our achievements, though performed at height, 21
The pith and marrow of our attribute. 22
So, oft it chances in particular men,
That for some vicious mole of nature in them, 24
As in their birth—wherein they are not guilty,
Since nature cannot choose his origin— 26
By their o'ergrowth of some complexion, 27
Oft breaking down the pales and forts of reason, 28
Or by some habit that too much o'erleavens 29
The form of plausive manners, that these men, 30
Carrying, I say, the stamp of one defect,

---

2 eager biting **3 lacks of** is just short of **5 season** time **6 held his wont** was accustomed. **6.1 *pieces*** i.e., of ordnance, cannon **8 wake** stay awake and hold revel. **takes his rouse** carouses **9 Keeps . . . reels** carouses, and riotously dances a German dance called the upspring **10 Rhenish** Rhine wine **12 The triumph . . . pledge** the celebration of his offering a toast. **15 manner** custom (of drinking) **16 More . . . observance** better neglected than followed **17 east and west** i.e., everywhere **18 taxed of** censured by **19 clepe** call. **with swinish phrase** i.e., by calling us swine **20 addition** reputation **21 at height** outstandingly **22 The pith . . . attribute** the most essential part of the esteem that should be attributed to us. **24 for . . . mole** on account of some natural defect in their constitutions **26 his** its **27 their o'ergrowth . . . complexion** the excessive growth in individuals of some natural trait **28 pales** palings, fences (as of a fortification) **29–30 o'erleavens . . . manners** i.e., infects the way we should behave (much as bad yeast spoils the dough). *Plausive* means "pleasing."

Being nature's livery or fortune's star, 32
His virtues else, be they as pure as grace, 33
As infinite as man may undergo, 34
Shall in the general censure take corruption 35
From that particular fault. The dram of evil 36
Doth all the noble substance often dout 37
To his own scandal.

Enter Ghost.

HORATIO. Look, my lord, it comes! 38

HAMLET.
Angels and ministers of grace defend us! 39
Be thou a spirit of health or goblin damned, 40
Bring with thee airs from heaven or blasts from hell, 41
Be thy intents wicked or charitable, 42
Thou com'st in such a questionable shape 43
That I will speak to thee. I'll call thee Hamlet,
King, father, royal Dane. Oh, answer me!
Let me not burst in ignorance, but tell
Why thy canonized bones, hearsèd in death, 47
Have burst their cerements; why the sepulcher 48
Wherein we saw thee quietly inurned 49
Hath oped his ponderous and marble jaws
To cast thee up again. What may this mean,
That thou, dead corpse, again in complete steel, 52
Revisits thus the glimpses of the moon, 53
Making night hideous, and we fools of nature 54
So horridly to shake our disposition 55
With thoughts beyond the reaches of our souls?
Say, why is this? Wherefore? What should we do?

[The Ghost] beckons [Hamlet].

HORATIO.
It beckons you to go away with it,
As if it some impartment did desire 59
To you alone.

MARCELLUS. Look with what courteous action
It wafts you to a more removèd ground.

---

32 Being . . . star (that stamp of defect) being a sign identifying one as wearing the livery of, and hence being the servant to, nature (unfortunate inherited qualities) or fortune (mischance) **33 His virtues else** i.e., the other qualities of *these men* (line 30) **34 may undergo** can sustain **35 in . . . censure** in overall appraisal, in people's opinion generally **36–8 The dram . . . scandal** i.e., The small drop of evil blots out or works against the noble substance of the whole and brings it into disrepute. To *dout* is to blot out. (A famous crux.) **39 ministers of grace** messengers of God **40 Be . . . health** Whether you are a good angel **41 Bring** whether you bring **42 Be thy intents** whether your intentions are **43 questionable** inviting question **47 canonized** buried according to the canons of the church. **hearsèd** coffined **48 cerements** grave clothes **49 inurned** entombed **52 complete steel** full armor **53 the glimpses . . . moon** i.e., the sublunary world, all that is beneath the moon **54 fools of nature** mere mortals, limited to natural knowledge and subject to nature **55 So . . . disposition** to distress our mental composure so violently **59 impartment** communication

But do not go with it.
HORATIO. No, by no means.
HAMLET.
It will not speak. Then I will follow it.
HORATIO.
Do not, my lord!
HAMLET. Why, what should be the fear?
I do not set my life at a pin's fee, 65
And for my soul, what can it do to that, 66
Being a thing immortal as itself?
It waves me forth again. I'll follow it.
HORATIO.
What if it tempt you toward the flood, my lord, 69
Or to the dreadful summit of the cliff
That beetles o'er his base into the sea, 71
And there assume some other horrible form
Which might deprive your sovereignty of reason 73
And draw you into madness? Think of it.
The very place puts toys of desperation, 75
Without more motive, into every brain
That looks so many fathoms to the sea
And hears it roar beneath.
HAMLET.
It wafts me still.—Go on, I'll follow thee.
MARCELLUS.
You shall not go, my lord. [*They try to stop him.*]
HAMLET. Hold off your hands!
HORATIO.
Be ruled. You shall not go.
HAMLET. My fate cries out, 81
And makes each petty artery in this body 82
As hardy as the Nemean lion's nerve. 83
Still am I called. Unhand me, gentlemen.
By heaven, I'll make a ghost of him that lets me! 85
I say, away!—Go on, I'll follow thee.

Exeunt Ghost and Hamlet.

HORATIO.
He waxes desperate with imagination.
MARCELLUS.
Let's follow. 'Tis not fit thus to obey him.
HORATIO.
Have after. To what issue will this come? 89
MARCELLUS.
Something is rotten in the state of Denmark.

---

65 fee value **66 for** as for **69 flood** sea **71 beetles o'er** overhangs threateningly (like bushy eyebrows). **his** its **73 deprive . . . reason** take away the rule of reason over your mind **75 toys of desperation** fancies of desperate acts, i.e., suicide **81 My fate cries out** My destiny summons me **82 petty** weak. **artery** blood vessel system through which the vital spirits were thought to have been conveyed **83 Nemean lion's nerve** as a sinew of the huge lion slain by Hercules as the first of his twelve labors **85 lets** hinders **89 Have after** Let's go after him. **issue** outcome

HORATIO.
Heaven will direct it.
MARCELLUS. Nay, let's follow him. 91

Exeunt.

1.5

Enter Ghost and Hamlet.

HAMLET.
Whither wilt thou lead me? Speak. I'll go no further.
GHOST.
Mark me.
HAMLET. I will.
GHOST. My hour is almost come,
When I to sulfurous and tormenting flames
Must render up myself.
HAMLET. Alas, poor ghost!
GHOST.
Pity me not, but lend thy serious hearing
To what I shall unfold.
HAMLET. Speak. I am bound to hear. 7
GHOST.
So art thou to revenge, when thou shalt hear.
HAMLET. What?
GHOST. I am thy father's spirit,
Doomed for a certain term to walk the night,
And for the day confined to fast in fires, 12
Till the foul crimes done in my days of nature 13
Are burnt and purged away. But that I am forbid 14
To tell the secrets of my prison house,
I could a tale unfold whose lightest word
Would harrow up thy soul, freeze thy young blood, 17
Make thy two eyes like stars start from their spheres, 18
Thy knotted and combinèd locks to part, 19
And each particular hair to stand on end
Like quills upon the fretful porcupine.
But this eternal blazon must not be 22
To ears of flesh and blood. List, list, oh, list!
If thou didst ever thy dear father love—
HAMLET. Oh God!

---

91 it i.e., the outcome
1.5 Location: The battlements of the castle.
7 bound (1) ready (2) obligated by duty and fate. (The Ghost, in line 8, answers in the second sense.) **12 fast** do penance by fasting **13 crimes** sins. **of nature** as a mortal **14 But that** Were it not that **17 harrow up** lacerate, tear **18 spheres** i.e., eyesockets, here compared to the orbits or transparent revolving spheres in which, according to Ptolemaic astronomy, the heavenly bodies were fixed **19 knotted . . . locks** hair neatly arranged and confined **22 eternal blazon** revelation of the secrets of eternity

GHOST.
Revenge his foul and most unnatural murder.
HAMLET. Murder?
GHOST.
Murder most foul, as in the best it is, 28
But this most foul, strange, and unnatural.
HAMLET.
Haste me to know't, that I, with wings as swift
As meditation or the thoughts of love,
May sweep to my revenge.
GHOST. I find thee apt;
And duller shouldst thou be than the fat weed 33
That roots itself in ease on Lethe wharf, 34
Wouldst thou not stir in this. Now, Hamlet, hear.
'Tis given out that, sleeping in my orchard, 36
A serpent stung me. So the whole ear of Denmark
Is by a forgèd process of my death 38
Rankly abused. But know, thou noble youth, 39
The serpent that did sting thy father's life
Now wears his crown.
HAMLET. Oh, my prophetic soul! My uncle!
GHOST.
Ay, that incestuous, that adulterate beast, 43
With witchcraft of his wit, with traitorous gifts— 44
Oh, wicked wit and gifts that have the power
So to seduce!—won to his shameful lust
The will of my most seeming-virtuous queen.
Oh Hamlet, what a falling off was there!
From me, whose love was of that dignity
That it went hand in hand even with the vow 50
I made to her in marriage, and to decline
Upon a wretch whose natural gifts were poor
To those of mine! 53
But virtue, as it never will be moved, 54
Though lewdness court it in a shape of heaven, 55
So lust, though to a radiant angel linked,
Will sate itself in a celestial bed 57
And prey on garbage.
But soft, methinks I scent the morning air.
Brief let me be. Sleeping within my orchard,
My custom always of the afternoon,
Upon my secure hour thy uncle stole, 62

28 in the best even at best **33 shouldst thou be** you would have to be. **fat** torpid, lethargic **34 Lethe** the river of forgetfulness in Hades **36 orchard** garden **38 forgèd process** falsified account **39 abused** deceived **43 adulterate** adulterous **44 gifts** (1) talents (2) presents **50 even with the vow** with the very vow **53 To** compared with **54 virtue, as it** just as virtue **55 shape of heaven** heavenly form **57 sate . . . bed** gratify its lustful appetite to the point of revulsion or ennui, even in a virtuously lawful marriage **62 secure hour** time of being free from worries

With juice of cursèd hebona in a vial, 63
And in the porches of my ears did pour 64
The leprous distillment, whose effect 65
Holds such an enmity with blood of man
That swift as quicksilver it courses through
The natural gates and alleys of the body, 68
And with a sudden vigor it doth posset 69
And curd, like eager droppings into milk, 70
The thin and wholesome blood. So did it mine,
And a most instant tetter barked about, 72
Most lazar-like, with vile and loathsome crust, 73
All my smooth body.
Thus was I, sleeping, by a brother's hand
Of life, of crown, of queen at once dispatched, 76
Cut off even in the blossoms of my sin,
Unhouseled, disappointed, unaneled, 78
No reckoning made, but sent to my account 79
With all my imperfections on my head.
Oh, horrible! Oh, horrible, most horrible!
If thou hast nature in thee, bear it not. 82
Let not the royal bed of Denmark be
A couch for luxury and damnèd incest. 84
But, howsoever thou pursues this act,
Taint not thy mind nor let thy soul contrive
Against thy mother aught. Leave her to heaven
And to those thorns that in her bosom lodge,
To prick and sting her. Fare thee well at once.
The glowworm shows the matin to be near, 90
And 'gins to pale his uneffectual fire. 91
Adieu, adieu, adieu! Remember me. [*Exit.*]

HAMLET.
O all you host of heaven! O earth! What else?
And shall I couple hell? Oh, fie! Hold, hold, my heart, 94
And you, my sinews, grow not instant old, 95
But bear me stiffly up. Remember thee?
Ay, thou poor ghost, whiles memory holds a seat
In this distracted globe. Remember thee? 98
Yea, from the table of my memory 99
I'll wipe away all trivial fond records, 100
All saws of books, all forms, all pressures past 101

---

63 hebona a poison. (The word seems to be a form of *ebony,* though it is thought perhaps to be related to *henbane,* a poison, or to *ebenus,* "yew.") **64 porches** gateways **65 leprous distillment** distillation causing leprosylike disfigurement **68 gates** entry ways **69–70 posset . . . curd** coagulate and curdle **70 eager** sour, acid **72 tetter** eruption of scabs. **barked** covered with a rough covering, like bark on a tree **73 lazar-like** leperlike **76 dispatched** suddenly deprived **78 Unhouseled . . . unaneled** without having received the Sacrament or other last rites including confession, absolution, and the holy oil of Extreme Unction **79 reckoning** settling of accounts **82 nature** i.e., the promptings of a son **84 luxury** lechery **90 matin** morning **91 his** its **94 couple** add. **Hold** hold together **95 instant** instantly **98 globe** (1) head (2) world (3) Globe Theater **99 table** tablet, slate **100 fond** foolish **101 All . . . past** all wise sayings, all shapes or images imprinted on the tablets of my memory, all past impressions

That youth and observation copied there,
And thy commandment all alone shall live
Within the book and volume of my brain,
Unmixed with baser matter. Yes, by heaven!
Oh most pernicious woman!
Oh villain, villain, smiling, damnèd villain!
My tables—meet it is I set it down
That one may smile, and smile, and be a villain.
At least I am sure it may be so in Denmark.
So, uncle, there you are. Now to my word:
It is "Adieu, adieu! Remember me."
I have sworn't.

Enter Horatio and Marcellus.

HORATIO. My lord, my lord!
MARCELLUS. Lord Hamlet!
HORATIO. Heavens secure him!
HAMLET. So be it.
MARCELLUS. Hillo, ho, ho, my lord!
HAMLET. Hillo, ho, ho, boy! Come, bird, come.
MARCELLUS. How is't, my noble lord?
HORATIO. What news, my lord?
HAMLET. Oh, wonderful!
HORATIO. Good my lord, tell it.
HAMLET. No, you will reveal it.
HORATIO. Not I, my lord, by heaven.
MARCELLUS. Nor I, my lord.
HAMLET.
How say you, then, would heart of man once think it?
But you'll be secret?
HORATIO, MARCELLUS. Ay, by heaven, my lord.
HAMLET.
There's never a villain dwelling in all Denmark
But he's an arrant knave.
HORATIO.
There needs no ghost, my lord, come from the grave
To tell us this.
HAMLET. Why, right, you are in the right.
And so, without more circumstance at all,
I hold it fit that we shake hands and part,
You as your business and desire shall point you—
For every man hath business and desire,
Such as it is—and for my own poor part,
Look you, I'll go pray.

---

108 My tables . . . down (Editors often specify that Hamlet makes a note in his writing tablet, but he may simply mean that he is making a mental observation of lasting impression.) **111 there you are** i.e., there, I've noted that against you. **116 secure him** keep him safe **119 Hillo . . . come** (A falconer's call to a hawk in air. Hamlet mocks the hallooing as though it were a part of hawking.) **127 once** ever **130 But . . . knave** (Hamlet jokingly gives a self-evident answer: every villain is a thoroughgoing knave.) **133 circumstance** ceremony, elaboration

HORATIO.
These are but wild and whirling words, my lord.
HAMLET.
I am sorry they offend you, heartily;
Yes, faith, heartily.
HORATIO. There's no offense, my lord.
HAMLET.
Yes, by Saint Patrick, but there is, Horatio, 142
And much offense too. Touching this vision here, 143
It is an honest ghost, that let me tell you. 144
For your desire to know what is between us,
O'ermaster't as you may. And now, good friends,
As you are friends, scholars, and soldiers,
Give me one poor request.
HORATIO. What is't, my lord? We will.
HAMLET.
Never make known what you have seen tonight.
HORATIO, MARCELLUS. My lord, we will not.
HAMLET. Nay, but swear 't.
HORATIO. In faith, my lord, not I. 153
MARCELLUS. Nor I, my lord, in faith.
HAMLET. Upon my sword. [*He holds out his sword.*] 155
MARCELLUS. We have sworn, my lord, already. 156
HAMLET. Indeed, upon my sword, indeed.
GHOST. (*cries under the stage*) Swear.
HAMLET.
Ha, ha, boy, say'st thou so? Art thou there, truepenny? 159
Come on, you hear this fellow in the cellarage.
Consent to swear.
HORATIO. Propose the oath, my lord.
HAMLET.
Never to speak of this that you have seen,
Swear by my sword.
GHOST. [*beneath*] Swear. [*They swear.*] 164
HAMLET.
Hic et ubique? Then we'll shift our ground. 165

[*He moves to another spot.*]

Come hither, gentlemen,
And lay your hands again upon my sword.

---

142 Saint Patrick The keeper of Purgatory **143 offense** (Hamlet deliberately changes Horatio's "no offense taken" to "an offense against all decency.") **144 honest** genuine **153 In faith . . . I** i.e., I swear not to tell what I have seen. (Horatio is not refusing to swear.) **155 sword** i.e., the hilt in the form of a cross **156 We . . . already** i.e., We swore *in faith.* **159 truepenny** honest old fellow **164 s.d.** ***They swear*** (Seemingly they swear here, and at lines 170 and 190, as they lay their hands on Hamlet's sword. Triple oaths would have particular force; these three oaths deal with what they have seen, what they have heard, and what they promise about Hamlet's *antic disposition.*) **165** ***Hic et ubique?*** Here and everywhere? (Latin.)

Swear by my sword
Never to speak of this that you have heard.
GHOST. [*beneath*] Swear by his sword. [*They swear.*]
HAMLET.
Well said, old mole. Canst work i'th'earth so fast?
A worthy pioneer!—Once more remove, good friends. 172

[*He moves again.*]

HORATIO.
Oh day and night, but this is wondrous strange!
HAMLET.
And therefore as a stranger give it welcome. 174
There are more things in heaven and earth, Horatio,
Than are dreamt of in your philosophy. 176
But come;
Here, as before, never, so help you mercy, 178
How strange or odd soe'er I bear myself—
As I perchance hereafter shall think meet
To put an antic disposition on— 181
That you, at such times seeing me, never shall,
With arms encumbered thus, or this headshake, 183
Or by pronouncing of some doubtful phrase
As "Well, we know," or "We could, an if we would," 185
Or "If we list to speak," or "There be, an if they might," 186
Or such ambiguous giving out, to note 187
That you know aught of me—this do swear, 188
So grace and mercy at your most need help you.
GHOST. [*beneath*] Swear. [*They swear.*]
HAMLET.
Rest, rest, perturbèd spirit!—So, gentlemen,
With all my love I do commend me to you; 192
And what so poor a man as Hamlet is
May do t'express his love and friending to you, 194
God willing, shall not lack. Let us go in together, 195
And still your fingers on your lips, I pray. 196
The time is out of joint. Oh cursèd spite 197
That ever I was born to set it right!

[*They wait for him to leave first.*]

Nay, come, let's go together. *Exeunt.* 199

---

172 pioneer foot soldier assigned to dig tunnels and excavations **174 as a stranger** i.e., needing your hospitality **176 your philosophy** this subject that is called "natural philosophy" or "science" (*your* is not personal.) **178 so help you mercy** as you hope for God's mercy when you are judged **181 antic** grotesque, strange **183 encumbered** folded **185 an if** if **186 list** wished. **There . . . might** There are those could talk if they were at liberty to do so. **187 note** indicate **188 aught** anything **192 commend . . . you** give you my best wishes **194 friending** friendliness **195 lack** be lacking **196 still** always **197 out of joint** in utter disorder. **199 let's go together** (Probably they wait for him to leave first, but he refuses this ceremoniousness.)

2.1

Enter old Polonius with his man [*Reynaldo*].

POLONIUS.
Give him this money and these notes, Reynaldo.

[*He gives money and papers.*]

REYNALDO. I will, my lord.
POLONIUS.
You shall do marvelous wisely, good Reynaldo, 3
Before you visit him, to make inquire 4
Of his behavior.
REYNALDO. My lord, I did intend it.
POLONIUS.
Marry, well said, very well said. Look you, sir,
Inquire me first what Danskers are in Paris, 7
And how, and who, what means, and where they keep, 8
What company, at what expense; and finding
By this encompassment and drift of question 10
That they do know my son, come you more nearer 11
Than your particular demands will touch it. 12
Take you, as 'twere, some distant knowledge of him, 13
As thus, "I know his father and his friends,
And in part him." Do you mark this, Reynaldo?
REYNALDO. Ay, very well, my lord.
POLONIUS.
"And in part him, but," you may say, "not well.
But if 't be he I mean, he's very wild,
Addicted so and so," and there put on him 19
What forgeries you please—marry, none so rank 20
As may dishonor him, take heed of that,
But, sir, such wanton, wild, and usual slips 22
As are companions noted and most known
To youth and liberty.
REYNALDO. As gaming, my lord.
POLONIUS. Ay, or drinking, fencing, swearing,
Quarreling, drabbing— you may go so far. 27
REYNALDO. My lord, that would dishonor him.
POLONIUS.
Faith, no, as you may season it in the charge. 29
You must not put another scandal on him
That he is open to incontinency; 31

2.1 Location: Polonius' chambers.
3 marvelous marvelously **4 inquire** inquiry **7 Danskers** Danes **8 what means** what wealth (they have). **keep** dwell **10 encompassment . . . question** roundabout way of questioning **11–12 come . . . it** you will find out more this way than by asking pointed questions (*particular demands*) **13 Take you** Assume, pretend **19 put on** impute to **20 forgeries** invented tales. **rank** gross **22 wanton** sportive, unrestrained **27 drabbing** whoring **29 season** temper, soften **31 incontinency** habitual sexual excess

That's not my meaning. But breathe his faults so quaintly 32
That they may seem the taints of liberty, 33
The flash and outbreak of a fiery mind,
A savageness in unreclaimèd blood, 35
Of general assault. 36
REYNALDO. But, my good lord—
POLONIUS.
Wherefore should you do this?
REYNALDO. Ay, my lord, I would know that.
POLONIUS. Marry, sir, here's my drift,
And I believe it is a fetch of warrant. 41
You laying these slight sullies on my son,
As 'twere a thing a little soiled wi'th'working, 43
Mark you,
Your party in converse, him you would sound, 45
Having ever seen in the prenominate crimes 46
The youth you breathe of guilty, be assured 47
He closes with you in this consequence: 48
"Good sir," or so, or "friend," or "gentleman,"
According to the phrase or the addition 50
Of man and country.
REYNALDO. Very good, my lord.
POLONIUS. And then, sir, does 'a this—'a does—what was I about to say?
By the Mass, I was about to say something. Where did I leave?
REYNALDO. At "closes in the consequence."
POLONIUS.
At "closes in the consequence," ay, marry.
He closes thus: "I know the gentleman,
I saw him yesterday," or "th'other day,"
Or then, or then, with such or such, "and as you say,
There was 'a gaming," "there o'ertook in 's rouse," 59
"There falling out at tennis," or perchance 60
"I saw him enter such a house of sale,"
Videlicet a brothel, or so forth. See you now, 62
Your bait of falsehood takes this carp of truth; 63
And thus do we of wisdom and of reach, 64
With windlasses and with assays of bias, 65
By indirections find directions out. 66
So by my former lecture and advice 67
Shall you my son. You have me, have you not? 68

---

32 quaintly artfully, subtly **33 taints of liberty** faults resulting from free living **35–6 A savageness . . . assault** a wildness in untamed youth that assails all indiscriminately. **41 fetch of warrant** legitimate trick. **43 wi'th'working** in the process of being made, i.e., in everyday experience **45 Your converse** The person you are conversing with. **sound** sound out **46 Having ever** if he has ever. **prenominate crimes** aforenamed offenses **47 breathe** speak **48 closes . . . consequence** takes you into his confidence, as follows **50 addition** title **59 o'ertook in 's rouse** overcome by drink **60 falling out** quarreling **62 Videlicet** namely **63 carp** a fish **64 reach** capacity, ability **65 windlasses** i.e., circuitous paths. (Literally, circuits made to head off the game in hunting.) **assays of bias** attempts through indirection (like the curving path of the bowling ball, which is biased or weighted to one side) **66 directions** i.e., the way things really are **67 former lecture** just-ended set of instructions **68 have** understand

REYNALDO.
My lord, I have.
POLONIUS. God b'wi'ye; fare ye well.
REYNALDO. Good my lord.
POLONIUS.
Observe his inclination in yourself. 71
REYNALDO. I shall, my lord.
POLONIUS. And let him ply his music.
REYNALDO. Well, my lord.
POLONIUS.
Farewell. *Exit Reynaldo.*

Enter Ophelia.

How now, Ophelia, what's the matter?
OPHELIA.
Oh my lord, my lord, I have been so affrighted!
POLONIUS. With what, i'th'name of God?
OPHELIA.
My lord, as I was sewing in my closet, 78
Lord Hamlet, with his doublet all unbraced, 79
No hat upon his head, his stockings fouled,
Ungartered, and down-gyvèd to his ankle, 81
Pale as his shirt, his knees knocking each other,
And with a look so piteous in purport 83
As if he had been loosèd out of hell
To speak of horrors—he comes before me.
POLONIUS.
Mad for thy love?
OPHELIA. My lord, I do not know,
But truly I do fear it.
POLONIUS. What said he?
OPHELIA.
He took me by the wrist and held me hard.
Then goes he to the length of all his arm,
And, with his other hand thus o'er his brow
He falls to such perusal of my face
As 'a would draw it. Long stayed he so. 92
At last, a little shaking of mine arm
And thrice his head thus waving up and down,
He raised a sigh so piteous and profound
As it did seem to shatter all his bulk 96
And end his being. That done, he lets me go,
And with his head over his shoulder turned
He seemed to find his way without his eyes,
For out o'doors he went without their helps,
And to the last bended their light on me.

71 in yourself in your own person (as well as by asking questions of others). **78 closet** private chamber **79 doublet** close-fitting jacket. **unbraced** unfastened **81 down-gyvèd** fallen to the ankles (like gyves or fetters) **83 in purport** in what it expressed **92 As** as if **96 As** that. **bulk** body

POLONIUS.
Come, go with me. I will go seek the King.
This is the very ecstasy of love, 103
Whose violent property fordoes itself 104
And leads the will to desperate undertakings
As oft as any passion under heaven
That does afflict our natures. I am sorry.
What, have you given him any hard words of late?

OPHELIA.
No, my good lord, but as you did command
I did repel his letters and denied
His access to me.

POLONIUS. That hath made him mad.
I am sorry that with better heed and judgment
I had not quoted him. I feared he did but trifle 113
And meant to wrack thee. But beshrew my jealousy! 114
By heaven, it is as proper to our age 115
To cast beyond ourselves in our opinions 116
As it is common for the younger sort
To lack discretion. Come, go we to the King.
This must be known, which, being kept close, might move 119
More grief to hide than hate to utter love. 120
Come.

Exeunt.

2.2

Flourish. Enter King and Queen, Rosencrantz, and Guildenstern [*with others*].

KING.
Welcome, dear Rosencrantz and Guildenstern.
Moreover that we much did long to see you, 2
The need we have to use you did provoke
Our hasty sending. Something have you heard
Of Hamlet's transformation—so call it,
Sith nor th'exterior nor the inward man 6
Resembles that it was. What it should be, 7
More than his father's death, that thus hath put him
So much from th'understanding of himself,
I cannot dream of. I entreat you both

---

103 ecstasy madness **104 property fordoes** nature destroys **113 quoted** observed **114 wrack** ruin, seduce. **beshrew my jealousy!** a plague upon my suspicious nature! **115 proper . . . age** characteristic of us (old) men **116 cast beyond** overshoot, miscalculate. (A metaphor from hunting.) **119 known** made known (to the King). **close** secret **119–20 might . . . love** i.e., might cause more grief (because of what Hamlet might do) by hiding the knowledge of Hamlet's strange behavior to Ophelia than unpleasantness by telling it.
2.2 Location: The castle. **2 Moreover that** Besides the fact that **6 Sith nor** since neither **7 that** what

That, being of so young days brought up with him,
And sith so neighbored to his youth and havior,
That you vouchsafe your rest here in our court
Some little time, so by your companies
To draw him on to pleasures, and to gather
So much as from occasion you may glean,
Whether aught to us unknown afflicts him thus
That, opened, lies within our remedy.

QUEEN.
Good gentlemen, he hath much talked of you,
And sure I am two men there is not living
To whom he more adheres. If it will please you
To show us so much gentry and good will
As to expend your time with us awhile
For the supply and profit of our hope,
Your visitation shall receive such thanks
As fits a king's remembrance.

ROSENCRANTZ. Both Your Majesties
Might, by the sovereign power you have of us,
Put your dread pleasures more into command
Than to entreaty.

GUILDENSTERN. But we both obey,
And here give up ourselves in the full bent
To lay our service freely at your feet,
To be commanded.

KING.
Thanks, Rosencrantz and gentle Guildenstern.

QUEEN.
Thanks, Guildenstern and gentle Rosencrantz.
And I beseech you instantly to visit
My too much changèd son.—Go, some of you,
And bring these gentlemen where Hamlet is.

GUILDENSTERN.
Heavens make our presence and our practices
Pleasant and helpful to him!

QUEEN. Ay, amen!

Exeunt Rosencrantz and Guildenstern [with some attendants].

Enter Polonius.

POLONIUS.
Th'ambassadors from Norway, my good lord,
Are joyfully returned.

KING.
Thou still hast been the father of good news.

11–12 That . . . havior that, seeing as you were brought up with him from early youth (see 3.4.209, where Hamlet refers to Rosencrantz and Guildenstern as "my two schoolfellows"), and since you have been intimately acquainted with his youthful ways **13 vouchsafe your rest** consent to stay **16 occasion** opportunity **18 opened** being revealed **22 gentry** courtesy **24 supply . . . hope** aid and furtherance of what we hope for **26 As fits . . . remembrance** as would be a fitting gift of a king who rewards true service. **27 of** over **28 dread** inspiring awe **30 in . . . bent** to the utmost degree of our capacity. (An archery metaphor.) **38 practices** doings **42 still** always

POLONIUS.
Have I, my lord? I assure my good liege
I hold my duty, as I hold my soul,
Both to my God and to my gracious king;
And I do think, or else this brain of mine
Hunts not the trail of policy so sure 47
As it hath used to do, that I have found
The very cause of Hamlet's lunacy.

KING.
Oh, speak of that! That do I long to hear.

POLONIUS.
Give first admittance to th'ambassadors.
My news shall be the fruit to that great feast. 52

KING.
Thyself do grace to them and bring them in. 53

[*Exit Polonius.*]

He tells me, my dear Gertrude, he hath found
The head and source of all your son's distemper.

QUEEN.
I doubt it is no other but the main, 56
His father's death and our o'erhasty marriage.

Enter Ambassadors [*Voltimand and Cornelius, with Polonius*].

KING.
Well, we shall sift him.—Welcome, my good friends! 58
Say, Voltimand, what from our brother Norway? 59

VOLTIMAND.
Most fair return of greetings and desires. 60
Upon our first, he sent out to suppress 61
His nephew's levies, which to him appeared
To be a preparation 'gainst the Polack,
But, better looked into, he truly found
It was against Your Highness. Whereat grieved
That so his sickness, age, and impotence 66
Was falsely borne in hand, sends out arrests 67
On Fortinbras, which he, in brief, obeys,
Receives rebuke from Norway, and in fine 69
Makes vow before his uncle never more
To give th'assay of arms against Your Majesty. 71
Whereon old Norway, overcome with joy,
Gives him three thousand crowns in annual fee
And his commission to employ those soldiers,
So levied as before, against the Polack,

---

47 policy statecraft **52 fruit** dessert **53 grace** honor. (Punning on *grace* said before a *feast,* line 52) **56 doubt** fear, suspect. **58 sift him** question Polonius closely **59 brother** fellow king **60 desires** good wishes **61 Upon our first** At our first words on the business **66 impotence** weakness **67 borne in hand** deluded, taken advantage of. **arrests** orders to desist **69 in fine** in conclusion **71 give th'assay** make trial of strength, challenge

With an entreaty, herein further shown,
[*giving a paper*]
That it might please you to give quiet pass
Through your dominions for this enterprise
On such regards of safety and allowance 79
As therein are set down.

KING. It likes us well, 80
And at our more considered time we'll read, 81
Answer, and think upon this business.
Meantime we thank you for your well-took labor.
Go to your rest; at night we'll feast together.
Most welcome home! *Exeunt Ambassadors.*

POLONIUS. This business is well ended.
My liege, and madam, to expostulate 86
What majesty should be, what duty is,
Why day is day, night night, and time is time,
Were nothing but to waste night, day, and time.
Therefore, since brevity is the soul of wit, 90
And tediousness the limbs and outward flourishes,
I will be brief. Your noble son is mad.
Mad call I it, for, to define true madness,
What is't but to be nothing else but mad?
But let that go.

QUEEN. More matter, with less art.

POLONIUS.
Madam, I swear I use no art at all.
That he's mad, 'tis true; 'tis true 'tis pity,
And pity 'tis 'tis true—a foolish figure, 98
But farewell it, for I will use no art.
Mad let us grant him, then, and now remains
That we find out the cause of this effect,
Or rather say, the cause of this defect,
For this effect defective comes by cause. 103
Thus it remains, and the remainder thus.
Perpend. 105
I have a daughter—have while she is mine—
Who, in her duty and obedience, mark,
Hath given me this. Now gather and surmise. 108
[*He reads the letter.*] "To the celestial and my soul's
idol, the most beautified Ophelia"—
That's an ill phrase, a vile phrase; "beautified" is a
vile phrase. But you shall hear. Thus: [*He reads.*]
"In her excellent white bosom, these, etc." 113

---

79 On . . . allowance i.e., with such considerations for the safety of Denmark and permission for Fortinbras **80 likes** pleases **81 considered** suitable for deliberation **86 expostulate** expound, inquire into **90 wit** sense or judgment **98 figure** figure of speech **103 For . . . cause** i.e., for this defective behavior, this madness, must have a cause. **105 Perpend** Consider **108 gather and surmise** draw your own conclusions. **113 "In . . . etc."** (The letter is poetically addressed to her heart, where a letter would be kept by a young lady.)

QUEEN. Came this from Hamlet to her?
POLONIUS.
Good madam, stay awhile, I will be faithful.

[*He reads.*]

"Doubt thou the stars are fire,
Doubt that the sun doth move,
Doubt truth to be a liar,
But never doubt I love.

O dear Ophelia, I am ill at these numbers. I have not art to reckon my groans. But that I love thee best, O most best, believe it. Adieu.
Thine evermore, most dear lady, whilst this machine is to him, Hamlet."

This in obedience hath my daughter shown me,
And, more above, hath his solicitings,
As they fell out by time, by means, and place,
All given to mine ear.
KING. But how hath she
Received his love?
POLONIUS. What do you think of me?
KING.
As of a man faithful and honorable.
POLONIUS.
I would fain prove so. But what might you think,
When I had seen this hot love on the wing—
As I perceived it, I must tell you that,
Before my daughter told me—what might you,
Or my dear Majesty your queen here, think,
If I had played the desk or table book,
Or given my heart a winking, mute and dumb,
Or looked upon this love with idle sight?
What might you think? No, I went round to work,
And my young mistress thus I did bespeak:
"Lord Hamlet is a prince out of thy star;
This must not be." And then I prescripts gave her,
That she should lock herself from his resort,
Admit no messengers, receive no tokens.
Which done, she took the fruits of my advice;
And he, repellèd—a short tale to make—
Fell into a sadness, then into a fast,

115 stay . . . faithful i.e., hold on, I will do as you wish. **118 Doubt** suspect **120 ill . . . numbers** unskilled at writing verses **121 reckon** (1) count (2) number metrically, scan **124 machine** i.e., body **126–8 And . . . ear** and moreover she has told me when, how, and where his solicitings of her occurred. **131 fain** gladly **136–7 If . . . dumb** If I had acted as go-between, passing love-notes, or if I had refused to let my heart acknowledge what my eyes could see **138 with idle sight** complacently or incomprehendingly. **139 round** roundly, plainly **140 bespeak** address **141 out of thy star** above your sphere, position **142 prescripts** orders

Thence to a watch, thence into a weakness, 148
Thence to a lightness, and by this declension 149
Into the madness wherein now he raves,
And all we mourn for.

KING [*to the Queen*]. Do you think 'tis this?

QUEEN. It may be, very like.

POLONIUS.
Hath there been such a time—I would fain know that—
That I have positively said "'Tis so,"
When it proved otherwise?

KING. Not that I know.

POLONIUS.
Take this from this, if this be otherwise. 156
If circumstances lead me, I will find
Where truth is hid, though it were hid indeed
Within the center.

KING. How may we try it further? 159

POLONIUS.
You know sometimes he walks four hours together
Here in the lobby.

QUEEN. So he does indeed.

POLONIUS.
At such a time I'll loose my daughter to him. 162
Be you and I behind an arras then. 163
Mark the encounter. If he love her not
And be not from his reason fall'n thereon, 165
Let me be no assistant for a state,
But keep a farm and carters.

KING. We will try it. 167

Enter Hamlet [*reading on a book*].

QUEEN.
But look where sadly the poor wretch comes reading.

POLONIUS.
Away, I do beseech you both, away.
I'll board him presently. Oh, give me leave. 170

Exeunt King and Queen [*with attendants*].

How does my good Lord Hamlet?

HAMLET. Well, God-a-mercy. 172

---

148 watch state of sleeplessness **149 lightness** lightheadedness. **declension** decline, deterioration. (With a pun on the grammatical sense.) **156 Take this from this** (The actor probably gestures, indicating that he means his head from his shoulders, or his staff of office or chain from his hands or neck, or something similar.) **159 center** center of the earth, traditionally an extraordinarily inaccessible place. **try** test **162 loose** (As one might release an animal that is being mated.) **163 arras** hanging, tapestry **165 thereon** on that account **167 carters** wagon drivers. **170 I'll . . . leave** I'll accost him at once. Please leave us alone; leave him to me. **172 God-a-mercy** God have mercy, i.e., thank you.

POLONIUS. Do you know me, my lord?
HAMLET. Excellent well. You are a fishmonger. 174
POLONIUS. Not I, my lord.
HAMLET. Then I would you were so honest a man.
POLONIUS. Honest, my lord?
HAMLET. Ay, sir. To be honest, as this world goes, is to be one man picked
out of ten thousand.
POLONIUS. That's very true, my lord.
HAMLET. For if the sun breed maggots in a dead dog, being a good kissing 181
carrion—Have you a daughter? 182
POLONIUS. I have, my lord.
HAMLET. Let her not walk i'th'sun. Conception is a blessing, but as your 184
daughter may conceive, friend, look to't.
POLONIUS [*aside*]. How say you by that? Still harping on my daughter. Yet he
knew me not at first; 'a said I was a fishmonger. 'A is far gone. And truly
in my youth I suffered much extremity for love, very near this. I'll speak
to him again.—What do you read, my lord?
HAMLET. Words, words, words.
POLONIUS. What is the matter, my lord? 191
HAMLET. Between who?
POLONIUS. I mean, the matter that you read, my lord.
HAMLET. Slanders, sir; for the satirical rogue says here that old men have
gray beards, that their faces are wrinkled, their eyes purging thick amber 195
and plum-tree gum, and that they have a plentiful lack of wit, together 196
with most weak hams. All which, sir, though I most powerfully and po-
tently believe, yet I hold it not honesty to have it thus set down, for your- 198
self, sir, shall grow old as I am, if like a crab you could go backward. 199
POLONIUS [*aside*]. Though this be madness, yet there is method in't.—Will
you walk out of the air, my lord? 201
HAMLET. Into my grave.
POLONIUS. Indeed, that's out of the air. [*Aside*] How pregnant sometimes 203
his replies are! A happiness that often madness hits on, which reason 204
and sanity could not so prosperously be delivered of. I will leave him 205
and suddenly contrive the means of meeting between him and my 206
daughter.—My honorable lord, I will most humbly take my leave of you.
HAMLET. You cannot, sir, take from me anything that I will more willingly
part withal—except my life, except my life, except my life. 209

Enter Guildenstern and Rosencrantz.

POLONIUS. Fare you well, my lord.
HAMLET. These tedious old fools!
POLONIUS. You go to seek the Lord Hamlet. There he is.

---

174 fishmonger fish merchant **181–2 a good kissing carrion** i.e., a good piece of flesh for kissing, or for the sun to kiss **184 i'th' sun** in public. (With additional implication of the sunshine of princely favors.) **Conception** (1) Understanding (2) Pregnancy **191 matter** substance. (But Hamlet plays on the sense of "basis for a dispute.") **195 purging** discharging. **amber** i.e., resin, like the resinous *plum-tree gum* **196 wit** understanding **198 honesty** decency, decorum **199 old** as old **201 out of the air** (The open air was considered dangerous for sick people.) **203 pregnant** quick-witted, full of meaning. **204 happiness** felicity of expression **205 prosperously** successfully **206 suddenly** immediately **209 withal** with

ROSENCRANTZ. [*to Polonius*]. God save you, sir!

[*Exit Polonius.*]

GUILDENSTERN. My honored lord!

ROSENCRANTZ. My most dear lord!

HAMLET. My excellent good friends! How dost thou, Guildenstern? Ah, Rosencrantz! Good lads, how do you both?

ROSENCRANTZ.
As the indifferent children of the earth. 218

GUILDENSTERN.
Happy in that we are not overhappy.
On Fortune's cap we are not the very button.

HAMLET. Nor the soles of her shoe?

ROSENCRANTZ. Neither, my lord.

HAMLET. Then you live about her waist, or in the middle of her favors? 223

GUILDENSTERN. Faith, her privates we. 224

HAMLET. In the secret parts of Fortune? Oh, most true, she is a strumpet. 225
What news?

ROSENCRANTZ. None, my lord, but the world's grown honest.

HAMLET. Then is doomsday near. But your news is not true. Let me question more in particular. What have you, my good friends, deserved at the hands of Fortune that she sends you to prison hither?

GUILDENSTERN. Prison, my lord?

HAMLET. Denmark's a prison.

ROSENCRANTZ. Then is the world one.

HAMLET. A goodly one, in which there are many confines, wards, and dun- 234
geons, Denmark being one o'th'worst.

ROSENCRANTZ. We think not so, my lord.

HAMLET. Why then 'tis none to you, for there is nothing either good or bad but thinking makes it so. To me it is a prison.

ROSENCRANTZ. Why then, your ambition makes it one. 'Tis too narrow for your mind.

HAMLET. Oh, God, I could be bounded in a nutshell and count myself a king of infinite space, were it not that I have bad dreams.

GUILDENSTERN. Which dreams indeed are ambition, for the very substance 243
of the ambitious is merely the shadow of a dream. 244

HAMLET. A dream itself is but a shadow.

ROSENCRANTZ. Truly, and I hold ambition of so airy and light a quality that it is but a shadow's shadow.

HAMLET. Then are our beggars bodies, and our monarchs and outstretched 248
heroes the beggars' shadows. Shall we to the court? For, by my fay, I can- 249
not reason.

---

218 indifferent ordinary, at neither extreme of fortune or misfortune **223 the middle . . . favors** i.e., her genitals. **224 her privates we** (1) we dwell in her privates, her genitals, in the middle of her favors (2) we are her ordinary footsoldiers. **225 strumpet** (Fortune was proverbially thought of as fickle.) **234 confines** places of confinement. **243–4 the very . . . ambitious** that seemingly very substantial thing that the ambitious pursue **248–9 Then . . . shadows** (Hamlet pursues their argument about ambition to its absurd extreme: if ambition is only a shadow of a shadow, then beggars [who are presumably without ambition] must be real, whereas monarchs and heroes are only their shadows—*outstretched* like elongated shadows, made to look bigger than they are.) **249 fay** faith

ROSENCRANTZ, GUILDENSTERN. We'll wait upon you.

HAMLET. No such matter. I will not sort you with the rest of my servants, for, to speak to you like an honest man, I am most dreadfully attended. But, in the beaten way of friendship, what make you at Elsinore?

ROSENCRANTZ. To visit you, my lord, no other occasion.

HAMLET. Beggar that I am, I am even poor in thanks; but I thank you, and sure, dear friends, my thanks are too dear a halfpenny. Were you not sent for? Is it your own inclining? Is it a free visitation? Come, come, deal justly with me. Come, come. Nay, speak.

GUILDENSTERN. What should we say, my lord?

HAMLET. Anything but to the purpose. You were sent for, and there is a kind of confession in your looks which your modesties have not craft enough to color. I know the good King and Queen have sent for you.

ROSENCRANTZ. To what end, my lord?

HAMLET. That you must teach me. But let me conjure you, by the rights of our fellowship, by the consonancy of our youth, by the obligation of our ever-preserved love, and by what more dear a better proposer could charge you withal, be even and direct with me whether you were sent for or no.

ROSENCRANTZ. [*aside to Guildenstern*]. What say you?

HAMLET. [*aside*]. Nay, then, I have an eye of you.—If you love me, hold not off.

GUILDENSTERN. My lord, we were sent for.

HAMLET. I will tell you why; so shall my anticipation prevent your discovery, and your secrecy to the King and Queen molt no feather. I have of late—but wherefore I know not—lost all my mirth, forgone all custom of exercises; and indeed it goes so heavily with my disposition that this goodly frame, the earth, seems to me a sterile promontory; this most excellent canopy, the air, look you, this brave o'erhanging firmament, this majestical roof fretted with golden fire, why, it appeareth nothing to me but a foul and pestilent congregation of vapors. What a piece of work is a man! How noble in reason, how infinite in faculties, in form and moving how express and admirable, in action how like an angel, in apprehension how like a god! The beauty of the world, the paragon of animals! And yet, to me, what is this quintessence of dust? Man delights not me—no, nor woman neither, though by your smiling you seem to say so.

---

251 wait upon accompany, attend. (But Hamlet uses the phrase in the sense of providing menial service.) **252 sort** class, categorize **253 dreadfully attended** waited upon in slovenly fashion. **254 beaten way** familiar path, tried-and-true course. **make** do **257 too dear a halfpenny** (1) too expensive at even a halfpenny, i.e., of little worth (2) too expensive *by* a halfpenny in return for worthless kindness. **258 free** voluntary **261 Anything but to the purpose** Anything except a straightforward answer. (Said ironically.) **263 color** disguise **265 conjure** adjure, entreat **266 the consonancy of our youth** our closeness in our younger days **267 better** more skillful **268 charge** urge. **even** straight, honest **271 of** on **271–2 hold not off** don't hold back **274–5 so . . . discovery** in that way my saying it first will spare you from having to reveal the truth **275 molt no feather** i.e., not diminish in the least. **279 brave** splendid **280 fretted** adorned (with fretwork, as in a vaulted ceiling) **281 congregation** mass. **piece of work** masterpiece **283 express** well-framed, exact, expressive **apprehension** power of comprehending **285 quintessence** very essence. (Literally, the fifth essence beyond earth, water, air, and fire, supposed to be extractable from them.)

ROSENCRANTZ. My lord, there was no such stuff in my thoughts.

HAMLET. Why did you laugh, then, when I said man delights not me?

ROSENCRANTZ. To think, my lord, if you delight not in man, what Lenten entertainment the players shall receive from you. We coted them on the way, and hither are they coming to offer you service.

HAMLET. He that plays the king shall be welcome; His Majesty shall have tribute of me. The adventurous knight shall use his foil and target, the lover shall not sigh gratis, the humorous man shall end his part in peace, the clown shall make those laugh whose lungs are tickle o'th'sear, and the lady shall say her mind freely, or the blank verse shall halt for't. What players are they?

ROSENCRANTZ. Even those you were wont to take such delight in, the tragedians of the city.

HAMLET. How chances it they travel? Their residence, both in reputation and profit, was better both ways.

ROSENCRANTZ. I think their inhibition comes by the means of the late innovation.

HAMLET. Do they hold the same estimation they did when I was in the city? Are they so followed?

ROSENCRANTZ. No, indeed are they not.

HAMLET. How comes it? Do they grow rusty?

ROSENCRANTZ. Nay, their endeavor keeps in the wonted pace. But there is, sir, an aerie of children, little eyases, that cry out on the top of question and are most tyrannically clapped for't. These are now the fashion, and so berattle the common stages—so they call them—that many wearing rapiers are afraid of goose quills and dare scarce come thither.

HAMLET. What, are they children? Who maintains 'em? How are they escotted? Will they pursue the quality no longer than they can sing? Will they not say afterwards, if they should grow themselves to common players—as it is most like, if their means are no better—their writers do them wrong to make them exclaim against their own succession?

289–90 Lenten entertainment meager reception (appropriate to Lent) **290 coted** overtook and passed by **293 tribute** (1) applause (2) homage paid in money. **of** from **foil and target** sword and shield **294 gratis** for nothing. **humorous man** eccentric character, dominated by one trait or "humor" **in peace** i.e., with full license **295 tickle o'th'sear** hair trigger, ready to laugh easily. (A *sear* is part of a gun-lock.) **296 halt** limp **298–9 tragedians** actors **300 residence** remaining in their usual place, i.e., in the city **302 inhibition** formal prohibition (from acting plays in the city) **302–3 late innovation** i.e., recent new fashion in satirical plays performed by boy actors in the "private" theaters; or the Earl of Essex's abortive rebellion in 1601 against Elizabeth's government. (A much debated passage of seeming topical reference.) **307 How . . . rusty?** Have they lost their polish, gone out of fashion? (This passage, through line 325, alludes to the rivalry between the children's companies and the adult actors, given strong impetus by the reopening of the Children of the Chapel at the Blackfriars Theater in late 1600.) **308 keeps . . . wonted** continues in the usual **309 aerie** nest. **eyases** young hawks **cry . . . question** speak shrilly, dominating the controversy (in decrying the public theaters) **310 tyrannically** vehemently **311 berattle . . . stages** clamor against the public theaters **311–2 many wearing rapiers** i.e., many men of fashion, afraid to patronize the common players for fear of being satirized by the poets writing for the boy actors. **312 goose quills** i.e., pens of satirists **314 escotted** maintained. **quality** (acting) profession **no longer . . . sing** i.e., only until their voices change. **315 common** regular, adult **316 like** likely **if . . . better** if they find no better way to support themselves **317 succession** i.e., future careers.

ROSENCRANTZ. Faith, there has been much to-do on both sides, and the na- 318
tion holds it no sin to tar them to controversy. There was for a while no 319
money bid for argument unless the poet and the player went to cuffs in
the question.

HAMLET. Is't possible?

GUILDENSTERN. Oh, there has been much throwing about of brains.

HAMLET. Do the boys carry it away? 324

ROSENCRANTZ. Ay, that they do, my lord—Hercules and his load too. 325

HAMLET. It is not very strange; for my uncle is King of Denmark, and those
that would make mouths at him while my father lived give twenty, forty, 327
fifty, a hundred ducats apiece for his picture in little. 'Sblood, there is 328
something in this more than natural, if philosophy could find it out.

A flourish [*of trumpets within*].

GUILDENSTERN. There are the players.

HAMLET. Gentlemen, you are welcome to Elsinore. Your hands, come then.
Th'appurtenance of welcome is fashion and ceremony. Let me comply 332
with you in this garb, lest my extent to the players, which, I tell you, must 333
show fairly outwards, should more appear like entertainment than yours. 334
You are welcome. But my uncle-father and aunt-mother are deceived.

GUILDENSTERN. In what, my dear lord?

HAMLET. I am but mad north-north-west. When the wind is southerly I 337
know a hawk from a handsaw.

Enter Polonius.

POLONIUS. Well be with you, gentlemen!

HAMLET. Hark you, Guildenstern, and you too; at each ear a hearer. That
great baby you see there is not yet out of his swaddling clouts. 341

ROSENCRANTZ. Haply he is the second time come to them, for they say an 342
old man is twice a child.

HAMLET. I will prophesy he comes to tell me of the players. Mark it—You 344
say right, sir, o'Monday morning, 'twas then indeed.

POLONIUS. My lord, I have news to tell you.

HAMLET. My lord, I have news to tell you. When Roscius was an actor in 347
Rome—

---

318 to-do ado **319 tar** incite (as in inciting dogs to attack a chained bear) **319–21 There . . . question** i.e., For a while, no money was offered by the acting companies to playwrights for the plot to a play unless the satirical poets who wrote for the boys and the adult actors came to blows in the play itself. **324 carry it away** i.e., win the day **325 Hercules . . . load** (Thought to be an allusion to the sign of the Globe Theatre, which allegedly was Hercules bearing the world on his shoulders.) **327 mouths** faces **328 ducats** gold coins. **in little** in miniature. **'Sblood** By God's (Christ's) blood **332 Th'appurtenance** the proper accompaniment **comply** observe the formalities of courtesy **333 garb** i.e., manner. **my extent** that which I extend, i.e., my polite behavior **334 show fairly outwards** show every evidence of cordiality **entertainment** a (warm) reception **337 north-north-west** just off true north, only partly **337–8 I . . . handsaw** (Speaking in his mad guise, Hamlet perhaps suggests that he can tell true from false. A *handsaw* may be a *hernshaw* or heron. Still, a supposedly mad disposition might compare hawks and handsaws.) **341 swaddling clouts** cloths in which to wrap a newborn baby **342 Haply** Perhaps **344–5 You say . . . then indeed** (Said to impress upon Polonius the idea that Hamlet is in serious conversation with his friends.) **347 Roscius** a famous Roman actor who died in 62 B.C.

POLONIUS. The actors are come hither, my lord.

HAMLET. Buzz, buzz!

POLONIUS. Upon my honor—

HAMLET. Then came each actor on his ass.

POLONIUS. The best actors in the world, either for tragedy, comedy, history, pastoral, pastoral-comical, historical-pastoral, tragical-historical, tragical-comical historical-pastoral, scene individable, or poem unlimited. Seneca cannot be too heavy, nor Plautus too light. For the law of writ and the liberty, these are the only men.

HAMLET. O Jephthah, judge of Israel, what a treasure hadst thou!

POLONIUS. What a treasure had he, my lord?

HAMLET. Why,

"One fair daughter, and no more,
The which he lovèd passing well."

POLONIUS [*aside*]. Still on my daughter.

HAMLET. Am I not i'th'right, old Jephthah?

POLONIUS. If you call me Jephthah, my lord, I have a daughter that I love passing well.

HAMLET. Nay, that follows not.

POLONIUS. What follows then, my lord?

HAMLET. Why,

"As by lot, God wot,"

and then, you know,

"It came to pass, as most like it was"—

the first row of the pious chanson will show you more, for look where my abridgement comes.

Enter the Players.

You are welcome, masters; welcome, all. I am glad to see thee well. Welcome, good friends. Oh, old friend! Why, thy face is valanced since I saw thee last. Com'st thou to beard me in Denmark? What, my young lady and mistress! By'r Lady, Your Ladyship is nearer to heaven than when I saw you last, by the altitude of a chopine. Pray God your voice,

---

350 Buzz (An interjection used to denote stale news.) **355 scene . . . unlimited** plays that are unclassifiable and all-inclusive. (An absurdly catchall conclusion to Polonius' pompous list of categories.) **Seneca** writer of Latin tragedies. **356 Plautus** writer of Latin comedy **356–7 law . . . liberty** dramatic composition both according to the rules and disregarding the rules. **357 these** i.e., the actors **358 Jephthah . . . Israel** (Jephthah had to sacrifice his daughter; see Judges 11. Hamlet goes on to quote from a ballad on the theme.) **362 passing** surpassingly **367 that follows not** i.e., just because you resemble Jephthah in having a daughter does not logically prove that you love her. **368 What . . . lord?** What does follow logically? (But Hamlet, pretending madness, answers with a fragment of a ballad, as if Polonius had asked, "What comes next?" See next note.) **370 lot** chance. **wot** knows **372 like** likely, probable **373 the first . . . more** the first stanza of this biblically based ballad will satisfy your stated desire to know *what follows* (line 368). **374 my abridgment** something that cuts short my conversation; also, a diversion **375 masters** good sirs **376 valanced** fringed (with a beard) **377 beard** confront, challenge. (With obvious pun.) **377–8 young lady** i.e., boy playing women's parts **378 By'r Lady** By Our Lady. **nearer to heaven** i.e., taller **379 chopine** thick-soled shoe of Italian fashion.

like a piece of uncurrent gold, be not cracked within the ring. Masters, you are all welcome. We'll e'en to't like French falconers, fly at anything we see. We'll have a speech straight. Come, give us a taste of your quality. Come, a passionate speech.

FIRST PLAYER. What speech, my good lord?

HAMLET. I heard thee speak me a speech once, but it was never acted, or if it was, not above once, for the play, I remember, pleased not the million; 'twas caviar to the general. But it was—as I received it, and others, whose judgments in such matters cried in the top of mine—an excellent play, well digested in the scenes, set down with as much modesty as cunning. I remember one said there were no sallets in the lines to make the matter savory, nor no matter in the phrase that might indict the author of affectation, but called it an honest method, as wholesome as sweet, and by very much more handsome than fine. One speech in't I chiefly loved: 'twas Aeneas' tale to Dido, and thereabout of it especially when he speaks of Priam's slaughter. If it live in your memory, begin at this line: let me see, let me see—

"The rugged Pyrrhus, like th'Hyrcanian beast"—

'Tis not so. It begins with Pyrrhus:

"The rugged Pyrrhus, he whose sable arms,
Black as his purpose, did the night resemble
When he lay couchèd in the ominous horse,
Hath now this dread and black complexion smeared
With heraldry more dismal. Head to foot
Now is he total gules, horridly tricked
With blood of fathers, mothers, daughters, sons,
Baked and impasted with the parching streets,
That lend a tyrannous and a damnèd light
To their lord's murder. Roasted in wrath and fire,
And thus o'ersizèd with coagulate gore,

---

380 uncurrent not passable as lawful coinage **cracked . . . ring** i.e., changed from adolescent to male voice, no longer suitable for women's roles. (Coins featured rings enclosing the sovereign's head; if the coin was sufficiently clipped to invade within this ring, it was unfit for currency.) **381 e'en to't** go at it **382 straight** at once. **quality** professional skill. **387 caviar to the general** i.e., an expensive delicacy not generally palatable to uneducated tastes. **388 cried in the top of** i.e., spoke with greater authority than **389 digested** arranged, ordered. **modesty** moderation, restraint. **389–90 cunning** skill. **390 sallets** i.e., something savory, spicy improprieties **391 indict** convict **393 handsome** well-proportioned. **fine** elaborately ornamented, showy. **395 Priam's slaughter** the slaying of the ruler of Troy, when the Greeks finally took the city **397 Pyrrhus** a Greek hero in the Trojan War, also known as Neoptolemus, son of Achilles—another avenging son. **th'Hyrcanian beast** i.e., the tiger. (On the death of Priam, see Virgil, *Aeneid,* 2.506 ff.; compare the whole speech with Marlowe's *Dido Queen of Carthage,* 2.1.214 ff. On the *Hyrcanian* tiger, see *Aeneid,* 4.366–7. Hyrcania is on the Caspian Sea.) **399 rugged** shaggy, savage. **sable** black (for reasons of camouflage during the episode of the Trojan horse) **401 couchèd** concealed. **ominous horse** fateful Trojan horse, by which the Greeks gained access to Troy **403 dismal** calamitous. **404 total gules** entirely red. (A heraldic term.) **tricked** spotted and smeared. (Heraldic.) **406 Baked . . . streets** roasted and encrusted, like a thick paste, by the parching heat of the streets (because of the fires everywhere) **407 tyrannous** cruel **408 their lord's** i.e., Priam's **409 o'ersizèd** covered as with size or glue

With eyes like carbuncles, the hellish Pyrrhus
Old grandsire Priam seeks."
So proceed you.

POLONIUS. 'Fore God, my lord, well spoken, with good accent and good discretion.

FIRST PLAYER. "Anon he finds him
Striking too short at Greeks. His antique sword,
Rebellious to his arm, lies where it falls,
Repugnant to command. Unequal matched,
Pyrrhus at Priam drives, in rage strikes wide,
But with the whiff and wind of his fell sword
Th'unnervèd father falls. Then senseless Ilium,
Seeming to feel this blow, with flaming top
Stoops to his base, and with a hideous crash
Takes prisoner Pyrrhus' ear. For, lo! His sword,
Which was declining on the milky head
Of reverend Priam, seemed i'th'air to stick.
So as a painted tyrant Pyrrhus stood,
And, like a neutral to his will and matter,
Did nothing.
But as we often see against some storm
A silence in the heavens, the rack stand still,
The bold winds speechless, and the orb below
As hush as death, anon the dreadful thunder
Doth rend the region, so, after Pyrrhus' pause,
A rousèd vengeance sets him new a-work,
And never did the Cyclops' hammers fall
On Mars's armor forged for proof eterne
With less remorse than Pyrrhus' bleeding sword
Now falls on Priam.
Out, out, thou strumpet Fortune! All you gods
In general synod take away her power!
Break all the spokes and fellies from her wheel,
And bowl the round nave down the hill of heaven
As low as to the fiends!"

POLONIUS. This is too long.

HAMLET. It shall to the barber's with your beard.—Prithee, say on. He's for a jig or a tale of bawdry, or he sleeps. Say on; come to Hecuba.

FIRST PLAYER.
"But who, ah woe! had seen the moblèd queen"—

---

410 carbuncles large fiery-red precious stones thought to emit their own light **415 antique** ancient, long-used **417 Repugnant** disobedient, resistant **419 fell** cruel **420 Th'unnervèd** the strengthless. **senseless Ilium** inanimate citadel of Troy **422 his** its **424 declining** descending. **milky** white-haired **426 painted** motionless, as in a painting **427 like . . . matter** i.e., as though suspended between his intention and its fulfillment **429 against** just before **430 rack** mass of clouds **431 orb** globe, earth **433 region** sky **435 Cyclops** giant armor makers in the smithy of Vulcan **436 proof** "proven" or tested resistance to assault **437 remorse** pity **440 synod** assembly **441 fellies** pieces of wood forming the rim of a wheel **442 nave** hub. **hill of heaven** Mount Olympus **446 jig** comic song and dance often given at the end of a play. **Hecuba** wife of Priam **447 who . . . had** anyone who had. (also in line 455.) **moblèd** muffled

HAMLET. "The mobled queen?"

POLONIUS. That's good. "Mobled queen" is good.

FIRST PLAYER.
"Run barefoot up and down, threat'ning the flames
With bisson rheum, a clout upon that head
Where late the diadem stood, and, for a robe,
About her lank and all o'erteemed loins
A blanket, in the alarm of fear caught up—
Who this had seen, with tongue in venom steeped,
'Gainst Fortune's state would treason have pronounced.
But if the gods themselves did see her then
When she saw Pyrrhus make malicious sport
In mincing with his sword her husband's limbs,
The instant burst of clamor that she made,
Unless things mortal move them not at all,
Would have made milch the burning eyes of heaven,
And passion in the gods."

POLONIUS. Look whe'er he has not turned his color and has tears in 's eyes. Prithee, no more.

HAMLET. 'Tis well; I'll have thee speak out the rest of this soon.—Good my lord, will you see the players well bestowed? Do you hear, let them be well used, for they are the abstract and brief chronicles of the time. After your death you were better have a bad epitaph than their ill report while you live.

POLONIUS. My lord, I will use them according to their desert.

HAMLET. God's bodikin, man, much better. Use every man after his desert, and who shall scape whipping? Use them after your own honor and dignity. The less they deserve, the more merit is in your bounty. Take them in.

POLONIUS. Come, sirs. [*Exit.*]

HAMLET. Follow him, friends. We'll hear a play tomorrow. [*As they start to leave, Hamlet detains the First Player.*] Dost thou hear me, old friend? Can you play *The Murder of Gonzago?*

FIRST PLAYER. Ay, my lord.

HAMLET. We'll ha 't tomorrow night. You could, for a need, study a speech of some dozen or sixteen lines which I would set down and insert in't, could you not?

FIRST PLAYER. Ay, my lord.

HAMLET. Very well. Follow that lord, and look you mock him not. (*Exeunt Players.*) My good friends, I'll leave you till night. You are welcome to Elsinore.

ROSENCRANTZ. Good my lord!

Exeunt [*Rosencrantz and Guildenstern*].

---

450 threat'ning the flames i.e., weeping hard enough to dampen the flames **451 bisson rheum** blinding tears. **clout** cloth **452 late** lately **453 all o'erteemed** utterly worn out with bearing children **456 state** rule, managing. **pronounced** proclaimed. **462 milch** milky, moist with tears. **burning eyes of heaven** i.e., stars, heavenly bodies **463 passion** overpowering emotion **464 whe'er** whether **467 bestowed** lodged. **468 abstract** summary account **472 God's bodikin** By God's (Christ's) little body, *bodykin.* (Not to be confused with *bodkin,* "dagger.") **after** according to **481 ha 't** have it **study** memorize

HAMLET.
Ay, so, goodbye to you.—Now I am alone.
Oh, what a rogue and peasant slave am I!
Is it not monstrous that this player here,
But in a fiction, in a dream of passion,
Could force his soul so to his own conceit
That from her working all his visage wanned,
Tears in his eyes, distraction in his aspect,
A broken voice, and his whole function suiting
With forms to his conceit? And all for nothing!
For Hecuba!
What's Hecuba to him, or he to Hecuba,
That he should weep for her? What would he do
Had he the motive and the cue for passion
That I have? He would drown the stage with tears
And cleave the general ear with horrid speech,
Make mad the guilty and appall the free,
Confound the ignorant, and amaze indeed
The very faculties of eyes and ears. Yet I,
A dull and muddy-mettled rascal, peak
Like John-a-dreams, unpregnant of my cause,
And can say nothing—no, not for a king
Upon whose property and most dear life
A damned defeat was made. Am I a coward?
Who calls me villain? Breaks my pate across?
Plucks off my beard and blows it in my face?
Tweaks me by the nose? Gives me the lie i'th'throat
As deep as to the lungs? Who does me this?
Ha, 'swounds, I should take it; for it cannot be
But I am pigeon-livered and lack gall
To make oppression bitter, or ere this
I should ha' fatted all the region kites
With this slave's offal. Bloody, bawdy villain!
Remorseless, treacherous, lecherous, kindless villain!
Oh, vengeance!
Why, what an ass am I! This is most brave,

---

492 But merely **493 force . . . conceit** bring his innermost being so entirely into accord with his conception (of the role) **494 from her working** as a result of, or in response to, his soul's activity. **wanned** grew pale **495 aspect** look, glance **496–7 his whole . . . conceit** all his bodily powers responding with actions to suit his thought. **503 the general ear** everyone's ear. **horrid** horrible **504 appall** (Literally, make pale.) **free** innocent **505 Confound the ignorant** i.e., dumbfound those who know nothing of the crime that has been committed. **amaze** stun **507 muddy-mettled** dull-spirited **507–8 peak . . . cause** mope, like a dreaming idler, not quickened by my cause **510 property** person and function **511 damned defeat** damnable act of destruction **512 pate** head **514 Gives . . . throat** calls me an out-and-out liar **516 'swounds** by his (Christ's) wounds **517 pigeon-livered** (The pigeon or dove was popularly supposed to be mild because it secreted no gall.) **518 To . . . bitter** to make things bitter for oppressors **519 region kites** kites (birds of prey) of the air **520 offal** entrails. **521 Remorseless** Pitiless. **kindless** unnatural **523 brave** fine, admirable. (Said ironically.)

That I, the son of a dear father murdered,
Prompted to my revenge by heaven and hell,
Must like a whore unpack my heart with words
And fall a-cursing, like a very drab, 527
A scullion! Fie upon't, foh! About, my brains! 528
Hum, I have heard
That guilty creatures sitting at a play
Have by the very cunning of the scene 531
Been struck so to the soul that presently 532
They have proclaimed their malefactions;
For murder, though it have no tongue, will speak
With most miraculous organ. I'll have these players
Play something like the murder of my father
Before mine uncle. I'll observe his looks;
I'll tent him to the quick. If 'a do blench, 538
I know my course. The spirit that I have seen
May be the devil, and the devil hath power
T'assume a pleasing shape; yea, and perhaps,
Out of my weakness and my melancholy,
As he is very potent with such spirits, 543
Abuses me to damn me. I'll have grounds 544
More relative than this. The play's the thing 545
Wherein I'll catch the conscience of the King. *Exit.*

3.1

Enter King, Queen, Polonius, Ophelia, Rosencrantz, Guildenstern, lords.

KING.
And can you by no drift of conference 1
Get from him why he puts on this confusion,
Grating so harshly all his days of quiet
With turbulent and dangerous lunacy?

ROSENCRANTZ.
He does confess he feels himself distracted,
But from what cause 'a will by no means speak.

GUILDENSTERN.
Nor do we find him forward to be sounded, 7
But with a crafty madness keeps aloof
When we would bring him on to some confession
Of his true state.

QUEEN. Did he receive you well?

527 drab whore **528 scullion** menial kitchen servant. (apt to be foul-mouthed.) **About** About it, to work **531 cunning** art, skill. **scene** dramatic presentation **532 presently** at once **538 tent** probe. **the quick** the tender part of a wound, the core. **blench** quail, flinch **543 spirits** humors (of melancholy) **544 Abuses** deludes **545 relative** cogent, pertinent

3.1 Location: The castle.

1 drift of conference course of talk **7 forward** willing. **sounded** questioned

ROSENCRANTZ. Most like a gentleman.
GUILDENSTERN.
But with much forcing of his disposition. 12
ROSENCRANTZ.
Niggard of question, but of our demands 13
Most free in his reply.
QUEEN. Did you assay him 14
To any pastime?
ROSENCRANTZ.
Madam, it so fell out that certain players
We o'erraught on the way. Of these we told him, 17
And there did seem in him a kind of joy
To hear of it. They are here about the court,
And, as I think, they have already order
This night to play before him.
POLONIUS. 'Tis most true,
And he beseeched me to entreat Your Majesties
To hear and see the matter.
KING.
With all my heart, and it doth much content me
To hear him so inclined.
Good gentlemen, give him a further edge 26
And drive his purpose into these delights.
ROSENCRANTZ.
We shall, my lord.

Exeunt Rosencrantz and Guildenstern.

KING. Sweet Gertrude, leave us too,
For we have closely sent for Hamlet hither, 29
That he, as 'twere by accident, may here
Affront Ophelia. 31
Her father and myself, lawful espials, 32
Will so bestow ourselves that seeing, unseen,
We may of their encounter frankly judge,
And gather by him, as he is behaved,
If 't be th'affliction of his love or no
That thus he suffers for.
QUEEN. I shall obey you.
And for your part, Ophelia, I do wish
That your good beauties be the happy cause
Of Hamlet's wildness. So shall I hope your virtues
Will bring him to his wonted way again,
To both your honors.
OPHELIA. Madam, I wish it may.

[*Exit Queen.*]

---

12 disposition inclination **13 Niggard of question** Laconic. **demands** questions **14 assay** try to win **17 o'erraught** overtook **26 edge** incitement **29 closely** privately **31 Affront** confront, meet **32 espials** spies

POLONIUS.
Ophelia, walk you here.—Gracious, so please you, 43
We will bestow ourselves. [*To Ophelia giving her a book*] Read on this 44
book,
That show of such an exercise may color 46
Your loneliness. We are oft to blame in this— 47
'Tis too much proved—that with devotion's visage 48
And pious action we do sugar o'er
The devil himself.

KING [*aside*]. O, 'tis too true!
How smart a lash that speech doth give my conscience!
The harlot's cheek, beautied with plastering art,
Is not more ugly to the thing that helps it 54
Than is my deed to my most painted word. 55
Oh, heavy burden!

POLONIUS.
I hear him coming. Let's withdraw, my lord. 57

[*The King and Polonius withdraw.*]

Enter Hamlet. [*Ophelia pretends to read a book.*]

HAMLET.
To be, or not to be, that is the question:
Whether 'tis nobler in the mind to suffer
The slings and arrows of outrageous fortune,
Or to take arms against a sea of troubles
And by opposing end them. To die, to sleep—
No more—and by a sleep to say we end
The heartache and the thousand natural shocks
That flesh is heir to. 'Tis a consummation
Devoutly to be wished. To die, to sleep;
To sleep, perchance to dream. Ay, there's the rub, 67
For in that sleep of death what dreams may come,
When we have shuffled off this mortal coil, 69
Must give us pause. There's the respect 70
That makes calamity of so long life. 71
For who would bear the whips and scorns of time,
Th'oppressor's wrong, the proud man's contumely, 73
The pangs of disprized love, the law's delay, 74
The insolence of office, and the spurns 75

---

43 Gracious Your Grace (i.e., the King) **44 bestow** conceal **46 exercise** religious exercise. (The book she reads is one of devotion.) **color** give a plausible appearance to **47 loneliness** being alone. **48 too much proved** too often shown to be true, too often practiced **54 to . . . helps it** in comparison with the cosmetic that fashions the cheek's false beauty **55 painted word** deceptive utterances. **57 *withdraw*** (The King and Polonius may retire behind an arras. The stage directions specify that they "enter" again near the end of the scene.) **67 rub** (Literally, an obstacle in the game of bowls.) **69 shuffled** sloughed, cast. **coil** turmoil **70 respect** consideration **71 of . . . life** so long-lived, something we willingly endure for so long (also suggesting that long life is itself a calamity) **73 contumely** insolent abuse **74 disprized** unvalued **75 office** officialdom. **spurns** insults

That patient merit of th'unworthy takes,
When he himself might his quietus make
With a bare bodkin? Who would fardels bear,
To grunt and sweat under a weary life,
But that the dread of something after death,
The undiscovered country from whose bourn
No traveler returns, puzzles the will,
And makes us rather bear those ills we have
Than fly to others that we know not of?
Thus conscience does make cowards of us all;
And thus the native hue of resolution
Is sicklied o'er with the pale cast of thought,
And enterprises of great pitch and moment
With this regard their currents turn awry
And lose the name of action.—Soft you now,
The fair Ophelia.—Nymph, in thy orisons
Be all my sins remembered.

OPHELIA. Good my lord,
How does Your Honor for this many a day?

HAMLET.
I humbly thank you; well, well, well.

OPHELIA.
My lord, I have remembrances of yours,
That I have longèd long to redeliver.
I pray you, now receive them. [*She offers tokens.*]

HAMLET.
No, not I, I never gave you aught.

OPHELIA.
My honored lord, you know right well you did,
And with them words of so sweet breath composed
As made the things more rich. Their perfume lost,
Take these again, for to the noble mind
Rich gifts wax poor when givers prove unkind.
There, my lord. [*She gives tokens.*]

HAMLET. Ha, ha! Are you honest?

OPHELIA. My lord?

HAMLET. Are you fair?

OPHELIA. What means Your Lordship?

HAMLET. That if you be honest and fair, your honesty should admit no discourse to your beauty.

OPHELIA. Could beauty, my lord, have better commerce than with honesty?

HAMLET. Ay, truly, for the power of beauty will sooner transform honesty from what it is to a bawd than the force of honesty can translate beauty

---

76 of . . . takes receives from unworthy persons **77 quietus** acquittance; here, death **78 a bare bodkin** a mere dagger, unsheathed. **fardels** burdens **81 bourn** frontier, boundary **86 native hue** natural color, complexion **87 cast** tinge, shade of color **88 pitch** height (as of a falcon's flight). **moment** importance **89 regard** respect, consideration. **currents** courses **90 Soft you** i.e., Wait a minute, gently **91–2 in . . . remembered** i.e., pray for me, sinner that I am. **105 honest** (1) truthful (2) chaste. **107 fair** (1) beautiful (2) just, honorable. **109 your honesty** your chastity **110 discourse to** familiar dealings with **111 commerce** dealings, intercourse

into his likeness. This was sometime a paradox, but now the time gives it proof. I did love you once.

OPHELIA. Indeed, my lord, you made me believe so.

HAMLET. You should not have believed me, for virtue cannot so inoculate our old stock but we shall relish of it. I loved you not.

OPHELIA. I was the more deceived.

HAMLET. Get thee to a nunnery. Why wouldst thou be a breeder of sinners? I am myself indifferent honest, but yet I could accuse me of such things that it were better my mother had not borne me: I am very proud, revengeful, ambitious, with more offenses at my beck than I have thoughts to put them in, imagination to give them shape, or time to act them in. What should such fellows as I do crawling between earth and heaven? We are arrant knaves all; believe none of us. Go thy ways to a nunnery. Where's your father?

OPHELIA. At home, my lord.

HAMLET. Let the doors be shut upon him, that he may play the fool nowhere but in 's own house. Farewell.

OPHELIA. Oh, help him, you sweet heavens!

HAMLET. If thou dost marry, I'll give thee this plague for thy dowry: be thou as chaste as ice, as pure as snow, thou shalt not escape calumny. Get thee to a nunnery, farewell. Or, if thou wilt needs marry, marry a fool, for wise men know well enough what monsters you make of them. To a nunnery, go, and quickly too. Farewell.

OPHELIA. Heavenly powers, restore him!

HAMLET. I have heard of your paintings too, well enough. God hath given you one face, and you make yourselves another. You jig, you amble, and you lisp, you nickname God's creatures, and make your wantonness your ignorance. Go to, I'll no more on't; it hath made me mad. I say we will have no more marriage. Those that are married already—all but one—shall live. The rest shall keep as they are. To a nunnery, go. *Exit.*

OPHELIA.

Oh, what a noble mind is here o'erthrown!
The courtier's, soldier's, scholar's, eye, tongue, sword,
Th'expectancy and rose of the fair state,
The glass of fashion and the mold of form,
Th'observed of all observers, quite, quite down!
And I, of ladies most deject and wretched,
That sucked the honey of his music vows,

---

114 his its **114–15 This . . . proof** This was formerly an unfashionable view, but now the present age confirms how true it is. **117–18 virtue . . . of it** virtue cannot be grafted onto our sinful condition without our retaining some taste of the old stock. **120 nunnery** convent. (With an awareness that the word was also used derisively to denote a brothel.) **121 indifferent honest** reasonably virtuous **123 beck** command **135 monsters** (An allusion to the horns of a cuckold.) **you** i.e., you women **138 paintings** use of cosmetics **139–41 You jig . . . ignorance** i.e., You prance about frivolously and speak with affected coynesss, you put new labels on God's creatures (by use of cosmetics); and you excuse your affectations on the grounds of pretended ignorance. **141 on't** of it **146 Th'expectancy and rose** the hope and ornament **147 The glass . . . form** the mirror of true self-fashioning and the pattern of courtly behavior **148 Th'observed . . . observers** i.e., the center of attention and honor in the court **150 music** musical, sweetly uttered

Now see that noble and most sovereign reason
Like sweet bells jangled out of tune and harsh,
That unmatched form and feature of blown youth 153
Blasted with ecstasy. Oh, woe is me, 154
T'have seen what I have seen, see what I see!

Enter King and Polonius.

KING.
Love? His affections do not that way tend; 156
Nor what he spake, though it lacked form a little,
Was not like madness. There's something in his soul
O'er which his melancholy sits on brood, 159
And I do doubt the hatch and the disclose 160
Will be some danger; which for to prevent,
I have in quick determination
Thus set it down: he shall with speed to England 163
For the demand of our neglected tribute.
Haply the seas and countries different
With variable objects shall expel 166
This something-settled matter in his heart, 167
Whereon his brains still beating puts him thus 168
From fashion of himself. What think you on't? 169

POLONIUS.
It shall do well. But yet do I believe
The origin and commencement of his grief
Sprung from neglected love.—How now, Ophelia?
You need not tell us what Lord Hamlet said;
We heard it all.—My lord, do as you please,
But, if you hold it fit, after the play
Let his queen-mother all alone entreat him
To show his grief. Let her be round with him; 177
And I'll be placed, so please you, in the ear
Of all their conference. If she find him not, 179
To England send him, or confine him where
Your wisdom best shall think.

KING. It shall be so.
Madness in great ones must not unwatched go.

Exeunt.

---

153 blown blossoming **154 Blasted with ecstasy** blighted with madness. **156 affections** emotions, feelings **159 sits on brood** sits like a bird on a nest, about to *hatch* mischief (line 160) **160 doubt** suspect, fear. **disclose** disclosure, hatching **163 set it down** resolved **166 variable objects** various sights and surroundings to divert him **167 This something . . . heart** the strange matter settled in his heart **168 still** continually **169 From . . . himself** out of his natural manner. **177 round** blunt **179 find him not** fails to discover what is troubling him

3.2

Enter Hamlet and three of the Players.

HAMLET. Speak the speech, I pray you, as I pronounced it to you, trippingly on the tongue. But if you mouth it, as many of our players do, I had as lief the town crier spoke my lines. Nor do not saw the air too much with your hand, thus, but use all gently; for in the very torrent, tempest, and, as I may say, whirlwind of your passion, you must acquire and beget a temperance that may give it smoothness. Oh, it offends me to the soul to hear a robustious periwig-pated fellow tear a passion to tatters, to very rags, to split the ears of the groundlings, who for the most part are capable of nothing but inexplicable dumb shows and noise. I would have such a fellow whipped for o'erdoing Termagant. It out-Herods Herod. Pray you, avoid it.

FIRST PLAYER. I warrant Your Honor.

HAMLET. Be not too tame neither, but let your own discretion be your tutor. Suit the action to the word, the word to the action, with this special observance, that you o'erstep not the modesty of nature. For anything so o'erdone is from the purpose of playing, whose end, both at the first and now, was and is to hold as 'twere the mirror up to nature, to show virtue her feature, scorn her own image, and the very age and body of the time his form and pressure. Now this overdone or come tardy off, though it makes the unskillful laugh, cannot but make the judicious grieve, the censure of the which one must in your allowance o'erweigh a whole theater of others. Oh, there be players that I have seen play, and heard others praise, and that highly, not to speak it profanely, that, neither having th'accent of Christians nor the gait of Christian, pagan, nor man, have so strutted and bellowed that I have thought some of nature's journeymen had made men and not made them well, they imitated humanity so abominably.

FIRST PLAYER. I hope we have reformed that indifferently with us, sir.

HAMLET. Oh, reform it altogether. And let those that play your clowns speak no more than is set down for them; for there be of them that will

---

3.2 Location: The castle.

2 our players players nowadays. **I had as lief** I would just as soon **7 robustious** violent, boisterous. **periwig-pated** wearing a wig **8 groundlings** spectators who paid least and stood in the yard of the theater. **9 capable of** able to understand **dumb shows and noise** noisy spectacle (rather than thoughtful drama) **10 Termagant** a supposed deity of the Mohammedans, not found in any English medieval play but elsewhere portrayed as violent and blustering **11 Herod** Herod of Jewry. (A character in *The Slaughter of the Innocents* and other cycle plays. The part was played with great noise and fury.) **15 modesty** restraint, moderation **16 from** contrary to **18 scorn** i.e., something foolish and deserving of scorn **18–9 and the . . . pressure** and the present state of affairs its likeness as seen in an impression, such as wax. **19 come tardy off** falling short **20 the unskillful** those lacking in judgment **20–1 the censure . . . one** the judgment of even one of whom. **21 your allowance** your scale of values **23 not . . . profanely** (Hamlet anticipates his idea in lines 25–26 that some men were not made by God at all.) **24 Christians** i.e., ordinary decent folk **nor man** i.e., nor any human being at all **25–6 journeymen** common workmen **27 abominably** (Shakespeare's usual spelling, *abhominably,* suggests a literal though etymologically incorrect meaning, "removed from human nature.") **28 indifferently** tolerably **30 of them** some among them

themselves laugh, to set on some quantity of barren spectators to laugh 31
too, though in the meantime some necessary question of the play be
then to be considered. That's villainous, and shows a most pitiful ambition in the fool that uses it. Go make you ready. [*Exeunt Players.*]

Enter Polonius, Guildenstern, and Rosencrantz.

How now, my lord, will the King hear this piece of work?

POLONIUS. And the Queen too, and that presently. 36

HAMLET. Bid the players make haste. [*Exit Polonius.*]
Will you two help to hasten them?

ROSENCRANTZ.
Ay, my lord. *Exeunt they two.*

HAMLET. What ho, Horatio!

Enter Horatio.

HORATIO. Here, sweet lord, at your service.

HAMLET.
Horatio, thou art e'en as just a man
As e'er my conversation coped withal. 42

HORATIO.
Oh, my dear lord—

HAMLET. Nay, do not think I flatter,
For what advancement may I hope from thee
That no revenue hast but thy good spirits
To feed and clothe thee? Why should the poor be flattered?
No, let the candied tongue lick absurd pomp, 47
And crook the pregnant hinges of the knee 48
Where thrift may follow fawning. Dost thou hear? 49
Since my dear soul was mistress of her choice
And could of men distinguish her election, 51
Sh' hath sealed thee for herself, for thou hast been 52
As one, in suffering all, that suffers nothing,
A man that Fortune's buffets and rewards
Hast ta'en with equal thanks; and blest are those
Whose blood and judgment are so well commeddled 56
That they are not a pipe for Fortune's finger
To sound what stop she please. Give me that man 58
That is not passion's slave, and I will wear him
In my heart's core, ay, in my heart of heart,
As I do thee.—Something too much of this.—
There is a play tonight before the King.
One scene of it comes near the circumstance
Which I have told thee of my father's death.
I prithee, when thou seest that act afoot,

31 barren i.e., of wit **36 presently** at once. **42 my . . . withal** my dealings encountered. **47 candied** sugared, flattering **48 pregnant** compliant **49 thrift** profit **51 could . . . election** could make distinguishing choices among persons **52 sealed thee** (Literally, as one would seal a legal document to mark possession.) **56 blood** passion. **commeddled** commingled **58 stop** hole in a wind instrument for controlling the sound

Even with the very comment of thy soul
Observe my uncle. If his occulted guilt
Do not itself unkennel in one speech,
It is a damnèd ghost that we have seen,
And my imaginations are as foul
As Vulcan's stithy. Give him heedful note,
For I mine eyes will rivet to his face,
And after we will both our judgments join
In censure of his seeming.

HORATIO. Well, my lord.
If 'a steal aught the whilst this play is playing
And scape detecting, I will pay the theft.

[Flourish.] Enter trumpets and kettledrums, King, Queen, Polonius, Ophelia, [Rosencrantz, Guildenstern, and other lords, with guards carrying torches].

HAMLET. They are coming to the play. I must be idle. Get you a place.
[The King, Queen, and courtiers sit.]

KING. How fares our cousin Hamlet?

HAMLET. Excellent, i'faith, of the chameleon's dish: I eat the air, promise-crammed. You cannot feed capons so.

KING. I have nothing with this answer, Hamlet. These words are not mine.

HAMLET. No, nor mine now. *[To Polonius]* My lord, you played once i'th'university, you say?

POLONIUS. That did I, my lord, and was accounted a good actor.

HAMLET. What did you enact?

POLONIUS. I did enact Julius Caesar. I was killed i'th'Capitol; Brutus killed me.

HAMLET. It was a brute part of him to kill so capital a calf there.—Be the players ready?

ROSENCRANTZ. Ay, my lord. They stay upon your patience.

QUEEN. Come hither, my dear Hamlet, sit by me.

HAMLET. No, good mother, here's metal more attractive.

POLONIUS *[to the King]*. Oho, do you mark that?

HAMLET. Lady, shall I lie in your lap?

[Lying down at Ophelia's feet.]

---

66 very . . . soul your most penetrating observation and consideration **67 occulted** hidden **68 unkennel** (As one would say of a fox driven from its lair.) **71 Vulcan's stithy** the smithy, the place of stiths (anvils), of the Roman god of fire and metalworking. **74 censure of his seeming** judgment of his appearance or behavior. **75 If 'a steal aught** If he gets away with anything **77 idle** (1) unoccupied (2) mad. **78 cousin** i.e., close relative **79 chameleon's dish** (Chameleons were supposed to feed on air. Hamlet deliberately misinterprets the King's *fares* as "feeds." By his phrase *eat the air* he also plays on the idea of feeding himself with the promise of succession, of being the *heir.*) **80 capons** roosters castrated and *crammed* with feed to make them succulent **81 have . . . with** make nothing of, or gain nothing from **are not mine** do not respond to what I asked. **82 nor mine now** (Once spoken, words are proverbially no longer the speaker's own—and hence should be uttered warily.) **86 i'th'Capitol** Caesar was assassinated in the Senate House on the Capitoline hill of Rome. (See *Julius Caesar,* 3.1.) **88 brute** (The Latin meaning of *brutus,* "stupid," was often used punningly with the name Brutus.) **part** (1) deed (2) role **calf** fool **90 stay upon** await **92 metal** substance that is *attractive,* i.e., magnetic, but with suggestion also of *mettle,* "disposition"

OPHELIA. No, my lord.

HAMLET. I mean, my head upon your lap?

OPHELIA. Ay, my lord.

HAMLET. Do you think I meant country matters?

OPHELIA. I think nothing, my lord.

HAMLET. That's a fair thought to lie between maids' legs.

OPHELIA. What is, my lord?

HAMLET. Nothing.

OPHELIA. You are merry, my lord.

HAMLET. Who, I?

OPHELIA. Ay, my lord.

HAMLET. Oh God, your only jig maker. What should a man do but be merry? For look you how cheerfully my mother looks, and my father died within 's two hours.

OPHELIA. Nay, 'tis twice two months, my lord.

HAMLET. So long? Nay then, let the devil wear black, for I'll have a suit of sables. O heavens! Die two months ago, and not forgotten yet? Then there's hope a great man's memory may outlive his life half a year. But, by'r Lady, 'a must build churches, then, or else shall 'a suffer not thinking on, with the hobbyhorse, whose epitaph is "For oh, for oh, the hobbyhorse is forgot."

The trumpets sound. Dumb-show follows. Enter a King and a Queen [*very lovingly*]*; the Queen embracing him, and he her.* [*She kneels, and makes show of protestation unto him.*] *He takes her up, and declines his head upon her neck. He lies him down upon a bank of flowers. She, seeing him asleep, leaves him. Anon comes in another man, takes off his crown, kisses it, pours poison in the sleeper's ears, and leaves him. The Queen returns, finds the King dead, makes passionate action. The Poisoner with some three or four come in again, seem to condole with her. The dead body is carried away. The Poisoner woos the Queen with gifts; she seems harsh awhile, but in the end accepts love.*

[*Exeunt players.*]

OPHELIA. What means this, my lord?

HAMLET. Marry, this' miching mallico; it means mischief.

---

98 country matters sexual intercourse. (With a bawdy pun on the first syllable of *country.*) **99 nothing** the figure zero or naught, suggesting the female sexual anatomy. (*Thing* not infrequently has a bawdy connotation of male or female anatomy, and the reference here could be male.) **106 only jig maker** very best composer of jigs, i.e., pointless merriment. (Hamlet replies sardonically to Ophelia's observation that he is merry by saying, "If you're looking for someone who is really merry, you've come to the right person.") **108 within's** within this (i.e., these) **110–11 suit of sables** garments trimmed with the dark fur of the sable and hence suited for a person in mourning. **113–14 suffer . . . on** undergo oblivion **114–15 "For . . . forgot"** (Verse of a song occurring also in *Love's Labor's Lost,* 3.1.27–8. The hobbyhorse was a character made up to resemble a horse and rider, appearing in the morris dance and such May-game sports. This song laments the disappearance of such customs under pressure from the Puritans.) **117 this' miching mallico** this is sneaking mischief

OPHELIA. Belike this show imports the argument of the play. 118

Enter Prologue.

HAMLET. We shall know by this fellow. The players cannot keep counsel; 119
they'll tell all.

OPHELIA. Will 'a tell us what this show meant?

HAMLET. Ay, or any show that you will show him. Be not you ashamed to 122
show, he'll not shame to tell you what it means.

OPHELIA. You are naught, you are naught. I'll mark the play. 124

PROLOGUE.

For us, and for our tragedy,
Here stooping to your clemency, 126
We beg your hearing patiently. [*Exit.*]

HAMLET. Is this a prologue, or the posy of a ring? 128

OPHELIA. 'Tis brief, my lord.

HAMLET. As woman's love.

Enter [*two Players as*] *King and Queen.*

PLAYER KING.

Full thirty times hath Phoebus' cart gone round 131
Neptune's salt wash and Tellus' orbèd ground, 132
And thirty dozen moons with borrowed sheen 133
About the world have times twelve thirties been,
Since love our hearts and Hymen did our hands 135
Unite commutual in most sacred bands. 136

PLAYER QUEEN.

So many journeys may the sun and moon
Make us again count o'er ere love be done!
But, woe is me, you are sick of late,
So far from cheer and from your former state,
That I distrust you. Yet, though I distrust, 141
Discomfort you, my lord, it nothing must. 142
For women's fear and love hold quantity; 143
In neither aught, or in extremity. 144
Now, what my love is, proof hath made you know, 145
And as my love is sized, my fear is so.
Where love is great, the littlest doubts are fear; 147
Where little fears grow great, great love grows there.

PLAYER KING.

Faith, I must leave thee, love, and shortly too;
My operant powers their functions leave to do. 150

---

118 Belike Probably. **argument** plot **119 counsel** secret **122 Be not you** Provided you are not **124 naught** indecent. (Ophelia is reacting to Hamlet's pointed remarks about not being ashamed to show all.) **126 stooping** bowing **128 posy . . . ring** brief motto in verse inscribed in a ring **131 Phoebus' cart** the sun-god's chariot, making its yearly cycle **132 salt wash** the sea. **Tellus** goddess of the earth, of the *orbèd* ground **133 borrowed** i.e., reflected **135 Hymen** god of matrimony **136 commutual** mutually. **bands** bonds. **141 distrust** am anxious about **142 Discomfort . . . must** it must not distress you at all. **143 hold quantity** keep proportion with one another **144 In . . . extremity** (women feel) either no anxiety if they do not love or extreme anxiety if they do love. **145 proof** experience **147 the littlest** even the littlest **150 My . . . to do** my vital functions are shutting down.

And thou shalt live in this fair world behind,
Honored, beloved; and haply one as kind
For husband shalt thou—

PLAYER QUEEN. Oh, confound the rest!
Such love must needs be treason in my breast.
In second husband let me be accurst!
None wed the second but who killed the first.

HAMLET. Wormwood, wormwood.

PLAYER QUEEN.
The instances that second marriage move
Are base respects of thrift, but none of love.
A second time I kill my husband dead
When second husband kisses me in bed.

PLAYER KING.
I do believe you think what now you speak,
But what we do determine oft we break.
Purpose is but the slave to memory,
Of violent birth, but poor validity,
Which now, like fruit unripe, sticks on the tree,
But fall unshaken when they mellow be.
Most necessary 'tis that we forget
To pay ourselves what to ourselves is debt.
What to ourselves in passion we propose,
The passion ending, doth the purpose lose.
The violence of either grief or joy
Their own enactures with themselves destroy.
Where joy most revels, grief doth most lament;
Grief joys, joy grieves, on slender accident.
This world is not for aye, nor 'tis not strange
That even our loves should with our fortunes change;
For 'tis a question left us yet to prove,
Whether love lead fortune, or else fortune love.
The great man down, you mark his favorite flies;
The poor advanced makes friends of enemies.
And hitherto doth love on fortune tend;
For who not needs shall never lack a friend,
And who in want a hollow friend doth try
Directly seasons him his enemy.

---

151 behind after I have gone **157 None** (1) Let no woman; or (2) No woman does. **but who** except the one who **158 Wormwood** i.e., How bitter. (Literally, a bitter-tasting plant.) **159 instances** motives. **move** motivate **160 base . . . thrift** ignoble considerations of material prosperity **165 Purpose . . . memory** Our good intentions are subject to forgetfulness **166 validity** strength, durability **167 Which** i.e., purpose **169–70 Most . . . debt** It's inevitable that in time we forget the obligations we have imposed on ourselves. **174 enactures** fulfillments **175–6 Where . . . accident** The capacity for extreme joy and grief go together, and often one extreme is instantly changed into its opposite on the slightest provocation. **177 aye** ever **181 down** fallen in fortune **182 The poor . . . enemies** When one of humble station is promoted, you see his enemies suddenly becoming his friends. **183 hitherto** up to this point in the argument, or, to this extent. **tend** attend **184 who not needs** he who is not in need (of wealth) **185 who in want** he who, being in need. **try** test (his generosity) **186 seasons him** ripens him into

But, orderly to end where I begun,
Our wills and fates do so contrary run 188
That our devices still are overthrown; 189
Our thoughts are ours, their ends none of our own. 190
So think thou wilt no second husband wed,
But die thy thoughts when thy first lord is dead.

PLAYER QUEEN.
Nor earth to me give food, nor heaven light, 193
Sport and repose lock from me day and night, 194
To desperation turn my trust and hope,
An anchor's cheer in prison be my scope! 196
Each opposite that blanks the face of joy 197
Meet what I would have well and it destroy! 198
Both here and hence pursue me lasting strife 199
If, once a widow, ever I be wife!

HAMLET. If she should break it now!

PLAYER KING.
'Tis deeply sworn. Sweet, leave me here awhile;
My spirits grow dull, and fain I would beguile 203
The tedious day with sleep.

PLAYER QUEEN. Sleep rock thy brain,
And never come mischance between us twain!

[*He sleeps.*] *Exit* [*Player Queen*].

HAMLET. Madam, how like you this play?
QUEEN. The lady doth protest too much, methinks. 207
HAMLET. Oh, but she'll keep her word.
KING. Have you heard the argument? Is there no offense in't? 209
HAMLET. No, no, they do but jest, poison in jest. No offense i'th'world. 210
KING. What do you call the play?
HAMLET. *The Mousetrap.* Marry, how? Tropically. This play is the image of 212
a murder done in Vienna. Gonzago is the Duke's name, his wife, Baptista. 213
You shall see anon. 'Tis a knavish piece of work, but what of that? Your
Majesty, and we that have free souls, it touches us not. Let the galled jade 215
wince, our withers are unwrung. 216

Enter Lucianus.

---

188 Our . . . run What we want and what we get go so contrarily **189 devices still** intentions continually **190 ends** results **193 Nor** Let neither **194 Sport . . . night** May day deny me its pastimes and night its repose **196 anchor's cheer** anchorite's or hermit's fare. **my scope** the extent of my happiness **197–8 Each . . . destroy!** May every adverse thing that causes the face of joy to turn pale meet and destroy everything that I desire to see prosper! **199 hence** in the life hereafter **203 spirits** vital spirits **207 doth . . . much** makes too many promises and protestations **209 argument** plot **210 jest** make believe. **offense** crime, injury. (Hamlet playfully alters the King's use of the word in line 209 to mean "cause for objection.") **212 Tropically** Figuratively. (The First Quarto reading, *trapically,* suggests a pun on *trap* in *Mousetrap.*) **213 Duke's** i.e., King's. (An inconsistency that may be due to Shakespeare's possible acquaintance with a historical incident, the alleged murder of the Duke of Urbino by Luigi Gonzaga in 1538.) **215 free** guiltless **galled jade** horse whose hide is rubbed by saddle or harness. **216 withers** the part between the horse's shoulder blades **unwrung** not rubbed sore.

This is one Lucianus, nephew to the King.
OPHELIA. You are as good as a chorus, my lord. 218
HAMLET. I could interpret between you and your love, if I could see the 219
puppets dallying. 220
OPHELIA. You are keen, my lord, you are keen. 221
HAMLET. It would cost you a groaning to take off mine edge.
OPHELIA. Still better, and worse. 223
HAMLET. So you mis-take your husbands.—Begin, murderer; leave thy 224
damnable faces and begin. Come, the croaking raven doth bellow for
revenge.

LUCIANUS.
Thoughts black, hands apt, drugs fit, and time agreeing,
Confederate season, else no creature seeing, 228
Thou mixture rank, of midnight weeds collected,
With Hecate's ban thrice blasted, thrice infected, 230
Thy natural magic and dire property 231
On wholesome life usurp immediately.

[He pours the poison into the sleeper's ear.]

HAMLET. 'A poisons him i'th'garden for his estate. His name's Gonzago. 233
The story is extant, and written in very choice Italian. You shall see anon
how the murderer gets the love of Gonzago's wife.

[Claudius rises.]

OPHELIA. The King rises.
HAMLET. What, frighted with false fire? 237
QUEEN. How fares my lord?
POLONIUS. Give o'er the play.
KING. Give me some light. Away!
POLONIUS. Lights, lights, lights!

Exeunt all but Hamlet and Horatio.

HAMLET.
"Why, let the strucken deer go weep, 242
The hart ungallèd play. 243
For some must watch, while some must sleep; 244
Thus runs the world away." 245

---

218 chorus (In many Elizabethan plays, the forthcoming action was explained by an actor known as the "chorus"; at a puppet show, the actor who spoke the dialogue was known as an "interpreter," as indicated by the lines following.) **219 interpret** (1) ventriloquize the dialogue, as in puppet show (2) act as pander **220 puppets dallying** (With suggestion of sexual play, continued in *keen,* "sexually aroused," *groaning,* "moaning in pregnancy," and *edge,* "sexual desire" or "impetuosity.") **221 keen** sharp, bitter **223 Still . . . worse** More keen, always *bettering* what other people say with witty wordplay, but at the same time more offensive. **224 So** Even thus (in marriage). **mis-take** take falseheartedly and cheat on. (The marriage vows say "for better, for worse.") **228 Confederate . . . seeing** the time and occasion conspiring (to assist me), and also no one seeing me **230 Hecate's ban** the curse of Hecate, the goddess of witchcraft **231 dire property** baleful quality **233 estate** i.e., the kingship. **His** i.e., the King's **237 false fire** the blank discharge of a gun loaded with powder but no shot. **242–45 Why . . . away** (Perhaps from an old ballad, with allusion to the popular belief that a wounded deer retires to weep and die; compare with *As You Like It,* 2.1.33–66.) **243 ungallèd** unafflicted **244 watch** remain awake **245 Thus . . . away** Thus the world goes.

Would not this, sir, and a forest of feathers—if the rest of my fortunes turn Turk with me—with two Provincial roses on my razed shoes, get me a fellowship in a cry of players?

HORATIO. Half a share.

HAMLET. A whole one, I.

"For thou dost know, O Damon dear,
This realm dismantled was
Of Jove himself, and now reigns here
A very, very— pajock."

HORATIO. You might have rhymed.

HAMLET. Oh, good Horatio, I'll take the ghost's word for a thousand pound. Didst perceive?

HORATIO. Very well, my lord.

HAMLET. Upon the talk of the poisoning?

HORATIO. I did very well note him.

Enter Rosencrantz and Guildenstern.

HAMLET. Aha! Come, some music! Come, the recorders.

"For if the King like not the comedy,
Why then, belike, he likes it not, perdy."

Come, some music.

GUILDENSTERN. Good my lord, vouchsafe me a word with you.

HAMLET. Sir, a whole history.

GUILDENSTERN. The King, sir—

HAMLET. Ay, sir, what of him?

GUILDENSTERN. Is in his retirement marvelous distempered.

HAMLET. With drink, sir?

GUILDENSTERN. No, my lord, with choler.

HAMLET. Your wisdom should show itself more richer to signify this to the doctor, for for me to put him to his purgation would perhaps plunge him into more choler.

GUILDENSTERN. Good my lord, put your discourse into some frame and start not so wildly from my affair.

HAMLET. I am tame, sir. Pronounce.

---

246 this i.e., this success with the play I have just presented. **feathers** (Allusion to the plumes that Elizabethan actors were fond of wearing.) **247 turn Turk with** turn renegade against, go back on **Provincial roses** rosettes of ribbon, named for roses grown in a part of France. **razed** with ornamental slashing **248 fellowship . . . players** partnership in a theatrical company. **cry** pack (of hounds, etc.) **251 Damon** the friend of Pythias, as Horatio is friend of Hamlet; or, a traditional pastoral name **252–4 This realm . . . pajock** i.e., Jove, representing divine authority and justice, has abandoned this realm to its own devices, leaving in his stead only a peacock or vain pretender to virtue (though the rhyme-word expected in place of *pajock or* "peacock" suggests that the realm is now ruled over by an "ass"). **252 dismantled** stripped, divested **263 perdy** (A corruption of the French *par dieu,* "by God.") **269 retirement** withdrawal to his chambers **distempered** out of humor. (But Hamlet deliberately plays on the wider application to any illness of mind or body, as in line 300, especially to drunkenness.) **271 choler** anger. (But Hamlet takes the word in its more basic humoral sense of "bilious disorder.") **273 purgation** (Hamlet hints at something going beyond medical treatment to bloodletting and the extraction of confession.) **275 frame** order. **276 start** shy or jump away (like a horse; the opposite of *tame* in line 277)

GUILDENSTERN. The Queen, your mother, in most great affliction of spirit, hath sent me to you.

HAMLET. You are welcome.

GUILDENSTERN. Nay, good my lord, this courtesy is not of the right breed. If 281
it shall please you to make me a wholesome answer, I will do your
mother's commandment; if not, your pardon and my return shall be the 283
end of my business.

HAMLET. Sir, I cannot.

ROSENCRANTZ. What, my lord?

HAMLET. Make you a wholesome answer; my wit's diseased. But, sir, such answer as I can make, you shall command, or rather, as you say, my mother. Therefore no more, but to the matter. My mother, you say—

ROSENCRANTZ. Then thus she says: your behavior hath struck her into
amazement and admiration. 291

HAMLET. Oh, wonderful son, that can so stonish a mother! But is there no sequel at the heels of this mother's admiration? Impart.

ROSENCRANTZ. She desires to speak with you in her closet ere you go to 294
bed.

HAMLET. We shall obey, were she ten times our mother. Have you any further trade with us?

ROSENCRANTZ. My lord, you once did love me.

HAMLET. And do still, by these pickers and stealers. 299

ROSENCRANTZ. Good my lord, what is your cause of distemper? You do
surely bar the door upon your own liberty if you deny your griefs to 301
your friend.

HAMLET. Sir, I lack advancement.

ROSENCRANTZ. How can that be, when you have the voice of the King himself for your succession in Denmark?

HAMLET. Ay, sir, but "While the grass grows"—the proverb is something 306
musty.

Enter the Players with recorders.

Oh, the recorders. Let me see one. [*He takes a recorder.*] To withdraw 308
with you: why do you go about to recover the wind of me, as if you 309
would drive me into a toil? 310

GUILDENSTERN. Oh, my lord, if my duty be too bold, my love is too unman- 311
nerly. 312

HAMLET. I do not well understand that. Will you play upon this pipe? 313

GUILDENSTERN. My lord, I cannot.

HAMLET. I pray you.

---

281 breed (1) kind (2) breeding, manners. **283 pardon** permission to depart **291 admiration** bewilderment. **294 closet** private chamber **299 pickers and stealers** i.e., hands. (So called from the catechism, "to keep my hands from picking and stealing.") **301 liberty** i.e., being freed from *distemper,* line 300; but perhaps with a veiled threat as well. **deny** refuse to share **306 "While . . . grows"** (The rest of the proverb is "the silly horse starves"; Hamlet implies that his hopes of succession are distant in time at best.) **something** somewhat. **307.1** ***Players*** actors **308 withdraw** speak privately **309 recover the wind** get to the windward side (thus allowing the game to scent the hunter and thereby be driven in the opposite direction into the *toil* or net) **310 toil** snare. **311–2 if . . . unmannerly** if I am using an unmannerly boldness, it is my love that occasions it. **313 I . . . that** i.e., I don't understand how genuine love can be unmannerly.

GUILDENSTERN. Believe me, I cannot.
HAMLET. I do beseech you.
GUILDENSTERN. I know no touch of it, my lord.
HAMLET. It is as easy as lying. Govern these ventages with your fingers and 319
thumb, give it breath with your mouth, and it will discourse most eloquent music. Look you, these are the stops.
GUILDENSTERN. But these cannot I command to any utterance of harmony. I have not the skill.
HAMLET. Why, look you now, how unworthy a thing you make of me! You would play upon me, you would seem to know my stops, you would
pluck out the heart of my mystery, you would sound me from my lowest 326
note to the top of my compass, and there is much music, excellent voice, 327
in this little organ, yet cannot you make it speak. 'Sblood, do you think I 328
am easier to be played on than a pipe? Call me what instrument you
will, though you can fret me, you cannot play upon me. 330

Enter Polonius.

God bless you, sir!
POLONIUS. My lord, the Queen would speak with you, and presently. 332
HAMLET. Do you see yonder cloud that's almost in shape of a camel?
POLONIUS. By the Mass and 'tis, like a camel indeed.
HAMLET. Methinks it is like a weasel.
POLONIUS. It is backed like a weasel.
HAMLET. Or like a whale.
POLONIUS. Very like a whale.
HAMLET. Then I will come to my mother by and by. [*Aside*] They fool me 339
to the top of my bent.—I will come by and by. 340
POLONIUS. I will say so. [*Exit.*]
HAMLET. "By and by" is easily said. Leave me, friends.

[*Exeunt all but Hamlet.*]

'Tis now the very witching time of night, 343
When churchyards yawn and hell itself breathes out
Contagion to this world. Now could I drink hot blood
And do such bitter business as the day
Would quake to look on. Soft, now to my mother.
O heart, lose not thy nature! Let not ever 348
The soul of Nero enter this firm bosom. 349
Let me be cruel, not unnatural;
I will speak daggers to her, but use none.
My tongue and soul in this be hypocrites:

---

319 ventages finger-holes or *stops* (line 321) of the recorder **326 sound** (1) fathom (2) produce sound in **327 compass** range (of voice) **328 organ** musical instrument **330 fret** irritate. (With a quibble on the *frets* or ridges on the fingerboard of some stringed instruments to regulate the fingering.) **332 presently** at once **339–40 They . . . bent** They humor my odd behavior to the limit of my ability or endurance. (Literally, the extent to which a bow may be bent.) **343 witching time** time when spells are cast and evil is abroad **348 nature** natural feeling. **349 (Nero** This infamous Roman emperor put to death his mother Agrippina who had murdered her husband, Claudius.)

How in my words so ever she be shent,
To give them seals never my soul consent! *Exit.*

3.3

Enter King, Rosencrantz, and Guildenstern.

KING.
I like him not, nor stands it safe with us
To let his madness range. Therefore prepare you.
I your commission will forthwith dispatch,
And he to England shall along with you.
The terms of our estate may not endure
Hazard so near 's as doth hourly grow
Out of his brows.

GUILDENSTERN. We will ourselves provide.
Most holy and religious fear it is
To keep those many many bodies safe
That live and feed upon Your Majesty.

ROSENCRANTZ.
The single and peculiar life is bound
With all the strength and armor of the mind
To keep itself from noyance, but much more
That spirit upon whose weal depends and rests
The lives of many. The cess of majesty
Dies not alone, but like a gulf doth draw
What's near it with it; or it is a massy wheel
Fixed on the summit of the highest mount,
To whose huge spokes ten thousand lesser things
Are mortised and adjoined, which, when it falls,
Each small annexment, petty consequence,
Attends the boisterous ruin. Never alone
Did the King sigh, but with a general groan.

KING.
Arm you, I pray you, to this speedy voyage,
For we will fetters put about this fear,
Which now goes too free-footed.

ROSENCRANTZ. We will haste us.

Exeunt gentlemen [Rosencrantz and Guildenstern].

353–4 How . . . consent! However much she is to be rebuked by my words, may my soul never consent to ratify those words with deeds of violence!
3.3 Location: The castle.
1 him i.e., his behavior **3 dispatch** prepare, cause to be drawn up **5 terms of our estate** circumstances of my royal position **7 Out . . . brows** i.e., from his brain, in the form of plots and threats. **We . . . provide** We'll put ourselves in readiness. **8 religious fear** sacred concern **11 single and peculiar** individual and private **13 noyance** harm **14 weal** well-being **15 cess** decease, cessation **16 gulf** whirlpool **17 massy** massive **20 mortised** fastened (as with a fitted joint). **when it falls** i.e., when it descends, like the wheel of Fortune, bringing a king down with it **21 Each . . . consequence** i.e., every hanger-on and unimportant person or thing connected with the King **22 Attends** participates in **24 Arm** Provide, prepare

Enter Polonius.

POLONIUS.
My lord, he's going to his mother's closet.
Behind the arras I'll convey myself 28
To hear the process. I'll warrant she'll tax him home, 29
And, as you said—and wisely was it said—
'Tis meet that some more audience than a mother, 31
Since nature makes them partial, should o'erhear
The speech of vantage. Fare you well, my liege. 33
I'll call upon you ere you go to bed
And tell you what I know.

KING. Thanks, dear my lord.

Exit [Polonius]

Oh, my offense is rank! It smells to heaven.
It hath the primal eldest curse upon't, 37
A brother's murder. Pray can I not,
Though inclination be as sharp as will; 39
My stronger guilt defeats my strong intent,
And like a man to double business bound 41
I stand in pause where I shall first begin,
And both neglect. What if this cursèd hand
Were thicker than itself with brother's blood,
Is there not rain enough in the sweet heavens
To wash it white as snow? Whereto serves mercy 46
But to confront the visage of offense? 47
And what's in prayer but this twofold force,
To be forestallèd ere we come to fall, 49
Or pardoned being down? Then I'll look up.
My fault is past. But oh, what form of prayer
Can serve my turn? "Forgive me my foul murder"?
That cannot be, since I am still possessed
Of those effects for which I did the murder:
My crown, mine own ambition, and my queen.
May one be pardoned and retain th'offense? 56
In the corrupted currents of this world 57
Offense's gilded hand may shove by justice, 58
And oft 'tis seen the wicked prize itself 59
Buys out the law. But 'tis not so above.

---

28 arras screen of tapestry placed around the walls of household apartments. (On the Elizabethan stage, the arras was presumably over a door or in the tiring-house facade.) **29 process** proceedings. **tax him home** reprove him severely **31 meet** fitting **33 of vantage** from an advantageous place, or, in addition. **37 the primal eldest curse** the curse of Cain, the first murderer; he killed his brother Abel **39 Though . . . will** though my desire is as strong as my determination **41 bound** (1) destined (2) obliged. (The King wants to repent and still enjoy what he has gained.) **46–7 Whereto . . . offense?** What function does mercy serve other than to meet sin face to face? **49 forestallèd** prevented (from sinning) **56 th'offense** the thing for which one offended **57 currents** courses of events **58 gilded hand** hand offering gold as a bribe. **shove by** thrust aside **59 wicked prize** prize won by wickedness

There is no shuffling, there the action lies 61
In his true nature, and we ourselves compelled, 62
Even to the teeth and forehead of our faults, 63
To give in evidence. What then? What rests? 64
Try what repentance can. What can it not?
Yet what can it, when one cannot repent?
O wretched state, O bosom black as death,
O limèd soul that, struggling to be free, 68
Art more engaged! Help, angels! Make assay. 69
Bow, stubborn knees, and heart with strings of steel,
Be soft as sinews of the newborn babe!
All may be well. [*He kneels.*]

Enter Hamlet.

HAMLET.
Now might I do it pat, now 'a is a-praying; 73
And now I'll do't. [*He draws his sword.*] And so 'a goes to heaven,
And so am I revenged. That would be scanned: 75
A villain kills my father, and for that,
I, his sole son, do this same villain send
To heaven.
Why, this is hire and salary, not revenge.
'A took my father grossly, full of bread, 80
With all his crimes broad blown, as flush as May; 81
And how his audit stands who knows save heaven? 82
But in our circumstance and course of thought 83
'Tis heavy with him. And am I then revenged,
To take him in the purging of his soul,
When he is fit and seasoned for his passage? 86
No!
Up, sword, and know thou a more horrid hent. 88

[*He puts up his sword.*]

When he is drunk asleep, or in his rage, 89
Or in th'incestuous pleasure of his bed,
At game, a-swearing, or about some act 91
That has no relish of salvation in't— 92
Then trip him, that his heels may kick at heaven,
And that his soul may be as damned and black

---

61 There . . . lies There in heaven can be no evasion, there the deed lies exposed to view **62 his** its **63 to the teeth and forehead** face to face, concealing nothing **64 give in** provide. **rests** remains. **68 limèd** caught as with birdlime, a sticky substance used to ensnare birds **69 engaged** entangled. **assay** trial. (Said to himself, or to the angels to try him.) **73 pat** opportunely **75 would be scanned** needs to be looked into, or, would be interpreted as follows **80 grossly, full of bread** i.e., enjoying his worldly pleasures rather than fasting. (See Ezekiel 16:49.) **81 crimes broad blown** sins in full bloom. **flush** vigorous **82 audit** account. **save** except for **83 in . . . thought** as we see it from our mortal perspective **86 seasoned** matured, readied **88 know . . . hent** await to be grasped by me on a more horrid occasion. (*Hent* means "act of seizing.") **89 drunk . . . rage** dead drunk, or in a fit of sexual passion **91 game** gambling **92 relish** trace, savor

As hell, whereto it goes. My mother stays.
This physic but prolongs thy sickly days. *Exit.*

KING.
My words fly up, my thoughts remain below.
Words without thoughts never to heaven go. *Exit.*

3.4

Enter [Queen] Gertrude and Polonius.

POLONIUS.
'A will come straight. Look you lay home to him. Tell him his pranks
have been too broad to bear with,
And that Your Grace hath screened and stood between
Much heat and him. I'll silence me even here.
Pray you, be round with him.

HAMLET (*within*). Mother, mother, mother!

QUEEN. I'll warrant you, fear me not.
Withdraw, I hear him coming.

[*Polonius hides behind the arras.*]
Enter Hamlet.

HAMLET. Now, mother, what's the matter?

QUEEN.
Hamlet, thou hast thy father much offended.

HAMLET.
Mother, you have my father much offended.

QUEEN.
Come, come, you answer with an idle tongue.

HAMLET.
Go, go, you question with a wicked tongue.

QUEEN.
Why, how now, Hamlet?

HAMLET. What's the matter now?

QUEEN.
Have you forgot me?

HAMLET. No, by the rood, not so:
You are the Queen, your husband's brother's wife,
And—would it were not so!—you are my mother.

QUEEN.
Nay, then, I'll set those to you that can speak.

HAMLET.
Come, come, and sit you down; you shall not budge.

---

95 stays awaits (me). **96 physic** purging (by prayer), or, Hamlet's postponement of the killing

3.4. Location: The Queen's private chamber.

1 lay home reprove him soundly **2 broad** unrestrained **4 Much heat** i.e., the King's anger. **I'll silence me** I'll quietly conceal myself. (Ironic, since it is his crying out at line 24 that leads to his death. Some editors emend *silence* to "sconce." The First Quarto's reading, "shroud," is attractive.) **5 round** blunt **10 thy father** i.e., your stepfather, Claudius **12 idle** foolish **15 forgot me** i.e., forgotten that I am your mother. **rood** cross of Christ **18 speak** i.e., speak to someone so rude

You go not till I set you up a glass
Where you may see the inmost part of you.

QUEEN.
What wilt thou do? Thou wilt not murder me?
Help, ho!

POLONIUS [*behind the arras*]. What ho! Help!

HAMLET [*drawing*].
How now? A rat? Dead for a ducat, dead!

[*He thrusts his rapier through the arras.*]

POLONIUS [*behind the arras*].
Oh, I am slain! [*He falls and dies.*]

QUEEN. Oh, me, what hast thou done?

HAMLET. Nay, I know not. Is it the King?

QUEEN.
Oh, what a rash and bloody deed is this!

HAMLET.
A bloody deed—almost as bad, good mother,
As kill a king, and marry with his brother.

QUEEN.
As kill a king!

HAMLET. Ay, lady, it was my word.

[*He parts the arras and discovers Polonius.*]

Thou wretched, rash, intruding fool, farewell!
I took thee for thy better. Take thy fortune.
Thou find'st to be too busy is some danger.—
Leave wringing of your hands. Peace, sit you down,
And let me wring your heart, for so I shall,
If it be made of penetrable stuff,
If damnèd custom have not brazed it so
That it be proof and bulwark against sense.

QUEEN.
What have I done, that thou dar'st wag thy tongue
In noise so rude against me?

HAMLET. Such an act
That blurs the grace and blush of modesty,
Calls virtue hypocrite, takes off the rose
From the fair forehead of an innocent love
And sets a blister there, makes marriage vows
As false as dicers' oaths. Oh, such a deed
As from the body of contraction plucks
The very soul, and sweet religion makes

25 Dead for a ducat i.e., I bet a ducat he's dead; or, a ducat is his life's fee. **34 busy** nosey **38 damnèd custom** habitual wickedness. **brazed** brazened, hardened **39 proof** impenetrable, like *proof* or tested armor. **sense** feeling **45 sets a blister** i.e., brands as a harlot **47 contraction** the marriage contract **48 sweet religion makes** i.e., makes marriage vows

A rhapsody of words. Heaven's face does glow
O'er this solidity and compound mass
With tristful visage, as against the doom,
Is thought-sick at the act.

QUEEN. Ay me, what act,
That roars so loud and thunders in the index?

HAMLET [*showing her two likenesses*].
Look here upon this picture, and on this,
The counterfeit presentment of two brothers.
See what a grace was seated on this brow:
Hyperion's curls, the front of Jove himself,
An eye like Mars to threaten and command,
A station like the herald Mercury
New-lighted on a heaven-kissing hill—
A combination and a form indeed
Where every god did seem to set his seal
To give the world assurance of a man.
This was your husband. Look you now what follows:
Here is your husband, like a mildewed ear,
Blasting his wholesome brother. Have you eyes?
Could you on this fair mountain leave to feed
And batten on this moor? Ha, have you eyes?
You cannot call it love, for at your age
The heyday in the blood is tame, it's humble,
And waits upon the judgment, and what judgment
Would step from this to this? Sense, sure, you have,
Else could you not have motion, but sure that sense
Is apoplexed, for madness would not err,
Nor sense to ecstasy was ne'er so thralled,
But it reserved some quantity of choice
To serve in such a difference. What devil was't
That thus hath cozened you at hoodman-blind?
Eyes without feeling, feeling without sight,
Ears without hands or eyes, smelling sans all,
Or but a sickly part of one true sense

---

49 rhapsody senseless string **49–52 Heaven's . . . act** Heaven's face blushes at this solid world compounded of the various elements, with sorrowful face as though the day of doom were near, and is sick with horror at the deed (i.e., Gertrude's marriage). **53 index** table of contents, prelude or preface **55 counterfeit presentment** representation in portraiture **57 Hyperion's** the sun-god's. **front** brow **58 Mars** god of war **59 station** manner of standing. **Mercury** winged messenger of the gods **60 New-lighted** newly alighted. **heaven-kissing** reaching to the sky **62 set his seal** i.e., affix his approval **65 ear** i.e., of grain **66 Blasting** Blighting **67 leave** cease **68 batten** gorge. **moor** barren or marshy ground (suggesting also "dark-skinned"). **70 The heyday . . . blood** (The blood was thought to be the source of sexual desire.) **72 Sense** Perception through the five senses (the functions of the middle or sensible soul) **74 apoplexed** paralyzed. **err** so err **75–7 Nor . . . difference** Nor could your physical senses ever have been so enthralled to *ecstasy* or lunacy that they could not distinguish to some degree between Hamlet Senior and Claudius. **78 cozened** cheated. **hoodman-blind** blindman's buff. (In this game, says Hamlet, the devil must have pushed Claudius toward Gertrude while she was blindfolded.) **80 sans** without

Could not so mope. O shame, where is thy blush?
Rebellious hell,
If thou canst mutine in a matron's bones,
To flaming youth let virtue be as wax
And melt in her own fire. Proclaim no shame
When the compulsive ardor gives the charge,
Since frost itself as actively doth burn,
And reason panders will.

QUEEN. Oh, Hamlet, speak no more!
Thou turn'st mine eyes into my very soul,
And there I see such black and grainèd spots
As will not leave their tinct.

HAMLET. Nay, but to live
In the rank sweat of an enseamèd bed,
Stewed in corruption, honeying and making love
Over the nasty sty!

QUEEN. Oh, speak to me no more!
These words like daggers enter in my ears.
No more, sweet Hamlet!

HAMLET. A murderer and a villain,
A slave that is not twentieth part the tithe
Of your precedent lord, a vice of kings,
A cutpurse of the empire and the rule,
That from a shelf the precious diadem stole
And put it in his pocket!

QUEEN. No more!

Enter Ghost [*in his nightgown*].

HAMLET. A king of shreds and patches—
Save me, and hover o'er me with your wings,
You heavenly guards! What would your gracious figure?

QUEEN. Alas, he's mad!

HAMLET.
Do you not come your tardy son to chide,
That, lapsed in time and passion, lets go by
Th'important acting of your dread command?
Oh, say!

GHOST.
Do not forget. This visitation

82 mope be dazed, act aimlessly. **84 mutine** mutiny **85–6 To . . . fire** when it comes to sexually passionate youth, let virtue melt like a candle or stick of sealing wax held over a candle flame. (There's no point in hoping for self-restraint among young people when matronly women set such a bad example.) **86–9 Proclaim . . . will** Call it no shameful business when the compelling ardor of youth delivers the attack, i.e., commits lechery, since the *frost* of advanced age burns with as active a fire of lust and reason perverts itself by fomenting lust rather than restraining it **92 grainèd** ingrained, indelible **93 leave their tinct** surrender their dark stain. **94 enseamèd** saturated in the grease and filth of passionate lovemaking **95 Stewed** soaked, bathed. (with a suggestion of "stew," brothel.) **96 Over . . . sty** (Like barnyard animals.) **100 tithe** tenth part **101 precedent lord** former husband. **vice** (From the morality plays, a model of iniquity and a buffoon.) **105.1 nightgown** a robe for indoor wear **106 A king . . . patches** i.e., a king whose splendor is all sham; a clown or fool dressed in motley **111 lapsed . . . passion** having let time and passion slip away **112 Th'important** the importunate, urgent

Is but to whet thy almost blunted purpose.
But look, amazement on thy mother sits. 116
Oh, step between her and her fighting soul!
Conceit in weakest bodies strongest works. 118
Speak to her, Hamlet.

HAMLET. How is it with you, lady?

QUEEN. Alas, how is't with you,
That you do bend your eye on vacancy,
And with th'incorporal air do hold discourse? 122
Forth at your eyes your spirits wildly peep,
And, as the sleeping soldiers in th'alarm, 124
Your bedded hair, like life in excrements, 125
Start up and stand on end. O gentle son,
Upon the heat and flame of thy distemper 127
Sprinkle cool patience. Whereon do you look?

HAMLET.
On him, on him! Look you how pale he glares!
His form and cause conjoined, preaching to stones, 130
Would make them capable.—Do not look upon me, 131
Lest with this piteous action you convert 132
My stern effects. Then what I have to do 133
Will want true color—tears perchance for blood. 134

QUEEN. To whom do you speak this?

HAMLET. Do you see nothing there?

QUEEN.
Nothing at all, yet all that is I see.

HAMLET.
Nor did you nothing hear?

QUEEN. No, nothing but ourselves.

HAMLET.
Why, look you there, look how it steals away!
My father, in his habit as he lived! 141
Look where he goes even now out at the portal!

Exit Ghost.

QUEEN.
This is the very coinage of your brain. 143
This bodiless creation ecstasy 144
Is very cunning in. 145

HAMLET. Ecstasy?
My pulse as yours doth temperately keep time,
And makes as healthful music. It is not madness

116 amazement distraction **118 Conceit** Imagination **122 th'incorporal** the immaterial **124 as . . . th'alarm** like soldiers called out of sleep by an alarum **125 bedded** laid flat. **like life in excrements** i.e., as though hair, an outgrowth of the body, had a life of its own. (Hair was thought to be lifeless because it lacks sensation, and so its standing on end would be unnatural and ominous.) **127 distemper** disorder **130 His . . . conjoined** His appearance joined to his cause for speaking **131 capable** capable of feeling, receptive. **132–3 convert . . . effects** divert me from my stern duty. **134 want . . . blood** lack plausibility so that (with a play on the normal sense of *color*) I shall shed colorless tears instead of blood. **141 habit** clothes. **as** as when **143 very** mere **144–5 This . . . in** Madness is skillful in creating this kind of hallucination.

That I have uttered. Bring me to the test,
And I the matter will reword, which madness 150
Would gambol from. Mother, for love of grace, 151
Lay not that flattering unction to your soul 152
That not your trespass but my madness speaks.
It will but skin and film the ulcerous place, 154
Whiles rank corruption, mining all within, 155
Infects unseen. Confess yourself to heaven,
Repent what's past, avoid what is to come,
And do not spread the compost on the weeds 158
To make them ranker. Forgive me this my virtue; 159
For in the fatness of these pursy times 160
Virtue itself of vice must pardon beg,
Yea, curb and woo for leave to do him good. 162

QUEEN.
Oh, Hamlet, thou hast cleft my heart in twain.

HAMLET.
Oh, throw away the worser part of it,
And live the purer with the other half.
Good night. But go not to my uncle's bed;
Assume a virtue, if you have it not.
That monster, custom, who all sense doth eat, 168
Of habits devil, is angel yet in this, 169
That to the use of actions fair and good
He likewise gives a frock or livery 171
That aptly is put on. Refrain tonight, 172
And that shall lend a kind of easiness
To the next abstinence; the next more easy;
For use almost can change the stamp of nature, 175
And either . . . the devil, or throw him out 176
With wondrous potency. Once more, good night;
And when you are desirous to be blest, 178
I'll blessing beg of you. For this same lord, 179

[pointing to Polonius]

I do repent; but heaven hath pleased it so
To punish me with this, and this with me, 181
That I must be their scourge and minister. 182

---

150 reword repeat word for word **151 gambol** skip away **152 unction** ointment **154 skin** grow a skin over **155 mining** working under the surface **158 compost** manure **159 this my virtue** my virtuous talk in reproving you **160 fatness** grossness. **pursy** flabby, out of shape **162 curb** bow, bend the knee. **leave** permission **168 who . . . eat** which consumes and overwhelms the physical senses **169 Of habits devil** devil-like in prompting evil habits **171 livery** an outer appearance, a customary garb (and hence a predisposition easily assumed in time of stress) **172 aptly** readily **175 use** habit. **the stamp of nature** our inborn traits **176 And either** (A defective line, often emended by inserting the word "master" after *either,* following the Third Quarto and early editors, or some other word such as "shame," "lodge," "curb," or "house.") **178–9 when . . . you** i.e., when you are ready to be penitent and seek God's blessing, I will ask your blessing as a dutiful son should. **181 To punish . . . with me** to seek retribution from me for killing Polonius, and from him through my means **182 their scourge and minister** i.e., agent of heavenly retribution.

I will bestow him, and will answer well 183
The death I gave him. So, again, good nigh.
I must be cruel only to be kind.
This bad begins, and worse remains behind 186
One word more, good lady.

QUEEN. What shall I do?

HAMLET.
Not this by no means that I bid you do:
Let the bloat king tempt you again to bed, 189
Pinch wanton on your cheek, call you his mouse, 190
And let him, for a pair of reechy kisses, 191
Or paddling in your neck with his damned fingers, 192
Make you to ravel all this matter out 193
That I essentially am not in madness,
But mad in craft. 'Twere good you let him know, 195
For who that's but a queen, fair, sober, wise,
Would from a paddock, from a bat, a gib, 197
Such dear concernings hide? Who would do so? 198
No, in despite of sense and secrecy, 199
Unpeg the basket on the house's top, 200
Let the birds fly, and like the famous ape, 201
To try conclusions, in the basket creep 202
And break your own neck down. 203

QUEEN.
Be thou assured, if words be made of breath,
And breath of life, I have no life to breathe
What thou hast said to me.

HAMLET.
I must to England. You know that?

QUEEN. Alack,
I had forgot. 'Tis so concluded on.

HAMLET.
There's letters sealed, and my two schoolfellows,
Whom I will trust as I will adders fanged,
They bear the mandate; they must sweep my way 211
And marshal me to knavery. Let it work. 212
For 'tis the sport to have the engineer 213

---

183 bestow stow, dispose of. **answer** account or pay for **186 This** i.e., the killing of Polonius. **behind** to come. **189 bloat** bloated **190 Pinch wanton** i.e., leave his love pinches on your cheeks, branding you as wanton **191 reechy** dirty, filthy **192 paddling** fingering amorously **193 ravel . . . out** unravel, disclose **195 in craft** by cunning. **good** (Said sarcastically; also the following eight lines.) **197 paddock** toad. **gib** tomcat **198 dear concernings** important affairs **199 sense and secrecy** secrecy that common sense requires **200 Unpeg the basket** Open the cage, i.e., let out the secret **201 famous ape** (In a story now lost.) **202 try conclusions** test the outcome (in which the ape apparently enters a cage from which birds have been released and then tries to fly out of the cage as they have done, falling to its death) **203 down** in the fall **211–12 sweep . . . knavery** sweep a path before me and conduct me to some *knavery* or treachery prepared for me. **212 work** proceed. **213 engineer** maker of *engines* of war

Hoist with his own petard, and 't shall go hard
But I will delve one yard below their mines
And blow them at the moon. Oh, 'tis most sweet
When in one line two crafts directly meet.
This man shall set me packing.
I'll lug the guts into the neighbor room.
Mother, good night indeed. This counselor
Is now most still, most secret, and most grave,
Who was in life a foolish prating knave.—
Come, sir, to draw toward an end with you.—
Good night, mother.

Exeunt [*separately, Hamlet dragging in Polonius*].

4.1

Enter King and Queen, with Rosencrantz and Guildenstern.

KING.
There's matter in these sighs, these profound heaves.
You must translate; 'tis fit we understand them.
Where is your son?

QUEEN.
Bestow this place on us a little while.

[*Exeunt Rosencrantz and Guildenstern.*]

Ah, mine own lord, what have I seen tonight!

KING.
What, Gertrude? How does Hamlet?

QUEEN.
Mad as the sea and wind when both contend
Which is the mightier. In his lawless fit,
Behind the arras hearing something stir,
Whips out his rapier, cries, "A rat, a rat!"

---

214 Hoist with blown up by. **petard** an explosive used to blow in a door or make a breach **214–5 't shall . . . will** unless luck is against me, I will **215 mines** tunnels used in warfare to undermine the enemy's emplacements; Hamlet will countermine by going under their mines **217 in one line** i.e., mines and countermines on a collision course, or the countermines directly below the mines. **crafts** acts of guile, plots **218 set me packing** set me to making schemes, and set me to lugging (him), and, also, send me off in a hurry. **223 draw . . . end** finish up. (With a pun on *draw,* "pull.")
4.1 Location: The castle.
0.1 *Enter . . . Queen* (Some editors argue that Gertrude does not in fact exit at the end of 3.4 and that the scene is continuous here. It is true that the Folio ends 3.4 with *"Exit Hamlet tugging in Polonius,"* not naming Gertrude, and opens 4.1 with *"Enter King."* Yet the Second Quarto concludes 3.4 with a simple *"Exit,"* which often stands ambiguously for a single exit or an exeunt in early modern texts, and then starts 4.1 with *"Enter King, and Queene, with Rosencaus and Guyldensterne."* The King's opening lines in 4.1 suggest that he has had time, during a brief intervening pause, to become aware of Gertrude's highly wrought emotional state. In line 35, the King refers to Gertrude's *closet* as though it were elsewhere. The differences between the Second Quarto and the Folio offer an alternative staging. In either case, 4.1 follows swiftly upon 3.4.) **1 matter** significance. **heaves** heavy sighs.

And in this brainish apprehension kills 11
The unseen good old man.

KING. Oh, heavy deed! 12
It had been so with us, had we been there. 13
His liberty is full of threats to all—
To you yourself, to us, to everyone.
Alas, how shall this bloody deed be answered? 16
It will be laid to us, whose providence 17
Should have kept short, restrained, and out of haunt 18
This mad young man. But so much was our love,
We would not understand what was most fit,
But, like the owner of a foul disease,
To keep it from divulging, let it feed 22
Even on the pith of life. Where is he gone?

QUEEN.
To draw apart the body he hath killed,
O'er whom his very madness, like some ore 25
Among a mineral of metals base, 26
Shows itself pure: 'a weeps for what is done.

KING.
Oh, Gertrude, come away!
The sun no sooner shall the mountains touch
But we will ship him hence, and this vile deed
We must with all our majesty and skill
Both countenance and excuse.—Ho, Guildenstern! 32

Enter Rosencrantz and Guildenstern.

Friends both, go join you with some further aid.
Hamlet in madness hath Polonius slain,
And from his mother's closet hath he dragged him.
Go seek him out, speak fair, and bring the body 36
Into the chapel. I pray you, haste in this.

[*Exeunt Rosencrantz and Guildenstern.*]

Come, Gertrude, we'll call up our wisest friends
And let them know both what we mean to do
And what's untimely done 40
Whose whisper o'er the world's diameter, 41
As level as the cannon to his blank, 42
Transports his poisoned shot, may miss our name
And hit the woundless air. Oh, come away! 44
My soul is full of discord and dismay. *Exeunt.*

---

11 brainish apprehension frenzied misapprehension **12 heavy** grievous **13 us** i.e., me. (The royal "we"; also in line 15.) **16 answered** explained. **17 providence** foresight **18 short** i.e., on a short tether. **out of haunt** secluded **22 from divulging** from becoming publicly known **25 ore** vein of gold **26 mineral** mine **32 countenance** put the best face on **36 fair** gently, courteously **40 And . . . done** (A defective line; conjectures as to the missing words include "So, haply, slander" [Capell and others]; "For, haply, slander" [Theobald and others]; and "So envious slander" [Jenkins].) **41 diameter** extent from side to side **42 As level** with as direct aim. **his blank** its target at point-blank range **44 woundless** invulnerable

4.2

Enter Hamlet.

HAMLET. Safely stowed.

ROSENCRANTZ, GUILDENSTERN (*within*). Hamlet! Lord Hamlet!

HAMLET. But soft, what noise? Who calls on Hamlet? Oh, here they come.

Enter Rosencrantz and Guildenstern.

ROSENCRANTZ.
What have you done, my lord, with the dead body?

HAMLET.
Compounded it with dust, whereto 'tis kin.

ROSENCRANTZ.
Tell us where 'tis, that we may take it thence
And bear it to the chapel.

HAMLET. Do not believe it.

ROSENCRANTZ. Believe what?

HAMLET. That I can keep your counsel and not mine own. Besides, to be demanded of a sponge, what replication should be made by the son of a king?

ROSENCRANTZ. Take you me for a sponge, my lord?

HAMLET. Ay, sir, that soaks up the King's countenance, his rewards, his authorities. But such officers do the King best service in the end. He keeps them, like an ape, an apple, in the corner of his jaw, first mouthed to be last swallowed. When he needs what you have gleaned, it is but squeezing you, and, sponge, you shall be dry again.

ROSENCRANTZ. I understand you not, my lord.

HAMLET. I am glad of it. A knavish speech sleeps in a foolish ear.

ROSENCRANTZ. My lord, you must tell us where the body is and go with us to the King.

HAMLET. The body is with the King, but the King is not with the body. The King is a thing—

GUILDENSTERN. A thing, my lord?

HAMLET. Of nothing. Bring me to him. Hide fox, and all after!

Exeunt [*running*].

4.2 Location: The castle.
10 That . . . own i.e., Don't expect me to do as you bid me and not follow my own counsel. **11 demanded of** questioned by **replication** reply **14 countenance** favor **15 authorities** delegated power, influence. **20 sleeps in** has no meaning to **23 The . . . body** (Perhaps alludes to the legal commonplace of "the king's two bodies," which drew a distinction between the sacred office of kingship and the particular mortal who possessed it at any given time. Hence, although Claudius' body is necessarily a part of him, true kingship is not contained in it. Similarly, Claudius will have Polonius' body when it is found, but there is no kingship in this business either.) **26 Of nothing** (1) of no account (2) lacking the essence of kingship, as in lines 23 and note **Hide . . . after** (An old signal cry in the game of hide-and-seek, suggesting that Hamlet now runs away from them.)

4.3

Enter King, and two or three.

KING.
I have sent to seek him, and to find the body.
How dangerous is it that this man goes loose!
Yet must not we put the strong law on him.
He's loved of the distracted multitude, 4
Who like not in their judgment, but their eyes, 5
And where 'tis so, th'offender's scourge is weighed, 6
But never the offense. To bear all smooth and even, 7
This sudden sending him away must seem
Deliberate pause. Diseases desperate grown 9
By desperate appliance are relieved, 10
Or not at all.

Enter Rosencrantz, [Guildenstern,] and all the rest.

How now, what hath befall'n?

ROSENCRANTZ.
Where the dead body is bestowed, my lord,
We cannot get from him.

KING. But where is he?

ROSENCRANTZ.
Without, my lord; guarded, to know your pleasure. 14

KING.
Bring him before us.

ROSENCRANTZ [*calling*]. Ho! Bring in the lord.

They enter [with Hamlet]

KING. Now, Hamlet, where's Polonius?

HAMLET. At supper.

KING. At supper? Where?

HAMLET. Not where he eats, but where 'a is eaten. A certain convocation
of politic worms are e'en at him. Your worm is your only emperor for 20
diet. We fat all creatures else to fat us, and we fat ourselves for maggots. 21
Your fat king and your lean beggar is but variable service—two dishes, 22
but to one table. That's the end.

KING. Alas, alas!

HAMLET. A man may fish with the worm that hath eat of a king, and eat of 25
the fish that hath fed of that worm.

4.3. Location: The castle.

4 of by. **distracted** fickle, unstable **5 Who . . . eyes** who choose not by judgment but by appearance **6–7 th'offender's . . . offense** i.e., the populace often takes umbrage at the severity of a punishment without taking into account the gravity of the crime. **7 To . . . even** To manage the business in an unprovocative way **9 Deliberate pause** carefully considered action. **10 appliance** remedies **14 Without** Outside **20 politic worms** crafty worms (suited to a master spy like Polonius). **e'en** even now. **Your worm** Your average worm. (Compare *your fat king and your lean beggar* in line 22.) **21 diet** food, eating. (With a punning reference to the Diet of Worms, a famous *convocation* held in 1521.) **22 service** food served at table. (Worms feed on kings and beggars alike.) **25 eat** eaten. (Pronounced *et.*)

KING. What dost thou mean by this?

HAMLET. Nothing but to show you how a king may go a progress through the guts of a beggar.

KING. Where is Polonius?

HAMLET. In heaven. Send thither to see. If your messenger find him not there, seek him i'th'other place yourself. But if indeed you find him not within this month, you shall nose him as you go up the stairs into the lobby.

KING [*to some attendants*]. Go seek him there.

HAMLET. 'A will stay till you come. [*Exeunt attendants.*]

KING.
Hamlet, this deed, for thine especial safety—
Which we do tender, as we dearly grieve
For that which thou hast done—must send thee hence
With fiery quickness. Therefore prepare thyself.
The bark is ready, and the wind at help,
Th'associates tend, and everything is bent
For England.

HAMLET. For England!

KING. Ay, Hamlet.

HAMLET. Good.

KING.
So is it, if thou knew'st our purposes.

HAMLET. I see a cherub that sees them. But come, for England! Farewell, dear mother.

KING. Thy loving father, Hamlet.

HAMLET. My mother. Father and mother is man and wife, man and wife is one flesh, and so, my mother. Come, for England! *Exit.*

KING.
Follow him at foot; tempt him with speed aboard.
Delay it not. I'll have him hence tonight.
Away! For everything is sealed and done
That else leans on th'affair. Pray you, make haste.

[*Exeunt all but the King.*]

And, England, if my love thou hold'st at aught—
As my great power thereof may give thee sense,
Since yet thy cicatrice looks raw and red
After the Danish sword, and thy free awe
Pays homage to us—thou mayst not coldly set
Our sovereign process, which imports at full,
By letters congruing to that effect,
The present death of Hamlet. Do it, England,

---

28 progress royal journey of state **33 nose** smell **38 tender** regard, hold dear. **dearly** intensely **41 bark** sailing vessel **42 tend** wait. **bent** in readiness **48 cherub** (Cherubim are angels of knowledge. Hamlet hints that both he and heaven are onto Claudius' tricks.) **53 at foot** close behind, at heel **56 leans on** bears upon, is related to **57 England** i.e., King of England. **at aught** at any value **58 As . . . sense** for so my great power may give you a just appreciation of the importance of valuing my love **59 cicatrice** scar **60 free awe** unconstrained show of respect **61 coldly set** regard with indifference **62 process** command. **imports at full** conveys specific directions for **63 congruing** agreeing **64 present** immediate

For like the hectic in my blood he rages, 65
And thou must cure me. Till I know 'tis done,
Howe'er my haps, my joys were ne'er begun. *Exit.* 67

4.4

Enter Fortinbras with his army over the stage.

FORTINBRAS.
Go, Captain, from me greet the Danish king.
Tell him that by his license Fortinbras 2
Craves the conveyance of a promised march 3
Over his kingdom. You know the rendezvous.
If that His Majesty would aught with us,
We shall express our duty in his eye; 6
And let him know so.

CAPTAIN. I will do't, my lord.

FORTINBRAS. Go softly on. *[Exeunt all but the Captain.]* 9

Enter Hamlet, Rosencrantz, [Guildenstern,] etc.

HAMLET. Good sir, whose powers are these? 10

CAPTAIN. They are of Norway, sir.

HAMLET. How purposed, sir, I pray you?

CAPTAIN. Against some part of Poland.

HAMLET. Who commands them, sir?

CAPTAIN.
The nephew to old Norway, Fortinbras.

HAMLET.
Goes it against the main of Poland, sir, 16
Or for some frontier?

CAPTAIN.
Truly to speak, and with no addition, 18
We go to gain a little patch of ground
That hath in it no profit but the name.
To pay five ducats, five, I would not farm it; 21
Nor will it yield to Norway or the Pole
A ranker rate, should it be sold in fee. 23

HAMLET.
Why, then the Polack never will defend it.

CAPTAIN.
Yes, it is already garrisoned.

HAMLET.
Two thousand souls and twenty thousand ducats

---

65 hectic persistent fever **67 Howe'er . . . begun** Whatever else happens, I cannot begin to be happy.
4.4 Location: The coast of Denmark.
2 license permission **3 conveyance** unhindered passage **6 We . . . eye** I will come pay my respects in person **9 softly** slowly, circumspectly **10 powers** forces **16 main** main part **18 addition** exaggeration **21 To pay** i.e., For a yearly rental of. **farm it** take a lease of it **23 ranker** higher. **in fee** fee simple, outright.

Will not debate the question of this straw. 27
This is th'impostume of much wealth and peace, 28
That inward breaks, and shows no cause without 29
Why the man dies. I humbly thank you, sir.

CAPTAIN.
God b'wi'you, sir. [*Exit.*]

ROSENCRANTZ. Will't please you go, my lord?

HAMLET.
I'll be with you straight. Go a little before.

[*Exeunt all except Hamlet.*]

How all occasions do inform against me 33
And spur my dull revenge! What is a man,
If his chief good and market of his time 35
Be but to sleep and feed? A beast, no more.
Sure he that made us with such large discourse, 37
Looking before and after, gave us not 38
That capability and godlike reason
To fust in us unused. Now, whether it be 40
Bestial oblivion, or some craven scruple 41
Of thinking too precisely on th'event— 42
A thought which, quartered, hath but one part wisdom
And ever three parts coward—I do not know
Why yet I live to say "This thing's to do,"
Sith I have cause, and will, and strength, and means 46
To do't. Examples gross as earth exhort me: 47
Witness this army of such mass and charge, 48
Led by a delicate and tender prince, 49
Whose spirit with divine ambition puffed
Makes mouths at the invisible event, 51
Exposing what is mortal and unsure
To all that fortune, death, and danger dare, 53
Even for an eggshell. Rightly to be great 54
Is not to stir without great argument, 55
But greatly to find quarrel in a straw 56
When honor's at the stake. How stand I, then, 57
That have a father killed, a mother stained,
Excitements of my reason and my blood, 59
And let all sleep, while to my shame I see
The imminent death of twenty thousand men

---

27 debate . . . straw settle this trifling matter **28 th'impostume** the abscess **29 inward breaks** festers within. **without** externally **33 inform against** denounce; take shape against **35 market of** profit of **37 discourse** power of reasoning **38 Looking before and after** able to review past events and anticipate the future **40 fust** grow moldy **41 oblivion** forgetfulness. **craven** cowardly **42 precisely** scrupulously. **th'event** the outcome **46 Sith** since **47 gross** obvious **48 charge** expense **49 delicate and tender** of fine and youthful qualities **51 Makes mouths** makes scornful faces. **invisible event** unforeseeable outcome **53 dare** could do (to him) **54–7 Rightly . . . stake** True greatness is not a matter of being moved to action solely by a great cause; rather, it is to respond greatly to an apparently trivial cause when honor is at the stake. **59 blood** (the seat of the passions.)

That for a fantasy and trick of fame
Go to their graves like beds, fight for a plot
Whereon the numbers cannot try the cause,
Which is not tomb enough and continent
To hide the slain? Oh, from this time forth
My thoughts be bloody or be nothing worth! *Exit.*

4.5

Enter Horatio, [Queen] Gertrude, and a Gentleman.

QUEEN.
I will not speak with her.

GENTLEMAN. She is importunate,
Indeed distract. Her mood will needs be pitied.

QUEEN. What would she have?

GENTLEMAN.
She speaks much of her father, says she hears
There's tricks i'th'world, and hems, and beats her heart,
Spurns enviously at straws, speaks things in doubt
That carry but half sense. Her speech is nothing,
Yet the unshapèd use of it doth move
The hearers to collection; they yawn at it,
And botch the words up fit to their own thoughts,
Which, as her winks and nods and gestures yield them,
Indeed would make one think there might be thought,
Though nothing sure, yet much unhappily.

HORATIO.
'Twere good she were spoken with, for she may strew
Dangerous conjectures in ill-breeding minds.

QUEEN. Let her come in. [*Exit Gentleman.*]
[*Aside*] To my sick soul, as sin's true nature is,
Each toy seems prologue to some great amiss.
So full of artless jealousy is guilt,
It spills itself in fearing to be spilt.

Enter Ophelia [*distracted*].

---

62 fantasy fanciful caprice, illusion. **trick** trifle, deceit **63 plot** plot of ground **64 Whereon . . . cause** on which there is insufficient room for the soldiers needed to fight for it **65 continent** receptacle, container

4.5 Location: The castle.

2 distract out of her mind. **5 tricks** deceptions. **hems.** clears her throat, makes "hmm" sounds. **heart** i.e., breast **6 Spurns . . . straws** kicks spitefully, takes offense at trifles. **in doubt** of obscure meaning **8 unshapèd use** incoherent manner **9 collection** inference, a guess at some sort of meaning. **yawn** gape, wonder; grasp. (The Folio reading, "aim," is possible.) **10 botch** patch **11 Which** which words. **yield** deliver, represent **12–13 there might . . . unhappily** that a great deal could be guessed at of a most unfortunate nature, even if one couldn't be at all sure. **15 ill-breeding** prone to suspect the worst and to make mischief **18 toy** trifle. **amiss** calamity. **19–20 So . . . spilt** Guilt is so burdened with conscience and fear of detection that it reveals itself through apprehension of disaster. **20.1 *Enter Ophelia*** (In the First Quarto, Ophelia enters, "*playing on a lute, and her hair down, singing.*")

OPHELIA.
Where is the beauteous majesty of Denmark?
QUEEN. How now, Ophelia?
OPHELIA (*she sings*).
"How should I your true love know
From another one?
By his cockle hat and staff,
And his sandal shoon."
QUEEN. Alas, sweet lady, what imports this song?
OPHELIA. Say you? Nay, pray you, mark.
"He is dead and gone, lady, (*Song.*)
He is dead and gone;
At his head a grass-green turf,
At his heels a stone."
Oho!
QUEEN. Nay, but Ophelia—
OPHELIA. Pray you, mark.
[*Sings*] "White his shroud as the mountain snow"—

Enter King.

QUEEN. Alas, look here, my lord.
OPHELIA.
"Larded with sweet flowers; (*Song.*)
Which bewept to the ground did not go
With true-love showers."
KING. How do you, pretty lady?
OPHELIA. Well, God 'ild you! They say the owl was a baker's daughter. Lord, we know what we are, but know not what we may be. God be at your table!
KING. Conceit upon her father.
OPHELIA. Pray let's have no words of this; but when they ask you what it means, say you this:
"Tomorrow is Saint Valentine's day, (*Song.*)
All in the morning betime,
And I a maid at your window,
To be your Valentine.
Then up he rose, and donned his clothes,
And dupped the chamber door,
Let in the maid, that out a maid
Never departed more."
KING. Pretty Ophelia—
OPHELIA. Indeed, la, without an oath, I'll make an end on't:
[*Sings*] "By Gis and by Saint Charity,
Alack, and fie for shame!

---

25 cockle hat hat with cockleshell stuck in it as a sign that the wearer had been a pilgrim to the shrine of Saint James of Compostella in Spain **26 shoon** shoes. **33 Oho!** (Perhaps a sigh.) **38 Larded** strewn, bedecked **40 showers** i.e., tears **42 God 'ild** God yield or reward. **owl** (Refers to a legend about a baker's daughter who was turned into an owl for being ungenerous when Jesus begged a loaf of bread.) **45 Conceit** Fancy, brooding **49 betime** early **53 dupped** did up, opened **58 Gis** Jesus

Young men will do't, if they come to't;
By Cock, they are to blame. 61
Quoth she, 'Before you tumbled me,
You promised me to wed.' "

He answers:
" 'So would I ha' done, by yonder sun,
An thou hadst not come to my bed.' " 66

KING. How long hath she been thus?

OPHELIA. I hope all will be well. We must be patient, but I cannot choose but weep to think they would lay him i'th'cold ground. My brother shall know of it. And so I thank you for your good counsel. Come, my coach! Good night, ladies, good night, sweet ladies, good night, good night.

[*Exit.*]

KING [*to Horatio*].
Follow her close. Give her good watch, I pray you.

[*Exit Horatio.*]

Oh, this is the poison of deep grief; it springs
All from her father's death—and now behold!
Oh, Gertrude, Gertrude,
When sorrows come, they come not single spies, 76
But in battalions. First, her father slain;
Next, your son gone, and he most violent author
Of his own just remove; the people muddied, 79
Thick and unwholesome in their thoughts and whispers
For good Polonius' death—and we have done but greenly, 81
In hugger-mugger to inter him; poor Ophelia 82
Divided from herself and her fair judgment,
Without the which we are pictures or mere beasts;
Last, and as much containing as all these, 85
Her brother is in secret come from France,
Feeds on this wonder, keeps himself in clouds, 87
And wants not buzzers to infect his ear 88
With pestilent speeches of his father's death,
Wherein necessity, of matter beggared, 90
Will nothing stick our person to arraign 91
In ear and ear. Oh, my dear Gertrude, this, 92
Like to a murdering piece, in many places 93
Gives me superfluous death. *A noise within.* 94

---

61 Cock (A perversion of "God" in oaths; here also with a quibble on the slang word for penis.) **66 An** if **76 spies** scouts sent in advance of the main force **79 remove** removal. **muddied** stirred up, confused **81 greenly** foolishly **82 hugger-mugger** secret haste **85 as much containing** as full of serious matter **87 Feeds . . . clouds** feeds his resentment on this whole shocking turn of events, keeps himself aloof and mysterious **88 wants** lacks. **buzzers** gossipers, informers **90 necessity** i.e., the need to invent some plausible explanation. **of matter beggared** unprovided with facts **91–2 Will . . . ear** will not hesitate to accuse my (royal) person in everybody's ears. **93 murdering piece** cannon loaded so as to scatter its shot **94 Gives . . . death** kills me over and over.

QUEEN. Alack, what noise is this?
KING. Attend! 96
Where is my Switzers? Let them guard the door. 97

Enter a Messenger.

What is the matter?
MESSENGER. Save yourself, my lord!
The ocean, overpeering of his list, 99
Eats not the flats with more impetuous haste 100
Than young Laertes, in a riotous head, 101
O'erbears your officers. The rabble call him lord,
And, as the world were now but to begin, 103
Antiquity forgot, custom not known, 104
The ratifiers and props of every word, 105
They cry, "Choose we! Laertes shall be king!"
Caps, hands, and tongues applaud it to the clouds, 107
"Laertes shall be king, Laertes king!"
QUEEN.
How cheerfully on the false trail they cry!
A noise within.
Oh, this is counter, you false Danish dogs! 110

Enter Laertes with others.

KING. The doors are broke.
LAERTES.
Where is this King?— Sirs, stand you all without.
ALL. No, let's come in.
LAERTES. I pray you, give me leave.
ALL. We will, we will.
LAERTES. I thank you. Keep the door. [*Exeunt followers.*]
Oh, thou vile king,
Give me my father!
QUEEN [*restraining him*]. Calmly, good Laertes.
LAERTES.
That drop of blood that's calm proclaims me bastard,
Cries cuckold to my father, brands the harlot
Even here between the chaste unsmirchèd brow 120
Of my true mother.
KING. What is the cause, Laertes,
That thy rebellion looks so giantlike? 122
Let him go, Gertrude. Do not fear our person. 123

---

96 Attend! Guard me! **97 Switzers** Swiss guards, mercenaries **99 overpeering of his list** overflowing its shore, boundary **100 flats** i.e., flatlands near shore. **impetuous** violent (perhaps also with the meaning of *impiteous* [*impitious,* Q2], "pitiless") **101 riotous head** insurrectionary advance **103–5 And . . . word** and, as if the world were to be started all over afresh, utterly setting aside all ancient traditional customs that should confirm and underprop our every word and promise **107 Caps** (The caps are thrown in the air.) **110 counter** (A hunting term, meaning to follow the trail in a direction opposite to that which the game has taken.) **120 between** amidst **122 giantlike** (Recalling the rising of the giants of Greek mythology against Olympus.) **123 fear our** fear for my

There's such divinity doth hedge a king 124
That treason can but peep to what it would, 125
Acts little of his will. Tell me, Laertes, 126
Why thou art thus incensed. Let him go, Gertrude.
Speak, man.

LAERTES. Where is my father?

KING. Dead.

QUEEN.
But not by him.

KING. Let him demand his fill.

LAERTES.
How came he dead? I'll not be juggled with. 131
To hell, allegiance! Vows, to the blackest devil!
Conscience and grace, to the profoundest pit!
I dare damnation. To this point I stand, 134
That both the worlds I give to negligence, 135
Let come what comes, only I'll be revenged
Most throughly for my father. 137

KING. Who shall stay you?

LAERTES. My will, not all the world's. 139
And for my means, I'll husband them so well 140
They shall go far with little.

KING. Good Laertes,
If you desire to know the certainty
Of your dear father, is't writ in your revenge
That, swoopstake, you will draw both friend and foe, 144
Winner and loser?

LAERTES. None but his enemies.

KING. Will you know them, then?

LAERTES.
To his good friends thus wide I'll ope my arms,
And like the kind life-rendering pelican 149
Repast them with my blood.

KING. Why, now you speak 150
Like a good child and a true gentleman.
That I am guiltless of your father's death,
And am most sensibly in grief for it, 153
It shall as level to your judgment 'pear 154
As day does to your eye. *A noise within.*

LAERTES.
How now, what noise is that?

---

124 hedge protect, as with a surrounding barrier **125 can . . . would** can only peep furtively, as through a barrier, at what it would intend **126 Acts . . . will** (but) performs little of what it intends. **131 juggled with** cheated, deceived. **134 To . . . stand** I am resolved in this **135 both . . . negligence** i.e., both this world and the next are of no consequence to me **137 throughly** thoroughly **139 My will . . . world's** I'll stop (*stay*) when my will is accomplished, not for anyone else's. **140 for** as for **144 swoopstake** i.e., indiscriminately. (Literally, taking all stakes on the gambling table at once. *Draw* is also a gambling term, meaning "take from.") **149 pelican** (Refers to the belief that the female pelican fed its young with its own blood.) **150 Repast** feed **153 sensibly** feelingly **154 level** plain

Enter Ophelia.

KING. Let her come in.

LAERTES.
O heat, dry up my brains! Tears seven times salt
Burn out the sense and virtue of mine eye!
By heaven, thy madness shall be paid with weight
Till our scale turn the beam. O rose of May!
Dear maid, kind sister, sweet Ophelia!
Oh, heavens, is't possible a young maid's wits
Should be as mortal as an old man's life?
Nature is fine in love, and where 'tis fine
It sends some precious instance of itself
After the thing it loves.

OPHELIA.
"They bore him barefaced on the bier, (*Song.*)
Hey non nonny, nonny, hey nonny,
And in his grave rained many a tear —"
Fare you well, my dove!

LAERTES.
Hadst thou thy wits and didst persuade revenge,
It could not move thus.

OPHELIA. You must sing "A-down a-down," and you "call him a-down-a." Oh, how the wheel becomes it! It is the false steward that stole his master's daughter.

LAERTES. This nothing's more than matter.

OPHELIA. There's rosemary, that's for remembrance; pray you, love, remember. And there is pansies; that's for thoughts.

LAERTES. A document in madness, thoughts and remembrance fitted.

OPHELIA. There's fennel for you, and columbines. There's rue for you, and here's some for me; we may call it herb of grace o'Sundays. You must wear your rue with a difference. There's a daisy. I would give you some

---

158 virtue faculty, power **159 paid with weight** repaid, avenged equally or more **160 beam** crossbar of a balance. **164–6 Nature . . . loves** Human nature is exquisitely sensitive in matters of love, and in cases of sudden loss it sends some precious part of itself after the lost object of that love. (In this case, Ophelia's sanity deserts her out of sorrow for her lost father and perhaps too her love for Hamlet.) **173 You . . . a-down-a** (Ophelia assigns the singing of refrains, like her own "Hey non nonny," to others present.) **174 wheel** spinning wheel as accompaniment to the song, or refrain **false steward** (The story is unknown.) **176 This . . . matter** This seeming nonsense is more eloquent than sane utterance. **177 rosemary** (Used as a symbol of remembrance both at weddings and at funerals.) **178 pansies** (Emblems of love and courtship; perhaps from French *pensèes,* "thoughts.") **179 document** instruction, lesson **180 There's fennel . . . columbines** (*Fennel* betokens flattery; *columbines*, unchastity or ingratitude. Throughout, Ophelia addresses her various listeners, giving one flower to one and another to another, perhaps with particular symbolic significance in each case.) **182 rue** (Emblem of repentance—a signification that is evident in its popular name, *herb of grace.*) **with a difference** (A device used in heraldry to distinguish one family from another on the coat of arms, here suggesting that Ophelia and the others have different causes of sorrow and repentance; perhaps with a play on *rue* in the sense of "ruth," "pity.") **daisy** (Emblem of love's victims and of faithlessness.)

violets, but they withered all when my father died. They say 'a made a 183
good end—
[*Sings*] "For bonny sweet Robin is all my joy."

LAERTES.
Thought and affliction, passion, hell itself, 186
She turns to favor and to prettiness. 187

OPHELIA.
"And will 'a not come again? (*Song.*)
And will 'a not come again?
No, no, he is dead.
Go to thy deathbed,
He never will come again.

"His beard was as white as snow,
All flaxen was his poll. 194
He is gone, he is gone,
And we cast away moan.
God ha' mercy on his soul!"
And of all Christian souls, I pray God. God b'wi'you.

[*Exit, followed by Gertrude.*]

LAERTES. Do you see this, O God?

KING.
Laertes, I must commune with your grief,
Or you deny me right. Go but apart,
Make choice of whom your wisest friends you will, 202
And they shall hear and judge twixt you and me.
If by direct or by collateral hand 204
They find us touched, we will our kingdom give, 205
Our crown, our life, and all that we call ours
To you in satisfaction; but if not,
Be you content to lend your patience to us,
And we shall jointly labor with your soul
To give it due content.

LAERTES. Let this be so.
His means of death, his obscure funeral—
No trophy, sword, nor hatchment o'er his bones, 212
No noble rite, nor formal ostentation— 213
Cry to be heard, as 'twere from heaven to earth,
That I must call't in question.

KING. So you shall, 215
And where th'offense is, let the great ax fall.
I pray you, go with me. *Exeunt.*

---

183 violets (Emblems of faithfulness.) **186 Thought** Melancholy. **passion** suffering **187 favor** grace, beauty **194 poll** head. **202 whom** whichever of **204 collateral hand** indirect agency **205 us touched** me implicated **212 trophy** memorial. **hatchment** tablet displaying the armorial bearings of a deceased person **213 ostentation** ceremony **215 That** so that. **call't in question** demand an explanation.

4.6

Enter Horatio and others.

HORATIO.
What are they that would speak with me?
GENTLEMAN. Seafaring men, sir. They say they have letters for you. 2
HORATIO. Let them come in. [*Exit Gentleman.*]
I do not know from what part of the world
I should be greeted, if not from Lord Hamlet.

Enter Sailors.

FIRST SAILOR. God bless you, sir.
HORATIO. Let him bless thee too.
FIRST SAILOR 'A shall, sir, an't please him. There's a letter for you, sir it came 8
from th'ambassador that was bound for England if your name be 9
Horatio, as I am let to know it is. [*He gives a letter.*]
HORATIO [*reads*]. "Horatio, when thou shalt have overlooked this, give 11
these fellows some means to the King; they have letters for him. Ere we 12
were two days old at sea, a pirate of very warlike appointment gave us 13
chase. Finding ourselves too slow of sail, we put on a compelled valor,
and in the grapple I boarded them. On the instant they got clear of our
ship, so I alone became their prisoner. They have dealt with me like
thieves of mercy, but they knew what they did: I am to do a good turn 17
for them. Let the King have the letters I have sent, and repair thou to me 18
with as much speed as thou wouldest fly death. I have words to speak in
thine ear will make thee dumb, yet are they much too light for the bore 20
of the matter. These good fellows will bring thee where I am.
Rosencrantz and Guildenstern hold their course for England. Of them I
have much to tell thee. Farewell.
He that thou knowest thine, Hamlet."
Come, I will give you way for these your letters, 24
And do't the speedier that you may direct me
To him from whom you brought them. *Exeunt.*

4.7

Enter King and Laertes.

KING.
Now must your conscience my acquittance seal, 1
And you must put me in your heart for friend,
Sith you have heard, and with a knowing ear, 3
That he which hath your noble father slain

4.6. Location: The castle.
2 letters a letter **8 an't** if it **9 th'ambassador** (Evidently Hamlet, concealing his identity). **11 overlooked** looked over **12 means** means of access **13 appointment** equipage **17 thieves of mercy** merciful thieves **18 repair** come **20 bore** caliber, i.e., importance **24 way** means of access
4.7 Location: The castle.
1 my acquittance seal confirm or acknowledge my innocence **3 Sith** since

Pursued my life.
LAERTES. It well appears. But tell me
Why you proceeded not against these feats 6
So crimeful and so capital in nature, 7
As by your safety, greatness, wisdom, all things else,
You mainly were stirred up. 9
KING. Oh, for two special reasons,
Which may to you perhaps seem much unsinewed, 11
But yet to me they're strong. The Queen his mother
Lives almost by his looks, and for myself—
My virtue or my plague, be it either which—
She is so conjunctive to my life and soul 15
That, as the star moves not but in his sphere, 16
I could not but by her. The other motive
Why to a public count I might not go 18
Is the great love the general gender bear him, 19
Who, dipping all his faults in their affection,
Work like the spring that turneth wood to stone, 21
Convert his gyves to graces, so that my arrows, 22
Too slightly timbered for so loud a wind, 23
Would have reverted to my bow again
But not where I had aimed them.
LAERTES.
And so have I a noble father lost,
A sister driven into desperate terms, 27
Whose worth, if praises may go back again, 28
Stood challenger on mount of all the age 29
For her perfections. But my revenge will come.
KING.
Break not your sleeps for that. You must not think
That we are made of stuff so flat and dull
That we can let our beard be shook with danger
And think it pastime. You shortly shall hear more.
I loved your father, and we love ourself;
And that, I hope, will teach you to imagine—

Enter a Messenger with letters.

How now? What news?
MESSENGER. Letters, my lord, from Hamlet:
This to Your Majesty, this to the Queen.

[*He gives letters.*]

---

6 feats acts **7 capital** punishable by death **9 mainly** greatly **11 unsinewed** weak **15 conjunctive** closely united. (An astronomical metaphor.) **16 his** its. **sphere** one of the hollow spheres in which, according to Ptolemaic astronomy, the planets were supposed to move **18 count** account, reckoning, indictment **19 general gender** common people **21 Work** operate, act. **spring** i.e., a spring with such a concentration of lime that it coats a piece of wood with limestone, in effect gilding and petrifying it **22 gyves** fetters (which, gilded by the people's praise, would look like badges of honor) **23 Too . . . wind** with too light a shaft for so powerful a gust (of popular sentiment) **27 terms** state, condition **28 go back** recall what she was **29 on mount** set up on high

KING. From Hamlet? Who brought them?

MESSENGER.
Sailors, my lord, they say. I saw them not.
They were given me by Claudio. He received them
Of him that brought them.

KING. Laertes, you shall hear them.—
Leave us. [*Exit Messenger.*]

[*He reads.*] "High and mighty, you shall know I am set naked on your kingdom. Tomorrow shall I beg leave to see your kingly eyes, when I shall, first asking your pardon, thereunto recount the occasion of my sudden and more strange return. Hamlet." What should this mean? Are all the rest come back? Or is it some abuse, and no such thing?

LAERTES.
Know you the hand?

KING. 'Tis Hamlet's character. "Naked!"
And in a postscript here he says "alone."
Can you devise me?

LAERTES.
I am lost in it, my lord. But let him come.
It warms the very sickness in my heart
That I shall live and tell him to his teeth,
"Thus didst thou."

KING. If it be so, Laertes—
As how should it be so? How otherwise?—
Will you be ruled by me?

LAERTES. Ay, my lord,
So you will not o'errule me to a peace.

KING.
To thine own peace. If he be now returned,
As checking at his voyage, and that he means
No more to undertake it, I will work him
To an exploit, now ripe in my device,
Under the which he shall not choose but fall;
And for his death no wind of blame shall breathe,
But even his mother shall uncharge the practice
And call it accident.

LAERTES. My lord, I will be ruled,
The rather if you could devise it so
That I might be the organ.

KING. It falls right.
You have been talked of since your travel much,
And that in Hamlet's hearing, for a quality

44 naked destitute, unarmed, without following **46 pardon** (for returning without authorization) **48 abuse** deceit. **no such thing** not what the letter says. **49 character** handwriting. **51 devise** explain to **55 Thus didst thou** i.e., here's for what you did to my father. **56 As . . . otherwise?** how can this (Hamlet's return) be true? Yet how otherwise than true (since we have the evidence of his letter)? **58 So** provided that **60 checking at** i.e., turning aside from (like a falcon leaving the quarry to fly at a chance bird). **that** if **62 device** devising, invention **65 uncharge the practice** acquit the stratagem of being a plot **68 organ** agent, instrument.

Wherein they say you shine. Your sum of parts
Did not together pluck such envy from him
As did that one, and that, in my regard,
Of the unworthiest siege.

LAERTES. What part is that, my lord?

KING.
A very ribbon in the cap of youth,
Yet needful too, for youth no less becomes
The light and careless livery that it wears
Than settled age his sables and his weeds
Importing health and graveness. Two months since
Here was a gentleman of Normandy.
I have seen myself, and served against, the French,
And they can well on horseback, but this gallant
Had witchcraft in't; he grew unto his seat,
And to such wondrous doing brought his horse
As had he been incorpsed and demi-natured
With the brave beast. So far he topped my thought
That I in forgery of shapes and tricks
Come short of what he did.

LAERTES. A Norman was't?

KING. A Norman.

LAERTES.
Upon my life, Lamord.

KING. The very same.

LAERTES.
I know him well. He is the brooch indeed
And gem of all the nation.

KING. He made confession of you,
And gave you such a masterly report
For art and exercise in your defense,
And for your rapier most especial,
That he cried out 'twould be a sight indeed
If one could match you. Th'escrimers of their nation,
He swore, had neither motion, guard, nor eye
If you opposed them. Sir, this report of his
Did Hamlet so envenom with his envy
That he could nothing do but wish and beg
Your sudden coming o'er, to play with you.
Now, out of this—

LAERTES. What out of this, my lord?

KING.
Laertes, was your father dear to you?

---

71 Your . . . parts All your other virtues **74 unworthiest siege** least important rank. **77 no less becomes** is no less adorned by **79–80 his sables . . . graveness** its rich robes furred with sable and its garments denoting dignified well-being and seriousness. **83 can well** are skilled **86 As . . . beast** as if, centaurlike, he had been made into one body with the horse, possessing half its nature. **87 topped** surpassed **88 forgery** fabrication **92 brooch** ornament **94 confession** testimonial, admission of superiority **96 For . . . defense** with respect to your skill and practice with your weapon **99 Th'escrimers** The fencers **104 sudden** immediate. **play** fence

Or are you like the painting of a sorrow,
A face without a heart?

LAERTES. Why ask you this?

KING.
Not that I think you did not love your father,
But that I know love is begun by time, 110
And that I see, in passages of proof, 111
Time qualifies the spark and fire of it. 112
There lives within the very flame of love
A kind of wick or snuff that will abate it, 114
And nothing is at a like goodness still, 115
For goodness, growing to a pleurisy, 116
Dies in his own too much. That we would do, 117
We should do when we would; for this "would" changes
And hath abatements and delays as many 119
As there are tongues, are hands, are accidents, 120
And then this "should" is like a spendthrift sigh, 121
That hurts by easing. But, to the quick o'th'ulcer: 122
Hamlet comes back. What would you undertake
To show yourself in deed your father's son
More than in words?

LAERTES. To cut his throat i'th'church.

KING.
No place, indeed, should murder sanctuarize; 126
Revenge should have no bounds. But good Laertes,
Will you do this, keep close within your chamber. 128
Hamlet returned shall know you are come home.
We'll put on those shall praise your excellence 130
And set a double varnish on the fame
The Frenchman gave you, bring you in fine together, 132
And wager on your heads. He, being remiss, 133
Most generous, and free from all contriving, 134
Will not peruse the foils, so that with ease,
Or with a little shuffling, you may choose
A sword unbated, and in a pass of practice 137
Requite him for your father.

LAERTES. I will do't,

---

110 begun by time i.e., created by the right circumstance and hence subject to change **111 passages of proof** actual well-attested instances **112 qualifies** weakens, moderates **114 snuff** the charred part of a candlewick **115 nothing . . . still** nothing remains at a constant level of perfection **116 pleurisy** excess, plethora. (Literally, a chest inflammation.) **117 in . . . much** of its own excess. **That** That which **119 abatements** diminutions **120 As . . . accidents** as there are tongues to dissuade, hands to prevent, and chance events to intervene **121 spendthrift sigh** (An allusion to the belief that sighs draw blood from the heart.) **122 hurts by easing** i.e., costs the heart blood and wastes precious opportunity even while it affords emotional relief. **quick o'th'ulcer** i.e., heart of the matter **126 sanctuarize** protect from punishment. (Alludes to the right of sanctuary with which certain religious places were invested.) **128 Will you do this** if you wish to do this **130 put on those shall** arrange for some to **132 in fine** finally **133 remiss** negligently unsuspicious **134 generous** noble-minded **137 unbated** not blunted, having no button. **pass of practice** treacherous thrust in an arranged bout

And for that purpose I'll anoint my sword.
I bought an unction of a mountebank 140
So mortal that, but dip a knife in it,
Where it draws blood no cataplasm so rare, 142
Collected from all simples that have virtue 143
Under the moon, can save the thing from death 144
That is but scratched withal. I'll touch my point
With this contagion, that if I gall him slightly, 146
It may be death.

KING. Let's further think of this,
Weigh what convenience both of time and means
May fit us to our shape. If this should fail, 150
And that our drift look through our bad performance, 151
'Twere better not assayed. Therefore this project
Should have a back or second, that might hold
If this did blast in proof. Soft, let me see. 154
We'll make a solemn wager on your cunnings— 155
I ha 't!
When in your motion you are hot and dry—
As make your bouts more violent to that end— 158
And that he calls for drink, I'll have prepared him
A chalice for the nonce, whereon but sipping, 160
If he by chance escape your venomed stuck, 161
Our purpose may hold there. [*A cry within.*] But stay, what noise?

Enter Queen.

QUEEN.
One woe doth tread upon another's heel,
So fast they follow. Your sister's drowned, Laertes.

LAERTES. Drowned! Oh, where?

QUEEN.
There is a willow grows askant the brook, 166
That shows his hoar leaves in the glassy stream; 167
Therewith fantastic garlands did she make
Of crowflowers, nettles, daisies, and long purples, 169
That liberal shepherds give a grosser name, 170
But our cold maids do dead men's fingers call them. 171
There on the pendent boughs her crownet weeds 172
Clamb'ring to hang, an envious sliver broke, 173

---

140 unction ointment. **mountebank** quack doctor **142 cataplasm** plaster or poultice. **143 simples** herbs. **virtue** potency **144 Under the moon** i.e., anywhere (with reference perhaps to the belief that herbs gathered at night had a special power) **146 gall** graze, wound **150 shape** part we propose to act. **151 drift . . . performance** intention should be made visible by our bungling **154 blast in proof** come to grief when put to the test. **155 cunnings** respective skills **158 As** i.e., and you should **160 nonce** occasion **161 stuck** thrust. (From *stoccado,* a fencing term.) **166 askant** aslant **167 hoar leaves** white or gray undersides of the leaves **169 long purples** early purple orchids **170 liberal** free-spoken. **a grosser name** (The testicle-resembling tubers of the orchid, which also in some cases resemble *dead men's fingers,* have earned various slang names like "dogstones" and "cullions.") **171 cold** chaste **172 pendent** overhanging. **crownet** made into a chaplet or coronet **173 envious sliver** malicious branch

When down her weedy trophies and herself 174
Fell in the weeping brook. Her clothes spread wide,
And mermaidlike awhile they bore her up,
Which time she chanted snatches of old lauds, 177
As one incapable of her own distress, 178
Or like a creature native and endued 179
Unto that element. But long it could not be
Till that her garments, heavy with their drink,
Pulled the poor wretch from her melodious lay 182
To muddy death.

LAERTES. Alas, then she is drowned?

QUEEN. Drowned, drowned.

LAERTES.
Too much of water hast thou, poor Ophelia,
And therefore I forbid my tears. But yet
It is our trick; nature her custom holds, 187
Let shame say what it will. [*He weeps.*] When these are gone, 188
The woman will be out. Adieu, my lord. 189
I have a speech of fire that fain would blaze,
But that this folly douts it. *Exit.*

KING. Let's follow, Gertrude. 191
How much I had to do to calm his rage!
Now fear I this will give it start again;
Therefore let's follow. *Exeunt.*

5.1

Enter two Clowns [with spades and mattocks].

FIRST CLOWN. Is she to be buried in Christian burial, when she willfully
seeks her own salvation? 2

SECOND CLOWN. I tell thee she is; therefore make her grave straight. The 3
crowner hath sat on her, and finds it Christian burial. 4

FIRST CLOWN. How can that be, unless she drowned herself in her own
defense?

SECOND CLOWN. Why, 'tis found so. 7

FIRST CLOWN. It must be *se offendendo,* it cannot be else. For here lies the 8
point: if I drown myself wittingly, it argues an act, and an act hath three

174 weedy i.e., of plants **177 lauds** hymns **178 incapable of** lacking capacity to apprehend **179 endued** adapted by nature **182 lay** ballad, song **187 It is our trick** i.e., weeping is our natural way (when sad) **188–9 When . . . out** When my tears are all shed, the woman in me will be expended, satisfied. **191 douts** extinguishes. (The Second Quarto reads "drowns.")

5.1 Location: A churchyard.

0.1. *Clowns* rustics **2 salvation** (A blunder for "damnation," or perhaps a suggestion that Ophelia was taking her own shortcut to heaven.) **3 straight** straightway, immediately. (But with a pun on *strait,* "narrow.") **4 crowner** coroner. **sat on her** conducted an inquest on her case **finds it** gives his official verdict that her means of death was consistent with **7 found so** determined so in the coroner's verdict. **8 *se offendendo*** (A comic mistake for *se defendendo,* a term used in verdicts of self-defense.)

branches—it is to act, to do, and to perform. Argal, she drowned herself wittingly.

SECOND CLOWN. Nay, but hear you, goodman delve—

FIRST CLOWN. Give me leave. Here lies the water; good. Here stands the man; good. If the man go to this water and drown himself, it is, will he, nill he, he goes, mark you that. But if the water come to him and drown him, he drowns not himself. Argal, he that is not guilty of his own death shortens not his own life.

SECOND CLOWN. But is this law?

FIRST CLOWN. Ay, marry, is't—crowner's quest law.

SECOND CLOWN. Will you ha' the truth on't? If this had not been a gentlewoman, she should have been buried out o'Christian burial.

FIRST CLOWN. Why, there thou say'st. And the more pity that great folk should have countenance in this world to drown or hang themselves, more than their even-Christian. Come, my spade. There is no ancient gentlemen but gardeners, ditchers, and grave makers. They hold up Adam's profession.

SECOND CLOWN. Was he a gentleman?

FIRST CLOWN. 'A was the first that ever bore arms.

SECOND CLOWN. Why, he had none.

FIRST CLOWN. What, art a heathen? How dost thou understand the Scripture? The Scripture says Adam digged. Could he dig without arms? I'll put another question to thee. If thou answerest me not to the purpose, confess thyself—

SECOND CLOWN. Go to.

FIRST CLOWN. What is he that builds stronger than either the mason, the shipwright, or the carpenter?

SECOND CLOWN. The gallows maker, for that frame outlives a thousand tenants.

FIRST CLOWN. I like thy wit well, in good faith. The gallows does well. But how does it well? It does well to those that do ill. Now thou dost ill to say the gallows is built stronger than the church. Argal, the gallows may do well to thee. To't again, come.

SECOND CLOWN. "Who builds stronger than a mason, a shipwright, or a carpenter?"

FIRST CLOWN. Ay, tell me that, and unyoke.

SECOND CLOWN. Marry, now I can tell.

FIRST CLOWN. To't.

SECOND CLOWN. Mass, I cannot tell.

Enter Hamlet and Horatio [*at a distance*].

---

10 Argal (Corruption of *ergo,* "therefore.") **12 goodman** (An honorific title often used with the name of a profession or craft.) **14–15 will he, nill he** whether he will or no, willy-nilly **19 quest** inquest **22 there thou sayst** i.e., that's right **23 countenance** privilege **24 even-Christian** fellow Christians. **ancient** going back to ancient times **25 hold up** maintain **28 bore arms** (To be entitled to bear a coat of arms would make Adam a gentleman, but as one who bore a spade, our common ancestor was an ordinary delver in the earth.) **31 arms** i.e., the arms of the body **33 confess thyself** (The saying continues, "and be hanged.") **37 frame** (1) gallows (2) structure **39 does well** (1) is an apt answer (2) does a good turn. **45 unyoke** i.e., after this great effort, you may unharness the team of your wits **48 Mass** By the Mass

FIRST CLOWN. Cudgel thy brains no more about it, for your dull ass will not mend his pace with beating; and when you are asked this question next, say "a grave maker." The houses he makes lasts till doomsday. Go get thee in and fetch me a stoup of liquor.

[*Exit Second Clown. First Clown digs.*]

Song.

"In youth, when I did love, did love,
Methought it was very sweet,
To contract—oh—the time for—a—my behove,
Oh, methought there—a—was nothing—a—meet."

HAMLET. Has this fellow no feeling of his business, 'a sings in grave-making?

HORATIO. Custom hath made it in him a property of easiness.

HAMLET. 'Tis e'en so. The hand of little employment hath the daintier sense.

FIRST CLOWN. *Song.*

"But age with his stealing steps
Hath clawed me in his clutch,
And hath shipped me into the land,
As if I had never been such."

[He throws up a skull.]

HAMLET. That skull had a tongue in it and could sing once. How the knave jowls it to the ground, as if 'twere Cain's jawbone, that did the first murder! This might be the pate of a politician, which this ass now o'erreaches, one that would circumvent God, might it not?

HORATIO. It might, my lord.

HAMLET. Or of a courtier, which could say, "Good morrow, sweet lord! How dost thou, sweet lord?" This might be my Lord Such-a-one, that praised my Lord Such-a-one's horse when 'a meant to beg it, might it not?

HORATIO. Ay, my lord.

HAMLET. Why, e'en so, and now my Lady Worm's, chapless, and knocked about the mazard with a sexton's spade. Here's fine revolution, an we had the trick to see't. Did these bones cost no more the breeding but to play at loggets with them? Mine ache to think on't.

---

52 stoup two-quart measure **53 In . . . love** (This and the two following stanzas, with nonsensical variations, are from a poem attributed to Lord Vaux and printed in *Tottel's Miscellany,* 1557. The *oh* and *a* [for "ah"] seemingly are the grunts of the digger.) **55 To contract . . . behove** i.e., to shorten the time for my own advantage. (Perhaps he means to *prolong* it.) **56 meet** suitable, i.e., more suitable. **57 'a** that he **58 property of easiness** something he can do easily and indifferently. **59–60 daintier sense** more delicate sense of feeling. **63 into the land** i.e., toward my grave (?) (But note the lack of rhyme in *steps, land.*) **66 jowls** dashes. (With a pun on *jowl,* "jawbone.") **67 politician** schemer, plotter **68 o'erreaches** circumvents, gets the better of **74 chapless** having no lower jaw. **75 mazard** i.e., head. (Literally, a drinking vessel.) **revolution** turn of Fortune's wheel, change. **76 trick** knack **cost . . . but** involve so little expense and care in upbringing that we may **77 loggets** a game in which pieces of hard wood shaped like Indian clubs or bowling pins are thrown to lie as near as possible to a stake

FIRST CLOWN. *Song.*

"A pickax and a spade, a spade,
For and a shrouding sheet; 79
Oh, a pit of clay for to be made
For such a guest is meet."

[*He throws up another skull.*]

HAMLET. There's another. Why may not that be the skull of a lawyer?
Where be his quiddities now, his quillities, his cases, his tenures, and his 83
tricks? Why does he suffer this mad knave now to knock him about the
sconce with a dirty shovel, and will not tell him of his action of battery? 85
Hum, this fellow might be in 's time a great buyer of land, with his 86
statutes, his recognizances, his fines, his double vouchers, his recoveries. 87
Is this the fine of his fines and the recovery of his recoveries, to have his 88
fine pate full of fine dirt? Will his vouchers vouch him no more of his 89
purchases, and double ones too, than the length and breadth of a pair of
indentures? The very conveyances of his lands will scarcely lie in this 91
box, and must th'inheritor himself have no more, ha? 92

HORATIO. Not a jot more, my lord.

HAMLET. Is not parchment made of sheepskins?

HORATIO. Ay, my lord, and of calves' skins too.

HAMLET. They are sheep and calves which seek out assurance in that. I 96
will speak to this fellow.—Whose grave's this, sirrah? 97

FIRST CLOWN. Mine, sir.

[*Sings*] "Oh, pit of clay for to be made
For such a guest is meet."

HAMLET. I think it be thine, indeed, for thou liest in't.

FIRST CLOWN. You lie out on't, sir, and therefore 'tis not yours. For my part, I do not lie in't, yet it is mine.

HAMLET. Thou dost lie in't, to be in't and say it is thine. 'Tis for the dead,
not for the quick; therefore thou liest. 105

FIRST CLOWN. 'Tis a quick lie, sir; 'twill away again from me to you.

HAMLET. What man dost thou dig it for?

FIRST CLOWN. For no man, sir.

HAMLET. What woman, then?

FIRST CLOWN. For none, neither.

HAMLET. Who is to be buried in't?

---

79 For and and moreover **83 his quiddities . . . quillities** his subtleties, his legal niceties **tenures** the holding of a piece of property or office, or the conditions or period of such holding **85 sconce** head **action of battery** lawsuit about physical assault. **86–7 his statutes** his legal documents acknowledging obligation of a debt **87 recognizances** bonds undertaking to repay debts **fines** procedures for converting entailed estates into "fee simple" or freehold. **double vouchers** vouchers signed by two signatories guaranteeing the legality of real estate titles. **recoveries** suits to obtain the authority of a court judgment for the holding of land. **88–9 Is this . . . dirt?** Is this the end of his legal maneuvers, to have the skull of his elegant head filled full of minutely sifted dirt? (With multiple wordplay on *fine* and *fines.*) **89–91 Will . . . indentures?** Will his vouchers, even double ones, guarantee him no more land than is needed to bury him in, being no bigger than the deed of conveyance? (An *indenture* is literally a legal document drawn up in duplicate on a single sheet and then cut apart on a zigzag line so that each pair was uniquely matched.) **92 box** (1) deed box (2) coffin. **th'inheritor** the acquirer, owner **96 assurance in that** safety in legal parchments **97 sirrah** (A term of address to inferiors.) **105 quick** living

FIRST CLOWN. One that was a woman, sir, but, rest her soul, she's dead.

HAMLET. How absolute the knave is! We must speak by the card, or equivocation will undo us. By the Lord, Horatio, this three years I have took note of it: the age is grown so picked that the toe of the peasant comes so near the heel of the courtier he galls his kibe.—How long hast thou been grave maker?

FIRST CLOWN. Of all the days i'th'year, I came to't that day that our last king Hamlet overcame Fortinbras.

HAMLET. How long is that since?

FIRST CLOWN. Cannot you tell that? Every fool can tell that. It was that very day that young Hamlet was born—he that is mad and sent into England.

HAMLET. Ay, marry, why was he sent into England?

FIRST CLOWN. Why, because 'a was mad. 'A shall recover his wits there, or if 'a do not, 'tis no great matter there.

HAMLET. Why?

FIRST CLOWN. 'Twill not be seen in him there. There the men are as mad as he.

HAMLET. How came he mad?

FIRST CLOWN. Very strangely, they say.

HAMLET. How strangely?

FIRST CLOWN. Faith, e'en with losing his wits.

HAMLET. Upon what ground?

FIRST CLOWN. Why, here in Denmark. I have been sexton here, man and boy, thirty years.

HAMLET. How long will a man lie i'th'earth ere he rot?

FIRST CLOWN. Faith, if 'a be not rotten before 'a die—as we have many pocky corpses nowadays, that will scarce hold the laying in—'a will last you some eight year or nine year. A tanner will last you nine year.

HAMLET. Why he more than another?

FIRST CLOWN. Why, sir, his hide is so tanned with his trade that 'a will keep out water a great while, and your water is a sore decayer of your whoreson dead body. [*He picks up a skull.*] Here's a skull now hath lien you i'th'earth three-and-twenty years.

HAMLET. Whose was it?

FIRST CLOWN. A whoreson mad fellow's it was. Whose do you think it was?

HAMLET. Nay, I know not.

FIRST CLOWN. A pestilence on him for a mad rogue! 'A poured a flagon of Rhenish on my head once. This same skull, sir, was, sir, Yorick's skull, the King's jester.

---

113 absolute strict, precise **by the card** i.e., with precision. (Literally, by the mariner's compass-card, on which the points of the compass were marked.) **113–4 equivocation** ambiguity in the use of terms **114 took** taken **115–6 the age . . . kibe** i.e., the age has grown so finical and mannered that the lower classes ape their social betters, chafing at their heels. (*Kibes* are chilblains on the heels.) **134 ground** cause. (But, in the next line, the gravedigger takes the word in the sense of "land," "country.") **139 pocky** rotten, diseased. (Literally, with the pox, or syphilis.) **hold the laying in** hold together long enough to be interred. **139–40 last you** last. (*You* is used colloquially here and in the following lines.) **143 sore** keen, veritable. **143–4 whoreson** (An expression of contemptuous familiarity.) **144 lien you** lain. (See the note at line 139.) **150 Rhenish** Rhine wine

HAMLET. This?

FIRST CLOWN. E'en that.

HAMLET. Let me see. [*He takes the skull.*] Alas, poor Yorick! I knew him, Horatio, a fellow of infinite jest, of most excellent fancy. He hath bore me on his back a thousand times, and now how abhorred in my imagination it is! My gorge rises at it. Here hung those lips that I have kissed I know not how oft. Where be your gibes now? Your gambols, your songs, your flashes of merriment that were wont to set the table on a roar? Not one now, to mock your own grinning? Quite chopfallen? Now get you to my lady's chamber and tell her, let her paint an inch thick, to this favor she must come. Make her laugh at that. Prithee, Horatio, tell me one thing.

HORATIO. What's that, my lord?

HAMLET. Dost thou think Alexander looked o'this fashion i'th'earth?

HORATIO. E'en so.

HAMLET. And smelt so? Pah! [*He throws down the skull.*]

HORATIO. E'en so, my lord.

HAMLET. To what base uses we may return, Horatio! Why may not imagination trace the noble dust of Alexander till 'a find it stopping a bunghole?

HORATIO. 'Twere to consider too curiously to consider so.

HAMLET. No, faith, not a jot, but to follow him thither with modesty enough, and likelihood to lead it. As thus: Alexander died, Alexander was buried, Alexander returneth to dust, the dust is earth, of earth we make loam, and why of that loam whereto he was converted might they not stop a beer barrel?

Imperious Caesar, dead and turned to clay,
Might stop a hole to keep the wind away.
Oh, that that earth which kept the world in awe
Should patch a wall t'expel the winter's flaw!

Enter King, Queen, Laertes, and the corpse [of Ophelia, in procession, with Priest, lords, etc.].

But soft, but soft awhile! Here comes the King,
The Queen, the courtiers. Who is this they follow?
And with such maimèd rites? This doth betoken
The corpse they follow did with desperate hand
Fordo it own life. 'Twas of some estate.
Couch we awhile and mark.

[He and Horatio conceal themselves. Ophelia's body is taken to the grave.]

LAERTES. What ceremony else?

HAMLET [*to Horatio*].
That is Laertes, a very noble youth. Mark.

---

155 bore borne **157 My gorge rises** i.e., I feel nauseated **158 gibes** taunts **160 chopfallen** (1) lacking the lower jaw (2) dejected. **161 favor** aspect, appearance **170 bunghole** hole for filling or emptying a cask **171 curiously** minutely **172–3 with . . . lead it** with moderation and plausibility. **175 loam** a mixture of clay, straw, sand etc. used to mold bricks, or, in this case, bungs for a beer barrel **177 Imperious** Imperial **180 flaw** gust of wind **181 soft** i.e., wait, be careful **183 maimèd** mutilated, incomplete **185 Fordo it** destroy its. **estate** rank. **186 Couch we** Let's hide, lie low

LAERTES. What ceremony else?
PRIEST.
Her obsequies have been as far enlarged
As we have warranty. Her death was doubtful, 191
And but that great command o'ersways the order 192
She should in ground unsanctified been lodged 193
Till the last trumpet. For charitable prayers, 194
Shards, flints, and pebbles should be thrown on her. 195
Yet here she is allowed her virgin crants, 196
Her maiden strewments, and the bringing home 197
Of bell and burial. 198
LAERTES.
Must there no more be done?
PRIEST. No more be done.
We should profane the service of the dead
To sing a requiem and such rest to her 201
As to peace-parted souls.
LAERTES. Lay her i'th'earth, 202
And from her fair and unpolluted flesh
May violets spring! I tell thee, churlish priest, 204
A ministering angel shall my sister be
When thou liest howling.
HAMLET [*to Horatio*]. What, the fair Ophelia! 206
QUEEN [*scattering flowers*]. Sweets to the sweet! Farewell.
I hoped thou shouldst have been my Hamlet's wife.
I thought thy bride-bed to have decked, sweet maid,
And not t'have strewed thy grave.
LAERTES. Oh, treble woe
Fall ten times treble on that cursèd head
Whose wicked deed thy most ingenious sense 212
Deprived thee of! Hold off the earth awhile,
Till I have caught her once more in mine arms.

[*He leaps into the grave and embraces Ophelia.*]

Now pile your dust upon the quick and dead,
Till of this flat a mountain you have made
T' o'ertop old Pelion or the skyish head 217
Of blue Olympus.
HAMLET [*coming forward*]. What is he whose grief
Bears such an emphasis, whose phrase of sorrow 220

---

191 warranty i.e., ecclesiastical authority. **192 order** (1) prescribed practice (2) religious order of clerics **193 She should . . . lodged** she should have been buried in unsanctified ground **194 For** In place of **195 Shards** broken bits of pottery **196 crants** garlands betokening maidenhood **197 strewments** flowers strewn on a coffin **197–8 bringing . . . burial** laying the body to rest, to the sound of the bell. **201 such rest** i.e., to pray for such rest **202 peace-parted souls** those who have died at peace with God. **204 violets** (See 4.5.183–4 and note.) **206 howling** i.e., in hell. **212 ingenious sense** a mind that is quick, alert, of fine qualities **217 Pelion** a mountain in northern Thessaly; compare *Olympus* and *Ossa* in lines 218 and 251. (In their rebellion against the Olympian gods, the giants attempted to heap Ossa on Pelion in order to scale Olympus.) **220 emphasis** i.e., rhetorical and florid emphasis. (*Phrase* has a similar rhetorical connotation.)

Conjures the wandering stars and makes them stand
Like wonder-wounded hearers? This is I,
Hamlet the Dane.

LAERTES [*grappling with him*]. The devil take thy soul!

HAMLET. Thou pray'st not well.
I prithee, take thy fingers from my throat,
For though I am not splenitive and rash,
Yet have I in me something dangerous,
Which let thy wisdom fear. Hold off thy hand.

KING. Pluck them asunder.

QUEEN. Hamlet, Hamlet!

ALL. Gentlemen!

HORATIO. Good my lord, be quiet.

[*Hamlet and Laertes are parted.*]

HAMLET.
Why, I will fight with him upon this theme
Until my eyelids will no longer wag.

QUEEN. Oh my son, what theme?

HAMLET.
I loved Ophelia. Forty thousand brothers
Could not with all their quantity of love
Make up my sum. What wilt thou do for her?

KING. Oh, he is mad, Laertes.

QUEEN. For love of God, forbear him.

HAMLET.
'Swounds, show me what thou'lt do.
Woo't weep? Woo't fight? Woo't fast? Woo't tear thyself?
Woo't drink up eisel? Eat a crocodile?
I'll do't. Dost come here to whine?
To outface me with leaping in her grave?
Be buried quick with her, and so will I.
And if thou prate of mountains, let them throw
Millions of acres on us, till our ground,
Singeing his pate against the burning zone,
Make Ossa like a wart! Nay, an thou'lt mouth,

---

221 wandering stars planets **222 wonder-wounded** struck with amazement **223 the Dane** (This title normally signifies the King; see 1.1.17 and note.) **224 s.d. *grappling with him*** The testimony of the First Quarto that *"Hamlet leaps in after Laertes"* and the ballad "Elegyon Burbage," published in *Gentleman's Magazine* in 1825 ("Oft have I seen him leap into the grave") seem to indicate one way in which this fight was staged; however, the difficulty of fitting two contenders and Ophelia's body into a confined space (probably the trapdoor) suggests to many editors the alternative, that Laertes jumps out of the grave to attack Hamlet.) **227 splenitive** quick-tempered **235 wag** move. (A fluttering eyelid is a conventional sign that life has not yet gone.) **241 forbear him** leave him alone. **242 'Swounds** By His (Christ's) wounds **243 Woo't** Wilt thou **243–4 Woo't . . . eisel?** Will you drink up a whole draft of vinegar? (An extremely self-punishing task as a way of expressing grief.) **244 crocodile** (Crocodiles were tough and dangerous, and were supposed to shed crocodile tears.) **247 quick** alive **250 his pate** its head, i.e., top. **burning zone** zone in the celestial sphere containing the sun's orbit, between the tropics of Cancer and Capricorn **251 an thou'lt mouth** if you want to rant

I'll rant as well as thou.

QUEEN. This is mere madness,
And thus awhile the fit will work on him;
Anon, as patient as the female dove
When that her golden couplets are disclosed,
His silence will sit drooping.

HAMLET. Hear you, sir.
What is the reason that you use me thus?
I loved you ever. But it is no matter.
Let Hercules himself do what he may,
The cat will mew, and dog will have his day.

Exit Hamlet.

KING.
I pray thee, good Horatio, wait upon him.

[*Exit*] *Horatio.*

[*To Laertes*] Strengthen your patience in our last night's speech;
We'll put the matter to the present push.—
Good Gertrude, set some watch over your son.—
This grave shall have a living monument.
An hour of quiet shortly shall we see;
Till then, in patience our proceeding be. *Exeunt.*

5.2

Enter Hamlet and Horatio.

HAMLET.
So much for this, sir; now shall you see the other.
You do remember all the circumstance?

HORATIO. Remember it, my lord!

HAMLET.
Sir, in my heart there was a kind of fighting
That would not let me sleep. Methought I lay
Worse than the mutines in the bilboes. Rashly,
And praised be rashness for it—let us know
Our indiscretion sometimes serves us well
When our deep plots do pall, and that should learn us

---

252 mere utter **255 golden couplets** two baby pigeons, covered with yellow down. **disclosed** hatched **259–60 Let . . . day** i.e., (1) Even Hercules couldn't stop Laertes' theatrical rant (2) I, too, will have my turn; i.e., despite any blustering attempts at interference, every person will sooner or later do what he or she must do. **262 in** i.e., by recalling **263 present push** immediate test. **265 living** lasting. (For Laertes' private understanding, Claudius also hints that Hamlet's death will serve as such a monument.) **266 hour of quiet** time free of conflict

5.2 Location: The castle.

1 see the other hear the other news. (See 4.6.19–21.) **6 mutines** mutineers. **bilboes** shackles. **Rashly** On impulse. (This adverb goes with lines 12 ff.) **7 know** acknowledge **8 indiscretion** lack of foresight and judgment (not an indiscreet act) **9 pall** fail, falter, go stale. **learn** teach

There's a divinity that shapes our ends,
Rough-hew them how we will—
HORATIO. That is most certain.
HAMLET. Up from my cabin,
My sea-gown scarfed about me, in the dark
Groped I to find out them, had my desire,
Fingered their packet, and in fine withdrew
To mine own room again, making so bold,
My fears forgetting manners, to unseal
Their grand commission; where I found, Horatio—
Ah, royal knavery!—an exact command,
Larded with many several sorts of reasons
Importing Denmark's health and England's too,
With, ho! such bugs and goblins in my life,
That on the supervise, no leisure bated,
No, not to stay the grinding of the ax,
My head should be struck off.
HORATIO. Is't possible?
HAMLET [*giving a document*].
Here's the commission. Read it at more leisure.
But wilt thou hear now how I did proceed?
HORATIO. I beseech you.
HAMLET.
Being thus benetted round with villainies—
Ere I could make a prologue to my brains,
They had begun the play—I sat me down,
Devised a new commission, wrote it fair.
I once did hold it, as our statists do,
A baseness to write fair, and labored much
How to forget that learning, but, sir, now
It did me yeoman's service. Wilt thou know
Th'effect of what I wrote?
HORATIO. Ay, good my lord.
HAMLET.
An earnest conjuration from the King,
As England was his faithful tributary,
As love between them like the palm might flourish,
As peace should still her wheaten garland wear
And stand a comma 'tween their amities,

---

11 Rough-hew shape roughly **13 sea-gown** seaman's coat. **scarfed** loosely wrapped **14 them** i.e., Rosencrantz and Guildenstern **15 Fingered** pilfered, pinched. **in fine** finally, in conclusion **20 Larded** garnished. **several** different **21 Importing** relating to **22 With . . . life** i.e., with all sorts of warnings of imaginary dangers if I were allowed to continue living. (*Bugs* are bugbears, hobgoblins.) **23 That . . . bated** that on the reading of this commission, no delay being allowed **24 stay** await **30–1 Ere . . . play** before I could consciously turn my brain to the matter, it had started working on a plan **32 fair** in a clear hand. **33 statists** politicians, men of public affairs **34 A baseness** beneath my dignity **38 conjuration** entreaty **40 palm** (An image of health; see Psalm 92:12.) **41 still** always. **wheaten garland** (Symbolic of fruitful agriculture, of peace and plenty.) **42 comma** (Indicating continuity, link.)

And many suchlike "as"es of great charge,
That on the view and knowing of these contents,
Without debatement further more or less,
He should those bearers put to sudden death,
Not shriving time allowed.

HORATIO. How was this sealed?

HAMLET.
Why, even in that was heaven ordinant.
I had my father's signet in my purse,
Which was the model of that Danish seal;
Folded the writ up in the form of th'other,
Subscribed it, gave't th'impression, placed it safely,
The changeling never known. Now, the next day
Was our sea fight, and what to this was sequent
Thou knowest already.

HORATIO.
So Guildenstern and Rosencrantz go to't.

HAMLET.
Why, man, they did make love to this employment.
They are not near my conscience. Their defeat
Does by their own insinuation grow.
'Tis dangerous when the baser nature comes
Between the pass and fell incensèd points
Of mighty opposites.

HORATIO. Why, what a king is this!

HAMLET.
Does it not, think thee, stand me now upon—
He that hath killed my king and whored my mother,
Popped in between th'election and my hopes,
Thrown out his angle for my proper life,
And with such cozenage—is't not perfect conscience
To quit him with this arm? And is't not to be damned
To let this canker of our nature come
In further evil?

HORATIO.
It must be shortly known to him from England
What is the issue of the business there.

HAMLET.
It will be short. The interim is mine,
And a man's life's no more than to say "one."
But I am very sorry, good Horatio,

---

43 "as"es (1) the "whereases" of a formal document (2) asses. **charge** (1) import (2) burden (appropriate to asses) **47 shriving time** time for confession and absolution **48 ordinant** directing. **49 signet** small seal **50 model** replica **51 writ** writing **52 Subscribed** signed (with forged signature). **impression** i.e., with a wax seal **53 changeling** i.e., substituted letter. (Literally, a fairy child substituted for a human one.) **54 was sequent** followed **58 defeat** destruction **59 insinuation** intrusive intervention, sticking their noses in my business **60 baser** of lower social station **61 pass** thrust. **fell** fierce **62 opposites** antagonists. **63 stand me now upon** become incumbent on me now **65 th'election** (The Danish monarch was "elected" by a small number of high-ranking electors.) **66 angle** fishhook. **proper** very **67 cozenage** trickery **68 quit** requite, pay back **69 canker** ulcer **69–70 come In** grow into **74 a man's . . . "one"** one's whole life occupies such a short time, only as long as it takes to count to 1.

That to Laertes I forgot myself,
For by the image of my cause I see
The portraiture of his. I'll court his favors.
But, sure, the bravery of his grief did put me
Into a tow'ring passion.

HORATIO. Peace, who comes here?

Enter a Courtier [*Osric*].

OSRIC. Your Lordship is right welcome back to Denmark.

HAMLET. I humbly thank you, sir. [*To Horatio*] Dost know this water fly?

HORATIO. No, my good lord.

HAMLET. Thy state is the more gracious, for 'tis a vice to know him. He hath much land, and fertile. Let a beast be lord of beasts, and his crib shall stand at the King's mess. 'Tis a chuff, but, as I say, spacious in the possession of dirt.

OSRIC. Sweet lord, if Your Lordship were at leisure, I should impart a thing to you from His Majesty.

HAMLET. I will receive it, sir, with all diligence of spirit. Put your bonnet to his right use; 'tis for the head.

OSRIC. I thank Your Lordship, it is very hot.

HAMLET. No, believe me, 'tis very cold. The wind is northerly.

OSRIC. It is indifferent cold, my lord, indeed.

HAMLET. But yet methinks it is very sultry and hot for my complexion.

OSRIC. Exceedingly, my lord. It is very sultry, as 'twere—I cannot tell how. My lord, His Majesty bade me signify to you that 'a has laid a great wager on your head. Sir, this is the matter—

HAMLET. I beseech you, remember.

[*Hamlet moves him to put on his hat.*]

OSRIC. Nay, good my lord; for my ease, in good faith. Sir, here is newly come to court Laertes—believe me, an absolute gentleman, full of most excellent differences, of very soft society and great showing. Indeed, to speak feelingly of him, he is the card or calendar of gentry, for you shall find in him the continent of what part a gentleman would see.

HAMLET. Sir, his definement suffers no perdition in you, though I know to divide him inventorially would dozy th'arithmetic of memory, and yet but yaw neither in respect of his quick sail. But, in the verity of

---

79 bravery bravado **85–6 Let . . . mess** I.e., if a man, no matter how beastlike, is as rich in livestock and possessions as Osric, he may eat at the King's table. **85 crib** manger **86 chuff** boor, churl. (The Second Quarto spelling, "chough," is a variant spelling that also suggests the meaning here of "chattering jackdaw.") **90 bonnet** any kind of cap or hat. **91 his** its **94 indifferent** somewhat **95 complexion** constitution. **100 for my ease** (A conventional reply declining the invitation to put his hat back on.) **101 absolute** perfect **102 differences** special qualities **soft society** agreeable manners. **great showing** distinguished appearance. **103 feelingly** with just perception **the card . . . gentry** the model or paradigm (literally, a chart or directory) of good breeding **104 the continent . . . see** one who contains in himself all the qualities a gentleman would like to see. (A *continent* is that which contains.) **105–7 his definement . . . sail** the task of defining Laertes' excellences suffers no diminution in your description of him, though I know that to enumerate all his graces would stupify one's powers of memory, and even so could do no more than veer unsteadily off course in a vain attempt to keep up with his rapid forward motion. (Hamlet mocks Osric by parodying his jargon-filled speeches.)

extolment, I take him to be a soul of great article, and his infusion of such dearth and rareness as, to make true diction of him, his semblable is his mirror and who else would trace him his umbrage, nothing more.

OSRIC. Your Lordship speaks most infallibly of him.

HAMLET. The concernancy, sir? Why do we wrap the gentleman in our more rawer breath?

OSRIC. Sir?

HORATIO. Is't not possible to understand in another tongue? You will do't, sir, really.

HAMLET. What imports the nomination of this gentleman?

OSRIC. Of Laertes?

HORATIO [*to Hamlet*]. His purse is empty already; all 's golden words are spent.

HAMLET. Of him, sir.

OSRIC. I know you are not ignorant—

HAMLET. I would you did, sir. Yet in faith if you did, it would not much approve me. Well, sir?

OSRIC. You are not ignorant of what excellence Laertes is—

HAMLET. I dare not confess that, lest I should compare with him in excellence. But to know a man well were to know himself.

OSRIC. I mean, sir, for his weapon; but in the imputation laid on him by them, in his meed he's unfellowed.

HAMLET. What's his weapon?

OSRIC. Rapier and dagger.

HAMLET. That's two of his weapons—but well.

OSRIC. The King, sir, hath wagered with him six Barbary horses, against the which he has impawned, as I take it, six French rapiers and poniards, with their assigns, as girdle, hangers, and so. Three of the carriages, in faith, are very dear to fancy, very responsive to the hilts, most delicate carriages, and of very liberal conceit.

107–10 But . . . more But, in true praise of him, I take him to be a person of remarkable value, and his essence of such rarity and excellence as, to speak truly of him, none can compare with him other than his own mirror; anyone following in his footsteps can only hope to be the shadow to his substance, nothing more. **112 concernancy** import, relevance **113 rawer breath** unrefined speech that can only come short in praising him. **115 Is't . . . tongue?** i.e., Is it not possible for you, Osric, to understand and communicate in any other tongue than the overblown rhetoric you have used? (Alternatively, Horatio could be asking Hamlet to speak more plainly.) **You will do't** i.e., You can if you try, or, you may well have to try (to speak plainly). **117 nomination** naming **123–4 I would . . . approve me** (Responding to Osric's incompleted sentence as though it were a complete statement, Hamlet says, with mock politeness, "I wish you did know me to be not ignorant [i.e., to be knowledgeable] about matters," and then turns this into an insult: "But if you did, your recommendation of me would be of little value in any case.") **126–7 I dare . . . himself** I dare not boast of knowing Laertes' excellence lest I seem to imply a comparable excellence in myself. Certainly, to know another person well, one must know oneself. **128–9 I mean . . . unfellowed** I mean his excellence with his rapier, not his general excellence; in the reputation he enjoys for use of his weapons, his merit is unequaled. **132 but well** but never mind. **134 he** i.e., Laertes. **impawned** staked, wagered **poniards** daggers. **135 assigns** appurtenances **hangers** straps on the sword belt (*girdle*), from which the sword hung. **and so** and so on. **135–7 Three . . . conceit** Three of the hangers, truly, are very pleasing to the fancy, decoratively matched with the hilts, delicate in workmanship, and made with elaborate ingenuity.

HAMLET. What call you the carriages?

HORATIO [*to Hamlet*]. I knew you must be edified by the margent ere you had done.

OSRIC. The carriages, sir, are the hangers.

HAMLET. The phrase would be more germane to the matter if we could carry a cannon by our sides; I would it might be hangers till then. But, on: six Barbary horses against six French swords, their assigns, and three liberal-conceited carriages; that's the French bet against the Danish. Why is this impawned, as you call it?

OSRIC. The King, sir, hath laid, sir, that in a dozen passes between yourself and him, he shall not exceed you three hits. He hath laid on twelve for nine, and it would come to immediate trial, if your lordship would vouchsafe the answer.

HAMLET. How if I answer no?

OSRIC. I mean, my lord, the opposition of your person in trial.

HAMLET. Sir, I will walk here in the hall. If it please His Majesty, it is the breathing time of day with me. Let the foils be brought, the gentleman willing, and the King hold his purpose, I will win for him an I can; if not, I will gain nothing but my shame and the odd hits.

OSRIC. Shall I deliver you so?

HAMLET. To this effect, sir—after what flourish your nature will.

OSRIC. I commend my duty to Your Lordship.

HAMLET. Yours, yours. [*Exit Osric.*]
'A does well to commend it himself; there are no tongues else for's turn.

HORATIO. This lapwing runs away with the shell on his head.

HAMLET. 'A did comply with his dug before 'a sucked it. Thus has he—and many more of the same breed that I know the drossy age dotes on—only got the tune of the time and, out of an habit of encounter, a kind of yeasty collection, which carries them through and through the most fanned and winnowed opinions; and do but blow them to their trial, the bubbles are out.

Enter a Lord.

---

138 What call you What do you refer to when you say **139 margent** margin of a book, place for explanatory notes **147 laid** wagered **passes** bouts. (The odds of the betting are hard to explain. Possibly the King bets that Hamlet will win at least five out of twelve, at which point Laertes raises the odds against himself by betting he will win nine.) **150 vouchsafe the answer** be so good as to accept the challenge. (Hamlet deliberately takes the phrase in its literal sense of replying.) **154 breathing time** exercise period. **Let** i.e., If **157 deliver you** report what you say **159 commend** commit to your favor. (A conventional salutation, but Hamlet wryly uses a more literal meaning, "recommend," "praise," in line 161.) **161 for's turn** for his purposes, i.e., to do it for him **162 lapwing** (A proverbial type of youthful forwardness. Also, a bird that draws intruders away from its nest and was thought to run about with its head in the shell when newly hatched; a seeming reference to Osric's hat.) **163 comply . . . dug** observe ceremonious formality toward his nurse's or mother's teat **163–8 Thus . . . are out** Thus has he—and many like him of the sort our frivolous age dotes on—acquired the trendy manner of speech of the time, and, out of habitual conversation with courtiers of their own kind, have collected together a kind of frothy medley of current phrases, which enables such gallants to hold their own among persons of the most select and well-sifted views; and yet do but test them by merely blowing on them, and their bubbles burst.

LORD. My lord, His Majesty commended him to you by young Osric, who
brings back to him that you attend him in the hall. He sends to know if
your pleasure hold to play with Laertes, or that you will take longer 171
time.

HAMLET. I am constant to my purposes; they follow the King's pleasure. If 173
his fitness speaks, mine is ready; now or whensoever, provided I be so 174
able as now.

LORD. The King and Queen and all are coming down.

HAMLET. In happy time. 177

LORD. The Queen desires you to use some gentle entertainment to 178
Laertes before you fall to play.

HAMLET. She well instructs me. [*Exit Lord.*]

HORATIO. You will lose, my lord.

HAMLET. I do not think so. Since he went into France, I have been in continual practice; I shall win at the odds. But thou wouldst not think how ill all's here about my heart; but it is no matter.

HORATIO. Nay, good my lord—

HAMLET. It is but foolery, but it is such a kind of gaingiving as would per- 186
haps trouble a woman.

HORATIO. If your mind dislike anything, obey it. I will forestall their repair 188
hither and say you are not fit.

HAMLET. Not a whit, we defy augury. There is special providence in the fall 190
of a sparrow. If it be now, 'tis not to come; if it be not to come, it will be
now; if it be not now; yet it will come. The readiness is all. Since no man 192
of aught he leaves knows, what is 't to leave betimes? Let be. 193

A table prepared. [*Enter*] *trumpets, drums, and officers with cushions; King, Queen,* [*Osric,*] *and all the state; foils, daggers,* [*and wine borne in;*] *and Laertes.*

KING.
Come, Hamlet, come and take this hand from me.

[*The King puts Laertes' hand into Hamlet's.*]

HAMLET [*to Laertes*].
Give me your pardon, sir. I have done you wrong,
But pardon't as you are a gentleman.
This presence knows, 197
And you must needs have heard, how I am punished 198
With a sore distraction. What I have done
That might your nature, honor, and exception 200
Roughly awake, I here proclaim was madness.
Was't Hamlet wronged Laertes? Never Hamlet.
If Hamlet from himself be ta'en away,
And when he's not himself does wrong Laertes,

171 play fence. **that** if **173–4 If . . . ready** If he declares his readiness, my convenience waits on his **177 In happy time** (A phrase of courtesy indicating that the time is convenient.) **178 entertainment** greeting **186 gaingiving** misgiving **188 repair** coming **190 augury** the attempt to read signs of future events in order to avoid predicted trouble. **192–3 Since . . . Let be** Since no one has knowledge of what he is leaving behind, what does an early death matter after all? Enough; forbear. **193.1 *trumpets, drums*** trumpeters, drummers **193.2 *all the state*** the entire court **197 presence** royal assembly **198 punished** afflicted **200 exception** disapproval

Then Hamlet does it not, Hamlet denies it.
Who does it, then? His madness. If't be so,
Hamlet is of the faction that is wronged; 207
His madness is poor Hamlet's enemy.
Sir, in this audience
Let my disclaiming from a purposed evil
Free me so far in your most generous thoughts
That I have shot my arrow o'er the house
And hurt my brother.

LAERTES. I am satisfied in nature, 213
Whose motive in this case should stir me most 214
To my revenge. But in my terms of honor
I stand aloof, and will no reconcilement
Till by some elder masters of known honor
I have a voice and precedent of peace 218
To keep my name ungored. But till that time 219
I do receive your offered love like love,
And will not wrong it.

HAMLET. I embrace it freely,
And will this brothers' wager frankly play.— 222
Give us the foils. Come on.

LAERTES. Come, one for me.

HAMLET.
I'll be your foil, Laertes. In mine ignorance 224
Your skill shall, like a star i'th'darkest night,
Stick fiery off indeed.

LAERTES. You mock me, sir. 226

HAMLET. No, by this hand.

KING.
Give them the foils, young Osric. Cousin Hamlet,
You know the wager?

HAMLET. Very well, my lord.
Your Grace has laid the odds o'th'weaker side. 230

KING.
I do not fear it; I have seen you both.
But since he is bettered, we have therefore odds. 232

LAERTES.
This is too heavy. Let me see another.

[*He exchanges his foil for another.*]

HAMLET.
This likes me well. These foils have all a length? 234

[*They prepare to fence.*]

---

207 faction party **213 in nature** i.e., as to my personal feelings **214 motive** prompting **218 voice** authoritative pronouncement. **of peace** for reconciliation **219 name ungored** reputation unwounded. **222 frankly** without ill feeling or the burden of rancor **224 foil** thin metal background which sets a jewel off. (With pun on the blunted rapier for fencing.) **226 Stick fiery off** stand out brilliantly **230 laid . . . side** backed the weaker side. **232 is bettered** is the odds-on favorite. (Laertes' handicap is the "three hits" specified in line 148.) **234 likes** pleases

OSRIC. Ay, my good lord.

KING.
Set me the stoups of wine upon that table.
If Hamlet give the first or second hit,
Or quit in answer of the third exchange, 238
Let all the battlements their ordnance fire.
The King shall drink to Hamlet's better breath, 240
And in the cup an union shall he throw 241
Richer than that which four successive kings
In Denmark's crown have worn. Give me the cups,
And let the kettle to the trumpet speak, 244
The trumpet to the cannoneer without,
The cannons to the heavens, the heaven to earth,
"Now the King drinks to Hamlet." Come, begin.

Trumpets the while.

And you, the judges, bear a wary eye.

HAMLET. Come on, sir.

LAERTES. Come, my lord. [*They fence. Hamlet scores a hit.*]

HAMLET. One.

LAERTES. No.

HAMLET. Judgment.

OSRIC. A hit, a very palpable hit.

Drum, trumpets, and shot. Flourish. A piece goes off.

LAERTES. Well, again.

KING.
Stay, give me drink. Hamlet, this pearl is thine.

[*He drinks, and throws a pearl in Hamlet's cup.*]

Here's to thy health. Give him the cup.

HAMLET.
I'll play this bout first. Set it by awhile.
Come. [*They fence.*] Another hit; what say you?

LAERTES. A touch, a touch, I do confess't.

KING.
Our son shall win.

QUEEN. He's fat and scant of breath. 260
Here, Hamlet, take my napkin, rub thy brows. 261
The Queen carouses to thy fortune, Hamlet. 262

HAMLET. Good madam!

KING. Gertrude, do not drink.

QUEEN.
I will, my lord, I pray you pardon me. [*She drinks.*]

KING [*aside*].

---

238 Or . . . exchange or draws even with Laertes by winning the third exchange **240 better breath** improved vigor **241 union** pearl. (So called, according to Pliny's *Natural History,* 9, because pearls are *unique,* never identical.) **244 kettle** kettledrum **253.1 A piece** A cannon **260 fat** not physically fit, out of training **261 napkin** handkerchief **262 carouses** drinks a toast

It is the poisoned cup. It is too late.

HAMLET.
I dare not drink yet, madam; by and by.

QUEEN. Come, let me wipe thy face.

LAERTES [*to King*].
My lord, I'll hit him now.

KING. I do not think't.

LAERTES [*aside*].
And yet it is almost against my conscience.

HAMLET.
Come, for the third, Laertes. You do but dally.
I pray you, pass with your best violence;
I am afeard you make a wanton of me.

LAERTES. Say you so? Come on. [*They play.*]

OSRIC. Nothing neither way.

LAERTES.
Have at you now!

[Laertes wounds Hamlet; then, in scuffling, they change rapiers, and Hamlet wounds Laertes.]

KING. Part them! They are incensed.

HAMLET.
Nay, come, again.

[The Queen falls.]

OSRIC. Look to the Queen there, ho!

HORATIO.
They bleed on both sides. How is it, my lord?

OSRIC. How is't, Laertes?

LAERTES.
Why, as a woodcock to mine own springe, Osric;
I am justly killed with mine own treachery.

HAMLET.
How does the Queen?

KING. She swoons to see them bleed.

QUEEN.
No, no, the drink, the drink—Oh, my dear Hamlet—
The drink, the drink! I am poisoned. [*She dies.*]

HAMLET.
Oh villainy! Ho, let the door be locked!
Treachery! Seek it out. [*Laertes falls. Exit Osric.*]

LAERTES.
It is here, Hamlet. Hamlet, thou art slain.
No med'cine in the world can do thee good;
In thee there is not half an hour's life.

---

272 pass thrust **273 make . . . me** i.e., treat me like a spoiled child, trifle with me. **276.1 *in scuffling, they change rapiers*** (This stage direction occurs in the Folio. According to a widespread stage tradition, Hamlet receives a scratch, realizes that Laertes' sword is unbated, and accordingly forces an exchange.) **280 woodcock** a bird, a type of stupidity or as a decoy. **springe** trap, snare

The treacherous instrument is in thy hand,
Unbated and envenomed. The foul practice
Hath turned itself on me. Lo, here I lie,
Never to rise again. Thy mother's poisoned.
I can no more. The King, the King's to blame.

HAMLET.
The point envenomed too? Then, venom, to thy work.
[He stabs the King.]

ALL. Treason! Treason!

KING.
Oh, yet defend me, friends! I am but hurt.

HAMLET [*forcing the King to drink*].
Here, thou incestuous, murderous, damnèd Dane,
Drink off this potion. Is thy union here?
Follow my mother. *[The King dies.]*

LAERTES. He is justly served.
It is a poison tempered by himself.
Exchange forgiveness with me, noble Hamlet.
Mine and my father's death come not upon thee,
Nor thine on me! *[He dies.]*

HAMLET.
Heaven make thee free of it! I follow thee.
I am dead, Horatio. Wretched Queen, adieu!
You that look pale and tremble at this chance,
That are but mutes or audience to this act,
Had I but time—as this fell sergeant, Death,
Is strict in his arrest—oh, I could tell you—
But let it be. Horatio, I am dead;
Thou livest. Report me and my cause aright
To the unsatisfied.

HORATIO. Never believe it.
I am more an antique Roman than a Dane.
Here's yet some liquor left.

[He attempts to drink from the poisoned cup. Hamlet prevents him.]

HAMLET. As thou'rt a man,
Give me the cup! Let go! By heaven, I'll ha 't.
Oh, God, Horatio, what a wounded name,
Things standing thus unknown, shall I leave behind me!
If thou didst ever hold me in thy heart,
Absent thee from felicity awhile,
And in this harsh world draw thy breath in pain
To tell my story. *A march afar off* [*and a volley within*].
What warlike noise is this?

292 Unbated Not blunted with a button. **practice** plot **300 union** pearl. (See line 241; with grim puns on the word's other meanings: marriage, shared death.) **302 tempered** mixed **308 chance** mischance **309 mutes** silent observers. (Literally, actors with nonspeaking parts.) **310 fell sergeant** remorseless arresting officer **311 strict** (1) severely just (2) unavoidable. **arrest** (1) taking into custody (2) stopping my speech **315 Roman** (Suicide was an honorable choice for many Romans as an alternative to a dishonorable life.)

Enter Osric.

OSRIC.
Young Fortinbras, with conquest come from Poland,
To th'ambassadors of England gives
This warlike volley.

HAMLET. Oh, I die, Horatio!
The potent poison quite o'ercrows my spirit. 328
I cannot live to hear the news from England,
But I do prophesy th'election lights
On Fortinbras. He has my dying voice. 331
So tell him, with th'occurrents more and less 332
Which have solicited—the rest is silence. [*He dies.*] 333

HORATIO.
Now cracks a noble heart. Good night, sweet prince,
And flights of angels sing thee to thy rest!

[March within.]

Why does the drum come hither?

Enter Fortinbras, with the [English] Ambassadors [with drum, colors, and attendants].

FORTINBRAS.
Where is this sight?

HORATIO. What is it you would see?
If aught of woe or wonder, cease your search.

FORTINBRAS.
This quarry cries on havoc. O proud Death, 339
What feast is toward in thine eternal cell, 340
That thou so many princes at a shot
So bloodily hast struck?

FIRST AMBASSADOR. The sight is dismal,
And our affairs from England come too late.
The ears are senseless that should give us hearing,
To tell him his commandment is fulfilled,
That Rosencrantz and Guildenstern are dead.
Where should we have our thanks?

HORATIO. Not from his mouth, 347
Had it th'ability of life to thank you.
He never gave commandment for their death.
But since, so jump upon this bloody question, 350
You from the Polack wars and you from England
Are here arrived, give order that these bodies
High on a stage be placèd to the view, 353

---

328 o'ercrows the triumphs over (like the winner in a cockfight) **331 voice** vote **332 occurrents** the events, incidents **333 solicited** moved, urged. (Hamlet doesn't finish saying what the events have prompted—presumably, his acts of vengeance, or his reporting of those events to Fortinbras.) **339 This . . . havoc** This heap of dead bodies loudly proclaims a general slaughter. **340 feast** i.e., Death feasting on those who have fallen. **toward** in preparation **347 his** Claudius' **350 so jump . . . question** so hard on the heels of this bloody business **353 stage** platform

And let me speak to th' yet unknowing world
How these things came about. So shall you hear
Of carnal, bloody, and unnatural acts,
Of accidental judgments, casual slaughters, 357
Of deaths put on by cunning and forced cause, 358
And, in this upshot, purposes mistook
Fall'n on th'inventors' heads. All this can I
Truly deliver.

FORTINBRAS. Let us haste to hear it,
And call the noblest to the audience.
For me, with sorrow I embrace my fortune.
I have some rights of memory in this kingdom, 364
Which now to claim my vantage doth invite me. 365

HORATIO.
Of that I shall have also cause to speak,
And from his mouth whose voice will draw on more. 367
But let this same be presently performed, 368
Even while men's minds are wild, lest more mischance
On plots and errors happen. 370

FORTINBRAS. Let four captains
Bear Hamlet, like a soldier, to the stage,
For he was likely, had he been put on, 372
To have proved most royal; and for his passage, 373
The soldiers' music and the rite of war
Speak loudly for him. 375
Take up the bodies. Such a sight as this
Becomes the field, but here shows much amiss. 377
Go bid the soldiers shoot.

Exeunt [marching, bearing off the dead bodies; a peal of ordnance is shot off].

---

357 judgments retributions. **casual** occurring by chance **358 put on** instigated. **forced cause** contrivance **364 of memory** traditional, remembered, unforgotten **365 vantage** favorable opportunity **367 voice . . . more** vote will influence still others. **368 presently** immediately **370 On** on top of **372 put on** i.e., invested in royal office and so put to the test **373 for his passage** to mark his passing **375 Speak** (let them) speak **377 Becomes the field** suits the field of battle

---

Analyzing the Text

1. In addition to the obvious conflict with Claudius, what are the internal and external conflicts that Hamlet must resolve? How well does he do this?
2. In the classical conception of tragedy, the main character is destroyed through a "tragic flaw" in his character or through a tragic error. In your own view, what is the nature of Hamlet's tragic flaw and how does it contribute to his demise?

Understanding Shakespeare's Techniques

1. Shakespeare is quite careful in creating a style of dialogue through which each character reveals something important about himself or herself. What can we infer, for example, about Polonius, Ophelia, and Laertes?

2. *Hamlet* is a play strongly marked by irony. Discuss a few key episodes where irony plays an important role.
3. How does Shakespeare use specific soliloquies, or speeches, to suggest that Hamlet makes discoveries about himself and the world in which he must confront evil, as the play unfolds?

Arguing for an Interpretation

1. We often think of tragedies as being unremittingly sad, yet there are many occasions where humor plays an important role in *Hamlet.* Where in the play does Shakespeare use humor, and for what purpose?
2. In his journey from naive innocence to disillusioned adulthood, Hamlet confronts many of the universal problems that plague everyone. What are some of these problems, and how does Hamlet react to them?
3. Rent a video or DVD of the 2000 version of *Hamlet* (starring Ethan Hawke as Hamlet), and after watching this modern-day version, write an essay comparing and contrasting it to the play in terms of significant cultural differences.

Connections

1. In what way does the idea of religious hypocrisy play a key role in Langston Hughes's essay "Salvation" and in Premchand's story "Deliverance"?
2. How do Naguib Mahfouz and Olaf Stapledon use unusual shifts in perspective and scale to emphasize the ephemeral nature of human life?
3. Compare Edgar Allan Poe's story ("The Masque of the Red Death") with William Faulkner's story ("A Rose for Emily") in terms of the protagonists' attempt to deny time and mortality.
4. Discuss how the "tragic flaws" of Okonkwo in Chinua Achebe's story and Prince Hamlet in *Hamlet* lead to needless suffering and destruction.
5. How do Machado de Assis and Anna Kamieńska use birds in their works to symbolize a dispassionate perception of human life?
6. In what ways do both Olaf Stapledon and William Butler Yeats incorporate elements of prophecy as to encroaching evil events as a major theme in their works?
7. Compare the differences in tone and choices of metaphors between Alfred Jarry's recasting of the crucifixion of Jesus with Gerard Manley Hopkins' treatment of the same theme.
8. How do the poems by Vasko Popa ("The Lost Red Boot"), Bella Akhmadulina ("The Garden"), and Les A. Murray ("Poetry and Religion") offer different perspectives on the meaning of poetry and the spiritual life?
9. In what respects do the windhover in Gerard Manley Hopkins's poem and the falcon in William Butler Yeats's poem symbolize opposite values?
10. In what ways do the poems by Dylan Thomas, Jorge Luis Borges, and Mary Oliver explore coming to terms with mortality?
11. How is the theme of failing sight given very different treatments in the poems by John Milton and Jorge Luis Borges?
12. What complementary perspectives on nature and identity are apparent in the poems by Walt Whitman, William Wordsworth, and Henry Wadsworth Longfellow?

13. How does the story by Carmen Naranjo ("And We Sold the Rain") and Ursula K. Le Guin's essay ("A Very Warm Mountain") use the theme of nature turned against humanity?
14. In what ways do both Aldo Leopold (in "Thinking Like a Mountain") and Ursula K. Le Guin (in "A Very Warm Mountain") anthropomorphize mountains, and for what purposes?
15. Why do you think Chinua Achebe used the phrase "things fall apart" from William Butler Yeats's poem "The Second Coming" as the title for his novel?
16. In what way does the structure of *Hamlet* reveal a shift from metaphysical speculation to real confrontation, in the here and now, that parallels the shape of the narrator's journey in the Epilogue from Olaf Stapledon's *Star Maker?*

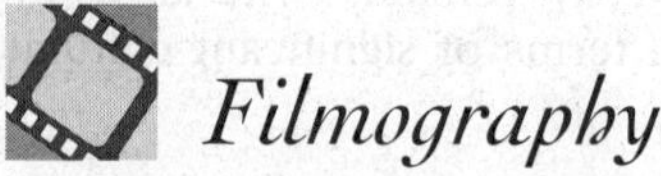

Filmography

Dracula (1931) Director: Tod Browning. Performer: Bela Lugosi.
The classic adaptation of Bram Stoker's novel about a vampire who terrorizes the countryside.

The Razor's Edge (1946) Director: Edmund Goulding. Performers: Tyrone Power, Gene Tierney, Clifton Webb, Anne Baxter.
Based on W. Somerset Maugham's novel, this sublime film charts the spiritual evolution of a rich young man who searches for real values and finds the true meaning of life with a sage in the Himalayas.

It's a Wonderful Life (1946) Director: Frank Capra. Performers: James Stewart, Donna Reed.
An American classic about a man on the verge of suicide who is saved by an angel and learns how important he has been in the lives of others.

Hamlet (1948) Director: Lawrence Olivier. Performer: Lawrence Olivier.
A skillful adaptation of Shakespeare's play that follows Hamlet as he pursues his quest to avenge his father's murder.

The Red Shoes (1948) Director: Emeric Pressburger. Performer: Moira Shearer.
Inspired by Hans Christian Anderson's fairy tale, this film tells the story of a young ballerina who is caught between love and the desire for success.

Moby Dick (1956) Director: John Huston. Performer: Gregory Peck.
This film, based on Herman Melville's classic saga, is a panoramic and compelling dramatization of Captain Ahab's all-consuming desire for revenge against the great white whale.

The Seventh Seal (1956) Director: Ingmar Bergman. Performers: Max Von Sydow, Gunnar Bjornstrand.
The allegorical figure of death visits medieval Sweden only to be challenged to a game of chess by a man who wants to keep on living. [Sweden]

Psycho (1960) Director: Alfred Hitchcock. Performers: Anthony Perkins, Janet Leigh.
Based on Robert Bloch's novelization of an actual murder, this film, acclaimed as the greatest horror film of all time, tells the story of a woman who is running from the law and checks in to the Bates Motel, which is run by the mentally deranged owner.

The Masque of the Red Death (1965) Director: Roger Corman. Performer: Vincent Price.

Loosely based on Edgar Allan Poe's story of the same name, about an evil prince who traffics with the devil while the plague afflicts those outside his castle walls.

Rosemary's Baby (1968) Director: Roman Polanski. Performers: Mia Farrow, Ruth Gordon, John Cassavetes.

An innocent young woman and her ambitious husband move to a new apartment, where she becomes pregnant and realizes she has fallen into a coven of witches and is carrying the Antichrist.

The Exorcist (1973) Director: William Friedkin. Performers: Linda Blair, Ellen Burstyn.

In one of the scariest films of all time, a young girl is possessed by a malevolent spirit.

The Last Wave (1977) Director: Peter Weir. Performers: Richard Chamberlain, Olivia Hamnett.

An attorney investigating the murder of an aborigine enters "dream time" and envisages an apocalyptic future of the continent under water. [Australia]

Resurrection (1980) Director: Daniel Petrie. Performers: Ellen Burstyn, Eva le Gallienne, Sam Shepard.

After being in a coma as the result of a car accident that has killed her husband, a woman finds she has miraculous powers to heal.

E. T.—The Extra-Terrestrial (1982) Director: Steven Spielberg. Performers: Dee Wallace, Peter Coyote, Henry Thomas.

A family tries to protect a stranded alien from being discovered by the government.

Koyaanisqatsi (1983) Director: Godfrey Reggio.

With an intense score by contemporary composer Philip Glass, this film creates a hynotic survey of modern life. The movie's title is the Hopi word for "life out of balance," and examines the disjunction between the urban landscape and the natural world.

The Purple Rose of Cairo (1985) Director: Woody Allen. Performers: Mia Farrow, Jeff Daniels, Danny Aiello.

During the Great Depression, a young woman's matinee idol literally steps off the screen and into her life in this magic realist film.

Hamlet (1996) Director: Kenneth Branagh. Performer: Kenneth Branagh.

This four-hour-long version relies on the complete text and situates the action in the nineteenth century to emphasize the political intrigues of the court and Hamlet's off-stage romance with Ophelia.

The Truman Show (1998) Director: Peter Weir. Performers: Jim Carrey, Laura Linney.

A naïve young man discovered that his entire life has been nothing but an elaborate television program.

Simone (2002). Director: Andrew Niccol. Performer: Al Pacino.

A down-on-his-luck filmmaker regains prominence with an ingénue who the public adores, but does not know is digitally created.

Appendix A

Critical Approaches to Literature

Several useful strategies for studying literary works have evolved over the last hundred years, and it may prove useful to be familiar with them. Each reflects certain assumptions as to the best way in which one should study a work of literature. These critical approaches are quite broad, and to some extent they may overlap. But each can heighten one's awareness of certain features of the work, which otherwise might go unnoticed.

1. Formalist Criticism (New Criticism)

Formalism is a broad term encompassing several kinds of criticism that began in the 1920s and 1930s. Also known as the *New Criticism,* it received a great deal of attention, especially in America, during the 1940s and 1950s. Formalist critics (although the term "formalism" was first coined by critics to disparage the objectives of this movement) study literary works without reference to anything external to the work itself, such as the historical period in which it was written, the politics of the times, the philosophical or theological values of the era, or even the psychological makeup or background of the author. In fact, this movement arose as a reaction to such outside considerations. Instead, formalist critics restrict their analysis to the grammatical or rhetorical structure within the work and the interrelationship between the text's basic elements, such as syntax and literary devices (diction, metaphor, irony, paradox, symbolism) that create or develop the work's impact. Formalists also pay particular attention to the way plot, characterization, and setting are used in the work. Given this emphasis on specific structural elements and their relationship to complex patterns of words and images, it is not surprising that analyses using this method involve a detailed study of the text. For example, notice how the following analysis uses this approach in a close reading that concentrates on relationships within a short section of James Joyce's *Ulysses* (New York: Random House, 1961. 720–23):

Bloom Revealed Through the Contents of His Secret Drawers

In the "Ithaca" chapter of James Joyce's *Ulysses,* Bloom opens one of two locked drawers immediately on returning home to add a fourth letter he has received, under the pseudonym of Henry Flower, from Martha Clifford.[1] The passages enumerating the contents of these locked drawers serve several important functions at this point in the novel; the interrelationship between items provides a refinement of the major elements in the novel by revealing Bloom's character through a recapitulation of the central themes of *Ulysses.* The first drawer contains artifacts representative of Bloom's fantasies of wealth, sexual fulfillment, and the recognition denied him in reality. Over half of the keepsakes in this drawer apply to Bloom's real or imagined relationships with women. A handwriting copybook of Milly's with drawings of *Papli* (her childish name for Bloom), the pink ribbon from an Easter egg when Milly was ten years old, and an infantile letter she wrote to him betray Bloom's desire to regress to happier times.

The photographs Bloom has of Queen Alexandra and Maud Branscombe fulfill Bloom's need for an ideal woman who is talented, beautiful, dignified, and famous. In reality, of course, Bloom is not an overwhelming success with women, and significantly this drawer does not contain any memento relating to his deeply disturbing relationship with Molly. In fact, Bloom's wistful indulgence about authority in the home is answered by the sealed prophecy he keeps concerning the proposed Home Rule Bill of 1886, which significantly never passed! The bazaar ticket, Austrian-Hungarian coins, and two coupons from the Hungarian lottery tell of Bloom's longings for wealth. Bloom's need for self-revitalization finds expression in the chart he has kept of his measurements compiled before, during and after two months of using Sandow-Whitely's Pully Exercises, the press cutting of a recipe for renovation of old tan boots, and the prospectus for Wonder-worker, a suppository he has sent for in Molly's name, which promises to "make a new man of you and life worth living." The items associated with Christianity (the pink ribbon of an Easter egg, Christmas card, and red sealing wax) emphasize Bloom's desire for spiritual as well as physical renewal.

By contrast, the items in the second drawer destroy Bloom's sustaining illusions by exposing him to the harsh reality of the past, with its unhappy memories of death, guilt, failure and regret. The contrast between the legal documents of the second drawer (an insurance policy payable at death, a bank passbook from 1903, a certificate of Canadian stock, and the docket for a grave plot originally purchased for his dead son, Rudy) and Milly's and Martha's letters in the first drawer oppose the impersonal bondage of the law and the ultimate reality of death to the encompassing spirit of love. The photograph of the Queen's hotel in Ennis, and the envelope addressed *To my Dear Son Leopold* remind Bloom of the fact that his father committed suicide to escape a painful and empty life. The local

[1] Martha Clifford, who was flirting with Bloom through a pseudonym by mail, is, according to Patrick Hogan in the *James Joyce Literary Supplement* (Fall 1992) most likely Nurse Callan, who is unmarried, has access to a typewriter, but is not used to typing, hence the typo of "patience/patients."

press-cutting concerning the change of his father's name (from Virag to Bloom), the daguerreotypes of his father and grandfather, the ancient Passover haggadah book, and his father's horn-rimmed spectacles all remind Bloom of the Jewish heritage he feels guilty about deserting for Molly. The happy family memories associated with Bloom's employment at Hely's recede as the painful memories of Rudolph Virag become dominant, and the Passover emphasis on the death of the first born (Rudy) focuses attention on the passion instead of on the resurrection. His father's suicide and the death of his son underscore the fact that father-son relationships are not permanent or fulfilling. Since none of the opposing forces in Bloom's nature proves strong enough to urge him to meaningful action, it would seem that the antithetical nature of the drawers is ultimately indicative of the irreconcilable forces contending within Bloom's personality.

This close reading identifies observable patterns and treats the text as self-contained—although in the context of Joyce's novel. A formalist approach is designed to increase the reader's appreciation of the inherent value of literary texts, almost as if they were objects of art in themselves. The *New Critics* further stipulated that literary criticism should seek to avoid two fallacies or mistaken assumptions in the study of literature. These are (1) the "intentional fallacy," which attempts to understand the work in terms of the author's intentions (whether stated or implied), and (2) the "affective fallacy," which equates the meaning of a work with the emotional response it elicits from the audience. To use this approach, analyze the basic literary techniques or formal elements (characterization, setting, point of view, language, tone, style, imagery, plot, and conflict, discussed in Chapter 2) and explain how these elements create and develop an identifiable theme within the work.

New Criticism radically differs from the interpretative strategies that follow and has been faulted for excluding potentially useful insights.

2. Biographical Criticism (Psychoanalytic Criticism)

In contrast to the *Formalist's* tendency to separate the literary text from salient events in the author's life, *Biographical Criticism* takes the opposite approach. These critics do not necessarily insist that there is a one-to-one relationship between the author's experiences and those of the characters. However, they believe that many fruitful insights into the meaning of the work can be gained by looking closely at the author's life and speculating about the psychological motives and desires (conscious or unconscious) that underlie conflicts presented in the work. This *Psychoanalytic* approach to literature originated with Sigmund Freud (1856–1939), who investigated the ways in which repressed thoughts and desires surfaced in the disguised language of dreams. Freud analyzed literary works including Sophocles' *Oedipus Rex* and Shakespeare's *Hamlet* as instances where the authors projected their own deep-seated anxieties and repressed wishes onto their characters. For example, after years of research with children, Freud concluded that Sophocles' play reveals a recurrent childhood dream to displace the parent of the same sex and to be the sole recipient of the affections of the parent of the opposite sex.

Freud discovered the same "Oedipal complex" in *Hamlet.* According to Freudians, Hamlet finds it nearly impossible to kill Claudius because he identifies with him in that Claudius had carried out Hamlet's deepest wish—that is, to displace his father and marry his mother. Although we may not agree with this particular interpretation, we can still benefit from this approach to explore the author-text interactions. For example, a psychoanalytic reading of the gravedigger's scene (V.i.) in *Hamlet* might suggest that Shakespeare wrote this, in part, to voice his deep-seated anxieties concerning his father's death:

Who Is the Tanner in the Gravedigger's Scene?

In *Hamlet* (V.i.) the gravediggers' banter before Hamlet and Horatio enter and their subsequent conversations may well refer to the recent passing of Shakespeare's father who was laid to rest on September 8, 1601.[1] The phrases, "ancient gentleman," "profession," and the query whether Adam could "dig without arms," taken together, may allude to the gentleman's coat of arms that Shakespeare used his influence to procure, in 1596, for his father, probably at the request of the latter.[2] John Shakespeare had repeatedly applied in previous years for a coat of arms and later sought to have it displayed with the Arden family crest.

During the 1580s, John Shakespeare, who was once a well-off manufacturer of gloves and other leather goods, went bankrupt and was subsequently ousted as alderman from the Stratford municipal office. Thus, the quest for a coat of arms may well be seen as an effort to retrieve lost social standing. The futility of worldly ambitions is a strong note in this scene, but does not simply refer to Shakespeare's father. Phrases reflecting the legal terminology of the time, especially concerning the acquisition of property, become ironic since Shakespeare used revenues he had acquired from his share in the Globe to purchase New Place, a fine house in Stratford, in 1597. Although his father left no legal will, Shakespeare inherited the two Henley Street homes his father owned. Legal documents from 1602 (during the time that Shakespeare was most likely revising *Hamlet*) show him to be involved in the effort to acquire surrounding properties and enlarge his holdings. Ironically, the joke about the previous tenant of the grave, which speculates he might have been "a great buyer of land" (V.i. 86) would seem to be a self-mocking reference to his own ambition. The few square feet of land is now the only thing he possesses, and that, not for long. The joke becomes macabre when Hamlet speculates there scarcely would be room for the corpse if one were to bury all his legal contracts with him (V.i. 91–2).

This leads Hamlet to the thought that contracts are made of parchment made from sheepskins (a phrase that still refers to college diplomas) and parchment is very likely the material on which Shakespeare wrote the play. The father-son connection becomes clear with the curious query as to whether parchment could also be made of calfskin (1.95). John Shakespeare was a glover, that is, he had made his living from the processing, cutting, and fashioning of calfskin gloves and other leather articles in a shop he operated from home. Thus, in one scene, we have an in-

[1] Biographical data are drawn from Park Honan's *Shakespeare: A Life,* Oxford University Press, 1998. 13, 21, 39, 228, 231, 235, 275.

[2] Quotes from *Hamlet* are drawn from the edition of the play reprinted in Chapter 9.

terrogation of the nature of ambition, the futility of aspirations for social status, and the desire for property and prestige that links father and son. That his father's death is at the heart of this scene can be adduced from Hamlet's question "how long will a man lie in the earth ere he rot"? (1.137) and the clown's answer, "a tanner will last you nine year" (1.140) because "his hide is so tanned with his trade that 'a will keep out water a great while" (1.142–3). As a tanner of calfskins, John Shakespeare owned a barn in the Gild Pits and in 1556 acquired work space in Green Hill Street in Stratford in which he kept the vats of chemicals used to process and treat calfskin. The futility of such worldly ambition gives rise to the ironic confrontation between Hamlet and the skull of the King's jester. Since Shakespeare's career as entertainer is analogous to that of a jester, the reference becomes self-mocking and continues the mood of self-deprecation that is such a powerful element in this scene. The original form of Hamlet's name in Danish history is Amleth, who in folklore, is a trickster or jester.[3] The scene becomes more poignant if we recall that Shakespeare's eleven-year-old son, Hamnet, had died in 1596—leaving Shakespeare without a male heir. So, it is at this particular moment in Shakespeare's life when he is compelled to come to terms with his father's death that he chose to dramatize a story in which he could sublimate and confront deep-seated anxieties about his father's death and the futility of ambition.

3. Historical Criticism (Marxist Criticism and the New Historicism)

The presumption underlying *Historical Criticism* is that the literary text is accorded equal weight with non-literary texts of the same historical period. As distinct from the *Formalist's* assumptions about the universal or timeless significance of the text, *Historicists* view the literary text as another kind of evidence that offers insight into the social and political forces of a particular era. For example, Luisa Valenzuela's short story "The Censors" (in Chapter 7) might be seen as more than simply an ironic fable about the corrupting effect of power. It could also be taken as a thinly disguised description of life under the military regime in Argentina during the late 1970s, when civil liberties disappeared and censorship became a routine feature of everyday life. To understand what *New Historicists* do, we might juxtapose Irene Zabytko's story "Home Soil" (in Chapter 7) with Tim O'Brien's essay, "If I Die in a Combat Zone" (in Chapter 7) and read her work of fiction using insights gained from the nonfiction text in terms of their complementary perspectives on the soldiers who served during the war in Vietnam.

Marxist critics look below the surface of the literary work (much as *Psychoanalytic critics* do) to discover the social and political forces, especially those related to class struggle, that have shaped the characters and incidents in the work. Moreover, they view literature itself as wholly determined by these forces, and investigate the way it serves unspoken class agendas. For example, in Chapter 6, Catherine Lim's "Paper" might be seen as a critique of capitalism,

[3] Harold Bloom in *Shakespeare: The Invention of the Human,* Riverhead Books, 1998, p. 390, informs us that "the name Amleth derives from the Old Norse for an idiot, or for a tricky Fool who feigns idiocy."

as might Marge Piercy's poem "The Nine of Cups." The superficiality of bourgeois aspirations might be the true subject of F. Scott Fitzgerald's "Winter Dreams" (Chapter 6). Writers who explicitly adopt a Marxist approach include Bertolt Brecht, in his poem "A Worker Reads History," and Dario Fo, in his play *We Won't Pay! We Won't Pay!* in Chapter 6.

4. Cultural Criticism (Postcolonial Criticism)

This approach looks very carefully at how and why particular literary texts come to play a role in both the high culture and popular culture of a particular society. For example, Bruce Springsteen's song lyrics "Streets of Philadelphia" (Chapter 8) might be viewed as a cultural document for what it suggests about Springsteen's strategic reformulation of his macho blue-collar *persona* to publicize the AIDS crisis. *Postcolonial Criticism* looks at literary works, especially those written by writers in countries that at one time or another have been under the control of European colonial powers. They analyze texts to rediscover the suppressed identity of those who have been colonized and to puncture the myths and stereotypes that have been perpetrated about non-European cultures (and used to justify economic exploitation). In this respect, *Postcolonial Criticism* aims at correcting the widespread misrepresentation of other cultures to serve political ends. For example, this approach can be applied to Léon Damas's poem "Hiccup" (in Chapter 6) to discover how the poem voices cultural resistance to France's occupation of the South American country, French Guiana. We might also analyze whether Albert Camus, in "The Guest" (Chapter 8), portrays the culture of Algeria (a country colonized by the French) from a European perspective. In a broad sense, these critics point out the limitations of traditional Western literature in its representation of people from other cultures, and they explore the latent tensions between the colonizers and those who are colonized.

5. Gender Criticism (Feminist Criticism, Gay and Lesbian Criticism)

The presumption that underlies *Gender Criticism* is that culture determines what we regard as the proper roles for men and women and how we think about masculinity and femininity. For example, we might analyze the way Margaret Atwood in "Happy Endings" (Chapter 5) depicts (and satirizes) the permissible roles men and women play in society and the extent to which these roles are culturally constructed. *Feminist critics* examine the representations of women in literature by both sexes, in order to understand the underlying power relationships, and to critique the way women are depicted as inferior, as the "other," and as part of nature (and thus incapable of dealing with the world). *Feminist critics* also question whether women writers use language in ways that are qualitatively different from male authors. These concerns are illustrated in Charlotte Perkins Gilman's story "The Yellow Wallpaper" (in

Chapter 5), and provide a useful perspective on Susan Glaspell's play, *Trifles* (in Chapter 5). Both works can be understood as political texts in that they show the extent to which patriarchal societies diminish women and their experiences. *Feminist critics* also examine the way canonical or mainstream authors represent women under the guise of neutrality. For example, they might note that the girl (Jig) in Ernest Hemingway's story "Hills Like White Elephants" (in Chapter 5) is depicted, albeit sympathetically, as someone who is dependent, subservient, and acquiescent to her male companion's demands.

Gay and Lesbian criticism examines how homosexuals are represented in works of literature and challenges stereotypes and homophobia. This approach might prove useful when reading the essays by Paul Monette ("Borrowed Time: An AIDS Memoir" in Chapter 8) and Luis Sepulveda ("Daisy" in Chapter 7).

6. Structuralism (Archetypal Criticism, Myth Criticism)

Structuralism views literature as an element within human culture that can be thought of as part of a system of signs that can be studied to discover the deep structures that determine their meaning. Rather than focusing on the specific content of a text, as a *Formalist* might, a *Structuralist* looks at the larger pattern of the narrative and tries to identify how it functions as an *archetype* for that society. For example, in Inés Arredondo's "The Shunammite" (in Chapter 3), the archetypal conflict between the flesh and the spirit might be understood as ultimately resolved through the mediating influence of love and forgiveness. Critics who adopt a *mythological* approach can also look at these *archetypes* to discover a series of parallels in many different cultures. For example, Bessie Head's story "Looking for a Rain God" (in Chapter 3) can be analyzed in terms of the ancient Greek myth depicted in Sophocles' *Oedipus Rex* (where the king became a scapegoat and restored fertility to the city of Thebes, which was threatened by plague and drought). The scapegoat motif also underlies Joyce Carol Oates's "Where Are You Going, Where Have You Been?" (in Chapter 4) in the depiction of the main character, Connie, as almost a Christ figure who risks her life to save her family and, in the process, renews her own life.

7. Deconstruction (Post-Structuralist Criticism)

Post-Structuralism and its applied form *Deconstruction* quarrel with the *Structuralist* assumption that writers are essentially in control of the linguistic systems they employ when they create their works. They also challenge *Formalist* assumptions that works of literature are self-sufficient, and that any ambiguities within a text ultimately can be resolved by showing how they contribute to a sense of unity. By contrast, for *Post-Structuralists,* language is a slippery and imprecise labyrinth of associations, and the unity of a text is a contrived illusion. To demonstrate this, they "deconstruct" literary works by reading against the supposed intention of the author. They look at tensions that appear to be resolved, but point to images and metaphors that suggest quite the opposite. *Post-Structuralists* reveal inconsistencies and contradictions that are normally glossed over, and probe for evidence of these gaps. For example, Christopher Durang's play *For Whom the Southern Belle Tolls* (Chapter 4) might be analyzed as an example of a rather playful deconstruction of the social values and character types depicted in Tennessee Williams's *The Glass Menagerie* (in Chapter 4). This approach might also be useful in analyzing the conclusion of Gregory Corso's poem "Marriage" (Chapter 5) where the speaker's triumphant affirmation is undercut by the image of an implausible pop culture heroine (in an ancient setting) that represents the girl he intends to marry.

8. Eco-Criticism

Eco-Criticism studies literature from an ecological or environmental perspective. These critics explore the aesthetic and symbolic values of the natural world and are alarmed by our increasing alienation from nature. *Feminist Criticism* provides a model for *Eco-critics,* who seek to discover the ways in which nature has been portrayed in literature, and bring to light a perception of the environment as a supportive and expressive ground for human existence. These critics might observe that both Ted Hughes (in his poem "Pike" in Chapter 1) and Ernest Hemingway (in his story "Hills Like White Elephants" in Chapter 5) portray nature in ways that deepen our awareness of the interrelationship between human beings and the natural world. Several of the works in Chapter 9 ("Nature and the Spirit") lend themselves to this approach, especially the essays by Aldo Leopold ("Thinking Like a Mountain") and Ursula K. Le Guin ("A Very Warm Mountain"), stories by Carmen Naranjo ("And We Sold the Rain") and Olaf Stapledon ("Star Maker"), and the poems by Henry Wadsworth Longfellow ("The Sound of the Sea") and Walt Whitman ("When I Heard the Learn'd Astronomer").

9. Reader Response Criticism

This school of criticism takes issue with the tenets of *Formalism,* which holds that the meaning of a work resides exclusively in the text. Advocates of the *Reader Response* approach argue that, in a very real sense, the meaning of a work of literature exists only within the mind of the reader as an ever-changing response to cues in the text. The writer may have intended the work to be read by one type of reader, but the reader's response is conditioned, to a greater degree than critics have previously recognized, by needs and expectations quite unique to that reader. Thus, this form of criticism not only studies the interpretive strategies that many readers use to make sense of what they read, but also looks at the kaleidoscopic range of responses readers from different backgrounds will have to the text.

For example, it is quite likely that most people who read Sembene Ousmane's "Her Three Days" (in Chapter 5), about a third wife in a society where polygamy is practiced, would bring very different personal and cultural expectations to the story than would someone who was part of that society.

Any of the critical strategies previously discussed will dramatically change the nature of the reading experience and fundamentally enhance your connection to the text.

10. Film Criticism

Although film is a radically different medium from fiction, poetry, or drama, useful analogies can be drawn from many of the approaches we described in "Topics for Literary Analysis" (Chapter 2) that you can apply to writing about film. Films can be studied using VCRs to freeze the action in individual frames; DVDs allow you to stop, slow, reverse, or enlarge particular scenes, and sometimes provide commentary by the director and screenwriter as well as scenes omitted from the final version of the film. Sometimes, of course, it will only be possible to see a film in a theater, and you will have to jot down your observations as soon as you can before you forget them. The most immediate response is often to the actors who play the leading roles. Consider, for example, how modern film versions of Shakespeare's *Hamlet* (with Laurence Oliver [1948], Richard Burton [1964], Kenneth Branagh [1996], or Ethan Hawke [2000]) elicit different reactions from audiences.

Film Versus Drama

First, let's consider how the filmmaker's way of telling a story differs from that of the playwright. In drama we listen to conversations between characters and witness events as they unfold. Usually, no narrator (or speaker) comments on events or characters, explains their motivation, or interprets the significance of the characters' actions as in fiction and poetry. We draw conclusions about what the characters think and feel based solely on what they do and say.

Unlike a staged play, the way scenes are shot in a film determines how much of the action we can see, from which angle we see it, the number of characters included in the shot, and how long the image remains on the screen. In films, the camera angle not only dictates the point of view from which the scene is shot, but establishes our sense of closeness to or distance from the characters.

In one shot, we may see events as they appear from a particular actor's perspective. A succeeding shot may show us the action from above as if we were looking down from an aerial view. In the space of a few moments, we can be transported from an intimate close-up to a panoramic long shot.

Montage as the Key Principle in Films

Montage (in which two or more images are juxtaposed to achieve an emotional effect that is more significant than any of the individual shots) is the basis of storytelling in film. For example, in Alfred Hitchcock's classic 1965 film, *Psycho,* the shower scene, in which the knife never actually strikes the character played by the actress Janet Leigh, was achieved through skillful film editing. *Montage* engages the audience's imagination through images that the audience is compelled to link together. In addition to *montage,* filmmakers use camera movement, sound, rhythm, and pacing to tell stories.

Camera Movements and Time

Directors use a number of techniques to suggest the passage of time. In a "dissolve," one image gradually fades into another, and suggests that some length of time has passed. Directors can use "wipes" to replace one image with another and create a sharp break with the earlier image. By using a "fade-out," the image gradually fades to black; with "fade-ins," the image gradually appears from an empty screen. Quick "cuts" stop a sequence to show a new image and create the feeling that many things are occurring simultaneously. For example, action films depend on quick cuts to accelerate the pace. Conversely, scenes shot in slow motion can be used to accentuate particular aspects of a person's character or to suggest great effort.

Camera Movements and Space

The audience's perception of distance and space can be achieved in a number of ways. In a "defocus shot," a scene ends by moving out of focus as a new scene moves into clear focus, to suggest that the two scenes are linked. With a "pan," the camera travels across a person, object, or scene, from a stationary position. In a "tracking" shot, the camera moves to follow a moving object or person. To move in toward or away from a scene, the camera moves closer or farther in a "dolly-in" or a "dolly-out." Other camera movements and angles can affect the audience's reactions. For example, a low camera angle shooting up imbues the subject with a sense of size, power, and importance. Conversely, a high camera angle shooting down can suggest powerlessness and vulnerability.

Lighting

The audience's emotional response to any of these camera movements is intensified by the way the scene is lit. A dim or diffused light can suggest suspense, ambiguity, or supernatural qualities. Conversely, a brightly lit scene can suggest innocence, optimism, or a new beginning. If the light is excessively bright, our impression may be of a harsh reality that is hard to look at. Flashing lights or strobe lights can be used to create an eerie mood. Color (of the scene, costumes, and any special effects)—or the absence of it—underscores the mood the filmmaker wishes to create, and can be used in a strictly realistic or purely symbolic way. For example, the director Steven Spielberg uses a momentary flash of color in a black and white film, *Schindler's List* (1993), to accentuate the humanity and pathos of a child amidst the bleak horror of the concentration camp.

Sound

Filmmakers use sound to communicate information and emotions that enhance the effects of the visual images. Dialogue and voice-overs (superimposed comments on the action) let us know what characters are thinking and narrate the events. The score or musical sound track often plays a crucial role in intensifying our emotional response to the scene, as do sound effects such as thunder, footsteps, or gunshots.

In the following sample analysis taken from *Media Sexploitation* (Upper Saddle River, N.J.: Prentice-Hall, 1976. 110–15.), Wilson Bryan Key attributes the horrific effects of the 1972 film, *The Exorcist,* to director William Friedkin's skillful subliminal use of the sounds of pigs squealing and the buzzing of angry bees in the movie's sound track.

WILSON BRYAN KEY

The Exorcist *Massage Parlor*

Auditory Archetypes

The Exorcist was remarkable in the way both audio and visual were integrated and mutually reinforced. The sound track, for which the movie won an Academy Award, was a brilliant example of creative subliminal sound engineering. Similar techniques have been used for years in other movies and by the popular music recording industry.

In several dozen interviews with theater employees—refreshment stand attendants, ushers, and ticket takers who had only heard the movie's sound track for several days before actually viewing the film, all reported extreme discomfort from the sound. The discomfort could not be verbally explained, but all agreed it was directly related to the sound track. Each of the theater staffs interviewed reported employees who became ill after finally seeing the film in its entirely—from mild to extreme nausea and hysteria.

Friedkin openly admitted he had used several natural sound effects in the movie's auditory background. One of these, he explained, was the sound of angry, agitated bees. After provoking a jar of bees into excited anger, he recorded their buzzing, then rerecorded the buzzing at sixteen different frequencies. He finally mixed the sixteen frequencies of buzzing together in what might be consciously heard as a single sound—a super buzzing of infuriated bees virtually unrecognizable at conscious levels. This sound of angry bees wove in and out of scenes throughout the film.

Virtually all humans (some much more strongly than others) respond with hysteria, fear, and intense anxiety to the sound of angry, buzzing bees, even if they have never in their lives experienced the actual sound. Many animals respond similarly. Perhaps the strongest verbally definable emotion triggered by the bee buzzing is fear or fright—a near panic-filled desire to run, flee, and escape from the threat. Carl Jung's theory of archetypes suggests that this sound—as the emotional reaction appears to cross cultures—could qualify as an archetypal symbol.

In many cultures the bee has been symbolically associated with death and immortality. In several ancient civilizations, dead bodies were smeared with honey as food for the soul. Indeed, honey was often used as an embalming fluid. Over many centuries in Europe, bees were prohibited from use in barter for fear they might take offense and destroy crops and flocks in retribution. Bees appeared as symbols of death, fear, and power in ancient Egypt, Germany, China, Greece, Italy, and Japan, in early Christian art, in both Hebrew and Moslem traditions, and in Norse mythology. The Hindu god Krishna was often described as hovering in the form of a bee. Souls have often been thought to swarm as bees migrating from hives.

There is never any conscious awareness, of course, within *The Exorcist* audience of angry bees buzzing. However, there are easily observable levels of anxiety produced by the sound as it weaves in and out of various scenes. The bee sound appeared, for example, in the scene where Father Merrin first visits Regan's bedroom while he removed various objects from a pouch, symbolically letting the invisible bees out of the bag.

Symbols of Evil

Another auditory archetype mixed subtly into the sound track was the terrified squealing of pigs while they were being slaughtered. Few sounds strike terror so deeply into the heart of man. This sound will affect virtually all humans even though they may never have experienced the squealing or sight of an actual pig. The expression "squealing like a stuck pig" has even gone into the language.

Pigs have been portrayed in various symbolic relationships with man for at least half a million years. Even today, the pig is considered one of the most intelligent of domestic animals—by human standards, of course. The pig, at least for modern man, was cursed by bad table manners that emphasize the pig's filth, greed, gluttony, and lethargy. Nevertheless, in many ancient cultures, pigs were often substituted for human victims during religious sacrifices. A black pig has often been symbolic in Christian art of the devil and Satan. In many civilizations the pig was thought to be a demon that injured fertility heroes in the groin, rendering them sterile. In Celtic mythology pigs were even portrayed as returning to life after being eaten. And, of course, in one of the New Testament's most celebrated exorcisms, Christ drove a legion of devils into a herd of swine which, maddened, threw themselves into a lake much as Father Karras flung his possessed body out the window.

In addition to the pigs' squealing hidden in *The Exorcist* sound track, Regan's grotesque, filthy face during the exorcism scene often resembled that of a pig. Further, subliminal reinforcement for the pig symbol is obtained by the word PIG written as graffiti on a ledge at the left side of the stairs looking down behind the house where the deaths occurred. This staircase, and the consciously unnoticed word PIG, appeared many times throughout the movie. Friedkin explained how the sound track often mixed the angry bee buzz with the pig squeals. The two sounds wove in and out of the film, coordinating with the visual.

Embedded in the sound, under the voices and surface sounds apparent in the exorcism scene, was what seemed to be the roaring of lions or large cats. A third of the audience surveyed described a feeling of being devoured or struggling against being devoured. There were also orgasmic sexual sounds in the exorcism scene that appeared to involve both males and females.

Sound is extremely important in the management and control of any group of individuals, certainly for those in a theater. Famed movie director Alfred Hitchcock ranked sound as more vital to the success of his famous suspense movies than his visual illusions.

In a recent Muzak Corporation advertisement, the company actually presented its services, background music for stores and offices, as an "environmental management" technique.

In Western society surprisingly little is publicly known about sound and its effect upon behavior. The consciously available portion of sound frequency ranges from 20 to 20,000 cycles per second—or so advertise the high-fidelity appliance manufacturers. Most theaters have sound equipment that will produce audible sound in this range. As a practical matter, however, few individuals can consciously hear over 17,000 cps or under 200 cps, especially young people whose hearing has been permanently dampened by high-volume electronic amplification.

Sound, nevertheless, can be perceived at each end of the spectrum beyond the consciously perceived frequencies. Resonance and other sound qualities also play parts in the subliminal perception of sound. To illustrate, some Moog synthesizers are capable of producing sound at 20,000 cps or higher and under 20 cps. You can consciously hear nothing at these high or low frequencies, but if volume or resonance is increased, most people become extremely agitated. If information is included in these subliminal frequencies, it will instantly be perceived at the unconscious level.

Hypnotic Inductions

When normal voice volume levels in *The Exorcist* were reduced, the audience was required to strain or increase attention or concentration upon the dialogue. This is almost a standard hypnotic induction technique, compelling the subject to concentrate upon one sensory data source. The audience uniformly leaned forward in their seats to hear, for example, the charming conversation between mother and daughter in the bedroom scene at the film's beginning. Similarly, many scenes throughout the movie were momentarily out of focus. Again, the audience—like puppets being manipulated with strings—leaned forward, concentrating on the visual images as they tried to correct for the blurred focus. Much of the dialogue between shock scenes was muted or whispered, so as to regain audience involvement.

When humans are led toward hypnosis, they become highly suggestible. Their emotions become more easily manipulated, managed, and controlled the further they proceed along the induction path.

Friedkin utilized little music in the sound track, though he credited works by Hans Werner Henzle, George Crumb, Anton Webern, and five other composers. Like all good background music, the themes were purposely designed for subliminal consumption. The consumption of music and sound generally followed two patterns. One pattern built slowly from plateau to plateau, always intensifying the audience's emotional response. Indeed, in a sample of roughly fifty women who had seen the movie, over half candidly admitted *The Exorcist* excited them sexually. Most cited the sound track as the apparent source of this excitement.

The other general sound pattern abruptly jarred the audience into a tension state. Loud, sharp noises—bells ringing, doors slamming, dogs barking—preceded and followed by extended periods of electronic silence. The sound would gradually increase to a crescendo, then abruptly trail off to nothingness, or cut off sharply. This technique is primarily an attention-holding-tension-building device. Physiological tension was also increased by silences. For example, the early scene in the attic—which was abruptly broken by a loud, sharp noise.

Jumping the sound from one scene to the next—as a continuity and tension-building device, quite similar to the pink roses used visually—was done throughout the film. An important sound jump occurred during

Father Karras's first visit to the house. During the preceding scene, in the dream sequence where Karras's mother climbs the subway stairs, the street sound was unrecognizable as a rather high frequency, moderately loud-volume sound. In the next scene where Karras visited the house, the sound was the same except a truck gear shift was heard and the sound increased in frequency. The gear shift identified the background noise, reducing audience tension for the priest's first visit with Regan, where the tension again built toward a tense climax.

Loud Silences

The Exorcist silences were not completely silent. They were electronic silences, with low-frequency background hums. The silences were only silent in contrast to high and increasing volume sequences. These silences also formed a series of plateaus which gradually increased in volume and decreased in time interval as the story moved toward various climactic situations. Silences, like the sounds, were used to produce within the audience a series of emotional plateaus. These silences became louder and louder and more and more rapid as each segment progressed. The tension and release, tension and release, tension and release, always building higher and higher and higher, induced—by itself—exhaustion and even nausea for many in the audience.

Another manifestation of tension management in the audience was coughing. The audience coughed heavily at predictable intervals throughout the movie. Audience coughing was recorded at several theaters and always appeared at roughly the same point in the story. This was compared with cough reactions in several other action-type films, *The Sting, Executive Decision,* and *Papillon. The Exorcist,* in comparison, produced notably stronger and more predictable cough patterns. There were, apparently, subliminal cues in the visual or auditory stimuli that motivated the coughing.

Coughing is a tension release and appeared to occur roughly within thirty seconds after the auditory tension peaks were released. The first sounds of the evil force in the attic sounded like coughing, followed by a rasping bronchial sound. Coughing, of course, can lead to an upset stomach.

The changes of Regan's voice—from that of a twelve-year-old girl to that of the devil—were carefully synthesized with the visual changes in her appearance. At some point during this transition, the girl's voice was replaced by the voice of Mercedes McCambridge, an actress with a deep husky voice. Friedkin admitted to putting the actress's voice through a filter to produce a voice unidentifiable as either male or female.

In other words, the devil's voice was consciously perceived as androgenous, or hermaphroditic. This voice quality would not be meaningful at the conscious level, but would be subliminally apparent. No matter how natural voices are disguised, hypnotized humans are able to identify male or female characteristics. It would not be an exaggeration to state that *The Exorcist* visual effects were only props for the sound. A large proportion of the audience recalled the sound with great discomfort weeks after leaving the theater.

Appendix B

Documenting Sources

You must document any evidence you cite, whether in the form of quotes, paraphrases, or summaries from a source. Not to do so is to commit plagiarism, that is, appropriating the language, ideas, and thoughts of someone else and presenting them as if they were your own. This is especially true when you paraphrase, that is, when you attempt to restate an author's ideas in your own words. Your paraphrase must be different enough from your original so that it conveys the meaning of the passage, but without using the author's original words. For example, here is a sentence from Octavio Paz's essay "Fiesta" in Chapter 1:

> It is governed by its own special rules, that set it apart from other days, and it has a logic, an ethic and even an economy that are often in conflict with everyday norms.

The following paraphrase would convey the meaning of Paz's original sentence, but would not constitute plagiarism:

> Fiestas operate on a different level from ordinary existence and permit behavior and expenditures that would be unacceptable at other times.

The ease with which material can be retrieved, downloaded, and integrated into papers, from the Internet, has made the problem of plagiarism worse. The aura of availability has made it easy to forget that this material must be documented in the same way as you do print sources of information. In fact, new online services (such as<www.turnitin.com/>) are available to instructors to help them identify and prevent plagiarism from the Web.

In addition to in-text citations of sources you quote, paraphrase, or summarize, you should also provide a "Works Cited" page at the end of your essay.

The style of citation we describe is drawn from the *MLA Handbook for Writers of Research Papers,* 6th ed. (New York: Modern Language Association of America, 2003) and the MLA Web site<http://www.mla.org>. In essence, the

MLA system of documentation has two complementary parts: (1) Parenthetical in-text citations signal the source of a quotation, paraphrase, or summary in your paper; (2) These in-text citations correspond to a *List of Works Cited* that appears at the end of your paper and provides full publication information.

In-Text Citations

If you identify the author's name to introduce a quote, you do not have to repeat the name in a parenthetical citation. Simply cite the page number in parentheses at the end of the quotation. The abbreviations *p., pg.,* and *pp.* are no longer used in citing pages. One further point: electronic sources such as Web pages and CD-ROMs usually do not contain numbered pages, so therefore your parenthetical citation will only contain the author's last name (or if the work is anonymous, the identifying title).

Source with One Author (Where the Author Is Identified)

> Olaf Stapledon writes that "in imagination I saw, behind our own hills' top the farther and unseen hills" (251).

Source with One Author (Where the Author Is Not Identified)

If you do not identify the author's name to introduce a quote, put the name and the page number(s) in parentheses.

> The author writes that "in imagination I saw, behind our own hills' top the farther and unseen hills" (Stapledon 251).

Source with One Author (Where the Work Has Not Been Previously Identified)

If you cite another work by the same author elsewhere in your paper, use the title word before the page number(s):

> Olaf Stapledon writes that "in imagination I saw, behind our own hills' top the farther and unseen hills" (*Star Maker* 251).

Source with One Author (Where the Author's Name and the Work Have Not Been Identified)

If you do not identify the author's name to introduce a quote and you cite another work by the same author elsewhere in your paper, use both the name and title word before the page number(s):

> The author writes that "in imagination I saw, behind our own hills' top the farther and unseen hills" (Stapledon, *Star Maker* 251).

Source with Two or Three Authors

The same rules apply when citing a work with two or three authors or from an indirect source as with one author, for example:

> Readers are quickly made aware of the kind of education Native Americans received: "It is almost impossible to explain to a sympathetic white person what a typical old Indian boarding school was like" (Crow Dog and Erdoes 28).

An Indirect Source

> The author reports that on the question of female circumcision Mahomet the Prophet stated "the woman will have a bright and happy face, and is more welcome to her husband, if her pleasure is complete" (qtd. in El Saadawi 122).

Notice that in all of these cases, the final period comes after the parenthetical citation. The only exception is when the quotation is more than four lines and thus, is set off by being indented ten spaces from the left margin. In that case, end the quotation with the normal punctuation (whether period, question mark, or exclamation point), and insert two spaces and put the page number(s) in parentheses. However, do not put a period at the end of the parenthetical citation.

List of Works Cited

At the end of your paper, on a separate page, include all sources quoted, paraphrased, or summarized in your paper. Begin each entry on a separate line. Alphabetize the list by the author's last name and provide full publishing information. Don't forget to indicate the date you accessed any online sources. If the entry uses more than one line, indent all subsequent lines 1/2 inch from the left margin. Double-space all lines. Notice that footnotes are no longer used; instead, parenthetical citations correspond to the List of Works Cited at the end of your paper. In this list, you provide in alphabetical order (last name first) all the secondary sources you have used, that is, all the authors and titles that you have quoted, paraphrased, or otherwise referred to in your paper.

The most commonly used forms are:

Book by One Author or Editor

Stapledon, Olaf. *Star Maker*. Los Angeles: Tarcher, 1987.

Whitely, Sheila, ed. *Sexing the Groove*. London: Routledge, 1997.

Book by Two or Three Authors or Editors

Crow Dog, Mary, and Richard Erdoes. *Lakota Woman.* New York: Grove, 1990.

Note that only the first author's name is reversed.

Hirschberg, Stuart, and Terry Hirschberg, eds. *Reflections on Language.* New York: Oxford UP, 1999.

Note the abbreviation "UP" is used for "University Press."

Book by More Than Three Authors or Editors

Abrams, M. H., et al., eds. *The Norton Anthology of English Literature.* 5th ed. 2 vols. New York: Norton, 1986.

The abbreviation *et al.* means "and others."

An Introduction, Preface, Foreword, or Afterword

O'Prey, Paul. Introduction. *Heart of Darkness.* By Joseph Conrad. New York: Viking, 1983. 7–24.

A Translated Book

Akhmadulina, Bella. *The Garden: New and Selected Poetry and Prose.* Trans. F. D. Reeve. New York: Henry Holt, 1990.

A Single Work in a Collection or Anthology

Pagels, Elaine. "The Social History of Satan." *Past to Present: Ideas That Changed Our World.* Ed. Stuart Hirschberg and Terry Hirschberg. Upper Saddle River, NJ: Prentice Hall, 2003. 256–67.

Edited Book Other Than an Anthology

Ruskin, John. *The Stones of Venice.* Ed. J. G. Links. London: Collins, 1960.

Revised Edition of a Book

Hirschberg, Stuart. *Strategies of Argument.* 2nd rev. ed. New York: Allyn & Bacon, 1996.

A Book in Several Volumes

Graves, Robert. *The Greek Myths*. 2 vols. New York: Braziller, 1967. Vol. 2.

When you use more than one volume of a multivolume work, give the total number of volumes after the title. In each parenthetical citation, give both the volume and page numbers of the volume you use.

Article in an Encyclopedia, Dictionary, or Other Reference Work

"Ceres." *The Concise Columbia Encyclopedia*. 2nd ed. 1989.

"Ceres." *The Random House Dictionary of the English Language: College Edition*. 1968.

Article in a Newspaper

Hoffman, Allan. "Official Puts Campus Music-swappers on Notice." *The Star-Ledger* 2 Sept. 2002: 37.

Since newspapers usually consist of several sections, a section number or letter may precede the page number, if applicable.

Article in a Weekly Magazine

Deane, Daniela. "The Little Emperors." *Los Angeles Times Magazine* 26 July 1992: 17-21.

Article in a Monthly Magazine

Oates, Joyce Carol. "Happy." *Vanity Fair* Dec. 1984: 34+.

A plus sign shows that the article is not printed on consecutive pages; if it were, a page range would be given: 34-36, for example.

Article in a Scholarly Journal

Hirschberg, Stuart. "Who is George Spelvin in Christopher Durang's *The Actor's Nightmare?*" *Notes on Contemporary Literature* 32.2(2002): 11-12.

The publication information for scholarly and professional journals should include the volume number (and the issue number if the journal paginates each issue separately—32.2, for example).

Film or Videotape

Hamlet. Dir. Michael Almereyda. Perf. Ethan Hawke. Miramax, 2000.

If the work of a particular person is the reason for the entry, it can start with the person's name, as do entries for print sources.

Television Program

The Mahabharata. Perf. Bruce Myers. PBS, New York. 28 Feb. 1999.

Lecture

Hughes, Ted. "Myth in Poetry." Seton Hall University, South Orange, NJ, 17 Mar. 1995.

Letter, E-Mail, or Interview

Lund, Diane. Letter to the author. 31 Aug. 2002.

Pepin, Jacques. E-mail to the author. 2 Dec. 2001.

Radziewcicz, Josie Mendez. Personal interview [or Telephone interview]. 17 Mar. 2002.

CD-ROMs Published as a Single Edition

"Surrealism." *The Oxford English Dictionary*. 2nd ed. CD-ROM. Oxford: Oxford UP, 1992.

CD-ROM publications in this form are not continually revised but issued a single time. The work is cited as you would a book, but with the word "CD-ROM" before the publication information.

CD-ROMs Published Periodically

Aaron, Belen V. "The Death of Theory." *Scholarly Book Reviews* 4.3 (1997): 146-47. ERIC. CD-ROM. SilverPlatter. Dec. 1997.

CD-ROM publications in this form are continually revised. The work is cited as you would a print periodical, but include the title of the CD-ROM, the word "CD-ROM," the vendor or distributor, and the release date of the electronic publication. These CD-ROMs often contain reprints and abstracts of the printed works, in which case, you should also include the publisher and the date for the print version before the information about the electronic version.

Electronic Sources

Web source documentation contains the same information as that for traditional print sources, such as author, title of document, and date of publication. However, entries for electronic sources also need to include the date of access and the URL enclosed in angle brackets < >. (If a URL will not fit on one line, break it only after a slash or a period.) The sequence to follow for citing online sources is as follows:

- The author of the Web site should go first, if the name is available.
- Title of the Web site—if the author's name is unavailable, begin with the title of the Web site.
- The date the Web site was last revised, posted, or modified; if not available, give the original publication date.
- If the Web site is an online version of a published journal, list the original publication date first and the online publication date next. (If no date is given, indicate this with *n.d.*)
- The date the site was accessed, or the date specified on an e-mail or posting, in parentheses.
- Web site address (URL) that shows the name of the institution/organization that supports the site.

Below are examples of common forms for electronic sources: you can find suggestions for other sources on the MLA Website <http://www.mla.org>.

Article in an Online Reference Book

"Barthes, Roland." *Encyclopaedia Britannica Online.* Vers. 99.1. 1994-2000. Encyclopaedia Britannica. (19 June 2000). <http://search.eb.com/bol/topic?eu=13685&sctn=1&pm=1>

Article in an Online Journal

Caesar, Terry. "In and Out of Elevators in Japan." *Journal of Mundane Behavior* 1.1 (2000): 6 pars. (12 Mar. 2000). <http://www.mundanebehavior.org/issues/v1n1/caesar.htm>.

If the pages or paragraphs are numbered, include that information. The abbreviation for *pages* is *pp.,* and the abbreviation for *paragraphs* is *pars.*

Article in an Online Magazine

Ollivier, Debra S. "Mothers Who Think: Les birds et les bees." *Salon* 12 May 1998:9 pars. (19 June 2000). <http://www.salon.com/mwt/feature/1998/05/12feature2.html>

Newsgroup

Kathman, David. "Shakespeare's Literacy—or Lack of." 3 Mar. 1998. (11 Mar. 1998). Newsgroup <humanities .lit.authors.Shakespeare>

Web Site

EyeWire Studios. Grand Prairie, TX. April 1999. (28 Aug. 2002) <http://www.eyewire.com>

An example of a *List of Works Cited* drawn from the above discussions would appear as follows (although no single paper would draw from such diverse sources).

Akhmadulina, Bella. *The Garden: New and Selected Poetry and Prose.* Trans. F. D. Reeve. New York: Henry Holt, 1990.

"Barthes, Roland." *Encyclopaedia Britannica Online.* Vers. 99.1. 1994–2000. Encyclopaedia Britannica. (19 June 2000) <http://search.eb.com/bol/topic?eu=13685&sctn=1&pm=1>.

Crow Dog, Mary, and Richard Erdoes. *Lakota Woman.* New York: Grove, 1990.

Deane, Daniela. "The Little Emperors." *Los Angeles Times Magazine* 26 July 1992: 17–21.

Hirschberg, Stuart. "Who is George Spelvin in Christopher Durang's *The Actor's Nightmare?*" *Notes on Contemporary Literature* 32:2(2002): 11–12.

Stapledon, Olaf. *Star Maker.* Los Angeles: Tarcher, 1987.

Glossary of Literary Terms

Abstract Language describes ideas, concepts, or qualities rather than specific persons, places, or things.

Action the process by which characterization and plot develop, including physical and psychological events, that is, words and deeds as well as characters' expressed inner thoughts.

Allegory a type of narrative in which characters, events, and even the setting represent particular qualities, ideas, or concepts. For example, in Machado de Assis's "A Canary's Ideas" the ornithologist and the canary represent the abstract ideas of obsession and narcissism. (See Fable, Parable, and Symbol.)

Alliteration the repetition of similar or identical sounds at the beginning of words or in accented syllables. Alliteration is used to underscore similarities and contrasts. For example, from "*st*em to *st*ern."

Allusion a brief reference in a literary work to a real or fictional person, place, thing, or event that the reader might be expected to recognize. Jimmy Santiago Baca's poem "Spliced Wire" alludes to an electrical connection. (See Context and Reader Expectation.)

Ambiguity a phrase, statement, or situation that may be understood in two or more ways. The title of Liliana Heker's story "The Stolen Party" has several meanings.

Anagnorisis the moment of recognition or discovery, especially in tragedy when the hero gains insight into the cause of his or her downfall.

Analogy a comparison drawn between two basically different things that have some points in common, often used to explain a more complex idea in terms of a simpler and more familiar one. Rahel Chalfi draws an analogy between the speaker and a wary, prickly fish in "Porcupine Fish." (See Metaphor and Symbol.)

Analysis the division of a literary work into its various parts or elements in order to better understand the entire work.

Anapest a metrical foot consisting of two unaccented syllables followed by an accented one, as in "lĭke ă chíld/frŏm thĕ wómb,/lĭke ă ghóst/frŏm thĕ tómb" from Percy Bysshe Shelley's "Cloud."

Antagonist a character who opposes the protagonist's completion of his or her goal. In *Hamlet,* Claudius is the antagonist to Hamlet.

Apostrophe a figure of speech in which an absent person, an abstract concept, or an inanimate object, is directly addressed, as in William Blake's "Ah! Sun-flower."

Archetypes themes, images, and narrative patterns that are universal and embody recurring features of human experience. Archetypal characters are, e.g., hero and scapegoat; an archetypal situation is, e.g., a quest. The quest motif of the journey underlies Eudora Welty's "A Worn Path." (See Myth and Symbol).

Argument a process of reasoning and putting forth evidence to support an interpretation, as in Nawal El Saadawi's essay "The Mutilated Half" and in Wing Tek Lum's "Minority Poem."

Aside a staging device in which a character makes a short speech heard by the audience, but not by the other characters in the play. For example, in Act II, Scene 2, line 186 of *Hamlet,* Polonius directs the statement "How say you by that? Still harping on my daughter" to the audience.

Assonance the repetition of vowel sounds in a line, stanza, or sentence, as in "*a*n *A*rab" and "*o*n the *o*pposite" in Yehuda Amichai's "An Arab Shepherd Is Searching for His Goat on Mount Zion."

Assumptions the knowledge, values, and beliefs a reader brings to a text.

Audience the group of spectators, listeners, viewers, or readers that a performance or written work reaches.

Autobiography an author's own life history or memoir. For example, Mary Crow Dog's "Civilize Them with a Stick" is drawn from her memoir *Lakota Woman.*

Ballad a narrative passed on in the oral tradition that often makes use of repetition and dialogue. Also known as a folk ballad when the author is unknown, as in "Edward, Edward."

Biographical Context the facts and circumstances of the author's life that are relevant to the work.

Blank Verse unrhymed iambic pentameter, a line of five feet. For example, the play *Hamlet* is written in blank verse.

Blanks (See Gaps.)

Caesura a pause introduced into the reading of a line of poetry that can be indicated by punctuation, or the grammatical construction of a sentence, or the placement of lines on a page. It was a particularly important device in Anglo-Saxon poetry, where each line had a caesura in the middle, but it is found in most forms of poetry, such as the sonnet, and in blank verse as in the line "what is it, what?" in Eleni Fourtouni's "Child's Memory."

Canon collectively, the classic works of literature from Old English and Medieval works through the modern period. Contemporary critics have addressed the issue of exclusion or underrepresentation of women, minorities, and non-Western authors.

Catharsis means purgation, and refers to the vicarious experience of pity and fear by audiences who witness a tragedy, first described by Aristotle in *Poetics.* (See Tragedy.)

Causal Analysis a method of analysis that seeks to discover why something happened or will happen.

Characterization technique a writer uses to create and reveal personalities of characters in a work of literature, usually by describing the characters' appearance, by directly ascribing character "traits," by presenting characters' actions, by revealing the characters' thoughts, or by showing the reactions of other characters to them. In fiction, the *narrator* is a particular kind of character who relates events without necessarily participating in them. In poetry, the *speaker* performs much the same function. (See Dynamic Characters, Flat Characters, Narrator, Round Characters, Speaker, Static Character, and Stock Character.)

Claim the assertion or interpretation the writer puts forward and supports with evidence and reasons. (See Thesis.)

Cliché a timeworn expression that through overuse has lost its power to evoke concrete images, as in the phrase "cool as a cucumber."

Climax the turning point of emotional intensity in a work of literature. Hamlet's failure to kill Claudius at prayer in Act III is the climax of the play, after which Hamlet's fortunes begin to decline.

Comedy a work in which the audience (or reader) is amused by situations that are humorous without involving disasters or an unhappy outcome for the main character(s). When comedy is used to educate the audience about social conditions and human foibles, it becomes satire. Tewfik al-Hakim's play, *The Donkey Market* is both comic and satiric. (See Satire.)

Commedia dell' Arte broadly humorous farce developed in sixteenth-century Italy, featuring stock characters, humorous situations, and improvised dialogue. Dario Fo's *We Won't Pay! We Won't Pay!* reflects this tradition.

Comparison/Contrast rhetorical technique for pointing out similarities or differences; writers may use a point-by-point or subject-by-subject approach.

Complication the introduction of an obstacle that impedes the objectives of the protagonist.

Conflict the opposition between a character and an obstacle (another character, society or fate) or within a character's mind.

Connotation the emotional implications a word may suggest, as opposed to its literal meaning. The word *fireplace,* for example, might connote feelings of warmth, hospitality, and comfort, whereas it denotes the portion of a chimney in which fuel is burned. (See Denotation.)

Consonance repetition of the final consonant sounds and stressed syllables that are preceded by different vowel sounds, as in "pai*n* of a thor*n*" in Chenjerai Hove's "You Will Forget." (See Assonance.)

Context the surrounding situation that affects a literary work, including the writer's life and the political, historical, and social environment. (See Biographical Context, Historical Context, Literary Context, Psychological Context, Social Context.)

Contextual Symbols a person, object, or event that acquires a more than literal meaning solely from the context of the work, also known as private, authorial, or personal symbols. Vasko Popa's poem "The Lost Red Boot" explores the private meanings this personal symbol has for the speaker.

Controlling Image an image or metaphor that determines the organization of an entire poem. For example, Lennart Sjögren's poem "The Roses" uses the flower as a controlling image. (See Figurative Language and Metaphor.)

Couplet a stanza of two lines, that usually rhyme.

Crisis the point of highest tension in a work that precipitates an irrevocable outcome; often the result of a choice made by the protagonist. (See Climax.)

Culture the totality of practices and institutions and the entire way of life of the people who produce them. In a narrow sense, specific aesthetic productions of literature, art, and music.

Denotation the explicit, primary, or literal meaning of a word as found in the dictionary, as distinct from its associative meanings. (See Connotation.)

Description writing that reports how a person, place, or thing is perceived by the senses. *Objective* description recreates the appearance of objects, events, scenes, or people. *Subjective* description emphasizes the writer's feelings and reactions to a subject.

Descriptive Poetry poetry in which the external world is presented in visual terms of color, shape, form, and depth.

Dialogue a conversation between characters. Dialogue can serve to characterize the speakers, create a mood or atmosphere, advance the plot, or develop the theme or main idea of the work (See Monologue.)

Diction the choice of words in a work of literature and an element of style important to the work's effectiveness. In William Faulkner's "A Rose for Emily" the characters speak in ways that are appropriate to their education and social class. (See Connotation, Denotation, Style, Tone.)

Drama a literary work written to be acted on a stage.

Dramatic Monologue a lyric poem in which the speaker addresses someone whose replies are not recorded, as in Robert Browning's "My Last Duchess."

Dramatic Poetry poems in which characters in addition to the speaker appear that include dialogue.

Dramatic Point of View action presented without a narrator commenting on the events or characters; also called the objective point of view.

Dynamic Characters characters whose behavior appears to change in response to events and experiences as opposed to static characters who change little, if at all.

Elegy a solemn reflective poem, usually about death. Dylan Thomas's "Do Not Go Gentle into That Good Night" and Mary Oliver's "When Death Comes" are poems that reflect this tradition.

Enjambment (from the French word meaning "to stride") the running over of a sentence or thought into the next line without a pause; a run-on line. For example, Margaret Atwood uses this technique throughout "At First I Was Given Centuries."

Epic a long narrative poem dealing with gods, heroes, and adventures, framed in a worldwide or national or cosmic setting, sometimes involving supernatural forces. *Beowulf*, Homer's *The Iliad* and *The Odyssey* are epic poems, and John Milton's *Paradise Lost* is a book-length epic poem.

Epigraph a brief quotation at the beginning of a literary work. For example, Margaret Sanger precedes her essay "The Turbid Ebb and Flow of Misery" with a quote from William Blake.

Epiphany an incident or event that evokes a sudden insight where the character(s) discovers something significant about himself or herself. James Joyce created his stories to incorporate this effect, as in "Araby" and "Eveline."

Essay a relatively brief prose discussion on a particular theme or subject.

Euphemism from the Greek phrase meaning "to speak well of" or "to use words of good omen"; the substitution of an inoffensive, indirect, or agreeable expression for a word or phrase that would be perceived as socially unacceptable or unnecessarily harsh. For example, in Victorian times, trousers were called "unmentionables" and the birth of a baby was referred to as the "arrival of the little stranger."

Examples specific incidents that clarify, illustrate, or support a writer's thesis or claim.

Expatriates artists and authors, including Ernest Hemingway and F. Scott Fitzgerald, who chose to live in Paris during the 1920s and 1930s in a freer bohemian society. They were referred to as the "lost generation" (a term coined by Gertrude Stein).

Explication a line-by-line interpretation of the meaning of a text.

Exposition the presentation of background material about the characters or the situation in a story, play, or poem, which supplies information necessary to understand events that follow; may appear either at the beginning or progressively throughout the work.

Fable a short tale that illustrates a moral whose characters are frequently animals who speak and act like human beings. (See Allegory.)

Fairy Tale a story, frequently from the oral tradition, that involves the help or hindrance of magical persons such as fairies, goblins, trolls, and witches.

Farce a type of comedy, usually satiric, that relies on exaggerated character types, slapstick, and other kinds of ridiculous behavior and situations that result from a contrived plot that makes use of surprises and coincidences, as in Christopher Durang's play *For Whom the Southern Belle Tolls.*

Feminine Rhyme a rhyme of two or more syllables, with the stress on a syllable other than the last, as in "ǵraditŭde/áttitŭde."

Fiction a mode of writing that constructs models of reality in the form of imaginative or mental experiences that are not literally true in the sense that they did not actually occur in the "real" world.

Figurative Language the use of words outside their literal or usual meanings, used to add freshness, and suggest associations and comparisons that create effective images; includes figures of speech such as hyperbole, irony, metaphor, personification, simile, and synechdoche.

First Person Narrator a narrator who is part of the story and refers to himself or herself as "I."

Flashback an interruption in the major action of a story, play, or essay to show an episode that happened at an earlier time, used to shed light on characters and events in the present by providing background information.

Flat Characters characters presented in terms of a single behavioral trait. The father in John Cheever's "Reunion" is presented this way. (See Round Characters.)

Folktale a traditional story about common people from a culture's oral tradition.

Foot a group of syllables in verse usually consisting of one accented syllable and the unaccented syllable(s) associated with it. (See Rhythm.)

Foreshadowing the technique of giving the reader, listener, or viewer of a story or play a hint, or clue, of what is to come next. For example, in the first sentence of "The Red Convertible," Louise Erdrich provides clues to the story's outcome.

Free Verse poetry that uses no set patterns of rhyme, meter, or line length, but uses rhythm and other poetic devices, as in Gregory Corso's "Marriage."

Gaps absences of or missing information in a text that different readers will fill in or complete in different ways.

Genre a type of literary work defined by particular characteristics of form or technique; for example, the short story, novel, screenplay, poem, play, or essay.

Historical Context refers to when the work was written and the time period in which the work is set in terms of the then current economic, social, political and cultural values.

Humor writing that expresses the faculty of perceiving or appreciating what is amusing or comical. Often consisting in the recognition and expression of incongruities in a situation or character. See Jhumpa Lahiri's story "This Blessed House."

Hyperbole a figure of speech involving great exaggeration used to emphasize strong feeling and to create a satiric or comic effect, not intended to be taken literally ("to wait an eternity").

Hypertext a kind of fiction that gives the impression of an inexhaustible text since it can be read in a nonsequential way and the reader can freely move from one place in the text to another to trace an idea or follow a character. Also called Hyperfiction. Milorad Pavic's story "The Wedgwood Tea Set" simulates this effect, although most hyperfiction is published on CD-ROMs.

Hypothesis (pl.: hypotheses) the reader's provisional conjecture or anticipation of what will happen next; an essential element in the reader's interaction with the text. (See Reader Expectation.)

Iambic Pentameter the most common meter in English poetry. A line or verse having five metrical feet; each foot consists of one unaccented syllable followed by one accented syllable. For example, "Ĭ lóve tŏ héar hĕr spéak, yĕt wéll Ĭ knów" in Shakespeare's "Sonnet 130: My Mistress' Eyes Are Nothing Like the Sun" is written in iambic pentameter.

Imagery in a basic sense, the use of language to convey sensory experience in order to arouse emotions or feelings which abstract language cannot accomplish; most often refers to a creation of pictorial images through figurative language. (See Figurative Language.)

Inference a reasonable conclusion about the behavior of a character or the meaning of an event drawn from the few details supplied by the author.

Intertextuality the influences of one literary text upon another, or references to a text that occurs in another. Muriel Rukeyser's "Myth" refers to *Oedipus Rex* by Sophocles.

Irony, Ironic (from the Greek *eiron,* a stock comic character who misled his listeners) a contrast between appearance and reality, what is and what ought to be. *Dramatic irony* occurs when the reader or viewer can derive meaning from a character's words or actions that are unintended by the character, or when two individuals have different levels of understanding or different points of view, as in Dario Fo's play *We Won't Pay! We Won't Pay! Situational irony* occurs when circumstances turn out contrary to what is expected, as in Inés Arredondo's story "The Shunammite." *Verbal irony* is the contrast between what is said and what is actually meant, frequently used as a device in satire, as in Jonathan Swift's "A Modest Proposal."

Limited Omniscient Point of View narrative restricted to the perspective of a single major or minor character; sometimes called third person limited omniscient point of view. Most modern fiction uses this technique. For example, see Joyce Carol Oates's "Where Are You Going, Where Have You Been?"

Literary Context literary works by others that have influenced that author; also includes the literary conventions prevailing at the time the work was composed that may have influenced the author's conception of plot, character, and other elements. *Hamlet* is an example of the revenge tragedy.

Literature a term that has come to stand for imaginative writing of high quality, although it should be recognized the term is an evaluative designation, not an absolute category.

Lyric, Lyric Poetry a short poem expressing an intense, basic personal emotion, such as grief, happiness, or love; poetry in which we seem to overhear the thoughts and feelings of the speaker. It may be rhymed or unrhymed. W. B. Yeats's "A Prayer for My Daughter" is a lyric poem. The sonnet and the ode are two types of lyric poems.

Magical Realism works in which mundane reality is displaced by fantastic, bizzare, or supernatural occurrences. "Half a Day" by Naguib Mahfouz and Carmen Naranjo's "And We Sold the Rain" contain these elements.

Metaphor a figure of speech that implies comparison between two fundamentally different things without the use of "like" or "as." It works by ascribing the qualities of one to the other, linking different meanings together, such as abstract and concrete, and literal and figurative. For example, Anne Bradstreet in "The Author to Her Book" compares her book to a child. (See Figurative Language.)

Meter recurrent patterns of accented and unaccented or stressed and unstressed syllables that create patterns of rhythm and emphasis. Meter is measured in units called feet, of which the most typical types in English are *iambic* (in which an accented or stressed syllable is preceded by an unaccented or unstressed syllable); *trochaic* (a stressed syllable followed by an unaccented syllable); *anapestic* (two unstressed syllables followed by a stressed one); *dactylic* (a stressed syllable followed by two unstressed ones); *spondaic* (two accented syllables). A line of poetry with two feet is known as *dimeter;* with three feet, a *trimeter;* with four feet, *tetrameter;* with five feet, *pentameter. Iambic pentameter* is the most common English metrical pattern. Poetry without a recognizable metrical pattern is called *free verse.*

Modernism a literary and artistic movement that arose and flourished in Europe and America in the first half of the 20th century; a reaction to mass culture and middle-class Victorian values. Modernist techniques are illustrated in the works of Ernest Hemingway ("Hills Like White Elephants"), James Joyce ("Eveline" and "Araby") and William Faulkner ("A Rose for Emily").

Monologue a long speech by one character in a literary work. (See Soliloquy.)

Montage a French term that means "mounting"; refers to the way a film is edited to create meaning by juxtaposing contrasting shots. This technique was invented by the Russian film director Sergei Eisenstein (1898–1948), and can be seen in his classic 1925 film, *The Battleship Potemkin,* in the scene where a baby carriage rolls down the Odessa steps.

Mood the atmosphere and feeling that a writer creates through the choice of setting, imagery, details, descriptions, and evocative words. (See Tone.)

Myth ancient stories that set out a society's religious or social beliefs, that often embody and express a culture's assumptions and values as expressed through characters and images that are universal symbols. (See Archetypes.)

Narration a true or made-up story that relates events and/or experiences in either poetry or prose. Narrations tell what happened, when it happened, and to whom; relate events from a consistent point of view; organize a story with a clear beginning, middle, and end; and use events and incidents to dramatize important moments in the action. (See Action, Plot.)

Narrator refers to the ostensible teller of a story, who may be a character in the story (as in Hanan al-Shaykh's "The Persian Carpet"), the author (as in Amy Tan's "Two Kinds"), or an anonymous voice outside the story (as in Catherine Lim's "Paper"). The narrator's attitude toward the events gives rise to the work's tone. (See Persona, Point of View, Tone.)

Novel an extended fictional prose narrative concerning the experiences of a central character. For example, Chinua Achebe's novel *Things Fall Apart* focuses on the life of a prominent Ibo warrior named Okonkwo.

Objective Point of View (See Dramatic Point of View.)

Octave an 8-line stanza that can stand alone or as the first 8 lines of a 14-line sonnet. (See Sonnet.)

Ode a long lyric poem in a formal style and complex form often written to commemorate or celebrate a special quality, object, or occasion, as does William Wordsworth's "Ode: Intimations of Immortality' from Recollections of Early Childhood."

Omniscient Narrator a narrator who knows everything about the characters and events and can move about in time and place, as well as from character to character, and enter the mind of any particular character. Kate Chopin's story "Désirée's Baby" employs an omniscient narrator.

One-dimensional Character characters whose personalities are centered around one or two traits. (See Stereotype, Flat Characters.)

Onomatopoeia the use of words whose sounds suggest their sense. For example, "hiss," "smack," "buzz," and "hum."

Parable a short, simple story that is designed to teach a lesson, truth, or moral; unlike a fable in which the characters are animals or an allegory where the characters represent abstract qualities. St. Matthew's Parables of "The Sower and the Seed" and "The Laborers in the Vineyard" from The New Testament are renowned examples.

Paradox a seemingly self-contradictory statement that may nevertheless be true.

Parody a composition that imitates the defining features of a serious piece of writing for comic or satiric effect. W. H. Auden's poem "The Unknown Citizen" parodies the language of bureaucratic memorials.

Persona (literally means "actor's mask") refers to the voice, and implied personality, the author chooses to adopt in order to tell the story in poetry or fiction. The persona may serve as a projection of views quite different from the author's. Jonathan Swift uses this technique in "A Modest Proposal" and Bruce Springsteen adopts a persona in "Streets of Philadelphia." (See Speaker, Voice.)

Personification a figure of speech that endows abstractions, ideas, animals, or inanimate objects with human characteristics as in Lennart Sjögren's poem "The Roses": "Silence leaps up from his chair."

Plot a series of related events organized around a conflict that builds to a climax followed by a resolution. Conflicts may be between two or more characters (as between Jing-Mei Woo and her mother in Amy Tan's story "Two Kinds"); between a character and society (the imprisoned "Man" in Kōbō Abe's play *Friends*) or the forces of nature (as in Xu Gang's poem "Red Azalea on the Cliff"); or internal, between opposing emotions, such as duty and conscience (as in Panos Ioannides' story "Gregory"). (See Action, Complication, Conflict, Crisis, Exposition, Resolution, Structure.)

Poem a literary form that emphasizes rhythm and figurative language. Often used to express emotions. (See Lyric, Meter, Rhyme.)

Point of View the perspective from which the events in a story are related; a story may be related in either the first person ("I") or the third person ("he," "she," or "they"). A first-person *narrator* is a character who tells the story he or she participated in or directly observed, as does the narrator in Louise Erdrich's "The Red Convertible." The observations and inferences of such a narrator may be reliable as far as they go, or unreliable as with the narrator in Charlotte Perkins Gilman's "The Yellow Wallpaper." A third-person *omniscient narrator* stands outside the events of the story, but allows the reader unlimited access to the characters' thoughts and feelings and may comment on the story or characters, as in Kate Chopin's "Désirée's Baby." So too, the third-person *limited omniscient narrator* is not directly involved in the story, but restricts the reader's access to the thoughts of one or two of the characters, as does the narrator in Monique Proulx's "Feint of Heart." The third-person *objective narrator* also stands outside the events of the story, but only reports, without comment, what the characters say and do without giving the reader access to any of the character's thoughts, as in Ernest Hemingway's "Hills Like White Elephants." (See Dramatic Point of View, First Person Narrator, Limited Omniscient Point of View, Omniscient Narrator.)

Post-modernism a term that refers to works that undercut or subvert traditional models of unity and coherence that employ irony and allusion to create a sense of discontinuity. Became popular in the last half of the 20th century and is associated with deconstructionist forms of criticism. Robert Fox's "Fable," Raymond Carver's "Neighbors," Nabil Mahfouz's "Half a Day," and Carmen Naranjo's "And We Sold the Rain" are examples of post-modernism.

Prosody includes the theory and principles of the elements that make up poetry; refers to accent, rhythm, meter, rhyme, and stanza form.

Protagonist the main character in a short story, play, or novel opposed by an adversary, or antagonist, who may be another character, the forces of fate, chance, nature, or any combination of these.

Pseudonym (literally "false name") an alias used by a writer who does not desire to use his or her real name; sometimes called a *nom de plume* or "pen name." Eric Blair used the name George Orwell.

Psychological Context the relevant conscious or unconscious motivations of the writer as these impulses, desires, and feelings influence the portrayal of emotions and behavior in the depiction of the characters. For example, F. Scott Fitzgerald's real-life pursuit of Zelda Sayre is reflected in the character Dexter's pursuit of Judy Jones in "Winter Dreams."

Pun a play on words that are similar in sound but have different meanings. For example, "don't put all your Basques in one exit" is a play on the phrase "don't put all your eggs in one basket."

Purpose the writer's objective; also, the goals of the four types of prose writing: narration (to tell or relate), description (to represent or delineate), exposition (to explain or clarify), and argument (to persuade).

Reader Expectation the mental process by which readers form hypotheses and fill in gaps in the text. For example, the point at which the reader understands that Peyton Farquhar's experiences are not literally happening in Ambrose Bierce's "An Occurrence at Owl Creek Bridge" illustrates this concept (See Assumptions, Hypothesis, Inference.)

Realism a 19th-century literary movement that aims to depict life as it is without artificiality or exaggeration. It uses ordinary language and focuses on ordinary people, events, and settings, all of which are described in great detail, as in Anton Chekhov's "The Lady with The Pet Dog." (See Romanticism.)

Resolution the unfolding of consequences that follow the climax; also called *denouement.*

Response Statement an essay that records the reader's reactions to a text, and explores the personal, literary, and cultural assumptions underlying those reactions.

Rhetoric in ancient Greece and Rome, the art of using language to influence or persuade others. Today, the term also refers to the specialized literary uses of language to express oneself effectively.

Rhyme the exact repetition of similar or identical sounds to unify parts of a poem to emphasize important words or lines, as "al*one*/st*one*" in Sara Teasdale's "The Solitary."

Rhythm the arrangement of stressed and unstressed sounds into patterns in speech and writing. Rhythm, or meter, may be regular or it may vary within a line or work. (See Meter.)

Romanticism a movement in the late 18th and early 19th centuries that was concerned with the individual's aspirations toward realizing an ideal self in an ideal world. William Wordsworth's "Ode: Intimations of Immortality from Recollections of Early Childhood" illustrates this philosophy. (See Realism.)

Round Characters characters presented in terms of a complex variety of personality traits as opposed to a single behavioral trait. Rounded characters are psychologically complex in that they often embody conflicting impulses that make them seem more real. The protagonist, Nunez, in H. G. Wells's story "The Country of the Blind" is a round character.

Satire a technique that ridicules both people and social institutions, often in an effort to bring about social reform. Exaggeration, wit, and irony are frequent devices used by satirists. Jonathan Swift in "A Modest Proposal" and Carmen Naranjo in "And We Sold the Rain" employ satiric techniques.

Scansion the marking off of lines of poetry into feet, indicating the stressed and unstressed syllables. (See Rhythm.)

Scene a division of an act in a play that may be long or short, serve as a transition, or even have an inner dramatic structure of setting up and resolving a conflict comparable to the dramatic structure of the play itself. For example, Scene I of Tewfik al-Hakim's *The Donkey Market* sets up a conflict as to how two laborers will gain employment and resolves it when they persuade a farmer to take one of them home as the donkey he just bought.

Science Fiction works of fiction usually set in the future or some remote region of the universe that use scientific discoveries or advanced technology, real or imaginary, in the plot. H. G. Wells in the 19th century (see "The Country of the Blind") and Olaf Stapledon in the 20th century (see "Star Maker") are pioneers in this genre.

Screenplay a motion picture script, in the form of a play written as the basis for a film, which gives the sequence of actions making up the plot, the dialogue, and descriptions of camera angles, settings, music, and sound effects.

Script the printed text of a play, including dialogue and stage directions.

Sestet a six-line stanza, or the last six lines of an Italian sonnet, as observable in John Milton's "When I consider how my light is spent."

Setting the time period and location in which the action of a story or play takes place. It may serve simply as a background or it may help create the atmosphere from which the story evolves, and may even alter the plot's development. Setting plays a crucial role in Bessie Head's story "Looking for a Rain God" and in William Wordsworth's poem "Ode: Intimations of Immortality from Recollections of Early Childhood."

Short Story a short work of narrative prose fiction that generally involves a small number of characters in a limited number of settings.

Simile a figure of speech involving a direct comparison between two unlike things and using the words "like" or "as." The phrase "her face like a strained flag" in William Faulkner's "A Rose for Emily" is a simile. (See Metaphor.)

Social Context the relevant social conditions and the effect of social forces as they influence the depiction of characters and classes of people in literary works; it includes economic and political circumstances as well as the effects of culture, race, class, power, and gender.

Soliloquy a long speech to the audience by one character in the absence of other characters, in which he or she shares private thoughts and feelings. A famous example is Hamlet's "To be or not to be" soliloquy. (See Monologue.)

Sonnet a lyric poem of 14 lines written in iambic pentameter. Sonnets fall into two groups, the Italian sonnet that establishes some issue in the first eight lines (octave) and then resolves it in the next six lines (sestet), as does John Milton in "When I consider how my light is spent," and the English sonnet that develops an idea in three stages and brings it to a conclusion in a couplet, as does Shakespeare in Sonnet 130: "My Mistress' Eyes Are Nothing Like the Sun."

Speaker the narrator of a poem; often a separate character created for the purpose of relating the events in a poem from a consistent point of view. (See Persona.)

Stanza the grouping of a fixed number of verse lines in a recurring metrical and rhyme pattern.

Static Character a character who changes little, if at all, over the course of the work. Mathilde's husband in Guy de Maupassant's story "The Necklace" is presented this way.

Stereotype a conventional character, who is defined in terms of one oversimplified, often exaggerated, personality trait, as is Ginny in Christopher Durang's play *For Whom the Southern Belle Tolls.*

Stock Character conventional character types who appear through the ages in many different forms of literature; such as the cruel stepmother, the servant-confidante, or the court jester. The bumbling police lieutenant in Dario Fo's *We Won't Pay! We Won't Pay!* is a stock character.

Stream of Consciousness the literary re-creation of a character's thoughts, psychological associations, perceptions, and memories in a seemingly random, but actually controlled, pattern. A narrative technique developed in the 19th century and made famous in the 20th century by James Joyce, William Faulkner, and Virginia Woolf. This technique is used in Olaf Stapledon's "Star Maker" and in Robert Desnos's poem "Midway."

Structure the fundamental organization or framework of a piece of writing; including both the principles underlying the form and the form itself. For example, in stories, the plot is the structural element; in plays, the divisions into acts and scenes express the inner dramatic structure; and in poetry, the formal arrangement into stanzas that develop a specific sequence of images and ideas forms the structure.

Style the author's characteristic manner of expression. Style includes the types of words used, their placement, as well as the distinctive features of tone, imagery, figurative language, sound, and rhythm.

Subplot a subordinate set of events in a novel or drama that reinforces or contrasts with the main plot. There may be more than one subplot. (See Plot.)

Support in argument, all the evidence the writer brings forward to enhance the probability of a claim being accepted; can include evidence in the form of summary, paraphrases, quotes drawn from the text, examples from personal experience, hypothetical cases, the testimony of experts, appeals to the audience's emotions and values, and the writer's own character or personality.

Surrealism a movement in modern literature and art that emphasizes the expression of the imagination as manifested in dreams; stresses the subconscious, often through the unexpected juxtaposition of symbolic objects in mundane settings. Alfred Jarry's poem "The Passion of Jesus Considered as an Uphill Race" is an example of surrealism.

Suspense the feeling of psychological tension experienced by the reader or spectator in anticipation of learning the outcome of a developing sequence of events.

Symbol something concrete, such as an object, person, place, or event, that stands for or represents something abstract, such as an idea, quality, concept, or condition. The symbol can be emphasized by repetition and position. In Barbara Kingsolver's poem "This House I Cannot Leave" the house symbolizes the speaker's self. (See Contextual Symbols, Archetypes.)

Synecdoche a figure of speech in which a part stands for the whole, for example, "all hands on deck" for everyone, or a whole for the part, for example, the "law" for police officers.

Synesthesia images drawn from one sense applied to another sense, as when descriptions of a certain sound are applied to a color. The phrase "the dreams—writhed in and about, taking hue from the rooms, and causing the wild music of the orchestra to seem as the echo of their steps" in Edgar Allan Poe's "The Masque of the Red Death" expresses this fusion of senses.

Syntax the pattern or structure of the word order in a sentence or phrase; the study of grammatical structure.

Text in the literal sense, the work itself, whether novel, poem, play, or story; can also include the work and its interpretations, which change from reader to reader or for the same reader over time.

Theater of the Absurd a movement in the theater that dramatizes the contrast between humanity's desire for a sense of meaning and purpose and the incoherence, purposelessness, and illusion of everyday life; a kind of theatre that challenges conventional assumptions underlying realistic drama. Kōbō Abe's play *Friends* is considered an absurdist drama.

Theme an underlying important idea in a literary work that may be mythical, moral, or psychological. It may be stated or implied. Literary works commonly have more than one theme. The reader's reactions determine in large part which themes are perceived as important. The loss of innocence is an important theme in James Joyce's "Araby."

Thesis the position taken by a writer, often expressed in a single sentence, that an essay develops or supports. (See Claim.)

Tone the writer's attitude toward the subject or audience, which may or may not be identical with the work's emotional atmosphere. Premchand's tone in "Deliverance" is one of barely controlled outrage toward the abuses of the caste system in India. (See Mood.)

Topic the subject the writer addresses, as distinct from the writer's thesis (opinion) about the subject. In Kelly Cherry's poem, "Alzheimer's," the topic or subject is Alzheimer's disease, whereas the thesis might be that "identity is equal to memory."

Tragedy a drama about a noble person whose character is flawed by a single weakness, which inevitably leads to his or her downfall or destruction. *Hamlet* is an often-cited example of a tragedy.

Tragic Flaw a psychological weakness in the character of the protagonist that leads to his or her downfall as, for example, Okonkwo's desire to appear strong leads to tragic consequences, in Chinua Achebe's "Things Fall Apart."

Tragicomedy a drama in which threatening and dangerous situations and serious consequences are combined with humor, and sometimes even a happy conclusion for some of the characters, as in Kōbō Abe's play *Friends.*

Transition a signal word or phrase that connects two sentences, paragraphs, or sections of an essay to produce coherence. Can include pronoun references, parallel clauses, conjunctions, restatements of key ideas, and terms such as "furthermore," "moreover," "by contrast," "therefore," "consequently," "accordingly," and "thus."

Turning Point (See Crisis.)

Understatement a form of verbal irony, often used for humorous effect, in which an opinion is expressed less emphatically than it might be, as in Portia's observation in the *Merchant of Venice* (I.2.106) "I dote on his very absence" (See Irony.)

Universal Symbols (See Archetypes).

Utopian Fiction a prose narrative that presents a detailed picture of an ideal society or an alternative world. By contrast, dystopian fiction presents a hellish society or vision of the future. H. G. Wells's "The Country of the Blind" is in the utopian tradition and has elements of a dystopia as well.

Villanelle a form of poetry normally consisting of 19 lines written in five tercets and a final quatrain, rhyming *aba aba aba aba aba* and *abaa.* Dylan Thomas's "Do Not Go Gentle into That Good Night" is one of the few examples of this form.

Voice an imagined projection of a speaker in a literary work (usually in a poem), sometimes identified with the author. (See Persona and Speaker.)

Wit purely intellectual manifestation of cleverness and quick thinking, chiefly in discovering analogies between things that are unlike each other, and expressing them in brief sharp observations, as does Maurice Kenny in his poem "Sometimes Injustice."

Acknowledgments

Kōbō Abe, *Friends,* translated by Donald Keene. Copyright © 1969 by Grove Press, Inc. Reprinted with the permission of Grove/Atlantic, Inc.

Chinua Achebe, excerpt from *Things Fall Apart.* Copyright © 1958 by Chinua Achebe. Reprinted with the permission of Heinemann Educational Publishers.

Bella Akhmadulina, "The Garden" from *The Garden: New and Selected Poetry and Prose,* translated by F. D. Reeve (New York: Henry Holt, 1990). Copyright © 1990 by F. D. Reeve. Reprinted with the permission of the author and translator.

Tewfik al-Hakim, *The Donkey Market* translated by Denys Johnson-Davies from *Egyptian One-Act Plays* (London: Wm. Heinemann, 1981). Copyright © 1981 by Denys Johnson-Davies. Reprinted with the permission of the translator.

Hanan al-Shaykh, "The Persian Carpet" from *Modern Arabic Short Stories,* translated by Denys Johnson-Davies (Washington, D.C.: Three Continents Press, 1988). Copyright © 1988 by Denys Johnson-Davies. Reprinted with the permission of the translator.

Dorothy Allison, "I'm Working on My Charm" from *Trash* (New York: Plume, 2002). Copyright © 1988, 2002 by Dorothy Allison. Reprinted with the permission of the author c/o Frances Goldin Literary Agent.

Yehuda Amichai, "An Arab Shepherd Is Searching for His Goat on Mount Zion" from *The Selected Poetry of Yehuda Amichai, Newly Revised and Expanded Edition,* translated by Chana Bloch and Stephen Mitchell. Copyright © 1986, 1996 by Chana Bloch and Stephen Mitchell. Reprinted with the permission of the University of California Press.

Gloria Anzaldúa, "Cervicide" from *Borderlands/La Frontera: The New Mexico.* Copyright © 1987 by Gloria E. Anzaldúa. Reprinted with the permission of Aunt Lute Books.

Inés Arredondo, "The Shunammite" from *The Underground River and Other Stories,* translated by Cynthia Steele and edited by Elena Poniatowska. Copyright © 1996 by the University of Nebraska Press. Reprinted with the permission of the publishers.

Machado de Assis, "A Canary's Ideas" from *The Devil's Church and Other Stories,* translated by Jack Schmitt and Lorie Ishimatsu. Copyright © 1977. Reprinted with the permission of the University of Texas Press.

Margaret Atwood, "Fiction: Happy Endings" from *Good Bones and Simple Murders.* Copyright © 1983 by O. W. Toad, Inc. Reprinted with the permission of Doubleday, a division of Random House, Inc. and McClelland & Stewart, Ltd., The Canadian Publishers. "At First I Was Given Centuries" from *Power Politics.* Copyright © 1971 by Margaret Atwood. Reprinted with the permission of House of Anansi Press in association with Stoddart Publishing Company.

W. H. Auden, "The Unknown Citizen" from *W. H. Auden: Collected Poems,* edited by Edward Mendelson. Copyright 1940 and renewed © 1968 by W. H. Auden. Reprinted with the permission of Random House, Inc.

Jimmy Santiago Baca, "Spliced Wire" from *What's Happening.* Copyright © 1982 by Jimmy Santiago Baca. Reprinted with the permission of Curbstone Press.

James Baldwin, excerpt from "My Dungeon Shook: Letter to My Nephew on the One Hundredth Anniversary of the Emancipation" from *The Fire Next Time* (New York: The Dial Press, 1963). Copyright © 1962, 1963 by

James Baldwin, copyright renewed. Reprinted with the permission of The James Baldwin Estate.

Miriam Baruch, "Sunflowers," translated from the Hebrew by Rahel Chalfi. Reprinted with the permission of the author.

Jorge Luis Borges, "Afterglow" from *Selected Poems 1923-1967,* translated by Norman Thomas Di Giovanni. Copyright © 1968, 1969, 1970, 1971, 1972 by Jorge Luis Borges, Emece Editores, S.A. and Norman Thomas Di Giovanni. Reprinted with the permission of Dell Publishing, a division of Random House, Inc.

Tadeusz Borowski, "Silence" from *This Way for the Gas, Ladies and Gentlemen.* Copyright © 1959 by Maria Borowski. English translation copyright © 1967 by Penguin Books, Ltd. Reprinted with the permission of Viking Penguin, a division of Penguin Putnam Inc. and Penguin Books Ltd.

Bertolt Brecht, "A Worker Reads History" from *Selected Poems,* translated by H. R. Hays. Copyright 1947 by Bertolt Brecht and H. R. Hays and renewed © 1975 by H. R. Hays and Stephen S. Brecht. Reprinted with the permission of Harcourt, Inc.

Grace Caroline Bridges, "Lisa's Ritual, Age 10" from *Looking for Home: Women Writing About Exile* (Minneapolis: Milkweed Editions, 1990). Copyright © 1990 by Grace Caroline Bridges. Reprinted with the permission of the author.

Albert Camus, "The Guest" from *Exile and the Kingdom,* translated by Justin O'Brien. Copyright © 1957, 1958 by Alfred A. Knopf, Inc. Reprinted with the permission of Alfred A. Knopf, a division of Random House, Inc.

Ernesto Cardenal, "The Swede," translated by John Lyons. Copyright © 1965 by Ernesto Cardenal. Copyright © 1992 by John Lyons. Reprinted with the permission of the translator.

Raymond Carver, "Neighbors" from *Where I'm Calling From: New and Selected Stories.* Copyright © 1986, 1987, 1988 by Raymond Carver. Reprinted with the permission of Grove/Atlantic.

Rahel Chalfi, "Porcupine Fish," from *Contemporary Israeli Literature,* edited by Elliott Anderson, translated by Robert Friend (1977). Reprinted with the permission of the author.

John Cheever, "Reunion" from *The Stories of John Cheever.* Copyright © 1962 by John Cheever. Reprinted with the permission of Alfred A. Knopf, a division of Random House, Inc.

Anton Chekhov, "The Lady with the Pet Dog" from *The Portable Chekhov,* edited and translated by Avrahm Yarmolinsky. Copyright 1947, © 1968 by Viking Penguin, Inc. Reprinted with the permission of Viking Penguin, a division of Penguin Putnam Inc.

Kelly Cherry, "Alzheimer's" from *Death and Transfigurations.* Copyright © 1997 by Kelly Cherry. Reprinted with the permission of Louisiana State University Press.

Kate Chopin, "The Story of an Hour" from *The Complete Works of Kate Chopin,* edited by Per Seyersted. Copyright © 1969 Louisiana State University Press. Reprinted with the permission of the publishers.

Judith Ortiz Cofer, "The Myth of the Latin Woman: I Just Met a Girl Named Maria" from *The Latin Deli: Prose & Poetry.* Copyright © 1993 by Judith Ortiz Cofer. Reprinted with the permission of The University of Georgia Press.

Gregory Corso, "Marriage" from *The Happy Birthday of Death.* Copyright © 1960 by New Directions Publishing Corporation. Reprinted with the permission of the publishers.

Mary Crow Dog and Richard Erdoes, "Civilize Them With a Stick" from *Lakota Woman.* Copyright © 1990 by Mary Crow Dog and Richard Erdoes. Reprinted with the permission of Grove/Atlantic, Inc.

Léon Damas, "Hiccup" from *Negritude: Black Poetry from Africa and the Caribbean,* edited and translated by Norman Shapiro (Stonington, Conn.: October House, 1970). Copyright © 1970 by Norman R. Shapiro. Reprinted with the permission of the translator.

Diana Der Hovanessian, "Looking at Cambodian News Photos" from *Selected Poems of Diana Der Hovanessian* (New York: Sheep Meadow Press, 1994). Copyright © 1994 by Diana Der Hovanessian. Reprinted with the permission of the author.

Robert Desnos, "Midway" translated by William Kulik, from Carolyn Forché and William Kulik, eds., *The Selected Poems of Robert Desnos* (New York: The Ecco Press, 1991). Copyright © 1991 by William Kulik. Reprinted with the permission of the translator.

Mahasweta Devi, "Giribala" from *Of Women, Outcasts, Peasants, and Rebels: A Selection of Bengali Short Stories,* edited by Kalpana Bardhan. Copyright © 1990 by The Regents of the University of California. Reprinted with the permission of the University of California Press.

Emily Dickinson, "Tell All the Truth but Tell It Slant" from *The Poems of Emily Dickinson,* edited by Thomas H. Johnson. Copyright 1945, 1951, © 1955, 1979, 1983 by the President and Fellows of Harvard College. Reprinted with the permission of The Belknap Press of Harvard University Press.

Rita Dove, "The Wake" from *Grace Notes.* Originally in *Poetry.* Copyright © 1989 by Rita Dove. Reprinted with the permission of the author and W. W. Norton & Company, Inc.

Christopher Durang, *For Whom the Southern Belle Tolls.* Copyright © 1995 by Christopher Durang. Reprinted with the permission of Helen Merrill, Ltd. on behalf of the author.

Nawal El Saadawi, "The Mutilated Half" from *The Hidden Face of Eve,* edited and translated by Dr. Sherif Hetata. Copyright © 1980. Reprinted with the permission of Zed Books.

Louise Erdrich, "The Red Convertible" from *Love Medicine, New and Expanded Version.* Copyright © 1984, 1993 by Louise Erdrich. Reprinted with the permission of Henry Holt & Company, LLC.

Martín Espada, "Jorge the Church Janitor Finally Quits" from *Rebellion Is the Circle of a Lover's Hands.* Copyright © 1990 by Martín Espada. Reprinted with the permission of Curbstone Press. Distributed by Consortium.

William Faulkner, "A Rose for Emily" from *The Collected Stories of William Faulkner.* Copyright © 1930, renewed 1958 by William Faulkner. Reprinted with the permission of Random House, Inc.

Dario Fo, *We Won't Pay! We Won't Pay!* translated by Ron Jenkins. Copyright © 1980, 1984, 2001 by Dario Fo and Ron Jenkins. Reprinted with the permission of Theatre Communications Group.

Carolyn Forché, "The Colonel" from *The Country Between Us.* Originally appeared in *Women's International Resource Exchange.* Copyright © 1981 by Carolyn Forché. Reprinted with the permission of HarperCollins Publishers, Inc.

Eleni Fourtouni, "Child's Memory" from *Watch the Flame.* Originally published in an earlier version in *Greek Women Poets* (New Haven, Conn.: Thelphini Press, 1978). Copyright © 1978 by Eleni Fourtouni. Reprinted with the permission of the author.

Robert Fox, "A Fable" from *The Midwestern University Quarterly* (1966), no. 3. Copyright © 1966, 1977, 1986 by Robert Fox. Reprinted with the permission of the author.

Robert Frost, "The Road Not Taken" from *The Poetry of Robert Frost,* edited by Edward Connery Lathem. Copyright 1916 and renewed 1944 by Robert Frost. Reprinted with the permission of Henry Holt and Company, LLC.

Nikki Giovanni, "Nikki-Rosa" from *Black Feeling, Black Talk, Black Judgement.* Copyright © 1968, 1970 by Nikki Giovanni. Reprinted with the permission of William Morrow & Company, a division of HarperCollins Publishers, Inc.

Nabil Gorgy, "Cairo Is a Small City" from *Modern Arabic Short Stories,* translated by Denys Johnson-Davies (Washington, D.C.: Three Continents Press, 1988). Copyright © 1988 by Denys Johnson-Davies. Reprinted with the permission of the translator.

Václav Havel, *Protest* from *The Vanck Plays,* translated by Vera Blackwell (New York: Faber and Faber, 1990). Copyright © 1978 by Václav Havel. Copyright © 1984 by Vera Blackwell. Reprinted with the permission of the Aura-Pont Agency, Prague.

Robert Hayden, "Those Winter Sundays" from *Angle of Ascent: New and Collected Poems.* Copyright © 1962 by Robert Hayden. Reprinted with the permission of Liveright Publishing Corporation.

Bessie Head, "Looking for a Rain God" from *The Collector of Treasures and Other Botswana Village Tales* (London: Wm. Heinemann, 1977). Copyright © 1977 by the Estate of Bessie Head. Reprinted with the permission of John Johnson, Authors' Agent, Ltd.

Liliana Heker, "The Stolen Party" from *Other Fires: Short Fiction by Latin-American Women,* edited by Alberto Manguel. Copyright © 1982 by Liliana Heker. Translation copyright © 1986 by Alberto Manguel. Reprinted with the permission of Clarkson Potter Publishers, a division of Random House, Inc. and the Lucinda Vardey Agency.

Ernest Hemingway, "Hills Like White Elephants" from *Men Without Women.* Copyright 1927 by Charles Scribner's Sons, renewed © 1955 by Ernest Hemingway. Reprinted with the permission of Scribner, a division of Simon & Schuster, Inc.

Linda Hogan, "Workday" from *Savings* (Minneapolis: Coffee House Press, 1988). Copyright © 1988 by Linda Hogan. Reprinted with the permission of the author.

Garrett Hongo, "Who Among You Know the Essence of Garlic?" from *Yellow Light.* Copyright © 1982 by Garrett Hongo. Reprinted with the permission of Wesleyan University Press

Chenjerai Hove, "You Will Forget" from *Red Hills of Home* (Gweru, Zimbabwe: Mambo Press, 1990). Copyright © 1990. Reprinted by permission.

Langston Hughes, "Salvation" from *The Big Sea.* Copyright 1940 by Langston Hughes, renewed © 1968 by Arna Bontemps and George Houston Bass. Reprinted with the permission of Hill and Wang, a division of Farrar, Straus & Giroux, LLC.

Ted Hughes, "Pike" from *Lupercal.* Originally published in *Audience* (Summer 1959). Copyright © 1959 and renewed 1988 by Ted Hughes. Reprinted with the permission of Faber and Faber, Ltd.

Panos Ioannides, "Gregory," translated by Marion Byron and Catherine Raizis, from *The Charioteer: A Review of Modern Greek Literature.* Copyright © 1989 by Panos Ioannides. English translation copyright © 1989 by Marion Byron and Catherine Raizis. Reprinted with the permission of Pella Publishing, New York, N.Y.

Kazuo Ishiguro, "A Family Supper" from *Firebird 2* (London: Penguin, 1982). Copyright © 1982 by Kazuo Ishiguro. Reprinted with the permission of Rogers Coleridge & White Ltd. 20 Powis Mews, London W11 1JN.

David Ives, "Sure Thing" from *All in the Timing: Fourteen Plays* (New York: Vintage Books, 1995). Reprinted with the permission of the author.

Alfred Jarry, "The Passion of Jesus Considered as an Uphill Race," translated by Gary Fletcher, from *Poems for the Millennium, Volume I,* edited by Jerome Rothenberg and Pierre Joris (Berkeley: University of California Press, 1995). Reprinted with the permission of the translator.

P'an Jen-mu, "A Pair of Socks with Love," translated by Chen I-djen, from Ann C. Carver and Sun-sheng Yvonne Chang, eds., *Bamboo Shoots After the Rain: Contemporary Stories by Women Writers of Taiwan* (New York: The Feminist Press, 1990). Originally published in *The Chinese Pen* (Winter, 1986). Reprinted by permission.

Mascha Kaléko, "Mannequins," translated by Susan L. Cocalis, from *The Defiant Muse: German Feminist Poems from the Middle Ages to the Present.* Copyright © 1986 by Susan L. Cocalis. Reprinted with the permission of The Feminist Press at the City University of New York, www. feministpress.org.

Anna Kamieńska, "Funny," translated by Mieczyslaw Jastrun, from Slanislaw Branczak and Clare Cavanagh, eds., *Polish Poetry of the Last Two Decades of Communist Rule.* Copyright © 1991 by Northwestern University Press. Reprinted with the permission of *Translation Magazine.*

Mahdokht Kashkuli, "The Button" from *Stories by Iranian Women Since the Revolution,* translated by Soraya Sullivan (Austin: Center for Middle Eastern Studies, University of Texas at Austin, 1991). Reprinted with the permission of Center for Middle Eastern Studies, The University of Texas at Austin.

Betty Keller, *Tea Party* from *Improvisations in Creative Drama.* Copyright © 1988 by Meriwether Publishing, Ltd. Reprinted with the permission of the publishers, 885 Elkton Drive, Colorado Springs, CO 80907.

Maurice Kenny, "Sometimes . . . Injustice" from *The Mama Poems.* Copyright © 1984 by Maurice Kenny. Reprinted with the permission of White Pine Press.

Wilson Bryan Key, "*The Exorcist* Massage Parlor" from *Media Sexploitation.* Copyright © 1976 by Wilson Bryan Key. Reprinted with the permission of Wilson Bryan Key.

Barbara Kingsolver, "This House I Cannot Leave" from *Another America, Second Edition.* Copyright © 1991, 1998 by Barbara Kingsolver. Reprinted with the permission of the publisher, Seal Press.

Jerzy Kosinski, "The Miller's Tale" from *The Painted Bird.* Copyright © 1965 by Jerzy Kosinski, renewed 1993 by Katherina Kosinski. Reprinted with the permission of Scientia-Factum, Inc.

Jhumpa Lahiri, "This Blessed House" from *Interpreter of Maladies.* Copyright © 1999 by Jhumpa Lahiri. Reprinted with the permission of Houghton Mifflin Company. All rights reserved.

Ursula K. Le Guin, "A Very Warm Mountain" from *In the Red Zone.* Originally published in *Parabola* (1980). Copyright © 1980 by Ursula K. Le Guin. Reprinted with the permission of the author and the authors agents, the Virginia Kidd Agency, Inc.

Aldo Leopold, "Thinking Like a Mountain" from *A Sand County Almanac and Sketches Here and There.* Copyright 1949, © 1977 by Oxford University Press, Inc. Reprinted with the permission of the publisher.

Catherine Lim, "Paper" from *Little Ironies: Stories of Singapore.* Copyright © 1986. Reprinted with the permission of Heinemann Asia/Reed International (Singapore) Pte. Ltd.

Naguib Mahfouz, "Half a Day" from *The Time and the Place and Other Stories.* Copyright © 1991 by the American University in Cairo Press. Reprinted with the permission of Doubleday, a division of Random House, Inc.

Guy de Maupassant, "The Necklace" translated by Marjorie Laurie from *Short Stories of Guy de Maupassant* (New York: E. P. Dutton, 1934). Reprinted with the permission of Everyman Publishers Plc, 140a Shaftesbury Avenue, London WC2H 8HD.

Edna St. Vincent Millay, "What Lips My Lips Have Kissed" from *Collected Poems.* Copyright 1923, 1951 by Edna St. Vincent Millay and Norma Millay Ellis. Reprinted with the permission of Elizabeth Barnett, Literary Executor.

Czeslaw Milosz, "My Faithful Mother Tongue" from *The Collected Poems, 1931–1987.* Copyright © 1988 by Czeslaw Milosz Royalties, Inc. Reprinted with the permission of HarperCollins, Inc.

Paul Monette, "Borrowed Time: An AIDS Memoir" from *Borrowed Time: An AIDS Memoir.* Copyright © 1988 by Paul Monette. Reprinted with the permission of Harcourt, Inc.

Alberto Moravia, "Jewellery," translated by Angus Davidson, from *Roman Tales.* Copyright © 1956, 1957 and renewed 1985 by Valentino Bompiani & Co. Reprinted with the permission of Bompiani, Milan.

Les A. Murray, "Poetry and Religion" from *The Daylight Moon and Other Poems.* Copyright © 1988. Reprinted with the permission of Persea Books, Inc. (New York).

Carmen Naranjo, "And We Sold the Rain," translated by Jo Anne Engelbert, from *And We Sold the Rain: Contemporary Fiction from Central America,* edited by Rosario Santos. Copyright © 1989. Reprinted with the permission of Seven Stories Press.

Jill Nelson, "Number One!" from *Volunteer Slavery* (Chicago: The Noble Press, 1993). Copyright © 1993 by Jill Nelson. Reprinted with the permission of the author.

John Frederick Nims, "Love Poem" from *Selected Poems.* Copyright © 1982 by John Frederick Nims. Reprinted with the permission of The University of Chicago Press.

Naomi Shihab Nye, "Where Children Live" from *Hugging the Jukebox* (Portland, Ore.: Breitenbush Books, 1984). Reprinted with the permission of the author.

Joyce Carol Oates, "Where Are You Going, Where Have You Been?" from *The Wheel of Love and Other Stories*. Copyright © 1970 by Joyce Carol Oates. Reprinted with the permission of John Hawkins & Associates, Inc.

Tim O'Brien, "If I Die in a Combat Zone" from *If I Die in a Combat Zone: Box Me Up and Ship Me Home.* Copyright © 1973 by Tim O'Brien. Reprinted with the permission of Dell Publishing, a division of Random House, Inc.

Sharon Olds, "The Planned Child" from *The Wellspring.* Copyright © 1995 by Sharon Olds. Reprinted with the permission of Alfred A. Knopf, a division of Random House, Inc.

Mary Oliver, "When Death Comes" from *New and Selected Poems.* Copyright © 1992 by Mary Oliver. Reprinted with the permission of Beacon Press, Boston.

George Orwell, "Shooting an Elephant" from *Shooting an Elephant and Other Essays.* Copyright by Sonia Brownell Orwell and renewed © 1974 by Sonia Orwell. Reprinted with the permission of Harcourt, Inc. and A. M. Heath & Co., Ltd. On behalf of Bill Hamilton as the Literary Executor of the Estate of the Late Sonia Brownell Orwell and Martin Secker & Warburg, Ltd.

Sembene Ousmane, "Her Three Days" from *Tribal Scars and Other Stories* (Portsmouth, New Hampshire: Heinemann, 1974). Reprinted with the permission of Societe Nouvelle Presence Africaine.

Linda Pastan, "Ethics" from *PM/AM: New and Selected Poems.* Copyright © 1982 by Linda Pastan. Reprinted with the permission of W. W. Norton & Company, Inc.

Milorad Pavić, "The Wedgwood Tea Set," translated by Darka Topali, from *The Prince of Fire: An Anthology of Contemporary Serbian Short Stories,* edited by Radmila J. Gorup and Madezda Obradovic. Copyright © 1998 by the University of Pittsburgh Press. Reprinted with the permission of the publishers.

Octavio Paz, "The Street," translated by Willis Knapp Jones, from *Spanish-American Literature in Translation.* Copyright © 1963 by Crossroad/Continuum Publishing Company. Reprinted with permission. "Fiesta" (editor's title) originally titled "The Day of the Dead" from *The Labyrinth of Solitude,* translated by Lysander Kemp. Copyright © 1962 by Grove Press, Inc. Reprinted with the permission of Grove/Atlantic, Inc.

Fritz Peters, "Boyhood with Gurdjieff" from *My Journey with a Mystic.* Copyright © 1964 by Fritz Peters. Reprinted with the permission of Tale Weaver Publishing.

Marge Piercy, "The Nine of Cups" from *Circles on the Water.* Copyright © 1982 by Marge Piercy. Reprinted with the permission of Alfred A. Knopf, a division of Random House, Inc.

Vasco Popa, "The Lost Red Boot" from *Vasco Popa Complete Poems,* translated by Anne Pennington, expanded and revised by Francis R. Jones. Copyright © 1996. Reprinted with the permission of Anvil Press Poetry Ltd.

Premchand, "Deliverance" from *Deliverance and Other Stories,* translated by David Rubin (Penguin Books India Pvt., Ltd., 1988). Reprinted with the permission of the publishers and translator.

Monique Proulx, "Feint of Heart" from *Intimate Strangers,* translated by Sheila Fischman (Toronto: Penguin Books Canada, 1986). Originally published in *Sans couer sans reproche* (Montreal: Quebec/Amerique, 1983). Reprinted with the permission of the author.

Sabine Reichel, "Learning What Was Never Taught" from *What Did You Do in the War, Daddy?* (New York: Hill & Wang, 1989). Copyright © 1989 by Sabine Reichel. Reprinted with the permission of the author.

Muriel Rukeyser, "Myth" from *A Muriel Rukeyser Reader,* edited by Jan Heller Levi (New York: W. W. Norton & Company, 1994). Copyright © 1973 by Muriel Rukeyser. Reprinted with the permission of International Creative Management, Inc.

Ira Sadoff, "Nazis" from *Emotional Traffic.* Copyright © 1992 by Ira Sadoff. Reprinted with the permission of David R. Godine, Publisher, Inc.

Tayeb Salih, "A Handful of Dates," translated by Denys Johnson-Davies, from *The Wedding of Zein and Other Stories* (London: Heinemann Educational, 1968 and Washington, D.C.: Three Continents Press, 1985). Reprinted with the permission of the translator.

Mark Salzman, "Lessons" from *Iron and Silk.* Copyright © 1986 by Mark Salzman. Reprinted with the permission of Random House, Inc.

Margaret Sanger, "The Turbid Ebb and Flow of Misery" from *The Autobiography of Margaret Sanger* (New York: W. W. Norton & Company, 1938). Copyright 1938 by Margaret Sanger. Reprinted with the permission of Sanger Resources and Management, Inc.

Luis Sepulveda, "Daisy" from *Full Circle.* Copyright © 1996. Reprinted with the permission of Lonely Planet Publications Pty. Ltd.

Notes to "Hamlet" from *The Complete Works of Shakespeare, Fifth Edition,* edited by David Bevington. Copyright © 2004 by Addison-Wesley Educational Publishers, Inc. Reprinted with the permission of Pearson Education, Inc.

Lennart Sjögren, "The Roses," translted by Robin Fulton, from *Four Swedish Poets.* Reprinted with the permission of White Pine Press.

Cathy Song, "The Youngest Daughter" from *Picture Bride.* Copyright © 1983 by Cathy Song. Reprinted with the permission of Yale University Press.

Natsume Soseki, excerpt from *I Am a Cat,* translated by Katsue Shibata and Motonari Kai. English translation copyright © 1961 by Kenkyusha Ltd. Tokyo. Reprinted with the permission of Peter Owen, Ltd.

Gary Soto, "Dirt." Reprinted with the permission of Gary Soto.

Bruce Springsteen, "Streets of Philadelphia." Copyright © by Bruce Springsteen, ASCAP. Reprinted by permission.

Olaf Stapledon, "The Ultimate Cosmos and the Eternal Spirit" from *Star Maker* (London: Methuen, 1937). Copyright 1937 by Olaf Stapledon. Reprinted with the permission of the Estate of Olaf Stapledon.

Amy Tan, "The Language of Discretion" from *The State of the Language,* edited by C. Ricks and L. Michaels. Copyright © 1990 by Amy Tan. Reprinted with the permission of Sandra Dijkstra Literary Agency. "Two Kinds" from *The Joy Luck Club.* Copyright © 1989 by Amy Tan. Reprinted with the permission of G. P. Putnams Sons, a division of Penguin Putnam Inc.

Sara Teasdale, "The Solitary" from *The Collected Poems of Sara Teasdale.* Copyright 1926 by The Macmillan Company, renewed 1954 by Marnie T. Wheless. Reprinted with the permission of Scribner, a division of Simon & Schuster, Inc.

Dylan Thomas, "Do Not Go Gentle into That Good Night" from *The Poems of Dylan Thomas.* Copyright 1946 by New Directions Publishing Corporation. Copyright 1952 by Dylan Thomas. Reprinted with the permission of New Directions Publishing Corporation and David Higham Associates, London, as agents for the Trustees of the Copyrights of Dylan Thomas.

James Thurber, cartoon. Copyright 1943, renewed © 1971. Reprinted with the permission of The Barbara Hogenson Agency, Inc.

Fadwa Tuqan, "I Found It," translated by Naomi Shihab Nye and Salma Khadra Jayyusi, from *A Mountainous Journey: A Poet's Autobiography* (St. Paul: Graywolf Press, 1990). Reprinted with the permission of Naomi Shihab Nye on behalf of Fadwa Tuqan.

Luis Alberto Urrea, "Border Story" (editors' title, originally titled "My Story") from *Across the Wire: Life and Hard Times on the Mexican Border.* Copyright © 1993 by Luis Alberto Urrea. Reprinted with the permission of Doubleday, a division of Random House, Inc.

Luisa Valenzuela, "The Censors," translated by David Unger. Copyright © 1982 by David Unger. Reprinted with the permission of the translator.

Kurt Vonnegut, Jr., "Who Am I This Time?" from *Welcome to the Monkey House.* Copyright © 1961 by Kurt Vonnegut, Jr. Reprinted with the permission of Dell Publishing, a division of Random House, Inc.

Diane Wakowski, "The Orange" from *Medea the Sorceress.* Copyright © 1991 by Diane Wakowski. Reprinted with the permission of Black Sparrow Press.

Alice Walker, "The Flowers" from *In Love and Trouble: Stories of Black Women*. Copyright © 1973, renewed 2001 by Alice Walker. Reprinted with the permission of Harcourt, Inc.

Eudora Welty, "A Worn Path" from *A Curtain of Green and Other Stories.* Copyright 1941 and renewed © 1969 by Eudora Welty. Reprinted with the permission of Harcourt, Inc.

Tennessee Williams, *The Glass Menagerie.* Copyright 1945 by Tennessee Williams and Edwina D. Williams, renewed © 1973 by Tennessee Williams. Reprinted with the permission of Random House, Inc.

Wing Tek Lum, "Minority Poem" from *Expounding the Doubtful Points* (Bamboo Ridge Press, 1987). Copyright © 1987 by Wing Tek Lum. Reprinted with the permission of the author.

Xu Gang, "Red Azalea on the Cliff" from *The Red Azalea: Chinese Poetry Since the Cultural Revolution,* edited by Edward Morin. Copyright © 1990. Reprinted with the permission of the University of Hawaii Press.

Wakako Yamauchi, "And the Soul Shall Dance," translated by Garrett Hongo, from *Songs My Mother Taught Me.* Reprinted with the permission of The Feminist Press at the City University of New York, www.feministpress.org.

W. B. Yeats, "The Second Coming" from *The Poems of W. B. Yeats: A New Edition,* edited by Richard J. Finneran. Copyright 1924 by Macmillan Publishing Company, renewed 1952 by Bertha Georgie Yeats. Reprinted with the permission of Simon & Schuster, Inc.

Irene Zabytko, "Home Soil" from *The Perimeter of Light: Writings About the Vietnam War,* edited by Vivian Vie Balfour. Reprinted with the permission of the author.

Special Indexes

Essays by Rhetorical Patterns

Short Fiction by Point of View

The following extends the discussion in Chapter 2 ("Writing About Point of View," pp. 159-161). We have added some additional refinements to the four basic vantage points (Omniscient, Limited Omniscient, First Person, Objective or Dramatic) from which stories are traditionally told and have arranged them as either First Person or Third Person narratives.

First Person

Narrator as the Protagonist or a Major Character

Narrator as an Observer and/or Participant

Unnamed Narrator Who Is Not a Participant

The First Speaker in the Story Quotes the First Person Narrative of Another

First Person Narratives or Letters Within a Story

Third Person

Limited Omniscient Point of View in Which a Major Character Is the Focus of the Narrative Along with Selected Thoughts of this Character

Limited Dramatic Point of View in Which the Major Character(s) Are the Focus of the Narrative, with Minimal Revelations of the Character's Thoughts

Omniscient Point of View of an All-Knowing Narrator Who Has Access to All the Character's Thoughts and Feelings

Dramatic or Objective Point of View Where No Single Character Is the Focus of the Narrative and There Are No Revelations of Any Character's Thoughts

Poems by Type

The following extends the discussion in Chapter 1 ("Kinds of Poetry," pp. 34–35).

Lyric or Reflective Poetry

These subjective personal poems focus on the feelings and perceptions of the speaker. They often relate crises of a personal nature although in some poems the speaker may represent a group rather than an individual.

Narrative Poems

This kind of poetry tells a story as in a short work of fiction and harks back to older forms of epics, romances, and ballads.

Descriptive Poetry

These poems emphasize colors, shapes, and sensory reactions with great intensity.

Dramatic Poetry

This kind of poetry includes voices and characters in addition to or along with the speaker and are constructed to lead up to a dramatic climax.

Geographical Index

South America

Southeast Asia

Chronological Index

Index of First Lines of Poetry